THIRD EDITION

COUNSELING ETHICS AND DECISION MAKING

R. ROCCO COTTONE
University of Missouri–St. Louis

VILIA M. TARVYDAS
The University of Iowa

PEARSON

Merrill
Prentice Hall

Upper Saddle River, New Jersey
Columbus, Ohio

Dedications

This book is dedicated to Francesca Cottone, who stood by her husband, my father, to the end through a debilitating and extended illness, with unconditional love and care. R.R.C.

For all those in my family across the generations who have struggled to do the right thing despite the consequences. They have all taught me that living a life of character is never easy, but always brings peace and respect.   V.M.T.

Library of Congress Cataloging-in-Publication Data

Cottone, R. Rocco.
   Counseling ethics and decision making / R. Rocco Cottone, Vilia M. Tarvydas.—3rd ed.
    p. cm.
   Rev. ed. of: Ethical and professional issues in counseling. 2nd ed. c2003.
   Includes bibliographical references and indexes.
   ISBN 0-13-171005-2
   1. Counselors—Professional ethics.   2.   Decision making.   I.   Tarvydas, Vilia M.   II.
  Cottone, R. Rocco. Ethical and professional issues in counseling.   III.   Title.
   BF637.C6C625 2007
   174'.91583—dc22

2005033049

Vice President and Executive Publisher: Jeffery W. Johnston
Publisher: Kevin M. Davis
Editorial Assistant: Sarah N. Kenoyer
Production Editor: Mary Harlan
Production Coordinator: Mary Tindle, Carlisle Editorial Services
Design Coordinator: Diane C. Lorenzo
Text Design: Carlisle Editorial Services

Cover Design: Candace Rowley
Cover Image: SuperStock
Production Manager: Laura Messerly
Director of Marketing: David Gesell
Marketing Manager: Autumn Purdy
Marketing Coordinator: Brian Mounts

This book was set in Garamond by Carlisle Editorial Services. It was printed and bound by Hamilton Printing Company. The cover was printed by The Lehigh Press, Inc.

Earlier editions entitled *Ethical and Professional Issues in Counseling.*

Pearson Prentice Hall™ is a trademark of Pearson Education, Inc.
Pearson® is a registered trademark of Pearson plc
Prentice Hall® is a registered trademark of Pearson Education, Inc.
Merrill® is a registered trademark of Pearson Education, Inc.

Pearson Education Ltd.
Pearson Education Singapore Pte. Ltd.
Pearson Education Canada, Ltd.
Pearson Education–Japan

Pearson Education Australia Pty. Limited
Pearson Education North Asia Ltd.
Pearson Educación de Mexico, S.A. de C.V.
Pearson Education Malaysia Pte. Ltd.

10 9 8 7 6 5 4 3 2
ISBN: 0-13-171005-2

Preface

We welcome you to the third edition of *Counseling Ethics and Decision Making*. Don't be confused—the title has changed. This text, in its previous editions, was titled *Ethical and Professional Issues in Counseling*. Based on feedback from readers and instructors using the prior editions, we changed the name to build on the strengths of the book—counseling ethics and decision making. This edition of *Counseling Ethics and Decision Making* enhances the strengths of the prior editions but keeps the same format and structure. There are significant additions to make the book even more useful in the classroom and on the desktops of professional counselors and counseling psychologists.

CHANGES TO THE THIRD EDITION

Significant changes are as follows:

1. The new edition references the new 2005 American Counseling Association (ACA) Code of Ethics. We were honored to have been involved in the revision of the code. So this new edition contains up-to-date references to the 2005 ACA Code of Ethics. The code is reprinted in Appendix A.
2. Reviews of the prior versions of the text lauded the book's coverage of decision making. We received positive reviews of our summary of decision-making models and the extensive presentation of two models of ethical decision making. Decision making has become a theme of the text, and every chapter now provides insights into decision-making processes. Case scenarios have been added to address decision-making processes. Some chapters address these scenarios in a structured way; however, we attempted to provide some unique approaches to presenting decision-making material in several chapters. In this way, we hope to engage the reader by providing different methods for presenting decision-making material.
3. Instructors will be pleased with the PowerPoint® presentations for each chapter. They can be downloaded from the Merrill Prentice Hall Companion Web site at **www.prenhall.com/cottone.** Also, we have taken care to provide an up-to-date test item bank for instructors. The online *Instructor's Manual*, which has been revised, instructs the user how to use a CD-ROM presenting ethical scenarios in order to enliven classroom discussion.
4. We have maintained and revised the chapters that address ethical issues in the specialties of counseling. We have received feedback that professors find these chapters useful, as they are able to choose chapters that address specialties aligned with coursework at their universities. For example, at a university with rehabilitation counseling, mental health counseling, and school counseling degree programs, the rehabilitation, mental health, and school counseling specialty chapters would be assigned. At another university with programs in chemical dependency, couple and family, and school counseling, those respective chapters would be assigned. In this way, faculty members can choose specialty chapters that are relevant to the focus of degree programs. These specialty chapters build on the material in the first sections of the book. They also provide information beyond the "context" of the specialties; for example, the school counseling chapter addresses ethical concerns related to counseling children and adolescents. The chapter on chemical dependency addresses how alcohol and drug use affect the process of counseling in many contexts.

Overall, we believe the new edition is up to date, comprehensive, and reader friendly and will provide instructors with the resources they need to enhance classroom presentation.

ACKNOWLEDGMENTS

We have learned over the years that relationships (professional, social, familial) are so important to everything we do. This textbook is no exception. We are so fortunate to have the opportunity to teach at universities that afford us the time and resources to complete this work. At the University of Missouri–St. Louis, Dean Charles Schmitz and the faculty of the Division of Counseling and Family Therapy (Dr. Therese Cristiani, Chair, and Drs. Kent Butler, Angela Coker, Jan Munro, Mark Pope, Susan Kashubeck-West, Matthew Lemberger, and Dawn Szymanski) have been highly supportive of this work. Also, a number of friends in St. Louis have given emotional and personal support through the term of this project, including Drs. Ricardo Moreno, James Lane,

Judy McGee, Carl Bassi, and Sherry Bassi, Dr. and Mrs. Paul Spezia, and Mr. and Mrs. Rich Wallut. Rock's wife, Molly, has been very understanding and loving through the late nights and lost holidays devoted to this revision. And his kids (Chris, Kristina, Maria, Torre, and Cristiana) have been anxiously awaiting the arrival of the new "box of books." A special thanks to the students of the Division of Counseling and Family Therapy for their support and help, especially doctoral research assistants, Jennifer McAfee and Robin Moore-Chambers, who worked hard to support revision efforts over the course of the last year, especially related to research updates and the PowerPoint® presentations for each chapter.

At the University of Iowa, the support of Dean Sandra Damico and the encouragement and friendship of Dennis R. Maki, Chair of the Department of Counseling, Rehabilitation and Student Development, for Vilia have been exceptional. The faculty of the department has facilitated the work in ways known and unknown to them and deserve appreciation. Inspiration, sage advice, and personal concern of colleagues Drs. Michael Leahy (Michigan State University) and James T. Herbert (Pennsylvania State University) have permitted Vilia to retain focus and a sense of purpose throughout her work. For both Vilia and Rock, the countless hours of work with some of the most committed and knowledgeable experts in counseling ethics on our ACA Code of Ethics Revision Taskforce was both a professional joy and an occasion for professional growth and refinement of our thinking. We thank the members of this the "cyberdonut and coffee club" for their contributions to the profession and our learning: Drs. Michael Kocet (Chair), John Bloom, Tammy Bringaze, Harriet Glosoff, Barbara Herlihy, Judy Miranti, Courtland Lee, and Christine Moll. As she has been challenged to explore complex problems in ethics, Vilia has been fortunate to have received the sage counsel of several of the most cogent and compassionate scholars in clinical ethics: Drs. John Banja (Emory University), Carol Gill (University of Illinois at Chicago), and Kristi Kirschner (Northwestern University, Rehabilitation Institute of Chicago). The unstinting support, insights, enthusiasm, and dedicated work of Drs. Christine Urish and Bobbi O'Rourke in updating the research and concepts of this book are critical to its excellence in this edition, as it has been in earlier versions. A special appreciation is due to Dr. Darcie Davis-Gage (University of Northern Iowa) for her generous willingness to evaluate the usefulness of the book from the instructional standpoint, and for her work in creating the excellent PowerPoint® presentations and enriching the learning activities for many book chapters.

We are thankful for our contributing authors, who have provided their expertise in areas of specialty practice and current interests. Their work has enhanced the textbook and increased our understanding and respect for the intricacies of ethical practice in specialized areas.

We are grateful to the following reviewers for their valuable suggestions: Charles Degeneffe, San Diego State University, Fresno; Yolanda V. Edwards, University of Maryland; Kevin Fall, Loyola University, New Orleans; James Slate Felming, University of Nebraska at Kentucky; and Frances Y. Mullis, Georgia State University.

Finally, a work effort of this magnitude always affects those with whom you live and love; your family. Vilia is deeply grateful for the unlimited support, patience, and care of her family, who often sacrificed themselves for the sake of her work—her husband, George; mother, Lucia; son, Ted; and new daughter, Julie.

We have also been fortunate to have an editor and an editorial staff who have been very supportive and patient. Kevin Davis, of Merrill/Prentice Hall, and his staff have provided us with much guidance and good advice. We also thank Sarah Kenoyer for her help in coordinating the third edition. It has been a pleasure to work with Kevin, Sarah, and others on the Merrill/Prentice Hall staff.

And to the readers, thank you for allowing us the opportunity to revise this book. We hope it will be a mainstay text in the area of professional ethics and decision making in counseling and counseling psychology.

About the Authors

R. Rocco Cottone, Ph.D., is a Professor of Counseling and Family Therapy and the Coordinator of Doctoral Programs in the Division of Counseling and Family Therapy at the University of Missouri–St. Louis. He earned his Ph.D. at Saint Louis University and M.Ed. and A.B. degrees at the University of Missouri–Columbia. He is certified in rehabilitation counseling, family therapy, and professional psychology. He is a member of the American Counseling Association (ACA) and served on the ACA Code of Ethics Revision Task Force from 2002 to 2005. He is a member of the ACA and the American Psychological Association, and he is a Clinical Member of the American Association for Marriage and Family Therapy. He holds licenses in counseling and psychology.

Vilia M. Tarvydas, Ph.D., LMHC, CRC, is a Professor and Program Coordinator of the Graduate Programs in Rehabilitation at the University of Iowa, where she is Director of the Institute on Ethics in Disability Policy and Rehabilitation Practice. She has a Ph.D. in rehabilitation psychology from the University of Wisconsin–Madison and an M.S. in rehabilitation counseling from the University of Wisconsin–Milwaukee. She is a licensed mental health counselor in Iowa. She was a program director for a brain injury rehabilitation center and has practiced as a psychologist in a hospital setting. Dr. Tarvydas is a past president of the American Rehabilitation Counseling Association and the National Council on Rehabilitation Education, and she was vice-chair of the Commission on Rehabilitation Counselor Certification (where she served as chair of the ethics committee). She has been awarded the Eda Holt Lifetime Achievement in Rehabilitation Award. Dr. Tarvydas is currently chair of the Iowa State Board of Behavioral Science Examiners and its disciplinary committee and a member of the American Counseling Association's Ethics Committee, and she served as a member of the ACA Code of Ethics Revision Task Force from 2002 to 2005.

CONTRIBUTORS

Janine M. Bernard, Ph.D., NCC, ACS, is Professor and Chair of the Counseling and Human Services Department at Syracuse University. Dr. Bernard received her Ph.D. in counselor education from Purdue University and her M.A. in counseling and personnel services from the University of Connecticut. Dr. Bernard is an Approved Clinical Supervisor and has written extensively in the area of clinical supervision. She is also a past chair of the National Board for Counselor Certification.

Ronald E. Claus, Ph.D., is a Research Assistant Professor at the Missouri Institute of Mental Health (part of the University of Missouri School of Medicine). He received his Ph.D. in Counseling from the University of Missouri–St. Louis. His research interests center around addiction and recovery from alcohol and drug problems. In particular, his interests include motivation and processes of change during and following treatment, self-help and spirituality in individuals with substance use disorders, and the relation of psychiatric comorbidity with the treatment and course of substance use disorders.

Julie Hautamaki, M.S., is a doctoral student in clinical rehabilitation psychology at the Illinois Institute of Technology. She received her master's degree in rehabilitation counseling from the Illinois Institute of Technology, Chicago, Illinois. She works at the Rehabilitation Institute of Chicago as a job placement specialist.

Donna A. Henderson, Ph.D., is a Professor in the counselor education program at Wake Forest University. She has a Ph.D. from the University of Tennessee at Knoxville in counselor education and an M.A. in teaching from James Madison University. She is a licensed professional counselor and a licensed school counselor in North Carolina. Dr. Henderson is also the immediate past president of the Association of Counselor Education and Supervision. She is a former high school counselor and has taught English and language arts in grades 7–12.

Dennis R. Maki, Ph.D., CRC, LMHC, ACS, is a Professor in the Graduate Programs in Rehabilitation and Chair of the Division of Counseling, Rehabilitation, and Student Development at the University of Iowa. Dr. Maki received his Ph.D. from the University of Wisconsin–Madison in Rehabilitation Counseling Psychology and his M.A. degree in Rehabilitation Counseling from Michigan State University. He is a past president of the American Rehabilitation Counseling Association and current president of the Council on Rehabilitation Education. Dr. Maki is an Approved Clinical Supervisor and is a contributor to the professional literature in the areas of clinical supervision, assessment, rehabilitation counselor education, and cross-cultural issues related to disability and rehabilitation.

Susan McGuire, M.Ed., NCC, MAC, is President of McGuire Counseling Services of St. Charles, Missouri. She is a specialist working in the area of addictions, with special emphasis on gambling addictions and ex-offender rehabilitation. She is a Licensed Professional Counselor.

Barbara Wolf O'Rourke, Ph.D., RN, LMHC, LP, is an adjunct Assistant Professor with the University of Iowa Graduate Programs in Rehabilitation. Dr. O'Rourke has a Ph.D. in rehabilitation psychology, an M.A. in counseling and human development, and a B.S.N. in nursing, all from the University of Iowa. She is involved in private practice as a rehabilitation psychologist and practiced for many years as a psychiatric nurse. Currently, she is a mental health counseling member of the Iowa Board of Behavioral Science Examiners.

David B. Peterson, Ph.D., CRC, NCC, Licensed Clinical Psychologist, is an Associate Professor in the Institute of Psychology at the Illinois Institute of Technology, Chicago. Dr. Peterson has studied and worked at several graduate programs in rehabilitation counseling and psychology. He completed his Ph.D. in Rehabilitation Psychology at the University of Wisconsin–Madison. He began his academic career at the Graduate Programs in Rehabilitation at the University of Iowa and later served as director of the Graduate Programs in Rehabilitation Counseling at New York University. In addition to a master's degree in deafness rehabilitation counseling, he was also trained and employed as an electronic engineer technician for an aerospace power systems firm. His research interests include computer-based training in clinical problem solving (ethical decision making) and its clinical implementation.

Mark Pope, Ed.D., NCC, MCC, NCCC, MAC, ACS, is a Professor of Counseling in the Division of Counseling and Family Therapy at the University of Missouri–St. Louis. He has served as President of both the American Counseling Association and the National Career Development Association (NCDA). He is a Fellow of the Society of Counseling Psychology, the American Psychological Association, and the National Career Development Association. He has received an NCDA Presidential Recognition Award for his work on innovations in the teaching of career counseling, an NCDA President's Award for his "passionate commitment" to career counseling, and the Robert Swan Lifetime Achievement Award for Career Development. He serves as editor of *The Career Development Quarterly.* He holds licenses in counseling and psychology.

Tarrell Awe Agahe Portman, Ph.D., LMHC, NCC, is an Assistant Professor in the Department of Counseling, Rehabilitation, and Student Development at the University of Iowa. She teaches in the M.A. school counseling program and the Ph.D. Counselor Education program. She is a licensed teacher and K–12 school counselor in Missouri and Iowa. Dr. Portman's research is in the area of multiculturalism, specifically with American Indian women.

Christine Urish, Ph.D., OTR/L, received her Ph.D. in rehabilitation counselor education from the University of Iowa. Dr. Urish has an M.S. in occupational therapy from Western Michigan University and is an Assistant Professor of occupational therapy at St. Ambrose University, Davenport, Iowa.

Jessica L. Walton, B.A., received her bachelor's degree from Loyola University, New Orleans. She is currently a doctoral student in clinical psychology specializing in rehabilitation at the Illinois Institute of Technology. She is currently working as a job coach for the Rehabilitation Institute of Chicago.

Discover the Companion Website Accompanying This Book

THE PRENTICE HALL COMPANION WEBSITE: A VIRTUAL LEARNING ENVIRONMENT

Technology is a constantly growing and changing aspect of our field that is creating a need for content and resources. To address this emerging need, Prentice Hall has developed an online learning environment for students and professors alike—Companion Websites—to support our textbooks.

In creating a Companion Website, our goal is to build on and enhance what the textbook already offers. For this reason, the content for each user-friendly website is organized by chapter and provides the professor and student with a variety of meaningful resources.

Common features of a Companion Website include:

- **Chapter Objectives**—outline key concepts from the text
- **Interactive Self-quizzes**—complete with hints and automatic grading that provide immediate feedback for students. After students submit their answers for the interactive self-quizzes, the Companion Website **Results Reporter** computes a percentage grade, provides a graphic representation of how many questions were answered correctly and incorrectly, and gives a question-by-question analysis of the quiz. Students are given the option to send their quiz to up to four email addresses (professor, teaching assistant, study partner, etc.).
- **Essay Questions**—allow students to respond to themes and objectives of each chapter by applying what they have learned to real classroom situations.
- **Web Destinations**—links to www sites that relate to chapter content

To take advantage of these and other resources, please visit the *Counseling Ethics and Decision Making* Companion Website at

www.prenhall.com/cottone

Contents

CHAPTER 11
Ethics and Multiculturalism   212

PART 5

ETHICAL PRACTICE WITH COUNSELING
SPECIALITIES   227

CHAPTER 12
Couple and Family Counseling   228

CHAPTER 13
School Counseling   241

CHAPTER 14
Mental Health Counseling
and Assessment   268

CHAPTER 15
Career Counseling   283

PART 1

Overview of Ethical, Professional, and Legal Issues in Counseling

CHAPTER 1

Introduction to Ethical Issues and Decision Making in Counseling

OBJECTIVES

After reading this chapter, you should be able to:

- Understand ethical terminology and define an ethical dilemma.
- Distinguish philosophical ethics and morality from professional ethics and morality.
- Distinguish professionally mandated ethics from legally mandated ethical standards.
- Explain the importance of professional organizations, especially those that define and enforce ethical standards.

- Define the terms *licensure* and *accreditation* and identify acceptable certification and accreditation bodies in counseling and psychology.
- Explain the system of ethics governance in counseling.
- Define skills necessary to become a professional decision maker.

INTRODUCTION

Aside from counseling theory, there is probably no other area of study that is more related to the everyday practice of counseling than the area of professional ethics. Counselors are frequently confronted with ethical dilemmas. An **ethical dilemma**[1] is a circumstance that stymies or confuses the counselor because (a) there are competing or conflicting ethical standards that apply, (b) there is a conflict between what is ethical and moral, (c) the situation is such that complexities make application of ethical standards unclear, or (d) some other circumstance prevents a clear application of standards. Counselors who are faced with an ethical dilemma must be alert to ethical and legal standards. They must be educated as to what is considered

acceptable and competent counseling practice. They should be educated about the ethical nuances involved in practice with special populations or in types of specialty practice. They must have a sense of their own morals and how those morals interplay with professional standards. Counselors must know when serious ethical dilemmas arise so that they may make informed and ethical decisions. In day-to-day practice, this means counselors must, from the very beginning of each case, act in a way that is ethically sensitive.

The goal of this textbook is to help you to become ethically sensitive—so that you know when you face a dilemma—and to give you direction on how to handle a dilemma in a professional way. This textbook will expand your knowledge of counseling ethics and illustrate ways to make ethical decisions. Practicing counselors make many decisions throughout any single day

---
[1]Boldfaced terms are defined in the Glossary.

of practice. By studying decision-making processes and models, your decisional power should be enhanced. So, the intent is to give you, the reader, the knowledge to understand professional ethics and the means to make wise professional decisions when faced with an ethical challenge.

Ethical standards are the rules that apply to counseling practice. Ethical standards do not arise in a vacuum. They derive from the judgments of individuals who are members of established and respected professional associations, such as the American Counseling Association (ACA) or the American Psychological Association (APA). These professional associations act much like the guilds of old, representing individuals of related professional interests. Professional organizations not only provide a meeting ground for practitioners, educators, and researchers but also play a political role in advocating for the profession. These organizations must communicate to many audiences that the represented professionals are competent, needed, and guided by standards (e.g., ethical codes) that act to minimize or to prevent harm to the individuals they serve. A profession without enforceable ethical standards is a questionable profession. Therefore, counselors must be alert to political and professional issues in counseling, psychology, and the other mental health professions.

This text focuses on ethical and professional issues in counseling (as a separate profession) and counseling psychology (as a specialty within the profession of psychology). Part I introduces ethical and professional issues, presents definitions and case-related scenarios, and introduces several key legal issues. Part II focuses on values and ethical decision making and presents a review of ethical decision-making models. Two ethical decision-making models are described in detail. Part III introduces issues that arise in work settings: ethical climate in the workplace and administrative practices as they relate to ethical and legal issues. Part IV presents emerging issues and current challenges in the field, including technology issues and those that arise in medical or behavioral health settings. Part V provides detailed and targeted summaries of ethical issues and standards in several of the major specialties of counseling, such as school, marriage and family, rehabilitation, career, addictions, and mental health counseling. Part VI reviews the role of the counselor as an ethical practitioner, including the counselor's duties and responsibilities in ethically compromising circumstances. This text provides the professional counselor with more than a cursory review of ethical issues; its purpose is to instill ethical responsibility through informed practice.

DEFINING ETHICS

The terminology related to ethics is sometimes confusing because the technical definitions used by philosophers and the definitions used by the lay public and mental health professionals do not match perfectly. **Ethics** in philosophy generally refers to theories about what is acceptable behavior. When the term **philosophical ethics** is used, it implies a discussion of theory. Many theories are related to ethics, and the behaviors that are defined as "good" or "right" that derive from one theory may be quite different than those that derive from another theory. For example, Friedrich Nietzsche, a 19th-century German philosopher, developed an ethics theory of *evolutionary naturalism*, wherein right and wrong result from what is naturally selected (following Darwin's theory of evolution). What is "weak" in terms of survival is not valued by a literal interpretation of Nietzsche's (1888/1968a; 1891/1968b) work. In *The Antichrist*, Nietzsche (1888/1968a) stated: "The weak and the failures shall perish. . . . And they shall even be given every possible assistance" (p. 570). Immanuel Kant's (undated, 1949) *categorical imperative* stands in contrast. In his view, the decision maker must consider that the decision may become a universal standard—even applying to the decision maker. Kant's categorical imperative has been trivialized to the golden rule—do unto others as you would have others do unto you. Consider how a person with a serious disability would view these two philosophies. By one philosophy, the disabled person would be viewed as dispensable; by the other philosophy, the person may be viewed as valuable. In some ways, what is good according to Nietzsche's theory is in conflict with Kant's. So what is right or valuable by one theory may not be right or valuable by another theory. Ethical theory ultimately directs interpretation of what is good or bad. These examples demonstrate that *philosophical ethics is theoretical*. The study of philosophical ethics shows that what is defined as a "good act" clearly derives from the theoretical orientation.

In philosophy, the term **morality** stands in contrast to ethics. Morality relates more to the application of ethical principles than to actual specified actions. Johnson (1999) stated:

> Philosophers have generally, for purposes of clarity, confined the usage of the terms *morals* and *morality* to the realm of practice. When they say that someone is morally good, they mean that the actions of that person are praiseworthy. *Ethics* is a term that refers not directly to practice but rather to theory. Philosophers would not

ordinarily say that someone is an ethically good person, but rather a good ethicist, meaning that the person's theories about ethics are worthy of serious consideration. This difference in usage, although generally accepted in philosophical circles, is not followed by people in general. In particular, the terms *ethics* and *ethical* are often used in place of *morality* and *moral*. For instance, we commonly speak of business *ethics* rather than business *morality* and we ask of someone's action "Was that *ethical?*" rather than "*Was that moral?*". (p. 2)

So, in philosophy, when an act is in question, it is a moral question. Whether the act is considered moral depends on the ethical theory that is applied.

Outside of philosophical circles, ethics and morality are intermixed and difficult to distinguish (Johnson, 1999). This is especially true when considering the professional ethics of counselors and psychologists. In fact, the philosophical definitions just described almost seem at odds with the application of these terms in professional ethics. One often hears the term **professional ethics**, meaning that a practitioner is acting according to standards of practice defined as acceptable by the profession. (Remember, actions in philosophy were reserved for *morals*) The term *moral* often implies that a person has a firm philosophical foundation, sometimes based in religious dogma or standards. In common parlance, when one says someone has morals, it means the person is guided by higher principles. So, in common usage, the terms ethics and morals are almost used to mean the opposite of what is acceptable in the academic discipline of philosophy.

For clarity, when this text uses the term ethics as it applies to the discipline of philosophy, the term will be identified as philosophical ethics. In those cases, the discussion will center on ethics as theory (as in the case of Nietzsche or Kant). When the term ethics is used without the qualifier (philosophical), it is used to mean professional ethics. Thus, when the term ethics stands alone, the reference is to professional ethics and the actions of professionals according to standards applied by the profession. When the term morality is used to apply to the discipline of philosophy, it is identified as philosophical morality. When the term morality (or morals) is used without the qualifier (philosophical), it is used to mean morality in the everyday sense. So when the term morals (or morality) stands alone, the reference is to principles or beliefs that guide an individual, sometimes deriving from a religious standard. The definitions, then, are as follows:

- *Philosophical ethics*—the theoretical analysis of what is good, right; or worthy.

- *Professional ethics or ethics*—acceptable or good practice according to agreed-upon rules or standards of practice established by a profession, as in counseling or psychology.
- *Philosophical morality*—assessment of actions of a person against a theory in philosophical ethics. Philosophical morality always refers to an act.
- *Morality*—the principles that guide an individual, sometimes deriving from a religious standard; sometimes referred to as moral principles.

In this text, the terms ethics and morality are addressed more often than are their philosophical alternatives. This is a text on professional ethics and practice, and, although reference is made to philosophical ethics and philosophical morality, the focus is clearly on the applied practice of ethics in counseling and psychology.

To further clarify the use of these terms, consider the following examples. What is ethical (even legal) practice in medicine may be immoral by certain religious standards (e.g., abortion). What is ethical in counseling practice also may be immoral by certain religious standards. For example, a fundamentalist Christian may be faced with a dilemma in counseling gay partners about their sexuality. A Roman Catholic counselor may be uncomfortable providing birth control information to a teenage client. In professional practice in the United States, ethics is separated from morality at the level of professional and legal directives. Consider the situation presented in Box 1–1 to assist in exploring your moral positions. Professional and legal standards tend to correspond to what is ethical. However, individual professionals may choose not to separate the moral from the ethical; for example, some physicians may refuse to perform abortions on moral grounds.

PROFESSIONAL ETHICS VERSUS LEGALLY MANDATED ETHICS

Now that the terms ethics and morals have been clarified, a distinction also must be drawn between what is considered **Professional ethics** and **legally mandated ethics**. In the United States, professionals such as counselors or psychologists are directed and bound by the ethical standards of the professional organizations to which they belong. Most counselors are members of the ACA. Counseling psychologists may have membership in the ACA, the APA, or both. The ACA and the APA are professional organizations that provide a forum for counselors to address their educational,

Box 1–1 • A Clarification-of-Morals Exercise

What are your morals? As part of the self-exploration process that is critical to anticipating how you will handle ethical dilemmas, take a few minutes to define and assess some of your basic moral principles—those principles that guide you broadly in your daily life. Consider also that these moral principles may translate to specific actions as you are faced with difficult choices as a counselor. For example, what is your stand on abortion? Is it guided by a religious standard? Would you counsel someone considering an abortion? Consider another moral issue: the taking of another person's life. What is your moral stance? Is it ever justifiable to take another person's life? If you believe taking a life can be justified, under what circumstances is it justified? Under what conditions would you counsel a client who has taken someone's life in a way that you do not believe is justifiable? Consider sexual relations outside of marriage. Are they acceptable or unacceptable? Does your religion guide you on this matter? Would you "keep the secret" from a spouse while counseling a person who admits, without remorse, to an extramarital sexual relationship? Attempt to define several guiding and absolute principles that influence you in your day-to-day life. What are the foundations of these beliefs? Finally, consider circumstances that would modify your stance.

personal, and professional needs. Both the ACA and the APA have divisions devoted to specialty interests. For example, two divisions of the ACA are the American Rehabilitation Counseling Association (ARCA) and the International Association for Marriage and Family Counseling (IAMFC). Rehabilitation counselors and marriage and family counselors attend the ACA conference and also attend meetings and professional presentations sponsored by their respective specialty groups. The APA is similar—divisions of the association (e.g., counseling psychology, rehabilitation psychology, or family psychology) organize activities and presentations for the national APA conference. The ACA and APA also make malpractice and other types of personal insurance available to members. Additionally, the ACA and the APA have established professional standards through committees that oversee ethical rules (including disciplinary procedures) and practice.

The ACA and APA codes of ethics direct members who are faced with an ethical concern or ethical dilemma (see Appendix A and B). Such a circumstance requires a professional to decide if an action is right or wrong (before or at the time of the act) when competing or mutually exclusive ethical, moral, or legal standards are involved. (Recall the definition of an ethical dilemma discussed in the first paragraph of this chapter.) It is possible that competing standards of right and wrong may be at the root of ethical dilemma. The ACA and APA codes of ethics are professional ethical standards.

Counselors who are licensed to practice counseling by one of the licensing states (48 of the 50 states in the United States as of this writing) and psychologists licensed to practice psychology (in all 50 states) are also directed by the ethical code referenced in the relevant state's licensure statute. In fact, one of the main reasons for the licensure of professions is to protect the public from unqualified or unethical practitioners. Counselors or counseling psychologists who act unethically, as judged by a licensure authority according to the authority's accepted standards, are subject to penalties as severe as suspension or revocation of a professional license. **Licensure** allows a person to practice a profession and prevents the practice of a profession by those who are unlicensed (Anderson, 1996; Dorken, 1976). **Revocation** of a license, therefore, is a loss of the right to practice in the state's jurisdiction. **Suspension** of a license is a temporary loss of the right to practice the profession within the jurisdiction. Licenses are not easy to attain. To be licensed as a professional counselor in most states requires a master's degree with one or more years of supervised professional (postdegree) practice; licensure candidates must also pass a stringent examination. The standards in psychology are similar, except a doctoral degree is almost always required. Consequently, the prospect of losing a professional license means the loss of livelihood. Whereas a breach of the code of ethics of a professional organization (such as the ACA or APA) can result in professional censure or even loss of membership, the breach of an ethical standard required by regulatory law (legally mandated) may result in the loss of a license to practice or other legal penalty. The distinction, therefore, between professional and legally mandated ethical standards is a crucial one.

In some cases, state licensure statutes or regulations simply reference the professional association's code of ethics. Most states develop their own standards, but ethical standards in licensure statutes are usually similar to (or based in large part on) those of the professional association. In counseling, the American Association of State Counseling Boards (AASCB) provides guidance to individual state licensure boards on matters related to ethical standards and enforcement. Members of the AASCB are representatives from state licensure boards. In other words, it is the professional association for the state licensure boards and the members of those boards. This organization works to enhance the consistency of standards in licensing counselors among all states. It also addresses issues of **reciprocity** of licensure, or what is called **portability** (Altekruse, 2001). Licensing reciprocity is a process whereby a licensed counselor's credentials in one state are recognized by another state for licensure purposes without additional imposed requirements. In psychology, the Association for State and Provincial Psychology Boards (ASPPB), a group made up of state psychology licensing board representatives, has its own code of ethics. (See Sinclair [2004] for a comparison of the ASPPB code of conduct and the APA and Canadian Psychological Association codes of ethics.) The ASPPB has also set up a credential bank

for individuals who meet quality licensure standards to facilitate reciprocity between states—the Certificate of Professional Qualification (CPQ) in psychology. The CPQ is accepted by many states as a credential that meets licensure standards. These important license-related organizations establish the ethical and professional training standards required to be admitted and retained in the professions.

Counselors need to know both the professional and legal ethical standards that direct their practices. Professionals are obligated to know these standards beyond the knowledge gained by a cursory reading of a code. Counselors should commit to memory the general principles that operate in ethical practice, and they should regularly discuss with other counselors or psychologists how such principles apply to professional practice. (See Box 1–2 for a statement made by a counselor who volunteered to share his own experience related to a serious breach of professional ethics.) Chapter 3 will be helpful in describing ethical standards because it provides a summary of ethical issues and describes broad ethical principles and associated ethical standards. Chapter 3 provides case scenarios with practice-relevant contexts for understanding these standards. Chapter 4 contains a summary of crucial legal issues.

Box 1–2 • Ethical Errors: Serious and Painful—A Letter From a Counselor Accused of Serious Ethical Misconduct

I remember the day all too well. It was the worst day of my professional life. "My God! What have I done?" Panic surged through my body. My mind raced with worry on the day my boss confronted me with my worst nightmare. He informed me that a former client of mine had accused me of the most serious of ethical violations. Specifically, I was being accused of having a harmful non-professional relationship with this client—a sexual relationship. My boss had tears in his eyes as if he was saying, "Please tell me it isn't true." But, I could not deny the truth. I had been denying the truth for 10 months. It was time to come clean and try to salvage what little integrity I had left. This is my story. It is serious and extraordinarily painful. I hurt many people. My behavior was completely irresponsible. I have lived through it, and I keep what I did in front of me as a teaching tool. I can never forget what I did, or I may become vulnerable again. It doesn't really matter what is known intellectually about ethical errors. Anyone can read and understand that there are certain things that must not be done, and there are many gray areas as well. But what happens

when the human, vulnerable side surfaces? What happens when buttons get pushed and countertransference issues arise? I hope what happens is that the truth is faced, that a boss or trusted colleague is consulted, or that personal counseling is undertaken. I didn't face the truth. As a result, I had to talk to a lawyer, to an ethics committee, and to my insurance company. I lost my job, my license, and lots of money. This was certainly an expensive lesson. What I did was wrong. My punishment was deserved.

What I gained from this ordeal was something very important: I gained myself. I'm sure most students of counseling and most practicing professionals have heard the many reasons why people pursue counseling professionally, including meeting one's own personal needs. This was certainly true for me. My need was to be needed. Therefore, I've been vulnerable to needy clients. When clients were hurting, I wanted to rescue and take care of them. I knew this prior to acting out, but I didn't know how strong this need was and how I could lose myself and my professional boundaries.

Box 1–2 • Ethical Errors: Serious and Painful—A Letter From a Counselor Accused of Serious Ethical Misconduct—*continued*

One of the many ironies is that I could see what was happening. I remember reviewing the ethical guidelines concerning romantic and sexual relationships. I even informed my spouse that I was attracted to a client prior to acting out. But I was blinded by needs. I needed help but was ashamed to ask for it. My denial took over and deception began. I held this shameful secret inside. My strong word of caution: Don't keep secrets. Secrets have powerful and destructive energy.

All counselors will be faced with ethical dilemmas throughout their careers. There are no simple answers and no complete guidebook to inform you about how to respond to the many difficult and ambiguous situations. Experience is a great teacher, but it cannot help with every possible concern. Furthermore, experience often teaches the hard way, by giving the test first, followed by the lesson.

There is little guidance to help those who have been cited for ethical misconduct or legal wrongdoing. A legal specialist for psychologists and counselors informed me that approximately 50% of mental health professionals will face some ethical or legal hardship during the course of their careers. How does one prepare for this behaviorally and emotionally? It is all too easy to say, "Just don't make any ethical mistakes." This statement is unrealistic and naive. Like shadows, mistakes lurk in the darkness and catch a person off guard, when one is most vulnerable.

If for some reason you are accused of some wrongdoing, whether you are guilty or not, it will most likely shock your system. Be prepared for an emotional roller coaster. Get help, but be cautious. Get a lawyer if necessary; inform your insurance company if your lawyer recommends that you do so (make sure you carry insurance); and be careful about what you tell friends, family, and colleagues. By all means, talk to a therapist if you are personally struggling.

I experienced a plethora of emotions. That dear old question, "How did it make you feel?" certainly became real for me. I was angry at my client, at first, for turning me in; after all, my client was a willing participant who encouraged my involvement. My denial was still strong for the only person I should have been angry at—myself. A client places a counselor in an authority position whether welcomed or not. I abused my position. I should have been angry at myself for allowing this to happen.

Once I was able to accept complete responsibility for what I did, I could begin to grieve. These were extraordinarily tough days. I had to endure many losses. I experienced many days of depression. For months I was completely ashamed of myself as a human being and could not imagine ever counseling again. Eventually, I realized that although I did a terrible thing, I was not a terrible person. I was a counselor who let personal issues get in the way of my professional responsibilities. Today I am very remorseful for what I did, and I am fortunate that I received a great deal of support when I began to tell the truth.

Not all people forgave me for what I did, and I understand this. I am very sorry for my behavior and I wish I could make amends to all those who suffered. I have developed many resources to help me personally, especially when I'm feeling stressed and overwhelmed, and I use my resources rather than just talk about them. I encourage all counselors to do the same. My resources are personal therapy, a 12-step program, my spouse, and a personal accountability program. It is very easy for counselors to talk and to listen, but more difficult for them to do their own personal work. Frankly, I believe that many counselors are compulsive about their jobs while neglecting themselves personally. Regardless, counselors owe it to their clients, to their profession, to their families, and most of all to themselves to take care of themselves.

Well, that is my story. I wouldn't wish it upon anyone. I have to live with myself every day knowing what I did. Sometimes it is very difficult and painful for me. But it is important for me to keep my pain and my story in front of me. I need to remind myself of what I did so I can prevent myself from ever doing it again. Mistakes are best prevented by taking an honest accounting of one's life and one's situation. Be alert to "red flags," and consult supervisors, colleagues, friends, or a therapist if personal needs begin to blind you to your professional responsibilities.

I wish you well on your journey.

ETHICS GOVERNANCE[2]

Some means to govern ethical practice are necessary to give meaning to professional standards and to enhance the societal stature of the profession. Because counselors are professionals and have professional responsibility, they are subject to discipline if they breach ethical standards. The process of ethical governance is intimately linked to the process of professional discipline. If counselors do not practice within the proscribed standards, ethical governance processes may be engaged to discipline them. Ethical standards of practice can be thought of as being either **mandatory**

[2]This section was adapted from "Ethics" by Vilia Tarvydas in D. R. Maki & T. F. Riggar (Eds.) (2004). *Handbook of Rehabilitation Counseling.* Copyright 2004 by Springer Publishing Co. Used by permission of Springer Publishing Company, Inc., New York, 10012.

or **aspirational** in the level of direction they provide the practitioner (Corey, Corey, & Callanan, 2003). The most basic level of ethical functioning is guided by mandatory ethics, wherein individuals focus on compliance with the law and the dictates of the professional codes of ethics that apply to their practice. At this level, counselors are concerned with remaining safe from legal action and professional censure. At the more ethically sophisticated level, the aspirational level, individuals additionally reflect on the effects of the situation on the welfare of their clients and the effects of their actions on the profession as a whole.

These same concepts of mandatory and aspirational ethics can be applied to counseling's standards of practice. It is important to reiterate that specific codes of ethics are binding only on persons who hold that particular credential or membership. If a credential holder or a member of a professional group violates an applicable code of ethics, the organization has the responsibility to provide a disciplinary procedure to enforce its standards. In the case of a professional association, the ultimate sanction would typically be loss of membership, with possible referral of the findings of an ethics committee to other professional or legal jurisdictions. This referral may be accomplished by providing information to ASPPB for dissemination to member psychology licensing boards. For a credentialing body such as the National Board of Certified Counselors (NBCC), the largest certifying body for professional counselors, or for a counselor licensure board in one of the licensing states, violators could face the more serious option of certificate or license revocation, thus possibly removing their ability to practice. Less serious levels of sanction, such as a reprimand or a period of probation, are also utilized. In the case of a reprimand or probation, there is often an additional requirement for educational or rehabilitative remedies, meaning the sanctioned counselor might be required to take an educational course on ethics, treat an addiction, be further supervised in practice, or follow other remedies to assist in regaining an appropriate level of functioning ethically or personally. The assessment of the level of seriousness of the ethical violation will affect the actual choice of sanction once an individual is found to be in violation of the code of ethics. Factors often considered include whether the act was intentional, the degree of risk or actual harm to the client, the motivation or ability of the violator to change, and the recidivism of the violator (Koocher & Keith-Spiegel, 1998).

Responsible practitioners supplement the mandatory level of ethics awareness with advanced knowledge of the scholarly literature on accepted ethical practice. They also consult colleagues who may have experience addressing challenging ethical circumstances and who are respected in the community as ethically wise practitioners. In addition, they may gain guidance from other codes of ethics and specialty guidelines. Sophisticated practitioners will seek these sources to supplement the required mandatory ethical standards with the more aspirational principles. In fact, for certain situations, the course of action suggested by the aspirational guidelines may contradict or exceed those required by mandatory standards. Such situations create stressful ethical dilemmas and place practitioners in need of means to reconcile them responsibly (see Chapter 6 for further guidance on making ethical decisions when involved in ethical dilemmas).

There are several levels of ethics governance for counselors, and various organizations are involved at different levels. These organizations, taken as a whole, constitute an interconnected network that performs a diversity of functions. Each entity plays a role in the creation of a system of ethics governance.

Colleges and universities provide professional education and research services. Professional programs at universities or colleges in counseling or psychology usually operate under the review of professional accrediting organizations. **Accreditation** allows for clear recognition of a program (its nature, intent, and quality). The accreditation review process is a means to certify that the school program meets standards set by the accrediting body. **Professional accreditation** is the process whereby a college or university professional program (e.g., counseling or psychology) voluntarily undergoes review by an accrediting body, such as the Council on Rehabilitation Education (CORE), the Commission on the Accreditation of Counseling and Related Educational Programs (CACREP), or the APA (2000). CORE, CACREP, and the APA are **professional accrediting bodies** that evaluate graduate education programs in rehabilitation counseling, counseling, and counseling psychology, respectively. Professional accrediting bodies essentially qualify educational programs as meeting standards beyond those required of colleges or universities to offer degrees; they certify that the educational institution meets these high professional standards. Professional accrediting bodies have the broadest function to provide aspirational educational guidance in ethics. They help to establish the structural foundation for ethical governance. Additionally, they help to build the theoretical and research base for understanding ethical issues, decision-making processes, and ethical educational methods. These aspects of the aspirational knowledge base are needed to support ethical development of a profession. Colleges and universities also ensure that proper preservice education and professional socialization occur to inculcate future practitioners and educators with the proper ethics base. Educators play an important part in role modeling and supporting ethical analysis and ethical behavior in teaching, supervision, and actual clinical practice. Educational institutions also serve as a resource to other professional organizations and regulatory bodies to provide teaching, research, and service that support aspirational and mandatory ethical practice.

The next level consists of the professional organizations with aspirational codes of ethics but with no internal mandatory enforcement mechanisms. The IAMFC and the Association for Specialists in Group Work (ASGW), as divisions of the ACA, are examples. For such organizations, the primary task is to encourage aspirational ethical practice of their members and the application of ethical standards in specific specialty contexts. Mandatory enforcement is not undertaken by such professional organizations due to factors such as lack of (a) appropriate consumer access and protection in the disciplinary process, (b) appropriate remedies for serious infractions, and (c) substantial financial, staff, and professional resources necessary for responsible enforcement. In some cases, the mandatory enforcement function of the organization is referred to a parent organization (e.g., to ACA in the case of the IAMFC or the ASGW) or the complainant is referred to another appropriate jurisdiction (e.g., a state licensure board) to initiate a disciplinary process.

Nonetheless, professional organizations with aspirational codes perform several significant functions within the ethics governance structure. They typically provide their members with supplemental codes of ethics that extend and illuminate other, more general codes. Such documents provide guidelines for ethical practice for particular, frequently encountered ethical issues or professional activities. For couple and family counselors such issues might be (a) confidentiality issues when more than one person is seen in counseling, (b) different modes of service delivery, (c) value issues, such as handling discussion of divorce or dissolution of a marriage, and (d) the responsibility to relationships rather than one individual in counseling. A supplemental code may take the form of guidelines for practice that address specialty setting or function-specific issues, as is done by the IAMFC. The IAMFC (2005) has an aspirational ethics code, which gives guidance to couple and family counselors. In addition

to maintaining supplementary, specialty ethical standards or guidelines, some professional organizations at the aspirational level collect information regarding ethical trends and needs for revision of either the specialty or generalist ethics codes. Their leaders also participate in revision and writing of both types of codes. These organizations identify and supply qualified professionals to serve on the various mandatory enforcement bodies. They provide educational programs to extend the knowledge base and to define better quality ethical practice, performing significant educational and socialization functions. A new and innovative role for these organizations, one that is potentially most meaningful, is identifying or providing remediation or rehabilitation programs for impaired professionals who have been found in violation (or are at risk for violation) of ethical standards.

At the third level of ethical governance are professional organizations that maintain and enforce a mandatory code of ethics (such as the ACA or the APA). These organizations provide an entry-level mandatory code and enforcement process for their members and, in the case of the ACA, enforce the standards or guidelines of division (specialty or special interest groups). Organizations at this level consult with certification and licensing bodies and the specialty professional organizations to ensure active participation of all parties in ethics enforcement. They also provide educational programs to increase practitioner knowledge.

The next level of ethics governance includes professional regulatory bodies that either certify or license professionals and those that constitute the preeminent enforcers of a mandatory code. National certification bodies, such as the NBCC and Commission on Rehabilitation Counselor Certification (CRCC), as well as state counselor and psychology licensure boards, operate at this level. They perform a pivotal role in the promulgation and enforcement of ethical standards. They do not develop completely novel internal standards; rather, they draw their specific codes of ethical standards from the organizations that constitute the professional body or their constituent counseling communities and then regulate based on the profession's own internal standards. They also may provide information and consultation to professional organizations in revising and maintaining current codes of ethics. Beyond their ethical regulatory function, these bodies encourage ethical proficiency of their licensees and certificate holders by requiring graduate degree program education and continuing (postgraduate) education, often in the area of ethics. (See Box 1–3.)

Box 1–3 • Ethics Governance and One State's Standard

To consider ethics governance related to mandatory licensure standards, consider a State of Missouri dictate that addresses sexual intimacies with clients. The ethics code referenced in the rules and regulations of the Missouri State Committee for Professional Counselors has a stipulation that bans "sexual intimacies" with clients. The standard, however, defines "sexual intimacies" very broadly, including sexual intercourse and sodomy, of course, but also including "hugging or caressing by either the licensed professional counselor or the client" or "touching" a person's "legs, stomach, chest, breasts, genitals or buttocks." Has the Missouri dictate gone too far, or is it right on target? If a counselor touches someone's knee, should that be considered unethical? How about a hug abruptly initiated by a client leaving the office—is that unethical? How about a counselor hugging a distressed child in a school context? Remember, this is a mandatory standard, and a person's license is at risk if there is a breach of ethical standards.

The courts are at the pinnacle of the ethics governance hierarchy. One of the primary mechanisms for this type of governance is adjudication of **malpractice** in the civil courts. In malpractice actions, establishing a violation of duty is one of the central points. The standard for determining what constitutes good professional practice, as applied to the matter at hand, is required. Good professional practice is sometimes hard to define and requires many types of considerations. It is not unusual to call various expert witnesses to testify regarding such practices. Additionally, one party to the action might attempt to establish that a blatant violation of the general rules of the profession occurred by reference to the profession's ethical standards (Thompson, 1990).

Another standard of practice applied in court may be consideration of whether the action or service in question was within the **scope of practice** of both the profession and the individual, the extent and limits of activities considered acceptable by individuals licensed or certified in a profession or specialty. Licensed counselors or psychologists in many states are governed by the scope of practice described in state statutes, and licensees may be required to declare their personal scopes of practice at the time they are licensed or when renewing a license (e.g., marriage and family counseling or counseling psychology). Practitioners are ethically bound to limit their own scope of practice to areas within those of the profession and in specialties within which they have obtained appropriate training and supervision. They must be able to demonstrate that they are competent to practice by virtue of appropriate education, supervision, and professional experience.

This five-level professional governance structure constitutes a network of mandatory and aspirational ethics. An interactive system of research, education, and enforcement shapes and regulates the ethical practice of counselors. This structure provides a system of knowledge, traditions, rules, and laws but does not provide practitioners with possibly the most crucial tool for ethical practice—knowledge and experience in applying their ethical decisions.

Although professionals may sometimes become caught up in the technicalities of ethics governance, it is important to keep in mind that preventing harm to others and benefiting them through a professional relationship is what professional ethics is all about. Lest readers lose sight of the powerful influence they have on people's lives, it is crucial to keep the client's welfare in mind. Box 1–4 is a statement by a former client of a psychologist who breached the detrimental relationship ban of his profession. The statement was volunteered by the victim and is published with her full permission. It is disguised to prevent identification but is a true account of her feelings through the process of her personal relationship with the psychologist.

DECISION-MAKING SKILLS

Professional counselors are highly educated professionals who have advanced college degrees. Decision making is a very important part of professionalism. Highly trained professionals are decision makers. Unlike individuals employed in the trades or unskilled labor, skilled professionals must develop, hone, and apply decision-making skills.

In practice, counselors face life-relevant situations, and each decision must be made in a way that will maximize the benefit to clients while minimizing potential harm. In effect, counselors must be viewed as intellectuals—individuals who apply higher level knowledge to solve complex human problems. At the foundation of decision making is an intellectual attitude. Counselors must believe that they can make

Box 1–4 • A Client's Story

For about a year, I sat "in the chair," trying to understand what had brought me to therapy. Across from me sat my therapist, my confidant, my partner in piecing together the puzzle that had become my life. I began by explaining that I was hurting inside because of the young woman I had become. I felt angry, defensive, alone. I had detached myself from all those who were dear to me, except for my family. They, however, were kept at arm's length. My temper had become short and my list of reasons for not going out with my friends had become long. I was confused by these changes in myself because I was unable to identify the source. I was sad about the changes because I did not like living such a negative, unpeopled existence. This existence was nothing like what I had lived the previous 22 years.

The day I realized why I was "in the chair" remains etched vividly in my mind. With bowed head and long curls hiding my face, I choked out the words with humiliation, shame, fear, and pain: I was raped. I told the therapist the story from the beginning—a story that began as one of friendship, laughter, and fun. Then I recounted how suddenly, without warning, the man I had chosen to call friend turned into someone I no longer knew. I told of the day he hovered above my head with eyes full of hate as he spoke with venom and how, because of shock and fear, I could not move. He hurt me with his body and he hurt me with his words. I described how it seemed like hours later that he dropped me off in front of my apartment. It was at that time that he grabbed the back of my head once again, pressed his mouth angrily onto mine, and told me he'd like to do that again sometime—that it was fun.

The pain I went through by finally acknowledging the rape was deep. Making sense of how it had affected my life forced me to open myself up to feel all that the experience was for me. I told the therapist that I felt robbed. I was robbed of my virginity and robbed of my innocence. Perhaps most critical, however, was that I felt I was robbed of my confidence. I felt I could no longer judge who or what was safe. This rapist had been my friend for months. I had gone willingly to his apartment. I completely trusted the boundary I felt existed between us. Then he raped me. Then he acted like it wasn't rape. Instead, he acted as if I had an equal role in creating what had happened.

My sense of industry and self-power were badly shaken. I trudged through it all with the therapist. He was the only one who knew my secret and as such, I funneled my only bit of trust into the therapeutic relationship. As I worked through the details of the rape, I began focusing on self and my interaction with others. In an attempt to learn to trust again, but this time with wisdom, I opened my life completely to the therapist. I chiseled away at the walls that I had built as a means of protection.

After several years of being in and out of therapy with this man, in one session, he said he'd like to have a beer with me. At this point, I trusted him implicitly. He had validated my feelings through the therapeutic relationship and I felt very connected to him. I agreed to have a beer with him. A decision could not be made as to where we would go that next week, so he suggested we just meet in his office. The following week, he brought a six-pack of beer and I sat "in the chair." I remember feeling drawn to him on some level. I think the connection was so strong for me because of the work we had done together in therapy. He had become the only man I trusted aside from those in my family. On another level, I knew it was wrong for me to have a beer with my therapist. I also felt it was wrong for me to feel an attraction to him.

I continued seeing him therapeutically after that, but there was no more alcohol involved. After several months, I terminated the therapeutic relationship for good. I felt I was ready to build healthy relationships without being too fearful of making a decision that was unsafe or wrong for me.

Several years later, I wrote my then ex-therapist a note explaining my marriage was ending. After getting the note, my ex-therapist called and asked me to have a beer with him. Again, the decision was made to meet at his office. Again, he brought the beer. Again, I sat "in the chair." After catching up for several hours, it was time to go. We stood up and hugged one another, which we had never done before. After a few minutes, he looked down on me and kissed me. The embrace became very sexual very quickly. As his hands moved to places previously associated with pain, I was not sure how to respond. I was certainly shocked and a little scared that he was touching me in this way. I kept my arms around his waist, not touching him in a sexual way. In addition to feeling shocked and a bit scared, because of my past, I also wanted so desperately for someone I trusted to touch me in a loving way that was full of care and tenderness. Based upon the words he whispered in my ear, it seemed he wanted to show me what tender, loving touch was like. I did not stop him from touching me. I was a willing participant, but also felt uneasy for I knew it was wrong for both of us to be doing.

I could not sleep that night. I was so full of self-condemnation—it horrified me to consider what my loved ones would think if they knew I had engaged in this type of relationship with my ex-therapist. For days afterward,

continued

Box 1–4 • A Client's Story—*continued*

when it entered my mind, a chill ran through my body. I was shocked that it had even happened.

After a few weeks, he called again. This time, he would come to my apartment. His visits became weekly. By this time, we were in a mutually sexual relationship. I could hardly fathom the fact that my ex-therapist and I were touching one another in a sexual way. It seemed the more he needed to be with me, the less comfortable I felt with what was happening. It seemed strange inside to think that the person I had needed for so long in therapy could somehow need something from me.

Several times, I expressed my difficulty with the situation and that I felt it wasn't right. His response at those times was related to us both being adults and it said implicitly that we were making the choice to be there with one another. As his comfort level began to increase as the relationship wore on, he began to speak his mind and act more freely. My unease became increasingly worse. Eventually, there were times when he touched me in a way that was painful, and he spoke to me in language that was crude. None of this felt loving. When I continued to bring up my uneasiness, he continued to tell me that we were adults. At this point, he was clearly no longer validating my experience. It was as if I was not allowed to discuss this with him. The power differential was still present, despite the fact that the therapeutic relationship had ended. I couldn't help but feel that if I had received these types of responses from a man other than my ex-therapist, my response or action would have been much different.

I finally recognized the physical and emotional pain I was in due to this relationship. I ended my involvement with my ex-therapist and was overwhelmed by the fallout. I felt angry, defensive, alone. I had detached myself from other individuals who were dear to me. I was ashamed, humiliated, full of guilt, and full of pain. Perhaps most importantly, however, was that my sense of being able to judge who or what was safe for myself was shaken. This man had been my therapist. I had trusted him for years. I completely trusted the boundary I thought existed between us. In this case, it was a trust that I was safe from harm with him. I don't think he intended to hurt me, but

his involvement with me reinjured me related to my original therapeutic issues.

The torment I have put myself through for getting involved with my ex-therapist is enormous. The anger I felt once I understood the clearly existing power differential has left me feeling victimized to some degree. Even as I was ending the relationship, I felt unable to share the full range of my feelings and the impact the relationship had on me and my life. It was as if I could not talk to him in that way because of who he was.

I am not comfortable simply labeling myself as a victim in this incident. I engaged in the relationship willingly. However, as my ex-therapist, he was well aware of my need for loving, physical touch. He was well aware of my fear of trusting men, as well as trusting myself to make good choices about men. I am being honest in saying I feel that a seduction occurred. The very issues that brought me to therapy were those that he sought to fill through a physical relationship with me. Despite my willingness to become involved with this man, he had an ethical responsibility to keep it from happening, whether he was attracted to me or not. The legal ethical guidelines for psychologists in his state ban sexual intimacies with former clients for 5 years. Our relationship occurred well within 5 years of our last official therapeutic contact.

In my opinion, this type of relationship should never occur between a previous client and therapist, regardless of the elapsed time. The therapist potentially knows everything about the client—strengths and vulnerabilities. The difference in power exists long after the therapeutic relationship ends. Although my ex-therapist suggested that I had an equal role in the choice to get involved by saying we were both adults, I now believe the responsibility weighs more heavily on his shoulders, as the professional.

So I write this story now—a story that began as one of trust, professionalism, and growth. Then, the man I had called "confidant" and "therapist" turned into someone I no longer knew. He became a lover. He hurt me with his words and he hurt me with his body. Together, we shattered what had become whole in me. I am on a new path to putting the pieces back together, but I am no longer "in the chair."

---

educated and informed decisions in a systematic and deliberate way.

To make wise decisions, counselors must have information available to them. They must have research skills to be able to define the critical issues and to search

for up-to-date information related to the decision to be made. That is why professional organizations typically publish journals—so that practitioners have current information on contemporary approaches to practice. Counseling journals are a source of information about what is currently accepted as ethical practice, and oftentimes counseling journals have sections that specifically address ethical issues and how dilemmas should be best approached by practicing professionals.

Counselors must also have a framework for making ethical decisions. One of the themes of this book is that decision making and daily practice go hand in hand. Competent professionals are competent decision makers. One must always consider that a professional decision can be challenged, and, as a professional, one must always be able to defend a decision. If an accepted decision-making model is used and a counselor can demonstrate adherence to an accepted decision-making process, then it becomes much easier to defend the decision. On the other hand, hodgepodge practice, practice without a framework or theory to guide decisions, is indefensible. Counselors should embrace a well-respected decision-making model, and they should use the model regularly until it becomes routine. Decision-making models can become habitual and effortless—you commit a decision-making process to memory. In this way, practicing an acceptable decision-making model becomes second nature.

Counselors also must be invested in their profession. This means they respect the profession to the degree they associate with other counselors through professional organizations. They, in other words, must embrace professionalism and work for the benefit of their clients and the profession. This means accepting, to large degree, the ethical dictates of the profession. Not all ethical standards may be viewed as fair—there may be some standards that are ill-conceived or out of date. But counselors must be willing to adhere to the ethical standards of the profession, and when standards need to be changed, they need to become politically active in facilitating the change. This is what is meant by embracing professionalism. Professional status is an honor, but it is also a responsibility.

CHAPTER SUMMARY

Knowledge of professional ethics is crucial to the everyday practice of counseling. Counselors who are faced with an ethical dilemma must be alert to ethical and legal standards. Professional organizations provide standards and codes that guide mental health professionals.

Philosophical ethics is the theoretical analysis of what is good, right, or worthy. Professional ethics is acceptable or good practice according to agreed-on rules or standards of practice established by a profession. Philosophical morality is the assessment of actions of a person against a theory in philosophical ethics and always refers to an act. Morality refers to the principles that guide an individual and often derive from a religious standard.

Licensure allows a person to practice a profession and prevents the practice of a profession by those who are unlicensed. Licenses can be revoked or suspended for violation of codes of ethics.

A five-level professional structure governs ethics for counselors: (1) colleges and universities; (2) professional organizations with aspirational codes of ethics but without internal enforcement mechanisms; (3) professional organizations that maintain and enforce a mandatory code of ethics; (4) professional regulatory bodies that are enforcers of mandatory codes; and (5) the courts.

Finally, decision making is a cornerstone of professionalism. Counselors must be viewed, and must view themselves, as intellectuals—highly educated problem solvers. They must have a higher level understanding of the complexities involved in solving human problems. They must seek out current information related to practical dilemmas that arise. They must be guided by decision-making models that become habitual and ingrained in their daily practice. They must also invest in their profession and be actively engaged in professional activities that better the profession and those served by the profession.

REFERENCES

Altekruse, M. K. (2001). *Counselor portability*. Presentation made to the American Association of State Counseling Boards. (Available from Dr. Altekruse at NTU, P.O. Box 311337, Denton, TX 76203-1337.)

American Counseling Association (2005). *Code of Ethics*. Alexandria, VA: Author.

American Psychological Association, Office of Program Consultation and Accreditation. (2000). *Guidelines and principles for accreditation of programs in professional psychology (Amendments effective January 1, 2000)*. Washington, DC: Author. (Available on-line at http://www.apa.org/ed/gp2000.html)

American Psychological Association (2002). Ethical principles of psychologists and code of conduct. *American Psychologist, 51,* 1060–1073.

Anderson, B. S. (1996). *The counselor and the law* (4th ed.). Alexandria, VA: American Counseling Association.

Corey, G., Corey, M. S., & Callanan, P. (2003). *Issues and ethics in the helping professions* (6th ed.). Pacific Grove, CA: Brooks/Cole.

Dorken, H. (1976). *The professional psychologist.* San Francisco: Jossey-Bass.

International Association of Marriage and Family Counselors. (2005). Ethical code for the International Association of Marriage and Family Counselors. Retrieved 10/18/05 from http://www.iamfc.com/ethical_codes.html

Johnson, O. A. (1999). *Ethics: Selections from classical and contemporary writers.* Fort Worth, TX: Harcourt Brace.

Kant, I. (undated, 1949). *Critique of practical reason and other writings in moral philosophy* (L. W. Beck, Trans.). Chicago: University of Chicago Press.

Koocher, G. P., & Keith-Spiegel, P. (1998). *Ethics in psychology* (2nd ed.). New York: Oxford University Press.

Nietzsche, F. (1968a). The Antichrist. In W. Kaufmann (Ed. & Trans.), *The portable Nietzsche* (pp. 565–656). New York: Penguin. (Original work written in 1888).

Nietzsche, F. (1968b). Thus spake Zarathustra. In W. Kaufmann (Ed. & Trans.), *The portable Nietzsche* (pp. 565–656). New York: Penguin. (Original work written in 1891).

Sinclair, C. (2004). *Code comparisons: The Canadian Code of Ethics for Psychologists compared with the APA and ASPPB codes.* Canadian Psychological Association. Retrieved from http://www.cpa.ca/documents/Code_Comparison.pdf

Thompson, A. (1990). *Guide to ethical practice in psychotherapy.* New York: Wiley.

CHAPTER 2

Counseling and the Mental Health Professions

OBJECTIVES

After reading this chapter, you should be able to:

- Provide a brief history of the counseling profession.
- Distinguish counseling from counseling psychology.
- Summarize education requirements, postdegree training, licensure, certification, and scope of practice for the mental health professions.

INTRODUCTION

Membership in a profession offers an individual status and responsibility. Law and medicine, both considered models of professionalism, are founded on a body of knowledge, technique, and practice. They are grounded in academic studies, have a scholarly base, and provide guidance to practitioners in the form of ethical and moral standards (e.g., medicine's Hippocratic oath). They allow practitioners several avenues of practice, even independent or freestanding practice. Over time, both psychology and counseling have become established as independent professions, technically on par with established professions such as medicine and law. To present oneself as a counselor or psychologist means that the individual has accomplished much—graduate education, postgraduate training, admission to the profession by competitive examination, and linkage to a professional community with strict ethical standards. There is pride in such accomplishment.

Today, counseling and psychology are not alone in the mental health enterprise. There are a number of competitive mental health professions, each with its own history and traditions. It is important for any practicing mental health professional to be alert to the mental health professions and the standards of each.

Medicine's specialty of psychiatry is the oldest established mental health profession. The youngest, in terms of pervasive legislative support, is marriage and family therapy. Social work and psychiatric nursing are two other mental health professions. Professionals with these affiliations make up the core of mental health providers.

In the mental health service arena, the core mental health professions both compete and cooperate. In all types of practice, it is likely that counselors will work with other mental health professions in the best interest of their clients. For example, many clients served by counselors in private practice may receive medication from a physician (either a primary care provider or a psychiatrist). It is crucial for independently practicing counselors to have working relationships with the prescribing physician. Many managed care organizations require nonphysician providers to have established cooperative service arrangements with board certified psychiatrists. Counselors working in agencies often work with a team of professionals assigned to the care of individual clients. Team members need to be alert to the limits of practice of other professionals. They also need to know the specialized skills associated with professional affiliation. It is unlikely that counselors will be involved in cases in which they are the only provider of mental health services.

COUNSELING AND COUNSELING PSYCHOLOGY

Counseling and counseling psychology were once considered sister occupations. They developed side by side as advances occurred in measurement and assessment, counseling theory, and mental health services. Counseling emerged from (and is still deeply embedded in) the educational setting, whereas psychology emerged as an academic discipline with applications in mental health settings. The first psychological clinic was founded in 1896 at the University of Pennsylvania (Fowler, 1996). Psychology's professional development preceded counseling by approximately 20 or 30 years, especially as related to licensure and independent mental health practice. The psychology specialty of counseling psychology is a bridge that spans the two professions; counseling psychology also acts as a boundary marker between them. If there is any doubt that the professions of counseling and psychology overlap in regard to activities and scope of practice, counseling psychology acts as a symbol of their similarity. On the other hand, if there are any doubts that the former sister occupations have emerged as discrete and competitive mental health professions, licensure standards of the two groups stand as distinguishing criteria. For example, Heppner, Casas, Carter, and Stone (2000), reported on a personal communication with Norm Gysbers, former president of what is now the ACA, about actions that caused some divergence of the ACA and APA on matters that would be relevant to counseling psychology; they stated:

> Norm Gysbers noted that a major shift occurred between the two organizations as third-party payments became more prevalent in the early 1980s, which placed increasing emphasis on accreditation and licensure as entrance into the psychology profession. In essence, the APA began to focus on credentialing *psychologists,* while the ACA then concentrated on credentialing *counselors.* (p. 23) [italics in original quote]

Although counseling psychologists may qualify for licenses in either psychology or counseling, requisite coursework or other requirements may be different between the two professions, requiring the licensure applicant to seek training beyond courses required for a degree. Master's-level counselors do not meet licensure

standards for psychology in states that adopt APA standards, which require a doctoral degree in psychology. Even doctoral-level-trained counselors find it difficult to meet psychology licensure standards, as degree requirements for psychology clearly require a degree title in psychology (counseling, education, or counselor education doctorates do not qualify). The provinces of the professions have been defined.

Gelso and Fretz (1992) defined several unifying themes of counseling psychology that apply to counseling as well: (a) "the focus on intact, as opposed to severely disturbed, personalities"; (b) "the focus on people's assets and strengths and on positive mental health regardless of the degree of disturbance"; (c) an emphasis on brief interventions; (d) "an emphasis on person–environment interactions, rather than an exclusive focus on either the person or the environment"; and (e) "an emphasis on educational and career development of individuals and on educational and vocational environments" (pp. 7–9). These themes may act as points in common shared by counselors and counseling psychologists.

In regard to practice, there is little that differentiates the licensed professional counselor from the licensed psychologist. Both provide counseling (or psychotherapy). Both professional licenses typically allow for assessment of individuals with standardized measurement instruments, such as intelligence tests or personality tests. Both licensed professional counselors and licensed psychologists provide individual or group treatments. The two professions compete in the same market of mental health services. Of all the mental health professions, counseling and psychology are probably the most similar in philosophy and practice. As Fretz and Simon (1992) stated:

> Ideally, attention will continue to be devoted to recognizing the legitimate overlap of functions of various levels and specialties of counselors and psychologists, as well as the meaningful differences in philosophy and practice that can support the continuing viability of the variety of mental health professions. A high degree of overlap in professional role functioning does not have to lead to hegemony by one profession; a clear specification of both unique and complementary professional roles can lead to a collaboration of professions that can benefit consumers as well as acknowledge unique professional competencies. (p. 23)

Counseling is not as closely aligned, either philosophically or historically, to the other mental health professions: psychiatry, social work, marital and family therapy, and psychiatric nursing.

THE MENTAL HEALTH PROFESSIONS

Beyond having a good understanding of the ethical principles that direct the professions of counseling and psychology, it is important to be well acquainted with the other mental health professions. It is especially important to know each profession's credentials and **limits of practice** (the boundaries that demarcate the acceptable activities associated with a profession).

Counseling

Counseling is an emerging mental health profession that developed from the field of professional education. At the time of this writing, 48 states and the District of Columbia regulate the independent practice of counseling, which essentially enables practice outside of schools or other educational settings. Because of counseling's historical linkage to schools, most professional counselors are educated in college or university departments or schools of education (where they usually have the option of receiving training to become school or nonschool community counselors).

The standard educational credential is the master's degree in counseling. Typically, the specific degree titles are the Master of Education (M.Ed.), the Master of Arts (M.A.) in education or counseling, the Master of Science (M.S.) in education or counseling, or the Master of Counseling (M.C.) degree. Doctoral-level practitioners may hold the Doctor of Philosophy (Ph.D.) in education or counseling. The Ph.D. is considered the highest academic degree in the United States and traditionally has been viewed as a research degree and a practitioner degree in the mental health field. Some practitioners may hold the Doctor of Education (Ed.D.) in counseling, which is considered a professional degree in education, much like the Doctor of Medicine (M.D.) credential is a professional degree in medicine. Most schools or colleges at research universities offer the Ph.D. or the Ed.D. with an option of the Ph.D. Although there is a trend away from the Ed.D. at large research universities, it is offered by increasing numbers of comprehensive (nonresearch) universities (Osguthorpe & Wong, 1991).

In most states, certified school counselors must have a master's degree plus documentation of specific coursework in education. Certification is usually granted to individual school counselors and is regulated by the state's department of education. Certification as a school counselor by such a department usually allows counseling practice only within elementary, middle, and secondary schools within the state. School certification in no way implies that the counselor has been credentialed to practice counseling independently (i.e., in private practice for a fee).

The independent practice of counseling is typically regulated by state licensure statutes. Licensure is a type of regulation that may restrict both the use of a professional title, such as counselor, and the practice of counseling in fee-for-service, independent practice. **Independent practice** is the practice of counseling outside of an exempt institutional or other setting (exempt from oversight by the licensure authority). For example, counselors working for a state government may be exempt from the licensing requirement. Because the state hires counselors based on some standard, and their practice is supervised and monitored by the authority of the state agency, it may be unnecessary to require that these employees meet additional state licensure requirements. Exemptions from licensure, if any, vary from state to state, and counselors should know the generally accepted exemptions to identify counselors who are practicing legally or illegally. In many states, counselors employed by a state's mental health, vocational rehabilitation, or family services agency may not be required by statute to be licensed by the regulatory board. They may practice counseling consistent with and within the bounds of their employment; however, a counselor who works in an exempt setting as an employee is not able to practice independently for a fee outside of that employment. A private practice as a second job, no matter how small the practice, remains under the jurisdiction of the licensure authority.

Each licensure statute defines the nature and limits of counseling practice controlled by the law and defines exceptions (exempt practice). For example, Christian Science practitioners are often exempted—as long as they practice within the bounds of religious doctrine, they may counsel Christian Scientists about religious and personal issues. Typical exemptions include pastoral counselors, state or federal employees, school counselors (as long as they are certified by the state's department of education), hypnotists, and substance abuse treatment personnel. Each state's exemptions may be unique to the politics involved in passing the licensure statute in that state. Exemptions are usually listed in the statute itself.

Counselor licensure for independent practice in most states requires a relevant master's degree from an acceptable educational institution with coursework in identified core areas (such as assessment, group counseling, counseling ethics, and counseling theories). States often require 1 or 2 years of post-master's degree supervised experience. Additionally, the license candidate must pass an examination of knowledge in the core areas of counseling by achieving an acceptable passing, or cut, score, which is usually at or near the national mean. The newly licensed professional counselor (often designated L.P.C. or other letters representing the state's title) is then allowed to charge clients for providing counseling services independent of any institutional oversight. Although practice is considered independent, licensed professional counselors are obligated to follow ethical and legal rules set forth by the state's licensure board, which has the right to suspend or revoke the license for unethical or illegal practice. Additionally, some licensure boards require continuing education of licensed professionals and may impose other requirements to maintain a license. Licensure boards often adopt nationally accepted ethical codes, often the ACA's code or some derivative, and adopt administrative or disciplinary rules that constitute mandatory standards of practice to protect consumers.

In addition to licensure of independent practice and state regulation or certification of counselors in the schools, another type of credential is sought by mental health professionals—specialty certification.

Specialty certification (such as in the specialties of rehabilitation, mental health, family, or addiction counseling) is a voluntary means for professionals to identify themselves as trained and qualified specialists. Overseen by freestanding, nongovernmental, and national specialty certification boards, specialty certification identifies professionals who hold specialized training or experience in a circumscribed practice of counseling, usually assisting a unique subpopulation of clients. As examples, Certified Rehabilitation Counselors (C.R.C.s) specialize in assisting individuals with disabilities; marriage or family counseling specialists serve couples or families; addiction counselors work with individuals with chemical dependencies or other addictions. Specialists often limit their practices to clients who need their particular type of treatment. In effect, specialty certification is a means to identify and to designate counselors who have met specialty standards and who, to some degree, limit their practices to those activities consistent with the specialty.

Many specialty certification boards are given approval or credibility by a large, national professional association. In counseling, the Commission on Rehabilitation Counselor Certification (CRCC) certifies rehabilitation counselors. CRCC was organized with the support of the American Rehabilitation Counseling Association, an affiliate of what is now the ACA, and in conjunction with the National Rehabilitation Counseling Association (NRCA), a division of the National Rehabilitation Association. These organizations currently have seats on the commission. The C.R.C. credential is the oldest and most widely recognized professional counseling specialty designation. The NBCC is the largest recognized specialty board in professional counseling. NBCC certifies general counselor and several specialty practitioners, such as addiction counselors and mental health counselors. (See Box 2–1 for information on contacting the ACA, NBCC, CRCC, and AASCB.)

Ordinarily, specialty certification requirements are equivalent to or more stringent than licensure standards. However, some counselors may be certified by a specialty board but may not be licensed to practice independently. Specialty certification is simply a way of identifying a practitioner's level of training and limits of practice; it is not a legal right to practice for a fee. Many counselors employed by a state government's vocational rehabilitation agency (usually a license-exempt setting) attain the C.R.C.

Box 2–1 • Counseling Professional Organizations and Credentialing Bodies

The largest professional group representing professional counselors is the American Counseling Association (ACA), 5999 Stevenson Avenue, Alexandria, VA 22304-3300; phone 703-823-9800 or toll free 800-347-6647; the ACA Web site is www.counseling.org. The National Board of Certified Counselors (NBCC) is located at Post Office Box 77699, Greensboro, NC 27417-7699; phone 336-547-0607; the NBCC Web site is www.nbcc.org. The address of the Commission on Rehabilitation Counselor Certification (CRCC) is 1835 Rohlwing Road, Suite E, Rolling Meadows, IL 60008; phone 847-394-2104; the CRCC Web site is www.crccertification.com. The address of the American Association of State Counseling Boards (AASCB) is 3-A Terrace Way, Greensboro, NC 27403-3660; phone 336-547-0914; the AASCB Web site is www.aascb.org.

credential to demonstrate their commitment and allegiance to their specialty, even though they may be required by law to restrict their practice to their state government job (if they are not licensed).

The mental health field has seen a proliferation of questionable certifications. Anyone can set up a specialty certification by incorporating a "board," getting a post office box, and developing application forms. A number of boards advertised in professional newspapers and journals have questionable or nonexistent connections to legitimate professional organizations. These boards may charge exorbitant fees to provide impressive-sounding credentials. However, most professionals consider such certification as worthless, except perhaps in deceiving the public. Wise and ethical practitioners seek certification only by specialty boards that are well respected in the professional community and have established relationships with recognized organizations that represent a profession (such as the ACA). Practitioners who purchase credentials from freestanding and unrecognized certification bodies to imply a level of expertise or training may be considered unethical if such an action misrepresents their professional qualifications. The terms most commonly used to describe specialty designation in the counseling and mental health professions are **certification, board certification,** or **diplomate** (such as the diplomate of the American Board of Professional Psychology).

Psychiatry

Psychiatry, the oldest recognized mental health profession, is a medical specialty. All psychiatrists must be physicians and, therefore, must have a medical or equivalent degree. Two academic-professional degrees in the United States allow for licensure as a fully qualified physician—the Doctor of Medicine (M.D.) and the Doctor of Osteopathy (D.O.). The Doctor of Chiropractic (D.C.) degree, which sometimes allows for the title of Chiropractic Physician, is not consistent with licensure for the full range of treatments typically associated with medical practice (e.g., chiropractors in most states are not allowed to prescribe medication). Graduates of medical schools outside the United States may have the M.D. degree or some variation, but once they pass a state's licensure standards for the Doctor of Medicine, they may legitimately use the M.D. designation after their names.

The D.O. degree is awarded by schools of osteopathy. Such schools are typically not associated with universities. Osteopathy is considered an alternative to the traditional training model of the profession of medicine, which is technically called allopathy. It is a relatively young profession, developed as an offshoot of medicine based on philosophical differences. Osteopaths believe that physical structure is often implicated in the disease process, and physical manipulation is a primary osteopathic treatment. Additionally, osteopaths focus on the individual patient more holistically and view medication as an adjunct to other treatments. There is separate licensure for osteopathic physicians. Regardless, osteopaths are licensed to provide the full range of medical treatment, including surgery and the prescription of medication. In a substantial portion of academic curricula and in actual practice, there may be little that distinguishes an osteopathic physician from an allopathic physician. In fact, some D.O.s specialize in psychiatry, seeking additional residency training after the education required for licensure as an osteopath.

A licensed physician must have the appropriate degree from an accepted school of medicine or osteopathy. Additionally, a 1-year, general medical internship must be completed in a hospital. Candidates are granted a license to practice as a physician upon completion of the internship and after passing the required licensure examinations (sometimes called state board examinations). This license allows the physician to perform all medical procedures and to prescribe medicine. Licensed physicians can practice independently—that is, in private practice. However, many hospitals will not grant a physician **hospital privileges** (the right to admit patients to and treat patients in the hospital) without postinternship training. Hospitals usually require a physician to show evidence of 3 or more years of additional training in a specialty—a residency. A **specialty residency** is a 3-year or more, hospital-based training program that prepares the physician to practice diagnosis, general treatment, and specialty procedures in a specific area of medical practice, such as orthopedic surgery, internal medicine (diagnostics), pediatrics, dermatology, family practice, or psychiatry. There are many specialties in medicine and osteopathy. Physicians who have completed a specialty residency can legitimately claim to be specialists and can perform procedures, usually within hospitals where they have been granted hospital privileges. Many physicians who have completed specialty residencies also seek **specialty designation**—certification through a national specialty certifying board. Specialty designation through such a board has become the benchmark for advanced specialty practice.

Box 2–2 • Psychiatry Professional Organizations and Credentialing Bodies

The largest professional association representing psychiatrists is the American Medical Association (AMA). Specifically related to psychiatry, however, the American Psychiatric Association (APA) is the largest professional group representing psychiatrists. The American Psychiatric Association is located at 1000 Wilson Boulevard, Suite 1825, Arlington, VA 22209-3901; phone 703-907-7300; the APA Web site is www.psych.org. The American Board of Psychiatry and Neurology (ABPN) address is 500 Lake Cook Road, Suite 335, Deerfield, IL 60015-5249; phone 847-945-7900; the ABPN Web site is www.abpn.com.

The national certifying body in psychiatry is the American Board of Psychiatry and Neurology (ABPN; see Box 2–2). Physicians who have been licensed and have completed an approved (by the relevant specialty board) specialty residency may then sit for a specialty examination, a rigorous test of knowledge within the specialty. Upon passing the test, physicians are granted diplomate status—essentially receiving a diploma of completion of specialty training. Diplomates of a specialty board may describe themselves as board certified specialists.

It is not necessary to be a board certified specialist to practice a specialty. However, to legitimately and ethically practice a specialty, a physician should have at least completed an approved specialty residency. Many psychiatrists practice without the ABPN designation.

Board certification is no guarantee of competence, just as not having board certification is no indication of incompetence. However, board certification helps to identify duly trained and knowledgeable specialty practitioners.

Psychiatrists can perform physically intrusive procedures (e.g., surgery or blood tests), electroconvulsive therapy (ECT), psychotherapy, and medicinal treatment or pharmacotherapy. Additionally, by virtue of their general medical training, they may practice any and all procedures within general medicine. This training allows the psychiatrist to be uniquely qualified to understand and address the biochemical and medical aspects of mental disorders. By nature of their training, psychiatrists have a knowledge base to understand and to treat any comorbid physical illness in individuals with mental disorders.

Psychology

Psychologists, unlike psychiatrists, cannot prescribe medications or perform other treatments or diagnostic procedures that are intrusive or invasive of the physical structure of the body. (It is noteworthy, however, that some psychologists, at the direction of some leaders of the APA, are actively petitioning state legislatures for the right to prescribe medication; two states, at the time of this writing, have granted psychologists the right to prescribe medication—New Mexico and Louisiana.) Psychologists, like counselors, can assess individuals with normative tests (such as IQ, aptitude, personality, or interest tests). Psychiatrists are not typically trained in psychometrics or psychological testing procedures and interpretation, and they should not be involved in such activity without appropriate training and supervision. Psychiatrists, psychologists, and counselors, however, are trained and licensed to perform psychotherapy or counseling.

Psychologists must be educated to the level of the academic doctorate Ph.D.; Ed.D.; or Doctor of Psychology, (Psy.D.). The Psy.D. is usually awarded by freestanding, nonuniversity-affiliated schools of psychology; as such, institutions granting the Psy.D. degree typically do not seek to prepare psychologists for potential research or academic roles. Freestanding schools of psychology primarily train individuals for clinical practice. The Ph.D. is usually awarded in clinical psychology or counseling psychology at university colleges of arts and science. Schools of education at universities or colleges may award the Ph.D. or the Ed.D. in counseling, educational, or school psychology. Any of these psychology degrees, if obtained from a legitimately accredited college or university, may signify doctoral-level training in psychology. Increasingly, however, the preferred national standard for academic psychology programs is accreditation through the APA's Committee on Accreditation.

To become licensed as a psychologist, candidates must complete the doctorate from an appropriately accredited program and perform 1 or 2 years of postdoctoral experience supervised by a licensed psychologist in a psychology service delivery program that is accepted or approved by the state licensure authority. Additionally, candidates must pass a stringent licensure examination. Once licensed, psychologists can independently provide the full range of psychological delivery services for a fee.

Psychologists may become board certified through the American Board of Professional Psychology (ABPP),

---

Box 2–3 • Psychology Professional Organizations and Credentialing Bodies

The address of the American Psychological Association (APA) is 750 First Street, N.E., Washington, DC 20002-4242; phone 800-374-2721; the APA Web site is www.apa.org. The American Board of Professional Psychology (ABPP) is located at 300 Drayton Street (3rd Floor), Savannah, GA 31401; phone 912-234-5477 or toll free 800-255-7792; the ABPP Web site is www.abpp.org. The address of the American Board of Psychological Specialties (ABPS) is C/O the ACFE, 2750 E. Sunshine, Springfield, MO 65804; phone 417-881-3818 or toll free 800-423-9737; the ABPS Web site is www.acfe.com.

---

which has linkage to the APA, or by the American Board of Psychological Specialties (ABPS), which has linkage to the American College of Forensic Examiners (see Box 2–3). Forensics is a term that pertains to legal issues or testimony in legal proceedings as an expert witness. The ABPP is the older, more recognized and respected clinical credential, whereas the ABPS primarily identifies a specialist in expert witness testimony. Specialties designated by either the ABPP or the ABPS include clinical, counseling, family, rehabilitation, and neuropsychology. ABPP specialty certification requires up to 5 years of postdoctoral specialized experience under the supervision of a board certified specialist, plus an acceptable score on an examination of knowledge in the specialty.

The largest professional association representing psychologists in the United States is the APA.

Marriage and Family Therapy

Marriage and family therapists are licensed in 46 states and the District of Columbia (as of this writing). Marital therapy focuses on concerns experienced by couples. The focus is on the relationship itself, with an implied obligation to assist the partners to solve problems so they can maintain their relationship. Family therapy is a treatment approach that treats social concerns or individual problems (including psychopathology) within the context of the family (whether defined by genetics, law, common law, or choice) or recognized household. Other individuals may be involved in a family's problem and may be asked to participate in treatment; for example, a dating partner of a household member may be asked to attend a session.

Marriage and family therapists are trained to treat relationships from a dyad (a two-person system) to a family system of three (a triad) or more individuals. Unlike other mental health professions that focus primarily on individual treatment, marriage and family therapists are trained in theories of relationships and relationship treatment, which typically are grounded in social systems theory (Cottone, 1992). This unique theoretical and clinical training constitutes a critical difference in how therapists conceptualize and practice their profession; relationships clearly become the focus.

There is controversy over the existence of marriage and family therapy as a separate or independent mental health profession. Larger, more inclusive professions, such as psychology and counseling, have taken the stance that marital therapy and family therapy are actually treatment approaches that counselors or psychologists may choose with appropriate training and experience. They argue that marriage and family therapy is not a profession unto itself, but rather reflects a body of specialized techniques. Accordingly, freestanding licenses for marriage and family therapists are criticized by some psychologists and counselors who believe that any trained psychiatrist, psychologist, or counselor with specialty training can practice marriage and family therapy. Because marriage and family therapy is within the scope of practice of the other mental health professions in many states (e.g., counseling or psychology), it is considered a specialty of those professions rather than a separate profession. In fact, a number of individuals affiliated with the ACA helped to establish the National Credentialing Academy, which certifies counselors as meeting criteria to be Certified Family Therapists.

Marriage and family therapists represented by the American Association for Marriage and Family Therapy (AAMFT; see Box 2–4) have taken the position that specialty training and specialty designation are not enough. They argue that in-depth, master's-level professional training is needed, primarily with grounding in social systems theory. Further, they have argued convincingly before state legislators that marriage and family therapy should be licensed as a freestanding mental health profession. As a result, many states license marriage and family therapy separately from other mental health professions.

To be licensed as a marriage and family therapist requires a master's degree in marriage and family therapy (or a closely related degree) with specialized coursework in systems theory, marriage and family

---

Box 2–4 • Marriage and Family Therapy Professional Organizations and Credentialing Bodies

The address of the American Association for Marriage and Family Therapy (AAMFT) is 112 South Alfred Street, Alexandria, VA 22314-3061; phone 703-838-9808; the AAMFT Web site is www.aamft.org. The International Association of Marriage and Family Counselors is an affiliate of the American Counseling Association and can be contacted through the ACA at 5999 Stevenson Avenue, Alexandria, VA 22304-3300; phone 703-823-9800 or toll free 800-347-6647; the ACA Web site is www.counseling.org. The National Credentialing Academy, NCA, (for Certified Family Therapists, CFTs) is located at 13566 Camino De Plata, Corpus Christi, TX 78418; the NCA Web site is www.natlacad.4t.com.

---

treatment approaches, and marriage and family therapy ethics, among more general areas. The college or university degrees most often awarded are the M.S. or M.A. One or 2 years of post-master's supervision of practice is also required. Upon completion of the supervised experience, applicants must pass an examination covering core knowledge areas.

Currently, there are no formally credentialed subspecialties of marriage and family therapy and, consequently, there are no specialty designations. In time, there will likely be specialty boards in marriage counseling, family work, children's issues, and other areas addressed by marriage and family therapists.

The AAMFT has a restricted membership composed of already licensed or highly trained and supervised professionals. The AAMFT offers an advanced membership level (clinical member), which acts much like a credential because the criteria for clinical membership are stringent. Interestingly, no examination is required to become a clinical member of the AAMFT. Rather, it requires 2 years of close supervision by an AAMFT-approved supervisor once candidates have completed basic master's-level coursework. The emphasis on the supervisory relationship, rather than on an examination, appears to reflect the overall emphasis of the profession on relationship.

Psychiatric Nursing

Psychiatric nursing has established itself as a mental health specialty through general certification in psychiatric and mental health nursing and through advanced clinical specialist certification as a mental health nurse. Training for the general practice of nursing requires at least 2 years of college-level preparation leading to state registration as a nurse (a registered nurse, R.N.). This registration is akin to state licensure of other health professions. To become a registered nurse, an individual must have an acceptable degree in nursing and must

pass an examination over nursing theory and practice and meet other registration requirements. There are three educational routes to meet educational requirements: the 2-year associate's degree; the 3-year diploma from a hospital-based school of nursing; and the bachelor's degree in nursing from a college- or university-affiliated nursing school. There is a trend away from the associate's degree and toward the bachelor of nursing degree as an entry-level training requirement.

Registered nurses are allowed to provide the full range of nursing services, primarily treating patients under the direction of a physician. However, in the psychiatric nursing area, certified clinical specialists in mental health nursing are master's-degree-trained nurses who have completed specialized coursework in psychotherapeutic approaches. Certified clinical specialists in mental health nursing make the case that they are trained to the level necessary to provide mental health treatments independent of physician oversight. Nurses are not licensed to administer psychological or educational tests or to independently prescribe medications.

The primary certifying body for professional nurses is the American Nurses Credentialing Center (ANCC; see Box 2–5). The ANCC was established under the auspices of the American Nurses Association (ANA). Over 90,000 nurses are certified by the ANCC. The ANCC certifies only those nurses holding the baccalaureate in nursing, regardless of state registration to practice nursing. Synopses of the two certifications in mental health nursing provided by the ANCC are as follows:

1. *Psychiatric and mental health nurse certification.* Generally, this level of certification requires the R.N., documented experience in psychiatric nursing, 30 contact hours of continuing education in coursework relevant to mental health practice, and a passing score on an examination over topics including theories and concepts, psychopathology, treatment modalities and

---

Box 2–5 • Nursing Professional Organizations and Credentialing Bodies

The address of the National League for Nursing (NLN) is 61 Broadway, New York, NY 10006; phone 212-363-1656 or toll free 800-669-1656; the NLN Web site is www. nln.org. The American Nurses Association (ANA) and the American Nurses Credentialing Center (ANCC) are located at 8515 Georgia Ave, Suite 400, Silver Spring, MD 20910-3492; phone 800-284-2378; the ANA and ANCC Web site is www.nursingworld.org.

Box 2–6 • Social Work Professional Organization and Credentialing Body

The address of the National Association for Social Work (NASW) is 750 First Street N.E., Suite 700, Washington, DC 20002-4241; phone 202-408-8600 or toll free 800-638-8799; the NASW Web site is www.naswdc.org.

---

nursing interventions, and professional issues and trends.

2. *Clinical specialist certification in either adult or child/adolescent psychiatric and mental health nursing.* Generally, this level of certification requires the R.N., documented experience in psychiatric nursing, documentation of experience in treatment modalities, a master's degree in psychiatric nursing or a closely related field, post-master's experience in psychiatric nursing, and a passing score on an examination that includes theories, psychopathology, treatment modalities, trends and issues, and other areas.

In addition to the ANA, the National League for Nursing (NLN) is respected as a professional nursing organization.

Social Work

Generally, social workers trained to the level of the master's degree specialize in one of two areas: public policy or clinical social work. In the mental health field, the clinical or psychiatric social worker is trained to practice as an independent mental health professional.

The degree required for independent practice in clinical social work is the Master of Social Work (M.S.W.) degree, which generally requires 60 to 72 semester hours of graduate coursework. Individuals seeking to be mental health professionals usually follow a graduate coursework track that focuses on psychotherapeutic treatment (rather than on social policy). Social workers often are trained to provide group and family treatments as well as individual psychotherapy, depending on the focus of the degree program. Social workers are not trained or licensed to administer psychological or educational tests or to prescribe psychotropic medications.

Licensure of social workers generally requires the M.S.W. and 1 to 2 years of post-master's supervised experience. A passing score on a licensure examination covering social work theory and practice often is required. Psychotherapy, group therapy, and couple or family therapy are all within the scope of practice of most social work licenses.

Master's-level-trained social workers who wish to be certified may seek credentialing through the Academy of Certified Social Workers (ACSW), which then allows its initials to be used after a social worker's name to designate advanced certification. The ACSW is a widely recognized and respected social work credential and is awarded under the direction of the National Association of Social Workers (NASW; see Box 2–6). The NASW is the largest national organization representing social workers. To be an ACSW, one must have a master's degree in social work, 2 years of post-master's paid experience in social work practice under supervision of a social worker, and an acceptable score on an examination over social work knowledge in assessment and service planning, intervention, professional development, ethical standards, and administration. The ACSW is a generic credential and does not necessarily reflect qualifications in clinical practice.

Social workers who are specialists in clinical practice may seek listing in the NASW Register of Clinical Social Workers. There are two levels of certification in the clinical category: the Qualified Clinical Social Worker and the Diplomate in Clinical Social Work. Both clinical credentials require a master's or doctoral degree in social work from a program accredited by the Council on Social Work Education, the social work accrediting body. Additionally, the ACSW credential or state licensure in social work and 2 years of supervised experience in clinical social work are needed. No examination is needed for the Qualified Clinical Social Worker credential, but candidates must pass an advanced examination to be a Diplomate. The diplomate credential also requires 3 additional years of practice.

There is one other social work certification—the School Social Work Specialist. This specialist must have a master's degree in social work from an accredited program, 2 years of postgraduate supervised school social work experience, and a passing score on a specialty test for school social workers. The ACSW is not needed.

Social work has established itself as a viable mental health profession. In fact, by level of education, it is the profession that competes most closely with master's-level professional counseling. Counselors and social workers may compete for similar jobs in mental health centers, hospitals, educational institutions, and other settings not requiring doctoral-trained professionals.

CHAPTER SUMMARY

Psychiatrists are licensed physicians that hold either the M.D. or D.O. degree. Candidates are granted a license to practice as a physician upon completion of an internship and after passing licensure (state board) exams. A specialty residency is usually a 3-year, hospital-based training program that prepares the physician to practice diagnosis, general treatment, and specialty procedures. A specialty designation is certification through a national specialty certifying board. Professional organizations and credentialing bodies for psychiatrists include the AMA, the American Psychiatric Association and the ABPN.

Psychologists treat individuals with psychotherapy and counseling and assess individuals with intelligence, aptitude, personality, and interest tests. They cannot prescribe medications or perform treatments or intrusive diagnostic procedures. Psychologists must be educated to the level of the academic doctorate and must perform 1 or 2 years of postdoctoral experience supervised by licensed psychologists. They must pass a stringent licensure exam. Counseling psychologists provide counseling and psychotherapy and assess individuals with standardized measurement instruments, such as intelligence tests and personality tests in both individual and group treatment. Professional counselors hold a master's degree in counseling. Doctoral-level practitioners may hold a Ph.D. in education or counseling; some practitioners may hold an Ed.D. in counseling. Certified school counselors require a master's degree plus specific coursework in education. Licensure is a type of regulation that restricts both the use of a professional title and the practice of counseling in fee-for-service independent practice. Specialty certification is a voluntary means for professionals to identify themselves as trained and qualified specialists that is overseen by national specialty certification boards. Professional organizations and credentialing bodies for counselors include the ACA, the NBCC, and the CRCC. Professional organizations and credentialing bodies for psychologists include the APA, the ABPP, and the ABPS.

Marriage and family therapists focus on relationship concerns experienced by couples or families. A master's degree, specialized coursework, 1 or 2 years of post-master's supervision of practice, and successful completion of an exam are required. Professional organizations and credentialing bodies for marriage and family therapists include the AAMFT, the ACA, and the NACFT.

Psychiatric nurses are master's-degree-trained nurses with specialized coursework in psychotherapeutic approaches. Two certifications are provided: psychiatric and mental health nurse, and clinical specialist. Professional organizations and credentialing bodies for psychiatric nurses include the NLN and the ANA.

Social workers generally specialize in public policy or clinical social work. A master's degree and 1 to 2 years of post-master's degree supervised experience are required. The NASW is the professional organization and credentialing body for social workers.

REFERENCES

Cottone, R. R. (1992). *Theories and paradigms of counseling and psychotherapy.* Needham Heights, MA: Allyn & Bacon.

Fowler, R. D. (1996, June). Clinical psychology celebrates its 100th. *The APA Monitor, 27* (6), 3.

Fretz, B. R., & Simon, N. P. (1992). Professional issues in counseling psychology: Continuity, change, and challenge. In

S. D. Brown & R. W. Lent (Eds.), *Handbook of counseling psychology* (2nd ed). New York: John Wiley & Sons.

Gelso, C. J., & Fretz, B. R. (1992). *Counseling psychology.* Fort Worth, TX: Harcourt Brace Jovanovich.

Heppner, P. P., Casas, J. M., Carter, J., & Stone, G. L. (2000). The maturation of counseling psychology: Multifaceted perspectives,

1978–1998. In S. D. Brown & R. W. Lent (Eds.), *Handbook of counseling psychology* (3rd ed). New York: John Wiley & Sons.

Osguthorpe, R. T., & Wong, M. J. (1991). *The Ph.D. versus the Ed.D.: Time for a decision.* Provo, UT: Brigham Young University. (ERIC Document Reproduction Services No. ED 339685)

CHAPTER 3

Introduction to Ethical Principles and Standards in Counseling

OBJECTIVES

After reading this chapter, you should be able to:

- Explain the five ethical principles that guide the helping professions: autonomy, nonmaleficence, beneficence, justice, and fidelity.
- Understand the specific standards commonly found in ethical codes that guide practices in counseling

and psychology, including confidentiality, privacy, privileged communication, avoiding potentially detrimental counselor–client relationships, informed consent, responsibility, and competence.

INTRODUCTION

Counselors must deal with a variety of ethical issues and dilemmas. Specific standards guide their practice, including confidentiality and privacy, privileged communication, avoidance of potentially detrimental counselor–client relationships, informed consent, professional responsibility, and competence. Several more basic ethical guidelines, defined as **ethical principles,** have evolved in the helping professions, primarily deriving from the field of biomedical ethics. Five ethical principles underlie *ethical standards* in the field of counseling; they are: autonomy, nonmaleficence, beneficence, justice, and fidelity. (See Box 3–1.)

ETHICAL PRINCIPLES

Background

In the most recent edition of *Principles of Biomedical Ethics*, Beauchamp and Childress (2001) described four general principles of ethical medical practice. They stated:

> The four clusters of principles are (1) *respect for autonomy* (a norm of respecting the decision-making capacities of

autonomous persons), (2) *nonmaleficence* (a norm of avoiding the causation of harm), (3) *beneficence* (a group of norms for providing benefits and balancing benefits against risks and costs), and (4) *justice* (a group of norms for distributing benefits, risks and costs fairly). (p. 12) [italics in original quote]

These four ethical principles have been applied to other human service professions since the first edition of Beauchamp and Childress (1979). In counseling, the principles are recognized as foundational guidelines for the specific ethical standards that address everyday practice. In fact, Kitchener (1984) published a seminal work applying the four ethical principles plus the ethical rule of fidelity to counseling psychology. According to Beauchamp and Childress, fidelity involves being true to one's word, and it also implies trust in the professional providing services and loyalty to the person being served. For example, Beauchamp and Childress stated: "Abandonment is a breach of fidelity, an infidelity amounting to disloyalty" (p. 313). A counselor should not abandon (discontinue services without adequate cause) a client in the middle of a

25

Box 3–1 • A Simplified Summary of the Five Ethical Principles

Autonomy—To allow opportunity for self-determination and unfettered decision making; to honor the right to individual decision making.

Nonmaleficence—"Primum non nocere" ("First let us do no harm"); to act so that harm is not done to clients.

Beneficence—To do good; to help clients and benefit them.

Justice—To be fair and egalitarian.

Fidelity—To be loyal, to be honest, and to keep promises.

---

contracted service. Kitchener believed that the four ethical principles (autonomy, nonmaleficence, beneficence, and justice) and the ethical rule of fidelity were foundational to ethical standards in counseling. In the literature of counseling, there has been widespread acceptance of these foundational principles, and, following Kitchener's lead, the rule of fidelity has been uncritically incorporated as an equal principle to the other four principles originally defined by Beauchamp and Childress.

Ethical principles constitute *high standards for ethical behavior.* Counseling and psychology have largely espoused **principle ethics,** the model of ethical reasoning traditionally dominant in medicine and bioethics. *Principle ethics involves objectively applying a system of ethical principles to determine the right decision when a counselor is faced with an ethical dilemma.* Principle ethics are in contrast to what is termed virtue ethics, which will be described in Chapter 5. One major difference between principle ethics and virtue ethics is that virtue ethics emphasize "the person taking action rather than the actions taken by that person" (Cottone, Kocet, & Glosoff, 2005).

Principle ethics involve reasoning about the dilemma or choice by specifying and balancing the ethical principles in an analysis to arrive at an ethical solution to the dilemma. **Specifying** involves determining and naming the principles that are involved in the situation being considered. **Balancing** involves weighing which principles are more applicable or important in the analysis (Meara, Schmidt, & Day, 1996). Several principles are usually involved in a dilemma. These principles are said to have **prima facie** merit in the analysis; that is, these principles *must be considered in every case and, if set aside, valid and compelling reasons must be given.* Such reasons are usually based on the specific facts in the situation and the greater importance of other core principles to the issue. This process allows for maintaining the general structure of obligations within a society without thoughtlessly forcing its members into slavish, absolutist compliance with stan-

dards that do not fit specific situations. The five ethical principles (autonomy, beneficence, nonmaleficence, justice, and fidelity) form the substrate on which enduring professional ethical obligations are based.

The Principles

Autonomy **Autonomy** is a right to self-determination of choice and freedom from the control of others. Kitchener (1984) noted that there is a difference between freedom of action and freedom of choice: Although people should have freedom to make choices, their ability to act on these choices is limited by the autonomy of others. If person X's choice abridges the freedom or autonomy of person Y, as in murder, it would be ethical to deny the autonomy of person X in that instance. Counselors create conditions of autonomy for their clients when they do not interfere unnecessarily in the decisions of clients; when they provide all necessary information to their clients in a manner clients can understand; and when it is determined that the clients have the ability to use this information to assess their choices, plan them, and carry them out (Howie, Gatens-Robinson, & Rubin, 1992). *The necessary conditions for autonomy are voluntariness, competence, and full disclosure of information.*

CASE SCENARIO 3–1

Autonomy

A counselor at a community mental health center has been seeing a client for approximately 6 months. The counselor's client initially presented substance use concerns but has not been complying with treatment goals for reducing substance use. The psychiatrist who manages the client's medications has suggested to the counselor that this client needs to be in a structured treatment program. At the client's next appointment, the counselor tells the client that arrangements for the client to participate in the agency's treatment program have been made "for her own good." The client is visibly upset at this news and replies that she has no desire to be in the program. The counselor tells the client, "It's too bad, you're already in it." Is this a violation of the client's autonomy?

YES. The counselor has ignored the client's right to self-determination or autonomy by making a treatment decision for the client without presenting information to the client in order for the client to make her own decisions.

Beneficence and Nonmaleficence.   The principles of beneficence and nonmaleficence are closely related, and in some ways represent different aspects of the same concept. **Beneficence** involves a more active concept of contributing to the well-being of others, whereas **nonmaleficence** involves being passive or refraining from taking some action that might harm another. At its most basic level, beneficence involves the general social obligation to provide mutual aid to members of our society who are in need of assistance. This obligation for mutual aid applies as long as (a) doing so involves a significant need on the part of the other; (b) the person who might assist the other has some particular qualification, such as knowledge or skill to assist the other; (c) the action would have a high probability of succeeding; and (d) the risk or burden to the person rendering aid is not greater than that to the person needing aid (Beauchamp & Childress, 1983).

The entire existence of a profession is based on the society's recognition of special skills and knowledge, as well as a purpose to help members of the society with certain types of problems and situations. Important professional duties stemming from beneficence include the obligation to ensure that professionals establish, reach, and maintain an appropriate level of competency in terms of their knowledge, skills, and ethical practices. They must balance their decisions to influence the client or actively undertake a course of action that, in their professional judgment, will result in the client's increased growth or well-being against the possibilities that they might, at the same time, sacrifice some of the client's autonomy or do harm to the client. Counselors must not assume a paternalistic or parent-like stance toward their clients. When working with clients of different backgrounds, classes, races, religions, or abilities, counselors must be ever cautious about assuming that they know better than the clients or their families what is in the best interests of clients. Howie, Gatens-Robinson, and Rubin (1992) (Figure 5–5), offered specific guidelines for determining when paternalistic beneficent action

might be justified. Being an expert does not automatically entitle the professional to the moral authority to take paternalistic action on behalf of a client. Counselors may be making a morally wrong action if they discuss only traditional career choices with female clients. If they assume that female clients would benefit more from traditional career choices than from the challenges of a nontraditional career, they are acting paternalistically.

Nonmaleficence is one of the oldest moral principles in the professions, probably best known as the cornerstone of the Hippocratic oath taken by ancient Greek physicians to "above all, do no harm." Nonmaleficence is refraining from any action that might cause harm, in addition to not intentionally harming others. This principle is often considered the most pressing obligation for professionals because their activities have the potential to do either good or harm. As a result of the client's trust and the counselor's advanced knowledge, the counselor often has access to special information or opportunities to injure clients either intentionally or unintentionally.

Kitchener (1984) discussed the responsibilities involved in diagnosis of clients as an especially powerful occasion to help or to harm the client. In conjunction with the client, the counselor must determine whether the benefits of diagnosis outweigh the possible harm of going through the assessment and diagnostic processes. Because diagnosis is related closely to treatment planning, funding, and the effects of labeling, these are important concerns. Kitchener noted that the experience of distress or discomfort is often unavoidable—even necessary—during diagnosis and treatment. This realization may make it difficult to discern what constitutes a sufficient level of harm to justify nonpursuit of a particular course in counseling. Psychiatrists, psychologists, counselors, and other mental health professionals who assign diagnoses often must rely on a variety of records, comments, evaluations, and judgments that are conveyed to them to assist in making an appropriate diagnosis. Counselors must ensure that their observations are included in this process or that an inappropriate diagnosis is reevaluated. The increased use of managed health care and the medical model to access psychotherapy have resulted in heavy pressures on mental health professionals to provide diagnoses for funding of care. These pressures are likely to increase the incidence of misdiagnosis or overdiagnosis, while increasing the possibility of harm to clients.

CASE SCENARIO 3–2

Beneficence

A client comes to a university counseling center with an eating disorder. No one on staff has expertise in this area, but the client is in need of services and is assigned to a female counselor. The counselor is aware that she lacks the knowledge and skills to work effectively with this client's issues and seeks consultation and supervision from a private practitioner who specializes in eating disorders. Is the counselor acting in the best interest of her client?

YES. This scenario illustrates the principle of beneficence. Counselors are obligated to possess appropriate levels of competence in terms of knowledge and skills to work with particular client issues. When no other qualified counselor is available within a particular agency, it is appropriate and the counselor's ethical obligation to seek consultation and supervision.

CASE SCENARIO 3–3

Nonmaleficence

A counselor in private practice utilizes a particular therapy technique only with his female clients. He firmly believes that clients with past sexual abuse issues can make progress in treatment only if they have sex with a caring male counselor. He regularly encourages his female clients to consider, as part of the treatment plan, engaging in sexual relations with him to "work through past trauma." Is this ethical?

NO. This scenario illustrates a violation of the principle of nonmaleficence. There is absolutely no research evidence to suggest that counselor–client sexual relations are therapeutic. Quite to the contrary, sexual relations between client and counselor are considered to be harmful to the client and are a clear ethical violation.

Justice. The concept of **justice** involves fairness and equality in access to resources and treatment. Counselors are obligated to ensure that their processes, agencies, and services do not discriminate. They must not operate in a manner that advances discrimination at the hands of others. Distributive justice involves access to resources and services that may be considered scarce (Howie, Gatens-Robinson, & Rubin, 1992). All of the policies and rules of agencies, institutions, eligibility criteria, laws, and social policies that affect the mental health practice should meet acceptable criteria for just distribution. If counselors determine that serious inequalities exist, they must determine what types of advocacy (both within and outside of the given system) are needed to address the injustice and undertake advocacy efforts to remedy the situation.

Some criteria for distributive justice that might be considered include (a) equal shares, (b) distribution by need, (c) distribution by motivation or effort, (d) distribution by contribution of person, (e) free market exchange or purchase, and (f) fair opportunity, or equalizing unequal opportunity (Howie, Gatens-Robinson, & Rubin, 1992). The process of determining a model of justice for a particular purpose and justifying that particular approach is a complex and important aspect of enacting the ideal of justice. Counseling practices such as due process considerations, access to grievance processes, and techniques of systems intervention and advocacy are examples of activities related to this principle.

The principle of justice requires that counselors act in a way that is fair to clients, especially in avoiding prejudicial decisions or favoritism.

CASE SCENARIO 3–4

Justice

Agency X is located in a small community and provides a variety of psychological, social, and vocational services for its clients. One staff member in particular has expertise in the area of vocational and career counseling. She sees two new clients, both with work-related problems. One client, a well-respected member of the community, is a department head at the county courthouse. The other client works as a night custodian at a local factory and has had some legal difficulties. The counselor recommends a full career assessment for the first client in response to the client's request for career exploration. She tells the second client that career counseling services are not offered at this agency, only job placement. She also tells him that he is experiencing job stress that will soon pass if he "just works hard enough." Is this discriminatory?

YES. This scenario illustrates a violation of the principle of justice. By not making the same recommendation for both clients in response to similar requests for career counseling, the counselor is discriminating against the second client based on his personal characteristics. The counselor is ethically obligated to provide equal access to resources and services to all clients.

Fidelity. Keeping promises, keeping commitments, honesty, and loyalty are characteristics of the principle of **fidelity.** Because the bond of trust in the counseling relationship is considered to be of utmost importance to its effectiveness, this principle holds particular meaning for individuals in counseling and the related professions. Indeed, many theorists, such as Rogers (1951), place particular importance on the healing characteristics engendered by the very qualities nurtured by fidelity. Some interpretations of fidelity emphasize the nature of the promises made to clients and the social contract between professional and client. However, reducing this concept to a legalistic concern that recognizes only specific, direct promises, and not those implied within the nature of the relationship, is inappropriate to the richness of the counselor–client relationship. Counseling practices, such as professional disclosure, informed consent, maintenance of confidentiality, and avoiding detrimental relationships are obligations that flow from the important principle of fidelity.

CASE SCENARIO 3–5

Fidelity

A client in need of a more structured living environment does not fully meet the criteria for admission to the local care facility or hospital. The client has been suicidal in the past and has been recently faced with some extraordinary situational stressors. The client has been very compliant with treatment, has been working hard to improve, and has expressed real discomfort to the counselor about the prospect of being hospitalized. Two staff members in a community agency consult with one another and decide to say that the client is in need of hospitalization for suicidal ideation. The underlying purpose is to have him meet the qualifications for admission into the care facility. Is this in the client's best interest?

NO. This scenario illustrates a violation of the principle of fidelity. Although it may be in the client's best interests to be in the care facility, the staff members are misrepresenting the truth to justify the client's admission and they are doing so knowing that the client has communicated a desire to stay out of the hospital.

Principles, Practices, and Codes of Ethics

The five ethical principles are drawn from broader, sociocultural understandings of what is right and good. Therefore, they have great explanatory power regarding how certain professional practices and rules, such as professional codes of ethics, agree with the common sense and general sense of the moral of U.S. society. They are at the heart of any well-written ethical standard or common clinical practice. (See Box 3–2.)

Even though the various professions and professional specialties in counseling have many codes of ethics, all can be analyzed in terms of the ethical principles underlying the specific ethical standards of the codes. **Ethical standards** are *specific profession-relevant directives or guidelines that reflect the best*

ethical practice of professionals. In other words, an ethical standard is an established guideline defined by a professional group to direct professionals when they are addressing ethical dilemmas. Codes of ethics usually are a compendium of ethical standards. Interestingly, the codes of the mental health professions are surprisingly similar in their basic conceptualizations of ethical practices. Although differences exist in specific areas and in how the details of the core obligations are discharged, all mental health professions endorse the core ethical obligations embodied in these five ethical principles.

It is useful to select a particular standard from a code of ethics to delimit the ethical principles that support it. This activity has been used by the Ethical Case Management Practice Training Program developed by Rubin and associates (Wilson, Rubin, & Millard, 1991). This analysis is helpful in strengthening the counselor's levels of familiarity and comfort with the application of the specific ethical principles. It also strengthens the ability to discern the underlying principles behind any number of ethically charged rules, policies, or client situations. Of course, the application of the ethical principles is also a critical stage of the ethical decision-making process as described by many authorities (see Chapter 6).

Consider the five foundational principles listed in Box 3.1 as you read the following section, which describes the ethical standards of counseling. Each ethical standard is, to some degree, an application of one or more of the guiding ethical principles.

ETHICAL STANDARDS IN COUNSELING

Confidentiality and Privacy

The APA and ACA codes of ethics address the issue of privacy as related to confidentiality. The concepts are related, but there are differences. Privacy is a broader issue—counselors and psychologists, by nature of their work, are privy to the most personal and intimate information about their clients. U.S. culture generally respects the fact that individuals have a right to maintain certain personal information as private—meaning it is not to be shared in an open forum. **Privacy** is the client's right to keep the counseling relationship a secret. Privacy relates not only to communications made to and by counselors, but also to issues such as: the disposal of client records, the provision of a private waiting room area, the security of tape recordings of counseling sessions or digitized communications (faxes), the use of credit cards for billing, the use of computer services for scoring of tests, billing, or e-mail, and other documentary or

Box 3–2 • Counseling Practices and the Ethical Principles That Underlie Them

Everyday counseling practice involves actions that are based on ethical principles. Inspect the following list of principles and practices (associated with each principle). Can you think of other practices that represent some of the principles? Are there other principles (not included in the five listed principles) that may be operating in counseling practice?

Autonomy
Obtaining informed consent.
Obtaining an evaluation of a client's competency (to make decisions).
Obtaining client consent/assent to treatment plans.
Respecting a client's freedom of choice related to participation in counseling, in general, or in certain procedures.

Nonmaleficence
Avoiding counseling in areas where one is not competent.
Avoiding harmful roles or relationships with clients.
Informing clients of risks associated with procedures and freedom of choice to undertake procedures.

Beneficence
Doing the best one can for one's clients within counseling parameters.

Working within one's limits of competence and training.
Heeding the duty to warn or protect endangered parties.
Terminating counseling or referring clients who are not benefiting from services.

Justice
Advocating against discrimination or against practices or rules that discriminate.
Respecting cultural differences.
Doing some work for the needy for no charge (pro bono publico).
Assuring that services are accessible to those with limitations.

Fidelity
Being loyal to clients and employees and keeping promises.
Being truthful and honest with clients.
Advocating for clients.
Respecting a client's privacy and confidentiality.
Being loyal to one's colleagues and the profession of counseling.

business activities of the counselor. For example, if a client pays for services with a credit card, and the counselor lists a counseling agency name or profession on the receipt, the credit card company effectively has information that the individual paid for services to a counselor, which is a breach of privacy. If sessions are scheduled in a way that others may observe clients in a waiting room, privacy may be compromised. Both the ACA and APA codes of ethics state that an individual's privacy should be respected. Counselors must be mindful of this overriding standard.

In 1996, the Public Law 104-191, the federal Health Insurance Portability and Accountability Act (HIPAA) was signed into law. The HIPAA law was designed to improve the continuity of health insurance coverage and to ensure that individuals could obtain insurance in a way that health insurance companies would not abuse information in health records. This law has a provision that is very specifically targeted to mental health professionals. Beyond standard and strict provisions for the exchange of information for billing, insurance, and other purposes, there is a restriction on the sharing of psychotherapy notes (U.S. Department of Health and Human Services, U.S. DHHS, 2003). On April 14, 2001, the U.S. DHHS instituted rules related to the HIPAA law,

providing new federal standards for the privacy of health records. Information about medication prescription, medication monitoring, start and stop times of counseling sessions, type and frequency of treatment, and test results and summaries may be released with a standard request. Psychotherapy notes, which contain very intimate information about clients, cannot be shared as standard procedure when a client gives permission generally to release information (New Patient Records Privacy Rule, 2001). Psychotherapy notes can be shared only with a client's permission on a detailed release form that addresses the release of psychotherapy notes specifically. In other words, general release-of-information forms are not acceptable for the sharing of psychotherapy notes. This law helps to protect clients from undue invasion of privacy by individuals who really do not need to know the private information relayed during counseling sessions. The central aspect of the privacy rule is minimum necessary disclosure (U.S. DHHS, 2003, p. 10); in this way, individuals are assured that only what is necessary is shared in order to address their health and disability concerns.

Confidentiality is a bit different from privacy. Confidentiality more specifically addresses information communicated in the counseling context and was developed as something akin to an antigossip guarantee. **Confidentiality** is "the obligation of professionals to respect the privacy of clients and the information they provide" (Handelsman, 1987, p. 33). When information is communicated in the privacy of the formal counselor–client relationship, it is to be maintained as a secret within that relationship. Confidentiality is an ethical concept almost universally referenced in both professional association codes of ethics and legal ethical standards. When confidentiality is referenced by law or statute, it is referred to as *legal confidentiality*. Legal confidentiality is a mandate that prevents the discussion of private communications (with a counselor in a professional context) from being revealed to other individuals without potential penalty of law. Confidentiality guaranteed by a professional association alone (nonlegal confidentiality) does not carry the weight of law; however, it does carry the weight of the professional association, which can censure members or remove them from association membership. Confidentiality is a guarantee to clients that what they communicate privately in professional counseling will be held in confidence—for the ears and eyes of the counselor alone, unless clients specifically release the counselor from the promise.

There are limits and exceptions to both professionally mandated and legal confidentiality. In a classic court case, *Tarasoff v. the California Board of Regents* (1974); (VandeCreek & Knapp, 1993), a judgment was made that a psychologist had the duty to warn an endangered party when a counseling client made a direct threat on a life. In this case, the psychologist, a counselor at a University of California counseling center, warned the police of the threat. Unfortunately, he failed to warn the threatened individual, whom the client later murdered. The legal judgment that followed the incident stated that in such cases, confidentiality is overridden by the **duty to warn**—to inform endangered individuals of an identifiable threat (see the related discussion in Chapter 4). In fact, in 2004, the California State Supreme Court extended the duty to warn in a decision against a therapist (David Goldstein) who chose not to inform an endangered party (Keith Ewing) when the parents of Goldstein's client informed Goldstein that their son (Geno Colello) threatened to hurt Ewing. Goldstein, the therapist, felt he was immune from responsibility because the client did not tell him of the threat. But the courts ruled against Goldstein, even in this situation where a third party warned of a direct threat to an identified victim. The Court held Goldstein responsible for not breaking confidentiality and warning the endangered party. Some believe that the California Supreme Court went too far in this case because the credibility of third parties cannot

be assessed. The question becomes, "Have the courts gone too far in extending the duty to warn?" Certainly, counselors have an obligation to protect a person's confidentiality, but what constitutes the boundary between a choice of keeping a promise or protecting the public? The message of the California Supreme Court is clear. Threats to individuals should not be taken lightly; the authorities and the potential victim must be warned. Beyond warning endangered parties, counselors may also be obligated to act in a way that may protect an endangered party. For example, a counselor should encourage a client threatening harm to others to seek help at a hospital emergency room, thereby preventing direct or immediate contact with the threatened party without additional evaluation and medical treatment. Any reasonable professional action of the counselor, beyond a warning to a threatened party, that could prevent harm to another person is interpreted as a **duty to protect.** Most ethical codes in psychology and counseling incorporate the practices suggested by the original *Tarasoff* decision (when a client makes a direct threat), and counselors should be alert to this limit of confidentiality. Certainly, if information is communicated by a third party (known to be credible by the counselor) about a threat by a client to harm someone or to act against society, the counselor would be wise to use a formal decision-making model to assist in making a decision to break confidentiality. (See Box 3–3.)

Common limits to confidentiality typically referenced in professional codes or statutes involve the following:

1. Required revelation to authorities of any case of substantiated or suspected child abuse or neglect;
2. Required revelation to authorities of a client's communicated intent to do harm to an identified individual or to society (e.g., through an illegal act);
3. Required revelation of counseling information to a parent or legal guardian of a client who is a minor child, on the request of the parent or legal guardian; and
4. In-case consultation with other professionals or students of counseling (often, however, identifying information must be disguised).

Counselors should inform clients prior to counseling of any professional or legal limits to the confidential relationship. Otherwise, they may share confidential information with others only with the direct written consent of clients. Due to HIPAA, when psychotherapy notes are involved, special release-of-information procedures must be followed.

Box 3–3 ● Assessing Clients for Potential to Harm Self or Others

When a client poses a risk to self or others, it is imperative for the counselor to consider actions to protect the client (if threatening suicide or self-harm, for example), an endangered party (if threatening an identifiable third party), or potential innocent bystanders. This risk assessment is crucial to the concepts of duty to warn or duty to protect.

Generally, a counselor must assess the client first for either suicidal ideation (thoughts) or assault/homicidal ideation (thoughts). It is not unusual for a person to have fleeting suicidal thoughts when the person is under pressure or in difficult circumstances. Even the healthiest people sometimes have fleeting thoughts of self-harm or harm to others who have "done them wrong." In and of itself, suicidal ideation or assault/homicidal ideation is not a warning sign of impending action by a client. However, when suicidal or assault/homicidal ideation is accompanied by *plans* (they know *how* they are going accomplish harm to self or others) or *intentions* (they know *when* they are going to accomplish harm to self or others), then the concern reaches a level requiring the counselor to take direct and ethical action. A general rule of clinical practice is that if a client has intentions or plans to do self or other harm, the counselor must act to warn and to protect the client or the identified endangered party. But assessing suicide risk is not as simple as evaluating for intentions or plans. Carrier (2004) provided a detailed chapter on assessing suicide risk. In addition to assessing for plans, he recommended assessing for a number of other predictive factors, including: means and opportunity to carry out the plan; previous suicide attempts; a diagnosed mood disorder (e.g., depression, bipolar disorder);

drug or alcohol use; hopelessness; social isolation; gender (more women than men attempt suicide, but more men than women complete a suicide attempt); anger; psychosocial stressors (such as unemployment, financial or relationship problems); and a family history of suicide. With assault/homicidal threat, a number of those factors apply, plus the client must be assessed for a history of doing harm to others or to animals. Carrier provided a nice review of assessment instruments used to assess suicide potential, and his review is worth reading. In Chapter 14 (Mental Health Counseling and Assessment) of this text, information is provided on how to address a person who is threatening harm. If a counselor believes that a client is a risk for suicide or harm to others, the counselor must act to warn and to protect the endangered party. For suicide, the client should be taken to the nearest hospital emergency room, or precautions should be taken to ensure the client is never left alone. A "no suicide" or "no harm" contract, although recommended, is *not enough in such circumstances*, because people contemplating self or other harm may not be in a clear state of mind. If there is an identified endangered third party—a potential victim or victims—action should be taken to alert the endangered individuals and the authorities. The counselor would also be wise to use a well-known decision-making model to determine if others are in danger and should be warned (e.g., family members or bystanders). State laws may require additional actions in such circumstances, and counselors should be alert to legal precedent on matters of duty to warn and duty to protect in jurisdictions where they practice.

Confidentiality is not only a legal issue at the state level; federal laws and regulations also address it. A federal law prohibits the disclosure of information of individuals treated for chemical dependency (see Chapter 18). On June 13, 1996, the U.S. Supreme Court ruled that communications between psychotherapists and their clients are confidential and privileged (privileged communication is defined in the next section of this chapter). The decision specifically extended federal privilege, which, according to the ACA (1996), "already applies to psychiatrists and psychologists." The actual Supreme Court case extended privilege to a licensed social worker, which, according to the ACA (1996), "leave[s] the door open for inclusion of other providers of psychotherapy" (p. 10). The Supreme Court decision adds credence to a generally respected concept of confidentiality in counseling and psychology.

QUESTIONS FOR REFLECTION

What value is the counseling profession if counseled individuals cannot be assured of confidentiality? If confidentiality cannot be guaranteed for an individual (or a group of individuals), what is the risk of nontreatment? Will individuals choose not to seek counseling if their confidentiality is not guaranteed? What is the risk to society if such individuals do not seek counseling?

Although confidentiality appears to be a straightforward concept, challenging situations may arise that make judgments difficult. One area of contemporary concern is related to individuals with human immunodeficiency virus (HIV) who may transmit the virus to others through intimate relations. Should the counselor breach confidentiality and warn a partner of an HIV-positive individual? Does *Tarasoff* apply? What are a counselor's responsibilities? These questions have received attention in the literature (Cohen, 1990; Harding, Gray, & Neal, 1993; Schlossberger & Hecker, 1996; Stanard & Hazler, 1995), but there are no clear answers. The ACA and APA codes do not give uncontrovertable guidance. However, an evolving norm to break confidentiality appears to be emerging in recent legal case law if the following criteria are met: (a) there is an identifiable party at risk; (b) there is a significant risk of infection; (c) a warning is likely to be effective in preventing infection; and (d) efforts to get the infected individual to reveal the infection to the endangered party have failed (Reaves, 1999). Like all complicated legal matters, there have been exceptions to the prevailing case law. In a Texas Supreme Court ruling (*Santa Rosa Health Care Corporation v. Garcia* [1998]), a provider was not held responsible to inform the wife of a hemophiliac of her possible exposure to HIV. The issue becomes a balancing act. Which is most critical—the risk of a life, the risk to society, or the risk of a most basic ethical standard at the foundation of a profession?

Acceptable ethical standards are often established after a serious concern has been raised in the literature or in the courts. Counselors must remain current with the professional literature to ensure that they are alert to potential ethical dilemmas; by doing so they can act to prevent a breach of ethics before it happens.

CASE SCENARIO 3–6

Confidentiality

The mother of a 21-year-old female client calls, concerned about her daughter, and wishes to share information with the counselor in private practice about the daughter's status. In the course of the conversation between the mother and the counselor, the mother asks about the daughter's progress in counseling. Should the counselor answer?

NO. The counselor should not answer without specific written consent from the client that allows communications with the mother. In fact, counselor should not even acknowledge that they are seeing any clients to anyone over the phone, especially without the client's written consent. This is true of anyone seeking information about an individual's participation in counseling, even an identified lawyer or judge. Counselors should be leery about communicating about clients over the phone on incoming calls, but may more safely communicate to individuals on calls they place with the permission of their clients.

CASE SCENARIO 3–7

Confidentiality

A counselor at a party meets a social worker who referred a client to the counselor. The social worker begins to discuss the client with the counselor while other individuals are milling around. Should the counselor discuss the case?

NO. The counselor should communicate to the social worker that they should not talk about cases at the party. With appropriate permission from the client, they should talk about the case only in a private, professional (not social) context. At that time, they should discuss only information directly pertinent to the social worker's role in the case and allowed by client consent. It is also prudent in this day of advanced technology (e.g., e-mail and cellular phones) to evaluate the privacy of any professional conversation, however proper, to ensure that confidentiality or privacy is not unintentionally breached.

CASE SCENARIO 3–8

Confidentiality

The spouse of a counselor meets the counselor at the counselor's office and sees a client walk out of the counseling office. The spouse asks, "What's his problem?" Should the counselor discuss the case with the spouse?

NO. A counselor's confidentiality does not extend to a spouse. In some cases, it does extend to coworkers in agencies or to other professional colleagues, but even in these cases, the coworkers or colleagues must be informed of the confidential nature of the information and must guarantee that they will maintain confidentiality. Regardless, the service-providing counselor is ultimately responsible ethically if confidentiality is breached.

CASE SCENARIO 3–9

Confidentiality

A counselor has had a rough day and goes to a local cosmetology salon after work. The counselor begins discussing tough cases with the cosmetologist but is careful to disguise names and identifying information about specific clients. Has anything unethical occurred?

YES. If it is possible that someone can identify a client by context, confidentiality has been breached. If, for example, a relative or friend of a client overhears such a conversation and can piece together the information, thereby identifying the client, an unethical act has occurred. Only in certain professional situations can a general discussion of disguised cases be ethical, such as a professor's discussion of a case in a relevant college class. Even if the risk of identifying a client is not significant, any practice of public discussion of cases is generally harmful of the trust of confidentiality. It risks decreasing the confidence of the lay public in the profession of counseling and subjects both clients and other counselors to misunderstanding or even ridicule.

Privileged Communication

Privileged communication is a legal right of clients found in state or federal statutes. **Privileged communication** is a client's right to prevent the revelation of confidential information in a legal proceeding (e.g., in a legal hearing or courtroom). A counselor cannot be forced to testify on a client's case if the privilege stands. Privileged communication is owned by the client, and only the client can waive the privilege allowing testimony (Hummel, Talbutt, & Alexander, 1985; Reaves, 1999). Privileged communication, being a legal right, is not found in professional codes of ethics; it is statutory (in state or federal laws).

Like confidentiality, there are limits to privileged communication. In many states, stipulations override any psychotherapist or counselor privileged communication in cases of substantiated or suspected child abuse or neglect. In such cases, a judge can order a counselor to testify on otherwise confidential information. Such disclosure is not illegal, and the counselor is given immunity from prosecution (i.e., cannot be found guilty of breaching privileged communication). Privilege also may not stand when a client sues a counselor.

In some states, communications are privileged in civil but not criminal cases by licensure statute. If a client is charged with a felony and goes to criminal court, attorneys can request the counseling case files and the judge can order the counselor to testify. Such a request to testify is called a **subpoena,** an order to appear in a legal hearing with all requested information. On the other hand, when a civil court (not a criminal court) such as a divorce court subpoenas a counselor, the counselor must refuse to testify about a client's case on the grounds of the client's lawful right to privileged communication. Other examples of civil cases in which a counselor cannot testify include workers' compensation disability or injury hearings, social security disability hearings, child custody hearings, termination of parental rights hearings (unless there is an allegation of child abuse or neglect and an exemption to privileged communication), and other legal proceedings in which a crime allegedly has been committed. As with confidentiality, counselors must know the limits of privileged communication written into licensure laws or other state statutes. (See the general review of privileged communications laws across several mental health professions by Herlihy & Sheeley, 1987.) The ethics committee of a state counseling association or a licensure board of a state can help a counselor identify those laws that affect professional practice. Most ethical codes require that counselors respect the laws in the jurisdiction where they practice.

QUESTION FOR REFLECTION

Confidentiality and privileged communication are related concepts, although privileged communication applies strictly to legal settings (e.g., preventing revelation of confidential information before the courts). Which of the five ethical principles underpin the concepts of confidentiality and privileged communication (autonomy, nonmaleficence, beneficence, justice, or fidelity)?

The U.S. Supreme Court ruled in the *Jaffee v. Redmond* (1996) case that communications between licensed psychotherapists and their patients are privileged communications. This ruling was groundbreaking because it had federal implications (not limited to one state) and because it was liberal in its definition of psychotherapist and psychotherapy. The privilege was applied to a client who was seeing a licensed clinical social worker. Remley, Herlihy, and Herlihy (1997) stated:

> The *Jaffee* decision has created an interpretation and generalization problem because state statutes have established privilege for the clients of specified licensed mental health professionals, whereas the Supreme Court decision has created a privilege for the "patients" of "psychotherapists." Because there is no definition of "psychotherapist" in federal law, federal courts will probably review state statutes to determine whether licensed mental health professionals are psychotherapists when determining whether their clients have privilege. No state currently licenses psychotherapists; rather, licensure is accorded to counselors, psychiatrists, psychologists, social workers, and others who may provide psychotherapy services. Whether privilege will be extended to clients of licensed counselors in federal courts in the future may depend on whether licensed counselors are recognized by the courts as "psychotherapists." The *Jaffee* decision may force the counseling profession to formulate a clear answer to the currently debated questions of whether counseling and psychotherapy are synonymous or separate and distinct activities, and whether counselors are willing to call themselves psychotherapists. (p. 213)

Only time will tell the implications of the *Jaffee v. Redmond* decision for the counseling profession.

CASE SCENARIO 3–10

Privileged Communication

A vocational rehabilitation counselor is hired by a workers' compensation insurance company to assess an alleged injured worker. The insurance claims adjuster refers the case and is suspicious that the claimant is malingering (faking an injury or illness) to collect workers' compensation injury benefits. The claims adjuster requests that the counselor evaluate the client to plan and to recommend rehabilitation services, if necessary. The counselor does not explain any limits of confidentiality and does not have the claimant sign a waiver of privileged communication. Counseling clients in the counselor's state are afforded privileged communication in civil legal proceedings. Later, the counselor is asked to testify on the case by a workers' compensation administrative law judge. The counselor was hired by the workers' compensation insurance company, so the counseling information is owned by the insurance carrier. Therefore, the counselor must testify. True or false?

FALSE. The client/claimant owns the privilege, and only the client can waive the privilege in a civil case. If it appears that court testimony is going to be part of a case assessment, the counselor should obtain a written waiver of privileged communication before assessing the client. This issue also involves another ethical standard, informed consent, which we address later in this chapter.

CASE SCENARIO 3–11

Privileged Communication

A marriage counselor sees a husband and wife in counseling conjointly. The counselor is subpoenaed by a judge regarding divorce proceedings at the request of the husband's attorney. The husband claims that the counselor had evidence of the wife's mental instability from previous medical and hospital records as well as from observation of the wife in marriage counseling. The husband believes the marriage counselor can testify as to the effects of the wife's mental disorder on the marriage. The husband waives privileged communication. The counselor refuses to testify on the basis of the privileged communication of the wife. Is the counselor acting legally?

IT DEPENDS. In some states, privileged communication stands only in cases in which there has been one-on-one communication between a client and a therapist. If other persons are present (as in group counseling or marriage, couple, or family counseling), the privilege may not stand. Whether privilege stands depends on how the statute is written and on past case law. In some states, relationship theory and family counseling are referenced into the definition of practice in the psychology or counselor licensure statute. Therefore, it can be assumed by the law itself that privilege extends to circumstances involving relational treatment or family counseling. If there is no state case law on this issue, a final conclusion on this issue is not possible. A counselor who is unsure whether privileged communication applies should consult or hire an attorney before attending any legal proceeding, thereby seeking representation on that issue before the court.

CASE SCENARIO 3–12

Privileged Communication

An allegation of child abuse is made against a counselor's client, who is the parent of the child in question. The counselor is subpoenaed by a hearing officer to attend a parental rights termination hearing. The counselor must go to testify. True or false?

TRUE. In states where privileged communication is overridden by licensure or other statutes in cases of child abuse or neglect, the counselor should appear and be prepared to testify in those cases. However, the counselor should alert the judge or hearing officer of the client's right to privileged communication and should formally request that the privilege be overridden as a part of the record, based on the relevant statute.

Counselor Roles and Relationships with Clients

Historical Use of the Terms Dual and Multiple Relationships. The literature of the mental health professions historically associated the term **dual relationship** (a relationship in addition to the contracted counseling relationship) with a misuse of therapist power or authority. Such relationships were viewed as a second role with the client that was always viewed as harmful. This is reflected in the older codes of ethics; for example, the outdated AAMFT Code of Ethics stated that therapists "make every effort to avoid dual relationships with clients that could impair professional judgment or increase the risk of exploitation" (AAMFT, 1991). The ACA (1995) code stated that "dual relationships" should be avoided "when possible." The term dual relationship has lost favor in the recent literature because it is unclear and, to some degree, misleading. For example, every counselor in private practice is in a dual (or for that matter, multiple) relationship with clients by nature of counseling. The counselor is a professional helper and is also involved in a contracted financial arrangement and a record-keeping arrangement. The therapist in private practice is at least involved in three professional relationships with clients: helper, business service provider, and record keeper. The term dual relationship, therefore, is not necessarily a negative term, and most codes acknowledge this by qualifying any discussion of dual relationships with a statement addressing harm or exploitation of clients. A dual relationship that is harmful or an exploitive relationship is wrong. Across the board, codes of ethics place a ban on harm to clients. Unfortunately, the term dual relationship, in and of itself, holds an undeserved negative connotation, and the newer codes of ethics have begun to modify terminology in discussing these matters.

Historically, ethical breaches in this area of counseling were the most prevalent and potentially damaging to clients and the profession of counseling as a whole. Part of the problem may have been related to inexact terminology and unclear ethical guidance on the dual relationship issue. Accordingly, in the 2003 edition of this text, some sweeping recommendations were made related to terminology as applied to this area of ethics. It is important to note that the new version of the ACA Code of Ethics includes some of the recommendations made in the earlier edition of this text. Before describing the new standards, some history is warranted.

Part of the negative connotation associated with the outdated term dual relationship has to do with the associated concern of exploitive sexual relationships. Ethical codes in the mental health professions ban sexual relationships with current clients and, in the case of former clients, ban involvement for a period 2 to 5 years subsequent to professional involvement. There is unanimous agreement among ethical codes: Sexual intimacies with clients are unethical. In states where psychotherapeutic practice is regulated, such relationships are also illegal. They are considered a breach of the most basic trust between a mental health professional and a client. This ban is not just a moral issue; research evidence indicates that such relationships are damaging to clients (Bouhoutsos, Holroyd, Lerman, Forer, & Greenberg, 1983; Pope, 1988). There are no compelling reasons in defense of sexual relations with current or recent clients. Counselors would have difficulty defending themselves in cases of substantiated or acknowledged sexual activity of this sort. In any discussion of roles and relationships with clients or former clients, sexual intimacies stand alone and deserve to be addressed directly and unequivocally. Related to legal repercussions of sexual relations with clients, Reaves (1999) stated, "the largest civil judgments have been reserved for those professionals that engage in such heinous conduct" (p. 23). Both the ACA and APA codes of ethics make it clear in freestanding sections that sexual intimacies with clients are unethical. The codes ban sexual intimacy with former clients for a period of time, but allow for professional scrutiny even after that time has passed.

Licensure boards often report that mental health professionals have had licenses suspended or revoked on the basis of improper sexual intimacies with patients or trainees under their supervision. The sexual contact issue between patients and counselors is commonly the

charge that leads to suspension or revocation of a professional license on ethical grounds. The ASPPB, which keeps statistics on disciplinary actions of its boards, reported that the highest number of reported disciplinary actions against psychologists fit into the category of "sexual/dual relationship with patient"; 715 of 2,206 disciplinary actions were in the sexual/dual relationship category (ASPPB, 2001).

Aside from the issue of sexual intimacies with current or former clients, the term multiple relationships has gained favor recently, implying two or more therapist–client relationships. The term is used in the more recent ethical code revisions, for example the APA (2002) code of ethics. Typically, the term multiple relationship is linked to the issue of exploitation or harm to clients. Exploitive or harmful multiple roles are considered unethical.

Harmful Versus Nonharmful Interactions Although it is wise to avoid potentially harmful relationships with clients or trainees, not all relationships with clients outside of counseling are technically illegal or unethical (Anderson & Kitchener, 1998). Certainly an unplanned, accidental social contact is not unethical; for example, a counselor could hardly be blamed for running into a client at a party or athletic event. Other cases also may not be unethical:

1. A professor of counseling is impressed by a student. After the student graduates, she hires him to work in a counseling service that she owns.
2. A supervisor of counselor licensure candidates gets to know his supervisees over several years of supervision. Friendships develop that last beyond the formal supervision agreement.
3. A counselor encounters a former client whose counseling was terminated several years earlier. The counselor remembers that the client provided a professional service, which he currently needs. He then negotiates to purchase the services from the former client.

These relationships are not illegal or technically unethical, but still warrant scrutiny. Counselors generally know if a relationship holds the potential of harming the client or compromising the client's best interests or well-being (Kitchener, 1988). In fact, the term **exploitation** can be defined as *an action by a counselor that benefits the counselor while it compromises the best interest or well-being of a client.* Counselors should also consider the appearance of impropriety as well as the unintended level of coercion or influence they may have on impressionable clients. The general rule is: Avoid potentially harmful or exploitive relationships, or, if such a relationship is imminent, clearly examine the ethical or legal ramifications and act to minimize or rectify any harm.

Some have argued that a total ban on relationships outside the contracted therapeutic relationship is unjustified. Lazarus (2001) and Lazarus and Zur (2002) have been vocal critics of such bans in psychotherapy in general. Tomm (1993), in the specialty of marriage and family counseling, has also been adamant in arguing against a total ban on extratherapy interactions. Their positions are founded on personal experiences wherein clients or trainees actually benefited by interactions outside of the counseling or supervising process. Both have made compelling arguments that an outright ban on all nontreatment (or nonsupervision) interaction misses the point—the issue is really detriment or exploitation by unethical practitioners. They argue that the focus should be on banning exploitation or harmful interactions, not on banning all nonprofessional interactions. For example, should a counselor feel guilty about buying Girl Scout cookies from a client? By some, this could be viewed as unethical, but it certainly is not likely to be harmful, and in some sense, it might be beneficial to the client. Although buying cookies from a client can be viewed as a trite example, there are many examples wherein therapists are put in positions of interacting with clients in ways that are innocent to the therapeutic relationship and may actually be beneficial to the client—attending a ceremony or family funeral, accompanying a client on an anxiety-producing activity, purchasing a product or service in a way that does not compromise counseling, or attending a wedding or graduation ceremony. An outright ban appears to be unjustified.

However, there may be a slippery slope (one step on a slippery slope may lead to a fall). Haug (1993) made a case that involvement in interactions outside of counseling with a client may lead to potentially detrimental relationships (the fall on the slippery slope). By banning all extratherapeutic interactions, ethical authorities may act to prevent truly harmful ethical breaches.

Counselors and therapists are human. No licensure board or ethical authority can control feelings. Pope, Keith-Spiegel, and Tabachnick (1986) found that "attraction to clients is a prevalent experience among both male and female psychologists" (p. 155). Feelings may develop and may be uncontrollable, but there are controls on actions of professionals. In fact, there is evidence that psychologists frequently contemplate entering sexual relationships with clients (Lamb, Catanzaro & Moorman, 2004). In a survey of male counselors, Thoreson and his associates found that "although relatively few respondents (1.7%) reported having engaged in sexual misconduct with clients during a professional relationship, the prevalence rate increased to 17% when the definition of sexual misconduct was expanded to include (a) students and students under supervision and (b) occurrences of sexual misconduct after the professional relationship" (Thoreson, Shaughnessy, Heppner, & Cook, 1993, p. 429). In a later survey of female counselors, "Counselors viewed sexual contact in current professional relationships as less ethical than contact in subsequent relationships, although relationships with former clients were seen as less ethical than relationships with former trainees. Compared with male counselors from a previous study, female counselors were less likely to report sexual contact in their professional roles" (Thoreson, Shaughnessy, & Frazier, 1995, p. 84). Because sexual feelings and contemplation of sexual relationships with clients and trainees is fairly common, counselor trainees need to be alert to the issues. Educators should train mental health professionals about ethical ways to handle attraction and sexual feelings toward clients (Harris, 2001; Lamb et al., 2004; Vasquez, 1988). Certainly all nonprofessional roles with clients should be managed carefully (Younggren & Gottlieb, 2004).

As to whether there is danger of physical or emotional harm, a healthy friendship that develops during a formal counseling or supervisory relationship and lasts beyond the formal contracted services may not be considered harmful. Sexual intimacies are another matter. To reiterate, research shows that clients most usually are in danger of emotional harm when involved sexually with a counselor or therapist (Bouhoutsos et al., 1983; Pope, 1988). To cross the line of sexual intimacy is a misuse of power for the therapist. Clients must be viewed, to some degree, as emotionally vulnerable by nature of their status. Seduction by clients is considered a symptom of some emotional disorders. Counselors must take extra precautions against any semblance of nonprofessional relationships.

If there is any question that the therapist may be "set up" by a client, or if there is discomfort regarding a counseling relationship, the counselor should take reasonable precautions. Strategies to consider include leaving the door slightly opened so that a secretary or colleague can see in the office, but in a way that the voice is somehow screened to maintain confidentiality; taping all sessions with client consent; and inviting a second therapist to do cotherapy with the client's permission. Just as care must be taken to protect clients from potential harm from interactions with counselors, care must also be taken to protect counselors from the malicious intentions of some clients.

Controversy exists over the issue of potential harm related to the use of touch in therapy. Some psychotherapeutic techniques actually encourage touch between therapists and clients. Other techniques may involve deep muscle massage or physical contact. Therapists who use these techniques believe that touch is therapeutic. Regardless, the ethical codes clearly ban sexual intimacy—any sexual contact is unacceptable. Therapists who use touch as part of their therapeutic repertoire should use it cautiously and appropriately. Hand holding may be acceptable; touching a person's knee or thigh can be considered crossing the ethical line. Having a witness available during treatments may also prevent the misinterpretation of touch in therapy or may minimize the therapist's legal vulnerability. Counselors should review state statutes and standards related to physical contact between counselors and clients if they plan to use such modalities. Some state guidelines are stricter than others.

A Need for Clear Standards. The high number of past complaints, questions, and infractions in the category of dual or multiple roles in counseling may have been related to confusion over the terms. The terms dual and multiple relationships are inexact. Although there is historical linkage to these terms, in the 2003 edition of this text it was recommended that they should be abandoned. Inexact terminology and ambiguous or equivocal standards are problematic for the ethics committees of credentialing bodies. The new ACA Code of Ethics standards in Box 3–4 are more exacting, using behaviorally-specific terminology. The standards avoid the terms dual and multiple relationships. Nonprofessional relationships are separated from other professional relationships (such as counseling a group and an individual at the same time, or when there is a role change during the counseling process such as going from marriage counseling to individual counseling). Several standards that relate to interactions with clients, former clients, trainees, and research participants are consistent. There is less room for equivocation as to whether a counselor has impaired judgment. The focus becomes harm to clients. The recommended standards also allow for potentially beneficial relationships with clients other than the contracted therapeutic relationship, with the client's permission, clear forethought, and adequate consideration before the relationship is initiated (excepting of course sexual or romantic interactions or relationships).

In other words, the terms dual and multiple relationships have been deconstructed—analyzed and re-

defined for what they truly represent. By abandoning global terms, clearer guidance can be given to counselors in compromising situations. In effect, the terms dual and multiple relationships have been redefined as three separate and distinct kinds of interactions: (a) sexual and romantic interactions with clients or family members of clients; (b) non-professional interactions with clients (excepting sexual or romantic interactions), such as attending a client's wedding or a client's graduation or a party after such an event; (c) contiguous professional relationships (professional roles in addition to an existing contracted role; such roles are undertaken sequentially or simultaneously to the preexisting role).

Two professional codes of ethics have been rewritten without use of the terms dual or multiple relationships: the *Code of Professional Ethics for Rehabilitation Counselors* (Commission on Rehabilitation Counselor Certification, 2001) and the ACA *Code of Ethics* (ACA, 2005). Additionally, an analysis of the issue in the field of marriage and family therapy has been published, addressing deficiencies in the AAMFT (2001) *Code of Ethics* (Cottone, 2005). As Tammy Bringaze, a member of the ACA task force that rewrote the ACA code of ethics, stated during the February 5th, 2005, task force meeting: "Clients don't know what 'dual' or 'multiple' relationships are when they file ethics complaints." A similar argument can be made for the past use of the term *impaired professional judgment*, a term found in some codes of ethics. How does a client prove impaired professional judgment or even comprehend the concept when making an ethics complaint? These terms appear to have been used for the benefit of therapists rather than benefit of client's who may have a complaint.

No ethical standards can give absolute guidance in every case of an ethical dilemma. However, the newer standards may represent an improved way to communicate right and wrong when it comes to interaction with clients in and outside of the therapeutic relationship. And because the standards allow for certain interactions that are potentially beneficial to clients, they reflect a value on positive ethics—going beyond prohibitions and sanctions and considering promotion of positive behavior (Handelsman, Knapp, & Gottlieb, 2002).

Differences in the Revised Standards and Traditional Standards. The following differences exist between the traditional standards on the dual relationship issue and the ACA Code of Ethics (2005) standards in Box 3–4:

1. The 2005 standards expand the ban on sexual relationships to romantic interactions.

2. The 2005 standards unequivocally ban sexual or romantic interactions for a 5-year period for clients and former clients. There is no "gray area" of potential dispute over whether a client has been harmed or exploited after a period of 2 years since the last professional contact (past standards allowed for such behavior so long as it was not exploitive or harmful 2 years subsequent to the end of counseling).

3. The 2005 standards separate nonprofessional interactions and contiguous professional interactions (role changes), giving clarity on such matters. For example, if a client is involved in group counseling and is seen contiguously in individual counseling, ethical dilemmas may arise (see Chapter 16). If there is a change in counseling modality (from individual to group or family counseling), counselors need specific guidance on how to handle these contiguous professional relationships. In the past, contiguous professional relationships and nonprofessional relationships were not distinguished in the dual relationship language.

4. Although nonprofessional relations should be avoided, the 2005 standards do not ban relationships or

---

Box 3–4 • ACA Code of Ethics—Standards on Counselor Roles and Relationships With Clients

a. Current Clients. Sexual or romantic counselor–client interactions or relationships with current clients, their romantic partners, or their family members are prohibited.

b. Former Clients. Sexual or romantic counselor–client interactions or relationships with former clients, their romantic partners, or their family members are prohibited for a period of 5 years following the last professional contact. Counselors, before engaging in sexual or romantic interactions or relationships with clients, their romantic partners, or client family members after 5 years following the last professional contact, demonstrate forethought and document (in written form) whether the interactions or relationship can be viewed as exploitive in some way and/or whether there is still potential to harm the former client; in cases of potential exploitation and/or harm, the counselor avoids entering such an interaction or relationship.

c. Nonprofessional Interactions or Relationships (other than sexual or romantic interactions or relationships). Counselor–client nonprofessional relationships with clients, former clients, their romantic partners, or their family members should be avoided, except when the interaction is potentially beneficial to the client.

d. Potentially Beneficial Interactions. When a counselor–client nonprofessional interaction with a client or former client may be potentially beneficial to the client or former client, the counselor must document in case records, prior to the interaction (when feasible), the rationale for such an interaction, the potential benefit, and anticipated consequences for the client or former client and other individuals significantly involved with the client or former client. Such interactions should be initiated with appropriate client consent. Where unintentional harm occurs to the client or former client, or to an individual significantly involved with the client or former client, due to the nonprofessional interaction, the counselor must show evidence of an attempt to remedy such harm. Examples of potentially beneficial interactions include, but are not limited to, attending a formal ceremony (e.g., a wedding or graduation); purchasing a service or product provided by a client or former client (excepting unrestricted bartering); hospital visits to an ill family member; and mutual membership in a professional association, organization, or community.

e. Role Changes in the Professional Relationship. When a counselor changes role from the original or most recent contracted relationship, he or she obtains informed consent form the client and recognizes the right of the client to refuse services related to the change. Examples of role changes include: (1) changing from individual to relationship or family counseling or vice versa; (2) changing from a nonforensic evaluative role to a therapeutic role, or vice versa; (3) changing from a counselor to a researcher role (i.e., enlisting clients as research participants) or vice versa; and (4) changing from a counselor to a mediator role, or vice versa. Clients must be fully informed of any anticipated consequences (e.g., financial, legal, personal, or therapeutic) of counselor role changes.

interactions with clients that are potentially beneficial to clients (excepting sexual or romantic interactions), as long as there is forethought and the client provides consent. Counselors no longer need to be leery about overtures to clients if the proposed interaction is potentially beneficial and if precautions are taken to prevent a "slippery slope." Client permission, which is required of all professional activities, should be required in this area as well. However, counselors must not be relieved of any responsibility for inadvertent harm done by their actions in this regard.

Confronting Counselors in Harmful Relationships With Clients or Trainees. As with breaches of all ethical standards, counselors who are aware of colleagues who are involved in harmful relationships with clients or trainees are obligated to confront the counselor in question. Most ethical codes allow a counselor first to confront the suspected unethical practitioner to attempt to rectify the problem before being obligated to report the concern formally to a legal or ethical authority. Colleagues have great potential influence over perpetrators of unethical behavior by addressing ethical concerns openly and by reeducating (or educating, in some cases) the unethical parties of ethical obligations. However, colleagues should report to authorities serious infractions or persistent concerns subsequent to reeducating or warning the perpetrator. In most cases, the reporting party is legally or professionally protected from retribution (e.g., immunity from any sort of legal counter suit). It is a professional counselor's responsibility to confront an unethical colleague. Borderline ethical concerns or dilemmas warrant discussion of the concerns with the offending counselor, as well as consultation with an authority on ethical matters (e.g., a member of a professional association's ethical practice committee). Persistent infractions by a counselor, or concerns of a serious or sexual nature, warrant a formal report to authorities.

QUESTIONS FOR REFLECTION

How are the 2005 ACA standards in Box 3.4 different from the standards in the current APA ethics code on the topic of multiple relationships? Which standards do you prefer, those of the ACA or APA?

QUESTION FOR REFLECTION

Which ethical principle(s) is(are) at the root of the standards in Box 3.4 that relate to avoiding potentially harmful relationships with clients—autonomy, nonmaleficence, beneficence, justice, or fidelity?

Informed Consent

Informed consent is the client's right to agree to participate in counseling, assessment, or other professional procedures or services after such services are fully explained and understood. Caudill (1998) stated:

> The premise, established in the 1972 case of *Cobb versus Grant* and the 1980 case of *Truman versus Thomas,* behind informed consent is that a patient should have access to all meaningful information in order to formulate an intelligent decision about whether to proceed with a particular course of treatment of a medical or psychological condition. The doctrine was originally defined with reference to medical care, where the options were generally quite clear and susceptible to formula application. (There are only so many ways to set a broken bone or to treat an infection). (p. 7)

However, there may be complications when this concept is applied to counseling. Caudill (1998) continued:

> The application of informed consent to psychotherapy, however, has led to some degree of confusion and murkiness. One of the problems in this regard is that unlike medicine, in the field of psychotherapy there are over 100 theoretical orientations and schools of thought. Thus, a therapist with a Freudian theoretical orientation will approach a problem markedly differently than one with a cognitive behavioral orientation. (p. 7)

Regardless, clients have the right to know the potential benefits or detriments of therapy or counseling. They should be fully informed of significant facts about procedures, what typically occurs, and the probable outcomes before treatment. Clients should be informed of the credentials or training of treating professionals, especially as related to specialized procedures. There should be no counselor coercion involved in a decision to undergo treatment. Alternative treatments, or alternatives to treatment, should also be addressed (see Caudill [1998] and Handelsman & Galvin [1988] for specific issues related to content and format of informed consent procedures).

Counselors generally present this information to clients in writing. The information should be clear and presented at a level that the client can understand (Handelsman, Kemper, Kesson-Craig, McLain, & Johnsrud, 1986). Counselors should ensure that clients are intellectually and emotionally able to understand the information provided so that they can make a true voluntary judgment (Handelsman & Galvin, 1988). Essentially, clients have freedom of choice to participate in counseling services.

Handelsman and Galvin (1988) provided a format for informed consent that lists questions the client can pose to the therapist. This format fosters open discussion of therapeutic issues and helps to establish a professional relationship and rapport. More recently, Handelsman (2001) made a compelling argument that informed consent should be considered a process, not an event. The consent process should be incorporated into the treatment process.

Informed consent alone does not legitimize treatment approaches. Caudill (1998) stated:

> Of course, tile fact that informed consent is given does not legitimize treatment approaches which are illegal or unethical. For example, in California there was a case in which therapists allegedly used a technique that involved beating the patient. In fact, they had informed consent forms which purported to authorize such treatment. In *Rains versus Superior Court* (1984), a California appellate court essentially held that it didn't matter what the consent form said, no such treatment was permissible. In addition, the cases are quite clear that an informed consent form will not legitimize treatment by an individual who does not have the requisite professional license. (p. 7)

Informed consent provisions do not override the responsibility of counselors to be nonmaleficent and to provide competent services.

Obtaining informed consent is not as serious a concern when clients are of legal (adult) age to consent and when they voluntarily seek treatment. However, it becomes a more serious concern when a client is a minor, when clients may not be fully competent to consent to treatment, or when there is a third-party referral. A third-party referral source is another individual, an agency, or an organization that directs the client to the provider of services. Clients referred by a third party sometimes go willingly and voluntarily submit to treatment. Other times, therapy is compulsory, meaning it is required for some legal reason. Compulsory therapy is initiated by a third-party referral source, usually as a form of rehabilitation or ongoing assessment when (a) the client has been involved with, is accused of, or is guilty of an illegal or potentially harmful act or when (b) treatment is viewed as a means to return a person to gainful activity when the person is receiving benefits or services for disability or other conditions. Examples of compulsory counseling are (a) a judge-ordered referral of an ex-offender who, as part of rehabilitation, must undergo counseling; (b) a workers' compensation company-referred injured client who is at risk of losing benefits and is required to undergo vocational assessment; (c) a chemically dependent parent who is at risk of losing custody of children through parental rights termination unless there is sobriety; and (d) a misbehaving child who is required to undergo assessment or therapy as a condition for return to school or other settings. In all of these cases, a third party requests evaluation or correction of the client's problem or condition. It is a client's right to consent to counseling. Even in cases of compulsory counseling, clients have the right to refuse services. If legal issues are involved, clients have the right to know if their counselor will testify on the case. If a counselor may be called to testify, the client must waive privileged communication, if applicable, and must be informed of the possible outcomes before accepting counseling services.

QUESTION FOR REFLECTION

Which ethical principle(s) is(are) at the root of the ethical standard of informed consent—autonomy, nonmaleficence, beneficence, justice, or fidelity?

Minor children involved in counseling technically do not have the right to consent to treatment; their parents or legal guardians have the right to consent for them. This is true in most states, but there are exceptions. Some states (by statute) allow minor children to seek counseling related to birth control, venereal disease, pregnancy or abortion, or substance abuse or dependence treatment without the consent of a parent or legal guardian. Barring such exceptions, parents or legal guardians not only have the right to consent to their children's counseling, they also, in most cases, may have the right to know what occurs in counseling and they may request termination of counseling at any time.

It is therapeutically and ethically wise for the counselor to consult a minor about treatment issues and to enlist the minor's participation when parental or guardian consent is given, even if there are limits to the confidential relationship. The limits of confidentiality must be addressed with the minor in a way that the minor understands: The minor must know that what is discussed in counseling can be shared with the parent or legal guardian.

Some counselors attempt to get a verbal or written agreement from parents or legal guardians that they will respect the minor's right to confidentiality. This is no guarantee, however. Unless there is clear statutory provision and case law for a parent or legal guardian's ability to waive informed consent and access to case information, such agreements must be viewed as tenuous, or even potentially misleading. Separate agreements that waive parental rights to informed consent or access to files may not be upheld legally. Certainly a parent or legal guardian would have the right to cancel such an arrangement at any time.

Obtaining informed consent is even more complicated when elderly or disabled persons are involved (Pepper-Smith, Harvey, Silberfeld, Stein, & Rutman, 1992). Can an elderly person with serious mental deterioration (e.g., dementia) consent to psychological or counseling assessment or treatment? Can a relative be consulted or informed? Many elderly clients may have diminished capacity to make informed judgments, yet they may be considered legally competent. These clients may be in vulnerable circumstances if an unscrupulous practitioner is involved. It is wise to obtain consent to inform and to consult with involved family members or to do family intervention in most cases in which a person's ability to make judgments is diminished. Such a person's informed consent to treatment may be in order technically. However, ethically, the involvement of family members may be necessary to ensure appropriate treatment when there is no legal guardian.

CASE SCENARIO 3–13

Informed Consent

A physician writes an order for a counselor to assess the IQ of a geriatric patient at a hospital. The patient consents. The IQ test and a thorough mental status assessment produce results of diminished capacity, but overall the IQ is in the low borderline range of measured intelligence. The counselor sends the bill for the assessment to Medicare and sends a co-payment bill to the spouse of the patient, who protests both the rationale for the test and the bill itself. The spouse claims that she should have been informed. Was anything done unethically in this case?

IT DEPENDS. The question on this case is, "Were the IQ testing and mental status assessment necessary for diagnostic or treatment reasons?" If so, nothing was done illegally, although a professional consult with a second opinion would be recommended, and appropriate consultation with family members (with permission) seems justified.

CASE SCENARIO 3–14

Informed Consent

A husband and wife attend their first marriage counseling session. They are never informed about the potential length of treatment, the probable results, or alternative treatments. The counselor simply begins counseling. Is this ethical?

NO. Most codes of ethics either explicitly or indirectly require: (a) the counselor to formally present procedure-relevant information and (b) the client to formally consent before treatment is initiated.

Professional Responsibility

Professional responsibility is the counselor's obligation to clients and to the counseling profession. It relates to the appropriateness of professional actions. In all cases, a professional counselor's responsibility is to advance the welfare of clients (Margolin, 1982). Counselors must not discriminate against those who seek their services. They cannot subjugate their obligations to their clients for the sake of monetary or other rewards. Professional counselors are also obligated to end their services if it becomes clear they are not helping or benefiting their clients.

Professional counselors are obligated to their employers as well as to their clients. They have a responsibility to serve their employers in a way that demonstrates competence and ethical sensitivity. Sometimes, however, conflicts arise between employing institutions and the best interests of clients. If such conflicts jeopardize the integrity of professional services rendered to clients, the counselor has an obligation to attempt to remedy the compromising conditions. When a reconciliation of institutional and professional conflicts is not forthcoming, the counselor has an obligation to terminate the affiliation with the employing institution, rather than to persist or compound the injustice. Just as physicians should not compromise the health and safety of their patients in a hospital that provides less than minimal standard care, counselors should refuse to treat clients in settings where the best interests of clients are in conflict with institutional interests. Professional counselors should always seek to develop treatment (work) environments where the employing institution's goals and objectives are consistent with a primary responsibility for competent and timely service to clients. (See the related discussion in Chapter 8 on office and administrative practices.)

QUESTION FOR REFLECTION

Which ethical principle(s) is(are) at the root of the ethical standard of responsibility—autonomy, nonmaleficence, beneficence, justice, or fidelity?

As you will learn in Chapter 12 (Couple and Family Counseling), defining one's professional responsibility for clients becomes complicated when there is more than one person receiving services in the counseling session. For example, who is the counselor responsible for in a marital counseling situation where partners are at odds over a major marital problem (assuming one partner is not endangered)? Can the counselor take sides, for example, if there has been an infidelity? Can the counselor take the side of one partner at the expense of the other partner? Counselors doing couple or family therapy often inform clients, before the initiation of treatment, that they avoid taking sides in disagreements, taking a role of "relationships advocate" (Margolin, 1982). Relationship advocacy means the counselor's responsibility is to help couples to help themselves save the relationship. So, in effect, the responsibility issue becomes complicated depending on the setting and nature of counseling. Regardless, the primary responsibility of counselors is to their clients, whether counseling occurs with an individual, a couple, a family, or a group.

It is important to recognize that the client is the person who is served, not the person or institution paying the bill (Cottone, 1982). Inexperienced or uninformed counselors or counselors who are unduly influenced by their business interests often mistakenly feel that their obligation is to the paying party. The counselor's principal obligation is always to the person receiving services—the client or counselee—unless there is potential danger to another individual or to society. In such a case, the counselor has a duty to warn the endangered party and the authorities. The presence of a third party (a person or institution) paying for services does not diminish, redirect, or in any way compromise the counselor's primary obligation to the counselee.

There may be limits to confidentiality or privileged communication if there is a third-party payer. In such cases, clients must be fully informed prior to the onset of treatment of any limits to confidentiality or privileged communication to ensure informed consent. Clients have the right to refuse treatment, even with the presence of a third-party payer, and counselors must respect the rights of clients to refuse treatment. Counselors have a clear responsibility to persons who receive their counseling services.

Persons who refuse treatment when there is third-party oversight may suffer consequences directly related to the relationship between the client and the overseeing person or agency (e.g., a third-party referral source or payer). Those consequences should be clearly circumscribed to the client's relationship with the third-party and should not impinge on the client's relationship with the counselor. Counselors have a primary responsibility to assess or treat fully informed clients competently and to communicate their findings only with the client's consent.

CASE SCENARIO 3–15

Responsibility

A counselor receives a referral from a friendly caseworker at the state family services agency. The caseworker communicates with the counselor that he is counseling a woman who is "disturbed." He wants her evaluated presumably for treatment potential, but notes that the information is really needed for possible parental rights termination. The counselor receives many cases from the referring caseworker at the family services agency, and the counselor agrees to assess the referred individual, saying, "I'll see what I can do." The client comes with the full intention of later receiving counseling under the auspices of the family service agency. Instead, the client is evaluated and never scheduled for later treatment, and the counselor's report appears as evidence in a parental rights termination hearing. Is this unethical?

PROBABLY. Assuming that the counselor informed the client of limits to confidentiality and privileged communication, this is still a probable breach of responsibility. This is especially true if the findings were in any way influenced by the prior stated intent of the caseworker to seek parental rights termination. The client should have been fully informed of the intent of the evaluation and its potential uses. Additionally, the evaluation should be as objective as possible in its recommendations, using standard and accepted means of assessment.

CASE SCENARIO 3–16

Responsibility

A school counselor/evaluator is given a case referred by a teacher who is a close friend. The teacher communicates to the counselor that the student is a "BD" (behavior-disordered) student and the teacher wants this child "out of my classroom" and "placed in special education." The counselor finds that much of the problem may be "embedded in" and "specific to" the teacher–student relationship, meaning there is less evidence for a diagnosis of BD in other settings. Yet the teacher has documented well the misbehavior of this student. The counselor recommends to the special education panel that a diagnosis/classification of BD is warranted. Is this ethical?

POSSIBLY. The counselor has an obligation to assess, historically and otherwise, the student's behavior in other settings with other authority figures. If the counselor's recommendation is primarily based on the friend's documentation and without otherwise independent competent assessment of competing outcome/recommendations, there is a breach of responsibility and probably a case of professional incompetence.

CASE SCENARIO 3–17

Responsibility

A researcher does a follow-up study on a previously tested hypothesis. The outcome conflicts with the prior conclusion and statistical findings. The researcher writes an article on the initial findings, but fails to acknowledge the follow-up study. The researcher also fails to acknowledge the work of one of her students who collected the data during the original study. The report is later published. Is this unethical?

YES. There is a breach of responsibility on two counts. First, the researcher has an obligation to report the findings of the follow-up study, even if it means the article might not be published. This omission is a breach of responsibility to the profession. Secondly, there is a breach of responsibility to the student who assisted in the study. The student should receive acknowledgment formally on the manuscript.

Competence

Professional competence focuses on two aspects of professional practice: (a) the quality of provided services and (b) the boundaries or scope of professional activity. Boundaries of professional activities involve whether the professional is trained, experienced, and licensed appropriately to perform certain procedures or treatments. **Counselor competence,** in the ethical sense, means that the counselor or therapist is capable of performing a minimum quality of service and that the service provided is clearly within the limits of training, experience, and practice as defined in professional standards or regulatory statutes. A counselor who tells a client not to take prescribed medication is unethical and is practicing illegally (literally practicing medicine without a license). A counselor who uses hypnotic technique may be well within the ethical and legal bounds of the counseling profession, depending on the counselor's past training and experience with hypnotic technique and regulation of hypnosis by statute. Both the quality issue and the scope-of-practice issue are implied in any discussion of professional competence.

Similarly, professional counselors or therapists who may be licensed to practice certain procedures or techniques should not perform those activities without appropriate specialized training in the area of practice in question. Professional licenses often define a scope of practice that is very broad, giving the licensed professional much latitude in his or her practice. Just because a counselor is licensed to do testing procedures does not mean the counselor can start administering intelligence tests without proper training and supervision of that practice. The scope of practice of a license does not supercede the competency of the individual counselor to perform certain procedures. Counselors, who are faced with doing procedures that are new to them, or desire to expand their personal scopes of practice, should request a professional consultation with a specialist who is trained and competent in the area. A **professional consultation** is a paid, formal arrangement wherein a consulting counselor obtains a second opinion, professional advice, or even supervision (to the extent of possible cotherapy) on an issue of concern from a knowledgeable, competent colleague. A licensed counselor with a rehabilitation counseling degree who does marriage counseling without ever having had a course or supervision in marriage counseling is practicing unethically (literally crossing the border of professional competence). In such cases, the rehabilitation counselor has an obligation to refer the client to, or to consult with, an appropriately trained and credentialed marriage counselor. Likewise, a marriage counselor should not suddenly begin chemical dependency treatment with a substance-dependent client without specialized training in chemical dependency; referral to or consultation with an appropriately trained substance abuse counselor is in order. Just because a professional is licensed to perform a procedure does not mean he or she can ethically perform the procedure. All physicians are licensed to do brain surgery, yet only those who have specialized training or experience in the procedure should be actively and independently doing it.

QUESTION FOR REFLECTION

Which ethical principle(s) appear(s) foundational to the concept of professional competence—autonomy, nonmaleficence, beneficence, justice, or fidelity?

Competency, however, is not as simple as what a licensure statute says one can do, or the extent of one's training for providing quality services. There are other issues that are crucial to the profession of counseling. Both the ACA and the APA have defined the need for competency related to working with individuals with culturally diverse backgrounds. In the 1990s there were major publications on the need for multicultural counselor competencies. Notably, Sue, Arredondo, and McDavis (1992) published "Multicultural counseling competencies: A call to the profession" in the *Journal of Counseling and Development.* That article summarized work that began in April of 1991, when the Association for Multicultural Counseling and Development (AMCD) outlined the need for a multicultural perspective in counseling. Subsequently, multicultural competencies were defined. The Sue et al. work was an attempt to bring the actions of the AMCD membership to the attention of the broader ACA membership. It provided a rationale and a need statement related to a multicultural perspective. The standards were also outlined. Since that time, the multicultural counselor competencies have been embraced by the counseling and psychology professions. Subsequent publications have outlined how multicultural competencies can be integrated into counseling practice (Arredondo, 1998; Hansen, Pepitone-Arreola-Rockwell, & Green, 2000). Multicultural issues are more thoroughly addressed in Chapter 11 (Ethics and Multiculturalism).

As a sign of the "technology" times, there are also concerns that counselors must be competent in alternative means of service delivery, most notably through technology. Today, with technological advances, it is possible to do counseling by phone, internet, or by e-mail, as examples. Assessment may now be computer assisted. Records are often digital and stored by means of computers. Facsimile (fax) machines may transmit records instantaneously. The practice of counseling has been enhanced and complicated by technology. In 1999, the Association for Counselor Education and Supervision (ACES) published its "Technical Competencies for Counselor Education Students: Recommended Guidelines for Program Development" (ACES, 1999). The ACES document not only addressed the need for counseling program graduates to have knowledge of technological applications, but also to "Be knowledgeable of the legal and ethical codes which relate to counseling services via the internet" (ACES, 1999). Counseling can no longer be conceptualized as sitting in a private room with a client. Technology has had a pervasive influence on the way counseling is provided and the resources that can be accessed and used. Wireless phones, as a simple example, have made counselors available to clients even when counselors are not near a land-based phone; counselors may be providing counseling to clients while they are in transit. The ethical implications of advances of technology are staggering, and this text devotes a whole chapter (Chapter 10) to these issues.

Suffice it to say, related to competencies, that the practice of counseling is changing due to a number of developments (e.g., multiculturalism and technology), and counselors are obliged to keep abreast of these concerns and to ensure competent and ethical practice in line with these developments.

CASE SCENARIO 3–18

Professional Competence

A school counselor has a client who is showing excessive anxiety; the counselor later learns that the client has been diagnosed by a psychiatrist as having "generalized anxiety disorder." The school counselor begins to arrange individual sessions of counseling and performs a technique called systematic desensitization, a behavioral technique used to ameliorate symptoms such as phobic anxiety when the anxiety results from the presentation of a specific object or situation. Is the counselor practicing unethically?

POSSIBLY NOT. If the anxiety is specifically school related and the counselor has been trained and supervised successfully in systematic desensitization, this activity is within the realm of competent practice. School anxieties, such as a phobia to testing or speaking in public, are treatable ethically by appropriately trained school counselors. On the other hand, if the phobia is not school-related, or if the counselor is attempting to treat the generalized anxiety disorder, this is questionable practice. It is generally understood that generalized anxiety disorder is not best treated by systematic desensitization. Also, the psychiatrist, if he or she was treating the client actively, should have been consulted, even regarding treatment of a circumscribed school phobia.

CASE SCENARIO 3–19

Professional Competence

A marriage counselor is counseling a couple that is having sexual difficulties. The problem is a complicated one, and the counselor's interventions have not produced a desirable outcome. The counselor has explained to the couple that although he has training to address certain sexual problems, he does not view himself as a sex therapist. Regardless, the husband and wife implore the counselor to continue treatment. They do not want to start over with another professional. The counselor continues to counsel the couple. Is this unethical?

PROBABLY. If other trained sex therapists are available, the counselor should either refer the couple to a sex therapist or professionally consult with one. On the other hand, if no other professional is available, the counselor has an obligation to immediately seek appropriate training or guidance and to serve the couple as best as possible.

DECISION MAKING IN CONTEXT

As you will learn in Chapter 6, professional decision making does not occur out of the context of a set of principles and standards for a profession. This chapter has laid out the ethical principles that have been historically linked to the professions of counseling and psychology. Also, ethical standards referenced in ethics codes for the professions of counseling and psychology have been delineated. These standards require critical analysis and evaluation. They are not defined by some omnipotent authority. Rather, they result from the consensual process of professionals, enlisted as "experts" by a professional association, who make a sincere effort to ensure that clients are being well served and not harmed by the profession. The principles act as global guides. The standards act as specific guidelines. Together, ethical principles and standards provide counselors with guidance as they face ethical dilemmas or as they address concerns by applying a decision-making model.

CHAPTER SUMMARY

Five principles guide ethical standards in the helping professions: autonomy, nonmaleficence, beneficence, justice, and fidelity. Counselors must abide by the ethical standards of confidentiality/privacy, privileged communication, avoidance of harmful relationships, informed consent, professional responsibility, and competence.

Confidentiality is the obligation of professionals to respect the privacy of clients and the information they provide. Counselors cannot reveal to others what is communicated in counseling without potential penalty of law, where there is legal confidentiality.

Privileged communication is a client's right to prevent the revelation of confidential information in a legal proceeding. A counselor cannot be forced to testify on a client's case if the privilege stands.

Harmful counselor–client relationships may involve: (1) sexual or romantic counselor–client interaction or (2) other avoidable nonprofessional relationships. Mental health professionals engaged in such relationships may face license suspension or revocation and legal consequences.

Informed consent is the client's right to agree to participate in counseling, assessment, or other professional procedures and services after such services are fully explained and understood. Clients must be fully informed of significant facts about procedures and possible outcomes before treatment.

Professional responsibility is the counselor's obligation to clients and to the counseling profession. Counselors have a primary responsibility to advance the welfare of their clients. They also bear responsibility to serve their employers in a way that demonstrates competence and ethical sensitivity.

Counselor competence means that the counselor or therapist is capable of performing a minimum quality of service and that the service is clearly within the limits of the counselor's training, experience, and practice as defined in professional standards or regulatory statutes. Counselors without specialized training in a particular area should refer clients to appropriately trained professionals.

REFERENCES

American Association for Marriage and Family Therapy. (1991). *Code of ethics.* Washington, DC: Author.

American Counseling Association. (1995, June). Code of ethics and standards of practice. *Counseling Today, 37*(12), 33–40.

American Counseling Association. (1996, July). Supreme Court extends confidentiality privilege. *Counseling Today, 39*(1), 1, 6, 10.

American Counseling Association. (2005). *Code of ethics.* Alexandria, VA: Author.

American Psychological Association. (2002). Ethical principles of psychologists and code of conduct. *American Psychologist, 57,* 1060–1073.

Anderson, S. K., & Kitchener, K. S. (1998). Nonsexual posttherapy relationships: A conceptual framework to assess ethical risks. *Professional Psychology: Research and Practice, 29,* 91–99.

Arredondo, P. (1998). Integrating multicultural counseling competencies and universal helping conditions in culture-specific contexts. *The Counseling Psychologist, 26,* 592–602.

Association for Counselor Education and Supervision. (1999). *Recommended technical competencies for counselor education students.* Alexandria, VA: Author.

Association of State and Provincial Psychology Boards. (2001). *Ethics, law and avoiding liability in the practice of psychology.* Montgomery, AL: Author.

Beauchamp, T. L., & Childress, J. F. (1979). *Principles of biomedical ethics* (1st ed.). New York: Oxford University Press.

Beauchamp, T. L., & Childress, J. F. (1983). *Principles of biomedical ethics* (2nd ed.). New York: Oxford University Press.

Beauchamp, T. L., & Childress, J. F. (2001). *Principles of biomedical ethics* (5th ed.). New York: Oxford University Press.

Bouhoutsos, J., Holroyd, J., Lerman, H., Forer, B. R., & Greenberg, M. (1983). Sexual intimacy between psychotherapists and patients. *Professional Psychology: Research and Practice, 14,* 185–196.

Carrier, J. W. (2004). Assessing suicidal risk. In D. Capuzzi (Ed.), *Suicide across the life span: Implications for counselors,* (pp. 139–162). Alexandria, VA: American Counseling Association.

Caudill, O. B. (1998, February/March). The hidden issue of informed consent. *Family Therapy News,* p. 7.

Cohen, E. D. (1990). Confidentiality, counseling, and clients who have AIDS: Ethical foundations of a model rule. *Journal of Counseling and Development, 68,* 282–286.

Cottone, R. R. (1982). Ethical issues in private for-profit rehabilitation. *Journal of Applied Rehabilitation Counseling, 13*(3), 14–17, 24.

Cottone, R. R. (2005). Detrimental therapist—client relationships—Beyond thinking of "dual" or "multiple" roles: Reflections on the 2001 AAMFT Code of Ethics. *The American Journal of Family Therapy, 33,* 1–77.

Cottone, R. R., Kocet, M. M., & Glosoff, H. L. (2005). *Building a foundation for ethical* practice. On-line course. American Counseling Association.

Handelsman, M. M. (1987). Confidentiality: The ethical baby in the legal bathwater. *Journal of Applied Rehabilitation Counseling, 18*(4), 33–34.

Handelsman, M. M. (2001). Accurate and effective informed consent. In E. Welfel & E. Ingersoll (Eds.), *The mental health desk reference: A sourcebook for counselors and therapists.* New York: Wiley.

Handelsman, M. M., & Galvin, M. D. (1988). Facilitating informed consent for outpatient psychotherapy: A suggested written format. *Professional Psychology: Research and Practice, 19*, 223–225.

Handelsman, M. M., Kemper, M. B., Kesson-Craig, P., McLain, J., & Johnsrud, C. (1986). Use, content, and readability of written informed consent forms for treatment. *Professional Psychology: Research and Practice, 17*, 514–518.

Handelsman, M. M., Knapp, S., & Gottlieb, M. C. (2002). In C. R. Snyder & S. J. Lopez (Eds.), *Handbook of positive psychology* (pp. 731–744). New York: Oxford University Press.

Hansen, N. D., Pepitone-Arreola-Rockwell, F., & Green, A. F. (2000). Multicultural competence: Criteria and case examples. *Professional Psychology: Research and Practice, 31*, 652–660.

Harding, A. K., Gray, L. A., & Neal, M. (1993). Confidentiality limits with clients who have HIV: A review of ethical and legal guidelines and professional policies. *Journal of Counseling and Development, 71*, 297–305.

Harris, S. M. (2001). Teaching family therapists about sexual attraction in therapy. *Journal of Marital and Family Therapy, 27*, 123–128.

Haug, I. (1993). *AAMFT luncheon plenary on "Dual Relationships: Sex, Power, and Exploitation."* (Audiotape cassette recording published through the AAMFT Resource Link). Norcross, GA (1-800-241-7785).

Herlihy, B., & Sheeley, V. L. (1987). Privileged communication in selected helping professions: A comparison among statutes. *Journal of Counseling and Development, 65*, 479–483.

Howie, J., Gatens-Robinson, E. & Rubin, S. E. (1992). Applying ethical principles in rehabilitation counseling. *Rehabilitation Education, 6*, 41–55.

Hummel, D. L., Talbutt, L. C., & Alexander, M. D. (1985). *Law and ethics in counseling.* New York: Van Nostrand Reinhold.

Jaffee v. Redmond et al. 1996 WL 315841 (U.S. June 13, 1996).

Kitchener, K. S. (1984). Intuition, critical evaluation, and ethical principles: The foundations for ethical decisions in counseling psychology. *Counseling Psychologist, 12*, 43–55.

Kitchener, K. S. (1988). Dual role relationships: What makes them so problematic? *Journal of Counseling and Development, 67*, 217–221.

Lamb, D. H., Catanzaro, S. J., & Moorman, A. S. (2004). A preliminary look at how psychologists identify, evaluate, and proceed when faced with possible multiple relationship dilemmas. *Professional Psychology: Research and Practice, 35*, 248–254.

Lazarus, A. A. (2001, January/February). Not all "dual relationships" are taboo: Some tend to enhance treatment outcomes. *The National Psychologist, 10*(1), 16.

Lazarus, A. A., & Zur, O. (Eds.). (2002). *Dual relationships and psychotherapy.* New York: Springer.

Margolin, G. (1982). Ethical and legal considerations in marital and family therapy. *American Psychologist, 37*, 788–801.

Meara, N. M. Schmidt, L. P., & Day, J. D. (1996). Principles and virtue: A foundation for ethical decisions, policies, and character. *The Counseling Psychologist, 24*, 4–77.

New patient records privacy rule takes effect. (2001, Spring). *Practitioner Update, 9*(1), 1, 4.

Pepper-Smith, R., Harvey, W. R., Silberfeld, M., Stein, E., & Rutman, D. (1992). Consent to a competency assessment. *International Journal of Law and Psychiatry, 15*, 13–23.

Pope, K. S. (1988). How clients are harmed by sexual contact with mental health professionals: The syndrome and its prevalence. *Journal of Counseling and Development, 67*, 222–226.

Pope, K. S., Keith-Spiegel, P., & Tabachnick, B. G. (1986). Sexual attraction to clients: The human therapist and the (sometimes) inhuman training system. *American Psychologist, 41*, 147–158.

Public Law 104–191. (1996). *Health Insurance Portability and Accountability Act.* Retrieved July 8, 2004 from http://aspe.hhs.gov/admnsimp/101104191.htm.

Reaves, R. P. (1999). *Avoiding liability in mental health practice.* Montgomery, AL: Association of State and Provincial Psychology Boards.

Remley, T. P., Herlihy, B., & Herlihy, S. B. (1997). The U. S. Supreme Court decision in *Jaffee v. Redmond:* Implications for

counselors. *Journal of Counseling and Development, 75*, 213–218.

Rogers, C. R. (1951). *Client-centered therapy.* Boston, MA: Houghton-Mofflin.

Santa Rosa Health Care Corporation v. Garcia, 964 S.W. 2nd 940 (Texas, 1998).

Schlossberger, E., & Hecker, L. (1996). HIV and family therapists' duty to warn: A legal and ethical analysis. *Journal of Marital and Family Therapy, 22*, 27–40.

Stanard, R., & Hazler, R. (1995). Legal and ethical implications of HIV and duty to warn for counselors: Does *Tarasoff* apply? *Journal of Counseling and Development, 73*, 397–400.

Sue, D. W., Arredondo, P., & McDavis, R. J. (1992). Multicultural counseling competencies: A call to the profession. *Journal of Counseling and Development, 70*, 477–486.

Tarasoff v. the California Board of Regents, 13C. 3d 177, 529 P. 2d 553, 118 Cal. Rptr. 129 (1974).

Thoreson, R. W., Shaughnessy, P., & Frazier, P. A. (1995). Sexual contact during and after professional relationships: Practices and attitudes of female counselors. *Journal of Counseling and Development, 74*, 84–89.

Thoreson, R. W., Shaughnessy, P., Heppner, P. P., & Cook, S. W. (1993). Sexual contact during and after the professional relationship: Attitudes and practices of male counselors. *Journal of Counseling and Development, 71*, 429–434.

Tomm, C. (1993). *AAMFT luncheon plenary on "Dual Relationships: Sex, Power, and Exploitation."* (Audiotape cassette recording published through the AAMFT Resource Link). Norcross, GA (1-800-241-7785).

United States Department of Health and Human Services (2003). *Summary of the HIPAA privacy rule.* Washington, DC: Author.

VandeCreek, L., & Knapp, S. (1993). *Tarasoff and beyond: Legal and clinical considerations in the treatment of life-endangering patients* (2nd ed.). Sarasota, FL: Professional Resource Press.

Vasquez, M. J. T. (1988). Counselor–client sexual contact: Implications for ethics training. *Journal of Counseling and Development, 67*, 238–241.

Wilson, C. A. Rubin, S. E., & Millard, R. P. (1991). Preparing rehabilitation educators to deal with ethical dilemmas. *Journal of Applied Rehabilitation Counseling, 22*(1), 30–33.

Younggren, J. N., & Gottlieb, M. C. (2004). Managing risks when contemplating multiple relationships. *Professional Psychology: Research and Practice, 35*, 255–260.

CHAPTER 4

Ethics and the Law

OBJECTIVES

After reading this chapter, you should be able to:

- Describe the complex relationship between ethics and the law.
- Identify the legal mechanisms that are relevant to the practice of counseling.
- Explain the key challenges facing counselors during the four phases of the counseling

relationship, including: counselor competency, informed consent, confidentiality and privileged communication, exceptions to confidentiality, recordkeeping, dangerousness and crisis concerns, and termination issues.

INTRODUCTION

Many counselors find the relationship between their clinical practices and the dictates of the law unsettling, and this relationship makes them feel vulnerable. In the past, it was not uncommon for counselors simply to hope that their basically sound clinical methods would be congruent with appropriate legal practices. Such a passive, reactive approach will not work for professional counselors, who need to understand and actively manage the legal aspects of their practices.

Counseling is a dynamic, well-recognized profession. The standing of counselors as independent and responsible professionals has been recognized legally by 48 states and the District of Columbia through counselor licensure (at the time of this writing). It is not unusual for counselors to be involved in such highly charged events such as diagnosing their clients as having a serious mental disorder, recommending that custody of a child be terminated, testifying at a hearing

regarding the effects of spousal abuse, or counseling an adult with mild mental retardation regarding reproductive rights and options. Counselors also provide forensic services related to their counseling expertise in countless civil, criminal, and administrative hearings. It is only reasonable to assume that with increased visibility and professional status, counselors will be held legally accountable for their actions. More importantly, counselors must understand and protect the legal rights of their clients.

QUESTION FOR REFLECTION

Examine the current ACA and APA codes of ethics related to law. They address the relationship between ethics and law. How are practitioners directed by these codes?

Counselors must approach the relationship between law and ethics with a constructive and clear-headed perspective. Many years ago, Ware (1971) considered the relationship between law and professional judgment in reconciling legislated and ethical standards of conduct. She noted that both tend to remain broad and open to situational interpretation, and she provided advice that continues to be meaningful to the profession's contemporary legal environment: Beware the tendency to look to other professions for standards to reconcile these conflicts. Noting counselors' emerging interest in the law, Ware described the phenomenon as a function of two factors: (1) a hope that the law would relieve counselors from the pressure to resolve complex or vague professional dilemmas; and (2) a fear that counselors might be sued regarding some legal violation. Ware concluded that although knowledge of legal standards is necessary to address issues in a balanced way, it would be unwise to rest too much hope on legal remedy or to fear the law too greatly. Balancing knowledge and respect with all clinically relevant factors not just the law is the approach taken by wise decision makers.

THE RELATIONSHIP BETWEEN LAW AND ETHICS

Both law and ethics have effects on the counselor–client relationship. Generally, the law is supportive or neutral in dealing with professional ethical codes and standards. The legal structure is neutral in most instances, allowing the profession to govern its practitioners' conduct and practices. Only in instances in which public health, safety, or welfare is threatened does the legal system tend to intervene and override the ethical codes of the profession. Counselors must have a situation-specific interpretation of both legal and ethical regulatory standards to conduct well-informed practice. Codes of ethics are not intended to supersede the law, but rather to clarify existing law and policy. (This close relationship between societal morals and values and professional values will receive detailed discussion in Chapter 5.) When instances occur in which ethical standards conflict with the law, it is difficult to reconcile legislated and ethical standards of conduct. Both standards are broad and open to situational interpretation, so counseling organizations need to work with bar associations, legislatures, the judiciary, and their own memberships to educate and to achieve better standards.

Counselors must think dynamically about the relationships among the law, the ethical standards of their profession, and their individual professional ethical and moral consciences. On rare occasions, counselors may be required to exercise personal and professional judgment when the legal and ethical requirements are at odds. Counselors should not be shocked at the possibility of at least considering this option. Other professions regularly grapple with this dynamic and daunting possibility as part of their ethical obligations. For example, traditionally journalists have considered being held in contempt of court and even being imprisoned rather than name their confidential sources if they have promised them confidentiality in order to gather valuable and often sensitive information.

The codes of ethics for the mental health professions offer relatively limited guidance in the instance when the apparent dictates of law and ethics conflict. The APA code of ethics provides no overall requirement to abide by any legal statute or administrative rule. It does contain several specific standards requiring conformity with legal requirements related to referral practices, fee practices, research and practices with research animals, and familiarity with rules concerning forensic work. Typically, ethical standards generally state that in cases of conflict, practitioners should make the parties aware of the conflict and their commitment to the ethical standards and attempt to resolve the conflict in a responsible manner. Other codes of ethics sometimes defer to the law (Remley, 1996).

Even when the code of ethics states that the professional should abide by the dictates of the law, the problem of what should be done in a specific instance of conflict is not resolved for two reasons:

1. It is the responsibility of the professional to weigh all aspects of a situation, determine which ethical and legal standards apply in general, and decide how they apply in this instance. Clients vary and each set of circumstances adds situational complexity to the interpretation. Counselors must exercise their judgment regarding the issues and concerns embedded in the situation. Through this interpretation, counselors can assess the appropriateness and applicability of the ethical and legal standards. It can be argued that the norm of engaging in such a level of independent judgment with the intent of upholding the principles and standards of the profession distinguishes a true profession from a skilled occupation.

2. Even after thorough efforts to resolve the conflict lawfully, the legal option for action may not be in the best ethical interests of the client—the counselor's

primary ethical obligation. Authorities on moral development and ethical decision-making theory recognize that the best solution to an ethical dilemma may violate the law in the interests of a higher moral or conscience level of analysis (Kohlberg, 1964, 1981; Van Hoose & Paradise, 1979).

These models are discussed in greater detail in Chapter 6. It is generally accepted that counselors and other professionals have a strong **prima facie** obligation to abide by the legal requirements of a situation. Prima facie, a Latin phrase, means that the obligation in question must be considered in every case and set aside only if valid and compelling reasons to do so are present in a specific instance. These reasons would involve ethical or legal reasons of greater importance than the specific legal rule in question.

Thompson (1990) noted that there are six interactions between ethics and the law. The examples listed in Table 4–1 illustrate the distinctions.

When counselors are faced with an apparent conflict between ethics and the law, they must take steps to resolve it. They must recognize that forces other than law and ethics may clash to create conflict. For example, employer policies and procedures, accreditation rules, or funding source rules might be at issue rather than the law. Remley (1996) recommended the following steps to guide the counselor in such conflicts.

1. Identify the force that is at issue regarding the counselor's behavior . . .
2. If a legal question exists, legal advice should be obtained . . .
3. If there is a problem in applying an ethical standard to a particular situation or in understanding the requirements of an ethical standard, the best action a counselor could take is to consult with colleagues and with those perceived to be experts in the counseling field . . .
4. If a force other than law or ethics (for example, an employer, an accrediting body, or a funding agency) is suggesting that a counselor take some action he or she perceives to be illegal, the counselor should seek legal advice to determine whether such action is indeed illegal. (p. 288)

Counselors must involve themselves in efforts to change laws that they believe place their clients at risk or cause them injury or harm. This determination often is not easy for counselors to make. For example, state law might force counselors to report the physical abuse of children as soon as they become aware of the abuse. This action might be taken despite the fact that the child must return home at the end of the session pending an investigation and might be in even more danger

TABLE 4–1 Interactions Between Ethics and the Law

	Example	
1. Ethical & Legal	Following a just law	Keeping a client's confidences that are also protected by law from disclosure
2. Ethical & Illegal	Disobeying an unjust law	Refusing to breach promised confidentiality even though ordered to by court
3. Ethical & Alegal	Doing good where no law applies	Offering free service to poor clients
4. Unethical & Legal	Following an unjust law	Following the Federal Trade Commission's edict that ethical codes cannot prohibit the use of testimonials in ads for counseling services
5. Unethical & Illegal	Breaking a just law	Disclosing confidential information protected by law from disclosure
6. Unethical & Alegal	Doing harm that no law prohibits	Promoting client dependency to enhance one's own feeling of power

Note: Adapted from *Guide to Ethical Practice in Psychotherapy* by A. Thompson, 1990, New York: John Wiley & Sons. Copyright 1990 by John Wiley & Sons. Adapted by permission.

of serious harm in retaliation for reporting the abuse to the counselor.

At its best, the legal system has stimulated the mental health professions to enhance their ethical standards. The careful ethical practices commonly used by counselors to warn and to protect potential victims of their dangerous clients are owed to the lessons learned in the landmark decisions surrounding the *Tarasoff v. the Regents of the University of California* (1974) court case (see Chapter 3). That decision and the related rulings that followed it are now collectively known as the *Tarasoff doctrine*. They have occasioned intense professional review and, in general, have positively influenced the growth of ethical standards and counseling interventions with dangerous clients for almost the past three decades.

LEGAL MECHANISMS

Society holds all mental health professionals accountable for maintaining proper clinical and ethical standards of practice through four legal mechanisms: professional ethics committees, state licensure boards, criminal courts, and civil courts (Pope & Vasquez, 1998).

Counselors and other mental health professionals are not expected to have expert knowledge of legal concepts and mechanisms and how they apply to their work at the same level as would an attorney. In fact, they are expected to have no special legal knowledge beyond that of a competent layperson (Shea, 1985), but they must seek legal opinions as needed. Nevertheless, counselors are aided by knowledge of the basic legal mechanisms that govern their practices. Such knowledge might allow them to avoid important missteps, anticipate possible legal entanglements, and react more appropriately to legal processes should the need arise.

The U.S. Constitution and federal, state, and local levels are the essential levels of legal authority (Remley, 1996). Laws pertaining to particular matters often differ from jurisdiction to jurisdiction. These differences can be quite striking from state to state, potentially leading to radically different implications for lawful, proper conduct in the same situation. For instance, the issues of privacy and confidentiality for clients who are HIV positive receive radically different treatment in the laws of various state jurisdictions. (See Burris [2001] for an excellent discussion of legal considerations that relate to working with clients who are HIV positive.)

A number of useful resources about state statutes, federal law, and court rulings that are relevant to counselors and other mental health professionals are available. Helpful references include the series of volumes published by the APA on state laws for mental health professionals, additional information on legal aspects of practice offered by Remley and Herlihy (2005), and a comprehensive overview of legal issues for the helping professions by Swenson (1997). In addition, the internet provides a number of useful sites to research state and other legal information. These resources allow counselors to become more intelligent consumers of legal services to understand their clients' legal situations.

Legal consultation is often imperative to understand the "terms of art" used in law, whose meanings vary from common understanding. The law itself varies from state to state—either in terms of the specific laws enacted by state legislatures or the way the courts within local jurisdictions have interpreted it in specific cases. The body of court rulings that interpret a law establishes what is known as case law. **Case law** provides precedents that are relevant to the law's interpretation in specific circumstances and jurisdictions and contributes to the evolution of a legal concept. Counselors must determine what laws and interpretations are relevant for any legal issues raised in the state and local jurisdictions in which they practice. For instance, all 50 states have some form of law that requires mandatory reporting of child abuse by mental health and other professionals. However, the definition of child abuse, the evidence necessary to report it, and the manner and timing of its reporting vary. Some states do not differentiate between neglect and abuse, but others do (Fischer & Sorenson, 1985; Remley & Herlihy, 2005). Although counselors are not expected to have advanced legal knowledge, they are obligated to have basic knowledge of their own state statutes and case law related to their profession.

Laws are also classified as civil or criminal. **Civil law** involves the obligation of citizens to one another. The obligation must be asserted by the individual before the obligation is enforced by the government (Remley, 1996). A civil matter involves an offense to an individual. The remedy is some form of compensation to the victim (Keary, 1985). Malpractice, the most common cause of legal liability for mental health practitioners, is a type of civil action (see Chapter 1). There are four legal elements or factors that must be proven if the plaintiff is to prevail or prove malpractice. They are:

- The counselor and client have entered into a professional relationship with one another and as a result, the counselor owes the client a duty of care.

- The counselor fails in this duty of care either as the result of negligent or substandard care.
- The client is either physically or materially harmed by this care.
- The conduct of the counselor was the *proximate cause* of the harm or injury to the client.

That is, the conduct of the counselor can be proven to have a close causal connection to the harm or injury (Swenson, 1997). In reviewing these four elements, it is clear that it is not easy to prove all four conditions exist in a particular case, especially the last element of proximate cause. For example, it may be very clear from evidence presented that a client who committed suicide was in a counseling relationship with a counselor, and that obviously he did suffer the ultimate harm when he shot himself. It may also be debatable in expert testimony whether the counselor used the best possible judgment in accepting the client's no-harm contract as assurance the client was safe to return to the community. However, what might be most unclear is whether the counselor's behavior in the counseling session, or the statement of the client's supervisor that he might be laid off at work the hour after he returned from his counseling session was the most likely explanation for why the client committed suicide. The difficulty of proving malpractice cases, as well as the attractive possibility of removing from practice a practitioner seen as dangerous, may account for the increase of ethical grievances being filed with state licensure board disciplinary committees (Welch, 2005). See Box 4–1 for information about the most common administrative and clinical areas for malpractice actions with mental health professionals.

Criminal law involves conduct required of all citizens or prohibited to all and is enforced by the government's legal authorities. In criminal matters, the state punishes the violator; punishments may involve imprisonment, fines, or death (Remley, 1996). Criminal actions against counselors in matters unrelated to their professional roles are likely just as common as those for members of the general public. The most frequent type of professionally related criminal offense for psychotherapists is fraud related to third-party billings (Pope & Vasquez, 1998). Engaging in sexual intimacy with a client is also a criminal offense in some states, including the following 13 states: California, Colorado, Connecticut, Florida, Georgia, Iowa, Maine, Michigan, Minnesota, New Mexico, North Dakota, South Dakota, and Wisconsin, and this trend toward criminalization of sexual contact between client and therapist seems to be growing (Kane, 1995).

The legal system embodies what society considers a minimum level of acceptable behavior on the part of its citizens. Professional organizations generally wish to strive for higher standards of behavior in professional practice and enforce these standards upon their members. However, no society will delegate all authority for such enforcement solely to the profession because it must continue to protect the rights and well-being of its citizenry. Thus, ethical and legal standards should be complementary in most instances, although both require different interpretations to be fully understood.

Box 4–1 • **Most Common Types of Malpractice for Mental Health Professionals (Welch, 2003)**

Administrative Risks
1. Improper record-keeping policies and procedures
2. Impact of HIPAA
3. Disclosure and informed consent
4. Responding to subpoenas
5. Staying in touch with ethical principles
6. Purchasing adequate licensing board insurance

Treatment Risks
1. Patient suicide
2. Family treatment and forensic situations
3. Clients with borderline personality disorder
4. Handling state licensing boards and ethics committees
5. Managed care and treatment limitations
6. Personal events in the life of the professional

Note: Adapted from "After Five Years, Fresh Insight" by Bryant Welch, 2005. *Insight: Safeguarding Psychologists Against Liability Risks*, Edition 3, 2005, p. 1.

COMMON LEGAL CONCERNS

Any number of possible legal issues exist that may affect counselors in the course of their service to clients. The most frequent legal concerns are fewer and more predictable due to counselors' increased awareness of the ethical aspects of counseling practice. Practitioners should recognize the more frequent issues and develop a well-informed approach to handling them—a series of conceptual templates for legal risk situations. By doing so, inexperienced counselors can anticipate and handle many of the standard issues more capably and know the initial steps to take when confronted with the more serious, complex situations. Such a proactive mental structure is important for better management of legal risk and liability exposure. DePauw (1986) provided a useful template for anticipating important ethical concerns in counseling practice, proposing that counselors adopt a standard, natural timeline perspective for ethical considerations. The timeline approach alerts the counselor to specific problems as they may arise within the stages of client service. This approach allows counselors to anticipate the natural rhythm of issues in their individual relationships with clients. DePauw incorporated many of the key challenges in client services and noted ethical matters in four phases of the counseling relationship:

1. Initiation phase issues;
2. Ongoing counseling issues;
3. Dangerousness and crisis concerns;
4. Termination phase issues.

Figure 4–1 presents the issues considered within each phase.

Initiation Phase Issues

The initiation phase includes the areas of precounseling, service provision, and informed consent. During this phase, counselors reach out to potential clients and ready them to enter into counseling relationships appropriately prepared and informed.

Counselor Competency.   It is critical for the well-being of clients that counselors possess adequate skills, experience, and training to serve them competently. Additionally, it is important that counselors assure themselves and their clients that they have these necessary qualities. By doing so, counselors limit their

I. *Initiation Phase Issues*
  A. Precounseling considerations
    1. advertising
    2. avoiding misuse of institutional affiliations
    3. financial arrangements
    4. donated services
  B. Service provision issues
    1. adequacy of counselor skills, experience, and training (competency)
    2. better service option for client
    3. concurrent counselor involvement
    4. conflicting dual relationships
  C. Informed consent issues
    1. structures to educate regarding purposes, goals, and techniques
    2. explanation of rules of procedure and limitations
    3. supervision and consultation release concerns
    4. experimental methods of treatment
II. *Ongoing Counseling Issues*
  A. Confidentiality
  B. Special issues of confidentiality
    1. children
    2. groups
  C. Consultation
  D. Record keeping
III. *Dangerousness and Crisis Concerns*
  A. Threat to self
  B. Threat to others
  C. Child abuse
  D. Gray areas (e.g., HIV/AIDS and dying client issues)
IV. *Termination Phase Issues*

FIGURE 4–1.   Timeline Perspective on Ethical and Legal Considerations

Note: From "Avoiding Ethical Violations: A Timeline Perspective for Individual Counseling" by M. E. DePauw, 1986. *Journal of Counseling & Development, 64*(5), 303–305. Copyright 1986 by American Counseling Association. Reprinted by permission.

liability and observe any regulations that require them to practice only within a specific scope of practice.

Counseling and other professional licensure laws commonly include definitions of the profession, as well as the practice and procedures of the profession. Taken together, these statutory definitions, and any regulations that may pertain to them, define the scope of practice for the profession within a jurisdiction. The definitions are usually drawn from those established by the profession's organizations at the national level. For example, since the 1980s the ACA has used its model counselor licensure bill to encourage a more regularized structure for individual state laws. In addition, ACA and the AASCB have had discussions to establish shared standards for counselor qualifications to be used by AASCB as it establishes a National Credentials Registry. Once established, the National Credentials Registry would assist counselors licensed in one state who register with the AASCB registry program and establish a credentials file in being able to more efficiently establish their credentials as they move from state to state throughout the courses of their careers if they select states that will accept the National Credentials Registry program (AASCB, 2005); this mechanism is called portability. Enhancing portability of counselor licensure credentials is a critical issue for the progress of counselor professionalization that hinges on a shared understanding of the counselor's scope of practice and the core requirements for counselor licensure.

A scope of practice is a statement of the extent and limit of practices considered acceptable to become licensed or certified professionals. More broadly defined,

it is a recognized area of proficiency or competence gained through appropriate education and experience. In most cases, the scope of practice is related closely to the profession's definition of its areas of competency. Professionals licensed under a specific law may operate within the limits of the scope of practice as described within that jurisdiction's law and regulations.

The professional scope of practice is different than the individual counselor's scope of practice, although they do overlap. An individual's scope of practice is based on one's own knowledge and skills gained through education and professional experience (see Figure 4–2 which graphically illustrates the relationship between the profession's and individual's identities and scopes of practice). Counselors are bound ethically to limit their practice to the scope of practice for which they are prepared within the profession's larger scope. In addition, the licensure regulations of many states require that professionals must identify their personal scope of practice and stipulate that they will practice within this area. Sometimes this includes the provision of a written statement of the scope of

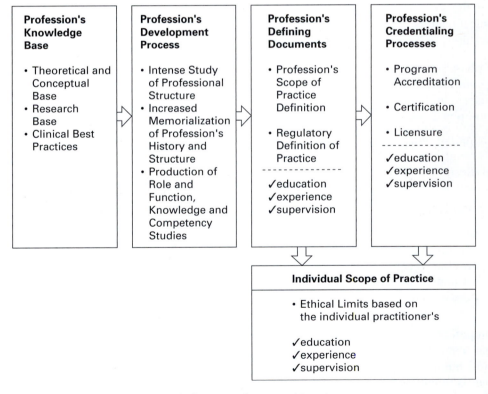

FIGURE 4–2. Your Professional Identity and Scope of Practice

practice to the licensure board. This statement then constitutes the appropriate legal and ethical limitations to the counselor's practice.

Counselors should not provide or supervise services to clients outside their area of expertise. Their scopes of practice should be made clear to prospective clients before they are accepted into practice. Referral to another professional is appropriate if the client's problem falls outside the counselor's scope of practice (Anderson, 1996). If counselors work with clients or techniques outside their areas of competency, they could be disciplined if the licensure board becomes aware of it, or the work might become a negative factor in a malpractice lawsuit if it can be demonstrated that the counselors used techniques for which they were not trained that resulted in harm to the clients.

Another important concern for all counselors, regardless of their level of skill or experience, is to responsibly maintain or add to their levels of competence. Both new counselors and experienced counselors may need to add a skill or area of practice to their professional practice capabilities. Licensing and certification bodies expect counselors who hold their credentials to engage in continuing education to maintain or add knowledge and skills, learn new procedures, and learn about needs of changing client populations. Counselors often enter into new practice areas with some concern and trepidation about how to gain the necessary competencies without unduly exposing their clients to risk or ineffective service. An individualized, systematic, and developmental continuing education program that includes specific personal professional goals and activities to meet these goals is an indispensable tool to enhance competency levels. Responsible professionals have a rich number of in-service, continuing education workshops, university courses, and programs to form an initial basis of learning new information. Many of these activities are offered through distance education programs for those who cannot participate through traditional means such as conferences and on-location workshops. In addition, it is critical to practice new skills until they are mastered with the supervision or collaboration of a colleague who is skilled in the new area of competence. It is important to look for a balance of didactic and practice activities, as well as proper supervision, to assure that the counselor has adequately achieved the desired level of competency in the new skill area.

QUESTION FOR REFLECTION

What should a classically trained school counselor, supervised in a school setting and licensed to practice independently in a state, do before setting up a private practice in marriage counseling?

Informed Consent Issues.   Clients have the right to make informed choices about their care. Counselors have the legal duty to provide their clients with sufficient information and to make sure they fully understand it before making their decisions. This practice originated within medical treatment settings and is known as informed consent—the client's right to agree to participate in counseling assessment, or professional procedures or services after such services are fully described and explained in a manner that is comprehensible to the client.

As the counselor and the client enter into the counseling relationship, they enter into a contractual relationship as well. This contract may be formal if it is written, or it may be spoken between the two parties. Both parties to the relationship must understand the basic aspects of the situation into which they may enter. Documentation is important to clarify what the counselor is, and is not, promising to do for the client. If one party thinks that the other party has not provided the items that were agreed on, that person may consider the contract violated—a legal charge called **breach of contract.**

Counselors should begin the informed consent process by engaging in a screening or precounseling consultation—this might be an aspect of the initial intake meeting. An initial precounseling consultation is an excellent tool to ensure that adequate and attentive initial preparation is available to both parties. At that time, certain basic information about the client's issues and objectives for counseling and the counselor's competency must be discussed to ascertain if the counselor is the appropriate helper for this individual client (Anderson, 1996).

Although there are many types of information that the counselor would be wise to provide to the client, some basic issues should be part of a thorough precounseling consent process. Discussing the common limits to confidentiality is particularly important at this initiation of counseling stage (see Chapter 3). Bertram and Wheeler (1994) included 20 topics on their checklist for a written informed consent for treatment (see

Appendix C). This document provides a thorough and useful format. Additionally, the counselor should discuss the same information with the client to reinforce the client's understanding of what is likely to occur in counseling. Generally, a written consent to treatment or a related document (i.e., professional disclosure statement or therapeutic contract) should address areas such as: (a) the therapeutic process, (b) background of the therapist, (c) costs involved in therapy, (d) length of therapy and termination, (e) consultation with colleagues, (f) interruptions in therapy (e.g., vacations, illness), (g) client's right of access to files, (h) rights pertaining to diagnostic labeling, (i) nature and purpose of confidentiality, (j) audiotape or videotape recording, (k) the benefits and risks of treatment, and (l) alternatives to traditional therapy (Corey, Corey, & Callanan, 2003). Many of these areas are ethically required according to professional codes of ethics. For example, among some of the types of information the ACA Code of Ethics (ACA, 2005) obliges the counselor to disclose are: (a) the purposes, goals, techniques, procedures, limitations, and potential risks of counseling, (b) the counselor's qualifications, credentials, and relevant experience, (c) the limitations of confidentiality, (d) how counseling services will be provided in the event of the counselor's incapacitation or death, (e) when the counselor changes roles from the original or most recent role and informs the client of the right to refuse services, (f) the limitations and conditions of services provided through use of technology, (g) limitations of confidentiality and foreseeable situation in which confidentiality must be breached, and (h) the nature and purposes of assessment and the specific use of results by potential recipients of the results. Professional disclosure statements are important, useful documents for both the counselor and the client; they constitute a legal contract and are often signed by both parties (Remley & Herlihy, 2005). In addition, any written contract or document should be periodically discussed and updated to fit the current nature of the agreed-upon work in which the counselor and client are engaged.

QUESTIONS FOR REFLECTION

How do the current ACA and APA codes of ethics address requirements of informed consent? What specifically must be addressed in the informed consent process?

Shaw and Tarvydas (2001) noted several benefits of using professional disclosure forms, including: (a) pro-moting client comprehension, (b) increasing client responsibility, (c) reducing the likelihood of client exploitation through a "contract" format, (d) reducing future conflicts because of misperceptions, (e) protection of counselors against malpractice suits, (f) encouraging self-scrutiny by health care professionals, and (g) increasing the autonomy of clients by making them less dependent on the counselor for information. Yet, in reviewing the literature on utilization of these forms in the mental health professions, Shaw and Tarvydas also found that many professionals do not use them. Informed consent requires the presence of three legal elements: capacity, comprehension of information, and voluntariness. The person must (1) possess the ability to make a rational decision **(capacity);** (2) have sufficient information and be able to understand it **(comprehension);** and (3) give consent by acting freely in the decision-making process **(voluntariness)** (Bray, Shepard, & Hayes, 1985). Counselors should obtain written, informed consent before proceeding with the client and make every effort to ensure that this consent is genuine and valid.

Several issues may arise that call this consent into question. **Client competence** is not an all-or-nothing quality; clients must be competent to make decisions for themselves, a precondition for being able to consent autonomously (Beauchamp & Childress, 1994). The criteria for the ability to make a decision also vary by the context or criteria of the decision to be made (Beauchamp & Childress). For example, an individual may be able to think rationally enough to decide whether to wear a coat on a given day, but may not be competent to decide whether to sell the family business. Limitations in competency may be temporary or permanent. Factors that might affect competency temporarily include intoxication or a severe psychological trauma, such as rape. More permanent conditions that affect a person's competency might include dementia (a loss of intelligence due to physical–organic factors) or severe mental retardation. Other cognitive or emotional states have less consistent or unclear effects on competency, such as major depression or judgment deficits after a traumatic brain injury. If counselors are in doubt about the ability of clients to make rational decisions, and evaluation of competency is not within their scopes of counseling practice, they should seek consultation with other professionals able to make such determinations. If a person is judged to be incompetent, a legal guardian or parent can provide consent. Counselors should always determine if their clients have guardians who must be involved in decision making, and the type of guardianship involved. A guardianship may extend to all areas of a client's life or may be specific to one area, such as financial or medical matters. If the client is not legally able to give consent, the counselor still has the ethical obligation to gain his or her **assent,** or indication or agreement with the plan or services. Counselors should explain the issues at hand to the clients in a manner that maximizes their ability to understand the situation and issues involved and include them in the decision-making process (ACA, 2005). After this process of preparation and discussion if the client does not agree to the service or plan, then the counselor must ask serious ethical questions about whether they should proceed in the face of this lack of agreement, even if it is legally possible to do so.

Several informed consent issues beyond client competency are of concern. Counselors have a major responsibility for the client's comprehension or understanding of the matter at hand. Counselors must ensure they provide information in a manner that maximizes the client's ability to understand it and its implications. The counselor must know the client's communication and learning styles and the conditions necessary for the individual to understand the information. The counselor must tailor the discussion to meet those needs. Some issues to be considered include the client's (a) verbal (oral and reading) and cognitive abilities, (b) ability to see or hear, (c) emotional state, (d) language of first choice, (e) degree of fatigue or illness, and (f) distractibility or attentional ability. The same information may need to be presented several ways (e.g., discussed, demonstrated, or written), repeated several times or on different occasions, or even provided by different persons. Counselors should be increasingly focused on awareness of the needs of clients from diverse cultural backgrounds to assure they obtain informed consent. Some cultures are more collectivistic in their worldview. A client arriving at an individual choice without consulting elders or other family members may violate the norms of the client's culture and place the counseling relationship in a precarious state (Remley & Herlihy, 2005).

Counselors must take special care with any forms used. They must be free of jargon, written at an appropriate reading level, and legible. The client must be literate in the language used on the form. An analysis of mandated consent to psychotherapy forms used in Colorado (Handelsman, Martinez, Geisendorfer, & Jordan, 1995) found that the forms' average readability

level reached upper college grades. Additionally, the majority of the forms contained legally mandated information, but fewer contained ethically desirable information.

Counselors must realize that no specific approach to informed consent works for all clients. They must use their professional sensitivity and judgment to find the correct method in each case. The client is dependent upon the counselor in this matter. Research has shown some positive results of proper informed consent procedures in counseling and psychotherapy. Results include clients' decreased anxiety, increased compliance with treatment, increased alertness to problems in treatment, and more rapid recovery (Pope & Vasquez, 1998; Shaw & Tarvydas, 2001). Clients can be encouraged to use a written list of questions to discuss informed consent and their care with their counselors to enhance their comfort and involvement in the informed consent process. Pomerantz and Handelsman (2004) developed a revised list of such questions (see Appendix D) that address new issues regarding insurance and managed care and psychopharmacology in addition to the basic issues clients should understand about their services.

Ongoing Counseling Issues

At this point in the process, the counselor and client are engaged in the ongoing work they have outlined. Two common issues with legal aspects are especially important in this phase: confidentiality and record keeping (consult Chapter 8 for further information about the proper maintenance of records and files used in counseling).

Confidentiality and Privileged Communication. Confidentiality and privileged communication are among the most troublesome areas of practice for mental health professionals (see Chapter 3). A national study found that almost two thirds of psychologists (61.9%) unintentionally violated client confidentiality (Pope, Tabachnick, & Keith-Spiegel, 1987). Anderson (1996) described the issues of confidentiality as confusing and of concern to counselors, and this perception has been exacerbated by the recent passage of HIPAA. The requirements of HIPAA are discussed at length in Chapters 9 and 10.

The ethical obligations of confidentiality and privileged communication derive from the ethical principles of fidelity, autonomy, and nonmaleficence. These principles support the counselor's duty to keep client information private and not reveal what is said or done within the counseling relationship. This promise of privacy to the client allows for the openness of communication and trust—the most basic and essential component of the therapeutic relationship.

The related concept of privileged communication provides clients the legal right that their confidential communications cannot be revealed in a legal proceeding. It derives from English common law in recognizing that clients must have the ability to talk freely to their attorneys if they are to defend themselves effectively in criminal legal proceedings (Anderson, 1996). Additionally, state statutes have established privileged communication similar to that of the attorney–client privilege for some professionals. Over time, privileged communication has been applied through common law or state statute to limited types of relationships, beginning with priest–penitent, attorney–client, and husband–wife relationships and gradually extending to physician–patient, psychologist–client, social worker–client, and counselor–client relationships. In the case of the mental health professions, privilege applies only to licensed professionals. Recent studies have documented that counselor–client privilege exists in all but one state that licenses counselors (Glosoff, Herlihy, & Spence, 2000), and in all 50 states for psychologists (Glosoff, Herlihy, Herlihy, & Spence, 1997). In that sense, counselor licensure statutes that include proper protections are an important tool to assist the counselor in protecting client confidentiality.

This extension of the protection to mental health professionals appears to have continued with the recent Supreme Court decision in *Jaffee v. Redmond* (1996) (Remley, Herlihy, & Herlihy, 1997). This decision upheld the ability of licensed psychotherapists to maintain the confidences of their clients in federal court cases. The case involved the ability of a clinical social worker licensed in Illinois to assert privilege for communications between herself and her client in a lawsuit. The client, Mary Lu Redmond, was a police officer who killed Ricky Allen, Sr. after responding to reports of a fight in progress. She found Allen allegedly poised to stab another individual. Carrie Jaffee, the administrator of the Allen estate, brought the lawsuit against Redmond, the City of Hoffman Estates, and its police department, alleging excessive force had been used in the incident. In the course of the legal proceedings, the family petitioned to obtain notes made

by the therapist in counseling sessions with Redmond after the incident. Redmond and the therapist refused to provide the notes. The judge instructed the jury to assume the notes were unfavorable to Redmond, and the plaintiff won the case. On appeal in the U.S. Court of Appeals for the 7th Circuit, the jury verdict was thrown out and the case was remanded for new trial. The court opinion stated that the trial court had erred by not offering protection to confidential communications. Jaffee appealed this decision to the U.S. Supreme Court, which upheld a strict standard of privileged communication in its June 13, 1996 ruling. The arguments made before the highest court by ACA and APA in friend-of-the-court briefs stem from four longstanding criteria that support the granting of privilege in the legal system. According to Wigmore (1961), the four criteria are:

1. The communications must originate in confidence that they will not be disclosed.
2. This element of confidentiality must be essential to the full and satisfactory maintenance of the relationship between the parties.
3. The relationship must be one that, in the opinion of the community, ought to be fostered.
4. The injury that would be inflicted to the relationship by the disclosure of the communications must be greater than the benefit gained for the correct disposal of litigation.

The *Jaffee v. Redmond* ruling applies only within the federal court system, but it does extend psychotherapist privilege to another group of licensed professionals—clinical social workers. Leadership in the counseling profession noted the following:

> With this recognition of licensed clinical social workers and the previous recognition of clinical psychologists and psychiatrists, counselors are the largest remaining group of licensed professionals providing psychotherapeutic services that is not explicitly recognized by federal courts. The Supreme Court used the term psychotherapist in its decision and counselors must be considered psychotherapists if they are to be covered by the *Jaffee* ruling. (NBCC, 1996, p. 4)

The Supreme Court mentioned state licensure of clinical social workers as a key factor in its decision. State licensure, inclusion of the profession in the privilege statutes of each state, and establishment of uniform qualifications for professionals to be considered psychotherapists appear to be important elements in advancing privileged communication status to counselors in the future (NBCC, 1996). Some authorities predict this landmark ruling may establish further privilege for licensed counselor–client relationships in future cases (Remley & Herlihy, 2005).

Special Issues and Exceptions to Confidentiality. The ethical obligation of counselors to assure clients of confidentiality and the clients' related legal right of privilege are basic to counseling. Many circumstances vary for counseling in different specialized areas of practice, and issues of confidentiality and privilege express themselves somewhat differently across these situations. Special circumstances related to confidentiality and privilege include counseling with persons who have HIV or AIDS (see Chapter 9), families or couples (see Chapter 12), minors or school settings (see Chapter 13), people with disabilities (see Chapters 14 and 17), groups (see Chapter 16), and clients in drug or alcohol treatment facilities (see Chapter 18). The rapid increase and extensive use of electronic and other technological devices in counseling settings have also created challenging problems for maintaining client confidentiality (see Chapter 10).

There are several commonplace exceptions to the general requirement of counselors to hold client communications confidential; Arthur and Swanson (1993) noted the following:

1. Client is dangerous to self or others.
2. Client waives confidentiality and privilege by requesting a release of information.
3. Counselor receives a court order requiring the release of information.
4. Counselor is involved in systematic clinical supervision.
5. Client's information and paperwork are processed by clerical workers for routine purposes, and client has been informed of this arrangement prior to counseling.
6. Client is informed of counselor-required legal or clinical consultation before counseling.
7. The issue of the client's mental health is raised by client in a legal proceeding, such as a custody lawsuit.
8. Counseling occurs with a third party in the room, as in group or family counseling.
9. Client is a minor (younger than age 18).
10. Client information is made available within the agency or institution as part of the treatment process, with the client receiving precounseling notification of this practice.
11. Information is shared within a penal institution as part of the operation of the institution or the case process.
12. Client discloses the information to advance a criminal or fraudulent activity.
13. Child abuse is suspected by the counselor.

Other exceptions to confidentiality exist for psychologists and counselors who serve in the military. In this highly specialized setting, the mental health professional is obliged to report threats to military installations, weapons, and military integrity, even when these do not imply specific threats to specific persons. These limitations to confidentiality when working with military personnel are of even greater concern when national security or war actions are underway. Military mental health providers are placed in unusually powerful positions in relationship to their clients, and also in potentially ethically conflicted positions, having to balance their obligations to their clients and the requirements of the Department of Defense (Orme & Doerman, 2001). As a result, they may be forced to compromise in the areas of "confidentiality, maintenance of records, competence, multiple relationships, misuse of clinical data by the larger organization, and the more global issue of sacrificing the client's best interests in the service of the military mission" (Johnson, 1995, p. 282).

Two additional concerns arise for all counselors who are faced with the legal system's demands for information they view as confidential: subpoenas and court appearances. A legally inexperienced counselor's first impulse upon receiving a subpoena might be to surrender all materials requested in the subpoena. This well-meaning response would not be proper because the ethical and legal duty to protect a client's confidentiality requires that the counselor make appropriate attempts to preserve client privacy.

A subpoena (see Chapter 3) is a court order to appear in a legal hearing—a court appearance or a deposition—with all requested information. The counselor might be questioned or subpoenaed documents might be examined. Often, subpoenas are drafted broadly to capture any information that might be of assistance to a party to the legal proceeding requesting the information—a "fishing trip" for anything potentially helpful. Counselors should be familiar with state statutes regarding privilege that might apply in their jurisdiction (Anderson, 1996). Arthur and

1. Do not respond to the subpoena automatically. Be sure that all staff members know proper procedures for responding.
2. Determine if the subpoena was requested by a current or former client or his or her attorney. Legally, this would require you to produce the documents or testify as directed. However, it is ethically important that you review any concerns you might have about detrimental aspects of this information with these parties so that they may exercise truly informed judgment about proceeding with this request.
3. Consult with your attorney and the client's attorney, after obtaining the client's permission to do so, regarding the situation. If the judgment is that you should respond to the subpoena, obtain written release of information forms specifying what will be released, and to whom, from all clients whose information will be revealed.
4. If it is determined that you should not respond, ask the client's attorney to file a motion to quash the subpoena. In this case, a judge will hear the concerns about the detrimental effects of revealing the materials and privately view them to rule on whether the counselor should be compelled to respond to the subpoena or to further limit the information provided.
5. NEVER ignore a subpoena or defy it without taking some of the measures described here and without legal assistance.
6. Be sure to keep thorough documentation in the client's record of all interactions with the client or the client's attorney in this matter, as well as copies of all subpoenas, releases of information, court rulings, and official communications.

FIGURE 4–3. Considerations in Responding to a Subpoena

Swanson (1993) and Anderson provided more specific recommendations to respond to a subpoena (see Figure 4–3).

An order to appear in court if the counselor's client is a defendant in a lawsuit presents a similar set of challenges. Counselors should protect their clients' confidences in a manner consistent with the earlier information. Judges can compel counselors to answer questions in legal proceedings even though counselors may argue that it is their ethical responsibility to preserve client confidentiality. If that occurs, Anderson (1996) had several additional suggestions: (a) answer

■ Document that something needs to be done; then do not do it.
■ Do not keep records current.
■ Do not obtain complete assessments or develop a comprehensive treatment plan.
■ Establish policies and procedures, but do not follow them.
■ Do not review or audit your records.
■ Nurture a dependent relationship and then cut it off quickly.
■ Combine a suicidal client with a provider who has a reputation for sexual impropriety.

FIGURE 4–4. Ways to Guarantee a Lawsuit
Note: Taken from *Documentation in Counseling Records* (p. 11) by R. Mitchell, 2001, Alexandria, VA: American Counseling Association. Copyright 2001 by American Counseling Association. Reprinted by permission.

truthfully, but do not volunteer information beyond what is specifically requested, (b) the counselor should be protected in the hearing by an attorney (the counselor's or the client's) and should follow the attorney's direction, and (c) discuss the concerns regarding confidentiality with the attorney before the hearing and prepare for the actual testimony to be provided.

Record Keeping. The importance of observing minimum acceptable standards of clinical record keeping should be obvious. Case records have been reported to be one of the top five areas of legal liability for counselors (Snider, 1987). Mitchell (2001) described common ways to guarantee a lawsuit, many of which are documentation related (see Figure 4–4).

Unfortunately, formal training in case-recording methods and procedures is usually limited in the professional education of most counselors. These matters are considered to be primarily a part of students' clinical experiences. Although good methods may certainly be learned in this manner, the resulting training is typically varied in terms of content, depth, and method. Counselors must educate themselves on the best practices in record keeping in mental health professions and thoroughly acquaint themselves with the methods and requirements of the system and practices used in their own setting. Good, basic introductions to client case-recording methods are provided by Mitchell (2001), Remley and Herlihy (2005), and Piazza and Baruth (1990). Counselors working in schools that receive federal funding should be aware that educational and other records are covered by the Family Educational Rights and Privacy Act (FERPA), which provides rights of access to educational records to students and their parents and defines educational record as any record kept by employees of an educational institution. Anderson (1996) further stated that "records made by and kept in the sole possession of" a professional such as a physician, psychologist, or other recognized professional "are excluded from the disclosure requirements, except that notes may be provided to other treating professionals or reviewed by a physician of the student's choice" (p. 38). For further information regarding issues of confidentiality in the schools, refer to Chapter 13.

The issue of adequate record keeping is considered so important in the practice of psychology that the APA (1993) adopted record-keeping guidelines. In addition to considering the principles and purpose underlying clinical records, the guidelines provide specific recommendations in the following areas: content, construction and control, retention of records, procedures with outdated records, and disclosure of record-keeping procedures. The considerations relevant to electronic record keeping are discussed in Chapter 10.

It is beyond the scope of this discussion to introduce the technical methods involved in good clinical record-keeping practices. However, Arthur and Swanson (1993) made several legally relevant points: (1) Security of files must be maintained; files must not be left where they can be accessed by unauthorized persons. (2) Notes should be written in nontechnical, clear, and objective statements with behavioral descriptions. Any subjective or evaluative statements involving professional judgments should be so designated and written in a separate section clearly set aside from factual content. (3) All client records should be written with the understanding that they might be seen by the client, a court, or some other authorized person. (4) Only information that is necessary and appropriate to the reason the client is receiving services should be documented. Remley (1990) cautioned that counselors should document critical incidents or interactions with clients extensively. Examples include emergencies; circumstances in which clients will not follow recommendations, thereby risking a negative outcome or endangering themselves; or when litigation appears possible.

Good recording practices enhance the quality of clinical analysis and service and protect both the client and the counselor.

Dangerousness and Crisis Concerns

At any point in working with a client, even as early as the first contact, crises and dangerous circumstances may arise. Such situations need to be dealt with effectively to prevent harm to the client and any other parties at risk. The *Tarasoff* court decision (see Chapter 3) and other related cases have shaped our understanding of how counselors should proceed. The *Tarasoff* case is arguably the best known case in mental health and counseling history. Prior to this decision, the strong ethical tendency was preserving client confidentiality. The results of this case made it clear that therapists had a legal obligation to third parties who are at risk of serious harm from dangerous clients. The California Supreme Court noted in its decision that "the protective privilege ends where the public peril begins" (*Tarasoff v. Regents of the University of California*, 1976, p. 347). As a result of the original *Tarasoff* decision (1974), the court held that an affirmative duty existed to warn the identifiable victim despite the client's right to confidentiality. This ruling established that "liability would attach where the psychotherapist *reasonably believed, or should have believed*, that the client posed a serious danger to an identifiable potential victim" (Anderson, 1996, p. 29, italics in original). This doctrine has come to be known as the duty to warn. The *Tarasoff* decision is binding only in California—other state courts do not have to follow its dictates. However, it has been an influential case; many other state and federal courts follow this ruling. Because determining the specific duty imposed on the psychotherapist in a particular jurisdiction is so confusing, 23 states have passed laws to define how the duty to warn and protect should be discharged. These laws generally establish: (a) when the duty arises, (b) the manner in which the psychotherapist may fulfill this duty, and (c) established immunity to the professional for violating client confidences to discharge the duty to protect (see Burris [2001] for a detailed presentation of these laws). Counselors should educate themselves about the legal requirements in their local jurisdictions for the duty to warn and protect others from dangerous clients. Although the legal decisions surrounding duty to warn potential victims of dangerous clients are complex, Remley and Herlihy (2005) summarized the essential guidance from these legal requirements thus: "Because of the *Tarasoff* case, when you determine that a client might harm an identifiable or foreseeable person, you must directly or indirectly warn that individual of the danger, except in Texas" (p.163). Clearly, this body of law has become very influential in the practice of all mental health professionals, and it is useful for counselors to understand more details about some of the rulings.

The 1976 *Tarasoff* ruling (known as *Tarasoff II*) was an appeal of the original 1974 *Tarasoff* decision (*Tarasoff I*). The defendants alleged that the parents of the client did not have a legal claim in the matter but rather were private third parties and not clients of the therapist. The California Supreme Court reconsidered the case and found that the parents could sue the defendants. *Tarasoff II* effectively expanded the original decision from the more limited duty to warn to a more inclusive duty to protect. In the **duty to protect** standard, warning the intended victim is only one option available to the therapist to protect others from a dangerous client (VandeCreek, Bennett, & Bricklin, 1994). Other interventions with the potential to be equally effective may be used to control the potential of dangerous behavior. These interventions include (a) voluntary or civil commitment of the client, (b) an increase or change in medication to control the condition creating the danger, (c) an increase in the frequency of sessions or supervision, or (d) referral of the client to another provider with better potential to control the violent behavior. Clearly, this does not absolve the therapist from the responsibility to exercise due care and proper professional judgment in assessing and attempting to protect potential victims from dangerous clients. It does expand the range of options to meet the needs of the public for protection and of the client to receive care that does not automatically expose the therapeutic relationship to the same level of potential harm (VandeCreek et al.). Assessing the degree of dangerousness or risk presented by a client has always been acknowledged as a difficult and not necessarily successful task, even for skilled therapists. Counselors must carefully determine whether they possess the clinical skills and competency to do so. If they do not, they must immediately involve supervisors or other appropriately skilled colleagues in such a manner as to ensure safety of all parties concerned. Efforts to accurately gather important information and consultation are very important for any clinician, regardless of skill

- As in all other situations, discuss the issue fully and openly with clients.
- Inform clients of the counselor's legal responsibility to warn others.
- Inform your supervisor of the potentially dangerous situation. If there is no supervisor, consult with another professional.
- Notify the person who might be responsible for the client or contact the police.
- Notify the intended victim.
- Explore other options, which may include commitment to an appropriate psychiatric facility.

FIGURE 4–5. Steps to Protect Others When Working With a Dangerous Client

Note: From *The ACA Legal Series: Confidentiality and Privileged Communication* (p. 22) by G. L. Arthur & C. D. Swanson, 1993; Alexandria, VA: American Counseling Association. Copyright 1993 by American Counseling Association. Reprinted by permission.

and experience level, to most accurately assess the degree of risk (Kitchener, 2000). When assessing the potential for harm, many ethicists use a model of risk assessment developed by Beauchamp and Childress (1994). This approach assesses two elements of harm: the probability of harm (high or low) and the magnitude of harm (major or minor) likely. The need to breach confidentiality to protect others is highest when there is a high probability for harm and the magnitude of the harm is major. Conversely, if the probability of harm is low and the magnitude of harm is minor, the counselor is in a clearer position to preserve client confidentiality while resolving the situation. Figure 4–5 presents recommended steps for the counselor to take if the client has been assessed as dangerous.

Several subsequent court decisions have expanded and clarified the duty to protect from dangerous clients. For example, victims who are not specifically identified but are foreseeable, likely targets of client violence, such as family members and others in close proximity to an identifiable victim, should be warned (*Hedlund v. Superior Court*, 1983; *Jablonski v. United States*, 1983). Counselors should educate themselves on additional rulings that influence their duty to protect their clients and people around them from harm. State and federal courts continue to struggle with how this important issue should be resolved in particular circumstances. Costa and Altekruse (1994) provided a set of practical guidelines for dealing with duty-to-warn situations, emphasizing practical issues in their application.

Another court case has established that a parallel duty exists to violate confidentiality if a client is judged to be at risk for self-harm. *Eisel v. Board of Education of Montgomery County* (1991) was a decision by the Maryland Court of Appeals that established the duty to protect for school counselors. This case involved a child who threatened suicide in the presence of schoolmates, who reported the threats to their parents, who notified the school counselors. The counselors interviewed the child, who denied the threats. Counselors did not notify the child's parents or school administration. After the child did commit suicide, the father sued the counselors and the school, alleging breach of duty to intervene to prevent the suicide (Anderson, 1996). This case and others led Anderson (1996) to caution that counselors do have a duty to protect their clients from harming themselves if it is foreseeable. Generally, a review of case law regarding malpractice suits demonstrates that courts are reluctant to punish practitioners for honest mistakes and failures (Baerger, 2001). However, it is prudent to keep in mind the

most common failure scenarios in cases of outpatient suicide that leave therapists vulnerable to lawsuits alleging malpractice. Bongar, Maris, Berman, and Litman (1998) described these risk scenarios involving failure(s) to: (a) properly evaluate the need to psychopharmacological intervention or use of unsuitable phamacotherapy, (b) specify criteria for hospitalization and failure to implement hospitalization, (c) maintain appropriate clinician–patient relationship, (d) properly supervise and consult, (e) evaluate for suicide risk at intake, (f) evaluate for suicide risk at management transitions, (g) secure records of prior treatments or inadequate history taking, (h) conduct a mental status exam, (i) establish a formal treatment plan, (j) safeguard the environment, and (k) adequately document clinical judgments, rationales, and observations. When working with their clients, counselors are wise to consistently follow a specific set of guidelines and document their steps promptly and thoroughly (see the guidelines in Figure 4–6 for dealing with suicidal clients and review Remley & Herlihy, 2005 for additional recommendations).

In more recent years, a significant amount of legal attention has focused on whether or not confidentiality of an HIV-positive client can be breached if the client's behavior puts unknowing others at serious risk for infection. Because social stigma and discrimination may cause serious harm to people with HIV disease, many states have passed stringent laws to protect the confidentiality and privacy of people who are HIV positive. Release of information may be permitted under narrowly defined circumstances, often only by physicians and often related to threats posed by the client. A state statute may impose a duty to warn (as in 23 states) and a state law may require nondisclosure of HIV-related information (Burris, 2001). The complexities of how to proceed in such contradictory instances when both legal dictates exist make it clear that counselors should obtain legal counsel to assist them in understanding their legal obligations. Counselors should review how the laws and cases in their own jurisdictions are pertinent to their work with people who are HIV positive *before* they are directly faced with them in the counseling relationship. Information about how counselors should work with ethical issues of people who have HIV disease is discussed more fully in Chapter 9, which deals with ethical issues involving clients' health.

1. Conduct a comprehensive examination of the client at intake.
2. If the client is at risk (e.g., likely to attempt to harm him or herself in the near future), hospitalization should be seriously considered and only rejected in the event of a comprehensive safety plan.
3. Review the level of risk a client presents at particularly stressful times in the client's life.
4. Maintain accurate records that explain significant treatment decisions and clearly delineate the reasons for rejecting hospitalization for at-risk outpatients and the reasons for choosing discharge for at-risk inpatients.
5. Take special precautions against suicide when treating the at-risk client including—where appropriate—involving the patient's family or friends in safety or discharge plans.

FIGURE 4–6. Recommendations for Working With a Suicidal Client to Minimize Malpractice Liability

Note: From "Risk Management with the Suicidal Patient: Lessons from Case Law" by D.R. Baerger, 2004. *Professional Psychology: Research and Practice, 32*(4), 359–366. Copyright 2004 by American Psychological Association. Reprinted by permission.

Termination Phase Issues

In the final phase of counseling, the focus shifts to ensuring that the client is prepared for the transition out of counseling or into a new relationship if a referral is made. Clearly, termination is a right of both the counselor and the client. The stage should have been set for the length and nature of the relationship, beginning with the process of informed consent and continuing through the therapy and subsequent reevaluations of the nature of the counseling relationship. If a client requires additional therapy or counseling beyond the counselor's scope of competence, the counselor is ethically responsible to refer the client properly and ensure that counseling needs are met after the conclusion of the first relationship. The counselor might consider documenting the referral arrangements in a follow-up letter summarizing the arrangements or names of individuals to whom referral might be made to record the transition precautions.

Counselors should take particular caution in two instances at termination. First, clients with serious, unresolved clinical conditions that require further intervention should not be terminated. If their care is beyond the abilities of the counselor, a referral may be made, but counseling must be continued until the referral transition occurs. Second, caution must be exercised in situations in which the counselor works for an institution, such as a managed care system, that mandates termination after a specified number of sessions, whether or not the client's condition is resolved sufficiently. If a client is terminated prematurely by the counselor, a malpractice suit may be filed for abandonment or failure to treat or refer. The counselor should seek to continue treatment, at least until appropriate alternate treatment can be arranged (Bennett, Bryant, VandenBos, & Greenwood, 1990).

Pressure on counselors and mental health professionals to terminate services prematurely may become one of the most prominent ethical and legal issues in mental health care (see Chapter 8 for discussion of the administrative aspects of financial and termination issues). The temptation to terminate a client may be great when a provider's fees run out, the client cannot afford further care, or the client amasses an increasingly large bill. If the client is in need of further treatment, the therapist is obligated to meet that need until it is resolved or a referral can be arranged. The more appropriate route to dealing with this issue is for the counselor and the client to fully understand the financial conditions and limitations involved and determine whether the client's resources will be sufficient for the duration of the counseling relationship. Counselors are not obligated to accept a client into counseling if this situation does not seem workable at the outset. The potential client may be better served by seeking counseling with an agency that has the potential to carry out a reasonable treatment plan.

CHAPTER SUMMARY

Counselors must have a situation-specific interpretation of both legal and ethical regulatory standards to conduct well-informed practice. They must weigh all aspects of a situation, determine which ethical and legal standards apply in general, and decide how they apply in a particular instance. Society holds all mental health professionals accountable for maintaining proper clinical and ethical standards of practice through four mechanisms: professional ethics committees, state licensure boards, criminal courts, and civil courts.

The counseling relationship has four phases: (1) initiation phase, (2) ongoing counseling phase, (3) dangerousness and crisis concerns phase, and (4) termination phase. Each phase faces key challenges, including counselor competency, informed consent, confidentiality and privileged communication, exceptions to confidentiality, record keeping, dangerousness, and termination issues.

INTERNET RESOURCES

Counselors who wish to gather current information on the internet should search under the following key terms: counselor liability, (counselor or psychologist) malpractice, ethics disciplinary actions and counseling or psychology, scope of practice (counseling), breach of contract, client/patient competency, privileged communication, dangerousness assessment, duty to warn, duty to protect.

REFERENCES

American Association of State Counseling Boards. (2005). Licensing portability for counselors—A new model. *The Liaison: Official Publication of the American Association of State Counseling Boards, 17* (Spring), 2.

American Counseling Association. (2005). *ACA Code of ethics*. Alexandria, VA: Author.

American Psychological Association. (1993). Record keeping guidelines. *American Psychologist, 48*, 984–986.

Anderson, B. S. (1996). *The counselor and the law* (4th ed.). Alexandria, VA: American Counseling Association.

Arthur, G. L., & Swanson, C. D. (1993). *The ACA legal series: Confidentiality and privileged communication*. Alexandria, VA: American Counseling Association.

Baerger, D. R. (2001). Risk management with the suicidal patient: Lessons from case law. *Professional Psychology: Research and Practice, 32*, 359–366.

Beauchamp, T. L., & Childress, J. F. (1994). *Principles of biomedical ethics* (5th ed.). Oxford: Oxford University Press.

Bennett, B. E., Bryant, B. K., VandenBos, G. R., & Greenwood, A. (1990). *Professional liability and risk management*. Washington, DC: American Psychological Association.

Bertram, B., & Wheeler, A. M. (1994). *Legal aspects of counseling: Avoiding lawsuits and legal problems*. Workshop materials. Alexandria, VA: American Counseling Association.

Bongar, B., Maris, R. W., Berman, A. L., & Litman, R. E. (1998). Outpatient standards of care and the suicidal patient. In B. Bongar, A. L. Berman, R. W. Maris, M. M. Silverman, E. A. Harris, & W. L. Packman (Eds.), *Risk management with suicidal patients* (pp. 4–33). New York: Guilford.

Bray, J. H., Shepard, J. N., & Hayes, J. R. (1985). Legal and ethical issues in informed consent to psychotherapy. *The American Journal of Family Therapy, 13* (2), 56–60.

Burris, S. (2001). Clinical decision making in the shadow of law. In J. R. Anderson & B. Barret (Eds.), *Ethics in HIV-related psychotherapy: Clinical decision making in complex cases* (pp. 99–129). Washington, DC: American Psychological Association.

Corey, G., Corey, M., & Callanan, P. (2003). *Issues and ethics in the helping professions* (6th ed.). Pacific Grove, CA: Brooks/Cole.

Costa, L., & Altekruse, M. (1994). Duty-to-warn guidelines for mental health counselors. *Journal of Counseling & Development, 72,* 346–350.

DePauw, M. E. (1986). Avoiding ethical violations: A timeline perspective for individual counseling. *Journal of Counseling & Development, 69*, 3–36.

Eisel v. Board of Education of Montgomery County, 324 Md. 376, 597 A, 2d 447 (Md. Ct. App. 1991).

Fischer, L., & Sorenson, G. P. (1985). *School law for counselors, psychologists, and social workers*. New York: Longman.

Glosoff, H. L., Herlihy, B., & Spence, B. (2000). Privileged communication in the counselor–client relationship. *Journal of Counseling & Development, 78*, 454–462.

Glosoff, H. L., Herlihy, S., Herlihy, B., & Spence, B. (1997). Privileged communication in the psychologist–client relationship. *Professional Psychology: Research and Practice, 28*, 573–581.

Handelsman, M. M., Martinez, A., Geisendorfer, S., & Jordan, L. (1995). Does legally mandated consent to psychotherapy ensure ethical appropriateness? *Ethics and Behavior, 5* (2), 119–129.

Hedlund v. Superior Court of Orange County, 669 P. 2d 41, 191 Cal. Rptr. 805 (1983).

Jablonski v. United States, 712 F. 2d 391 (9th Cir., 1983).

Jaffee v. Redmond et al., WL 315841 (U.S. June 13, 1996).

Johnson, B. W. (1995). Perennial ethical quandaries in military psychology: Toward American Psychological Association–Department of Defense collaboration. *Professional Psychology: Research and Practice, 26*, 281–287.

Kane, A. W. (1995). The effects of criminalization of sexual misconduct by therapists. In J. C. Gonsiorek (Ed.), *Breaches of trust: Sexual exploitation by health care professionals and clergy* (pp. 317–332). Thousand Oaks, CA: Sage.

Keary, A. O. (1985). Criminal law and procedure. In N. T. Sidney (Ed.), *Law and ethics: A guide for the health professional* (pp. 63–102). New York: Human Sciences.

Kitchener, K. S. (2000). *Foundations of ethical practice, research, and teaching in psychology*. Mahwah, NJ: Lawrence Erlbaum Associates.

Kohlberg, L. (1964). Development of moral character and moral ecology. In M. L. Hoffman & L. W. Hoffman (Eds.), *Review of child development research*: Vol. I. New York: Russell Sage Foundation.

Kohlberg, L. (1981). *Philosophy of moral development*. San Francisco: Harper & Row.

Mitchell, R. W. (2001). *Documentation of counseling records* (2nd ed.). (AACD Legal Series). Alexandria, VA: American Counseling Association.

National Board for Counselor Certification. (1996, Summer). *Jaffee v. Redmond:* A primer on privilege. *NBCC NewsNotes, 13*, 1–4.

Orme, D. R., & Doerman, A. L. (2001). Ethical dilemmas and U.S. Air Force clinical psychologists: A survey. *Professional Psychology: Research and Practice, 32*, 305–311.

Piazza, N. J., & Baruth, N. E. (1990). Client record guidelines. *Journal of Counseling & Development, 68*, 313–316.

Pomerantz, A. M., & Handelsman, M. M. (2004). Informed consent revisited: An updated written question format. *Professional Psychology: Research and Practice, 35*, 201–205.

Pope, K., Tabachnick, B., & Keith-Spiegel, P. (1987). Ethics of practice: The beliefs and behavior of psychologists as therapists. *American Psychologist, 42*, 993–1006.

Pope, K., & Vasquez, M. J. T. (1998). *Ethics in psychotherapy and counseling* (2nd ed.). San Francisco: Jossey-Bass.

Remley, T. P., Jr. (1990). Counseling records: Legal and ethical issues. In B. Herlihy & L. Golden (Eds.), *ACA ethical standards casebook* (4th ed., pp. 162–169). Alexandria, VA: American Counseling Association.

Remley, T. P., Jr. (1996). The relationship between law and ethics. In B. Herlihy & G. Corey (Eds.), *ACA ethical standards casebook* (5th ed., pp. 285–292). Alexandria, VA: American Counseling Association.

Remley, T. P., & Herlihy, B. (2005). *Ethical, legal, and professional issues in counseling* (2nd ed.). Upper Saddle River, NJ: Merrill/Prentice Hall.

Remley, T. P., Jr., Herlihy, B., & Herlihy, S. B. (1997). The U.S. Supreme Court decision in *Jaffee v. Redmond:* Implications for counselors. *Journal of Counseling and Development, 75*, 213–218.

Shaw, L. R., & Tarvydas, V. (2001). The use of professional disclosure in rehabilitation counseling. *Rehabilitation Counseling Bulletin, 45*, 40–47.

Shea, T. E. (1985). Finding the law: Legal research and citation. In N. T. Sidney (Ed.), *Law and ethics: A guide for the health professional* (pp. 411–424). New York: Human Sciences.

Snider, P. D. (1987). Client records: Inexpensive liability protection for mental health counselors. *Journal of Mental Health Counseling, 9,* 134–141.

Swenson, L. C. (1997). *Psychology and law: For the helping professions.* Pacific Grove, CA: Brooks/Cole Publishing Co.

Tarasoff v. Regents of University of California, 13 C.3d 177, 529 P. 2d 553, 118 Cal. Rptr. 129 (1974).

Tarasoff v. Regents of University of California, 17 Cal. App. 3d 425, 551 P. 2d 334 (1976).

Thompson, A. (1990). *Guide to ethical practice in psychotherapy.* New York: John Wiley & Sons.

VandeCreek, L., Bennett, B. E., & Bricklin, P. M. (1994). *Risk management with potentially dangerous patients.* Washington, DC: APA Insurance Trust.

Van Hoose, W. H., & Paradise, L. V. (1979). *Ethics in counseling and psychotherapy: Perspectives in issues and decision making.* Cranston, RI: Cranston Press.

Ware, M. L. (1971). The law and counselor ethics. *Personnel and Guidance Journal, 50,* 305–310.

Welch, B. (Edition 3, 2005). After five years, fresh insight. *Insight: Safeguarding psychologists against liability risks.* Amityville, NY: American Professional Agency, Inc.

Wigmore, J. H. (1961). Evidence in trials at common law. In J. T. McNanghton (Ed.), *Rules of evidence* (Vol. 8, rev. ed.). Boston: Little, Brown.

PART 2

Values and Decision Making

CHAPTER 5

Values, Virtues, and Care in Counseling

OBJECTIVES

After reading this chapter, you should be able to:

- Explain the value-laden nature of counseling.
- Define and contrast the concepts of ethics, morals, and values.
- Explain the historical and ongoing role of values in the counseling process.
- Identify and discuss the three processes used to examine and work with value systems: values clarification, values conflict resolution and valuing processes, and moral discussion.
- Discuss the differences between principle ethics, virtue ethics, and the ethics of care.
- Identify the characteristics of approaches categorized as relational ethics.

INTRODUCTION

Counselors and their clients focus on issues of value and the meaning of life as they solve problems, develop strategies, and work toward goals. They use their unique interpretations of what is good, bad, right, wrong, joyous, and painful in their experiences to guide them. These understandings, called values, are abstract and difficult to define and communicate. Values must be experienced to be truly grasped. They are powerful and drive our choices about what we wish to do and what we would like to have. They focus our energies and choices. Reflect on the strong emotion and sense of rightness you experience when you hug your child after returning from a long journey; the confusion and disgust you feel as you watch the beating of an individual on television news; or the sense of calm and joy you experience when you see a beautiful sunrise or feel gentle, pine-scented breezes. The beliefs and preferences that underlie these values can be articulated—love of family, respect for life and personal freedom, and respect for nature and our responsibility to care for these resources. Values are formed over the years through our experience of the beliefs, choices, and actions of significant others and through exposure to cultural institutions such as school and places of worship.

Both clients and counselors hold values, whether or not they are able to articulate them in the moment. When clients come to counselors for assistance in making choices or changing their lives, both parties enact values, either knowingly or unknowingly.

Value analysis and choice in ethical decision making are increasingly important. New developments in ethics, such as virtue ethics, multiculturalism, and feminist streams of thought, illustrate how values and worldview-based analysis can be reframed to accommodate the diverse lives and perspectives of all people in counseling.

THE BASIC CONCEPTS OF VALUES

In a sermon given in Georgia on February 4, 1968, during the height of the Civil Rights movement, the Reverend Martin Luther King, Jr. spoke eloquently about what it takes to truly be a helper:

> Everybody can be great because anybody can serve (the Civil Rights movement). You don't have to have a college degree to serve, you don't have to make your subject and verb agree to serve, you don't have to know about Plato and Aristotle to serve, you don't have to know Einstein's "Theory of Relativity" to serve, you don't have to know the Second Theory of Thermodynamics and Physics to serve. . . . You only need a heart full of grace, a soul generated by love. (King, 1968)

The issues that surround ethical judgment involve a complex interplay of morals, values, and priorities that people hold in relationship to themselves, their colleagues, and other professionals. Ethical principles of practice are interrelated with, but distinguishable from, concepts such as morals, values, and codes of ethics. Taken together, they form the heart and soul of counseling.

Ethics and Morals

Ethics has been variously defined. In Chapter 1, the difficulty of distinguishing the concepts of ethics and morality in the arenas of philosophy and professional practice was discussed. In discussing the practice of professional counseling and psychology, the term professional ethics carries a meaning more closely related to the concept of philosophical morals; that is, *acting* in accord with standards of professional practice. When reading the professional counseling and psychology literature, the meaning of ethics and morality becomes even more confusing because authors do not have a clear agreement on definition. For example, in the professional counseling and psychology literature, ethics is defined as "a branch of study in philosophy concerning how people ought to act toward each other, pronouncing judgments of value about those actions" (Kitchener, 1984, p.18); and "a hierarchy of values that permits choices to be made based on distinguished levels of right or wrong" (Shertzer & Linden, 1979, p. 510). In describing morals in the professional literature, the nature of the concepts takes on a clear connotation of the goodness or badness of human behavior or character (Van Hoose & Kottler, 1985) and implies an element of coercion (Mowrer, 1967). Although ethics also deals with the appropriateness of human action, it connotes more of a basis in reason and objectivity (Van Hoose & Kottler). In differentiating between ethics and morals, Kitchener noted that morals are more related to the individual's belief structure, whereas ethics involve the study and evaluation of this belief structure. The importance of this distinction and the evaluative component of ethics become clear when one realizes that "it is critical to differentiate between saying 'X' *believes* a certain action is right or good and that action is right or good" (Kitchener, p. 16). It is not difficult to think of examples of people who are steeped in personally or environmentally distorted thinking: Recall the scientists in charge of the Tuskegee experiment that left black men with syphilis intentionally untreated for decades, or the Reverend Jim Jones, who led the mass suicide of his cult in Guyana. The individuals involved in these, and countless other tragic circumstances, may have acted consistently with their personal moral code, but not ethically, as based on a broader analysis of appropriate behavior. The need for evaluation of personal actions against a broader standard of what is right and good is imperative for the well-being of all.

Values

Counselors are required to distinguish their personal moral codes from and reconcile them with the profession's values to behave in an ethical manner. However, some experts in the field maintain that the stated attempt to separate moral outlook and choices from professional skills and practices is both deceptive and deleterious to one of psychotherapy's major sources of legitimacy, direction, and power (Frank, 1961; London, 1986). In fact, Doherty (1995) advocated counseling that actively incorporates a moral development perspective. He argued that counselors should urge their clients to adopt a sense of moral responsibility, and that counselors should ascribe to the ideals of commitment, justice, truthfulness, and community in their work with clients. Others have suggested that counseling be seen as an opportunity for moral reflection and encouragement of character development (Griffith & Duesterhaus, 2000). Clearly, counselors must give much thought to understanding the role of morals and values in their work. Most professionals agree that all counseling involves values, no matter how directly or indirectly they are expressed.

Rokeach (1973) defined value as "an enduring belief that a specific mode of conduct or end-state of existence

Box 5–1 • End-of-Life Choices as Enacted Values

Anyone who has worked with or been close to someone who is near death knows that the final choices about how one dies take on stark personal meaning. Being near death is sometimes referred to as "instant values clarification." It is important to discuss your final wishes about terminal care with medical caregivers and family while you are healthy and able to express your desires. By making these decisions before you become ill with a life-threatening condition, your choices will be based on clear thinking and on your personal values about the end of life. An Extended Values History is a tool to assist you and your loved ones in making decisions about the quality of care you desire (or do not desire) if you become terminally ill. Although the document is not legally binding, it is used in conjunction with a legally executed living will or durable power of attorney for health care. Go to www.euthanasia.org/vh.html and complete the Extended Values History. Discuss your choices and answers with those closest to you. In class, discuss what you discovered about yourself and your values in doing this important bit of personal business.

is personally or socially preferable to an opposite or converse mode of conduct or end-state of existence" (p. 5). **Values** involve that which is intrinsically worthwhile or worthy of esteem for its own sake and reflect the value holder's worldview, culture, or understanding of the world. Values arise from individuals' experiences and interactions with their culture, the world, and the people around them, such as their parents, friends, religious leaders, and neighbors. Thus, values vary among individuals, but are likely to vary less among persons growing up within similar systems, such as specific cultures or religions. A **value system** is a hierarchical ranking of the degree of preference for the values expressed by a particular person or social entity.

Values are often mistakenly thought of as involving a simple expression of personal interest or preference, such as a preference for an automatic rather than a standard transmission in a new car. Actually, values are more complex—they involve a set of beliefs that include evaluative, emotional, and existential aspects. There are elements of goodness, obligation, or requirement; positive or negative affective orientation; and a sense of the meaningfulness of the situation or choice attached to the object of the valuing process. Values are not directly observable, but they guide human choice and action through the value preferences expressed in human choices and goals, and they may also be expressed verbally (see activity in Box 5–1).

There are many systems for describing values, including Rokeach's (1973) 18 values that reflect desirable end-states. Allport, Vernon, and Lindzey (1960) saw six basic values or evaluative attitudes reflected in personality types: theoretical, economic, aesthetic, social, political, and religious. Similarly, Frankena (1963) identified eight distinct realms of value, only one of which is related to ethics: morality, art, science, religion, economics,

politics, law, and manner or custom. In all of these systems, values can be either moral or nonmoral in nature—they may or may not involve preferences concerning what is morally right or wrong. For example, a person's choice to become a vegetarian might be based on nonmoral or moral value grounds. It might stem from belief in the importance of social status and a wish to follow the lead of a charismatic friend, or to be "politically correct" (nonmoral values of manner or custom); or the choice might be based on a spiritual belief that all forms of life should be respected and protected from discomfort and violence (moral). Thus, any situation, choice, or action may be valued or prized in a number of disparate and possibly competing ways by different individuals or groups. It also is possible for one individual to hold two or more conflicting values about a particular object or situation, resulting in some level of dissonance if the person becomes aware of the conflicting values. The vegetarian who believes in the sanctity of all life forms may also value respect for family tradition and a mother's wishes (thus eating Thanksgiving turkey once a year at the family gathering).

The process of socializing new students into a profession can also be thought of as introducing them to the profession's specific core values. For example, new students will learn the high value that counselors place on protecting clients' privacy by hearing instructors and fellow students discuss it in class and then observing their clinical supervisors struggle to keep client information confidential by claiming privilege in the face of a subpoena. This socialization process can be seen as a way of assisting these individuals in adopting a specific subculture or worldview that will enhance their professional perspective, judgment, and ability to function responsibly in their new roles. Rokeach and Regan (1980) noted two dimensions of values that are relevant to counseling: (a) standards of competency and standards of morals, and (b) terminal (desirable end-states) and instrumental (behaviors useful to reach end-state) values. Wisdom (more desirable than foolishness), truthfulness (more desirable than deceit), and freedom (more desirable than enslavement) are examples of terminal values. Instrumental values concern those idealized or desirable types of behavior that are useful in attaining the end-state, such as being organized or industrious. They are not necessarily good in and of themselves. For example, the instrumental value of industriousness may serve either a thief or Mother Theresa, but to very different ends. These dimensions add richness to the consideration of ethics concepts. Thus, unethical practices can be seen as stemming from either ignorance or inadequate training and supervision (violations of the value concerning standards of competency), as well as from personal profit motive, need for self-enhancement, or the need to maintain power and status (terminal values). These latter motivations may be related to personal values that are nonmoral values and are in conflict with the moral values embedded in the profession's values as reflected in its standards regarding particular situations.

Another important differentiation involves acknowledging that some values can be seen as universal, but not necessarily absolute. Historically, anthropologists see such values as the prohibition against killing, a prohibition on marriage or sexual intercourse between members of the immediate family, respect for ownership of property, and truthfulness as values shared by most human cultures (Brandt, 1959; Kluckhorn, 1951). Nevertheless, culturally permissible exceptions under specific circumstances are allowed, such as killing to defend one's own life or in battle in a war. This acknowledgment is not tantamount to ethical relativism or situational ethics. These exceptions are related to limited circumstances that make the exception permissible. Further, these exceptions are widely understood and supported by the entire cultural group for all people in similar circumstances. In more recent work, the quest to identify universal values relevant to counseling while still respecting human diversity continues. After reviewing the scholarly and religious literature concerning universal values and values central to the major streams of world culture, Kinnier, Kernes, and Dautheribes (2000) compiled a list of universal moral values to use in counseling to assist clients in examining the implications of their value conflicts. Examine these values as presented in Figure 5–1 and think about whether you agree that

I. Commitment to something greater than oneself
   To recognize the existence of and be committed to a Supreme Being, higher principle, transcendent purpose, or meaning to one's existence
   To seek the truth (or truths)
   To seek justice
II. Self-respect, but with humility, self-discipline, and acceptance of personal responsibility
   To respect and care for oneself
   To not exalt oneself or overindulge—to show humility and avoid gluttony, greed, or other forms of selfishness or self-centeredness
   To act in accordance with one's conscience and to accept responsibility for one's behavior
III. Respect and caring for others (i.e., the Golden Rule)
   To recognize the connectedness between all people
   To serve humankind and to be helpful to individuals
   To be caring, respectful, compassionate, tolerant, and forgiving of others
   To not hurt others (e.g., do not murder, abuse, steal from, cheat, or lie to others)
IV. Caring for other living things and the environment

FIGURE 5–1. The Short List of Universal Moral Values
Source: From "A Short List of Universal Moral Values" by R. T. Kinnier, J. L. Kernes, and T. M. Dautheribes, 2000, *Counseling and Values, 45,* 4–16. Copyright 2000 by American Counseling Association. Reprinted by permission.

they are universal. How do you feel about using them in counseling? Are they "universal" enough to be used with clients of diverse cultural, ethnic, and religious backgrounds? How might examining them assist both counselor and client in resolving the issues presented in counseling?

VALUES IN COUNSELING

Historical Perspective

Do all members of the human race share common values? To what degree should a counselor's values influence clients? These questions constitute some of the most troublesome debates in counseling and date to the beginning of psychotherapy's development with Sigmund Freud's psychodynamic approach. In his system of therapy, the therapist was to work assiduously to maintain an absolute neutrality of response to the patient, thus providing a "blank screen" on which the patient could project and play out intrapsychic conflicts. The desired result of this process was transference reaction. Patients would project the persona of an important figure from their earlier psychic development and engage this persona in reparatory work by playing out conflicts with this figure in the therapist–patient relationship. It was essential that characteristics of the therapist, including values and morals, were not conveyed to the patient, thereby encouraging the projection process.

The substance of orthodox Freudian psychodynamic therapy as well as the enthusiastic adoption of the objective, scientific paradigm continued to influence the development of all psychotherapy. This legacy resulted in a long-term supposition that counselors and therapists could and should be value-neutral, a belief that persisted into the 1950s (Ginsberg & Herma, 1953; Walters, 1958). Later, professionals began acknowledging the value-based nature of counseling (Bergin, 1985; London, 1986; Pietrofesa, Hoffman, Splete, & Pinto, 1978). Education and research have continued to value and develop the scientific and technical aspects of professional practice in subsequent decades. However, it is just as critical for counselors to acknowledge and develop the ability to address the moral and value dimensions of their expertise (Corey, Corey, & Callanan, 2003; London, 1986). Herr and Niles (1988) noted that the counselor's values determine the *process* of counseling, whereas the client's values determine the *content* of counseling. In addition, the content of the problem the client brings to counseling may be value laden in and of itself for both the counselor and client, such as whether or not to have premarital sex. Clients also may attempt to camouflage or avoid certain issues due to struggles with their value systems, such as refusing to discuss their struggles with issues of gender identity. Figure 5–2 provides examples of the myriad value-charged issues that clients may bring to counseling. Counselors should examine their own values and biases in these areas.

QUESTION FOR REFLECTION

Your 16-year-old client informs you that she is pregnant by her 17-year-old boyfriend. She tells you that she does not love her boyfriend and was thinking about ending the relationship prior to the pregnancy. She wants to have an abortion and needs your help. You are pro-life and do not support abortion; however, you work in a public school that does not have a policy prohibiting counselors from working with students considering abortion. What do you do?

A counselor's personal and professional value systems will influence the course of the counseling interaction through a wide range of mechanisms: (a) if and how the client will be diagnosed, (b) whether certain topics will be focused on or discussed at all through specific direction or more subtle verbal or nonverbal reinforcement, (c) which goals are considered possible or appropriate for the counseling work they will do, and (d) how they will be evaluated (Strupp, 1980).

Counselors' Values in the Relationship

Counselors should become intensely involved in assessing their own values and how they affect the counseling process (Corey, Corey, & Callanan, 2003; Herr & Niles, 1988). It is highly unethical for counselors to impose their values on a client (Corey, Corey, & Callanan). For example, some counselors have pressured homosexual clients who are content with that status to become involved in conversion or reparative role recovery therapy. Practitioners of reparative therapy believe that homosexuality is a mental illness rather than a variation within the normal spectrum of human sexual, affectional expression. The counselor who imposes this value upon a client has acted unethically for three reasons. First, the counselor has used a position of trust with the client to coerce the client into undergoing therapy that is not desired. Second, the counselor has

abortion	assisted suicide	pre- or extramarital sex
sexual identity issues	child custody	spousal abuse
substance abuse	illegal means of support	interracial relationships
cross-racial adoption	unsafe sexual activity	child neglect/abuse
controversial religious beliefs	racist behavior/attitudes	dishonesty
birth control	unwed pregnancy	discipline of children
infertility/childlessness	cosmetic surgery	death and dying
unusual sexual practices	gang membership	suicide

FIGURE 5–2. Value-Charged Issues in Counseling

ignored the findings of the psychological and medical communities that homosexuality is not a mental illness and thus needs no treatment. Third, the counselor has recommended a course of action that at best is ineffective and, in the majority of cases, has proven to be harmful. Although homosexuality may be considered a controversial issue in some social or religious arenas, there is no such controversy in the medical and psychological arenas. The National Rehabilitation Association, the American Medical Association, the American Academy of Pediatrics, the ACA, the American Psychiatric Association, the APA, the National Association of School Psychologists, and the NASW, represent over a million health and mental health professionals. All of these organizations recognize homosexuality as a healthy expression of human sexuality rather than a mental illness, and thus it needs no "cure." In addition, these organizations have classified reparative therapy as a harmful and therefore unethical practice. Counselors who hold the personal value that homosexuality is a mental illness are ethically obligated to inform their clients who have issues concerning sexual identity that the counselor's values are at odds with counseling, psychological, and health care professional organizations. They should then assist their clients in locating another professional who can work positively with them. It is important to note that homosexual clients who are not content with their sexual orientation are candidates for therapy to come to acceptance of their sexuality identity. This is particularly true of young clients who are at elevated risk for suicide.

Recent recommendations urge counselors to disclose their values and philosophical orientations directly to clients. This discussion might occur either within the context of specific issues that arise within the course of counseling or as part of the process of informed consent and professional disclosure at the outset of counseling (Tjelveit, 1986). As with any advanced counseling technique, such as confrontation, the counselor should disclose values carefully. This disclosure should be intentional, focused on enhancing the client's process, and presented in an open, nonjudgmental manner that carries with it the sense that these values may be accepted or rejected without risking the counseling relationship.

QUESTION FOR REFLECTION

Your client makes this statement in session: "I hate Jews. It's too bad Hitler wasn't able to finish what he started." You are Jewish. What, if anything, do you say in response to this statement?

The client might experience the same personal values held by the counselor, as well as a more general body of shared values. Traditionally, these shared values have been described as *mental health values* (Jensen & Bergin, 1988) or *essential therapeutic values* (Strupp, 1980). A national survey by Jensen and Bergin examined counselors' degree of consensus with key mental health values including autonomy and independence, skill in interpersonal communication, honesty, and self-control. They found a substantial consensus among surveyed counselors that these are central counseling values. The essential therapeutic values described by Strupp are that people (a) have rights, privileges, and responsibilities; (b) have the right to personal freedom; (c) have responsibilities to others; (d) should be responsible for conducting their own affairs, as much as they are able; (e) should have their individuality respected; (f) should not be dominated, manipulated, coerced, or indoctrinated; and (g) are entitled to make their own mistakes and learn from them. Values may be observed interpersonally within the counseling relationship through studying the perceived operations of (a) **support,** the receiving of encouragement, understanding, and kindness from others; (b) **conformity,** the following of rules and observation of societal regulations; (c) **recognition,** the attraction of favorable notice and being considered important; (d) **independence,** seeing oneself as being free to make one's own decisions and acting autonomously; (e) **benevolence,** the experience of sharing, helping, and acting generously toward others; and (f) **leadership,** the sense of having responsibility, power, and authority over others (Gordon, 1976). Clearly, the values of counselors are expressed through specific behaviors that affect the client in the counseling relationship.

In addition to these more global value orientations, some theoretical orientations embody and promulgate specific philosophical or value positions as part of the therapeutic system. To the degree that counselors follow these specific systems of therapy, they will directly influence the philosophy and values of their clients, hopefully with the client's direct awareness and consent. Examples of such approaches and associated values include (a) Adlerian Psychotherapy's emphasis on social striving and social interest; (b) Reality Therapy and its focus on personal responsibility and the quality of the individual lifestyle; (c) Existential Therapy and its emphasis on learning this particular philosophical system, including such concepts as self-determination and freedom with responsibility; and (d) Ellis's Rational–Emotive

Behavior Therapy and its goal of indoctrinating the client with a new set of rational beliefs and values. A counselor's theoretical approach, philosophy, and underlying value system also have an influence on clients. Therefore, the counselor should include these beliefs in the informed consent procedures at the outset of the relationship. These issues should be thoroughly discussed in terms that prospective clients can understand to ensure that they comprehend these aspects of counseling, how the issues might influence their treatment, and whether the values are compatible with their own value system.

When there appears to be serious value incompatibilities or extreme levels of discomfort, counselors must determine if they should continue working with a client or refer the client to someone else who might have a better level of ability or compatibility with which to assist the client. If the counselor is in serious danger of imposing values on the client or is unable to remain objective, the counselor should consider referring the client elsewhere. Counselors often either over- or underestimate their ability to work with clients who cause such reactions in them. In such instances, counselors must make every effort to be honest with themselves. Supervision by a skilled senior colleague is invaluable in this determination. If the counselor is actually placing the client at risk or impeding progress, an appropriate referral made in a positive, constructive manner is necessary. In other instances, proper safeguards such as a skilled supervisor, consultant, or cotherapist can be arranged. Then, with client consent, counseling can proceed effectively. Such situations help counselors increase their ability to understand the viewpoints of others that may be challenging to them.

Research has demonstrated that the degree to which the values of the counselor and client are congruent influences the outcome of the counseling process. For example, clients who adopt values like those of their counselors tended to have more positive outcomes (Beutler, Pollack, & Jobe, 1978; Landfield & Nawas, 1964; Welkowitz, Cohen, & Ortmeyer, 1967). This important effect of differing counselor and client value systems demonstrates the increasing importance of the counselor being culturally sensitive. Counselors must become aware of the value systems of their clients from different cultures and of their own cultural assumptions and biases. They also must be willing and able to apply the skills necessary to accommodate and work across these diverse cultural perspectives (Arredondo & Toporek, 2004; Pederson, 1985; Sue, 1996).

QUESTION FOR REFLECTION

Your client, a member of the Lakota Sioux, recently lost her husband in an automobile accident and is seeing you for counseling. She reports that she saw her deceased husband and he told her to "watch for the eagle." She has been maintaining evening vigils in wait of her husband's request. You become concerned because she seems to be experiencing hallucinations. What will you do?

Values, Cultural Worldviews, and Multiculturalism

A deep appreciation and understanding of the values of various cultural, social, and racial groups may provide a window into the relationship with a client who is from a nonmajority group. (Many of the basic concepts of multiculturalism and the ethical obligations to diverse clients are discussed in Chapter 11.) Counselors must understand how individuals from different cultures see the world and how they value different situations or ways of being—their **worldview.** In our diverse society, we can no longer presume that all people hold common, universal values that will be expressed in the same way. Even when people from diverse cultures do hold common values, they may apply them to specific circumstances very differently. The actual choices and behaviors they choose are more likely culture specific.

The values of different cultures have been described using a variety of dimensions upon which cultural groups may differ. Although these various descriptors may be confusing, they do reflect the rich differences in what human beings value and how they see the world. Themes or dimensions for cultural values include nature, time, social relations, activity, humanity, customs, traditions, and religion (Hopkins, 1997). In contrast, Hofstede (1980) researched cultural differences relevant to public life and work behavior and found four major cultural dimensions: (a) power distances, (b) uncertainty avoidance, (c) individualism/collectivism, and (d) masculinity/femininity, or valuing assertiveness and materialism rather than concern for people and quality of life.

Becoming culturally sensitive is not an easy pursuit for counselors and constitutes a lifelong area for personal and professional development. Corey, Corey, and Callanan (2003), strident proponents of this type of value learning and exploration, noted that often counselors must challenge the stereotypical beliefs that are common legacies of a Eurocentric majority culture. The stereotypical assumptions they called attention to are that clients: (a) are ready to engage in and value self-disclosure; (b) will be better off if they behave in an assertive manner; (c) believe that self-actualization is important, and that a trusting relationship can be quickly formed; (d) have nonverbal behaviors we can readily understand; and (e) value directness (Corey, Corey, & Callanan). Counselors must continuously strive to learn more about different cultures and varying value systems related to their clients' lives. Learning about these value themes or dimensions by listening to clients with openness and a desire to enter into their frame of reference is an important obligation.

VALUES CLARIFICATION, VALUING, AND MORAL DISCUSSION

How can counselors best prepare themselves to recognize their values and the implications of these values in their work? This task can be daunting. Three general processes have been developed to assist in this task: (a) values clarification, (b) the valuing process, and (c) moral discussion.

Values Clarification

The work of Raths, Harmin, and Simon (1966, 1978) sparked a tremendously successful movement among educators, counselors, other helping professionals, and even the public that focused attention on the importance and understanding of values. These scholars addressed the vacuum that many people felt in the 1950s in terms of establishing a sense of meaning and the importance of values within their lives and work. This movement appeared to be a reaction to the value-neutral influence of the scientific tradition and the increasing popularity of the humanistic philosophical and therapeutic movements of the late 1950s to the 1970s. The contemporary work of Rogers, Perls, Maslow, and others encouraged self-determination, examination of one's own perspectives, and the search for personal meaning and truth through self-examination (Kinnier, 1995). It is within that context that Raths, Harmin, and Simon (1966) noted that many individuals are unaware of the values they hold and suffer from this lack of focus in their personal and professional relationships and even in the sense of who they are.

Values clarification helps individuals clarify their beliefs through a method that focuses on the process surrounding assigning value rather than on the content of what is valued (Raths, Harmin, & Simon, 1978).

Distinct steps in the values clarification process involve the three main functions of prizing, choosing, and acting on one's values. Values chosen through this process are considered clarified values.

Kirschenbaum (2000) became convinced that values clarification should be an element in a more comprehensive approach that includes the original seven valuing processes described by Raths, Harmin, and Simon (1978) that are contained in the facilitating stage of the new model, but also adds the processes of inculcation of positive values and character, modeling of values and character, and skill building necessary to live a satisfying and constructive life (Kirschenbaum; see Figure 5–3). This recent revision addresses the criticisms of those authorities who faulted values clarification for being concerned only with the process rather than the outcome of the process. Kirschenbaum's more recent revision concerns itself with both the process and the hoped-for outcomes of values education. Box 5–2 lists activities that are consistent with this tradition.

Values Conflict Resolution

Clearly, the ways in which human experience can be explored through values clarification are vast. Nevertheless,

I. Inculcating
II. Modeling
III. Facilitating
    A. Prizing beliefs and behaviors
      1. prizing and cherishing
      2. publicly affirming, when appropriate
    B. Choosing beliefs and behaviors
      3. choosing from alternatives
      4. choosing after consideration of consequences
      5. choosing freely
    C. Acting on beliefs
      6. acting
      7. acting with a pattern, consistency and repetition
IV. Value-laden skill building

FIGURE 5–3.   The Comprehensive Values Education Process (Includes the Seven Values Clarification Steps in the Facilitation Process)

Source: Adapted from "From values clarification to character education: A personal journey" by H. Kirschenbaum, 2000, *Journal of Humanistic Counseling, Education and Development, 39,* 20. Copyright 2000 by the American Counseling Association. Reprinted by permission.

Box 5–2 • What Are Some of My Values?

The following activities are consistent with the values clarification tradition. After completing the activities, discuss your answers in a group. Conduct an open, thought-provoking discussion with your peers, examine the consequences of your position, and publicly affirm your beliefs.

Activity 1. Imagine that your doctor has told you that you have a virulent form of cancer and you will be dead soon. You have decided to write your own eulogy. What are the unique traits or meaningful accomplishments that you especially want to include? Why are they particularly important to you? Which one is the most important to you? Why? Which one is most important to your parents? Which one is most important to your spouse, partner, or closest friend? Do these perspectives differ? Why or why not?

Activity 2. Imagine you are in a longstanding relationship with your partner that is very happy, except for one thing—you and your partner are not able to have a biological child despite wanting one badly. You have decided to adopt a child, but are not able to receive a healthy infant of your own race. You are offered the opportunity to choose from among the following babies: a biracial baby, a baby that is moderately mentally retarded, a baby whose biological mother is HIV positive, a 2-year-old who appears to be hyperactive, a child with facial deformities that can be only partially corrected by surgeries, and a toddler who survived the murder–suicide of his biological parents. Would you adopt one of these children or choose not to have a child? If you would adopt, which child would you select and why? For each of the children you did not select, what was your reasoning?

Countless individuals have taken part and benefited from this type of encounter. This approach offers opportunities to examine countless aspects of our personal and professional relationships and lifestyle choices. It is likely to stimulate lively discussion and serious self-examination. The activities can be tailored to the concerns and needs of quite disparate types of people, including counselors. For example:

- What is your ideal type of client to work with? Why? Your most dreaded? Why?
- What makes you happiest about your work as a counselor? Over what do you become the most upset or afraid?
- Who is the living person who has most influenced your work? Why and how?
- What historical or prominent celebrity figure has most influenced your work? Why and how?
- What is the greatest boost to your effectiveness and why?
- What is the biggest threat to your effectiveness and why?
- What are you proudest of about yourself as a counselor? Ashamed of?

values clarification began to lose favor during the 1980s. The most common area of concern involves the apparently value-neutral position of the group leader or teacher. Many have voiced concern that this experience may create a permissive, self-absorbed atmosphere, and in its extreme, allow abusive or abhorrent values to go unchallenged. Kinnier (1995) suggested that religious conservatism, political conservatism, a therapeutic paradigm shift away from humanistic philosophy, and the inherent flaws within the theory itself are the major forces that have dampened earlier enthusiasm for values clarification. He noted that the core concepts are worth retaining and recommended several changes to resolve specific problems and to extend the usefulness of this approach. Kinnier forwarded the idea of focusing on one concrete and specific values conflict at a time in a specific area of the person's life because people do not effectively evaluate values in single, abstract form. The emphasis should not be on rank ordering values, but rather on determining which values are in conflict and the degree of conflict, as well as arriving at an overall statement of how the key values in conflict can be reconciled. This would provide a more specific goal to the process—resolution of a specified values conflict—and, thus, Kinnier suggested how more effective interventions could be tailored to assist in this conflict resolution (Table 5–1). The interventions are divided between rational and intuitive-type foci to accommodate differing personal styles of those in conflict.

In addition to these concerns about how the process was conceptualized and applied, several authorities reviewed the effectiveness of values clarification in values or moral education. Based on their critical review of the literature in this area, two leading proponents of moral education (Leming, 1993; Lickona, 1991) considered the moral discussion approach of Lawrence Kohlberg (1981) rather than values clarification (Raths, Harmin, & Simon, 1966) to be successful in moral education.

TABLE 5–1   Strategies for Intrapersonal Values Conflict Resolution

Rational	Intuition Enhancing
Defining the conflict clearly	Emotional focusing
Gathering information systematically	Brainstorming/free association
Comparing alternatives and considering consequences logically	Life review
Eliminating alternatives systematically	Psychodrama Guided imagery into hypothetical focus
Being vigilant for maladaptive affect regarding the conflict, resolution, or both (e.g., worry, postdecisional regret, irrational beliefs) and using cognitive restructuring, emotional inoculation, or stress-reduction techniques to counter maladaptive affect	Personal rituals Incubation (e.g., Vision Quest, Incubation (e.g., Vision Quest meditation) Self-confrontational exercises such as the devil's advocate or the two-chair exercise, and confrontation with one's own mortality that involves both rational discourse and a focus on affective reactions

Source: From "A Reconceptualization of Values Clarification: Values Conflict Resolution" by R. T. Kinnier, 1995, *Journal of Counseling & Development, 74,* 18–24. Copyright 1995 by American Counseling Association. Reprinted by permission.

Valuing

Other issues have arisen as counselors attempt to apply the individualistically oriented concepts of values clarification to group or marriage and family counseling issues. The role of interdependence in healthy human relationships and the social, political, and cultural context of the individual's experience are an important aspect of the counseling therapeutic and theoretical worldviews that are beyond the scope of more limited specialty area perspectives. For example, Sue (1996) noted that counseling practices that impose monocultural value systems or biases on clients from diverse cultural backgrounds are discriminatory and unethical.

Marriage and family counselors have long struggled with issues of reconciling the conceptualization of the individual's values with those in the relationships of the group or family as a wholistic entity. Doherty and Boss (1991) reviewed the literature on value issues and ethics in the practice of marriage and family. They noted that the idea of value neutrality on the part of the therapist is no longer viable and the emphasis in the field should be on accommodating values within the therapeutic process. Thomas (1994) provided a model of value analysis within marriage and family counseling that attempts to meld personal and systemically oriented value systems in addressing value dilemmas. He noted that counselors must analyze and reconcile values at (a) the individual level of the counselor microsystem, (b) the family level of the client's microsystem, and (c) the level of the overlapping counseling process itself (mesosystem). These operations are embedded in the context of societal values surrounding the dilemma (macrosystem). Although this analysis may be couched in the marriage and family counseling paradigm, it is important for counselors in all settings to consider contextual or hierarchical levels that affect their ethical and values analysis (Tarvydas & Cottone, 1991). Authorities such as Sue (1996) and Coyne and Cook (2004) have called for a recognition that systems interventions will be necessary for ethical practice as counselors recognize that clients often have experiences embedded in the systems in which they are nested.

Valuing, or the negotiation of values, is a model and practice that has grown out of these concerns for reconciling disparate and often competing values orientations. This model better accommodates forces of social change as expressed in various social and cultural value changes (Huber, 1994). Huber described the valuing process as one in which the counselor:

Negotiates with a client in emphasizing certain values previously de-emphasized, and at the same time in relegating other values to the background. Within the context of the therapist–client negotiation, values evolve with accompanying behavioral changes that are compatible with values changes. Essentially, the therapist and client come together in negotiating a common world of less pain and conflict . . . Valuing recognizes that when therapist and client come together, they can negotiate a new, common system containing elements or both subsystems as well as unique properties arising from their interactions. (pp. 235–236)

Counselors must acknowledge several implications in their practice to enact such an approach to reconciling values. Taken together, these assumptions constitute a valuing perspective and worldview that create the conditions for this more interactive alliance around a particular values perspective. Huber (1994) described these key assumptions based on the earlier work of Dell (1983). The practitioner must recognize that:

1. No such *phenomenon as an absolute value* exists that is objectively true or good. Rather, values are a result of the person's processing or reaction of a system's values.
2. All persons must *take responsibility* for selecting, interpreting, and holding their own values; thus, no one can be held ultimately responsible for changing another's values.
3. Therapists must accept responsibility for the tendency to *pathologize their clients,* or to see them in terms of their pathologies or problems, thus de-emphasizing the role of their own values in the process.
4. Counselors must accept that "*what is, is.*" They must allow clients to be accepted for who they are, rather than being judged as bad or sick because of behaviors that do not conform to the counselor's values or preferences.

In addition to these assumptions, values negotiation or valuing involves several process-related components.

The value assumptions just described are only working assumptions and must be examined critically. Nevertheless, these principles, if acknowledged and incorporated within the work of the valuing process, will allow valuing to occur in a constructive and productive manner. The core components of valuing are (a) recognition of mutual obligations and entitlements within the relationships among the parties, or the "give and take" of human interactions; (b) the acknowledgment of those things to which others are entitled and the valid claims of others; and (c) the balance of fairness (Huber, 1994). If obligations, entitlements, and claims are all taken together and are in relative balance, the climate will facilitate the balance of fairness in terms of values issues in the relationship. Although attending to these principles and the valuing process within the counseling relationship may appear to add greatly to its complexity, in reality these considerations recognize and respect the truly shared nature of this important relationship between diverse, autonomous beings. Values issues that arise between counselor and client from the dazzlingly numerous sources of interpersonal diversity

are not only accommodated, but have the potential to enrich the counselor and the client, and their relationship, if they are directly addressed within the valuing process.

Moral Discussion and Levels of Development

Kohlberg (1964; 1971), one of the key figures in developmental psychology and the philosophy of morality, has led in the current understanding of the moral development of children and adults. His work provides a way to extend and enrich the important process of values education or clarification by understanding the moral perspectives that underlie these value choices. Kohlberg's work presents a theoretical understanding of how moral reasoning develops and relates values to moral growth. The Kohlberg system removes concerns about the seeming relativity of values in the values clarification by interpreting moral choice within a particular, developmental moral system that holds justice as its core concept. Kohlberg's theory explains value choices within the context of how people develop higher levels of moral judgment (Reimer, Paolitto, & Hersch, 1983).

Kohlberg's work (1964; 1971) is drawn from Piaget's developmental psychology, which focused on the reasoning processes underlying the behavior involved in children's cognitive developmental stages. Similarly, Kohlberg focused specifically on the reasoning processes underlying the behaviors associated with moral development. He also assumed a universal, absolute core of morality that provides structure to this reasoning process. Kohlberg maintained that all human societies believe in certain core moral values, even though there may be moral debates and cultural differences regarding their interpretations: (a) laws and values, (b) conscience, (c) personal roles of affection, (d) authority, (e) civil rights, (f) contract, trust, and justice in exchange, (g) punishment, (h) the value of life, (i) property rights and values, and (j) truth. Kohlberg spent his career studying how moral stages are organized and learned. He proposed that children form their own moral philosophies and systems as they are exposed to and grapple with moral experiences and dilemmas. This process is creative and is an attempt to make sense out of the information, experiences, and culture that surround the individual. It is considered optimal to expose people to these situations and assist them in processing them for themselves within the context of the moral system. Kohlberg and Wasserman

(1980) recommended that ethical behavior can best be encouraged by (a) exposing people to the higher stages of moral development; (b) introducing them to irreconcilable ethical dilemmas, thus stimulating awareness and dissatisfaction with the lower, less sophisticated levels of reasoning; and (c) providing a supportive, therapeutic environment in which the situations and analyses can be processed freely. Van Hoose and Kottler (1985) noted that the counseling session is a likely environment for this process.

QUESTION FOR REFLECTION

You counseled a couple for approximately 1 year and the marriage ended in divorce. The husband is suing his wife for custody of their two children. You have received a subpoena from the husband's attorney to appear in court to testify about the wife's emotional instability. Although there was evidence of the wife's emotional instability during counseling, you do not think it is serious enough to warrant an "unfit mother" verdict. To complicate matters, you find out that the wife has employed the most incompetent attorney in the city and you are afraid he will not represent her well. What will you do?

Kohlberg's system of moral development stages has been described as Kohlberg's greatest contribution to the study of ethics (Van Hoose & Kottler, 1985). Van Hoose and Paradise (1979) adapted these stages to describe the stages of ethical orientation for counselors (Figure 5–4). They assumed that counselors, like all persons, initially mature through stages of development within the context of age and situation-specific experiences. They challenged counselors to identify and explore their rationales for particular value or ethical choices. Through insight and self-awareness, counselors reach more sophisticated levels of ethical reasoning. These stages of ethical orientation presented by Van Hoose and Paradise are (a) punishment, (b) institutional, (c) societal, (d) individual, and (e) principle or conscience. (See Figure 5–4 for descriptions of the stages' characteristics. You may wish to think about the last ethical dilemma you faced, how you responded to it, and your level of thinking on this matter.) The individual's level of ethical orientation can be thought of as forming that person's intuitive sense of moral judgment. The counselor would use this dominant general level of orientation or moral thinking to consider ethical dilemmas as described by Kitchener (1984) and discussed within the decision-making arena described in Chapter 6.

In the context of this theoretical framework, a number of assumptions regarding ethical behavior follow: (a) The counselor's functioning is not solely at one stage—this functioning may be affected by situational, educational, and other variables; (b) the orientations are qualitatively discrete stages that reflect a continuum of ethical reasoning; (c) the basis for ethical judgment is characterized by the dominant stage of ethical orientation; (d) stages are continuous and

Stage I. Punishment Orientation Counselor decisions, suggestions, and courses of action are based on a strict adherence to prevailing rules and standards, i.e., one must be punished for bad behavior and rewarded for good behavior. The primary concern is the strict attention to the physical consequences of the decision.

Stage II. Institutional Orientation Counselor decisions, suggestions, and courses of action are based on a strict adherence to the rules and policies of the institution or agency. The correct posture is based on the expectations of higher authorities.

Stage III. Societal Orientation The maintenance of standards, approval of others, and the laws of society and the public characterize this stage of ethical behavior. Concern is for duty and societal welfare.

Stage IV. Individual Orientation The primary concern of the counselor is for the needs of the individual while avoiding the violation of laws and the rights of others. Concern for law and societal welfare is recognized, but is secondary to the needs of the individual.

Stage V. Principle or Conscience Orientation Concern for the individual is primary with little regard for the legal, professional, or societal consequences. What is right, in accord with self-chosen principles of conscience and internal ethical formulations, determines counselor behavior.

FIGURE 5–4.   Stages of Ethical Orientation

Source: From *Ethics in Counseling and Psychotherapy: Perspectives in Issues and Decision Making* (p. 117) by W. H. Van Hoose and L. V. Paradise, 1979, Cranston, RI: The Carroll Press.

overlapping, suggesting development toward higher levels; (e) development in ethical judgment is forward and irreversible, but specific ethical actions need not be so; and (f) internalized ethical conflict may be generated by discrepancies between ethical reasoning and action associated with situational influences (Van Hoose & Paradise, 1979). Although all stage theories can be criticized for certain structural limitations (e.g., not accommodating individual variations in patterns of movement between stages), the stages of ethical orientation for counselors presented by Van Hoose and Paradise continue to provide a useful framework for counselors to think about their moral development. Counselors may be assisted by realizing that there are hierarchically and developmentally ordered benchmarks against which they measure their current ethical reasoning abilities. Additionally, because the theory is oriented toward continued moral development through ongoing education within a specific moral and principled framework, it provides a positive, structured model for professional education and improvement.

PRINCIPLE ETHICS, VIRTUE ETHICS, AND THE ETHICS OF CARE

Principle ethics and analysis as introduced in Chapter 3, are powerful tools that the counselor must learn to employ in the ethical decision-making process. Recent trends question the exclusive reliance on principle ethics, most notably those of feminist scholars and authorities in cross-cultural or multicultural studies. This critique is related to the perception that the cultural assumptions in principle ethics are based heavily on Western, scientific thought and a general individualistic, male-oriented worldview (see Chapter 11). Since the late 1980s, the study of ethical discourse has been enriched by writings on the ethics of care and virtue ethics. These two perspectives offer alternative perspectives for considering ethical reasoning. Both hold the potential to better accommodate the positions of nonmainstream people, women, and persons from culturally diverse backgrounds. Virtue ethics, the ethics of care, and the multicultural perspective can complement the traditional processes of principle ethics that have provided the bulk of ethical tradition within counseling.

Traditional principle ethics approaches analysis of problematic ethical questions through application of a set of ethical principles that constitute prima facie obligations owed to others. Principle ethics requires the use of a rational, linear, logical, universal, and objective analysis to determine what one's ethical duty is in a particular situation. This process requires weighing how the principles apply to the case at hand through an impartial analysis. This approach essentially requires the counselor to ask the question "what shall I do?" to resolve the ethical dilemma (Meara, Schmidt, & Day, 1996). In terms of ethical approaches to research participation, principle ethics approaches tend to focus on a contractual model.

Relational Ethics

Relational ethics has developed and been nurtured by the feminist ethics tradition and can be seen as broadly encompassing such major areas as virtue ethics, ethics of care, and feminist ethics. The movement to consider ethical issues from the viewpoint of relational or virtue ethics and those implications is full of difficulty as well as great potential (Fisher, 2000). The broad area of **relational ethics** addresses ethical reasoning primarily through development of character traits or virtues and concerns itself with cultural, contextual, relational, and emotional-intuitive responses to ethical dilemmas. Relational ethics addresses the question of "who should I be?" that will inform my ethical reasoning and actions within the context of the particular relationships I have with others. As such, relational ethics approaches may have greater potential to accommodate the consideration of the concerns present by nonmainstream people, women, and people from culturally diverse backgrounds. In this paradigm, counselors and clients may choose to enter into a relationship in which they would collaboratively discuss the benefits and concerns that would be relevant to their respective needs and interests in the situation. The ethical traditions of virtue ethics, ethics of care, and feminist ethics offer rich streams of thought to broaden out the consideration of the ethical dilemmas that occur within counseling practice.

There is a natural tendency among many behavioral scientists and traditional practitioners to reject the use of the concepts of virtue and relational/contextual foci in ethical considerations. This tendency originates in a long history of valuing the scientific tradition. Scientific communities historically have called into question the focus on nonempirical aspects of a situation that are not considered scientific evidence; in short, they prefer dealing with what are seen as facts rather than values (Tjeltveit, 2003). Virtues and relational ethics are closely related to the determination of what constitutes good in the context of specific communities and relationships. Addressing ethical dilemmas under conditions where there is no explicit dialogue about what is good or virtuous in a professional community is difficult. In these conditions there may be divergent interpretations of what is good, as well as diverse and multiple communities involved as stakeholders in the ethical situation. Therefore, it is likely that there will be major obstacles in gaining a satisfying resolution to the important ethical questions, especially if conditions arise in which open consideration and nonhierarchical discussion about these issues are not encouraged. It is for that reason that the narratives, beliefs, and traditions of clients and their communities must be considered. Approaches to ethical decision making are beginning to provide clear inclusion of both relational and principle ethical consideration (Cottone, 2000; Kitchener, 1996; Tarvydas, 2004). There is recognition that such integrative approaches may enhance the ability of models to address transcultural dilemmas in responsible approaches to ethical decision making (Garcia, Cartwright, Winston, & Borzuchowska, 2003). The broader consideration of contextual, environmental factors, while including explicit discussion of what constitutes virtue and what aspects of relationship are critical and constitute a shared sense of goodness, is necessary to develop a collaborative sense of the ethical obligation that will serve the needs of the diverse communities involved (Tjeltveit, 2003).

Virtue Ethics

Virtue ethics is very often discussed by contrasting it to the prevailing tradition of principle ethics. In **virtue ethics,** professionals are called upon to aspire toward ideals and develop virtues or traits of character to achieve these ideals (Meara, Schmidt, & Day, 1996). It is the qualities of the person that have merit or work in some particular context; these qualities are often related to matters of right conduct or morality. Virtue ethics focuses on the agent or individual rather than on the action or decision made, as in principle ethics—not "what shall we do?" but rather "who shall we become?" (Kleist & White, 1997, p. 129).

Virtue ethics has two general goals: (1) achieving and maintaining professional competence, and (2) striving for the common good. To accomplish these ends, the professional should cultivate such virtues as prudence, integrity, and respectfulness. Virtuous professionals (a) are motivated to do what is good; (b) possess vision and discernment; (c) realize the role of affect or emotion in assessing or judging proper conduct; (d) have a high degree of self-understanding and awareness; and, most importantly, (e) connect with and understand the mores of their communities and the importance of community in moral decision making, policy setting, and character development; and are alert to the legitimacy of client diversity in these respects (Meara, Schmidt, & Day, 1996). Virtuous professionals strive to do what is right because they judge it to be right rather than being concerned about a particular outcome. (See Box 5–3.) Some authorities see virtue ethics as enhancing ethical practice in multicultural contexts: Practitioners are more sensitive in their conduct because they are rooted in a particular community's wisdom and moral sense (Ibrahim, 1996; Vasqeuz, 1996).

It is important to evaluate critically how virtue ethics can contribute to the ethical tradition of the counseling profession, as well as to consider related concerns. The communities that are a crucial medium for the development of a virtuous ethic can themselves be insular and ethnocentric, thus becoming harmful to others (Kitchener, 1996). Also, the virtue ethics tradition is seen as irrelevant to the adjudication of ethics complaints by licensure boards and ethics committees (Bersoff, 1996). Finally, the professional community has raised concerns that it may be impossible to teach virtues and that selection of virtuous individuals into the professional community may be the necessary approach (Bersoff; Kitchener, 1996). Nonetheless, many scholars believe that principles and virtues cannot be separated—neither is primary, but each serves to balance the other. Professionals are called upon to perform certain actions for certain kinds of people.

Ethics of Care

The **ethics of care,** which springs from the feminist scholar Carol Gilligan's (1977) critique of Kohlberg's (1971) work on moral development, is not necessarily a new approach. Her groundbreaking critique noted that Kohlberg's work was based on male, and not female, research participants. Women were generally seen in Kohlbergian research as performing at a lower state of moral maturity—that of conventional-level development. Gilligan stated that because women attend to the influences of relationships in their reasoning, their approach is essentially accommodated by a system of moral development that is relationally—and not justice—based. Thus, caring for others is not interpreted as consistent with the highest level of moral development. As a result, Gilligan and other scholars working in this new perspective developed an approach to ethics: the ethics of care that operates in contrast to the

Box 5–3 • Qualities of a Virtuous Counselor

Many personal qualities could be considered characteristic of a virtuous professional. These can be most simply thought of as habits that are nurtured and mature within the process the person goes through in interacting with the community during childhood and throughout life. These are four virtues discussed by Meara, Schmidt, and Day (1996) and others as being characteristic of a virtuous therapist:

Prudence   Respectfulness
Discernment   Benevolence
Integrity

Examine this list of virtues, think about them, and consider the following questions:

1. How would you define these virtues in your own words?

2. In your viewpoint, is this list complete? What virtue would you add? Why?

3. Give one or two examples of choices or actions for each virtue that you might take as a counselor motivated by that virtue.

4. How would clients be affected by these demonstrations of virtue?

5. In which of these virtues are you strongest?

6. In which of these virtues are you weakest?

7. Think about one or two of the most influential events in your life that you can remember as teaching you these virtues. Describe the event and the situation that was involved. Who was involved? Who influenced you the most in the situation and why?

---

prevailing ethic of justice, or principle ethics. Although many of these scholars were feminists, the area is more properly thought of as the ethics of care rather than *feminist ethics* due to its content, applicability across genders, and much broader influence on the study of ethics, such as to the study of ethics within a multicultural context.

Within the ethics of care, the world is seen through a particular "way of knowing" or interpreting experience that emphasizes human connectedness, or a relational perspective, as opposed to seeing it through a lens of scientific knowledge and the laws of nature and man. It emphasizes the social construction of understanding, knowledge, and the participation of a community of "knowers." Within this perspective, great importance is placed on communication with others and honoring relational aspects, obligations or obligations of care inherent in the relationships between people. To fulfill this obligation, one person must be able to take the perspective of and understand the other. This perspective calls upon one not to leave out others to whom one owes social obligation or exclude them from consideration (Noddings, 1992). Although the ethics of care has had wide influence, particularly in nursing scholarship, it has received a number of criticisms as well. For example, some feel it could lead to neglecting the care of strangers (Crowley, 1994), exploitation of the caregiver, not distinguishing between right and wrong sufficiently because care is blind (Nel-

son, 1992), and not having a coherent definition of the ethic of care (Veatch, 1998). The Feminist Therapy Code of Ethics of the Feminist Therapy Institute attempts to use these concepts to guide the work of counselors who wish to use feminist standards (see Appendix E). The influence of the ethics of care continues to grow, possibly because, in addition to its potential to respond to the influences of social constructivism and multiculturalism on the professions, it has a compelling human appeal. This appeal is well reflected in the remarks of Tong (1998) when she stated that practitioners are required "to at least *try* to develop caring feelings as well as conscientious desires and empathic skills . . . In my hours of greatest vulnerability, I will need more than skilled hands. I will also need a *caring* heart" (p. 151).

These newer areas of ethics scholarship have done much to enrich the dialogue about ethics, as well as humanizing and diversifying the practice of applied ethics. Any serious area of study requires that scholars and practitioners be alert to new trends and information that result in updating or changing the knowledge base and skills of the field. The multiculturalism movement, virtue ethics, and the ethics of care perform such a service for the study of ethics and substantially enrich counselors' understanding of practicing the profession ethically. In Chapter 6 you will be introduced to two models of ethical decision making that attempt to respond to these new ways of viewing ethics. Tarvydas' Integrative Decision-Making Model of Ethical Behavior, and Cottone's Social Constructivism Model of Ethical Decision Making. Tarvydas' model incorporates the influences of virtue ethics within the important attitudinal assets that are discussed as permeating the ethical decision making process, and the influence of the ethics of care can be seen in the careful consideration of the perspective of the other and the stakeholders in Stage I, as well as the infusion of contextual analysis throughout Stages III and IV. Cottone's Social Constructivism model is wholly grounded in a foundational theory that views relationships and relational systems as the core of understanding for ethical analysis. These constructivism models are yet another illustration of how virtue ethics and the ethics of care have stimulated new thinking in the understanding of ethics.

CHAPTER SUMMARY

The issues surrounding ethical judgment involve a complex interplay of morals, values, and priorities that people hold in relationship to themselves, their colleagues, and other professionals. Ethics is a branch of study in philosophy concerning how people ought to act toward one another. Morals involve the goodness or badness of human behavior or character. Values are enduring beliefs of what is worthwhile and reflect the value holder's worldview, culture, or understanding of the world. Values clarification, the valuing process, and moral discussion are general processes that assist counselors in working with clients' value systems. Values clarification involves three steps: prizing, choosing, and acting on one's values. Values chosen through this process are called clarified values. Valuing, or negotiation of values, accommodates forces of social change as expressed in social and cultural value changes.

INTERNET RESOURCES

Those wishing to investigate these topics further should search the internet using the following keywords: values, morals, values clarification, values conflict resolution, valuing, moral discussion, moral development, character education, principle ethics, virtues, virtue ethics, relational ethics, ethics of care, and feminist ethics.

REFERENCES

Allport, G. W., Vernon P. E., & Lindzey, G. (1960). *The study of values.* Boston: Houghton-Mifflin.

Arredondo, P., & Toporek, R. (2004). Multicultural counseling competencies = Ethical practice. *Journal of Mental Health Counseling, 26,* 44–55.

Bergin, A. E. (1985). Proposed values for guiding and evaluating psychotherapy. *Counseling and Values, 29,* 99–116.

Bersoff, D. N. (1996). The virtue of principle ethics. *The Counseling Psychologist, 24,* 86–91.

Beutler, L. E., Pollack, S., & Jobe, A. (1978). Acceptance, values, and therapeutic change. *Journal of Consulting and Clinical Psychology, 46,* 198–199.

Brandt, R. (1959). *Ethical theory.* Upper Saddle River, NJ: Prentice Hall.

Corey, G., Corey, M. S., & Callanan, P. (2003). *Issues and ethics in the helping professions* (6th ed.). Pacific Grove, CA: Brooks/Cole.

Cottone, R. R. (2000). A social constructivism model of ethical decision making in counseling. *Journal of Counseling and Development, 79,* 39–45.

Crowley, M. A. (1994). The relevance of Noddings' ethics of care to the moral education of nurses. *Journal of Nursing Education, 33*(2), 20–34.

Coyne, R. K., & Cook, E. P. (2004). *Ecological counseling: An innovative approach to conceptualizing person–environment interaction.* Alexandria, VA: American Counseling Association.

Dell, P. (1983). From pathology to ethics. *The Family Therapy Networker, 7*(6), 29–31, 64.

Doherty, W. J. (1995). *Soul searching: Why psychotherapy must promote moral responsibility.* New York: Basic Books.

Doherty, W., & Boss, P. (1991). Values and ethics in family therapy. In A. S. Gurman & D. P. Kniskern (Eds.), *Handbook of family therapy: vol. 2.* New York: Brunner/Mazel.

Fisher, C. B. (2000). Relational ethics in psychological research: One feminist's journey. In M. M. Brabeck (Ed.), *Practicing feminist ethics in psychology.* Washington, DC: American Psychological Association.

Frank, J. (1961). *Persuasion and healing.* New York: Schoken.

Frankena, W. K. (1963). *Ethics.* Upper Saddle River, NJ: Prentice Hall.

Gilligan, C. (1997). In a different voice: Women's conception of the self and of morality. *Harvard Educational Review, 47,* 481–517.

Garcia, J., Cartwright, B., Winston, S. M., & Borzuchowska, B. (2003). A transcultural integrative ethical decision-making model in counseling. *Journal of Counseling & Development, 81,* 268–277.

Ginsberg, S. W., & Herma, J. L. (1953). Values and their relationship to psychiatric principles and practice. *American Journal of Psychotherapy, 7,* 536–573.

Gordon, L. V. (1976). *Survey of interpersonal values: Revised manual.* Chicago: Science Research Associates.

Griffith, B. A., & Duesterhaus, M. (2000). Integrating a moral conversation: A framework for counselors. *Journal of Humanistic Counseling, Education and Development, 39,* 47–55.

Herr, E. L., & Niles, S. (1988). The values of counseling: Three domains. *Counseling and Values, 33,* 4–17.

Hofstede, G. (1980). *Culture's consequences: International differences in work values.* Beverly Hills, CA: Sage Publications.

Hopkins, W. E. (1997). *Ethical dimensions of diversity.* Thousand Oaks, CA: Sage Publications.

Huber, C. H. (1994). *Ethical, legal, and professional issues in the practice of marriage and family therapy* (2nd ed.). Upper Saddle River, NJ: Merrill/Prentice Hall.

Ibrahim, F. A. (1996). A multicultural perspective on principle and virtue ethics. *The Counseling Psychologist, 24,* 78–85.

Jensen, J. P., & Bergin, A. E. (1988). Mental health values of professional therapists: A national interdisciplinary study. *Professional Psychology: Research and Practice, 19,* 290–297.

King, M. L., Jr. (1968, February 4). *Drum Major Instinct Sermon.* Given at Ebenezer Baptist Church, Atlanta, GA.

Kinnier, R. T. (1995). A reconceptualization of values clarification: Values conflict resolution. *Journal of Counseling & Development, 74,* 18–24.

Kinnier, R. T., Kernes, J. L., & Dautheribes, T. M. (2000). A short list of universal moral values. *Counseling and Values, 45,* 4–16.

Kirschenbaum, H. (2000). From values clarification to character education: A personal journey. *Journal of Humanistic Counseling, Education and Development, 39,* 4–20.

Kitchener, K. S. (1984). Ethics in counseling psychology: Distinctions and directions. *Counseling Psychologist, 12*(3), 43–55.

Kitchener, K. S. (1996). There is more to ethics than principles. *The Counseling Psychologist, 24,* 92–97.

Kleist, D. M., & White, L. J. (1997). The values of counseling: A disparity between a philosophy of prevention in counseling and counselor practice and training. *Counseling and Values, 41,* 128–140.

Kluckhorn, C. (1951). Values and value orientations in the theory of action: An exploration in definition and clarification. In T. Parsons & E. A. Shils (Eds.), *Toward a general theory of action* (pp. 338–433). Cambridge, MA: Harvard University Press.

Kohlberg, L. (1964). Development of moral character and moral ecology. In M. L. Hoffman & L. W. Hoffman (Eds.), *Review of child development research.* Vol. I. New York: Russell Sage Foundation.

Kohlberg, L. (1971). Moral development and the education of adolescents. In R. Purnell (Ed.), *Adolescents and the American high school.* New York: Holt, Rinehart & Winston.

Kohlberg, L. (1981). *Philosophy of moral development.* San Francisco: Harper & Row.

Kohlberg, L., & Wasserman, E. R. (1980). The cognitive-developmental approach and the practicing counselor: An opportunity for counselors to rethink their roles. *Personnel and Guidance Journal, 59,* 559–568.

Landfield, A. W., & Nawas, M. M. (1964). Psychotherapeutic improvement as a function of communication and adoption of therapist's values. *Journal of Counseling Psychology, 11,* 336–341.

Leming, J. S. (1993). *Character education: Lessons from the past, models for the future.* Camden, ME: The Institute for Global Ethics.

Lickona, T. (1991). *Educating for character.* New York: Bantam.

London, P. (1986). *Modes and morals of psychotherapy* (2nd ed.). New York: Holt, Rinehart & Winston.

Meara, N. M., Schmidt, L. D., & Day, J. D. (1996). Principles and virtue: A foundation for ethical decisions, policies, and character. *The Counseling Psychologist, 24*(1), 4–77.

Mowrer, O. (1967). *Morality and mental health.* Chicago: Rand McNally.

Nelson, H. L. (1992). Against caring. *The Journal of Clinical Ethics, 3*(1), 8–14.

Noddings, N. (1992). In defense of caring. *The Journal of Clinical Ethics, 3*(1), 14–17.

Pederson, P. (Ed.). (1985). *Handbook of cross-cultural counseling and therapy.* Westport, CT: Greenwood.

Pietrofesa, J. J., Hoffman, A., Splete, H., & Pinto, D. (1978). *Counseling: Theory, research, and practice.* Chicago: Rand McNally.

Raths, L., Harmin, M., & Simon, S. (1966). *Values and teaching: Working with values in the classroom.* Upper Saddle River, NJ: Merrill/Prentice Hall.

Raths, L., Harmin, M., & Simon, S. (1978). *Values and teaching: Working with values in the classroom* (2nd ed.). Upper Saddle River, NJ: Merrill/Prentice Hall.

Reimer, J., Paolitto, D. P., & Hersch, R. H. (1983). *Promoting moral growth: From Piaget to Kohlberg.* New York: Longman.

Rokeach, M. (1973). *The nature of human values.* New York: Free Press.

Rokeach, M., & Regan, J. (1980). The role of values in the counseling situation. *Personnel and Guidance Journal, 58,* 576–583.

Shertzer, B., & Linden, J. (1979). *Fundamentals of individual appraisal: Assessment techniques for counselors.* Boston: Houghton-Mifflin.

Strupp, H. H. (1980). Humanism and psychotherapy: A personal statement of the therapist's essential values. *Psychotherapy: Theory, Research and Practice, 17,* 396–400.

Sue, D. W. (1996). Ethical issues in multicultural counseling. In B. Herlihy & G. Corey (Eds.), *ACA ethical standards casebook* (5th ed.). Alexandria, VA: American Counseling Association.

Tarvydas, V. M. (2004). Ethics. In D. R. Maki & T. F. Riggar (Eds.). *Handbook of rehabilitation counseling* (pp. 108–141). New York: Springer Publishing Co.

Tarvydas, V. M., & Cottone, R. R. (1991). Ethical responses to legislative, organizational, and economic dynamics: A four-level model of ethical practice. *Journal of Applied Rehabilitation Counseling, 22*(4), 11–18.

Thomas, V. (1994). Value analysis: A model of personal and professional ethics in marriage and family counseling. *Counseling and Values, 38,* 193–202.

Tjeltveit, A. C. (2003). Implicit virtues, divergent goods, multiple communities: Explicitly addressing virtues in the behavioral sciences. *American Behavioral Scientist, 47,* 395–414.

Tjelveit, A. C. (1986). The ethics of value conversion in psychotherapy: Appropriate and inappropriate therapist influence on client values. *Clinical Psychology Review, 6,* 515–537.

Tong, R. (1998): The ethics of care: A feminist virtue ethics of care for healthcare practitioners. *Journal of Medicine and Philosophy, 23*(2), 131–152.

Van Hoose, W. H., & Kottler, J. A. (1985). *Ethical and legal issues in counseling and psychotherapy.* (2nd ed.). San Francisco: Jossey-Bass.

Van Hoose, W. H., & Paradise, L. V. (1979). *Ethics in counseling and psychotherapy: Perspectives in issues and decision making.* Cranston, RI: The Carroll Press.

Vasquez, M. (1996). Will virtue ethics improve ethical conduct in multicultural settings and interactions? *The Counseling Psychologist, 24,* 98–104.

Veatch, R. M. (1998). The place of care in ethical theory. *Journal of Medicine and Philosophy, 23*(2), 210–224.

Walters, O. S. (1958). Metaphysics, religion, and psychotherapy. *Journal of Counseling Psychology, 5,* 243–252.

Welkowitz, J., Cohen, J., & Ortmeyer, D. (1967). Value system similarities: Investigation of patient/therapist dyads. *Journal of Consulting Psychology, 31*(1), 48–55.

CHAPTER 6

Ethical Decision-Making Processes

R. Rocco Cottone • Vilia Tarvydas • Ronald E. Claus

OBJECTIVES

After reading this chapter, you should be able to:

- Explain the decision-making process as a value-laden, but rational, process.
- Cite the literature on decision-making models.
- Summarize the models of ethical decision making.

- Apply two decision-making models—one based on an integration of current theory and practice, and the other based on a purely theoretical model.

INTRODUCTION

This chapter presents a scholarly review of ethical decision-making models. It also presents details of two decision-making models developed by the authors. Tarvydas developed the first model; it is an integration model that blends the best of what is known about decision making in counseling to the date of this writing. An extended example of how this model might be applied to resolve an ethical dilemma is provided. Cottone developed the second model; it is a theoretically based model designed using a social constructivism philosophy. Beyond showcasing the authors' models, it is hoped you will get a sense of their commitment to ethical practice and of their theoretical, philosophical, and empirical inclinations. Presenting both models also is intended to give students and professors some choice and flexibility in approaching ethical decision making in and outside of the classroom. The models are quite distinct. It is hoped readers will gain by comparative analysis of the models.

Parts of this chapter draw heavily and directly from two works published in the ACA *Journal of Counseling and Development*—Cottone (2001) and Cottone and Claus (2000) with permission of the ACA; and from "Ethics" by V. M. Tarvydas, 2004, in T. F. Riggar & D. R. Maki (Eds.), *Handbook of rehabilitation counseling,* Copyright 2004 by Springer Publishing Co. Used by permission. First authorship on this chapter is shared by Cottone and Tarvydas.

QUESTIONS FOR REFLECTION

Reflect on your last major decision, such as choosing an undergraduate or graduate program, becoming engaged or married, making a major purchase, or choosing a job. Think about the process you experienced as you made the decision. Did you do some background research? What individuals were involved in discussions about the decision? What values affected your decision? Who communicated these values to you during your personal development? What social or cultural factors may have influenced your decision? Was the process smooth or abrupt? What emotions did you experience? Did you have a chance to reflect or reconsider your decision after you made it? What actions did you take to implement the decision? Looking back, do you feel it was a wise decision? How could the decision-making process have been done better?

ETHICAL JUDGMENT

The practice of counseling is an art as well as a science, requiring the practitioner to make both value-laden and rational decisions. Rather than being incompatible stances, facts and values must be considered together if counselors are to make good decisions. Ethical deliberation blends such elements as (a) personal and moral sensitivity, (b) philosophy of practice, (c) clinical behavioral objectivity, and (d) the responsibility for efficient and competent care of clients.

An ethics code provides counselors with guidance for the specific situations they experience in their practices. However, authorities have long recognized that ethics codes must be general enough to apply across a wide range of practice settings. They also are reactive in nature; that is, they address situations that have already been part of the profession's experience (Kitchener, 1984; Mabe & Rollin, 1986). As a result, even with the knowledge of the profession's code of ethics, counselors may not find sufficient guidance to resolve a dilemma. They may find that the particular situation they face is not addressed in their code, is addressed by more than one code providing conflicting direction, or conflicting provisions within one code appear to apply to the situation. Thus, counselors must be prepared to exercise their ethical and professional judgment responsibly. *Ethical dilemmas are not so much a failure of ethical codes as a natural and appropriate indicator of the importance of professional judgment.* The need to use ethical judgment is affirmation that one is involved in the "practice of a profession," rather than "doing a job," however skilled.

To exercise professional judgment, counselors must be prepared to recognize underlying ethical principles and conflicts among competing interests, as well as to apply appropriate decision-making skills to resolve the dilemma and act ethically (Francouer, 1983; Kitchener, 1984; Tarvydas, 2004). Fortunately, professionals are assisted in this task by examination and refinement of their ordinary moral sense, as well as the availability of thoughtful models for the ethical decision-making process. Many components of ethical decision making involve teachable, learnable skills to supplement the professional's developing intuitive judgment.

Several models exist that explain and structure the process of ethical decision making. Some are highly theoretical; others are empirical or philosophical. Some are clinically sound approaches derived from practices that have been known to resolve significant ethical dilemmas. Others are based on anecdotal evidence alone—given credence in stories that have become ethical folklore. Because ethical decision making is so critical to the practice of the counseling profession, this chapter provides a thorough scholarly review of the literature on the topic. There are many ethical decision-making models in counseling, but only some are philosophically, empirically, or theoretically founded.

A REVIEW OF ETHICAL DECISION-MAKING MODELS

In 1984, Kitchener published a seminal work related to ethical decision making in counseling and counseling psychology. Kitchener argued that in the absence of clear ethical guidelines, relying on personal value judgments (as some other authors had proposed) was inadequate because "Independent of . . . external considerations, not all value judgments are equally valid" (p. 44). She argued that counseling professionals should "develop a deeper understanding of the basis for ethical decision making" (p. 44). She then presented a model that integrates Hare's (1981) work on levels of moral thinking (intuitive and critical evaluative), and Beauchamp and Childress's (1979) suggested ethical principles (autonomy, beneficence, nonmaleficence, and justice), and the ethical rule of fidelity. Subsequent to Kitchener's 1984 publication, there have been many publications on ethical issues in counseling.

Since Kitchener's (1984) article was published, Beauchamp and Childress's (1979) text, *Principles of Biomedical Ethics,* has been revised several times; it is a highly cited work in its fifth edition (2001) that has laid the groundwork for other authors. Although the Beauchamp and Childress (2001) text is a foundation text that provides guiding principles for ethical decision making, it fails to address decision-making models or processes with any depth. Instead, the authors provide a thorough analysis of ethical theory, including criteria of theory construction and an overview of widely recognized ethical theories (e.g., utilitarianism, Kantianism, and liberal individualism). In a work published in 1994, Beauchamp and Walters provided a "set of considerations" or "methods" for resolving moral disagreements as a way "of easing and perhaps settling controversies" (p. 4). The methods included: (a) "obtaining objective information," (b) "providing definitional clarity," (c) "adopting a code," (d) "using examples and counterexamples," and (e) "analyzing arguments" (pp. 4–7). Beauchamp and Walters did not present a review of decision-making processes, but they took a position and presented a basic model for judging ethical decisions. As with the Beauchamp and Childress (2001) and Beauchamp and Walters works, there was a lack of in-depth discussion of ethical decision-making processes in the literature. Rather, authors simply listed the actual act of making a decision as a step, or they did not list it as a step at all. In either case, they did not address an

Box 6–1   •   What Are They Thinking? . . . Inside the Minds of Ethics Committee Members

Counselors often wonder what ethics committee members are thinking when they adjudicate an ethics complaint and determine what the most fitting penalty might be for the counselor who has violated the code of ethics. Let's imagine that you are on the ethics committee of your state disciplinary committee and you have just found a licensee guilty of having initiated a sexual relationship with a counseling intern from the local counselor education program whom he was supervising in his practice. First answer the following two questions: What questions would you want answered to determine how severe the sanctions you would pose should be? What kind of information would you consider in favor of a less severe penalty? Finally, consider this question in connection with the ethical decision-making model of your choice: Which, if any, of these mitigating factors might have been highlighted or influenced by aspects of the decision-making model and how might this have changed the course of events experienced by the counselor now facing ethical disciplinary action?

explanatory framework for the decision process itself. Some models are exceptions (i.e., that explain the actual decision process), especially those involving theoretical and philosophical foundations. (See Box 6–1.)

Theoretically or Philosophically Based Models of Ethical Decision Making

Several authors made an attempt to ground ethical decision making on some theory or philosophy—notably, Hare's (1991) *The Philosophical Basis of Psychiatric Ethics,* which in its original 1981 form was used by Kitchener (1984) as a guiding work. Hare argued that absolute thinking (dealing with rights and duties) and utilitarian thinking (doing the greatest good for the greatest number; considering the interests of patients) were both involved in ethical decision making. He then invoked two levels of moral reasoning to address ethical dilemmas—the intuitive and critical levels:

> That we have a duty to serve the interests of the patient, and that we have a duty to respect his rights, can both perhaps be ascertained by consulting our intuitions at the bottom level. But if we ask which duty or which intuition ought to carry the day, we need some means other than intuition, some higher kind of thinking (let us call it 'critical moral thinking') to settle the question between them . . . (p. 35)

Hare believed that the "intuitive level, with its prima facie duties and principles, is the main locus of everyday moral decisions" (p. 35). However, he argued that it is "not sufficient" (p. 36), and must be superceded by critical (utilitarian) thinking when "no appeal to intuitions" can "settle the dispute" (p. 38). Although Hare's work was applied to psychiatry, it has direct relevance to counseling. Many have followed the lead

of Kitchener and incorporated his ideas in their works.

Rest (1984) produced another work that is cited often in the literature. He published extensively on the topic of developmental issues related to moral reasoning (Rest, Cooper, Coder, Maganz, & Anderson, 1974; Rest, Davison, & Robbins, 1978). His 1984 work, written specifically for the applied ethics of psychology, drew heavily on theories of moral development (Kohlberg, 1969, 1980) and research findings (Schwartz, 1977) to present a four-component model of "processes involved in the production of moral behavior" (p. 19). The components are: (a) "To interpret the situation in terms of how one's actions affect the welfare of others"; (b) "To formulate what a moral course of action would be; to identify the moral ideal in a specific situation"; (c) "To select among competing value outcomes of ideals, the one to act upon; deciding whether or not to try to fulfill one's moral ideal"; (d) "To execute and implement what one intends to do" (p. 20). The four components are not temporally linear, and they are not virtues or traits of individuals. Rather, "they are major units of analysis in tracing out how a particular course of action was produced in the context of a particular situation" (p. 20). Rest argued that "The four-component model provides a framework for ordering existing research on moral development, identifying needed research and deriving implications for moral education. There are many directives for the moral education of counselors that come from this research" (p. 27). For instance, he believed an assessment instrument could be developed for each component to assess counseling students entering training or the outcomes of training programs themselves. In a later work, Rest (1994) reviewed the works of Kohlberg and gave an up-to-date summary of research findings related to Kohlberg's theory. He also offered a revision of the four-component model. He defined the four components as "the major determinants of moral behavior" (p. 22), and he summarized the components as: (a) "Moral Sensitivity," (b) "Moral Judgment;" (c) "Moral Motivation," and (d) "Moral Character" (pp. 23–24). He stated:

> In summary, moral failure can occur because of deficiency in any component. All four components are determinants of moral action. In fact, there are complex interactions among the four components, and it is not supposed that the four represent a temporal order such that a person performs one, then two, then three, then four—rather the four components comprise a logical analysis of what it takes to behave morally. (p. 24)

Rest's model is clearly theoretically linked to cognitive theory through the works of Kohlberg, and he has one of the most empirically well-grounded approaches for analyzing moral behavior.

Gutheil, Bursztajn, Brodsky, and Alexander (1991), in a text on decision making in psychiatry and law, provided a chapter entitled, "Probability, Decision Analysis, and Conscious Gambling." The chapter reviewed the mechanistic and probabilistic paradigms in science and took a stand that decision making must account for some level of uncertainty (probability). They made an argument in favor of decision analysis as a formal decision-making tool:

> Decision analysis is a step-by-step procedure enabling us to break down a decision into its components, to lay them out in an orderly fashion, and to trace the sequence of events that might follow from choosing one course of action or another. This procedure offers several benefits. It can help us to make the best possible decision in a given situation. Moreover, it can help us to clarify our values, that is, the preferences among possible outcomes by which we judge what the best decision might be. Decision analysis can also be used to build logic and rationality into our intuitive decision making—to educate our intuition about probabilities and about the paths of contingency by which our actions, in combination with chance or "outside" events, lead to outcomes. (p. 41)

Decision analysis involves several approaches, including: (a) acknowledging the decision; (b) listing the pros and cons; (c) structuring the decision (including development of a decision tree to graph decisional paths and subsequent decisional branches); (d) estimating probabilities and values; and (e) calculating expected value. Estimating probabilities by means of a decision tree may involve calculating "the relative frequency with which the event in question occurs over a large number of trials in similar circumstances" (p. 46). The authors contrast decision analysis to decision making as gambling. Their model is clearly linked to nonmechanistic, probability theory in science (e.g., the uncertainty principle).

Two articles integrated Berne's (1972) transactional analysis therapeutic approach with ethical decision-making processes. For example, Chang (1994) identified a five-step model of making an ethical decision and emphasized three core values implicit in transactional analysis. These values affect the decision-making process through the assumptions that (a) people are born acceptable or "OK" (b) clients are capable of understanding their problems and are actively involved in healing; and (c) people can take charge of their lives. Chang addressed the interplay of transactional analysis values and other ethical standards or directives. McGrath (1994) believed that Kitchener's (1988) discussion of roles was relevant to transactional analysis (TA) because it was common to view TA supervisors also as therapists. Accordingly, role theory would have direct relevance to individual TA therapists making decisions.

Based on a theory of feminism, Hill, Glaser, and Harden (1995) proposed a model for ethical decision making. They valued the emotional responses of the counselor and the social context in which the therapeutic relationship takes place. In accord with feminist beliefs regarding power, the client is engaged as fully as possible in the decision-making process. At each step, the feminist model includes a rational-evaluative procedure with corresponding emotional and intuitive queries to assist the counselor. This model includes a review process in which the counselor considers the impact of personal values, the universality of the proposed solution, and the intuitive feel of the proposed solution. Because personal characteristics affect ethical decisions, the authors believed integration of this factor into their model improved the decision-making process.

Betan (1997) proposed a hermeneutic perspective of ethical decision making. He stated that "hermeneutics represents a shift in views of the nature of knowledge and the process of how we come to know" . . . because . . . "knowledge is situated in the context of human relationships in which the interpreter (as knowledge is interpretation) participates in narrating meaning" (p. 352). He advocated that hermeneutics adds to, rather than replaces, the principled approaches of Kitchener (1984) and Rest (1984): "The context of the therapeutic relationship and the clinician's psychological needs and dynamics are fundamental considerations in the interpretation and application of ethical principles" (p. 356). Further, he stated:

> A linear, logical-reductionistic approach to ethics, such as that offered by Kitchener (1984) and Rest (1984), can lead to a false dichotomy between the rational and the intuitive, and the universal and the subjective. The key in this hermeneutic approach is to acknowledge the dialectic of the universal and the subjective of human relations, in which each informs the other. That is, our sense of what is universal (in this regard, a standard or principle) is a product of shared subjective experiences, which in turn are embedded in a context of cultural interpretation. (p. 356)

The prima facie obligation of ethical principles asserted by Kitchener must instead, according to Betan, be applied in the context of personal and cultural values. That an ethical truth is constructed in the framework of one's conception of self, others, and the world holds implications for counselor training; counselors must work to gain awareness of ethical dilemmas, their own personal and moral values, and the interaction between ethical principles and context.

Cottone (2001, 2004) took an even more radical relational position than that of Betan (1997). Cottone (2001) proposed an ethical decision-making approach based on social constructivism. He argued that decision making is not a psychological process. Rather, decision making always involves interaction with other individuals. Building on the works of Gergen (1985) in social psychology and the works of Maturana (1978, 1988; Maturana & Varela, 1980) in the biology of cognition, Cottone (2001) argued that ethical decisions "are not compelled internally; rather, they are socially compelled" (p. 6). Further, he asserted that ethical decision making occurs in the interactive processes of negotiating, consensualizing, and arbitrating. An individual's psychological process is not involved. The social constructivism perspective of ethical decision making takes the decision out of the "head," so to speak, and places it in the interactive process between people. Cottone's model is presented later in this chapter.

Empirical Findings on Theoretically or Philosophically Based Models

Two empirical studies in the published literature had direct theoretical linkage. Cottone, Tarvydas, and House (1994) derived hypotheses about how counseling students in a graduate program make decisions based on social systems theory. According to social systems theory, they posited that "all thinking and decision making would be highly socially and relationally influenced, and both number and types of relationships would potentially influence how individuals act and think" (p. 57). They concluded:

> The results indicate that interpersonal relations influenced the ethical decision making of graduate counseling student participants when they were asked to reconsider a decision. In other words, relationships seem to influence ethical decision making linearly and cumulatively. Additionally, there seems to be an interaction between the number and type of consulted relationships in a way that eludes simple explanation. Although there was only a small interaction effect size, the results support a conclusion that ethical decision making in a reconsideration circumstance is a relatively complex issue, with at least the number and type of relationships interacting. (p. 63)

The results support a conclusion of social influence over ethical choice. The second study was a test of Janis and Mann's (1977) theory of decision making under stress by Hinkeldey and Spokane (1985). Hinkeldey and Spokane concluded that "consistent with Janis and Mann's theory, results showed that decision making was affected negatively by pressure but that participants relied little on legal guidelines in making responses to ethical conflict dilemmas" (p. 240).

Dinger (1997) presented dissertation findings on a study that compared Kitchener's (1984) Ethical Justification model to the A-B-C-D-E worksheet model of Sileo and Kopala (1993) and concluded that the Kitchener model better served participants in identifying the ethical issues presented in different scenarios.

Practice-Based Models of Ethical Decision Making

Some authors have proposed models based on pragmatic procedures derived largely from experience or intended primarily as practical guides for counselors. These models tend to be less theory specific or philosophically pure than those discussed previously. Table 6–1 summarizes practice-based, decision-making models and provides a step-by-step comparative layout. Although the steps may not align perfectly in the table, it does present a basic visual picture that allows for a comparative analysis. (For a more in-depth discussion of these approaches, see the article published by Cottone and Claus [2000].)

TABLE 6–1 Summary of Ethical Decision-Making Models

Corey, Corey, & Callanan (2003)	Forester-Miller & Davis (1996)	Hill, Glaser, & Harden (1995)	Keith-Spiegel & Koocher (1985)	Stadler (1986)	Steinman, Richardson, & McEnroe (1998)	Welfel (2002)
1. Identify the problem	1. Identify the problem	1. Recognize the problem	1. Describe the parameters	1. Identify competing principles	1. Identify the problem	1. Develop ethical sensitivity
2. Identify potential issues involved	2. Apply the ACA Code of Ethics	2. Define the problem	2. Define the potential issues	2. Secure additional information	2. Identify the relevant ethical standard	2. Define the dilemma & options
3. Review relevant ethical guidelines	3. Determine nature of dilemma	3. Consult if needed	3. Consult legal and ethical guidelines	3. Consult with colleagues	3. Determine possible ethical traps	3. Refer to professional standards
4. Know applicable laws and regulations			4. Evaluate the rights, responsibilities, & welfare of involved parties	4. Identify hoped-for outcomes	4. Frame preliminary response	4. Examine relevant laws and regulations
5. Obtain consultation	4. Generate potential courses of action	4. Develop solutions	5. Generate alternate decisions	5. Brainstorm actions to achieve outcomes	5. Consider consequences of that response	5. Search out ethics scholarship
6. Consider possible & probable courses of action	5. Consider potential consequences, determine course of action	5. Consult if needed	6. Enumerate the consequences of each decision	6. Evaluate effect of actions		6. Apply ethical principle to situation
7. Enumerate consequences of various decisions			7. Estimate probability for outcomes of each decision	7. Identify competing nonmoral values		7. Consult with supervisor & peers
8. Decide on best course of action	6. Evaluate selected course of action	6. Choose a solution	8. Make the decision	8. Choose a course of action	6. Prepare an ethical resolution	8. Deliberate and decide
		7. Review process		9. Test the course of action	7. Get feedback from peers & supervisor	
	7. Implement course of action	8. Implement plan and evaluate		10. Identify steps, take action, evaluate	8. Take action	9. Inform supervisor & take action
		9. Reflection				10. Reflect on the experience

TARVYDAS'S INTEGRATIVE DECISION-MAKING MODEL OF ETHICAL BEHAVIOR

The Tarvydas Integrative Decision-Making Model of Ethical Behavior incorporates the most prominent principle and virtue aspects of several decision-making approaches and introduces some contextual considerations into the process. Generally, ethical decision-making models can be thought of as having the characteristics of either principle or virtue ethics (Corey, Corey, & Callanan, 2003). Principle ethics focuses on the objective, rational, and cognitive aspects of the process. Practitioners who adhere to this perspective tend to view the application of universal, impartial ethical principles, rules, codes, and law as the core elements of ethics. Virtue ethics considers the characteristics of the counselors themselves as the critical element for responsible practice. Thus, proponents of virtue ethics approaches focus more on how counselors reflect on and clarify their moral and value positions. Additionally, they examine other personal issues that might influence their ethical practice, such as unresolved emotional needs that might negatively affect their work with clients. Many argue that it is preferable that ethical decision making include both aspects (Corey, Corey, & Callanan, 2003; Meara, Schmidt, & Day, 1996). Among other positive contributions of such a synergistic approach, Meara, Schmidt, and Day (1996) and Vasquez (1996) speculated that the addition of virtue ethical perspectives would improve ethical conduct in multicultural and diverse interactions and settings.

The Tarvydas Integrative Model (Table 6–2) emphasizes the constant process of interaction between the principle and virtue elements and places a reflective attitude at the heart of the process. The model also focuses on the actual production of ethical behavior within a specified context, rather than prematurely terminating analysis by merely selecting the best ethical course of action without following through on it.

Conceptual Origins

The Tarvydas Integrative Model builds on several well-known decision-making models used widely by professionals in the mental health and counseling communities. The works of Rest (1984) and Kitchener (1984) are foundational. Rest (1984) provided the Tarvydas Integrative Model, with its core understanding of ethical decision making, as a psychological process that involves distinct cognitive-affective elements interacting in each component. Cognitions and emotions are seen as unavoidably intertwined at each component of the decision-making process and in the execution of ethical behavior. Rest (1984) thought about ethical decision making as more than a direct expression of moral or value traits or a stage in a moral developmental process. He emphasized considering the completion of ethical behavior as the key point, rather than merely making a cognitive decision or having good intentions to do an ethical act. Therefore, Rest's (1984) ethical decision-making components and many of his considerations are the foundation of the Tarvydas Integrative Model.

Kitchener (1984) provided other core elements to the Tarvydas Integrative Model. She made a use of Hare's (1981) distinction between the **intuitive** and **critical-evaluative levels** of ethical decision making, thus providing a forum to incorporate the richness and influence of the everyday personal and professional moral wisdom into the individual professional's process of ethical decision making. This personal and professional wisdom informs the first level of the process—the intuitive level, where both nonconscious and conscious levels of awareness lead to decisions that call into play the individual's existing morals, beliefs, and experiences. These morals, beliefs, and experiences that constitute our ordinary moral sense also include professional learning and experiences. Kitchener noted that the intuitive level of process often is the professional's main decision-making tool when a situation is not perceived as novel, unusual, or requiring an unusual level of care. At this intuitive level, practitioners incorporate and rely on experiences and wisdom gained through the many problems they have encountered and solved in their years of practice. This accumulated intuitive process may make their ethical decision-making processes more efficient and sophisticated over time if they are thoughtful, reflective decision makers. The intuitive level of analysis always constitutes the first platform of decision making, even when the situation requires the more detailed level of analysis involved in the critical-evaluative level of consideration. Thus, a person's ordinary moral sense is relevant to one's ethical decision-making process, reinforcing the concerns raised by proponents of the virtue ethics perspective.

If the ethical issue is not resolved at the intuitive level, the counselor progresses to Kitchener's (1984) critical-evaluative level of ethical analysis. This level involves three hierarchical stages of examination to resolve the dilemma. At the first stage, the counselor

TABLE 6–2 The Tarvydas Integrative Decision-Making Model of Ethical Behavior

Themes or Attitudes in the Integrative Model

Maintain an attitude of **reflection.**

Address **balance** between issues and parties to the ethical dilemma.

Pay close attention to the **context(s)** of the situation.

Utilize a process of **collaboration** with all rightful parties to the situation.

Stage I. Interpreting the Situation Through Awareness and Fact Finding

Component 1	Enhance **sensitivity** and **awareness.**
Component 2	Determine the major **stakeholders** and their ethical claims in the situation.
Component 3	Engage in the **fact-finding** process.

Stage II. Formulating an Ethical Decision

Component 1	**Review** the problem or dilemma.
Component 2	Determine what **ethical codes, laws, ethical principles,** and **institutional policies and procedures** exist that apply to the dilemma.
Component 3	Generate possible and probable **courses of action.**
Component 4	Consider potential positive and negative **consequences** for each course of action.
Component 5	**Consult** with supervisors and other knowledgeable professionals.
Component 6	Select the best **ethical course of action.**

Stage III. Selecting an Action by Weighing Competing Nonmoral Values, Personal Blind Spots, or Prejudices

Component l	Engage in reflective recognition and analysis of **competing nonmoral values, personal blind spots,** or **prejudices.**
Component 2	Consider **contextual influences** on values selection at the collegial, team, institutional, and societal levels.
Component 3	Select the **preferred course of action.**

Stage IV. Planning and Executing the Selected Course of Action

Component 1	Figure out a reasonable **sequence of specific actions** to be taken.
Component 2	Anticipate and work out personal and contextual **barriers** to effective execution of the plan of action and effective countermeasures for them.
Component 3	**Carry out, document,** and **evaluate** the course of action as planned.

determines if any laws or ethical rules exist that would provide a solution for the dilemma. If they do not exist, or if they exist but provide conflicting dictates, the counselor progresses to the second stage by considering how the core ethical principles apply to the situation. The authoritative work of Beauchamp and Childress (1979) identified autonomy, beneficence, nonmaleficence, and justice as the core ethical principles that govern ethical behavior. Kitchener (1984) subsequently added fidelity to these core principles for helping professionals, resulting in five core ethical principles to be considered in ethical decision making.

If counselors are still uncertain as to the appropriate ethical course of action, they proceed to the third stage—assessing the positions suggested by ethical theory. Patterson (1992) recommended that counselors should be concerned with normative ethical theory and may benefit from considering whether they prefer their action be based on a general or a universal law. Kitchener (1984) suggested applying the "good reasons" approach, in which counselors attempt to make a decision based on what they would wish for themselves or someone dear to them. Another standard suggested by Kitchener is to take the action that will result in the least amount of harm.

The final conceptual influence on the Tarvydas Integrative Model is the *four-level contextual model* of ethical practice introduced by Tarvydas and Cottone (1991). This approach broadens consideration of the contextual forces acting on ethical practice beyond a singular focus on only the individual practitioner in relationship to the individual client. The four levels are hierarchical, moving to increasingly broader levels of social contexts within which ethical practice is influenced. The four levels are (1) the clinical counseling level, (2) the clinical interdisciplinary team level, (3) the institutional/agency level, and (4) the societal resource/public policy level. The relationships among the levels are seen as interactive. Peak ethical efficiency and lowest levels of ethical stress are reached when each level holds compatible values and standards or endorses a mutually acceptable mechanism for ethical dilemma resolution. The first (or micro) level in the hierarchy is the traditionally central clinical counseling core, in which the counselor–client relationship is the focus. The second level is the clinical interdisciplinary team interaction. At this point, practitioner-to-practitioner dynamics are considered. Team members may be physically dispersed, but functionally remain a team in terms of collaboration or coordinated work with respect to the client's care. Team communications often occur by telephone or electronic means, with only infrequent meetings or staffings. Nonetheless, the team is an important clinical and ethical force in the client's life. Team relationships and leadership, collaboration skills, and the interplay of the differing ethical codes and traditions are important to the process. At the third level, the institutional or agency context and its constraints enter into the process. Dictates of agency policy, practitioner-supervisor style and practices, and staffing patterns are factors that might have an influence. Corporate or administrative operations such as institutional goals, marketing strategies, and corporate oversight processes may also play a role. At the fourth (or macro) level, the effects of overall societal resources and public policy are considered. Social concern for scarce health care resources, trends in managed care, and the privatization of mental health care are examples of broad themes and related policies that may affect ethical practices at the practitioner level. Societal values related to such areas as independence and self-sufficiency, work and productivity; physical appearance, what constitutes an unacceptable lifestyle, and other types of behavior do influence the work of counselors extensively (Gatens-Robinson & Rubin, 1995). Societal values also are expressed in more concrete ways that may affect counselor practices through such influences as the climate created by local public opinion, local governance boards such as school boards, and various legislative and regulatory codes.

Themes and Attitudes

In addition to the specific elements or steps of the Tarvydas Integrative Model, four underlying themes or attitudes are necessary for the professional counselor. These attitudes involve mindfully attending to the tasks of (a) maintaining a *stance of reflection* concerning one's own conscious awareness of personal issues, values, and decision-making skills, as well as extending effort to understand those of all others concerned with the situation and their relationship to the decision maker; (b) addressing the *balance* among various issues, people, and perspectives within the process; (c) maintaining an appropriate level of *attention to the context* of the situation in question, allowing awareness of the counselor–client, treatment team, organizational, and societal implications of the ethical elements; and (d) seeking to use a process of *collaboration* with all rightful parties to the decision, but most especially the client.

By adopting these background attitudes of reflection, balance, context, and collaboration, counselors engage in a more thorough process that will help preserve the integrity and dignity of all parties involved. This will be the case even when outcomes are not considered equally positive for all participants in the process, as is often true in a serious dilemma when such attitudes can be particularly meaningful. Indeed, Betan and Stanton (1999) studied students' responses to ethical dilemmas, analyzing how emotions and concerns influence willingness to implement ethical knowledge. They concluded that "subjectivity and emotional involvement are essential tools for determining ethical action, but they must be integrated with rational analysis" (Betan & Stanton, p. 295).

Reflection is the overriding attitude of importance throughout the enactment of the specific elements of stages and components of the Tarvydas Integrative Model. Many complex decision-making processes easily become overwhelming, either in their innate complexity or in the real-life speed or intensity of events. In the current approach, the counselor is urged to always "stop and think!" at each point in the process. The order of operations is not critical or absolute. The order of steps is not as important as being reflective and invested in a calm, dignified, respectful, and thorough analysis of the situation. It is not until we recognize that we are involved in a highly meaningful process and appreciate its critical aspects that we can mobilize all the resources needed to assist the process and people within it. An attitude of mindful reflection will serve the counselor well at all stages of this process.

CASE SCENARIO 6–1

Themes and Attitudes

Jimmy W. is in fifth grade and has been sent to see you, his school counselor, by Mrs. James, his teacher. This has been a difficult year for you professionally and personally. You have felt overwhelmed by an increasing number of students assigned to you. You also have had difficulty concentrating since your rather acrimonious divorce, which was finalized during the summer. Jimmy has continued to do good work in class since his parents' divorce 8 months ago. However, Mrs. James has noticed that Jimmy tears up his worksheets and art projects as soon as they are graded and is not showing his usual enthusiasm for schoolwork. She has talked to him about the situation, but Jimmy denies that anything is wrong. Jimmy finally confides to you that his mother will no longer allow him to send letters and his completed school work to his father who lives in another state. He misses his father and his correspondence with him; he also thinks his work is meaningless and not important enough to be seen by his dad. He asks you if you will send his letters and school work to his father occasionally. Jimmy finally gives you permission to discuss his concerns with his mother. Mother angrily forbids you to communicate with Jimmy's father in any way. She informs you that she is the sole custodial parent and guardian and that Mr. W. moved away rather than "be bothered with the responsibility of Jimmy." She reluctantly allows you to continue counseling Jimmy about his "behavior problems" in school, but tells you not to raise his hopes about seeing or communicating with his father. Although you will continue to provide supportive counseling to Jimmy, you consider the matter of contact with Mr. W. closed. By the end of the school year, you have not heard from Mr. or Mrs. W. and Jimmy's problems have not worsened. Were you correct?

PROBABLY NOT. When you stop and reflect on this situation outside of the intense moments of the meeting with Jimmy and his mom, you realize that two factors probably clouded your thinking. The first factor was your own painful divorce and custody problems. The second factor involved recent situations in which your school principal criticized you before the school staff for refusing to reveal to him confidential information in a controversial case about a student's family financial matters. Your anger at your former spouse and your fear of the principal have blinded you to other questions you must explore. You may discover that either the mother has incorrectly reported the custody arrangements, or the father does have some legal right to the communication his son desires. Even if Mr. W. does not have a legal right to correspondence from his son, Jimmy's rights and desires must be considered primary, and his father may have some moral claim to continue contact with his son apart from the custody decree specifics. Although counseling must occur with parental consent, it might be possible to counsel Jimmy and his mom to preserve some

acceptable type and level of contact with Jimmy's father. A greater ability to communicate might facilitate Jimmy's adjustment and future cooperative communication regarding other aspects of Jimmy's welfare. These deeper considerations would include themes of balancing the moral claims of all parties regardless of the legal aspects of the situation. It also introduces the attitude of collaboration to the decisions involving Jimmy's well-being. None of these issues would have been available for your consideration unless you had first systematically practiced the attitude of reflection about a decision you initially thought was obvious.

Elements

The specific elements that constitute the operations within the Tarvydas Integrative Model have four main stages with several components and steps within each stage. As previously stated, the concepts summarized in the following sections are primarily from Rest (1984), Kitchener (1984), and Tarvydas and Cottone (1991).

Stage I: Interpreting the Situation Through Awareness and Fact Finding.

At this stage, the primary task of counselors is to be sensitive and aware of the needs and welfare of the people around them and the ethical implications of these situations. This level of awareness allows counselors to imagine and to investigate the effects of the situation on the parties involved and the possible effects of various actions and conditions. This research and awareness must also include emotional as well as cognitive and fact-based considerations. Three components constitute the counselors' operations in this stage.

Component 1 involves enhancing one's sensitivity and awareness. The counselor attempts to consider the perspective of each major party experiencing the dilemma—especially the client. As part of this process, the counselor seeks to apply the skills of empathic understanding or role taking. Counselors sensitize themselves to the thoughts, feelings, expectations, motivations, concerns, and reactions of these others. In *Component 2*, the counselor takes an inventory of the people who are major stakeholders in the outcome of the situation. It is important to reflect on any parties who will be affected and play a major role in the client's life, as well as considering what their exact relationship is ethically and legally to the person at the center of the issue—the client. In Case Scenario 6–1 Jimmy may be best served by some contact with his father, assuming that the father is interested and not abusive. Imagine dropping a rock into a pond: The point of impact is where the central figure, the client, is situated. However, the client is surrounded by people at varying levels of closeness, such as parents, foster parents, intimate partners, spouse, children, employer, friends, and neighbors. They radiate out from the client in decreasing levels of intimacy and responsibility to the client.

Figure 6–1 depicts how the spheres of influence of these stakeholders in the client's life, as well as the stakeholders at each of the four levels in the professional world of the counselor, may intersect. This figure visually reflects the intersection and interaction between the client's and professional's universes. This way of thinking about the relationships between the different stakeholders in the situation allows for a fuller appreciation of the specific people and contexts of the counselor's practice and the client's situation. A number of people and levels of the service hierarchy will (or should) play a part in the ethics decision. These social forces will create both positive and negative influences in the ethical situation and should be taken into account in the ethical analysis. The ethical claims of these parties on the counselor's level of duty are not uniform. Almost all codes of ethics in counseling make

it clear that the client is the person to whom the first duty is owed, but there are others to whom the counselor has lesser, but important, levels of duty. It is always important to determine whether any legal surrogate decision makers for the client exist, such as a guardian or person with power of attorney, so that they may be brought into the central "circle of duty" early in the process. In Case Scenario 6–1, the mother must be counseled. The noncustodial parent has many rights to contact his son and even decision-making authority in some jurisdictions. It is useful to be sensitive and proactive in working through situations in which the legal relationships involved do not coincide with the social and emotional bonds between the client and other people involved in the dilemma.

In the final element in Stage I, *Component 3*, the counselor undertakes an extensive fact-finding investigation of a scope appropriate to the situation. The nature of the fact-finding process should be carefully considered. It is not intended to be a formal investigative or quasi-legal process. The counselor should carefully review, understand the information at hand, and seek out new information. Only information that is appropriately available to a counselor should be involved. The scope and depth of information that would be rightfully available to the counselor is surprisingly great, but it is often underutilized. For example, information might be gained from such sources as further discussion with the client, contacts with family (with appropriate permission of the client), case records, expert consultation and reports, legal resources, or agency policy and procedures. In Case Scenario 6–1, the exact legal nature of the father–son relationship and the mother–father relationship should be explored.

Stage II: Formulating an Ethical Decision. Although this aspect of the process is most widely known by professionals, many may erroneously think it is the end of the process. The central task in this stage is to identify which of the possible ethical courses of action appears to come closest to the moral ideal in the situation under consideration (Rest, 1984). Many decision-making models in other areas of counseling can be applied as a template at this stage, but the following components are drawn from the work of Van Hoose and Kottler (1985).

Component 1 suggests that the counselor review the problem or dilemma to be sure that it is clearly understood in light of any new information obtained in Stage I. In *Component 2*, the counselor researches the standards of law and practice applicable to the situation.

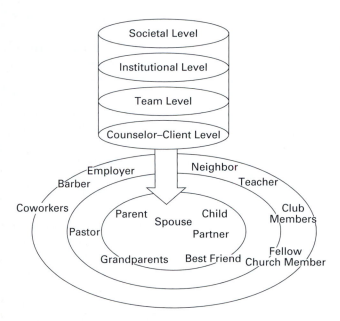

FIGURE 6–1. The intersection of the Client's Personal World with the Counselor's Professional Hierarchical Contexts

This component includes Kitchener's (1984) attention to ethical codes, laws, and ethical principles; and Tarvydas and Cottone's (1991) concern for the team and organizational context in the examination of institutional policies and procedures to make mention of other useful areas for consideration. If you were the counselor in Case Scenario 6–1, at this point you would need to ensure that you were familiar with the requirements of the Family Educational Rights and Privacy Act of 1974 (see Chapter 13). You need to be sure about the protection afforded to your counseling notes and which records about Jimmy would be released to Jimmy's parents upon their request. The counselor would also analyze which of the five core ethical principles (autonomy, beneficence, nonmaleficence, justice, and fidelity) are either supported or compromised by the types of actions that are being contemplated. This operation is formally known as principle analysis and is one of the most challenging, yet critical, aspects of the ethical analysis of a dilemma. The core, or main principle, analysis concerns the ethical obligations owed to the client rather than those owed to other parties in the situation. *Component 3* initiates the process of formally envisioning and generating possible and probable courses of action. As with all decision-making processes, it is important not to end this exploratory process by prematurely censoring the possibilities, or giving in to a sense of being too overwhelmed or too limited in options. Generally, reducing the possibilities to two opposing courses of action best facilitates further processing of the dilemma. Examples of such dual options might be to violate or not violate confidentiality; and to join the client outside of the office at a social function such as a graduation or not. *Component 4* is the logical outgrowth of considering these courses of action—positive and negative consequences are identified and assessed in light of the risks, as well as the material and personal resources available. In *Component 5*, the counselor is reminded to consult with supervisors and trusted, knowledgeable colleagues for guidance, if this has not been done before this point. Professional standards of practice emphasize the importance of appropriate collegial consultation to resolve difficult clinical and ethical dilemmas. Research has also demonstrated that such consultations can have a significant influence on those seeking such consultation (Cottone, Tarvydas, & House, 1994). At this time, it is valuable to review the reasoning employed so far in working through the ethical dilemma, and the solutions and consequences envisioned, to be sure that all potentially useful and appropriate considerations have been taken into account. Finally, the best ethical course of action is determined and articulated in *Component 6*. The ethical decision at this stage of the model should be contrasted with the actual decision made by the counselor—that is the product of Stage III.

Stage III: Selecting an Action by Weighing Competing Nonmoral Values, Personal Blind Spots, and Prejudices.

Many people would think the ethical decision-making process is concluded at the end of Stage II. This impression is limited by the realization that many additional forces may affect the counselor. As a result, the counselor may not actually execute the selected ethical course of action. *Component I* of Stage III interjects a period of reflection and active processing of what the counselor intends to do in view of competing nonmoral values (Rest, 1984). At this point, the counselor considers any personal factors that might intervene to pull him away from choosing the ethical action or cause that action to be modified substantially. Nonmoral values involve anything that the counselor may prize or desire that is not, in and of itself, a moral value (i.e., virtue, justice, or autonomy). Nonmoral values may include such things as valuing social harmony, spending time with friends or working on one's hobby, being wealthy or famous, or having political power; all potentially valuable and worthy, but not linked to moral qualities. In this component, counselors are also called upon to examine themselves to determine if they have some personal blind spots or prejudices that might affect their judgment or resolve to do the ethical thing, such as a fear of HIV infection or the conviction that men who are homosexual are also likely to molest children. These blind spots are personal reactions or beliefs of which counselors are not fully aware, but that may have a very powerful effect on their reactions and choices in ethical situations. This portion of the model provides an excellent opportunity for counselors to carefully evaluate whether they have adequately incorporated multicultural and diversity considerations and competencies in their work on this ethical dilemma. For example, they need to be sure that they are not operating from a culturally encapsulated or privileged frame of reference. In Case Scenario 6–1, the counselor might have realized upon reflection that her need to avoid controversy with the principal, or her identification with Jimmy's mother's anger with her ex-husband (a non-custodial parent), and her wish to be seen as supportive of the rights of a single mother may be competing with her knowledge of what is legally or ethically right.

It is important that counselors allow themselves to become aware of the strength and attractiveness of other values they hold that may influence whether they will discharge their ethical obligations. If they are self-aware, they may more effectively and honestly compensate for their conflicted impulses at this point. They may have a visceral distaste for homosexuals, an overriding need to protect minor children, or a sexual or emotional attraction to a particular client. Counselors may have strong needs for acceptance by peers or supervisors, prestige, influence, to avoid controversy, or to be financially successful. These value orientations may come into conflict with the course of action necessary to proceed ethically and must be reconciled with the ethical requirements if the client is to be served ethically. On the other hand, counselors may place a high value on being moral, ethical, and accepted as respected professionals with high ethical standards. They may value the esteem of colleagues who place a high value on ethical professional behavior. Those forces should enhance the tendency to select ethical behavioral options. (The influence of the ethical climate on the ethical behavior of the counselor is more fully explored in Chapter 7.) The importance of selecting and maintaining ethically sensitized and positive professional and personal cultures is critical to full professional functioning, as the next component suggests.

In *Component 2* of Stage III, counselors systematically inventory the contextual influences on their choices at the collegial, team, institutional, and societal levels. Although this is not a simple process of weighing influences, it should serve as an inventory of influences that may be either dysfunctional or constructive for selecting the ethical course over other types of values present in these other interactions. Counselors may also use this type of information to think strategically about the influences they will need to overcome to provide ethical service in the situation. Beyond the immediate situation, it is important to recognize that counselors should control their exposure to contexts that consistently reinforce values that run counter to the dictates of good ethical practices. In Case Scenario 6–1, Jimmy's counselor might be influenced in one direction if she spends most of her personal and professional time with staff who are concerned primarily with getting ahead in the school hierarchy and being seen favorably by the administration, in contrast with having a few strong relationships with colleagues who take great pride in their professional identities and reputations. This problem might result in terminating or curtailing certain relationships, changing employment, or selecting another aspect of counseling service to provide.

Component 3 is the final aspect of Stage III. At this time, the counselor selects the preferred course of action or the behavior that he or she plans to undertake. This decision may be a reaffirmation of the intention to take the ethical course of action as determined at the conclusion of Stage II. However, it may be some other course of action that may even be unethical or a modified version of the ethical course of action selected in Stage II. Whatever the choice, the counselor selects it after this more extensive reflection on personal competing values and blind spots, as well as the contextual influences in the situation in question.

Stage IV: Planning and Executing the Selected Course of Action. Rest (1984) described the essential tasks of this stage as planning to implement and execute what one plans to do. This operation includes *Component 1*, in which the counselor determines a reasonable sequence of specific actions to be taken. In *Component 2*, the task is to anticipate and work out all personal and contextual barriers to effectively executing the plan. It is useful to prepare countermeasures for barriers that may arise. In Case Scenario 6–1, if Jimmy's father indeed has a legal and ethical right, as well as a personal interest in Jimmy, what barriers might arise if Jimmy is given the opportunity to contact him? It is here that the earlier attention to other stakeholders and their concerns may suggest problems or allies to the process. Additionally, earlier consideration of the contextual influences in Stage III assist the counselor in this type of strategic planning. *Component 3* is the final step of this model. It provides for the execution, documentation, and evaluation of the course of action as planned. Rest (1984) noted that the actual behavioral execution of ethics is often not a simple task, frequently drawing heavily on the personal, emotional qualities and professional and interpersonal skills of the counselor. He mentions such qualities as firmness of resolve, ego strength, and social assertiveness. Countless skills such as persistence, tact, time management, assertiveness, team collaboration, and conflict resolution could be added to this list. Considerations are limited only by the characteristics and requirements of the counselor and the specific situation involved. To protect the interests of both counselor and client, document the entire plan and the rationale behind it thoroughly, and take ethical decision-making steps in response to the ethical dilemma as the process unfolds. The information gained in this documentation process will prove critical in evaluating the effectiveness of the entire ethical decision-making process.

Multiculturalism and the Tarvydas Integrative Model

The Tarvydas Integrative Model approach respects the importance of setting and environmental factors that are crucial in counseling. It encourages the use of a universalist philosophical approach. *Universalism* attends to and honors the role of cultural and diversity differences while applying the more universal ethical principles that are common in most cultures (Frame & Williams, 2005; Pedersen, 1995; Ponterotto & Casas, 1991). Through the Tarvydas Integrative Model's requirement that the contexts of the parties, the relationships, and individual perspectives of the stakeholders in the dilemma be considered, it provides a robust process that will encourage full consideration of the unique cultural understandings and values that the parties to the dilemma bring to it. Indeed, in reviewing the various approaches to ethical decision making, Garcia, Cartwright, Winston, and Borzuchowska (2003) observed that this model uses virtue ethics and behav-

ioral strategies that are consistent with a multicultural approach to counseling and ethical decision making. They proposed an Integrative Transcultural Ethical Decision-Making Model that is based primarily on the Tarvydas Integrative Model.

Practicing the Tarvydas Integrative Model

Like the basic counseling microskills, the skills of ethical decision making do not come automatically, or even easily, after merely reading concepts in a book (See Box 6–2.). A gradual progression in gaining practical skills and sensitive, accurate ethical knowledge is achieved by solving mock ethical dilemmas; working to address actual ethical dilemmas under the su-

---

Box 6–2 • Why Bother? . . . A Learner's Perspective

Discussions during the ethics course in my master's program quite often got heated: sometimes because none of the arguing parties were clear about their adherence to principle or virtue ethics, occasionally because we didn't really take the time to study definitions and explanations of principles we were talking about. Sometimes it was because we forgot about the "blind spots" and prejudices that all of us hold to a certain extent. But most of the time the issue occurred because we simply did not think that we would have ethical issues or dilemmas that need more than a 1-minute processing time before reaching an ethical decision once we were out in the field. Based on this presumption, we could not appreciate Tarvydas's nitty-gritty, step-by-step, take-it-slow-and-reflect. Integrative Decision-Making Model or that of any other model. In fact, the less we had to integrate different ideas, the happier we were, because the class took less out of us and ended sooner.

The everyday reality of counseling work was a rude awakening for all of us from the 1-minute ethical decision-making camp. When client's needs, supervisor's demands, insurance requirements, local interpersonal storms, and personal virtue ethics collide, it takes a lot longer than a 1-minute process to figure out where you stand and especially how to help, or at least not hurt, your client. The real work I was so eager to face ended up presenting me with ethical issues and dilemmas not just day to day but sometimes almost hour by hour. Dilemmas arose not just in my counselor–client therapeutic work, but seemingly in every interaction that involved at least two human beings.

However many ethical dilemmas I had to face, they all had one thing in common: They were not simple, and it took a whole lot more than 1 minute to reach a "course

of action." Even though I boxed up all my old manuals and placed them in the garage in the hope that I would never read them again, it felt very good to have an ethical decision-making model to dust off and go back to. I was so grateful to Dr. Tarvydas for her model's having such a strong emphasis on the constant interaction between virtue and principle ethics as well as reflective attitude.

In school, my peers used to tease me about being an ethics freak, as I was able to find an ethical issue in just about every human interaction. At the time it was a joke, but the joke stayed with me since then, causing indefinite hours of struggle, reflection, and short-lived moments of satisfaction.

This same passion for and obsession with ethics got me recruited onto a statewide ethics committee, reviewing ethics complaints of numerous counselors, supervisors, and clients. At first the number of ethics complaints I had to process was overwhelming. But the more cases I investigated, the deeper the weight of ethical decision making sunk in, as well as my personal responsibility in the process. At times it came down to my decision, reviewed by the ethics committee, if someone lost or kept a job or a licensure. Especially for paraprofessionals, that licensure meant the option between counseling and a lesser type of employment . . . or unemployment.

However unbelievable it sounds to you who are struggling through the seemingly too long and too detailed Tarvydas Integrative Model, at least trust the experience of one who has been in your shoes. The decision-making model is going to save you one day from long sleepless nights of struggles with ethical dilemmas . . . much longer nights than what you spend now writing midterm papers.

pervision of an ethically knowledgeable instructor, clinical supervisor, master counselor, or mentor; and incorporating ethical analysis into the clinical training process.

Case Scenario 6–2 presents a complex ethical case with a full ethical analysis using the Tarvydas Integrative Model and all of its stages and components. The analysis does not represent "the one and only" correct answer to the dilemma presented. Information discovered or concerns raised by other reasonable people can lead to important shifts in the elements of a case. Reasonable professionals can judge and weigh the same ideas or risks differently; there may be several valid conclusions to the same case. This process is not so much about getting the "hidden, correct answer" but rather about going through the process of decision making thoroughly and carefully while exercising due care and good, reasonable professional judgment throughout. By doing so, counselors are more likely to arrive at an explicable judgment that minimizes risk to the client, the counselor, and others. Counselors also benefit from increased confidence and peace of mind in knowing they did their best and used a thorough, thoughtful approach to solving a dilemma that may not have a satisfying solution for the parties involved.

CASE SCENARIO 6–2

ILLUSTRATION OF THE TARVYDAS INTEGRATIVE MODEL FOR ETHICAL BEHAVIOR

Narrative of Case Example

John, a 43-year-old man, is meeting with a counselor at the Department of Correctional Services (DCS). He has recently been released from prison on parole and is meeting with a counselor voluntarily to deal with some issues of depression. He is currently on medication for depression and has attempted suicide in the past. He was married to a woman for 9 years and they had two children together, now ages 7 and 5. She also had two children from a previous relationship, now ages 12 and 8, whom John also considers to be his children. He and his wife are recently divorced. At first she would not allow the children to visit their dad, but just recently John says they have been talking again, and his ex-wife has started to trust him again and lets the children visit whenever they want to. Just recently, his youngest girl confided in him that their mom and her new friends are still using drugs and also selling them from the house. She had found a syringe at the home that her mom thought was hidden. John is very adamant that he does not want to contact Department of Human Services (DHS) or any other similar agency about this. He had contacted DHS for a similar situation a few years ago and had a bad experience. DHS had "done nothing," and his ex-wife

had found out that he had made the report. She did not let him see the kids for a long time after the incident. He feels that at this point he can do the most good by keeping a close relationship with his children and a civil relationship with his ex-wife. He is now living a clean and drug-free life and feels that he is his ex-wife's best hope to straighten out. He says if a report is made, the only thing he is sure of is that his ex-wife will not let him see the children, and he does not know if he could live without being part of his children's lives. In this case, the client, John, has his reasons for not wanting to contact DHS, and client autonomy needs to be respected. The client also raises the issue that perhaps contacting the authorities really is not in the best interest of the children. John also made some statements regarding not being able to live without being a part of his children's lives, which need to be taken seriously given his suicidal history and current state of depression. On the other hand, the young children are involved in a dangerous situation. There is no report of physical or sexual abuse occurring, yet drug use in the home and young children coming across needles is definitely dangerous and could be considered abuse. At this point the counselor feels there may be a potential dilemma that needs to be explored further.

Stage I: Interpreting the Situation Through Awareness and Fact Finding

The counselor's primary task in Stage 1 is to be sensitive and aware of the needs and welfare of the people involved and the ethical implications of these situations. This level of awareness allows counselors to imagine and to investigate the effects of the situation on the parties involved and the possible effects of various actions and conditions. This research and awareness must also include emotional as well as cognitive and fact-based considerations.

Component 1: Sensitivity and Awareness At this point the counselor talks to the client and gets his impression of who will be affected by this situation and how they will be affected. The client clearly cares about his children and firmly believes that they will have their best chance if he continues to be a part of their lives. John has no guarantee what would happen if he did contact DHS, and he does not want to take that risk. Given what happened the last time he called, he is very distrustful of the system and his ex-wife's reaction. John also expressed some concerns for his ex-wife, and even though they parted on unfriendly terms, he still seems to care about her and wants what is best for her. He says that they are just starting to talk again, and he feels that he may be the only one who truly understands what she is going through with the drugs. John feels he might be able to help his ex-wife kick the habit. Although he admits that he worries about the environment his children are living in, John feels that this is the best chance they have.

The counselor also notes that there are four children of varying ages in the house. Whereas an 18-year-old might understand how dangerous finding a needle in the house really is, a 5-year-old most likely would not. Aside from needles being in the house, there is also the potential for danger from the people who are around the children. If their mother is dealing drugs from the home, it is likely that many of those she sells to are in the house also and around the children.

John says he understands all of this, but still feels that he is making progress with his ex-wife and that he is the best chance for his children. He acknowledges that he is taking on a lot of responsibility, but he says that he would do anything for his children and truly believes that he is doing the best for them in the long run.

Component 2: Major Stakeholders and Their Ethical Claims The counselor identifies the parties who will be affected and what their exact relationship is ethically and legally to the person at the center of the issue. There are often others to whom the counselor has lesser, but important, levels of duty, such as parents, intimate partners, spouse, children, employer, friends, neighbors, guardian, or persons with power of attorney. The following list shows all important parties with an ethical or legal claim in this situation.

Party	Ethical Claim
1. Client	He does not want to contact any authorities.
2. Children	They may be in danger and may not know all of their options or how they could get help.
3. DCS	The agency is responsible for its counselors and could be held liable for mistakes made by its employees.
4. Counselor	He may be held liable for any harm that befalls the children or the client.
5. Ex-wife	She could face an abuse investigation and the subsequent consequences.
6. Grandparents	They would most likely get custody of the children if DHS did find abuse.

Component 3: Fact-Finding Process The counselor undertakes an extensive fact-finding investigation of a scope appropriate to the situation by reviewing and understanding current information and seeking out new information. This investigation involves gathering information appropriately available to the counselor either through professional records and channels (with appropriately obtained releases of information) or through public domain information. Sources might include further discussion with the client, contacts with family (with the client's permission), current and old client records in one's own or another agency, expert consultation and reports, legal resources, or agency policy and procedures. List all facts or factual questions the counselor should reasonably be able to research or answer.

A call was made anonymously to DHS to find out if the situation in general fell under the guidelines for mandatory reporters, which it did not. DHS stated that it did not fall under mandatory guidelines because it was third-party information.

The counselor talked to the supervisor and found out that DCS has an unwritten rule, or policy, to convince the client to call authorities and report the situation himself.

The client stated that if DHS was contacted, an investigation was conducted, and action was taken to remove the children from their mother, the maternal grandparents would probably receive custody. The client stated that he has a good relationship with his ex-wife's parents. He thought that they would allow him to see the children if they did get custody.

The counselor was informed by a supervisor that DHS may not have done anything the last time John reported because there may have been some type of drug investigation going on. If there is a current investigation into drug trafficking or selling, DHS can postpone going into the house for a child abuse charge because the house is under supervision as part of a larger investigation.

Stage II: Formulating an Ethical Decision
The counselor's task in this stage is to identify which of the possible ethical courses of action appears to come closest to the ethical ideal in the situation under consideration.

Component 1: Review Problem or Dilemma Review the problem or dilemma to be sure it is clearly understood in light of any new information. This situation does not fall into the category of mandatory reporting, so the counselor is not legally bound to break the client's confidence. However, we now know that the unwritten policy of the counselor's institution (DCS) is to try to convince or coerce the client to call DHS on his own. Thus, we must decide whether to respect the client's wishes not to call DHS or try to coerce the client to call, in accordance with the institution's unwritten policy.

Component 2: Determine Ethical Codes, Laws, Principles The counselor must determine and research the standards of law (in any and all applicable local jurisdictions) and professional practices applicable to the situation. The latter material includes ethical codes and related standards of care, laws, ethical principles, and institutional policies and procedures. If the counselor is licensed or holds national certification, the codes of ethics that apply to that credential also must be consulted. List those here.

Ethical Codes List any rules of canons from applicable ethics code(s) and provide a summary of the dictates. For counselors, the ACA Code of Ethics and any applicable specialty standards are recommended. If the counselor is licensed or holds national certification, the codes of ethics that apply to that credential also must be consulted.

ACA Code of Ethics (2005):
Section A.1.a "Primary Responsibility. The primary responsibility of counselors is to respect the dignity and promote the welfare of the clients."
Section A.4.a "Avoiding Harm. Counselors act to avoid harming their clients, trainees, and research participants and to minimize or to remedy unavoidable or unanticipated harm."

Section B.2.a "Danger and Legal Requirements. The general requirement that counselors keep information confidential does not apply when disclosure is required to protect clients or identified others from serious and foreseeable harm or when legal requirements demand that confidential information must be revealed. Counselors consult with other professionals when in doubt as to the validity of an exception."

Section D.1.g "Employer Policies. The acceptance of employment in an agency or institution implies that counselors are in agreement with its general policies and principles. Counselors strive to reach agreement with employers as to acceptable standards of conduct that allow for changes in institutional policy conducive to the growth and development of clients."

Section D.1.h "Negative Conditions. Counselors alert their employers of inappropriate policies and practices. They attempt to effect changes in such policies or procedures through constructive action within the organization. When such policies are potentially disruptive or damaging to clients or may limit the effectiveness of services provided, and change cannot be affected, counselors take appropriate further action. Such action may include referral to appropriate certification, accreditation, or state licensure organizations, or voluntary termination of employment."

Laws/Legal Considerations List any laws or legal considerations that may apply. Research those relevant to your own jurisdiction. The example is provided based upon Iowa law, circa 2005. This example is not to be considered a legal opinion, only an example. For further information, consult legal counsel and resources in your own area.

Iowa Code:

Section 232.69 "Mandatory and permissive reporters-training required." A counselor is considered to be a mandatory reporter "who, in the scope of professional practice or in their employment responsibilities, examines, counsels, or treats a child and reasonably believes a child has suffered abuse."

Section 232.68 Included in the definitions of child abuse: "An illegal drug is present in a child's body as a direct and foreseeable consequence of the acts or omissions of the person responsible for the care of the child."

Ethical Principles List all ethical principles that describe relevant obligations. Describe the courses of action, the principles upheld, the principles compromised, and the obligations. Sometimes this process if referred to as *principle analysis*. This is a process wherein ethical principles are specified and subjected to balancing considerations.

Each of the two courses of action can be supported by one or more ethical principles. Contacting authorities could fall under the category of beneficence on the part of the children. Keeping John's confidence could fall under the category of autonomy, for honoring the right to individual decisions. There is also the possibility that both scenarios could fit into the category of nonmaleficence. Not telling anyone could lead to harm for the children in some way. Also, by telling, it is possible that John's fears could materialize and the ex-wife

could keep the children away from him. In this way, it may be harmful to John and also to the children if they are not allowed to see their father.

The ethical principles supporting the other course of action will be compromised. If the authorities are notified, the counselor is not respecting the client's autonomy. If authorities are not told, the counselor may be compromising the principles of nonmaleficence toward the children and the concept of beneficence in the same way.

In principle analysis, the principle obligations owed to your client are normally thought to outweigh those owed to others. Therefore, they are the only ones frequently considered; or if those obligations to others are considered, those owed to the client generally supercede them because the counselor incurs these primary obligations by virtue of entering into a professional relationship with the client. The exception to this case would involve obligations to vulnerable others (e.g., small children) or those situations in which there is a high degree of serious danger or risk. This reasoning is why this case is a particularly troublesome dilemma.

This situation is an ethical dilemma, not just an ethical issue. An ethical issue has a fairly identifiable course of action that is appropriate, even if taking that action is not necessarily easy in practice (i.e., as in the case of involuntarily committing a seriously suicidal individual).

Action A: Pressuring the Client

Principles Upheld	*Principles Compromised*
Beneficence (to children)	Beneficence (to client)
	Nonmaleficence (to client)
	Autonomy (of client)
	Fidelity (to client)

Action B: Not Pressuring the Client

Principles Upheld	*Principles Compromised*
Nonmaleficence (to client)	Beneficence (to children)
Beneficence (to client)	Nonmaleficence (to children)
Autonomy (to client)	
Fidelity (to client)	

Institutional/Agency Rules or Policies List any institutional/agency rules or policies that may apply. In the experience of the counselor, the unwritten policy of DCS is to try to coerce the client into reporting the possible child abuse to DHS.

Component 3: Courses of Action List all possible and probable courses of action. If you can boil this selection down to two opposing options, this strategy is recommended.

Action A: Attempt to coerce the client into reporting.

Action B: Do not try to coerce the client into reporting.

Component 4: Positive and Negative Consequences Consider potential positive and negative consequences for each course of action in light of the risks.

Action A: Pressure the Client

Positive Consequences	*Negative Consequences*
May protect the children from abuse	Does not respect client's autonomy or confidentiality
Follows unwritten DCS policy	Ex-wife may cut off child visitation
Hurts client's trust of counselor	
DCS would not step in to coerce the client	Negative relationship with ex-wife
Less time for other pressing issues of client	May evoke suicidal thoughts
Protects DCS from liability	

Action B: Do Not Pressure the Client

Positive Consequences	*Negative Consequences*
Respects client's autonomy and confidentiality	Does not protect children from possible abuse
Time for other client issues	Counselor is defying employer (DCS)
Does not evoke suicidal thoughts	DCS might step in and coerce client anyway
Child visitation is preserved	DCS might be liable (if child is harmed)
Positive relationship with ex-wife	

Component 5: Consult With Others Consult with supervisors and the following other knowledgeable professionals to review the situation and to obtain their suggestions and opinions.

1. ACA ethics committee
2. Counselors from other corrections agencies
3. Other colleagues
4. DHS anonymously again
5. Attorney

Component 6: Determine Best Ethical Action Select the best ethical course of action.

The best ethical course of action would be not to pressure the client to report to DHS for the following reasons:

1. More ethical principles support this course of action, especially for the client.
2. More positive than negative consequences are likely to result.
3. The Iowa Code does not consider this a situation of mandatory child abuse reporting because the counselor is not working directly with the children and the only information is "hearsay."

Stage III: Selecting an Action by Weighing Competing Nonmoral Values, Personal Blind Spots, or Prejudices

In this stage the counselor must realize the many additional forces that may affect him and tempt him actually not to execute the selected ethical course of action.

Component 1: Competing Values or Concerns The counselor engages in a period of reflection and active processing of personal competing values (e.g., need to be liked by coworkers or his supervisor, or a desire to be seen as a "team player" so as to be promoted by the supervisor), personal blind spots, or prejudices that may influence whether or not he will discharge his ethical obligations. These value orientations may either come into conflict with the course of action necessary to proceed ethically or enhance the tendency to select ethical professional behavior.

Conflicting Concerns	**Potential Effects**
1. Fear of a negative evaluation by employer if he does not follow unwritten policy	Loss of job, license, respect; financial consequences
2. The need to protect the children at all costs no matter what the situation	Loss of reputation and seen as a confidentiality risk
3. Fear of legal repercussions if abuse situation is not reported to DHS	Children are harmed, loss of license or job
4. Fear of harm to DCS	Personal mental health; financial impact on agency/self
5. Fear of losing respect of colleagues	Personal mental health, future relationships
6. Feeling that client should not be pressured and has autonomy in the decision	Harm to children; increased client confidence
7. Feeling that counseling session should be used to work on the client's problems (e.g., depression)	DHS not contacted and children are harmed; client benefits from counseling rather than using all of the time trying to convince client to call DHS

Component 2: Contextual Influences The counselor systematically inventories the contextual influences on his choices at the collegial, team, institutional, and societal levels. These influences might be either dysfunctional or constructive for selecting the ethical course over other types of values.

Level 1: Clinical

1. Counselor's professors/supervisors have recommended advocating for clients' autonomy in the past.

Level 2: Team

1. A few coworkers note that DHS said that the counselor is not required to report the situation to DHS because it is third-party information.

Level 3: Institutional/Agency

1. DCS has an unwritten policy of convincing the client to report abuse on his own.

2. Counselor's supervisor and the administrators support the institution's policy and feel that all counselors at DCS should adhere to both written and unwritten policies.

Level 4: Social Policy/General Cultural

1. Society values children and children's welfare.
2. Society has little tolerance for drug abuse or the selling of drugs, especially when children are involved.
3. There is a fear of transmitted diseases in society, especially HIV and AIDS, which can be passed through intravenous drug use.
4. Society has a prejudiced attitude toward ex-cons on parole and makes little distinction between those who are recovering successfully and those who are not.

Component 3: Select Preferred Action The counselor selects the preferred course of action.

This course of action is to attempt to convince the client to call DHS anonymously. Yet, the counselor still respects the client's autonomy and will not coerce him to report the situation to DHS.

Stage IV: Planning and Executing the Selected Course of Action

In this stage, the counselor plans to implement and execute the selected course of action.

Component 1: Possible Sequences of Actions The counselor determines a reasonable, practical sequence of concrete actions to be taken. List the action steps to be taken.

1. Talk with client about the consequences of his reporting versus not reporting the situation (anonymously, at least) to DHS.
2. Attempt to convince the client to call DHS anonymously for information about what would happen if the situation were reported.
3. If the client does not call, do not continue to attempt to convince him any further.
4. If the client does call and receives the information, give support for what he decides to do next.

Component 2: Contextual Barriers and Countermeasures The counselor will need to anticipate and work out all personal and contextual barriers to effectively execute the plan. It is useful to prepare countermeasures for any contextual barriers that may arise.

Possible Barriers	Possible Countermeasures
1. Client does not wish to call	Document the attempts to get client to call and do not press the issue any further
2. Supervisor may want the counselor to	Inform the supervisor of discomfort with the situation
continue to coerce the client to call	and apprise someone in authority over the supervisor
3. DCS may assign the case to someone else	No countermeasure unless client insists upon seeing the current counselor
4. Client's ex-wife may refuse to let him see the children if he reports the situation to DHS	Encourage the client to speak with an attorney about his rights with the children

Component 3: Carry Out, Document, and Evaluate This step provides for the execution, documentation, and evaluation of the course of action as planned. Describe here the planned goal(s) and potential types of measurements of plan effectiveness and sources of information.

The counselor would carry out the plan by talking to the client about the consequences of reporting versus not reporting the abusive situation to DHS and attempt to get the client to call for information. If the client decides to call, the counselor would support his next step. The counselor would document the ethical decision-making steps taken. Finally, the counselor would evaluate the effectiveness of the plan of action and the entire ethical decision-making process.

Goal	Measure
1. Review consequences of reporting or not reporting and attempt to get the client to call DHS for information	Weigh benefits and costs of client's decision; assess client's level of comfort with either decision
2. Support client if he decides to call	Assess what client needs from counselor
3. Prevent harm to children and help mother	Follow up with treatment referrals for mother and on the children's welfare

This case study was developed by Vilia Tarvydas, Ph.D., LMHC, CRC, and uses the Tarvydas Integrative Decision-Making Model for Ethical Behavior.

COTTONE'S SOCIAL CONSTRUCTIVISM MODEL OF ETHICAL DECISION MAKING

The social constructivism model of ethical decision making was first introduced in the literature in 2001. This model is based purely on philosophy, incorporating the ideas of the social constructivism movement into mental health services without integration of other ideas historically valued in the ethical decision-making literature. Whereas the Tarvydas model builds on the best that is known about ethical decision making as a psychological and social process to date, the Cottone model diverges by presenting a model that is incompatible with the emphasis of established models on psychological theory. It is a purely social-relational model.

The term **social constructivism** is used here to represent an intellectual movement in the mental health field that has emerged from both the psychological and systemic-relational paradigms of mental health services (see the related discussions in Lyddon [1995] and Cottone [1992]). Generally, social constructivism implies that what is real is not objective fact; rather, what is real evolves through interpersonal interaction and agreement as to what is "fact" (Ginter et al., 1996). The *radical constructivist* position, which represents an extreme view and a complete break from psychological theory, is derived from the works of von Foerster (1984), von Glasersfeld (1984), and specifically Maturana (Maturana, 1978, 1988; Maturana & Varela, 1980). The radical constructivism position has been embraced by theorists in the field as an offshoot of social systems theory (a comprehensive theory of relationships). It is a unique, biologically grounded theory (the biology of cognition) that ultimately allows for a *biosocial* interpretation of what is "real." In essence, biologically based social constructivism argues that all that is known is known through biological and social relationships (biosocial). Psychological processes are not involved. Knowledge derives from complex physiological relations wherein observing organisms interact socially to construct a reality. Literally, that means that when we are interacting with other people, we are physically and perceptually affected by the presence of the other person, while at the same time we are communicating socially. Our biology is engaged perceptually while, simultaneously, we are socially engaged. So, as an example, when two people look at a growth on a tree (a perceptual process) and define it as "fruit" (a social process), then it becomes understood as fruit within the confines of that relationship.

The social constructionist movement in psychology (Gergen, 1985) is more rooted in the social psychology literature and avoids in-depth theorizing about biological bases. However, the social constructionism movement (make note of the slightly different spelling of "constructionism" and "constructivism") has uncanny similarities to the ideas presented by the radical social constructivists. Gergen (1985, 1991, 1994), a social psychologist, has thrown down a broad theoretical gauntlet arguing for a social-relational interpretation of human understanding. Gergen (1991) stated: "The reality of the individual is giving way to relational reality" (p. 160). The term social constructivism, therefore, is used here to represent the biologically rooted but

radical constructivism deriving primarily from the works of Maturana, while acknowledging the seminal works of Gergen, which are grounded in social psychology.

The need for a social constructivism model of ethical decision making is threefold. First, it provides a distinct view of the decision-making process—it is based purely on a relational view of reality. Other models tend to portray the decision maker as a psychological entity that makes the decision alone or within some social context. For example, Kitchener, in her highly cited 1984 work, described ethical decisions as those involving the decision maker's intuitive and critical evaluative reasoning. In contrast, the social constructivism perspective places the decision in the social context itself, not in the head of the decision maker; decision making becomes an interpersonal process of negotiating, consensualizing, and arbitrating (three terms defined later in this chapter). A second rationale for developing a social constructivism model is that it may lead to empirical testing of social versus psychologically based ethical decision-making models. Because a constructivism approach is so unique theoretically, it provides a competitive perspective to more psychologically based models. Critical paradigm experiments (Cottone, 1989a, 1989b) may be designed to test the social perspective against the more traditional psychological perspective. Such experiments help researchers and practitioners weigh the relative merits of one approach against another, providing an empirical foundation that is sorely needed in this area of study. The third rationale for a social constructivism model is its appeal to practitioners as an alternative perspective for framing ethical decisions. Although there is a plethora of ethical decision-making models; this model provides an alternative to psychological or hybrid models for practitioners who are more aligned with a systemic or relational worldview. The model is parsimonious and does not involve complex steps or stages, so it may be easier for counselors to implement in the stressful times that accompany an ethical challenge.

In a follow-up article on the model, invited by the editors of the *Canadian Journal of Counselling,* Cottone (2004) stated:

> To truly appreciate a social constructivism model of ethical decision making, one must first transform one's thinking to accept a radical position: The psychology of the individual can be displaced by relational (biosocial) theory. Social constructivism is founded on ideas that allow for all conclusions about human functioning to be understood based on the biological and social forces

that affect behaviour. Psychology that focuses primarily on an individual can be viewed as excess baggage, a social creation itself that provides little or no descriptive power beyond biological and social factors. In other words, all behaviour can be viewed as biologically affected and manifested through social relationships. This is a difficult position for some people to accept. After all, many current mental health professionals have been inculcated with psychological theory. The thought that the psychology of the individual is superfluous is not easily accommodated. (p. 6)

To understand the model, one must be willing to set aside thinking in psychological terms—that is, thinking about people as individuals with free will and individual choice. One must be willing to suspend judgment long enough to accept that all that is known about ethical dilemmas derives from relationships, at many levels.

Understanding the Application of Social Constructivism to Ethical Decision Making

Objectivity in Parentheses.   What social constructivism means to ethical decision making is that decisions can no longer be viewed as occurring internally. Many other decision-making models portray the decision as the responsibility of the individual decision maker. For example, an individual is asked to decide on a best course of action (Corey, Corey, & Callanan, 2003), select an action by weighing competing values in a given context (Tarvydas model), make the decision (Keith-Spiegel & Koocher, 1985), or deliberate and decide (Welfel, 2002). From a constructivism perspective, decisions are moved out of the intrapsychic process and into the interpersonal realm. As Gergen (1985) wrote:

> From this perspective knowledge is not something people possess somewhere in their heads, but rather, something people do together. Languages are essentially shared activities. Indeed, until the sounds or markings come to be shared within a community, it is inappropriate to speak of language at all. In effect, we may cease inquiry into the psychological basis of language (which account would inevitably form but a subtext or miniature language) and focus on the performative use of language in human affairs. (p. 270)

Further, Gergen said: "The mind becomes a form of social myth; the self-concept is removed from the head and placed within the sphere of social discourse" (p. 271). From this vantage point, all that is done, all activity, and all to which language is applied is a reflection of what has been shared previously in the community. Language is not generated spontaneously; it is transmitted socially. All that is done (in language or otherwise) is bound to heritage. Decisions, therefore, cannot be located "in" the individual. Rather, they are in the social matrix. There is no free will or choice, because all decisions are biologically and socially compelled within a person's network of relationships.

The social constructivism position is contrary to the positions taken by ethicists in counseling who appear to be bound predominantly to psychological theorizing about how decisions are made. Decision-making models tend to lay out steps for ethical choice (Cottone & Claus, 2000), but almost across the board they fail to describe adequately how that choice occurs; it somehow disappears into the head (or mind) of the individual making the decision, either intuitively or based on utilitarian values (Hare, 1991). For example, how are values weighed by the individual? Few models actually answer that question. For example, Gutheil et al. (1991) grounded their decision model in probability theory and weighing probabilities. With most models, how a decision is made is a psychological mystery.

The social constructivism approach to ethical decision making places the ethical decision out in the open—in the interaction between individuals as they operate in what Maturana (1978) identified as the "consensual domain" (p. 47). A decision is never made in a social vacuum. A decision is always made in interaction with at least one other individual. The interactive aspects of a decision are undeniable. In professional ethics, a decision to enter into an intimate relationship with a client is a decision made in interaction with the client. Likewise, a decision to breach a client's confidentiality is a decision made in relation to a third party. Decisions are not compelled internally; rather, they are compelled socially. This is the social constructivism position.

Some decisions may be viewed as "good" within a social context, whereas others may be viewed as "bad" within a social context. But that is not to say that decisions are "relative." What differentiates the social constructivism approach from purely relative models of right or wrong (where right and wrong are relative truths held by individuals) is that the social constructivism approach defines the view within a social consensual domain as absolutely true within that social context. As Maturana (1988) described it, "objectivity" is "in parentheses," where the parentheses are the boundaries of human interaction. In other words, reality is viewed as socially constructed, and within the social context, it is an absolutist's view. To demonstrate this point, consider that there can be competitive social consensualities—competitive absolute truths, so to speak. Understanding that there can be competitive absolute truths (a logical contradiction) helps to clarify the distinction between social constructivism and objectivism (where there is one absolute truth) and relativism (where truth is relative to each individual). Social constructivism stands apart from objectivism and relativism in the primacy of relationships. In effect, there are *pockets of objectivities*, and each pocket is demarcated by the group that acts according to what is believed to be true. For example, according to social constructivism, there can be several competitive truths, even competitive "gods." Each of a number of competitive gods represents absolute truth within a social-consensual domain represented by the religion's adherents. Each such god effectively competes for what is absolutely true against other gods (other socially consensually constructed realities). Ironically, some people literally war over some religions; but there is no irony from a social constructivism perspective. In those cases, the warring individuals believe absolutely in the "truths" represented by their god and will fight to the death to preserve such principles. This demonstrates the power of shared beliefs—beliefs acknowledged within a social (in this case a religious) group.

Just as people fight wars over religion, so too can mental health professionals war over what is believed to be ethical practice. Past court cases have frequently represented the battlefield. The classic and well-known Tarasoff legal decision is a good example. In that case, a University of California therapist took what he believed were acceptable actions to warn authorities of a dangerous client. The therapist took actions that were, up to that moment, directed by the professional consensus as to obligations of counselors in that circumstance. The surprise was that the courts ruled in favor of a different view—siding with the family of the murdered individual targeted by the client—and the courts assessed liability. VandeCreek and Knapp (1993) explained:

> The decision was based, to a large extent, on the affirmative duty to act which arises out of the "special relationship" between a psychotherapist and a patient. According to the common law, an individual usually has no duty to control the behavior of another in order to protect a third party. Nevertheless, once a "special relationship" has been established, the law may require

affirmative obligations. These socially recognized relationships, such as parent to child or possessor of land to renter, imply a legal duty to attempt to protect others from harm, or to warn them of potential harm. (p. 5)

The professionals involved were essentially trying to protect the confidentiality of the client consistent with ethical standards to that date. But, in interaction with the legal system, the actions and the defense did not hold weight. Accordingly, serious implications for professional ethics in counseling derive from a social constructivism perspective because no single, socially constructed ethical stance can be considered inherently better than another—predominance only derives from negotiation, consensus building, or arbitration. As with the Tarasoff decision, the involved parties were acting according to what was directed socially by the consensus of their communities. The fact that there was an unresolved clash of consensualities led to arbitration.

Conflicting Consensualities. Professionals must identify the levels of consensus that operate around an action or a dilemma. The fact that there is a dilemma means there may be a disagreement—a conflict of consensualities—between groups of people with which the professional has interacted.

The codes of the ACA and the APA reflect consensualities as to what is acceptable practice; membership in either the APA or the ACA indicates interaction with the consensualizing process the association represents. Counselors also interact with clients and client families, lawyers, judges, physicians, and other mental health professionals. Each interaction may represent the coming together of two systems of thought. Each may represent a distinct consensus on an issue. When there is a disagreement over an ethically sensitive issue that is resistant to easy negotiation, there is a conflict of consensualities. Take, for example, one of the most salient cases of a breach of ethical standards—sexual intimacies with a client. The counselor who enters a sexual relationship with a client acts in a way that represents rejection of the professional standard banning sexual intimacies while acting in a way that represents acceptance of the risks of the social/sexual relationship. The sexual relationship may also represent linkage to a system, which may not fit well within the constraints of a secret, professionally banned relationship. For example, the client may have family, friends, or an attorney who advises that such a relationship is "wrong." When a disagreement arises between the professional and the client's system, a clash of consensualities may result (a disagreement over the nature or course of the relationship), with potential legal and professional threat to the counselor. The decision to enter into such a relationship is an act of vulnerability for the professional—the counselor's livelihood is at stake. Nothing professionally damaging may occur, but there is a possibility that the couple's initial consensus that the relationship exists (or may be acceptable at some level) may deteriorate under the strain of other relationships and competing consensualities that come to bear on their interaction. Of course, there is a consensus established in the professional literature that sexual intimacies with clients are unethical (the ACA and APA codes) and harmful (Bouhoutsos, Holroyd, Lerman, Forer, & Greenberg, 1983; Pope, 1988). Therefore, a counselor would be well served to avoid such a detrimental relationship. There is little support for an offending professional given current ethical and professional standards.

A decision to breach an ethical standard (as with an offending counselor) or the decision to challenge a professional's ethics (as with the educated client) is a decision that derives from past and present interactions. There are no psychological determinants, but only biological and social forces that affect interactions one way or another. In other words, *the actions of the client and the counselor can be completely conceptualized as resulting from physical and social forces,* not psychological needs. The action to mount an ethical challenge to the counselor also derives from physical and social factors impinging the client. What appears to be an ethical (or unethical) decision is simply an action taken in concert with the emerging social consensus of the moment.

Social constructivism ethical decision making means that the professional must avoid *linkages of vulnerability* and cultivate *linkages of professional responsibility.* Relationships should be cultivated in accord with the larger sociolegal consensus that pervades professional practice. Ethical decision making occurs well before a crisis of consensualities arises. It is implicit in the professional culture. It means a rich, professional network is established and actions are taken to prevent and to avoid contact with social networks where challenges of right and wrong must be answered.

So, social constructivism ethical decision making is not classic psychological decision making at all. It is linkage to professional culture. One either does or does not fully enter into a professional culture. Those interactions that help to engage a professional fully in the ethical professional climate are actions of ethical

choice. Such activity happens most basically in educational institutions where counselors are introduced by seasoned clinicians to a professional culture and to the rules that guide acceptable practice. At that level, the profession is responsible for conveying the importance of linkage to a professional culture so that communicating on ethical issues becomes an ongoing activity of the student professional.

The Interpersonal Processes of Negotiating, Consensualizing, and Arbitrating

Counseling practice is complex and ethical dilemmas arise as new challenges confront practitioners. Even a counselor who is closely aligned with an ethically sensitive professional community may face an ethical challenge. Should there be accusations of unethical practice, counselors must act to protect their own interests and the interests of their clients. In such cases, the social constructivism ethical decision-making alternative to psychologically based ethical decision making must occur. It does not occur internally or "in the head." Instead, social constructivism ethical decision making is a process of negotiating (when necessary), consensualizing, and arbitrating (when necessary) that occurs in the interpersonal process of relations that come to bear at critical moments of professional practice.

Negotiating is the process of discussing and debating an issue wherein at least two individuals indicate some degree of disagreement. For example, if a client's attorney contacts a counselor about testifying at a worker's compensation or disability hearing, the counselor should first request permission from the client to release confidential information (in order to talk to the attorney). Next, the counselor should consult with the attorney and negotiate as to whether the testimony is crucial to the client's case. If there is a formal request to testify, a waiver of privileged communication might be necessary, depending on laws in the jurisdiction. If there is a disagreement over the nature of the testimony or its potential effects, the counselor might refuse to testify, recognizing that a court-ordered subpoena might result. Negotiation, therefore, is a process of discussing and debating a position taken by the counselor; negotiation requires operation in language and some level of expressed disagreement.

Consensualizing is a process wherein at least two individuals act in agreement and in coordination on an issue. Consensus is viewed as an ongoing interactive process, not a final outcome or "thing." Cottone (1992) stated: "The idea of consensus must not be viewed solely as a formal language-based activity. In fact, consensus is probably best understood by the actions of individuals as they relate mutually, verbally and non-verbally, within certain interpersonal contexts" (p. 269). Where there is language, social interaction, and co-operation, there is an evolving consensuality. (Notice that the word "co-operation" is hyphenated; the hyphen is purposeful and indicates that individuals operate—act—in a coordinated fashion.) Maturana (1970) described this as the "consensual domain" (p. 50). Individuals who consensualize may have been involved in negotiation, but it is not necessary to negotiate to consensualize. Negotiation requires that there was some degree of disagreement, whereas consensualizing may or may not involve disagreement. For example, if an attorney requests that a counselor testify, the counselor may agree (with minimal discussion or no debate) and may just show up at the scheduled hearing ready to testify. In this case, the attorney and the counselor have consensualized by coordinated action as to the request to testify. Consensualizing is the process of socially constructing a reality. If there is disagreement or discordant action (consensualizing is not evident), arbitration may be necessary.

Arbitrating is a process whereby a negotiator or negotiators seek the judgment of consensually accepted individuals (alone or in groups) who are socially approved as representatives of sociolegal consensus—arbitrators. Arbitrators make judgments in interaction with each other, complainants, defendants, the authority of agreed-upon rules or law, and past judgments (e.g., case law). In most cases, the arbitrator has final say, unless, of course, there is an appeal to a higher consensually accepted arbitrator (e.g., a court of appeals). Arbitrating is the social process that imposes a socially constructed reality.

Response to a Challenge

When a professional is accused or questioned about ethical misconduct, he or she may respond in a way that acknowledges, disputes, or further questions the alleged or questionable behavior. The counselor's response probably derives as much from the nature of the relationship to the accuser or inquirer as to the nature of the alleged misconduct. To deny an accusation of a "nemesis" may prevent meaningful negotiation, even in the case of acceptable conduct, setting up an adversarial circumstance and a clash of consensualities to be settled by consensually agreed-upon higher authorities (e.g., the courts). Denial to a friendly colleague, on the other hand, may bring about negotiation as to whether a breach has occurred (against some agreed-upon standard, such as an ethical standard in a code of ethics). The moment of accusation or inquiry is a critical moment, and social forces influence what may appear to outsiders as a "decision."

The Social Constructivism Process of Ethical Decision Making When a Concern Arises. At critical moments, such as when a concern arises or when there has been an accusation or inquiry, the ethically sensitive professional operating from a social constructivism mode would take several steps: (a) obtain information from those involved; (b) assess the nature of the relationships operating at that moment in time; (c) consult valued colleagues and professional expert opinion (including ethics codes and literature); (d) negotiate when there is a disagreement; and (e) respond in a way that allows for a reasonable consensus as to what should happen or what really occurred. Every involved relationship must be examined for potential linkage to another (possibly adversarial) system of thought. Additionally, every involved relationship must be assessed for a potential conflict of opinion over what should or did happen. If consensus is not possible, further negotiation, interactive reflection, or arbitration may be necessary. (See Figure 6–2).

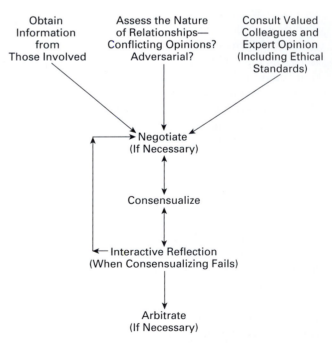

FIGURE 6–2. The Interactive Process of Socially Constructing an Outcome to an Ethical Dilemma

After information is obtained, the nature of relationships is assessed and valued colleagues and experts are consulted (Figure 6–2). The interactive process of socially constructing an outcome to an ethical dilemma involves negotiating (if necessary), consensualizing, and arbitrating (if necessary). The ultimate goal is to establish consensus among involved parties about what should or did happen in questionable circumstances. When consensualizing fails, parties may partake in *interactive reflection*, a process of conversation with trusted individuals to come to agreement as to whether arbitration should be sought or whether a position needs to be modified to reenter negotiation. If consensualizing fails after interactive reflection, arbitration is necessary.

"A Truth" Versus "The Truth". Conflicts between people can, hopefully, be addressed by open discussion or reasonable negotiation of what should happen (or what actually occurred). Unfortunately, "the truth" may be a matter of dispute. If, in fact, counselors plan to break the rules (or have broken the rules), they should accept the consequences of their actions imposed by the sociolegal consensus in the profession and the courts. Otherwise, they might act to protect their own professional interests by denying a wrongdoing, possibly at the expense of clients.

It may be that only a client and a professional know the actions that have occurred. When there is a difference of opinion about an act—a conflict of consensualities—arbitration may be the only answer. In such cases, "the truth" may never be known to others, even though a judgment may occur. Aside from arbitration, when there is a dispute (i.e., there are competing truths), only in cases of repeated offenses can "a truth" be established. Where there are repeated offenses, such "a truth" is established around the victims, whose stories combine to constitute a systemic imperative for legal or professional action. Some professionals may "come clean" in such a circumstance. Other professionals may resist acceptance of professional or legal mores (or possibly be the victims of a conspiracy, however unlikely). Whatever the professional's action, it reflects the physical and social forces affecting the counselor at that moment in time.

Once an ethical course of action has been chosen, it is wise for counselors to take additional steps in line with the recommendation of Tarvydas (see her model in this chapter) to engage in a period of reflection and active processing of what the counselor intends to do. From a social constructivism position, however, reflection is not a process of mind—rather it is a continued reappraisal of actions in context and in consultation with others who can provide a perspective that represents their linkage to the professional community. It is a continued process of seeking alternative opinions or perspectives. If different perspectives emerge that allow for different views and a negotiated settlement (prior to an arbitrated decision), it is not too late to reappraise the circumstance. In the constructivism model, such reflection takes the form of interactive reflection.

Case Scenario 6–3 is based on an actual case discussed in a graduate course on ethical issues in counseling. The case demonstrates the interactive processes involved in decision making. Terms associated with the social process of ethical decision making are bracketed as related to the flowchart shown in Figure 6–2.

CASE SCENARIO 6–3

Counseling is provided to a 12-year-old girl through a family counseling agency funded by both private and government funds. The girl lives with her grandmother, who signs the consent for treatment as the child's legal guardian. After several counseling sessions, the grandmother demands to know what the child reported. The child, in counseling, reports to the counselor that the grandmother is not her legal guardian, which is substantiated [assessment of the nature of relationships]. Her mother is identified as legal guardian [assessment of the nature of relationships]. The mother lives 60 miles from the counseling center and has not been involved with the child for some time. The counselor is faced with a dilemma—technically there has been no informed consent because the grandmother fraudulently signed the consent form as the legal guardian. Yet the counselor has an ethical responsibility to the child according to ethical standards. The counselor consults the executive director of the agency (a noncounselor) who informs her that counseling cannot continue without informed consent or procedures would be breached, threatening the service contract [consultation of colleagues]. The clinical service supervisor is consulted and informs the counselor that, aside from informed consent, she still has an obligation to the child [consultation of colleagues]. The counselor attempts to seek the mother's permission, but fails on several phone attempts [obtaining information from involved parties]. She even arranged through certified mail to meet the mother, drove 60 miles, and was disappointed when the mother did not show for the scheduled meeting at the arranged site [attempt to negotiate]. The counselor then sought the joint counsel of her clinical supervisor and the executive director [consultation with colleagues]. The executive director took a firm legal stance and directed her not to work with the child without legally executed informed consent by the responsible adult. An agreement was reached among the professionals to request the grandmother's assistance in procuring the informed consent of the mother [consensualizing]. The grandmother agreed [consensualizing], but faced with the non-cooperation of the mother [nonconsensus], the grandmother obtained legal custody of the child only after threatening the mother with charges of child neglect [threat of arbitration leading to renegotiation and coordinated action between the mother and grandmother]. Counseling was reinitiated with the consent of the grandmother as the legal guardian. The child was informed that the grandmother had legal access to information provided in counseling.

As Case Scenario 6–3 demonstrates, the outcome of an ethical dilemma is highly social and can be clearly conceptualized as an interactive, not intrapsychic, process.

How the Social Constructivism Model Interfaces with Multiculturalism

Because the social constructivism model of ethical decision making is based on relational theory and fully acknowledges the "communities of understanding" that each person represents, it is fully sensitive to cultural issues. In fact, the social constructivism model not only acknowledges cultural diversity (by accepting culturally derived truths) but it also helps to define the limits of multiculturalism (Cottone, 2004). The limits of multiculturalism are defined by the ethical constraints of a situation—those ethical consensualities established by the profession that define acceptable limits about permissible behavior in and out of the counseling context. In 2004, Cottone presented a case scenario that is helpful in describing both the model's facility at incorporating diversity issues, while delimiting ethical constraints on behaviors, no matter how culturally grounded those behaviors may be. Consider a hypothetical case of a young teenage African girl who lives in America with her parents, who are citizens of an African nation. The girl and the parents have temporary permission to live in the United States. The girl is enrolled in a school, where she reports to the counselor that she fears a planned visit to her homeland, because her parents plan to have her undergo a ritual female circumcision, a procedure that is common in her homeland. She fears the circumcision and does not want to go back to the homeland or to participate in the ritual. The counselor is faced with a dilemma— there are laws in the state of residence that would define such an act as child abuse, whereas the counselor

found (through researching the ritual) that, indeed, it is a culturally accepted practice in the child's homeland. The counselor followed a process that exemplified the social constructivism model, consulting the parents, the legal authorities, an ethics professor, and a professor of multicultural counseling. Although the parents disagreed, a consensus was established among the other consulted individuals—regardless of cultural tradition, in this case, state statutes protecting children prevailed. The counselor decided that, if the parents insisted that the child would have to undergo the procedure, the child abuse authorities in the state of current residence would be called.

In effect, multiculturalism has limitations. Counselors cannot condone certain actions that are dangerous to others, for example, no matter what cultural tradition directs a behavior. If a client is a part of a group that defines a behavior as acceptable, that alone does not allow for acceptance of that behavior, especially if the behavior is antithetical to ethical principles at the foundation of counseling practice. There are limits as to what can be defined as "accepted" behavior by nature of counseling ethical principles; for example, acceptance of a "hate group" philosophy, where such a hate group is known to act on the philosophy, would be antithetical to counseling practice. The social constructivism ethical decision-making model, therefore, brings all community mores and traditions to bear on a situation—those of the cultural traditions of the client *and* those of the professional culture of counseling. In the end, there is reconciliation of these consensualities around the defined acceptable limits of counseling practice as a counselor consults with others to define a course of action. If there is a clash of consensualities, as with the case example of the parents from an African nation, then the counselor must take a position that appear to be beneficent, nonmaleficent, just, faithful to the client, and respecting of the client's freedom of choice.

Concluding Words About Social Constructivism Ethical Decision Making

Gergen (1991) stated: "When individuals declare right and wrong in a given situation, they are only acting as local representatives for larger relationships in which they are enmeshed. Their relationships speak through them" (pp. 168–169). The social constructivism approach to ethical decision making is a purely social interpretation of the decision-making process. The social constructivism decision-making approach is a process of negotiating and consensualizing. All behavior occurs in a social context. From the constructivism perspective, decisions occur always in interaction. Professionals are less vulnerable to ethical challenges if they are linked to a rich professional culture, which is not supportive of a breach of ethical standards. When concerns arise at crucial moments of professional practice, the social constructivist obtains information from those involved, assesses the nature of relationships operating at that moment, consults valued colleagues and professional expert opinion (including ethical codes), negotiates when necessary, and responds in a way that allows for a reasonable consensus. Where negotiation must occur—when there is a conflict of consensualities—the counselor may accept or challenge an opposing position, knowing that an adversarial relationship may be established and judgment may occur in consensually agreed-upon courts of arbitration. The social constructivism model also acknowledges multiculturalism, and by nature of accepted ethical standards, it helps to define the limits of multiculturalism.

CHAPTER SUMMARY

Counselors must exercise their ethical and professional judgment responsibly. They must recognize an ethical dilemma and apply appropriate decision-making skills to resolve the dilemma. Several models exist that explain and structure the process of ethical decision making: (a) theoretically or philosophically based models; and (b) practice-based models.

Theoretically or philosophically based models ground ethical decision making on a theory or philosophy. These models include absolute thinking (Hare, 1981); moral reasoning (Rest, 1984, 1994); decision analysis (Gutheil et al., 1991); transactional analysis (Berne, 1972); feminist (Hill et al., 1995); hermeneutic (Betan, 1997); and social constructivism (Cottone, 2001).

Practice-based models are based on pragmatic procedures derived from experience or intended as practical guides for counselors. They are less theory specific or philosophically pure than theoretical models and have characteristics of either principle or virtue ethics. Principle ethics focuses on the objective, rational, and cognitive aspects of a process. Virtue ethics considers the characteristics of the counselors themselves as the critical element for responsible practice. The Tarvydas Integrative Model builds on the Rest (1984, 1994), and Kitchener (1984) models and has a four-level approach: (1) clinical counseling level, (2) clinical interdisciplinary team level, (3) institutional/agency level, and (4) societal resource/public policy level. The Tarvydas model has four underlying themes: stance of reflection, balance, attention to the context, and collaboration.

Cottone's social constructivism model provides an alternative to practitioners who are more aligned with a systemic or relational worldview. In this view, decisions are not viewed as occurring internally; decisions are moved out of the intrapsychic process and into the interpersonal realm. Social constructivism ethical decision making is a process of negotiating, consensualizing, and arbitrating. Negotiating is the process of discussing and debating an issue wherein at least two individuals indicate some degree of disagreement. Consensualizing is a process wherein at least two individuals act in agreement and in coordination on an issue. Arbitrating is a process whereby a negotiator seeks the judgment of consensually accepted individuals who are socially approved as representatives of sociolegal consensus. Overall, social constructivism ethical decision making directs counselors to avoid linkages of vulnerability while cultivating linkages of professional responsibility.

REFERENCES

American Counseling Association. (2005). *ACA code of ethics.* Alexandria, VA: Author.

Beauchamp, T. L., & Childress, J. F. (1979). *Principles of biomedical ethics.* Oxford, England: Oxford University Press.

Beauchamp, T. L., & Childress, J. F. (2001). *Principles of biomedical ethics* (5th ed.). New York: Oxford University Press.

Beauchamp, T. L., & Walters, L. (1994). *Contemporary issues in bioethics* (4th ed.). Belmont, CA: Wadsworth.

Berne, E. (1972). *What do you say after you say hello? The psychology of human destiny.* New York: Grove Press.

Betan, E. J. (1997). Toward a hermeneutic model of ethical decision making in clinical practice. *Ethics and Behavior, 7,* 347–365.

Betan, E. J., & Stanton, A. L. (1999). Fostering ethical willingness: Integrating emotional and contextual awareness with rational analysis. *Professional Psychology: Research and Practice, 30,* 295–301.

Bouhoutsos, J., Holroyd, J., Lerman, H., Forer, B. R., & Greenberg, M. (1983). Sexual intimacy between psychotherapists and patients. *Professional Psychology: Research and Practice, 14,* 185–196.

Chang, V. N. (1994). A transactional analysis decision-making model and ethical hierarchy. *Transactional Analysis Journal, 24,* 15–20.

Corey, G., Corey, M. S., & Callanan, P., (2003). *Issues and ethics in the helping professions* (6th ed.). Pacific Grove, CA: Brooks/Cole.

Cottone, R. R. (1989a). Defining the psychomedical and systemic paradigms in marital and family therapy. *Journal of Marital and Family Therapy, 15,* 225–235.

Cottone, R. R. (1989b). On ethical and contextual research in marital and family therapy: A reply to Taggart. *Journal of Marital and Family Therapy, 15,* 243–248.

Cottone, R. R. (1992). *Theories and paradigms of counseling and psychotherapy.* Needham Heights, MA: Allyn & Bacon.

Cottone, R. R. (2001). A social constructivism model of ethical decision making in counseling. *Journal of Counseling and Development, 79,* 39–45.

Cottone, R. R. (2004). Displacing the psychology of the individual in ethical decision making: The social constructivism model. *Canadian Journal of Counselling, 38,* 5–13.

Cottone, R. R., & Claus, R. E. (2000). Ethical decision-making models: A review of the literature. *Journal of Counseling & Development, 78,* 275–283.

Cottone, R. R., Tarvydas, V., & House, G. (1994). The effect of number and type of consulted relationships on the ethical decision making of graduate students in counseling. *Counseling and Values, 39,* 56–68.

Dinger, T. J. (1997, April). *Do ethical decision-making models really work?* An empirical study. Paper presented at the American Counseling Association world conference, Orlando, FL.

Forester-Miller, H., & Davis, T. E. (1996). *A practitioner's guide to ethical decision making.* Alexandria, VA: American Counseling Association.

Frame, M. W., & Williams, C. B. (2005). A model of ethical decision making from a multicultural perspective. *Counseling and Values, 49,* 165–179.

Francouer, R. T. (1983). Teaching decision making in biomedical ethics for the allied health student. *Journal of Allied Health, 12,* 202–209.

Garcia, J., Cartwright, B., Winston, S. M., & Borzuchowska, B. (2003). A transcultural integrative ethical decision-making model in counseling. *Journal of Counseling & Development, 81,* 268–277.

Gatens-Robinson, E., & Rubin, S. E. (1995). Societal values and ethical commitments that influence rehabilitation service delivery behavior. In S. E. Rubin & R. T. Roessler (Eds.), *Foundations of the vocational rehabilitation process* (pp. 157–174). Austin, TX: Pro-Ed.

Gergen, K. J. (1985). The social constructionist movement in modern psychology. *American Psychologist, 40,* 266–275.

Gergen, K. J. (1991). *The saturated self.* New York, NY: Basic Books.

Gergen, K. J. (1994). *Toward transformation in social knowledge* (2nd ed.). London: Sage.

Ginter, E. J. (chair), Ellis, A., Guterman, J. T., Ivey, A. E., Lock, D. C., & Rigazio-Digilio, S. A. (1996, April). *Ethical issues in the postmodern era.* Panel discussion conducted at the 1996 world conference of the American Counseling Association, Pittsburgh, PA.

Gutheil, T. G., Bursztajn, H. J., Brodsky, A., & Alexander, V. (1991). *Decision making in psychiatry and the law.* Baltimore, MD: Williams & Wilkins.

Hare, R. (1981). The philosophical basis of psychiatric ethics. In S. Block & P. Chodoff (Eds.), *Psychiatric ethics* (pp. 31–45). Oxford, England: Oxford University Press.

Hare, R. (1991). The philosophical basis of psychiatric ethics. In S. Block & P. Chodoff (Eds.), *Psychiatric ethics* (2nd ed., pp. 33–46). Oxford, England: Oxford University Press.

Hill, M., Glaser, K., & Harden, J. (1995). A feminist model for ethical decision making. In E. J. Rave & C. C. Larsen (Eds.), *Ethical decision making in therapy: Feminist perspectives* (pp. 18–37). New York: Guilford.

Hinkeldey, N. S., & Spokane, A. R. (1985). Effects of pressure and legal guideline clarity on counselor decision making in legal and ethical conflict situations. *Journal of Counseling and Development, 64,* 240–245.

Janis, I. L., & Mann, L. (1977). *Decision making: A psychological analysis of conflict, choice, and commitment.* New York: The Free Press.

Keith-Spiegel, P., & Koocher, G. P. (1985). *Ethics in psychology.* New York: Random House.

Kitchener, K. S. (1984). Intuition, critical evaluation and ethical principles: The foundation for ethical decisions in counseling psychology. *The Counseling Psychologist, 12*(3), 43–55.

Kitchener, K. S. (1988). Dual role relationships: What makes them so problematic? *Journal of Counseling and Development, 67,* 217–221.

Kohlberg, L. (1969). Stage and sequence: The cognitive-developmental approach to socialization. In D. Soslin (Ed.), *Handbook of socialization theory and research* (pp. 347–480). Chicago: Rand McNally.

Kohlberg, L. (1980). High school democracy and educating a just society. In R. L. Mosher (Ed.), *Moral education: A generation of research and development* (pp. 20–57). New York: Praeger.

Lyddon, W. J. (1995). Forms and facets of constructivist psychology. In R. A. Neimeyer & M. J. Mahoney (Eds.), *Constructivism in psychotherapy* (pp. 69–92). Washington, DC: American Psychological Association.

Mabe, A. R., & Rollin, S. A. (1986). The role of a code of ethical standards in counseling. *Journal of Counseling and Development, 64,* 294–297.

Maturana, H. R. (1970). Biology of cognition. In H. R. Maturana & F. J. Varela (1980). *Autopoiesis and cognition: The realization of the living.* Boston: D. Reidel.

Maturana, H. R. (1978). Biology of language: The epistemology of reality. In G. A. Miller & E. Lenneberg (Eds.), *Psychology and biology of language and thought* (pp. 27–63). New York: Academic Press.

Maturana, H. R. (1988). Reality: The search for objectivity or the quest for a compelling argument. *Irish Journal of Psychology, 9*(1), 25–82.

Maturana, H. R, & Varela, F. J. (1980). *Autopoiesis and cognition: The realization of the living.* Boston: D. Reidel.

McGrath, G. (1994). Ethics, boundaries, and contracts: Applying moral principles. *Transactional Analysis Journal, 24,* 6–14.

Meara, N. M., Schmidt, L. D., & Day, J. D. (1996). Principles and virtues: A foundation for ethical decisions, policies and character. *The Counseling Psychologist, 24,* 4–77.

Patterson, J. B. (1992). Ethics and ethical decision making in rehabilitation counseling. In R. M. Parker & E. M. Szymanski (Eds.), *Rehabilitation counseling: Basics and beyond* (pp. 165–193). Austin, TX: Pro-Ed.

Pedersen, P. B. (1995). Culture-centered ethical guidelines for counselors. In J. G. Ponterotto, J. M. Casas, L. A. Suzuki, & C. M. Alexander (Eds.), *Handbook for multicultural counseling.* Thousand Oaks, CA: Sage.

Ponterotto, J. G., & Casas, J. M. (1991). *Handbook of racial/ethnic minority counseling research.* Springfield, IL: Charles C. Thomas.

Pope, K. S. (1988). How clients are harmed by sexual contact with mental health professionals: The syndrome and its prevalence. *Journal of Counseling and Development,* 67, 222–226.

Rest, J. R. (1984). Research on moral development: Implications for training psychologists. *The Counseling Psychologist, 12*(3), 19–29.

Rest, J. R. (1994). Background: Theory and research. In J. R. Rest & D. Narvaez (Eds.), *Moral development in the professions: Psychology and applied ethics* (pp. 1–26). Hillsdale, NJ: Lawrence Erlbaum Associates.

Rest, J. R., Cooper, D., Coder, R., Maganz, J., & Anderson, D. (1974). Judging the important issues in moral dilemmas—an objective test of development. *Developmental Psychology, 10*(4), 491–501.

Rest, J. R., Davison, M. L., & Robbins, S. (1978). Age trends in judging moral issues: A review of cross-sectional, longitudinal, and sequential studies of the Defining Issues Test. *Child Development, 49*(2), 263–279.

Schwartz, S. H. (1977) Normative influences on altruism. In L. Berkowitz (Ed.), *Advances in experimental social psychology* (Vol. 10, pp. 221–279). New York: Academic Press.

Sileo, F. J., & Kopala, M. (1993). An A-B-C-D-E worksheet for promoting beneficence when considering ethical issues. *Counseling and Values, 37,* 89–95.

Stadler, H. A. (1986). Making hard choices: Clarifying controversial ethical issues. *Counseling and Human Development. 19,* 1–10.

Steinman, S. O., Richardson, N. F., & McEnroe, T. (1998). *The ethical decision-making manual for helping professionals.* Pacific Grove, CA: Brooks/Cole.

Tarvydas, V. M. (2004). Ethics. In T. F. Riggar & D. R. Maki (Eds.), *Handbook of rehabilitation counseling,* (pp. 108–141). New York: Springer.

Tarvydas, V. M., & Cottone, R. R. (1991). Ethical responses to legislative, organizational and economic dynamics: A four-level model of ethical practice. *Journal of Applied Rehabilitation Counseling. 22*(4), 11–18.

Van Hoose, W. H., & Kottler, J. A. (1985). *Ethical and legal issues in counseling and psychotherapy.* San Francisco: Jossey-Bass.

VandeCreek, L., & Knapp, S. (1993). *Tarasoff and beyond: Legal and clinical considerations in the treatment of life-endangering patients.* Sarasota, FL: Professional Resource Press.

Vasquez, M. J. T. (1996). Will virtue ethics improve ethical conduct in multicultural settings and interactions? *The Counseling Psychologist, 24,* 98–104.

von Foerster, H. (1984). On constructing a reality. In P. Watzlawick (Ed.), *The invented reality* (pp. 41–61). New York: W. W. Norton.

von Glasersfeld, E. (1984). An introduction to radical constructivism. In P. Watzlawick (Ed.), *The invented reality* (pp. 17–40). New York: W. W. Norton.

Welfel, E. R. (2002). Ethics in counseling *and psychotherapy: Standards, research, and emerging issues* (2nd ed.). Pacific Grove, CA: Brooks/Cole.

PART 3

Organizational and Administrative Issues

CHAPTER 7

Ethical Climate

Vilia M. Tarvydas • Barbara L. O'Rourke • Christine K. Urish

OBJECTIVES

After reading this chapter, you should be able to:

- Outline the concepts and elements of organizational culture and explain their effects on the ethical climate of an organization.
- Define *impaired professional* and describe the effects of impairment on professional practice.
- Explain counselor burnout, relate it to job stress, and describe the factors that may increase its incidence or assist in alleviating its detrimental effects.
- Describe professional boundary problems, the types of counselors who may be affected, and some strategies to limit potential problems with professional boundaries.
- Discuss the problems that accompany substance abuse among counselors.
- Explain mobbing behavior in the workplace and its effects on workers, its relationship to organizational characteristics, and ways to reduce its incidence.
- Discuss whistle-blowing and its consequences for the whistle-blower and others involved.

INTRODUCTION

Whether counselors realize it or not, they are profoundly influenced by the environments and work cultures in which they practice. If they are unaware of these influences, they are powerless to develop appropriate responses or strategies to respond intentionally to these work culture challenges or to draw upon the work culture's strengths. Work environments are cultures that create particular ethical climates that influence the quality of service provided to clients. Unethical individuals in the workplace have the ability to influence others to behave unethically, and vice versa.

Ivey (2003) asserted, "Intentionality is a core goal . . . [of effective counseling]" (p. 14). He stated the following:

> Intentionality is acting with a sense of capability and deciding from among a range of alternative actions. The intentional individual has more than one action, thought, or behavior to choose from in responding to changing life situations. The intentional individual can generate alternatives in a given situation and approach a problem from different vantage points, using a variety of skills and personal qualities, *adapting styles to suit different individuals and cultures.* (p. 14)

It is important to understand that an ethical perspective and process must also be skill based and intentional, or applied. Further, issues of morality and ethical decision making are ever present in the machinations of everyday counseling. Every counseling decision contains an ethical or moral aspect, and each of these decisions is embedded in an influencing context. To achieve a more complete approach to intentional counseling, counselors must be equally aware of and proactive about ethical choices in their communication techniques.

Research continues to explore significant factors that may influence counselors' degree of effectiveness in ethical decision making. Factors that have been examined include variables related to the individual counselor, such as moral orientation (Liddell, Halpin, & Halpin, 1992), the number and type of consulted relationships (Cottone, Tarvydas, & House, 1994), or level of ethics education (Tarvydas, 1994). Additionally, the effect of context-related factors on ethical decision making is being examined. The effect of working in a certain type of environment, such as within a school-based or health care team, or with particular people, such as individuals from numerous disciplines, may influence the ethics of practice. The need is great for ongoing research that will continue to identify, clarify, and define factors as they relate to sound, ethical decision making in counseling practice.

Applied ethics in counseling occurs within organizational or institutional settings; for example (a) hospitals, (b) community mental health centers, (c) small, mental health, private practice groups, (d) schools, (e) military settings, and (f) rehabilitation settings. An ethical or unethical climate has effects on the intentional ethical decision-making process of counselors. Counselors may face a significant environmental challenge by sharing a work environment with an unethical colleague.

ORGANIZATIONAL CULTURE

More and more, counseling occurs within the context of an organization or institution. To understand more clearly how ethical decision making can be affected by participation in an organizational setting, think of an organization as a type of culture. The use of a cultural perspective can help counselors realize the organization's complexity and the interaction between the characteristics of a setting as they influence decision making. This includes a need to understand the unique aspects of group or team experiences. The social, political, and cultural dynamics that occur in a larger organization, such as a hospital or managed care organization, also occur within smaller group settings such as a classroom within a school.

Culture

Conceptual models used to develop an understanding of multicultural and cross-cultural counseling suggest that counselors must fully examine the potential influence of their worldview upon their counseling practice (Ivey, 2003). Counselors must strive to understand how a developed worldview may influence (a) the decision making of members of any culture, (b) any individual who interacts with members of the culture, and (c) the effects of the interaction between an insider (a member of the culture) and an outsider. Multicultural models typically assume that the counselor is the outsider; however, the converse may also be true. If clients take an active decision-making role regarding their care within a health care team, or if students and their parents construct an education plan, the clients are working to gain acceptance within the team. The team is a cultural group with its own language and style of communicating. The client is the outsider and may feel very uncomfortable about this difference. Counselors' worldviews are shaped partially by their participation in a specific organizational culture. These worldviews may affect their decision making, including the ethical components of those decisions.

Schein (1990), an organizational psychologist, implied that a specified group of people who have had stability over time and a shared history of working together form a culture. The culture is what the group learns over a period of time in regard to problem solving. This type of learning is manifested as observable behaviors—ways of thinking about the world and ways of feeling. More specifically, Schein stated:

> Culture can [now] be defined as (a) a pattern of basic assumptions, (b) invented, discovered, or developed by a given group, (c) as it learns to cope with its problems of external adaptation and internal integration, (d) that has worked well enough to be considered valid, and therefore (e) is to be taught to new members as the (f) correct way to perceive, think, and feel in relation to those problems. (p. 111)

This description of a working culture clearly reflects experiences reported by counselors who have been part of a working group, whether on a school team with one or two members or on a larger team of health care workers. For example, a group of counselors assumes, based on recent complaints about services provided by one member of the group, that discussing appeal procedures with clients sets a tone that encourages client complaints. Consequently, the group falls into the practice of merely handing out the client rights brochure without discussing it further with the client. This practice becomes so routine that new staff members are told not to spend valuable time discussing appeal rights with clients. Over time, what effects will this change in the agency culture have on the atmosphere in the agency, on the counselor–client relationship, and on the rights of clients?

Any definable group with a shared history can have a culture within an organization. Therefore, an organization can have many subcultures. Specific units within an agency, or disciplines within the same organization, can have fully functioning subcultures complete with their own language and practices—and degrees of respect for ethical practice standards. They may also have their own set of ethical practice ideals and standards due to different ethical traditions, degrees of education, and exposure to ethical standards.

Ethics and Organizational Culture

Hospital-based practice is a specific type of organizational culture that generally manifests a model of practice reflected by a definable paradigm. The hospital practice model, typically known as the *medical model*, represents the organic paradigm (Cottone, 1992). This model is becoming increasingly prevalent in the behavioral health practices of counselors due to the influence of managed care on all mental health disciplines. The medical model culture is characterized as one in which the physician diagnoses and treats the disease of the client, and the client is relieved of blame. The role of the physician (expert) is often defined as autocratic. The role of both the client and the ancillary staff (including the counselor) is to trust and to cooperate with the physician (expert). The historical shaping of this paradigm was developed from the values and procedures of its religious and military roots. Historically, this paradigm contains a deference and deeply rooted respect for chain-of-command orders over and above individual beliefs. Therefore, this approach represents a parentalistic and hierarchically based framework that has potential for creating ethically based tension. The tension inherent in this culture is encountered when the "order" from the physician (expert) conflicts with the autonomous needs of the client or other caregivers.

Professional roles are constructed in response to institutional expectations and professional practices. Beauchamp and Childress (2001) stated that such roles also incorporate virtues and obligations. Roles encompass social expectations as well as standards and ideals. The hospital culture is an example of an environment or context with definitive ideas about how the helping process should occur.

CASE SCENARIO 7–1

A Cultural Setting

A rehabilitation counselor is asked by a client to represent her at a rehabilitation residential care treatment center's interdisciplinary team meeting. The client's desire is to remain in the center until she feels more able to manage her own care. After careful assessment, the counselor concurs with the client that a delayed discharge would be in her best interest. The client's psychiatrist orders that the client be prepared for discharge immediately. The implicit rule of the organization is that clients belong to the doctors and that the center and its staff are only assisting the physicians in the care of their clients. Dissenting opinions at team meetings are strongly discouraged due to their historically fruitless outcomes and the time they take from the staff. Should the counselor persist in forwarding the desire of the client? How?

YES. Ethical standards in counseling clearly define counselors' obligations to their clients, and the rehabilitation counselor's code of ethics also requires that the counselor assist clients in advocating for their needs and rights (CRCC, 2001). Further, collaboration is considered a necessary condition for ethical decision making.

Political and moral or ethical problems will arise and persist as long as some professionals make the decisions and order their implementation by others who have not participated in the decision making. Beauchamp and Childress (2001) pointed out that these conflicts are avoidable but must be anticipated and prevented by establishing practices that honor open and collaborative decision making. Obligations of fidelity must be made clear; open routes to collegial dialogue must be valued. If this is not the case, Beauchamp and Childress warned that compassion, although cherished as a core virtue, can cloud judgment and work against rational and effective decision making. Based on the levels of organizational practice discussed in Tarvydas and Cottone (1991), a useful, ethical decision-making model for use in the larger organizational context is provided in Chapter 6. Given guidelines such as those provided in this model, decision making that involves complexity and conflict can be broken down into manageable tasks that help facilitate collaborative discussion among all rightful parties.

The setting, including the people with whom counselors work, significantly influences ethical decision making. Doherty (1995) summarized this point well:

Unsupportive and alienating work settings inevitably affect therapists' ability to care, especially for difficult clients at the end of a long workday or workweek.

Having our work undermined by other professionals in positions of greater institutional power erodes motivation and investment in clinical care. Seeing too many clients during a workweek does the same, as does having to fit the client's needs to the rigidly enforced restrictions of managed care contracts. Therapists start to go through the motions, it shows, and we know it. We become negative about our clients, we hope for no-shows and cancellations, our natural caring declines, and our ethical caring begins to feel like martyrdom. When such conditions arise, it is time to change the context or get out, in my view, because we cannot sustain the fundamental virtue of caring. (p. 13)

Clearly, the work setting, whether it is an informal group or a more formal organizational structure, influences counselors' decision-making processes significantly.

ORGANIZATIONAL CLIMATE

Several authors have suggested that an organizational climate is the outward manifestation of its culture (Mohan, 1993; Schein, 1990). Climate is a metaphor that suggests an image wherein the environment, as the sum total of energy, presents atmospheric conditions as a type of aura. These conditions hold, support, create, and sustain the type of ethical decision making that occurs. An awareness of these conditions is particularly important when counselors confront a decision with an emotional component, such as one that presents an ethical dilemma. Using the atmospheric conditions of our weather example, the climate may be fair or stormy. Bellah, Madson, Sullivan, Swidler, and Tipton (1985) described this phenomenon as our *moral ecology.*

Organizational climate is how people characterize a system's practices and procedures, such as the sense of safety or fear of retribution that a counselor may feel when faced with big or small decisions within this context. Therefore, the concept of organizational climate—more specifically, the ethical climate—is one level of analysis that can help us understand and explain moral behavior as it is observed. An **ethical climate,** one facet of an organizational climate, describes the shared perceptions that colleagues hold concerning ethical procedures and practices within an organization. It upholds or erodes virtues such as compassion, discernment, truthfulness, and integrity.

The individual and organizational variables that contribute to the ethicality of the climate are complex and multilayered (Tarvydas & Cottone, 1991). The decision maker is faced with individual, client, team,

and organizationally contingent factors that must be considered. For example, decisions within an organization are often made by teams or groups rather than by individuals. Such decisions affect the workings of a team or group within the organization significantly. A growing body of literature is examining the dynamics inherent in team-based, ethical decision making (Agich, 1982; Klebe-Trevino, 1986; O'Rourke, 1996). A basic understanding of some of the identified variables, both for the individual and for the team, is essential to intentional ethical counseling within an organizational setting.

Two basic individual skills have been identified as essential to the collaborative process: (a) the ability to assert one's thoughts and ideas, and (b) the ability to clarify the content of others' contributions to the decision-making process (Weiss & Davis, 1985). These basic skills are useful in any decision-making process involving two or more individuals and are particularly important in a hierarchically structured context wherein one person has more power than others.

Given the potential inequities and complexities inherent in making team-based decisions, it is essential that a working team establish a due process in a particular form for its decision-making practices. The mechanism of such a due process must be sensitive to multiple disciplinary perspectives and cultural gender differences and must be able to facilitate the production of a group decision. Constructing a useful process that is both efficient and equitable is a complex task. For example, the following questions may arise: How do we proceed if a particular professional disagrees with a team decision? Is team consensus necessary to adopt a decision? How do we provide client confidentiality when decisions made about the client occur within a larger organization that has nonprofessional support staff and reporting or billing requirements? What is an appropriate appeals process that is truly accessible to clients? Like the construction of a group culture in group counseling that has established normative behavior, the working relationship of a team develops over time and must be shaped proactively from its beginning.

CASE SCENARIO 7–2

Confidentiality

A school counselor is working with a young woman who has had numerous behavioral problems, including shoplifting. The student has demonstrated significant improvement during the last semester in both her motivation toward school and in her social behavior. Trust was difficult to establish between the girl and her counselor, but they have developed a working relationship. During the annual Individualized Educational Plan meeting, one of the girl's teachers suggested that the student might benefit from having a job. There is an opening in the lost-and-found department of the school office. Should the counselor tell the team, which includes the student's mother, that she has concerns about the student's current ability to handle other people's property? What could this disclosure do to the trust that has been built with the client? Should the counselor voice her concerns? How would your thinking change if the organizational climate were a public school? A conservative religious school?

PROBABLY YES. The counselor has a responsibility to support the young woman and help her achieve her counseling goal of avoiding behavioral problems such as stealing. Allowing her to be placed prematurely in a setting that exposes her to overwhelming triggers for stealing behavior would present considerable therapeutic risk. Another concern involves the degree to which the team understands the critical importance of confidentiality and the team's shared responsibility for assisting the student's progress toward dealing with her behavioral problems. The team's opinions may be influenced by their personal and professional perspectives. It is possible that those might be influenced by or consistent with the position taken by the school administration in a religiously conservative school. The counselor must be an active participant in setting the climate for these team responsibilities and may have to engage in tactful, active teaching or reminders. This sets the stage for any appropriate client disclosures. If the team is truly to function as a treatment team, important observations should be shared—but with the shared responsibility to assure that the student's trust and confidentiality are not violated.

Lastly, but most importantly, the integrity of the student must be respected. The counselor must gain the student's permission (and even direct participation) in bringing this concern to the team and her mother. Her ability to directly evaluate the risk to herself and bring the issue to the team might have significant therapeutic benefits. At the outset of counseling, the student should have been informed that information and counselor judgments integral to her case would be shared with the treatment team, thus setting the stage for this discussion. If the student is reluctant and the counselor still thinks the opinion must be shared, the counselor should at least discuss her reasons for the disclosure and its perceived benefits and risks with the student before the team meeting.

Accountability to the Organization

The nature of the counseling environment plays a significant role in counselors' decision-making processes. Ethical standards mandate that counselors are accountable to both their clients and to the organizations in which they work. As a result, it is ethically sound practice for

counselors to explore fully and to commit to the mission and standards of practice of any organizations for which they work. Conversely, it is the organization's ethical obligation to fully disclose all relevant information about its mission and practices, including its provision of due process for resolution of conflicts with employees. Counselors who accept a position with an organization enter into a tacit agreement with that organization to honor its values and standards of practice. At the same time, counselors have an obligation to honor their professional code of ethics. Intentional practice is served by having a preexisting plan to resolve any conflicts between organizational and professional obligations. Institutions have attempted to be more intentional by constructing mechanisms to provide due process through working ethics committees and the use of case consultation meetings. Again, the Tarvydas and Cottone decisional models described in Chapter 6 are useful tools for any individual counselor seeking to reconcile professional and institutional aspects of ethical dilemmas.

Consider the effect of a specific, overarching philosophy that creates a hospital's climate, such as a religious affiliation. Clinical decisions concerning use of client service options, such as provision of pregnancy termination and birth control or withdrawal of nutrition and hydration from a client in a persistent vegetative state, become enmeshed in the ethical value climate of that particular institution. Extend this consideration to a school environment, such as a controversy in providing a support group for gay, lesbian, and bisexual students in a high school. An institution's values and moral orientation are often the overriding aspect of the concerns involved in these situations.

Organizational values and morality subsequently influence the ethical decision-making processes of members. This force is particularly evident when moral obligations and religious standards are in conflict with an institution's espoused ethical practices.

CASE SCENARIO 7–3

Accountability

A counselor is working with a client who has been treated for depression at a local Catholic mental health outpatient clinic. During the course of her treatment, the client disclosed that she had been raped several weeks earlier but is otherwise not sexually active. A pregnancy test reveals that she is pregnant. She is requesting information from the counselor about obtaining a therapeutic abortion. Should the counselor engage in a dialogue about this issue with the client, given that it is strictly forbidden by institutional values?

YES. As part of informed consent, the counselor must inform the client about the limits of their relationship and offer to help her identify her alternatives.

Climate Factors and Ethical Decisions

Factors in the work environment that influence the ethical decision-making climate of service organizations include the organization's socialization practices, interpersonal relationships with significant others in the workplace (peers and superiors), role perceptions, and individual levels of development of the service providers. Research has examined specific elements of an organizational environment that have shown influence on the ethical behavior of employees. These factors include (a) structure (centralized versus participatory management), (b) ethical climate (reinforceable values; e.g., beneficence), (c) task dimensions, (d) influence of significant others in the environment, (e) role perceptions, and (f) levels of personal development of the individual service provider (Wiles, 1993). These elements include the influence of significant others such as peers and superiors, the opportunity to behave ethically as guided by a code of ethics, and the use of rewards and punishments for both ethical and unethical behavior. Wiles reviewed the ethical climate literature and found that organizationally based ethics decision-making models include 11 specific factors, as noted in Figure 7–1.

Clearly, an ethical climate is a product of the interaction among the institution, the individual counselor, and numerous contributing influences from both sources. The ACA Code of Ethics recognizes these influences and clearly defines standards of practice regarding personnel administration. It is the responsibility of the individual counselor to address some of these influences before making a working covenant with the institution.

The remainder of this chapter examines factors related to the influence of significant individuals within counselors' work environments who may have been unethical in their behavior or impaired in their ability to practice.

IMPAIRED PROFESSIONALS

The impairment of professionals' ability to function in their professional roles is a growing concern in U.S. society. The term impairment should not be seen as being judgmental. Rather, it is a technical term that objectively describes the individual's ability to function

1. Environmental factors (external forces)
2. Organizational factors (organizational culture; organizational socialization; characteristics of the job/task; significant others in the organization)
3. Opportunity and situational factors
4. Individual factors (personal values; societal and familial socialization experiences; ego strength; locus of control; field dependence; personal knowledge and attitudes; age; education; gender; job tenure)
5. Stage of moral development
6. Characteristics of the moral issue
7. Recognition of the moral issue (moral sensitivity)
8. Moral evaluation (includes moral philosophy, ethical decision ideology, and phased decision process)
9. Intentions
10. Behavior
11. Evaluation of the behavior (ability to self-reflect)

FIGURE 7–1. Factors in Organizational Climates That Affect Individual Decision Making
Source: From "Socialization and Interpersonal Influence on Ethical Decision-Making Climate in Service Organizations" by J. Wiles, 1993, unpublished dissertation. Memphis, TN: University of Memphis.

and is distinct from a disability. A **disability** is an identifiable condition that may be stable and whose functional limitations, when manifested, are recognized and often overcome with appropriate changes, assistance, or accommodations. In contrast, an **impairment** is often a gradually recognized condition that manifests when an individual attempts to perform some activity. It is not immediately obvious and involves a level of diminished function (obtained by documented evidence). Impairments may be manifested on a continuum by varying degrees of loss of optimal function and can have many causes. A person with a disability may also become impaired, given this perspective. In fact, all counselors (as well as all people) are impaired to some degree at some time in their practice. Impairment may be the result of having a headache or the flu. The more dysfunctional and pervasive impairments that can disrupt professional performance typically include unrecognized or untreated chronic physical illness, substance abuse, and emotional or psychological factors such as burnout and sexual acting-out behaviors, Lamb, Cochran, and Jackson (1991) defined impairment broadly as it is applied to psychology interns in the following way:

An interference in professional functioning that is reflected in one or more of the following ways: (a) an inability or unwillingness to acquire and integrate professional standards into one's repertoire of professional behavior; (b) an inability to acquire professional skills and reach an accepted level. (p. 293)

Ethically, professional impairment is a matter of concern when it leads to a decreased level of professional competence. The term can be applied to people in various professional roles, including those of student, counselor, intern, supervisee, and supervisor. A retrospective study of the treatment records of 334 health professionals over 15 years examined the profiles of those who had sought treatment or evaluation for a professional impairment. Findings indicated the three most common problems leading to referral were: suicidal behavior, marital problems, and work problems. Further concerns identified in the study (in descending order of frequency) were boundary violations, alcohol and drug abuse, anger management,

and psychotic behavior (Katsavdakis, Gabbard, & Athey, 2004). Three of the more common issues related to the development of specific professional impairments are (a) burnout and job stress, (b) violation of professional boundaries, and (c) substance abuse. (See Box 7–1.)

Counselors who continue to provide professional services while impaired may be in violation of their ethical code. A counselor who is aware that a colleague or student is providing unethical services but fails to intervene may also be behaving unethically due to failure to address this issue. This failure to act may detract from the quality of client care or actually result in harm to a client.

Awareness that includes a working knowledge of practice standards and sensitivity to violation of these standards is key to ethical behavior. The impaired professional often provides clues over time that a pattern

---

Box 7–1 • Exploring the Code

Examine the current ACA and APA codes of ethics to learn about the ethical obligations that are part of the counselor's interpersonal professional environment.

What does the code of ethics say about therapist–client relationships after therapy has ended? Can they occur? When?

What should a professional do according to the code of ethics if they feel a colleague is impaired? Does the code define impairment? How does this relate to professional competence?

If a counselor is feeling as if they are burned out, what does the code state regarding monitoring their effectiveness? Does this relate to the subject of counselor burnout?

A counselor is supervising a student and suspects the student is impaired. Does the code offer guidance as to how the counselor should proceed with this student? Should they contact the educational program? Serve as the student's therapist? Both? Neither?

A supervisor of a large counseling agency suspects a counselor (one of their subordinates) of engaging in fraudulent behavior regarding billing practices. The supervisor confronts the counselor, who denies any wrongdoing. Who is the supervisor responsible to—the counseling agency, the clients this counselor is serving, the insurance companies to whom the fraudulent billing has occurred? What guidance does the code offer to this situation?

As a supervisor at a large counseling agency, you are responsible for the supervision of many counselors. Several counselors suspect a colleague is pursuing an inap-

propriate relationship with a client. You encourage them to confront their colleague, which they are unwilling to do. You begin to pay closer attention to this colleague and become aware that not only is he pursuing an intimate relationship with a client, but alcohol use (coming to work with alcohol on breath after lunch) has become an issue as well. You meet with this counselor and advise him that he must modify his behavior or his position will be terminated with the agency. You encourage this individual to seek counseling as a condition of maintaining employment. Is there anything else that you as the supervisor should do in this situation? Contact the licensing board regarding the staff member's behavior? Contact the ACA? What would you do?

Your colleague has confided in you that she is experiencing marital difficulties. These difficulties are significant and include a custody battle over her children. As a result, the counselor is frequently out of the office without authorization, misses appointments, and is behind in her documentation. Her caseload consists of individuals who have experienced work-related injuries. She has one client who, in addition to a crush injury to their hand, also has an Axis II diagnosis of borderline personality disorder. The counselor confides in you that she is being called into court and her records are being questioned with this particular client. The counselor reports to you that she has not kept up on her documentation due to what she calls excessive demands on her time. Do you feel that she is an impaired professional? How do you know? What would you do?

of problem behavior exists. Typically, the unethical behavior of an impaired colleague is not an isolated occurrence. For example, it is not difficult to imagine a colleague who comes in late frequently, is irritable with other staff members, and often cuts client sessions short. After some time, you and your colleagues are shocked, but not surprised, to discover that the supervisor has found this colleague has not been staying current with his charting and has even falsified some of these documents. Worse yet, there is speculation that he has been seeing one of his clients socially after work.

BURNOUT AND JOB STRESS

According to Skorupa and Agresti (1993), **burnout** is an emotional exhaustion in which the professional no longer has positive feelings, sympathy, or respect for clients. It is often associated with fatigue, frustration, and apathy that result from prolonged stress and overwork. Burnout is thought to have three distinct factors: (a) emotional exhaustion, including feeling emotionally overextended with work; (b) depersonalization, including having unfeeling or impersonal reactions to clients; and (c) a lack of personal accomplishment or feeling incompetent at your work (Maslach & Jackson, 1986).

Counseling and the work done in the helping and mental health professions are significantly stressful by their very nature. Counselors work to help clients in very intimate and personal ways. However, they work with clients whom they cannot and should not control and within institutions and financial and practical constraints over which they have similarly little control. These conditions create uncertainty and lack of control and often are coupled with witnessing the emotional ups and downs of clients' lives as well as working within crisis or traumatic situations. All counselors at some time experience some degree of the signs of burnout. Studies reviewed by Welfel (2002) have shown that about "1 to 5% of those sampled suffer from a full syndrome of burnout, but approximately one-third of the counselors scored high in emotional exhaustion in a number of these studies" (p. 59).

Burnout should be differentiated from *job stress*. Stadler (1990) noted that "impaired counselors have lost the ability to transcend stressful events" (p. 178). Not all stress is negative or rises to the level that it seriously affects the function of the individuals experiencing it. In fact, stress can be positive and, in its most basic sense, is the individual's reaction to challenges and changes. It can mobilize, focus, and energize the

individual's work and responses, hopefully leading to the satisfaction of a job well done or a difficult challenge resolved positively. There are quite a number of resources that counselors can use to enhance their personal and professional well-being in dealing with job stress and preventing burnout. Research has shown that some personal characteristics cast a protective influence over distress. For example, research has shown that for some individuals, the quality of personality hardiness can interrupt the stress-exhaustion process (Maddi & Kobasa, 1984). Nevertheless, preventative steps are important for the well-being of all helping professionals, either to increase their quality of life or to prevent some serious, negative reaction. Brems (2000) provided a personal and professional self-care plan for counselors, whether they are novices or seasoned professionals. She provided detailed information about the following self-care skills:

Professional Self-Care Skills

- Continuing education
- Consultation and supervision
- Networking
- Stress management strategies

Personal Self-Care Skills

- Healthy personal habits
- Attention to relationships
- Recreational activities
- Relaxation and centeredness
- Self-exploration and awareness

Studies suggest that certain client factors may contribute to therapist burnout. Among these are the number of contact hours with clients and the number of clients in a caseload that present with pervasive stressful behavior, such as aggression or limit testing (Hellman, 1986). These factors are of concern in the increasingly dominant environment of managed care. Interestingly, therapists who work in agency settings were more prone to burnout than those working in private settings (Hellman, 1986). These data indicate the importance of climate conditions on an individual. Implications for ethical practice may include (a) setting limits on the size of a caseload, (b) acknowledging a duty to understand the process of burnout and prevention techniques, (c) conducting research to determine how work settings can affect counselors, and (d) mediating untoward effects of workplace stress on the work of counselors.

CASE SCENARIO 7–4

Burnout?

A social worker with many years of experience is working as your colleague and mentor. You notice that she has become increasingly judgmental. She becomes anxious and rejects her clients when they start to place demands on her or when they "don't do what is good for them." You understand her job-related stresses: All of you are expected to take more and more clients, do more documentation of services, and are no longer offered overtime pay. What strategies can you offer your colleague to help her deal with this situation? Is her behavior severe enough to constitute burnout? Impairment?

YES AND NO. Yes, certainly these are signs of counselor fatigue and high levels of job stress. However, impairment is present only if your colleague's judgmental attitudes influence her actual practice. Approach her as a concerned colleague and remind her of the importance of managing her job-related stress. Support her in identifying and practicing strategies to increase her levels of personal and professional wellness. When you discover she wants to learn some stress management techniques, you invite her to join your evening meditation class at the Yoga Center.

PROFESSIONAL BOUNDARIES

Professionals who transgress boundaries with clients, students, or participants in research may be violating clearly stated ethical standards related to detrimental counselor–client relationships (basic concepts related to detrimental counselor–client relationships were discussed in Chapter 3). Supervisors and educators also have responsibilities to avoid conflicting relationships that are detrimental to their supervisees and students (see Chapter 19). Schoener (1995) described the types of individuals who may become boundary violators and might be more likely to be involved in such relationships. These six traits are: (1) psychotic and severe borderline disorders, (2) manic disorders, (3) impulse control disorders, (4) chronic neurosis and isolation, (5) situational offenders, and (6) deficits due to naivete (see Figure 7–2).

Treatment boundaries are defined and established by the professional to promote a trusting relationship and facilitate an effective therapeutic working alliance. Professional boundaries may include limitations about such relationship factors as: establishing fee structure for services, time and session length, personal disclosure, limits of touch, and the general tone of the professional relationship (The College of Psychologists of Ontario, 1998). Boundary problems and sexual misconduct rank the highest next to suicide as the reasons

1. Psychotic individuals. These professionals have difficulties with boundaries due to delusional thoughts.
2. Antisocial, narcissistic, and borderline traits. These individuals may appear high functioning on the surface but have the need for control and manipulation in relationships. These individuals may engage in exploitive behavior in relationships.
3. Chronic neurotic or character-disordered individuals. These individuals are susceptible to "lovesickness". These are socially isolated individuals who have significant emotional needs that are met through relationships with clients.
4. Individuals experiencing life crises. This can include individuals at midlife or late life and new clinicians. This can include life illness in the clinician as well.
5. Individuals experiencing life changes. Life transitions, including retirement or job change (promotion/loss) can make a clinician susceptible to boundary violations.

FIGURE 7–2. Predictive Features of Potential Boundary Violators

Adapted from: From "Boundary Violations and Personality Traits Among Psychiatrists." by P.E. Garfinkle, R.M. Bagby, E.M. Waring, B. Dorian, 1997, *Canadian Journal of Psychiatry, 43,* 758–763; and from "This Couldn't Happen to Me: Boundary Problems and Sexual Misconduct in the Psychotherapy Relationship." by D.M. Norris, T.G. Gutheil, L.H. Strasburger, 2003, *Psychiatric Services, 54*(4), 517–522.

for malpractice claims against mental health providers (Norris, Gutheil, & Strasburger, 2003).

Counselors should evaluate whether their current situations place them at risk for a boundary violation and keep these factors in mind as they proceed in professional practice. For example, life crises during midlife and late life appear as common precipitants in boundary violations with clients. Of course, early career practitioners are not immune from boundary violations; they may face such problems as developing their practices, feeling an excessive need to please clients, and balancing the demands of their professional and home lives. In general, counselors must be aware that life crises such as anxieties about aging, career disappointments, unfulfilled hopes, and marital conflicts can lead to boundary violations (Norris et al., 2003). Additionally, normal life transitions such as retirement and job change (e.g., promotion or job loss) can make the counselor susceptible to boundary violations. Financial stresses such as working in managed care, envy of client wealth, greed, and financial exploitation may be so significant for some professionals that financial boundary violations begin to outnumber sexual boundary violations. Illnesses of practitioners also place them at risk for boundary violations, because they may turn to the client inappropriately for solace and support, or clinician loneliness may lead to an impulse to confide in clients. Clinicians always should exercise caution in the area of personal self-disclosures, as they can lead to clinician confusion and uncertainty (Norris et al.).

The most common misconception in the area of boundary violations is "It couldn't happen to me" (Norris et al., 2003). Examine your own boundary awareness by doing the activities in Figure 7–3. Adequate educational opportunities to explore these issues and quality supervision are essential to their practice.

CASE SCENARIO 7–5

Boundary Issues

Last semester, as a graduate assistant, you were supervising a student on a project that reflects your own interests. You met outside of your scheduled supervisory hour on several occasions and began to know more about each other's personal lives. You really like this student and want to see him succeed. You have just received your class list for the course you are teaching next semester. This student's name is on the list. Do you have any ethical concerns? What actions can you take to ensure that you and the student remain ethical?

YES. Your friendship with this student has the potential either to make objective judgment difficult or to create the appearance of unfairness in the minds of other students. Raise this issue with both the student and the supervising faculty member so that alternate arrangements might be discussed, such as transfer of yourself or the student to another section. It might be possible for the student to continue in your class if you end your social relationship and arrange for more intense faculty review of your grading.

It is natural for counselors to be attracted to clients or to like their company at times. This reaction is not unusual in professionals who are highly interested in people and are motivated to help them. Some basic practices assist counselors in avoiding poor habits or patterns that may gradually facilitate boundary-violating behaviors. Counselors should try to adopt the following practices, which will provide client-centered care and maintain professionalism:

1. Provide individual care—Show compassion, meet the client's needs, and show interest in the client but do not promote or encourage a relationship that leads to dependence. Be mindful of cultural and ethnic characteristics.
2. Use good communication skills—Watch the level of disclosure (remember who is giving and who is receiving therapy!), ask colleagues for feedback, and seek feedback from an objective party.
3. Monitor physical boundaries—Watch clothing selection, watch type of touch (therapeutic touch versus sexual touch), and avoid potentially detrimental relationships.
4. Maintain emotional-psychological boundaries—Avoid enmeshment, power/control issues, and affection. Solve problems with the patient, not for the patient.
5. Remember your code of ethics—Above all, keep in mind that you are a professional who provides a professional service, and keep the focus of therapy as such.

Agencies can assist counselors in maintaining appropriate boundaries by developing an appropriate organizational climate through policy development. Policies that reinforce appropriate professional boundaries through proactive actions in hiring, the development of personnel policies, staff performance review, and staff education are important in setting the right climate (Sheets, 2001). In the hiring process employers may ask about past employment termination, ethical complaints, licensure complaints, or investigations of unprofessional conduct. Employers are directed to contact regulatory boards to verify credentials and history. Further, employers are directed to obtain written authorization from the potential employee to obtain references from previous employers and supervisors. Personnel policies should include new employee review and sign-off on relevant codes of ethics prior to beginning service within the agency. The agency should have in place specific and well-outlined processes for review of unprofessional conduct complaints. These policies should address confidentiality of information and due process. Staff performance reviews should address issues of professional accountability as well as boundary issues. The culture of the organization should expect employees to demonstrate competence and value personal accountability and constructive feedback among all staff members. Staff education should include new employee orientation with direct attention paid to reviewing relevant codes of ethics and a frank discussion of professional boundary issues. Ongoing employee education should consider professional boundaries as an annual topic at the

---

Activity 1: Identifying Boundary Crossings

Place a checkmark on the line if you feel that the behavior described in the statement is crossing a professional boundary. After you complete the checklist on your own, discuss your opinions with your classmates. Use the discussion points that follow to add others' perspectives to your thinking.

1. _____ You are spending a disproportionate amount of time with one client.
2. _____ You feel that you are the only one who "really understands" the client.
3. _____ A client's significant other brings treats such as cinnamon rolls, garden produce, and cookies to you on a regular basis.
4. _____ You tend to keep secrets with a client or make special plans.
5. _____ You are guarded or defensive when questioned about your interactions or relationship with a client.
6. _____ A client requests that you discuss with her your hospitalization for depression. You spend 30 minutes of the therapy session sharing your experience.
7. _____ You ask a client for personal advice in an area in which she is an expert (car dealer, financial planning).
8. _____ Your client wants to introduce her daughter to your son for the purpose of a social relationship.
9. _____ About 6 months after you have counseled a client, she asks you for a date to which you consent. On your first date, she makes sexual advances that you give in to.
10. _____ You give a client a ride home after her counseling session.
11. _____ Your client pages you to discuss bringing lunch to her home at her expense prior to a home therapy or case management session.

Discussion Points

1. You need to watch the amount of time you spend with your clients. You do not want to make clients overdependent on you. Meet their needs, but do not foster detrimental dependence.
2. You are not the only person who understands the client. This type of attitude can also foster detrimental dependence.
3. In this situation, you would be well advised to understand the facility/agency policy regarding accepting gifts. If the policy OKs accepting food from clients and family, share the gifts with other staff and other clients if possible. If other clients observe the gift giving, they may fear a lower level of care unless they, too, bring gifts. Also, evaluate the possible role of the client's cultural background in offering gifts. Make all reasonable attempts to be sensitive to traditions. Acknowledge the gift but do not make it the center of attention. Treat the gift giving in a culturally appropriate manner (if relevant in the situation). If your facility does not allow gift giving, graciously decline the gift and offer the family another option, such as donating the food to a homeless shelter or battered women's shelter.
4. Keeping secrets or making special plans with a client is not viewed as therapeutic. Your fellow clinicians may consider this behavior devious and deceitful.
5. Why are you so defensive? If you have nothing to hide, why the defensiveness? You need to check this out for yourself.
6. Who is giving and who is receiving therapy? Always be mindful of your role—meeting the client's needs, not the client meeting your needs.
7. Again, as in #6, who is giving and who is receiving therapy? You can generalize about the client's occupation and needs as they relate to therapy, but do not ask for or receive advice specifically for yourself at the client's expense.
8. This may be considered breaking a professional boundary and does not relate to therapy goals.
9. You are placing yourself in serious risk of a detrimental counselor–client relationship. What is your role? It is not that of the client's friend. Participating in a social relationship may be considered a boundary violation.
10. Is this part of your job description? In some places, counselors may transport clients in agency vehicles; however, if this is not a part of your job description, you need to consider the numerous liability issues that can arise.
11. Is one of your therapy goals lunch preparation or teaching/reinforcing independent living skills? If so, you need to plan ahead and work with the client. The client should not be buying your meal. If you do get the lunch, how will you bill for the services provided? You can't bill for eating with your client. What are the client's needs and goals for therapy?

continued

FIGURE 7–3. Boundary Awareness Activities

Activity 2: Test Your Boundary Awareness

Be prepared—your clients may make statements to you like those that follow. Pair up with another student and take turns role-playing counselor and client. The client starts out the interchange with one of the following client statements. After about 2 or 3 minutes of mock dialogue, discuss with your partner how each of you felt and the reactions each of you had during this interchange. Make a particular effort to talk about what conditions might make you, as the counselor, vulnerable to responding in an unprofessional manner and what you, as the client, might be seeking in these interchanges.

My doctor never talks to me!
Have you ever been depressed?
You make me mad.
I want to talk to your supervisor!
Is my case manager any good?
Do you go to church?
You were rude to me, I want another therapist!
You are not helping me!
Will you go to dinner with me?
I hate going to physical therapy.
You are the only person who understands me!
You don't understand me, you've never had cancer!

FIGURE 7–3.   Boundary Awareness Activities—*continued*

minimum. Special educational sessions may be held by supervisory staff following an incident of professional misconduct to assist the staff in learning from the experience (Sheets, 2001).

SUBSTANCE ABUSE

Although the etiology of substance dependence and abuse is varied, preexisting faulty coping mechanisms and certain predictive behaviors seem to precede professional impairment. Knowledge of risk factors related to chemical dependency can aid in early recognition and intervention. The following etiologic factors have been consistently cited in the literature: (a) genetic predisposition, (b) poor coping skills, (c) lack of education about impairment, (d) absence of effective prevention strategies, (e) drug and alcohol availability, (f) the context of a permissive environment, and (g) denial.

Ironically, as with any lethal malady, early diagnosis and intervention are critical, but the hallmark of chemical dependency continues to be denial. Waiting for spontaneous insight from an affected colleague is unconscionable—and unethical. Although the workplace is often the last area to be affected, professional competence is affected adversely. Barriers to early recognition of the chemical dependency of a colleague include (a) lack of training in recognition of early signs of abuse, (b) the insidious and confusing effect of the disease's progression on daily function that lends to signs that are easily rationalized away, and (c) the subsequent denial of both the impaired professional and the individual's colleagues.

The task of differentiating impairment from problematic behaviors is difficult. Acting on the conclusion that impairment is imminent is even more difficult. Relatively few counselors have received training in this area. The literature (Skorina, DeSoto, & Bissell, 1990) suggests that counselors tend to underestimate or fail to recognize impairment in colleagues. Therefore, intervention, and the colleague's recovery, may be delayed.

Suggestions for dealing intentionally with potential impairment among one's peers include primary, secondary, and tertiary levels of intervention based on the timing and need of the situation. Primary interventions include involvement in educational programs (e.g., graduate education or in-service programs). These educational programs provide (a) values clarification regarding impairment and the individual conditions that often cause the impairment (e.g., adopting an attitude of assistance and compassion versus one of blame); (b) knowledge of potential signs of impending impairment for each condition; and (c) enactment of prevention strategies that address each area of potential impairment (both individually and institutionally). Secondary interventions include the establishment and knowledge of sound practice standards. These standards include steps to obtain due process for both the individual who may be impaired as well as the individual's colleagues. Tertiary intervention involves understanding and involving the necessary resources to make a direct intervention with an impaired colleague.

CASE SCENARIO 7–6

Substance Abuse

The medical director of the treatment center where you work as a chemical dependency counselor has started to miss the morning staff meetings fairly regularly. He always has a rational explanation. Two weeks ago, an evening nurse confided in you that she thought she smelled alcohol on the doctor's breath as he attended to a client. Is this enough evidence to initiate an intervention with the physician?

NO. Impairment requires the documentation of significantly impaired function. However, there is enough evidence to discuss your concerns with the physician.

MOBBING

In the past decade, the concept of emotional abuse in the workplace began to be recognized, discussed, and treated in the United States. Increased numbers of high-profile, shocking incidents of violence in schools and the workplace caused scholars to consider factors that create negative, and sometimes unbearable, forces acting on individuals. Counselors and the settings in which they work are not immune to these forces. A recent text by Davenport, Distler Schwartz, and Pursell Elliott (1999) described **mobbing** as "workplace expulsion through emotional abuse" (p. 20). These authors noted that the term was derived from its root word, mob, meaning a disorderly crowd engaged in lawless violence. The first use of this term, as applied to human behavior, occurred in the 1960s by an Austrian ethnologist, Konrad Lorenz. Lorenz (1966) described human behavior as being similar to the behavior that animals show in scaring away an enemy.

Later, Heinesmann (1972), a Swedish physician, researched similar behavior among children that has subsequently been labeled *bullying.* His early work, *Mobbing: Group Violence Among Children,* was published in Sweden in 1972. Until 1982, this concept was used exclusively in the study of children. Leymann (1996) then used the term mobbing to describe similar violence among adults in the workplace. He found that work cultures created circumstances wherein marked individuals were labeled as difficult and pushed to the margins of the workgroup culture. Leymann's work has generated much interest in Europe.

According to Davenport et al. (1999), mobbing is an emotional assault that targets an individual via two types of hurtful conduct from work colleagues. One type of misconduct is overt and is considered to be active aggression. The other involves passive tactics that are more covert and often disguised between acts of occasional kindness. Mobbing is a process that happens insidiously over time. Leymann (1996) distinguished five phases in this process: conflict, aggressive acts, management involvement, branding (as "difficult" or "mentally ill"), and expulsion. Other terms have been used for these phenomena: bullying, workplace trauma, harassment, and emotional abuse in the workplace (Keashly, 1998). The unsent letter of a clinician who experienced mobbing to her supervisor provides a poignant picture of the very real and painful effects of this all-too-common phenomenon (see Box 7–2).

Mobbing is the process of an emotional assault (Davenport et al., 1999) that often begins with passive, insidious marking of an individual as a threat to the norms of the organizational culture. The mobbing process is like the process of marking among people with disabilities that has been so well described by Jones et al. (1984) in their classic text, *Social Stigma: The Psychology of Marked Relationships.* This stigmatizing process is always relational. In the classic case, the process begins when an individual's flaw or mark of deviance initiates a pronounced attribution process. The process of attributing certain negative characteristics to the person results in an attack on the person's basic integrity and often results in hostile rejection. The outcome is not necessarily based on who the person actually is, but whom the person may represent to the organizational culture. For example, a counseling intern frequently asks pointed questions about the billing practices of the supervisor and the other counselors in the agency. This intern may eventually be ostracized by all of the counselors as someone who is "holier than thou" and has no potential for the "real" work of counseling.

A distinguishable characteristic of mobbing is the organizational collusion that typically supports this insidious process. Davenport et al. (1999) identified organizational elements that make a working environment vulnerable to participation in mobbing: bad management (e.g., excessive bottom-line orientation at the expense of human resources), stress-intensive workplace, monotony, disbelief or denial by managers, unethical activities, flat organizations, and

Box 7–2   •   The Unmailed Plea: Mobbing Can Kill You

The following is a letter I would very much like to give to the director of this agency's clinical operations but to date have not decided if I could withstand the consequences.

As this may appear in a textbook, I have altered all proper noun identifiers, as well as the location of the agency, not because I do not want readers to know what has happened to me and where, but because I am still employed by this agency's call center and cannot afford to lose my job or be sued.

To: Ms. CA, Clinical Director
CounselingCare Agency

From: MW, Crisis Care Specialist

Up to and including today, I have worked 8 consecutive years at CounselingCare. During this time I have labored to build trust and a good working relationship with employees from many different departments and have been humbled by letters of gratitude from several of my clients. My professional priority has always been to do the right thing by my clients, knowing that this necessitates a high standard in employee-to-employee interactions. Should I sense that I have said or done anything hurtful to another employee, I seek them out and strive for reconciliation. I know that, one way or another, interpersonal negativity will work its way out onto the most vulnerable among us: our clients. I am by no means perfect in this, but this has always been my goal.

I believe a change in management is an urgent professional priority in the clinic. Currently administered under one department, the center may need to be put under a different department to accomplish this. It may take a professionally higher standard to make the necessary changes at the agency.

We have lost several strong employees already because of the work environment; it would be a shame for the program and the public to lose more. It grieves me to do so, yet I am compelled by the urgency of the situation and the ineffectiveness of multiple staff attempts to seek relief via the established chain of command.

I believe the people on that chain of command have truly desired to make the necessary changes but have been stopped by the person at the top of that chain, the CEO. This is what I have been told by people from different departments who have occasion to be in meetings with the CEO.

I myself went to the CEO a few years ago to discuss the presence of mobbing, or bullying, at CounselingCare. I gave him a book on the topic (Davenport et al., 1999) and explained why I thought

this was going on here. Unfortunately, I did not feel safe enough to disclose exactly who was doing the bullying.

His response was to tell me that he did not think CounselingCare had any such problem. Interestingly, the CEO and the manager of my department are seen frequently chatting at length in the hallway outside the department.

I write to you now because, to date, none of us has been willing to put anything in writing, nor were we asked to do so by the administrators we talked with.

My relationship with the agency started just a couple of months after it was created. I was there to serve our very first client. I worked very hard with the supervisor in question, DN. She and I were equals, just staff working to create a good program for CounselingCare and its community. The manager was happy to delegate responsibility to the supervisor.

DN frequently sought my professional opinions because I am experienced and have advanced training in crisis care. I had to make very painful decisions about some of my co-workers whom I was asked to supervise and who had come to the agency from other departments. These were staff members that I saw nearly every workday. During their probationary period in our department it became obvious to me that we would not be able to improve their weaknesses in crisis care with extra training, and worse yet, they posed a risk to client safety. I recommended to DN that they not pass their probation. They left with very bad feelings toward my department and have not spoken to me since.

This department has a hard-won reputation for excellence, but working with DN has always been, well, a challenge. She tends to be tense about any given topic or situation She was in a perpetually charged state of fearful, angry paranoia about perceived threats against the call center. If not angry with outsiders, she would become angry with me if I came to her with any concerns that she chose to interpret as a threat to her authority.

She would shout, while jabbing her finger in the air towards me, "Sit DOWN!" and would repeat this until I had, in fact, sat down and said nothing. I wondered a couple of times if she was going to hit me.

Then came the day 2–3 years ago when it all got worse. That was a day just like any other day. But it was the day we both knew that I was no longer buying into whatever DN told me. Since that day, she made my workdays an exercise in psychological torture. This supervisor has also managed to turn two of my

continued

Box 7–2 • The Unmailed Plea: Mobbing Can Kill You—*continued*

coworkers against me by telling them god knows what. DN is very good at splitting the staff. I know this because I observed it and because a few of the RNs chose to tell me.

One coworker had been told from day one not to dare talk to me or listen to anything I had to say about telephone crisis calls. She was afraid to even look at me until she was sure DN had left the building.

Yet DN would brag about me to new staff or professionals with glowing descriptions of my value as an experienced professional and as a "goodwill ambassador" for CounselingCare. It is very strange to be so publicly valued and so privately despised.

This behavior is always done behind closed doors. The door to the call center is kept closed for confidentiality. But when there are outside witnesses present, DN addresses us with a breathy, almost cooing voice, as one might speak to a baby you didn't wish to waken.

Did I mention that after angry outbursts to the staff there would be little gifts the next day on our desks? Candy . . . or something decorative, something seasonal. Sometimes gift certificates. Lots and lots of candy.

DN claimed inside knowledge of everyone in any position of authority or having anything to do with the department. Invariably her special knowledge led to proclamations labeled "the truth" and orders delivered

"solely for job protection." For example, she would say that a certain person was dangerous to the department and that staff should not talk to a certain person or jobs could be lost.

She portrayed the (then) manager of the department as dangerously incompetent. She also describes the director of community relations as "bovine." It was the first time in my life I had ever heard that word used to describe another human.

I cannot completely document here the constant, daily psychological assaults of 8 years with DN. Let me just say that since starting at CounselingCare, I've gained about 65 lbs, developed hypertension, had two knee surgeries and one shoulder surgery, and have required large doses of antidepressants and psychotherapy just to get through each working day.

There is a photo of me from 2 years ago that tells it all. On vacation in a Latin American country I had longed to visit for many years, I am standing in front of a magical lacey-white rain forest waterfall that starts several hundred feet above me. You would expect a facial expression of excitement or joy on the face of someone having "the vacation of a lifetime". I look like a battered woman.

My health has been so diminished that for the last few years I have been driven by only one thought—I cannot let this job kill me.

downsizing/restructuring/merging. These authors asserted that it is the culture of the organization that determines whether mobbing will be allowed to develop or will be extinguished, particularly the organization's ability to handle differences and conflict.

Within this vulnerable organizational context, Davenport et al. (1999) suggested that the complex dynamic that results in mobbing is the outcome of an interaction among five elements: (1) the psychology and the circumstances of the mobbers; (2) the organizational culture and structure; (3) the psychology of the mobbee's personality; (4) the circumstances of the mobbee; and (5) a triggering event, a conflict, and factors outside the organization (i.e., values and norms, in U.S. culture).

WHISTLE-BLOWING

A *whistle-blower* is one who "identifies an incompetent, unethical, or illegal situation in the workplace and

reports it to someone who may have the power to stop the wrong" (McDonald & Ahern, 2000, p. 314). Counselors are mandated by their codes of ethics and by state licensure guidelines to report questionable or unethical behavior, yet many are hesitant to become whistle-blowers. Collegial support may be mixed when a colleague reports the suspected behavior of a peer. There are two types of **whistle-blowing,** *internal whistle-blowing,* which is often called reporting (Nathaniel, 2002), and *external whistle-blowing,* including public disclosure by a person with inside information about a specific situation (Hunt, 1995).

Mixed support may be particularly evident in hierarchical organizations, such as large bureaucracies or hospitals, if the accused is an administrator, supervisor, or physician who also occupies a place on the upper level of the hierarchy, or if the whistle-blowing disrupts the immediate work team in any setting. On the other hand, whistle-blowing can be beneficial and override the negative risks by (a) providing a climate that supports the protection of current and future clients as well as coworkers, (b) facilitating communication among colleagues, and (c) encouraging constructive problem solving. Several laws have been designed to safeguard employees who suspect the unethical behavior of their colleagues. However, court actions suggest that legal protection for whistle-blowers is tentative. For example, a 1981 Michigan state law protects employees who expose illegal or dangerous employee activity from wrongful discharge from any government or private-sector organization. As stated in Chapter 3, counselors are obligated to their employers as well as to their clients, making the decisions concerning disclosure ethically complex. The actual experience of becoming a whistle-blower can be a life-changing event if the situation is serious enough. At times, the counselor

may receive sufficient support and the process may be difficult, but gratifying. In other instances, the experience can be harrowing even though the counselor may eventually be vindicated. Box 7–3 relates the story of two counselors who "did the right thing" and are proud of it, yet they paid a serious price. Note the characteristic mobbing behaviors that were directed against them in the process. With access to the internet on the rise, there are a number of watchdog organizations that provide "how to" information as well as encouragement for whistle-blowers. These Web sites provide information on the process as well as the type of retaliatory techniques that may be used against the whistle-blower. Other internet sites offer support to individuals who have blown the whistle or are in the process of exposing wrongdoing at the current time.

Box 7–3   •   Two Colleagues Make the Ultimate Ethical Decision

We live in an interdependent world where work and ethics are inextricably linked. Knowing that we are providing a useful service to others lets us routinely deal with difficulties and problems that are part of any job. In our place of work, routine circumstances led to a chain of events that uncovered fraudulent billing practices. We attempted to correct this by working within the corporation. Our attempts to correct unethical and fraudulent activities were "spun" by corporate managers as "politics," described as "trying to get workers" (those who were responsible for the fraudulent activities). We experienced firsthand how a system that had lost its moral compass protects itself through attacks on our professional credibility. We were threatened and isolated. One of us was fired, the other was forced out. Later we found ourselves unemployable. We worried that we had been blacklisted. We can attest that "whistle-blowers suffer certain and severe retaliation from management especially if their information proves to be significant, reveals systematic misconduct, and the practices exposed are part of the regular profit accumulation of the organization" (Rothschild & Miethe, 1999).

We are not experts, but when we found ourselves in a whistle-blower situation, we experienced firsthand the connection between work and ethical expression. We were dumbfounded when the corporation ignored the bad billing practices we had discovered. Instead of backing our efforts, the corporation criticized us for not getting along with subordinates. Overnight everything changed. We went from the model team to troublemakers.

We were disappointed by the behavior of some coworkers. Professional colleagues whom we had once

respected became overwhelmed by concerns for job security. We found silence where we had expected support from the organization and other members of the helping professions. We experienced the effects of extreme trauma, shame, fear, loss of confidence, and depression that impacted all of our relationships and family. Despite our own fear of what the future could bring, we summoned our courage and proceeded with integrity. We could do the right thing by having our case heard and decided in a court of law. We took the initiative with energy and conviction, persevering and being willing to hang in there, no matter what.

Having our case heard in a court of law made a big difference. Even if the case had not been won, having a trial was the right thing. The trial was based on evidence, and we had the documentation that made the difference. The procedures of the trial were daunting; however, the trial was our only opportunity to make our case to the public. By taking a stand, we were effectively cut off from the support systems one traditionally turns to in times of great stress.

Our former boss apparently forgot that he had nominated one of us for Employee of the Year when he testified that that person was always a problem. The CEO was angry and embarrassed when confronted by the evidence. One of our frustrations with the discovery process was that the only documentary evidence of the billing problem came from us. Despite our requests for documentation, the corporation seemed not to have any of the many memos we had generated on the subject. We were appalled to learn that one of the employees we had tried to

continued

Box 7–3 ● Two Colleagues Make the Ultimate Ethical Decision—*continued*

correct had searched our office and thrown many papers away. Realizing that our concerns about the organization practices needed to be supported by evidence, we carefully documented them in a report to the clinical supervisor as we sought for the identified issues to be addressed by appropriate supervisors in the organization. This report and retention of records of our repeated attempts to seek the support of organization officers in correcting these practices provided the evidence that made the difference. The money won in the lawsuit is a representation of some justice for the individuals involved.

Being a whistle-blower was a life-altering experience. In its entirety, the experience was painful. We had acted in good faith to seek remedies to fraudulent practices, but the system did not recognize or honor that effort. The experience also was an opportunity. It gave us a window in time to evaluate our ethics and our values. When work and life are rooted in ethical practice, you have the energy and the vision to do whatever is necessary. We all want to contribute and make a positive difference with our work. We are all drawn to what is good and right and each one

of us is capable of making this difference. We found that in our materialistic society, ethical and value-based action is not to be taken for granted and is the only thing that gives authenticity and substance to living and working.

A decision to step forward should not be taken without serious consideration. Sound legal advice and documentation is crucial as well. The role of whistle-blower was forced upon us. After the fact, we realized that even though we could not predict what the outcome of our actions might be, our response of finding justice through the legal system was the right and good thing to do. We did not know that it would work out to a positive conclusion. We only knew that it was the right action to take and did so without regrets. We could not turn a blind eye to our professional ethics or the rights of our clients to honest and ethical services. When life and work are guided by ethical values, we are empowered to act responsibly and compassionately, even in the midst of challenging circumstances. Each one of us has the ability to make this difference. Never forget what the priorities are.

Ethical codes for counseling disciplines do provide codified standards of behavior for addressing concerns regarding unethical behavior of a colleague. The APA and the ACA codes of ethics provide standards for informal resolution of ethical violations and for reporting ethical violations. They direct the professional first to attempt to resolve the situation by discussing it directly and informally with the other therapist, providing that confidentiality rights of the client are not violated in the process. If the violation is too serious, or is not resolved after this informal discussion, the professional will take further action including possible referral to licensure boards or professional organizations' ethics committees for adjudication. This last course of action would not be possible if there are violations of the client's confidentiality rights that cannot be resolved.

In a more general sense, Felie (1983) suggested several guidelines for whether, when, and how to blow the whistle on a colleague if informal routes prove to be ineffective and if the colleague is not of one's own discipline but works as a peer within an organizational setting. She outlined six steps for addressing the problem (Figure 7–4).

The act of taking a colleague to task for ethically inappropriate behavior is daunting. Nevertheless, counselors have an important obligation to their clients

and society at large to protect them and to uphold the trust placed in the profession.

LEGAL ISSUES

The Civil Rights Act of 1967, Title VII, made it unlawful for an employer to discriminate or to fire an individual based on race, color, religion, sex, or national origin. Subsequently, federal and state legislation extended this protection; for example, The Age Discrimination in Employment Act of 1967; The Vocational Rehabilitation Act of 1973; and The Americans with Disabilities Act of 1990. The Supreme Court ruled that Title VII is not limited to tangible discrimination but is also intended to be applied to people who may be subjected to a hostile work environment. For example, the claim of "hostile environment" has been used in litigation involving sexual harassment.

U. S. legislation has attempted to extend compensatory relief to individuals who have suffered significant mental injury as a result of a hostile working environment. Arizona, California, Iowa, Wisconsin, and Wyoming legally acknowledge that mental injury can result from excessive stress on the job—calling it *mental health injury.*

This changing legal landscape is also affecting the corporate world. Companies such as Levi Strauss & Co.

1. **Confirm the issue.** Conduct an objective assessment of the situation. Make certain that you are competent to make this determination and that your desire to make this report is not based on personal motives.
2. **Check your perceptions with peers.** Examine them against the norms of your institution and your discipline. Compare the activity against your state's practice guidelines and those of your institution. Does the situation truly exceed acceptable standards? Maintain a nonjudgmental attitude throughout the process.
3. **Involve others in an action plan.** Develop a plan of action for voicing your concerns. Respect your institution's chain of command. Multiple participants are more effective in providing a successful intervention. Have intervention goals established in advance. Anticipate possible reactions.
4. **Set deadlines.** They demonstrate that you are serious. Implement your plan after conferring with your immediate supervisor.
5. **Document details of your discussion.** Include time, date, and the basic content of the conversation. Timing of any intervention is crucial— soon after a precipitant crisis is optimal.
6. **If needed, take the problem upstairs.** If your supervisor dismisses or fails to address the situation, be prepared to move up the organizational ladder.

FIGURE 7–4.   Guidelines for Whistle-Blowing
Source: From "Thinking about Blowing the Whistle?" by A. G. Felie, 1983, *American Journal of Nursing, 83,* 1541–1542. Reprinted by permission of Lippincott-Raven Publishers, Philadelphia, PA.

1. Mission statement includes the organizational objectives on how employees are treated; vision and value statements align all employees.
2. Organizational structure includes clear reporting levels.
3. Job descriptions are defined in terms of duties and responsibilities.
4. Personnel policies are comprehensive, consistent, legal, and simple, including expected behaviors and standards of ethics.
5. Disciplinary issues are dealt with consistently, fairly, and expeditiously.
6. Employees buy into the goals and objectives of the organization. They have been educated regarding their role in the achievement of these goals.
7. New employees are selected not only based on their technical qualifications but also on the basis of their emotional intelligence, such as their capacity of dealing with diversity, working in self-directed teams, and managing conflict.
8. Training and staff development—highly valued for all employees. The system meets the needs of the changing organization. Training includes issues of human relations in addition to technical knowledge.
9. Communications are open, honest, effective, and timely.
10. Participation, teamwork, creativity, decision-making trust, and empowerment are structures that allow for the highest possible degree of employees' personal involvement in achieving the company's goals.
11. Conflict resolution/mediation is a mechanism for resolving conflict at all levels. There is a follow-up to ensure that the conflict has really been resolved.
12. EAPs (Employee Assistance Programs) or a comparable program includes behavioral risk assessment and management (Davenport et al., 1999, p. 142).

FIGURE 7–5.   Ways to Reduce Mobbing
Source: From *Mobbing: Emotional Abuse in the American Workplace* by N. Davenport, R. Distler Schwartz, & G. Pursell Elliott, 1999. Reprinted by permission of Civil Society of Publishing, Ames, IA.

and the Saturn Corporation are leading the way in establishing company philosophies that support an individual's right to a work environment that is free from mobbing. Davenport et al. (1999) offered a list of twelve components that can create this type of culture (Figure 7–5).

Counseling, mental health, rehabilitation, and other helping organizations that employ professionals who work directly with clients should take seriously the need to establish a nonthreatening, positive environment.

Mobbing and whistle-blowing often begin with the presence of an unresolved conflict and the admirable attempt of an individual to resolve the situation. One result of an unresolved situation of conflict may be the act of whistle-blowing. The conflict may actually provide a potentially explosive atmosphere with the fuel it needs to ignite. In turn, the whistle-blower can serve as a target for unresolved hostility, or mobbing.

DECISION MAKING IN CONTEXT

In thinking about ethical decision making, counselors and counselor educators often consider the ethical dilemma in a shortsighted way—focusing on only the relationship between the counselor and client as individuals. However, after only a moment's consideration it is both practically obvious and conceptually clear that the context or climate surrounding the situation is critical to understanding how to proceed in the ethical decision-making process. The following scenario will illustrate some ways in which consideration of the ethical climate surrounding a situation is incorporated into selected aspects of the Tarvydas Integrated Model and the Cottone Social Constructivism Model of Ethical Decision Making.

In this ethical dilemma you are the supervisor of many counselors at the local mental health center. Several of the counselors have approached you with concerns regarding one of their colleagues. They are concerned about this colleague due to the recent marital and emotional difficulties she has been experiencing. The counselors are concerned that her issues outside of work are impacting her clinical judgment and competence. You encourage the counselors to share their concerns with their colleague directly, which they are unwilling to do. You ask the counselors for specific examples of their concerns and begin to watch this counselor's work more closely. During this watching, you discover the counselor has not been documenting her sessions and has been overbilling insurance for the clients she is seeing. Counselors are to dictate their session notes at the end of each session and complete billing forms for the amount of time the client is seen. The counselor has been double billing clients for sessions and has been dictating two sentences, "Client seen for 50-minute session. Progress toward goals continues." When confronted, the counselor shows you her personal handwritten notes that need to be dictated. This level of documentation is not in line with agency policy, and fraudulent billing goes against agency standards. What should you do?

In the Tarvydas Integrative Model of Ethical Decision Making, you, the supervisor, may begin utilizing an acute awareness of your power to set an ethical climate in Stage I as you seek to interpret the situation through awareness and fact finding. At this point you would try to demonstrate sensitivity to the supervisee's situation. You might ask yourself if, from the supervisee's perspective, she feels there is anything to be concerned about regarding her work performance at this time or if she sees any changes in her performance. You also realize that the stakeholders in this situation will be affected by the ethical climate created. If the counselor is having personal issues and you, the counselor's colleagues, or the agency do not intervene and set a climate that does not support this conduct, her competence in the area of counseling will be affected for this and future clients. Also, insurance companies are likely to intervene—fraudulent billing is against the

law and there could be legal ramifications against the mental health center. The administration of your mental health center wants to create conditions that provide quality services and create confidence and pride in the work of the center, and it expects employees to perform according to established standards—in short, the administrative climate reinforces ethical conduct of the staff over financial gain to the agency. During fact finding you will seek to determine how long the counselor has been documenting this way, how many clients she may be seeing, and how many charts are incomplete. This will be important to assess the seriousness and depth of the misconduct, including what harm has occurred. You discover that she has experienced these problems only recently. It also appears that her clients have not experienced any serious decline in the quality of her services.

In Stage II, you consult with the administrator of the agency (your direct supervisor) to determine what course of action to follow and are pleased to experience support for a compassionate but direct intervention to address the counselor's issue. Possibilities could include suspension, mandated counseling, correction of billing errors, or reporting of unethical behavior to a licensure board. After reviewing the ACA Code of Ethics and thinking about the ethical principles of nonmaleficence, fidelity, and beneficence toward the client, you decide on either suspending the counselor for 2 weeks or allowing her to continue working under increased and supportive supervision while the billing errors are corrected if she will agree to mandated counseling. While considering the positive and negative consequences of these options, you decide on the mandated counseling while she continues to work. You think that this counselor can address issues in her personal situation that may be impacting her ability to function effectively within her daily work environment. It will offer the counselor time to reflect on her current situation and past work issues and to make a positive plan for the future. There are some negative consequences that are possible in that the counselor may attend required sessions but not internalize or benefit from counseling. She also may resent the fact that counseling was required for ongoing employment, and this reaction may yield ongoing resentment with the supervisor and agency. On balance, you do decide to offer the mandated counseling option to her as the right ethical solution.

In thinking about the matter in Stage III, you wonder whether you might have a personal blind spot affecting your judgment because you feel personally close to this counselor and you yourself experienced turmoil during your own divorce several years ago. Additionally, you do not want to go through the possible feeling of failure as a supervisor in the eyes of your staff if you directly address this counselor's problems rather than hoping that she will recover herself without intervention. However, after further contemplation, you realize that you should still proceed with the plan you set out during Stage II. This decision is further reinforced when you evaluate the contextual factors in Stages III and IV and realize not only that the team and administration seem to hold beliefs that are consistent with this intervention but also that the climate they created will enhance and assist in the intervention as you plan for it in Stage IV. This was demonstrated by their compassionate, but clear, concern when they brought this counselor's problem to your attention originally. Finally, you are pleased to think that a positive by-product of this intervention will further reinforce the value placed on ethics in the agency climate overall for all staff.

The Social Constructivist Model would also emphasize the issues in this dilemma that are part of the ethical climate from the standpoint of the social relationships that constitute the climate. You would consider that there are several social systems involved in this counselor's situation—the relationships between the counselor and clients, the counselor and her colleagues, the supervisor and the clients, the supervisor and the agency's administration, and finally between the agency and the insurance companies that rely on the integrity of their shared billing agreement. Through reviewing some of the issues and information raised in processing this dilemma through the Tarvydas Integrative Model, it would seem that most of the viewpoints of this situation would involve a nonadversarial consensus that the counselor's behavior does not meet their shared rules of conduct for professional behavior. This consensus was gained through an intricate series of consultations between all these parties that allowed the situation to be discussed and processed within the social boundaries of the team, supervisory, and administrative social systems. In these consultations, it seems that the parties shared consensualities, thus opening up the possibilities for a consensualized remedy to the situation that these parties could endorse.

The more interesting issue facing the supervisor in this model's process is whether or not the counselor will disagree with this interpretation and consensus that is shared by her supervisor and administration and consistent with team beliefs. She might remind the supervisor of her long-term and positive relationship with both the supervisor and team to present an alternative objective "truth" regarding the situation. For example, she might note that she is a "good counselor and team member" whose judgment is consistently valued and of a high ethical quality. Furthermore, she contends that the supervisor and team have avoided being harsh in applying sanctions to the behavior of other team members who are valued in the past, allowing them to self-correct their behavior once the problems have been called to their attention. She calls upon the supervisor to apply the team and agency norms fairly to her in this difficult situation, saying that she does not have the need, time, or money to go through mandatory counseling as a condition of her employment, feeling that this is discriminatory and overly harsh. She calls upon the supervisor to negotiate an alternative solution for her. Although she does not disagree with the facts in the situation, she does not recognize the fairness of the mandatory counseling and supervision. The supervisor and the counselor attempt to negotiate the situation but become deadlocked, at which time the supervisor asks the advise of the administrator. The administrator asks an office manager from another office of the agency to step in to see if he can arbitrate an agreement regarding how to handle the situation. After discussions between all parties have been held, and after all parties have agreed to abide by the decision of the arbitrator, he proposes the idea that the counselor obtain a psychological evaluation regarding whether she is experiencing any impairment in her work or needs any type of mental health intervention at present. He further proposes that all parties agree to be bound by the recommendations of this evaluation and that, in any case, the counselor should receive additional supervision for 6 months. This supervision would include assisting her in reviewing and correcting her billing and clinical records. After considerable thought, the counselor, supervisor, and administration agree to this arbitrated solution to the ethical dilemma.

CHAPTER SUMMARY

Counselors are profoundly influenced by the environments and work cultures in which they practice. Work environments are cultures that create a particular ethical climate that influences the quality of services provided to clients. Ethical and unethical colleagues influence their coworkers to behave ethically and unethically.

Organizational climate is how people characterize a system's practices and procedures, such as the sense of safety or fear of retribution that a counselor may feel. Ethical climate describes the shared perceptions that colleagues hold concerning ethical procedures and practices within an organization.

A disability is an identifiable condition that may be stable and is often overcome with appropriate changes, assistance, or accommodations. An impairment is a gradually recognized condition that manifests when an individual attempts to perform some activity. Chronic physical illness, substance abuse, burnout, and sexual acting-out behaviors are pervasive impairments that can disrupt professional performance. Substance abuse adversely affects professional competence. Early diagnosis and intervention are essential. Burnout is an emotional exhaustion in which the professional no longer has any positive feelings, sympathy, or respect for clients.

Boundary violations occur when professionals' ethical standards are loose with clients, students, or research participants. Those most likely to violate professional boundaries are those who have psychotic disorders, manic disorders, impulse control disorders, chronic neurosis and isolation, and naivete and those who are situational offenders.

Mobbing is an emotional assault that targets a work colleague. Organizational elements that contribute to mobbing include bad management, a stress-intensive workplace, monotony, disbelief or denial by managers, unethical activities, flat organizations, and downsizing or restructuring.

Whistle-blowing is the ethical reporting of unethical behavior. Whistle-blowing receives mixed support, particularly in hierarchical organizations. It can be beneficial and override the negative risks by providing a protective environment for clients and coworkers and facilitating communication. The experience of becoming a whistle-blower can be a life-changing event.

INTERNET RESOURCES

Readers seeking further information concerning the issues of ethical climate discussed in this chapter should try the following search key words: impaired professional, professional boundary, boundary violation and counseling, professional culture or climate, organizational climate, job stress, job burnout, substance abuse and professionals, mobbing, bullying, and whistle-blowing.

REFERENCES

Agich, G. J. (Ed.). (1982). *Responsibility in health care.* Boston: D. Reidel.

Beauchamp, T. L., & Childress, J. F. (2001). *Principles of biomedical ethics* (5th ed.). New York & Oxford, England: Oxford University Press.

Bellah, R. N., Madson, R., Sullivan, W. M., Swidler, A., & Tipton, S. M. (1985). *Habits of the heart: Individualism and commitment in American life.* New York: Harper & Row.

Brems, C. (2000). *Dealing with challenges in psychotherapy and counseling.* Pacific Grove, CA: Brooks/Cole.

The College of Psychologists of Ontario. (1998). Professional boundaries in health-care relationships. *The Bulletin, 25*(1), 1–7.

Commission on Rehabilitation Counselor Certification. (2001). *Code of professional ethics for rehabilitation counselors.* Rolling Meadows, IL: Author.

Cottone, R. R. (1992). *Theories and paradigms of counseling and psychotherapy.* Needham Heights, MA: Allyn & Bacon.

Cottone, R. R., Tarvydas, V., & House, G. (1994). The effect of number and type of consulted relationships on the ethical decision making of graduate students in counseling. *Counseling and Values, 39,* 56–68.

Davenport, N., Distler Schwartz, R., & Pursell Elliott, G. (1999). *Mobbing: Emotional abuse in the American workplace.* Ames, IA: Civil Society of Publishing.

Doherty, W. J. (1995). *Soul searching: Why psychotherapy must promote moral responsibility.* New York: Basic Books.

Felie, A. G. (1983). The risks of blowing the whistle. *American Journal of Nursing, 83,* 1387.

Heinesmann, P. (1972). *Mobbing: Group violence among children.* Stockholm, Sweden: Natur och Kutlur.

Hellman, J. (1986). The stresses of psychotherapeutic work: A replication and extension. *Journal of Clinical Psychology, 42,* 197–204.

Hunt, G. (1995). *Whistleblowing in the health service.* London: Edward Arnold.

Ivey, A. E. (2003). *Intentional interviewing and counseling: Facilitating client development in a multicultural society* (5th ed.). Pacific Grove, CA: Brooks/Cole.

Jones, E., Farina, A., Hastorf, A., Markus, H., Miller, D., & Scott, R. (1984). *Social stigma: The psychology of marked relationships.* New York: W. H. Freeman and Company.

Katsavdakis, K. A., Gabbard, G. O., Athey, G. I. (2004). Profiles of impaired health professionals. *Bulletin of the Menninger Clinic, 68*(1), 60–72.

Keashly, L. (1998). Emotional abuse in the workplace: Conceptual and empirical issues. *Journal of Emotional Abuse, 1*(1), 85–117.

Klebe-Trevino, L. (1986). Ethical decision making in organizations: A person-situation interactionist model. *The Academy of Management Review, 11,* 601–617.

Lamb, D. H, Cochran, D. J., & Jackson, V. (1991). Training and organizational issues associated with identifying and responding to intern impairment.

Professional Psychology: Research and Practice, 22, 291–296.

Leymann, H. (1996). The content and development of mobbing at work. *European Journal of Work and Organizational Psychology, 5*(2), 10–22.

Liddell, D. L., Halpin, G., & Halpin, W. G. (1992). The measure of moral orientation: Measuring the ethics of care and justice. *Journal of College Student Development, 33*, 325–330.

Lorenz, K. (1966). *On aggression* (1st ed.). New York: Harcourt, Brace and World.

Maddi, S. R., & Kobasa, S. C. (1984). *The hardy executive: Health under stress.* Homewood, IL: Dow Jones-Irwin.

Maslach, C., & Jackson, S. E. (1986). *Maslach Burnout Inventory: Manual* (2nd ed.). Palo Alto, CA: Consulting Psychologists Press.

McDonald, S., & Ahern, K. (2000). Physical and emotional effects of whistle-blowing by nurses. *Journal of Professional Nursing, 16*, 313–321.

Mohan, J.(1993). The business of medicine. *Sociology, 22*, 648–649.

Nathaniel, A. (2002). Moral distress among nurses. *Ethics and Human Rights Issues* Update, 1, 3.

Norris, D. M., Gutheil, T. G., Strasburger, L. H. (2003). This couldn't happen to me: Boundary problems and sexual misconduct in the psychotherapy relationship. *Psychiatric Services, 544,* 517–522.

O'Rourke, B. (1996). *Individual interdisciplinary team members' perception of ethics decision-making context: A descriptive study.* Unpublished doctoral dissertation, University of Iowa, Iowa City.

Rothschild, J., & Miethe, T. D. (1999, February). Whistle-blower disclosures and management retaliation: The battle to control information about organization corruption. *Work & Occupations, 26* (1), 107–128.

Schein, E. H. (1990). Organizational culture. *American Psychologist, 45*, 109–119.

Schoener, R. (1995). Assessment of professionals who have engaged in boundary violations. *Psychiatric Annals, 25*, 95–98.

Sheets, V. (2001). Professional boundaries: Staying in the lines. *Dimensions of Critical Care Nursing, 20*(5), 36–40.

Skorina, J. K., DeSoto, C. B., & Bissell, L. (1990). Alcoholic psychologists: Routes to recovery. *Professional Psychology: Research and Practice, 21*, 248–251.

Skorupa, J., & Agresti, A. (1993). Ethical beliefs about burnout and continued professional practice. *Professional Psychology: Research and Practice, 24*, 281–285.

Stadler, H. A. (1990). Counselor impairment. In B. Herlihy & L. Golden (Eds.), *Ethical standards casebook.* Alexandria, VA: American Association for Counseling and Development.

Tarvydas, V. M. (1994). Ethical orientations of masters' rehabilitation students. *Rehabilitation Counseling Bulletin, 37*, 202–214.

Tarvydas, V. M., & Cottone, R. R. (1991). Ethical responses to legislative, organizational, and economic dynamics: A four-level model of ethical practice. *Journal of Applied Rehabilitation, 22*(4), 11–17.

Weiss, S. J., & Davis, H. P. (1985). Validity and reliability of the collaborative practice scale. *Nursing Research, 34*, 299–305.

Welfel, E. R. (2002). *Ethics in counseling and psychology: Standards, research, and emerging issues* (2nd ed.). Pacific Grove, CA: Brooks/Cole.

Wiles, J. (1993). *Socialization and interpersonal influence on the ethical decision-making climate in service organizations.* Unpublished dissertation, University of Memphis, Memphis, TN.

CHAPTER 8

Office, Administrative, and Business Practices

OBJECTIVES

After reading this chapter, you should be able to:

- Discuss the ethical issues that typically arise from office, administrative, and business practices.
- Explain the major areas of concern that derive from the layout of the professional counseling office, such as privacy and confidentiality issues.
- Discuss how to oversee, manage, and monitor ethically sensitive activities in schools, agencies, and private practices.

- Explain procedures and policies that may be discriminatory or unfair to special populations of clients.
- Identify issues related to billing health insurance and working through managed care providers.
- Understand that the area of office, administrative, and business practices is highly amenable to ethical planning and forethought, as a means of preventing ethical dilemmas.

INTRODUCTION

One of the most overlooked areas of study in the ethics literature relates to business practices. Yet, business practice is one of the most challenging areas of ethical practice—and one of the areas most challenged by clients and other individuals served by professional counselors. Many of the complaints before licensure boards and certification bodies are about business, administrative, or office practices, such as inadequate recordkeeping or fraudulent acts (e.g., false billing; Association of State and Provincial Psychology Boards, 2001). Nothing will raise the ire of a client (or third-party payer) more than a bill for unsatisfactory services, a bill that does not reflect the actual services requested or provided, a bill that breaches confidentiality, or a bill that reflects financial irregularities. Generally, counselors are ill prepared to address these issues and to set standards and office procedures to prevent problems. Classic examples of problematic office practices include: (a) waiting rooms that do not

provide any privacy (secretaries discuss issues with clients in the open or there is no discreet entry or exit); (b) use of electronic equipment without adequate encryption (e.g., fax machines, cell phones, intercoms; see Chapter 10); (c) advertising (e.g., misrepresentation); (d) fee setting and collection of unpaid bills (e.g., unfair fee setting or surprise involvement of fee collectors); (e) inadequate maintenance of records and disposal of confidential records (e.g., shredding of records); (f) poor referral and termination procedures; (g) poor sound insulation in offices; (h) misrepresentation of credentials to the public (e.g., licensure status); and (i) fraudulent billing practices.

THE LAYOUT OF THE OFFICE

Privacy issues should be utmost in the design of a professional office. A professional supervisor recently visited a student intern at a reputable sex therapy clinic.

While waiting in the lobby area, the supervisor was able to overhear a secretary asking detailed, intimate questions of a prospective client over the phone. The secretary repeated the prospective client's name, phone number, and address as she recorded them, allowing everyone in the waiting area to hear. Sound-proofing or screening in such a situation is absolutely necessary. Waiting areas should be designed so that people entering or leaving the counseling suites can do so without passing other waiting clients. A separate exit door is ideal, or if space restrictions prevent a separate exit door, scheduling should be arranged so that a minimal number of people are in the waiting area at one time. Files should not be left out in the open where visitors in the waiting area can see them, and computer monitors should be turned so that confidential information is not easily viewed by the waiting public. These are basic issues of privacy. Nothing is more disturbing, for example, than waiting in a physician's office and having one's medical problems broadcast to everyone present. Counseling clients may have issues even more sensitive than those of patients in a physician's office. Counselors and administrators must be very sensitive to these common breaches of privacy, which can be prevented by careful planning. *Planning is decision making to prevent problems,* and it is absolutely crucial when it comes to administrative and office practices. Counselors are guided by the ACA and APA ethics codes, which make it clear that counselors must respect the privacy of their clients.

Offices should also be organized to provide for the safety of clients and staff. If safety concerns arise from the nature of the clientele, staff should be prepared to deal with emergency situations. Some professionals provide counsel to ex-offenders, individuals with anger or impulse control problems, or individuals with poor or impaired judgment. A rehabilitation counselor in a nonprofit agency was punched in the face by a client diagnosed as having paranoid schizophrenia. The client reported that he overheard the counselor make a racial slur while the counselor was on the phone trying to assist in job placement of the client. The client had a record of assaulting other individuals for racial slurs, even when no such slurs were heard by bystanders. The client was apparently hallucinating and became violent in response to the hallucinations. Given the client's record, precautions should have been taken in this case. When working with potentially dangerous or violent clients, counselors should establish safety and contingency plans. Procedures for warning or alerting others of potential, imminent, or active crises should be in place. Equipment might be purchased to help to ensure safety (door key pads, warning systems), or offices can be designed to allow visual access (counselor offices with windows to another secure office) so other professional staff can monitor activities. Counselors, staff, and clients should feel safe in the counseling setting, and administrative and professional staff should be alert to potential concerns and methods for preventing problems.

The common practice of sharing office space is another area of concern. Some counselors, by choice or by necessity, share office space—they may see clients at different times during the same day or on different days. In most cases, this arrangement is a matter of economics. Private practitioners in part-time, private practices may be unable to afford an individual office all their own; they may enter into an agreement with a colleague to share costs and space. Some agencies and schools are pressed for space and are unable to provide individual offices for professional staff. Whatever the arrangement, counselors who share space should have a clear agreement about the boundaries related to client information. Unless the counselors are employed by the same agency or school and have their clients' understanding of the organization's right to share information, they must make efforts to secure files and other case-relevant information. Separate storage areas (e.g., file cabinets) should be secured even from colleagues who share space; licenses should be displayed according to law for all of the people who use the office; and procedures for taking calls and messages must be established to provide for maximum security. A formal, written ethics agreement between parties sharing space is also recommended. Extra precautions should be taken to ensure that a client's rights are not compromised because of financial exigency.

Counselors must also be sensitive to accessibility issues—individuals with disabilities often have impairments that affect their mobility. "Offices should be planned with 'universal design' principles in mind so that they are accessible to all people, not just the able-bodied" ("Make Sure Your Office Layout is Legal," 1993, March). *Universal design* is a term that refers to standardized rules of architectural design so that buildings meet accessibility standards. Special parking spaces for those with mobility problems must be provided. Offices and buildings should be designed to maximize the accessibility of individuals with problems negotiating spaces. Elevators should be available in storied buildings, facilities should be wheelchair accessible, and bathrooms must be made accessible.

Special accommodations for the hearing or visually impaired should be in place. Sensitivity to disability-related concerns is important when serving individuals in need. In most states, the state department that provides rehabilitation services addresses accessibility issues in establishing and maintaining an office. Offices that receive federal funds must be in compliance with accessibility standards.

QUESTIONS FOR REFLECTION

You are a counselor in an agency with paper-thin walls. You are counseling a client, and both you and your client are able to overhear a very private counseling session from an adjoining room. What should you do?

Consider the options in this situation. Consult the ethical codes of the ACA and the APA. What is your first course of action? Is additional follow-up activity necessary?

FEE SETTING, BILLING, AND COLLECTIONS

Fee issues are among those that appear to produce the most variability of confidence when practitioners are asked to rate ethical acceptability (Gibson & Pope, 1993). Gibson and Pope (1993) citing their own findings and the work of Pope and Vasquez (1991), concluded, "The topic of fees is one that often evokes feelings of discomfort and may therefore be relatively neglected in training programs" (p. 334).

Counselors should follow some simple advice in establishing their billing and collections policies—be cautious and be fair. If clients or third-party payers feel cheated or slighted, there is potential for conflict. The ACA and APA ethics codes indicate counselors and psychologists should not be discriminatory in setting fees.

A classic area of debate related to fee setting among practicing professionals is the issue of **sliding fee scales.** In this system, individuals are required to pay a certain amount for a service based on their income. A person with a very low income may be required to pay an amount less than a person with a high income for an hour of counseling or psychotherapy. There are benefits and problems with this sort of fee setting (Lien, 1993). Some argue that it provides people with low incomes an opportunity to receive services they otherwise could not afford. Others argue that it is inherently unfair and prejudicial of the wealthy client or the client with insurance or other benefits. It also appears to be in conflict with the ethical code of the ACA, which requires that there be no discrimination against individuals on the basis of

socioeconomic status (see the ACA code section on Professional Responsibility). Some agencies have compromised by charging lower fees for the services of student counselors (pre-degree) or counselors in training (degreed, but unlicensed or provisionally licensed professionals working to meet licensure standards). Some still argue that this may provide an inferior (or at least a less clinically savvy) product to the poorer client. It is also possible that if practitioners receive a lower fee, they might be less conscientious.

The flat fee, variable collection procedure is another option. In this system, one fee is charged for all clients, say $100 per hour. All clients are required to pay at least 50% of the fee before they leave the office ($50). The remainder is billed to the client. Some clients may choose to pay the total amount at the time of the service; others have insurance that may cover the balance or even more of the full fee. If the insurance covers more than the 50% of unpaid fees, the client would get a refund or reduced co-payment at a subsequent session. The procedure is invariable in collection of at least a certain percentage of the fee at the time of service. However, the agency can use discretion in collection of the unpaid balance. Clients who have fewer resources may not be billed on the remainder as often, or may not be required to pay as much on the balance of their bill at each billing cycle. Some of these bills will go uncollected, so the agency has some flexibility in attempting to collect the balance. The unpaid balance is a private matter, and not one that is prejudicial of certain groups at the time of the service agreement. On the negative side, this approach may scare away clients who may not be able to afford the full fee; they may be hesitant to commit to services even with knowledge of the non-aggressive collection procedures. They may seek services from an agency with a lower or sliding scale.

Some counselors are willing to charge lower fees but require full payment at the time of service. They may serve only a clientele that has ready access to funds to pay for services. This method avoids all of the work and expense of billing. Others use credit or debit card payments. Although a small fee is charged to the counselor for use of credit or debit cards, this method allows immediate guaranteed payment for services.

Regardless of the fee and billing procedure, it is important that counselors have a clearly articulated fee schedule and stick to the schedule. Varying fees and billing practices may be viewed as prejudicial and could be grounds for legitimate complaints against an agency or professional.

Raising fees during counseling may prove uncomfortable for both the counselor and the client. Some counselors have a set fee for a particular client. If the client's case is terminated and then reopened, it is reopened at the current rate, even if that rate constitutes an increase over the previous rate. Once opened, the fee remains the same, no matter what changes occur in the fee schedule. Some professionals never raise a fee on a case once the client has initiated treatment—the fee always remains the same. This kind of policy helps to encourage future client contact with the professional. Other agencies or private practitioners raise fees regularly, even in the course of treatment of a client. Clients are (and should be) informed that rates are not permanent and may be increased during their treatment. No one fee-raising method is more ethical than another, but, certainly, clients should know the rules from the very beginning of counseling.

If arrangements are made about collections, such as hiring a collection agency or attorney to secure unpaid balances, these arrangements should be explained to clients when they initially agree to services (see the ACA and APA codes). Clients should agree to services with full knowledge of potential collection procedures by signing a written statement of the agreement. Also, remember, "time is the enemy of collections" (Roberts & Roberts, 1985), so quick and systematic billing procedure should be used to facilitate collections. If collections or payments are made through a credit or debit card, it is wise to use an agency name that does not imply mental health services, to avoid a potential breach of privacy. If the credit card company or bank receives a debit from Anita's Counseling and Psychotherapy Services, the credit world knows that the client received such services. If the name of the agency is abbreviated in some way to disguise the service (e.g., Anita's Services, or Anita, Inc.), it is less likely that individuals will be able to identify the service provided.

Counselors can take some simple actions to prevent breach of client privacy. Mailed envelopes should list only the return address, without the agency name, so that people picking up a client's mail (e.g., roommates or family members) do not know that there has been contact with a mental health service provider. Likewise, counselors, staff, or collection agencies should not leave detailed phone messages that imply counseling services on answering machines or with anyone other than the client. Leaving a name and return phone number is sufficient.

Fraudulent billing is another major issue. In many cases, medical insurance programs will not pay for certain types of counseling services unless they can be clearly defined as psychotherapy for a person diagnosed with a mental disorder. Counselors often provide services that technically do not meet the definition of psychotherapy in treatment of mental disorders. For example, marriage or family counseling is not technically medical psychotherapy. It is fraudulent billing practice to provide a service outside of the realm of medical psychotherapy and then to bill it as such. Clients may want services billed in a way that meets medical insurance standards to avoid paying out of pocket, but the consent of clients to bill insurance in no way protects the counselor in cases of fraudulent billing. If marriage counseling is provided, marriage counseling should be billed, regardless of reimbursement issues. Clients should also know that when medical insurance is billed, it requires a medical (psychiatric) diagnosis. Counselors should not diagnose mental disorders unless "they are qualified and competent" to render such diagnoses and licensed to do so (Anderson, 1996, p. 75). Some clients prefer to avoid communicating such diagnoses to third-party payers, and they may request to make other payment arrangements.

Billing for services that were not provided or justified is another fraudulent practice. A psychologist was sued for and found guilty of Medicare fraud when it was learned he was billing for the intelligence testing of nursing home residents who suffered from diagnosed dementia (loss of intelligence). In most cases, the tests were never given, or only cursory procedures were used to document attempts to test the patients. The testing was found to be unnecessary and, in most cases, there was no record of actual test administration. This was a clear case of fraudulent practice.

Some mental health professionals have been found guilty of double billing—for example, billing a government agency and then billing a client or client's family in full for services already reimbursed by a third party. This is obviously unacceptable practice.

Also there are instances of: (a) billing for an individual session when the client is seen in group; and (b) billing at a full credentialed rate for services rendered by students or a paraprofessional assistant. These are charges of fraud that are fairly common in the current managed care marketplace. Playing "get-rich schemes" at the expense of a third-party payer is a very dangerous game—such violations can result in felony convictions for insurance fraud, loss of a license to practice, or censure from a professional organization.

Another issue of concern is submitting forms to a third-party provider (such as a managed care company) requesting therapy for a client and purposefully overdiagnosing the client to ensure payment or permission to treat the patient for an extended period of time. (See the related discussion of upcoding and downcoding in Chapter 9.) **Overdiagnosis** is a diagnosis that is more severe than diagnostically justified to ensure adequate insurance coverage for the anticipated treatments (Cummings, 1998). Cummings stated:

> With indemnity insurance and in times past, providers characteristically underdiagnosed ostensibly for the protection of their patients. The most innocuous reimbursable diagnosis was overly used, whereas schizophrenia was seldom evoked as in many states the patient could suffer such consequences as loss of a driver's license or ineligibility for life insurance. In contrast, the era of managed care has seen the mushrooming of the use of severe diagnoses. Forced on many occasions to demonstrate concepts of "medical necessity" or "life threatening," practitioners' exaggeration of findings on evaluation has become widespread. (p. 61)

Obviously, it is unacceptable to overdiagnose for the purpose or reimbursement. In addition to constituting insurance fraud, overdiagnosing can do harm to clients. Diagnoses may follow clients for a lifetime, and a false diagnosis may affect the client's future insurability and future relations with mental health professionals.

Missed sessions are another issue. Should clients be billed when they miss appointments without giving adequate notice to allow rescheduling? Woody (1989) stated: "Missed sessions are troubling for both the client and the practitioner. If a client fails to show up for an appointment, the client suffers from lack of treatment, and the practitioner suffers from lack of income" (p. 150). Most practitioners have a general rule about billing missed appointments, and whatever policy is established, it should be communicated clearly (on informed consent forms) and implemented consistently. Missed appointments are usually not upsetting to the practitioner who has other work to fill the missed appointment time slot, but if the missed appointment is inconvenient and represents wasted time, it becomes problematic for the counselor. Legitimate emergencies that prevent attendance should be excused without penalty, and a policy about adequate advanced notice to cancel appointments should be clearly communicated to clients initiating treatment. Note that insurance companies do not pay for missed appointments—they pay only for services rendered, so bills for missed appointments go directly to the client.

Should counselors charge clients for phone contacts? Some charge one tenth of an hour for every 6 minutes on the phone. Others do not charge for phone contacts unless they represent an extended therapeutic interaction. As with other billing issues, clients should know how they are being charged well in advance. A surprise on a bill is likely to incite already fragile clients and create a conflict situation. Phone contacts are typically not reimbursed by insurance carriers.

Counselors have at least two options in dealing with clients who do not pay their fees. First, the counselor has the right to terminate the counseling relationship. The ACA code states that termination is appropriate when clients do not pay charged fees. If, however, it is clear that clients cannot pay fees, the counselor has the option of serving the client **pro bono publico,** for the public good, at no fee. The ACA code encourages such work. Counselors should know how much of their work is pro bono and if such an arrangement is acceptable to administrators and supervisors.

QUESTIONS FOR REFLECTION

You learn that one of your colleagues in a private agency is billing medical insurance for "medical psychotherapy" when, in fact, the counselor is providing career counseling services, including resume-writing guidance. It is obvious that the individuals receiving the counselor's services are not seeking treatment for a mental disorder. What are your obligations in this situation as a professional counselor? Why is this conduct unethical? What specific course of action should you take?

AGREEMENTS WITH NONPROFESSIONAL STAFF MEMBERS

Most agencies and schools employ nonprofessional staff members, such as clerical and janitorial staff. All nonprofessional staff members (as well as other professional and paraprofessional staff) must be fully aware of the ethical obligations of professional counselors and must be fully informed of their specific obligations to ensure the ethical rights of clients. Both the ACA and APA ethics codes state that counselors are ethically responsible to guarantee that there is no breach of ethics by staff members under their direction. In-service (in agency or within school) ethics training with staff members is highly recommended. A formal written agreement between counselors and their staff members is also recommended; this assigns a formality and importance to matters of ethical sensitivity. A breach of ethics could, and in some cases should, lead to termination of an employee who knowingly breaks the rules. Staff members should be especially sensitive to the client's right to privacy and confidentiality. Use of temporary staff or temporary agency workers should be avoided—such workers may work at the counseling site for short periods and may be replaced prior to adequate ethics training.

ADVERTISING

It was once considered unprofessional for highly educated professionals to advertise or solicit for clients. Professional codes of ethics banned lawyers and doctors from advertising. Legal challenges to these ethics code edicts were successful, and today radio and TV advertisements for doctors, lawyers, health service providers, and mental health professionals are common. A 1987 survey of psychologists found that about one fourth of the respondents advertised in newspapers and similar media (Pope, Tabachnick, & Keith-Spiegel, 1987). Interestingly, in a survey of consumer attitudes toward advertising by mental health professionals, Hite and Clawson (1989) found that respondents did not believe advertising would "lower the credibility, dignity, or image of the particular profession being promoted and that it could be done in good taste by mental health professionals" (p. 42). Any fears that advertising would have a negative effect on the credibility or image of the counselor may be unfounded.

Deception is the major issue related to advertising and soliciting clients. The ACA and APA codes caution practitioners and define deceptive advertising as unethical. Examples of deception include: (1) A master's-level, licensed professional counselor earns a doctoral degree from a bogus degree program (or a degree in a field unrelated to counseling) and lists the doctorate as a professional qualification (Dattilio, 1989). (2) A counselor who lists himself as a Ph.D. candidate or claims to have completed Ph.D. studies, although not technically a misrepresentation, certainly is being deceptive—such status does not necessarily lead to attainment of the degree and may mislead the public. (3) A counselor who lists bogus, unrelated, or unfinished degrees as credentials is deceptive and is misrepresenting his legitimate (acceptable), professional counseling training.

Additionally, the ACA code requires that client testimonials be solicited only from clients who are not vulnerable in any way related to consent. Counselors should avoid making global statements related to the nature or success of treatment, such as "loving care," "your way to health and happiness"—counselors cannot guarantee that they will care in a loving way for all of their clients, nor should they guarantee that all clients will be happy once services are provided (happiness may not be the acceptable outcome!). Trying to defend oneself against a client's claims that he or she did not feel happier after services, for example, could be a nightmare.

Cautions aside, and given the competitive nature of the health enterprise today, it may serve a counselor well to advertise. However, advertising should be prudent, tasteful, and free from global statements or guarantees that cannot be substantiated by professional literature or objective data.

If a counselor sells products in addition to providing services, such products should be advertised in a way that accurately depicts the product or service. It is quite legitimate for a counselor to sell relaxation audio- or videotapes to clients for use in the privacy of their homes. However, in many places a formal retail sales license is needed to sell products, and local laws must be examined to ensure that products are sold in a legal way. Counselors should limit the sale of products to those products within the purview of their professional license. Selling health aids for matters unrelated to mental health might be easily challenged by a client who is disenchanted by the product; such sales may constitute a potentially detrimental relationship. If a counselor sells vitamins or cleaning products as a sideline, selling such products to clients may infringe on the professional relationship. It is important to keep the role of the professional counselor clearly delineated.

Counselors employed in two or more settings should also avoid soliciting clients from one agency or setting of employment to another—for example, a counselor employed by a school should avoid soliciting clients for a private practice while in the role of a school counselor.

CREDENTIALS

For the professionally motivated individual, there is nothing more rewarding than earning a degree and being able to list degree initials after one's name. Once licensure status is earned, professionals can add additional letters after their names, such as L.P.C. for "licensed professional counselor." Professional certification by legitimate, professional certifying bodies offers a counselor another way of distinguishing himself or herself. The NBCC and the CRCC allow individuals to list N.C.C. or C.R.C. after their name to signify certification. It is common to see the initials M.A., L.P.C., N.C.C. after a counselor's name on correspondence, in case files, on letterhead, and on professional business cards. Counselors are proud to list such credentials. It is wise to list credentials in case file information to distinguish if services were provided by a counselor or other mental health professional, such as a psychiatric nurse, clinical psychologist, social worker, physician, or family therapist. In some cases, it is unnecessary to list all credentials—one does not have to present a resume with every letter of correspondence. A listing of basic credentials is sufficient. In case files, it may be sufficient and prudent to list initials or titles associated with the professional license, for example L.P.C. or Licensed Psychologist. Counselors must not misrepresent their credentials; also, it is unacceptable for a counselor to state that one is licensed without providing information on the type of license. There should be no question as to whether a person is a licensed counselor, psychologist, social worker, nurse, family therapist, or physician.

Although professional memberships can be announced in correspondence, membership itself should not be held out as a credential, unless the association has a special designated membership level. For example, the AAMFT has a "clinical member" category, which requires the member to have intense, approved supervision after receiving a degree. AAMFT clinical membership is a sought-after status and is a well-recognized credential.

Credentials in the mental health field are a dime a dozen. Literally anyone can set up a certification body and charge a fee for a fancy diploma. Use of such credentials to mislead the public about the competence or qualifications is highly dubious and reflects badly on the counselor and the profession (see Chapter 2). Such credentials may not stand the test of a court challenge in defense against incompetent practice or malpractice as a specialist. Generally, only credentials with linkages to legitimate professional organizations are valued in the mental health field. Beyond the NBCC and the CRCC, two examples of acceptable counseling credentials are those offered by (a) the National Credentialing Academy for Certified Family Therapists (which has linkage to the ACA through its affiliate), the IAMFC and (b) the Certificate in Clinical Hypnosis sponsored by the American Society of Clinical Hypnosis. Agency and school administrators should communicate which

credentials are acceptable or valued and how, when, and where acceptable professional credentials are to be displayed or listed.

QUESTIONS FOR REFLECTION

A counselor lists on his business card that he is a certified hypnotherapist but provides no further information. Is this unethical? If so, why?

MAINTENANCE OF RECORDS AND FILES

Offices sometimes become sloppy. It is not unusual to visit a professional counselor's office and to feel that it is "lived in" (to put it nicely). Although a professional office may feel like home to many, there are serious differences between professional and nonprofessional offices. Client records, unlike personal items, need to be protected. They should be filed in a safe place and locked away when not in use. Files should not be left out in the open, especially after work hours or when other clients are in close, visual contact.

It is standard procedure to destroy records a certain number of years after services have been terminated. Most licensure boards require that records be kept a certain period of time after services have been terminated for legal reasons (e.g., in case there is an ethics complaint). Records are generally kept for 5 to 7 years after services have been terminated. Disposal of records is not as simple as just throwing them in the trash— records should be destroyed in a way that removes identification or by shredding or burning. Old bills, office notes, and calendars should also be destroyed in a way that ensures privacy.

Counselors should have policies about removing files from the office. Some agencies have strict policies that forbid removal of files from the office, which can be a dangerous practice—a file in a briefcase can be stolen, files may be left in an unlocked automobile, and a counselor's family members may have access to files in the home setting. Obviously, this is not good ethical practice. Counselors should have a compelling reason to remove a file to an unsecured environment.

COMMUNICATIONS WITH OTHER PROFESSIONALS

Communication with other professionals can take several forms. Communication occurs among the professionals within an agency and with professionals outside of the agency. Schools also have internal and external means of communications, primarily between counselors and teachers or administrators.

Clear agency or school guidelines should be established for intraagency/intraschool communications, with the client's best interests at heart. Most agencies have general statements of confidentiality that allow for internal communications among professionals, such as counselors, psychologists, psychiatrists, and social workers on staff. Schools, however, may have policies that prevent the communication of sensitive counseling material to teachers or administrators without compelling educational or safety-related reasons. The prudent course of action is to keep confidential information as confidential as possible within a school or agency setting. Clients should never be the brunt of gossip in a teacher's lounge, nor should agency personnel know more than they need to know in regard to interactions with clients. However, there are cases that require cross-professional involvement—for example, between a psychiatrist and a counselor who are both involved with a client. Generally, clients should know when such interaction is necessary and the reasons for consultation. In most cases, special consent is not necessary for within-agency or school consultation; however, local and federal laws should be examined to assess if special obligations exist (see Chapters 13 and 18).

Communications with professionals outside of an agency or school are governed by rules of confidentiality and privacy. Formal consent should be obtained— confidentiality and privacy statements signed by the client at the outset of treatment should describe circumstances under which a counselor can communicate to other professionals in the best interests of the client (as in emergency situations). If ongoing formal consultation is requested, the counselor should have a formal agreement with the consultant allowing for such interaction— for example, a private practitioner might have an agreement with another private practitioner to discuss difficult cases. To ensure that professional feedback can occur without a breach of client rights, counselors can develop a consultant agreement that allows for detailed discussion of cases, perhaps without identifying client information. Such agreements are in no way reflective of a supervisory or controlling relationship and simply allow for professional communication on challenging cases.

When a counselor makes a referral, he or she cannot receive remuneration for the referral. Such payment could compromise professional judgment, leading to referral to the remunerating professional for less than professional reasons. Also, it is highly recommended that

counselors refer to a list of qualified professionals rather than to one professional and allow clients to choose from the list on their own after researching their options. Counselors must consider the legal ramifications of referrals. Attorneys sometimes "shotgun" lawsuit—broadly "shooting at" (suing) any involved professional. If a professional to whom a counselor referred a client does something wrong, the client's lawyer might sue the counselor as the referring agent.

QUESTION FOR REFLECTION

You are a professional school counselor employed in a secondary school. At lunch in the teachers' lounge you overhear one of your counseling colleagues and a teacher discussing the family problems of a student. There is some laughter involved. What should you do?

DISAGREEMENTS WITH EMPLOYERS OR SUPERVISORS

Professional counselors sometimes have disagreements with employers, administrators, or supervisors. It is important to have a clear understanding of the role of the supervisor and the role of the supervised counselor. If the supervision is for professional licensure or certification, both parties should sign a formal supervision agreement (Remley & Herlihy, 2001). Such an agreement should spell out the responsibilities of both parties, the amount of time and the place where supervision is to take place, the nature of job duties covered by the supervision, the ethical obligations of the supervisor and supervised counselor, the nature of legal responsibility for work that is accomplished, the requirement of malpractice insurance and coverage on the supervisor's policy, an agreement on how the supervision can end (e.g., the circumstances and actions that can lead to a negative recommendation by the supervisor regarding licensure or certification), and the length of the proposed supervision. Failure to clarify details on such matters can lead to difficulties if there are disagreements. Supervised counselors should also have some understanding about what to do if they question the ethical judgment of their supervisors. An arbitration arrangement to address disagreement is one way to avoid conflicts—that is, if there is disagreement, an arbitrator acceptable to both parties is consulted to make a judgment on the acceptable course of action (Remley & Herlihy, 2001, offer a Clinical Supervision Model Agreement that serves as an excellent example of licensure supervision).

Conflicts with administrators sometimes are more problematic. If a noncounselor administrator establishes policy that conflicts with the conventional ethical wisdom of the profession, counselors have an obligation to educate the administrator. Administrative policies are sometimes crucial to the effectiveness of counseling— for example, an administrator may require that a number of clients too large to accomplish effective group counseling should be scheduled for group sessions. Counselors may be assigned a caseload that is too large to provide competent services; equipment, tests, and supplies may be out of date; facilities may be inadequate. A number of administrative issues can become problematic; counselors are obligated to address the problems with the people in charge. If changes are not made to ensure adequate, competent, and ethical services, a counselor should examine other employment options. However, the counselor's primary responsibility is to try to inspire changes within the organization according to both the ACA and APA ethics codes.

Counselors also have an obligation to prevent discrimination. If it appears that administrative policies are such that certain constituents are singled out, denied services, or treated unfairly, it is the counselor's obligation to address concerns with the administration.

Both the ACA and the APA ethical codes have stipulations about nondiscrimination.

DECISION MAKING IN CONTEXT

The area of office, administrative, and business practices is an area of counseling practice that lends itself to planning. Planning is the best defense against ethical challenges in this area. Planning constitutes a first line of ethical decision making. It is preemptive. It is forward thinking. Counselors must make decisions from the outset of their practices, whether in organizational or private practice settings, to establish policies and procedures that ensure ethical safeguards. By reviewing the applicable codes of ethics, counselors can foresee problematic areas related to office, administrative, and business practices. The attitude of administrators is absolutely critical, as they will establish the ethical "tone" of the office related to policies and procedures. Ideally, when in an organizational setting, professional staff will be involved in defining the crucial ethical issues and will be able to have input into methods to ensure ethical practice. When feasible, following universal design guidelines is recommended, as this prevents the cost involved in modifying physical structures to meet accessibility standards.

Box 8–1 • Application of an Ethical Decision-Making Model to the Process of Planning Office, Administrative, and Business Practices

The application of a decision-making model to planning office, administrative, and business practices is a way of demonstrating how forethought on such matters can prevent serious ethical breaches. Assume that you work for an agency that employs a staff of six professional counselors. The agency has just signed a lease for new office space, and the administrator of the agency has asked the supervisor of counseling to consult with the professional staff to address the layout of the new office space. There are limitations, both financial and spatial, so counselors don't have unlimited options. Both the administrator of the agency and the counselor supervisor have confidence in the professional staff, and the supervisor has set up a half-day meeting to address basic office layout issues. The supervisor provided copies of the ACA and APA ethics codes and has also done a brief review on office practices in the mental health professions literature. The counseling staff has been asked to devise three acceptable office layout plans. The supervisor decided, in consultation, to apply the Social Constuctivism Model of Ethical Decision Making, presenting each ethical principle (autonomy,

beneficence, nonmaleficence, fidelity, and justice) as a framework for defining ethical problems. The counselors define fidelity (e.g. confidentiality/privacy), safety (nonmaleficence), and accessibility (justice) issues as critical ethical concerns related to the office layout. The counselors are to "consensualize" as to ethically acceptable office layouts. Once the plans are drawn in rough format, they will be presented to the administrator and the office building staff, who will then estimate the cost of the plans. If there is disagreement as to the cost, feasibility, or ethical sensitivity of the plans, then a process of negotiation will proceed, in which case the professional and construction supervisors will attempt to come to agreement (reasonable compromises). If there is an impasse, the agency administrator will be viewed as the final arbitor in the decision process.

In this very concrete example, one can see how a decision-making model can be used to plan to prevent ethical dilemmas related to office, administrative, and business practices. Remember, planning is preventative decision making.

Consultation is important in any decision-making model, and in some models that emphasize relational decision making, it is crucial. Gathering the important information related to ethical office, administrative, and business practices is a good starting point. Once issues have been identified, each can be addressed as an ethical challenge.

Unfortunately, some professionals do not use forethought related to office, administrative, and business practices. Because they have failed to plan, they must address the ethical dilemmas as they arise. Decision making in cases of nonaccommodating practice then becomes remediation. Such decision making must address the concern immediately, and it must correct the policy, procedure, or structural issues that lead to the dilemma. In such cases, where a dilemma could have been avoided with ethical forethought, resolution of ethical dilemmas must involve thoughtful application of a formal ethical decision-making model (see Box 8–1).

CHAPTER SUMMARY

Privacy issues should be utmost in the design of a professional office. Soundproofing, separate entry/exit doors, and maintaining privacy of client files are issues of importance. Offices should be organized to provide for the safety of clients and staff. In space-sharing arrangements, counselors must ensure the privacy of all client files and other case-relevant information. Formal, written ethics agreements between parties are recommended. Counselors must make provisions for individuals with disabilities: elevators in storied buildings, wheelchair accessible bathrooms, and accommodations for hearing or visually impaired clients. Offices that receive federal funds must be in compliance with accessibility standards.

Several systems are available for fee setting: (1) sliding fee scales; (2) flat fee, variable collection procedures; (3) low-fee cash-only service, and (4) credit/debit card payments. Regardless of the fee and billing procedures, counselors must have a clearly articulated fee schedule and stick to the schedule.

Clients must understand the procedures at initiation of treatment. Fraudulent billing is a major concern; billing for services that were not provided or justified is fraudulent practice. Double billing can result in felony convictions for insurance fraud, a loss of license to practice, and censure from a professional organization. Overdiagnosing also constitutes insurance fraud and can do harm to clients.

All nonprofessional staff must be fully aware of their ethical obligations. Counselors are ethically responsible to guarantee no breach of ethics by staff members under their direction.

Counselors must avoid deception in advertising. Client testimonials should be solicited only from clients who are not vulnerable in any way related to consent. Counselors should avoid global statements they cannot guarantee. Counselors must not misrepresent their credentials. Use of credentials to mislead the public about competence or qualifications is highly dubious.

It is standard practice to destroy case records a certain number of years after services have been terminated, generally 5 to 7 years. Records should be destroyed in a way that removes identification or by shredding or burning.

Communication with other professionals can occur among the professionals within an agency and with professionals outside the agency. Clear guidelines should be established with the client's best interests at heart. Most agencies have general statements of confidentiality that allow for internal communications. Communications outside an agency or school are governed by rules of confidentiality and privacy.

It is important to have a clear understanding of the roles of the supervisor and the supervised counselor in case of disagreements. Agreements should spell out the responsibilities of both parties.

The area of office, administrative, and business practices is highly amenable to ethical planning and forethought. By planning ahead, ethical dilemmas may be avoided. However, when faced with an ethical dilemma, counselors should apply an acceptable ethical decision making model.

REFERENCES

Anderson, B. S. (1996). *The counselor and the law* (4th ed.). Alexandria, VA: American Counseling Association.

Association of State and Provincial Psychology Boards. (2001). *Ethics, law and avoiding liability in the practice of psychology.* Montgomery, AL: Author.

Cummings, N. A. (1998). Moral issues in managed mental health care. In R. F. Small & L. R. Barnhill (Eds.), *Practicing in the new mental health marketplace: Ethical, legal, and moral issues.* Washington, DC: American Psychological Association.

Dattilio, F. M. (1989). Fraudulent degrees: A threat to the mental health counseling field. *Journal of Mental Health Counseling, 11,* 151–154.

Gibson, W. T., & Pope, K. S. (1993). The ethics of counseling: A national survey of certified counselors. *Journal of Counseling and Development, 71,* 330–336.

Hite, R. E., & Clawson, D. L. (1989). Consumer attitudes toward advertising by mental health professionals. *Journal of Marketing for Mental Health, 2,* 33–57.

Lien, C. (1993). The ethics of the sliding fee scale. *Journal of Mental Health Counseling, 15,* 334–341.

Make sure your office layout is legal. (1993, March). *Medical Economics, 70,* 111.

Pope, K. S., Tabachnick, B. G., & Keith-Spiegel, P. (1987). Ethics of practice: The beliefs and behaviors of psychologists as therapists. *American Psychologist, 42,* 993–1006.

Pope, K. S., & Vasquez, M. J. T. (1991). *Ethics in psychotherapy and counseling.* San Francisco: Jossey-Bass.

Remley, T. P., & Herlihy, B. (2001). *Ethical, legal and professional issues in counseling.* Upper Saddle River, NJ: Merrill/Prentice Hall.

Roberts, T., & Roberts, J. (1985). An integrative model of cash collections for mental health centers. *Community Mental Health Journal, 21,* 282–293.

Woody, R. H. (1989). *Business success in mental health practice.* San Francisco, CA: Jossey-Bass.

PART 4

Ethical Challenges and Emerging Issues

CHAPTER 9

Ethics and Client Health

Vilia M. Tarvydas • Barbara L. O'Rourke • Christine K. Urish

OBJECTIVES

After reading this chapter, you should be able to:

- Discuss the health care issues that affect counseling practices and the resources that assist counselors in helping their clients face these issues.

- Explain the basic forms of managed health care and the ethical impact of managed health care on counselor practice in the areas of counselor competence, informed consent and confidentiality, fidelity, integrity, diagnosis, conflict of interest, and business relationships.

- Define the term *biomedical ethics* and summarize information from the bioethical literature that is relevant to counseling.

- Discuss the ethical aspects of the bioethical issues involved in genetics, hastened death and end-of-life care (euthanasia, rational suicide), abortion, complementary and alternative medicine, and HIV.

INTRODUCTION

In recent years, we have seen a trend in westernized medicine toward a more holistic and comprehensive system of health care. This trend includes turning to types of care once considered alternative, as well as including family, community, and other aspects of an individual's life into health care. As this trajectory continues, counseling is seen as both healing art and science and is becoming a more integral part of traditional health care. At the same time, as the field of health care incorporates counseling as an important aspect of healing, counselors are integrating physical aspects of care into their practice. Counseling services now are acknowledged widely as being effective for clients who are experiencing a variety of physical and psychiatric problems.

Rehabilitation counselors, mental health counselors, and social workers have been educated to provide counseling service to people with acute and chronic health conditions and have been doing this type of work for years. In the precedent set by these disciplines, it is becoming more common to see counselors as part of a health care team in such a wide range of settings as family health agencies, rehabilitation facilities that assist in recovery from disabilities such as head or spinal injury, chemical dependency treatment centers, and pain clinics. Counselors in these settings provide counseling and supportive services such as training in stress management, teaching coping skills, and coordinating the educational needs of young clients. In fact, major funding sources such as insurance companies and other third-party payer systems are demanding a more comprehensive, interdisciplinary approach to treatment. Thus, the practices of both medicine and counseling are shifting, and the requisite skills and abilities needed by all disciplines for sound practice are also expanding.

Mental health care is practiced increasingly within the context of medicine and biomedicine whether or not counselors practice directly in a medical or health care setting. Additionally, community-based counselors are likely to encounter clients who are facing health or medically related issues. School counselors see students who are considering abortion. Employment and rehabilitation counselors see people who are HIV-positive and struggling to deal with employment discrimination. Most counselors see people with mental disorders who are on medications and are using some type of complementary medical therapy. In the future, all will see the unknown impacts of genetic advances on the lives of the clients they serve. This chapter will focus on: the impact of working in a managed care environment, important ethicolegal considerations when working with health care issues, developing counselors' understanding of bioethics as a specialty of ethics that affects our clients and society, and discussing several specific contemporary bioethical issues that counselors are most likely to face.

MANAGED CARE

Health care reform continues to evolve in response to the escalating and devastating costs of health care. Estimates of the U.S. General Accounting Office indicate that of the 70.5% of U.S. citizens who are younger than 65 years and have private health insurance, four of five are covered by a **managed care organization** (MCO; Office of Public Policy and Information, 1997). Beyond this startling figure, it is important to note that managed care health coverage also is increasing in public health care programs including both the Medicare and Medicaid programs since the passage of the Balanced Budget Act of 1997 (Office of Public Policy and Information). The purpose of managed care is to control the increasing health care costs in the United States (Chan, Lui, Rosenthal, Pruett, & Ferrin, 2001). **Managed care** is defined as "any system that combined the financing and delivery of health care services to control cost, quality, quantity, and access of health services" (Dombeck & Olsan, 2002, p. 222). MCOs use a variety of techniques to keep costs low, including: limited number of session, preauthorization review, utilization review, and a lengthy period of time clinicians and agencies must wait to obtain payment for services previously provided (Meier & Davis, 2001).

Cooper and Gottlieb (2000) presented a historical perspective of the emergence of the managed care movement, the evolution of managed mental health care, and the goals and key concepts involved in this health care reform. Managed care encompasses a variety of designs and reimbursement systems (Dombeck & Olsan, 2002).

Types of Managed Care

The types of service in **MCOs** typically take several forms. Organizations that participate in managed care include (a) health maintenance organizations **(HMOs),** which provide specified health services using a restricted group of providers at a fixed cost to the consumer; (b) preferred provider organizations **(PPOs),** which purchase health care from specific providers at a discounted rate; and (c) independent practice associations **(IPAs),** which allow consumers to choose independent practitioners but retain a portion of the fees from providers who may be reimbursed either on a fee-for-service or capitated basis (Shore, 1996). The aim of managed care is twofold: (a) to limit the treatment to that required to return a client to a reasonable level of functioning as soon as possible, but not necessarily to deal with the underlying clinical illness; and (b) to address the secondary goal of prevention, on the theory that preventative care will reduce the overall cost of health care. The presence of a managed care environment has created a unique ethical climate for counselors in which they must learn to practice. Counselors' responses to this climactic change are diverse.

Ethical Climate of Managed Care

Reactions to managed care systems in the health care industry have been mixed. Strong ethical concerns and considerations have been generated in the area of mental health (Cooper & Gottlieb, 2000; Glosoff, Garcia, Herlihy, & Remley, 1999). Benefits for managed care consumers and counselors have been identified as (a) limited cost of services compared to traditional indemnity plans, (b) increased access to necessary mental health services, (c) no exclusions due to a preexisting condition, (d) increased referral rate for some practitioners, and (e) establishment of quality control and monitoring of standards of practice (Lawless, Ginter, & Kelly, 1999). Chan et al. (2001) stated that case management interventions that occur at the time of illness or injury and focus on early medical intervention and conflict resolution can avoid the development of a negative relationship between the employee and the employer.

Disadvantages often noted include (a) a limited choice in health care providers, (b) an inability to consult a specialist directly, (c) a reduction in the variety of services available, (d) the potential for overuse of pharmacological interventions, (e) a limited treatment duration for some diagnoses, (f) the increased potential for overreliance on outpatient services, (g) the use of a gatekeeping system, (h) use of specific clinical guidelines that may not be appropriate for all clients with a specific condition; and (i) provider bonuses for clients who make specific improvements (outcomes) within a specified period of time. Moffic (2002) expressed concern that such provider bonus structures may "rush" the clinician or the clinician may be tempted to engage in fraudulent behavior by indicating the client has improved to obtain the bonus when client improvement may not have met the specified indicator. In the gatekeeper procedure, the managed care vendor often assigns the client to a care provider or dictates treatment options before their approval in an effort to control costs. Counselors also express difficulty in establishing treatment goals in a managed care environment, as the length of treatment is uncertain because it is often determined by utilization review that can vary from MCO to MCO (Meier & Davis, 2001). Further, some MCOs provide counselors with report cards that describe the average number of sessions for a client during a specified time frame. The message conveyed by this action to the counselor is that they should not exceed the MCO's criteria (Meier & Davis).

Nevertheless, managed care is a reality that is here to stay. The questions then become, "What form will it take?" and "How will this form affect client care?" Hersch (1995) said, "It is time to move beyond our hurt, fear, and anger. It is time to become creative and adaptive by fully using the substantial repertoire of professional skills available" (p. 16) to ensure quality client care. Counselors must be informed about managed care and involved in shaping the principles of managed care to provide sound, ethical care to clients. Counselors who provide services to clients under a managed care agreement need to be keenly aware of their obligations to the managed care plan and their clients and be knowledgeable of the professional code of ethics (Huber, 1995). Despite whatever dissatisfaction, ambivalence, or resistance to managed mental health care that counselors may have, they may find it difficult to survive financially if

they choose not to participate in such systems (Lawless et al. 1999). Although new clinicians may begin practice with limited choices regarding where they work or what type of clients they serve, it is important to note that managed care impacts everyone and beginning practice with an informed perspective is a wise decision (Alleman, 2001). Counselors seeking positions in which they can have long-term therapeutic relationships with clients, or who feel the need for personal power and control over the treatment provided to their client, may run in to difficulties when they encounter the environment of managed care (Alleman).

Managed care systems have a major impact on the ethical landscape of counseling. Miller (1998) of the National Coalition of Mental Health Professionals and Consumers identified eleven of the most common unethical managed care practices: (a) disregarding personal and medical privacy, (b) using false advertising, (c) using deceptive language, (d) violating traditional scientific ethics, (e) practicing outside of a professional's area of competence, (f) creating and intensifying conflicts of interest, (g) keeping secrets about financial conflicts of interest, (h) violating informed consent procedures, (i) using kickbacks to keep patients away from specialists, (j) squandering money entrusted to their care, and (k) disregarding information about harm to patients. It is important for clinicians to be aware of these unethical practices to prepare themselves if they are placed in a situation in which one of these unethical practices is occurring. These concerns surfaced in a study of 108 mental health counselors in four states. These counselors indicated managed care has negatively affected their work with clients. Within this study, client confidentiality and disclosure was identified as the most problematic ethical issue (Danzinger & Welfel, 2001). Additional problems identified by counselors in this study included: revised treatment plans to match MCO protocols (60%), premature termination of counseling relationship (44%), and inconsistent informed consent (36%). Disturbingly, only one third of the counselors surveyed reported using the ACA code of ethics to assist in solving ethical dilemmas as a result of managed care (Danzinger & Welfel). See Box 9–1.

Cooper and Gottlieb (2000) grouped ethical problems into several ethical issues in managed mental health care that must be addressed: (a) counselor competence, (b) informed consent and confidentiality, (c) fidelity, (d) conflict of interest, and (e) business relationships.

Box 9–1 • Exploring the Code

Examine the professional codes of ethics to which you are held accountable

1. Which areas would you need to be sensitive to when practicing in a managed care environment?
2. Does your professional code of ethics address counseling individuals who are considering donation of embryos for stem cell research? If so, in what area would this be considered? If this is not an area addressed by the code, should it be?
3. What are the differences between business ethics and professional ethics? Do these differing ethics facilitate conflicted loyalties in counselors who are employed at for-profit agencies?
4. You are working with the family of a patient who did not sign a power of attorney and does not have a living will. One family member wishes to discontinue life support, whereas other family members are fighting against this action. Does your professional code of ethics offer guidance in this area?
5. You work with a counselor who has completed Level I Reiki training and has presented to her colleagues at the pain clinic the desire to train others in this alternative medicine technique. You learn that individuals must complete Level III Reiki training before they are able to train others. This colleague is passing her credentials as being able to train others. What does your professional code indicate about competence and credentials in this area?

Counselor Competence

The obligation of counselor competence as mandated by the ACA and APA codes of ethics requires that counselors strive to maintain the highest level of professional services and neither claim nor imply professional qualifications exceeding those they possess. Counseling practice in a managed care setting may present relevant questions regarding several aspects of a counselor's competence. One implication is that counselors must be trained adequately to appropriately select, diagnose, and treat clients in a managed care situation. The counselor must be able to identify who is appropriate for services; for what kind of treatment, and under what circumstances. Typically, managed care has resulted in more medical services, including mental health services, being rendered on an outpatient or nonhospital basis. Moreover, briefer, more cost-effective therapy modalities are the treatment of choice for numerous conditions within managed care situations. With this context in mind, Meier and Davis (2001) offered some potential solutions for successful clinical services within a managed care environment. Counselors are encouraged to act as their clients' agent and not abandon their clients to the MCO. To this end, counselors are encouraged to consider the strategies presented in Figure 9–1.

Counselors who plan to practice in a managed care setting must demonstrate specific, requisite skills for being successful within that setting. Due to the advantages and disadvantages of managed care, counselors may

1. Limit goals to the most distressing current symptoms and postpone attention to contributing or less distressing issues.
2. Share the session issue with the client, as soon as appropriate, so that both individuals can help decide how far to proceed.
3. Help the client decide whether he or she will pay for therapy when insurance payments are exhausted.
4. Refer the client to a counseling agency with the ability to continue therapy post insurance.
5. Continue working with the client pro bono or at a significantly reduced rate.

FIGURE 9–1.   Strategies for More Successful Managed Care Service

Source: From "Managed care as an ethical issue" by S. T. Meier and S. R. Davis, 2001, in F. Flach (Ed.). *Ethical Issues in Professional Counseling* (pp. 27–36). Copyright 2001 by Hatherliegh Press. Adapted by permission.

be encouraged to provide services that are outside of their area of competency (Lawless et al., 1999). Counselors should remember their individual professional codes of ethics and strive to uphold the ethical standards in provision of services. Moreover, counselors should be aware of specific skills that would assist them in facilitating success within a managed care environment, including effective communication and knowledge of business principles. Being business savvy is a definite asset to a counselor who wishes to practice in managed care. Two specific skill areas in which counselors may or may not be proficient are often emphasized in managed care settings: diagnosis and use of brief therapies.

Diagnosis. Managed care has affected the very definition of mental illness. Counselors' moral and ethical responses to these changes are important, not only for the clients who sit in front of them, but also for all potential clients who may need their services in the future. The importance of diagnosis is heightened by managed care, and labeling through diagnosis can be damaging to the clients. The stigma associated with diagnosis and the use of diagnosis to reduce managed care responsibilities to clients are but two examples of possible damaging effects of assigning a diagnosis to someone. Damage to clients may extend into their futures and include such effects as a decreased ability to obtain a job and insurance coverage, or to have the diagnosis used negatively in a custody hearing or other legal matters. Nevertheless, diagnosis generally has come to be accepted as a necessary process and presents counselors with a significant challenge. Wylie (1995) stated "therapists are increasingly caught in a three-way crunch between diagnostic accuracy (often complicated by ambiguous symptoms), confidentiality, and the power wielded by the insurer, usually around problem diagnoses that are stigmatized" (p. 32). Part of the challenge of appropriate diagnosis to counselors is to clarify the philosophical and moral systems they themselves hold regarding the use of a labeling system in mental health. They must address questions such as whether to use a less severe diagnosis to reduce the effect of labeling on a client. Conversely, they must examine whether they have a tendency toward overreporting and overdiagnosing clients' problems to help them qualify for services and to justify gaining reimbursability for services (Bilynsky & Vernaglia, 1998). The counselor is cautioned that such behavior could constitute insurance fraud and result in legal action.

Counselors need to be aware of the temptation to upcode or downcode a client diagnosis when working in a managed care environment (Cooper & Gottlieb, 2000). A counselor who **upcodes** a client diagnoses the client with a more serious or severe diagnosis than the client presents with in an attempt to obtain an increased number of counseling sessions from the MCO. A counselor who **downcodes** a client gives the client a less serious or severe diagnosis to obtain treatment for that client. For example, if a managed care company does not pay for services for a diagnosis of personality

disorder, the counselor may omit reporting the diagnosis and just report the condition. Further, upcoding and downcoding are ethical violations of integrity (Daniels, 2001). Danzinger and Welfel (2001) reported 44% of the counselors they surveyed had changed a client's diagnosis to obtain managed care reimbursement or were willing to engage in this behavior. Both upcoding and downcoding are unethical and may be considered fraudulent (Cooper & Gottlieb).

The Health Care Finance Administration (HCFA), the U.S. Department of Justice (DOJ), the Office of Inspector General (OIG), and the DHHS have become keenly aware of the use of upcoding for certain diagnoses as well as the improper discharge of clients only to readmit them in a very short period of time (Berenson; 1999; Department of Health and Human Services, 2000; Hallam, 1999). Practitioners who have felt limited due to reimbursement rates for a specific diagnosis have been identified as misdiagnosing a client and overdiagnosing or upcoding to obtain an increased number of sessions with the client, or the same amount of sessions but more revenue due to the upcode. This latter practice is more questionable ethically—it appears practitioner self-interest is the primary motivation for this practice. Conversely, some practitioners have been observed as underdiagnosing clients to receive increased reimbursement and rewards from the MCO (Hallam). In a very stark sense, these pressures cause the counselor to struggle with the question of whose standards will establish the diagnosis—those of the professional or those of the MCO. Ethically, it is very clear that the responsibility for objective and honest professional diagnostic and treatment services rests with the counselor.

In defining *mental illness* as impaired functioning, the proponents of managed care have challenged the traditional definition and, subsequently, its traditional treatment goals. In some systems, this shift may deprive clients with certain diagnoses (such as personality disorder) of longer term services. The managed care treatment model opts for minimal levels of acceptable function over maximizing the quality of life as its desired outcome. *The Diagnostic and Statistical Manual, Fourth Edition* (DSM–IV-TR, 2000) classification system is the required, primary diagnostic schema used by managed care corporations. This requirement has been accused of providing a mechanism for narrowing and constricting treatment and has been adopted as the official justification for denying "medical necessity" (Wylie, 1995). Further, this system of diagnosis is incompatible with some orientations, such as systems theory and the psychosocial rehabilitation philosophy, which seeks to demedicalize or depathologize functional limitations and to focus on an asset-based model.

According to Kutchins and Kirk (1987), the original development of a diagnostic system in mental health was done for reasons of enhanced communication and not for economic purposes. However, the current thrust of the DSM system is fiduciary access. This means that payment of services often depends on the type of diagnosis according to this nomenclature. Moreover, to use this system of diagnosis accurately requires the evaluation and use of organic/physical information that is typically beyond the counselor's expertise. If these assumptions are true, diagnosis requires consultation or the collaborative effort of a physician or psychiatrist and a counselor when treating the client.

The DSM–IV-TR classification system's multiaxial approach was developed to facilitate this collaborative effort as a means to include the biological and psychosocial aspects of mental health. However, the reality in practice often results in an imbalance in the importance given to diagnoses placed under certain axes. For example, the use of V codes as "conditions that may be a focus of clinical attention" (DSM–IV-TR, 2000) is often not seen as significant for treatment and, therefore, is not reimbursable by managed care. This barrier to treatment may be applied to other diagnoses as well. Diagnoses that typically may not be reimbursable include adjustment disorders, personality disorders, and disorders that require long-term treatment such as post-traumatic stress disorder.

When an MCO questions or challenges a counselor's decision-making process with regard to diagnosis and treatment, the counselor must be prepared to present empirical support as evidence of clinical judgment. The counselor needs to present the information in language that can be easily understood and will be accepted by the MCO (Glosoff et al., 1999). Figure 9–2 lists the requisite knowledge and skills for competent counselors who practice in the managed care environment.

Even when the diagnosis itself is not in question, the current diagnostic system presents ethical challenges to counselors. For example, problems may arise concerning limitations of confidentiality and the ramifications of new technology with interconnecting computer data banks and internet networking capabilities. Wylie (1995) asserted that "many diagnoses can still shadow a client's life like hounds from hell and much more efficiently in the cyberspace age than ever before"

Counselors who work in a managed care environment should know:
1. The diagnostic categories within the *Diagnostic and Statistical Manual of Mental Disorders* (4th ed.) (DSM–IV)
2. The standards of professional practice for providing treatment of various clinical problems
3. Managed care terminology
4. The factors that impact client satisfaction with counseling and managed care services
5. The procedures for billing and reimbursement for services provided
6. The procedures to follow when a client's counselor is not available and the client requires services
7. How to balance the needs of the managed care organization in accessing confidential client medical records
8. How effective treatment plans develop
9. Record-keeping procedures that are consistent with the counselor's area of professional expertise and fulfill the requirements of the managed care organization
10. How to obtain ongoing training to demonstrate continued competence in the counselor's area of expertise
11. Effective practice management strategies in the areas of billing, reporting, and basic accounting procedures
12. How to collect and maintain outcome and effectiveness data
13. Counseling philosophy to provide to potential clients and the managed care organization
14. How to work as a part of a team in a cooperative manner

FIGURE 9–2. Counselor Knowledge and Skills Needed in a Managed Care Environment

Source: Adapted from "Managed care: Ethical considerations for counselors" by H. L. Glosoff, J. Garcia, B. Herlihy, and T. P. Remley, 1999. *Counseling and Values, 44*(1). Copyright 1999 by the American Counseling Association; and from "Managed care: What mental health counselors need to know" by L. Lawless, E. J. Ginter, and K. R. Kelly, 1999. *Journal of Mental Health Counseling, 21*(1). Copyright 1999 by the American Mental Health Counseling Association. Adapted by permission.

(p. 32). Clearly, counselors must work at all levels—personally and politically—to address these dilemmas. They also must know and understand their institutions' information management systems and policies so that they can best protect their clients' confidentiality and provide accurate informed consent.

Kutchins and Kirk (1987) offered counselors a list of time-honored suggestions to guide their use of the

- All diagnoses should be made with scrupulous regard for correct procedures. Know your boundaries of competence.
- Careful attention should be paid to organic conditions. Work in conjunction with a physician or carefully review all medical reports.
- A physician should be routinely consulted about the medical aspects of a diagnosis.
- Every diagnosis should be accurately reported to the client and to the insurer. Further, the client should be fully informed about the potential ramifications of using the diagnostic label before its use in formal documents.
- Patients should be advised, preferably in writing, that no diagnosis is meant to indicate a definitive judgment about any physical condition.
- Patients should be referred to physicians for the evaluation of any medical condition.

FIGURE 9–3. Procedures for Using DSM–IV System
Source: From "DSM–III-R and Social Work Malpractice" by H. Kutchins and S. Kirk, 1987, May, *Social Work.* Copyright 1987 by the National Association of Social Work. Adapted by permission.

DSM classification system. A modified version of their list is provided in Figure 9–3.

Brief Therapies. Many MCOs encourage the use of brief therapy strategies. Counselors should learn these techniques for use with their clients in the managed care environment (Lawless et al., 1999). However, not all clients may benefit from brief therapy approaches. Counselors must be able to evaluate clients critically to determine if brief services would be beneficial or if the client would be harmed more from brief services than if no therapy services were provided (Glosoff et al., 1999). Counselors must be aware of their own professional limitations and institute appropriate agency referrals for clients who require services outside of their professional competence.

Some counselors may view the time-limited therapeutic approach encouraged by many managed care companies as limiting, and others may try to view this from a different, possibly more positive perspective. The time limit may create a sense of urgency, accountability, and purpose, which can facilitate the client to be more committed to the therapeutic relationship, with the counselor and client being committed to making the treatment time that they have available as productive as possible (Alleman, 2001).

Not surprisingly, hospital and agency health care ethics committees are playing an increasing role in

resolving ethical decisions regarding managed care. Clinicians need to explore what resources are available to them in this area. For example, one survey of 45 hospitals in the Philadelphia area found that health care ethics committees were spending 7.6% of committee time on managed care issues (McGee & Spanogle, 2001). Counselors are encouraged to become politically active, join local, state, and national groups who are working on managed care issues, stay informed through consumption of professional publications that address managed care issues, utilize resources on the internet to self-educate, and seek assistance in navigating the managed care system (Meier & Davis, 2001).

Counselor competence for short-term treatments requires that counselors must be prepared and able to focus on achievable, specific treatment goals and to be active and more directive in conducting treatment. Short-term treatment should not be considered long-term therapy conducted in merely a more abbreviated time frame; it requires a unique set of skills. Clinicians must be trained for this approach and provide only treatment that falls within their personal scopes of practice as determined by appropriate training and experience. They also must be fully informed and competent in facilitating appropriate client referrals.

Informed Consent and Confidentiality

Clients need to be advised regarding what information will be shared with the MCO throughout therapy. This means informed consent does not occur once during therapy, rather it is an ongoing concern of the clinician (see Chapters 3 and 4). Although information management is always of critical importance to the counselor, it is even more so within the context of managed care and the passage of HIPAA. Data tracking is crucial to both accessing and using the managed care system. Consequently, this necessary exchange of information presents problems and limitations for counselor–client confidentiality, especially given the increasing use of computerized data and facsimile exchanges of information. Although accurate and full disclosure by both the client and the counselor is vital to the counseling process, disclosure must now occur in a climate where information can be used to withhold or dictate services. Record keeping is a formal process often dictated by managed care systems that threatens a client's autonomous rights by curtailing limits and decreasing an individual's freedom of choice. Counselors must provide their clients with comprehensive informed consent regarding limitations to confidentiality. Observers have noted that clients must become more assertive and carry greater responsibility for their own care under MCOs. The professional–client relationship requires more attention to maintain the necessary levels of trust needed to be effective under these more difficult conditions (Murphy, 1998). The potential limitations on a counselor's ability to retain confidentiality must be fully disclosed to the client before establishing a counseling relationship.

In the area of diagnosis and assessment, counselors with expertise in psychometrics may request information about the validity of assessments required by certain MCOs and may challenge the utility of these required outcome measures. Further, clinicians may wish to explain (if appropriate) to clients that managed care assessments may be used by the managed care company for utilization review and may have limited to no impact upon the treatment decisions of the counselor (Meier & Davis, 2001).

Due process is significant ethically in that it must include fully informed consent—for example, informed consent should include disclosure of all treatment alternatives that might be most beneficial to the client, regardless of cost or the payer's willingness to provide these services. Institutions must have an ethical grievance process that allows clients to challenge client care decisions in a timely and responsive manner. Patients must also be able to obtain assistance in resolving their problems at an earlier stage—for example, through the use of ombudsman and client assistance programs. There must be processes of appeal that address issues of discrimination and protect people who are disadvantaged within a context of client-centered care, wherein the client's preferences and values are important to the treatment outcome.

HIPAA.   What is HIPAA? It is a law that has three parts: administrative, security, and privacy and is administered by the Center for Medicare and Medicaid (Glomstad, 2005). Standards for entities dealing with health information to help them readily communicate with one another are addressed in the administrative portion of the law. The security portion of the act was recently implemented and established procedures for the confidentiality of electronic client information. The privacy regulations in HIPAA related to all protected health information affect clinicians most directly (Glomstad). *Privacy* is defined to include "all individually identifiable health information transmitted or maintained by a covered entity, regardless of form" (ACA, 2002, p. 3). Privacy regulations specifically define *use* as "the sharing, employment, application, utilization, examination, or analysis of such information within an entity that maintains such information" (ACA, 2002, p. 3). *Disclosure* is defined as "the release, transfer, provision of access to or divulging in any other manner of information outside the entity holding the information" (ACA, 2002, p. 3). It is important that clinicians understand the differences between the terms consent and authorization under HIPAA. HIPAA regulations state that *consent* "allows the use and disclosure of protected health information only for treatment, payment and healthcare operations" (ACA, 2002, p. 4), whereas *authorization* "allows the use and disclosure of protected health information for purposes other than treatment, payment, and healthcare operations" (ACA, 2002, p. 4). Due to these regulations, a common question for practitioners on a daily basis is to disclose or not disclose? (Glomstad). As a result of HIPAA, many practitioners err on the side of caution, sometimes to an excessive point.

Within HIPAA there are three categories of disclosure: disclosure in the context of treatment, disclosure related to payment, disclosure related to health care operations. Regardless of the type of disclosure, individuals must keep in mind the minimum necessary standard within HIPAA. Clinicians may wonder if the regulations in HIPAA override current regulations in the area of substance abuse and student records (FERPA). The answer is no, HIPAA does not override existing federal laws in these areas (ACA, 2002). Privacy regulations of HIPAA provide clients with important rights, including: the right to view and copy their health information, the right to have their health care records amended, the right to request restrictions on the use of their health information as well as a specific account for disclosures of their health information (ACA, 2002).

It is possible for counselors to keep their counseling process notes private through the provision in HIPAA that defines, *psychotherapy notes*. Psychotherapy notes are defined as "notes recorded (in any medium) by a health care provider who is a mental health professional documenting or analyzing the contents of conversation during a private counseling session or a group, joint, or family counseling session" (ACA, 2002, p. 5). Counselors must keep these notes private and they must be kept separate from the client's medical or treatment records and intended for the counselor's private use only. Mental health advocates were able to make the case that it is essential to exclude psychotherapy notes from the provisions that cover the medical record so counselors could protect sensitive personal information. The definition of psychotherapy notes does exclude the following information: "medication prescription and monitoring, counseling session start and stop times, the modalities and frequencies of treatment furnished, results of clinical tests, and any summary of the following items: diagnosis, functional status, the treatment plan, symptoms, prognosis and progress" (ACA, 2002, p. 5).

Why should clinicians be knowledgeable about HIPAA? First of all, because this is a law and there are penalties if the law is not followed. If clients feel you have violated their privacy rights, they can sue the practitioner (Glomstad, 2005). Clients can file a complaint with the DHHS Office of Civil Rights (OCR). If this office identifies a violation has occurred, they can impose a fine of up to $100.00 per violation up to $25,000.00 per year. The OCR may not impose a fine if they feel the violation was due to reasonable cause and the practitioner or covered entity takes corrective action. However, if a civil fine is imposed, the OCR can additionally refer cases to the DOJ for criminal prosecution. The DOJ can impose fines of up to $250,000.00 per year in addition to up to 10 years in jail to those who misuse individually identifiable health information (Glomstad). What is the best course of action in the case of HIPAA? Counselors should be knowledgeable of the law and ensure the policies and procedures within the agency in which they are employed follow HIPAA regulations. The ACA has materials to assist counselors in navigating the established HIPAA regulations. Further information can be obtained via the internet from the OCR within the DHHS as well as from the Centers for Medicare and Medicaid.

Fidelity

Ethically, counselors must make themselves aware of the potential effects that a managed care situation may have on the counselor–client relationship and on their own ethical obligation to fidelity. They must minimize any detrimental effects of this care system on the obligation of fidelity to the best of their abilities. The managed care process could have a significant effect on the client's level of trust in the counselor–client relationship. If the client perceives the counselor has a conflict of interest and is sharing private or negative information with insurers or employers through the managed care system, trust will be compromised. The principle of fidelity requires counselors to be concerned with issues of loyalty and faithfulness to the bonds created in

this trusting relationship. Similarly, they must honor confidentiality and avoid harming their clients. Given the specific needs of each client, it would be useful and ethically sound for counselors to consider carefully the potential effects of varying forces and intrusions imposed by managed care upon aspects of their relationships with each client. For example, managed care might have an effect on counselors' loyalties and diagnostic and termination practices. If consumers are dissatisfied with the rate of reimbursement, the way in which their case is being reviewed, or their course of treatment, they must be advised of their rights and due process under the policies and procedures of their health care provider and the law in relation to the health care services they receive.

Conflicted Loyalties. The possibility exists that the professional counselor's loyalty could no longer be to the client or even to a professional's peers, but rather to the managers or systems in charge of prior authorization and utilization review of services. The philosophy of managed care demands awareness of limited resources, thereby expanding the counselor's moral role to include concerns about distribution of resources to groups or populations of individuals, as well as to individual clients. Traditionally, counselors have been held to the ethical responsibility of considering their clients' needs above those of others unless direct risk or harm to others can be ascertained. Now mental health professionals are challenged to assume responsibility for population-based practice without losing concern for the individual.

This widening of ethical obligation to include broader concerns about distributive justice for society is a revolutionary emphasis for counselors. Managed care has been recognized as involving at least two conflicting interests: the need for counselors (a) to balance their clients' needs with those of other clients in the managed system; and (b) to balance clients' needs with cost containment and financial resources. In managed care, this balance is usually mediated by an individual in a gatekeeping role, often called the **case manager.** Some authorities maintain that it is important that professionals recognize the overall responsibility for determining such weighty moral questions by challenging the broader community to address these issues through debate and formation of political and social policy. Counselors should participate in this policy debate both individually and through their professional organizations.

Several authors have written about the potential intrusion of the gatekeeper's function into the counselor's ethical analysis and have described the situation as if the managed care representative was present psychologically in the counseling session. Haas and Cummings (1991) offered the opinion that "the symbolic presence of the manager or third party intensifies the issues in vulnerable therapist–client pairs" (p. 49) and stands to erode the trusting relationship in counseling. Almost two decades ago, Pellegrino (1986) warned that "this [gatekeeper] role is morally dubious because it generates a conflict between the responsibility of the [caregiver] as a primary advocate of the client and as guardian of society's resources" (p. 23).

Counseling codes of ethics are clear in their stance that counselors' commitments to their clients come first. Sections in the APA and ACA codes of ethics, for example, protect the welfare of the consumer. However, interpretation of such consumer mandates has become more difficult in the context of managed care. As pressures mount on counselors, the profession will be called on to further clarify ethical standards and practices in managed care settings.

Integrity, Fraud, and Malpractice. The DOJ has investigated managed care fraud in cases involving MCOs delaying their reports to Medicare regarding enrollment figures to obtain more capitation fees; embezzlement of capitation fees by MCO plans or subcontractors of the MCO; and specialists who receive kickback payments to keep referral rates low (Hallam, 1999). The government has developed new rules in the form of a voluntary compliance program. This program addresses such issues as the MCO's ability to enroll the healthiest individuals in the organization; use of physicians as marketing agents; MCO encouragement or initiation of disenrollment of clients from identified plans; quality of care including critical examination of underutilized services; and data collection and submission (Department of Health and Human Services, 2000; Hallam).

Termination. Ethical guidelines for terminating a counselor–client relationship state that counselors should not abandon their client unless the client (a) no longer needs services, (b) is not benefiting from services, or (c) is being harmed by continued service. Responsible counselors inform their clients of these possibilities before counseling begins. Nevertheless, a potential conflict may arise when counseling services are no longer sanctioned by the client's managed care system and the financial assistance for the service is terminated. This problem is particularly pressing if a financial burden is potentially harmful to the client. The counselor must

choose among several alternatives: (a) offer pro bono services, (b) provide alternatives that do not involve a financial burden (e.g., community or support groups), (c) negotiate referral, (d) challenge the managed care system, (e) offer continued services on a sliding scale fee or variable collection arrangement until the client is stabilized, or (f) continue services at the present fee or a reduced fee to be paid directly by the client.

The counselor's advocacy on behalf of the client and the client's self-advocacy are paramount when such conflicts of interest arise. Proficiency in these advocacy roles requires educating clients to learn to advocate for themselves through skill-training interventions, as well as building the professionals' knowledge and skill base so they might become more proficient in systems advocacy skills. Problems of inappropriate or premature termination may occur more frequently in the prevalent managed care system, and they will continue to impose moral dilemmas for both counselors and their clients. In many codes of ethics, the professional's obligation to advocate for clients with the MCO may not rise to the level of an enforceable ethical standard. However, some authorities on ethical issues in MCOs think that mental health professionals must become involved in both individual and systemic advocacy to improve the welfare of their clients, the public, and our professions (Acuff et al., 1999). In fact, the professional counselor must consider whether there may be a duty to appeal that would involve not just passively informing clients of their right to appeal adverse decisions within the MCO system, but rather to actively educate and support clients in appeals. From this more radical viewpoint, the counselor might initiate an appeal on behalf of the client when that approach is more effective or timely.

Revisions of current ethical codes will need to include guidelines for counseling practice that assist the counselor in allocating resources that facilitate client advocacy in these situations. The counseling profession and the governmental regulatory bodies must ensure that managed care techniques are implemented in a way that protects clients, the integrity of their relationship with their counselor, and the well-being of the profession itself.

Efforts to preserve the appropriate ethical role of the counselor include the development of appropriate procedures to reduce conflict in at least three ways: (a) developing practice guidelines that have been established at a higher policy-making level, (b) increasing the role of clients in the decision-making process, and (c) establishing a well-structured appeals process for clients who disagree with treatments or termination decisions.

Conflict of Interest and Business Relationships

In the managed care system, the counselor fulfills the role of the service provider as well as the MCO employee, even if the counselor is an independent practitioner. Working within a managed care environment places the counselor in the middle of potential competing interests (Cooper & Gottlieb, 2000). In this type of situation, the counselor is caught between advocating for the client who may require additional services and supporting the mission of the MCO to contain costs. In this ongoing situation, the practitioner has an ethical obligation to address conflict of interest issues with the client and the MCO to resolve the conflict.

Counselors must first clearly understand the difference between medical ethics and business ethics (Mariner, 1997). During their academic education, counselors are presented with information on professional ethics and medical ethics; however, they may have limited or no exposure to business ethics. Business ethics differ from medical ethics. Traditional medical ethics focus on the physician–patient relationship. However, in a managed care environment, these relationships are often much more complex. MCOs do much more than provide medical care. They are an intricate blending of insurance, management, and health care delivery. The managed care organization does not provide the care per se; rather, health care professionals do (Mariner).

Counselors need to be mindful of the fact that the MCO is just that—an organization, not an individual or a profession with a history of professional ethics (Mariner, 1997; Taryvdas, Peterson, & Michaelson, 2004). Therefore, ethical principles that are applied consistently to a variety of health care professionals are not applied easily to the MCO. Practitioners utilize evidence-based models of care. This differs from the managed care approach of utilizing actuarial models to examine health and illness.

To provide services in an MCO, counselors are typically required to sign a legally binding contract (Cooper & Gottlieb, 2000). These contracts may be filled with business and legal issues that are unfamiliar to the counselor. Counselors must read these documents with a critical eye and seek outside assistance in areas of uncertainty. Counselors are guided by professional ethical standards and need to make certain the MCO is aware of their ethical obligations. Should conflicts arise, counselors should take steps to resolve the dispute in a responsible and professional manner. Gag clauses, no-cause termination, utilization review, hold-harmless clauses, and indemnification clauses are all issues that the practitioner may have to deal with when working with an MCO. Counselors need to be aware of their professional rights and responsibilities in each of these situations (Cooper & Gottlieb).

Practitioner's Ethical Obligation to Self-Educate. Do you, as a counselor, understand the terms *capitation, utilization review, case rate, health maintenance organization, mixed model, management services organization,* and *independent practice association?* If not, you should consider updating your managed care language. Counselors are now required to have command of a new set of terms and acronyms such as PPO, PPA (preferred provider agreement), HMO, UR (utilization review), gag rules, risk sharing, and gatekeeper (Dombek & Olsan, 2002). With more frequency, counselors and clients are presented with these terms and abbreviations and may be unaware of their meanings or their importance.

A study completed by the Center for Studying Healthcare System Change found that only 30% of health care consumers were able to correctly identify four basic health plan features of their managed care organization (Greiner, 2001). These four basic plan features include (1) whether consumers must choose from a provider network; (2) whether payment is provided for any of the out-of-network care; (3) whether the consumer must sign up with a primary care provider; and (4) whether referrals must be obtained for specialty care. These results indicate that many health care consumers lack a basic understanding of how their managed care plan can be utilized to their benefit. That deficit may have an impact on their ability to make informed health care decisions. Therefore, practitioners not only have an ethical responsibility to have a solid understanding of managed care practices themselves, but also have an obligation to educate and inform their clients of the complex information they need to know about the MCO. This information can assist clients in making effective decisions about cost and quality of care. If clients fail to effectively understand how their individual health plan can work to their benefit, their satisfaction and ability to independently access care can be compromised (Greiner).

Counselors also should be aware and make their clients aware of documents useful in understanding the health care system and advocating for clients' needs, such as *Bill of Rights for Consumers Accessing Behavioral Health Services.* This document is available at the

Web site of the American Managed Behavioral Health-care Association and provides guidance to clients and counselors in such areas as: provider choice, confidentiality, determination of treatment, benefit usage, disclosure, discrimination, appeals, accountability, continuity of care, and external advocacy.

Practitioners must be cautious not to facilitate further unjustified negativity on the part of their clients. This attitude only fuels the public backlash directed toward MCOs, which reflects decreased trust due to cost constraints, explicit rationing, and negative media coverage (Mechanic, 2001).

Practitioners should be able to evaluate managed care contracts effectively prior to entering a managed care agreement. They must determine if the financial or other mechanisms present within the MCO are consistent with their ethics and values of providing competent and compassionate care (Jecker, 1998). This includes providing care to clients in a manner that is not time constrained. In addition, professionals should ensure that clients will not be denied clinically effective treatment services. If the organization indicates that payment will be on a capitated basis, professionals must determine if they will be able to provide quality care under these constraints.

Individuals who are considering practicing in a managed care environment may benefit from speaking with a colleague currently working in this environment. They may also benefit from review of the work of Cooper and Gottlieb (2000) and Acuff et al. (1999). These articles can provide the practitioner with a variety of situations that address informed consent, payment for services, approval/denial of services, and MCO involvement in treatment planning and implementation. Practitioners must be always mindful of their fiduciary relationship to their client.

BIOETHICAL ISSUES

The integration of health care services has created a new ethical landscape for all parties, including the counselor who participates in the health care system. Ethical, political, and social norms create a new complexity within this environment for counseling practice. Counselors who work in a health care setting are expected to operate within the prevailing biomedical model. All responsible counselors should be well informed about these far-reaching issues. Biomedical and health care advances—and, more importantly, the ethical challenges they pose—will be a profound force on contemporary society and culture during the 21st century. The ethical guidelines that have developed out of the traditions within the biomedical model are called biomedical ethics.

According to Beauchamp and Childress (2001), **biomedical ethics,** a relatively young field, is a way of understanding complexity and examining moral life as it pertains to the biological sciences, medicine, and health care. Biomedical ethics applies general ethical theories for specific forms of conduct or moral judgment to these areas. Thus, this field is a type of practical or applied ethics.

Biomedical issues may seem remote to counselors in practice. Even the word bioethics may distance counselors from the awareness that they must learn about these issues. This is a serious error in judgment—our clients want to, or do not want to, be pregnant; they have grave illness such as HIV or cancer and try to live with them, or consider dying; clients may consider genetic testing to prepare for an uncertain future, and in that future employers may begin to use employees' genetic information to select or track employees; and clients will self-select herbal, meditative, and other therapies rather than resorting to traditional medical treatments for their care. Bioethical issues *will* affect counselors with increased frequency in the future. To deal with these bioethical dilemmas, counselors should be aware of resources for assistance: bioethics centers, consultants, internal agency committees, and other professional colleagues with experience in bioethics.

The remainder of this chapter presents information on selected bioethical areas that are most likely to be influential in the lives of counseling clients: genetics, end-of-life care and hastened death and euthanasia, complementary and alternative medicine, HIV/AIDS care, and abortion. This information will help counselors anticipate these issues and the challenges that will confront future practice.

Genetics

Genetics is an area of science that presents serious ethical questions. Ongoing research in genetics provides new discoveries and challenges on virtually a daily basis. Although advances in genetics may have a positive impact on individuals and society in the future, genetics presently does not necessarily provide clear-cut answers, and it provides us with complex ethical questions (Dalzell, 2001).

The Human Genome Project (HGP) was initially undertaken by the U.S. Department of Energy and the National Institutes of Health. These agencies worked in conjunction with private U.S. and international entities to identify all of the approximately 30,000 genes within human DNA (Human Genome Project, 2001). **Genetics** is the study of inherited traits, and **genomics** is the study of the entire set of human genes, the assembly of the gene sequence, gene expression, and the relationship between the different gene sequences (Larson, 2000). Researchers are studying normal and abnormal genes to identify the importance of individual genes and the consequences of genetic dysfunction (Jegalian & Biesecker, 2000). By decoding the human genome, researchers will have the ability to uncover the numerous mysteries of various diseases (Larson; Rieger, 2000).

With the recent completion of the sequencing of the human genome, genetic testing will be requested by the general public for a greater number of medical conditions such as cancer, cardiovascular disease, and diabetes for which evidence-based interventions currently exist, as well as for conditions such as Alzheimer disease for which limited interventions are available (Wang Gonzalez & Merajver, 2004). It is predicted by 2010 that information contained within the HGP will be effectively utilized to identify individuals who are at highest risk for several diseases for which interventions currently exist, including cancer (Giarelli, 2001).

Genetic Testing and Counseling. The future of genomics and genetic testing necessitates that counselors become educated regarding current developments and be able to explain them to their clients (Larson, 2000). **Genetic testing** is a broad term that describes specific techniques that seek the presence of genetic mutations or altered gene proteins, which may indicate a genetic condition or a predisposition to disease (Rieger, 2000). In the past, genetic counseling was most often utilized with individuals interested in ascertaining genetic risks as they relate to reproduction. However, current genetic tests are utilized to ascertain predisposition to some forms of cancer as well as physical characteristics and behavioral traits that are within the range of normal human variation (Rieger; White, 1999). Despite these advances, genetic testing for cancer is not recommended at present because only 5 to 10% of cancer is inherited (Tufts University, 1998).

To assure that testing services are utilized in an appropriate fashion, comprehensive genetic counseling is essential both before and after testing. White and Calliff-Daley (1999) developed guidelines for pretest education, informed consent, and posttest counseling issues (see Figure 9–4).

- Obtain an accurate family history and confirm diagnosis before testing.
- Provide information about the natural history of the condition and the purpose of the test.
- Discuss the predictive value of the test, the technical accuracy of the test, and the meaning of a positive or negative test.
- Explore options for approximation of risk without genetic testing.
- Explore the patient's motives for undergoing the test, the potential impact of testing on relatives, and the risk of passing a mutation on to children.
- Discuss the potential risk of psychosocial distress to the patient and family, even if no mutation is found.
- Explain the logistics of testing and fees involved for testing and counseling.
- Discuss issues involving confidentiality and the risk of unemployment and insurance discrimination.
- Describe the patient's medical options, the efficacy of available surveillance and prevention methods, and recommendations for screening if test results are negative.
- Provide a written summary of the content of the counseling session.
- Obtain informed consent for testing.
- Provide test results in person and offer follow-up support.

FIGURE 9–4. Guidelines for Pretest Education, Informed Consent, and Posttest Counseling
Source: From "Genetic testing for disease susceptibility: Social, ethical and legal issues for family physicians" by M. T. White and F. Calliff-Daley, 1999, *American Family Physician, 60*(3). Copyright 1999 by the American Medical Association. Adapted by permission.

Physicians, social workers, and nurses can provide genetic counseling (Parens & Asch, 1999). It is most often performed by master's-degree-level professionals with specific education in genetic principles and training in brief psychosocial counseling. One of the most important ethical practices in the area of genetic testing and counseling is providing individuals with informed consent to engage in genetic testing. Counselors also assist clients in reaching an informed decision about testing and explain how to utilize test results (Parens & Asch, 1999). Counselors should be aware of the risks and benefits associated with genetic testing and prepared to share this information with their clients. Risks associated with genetic testing include psychological stress, increased difficulty within family relationships, confidentiality and disclosure issues, and the potential for employment and insurance discrimination. Benefits of genetic testing include emotional relief and reassurance, increased knowledge that may impact future decisions, increased awareness that may impact high-risk behavior, and positive behavior changes (White & Calliff-Daley, 1999).

Genetic counseling is a specific field that has a commitment to assist clients in discovering what course of action would be best for them after reflection (Parens & Asch, 2003). The goals of genetic services include counseling and testing. In the area of counseling, counselors are responsible for providing education and information, supporting and assisting clients in coping, and facilitating informed decision making. In the area of testing, counselors assist clients in framing subsequent decisions, examining past and current health behaviors, and considering current health status (Wang et al., 2004). Genetic counselors provide anticipatory guidance; that is, assisting clients in considering what may happen or how they will feel at some point in the future.

Each genetic decision is unique based upon individual responses to potential risk and uncertainty within the context of the client's personal values and specific circumstances (see Figure 9–5 to review some questions counselors may need to consider). The consequences of genetic decisions do not typically impact one individual—rather, they may affect family members directly and society as a whole indirectly. Advances in the diagnosis and treatment of genetic disorders may change perceptions of what is considered a genetic disease or disability (White, 1999).

The ethical principles of autonomy, beneficence, nonmaleficence, and justice can be examined from a genetic counseling perspective. The principle of autonomy is focusing on the client's right to determine when and if to have testing, as well as the right to privacy and the absence of coercion in the delivery of any medical services that may follow the testing (Giarelli, 2001). In the area of beneficence, the rights of the client to tell or not tell family members about the outcome of a genetic test may come into conflict with the duties the clinician may perceive as within their scope of practice (see Box 9–1). The principle of nonmaleficence is involved when considering whether or not to have a genetic test, the individual considers all possible effects of knowing their risk for the development of a disease. Justice issues related to genetic testing are the accessibility to testing and also the access to health care services, follow-up care, and insurance underwriting of procedures for a presymptomatic condition (Giarelli).

The National Society of Genetic Counselors provides a code of ethics for counselors who intend to practice in this area. Counselors who are interested in knowing more about the code of ethics for genetic counselors are directed to examine the code on-line.

Counselors who provide genetic counseling must understand the three components of the counseling process specific to this area: a comprehensive risk assessment, education, and psychosocial counseling (Jegalian & Biesecker, 2000). Counselors must have a clear understanding of the genetic foundation of the health problem to assist families in determining the risk that a disease will affect future generations (Jegalian & Biesecker). Upon completion of testing, counselors should provide services that focus on facilitating positive coping mechanisms and psychosocial adjustment within the family. They should also provide information about the disorder and help clients deal with the potential prognosis (Jegalian & Biesecker).

Genetic information has the ability to impact a client's sense of self and the most basic life decisions regarding career, marriage, and childbearing (Oktay, 1998). Individuals who are provided with negative genetic testing results may experience guilt that is disproportionate to that experienced with other diseases. They may apply religious or cultural interpretations to the information, such as viewing the disease as a curse on the family for some past transgression. Genetic counselors should assess their own values, use terms that are as value neutral as possible, provide unconditional support, understand

---

1. What is "normal" and what constitutes a disability, and who is to make this decision?
2. What are diseases, or disabilities, and should they be prevented or cured?
3. How can we meet the financial needs of individuals who desire gene therapy, which are beyond what many individuals can afford?
4. Who should obtain these services and at what cost?
5. Does the search for a cure for specific disabilities for individuals who may be diagnosed in the future have a negative impact on those currently living with a disability?

FIGURE 9–5.   Genetic Questions Counselors May Confront
Source: From "Gene therapy." By the *Human Genome Project,* 2001, available on-line at: http://www.ornl.gov/hgmis/medicine/genetherapy.html.

current genetic information, articulate this information clearly to individuals and families, and assist clients in taking action that is consistent with their own values (Parens & Asch, 1999; White, 1999). These factors are essential. Many clients find it quite difficult to make these decisions due to the unfamiliar terminology and the difficulty of comprehending it under increased stress (White).

Confidentiality of Genetic Information. One of the benefits of the HGP may be increased awareness of risk factors that an individual can address to prevent disease or disability. However, this information has potential value to employers and insurance companies who may wish to use the information to predict future illness, associated health care costs, and an individual's ability to perform a job (Fuller et al., 1999). Family members and the courts may want access to genetic information in child custody cases. Educational institutions may also want access to genetic information. Some individuals fear that genetic testing information may fuel a reemergence of the eugenics movement.

Genetic information has been used in discrimination against individuals in the areas of medical benefits and employment (Fuller et al., 1999). Legislation has attempted to protect genetic information by not having it placed in a client's regular medical record (Larson, 2000). The Americans with Disabilities Act includes provisions that prohibit any medical inquiries or examinations at the preemployment/offer stage. Therefore, genetic testing or requesting a genetic history of a potential employee would be excluded (Carnovale & Clanton, 2002). As genetic testing usually focuses on future health probabilities, it is improbable that the ADA would ever allow this in a preemployment position. Current genetic discrimination laws prevent the use of genetic information about an asymptomatic individual. According to the ADA, "an asymptomatic person who is discriminated against based on the knowledge of the genetic test results is a disabled person because the knowledge of the test leads to the perception that he or she has an impairment" (Wolbring, 2001, p. 1). Furthermore, HIPAA provisions "generally forbid sharing of identifiable data without patient consent. However they do not specifically address use or disclosure policies for human genetic data" (Lin, Owen, & Altman, 2004). HIPAA regulations do however restrict employer collection, use, and disclosure of genetic information that is gathered through the participation in an employer-sponsored group health plan (Lorber, 2004). The

Equal Employment Opportunity Commission, the federal agency charged with enforcing the ADA will "continue to respond aggressively to any evidence that employers are asking for or using genetic tests in a manner that violates the ADA" (Lorber, p. 2).

HIPAA does not allow the categorization of a genetic predisposition as a preexisting condition. It also prevents insurance carriers from using these factors to deny or limit health care coverage for members of a group insurance plan; and it denies insurance carriers the opportunity to charge different rates based on an individual's genetic information (Oktay, 1998). Genetic discrimination based on access to genetic information is wrong because individuals are unable to change their hereditary characteristics (Peters, 1996). States with specific state legislation that protects genetic information require written client consent for release of genetic test results. Legislation continues to be proposed and debated in Congress to prevent discrimination that results from genetic testing. However, lobbying efforts from the insurance industry, pharmaceutical manufacturers, and biotechnology companies often oppose such legislation (Oktay). As of this writing, in both the House of Representatives and Senate debate continues regarding genetic information and nondiscrimination. In 2003, the Senate passed genetic nondiscrimination legislation, but it failed to make it through the 108th Congress.

In 2000, President Clinton signed an executive order that (a) prohibits federal employers from requesting genetic testing as a preemployment requirement or as a method for obtaining benefits; (b) prohibits federal employers from using genetic information to classify employees in ways that may limit their professional advancement opportunities; and (c) provides privacy protections to genetic information used in medical treatment and research (HGP, 2001). Furthermore, the Ethical, Legal, and Social Implications (ELSI) subcommittee of the HGP has committed 5% of the subcommittee's annual budget toward the development and maintenance of ethical standards regarding genomic discoveries and information (HGP).

QUESTION FOR REFLECTION

Counselors must consider their ethical responsibilities related to a new potential variant of the duty to warn. Imagine that a client has genetic testing for a specific condition, tests positive, and has siblings. The client does not wish to inform her siblings of the test results about the hereditary genetic condition and the fact that they are likely carriers of the condition. As a result, the siblings do not know that the condition can potentially be treated with medication. In such a scenario, the counselor must examine beneficence related to the possibility of breaching confidentiality (Leung, 2000). What actions should be taken?

Eugenics.   **Eugenics** has been described as the use of a scientific strategy for orchestrating human evolution through methods of encouraging transmission of "desirable" traits and discouraging transmission of "undesirable" traits (Suzuki & Knudtson, 1990). The concept of eugenics dates back to the 1800s. This movement accelerated under the direction of Sir Francis Galton, a mathematician and the cousin of Charles Darwin, who began promoting the concept as early as the 1860s. Early proponents believed it was important to increase the number of people with desirable genetic traits through selective reproduction of individuals of high intelligence and moral character. Such a strategy was thought to reduce and possibly eliminate problems in the general population that were associated with low intelligence and moral character such as crime, alcoholism, and poverty (National Center for Genome Resources, 1997). By the late 1920s, 29 U.S. states had adopted legislation that forced sterilization on over 10,000 individuals who were identified as mentally retarded or alcoholic or who possessed criminal tendencies. The interest in eugenics that was prevalent in the early half of the 20th century declined as a result of the horrific genocide and genetic engineering activities of the Nazis during World War II (National Reference Center for Bioethics Literature, 2001).

Scientists and clinicians hope that current and future advances in gene therapy and genetic counseling, screening, and testing will enable them to facilitate positive changes in the lives of individuals. However, these great capabilities challenge our society never to repeat the destructive excesses of the eugenics movement. Such advances raise major moral and ethical questions related to changing human genes, performing genetic testing for a specific diagnosis when no cures exist, and performing genetic testing to determine the presence of a disabling condition in utero for purposes of aborting such a "defective" fetus, as well as ethical and legal issues in the confidentiality of genetic information (National Reference Center for Bioethics Literature, 2001). It is important that the disability community is involved in the development of ethical frameworks in this area. According to Wolbring (2001), disabled people feel "that it is mostly nondisabled people who develop ethical frameworks on

issues affecting disabled people. The negative attitude of many disabled people toward bioethical issues stems precisely from this fact" (p. 1).

Within the bioethics community, steps have been taken to hear the opinions of persons with disabilities on bioethical issues within the mainstream bioethics debate. This is apparent through the establishment of a disability interest group within the American Society for Bioethics and Humanities; however, there is still much more work to be done in this area (Wolbring, 2001).

End-of-Life Care and Hastened Death

End-of-life care has been gaining attention from both professionals in the medical and mental health communities and our society at large. Situations involving people who face end-of-life decisions and controversies have been increasingly prominent topics in our popular media and public discourse. Counselors may encounter end-of-life issues in their practices involving hastened death of two types: euthanasia and rational suicide.

Euthanasia and other forms of hastened death are significant and polarizing social issues (Albright & Hazler, 1995). **Hastened death** is a broad term that refers to any process by which people speed up the dying process, including suicide, rational suicide, euthanasia, and aid in dying (Werth & Holdwick, 2000). Historically, the first references to these practices occurred in the Hippocratic Oath (Emmanuel, 1994) and it has remained an issue with varying degrees of intensity since that time. Both the scholarly literature and codes of ethics in counseling have remained largely silent on these critical issues until recently.

The term **euthanasia** is derived from two Greek words that mean "good death" (Beauchamp & Walters, 1989). Inadequate and often unclear definitions of euthanasia have been noted throughout the literature. This definitional problem has affected public perception of the issues surrounding euthanasia, as well as research and professional writing. This problem also has encumbered the resolution of the ethical and legal status of this important issue. Terms that describe euthanasia typically have been based on three criteria: (1) the basis of intention to die, (2) the nature of the critical action involved in effecting the death, and (3) the consent of the person requesting death. Qualifying terms have been used to distinguish these elements: passive or indirect euthanasia and active euthanasia. Either of these approaches can be classified as voluntary or involuntary. Emmanuel (1994) argued that although such definitional distinctions may be useful, the joining of each qualifier with the emotionally charged word euthanasia confuses moral judgment and distorts subsequent public and political debates. However, a clear definition is important to professional counseling research and scope of practice.

Passive euthanasia is the practice of withdrawing or withholding life-sustaining treatments. Legal rulings consistently support such practices under certain conditions. According to Emmanuel (1994), the medical literature demonstrates a rising consensus supporting the ethical appropriateness of such actions. For example, the ethical principle of double effect has evolved. **Double effect** is the idea that unacceptable consequences such as death are deemed acceptable under certain circumstances. This stance supports the use of medication for pain relief in terminal conditions, even if it shortens a person's life. Such a decision highlights the propensity toward beneficence over nonmaleficence as the guiding ethical principle in these circumstances. Another example of this concept is the common practice of do-not-resuscitate (DNR) orders for certain terminal clients. However, as Beauchamp and Childress (2001) pointed out, the debate is not over. These authors suggest that the distinctions between treatment and nontreatment are untenable and should be replaced by the distinction between obligatory and optional means of treatment. Such a conceptual framework would serve to offer a more adequate rationale for any given choice of action.

Beauchamp and Childress (2001) also considered the omission–commission distinctions regarding treatment. They concluded that the decision to stop treatment is often perceived as more momentous and consequential to the caregiver than the withholding of treatment. For example, the initiation of treatment can create expectations and imply responsibility on the part of the caregiver. However, Beauchamp and Childress argued that the moral burden of proof is greater if the decision involves withholding rather than withdrawing treatments. They also noted that "claims of medical futility are often presented as objective and value-free, when in fact they are subjective and value-laden" (Beauchamp & Childress, p. 192). Either approach potentially can lead to the over-or undertreatment of clients. These authors suggested that such decisions should be based on the client's welfare and rights, which include a balanced consideration of the benefits and burdens of the treatment.

Advance directives are health-related decisions obtained from a person before that person's loss of competence. The initiation of this legal process is based on ethical and legal considerations of individual autonomy. There are two types of advance directives: "(1) **living wills,** which are specific substantive directives regarding medical procedures that should be provided or forgone in specific circumstances, and (2) **durable power of attorney (DPA) for health care,** or proxy directive" (Beauchamp & Childress, 2001, p. 152). The DPA allows individuals to select substitute decision makers who are empowered to make health care decisions on their behalf should they be incapacitated.

Active euthanasia or *mercy killing* or *assisted suicide,* is the intentional termination of life. Justifications for such actions are grounded in the principle of beneficence with regard to the person who delivers the lethal means, and in the principle of autonomy with regard to an individual's right to make the decision to end their own life. Conversely, it has been argued that such acts are violations of nonmaleficence. Assisted suicide is legal in the state of Oregon as a result of the Oregon Death with Dignity Act and subsequent U.S. circuit court and Supreme Court rulings. The Netherlands has permitted assisted suicide for a number of years (Werth & Holdwick, 2000). At the same time, acts of suicide or attempted suicide have been decriminalized throughout most of the United States, creating a paradoxical situation in the minds of some persons.

The voluntary-versus-involuntary distinction is a means to further qualify the dying individual's degree of contribution to the decision. Voluntary status assumes that individuals elect and actively seek their own time and manner of death. Involuntary decisions are much more controversial because the individuals facing death have no active part in the decision making, due to being comatose or otherwise incapacitated.

Ethical decisions regarding euthanasia and hastened death typically center on three key ethical principles: autonomy, beneficence, and nonmaleficence. Most discussions and writings in this area have been about the role of physicians or the role of a significant other. Either, or both, typically serve as the agent who delivers the means to death. However, counselors may be in a special position to understand the wants and needs of both the client and the client's family regarding this decision. Counselors are very likely to face issues of hastened death in their work. Surveys show that between one fourth and one third of nonpsychiatrist mental health professionals can expect to have at least one client die as a result of suicide during their careers (Rogers, Gueulette, Abbey-Hines, Carney, & Werth,

2001). Therefore, a counselor's contribution to a debate regarding the relevance of any guiding ethical principle to a client will be significant. The APA recently issued an important report that examines the role of psychology in end-of-life decisions and quality-of-care issues (APA, 2005) that provide extended consideration of the issues involved. Additionally, ACA added some direct guidance to counselors in its 2005 Code of Ethics (ACA, 2005).

Many dying clients and their families face inadequate counseling, emotional support, and pain control. Counselors must address these inadequacies, along with the ethical issue of euthanasia. First, counselors must identify and reconcile their personal biases and values regarding related issues (e.g., death and quality of life with chronic or terminal illnesses) before working with clients and their families. Decisions about euthanasia more often are shaped by the personal values of the parties to this ethical and personal dilemma rather than by law. The recognition and reconciliation of issues of diversity—cultural, familial, and individual—are vital to sound ethical practice. This recognition requires an ongoing effort by counselors to better understand cultural and religious views of life and death that may be different from their own. For example, some Eastern religious traditions view death as a means to enter a blissful spiritual state. Counselors must be intimately familiar with the decision-making context of any individual facing such a decision. In all forms of hastened death, the counselor must make one very critical assessment—determining whether the client is clinically depressed or suffering from any other serious mental or cognitive disorder that may impair judgment. Such disorders can seriously impair the client's ability to engage in rational decision making (Siegel, 1986). The counselor must ensure that the client's condition is evaluated properly, either directly by the counselor or by referral to a competent psychiatrist or psychologist. Counselors must clarify their own roles in providing assistance to clients and families as they consider euthanasia. Counselors' primary ethical charge is their obligation to respect the integrity and promote the welfare of the client. Understanding euthanasia and the arguments for and against it are important building blocks in a sound, ethical decision-making process in all areas of hastened considerations.

Arguments for Euthanasia.   According to Beauchamp and Childress (2001) and Emmanuel (1994), four basic claims currently support euthanasia as a legitimate health care intervention. These arguments are based on (1) the principle of autonomy as an a priori principle; (2) the primacy of the principle of beneficence; (3) the assertion that passive euthanasia is an acceptable practice and that no real distinction between active and passive euthanasia exists; and (4) the argument is based on utility, which supports rules that promote the most favorable consequences for the largest number of people.

According to the first claim, the cultural context of the United States is based on individualism and self-determination; the rights of an individual are viewed as paramount. In this culture, these rights, including the right to die, clearly are supported by the ethical principle of autonomy. The essence of this right is a belief that all individuals must be given the opportunity to determine what is good and valuable in life. This determination includes the right to determine the time and manner of one's own death. Enactment of this right rests on individual consent and assumes that obligations for action naturally follow this right. Put another way, rights form the justified basis of obligations.

Second, based on the duty to do good embedded in the principle of beneficence, euthanasia is seen as an acceptable way to end a life that would probably inflict more pain and suffering. In other words, euthanasia could be considered humane. This benevolent act has been sanctioned socially through the practice of refusing or not providing life-sustaining interventions. In fact, Brock (1992) claimed that such an opportunity may provide individuals with psychological insurance against anxiety over anticipated pain and suffering, and therefore is an integral part of a trusting relationship between a client and care providers. If this claim is accepted, euthanasia would not be considered separate from other alternatives of care. In fact, there has been discussion of broadening the claim of best interest to include the welfare of an individual's family, a controversial perspective.

The third argument proclaims that there is no distinction between active and passive euthanasia. An act and an omission are viewed as equivalent. Withholding life-sustaining care shares an equal intention of assisting in death. Arguably, there is no moral difference in the final results, except that passive euthanasia follows nature's course whereas active euthanasia hastens nature's course.

Finally, the utility argument suggests that rules should promote the greatest good. Proponents of this claim argue that bad consequences of euthanasia are remote and speculative. However, these proponents contend that tight procedures based on careful analysis and review will be necessary to prevent ill effects. Figure 9–6 presents safeguards for ethical euthanasia.

1. Requests should be made by a competent person on several occasions and in writing.
2. A thorough examination should be made to rule out or treat any prevailing psychological condition.
3. The act of assistance should be restricted to certified physicians who will not receive compensation for their work.
4. Careful documentation with reference to alternative treatments should be offered to the person.
5. All cases should be reported to an official body.

FIGURE 9–6. Elements of Ethical Procedural Safeguards for Euthanasia

Source: From "Euthanasia: Historical, Ethical, and Empirical Perspectives" by E. J. Emmanuel, 1994, September 12, *Archives of Internal Medicine, 154.* Copyright 1994 by the American Medical Association. Reprinted by permission.

Arguments Against Euthanasia. Six primary claims appear in the literature arguing against euthanasia as a sanctioned medical intervention. These arguments include (1) the overextension of the concept of autonomy, (2) the idea that legalization should not be promoted on the basis of beneficence, (3) the ethical distinction between active and passive euthanasia, (4) the potential to extend the practice to the noncompetent or nonconsenting, (5) the intrusion of the courts into the private realm, and (6) the potential for bias based on gender or disability.

John Stuart Mill (1910) warned that not all voluntary acts are justified by the principle of autonomy. Opponents of euthanasia use the analogy of voluntary slavery and argue that not all independent desires are justifiable. Further, they argue that satisfying preferences must not be confused with a legal right to autonomy. In other words, there can and should be boundaries of acceptable behavior. Consequently, withholding life-sustaining measures is clearly distinct from actively facilitating death.

Similarly, remote acts of beneficence that occur in rare cases of assisting the end of suffering do not justify the legalization of these acts in general. Opponents of euthanasia claim that traditional medical practice has not provided adequate treatment of pain and suffering. Therefore, the boundaries between acceptable and unacceptable conditions of pain and suffering have not been defined. In sum, an acceptable practice of euthanasia could undermine the pursuit of a health care goal of well-being.

In fact, some opponents say there is an ethical and true distinction between active and passive euthanasia based on the intentionality of the caregiver. Euthanasia could undermine the trust inherent in the healing relationship as well as the laborious provision of compassionate care. Potential healing might be supplanted by a view of killing as healing.

The potential exists for the natural and logical extension of arguments for euthanasia to include vulnerable and unprotected individuals such as incompetent, comatose, or mentally deficient clients; children; and other disempowered people. This is known as the **slippery slope argument.** Beauchamp and Childress (2001) described this effect as the "progressive erosion of moral restraints" (p. 146). They contended that a move in this permissive direction might be used as an argument to decrease the burden on a family or society, to eliminate individuals who have a perceived diminished quality of life based on a disability, and to consequently modify attitudes toward the respect for life. See Box 9–2.

The more direct political argument against legalizing practices of euthanasia parallels the abortion debates and warns against the intrusion of the courts into private matters of health and death. Such intrusions are deemed inevitable to ensure sound, procedural safeguards for such practices; therefore, they would be unavoidable if the practices of euthanasia were legalized.

Finally, there are serious concerns that hastened death may be a response the individual selects due to external influences, the expectations of others, or being seen as a severely damaged or devalued person. Wolf (1996) cautioned that the debate regarding the use of euthanasia has been incomplete and the actual practice must not precede a more complete analysis. Before deciding to legitimize a euthanasia process, several salient variables must be examined. Gender is prominent among these factors. Wolf began this analysis and observed that women may request euthanasia at a higher rate than men. Women also seem to seek euthanasia for different reasons. These choices may be more related to the needs of others than relief from personal pain—an aspect of the valorization of women's propensity to self-sacrifice. Wolf questioned how the image of a woman as the candidate for euthanasia may affect the public debate.

The public perception of persons with disabilities as a burden to society and the people around them has been a central concern of disability advocates and scholars for some time. Olkin (1999) reviewed "the burden literature" appearing since 1990 about people with disabilities and was struck by the volume of this work and the tendency to discuss the burden as attached to the person rather than the disability. This type of work

Box 9–2 • A Pause to Reflect: Is There a Slippery Slope?

Peter Singer, professor of bioethics, has come under fire from the disability community for his views and beliefs regarding disability. As evidenced by a documentary, *Singer: A Dangerous Mind,* the positions forwarded by this ethicist are viewed as controversial. Singer states, "Killing a disabled infant is sometimes not wrong. Given that the infant, like any infant, is not a person, as I see it, I think that it's ethically defensible to say we do not have to continue its life. It doesn't have a right to life" (Barney, 2003, p. 1). Singer goes on to state, "I don't think any newborn baby has a right to life, until they're capable of that, they are a being who has a future, who lives over time" (Barney, p. 1). Individuals within the disability community have challenged Singer's views as similar to Hitler's philosophy

with an academic approach. "Just what is having a disability 'really' like for people themselves and for their families? Just how much of a problem of disability is socially constructed? Is it reasonable to say that in a differently constructed social environment, what are now disabling traits would become more 'neutral' characteristics?" (Parens & Asch, 2003, p. 44).

What are your reactions to Singer's provocative statements? Do you think highlighting such positions in our literature begins to desensitize us and begins our movement down a slippery slope? What types of decisions might occur as a result? Do you think people with disabilities would have the same response to Singer as people who are not disabled? Why or Why not?

and that of the popular media may play into prejudices and set the stage for making individuals with disabilities view themselves and their very existence as an overwhelming burden, thus influencing them to select euthanasia. Another potential danger is a growing perception that life with a disability is a worthless and negative existence and a drain on limited resources, thus setting the stage for a climate that encourages people with severe disabilities to eliminate themselves. In such a cultural climate, parents who receive genetic tests that indicate their baby will have a serious disability may elect an abortion. Although movement from such general concerns to charges of genocide—targeting persons with disabilities—may sound rather far-fetched, one need only read Friedlander's (1995) chilling and fascinating account of the evolution of the Nazi genocide, in which thousands of persons with disabilities were subjected to "euthanasia." It is important to understand how such prejudices may develop into initially unthinkable results.

Implications for Counselors. Counselors may find themselves in a unique position of helping clients and their families during the decision-making process regarding euthanasia (Figure 9–7). Several authors have been particularly helpful in preparing counselors to engage in this process with clients (Albright & Hazler, 1995; Humphrey, 1991).

Rational Suicide. Much of the preceding discussion of euthanasia pertains to the area of rational suicide as well. In this form of contemplated death, the individual does not receive the means of death from the hands of another, but rather ends their own life. More specifically,

1. Keep current on the developing legal, social, and ethical information related to euthanasia.
2. Determine what culturally influenced moral theory, personal biases, and personal perspectives guide your practice. Continue to clarify personal beliefs and values.
3. Become adept at the skill of self-reflection. Assess your ethical decision-making process, understand it, and use it to deal consistently with issues.
4. Examine, understand, and reconcile institutional protocols, legal precedents, and liabilities.
5. Obtain differing professional perspectives.
6. Be knowledgeable about the potential course, prognosis, and all treatment alternatives related to a client's illness.
7. Be familiar with all contextual factors that may be influencing a client—e.g., who constitutes the client's support system and what are these individuals' perspectives?
8. Seek to understand clients by exploring their world.
9. Act as a resource person and empathic listener. Assist clients with psychic and physical pain. Provide support and maintain substantial autonomy.
10. Help clients understand the importance of various personal and formal documents associated with the end of life.
11. Be available to comfort significant others after a death has occurred.

FIGURE 9–7.   Counseling Implications of Euthanasia
Source: From "A Right to Die? Ethical Dilemmas of Euthanasia" by D. E. Albright and R. J. Hazler, 1995, *Counseling and Values, 39.* Copyright 1995 by the American Counseling Association. Reprinted by permission.

rational suicide is defined as "following a sound decision-making process, a person has decided, without being coerced by others, to end his or her life because of unbearable suffering associated with a terminal illness" (Werth & Holdwick, 2000, p. 513).

In their rulings on cases concerning physician-assisted suicide, the Ninth and Second Circuit Courts of Appeals ruled that laws prohibiting physician-assisted death were prohibited in the state of Washington (*Compassion in Dying v. Washington; Quill v. Vacco,* respectively). Those decisions were appealed to and ruled upon by the U.S. Supreme Court. At that time, ACA filed an amicus curia ("friend of the court") brief with the U.S. Supreme Court in conjunction with several other organizations. They took positions that spoke to the mental health issues involved in hastened death and supported the circuit court decisions (Werth, 1999). The U.S. Supreme Court eventually ruled that people who are terminally ill do not have a constitutional right to physician-assisted suicide, but that only the states could decide whether to allow such activities. For counselors, however, the ACA brief made an important statement—that clients who are terminally ill, mentally competent, and facing an imminent and inevitable death should be able "to choose the manner and hasten the timing of their death" (Brief of the WSPA et al., 1996, p. 2). Mental health professionals can play an important role in discussing this issue with people who are considering physician-assisted suicide. They can determine if the person has a mental disorder that would impair decision-making ability. Professionals can also determine if the person was unduly pressured by others to make this decision and if significant others were sufficiently involved in discussions leading up to the decision. These points closely parallel the necessary criteria for assessing if an individual is capable of making a decision concerning rational suicide (see Box 9–3).

In a survey of mental health counselors about their attitudes toward rational suicide, over 80% were moderately supportive of the idea that people can make decisions for themselves to undertake rational suicide as their best option (Rogers et al., 2001). A new ethical standard in the ACA code of ethics assists counselors who provide such care in fulfilling their ethical obligations to ensure such individuals receive expert and proper care (ACA, 2005). It also supports counselors' responsibility to respect the dignity, welfare, and autonomy of the client and permits counselors to carefully consider whether the specific circumstances require them to violate confidentiality when disclosure is needed to protect the client from clear and imminent danger through rational suicide. Counselors must think carefully about what strategies and resources they would employ in such instances. Werth (1999) offered excellent guidelines for these considerations.

Complementary and Alternative Medicine

Natural phenomena began to be measured, understood, and subsequently controlled in Galileo's time. Empirical science has now become the truth of Western civilization. According to Wilbur (1988), this approach became a privileged way of knowing and created a chasm between science and other ways of knowing. Wilbur argued that this gap has served to separate truth from meaning, and what we know about our bodies from whom we believe ourselves to be (our mind and spirit)—fracturing our holistic sense of self from our material body. In Western culture, this divide is exemplified in the current gap among traditional, institutionalized, and nontraditional health care.

Box 9–3 • Criteria for Assessing Adequacy of Rational Suicide Decision

1. Has the person met the general requirements for receiving aid in dying (e.g., in Oregon: a diagnosis, by two physicians, of a terminal illness with a prognosis of 6 months or less)?

2. (a) Does the individual have the capacity to form reasoned decisions about his or her health care? (b) Has the person engaged in a sound decision-making process, considering all alternatives?

3. Is the person making the decision voluntarily or are there subtle or overt coercive pressures influencing the decision?

4. Is it possible to facilitate conversation among the suffering person and his or her significant others to make the dying process easier on all involved?

Source: J. L. Werth, & D. J. Holdwick. (2000). A primer on rational suicide and other forms of hastened death. *The Counseling Psychologist, 28,* 511–539.

Nowhere is this chasm more apparent than when a person is faced with making an important health care decision. In Western culture, science has long been the centerpiece of this type of decision making—the contemporary paradigm of truth. Over the past several decades, the privileged position of science as the exclusive truth in health care has been challenged by practices outside the biomedical realm. Such practices have been dubbed **complementary medicine** (those that work with traditional medicine) and **alternative medicine** (those used instead of traditional medicine). Complementary and alternative medicine **(CAM)** approaches are becoming more popular in health care, resulting in a marked shake-up in the health care world. Recent research has documented the tremendous growth in their use, including the results of a national survey that appeared in the *Journal of the American Medical Association*. The survey revealed that 4 out of 10 people (42%) use some form of CAM (Marcus, 1999). Some of the most frequently used CAMs are relaxation techniques, herbal medicine, massage, chiropractic, spiritual healing, megavitamin therapy, self-help, imagery, energy healing, homeopathy, hypnosis, biofeedback, and acupuncture (Eisenberg et al., 1998).

Proponents of biomedicine (practices based on empirical science) or traditional medical practice have responded to this challenge to biomedical dominance. For some observers, this debate between medicine and nontraditional practices takes the appearance of a full-scale cultural war. Patients are often faced with the dilemma of an either/or choice in health care services. Some practitioners from both sides of the debate have taken entrenched positions, demanding that their patients declare their loyalty and limit their access to other health care practices. Box 9–4 describes the emotionally painful and potentially psychologically damaging effects

Box 9–4 • A Counselor in Training Learns About Complementary and Alternative Medicine

Working on a hematology/oncology inpatient unit has its inspirational and heartbreaking moments. I feel the best part of my job is the patients with whom I have the privilege to work. Cancer in itself is a word that strikes many emotions. Working with cancer patients has presented me the opportunity to experience the hardest of emotions and learn the importance of assisting people facing a life-threatening disease. Certainly, I have learned the importance of patients having a positive relationship with the medical staff. At times I can see the looks of fear and discontentment among the medical staff. It scares me to think of how these reactions affect the care patients receive. Not very long ago I was confronted with a situation in which staff let their personal beliefs and attitudes interfere with the care a patient received.

With every admission, information is conveyed to the floor that helps us provide the best environment for a given patient. In this case we admitted a 40-year-old female with metastasized breast cancer who had a history of the condition for over a year. As noted on her admission orders, she was to be seen for a first-time evaluation of her cancer, which seemed odd given her year-long history. On arrival, the patient was off to numerous diagnostic tests, and I served as her floor liaison, escorting her about the hospital. I had been informed of the specifics of her case, which usually entailed only the diagnosis and reason for admission. Before I left the floor, I got the impression that something was unique to this situation. As I inquired into the nurse's reaction to interviewing the patient, she revealed that the patient had been self-administering treatment for the past year. Nothing seemed odd about that until the nurse revealed the patient's occupation as a naturopathic healer. The immediate reactions of the staff were disbelief and criticism, for the patient's approach challenged every treatment principle practiced within our institution.

Walking into the room with a wheelchair, I met the fiancé of the patient. He diligently helped prepare the patient for her journey, lifting her by himself and putting her in the wheelchair. The patient could not stand or lift her legs without assistance. She displayed a flat affect and appeared physically and emotionally exhausted. The fiancé accompanied us to each test, and along the way we conversed about the hospital as well as about their long, 4-hour journey to the hospital. They remarked, on the massive size of the hospital and how it was the first time they had been to the area. It was clear to me they both felt overwhelmed and out of place, which is a typical feeling of first-time patients I have encountered. The patient's family was 4 hours away and relying upon information conveyed through the fiancé. At the final test, the fiancé left to contact the patient's family, and the two of us proceeded on to the diagnostic station.

continued

Box 9–4 • A Counselor in Training Learns About Complementary and Alternative Medicine—*continued*

As I waited for the completion of a test, the technician and I could not help but notice the unusually great number of doctors that were assembling about the diagnostic facility. It was hard not to be distracted by the gathering, for they were animatedly discussing the patient's case. The discussion was one of astonishment and skepticism. In their eyes, this patient had broken every principle by which they practiced. The comments were none too kind or sympathetic to the patient's condition. A consulting physician to the case conveyed his intention to confront the patient on the absurdity of her treatment approach and beliefs. It was clearly apparent to me that their skepticism would be conveyed to the patient. It was then that I left the situation to return to the floor, for my shift had just ended.

What followed was a clear display of unethical behavior by medical professionals. In fact, I left work that day shattered by the thought of the medical staff approaching the patient with the hostility and the disregard I had witnessed. On my return to work a few days later, the patient's situation was emotionally better because her family had visited and she continually received cards and words of encouragement from numerous supporters. The mocking never stopped, but her acceptance of medical treatment aided in decreasing her discomfort and increasing her quality of life. What kept this patient going through this whole ordeal was her supporters. Their strength and support showed me that she was not alone, and it made quite an impression upon the staff.

Personally, I may not have agreed with the patient's beliefs and alternative approach, but I felt that this opinion should not impede me from effectively assisting her at the current time. I feel she had already taken a big leap by coming to our institution and that our job was dependent upon establishing her need for consultation. In approaching this situation and others similar to it, I feel it is important to respect the wishes of the patients and become knowledgeable concerning their chosen approach as well as assist them in understanding the way in which I practice.

The use of CAMs is a very hot topic in the medical and professional world. In my experience working within this hospital setting, medical professionals who endorse CAMs are typically given a cold shoulder by those who practice traditional treatment regimens or are working independently outside the hospital environment. CAMs present a challenge to the traditional medical community, threatening their typical practices. In their opinion, such practices put patients in jeopardy of the advancement of their cancer. Their major concern tends to be the lack of empirical data or evidence to support these types of treatments. However, many of these practices may be safe and very helpful to clients who use them to supplement, not substitute, their traditional medical treatments. I feel that medical professionals are entitled to their opinions, yet when it comes to sharing that perspective, it must be done in such a way as to not threaten a patient's psychological and physical well-being.

I think the most important bit of advice I can lend in relation to CAMs is to acknowledge their existence. Learn more about them so you can understand the consumer's perspective. I learn something new each day, especially at work. My awareness of this patient's situation helped me understand the right approach and information I needed to have in order to assist her effectively. If I had shut her out and mocked her beliefs, it would only add to her pain and discontent. Shutting out the use of CAMs is no way to handle the situation, for it impedes the relationship, inviting stereotypes and bias to impede your judgment of what is best for your client's emotional and physical well-being. It is important to handle the situation professionally, meaning that you are aware of your personal values and beliefs and able to appropriately confront clients without doing emotional harm. I think it is important to express your beliefs in a manner that is constructive and conducive to assisting individuals without degrading their beliefs. It is my hope that by doing so, the consumer may come to accept my approach.

Know where you stand on the use of CAMs. This understanding is the first step towards the awareness of your consumer's needs. It is imperative to keep an open mind and not let assumptions or judgments interfere with the care one provides to consumers utilizing CAMs. Imposing your values upon these individuals will, I feel, be met with resistance and will derail any attempt you may have in assisting them to meet their needs. Know who you are and know your limitations. This will help in the conveyance of your approach and contribute to its acceptance by your consumers.

of such tensions in the life of one woman with a metastasized cancer and those who surround her. Counselors can play a significant role in assisting individuals who are negotiating their health care choices in this current climate of uneasy acceptance of CAMs.

History of the Health Care Debate. In Western culture and particularly in the United States, biomedicine has political power and influence through legal practices and regulatory statutes. These powers secure the dominance of traditional health care to the exclusion of nonsanctioned practices. Practitioners of biomedicine historically criticize and thwart practices outside of traditional medicine's defined methods, calling more esoteric therapies "unconventional" and "unorthodox" at best and "irrational" and "dangerous" at worst (Cohen, 2000). Despite biomedicine's central position, there have been overwhelming gains in the number of people utilizing nonbiomedical practices, also known as **holistic care,** in the United States since the 1960s. The Landmark Healthcare Study showed that 42% of Americans now use complementary and alternative methods of health care (Eisenberg et al., 1998).

In 1992, the U.S. Congress created The Office for Study of Unconventional Medical Practices, which mandated the documentation of esoteric health care practices. This enactment resulted in a document entitled The Chantilly Report (NIH, 1994), which systematically categorized these practices. As the use of nontraditional health care practices continued to rise through the 1990s, the Office for Study eventually became designated the Office of Complementary and Alternative Medicine (CAM). This type of health care was granted full legitimacy when the National Center for Complementary and Alternative Medicine at the National Institutes of Health was formed in 1998. It now seems undeniable that the use of nontraditional medical practices is here to stay and their use is on the rise.

The *1999 United States Census Reports* documented that the United States has increased greatly in racial and cultural diversity. With this diverse population has come a wide range of cultural health care practices, further enhancing the tension between traditional and nontraditional health care practices. The clash of cultures and shift of paradigms are creating significant concerns for those who assist individuals in making health care choices. Questions are arising, such as: Who is effective? What is safe? How can my healers work together? Whom do I trust? To answer these and other questions, consumers must address and understand the relevant legal, ethical, and moral issues.

Legal Issues Related to CAMs.   An increasing number of cases involving CAM practices are emerging in the court systems (Cohen, 2000; Studdert et al., 1998). As the legal system increasingly interfaces with health care in general, and CAM practices in particular, the landscape of healing practice is taking new shape.

One controversial part of the current health care landscape is the system of credentialing and sanctioning practitioners. Regulatory mechanisms such as certification and licensure can be an important avenue for a counselor in determining the legitimacy of a CAM practitioner to whom they may wish to refer a client. However, contemporary credentialing practices are creating some interdisciplinary tension among potential care providers. According to Cohen (2000), health care licensing laws are now being created to regulate CAM practices and are aimed at protecting the public. Such statutes ensure that only those who meet set criteria can legally practice; all others can be prosecuted. This seemingly beneficial move may serve to suppress other means of care, such as indigenous practices. Thus, the licensure system can be seen as creating a kind of paternalism that may fractionalize CAM and traditional medical practices, pitting one against another. Medicine's legal claim to sole authority to provide healing services is being challenged for these very reasons. Numerous CAM practitioners are also becoming involved in the credentialing process. Cohen asserted that the desire to protect the public (do no harm) must be balanced against the wish to grant every opportunity for healing (autonomous choice of beneficial care). These are compelling philosophical arguments for a practicing counselor to consider.

Another important legal consideration in our evolving health care environment is the issue of professional liability. This is a particularly salient concern given the relative dearth of evidence on the efficacy and safety of many of the CAM approaches. Two specific examples of liability issues related to CAM practices that the current medical community is facing are referral liability and vicarious liability, including institutional liability. As the medical profession pioneers this legal frontier, counselors should remain apprised of these and other emerging issues as they relate to their own practice.

Referral liability is not a new issue but is one that is further complicated by the lack of coordination between CAM care and traditional medical practices. According to Studdert et al. (1998), an estimated 90% of patients using CAM care are not referred by their physician but are, instead, self-referred. A major reason for this lack of referral is the physician's concern about exposure to liability. This area has brought a complex set of concerns to bear on the physician's decision-making process (Studdert et al.). The threat of liability lends substantial weight to the influence of medical paternalism. Physicians must choose between upholding the autonomous decision-making rights of their patients and protecting themselves against potential malpractice litigation.

The same complex dynamic can be extended to health care facilities in the form of **vicarious liability**—an organization's responsibility for the potential negligence of its employees' referrals. Studdert et al. (1998) noted that "hospitals and managed care organizations have a legal obligation to be diligent in selecting, retaining, and evaluating health care professionals; this same obligation will extend to their relationship with alternative medicine practitioners" (p. 1618). By and large, organizations tend to make more conservative choices, potentially sacrificing the rights of the individual to their choice of care options. Cohen (2000) asserted that the development of appropriate institutional protocols relating to CAM modalities includes creative, interdisciplinary rules and policies to govern these protocols.

A final and related legal concern that is relatively new to the courts is the area of third-party reimbursement. Managed care typically seeks to minimize the use of specialists and expensive testing. For example, an insurance plan that offers to cover CAM services may determine that participants should be referred to a chiropractor rather than to an orthopedic surgeon, given certain predetermined indicators. Conversely, failure to refer to and use complementary modalities could constitute legal negligence. Health care in Western culture is, by and large, a capitalist venture. The tension is real, and economic control is a major route through which a third party can provide self-protection. The actual cost of failure to include CAM care may be to the client in a diminished quality of care.

Ethical Issues Related to CAMs. The principle of autonomy involves the right of any individual to exercise self-determination. In bioethics, this right refers to the ability to reject unwanted treatment and to make informed choices among treatment options. To exercise the right to self-determine, an individual must have sufficient and reliable information. This type of information traditionally has meant professional disclosure, provision of comprehensive information about any treatment, a state of voluntary choice, and a discernable competence on the part of the client to consent. Practitioners on both sides of the health care debate—both traditional and CAM—are faced with an increasing responsibility to provide opportunities for informed choice by addressing all relevant and available information about a condition and its documented treatments—traditional or otherwise. This information should include discussion of such factors as benefits, risks, consequences, and full disclosure of options of care. Practitioners are urged to share this information in a manner that precludes their own biases and facilitates their clients' informed choices.

The obligation to disclose comprehensive information and to assist an individual in making an informed and autonomous choice is a benchmark of a trusting relationship between practitioners and their clients. The need to maintain a strong working relationship represents the ethical principle of fidelity. When practitioners are not open to a dialogue with clients about viable alternatives under the guise of beneficent care, they create the potential for undetected harm. In fact, Clark (2000) stated that the current status quo is oftentimes, "don't ask and don't tell" (p. 455) by physicians, leading to medical paternalism. Conversely, well-meaning CAM advocates may be denying the role of traditional medicine that may be beneficial or even lifesaving for their clients.

Moral Issues Related to CAMs. The creation of an atmosphere of dialogue and a sincere move to patient-centered care is essential for quality health care. Individuals must have sufficient and reliable information to make sound health care choices in an atmosphere that supports their personal goals, values, and beliefs.

This supportive atmosphere can be of particular concern for individuals with diverse backgrounds whose health care practices may be disparate from accepted health care practices. Issues of diversity can range from more obvious transcultural situations such as Aruvedic practices (Cohen, 2000), found among Indian cultures, to subcultural practices such as snake handling, which occurs among a population of Appalachian Christians (Covington, 1995). Conversely, adherence to traditional medicine can now be considered a radical approach.

Cancer and CAM Care. Because of cancer's lethal potential, the treatment of cancer patients has often been at the center of the debate between the use of traditional and nontraditional health care practices. Negotiating a diagnosis of cancer and the subsequent treatment stands as a touchstone for other health care decision-making practices. A cancer patient's decisions can literally mean the difference between life and death or between a life with a measure of quality versus a life bereft of meaning. According to Marwick (1998), "some 60% of the inquiries the OAM (Office of Alternative Medicine) receives deal with cancer. By far cancer is the largest single condition people ask about. National surveys show that half of cancer patients will use some kind of unconventional therapy" (p. 1554).

At a Symposium of the American Society of Clinical Oncology and the American Cancer Society in 1999, Dr. Wendy Harpham, an internal medicine physician and a cancer survivor, gave an address to a group of government and academic physicians who had joined to discuss the role of nontraditional approaches with cancer patients. In her address, Dr. Harpham attempted to personalize the current thinking about the use of CAM cares in the treatment of cancer by telling her own story and owning her own biases for biomedicine while seriously examining nontraditional options. This account was later published in *CA, A Cancer Journal for Clinicians* (Harpham, 2001).

The summary of this article provides a fascinating snapshot of the prevailing attitudinal environment faced by this courageous individual: "Despite her scientific training and experience in medical practice, after being diagnosed with an indolent non-Hodgkin's lymphoma, [Dr. Harpham] was subjected to intense pressure about alternative therapies from well-meaning friends and relatives. While insulated at first from these forces, disease recurrences and progression increased her vulnerability to the lure of seemingly gentler approaches. A data-driven study of alternative therapeutic methods, however, convinced [Dr. Harpham] that investigational strategies offered her a better chance of cure or improvement than unproven alternative methods. [Dr. Harpham] offers guidelines for physicians about what patients want, and emphasizes the importance of hope, caring, and information" (Harpham, 2001, p. 131). Dr. Harpham described the emotional and rational vicissitudes that were inherent in her decision-making process. From this experience, she was able to articulate six important factors for physicians (and other health care providers) to consider when helping patients make decisions about their health care. A modified version of these factors offers a good starting place for the development of a respectful approach integrating CAM and traditional health perspectives:

1. Patients want to get well. Establish your role as your patient's ally and advocate.
2. Patients want to avoid pain, distress, poverty, and uncertainty. Offer more than the cold statistics of conventional practices. Help the patient to access all resources to be well informed.
3. Patients want to enhance self-healing. Encourage these efforts. These may include providing information on exercise, nutrition, spirituality, etc.
4. Patients want to feel empowered. Encourage patient participation and active endeavors in their pursuits of health care.
5. Patients want the best possible treatment. Emphasize the strengths of the scientific method, acknowledge the limitations of this same method, and dedicate yourself to narrowing the gap between optimal and actual care.
6. Patients want hope (in fact, need hope). (Harpham, p. 135)

Dr. Harpham concluded that in the end, if physicians and those who share their biomedical worldview do not address the issue of CAM practices, they are, by their silence, unethically leaving their patients with an unbalanced input about treatment. Although her position represents one of known bias, her overarching goal is representative of sound moral, ethical, and legal practices—that is, the goal of safe, compassionate, and effective integration of health care practices.

Integrative care, which combines conventional and nonconventional therapies in a safe, effective, and appropriate way, is the answer to an ongoing dilemma between conventionality and its opponents. Cohen (2000) stated that "while firm proponents and staunch opponents of CAM represent the poles of belief about the role, safety, and efficacy of such therapies, the term integrative health care, as just defined, expresses an achievable and desirable goal in the future of U.S. health care" (p. 3). Counselors must be prepared to address the difficulties of this integration while concurrently addressing the moral, ethical, and legal needs of their clients.

HIV and AIDS Care

The HIV/AIDS epidemic has presented counselors with new ethical decision-making dilemmas. This uncharted territory has required counselors to carefully examine and consider prudent action on unresolved ethical issues. Legal and professional norms of practice have remained difficult to negotiate. These unresolved dilemmas are now embedded within a managed health care environment, rendering them even more complex. As counselors struggle to resolve these emerging ethical issues; they must have a working knowledge of the basic issues related to working with individuals touched by HIV/AIDS.

Ryan and Rowe (1988) identified some predictable ethical dilemmas that counselors may encounter in providing services to people who are HIV-positive: (a) personal conflicts with clients' values and behaviors,

(b) conflicts with colleagues whose personal biases or unresolved issues prevent them from serving clients appropriately, (c) concerns about a caregiver's right to know which clients are HIV-infected, (d) concerns about whether to reveal a client's positive status to sexual partners or partners sharing needles when the client refuses to inform others at risk, (e) conflicts with social service agencies that fail to provide appropriate training and supervision for caregivers or services for people who are HIV-positive, and (f) concerns about the increasing accountability of the counseling profession as an organization that should be advocating for people with HIV more effectively. Ryan and Rowe suggested two major areas of ethical concerns in working with people who have HIV: confidentiality and informed consent.

In general, counselors must provide the same sound ethical practice to people who have HIV/AIDS that they provide to any other client. Specifically, they must strive to protect the privacy of their clients while promoting their welfare. Counselors who practice with HIV-positive clients must have an appropriate degree of practitioner competence. The counselor's competency must include a working knowledge of potential cultural or lifestyle differences; the HIV disease process (e.g., etiology, prognosis, and treatment); and an explicit degree of self-awareness with regard to the counselor's own values, assumptions, and fears. According to Melton (1988), the need to be educated in working with people who are HIV-positive is founded firmly upon the principle of beneficence. Beneficent practice also extends professional responsibilities to include client advocacy. Previous attempts at advocacy have extended the Rehabilitation Act of 1973 and the Americans with Disabilities Act to protect people who are HIV-positive as they would protect any other individuals with disabilities from undue discrimination.

Four major issues deal with confidentiality and the person who is HIV-positive: (a) the presence of a special relationship between client and counselor and the duty to treat, (b) assessment of the impending degree of dangerousness of the client, (c) the presence of an identifiable victim of client danger, and (d) the articulation of appropriate counselor actions in working with persons who are HIV-positive (Knapp & VandeCreek, 1990; Lamb, Clark, Drumheller, Frizzell, & Surrey, 1989; Morrison, 1989; Totten, Lamb, & Reeder, 1990).

Special Relationship and the Duty to Treat. The Tarasoff outcome (see Chapter 3) and other prevailing evidence support the conclusion that entering into a professional relationship is a sufficient condition for counselors to assume some responsibility for their clients. As a result, the counselor assumes some degree of responsibility for any third parties the counselor reasonably knows to be in danger from that client. The conclusions based on Tarasoff and related decisions suggest that confidentiality is valued highly in the special relationship between the counselor and the client; however, it is not bound as an absolute. Under certain circumstances, the counselor is bound ethically to protect a potential victim in the face of certain harm (Stanard & Hazler, 1995). According to Melton (1988), most courts have considered the duties to third parties to be congruent with the Tarasoff logic. In this perspective, often referred to as the duty to warn, the counselor is charged with a duty to exercise reasonable care in warning a specific intended third party who has been threatened by a client. Tarasoff limited the definition of "reasonable foreseeable harm" to include cases that involve a specific, identifiable victim. This threat must be weighed carefully against the harm that the client may incur by any breach of confidentiality. People who are HIV-positive are particularly vulnerable to any breach of confidentiality and face unique social and emotional threats because of the public's fear and anxiety of contagion. An intrusion of privacy should be no greater than necessary to exert reasonable care (Melton).

Figure 9–8 suggests guidelines for counselors who make decisions about limiting the degree of client confidentiality (Cohen, 1990). Ethical practice dictates that boundaries of confidentiality must be clear to the counselor and to the client before the counseling process begins.

Although there always have been implicit risks for health care providers in the course of providing their services, the deadliness of the HIV/AIDS epidemic has heightened the debate regarding the counselor's duty to treat. Justification for refusal to treat a client has been based primarily on the risk of contagion or on the presence of values conflicts between counselor and client (Morrison, 1989). Some counselors who elect not to treat people who are HIV-positive may do so because the issues clients bring to treatment constitute a values conflict that the counselor may view as insurmountable. Others may simply feel uncomfortable with people who have HIV—the lifestyle choices related to the types of people or the life issues related to the decision. Although ethical codes of various disciplines suggest that counselors are obligated to respect clients and to protect the welfare of those seeking services, there is no

1. Counselors who receive information from clients who may have a communicable disease known to be fatal must disclose information to relevant third parties if, and only if, the counselors have reason to believe that:
   a. There is medical evidence.
   b. The clients bear specific relation (e.g., sexual or shared needles) to specified third parties at high risk of contagion.
   c. The clients have not already informed the third parties nor are they likely to make such disclosures in a timely manner.
2. In cases wherein the above conditions are met, counselors' general obligation to third parties is defined by:
   a. Within the counseling context, before disclosure, counselors must make all reasonable efforts to educate the clients about the disease and to provide the clients with the support, understanding, encouragement, and opportunity to disclose the information to third parties on their own.
   b. The counselor must make third-party disclosure in a timely fashion.
   c. Before disclosure, counselors must inform clients of their intention.
   d. Counselors must disclose the information only to the parties at risk or to the legal guardian (in the case of minors).
   e. Counselors must limit the third-party disclosure to general medical information, in earnest, communicate to the third party a willingness to provide support in the form of counseling or to make an appropriate referral.

FIGURE 9–8.   Limitations of Confidentiality
Source: From "Confidentiality, Counseling, and Clients Who Have AIDS: Ethical Foundations of a Model Rule" by E. D. Cohen, 1990, *Journal of Counseling and Development, 68,* 282–286. Copyright 1990 by the American Counseling Association. Reprinted by permission.

clearly stated duty to treat undesirable or difficult clients. Refusal to treat a client is a moral, ethical, and legal decision and must be viewed from this perspective. People with HIV/AIDS are legally protected from discrimination based on their illness. Although it may not be necessary for the counselor to assume an ethical responsibility to treat a person with HIV, the counselor is morally responsible to reflect on the reasons for this decision. Moreover, the counselor has an ethical obligation to assist any individual seeking services in fully

and respectfully obtaining appropriate referral services, even if this individual is not accepted as a client.

Assessment of Dangerousness.   The prediction of dangerousness is considered to be significantly unreliable. The reasons for this high degree of unreliability are complex (Morrison, 1989). Certain behaviors, such as a history of violence or assaultive behavior and the availability of weapons, have been shown to be related to future dangerousness but have not proven to be directly predictive. Moreover, the dynamics of inherent dangerousness involved in the transmission of a fatal disease such as HIV/AIDS are substantively different from other assumed types of danger. Therefore, determining the degree of dangerousness of a client who is HIV-positive is a significantly difficult task.

Counselors must consider several important factors before concluding that a client who is HIV-positive is an inherent danger to another individual: (1) Counselors must acknowledge the limit of their own competence in the diagnosis and prognosis of HIV. (2) Counselors must obtain reliable medical proof that such a condition exists for a client and gather current, valid, and expert medical information regarding the course and transmission of the disease at varying stages and in relationship to this individual client's disease stage. (3) Counselors must establish the extent to which this particular client is engaging in high-risk behaviors. (4) Counselors must identify a victim of any dangerous behavior. (5) Counselors must assess the degree to which any strategies are being used by the client to reduce the degree of danger to a third party. Historically, given the prognostic ambiguity in assessing a client's degree of dangerousness, mental health professionals tended to overpredict the degree of dangerousness—overprediction seemed a more prudent error than underprediction. According to most literature, the Tarasoff stance on the assessment of dangerousness has been upheld. However, counselors first must consider less intrusive means of diffusing any impending risk before violating the confidentiality and trusting relationship with their client. For example, including significant others in the counseling process or encouraging voluntary disclosure by the client to potential victims would protect others while not violating confidentiality.

Identifiable Victim.   According to legal rulings, a counselor is required to substantiate the presence of a specific, identified victim before breaching a client's confidentiality to warn a third party of danger. However, courts have extended the counselor's duty to protect unknown, but readily identifiable, others. For instance, a client may describe a specific person, such as a roommate, with whom the client shares an IV needle and not provide that person's name. With limited effort, the counselor may identify a specific, knowable person. However, a counselor cannot interrogate or independently investigate a client to obtain this information. The identification of a specific victim in impending danger comes solely from client disclosure. According to Lamb et al. (1989), the issue of an identifiable victim has several implications for counselors who work with people who have HIV (Figure 9–9).

Appropriate Counselor Actions. As more counselors work with people who have HIV, informed, ethical

practice must include thoughtful preparation for working with these clients. Counselors must consider and learn about the implications of HIV in all aspects of the counseling process, including prudent record-keeping procedures that protect the client's confidentiality, particularly in the context of managed care (Hughes & Friedman, 1994). Currently, membership in a high-risk group may be considered evidence for cancellation of a client's insurance benefits or may lead to the loss of a client's job. The client's record should contain all contacts with the client, a summation of the client's progress, documents that support informed consent, and all test data. Working notes should be kept separate from the client's record (Morrison, 1989). Clearly, counselors must use all aspects of good ethical and clinical practice in serving people who have HIV.

1. Become familiar and continually update medical information regarding HIV.
2. Be familiar with short- and long-term issues that may arise.
3. Be aware of one's own attitudes, biases, and prejudices as they relate to individuals with HIV.
4. Seek to inform and encourage all clients in high-risk groups to consider safe methods of having sex and using drugs.
5. Be prepared to refer clients to legal resources if warranted to protect their right to nondiscrimination.
6. Keep current regarding existing state and federal laws concerning the caregiver role in the spread of communicable diseases.
7. Articulate early in the therapeutic relationship the limitations of confidentiality, including the possible use of written formats to facilitate the informed consent process.
8. Determine mutual goals with the client as part of an ongoing assessment.
9. Remember that your principal duty is to your client.
10. Exercise your prerogative to refer or consult with other professionals as needed.
11. Maintain appropriate case notes that document confidentiality issues, understandings with your client, treatment goals and progress, and unusual events. Consider working notes separate from the formal client record.

FIGURE 9–9. General Counselor Implications for Working with People with AIDS

Source: From "Applying Tarasoff to AIDS-related Psychotherapy Issues" by D. H. Lamb, C. Clark, P. Drumheller, K. Frizzel, and L. Surrey, 1989, *Professional Psychology, 20.* Copyright 1989 by the American Psychological Association. Adapted by permission.

Abortion

Counselors who work in a variety of environments, including school, rehabilitation, and marriage and family practice settings, may be confronted with the issue of abortion during clinical practice. Abortion is a value-laden issue in society at large and also within the counseling setting. Without a massive shift in public opinion, abortion will remain one of the most divisive health care policy issues.

Because of the value-laden and emotional nature of the abortion issue, counselors must examine their own values and understand their clients' value systems (Wilcox, Robbennolt, & O'Keeffe, 1998). They must carefully analyze all relevant empirical research to ensure that all involved parties in the debate appropriately characterize the scientific knowledge base. They should encourage health care policy and institutional policy that are based upon evidence rather than assumptions alone (Wilcox et al.).

Counselors who consider providing services to individuals who are considering abortion must first examine the environment in which they are employed. Their agencies may have in place very specific procedures and guidelines as to whether the counselor can provide such counseling services, as well as the nature and direction of the services to be provided. Despite the fact that 70% of Americans feel that abortion should be legal in some form, there is a huge chasm regarding opinions about the circumstances under which it should be performed (Russo & Denious, 1998). Clearly, there is no simple answer.

Counselors may also find or seek employment in settings or agencies that provide counseling to clients considering alternatives to abortion. In those settings counseling focuses on such sensitive topics as: (a) garnering resources for young parents; (b) the prospect of single parenthood; or (c) the option of placing the child up for adoption. Counselors must be alert to the emotion-laden nature of such topics and pay special attention to the adjustment concerns of clients before and subsequent to the choices they make.

QUESTIONS FOR REFLECTION

1. What value or moral issues may arise within you as a professional when considering counseling clients in the area of genetics or donation of embryos for stem cell research?
2. Do you think that managed care will at some point in time provide research to strengthen the profession of counseling due to the outcome data which these companies are constantly collecting?
3. Is there any way to keep your values about complimentary and alternative medicine from impacting your relationship with clients who are using these approaches and may have difficulty with conventional counseling approaches?
4. How do you address differences in values or moral issues when you are employed at an agency that does not condone abortion and your views are considered prochoice? Could you ethically be employed in this type of setting?

Some facilities provide counseling services for abortion only under specific circumstances (e.g., in cases of rape or incest). Others provide counseling at all times for any circumstance, and some refer clients to other appropriate counseling agencies. The public debate presently is divided into two sides: One camp addresses abortion as a right related to individual freedom, control, and equality for women. The other position views this action as a threat to morality and social cohesion (Russo & Denious, 1998), or to the rights of the "unborn child".

Currently, some health care providers and advocates of women's health are concerned about the decrease in the number of physicians who perform abortions. This limited pool of providers has influenced the availability of such services (Henshaw, 1998). Counselors are also affected as clients seek advice on where they can obtain abortion services. At present, access is limited for women who are unable to pay, those living in nonurban areas, and those who are unwilling to face potential harassment at a large, urban clinic.

When a client makes the decision to have an abortion, she is protected, to a certain degree, by legislation that addresses the psychological and physical health risks of abortion and informed consent (Adler, Smith, & Tschann, 1998). Counselors who work with adolescents must be familiar with state regulations regarding parental consent. Many argue that parental consent legislation is in place because abortion carries with it a substantial risk and minors are incapable of making informed choices related to the risk.

Regardless of the client's age, it is the counselor's responsibility to address the client's competence to make the important decision about abortion and to provide meaningful informed consent (see Chapter 3). With adolescents and children, the counselor should focus on assessing competence to make an informed choice, whereas with adults, the counselor must provide information to ensure that the client is in a position to give informed consent and is making the decision of her free will (Koocher & DeMaso, 1990). The counselor is faced with a dilemma upon providing this information—there is no clear standard for determining when adolescents or adults have the capability of making an informed decision in this area (Adler et al., 1998).

Special Issues of Adolescents and Abortion. The issue of parental consent assumes the need to consult with a parent or guardian regarding an abortion decision. Zabin, Hirsch, Emerson, and Raymond (1992) found that 91% of adolescents did consult with a parent or other adult guardian after receiving a positive pregnancy test result. Another 4% of these adolescents discussed their pregnancy with an adult other than a parent or older sibling. Many question the necessity of consent laws because it appears that a high percentage of minors consult with their parents voluntarily (Adler et al., 1998). School counselors who think "this couldn't happen to me" should take notice of *Arnold v. Board of Education* of Escambia Country (Adler et al., 1998), in which a school counselor and principal were charged with not informing parents that their high-school-aged child was pregnant and that the school officials had urged the student not to tell her parents. Further, the parents claimed the school counselor had coerced the student into having an abortion. The trial court "concluded that the students were not deprived of their free will and had chosen to obtain an abortion, had chosen not to tell their parents, and that there was no coercion on the part of school officials" (Stone, 2002, p. 32).

Counselors may encounter adolescents who fear telling their parents or adult guardians of their pregnancies, let alone their consideration of abortion. They may fear the potential response from their parents. This fear may also make them feel ill at ease in trying to obtain a judicial bypass of consent laws from the state. Counselors need to be aware that these adolescents may be at risk in several ways: (a) they may attempt to obtain an illegal abortion; (b) they may attempt to self-induce an abortion; and (c) they risk complications due to the delay of the abortion procedure because of the time it may take for the judicial bypass procedure. Some clients appear for counseling services because certain states allow parental consent to be waived if the adolescent has obtained professional counseling (Adler et al., 1998). At present, more research is needed in the area of adolescent competence and decision making. Counselors during the course of their professional responsibilities may assist students with value-laden issues such as abortion if they are competent to provide this advice and proceed in a professional manner. However, counselors are urged to be well educated regarding school board policies. Some schools can and do adopt policies that forbid counselors from addressing certain topics and instruct the counselor to immediately contact the parents if specified topics are brought up by students. Counselors must at all times be prepared to demonstrate they behaved in the same manner that a reasonably competent professional would have behaved in this situation. Any coercion on the part of the counselor or attempt to impose personal values on a minor student would be inappropriate on the part of the counselor and would not be indicative of the behavior of a reasonable and competent counselor (Stone, 2002).

Risks of Abortion. Few studies show adverse effects to women who choose to have an abortion. However, adolescents have increased health risks, and many feel extra protection for adolescents is warranted (Adler et al., 1998).

Postabortion emotional distress has been linked to psychological risk factors including psychological difficulties prior to the procedure, ambivalence about the decision, limited coping skills, and an inadequate social support system (Adler et al., 1998), regardless of age. Counselors must be aware of the best counseling approaches available and know when to refer potential clients for additional services.

Counselors who provide abortion-relevant counseling services must be mindful of special issues that may emerge during abortion counseling: sexual abuse, assault, incest, multiple unintended pregnancies, religious reactions toward individuals who choose to have an abortion or are considering abortion, and special situations such as selective abortion to increase the viability of remaining fetuses (Fisher, Castle, & Garrity, 1998). Unintended pregnancy is a unique crisis that is often approached differently than other life decisions (Adler et al., 1998).

CHAPTER SUMMARY

The diversity of complex medical and health issues that confront people in modern society is awe inspiring. In the future, counselors will find their clients struggling with information and choices that are currently beyond our imagination. Professionals must be open to learning new perspectives that stimulate moral and ethical development.

Organizations that participate in managed care include: (1) health maintenance organizations (HMOs), which provide specified health services using a restricted group of providers at a fixed cost to the consumer; (2) preferred provider organizations (PPOs), which purchase health care from specific providers at a discounted rate; and (3) independent practice associations (IPAs), which allow consumers to choose independent practitioners but retain a portion of the fees from providers who may be reimbursed either on a fee-for-service or capitated basis.

Counselors who practice in managed care settings must have effective communication skills; knowledge of business practices; knowledge and skills in providing competent counseling; and knowledge of professional codes of ethics and ethical standards, including counselor competence, informed consent and confidentiality, integrity, conflict of interest, and business relationship.

Counselors confront a number of bioethical issues, including euthanasia, genetic testing, confidentiality, eugenics, abortion, HIV/AIDS, and rational suicide. To effectively deal with these emerging issues, counselors must have knowledge of biomedical ethics—understanding and examining moral life as it pertains to the biological sciences, medicine, and health care.

Complementary medical practices work with traditional medicine. Alternative medical practices are used instead of traditional medicine. CAM approaches are showing tremendous growth, and include relaxation techniques, herbal medicine, massage, chiropractic, spiritual healing, megavitamin therapy, self-help, imagery, energy healing, homeopathy, hypnosis, biofeedback, and acupuncture. Counselors must be prepared to address the legal, moral, and ethical issues that accompany these treatments.

INTERNET RESOURCES

A wealth of interesting information and ideas on health issues and ethics can be obtained by searching the internet, using some of the key words: managed care, rationing of care, managed care organization, capitation, fee for service, upcode, downcode, HIPAA, case management ethics, bioethics, genetic testing, genetic counseling ethics, eugenics, hastened death, euthanasia, advance directive, living will, durable power of attorney, rational suicide, abortion, holistic medicine, complimentary and alternative medicine, ethics of HIV care.

REFERENCES

Acuff, C., Bennett, B. E., Bricklin, P. M., Canter, M. B., Knapp, S. J., & Moldawsky, S. (1999). Considerations for ethical practice in managed care. *Professional Psychology: Research and Practice, 30*(6), 563–575.

Adler, N. E., Smith, L. B., & Tschann, J. M. (1998). Abortion and adolescents. In L. J. Beckman & S. M. Harvey (Eds.), *The new civil war: The psychology, culture and politics of abortion* (pp. 285–286). Washington, DC: American Psychological Association.

Albright, D. E., & Hazler, R. J. (1995). A right to die? Ethical dilemmas of euthanasia. *Counseling and Values, 39*, 177–189.

Alleman, J. R. (2001). Personal, practical, and professional issues in providing managed mental health care: A discussion for new psychotherapists. *Ethics & Behavior. 11*(4), 413–430.

American Counseling Association (2005). *American Counseling Association code of ethics.* Alexandria, VA: Author.

American Counseling Association (2002). *HIPAA and health information privacy: Frequently asked questions.* Alexandria, VA: Author.

American Psychiatric Association. (2000). *Diagnostic and statistical manual of mental disorders–IV-Text revision.* Washington, DC: Author.

American Psychological Association (2005). *Report from:* APA working group on assisted suicide and end-of-life decisions [On-line]. Available: http://apa.org/pi/aseol/section1.html.

Barney, S. (2003). *Singer: A dangerous mind.* Available: http://www.utilitarian.net/singer/interviews-debates/2003.htm

Beauchamp, T., & Childress, W. (2001). *Principles of biomedical ethics* (5th ed.). Baltimore, MD: Johns Hopkins University Press.

Beauchamp, T., & Walters, L. (Eds.). (1989). *Euthanasia and the prolongation of life. Contemporary issues in bioethics* (3rd ed.). Belmont, CA: Wadsworth.

Berenson, R. A. (1999). Testimony on the balanced budget act's impact on fee-for-service medicare before the senate finance committee [On-line]. Available: http://www.hfca.gov/testimony/1999/feefrol.htm

Bilynsky, N. S., & Vernaglia, E. R. (1998). The ethical practice of psychology in a managed case framework. *Psychotherapy, 35,* 54–68.

Brief of the Washington State Psychological Association; the American Counseling Association; the Association of Gay, Lesbian, and Bisexual Issues in Counseling; and the Coalition of Mental Health Professionals Supporting Individual Self-Determination in Decisions to Hasten Death. (1996, December). Filed with the Supreme Court of the United States, October 1996 term for *Washington v. Glucksberg* and *Vacco v. Quill.*

Brock, D. W. (1992). Voluntary active euthanasia. *Hastings Center Report, 22,* 10–22.

Carnovale, B. V., & Clanton, M. S. (2002). Genetic testing: Issues related to privacy, employment and health insurance. *Cancer Practice, 10*(2), 102–104.

Chan, F., Lui, J., Rosenthal, D., Pruett, S. R., & Ferrin, J. M. (2001). Managed care and rehabilitation counseling. *Journal of Rehabilitation Administration, 26*(2), 85–97.

Clark, P. A. (2000). The ethics of alternative medicine therapies. *Journal of Public Health Policies, 21*(4), 447–467.

Cohen, E. D. (1999). Confidentiality, counseling, and clients who have AIDS: Ethical foundations of a model rule. *Journal of Counseling and Development, 68,* 282–286.

Cohen, M. H. (2000). *Beyond complementary medicine: Legal and ethical perspectives on health care and human revolution.* Ann Arbor, MI: The University of Michigan Press.

Compassion in Dying v. Washington, 79 F. 3d 790 (9th Cir. 1996).

Cooper, C. C., & Gottlieb, M. C. (2000). Ethical issues with managed care: Challenges facing counseling psychology. *The Counseling Psychologist, 28*(2), 179–237.

Covington, D. (1995). *Salvation on Sand Mountain: Snake handling and redemption in Southern Appalachia.* New York: Penguin Books.

Dalzell, M. D. (2001, May). Genetic medicine: Powerful opportunities for good and greed. *Managed Care,* 1–10.

Daniels, J. A. (2001). Managed care, ethics, and counseling. *Journal of Counseling & Development, 79,* 119–122.

Danzinger, P. R., & Welfel, E. R. (2001). The impact of managed care on mental health counselors: A survey of perceptions, practice and compliance with ethical standards. *Journal of Mental Health counseling, 23*(2), 137–151.

Department of Health and Human Services. (2000). Office of the inspector general compliance program for individual and small group physician practices. *Federal Register, 65*(194), 59434–59452.

Dombeck, M. T., & Olsan, T. H. (2002). Ethics and managed care. *Journal of Interprofessional Care, 16*(3), 221–233.

Eisenberg, D. M., Davis, R. B., Ettner, S. L., Appel, S., Wilkey, S., Van Rompay, M., et al. (1998). Trends in alternative medicine use in the United States 1990–1997: Results of a follow-up national survey. *Journal of the American Medical Association, 280*(18), 1569.

Emmanuel, E. J. (1994, September 12). Euthanasia: Historical, ethical, and empirical perspectives. *Archives of Internal Medicine. 154,* 1890–1901.

Fisher, B., Castle, M. A., & Garrity, J. M. (1998). A cognitive approach to patient-centered abortion care. In L. J. Beckman & S. M. Harvey (Eds.), *The new civil war: The psychology, culture and politics of abortion* (pp. 308–321). Washington, DC: American Psychological Association.

Friedlander, H. (1995). *The origins of the Nazi genocide: From euthanasia to the final solution.* Chapel Hill, NC: University of North Carolina.

Fuller, B. P., Kahn, M. J., Barr, P. A., Biesecker, L., Crowley, E., Garber, J., et al. (1999). Privacy in genetics research. *Science, 285*(5432), 1359–1360.

Giarelli, E. (2001). Ethical issues in genetic testing. *Journal of Infusion Nursing, 24*(5), 301–310.

Glomstad, J. (2005). Navigating HIPAA. *Advance for Occupational Therapy Practitioners, 21*(10), 18–20.

Glosoff, H. L., Garcia, J., Herlihy, B., & Remley, T. P. (1999). Managed care: Ethical considerations for counselors. *Counseling & Values, 44*(1), 8–17.

Greiner, A (2001). Only one-third of consumers correctly identify basic managed care plan, features [On-line]. Available: http://www.hschange.org/content/297/?topic=topic06

Haas, L. J., & Cummings, N. A. (1991). Managed outpatient mental health plans: Clinical, ethical, and practical guidelines; for participation. *Professional Psychology: Research and Practice, 22*(1), 45–51.

Hallam, K. (1999). Sit up, take notice. *Modern Healthcare, 29*(25), 50.

Harpham, S. (2001). Alternative therapies for curing cancer: What do patients want? What do patients need? *CA, A Cancer Journal for Clinicians, 51*(2),131–136.

Henshaw, S. K. (1998). Barriers to access to abortion services. In L. J. Beckman & S. M. Harvey (Eds.), *The new civil war: The psychology, culture and politics of abortion* (p. 61). Washington. DC: American Psychological Association.

Hersch, L. (1995). Adapting to health care reform and managed care: Three strategies for survival and growth. *Professional Psychology: Research and Practice, 26*(1), 16–26.

Huber, C. H. (1995). Counselor responsibility with managed mental health care. *The Family Journal: Counseling and Therapy for Couples and Families, 3*(1), 42–44.

Hughes, R. B., & Friedman, A. L. (1994). AIDS-related ethical and legal issues for mental health professionals. *Journal of Mental Health Counseling, 16,* 445–458.

Human Genome Project (2001). Gene therapy [On-line]. Available: http://www.ornl.gov/hgmis/medicine/genetherapy.html

Humphrey, D. (1991). Final exit: *The practicalities of self-deliverance and assisted suicide for the dying.* New York: Dell Publishing.

Jecker, N. S. (1998). Ethics in medicine: Managed care [On-line]. Available: http://eduserv.hscer.washington.edu/bioethics/topics/manag.html

Jegalian, K., & Biesecker, L. (2000). The human genome project. *Exceptional Parent, 30*(3), 29–32.

Knapp, S., & VandeCreek, L. (1990). Application of the duty to protect HIV-positive clients. *Professional Psychology: Research and Practice, 21,* 161–166.

Koocher, G. P., & DeMaso, D. R. (1990). Children's competence to consent to medical procedures. *Pediatrician, 17,* 68–73.

Kutchins, H., & Kirk, S. (1987, May). DSM–III-R and social work malpractice. *Social Work,* 205–211.

Lamb, D. H., Clark, C., Drumheller, P., Frizzell, K., & Surrey, L. (1989). Applying Tarasoff to AIDS-related psychotherapy issues. *Professional Psychology: Research and Practice, 20,* 37–43.

Larson, L. (2000). Genomics. *Hospital & Health Networks, 74*(3), 76–81.

Lawless, L., Ginter, E. J., & Kelly, K. R. (1999). Managed care: What mental health counselors need to know. *Journal of Mental Health Counseling, 21*(1), 50–66.

Leung, W. C. (2000). Results of genetic testing: When confidentiality conflicts with a duty to warn relatives. *British Medical Journal, 321*(7274), 1464–1467.

Lin, Z., Owen, A. B., & Altman, R. B. (2004). Genomic research and human subject privacy. *Science, 305,* 183.

Lorber, L. Z. (2004). Genetic non-discrimination in the workforce. Federal testimony to the Committee on House Education and Workforce Subcommittee on Employer–Employee Relations. *FDCH Congressional Testimony, 07/22/2004.*

Marcus, C. (1999). Special report: Alternative medicine—the AMA reviews scientific evidence. *Clinical Reviews, 9*(2), 87–90.

Mariner, W. (1997). Business versus medical ethics: Conflicting standards for managed care. In J. W. Glaser & R. P. Hamel (Ed.), *Three realms of managed care* (pp. 92–111). Kansas City, MO: Sheed & Ward.

Marwick, C. (1998). Alterations are ahead at the OAM. *Journal of the American Medical Association, 280*(18), 1553–1554.

McGee, G., & Spanogle, J. P. (2001). Health-care ethics committees and managed care. *American Journal of Managed Care, 7*(8), 821–827.

Mechanic, D. (2001). The managed care backlash: Perceptions and rhetoric in health care policy and the potential for health care reform. *Milbank Quarterly, 79*(1), 14–18.

Meier, S. T. & Davis, S. R. (2001). Managed care as an ethical issue. In F. Flach (Ed). *Ethical issues in professional counseling* (pp. 27–36). New York: Hatherleigh.

Melton, G. B. (1988). Ethical and legal issues in AIDS-related practice. *American Psychologist, 43,* 941–947.

Mill, J. S. (1910). *Utilitarianism. In utilitarianism, or liberty, and representative government* (pp. 1–60). London: J. M. Dent. & Sons (original work published 1863).

Miller, I. (1998). Eleven unethical managed care practices every patient should know about. Available: http://www.nomanagedcare.org/eleven.html

Moffic, H. S. (2002). Quality still counts. *Psychiatric Times, 19*(6), 1–6.

Morrison, C. F. (1989). AIDS: Ethical implications for psychological interventions. *Professional Psychology: Research and Practice, 20,* 166–171.

Murphy, M. J. (1998). Evolution of practice and values of professional psychology. In R. F. Small & L. R. Barnhill (Eds.), *Practicing in the new mental health marketplace: Ethical, legal, and moral issues* (pp. 37–52). Washington, DC: American Psychological Association.

National Center for Genome Resources. (1997). *Eugenics.* Retrieved July 11, 2001 from the Charles Stuart University Web site: http://www.csu.edu.au/learning/ncgr/gpi/odyssey/dolly-cloning/eugenics.html

National Institutes of Health. (December, 1994). *Alternative medicine: Expanding medical horizons.* (A report to the National Institutes of Health on alternative medical systems and practices in the United States). NIH Publication 94-0666 [Chantilly Report].

National Reference Center for Bioethics Literature. (2001). *Scope note 28: Eugenics.* Retrieved. July 11, 2001 from the Joseph and Rose Kennedy Institute of Ethics, Georgetown University Web site: http://www.georgetown.edu/research/nrcbl/scopenote/sn28.htm

Office of Public Policy and Information. (1997). *Managed care: A primer on issues and legislation.* Alexandria, VA: American Counseling Association.

Oktay, J. S. (1998). Genetics cultural lag: What can social workers do to help? *Health and Social Work, 23*(4), 310–316.

Olkin, R (1999). *What psychotherapists should know about disability.* New York: Guilford.

Parens, E., & Asch, A. (2003). Disability rights critique of prenatal genetic testing: Reflections and recommendations. *Mental Retardation and Developmental Disabilities, 9,* 40–47.

Parens, E., & Asch, A. (1999): The disability rights critique of prenatal testing: Reflections and recommendations. *Special Supplement Hastings Center Report, 29*(5), S1–S22.

Pellegrino, E. D. (1986). Rationing health care: The ethics of medical gate keeping. *Journal of Contemporary Health, Law Policy, 2,* 23–45.

Peters, T. (1996). In search of the perfect child: Genetic testing and selective abortion. *Christian Century, 113*(31), 1034–1038.

Quill v. Vacco, 80F. 3d 716 (2d Cir. 1996).

Rieger, P. T. (2000). The gene genies. *American Journal of Nursing, 100*(10), 87–90.

Rogers, J. R., Gueulette, C. M., Abbey-Hines, J., Carney, J. V., & Werth, J. L. (2001). Rational suicide: An empirical investigation of counselor attitudes. *Journal of Counseling and Development. 79,* 365–372.

Russo, N. F., & Denious, J. E. (1998). Why is abortion such a controversial issue in the United States? In L. J. Beckman & S. M. Harvey (Eds.), *The new civil war: The psychology, culture and politics of abortion* (pp. 25–26). Washington, DC: American Psychological Association.

Ryan, C. C., & Rowe: M. J. (1988). AIDS: Legal and ethical issues. *Social Casework, 69,* 324–333.

Shore, M. (1996, January). Impact of managed care. *New England Journal of Medicine,* 116–118.

Siegel, K. (1986). Psycho-social aspects of rational suicide. *American Journal of Psychotherapy, 44,* 1053–1061.

Stanard, R., & Hazler, R. (1995). Legal and ethical implications of HIV and duty to warn for counselors: When does Tarasoff apply? *Journal of Counseling and Development, 73,* 397–400.

Stone, C. (2002). Negligence in academic advising, and abortion counseling: Courts rulings and implications. *Professional School Counseling, 6*(1), 28–36.

Studdert, D. M., Eisenberg, D. M., Miller, F. H., Curto, D. A., Daptchuk, T. J., & Brennan, T. A. (1998, November 11). Medical malpractice implications of alternative medicine. *Journal of the American Medical Association, 280*(18), 1610–1616.

Suzuki, D., & Knudtson, P. (1990). *Genethics: The clash between new genetics and human values.* Cambridge, MA: Harvard University Press.

Tarvydas, V. M., Peterson, D. M., & Michaelson, S. D. (2004). Ethical issues in case management. In F. Chan, M. L. Leahy, & J. L. Saunders (Eds.), *Case management for rehabilitation health professionals.* Gaithersburg, MD: Aspen Publishing.

Totten, G., Lamb, G., & Reeder, G. D. (1990). Tarasoff and confidentiality in AIDS-related psychotherapy. *Professional Psychology: Research and Practice, 21,* 155–160.

Tufts University. (1998). When genetic testing might be appropriate. *Tufts University Health & Nutrition Letter, 16*(1), 8.

Wang, C., Gonzalez, R., & Merajver, S. D. (2004). Assessment of genetic testing and related counseling services: Current research and future directions. *Social Science & Medicine, 58,* 1427–1442.

Werth, J. L. (1999). Mental health professionals and assisted death: Perceived ethical obligations and proposed guidelines for practice. *Ethics & Behavior, 1,* 159–163.

Werth, J. L, & Holdwick, D. J. (2000). A primer on rational suicide and other forms of hastened death. *The Counseling Psychologist, 28,* 511–539.

White, M. T. (1999). Making responsible decisions: An interpretive ethic for genetic decision making. *Hastings Center Report, 29*(1), 14–22.

White, M. T., & Calliff-Daley, F. (1999). Genetic testing for disease susceptibility: Social, ethical and legal issues for family physicians. *American Family Physician, 60*(3), 748–751.

Wilbur, K. (1988). *The marriage of sense and soul.* New York: Broadway Books.

Wilcox, B. L., Robbennolt, J. K., & O'Keeffe, J. E. (1998). In L. J. Beckman & S. M. Harvey (Eds.), *The new civil war: The psychology, culture and politics of abortion* (pp. 21–22). Washington, DC: American Psychological Association.

Wolbring, G. (2001). Disabled people's approach to bioethics. *The American Journal of Bioethics, 1*(3), 1–2.

Wolf, S. (Ed.). (1996). *Feminism and bioethics: Beyond reproduction.* New York and Oxford, England: Oxford University Press.

Wylie, M. S. (1995, May/June). The power of DSM–IV: Diagnosing for dollars. *Networker,* 22–32.

Zabin, L. S., Hirsch, M. B., Emerson, M. R., & Raymond, E. (1992). To whom do inner-city minors talk about their pregnancies? Adolescents' communication with parents and parent surrogates. *Family Planning Perspectives, 24,* 148–154, 173.

CHAPTER 10

Ethics and Technology

David B. Peterson • Julie B. Hautamaki • Jessica L. Walton

OBJECTIVES

After reading this chapter, you should be able to:

- Provide an overview of technology as it applies to counseling practice.
- Relate such technology to the ethical practice of counseling professionals in:
  - maintaining confidential records,
  - conducting confidential communication,
  - using technology to enhance counseling services,
  - using technology in place of direct counseling services,
  - using the internet as a counseling service modality, and
  - conducting assessments to enhance counseling practice.
- Review ethical standards of practice relevant to the use of technology in counseling.
- Explore the use of technology in counselor education.

INTRODUCTION

During the past 40 years, computer capabilities have dramatically increased while costs to implement such technology have decreased significantly (Ford, 1993; Sampson, 2000; Simons, 1985). Personal computers (PCs) have increased in sophistication, and PC-based programming languages are powerful and easy to use. These changes have increased the use of such technology in the counseling profession (Bloom & Walz, 2000, 2004; Colby, 1980; Ford, 1993; Kraus, Zack, & Stricker, 2004; Levitan, Willis, & Vogelgesang, 1985; Sampson, 2000).

Computer-based applications for clinical situations in counseling-related professions began as early as the 1960s, with computer-based test interpretation (Butcher, 1987; Fowler, 1985). During the 1970s, researchers expanded computer-assisted testing capabilities to include administration, scoring, and interpretation of psychological tests (Butcher, 1987). Computer-assisted assessments have increased in number throughout the 1980s and into the 21st century; and the use, assets, and limitations of such technologies have been well explored in the counseling literature (Bloom & Walz, 2000, 2004; Butcher, 1985, 1987; Eyde, 1987; Ford, 1993; Fowler; French, 1986; Matarazzo, 1985, 1986; Merrell, 1985; Sampson, 1990, 2000).

Computer-assisted therapy also originated in the 1960s, with much less success than computerized assessment applications (Colby, Gould, & Aronson, 1989;

Authors' notes: This chapter is a revision of Peterson (2003), found in the second edition of Cottone & Tarvydas (2003), *Ethical and Professional Issues in Counseling.* The authors wish to express thanks to and acknowledge the conceptual and editorial contributions of Fong Chan, University of Wisconsin–Madison, and the editorial contributions of Gerry Murray, The University of Arkansas-Little Rock, to the first edition of this chapter, as they continue to influence this work.

Colby, Watt, & Gilbert, 1966; Ford, 1993). Therapeutic applications received little further attention until the 1980s (Ford, 1993). Since then, various types of computer-assisted therapies have been used, including professional consultation programs, client therapeutic learning programs, and on-line therapy.

Unlike computer-assisted assessment, little has been written on the ethical issues related to the use of computer-assisted therapy until recently (Bloom & Walz, 2000, 2004; Kraus et al., 2004; Peterson, 2003; Peterson, Murray, & Chan, 1998; Sampson, Kolodinsky, & Greeno, 1997). In 2002, a panel of 62 psychotherapy experts projected that internet-based therapy services would be one of the largest growing service areas in the next 10 years (Norcross, Hedges, & Prochaska, 2002). This prediction calls for increased research and guidelines to facilitate ethical practice for implementing nontraditional forms of service provision.

As computer technology has become more affordable and desktop and laptop computers have grown in number, tasks once dedicated to paper, typewriter, or pen have been transferred to more convenient computerized technologies. The advent of facsimile machines (faxes), computer modems for phone line communication, computer networks (e.g., the internet), wireless satellite networks, and paperless technologies such as personal assistants (PAs; e.g., Palm and Visor technology) has resulted in new forms of electronic media that the counseling profession uses with increasing frequency. As a result of these technological developments, the counseling profession has had little time to address the resulting ethical and professional issues (Bloom & Walz, 2000, 2004; Ford, 1993; Krause, et al., 2004; Sampson, 2000; Sampson et al., 1997). The ethical codes of practice and the literature associated with counseling and the allied health professions have been hard pressed to keep pace with the dramatic changes in technology (Granello, 2000). Some ethical issues related to recent technological developments have been of concern to counselors and psychologists for many years. Other issues are unique to more recent technological developments. Several counseling-related organizations have addressed new standards of practice that will affect the standards and codes used today (ACA, 1999, 2005; AERA, APA, & NCME, 1999; APA, 1986, 1997; CRCC, 2001; NBCC, 2001).

It is essential for counseling professionals to remain current with efforts to develop and establish ethical standards and codes of conduct to protect and benefit their clients. Recent technological developments affect the practices and ethical decision-making processes of the counseling professional. As managed care continues to place new demands on the allied health professions, it is ethically essential that counseling-related professions explore the use of technology to facilitate ethical counseling practice (Bloom & Walz, 2000, 2004; Erdman & Foster, 1988; Sampson, 2000).

QUESTIONS FOR REFLECTION

- Consider your personal views in regards to technology. Do you welcome new technology into your daily routine?
- Are you comfortable using various forms of technology in general? In counseling, specifically?
- How might your views impact a counseling relationship over the internet?
- Does counseling using nontraditional modalities affect the therapeutic relationship?

ETHICAL MANAGEMENT OF ELECTRONIC MEDIA

Ethical codes addressing the maintenance of client records, such as those established by the APA, mandate that psychologists maintain appropriate confidentiality in creating, storing, accessing, transferring, and disposing of all manner of records in their care, including those received electronically. The ACA has a similar requirement—the ethical counseling professional must protect the client's right to confidentiality regardless of the type of electronic media. Counseling professionals use a variety of types of electronic media, including personal computers, faxes, e-mail, and cellular phones.

All forms of electronic media used in counseling may contain sensitive material protected by therapist–client confidentiality and privileged communication; therefore, it is important that ethical counselors are aware of how the use of electronic media influences professional practice (Figure 10–1). Protocols need to be in place to ensure that electronic media will be accessible only to ethically appropriate parties. Electronic media storage systems may not be immediately understandable or visible to the counseling professional; therefore, ethical management of such data may be easily overlooked.

Electronic Media on Personal Computers

Personal computer systems commonly used by counseling professionals are composed of hardware and software. Hardware consists of the electrical and

1. Ethical codes require that the same safeguards be used for both printed and electronic media.
2. Electronic media may appear deceptively simple and safeguarded from unethical access. Although privacy protocols are time consuming and costly, they are essential to ethical data management.
3. Fax transmissions of ethically sensitive material must be carefully controlled.
4. E-mail should not be considered a confidential form of communication.
5. Discussion of confidential matters should not occur over cellular phones.

FIGURE 10–1. Reminders for Ethical Use of Electronic Media

mechanical devices of the computer system. Electronic media can be safeguarded at the hardware level with a mechanical lock and key that prevent power from reaching the computer, thus maintaining confidentiality of the information within. Once turned on, such systems should not be left unattended unless protected at the software level.

Software includes the programs written for the CPU to perform various functions, or applications. Common computer applications used by counseling professionals include document production using word processing applications, financial and records management using spreadsheets, and record filing on databases. *Therapist Helper* by Brand Software, Inc., is a suite of software that helps to manage lists of clients and referral resources, diagnostic codes, insurance billing transactions, reporting capabilities, managed care authorizations, and progress notes.

Documents created by a word processor, spreadsheet, or database application can be printed to create a hard copy and stored as files on memory systems. In addition to the need to control access to printed matter generated from computers, the data stored on hard disks, floppy disks, JAZ or ZIP disks, memory keys, and CDs must be carefully controlled. Personnel with access to such data must be well trained regarding ethical management of electronic media. A Flash Drive Memory Key containing a gigabyte of confidential information is much less obvious than the tremendous paper equivalent of such stored information. A small computer disk can store information equivalent to many client charts and is much easier to remove from an office than a rack full of confidential records. Paper records and electronic information must be locked in tamper-proof surroundings.

The storage of confidential material on a hard drive may be even less obvious to the counselor. All staff members within a counseling organization must be oriented to the appropriate ethical procedures for storage of client records and the related access protocols. For hard drives on PCs, security software is available that will allow access to certain files only if a person has an access code or password. People who are issued access codes must protect their codes from misuse. If a PC in a counseling organization does not require a security code to access confidential information, large amounts of data are at risk of being viewed by people who should not have access to such information.

Organizations that use a server for a network of computers, sometimes called a *local area network* (LAN), need to establish protocols that limit access only to ethically relevant parties. Servers can be accessed by personal computers with modems over telephone lines, dramatically increasing the audience potentially having access to the secured data. Computer systems management specialists who set up systems for business organizations must be made aware of the location of sensitive confidential material. They can design the system with the appropriate safeguards and security protocols to maintain confidentiality through security software that requires pass codes and the requisite employee training. LAN administrators routinely back up or duplicate LAN files as archives in the event of a hardware or software malfunction that results in the loss of data. If a PC user on the network has stored files on the server (e.g., word processor documents, spreadsheet files, database files, e-mail), the archived files may contain confidential material. Even though a given file may be deleted locally by a network user, there may be an archived copy stored somewhere, accessible to potentially inappropriate parties. Protocols must be established with LAN administrators regarding the archiving of potentially confidential information.

Unfortunately, counseling professionals may not be motivated to purchase adequate systems of protection due to ignorance or the presumed unlikelihood of unethical file disclosure. Establishing a secure computer system can be time consuming and costly; nevertheless, confidential client information needs to be protected.

Faxes and E-mail

Fax machines allow the transmission of information either from paper or directly from a computer file. Generally, faxes are composed of printed matter, which can include any type of client information protected by therapist–client confidentiality. Counselors need to use caution when sending confidential information by fax. Many businesses have centrally located, public fax machines that are inappropriate for receiving confidential information. It is the counselor's responsibility to assure that confidential fax transmissions arrive in a secured environment. Faxes can be sent directly to a PC by modem. The security precautions mentioned for electronic media storage apply to fax transmissions sent to PCs. A quick phone call to assess the situation before sending a confidential fax is appropriate to ensure safe arrival of sensitive information. In the event that a destination PC or fax machine is not secure, the counselor should phone before transmitting documents to alert appropriate parties to intercept confidential information. Disclaimers placed on fax cover sheets are not sufficient protection against unscrupulous interception of confidential data.

Electronic mail, or e-mail, uses the internet to send and receive messages among individuals or groups, simulating the sending and receiving of letters through the mail. E-mail is increasingly sent via digital handheld devices that use wireless technology (e.g., Wi-Fi), in addition to traditional hard wire connections in organizational systems. A recent article in *Counseling Today* addresses the emerging use of technology in counseling service provision. Although it highlights some advantages to e-mail therapy, such as convenience, extra time to process information, increased opportunities for supervision, and writing as part of the therapeutic process, the disadvantages noted include a lack of immediacy, difficulties with verifying client identity, and the lack of utility for clients who have difficulty expressing ideas in written form (Kennedy, 2005). Not mentioned in the article is one serious concern, that the confidential information transmitted via e-mail is vulnerable to interception by people other than the designated recipient, even more so with wireless computer technology. Therefore, counselors must use caution when sending counseling-related information via e-mail. Because of frequent use of e-mail by counselors, it is important to emphasize the ethical vulnerability of such communication.

Cellular Phones

Although cellular phones are a tremendous convenience in today's fast-paced society, they are neither secure nor private forms of communication. One need only use such technology in a major metropolitan area

to discover the intrusion of unwelcome one- or two-way conversations. Discussion of confidential material should not occur over cellular phone networks.

Although the use of cellular phones presents some risk to confidentiality, some suggest there are benefits associated with telephone-based communication in counseling. Ellevan and Allen (2004) suggested that as a familiar and widely available technology, phones of all types may be easier to use for some clients than other more advanced technologies.

A Word on HIPAA

In its design, Congress employed HIPAA to encourage the use of electronic means of health information transmission as a way of increasing efficiency, creating uniform standards, while protecting the privacy of the insured. Thus it is relevant to the ethical management of electronic media in counseling.

When dealing with electronic management of data, or with data that may some day be managed electronically, conventional wisdom has been to assume that HIPAA will apply to your counseling practice in whole or in part at some point in the future.

HIPAA is basically comprised of three major rule sets: (1) the electronic transaction rule, (2) the privacy rule, and (3) the security rule. The electronic transaction rule covers the electronic transmission of protected health information between the counselor (or one of his or her agents) and an insurance company (or similar entity) in all manner of counseling service provision and related administration.

Protected health information (PHI) is information that identifies an individual, is created or received by a health care provider, and relates to the individual's physical or mental health. The privacy rule went into effect April 14, 2003, and requires that the counselor provide the client with written disclosure of policies and procedures related to the use and disclosure of PHI. The disclosure must occur by the end of the first treatment contact, and it has been recommended that if contact is by phone that the counselor mail the disclosure form to the client the same date. The client must acknowledge receipt of the information, which now tends to occur during the signing of the counselor–client agreement of informed consent forms.

The security rule went into effect April 20, 2005, and pertains to electronic transactions of PHI and the storing of such information. The rules allow for scalability to the context of a given counseling practice. Administrative standards of the security rule address office policies and procedures for maintaining PHI, including the training of staff. Physical standards delineate procedures to limit access to stored information, whereas technological standards address technical requirements to protect PHI. The vulnerabilities of electronic data storage reviewed previously are relevant to the administrative, physical, and technical standard requirements of HIPAA.

COMPUTER-ASSISTED COUNSELING

Computer-assisted counseling exists in a variety of forms. Some programs function as therapeutic consultants (Goodman, Gingerich, & Shazer, 1989). The advent of the internet and chat rooms has created the opportunity for direct, on-line communication between counselor and client (on-line counseling). Video teleconferencing allows communication between the counselor and client in real time (Elleven & Allen, 2004). Therapeutic software that is marketed to operate without therapist assistance is also available (Lawrence, 1986; Sampson, 1986). However, when using such technology, the counselor needs to ensure that the client is aware of potential vulnerabilities.

History

Computer-assisted therapy was first developed in the 1960s (Colby et al., 1966) but was relatively unsuccessful. Attempts to computerize psychotherapy were rejuvenated in the 1980s with the popularization of behavioral modes of therapy and the emphasis of bringing about change through education (Ford, 1993; Wagman, 1988). Early versions of counseling software that did not require counselor assistance included MORTON, which was based on cognitive behavior therapy and was designed primarily to treat mild forms of depression (Selmi, Klein, Greist, Johnson, & Harris, 1982). One experimental program, GURU, attempted to expand interactive conversation capabilities with the goal of increasing self-awareness (Colby, Colby, & Stoller, 1990).

More recently, virtual psychotherapy programs have been under development, such as Avatars (Duncan, 1997). This software depicts characterizations of the client via a computer image or graphic, with bubbles overhead to indicate ongoing dialogue. Another application, Palace, develops an "intranet," or closed internet system, allowing for virtual psychotherapy with a controlled audience (Duncan). Computer-assisted therapies have not gained a great

audience to date (Granello, 2000). These applications require further research to evaluate their effectiveness as a counseling practice.

Career Counseling

Computerized career counseling has been evaluated by Kilvingham, Johnston, Hogan, and Mauer (1994). They concluded that clients who were highly motivated and goal directed benefited from the System for Interactive Guidance and Information-Plus (SIGI-PLUS). However, they determined that clients with less clear goals and less motivation for independence did not benefit as much from the use of this program. Group or individual counseling was proposed as more appropriate in the latter case. In such a case, using computer career counseling software as an adjunct to individual and group counseling would be exemplary of good, ethical counseling practice.

Career counseling often involves a psychoeducational approach (information provision), which lends itself well to delivery through computer-assisted venues. A comprehensive review of research evaluating one of the most popular career guidance systems, DISCOVER, suggested that the computer-assisted format helped to increase self-efficacy and decision-making skills, increased planfulness, increased knowledge about specific occupations, and resulted in more targeted career goals (Taber & Luzzo, 1999). For a comparison of 15 well known computer-assisted guidance systems, see also Sampson et al. (1994).

Rehabilitation. As early as 1978, video games were used in the later phases of cognitive retraining for persons with a head injury. Cognitive retraining falls under the domain of therapy in a rehabilitation hospital setting. The novelty of the games made the monotonous, repetitive exercises that enhanced cognitive functioning more enjoyable (Caplan, 1987). A more sophisticated computerized testing application, the Computer Assisted Cognitive Retraining system (CACR), was developed in 1987 by the Brain Injury Rehabilitation Unit in Palo Alto, California. The CACR used various computer-driven exercises to enhance the individual's alertness, attention, concentration, fine motor skills, memory, and certain language abilities (e.g., spelling, reading, and word finding). Performance scores were recorded by the computer, and a graph indicated the client's progress.

Other Applications. A variety of theoretical orientations have been adapted to computer-assisted counseling, including behavioral, cognitive, educational, and psychodynamic approaches (Ford, 1993). On-line therapy has been shown to be effective in treating specific presenting problems, including anxiety (Cohen & Kerr, 1998), posttraumatic stress disorder (Lange, Schrieken, & van de Ven, 2000), eating disorders (Celio et al., 2002), and panic disorder with agoraphobia (Bouchard et al., 2000). Software has been developed to target AIDS education (Schinke & Orlandi, 1990; Schinke et al., 1989), the treatment of drug and alcohol abuse (Moncher et al., 1985), cognitive behavioral techniques (Wright, et al., 2002), obesity (Burnett, Magel, Harrington, & Taylor, 1989; Burnett, Taylor, & Agras, 1985; Taylor, Agras, Losch, Plante, & Burnett, 1991), personal distress (Wagman, 1980, 1988; Wagman & Kerber, 1980), sexual dysfunction (Binik, Servan-Schreiber, Freiwald, & Hall, 1988; Servan-Schreiber & Binik, 1989), smoking (Burling et al., 1989; Schneider, 1986; Schneider, Walter, & O'Donnell, 1990), and stress (Smith, 1987). Various clinical populations have benefited from computer-assisted counseling, including persons with depression (Selmi, Klein, Greist, Sorell, & Erdman, 1990), persons with phobia (Carr, Ghosh, & Marks, 1988; Salyer, 1997), people who are violent offenders (Ford & Vitelli, 1992), patients with burn pain (Salyer), and patients with head trauma who need cognitive retraining (Niemann, Ruff, & Baser, 1990). As computer technology continues to improve, so will the capabilities of computer-assisted therapy. The ethical implications of widespread use of such technology have not been adequately explored (Ford, 1993; Peterson et al., 1998; Sampson et al., 1997). Research is needed to compare the outcomes of in vivo counseling and newly developed computer-assisted counseling, how they may be used together to affect change, and what factors of such technology contribute to effective therapy.

Computer-Assisted Counseling: Real Therapy?

Counselors with a psychodynamic or humanistic orientation may be most resistant to the use of computer-assisted counseling in lieu of individual face-to-face therapy (Ford, 1993). Many counselors do wonder—is computer-assisted counseling "real therapy"? The concepts of counseling and psychotherapy are so inclusive that further clarification of computer-assisted counseling is necessary before the point can be argued successfully. Grencavage and Norcross (1990) suggested that psychotherapies do have commonalities: (a) development of a therapeutic alliance, (b) opportunity for catharsis, (c) acquisition and practice of new behaviors,

and (d) clients' positive expectations. The literature supports the contention that computer-assisted counseling can be used to practice new behaviors, test simulated situations, express feelings and emotions, receive feedback, develop insight, and learn how to better interact with others (Ford, 1993). Ford (1993) contended that if sharing a number of commonalities with recognized psychotherapy techniques is the criterion for determining the viability of computer-assisted psychotherapy, it can be argued strongly that such technology is, in fact, a form of psychotherapy. Cook and Doyle (2002) found on-line therapy to be an appealing method of receiving mental health assistance and developing a working alliance, and an empathic relationship that can be instituted regardless of the form of communication.

Face-to-Face Versus On-Line Counseling

Current research compares the outcomes of face-to-face to on-line counseling and how these two methods may be combined to produce effective outcomes. Day and Schneider (2002) discovered an increase in client participation for on-line versus face-to-face counseling. Cook and Doyle (2002) found participants that utilized on-line counseling felt a collaborative, bonding relationship with therapists and reported an overall positive experience with unique advantages over face-to-face counseling. In addition, current research supports the combination of both face-to-face counseling and on-line counseling for effective outcomes. In an informal survey conducted by Metanoia (2001), a large percentage of on-line clients reported that on-line counseling was their first experience with counseling and that they would not have otherwise considered seeking face-to-face counseling. After experiencing on-line counseling, almost 65% of the participants reported seeking face-to-face counseling. Findings from Mallen, Day, and Green (2003) suggested that on-line relationships may need more time to develop than in-person relationships.

Consumer Acceptance

Counselors have an ethical responsibility to use interventions that suit an individual client's needs. The acceptance of computer-assisted counseling interventions by the consumers of such services is a critical aspect of the overall ethical viability of such technology. The counselor should gauge the client's comfort level with technology and offer other potential options (Elleven & Allen, 2004). History has shown that, for many consumers, acceptance of the technology is not an issue (Erdman, Klein, & Greist, 1985; French & Beaumont, 1987; Harrell, Honaker, Hetu, & Oberwager, 1987; Rozensky, Honor, Rasinski, Tovian, & Herz, 1986; Wyndowe, 1987). In fact, some consumers prefer technological alternatives over face-to-face interventions (Cook & Doyle, 2002; Day & Schneider, 2002; Farrell, Camplair, & McCullough, 1987; Ford & Vitelli, 1992; Lukin, Dowd, Plake, & Kraft, 1985) with clients who express positive sentiments toward computer-assisted forms of counseling (Binik et al., 1988; Burda, Starkey, & Dominguez, 1991; Clarke & Schoech, 1984; Colby et al., 1989; Cook & Doyle, 2002; Ford, 1988; Matthews, De Santi, Callahan, Koblenz-Sulcov, & Werden, 1987; McLemore & Fantuzzo, 1982; Servan-Schreiber & Binik, 1989).

Independent Use

The use of computer-assisted therapy independent from a therapist presents another ethical quandary. Many counselors are opposed to using such technology as a replacement for human therapists (Bloom & Walz, 2000, 2004; Colby et al., 1989; Davidson, 1985; Ford, 1988, 1993; Ford & Vitelli, 1992; Hartman, 1986a; Krause, et al., 2004; Selmi, Klein, Greist, Sorell, & Erdman, 1990). However, many such programs are designed so that at least moderately functioning clients do not need assistance with administration (Ford, 1993; Sampson, 1986; Sampson & Krumboltz, 1991). One fact is clear: Counselors are necessary for the development and evaluation of effective computer-assisted counseling programs (Ford, 1993).

The ethical question facing counselors is, "How safe are these technologies for independent users?" There are certain benefits associated with making computer-assisted therapy available to independent users: "Cost, convenience, and privacy are just some of the advantages of self-help programs" (Ford, 1993, p. 391). "To the extent that it is possible to offer the public sound, effective programs that do not require professional intervention, it would be socially irresponsible to restrict unduly or to discourage psychologists from making such contributions" (Keith-Spiegel & Koocher, 1985, p. 217).

The criteria for determining whether a program should be used by someone who requires professional intervention remain a question. Due to the cost effectiveness of computer-assisted therapy, help can be made available to people who otherwise could not afford therapy provided by a counselor (Colby, 1980, 1986; Davidson, 1985; Ford, 1993; Ford & Vitelli, 1992; Sampson &

Krumboltz, 1991). However, making such technology available for those who may benefit from it also presents the potential for some to be harmed through its use.

Legal and ethical ramifications exist for improper use of computer-assisted therapy. Three probable malpractice complaints against counselors that may result from improper use of such technology are: (a) negligent rendering of services, (b) negligence that leads to suicide, and (c) improper supervision of a disturbed client (Ford, 1993). As malpractice suits unfold, perhaps the necessary laws, codes, and standards will evolve. With respect to independent use, it seems best that computer-assisted counseling should be an adjunct to the relationship between counselor and client, so that harm to the client will be avoided through careful supervision.

Computer-Assisted Counseling Technology Validation

The ethical codes of the APA and the ACA require that software developers provide empirical evidence of the safety and effectiveness of computer-assisted assessment products before making any claims as to their effectiveness. This is not the case with computer-assisted therapy—there are no laws or ethical standards in place to require evidence of validity and reliability before developers can make claims in marketing their self-help software (Ford, 1993; Sampson et al., 1997). Given the precedent set by codes associated with computer-assisted assessment, software developers must demonstrate treatment effectiveness of their computer-assisted therapy empirically. Research can be done through experiments using the software with a sample of the target population and a peer review process. Standards to require this suggestion should become a priority for the counseling profession.

Another important point to address regarding program effectiveness is the credibility that is so easily extended by lay people toward information conveyed by computers (Hartman, 1986b; Sampson, 1986). Ford (1993) proposed that it should be deemed unethical to capitalize on consumer naiveté as to the veracity of computer output. Appropriate training standards should be in place to ensure the appropriate use of computer-assisted counseling (Figure 10–2).

Access to Software

Companies that produce mental health software establish various levels of restricted access to therapeutic and testing software purchasers. However, there are few

1. Computer-assisted psychotherapy needs more evidence for validity and reliability. Potential applications and consumer acceptance argue for further development of this therapeutic modality.
2. It is unethical to capitalize on consumer naiveté as to the credibility or effectiveness of computer-assisted therapy.
3. Use of computer-assisted therapy software should be restricted to qualified professionals, much in the same way that testing materials are controlled by test publishers.

FIGURE 10–2.   Ideas for Reflection About Computer-Assisted Counseling

standards for access to such software, resulting historically in less-than-rigorous control over distribution (Ford, 1993). If software is designed for a client who should receive some type of therapy that is at least supervised by a clinician, the counseling profession must exercise some control over who has access to such software. Standards should be generated to make counseling-related software available only to qualified professionals, placing the liability for negligent use of the product on the practitioner (Ford, 1993; Schwitzgebel & Schwitzgebel, 1980).

Ethical Dilemmas in Computer-Assisted Counseling

There are at least four parties involved in computer-assisted counseling: (a) the client, (b) the counselor, (c) the software manufacturer, and (d) professional bodies such as the ACA, the APA, CRCC, and the NBCC. Responsibility for the ethical provision of electronic mental health services according to a specified set of standards is borne by the latter four parties at some level, and that responsibility must be given consideration by all participants involved.

The ACA (1999) established a standard that addresses the use of computer technology in counseling. In summary, counselors have an obligation to ensure that:

(1) the client is intellectually, emotionally, and physically capable of using the computer application; (2) the computer application is appropriate for the needs of the client; (3) the client understands the purpose and operation of the computer applications; and (4) clients are satisfied with the experience: a follow-up of client use of a computer application is provided to correct possible misconceptions, discover inappropriate use, and assess subsequent needs.

These standards do not support the autonomous use of computer-assisted counseling by all clients, and they acknowledge the potential for misunderstanding and the lack of contact between counselor and client inherent in such cases.

Before engaging in electronic delivery of counseling-related services, Glueckauf, Pickett, Ketterson, Loomis, and Rozensky (2003) proposed a self-study assessment for counselors to critically examine five domains related to such service provision: state regulatory and licensure issues, technology issues, ethical issues, professional relationship issues, and specific training requirements. The APA has yet to publish standards or codes that specifically address computer-assisted therapy, apart from the ethics statement in listed in Appendix F.

The use of computers to assist in the counseling process also introduces practical and financial ethical dilemmas. If a client is using a computer to assist with the therapeutic process, does this imply that services rendered are of a shorter duration than a face-to-face counseling modality? Counseling service providers must decide how to bill when computer applications are used as an adjunct to therapy. The client may ultimately save money because of less direct contact with the therapist (Cook & Doyle, 2002). The ACA requires that when establishing fees for professional counseling services, counselors need to consider the financial status of clients and locality. If the fee structure is deemed inappropriate for a client, it is the ethical responsibility of the counselor to assist the client in finding comparable services of acceptable cost (ACA, 2005). Conversely, if the therapist is maintaining ethical responsibility for the entire therapeutic process and chooses to closely monitor the use of computer technology, the difference in time used for therapy will merely be reappropriated to monitoring the technology introduced into therapy. The ethical codes and standards under development must address this financial issue.

Ford (1993) discussed the independent use of computer-assisted counseling services, specifically the legal issues that may arise out of litigation and legislation related to the electronic provision of counseling services. The lack of face-to-face monitoring of clients in computer-assisted telepsychology and cybercounseling sessions and issues related to Tarasoff liability (VandeCreek & Knapp, 1993) may result in malpractice lawsuits that shape legislative policy and ethical code development. Due to the nature of a fiduciary relationship established via electronic media, it is critical that counseling professionals using such technology remain aware of case law developments that affect practice. Legal issues ultimately may involve federal, state, and local legislation—and litigation. The literature that likely will be developed as a result of this new and technological enterprise will be of great importance to mental health professionals.

On-Line Counseling Forums

On-line forums of counseling can be found in the counseling research literature under a number of descriptors: psychotherapy in cyberspace (Stricker, 1996); counseling on the information highway (Sampson et al., 1997); behavioral telehealth (Glueckauf, et al., 2003; Heinlein, Welfel, Richmond, & O'Donnel, 2003; Nickelson, 1996); cybercounseling (Bloom & Walz, 2000; Duncan, 1997); telepsychology (Koocher & Morray, 2000); Web counseling (Alleman, 2002; Heinlen et al.; NBCC, 2001); on-line psychotherapy (Ragusea & VandeCreek, 2003); on-line counseling (Alleman; Elleven & Allen, 2004); on-line therapy (Cook & Doyle, 2002; Heinlen et al.); e-therapy (Alleman; Elleven & Allen; Heinlen et al.); e-counseling (Elleven & Allen); cybertherapy (Alleman; Elleven & Allen; Heinlen et al.); telecounseling (Elleven & Allen); computer-mediated psychotherapy (Alleman; Cook & Doyle); computer-assisted psychotherapy (Wright, et al., 2002); internet-based therapy (Heinlen et al); telepsychiatry (Heinlen et al.); virtual therapy (Norcross, et al., 2002); and, simply, counseling over the internet. On-line forums of counseling represent one of the most recent technological developments in computer applications for the counseling profession (Bloom & Walz 2000, 2004; Duncan; Sampson et al., 1997).

The Internet

Internet Bulletin Board Systems (BBSs) typically are organized around a topic of interest; people can read a posting or add their own. An example of a counseling BBS may contain "posted messages on the content and process of counseling from participants who conduct discussions through these postings" (Sampson et al., 1997, pp. 203–204). Discussions can be moderated or unmoderated (Berge, 1994), allowing for controlled quality of discussion groups or potentially inappropriate information exchanges, respectively. The confidentiality of information on BBSs is not protected, so counselors must use caution to protect confidentiality when posting material. Encryption software uses an algorithm to resequence data codes to disguise data from parties who do not have the algorithm key. More research is needed to develop ways to prevent computer "hackers" (amateur software developers) from breaking such codes and accessing ethically sensitive material.

E-mail uses the internet to send and receive messages. List servers are e-mail-type software that provide easy, international dissemination of discussion lists and electronic journals (Sampson et al., 1997). Mental health professionals who use e-mail should recognize the ethical vulnerability of such communication.

Internet relay chat (IRC), or chat mode of internet communication, allows two people to correspond in real time using a split screen—one side for each person (Duncan, 1997; Sampson et al., 1997). Computer conferencing allows groups of individuals to converse simultaneously through text, with one person potentially serving as moderator. In addition to the group counseling dynamic of such communication, the same limitations exist on the e-mail level of confidentiality. Chat rooms, a version of IRC with a little more privacy, are in frequent use.

Although the audience is more limited in a chat room, the same ethical questions arise on the World Wide Web (WWW). The WWW is composed of computer servers and graphical interfaces that are connected to the internet. Together they provide an avenue of information exchange, including audio and visual material and text-based information. Individuals and organizations can establish and maintain a home page on the WWW, which is accessed on the internet, to convey information about a specific person or organization. A Web site on the WWW comprises a home page with links, which are indicated by various graphical means. When activated (or "clicked" with a mouse), these links open up related home pages, Web sites, and multimedia files. The colloquialism "surfing the Net" implies searching for information on the WWW, which is connected via the internet: Various software packages facilitate connection with the WWW and the associated home pages, Web sites, and links (e.g., Netscape or Microsoft Explorer).

Counseling Applications on the Internet

BBSs serve counselors as information resources, allowing access to specialized and current information regarding mental health issues (Marino, 1996). List servers and information databases (e.g. ERIC, PSYCHLIT) assist counselors in accessing diverse information quickly (Walz, 1996). However, the professional who accesses this information should treat such information with the same healthy skepticism as any printed material. Career counselors use the WWW, BBSs, and Web sites (Sampson et al., 1997), which provide job vacancy listings and even assistance in assembling resumes and submitting them to prospective employers (Allen, 1995; Boles, 1996; Jandt & Nemnich, 1995; Kennedy, 1995; Riley, Roehm, & Oserman, 1996; Woods & Ollis, 1996; Woods, Ollis, & Kaplan, 1996). Career counseling has also benefited from the use of video conferencing. After using the WWW to locate jobs and create and submit resumes, the interview between employer and prospective employee can occur in real time using on-line video interviewing technology (Bloom & Walz, 2000; Magnusen & Magnusen, 1995).

E-mail is used by consumers to access mental health professionals and to ask specific questions about diverse mental health issues (Hannon, 1996). The information exchange is similar to that in radio, print media, and television forums of advice giving—the exchange is not in real time. A multitude of ethical concerns are associated with this type of counseling: misaddresses, the inability to see nonverbal behavior (Alleman, 2002; Ragusea & VandeCreek, 2003), increased opportunity for fraud, no guarantee of confidentiality (Alleman, Elleven & Allen, 2004; Ragusea & VandeCreek), and limited use for clients without high verbal ability (Duncan, 1997) or with psychological or physical impairments (Ragusea & VandeCreek).

The Information Highway: Future On-line Counseling

Sampson et al. (1997) predicted that the future information highway will be an integration of the internet, multimedia-based PCs, cable TV networks, and wired and wireless telephone networks. The application potential of such an information highway is tremendous—enhancing existing technologies and creating uses not yet conceived. The information highway has become a reality for many citizens in the United States (Bloom & Walz, 2000; Gates, Myhrvold, & Rinearson, 1995). Many cable service carriers have combined efforts with telephone services, allowing access to the information highway through television cable networks.

Multimedia presentation of counseling services has the potential to be quite creative and may allow for much more information dissemination than does a typical phone directory. With real-time video conferencing, clients can screen potential therapists before embarking on a therapeutic relationship. The counseling professional could potentially make suitability judgments as well. In the event that a referral is necessary, electronic media (e.g., e-mail) can be used to contact the referral sources and transfer associated records, given the proper encryption software is installed to ensure confidentiality.

Ultimately, the actual counseling sessions can occur in real time, using on-line computer technology on the information highway. The information highway allows "counselors to overcome problems of distance and time to offer opportunities for networking and interacting not otherwise available" (Walz, 1996, p. 417; see also Hufford, Glueckauf, & Webb, 1999). Orientation to counseling services can occur using computer-assisted instruction (Sampson, 1986), freeing up on-line and counselor time and, subsequently, lessening client expense. The protocols necessary to protect such communication over the internet, such as data encryption and video signal scrambling (as used for premium cable TV channels), need to be in place to guarantee confidential communication. Otherwise, such practice could be considered unethical.

Ethical Concerns with On-Line Counseling

Direct, on-line counseling services are increasingly prevalent on the internet (Bloom & Walz, 2000, 2004; Duncan, 1997; Sampson et al., 1997). A recent poll of on-line therapy sites found some sites that offered e-mail service at no cost, whereas others charged flat fees for e-mails ranging from $15 to $80. Others charged per minute for e-mail with costs as high as $2 per minute. In addition, some sites offered "combination packages" where they would charge a set fee for a limited amount of services. For chat or telephone sessions most sites charged on a per-minute basis (Heinlen, et al., 2003). A survey of the number of counseling-related home pages conducted between April 1996 and August 1996 suggested that counselors offered services that ranged from single-treatment interventions to 35 specialty services (Sampson et al., 1997).

The majority of e-therapy Web sites appear to have been developed by people identifying themselves as mental health professionals. However, Heinlen and associates (2003) found that 36% of individuals sampled did not explicitly state professional training or credentials. Previously, in the aforementioned survey conducted between April and August 1996, credentials of practitioners varied, including Ph.D., M.D., M.A., and L.P.C. Some individuals who indicated degree credentials after their names did not indicate the disciplines in which they received their degrees, and many "counselors" did not indicate any credentials or training (Sampson et al., 1997).

1. More research is needed to develop safeguards to confidentiality in venues of Internet-based counseling services.
2. Credentials vary for practitioners of Web-based counseling services, so the profession is obligated to educate the consumer as to the potential pitfalls of consuming services from unqualified practitioners.
3. Counseling professionals must also assume responsibility for providing equal access to on-line counseling services in order to empower rather than disenfranchise consumers of Internet-based counseling services.

FIGURE 10–3. Thinking About Cybercounseling Ethical Obligations

The ACA Code of Ethics requires that counselors identify their credentials in a manner that is not false, misleading, deceptive, or fraudulent. Psychotherapy in cyberspace brings with it a number of ethical concerns, including: (a) licensing criteria for such practice, (b) confidentiality issues, and (c) client safety issues (Stricker, 1996). People who offer counseling services over the internet should use technological safeguards to protect confidentiality. Such assurances should be sought out before using such services. If the providers are not using appropriate security measures, such practice should be deemed unethical (Figure 10–3).

Security. A fully functional information highway needs a solid data security system, including means of safely transferring money (Duncan, 1997; Gates et al., 1995). Data encryption must become more sophisticated to keep pace with the increasing sophistication of people who illegally break such codes. As biometric technology (e.g., voiceprints or thumbprints) becomes more reliable and cost effective, it will likely be used to control users at the receiving end of the information highway (Sampson et al., 1997).

Access to Services. U.S. Department of Commerce (1999) data suggest that socioeconomic status (SES) plays an important role in access to Web-based services. Households with incomes of $75,000 and higher are 20 times more likely to have access to the internet than those at the lowest income levels. Conversely, in a recent study by Cook and Doyle (2002), participants were well represented at all income levels. Ethnicity also appears to play a part—Caucasians are more likely to have access to the Web from home than are people of non-Caucasian ethnic backgrounds from any location.

Education levels may also play a part in who accesses on-line services. Cook and Doyle found individuals that accessed on-line services tended to be highly educated. Finally, location of residence also plays a part in access to services: Americans living in rural areas are half as likely to have access to the Web as their urban counterparts, even at the lowest income levels. To address disparities in access to technology, counselors can inform their clients of free public access points, such as public libraries, for using technology applications (ACA, 2005). However, these venues may preclude confidential communication. Socially responsible practitioners must make every effort to keep progressive technology in counseling equally accessible to all who need it, lest the technology itself becomes a vehicle of disenfranchisement rather than one of empowerment (see also Lee, 2000).

Cost to the Practitioner. Although many users have free access to the internet through organizations and educational institutions, enhanced technology for the information highway comes with a price. The counseling profession may be faced with cost-prohibitive factors of using such technology in some institutions. If the counseling profession becomes dependent on the free services currently available and cannot shift the resources to continue accessing the information highway when costs increase, the people hurt by such a change may be the consumers of on-line counseling services. Counselors are ethically responsible to assess their ability to maintain consumer access to this technology as costs increase, or they must be prepared to provide reliable referral sources when on-line counseling services become too expensive for consumers.

Although on-line technology removes some barriers of distance and time, the question remains whether counselors actually have the time and energy to accommodate the subsequent increase in client contact. The time constraints imposed by distance and circumstance allow counselors to process between client contacts, document interactions, and prepare for the next client. If counselors already have a full docket of clients, the remaining benefit of providing on-line counseling services is that of service availability to individuals who are remotely located or homebound. It may be presumptuous to assume that on-line technology will result in more people served per counselor, given the necessary time to process and document counseling interactions.

The reader is encouraged to remain current regarding ongoing research, including information from practicing professionals on ethical dilemmas encountered on the internet, and current updates on legal, technical, and practical aspects of Web counseling. The reader should periodically search the Web with key terms noted at the end of this chapter, leading to various Web sites and new publications that can help the professional counselor remain current with these developing technologies.

ETHICS AND POLICY DEVELOPMENTS IN ON-LINE MENTAL HEALTH SERVICES

The Emergence of Telehealth

One of the greatest potentials in using the internet to deliver mental health services is the ability to reach remote areas that were formerly without access to such services (Harris-Bowlsbey, 2000). **Telehealth services,** or remote, electronic consultation between consumers and providers in the health care professions (e.g., via videoconferencing), have received increasing attention throughout the helping professions over the past decade.

Health care providers that participate in telehealth services are eligible for Medicare reimbursement in rural areas determined by the federal government to have a shortage of health professionals (e.g., North Dakota and Montana), with fee schedules remaining the same as those for regular office visits. In 1997, the states of California and Louisiana passed laws requiring private insurance carriers to provide reimbursement for such services. The Federal Communications Commission (FCC) provided grants for public, nonprofit entities wishing to develop their potential in these areas; the FCC's Web site can provide useful guidance.

In addition to the federal and state support for telehealth, a number of professional organizations have responded to the presence of internet-based counseling services by developing policies and standards that can help guide counseling professionals through this new frontier. The trailblazer of this effort among counseling organizations is the NBCC.

NBCC and CCE Efforts

In 1995, the NBCC Board of Directors appointed a Web Counseling Task Force and, in cooperation with its affiliate, the Center for Credentialing and Education (CCE), created standards for the ethical practice of WebCounseling (NBCC, 2001; see Appendix G). The Board of Directors of NBCC established and adopted a code in 1997 that was unique to WebCounseling and WebCounselors. This group defined **WebCounseling** as "the practice of professional counseling and information delivery that occurs when client(s) and counselor are in separate or remote locations and utilize electronic means to communicate over the internet." New standards were adopted by NBCC in 2001 that provide guidance for the currently termed area of internet counseling. In addition to the recommendation to adhere to the NBCC code of ethics pertaining to the practice of professional counseling, the following is a summary of NBCC's suggestions to guide the practice of internet counseling:

1. Use code words or numbers to screen potential imposters and to correctly verify client identity.
2. Where parent/guardian consent is necessary, use similar technology to establish identity of consenting person.
3. Establish procedures for contacting internet counselor when he or she is off-line.
4. Provide solutions in the event of technical failure (phone numbers, collect calls, time zone differences, and response delays in e-mail correspondence).
5. Discuss the impact of the loss of visual cues where relevant and how to cope with misunderstandings.
6. Establish a counselor on call within the client's geographic region, as well as local crisis intervention hotline numbers.
7. Assist clients to identify free public access points to the internet in their community to access counseling, assessment, information, and instructional resources.
8. Make reasonable efforts to make the counselor's Web site accessible to clients with disabilities.
9. Consider the culture, language, time zone, and other local conditions that may impact clients.
10. Inform clients of encryption methods used to help insure confidentiality; clarify hazards of data that are not encrypted (e.g., unauthorized transmission or monitoring of records).
11. Inform clients how long treatment-related electronic data are preserved.
12. Follow appropriate procedures for release of confidential electronic information.
13. Review legal statutes (local, state, provincial, and national) and ethical codes as they pertain to internet counseling and supervision; review codes and laws in the counselor's as well as client's home locations due to questions about jurisdiction; clarify local customs regarding age of consent, child abuse, and neglect reporting.

14. Provide links to Web sites of all relevant certification bodies and licensure boards to facilitate consumer protection.

NBCC's code provided an opportunity to consider possible difficulties in implementing telehealth treatment paradigms. However, some of the proposed solutions were unclear, ambiguous, and perhaps premature. For instance, the concept of "counselor on call" appears unclear or unwieldy and highlights the volatility of a distant counseling relationship. Notwithstanding the lack of conclusive research available on the types of presenting problems that are inappropriate for telehealth contexts, NBCC's list of presenting problems and the associated efforts to establish standards of practice in this emerging area were commendable, and they were considered by other professional organizations embarking on similar missions. However, the ethical risks associated with **cybercounseling**—counseling on the internet—are profound. Standards of practice in this area will continue to evolve.

ACA Efforts

The ACA built upon the work of the NBCC through its ethics committee. This group attempted to educate ACA's members of the risks associated with providing counseling services over the internet (Hughs & Ruiz, 1998). ACA's Governing Council approved the Ethical Standards for Internet On-Line Counseling in October 1999 (see Appendix H). ACA described the standards as guidelines that "establish appropriate standards for the use of electronic communications over the internet to provide on-line counseling services, and should be used only in conjunction with the latest ACA Code of Ethics and Standards of Practice" (ACA, 1999). The standards are more detailed than those generated by the NBCC, and they appear to have benefited from NBCC's more general, yet trailblazing, efforts.

In 2005, the ACA integrated previous standards and adopted additional standards in order to further address important issues related to on-line counseling. As previously stated in the 1999 ACA code, counselors are responsible for educating clients about the benefits and limitations associated with the use of technology applications during the counseling process. The revised 2005 ACA code further expands on this idea by defining technology applications as (but not limiting it to) computer hardware and software, telephones, the World Wide Web, the internet, on-line assessment instruments, and other communication devices. The new code also states that counselors are responsible for educating clients about free access points (e.g., libraries) for the convenient use of such technological applications. More importantly, when providing technology-assisted distance counseling services, counselors are to ensure that clients are satisfied with their experiences (ACA, 2005).

Additionally, ACA, in collaboration with the ERIC/Counseling & Student Services (ERIC/CASS) Clearinghouse, developed edited texts called *Cybercounseling and Cyberlearning: Strategies & Resources for the Millennium* (Bloom & Walz, 2000) and an extension to this volume, *Cybercounseling and Cyberlearning: An Encore* (Bloom & Walz, 2004). These texts review the "state of the art" through the contributions of counselors who are working in this emerging area of practice. Although the newness of counseling cyberservices makes it difficult to produce texts that are not predominantly speculation and opinion, these texts contain very useful Web resource directories and some informative firsthand accounts of professionals engaging in cybercounseling and cyberlearning.

APA Efforts

Since 1997, the APA Board of Professional Affairs (BPA) has allocated resources to consider the ethical implications of "telepsychology." In November 1997, BPA sponsored an institute on telehealth, where a broad range of stakeholder representatives (i.e., APA, federal government, private sector, and experts in the field) explored the rapidly developing realm of telehealth applications in psychology. BPA then appointed a Work Group on Professional Practice Issues in Telehealth to make recommendations for policy development. The group's position to date has been that the current ethical code adequately addresses the use of any innovative technology in psychological practice.

APA first issued a statement regarding "Psychotherapy by Telephone" in 1993. Subsequently, in 1995 and again in 1997, the Ethics Committee of the APA issued a statement that addressed services by telephone, teleconferencing, and the internet (see Appendix F). The statement suggested that the current APA ethics code sufficiently addresses the ethical cautions associated with emerging areas of practice (APA, 1997).

However, Koocher and Morray (2000) suggested that professional ethical codes and guidelines do not go far enough—practitioners can avoid scrutiny by avoiding professional organizations that create enforceable standards or by using unregulated titles or service descriptions to elude regulatory authorities.

Many states have legislation that provides title-only provisions in credentialing legislation, so eluding authority is easy enough to achieve. State policies that address professional practice or function (rather than title only) will most likely be more effective in providing quality controls for ethical practice.

APA Practice Directorate staff also provided information regarding the unique needs of behavioral health consumers and practitioners through work groups that supported the federal Joint Working Group on Telemedicine (JWGT), an interagency work group deeply involved in federal administrative telehealth activity. APA's BPA appointed a Work Group on Professional Practice Issues in Telehealth to make recommendations for policy in this area. The group's work culminated in a set of 10 interdisciplinary principles for professional practice in telehealth (see Reed, McLaughlin, & Milholland, 2000). Additionally, APA's Division 31 sponsored, along with numerous division cosponsors, a 1999 APA Telehealth Miniconvention that addressed "innovative practice and research opportunities" according to "top telehealth experts" (APAGS, 1999). APA and its membership have made efforts to articulate and disseminate information regarding the emerging area of telepsychology, particularly as it applies to the broader area of telehealth and telemedicine.

The Executive Director for Practice at APA, Dr. Russ Newman (2001), provided a statement on "on-line therapy." He described numerous inquiries to APA regarding the official position "for" or "against" on-line therapy. He wrote that this technology is not a singular entity that argues for a singular position and applauded the work of BPA's Work Group on Professional Practice Issues in Telehealth. He stated that the current state of affairs argues for practitioners to answer three questions: (1) under what conditions; (2) for what problems; and (3) with which interventions, "does the application of internet technology facilitate the delivery of health care services?" (p. 56). "In the end" he concluded, "the profession must determine when the internet is useful and when it is not" (p. 56).

NCDA Efforts

The National Career Development Association (1997) contributed a set of standards for the helping profession's consumption as Web technology influences career-related endeavors. The guidelines begin with suggestions for use of internet delivery of career counseling and career planning services (see Appendix I). The next section reviews the ethical use of the internet for job posting and searching. The final section lists unacceptable counselor behaviors on the internet and ends with a brief discussion of the need for research in the area of Web-assisted counseling and guidance.

ISMHO Efforts

The International Society for Mental Health Online (ISMHO) was formed in 1997 to "promote the understanding, use and development of online communication, information and technology for the international mental health community" (ISMHO, 2005). Similar to the APA and ACA, this organization provides guidelines for on-line mental health services. The efforts of the organization are solely devoted to on-line counseling and provide a forum for those interested in practicing on-line services (ISMHO).

Regulation of Telepsychology

According to Duncan (1997), 20 states developed legislation related to on-line counseling services by 1997. Koocher and Morray (2000) conducted a survey of State Attorneys General (AGs) regarding legal and regulatory issues related to the delivery of behavioral health services via electronic means (i.e., teleconference, internet, and other electronic media). Questions included:

1. Which mental health professions are regulated by statute in your state: psychiatry, psychology, social work, marriage and family counseling, pastoral counseling, psychiatric nursing, rehabilitation counseling, and other fields?
2. Has your state enacted statutes regulating the practice of psychotherapy or counseling apart from the professions listed above?
3. Has your state enacted statutes regulating the practice of psychotherapy or counseling by means of telephone, internet, or other electronic means?
4. Have any of the statutory mental health licensing authorities in your state adopted rules limiting or otherwise regulating the practice of psychotherapy or counseling by electronic means? If no, is such regulation contemplated?
5. Have any of the statutory mental health licensing authorities in your state brought charges against a licensed mental health practitioner for delivering psychotherapy or counseling by electronic means?
6. Does your state claim regulatory authority over mental health practitioners residing outside your state who offer psychotherapy or counseling to

residents of your state via telephone, internet, or other electronic means? If no, do you contemplate seeking such authority? If yes, have you prosecuted such a case?

7. Has your office received complaints about psychotherapy or counseling services provided across state lines by electronic means?

AGs from 41 states and the District of Columbia replied. The survey suggested that, as of 1999, only 7% of states surveyed had enacted statutes addressing telehealth issues in the practice of psychotherapy or counseling by means just described. Additionally, 93% of the mental health licensing authorities had yet to adopt rules limiting or otherwise regulating such practice. Only 17% of those without policies in place contemplated future policy development in this area. This result may be explained by the fact that 85% of those surveyed indicated no charges had been brought against mental health professionals using telehealth modalities, with only 5% expressing the existence of such litigation. Clearly, case law review will continue to inform efforts to regulate practice in this innovative area.

Another interesting question addressed in the survey explored how states are handling practitioners who provide telehealth services across state jurisdictions. How will credentialing be addressed across jurisdictions? Is it possible for a practitioner to remain aware of all mandatory reporting laws as they vary across 51 jurisdictions (including the District of Columbia)? Under which state jurisdiction does the practitioner actually practice—his own or that of the recipient of services?

Although only 17% of those surveyed reported complaints about telehealth services provided across state lines, it appears that some states (particularly those with large rural areas that could benefit most from such services) have anticipated the emergence of such telepsychology practices. Forty-five percent of states surveyed claimed regulatory authority over mental health practitioners residing outside the state who offer mental health services to residents of that state, and 14% of those who responded described such policy development as pending. The financial implications for practitioners who need to be credentialed in multiple states to practice across jurisdictions could be profound, not to mention the bureaucratic burden presented to licensing boards. Some professions have begun to address the telehealth-across-jurisdictions dilemma (e.g., medicine), but counseling and psychology are behind

in this regard (Nickelson, 1996). One notable exception is the ASPPB, which established a credential of reciprocity that has experienced limited success in the United States.

Although consumer complaints regarding telepsychology or behavioral telehealth practices are rare, it is clear that policymakers are considering this emerging technology and that increased regulatory activity in this regard is imminent. It is only a matter of time before malpractice lawsuits involving behavioral telehealth become significant events in case law. As one AG respondent explained, his psychology licensing board issued a public statement suggesting that those who provide psychotherapy services via the internet should do so at their own risk (Koocher & Morray, 2000).

Given the lack of consensus that currently exists, Koocher and Morray (2000) offered the following recommendations with respect to telepsychology:

1. Before engaging in the remote delivery of mental health services via electronic means, practitioners should carefully assess their competence to offer the particular services and consider the limitations of efficacy and effectiveness that may be a function of remote delivery.

2. Practitioners should consult with their professional liability insurance carrier to ascertain whether the planned services will be covered. Ideally, a written confirmation from a representative of the carrier should be obtained.

3. Practitioners are advised to seek consultation from colleagues and to provide all clients with clear, written guidelines regarding planned emergency practices (e.g., suicide risk situations).

4. Because no uniform standards of practice exist at this time, thoughtful written plans that reflect careful consultation with colleagues may suffice to document thoughtful professionalism in the event of an adverse incident.

5. A careful statement on limitations of confidentiality should be developed and provided to clients at the start of the professional relationship. The statement should inform clients of the standard limitations (e.g., child abuse reporting mandates), any state-specific requirements, and cautions about privacy problems with broadcast conversations (e.g., overhead wireless phone conversations or captured internet transmissions).

6. Clinicians should thoroughly inform clients of what they can expect in terms of services offered, unavailable services (e.g., emergency or

psychopharmacology coverage), and access to the practitioner, emergency coverage, and similar issues.

7. If third parties are billed for services offered via electronic means, practitioners must clearly indicate that fact on billing forms. If a third-payer who is unsupportive of electronic service delivery is wrongly led to believe that services took place in vivo as opposed to on-line, fraud charges may ultimately be filed. (p. 505)

Another on-line activity affecting counselors is the use of on-line supervision and virtual practica, all of which fall under the umbrella of counselor education.

COMPUTER-ASSISTED ASSESSMENT

The application of computers to the area of assessment includes the ability to administer, score, and interpret most of the psychological assessment instruments and procedures that are used by clinicians—such as personality tests, cognitive tests, and structured interviews. Intelligence test scoring and interpretation applications were among the first commercially available programs for PCs and have been the primary focus of software developers (Honaker & Fowler, 1990). Recent development of the application of computerized cognitive and aptitude assessment includes: (a) subtests of the Wechsler Adult Intelligence Scale–III (French & Beaumont, 1992; Psychological Corporation, 1997), (b) Air Force flight performance tests (Park & Lee, 1992), (c) the Wonderlic Personnel Test (Kennedy, Baltzley, Turnage, & Jones, 1989), (d) memory subtests from the Wechsler Memory Scale–III and the Benton Tests (Youngjohn, Larrabee, & Crook, 1991), and (e) multidimensional assessment of elderly people (Stones & Kozma, 1989). At the beginning of the 1990s, computer programs involving personality assessment accounted for the largest single number of assessment software applications available—45% of all computerized assessment products (Honaker & Fowler, 1990). Such tests included the Minnesota Multiphasic Personality Inventory–2 (MMPI–2), the California Psychological Inventory (CPI), the Millon Clinical Multiaxial Inventory (MCMI), the 16 Personality Factor Test (16PF), the NEO Personality Inventory–Revised (NEO PI–R), and the Rorschach inkblot test. These tests continue to experience widespread use in their standard and computerized formats (Aiken, 2000; Hood & Johnson, 1997).

Benefits of Computer-Assisted Test Administration

One benefit of computerized test administration is rapid presentation of reliable and repetitive information, which can be taxing on both the client and the test administrator if administered orally (Argentero, 1989; Caplan, 1987). The storing and retrieval of test data can be simplified with computer applications, which allow the professional to attend to other important dynamics in the assessment and training process (Honaker & Fowler, 1990). Human error during data collection also can be minimized. Additionally, there is evidence of increased reliability in the scoring of intelligence tests administered in a computer format, which further increases the veracity of test results (Honaker & Fowler). However, the reliability of computer-assisted assessment depends on the competency of the administrator of the software. The administrator must understand the noncomputerized administration procedures of a given test and how these are influenced by computer technology (Drummond, 1996). A thorough understanding of an assessment tool (i.e., its development, validity, reliability, and theoretical framework) is essential before administration. Unfortunately, the ease of computer-assisted assessment is deceptive—this perception may encourage use by people who are not trained adequately in measurement and statistics or are operating outside a given area of competency, and may constitute unethical practice according to the codes established by the ACA, APA, and the NBCC.

Another benefit of the use of computer-administered assessment is the development of adaptive or tailored testing (Weiss, 1985; Wise & Plake, 1990). Computer technology allows the examinee's responses to determine which subsequent items are to be administered. The resultant number of items required generally is reduced by 50%, therefore reducing test time. For higher ability examinees, boredom is avoided by offering more challenging items. Lower ability examinees may avoid discouragement that can occur secondary to item difficulty. This provides for more equal and ethical test administration to examinees, regardless of ability level, thus optimizing a given person's performance (Wise & Plake).

The ethical administration of tests requires precision and consistency. Computerized administration of testing has the potential to improve precision and consistency, thus enhancing the ethical administration of tests. It is important that the counseling field continue to demonstrate the validity and reliability of computerized assessment tools and compare their performance with comparable and better established, paper-and-pencil tests.

Limitations of Computerized Administration

The benefits of this reported ease of administration and data collection can be misleading. Accurate interpretation of test performance also requires careful observation of the examinee during the administration of any test. Computerized test administration may encourage less vigilance on the administrator's part, possibly resulting in the absence of important clinical data. Specifically, situational factors related to the individual during the testing process may be overlooked. Interpreting a test without taking into account those factors (e.g., environmental stimuli, distracters, arousal level of the client during the assessment process, and fluctuations in performance related to such factors) beyond the basic test scores generated by a computer program may result in the unethical use of test data. Thus, the data gathered are essentially incomplete and may not present a holistic view of the person (Maki, 1986).

Some domains of assessment do not transfer well to computerized assessment. One such area is neuropsychological testing. The stimulus–response complexity of many neuropsychological tests is difficult to duplicate with current computer technology. Although computerized assessment has its place in the assessment process, it cannot replace the involvement of the professional. It can, however, serve as a useful adjunct to the assessment process (Binder & Thompson, 1994). Thus, the ethical use of computerized technology must be considered within the context of the discipline using such technology.

A social issue associated with computerized assessment is the limited access to such technology for people with socioeconomic limitations. In a publication addressing the ethical treatment of patients with brain injury, Ackerman and Banks (1990) highlighted the limitations that socioeconomic status of a consumer or providing institution can impose upon the availability of such technology. It is important that technology that improves outcomes in patient treatment is made available to all who need it, regardless of their ability to pay.

The use of computers to administer assessment instruments is not a replacement for the professional counselor. Counseling practice is essentially a human-to-human encounter that provides assistance to people in need of counseling interventions. The use of technology in assessment may facilitate such endeavors; however, implementation of technology in the counseling process also requires careful monitoring and supervision by experienced professionals to promote sound ethical practice (see Wall, 2000).

Computer-Generated Assessment Results and Reports

The use of PCs to assist in interpreting psychological test results is increasing and is known as *computer-based test interpretation* (CBTI). A great deal of controversy surrounds this area of technology. Programs have been developed to meet the demands of the counseling professional, including systems that schedule appointments, administer a battery of tests, perform statistical and data management functions, and produce results in the form of computer-generated reports. However, reliability and validity information for these integrated systems is limited. Although the sophistication of modular-integrated systems of assessment is increasing, some serious ethical considerations remain.

When a counseling professional has access to computer-generated test results from given test data, there is potential for overreliance on the computer to interpret the protocol. The computer is unable to incorporate qualitative data that are accessible to the counselor. Qualitative data can take exception to direct interpretation of the quantitative test data. Errors in data entry can also result in inaccurate test scores. Professionals who use such software are obligated ethically to carefully review the data entered. Computer-generated test reports must also be interpreted carefully to avoid unethical assessment practice. Such protocols generally request raw test data or data collected from a structured interview. The data are then incorporated into a template report that is adjusted, based on the data entered. The counselor must review the entire report for accuracy and correspondence to available test data. Individual test results do not always lend themselves to a predictable template interpretation. The professional must critically analyze the report content and edit and supplement the report accordingly. Computer-generated reports can be useful templates for producing reports but should not be provided to referral sources without careful scrutiny by the examiner.

Organizational pressures in today's mental health care settings from managed care and third-party payment sources may force many organizations to do more with less. Such pressure encourages the use of less qualified technicians who are paid less to perform assessment procedures. Overreliance on the ease of computer technology is of even greater concern when less qualified examiners are used in the assessment process. The temptation to take any information that a computer generates, be it data interpretation or a report, and accept it at face value is a reality with potentially serious consequences. Overconfidence in technology can overshadow reasonable interpretation of results. Technology can help make test administration, interpretation, and report generation a more efficient process. However, computerized assessment must be viewed in light of its assets and limitations.

Research Issues in Computerized Assessment

The update to the Standards for Educational and Psychological Testing (AERA et al., 1999) provides standards for the development of computer-administered tests, the use of computer-based testing in general, the use of computer-generated test interpretations, and the implementation of computer-adaptive testing.

The ethical appropriateness of using PCs to administer tests is being examined in research today. The APA (1986) Committee on Professional Standards, along with the Committee on Psychological Tests and Assessment, developed the *Guidelines for Computer-Based Tests and Interpretations.* The ethical codes of ACA and APA address the importance of ethical behavior regarding the application of any technology in the assessment of, and subsequent treatment of, clients. The APA addressed specific ethical obligations of psychologists when dealing with assessment technology: (a) psychologists select scoring and interpretation services (including automated services) on the basis of evidence of the validity of the program and procedures as well as on other appropriate considerations, and (b) psychologists retain responsibility for the appropriate application, interpretation, and use of assessment instruments, whether they score and interpret such tests themselves or use automated or other services.

Equivalence is a major issue addressed by the APA. The interchange of information between computer-based and conventional (paper-and-pencil) tests has been deemed allowable if: (a) the rank orders of scores tested in alternative modes closely approximate each other, and (b) the means, dispersions, and shapes of the score, distributions are approximately the same or have been made approximately the same by rescaling the scores from the computer mode. The computerized version must be psychometrically similar to the paper-and-pencil version; thus, the term **equivalence.**

Scholars also are exploring the possibility that the exchange of people, paper, and pencil for computer technology changes how the examinee responds to evaluation. For example, personally sensitive issues appear to be easier to divulge to a computer program than to an actual therapist, which may increase the amount of data available to the counselor (Honaker & Fowler, 1990; Sampson, 2000). The psychological constructs tapped by clinical interviews and the traditional methods of testing may be different from those tapped when a computer is used for these same purposes. Because of these potential differences, norms generated by non-computerized assessment tools may not generalize to the computer format.

To use a computer for ease of administration and then interpret the test by paper-and-pencil norms may not be ethical due to the potential error that can be introduced. More time is needed to establish appropriate norms for computerized test interpretation. Many computerized assessment instruments must be treated as experimental until further research clarifies the effect of the computer medium on the overall assessment process. Manuals that accompany any tests must be reviewed carefully to determine the appropriateness of the use of the instrument.

COMPUTER-ASSISTED COUNSELOR EDUCATION

On-Line Supervision and Virtual Practica

Cyberspace, or the internet, has been considered an alternative means of counselor supervision (Myrick & Sabella, 1995). Myrick and Sabella recommended the use of e-mail to share professional ideas and information with supervisees in remote and distant areas. Such technology also provides an opportunity for academic, organizational, or peer supervision. Myrick and Sabella also provided specific scenarios in which elementary school counselors were able to access timely assistance for complex cases, particularly when counselors were practicing in remote locations.

E-mail, or text-based supervision, has its limitations. Removing the one-to-one interaction between supervisor and supervisee limits the data to which supervisors may respond (e.g., body language or acceptance of constructive criticism). The development of satellite and computer technology that allows real-time video and audio interaction minimizes some limitations of text-based supervision. However, it is unclear how this technology compares with person-to-person supervision within the same space. The ethical issues identified in the on-line counseling section of this chapter also apply to on-line supervision and practica. Unless sufficient security protocols are in place, such activity could be considered unethical. Further research is needed regarding existing systems and protocols.

Distance Learning

Distance learning may be conceptualized as the use of technical equipment to guarantee consistent product quality in mass volumes and use of technical media (e.g., television, radio, and satellite broadcasting) in place of in vivo teachers to broaden accessibility (Stewart, 1992). New technologies are being used to deliver preservice and in-service training to counselors from various specialty areas (Davis & Yazak, 1995). Since the development of the British Open University in 1969, distance-learning programs have expanded worldwide. Distance learning is useful for persons in remote and rural areas, for learners who have limited mobility, and for professionals with busy schedules or economic limitations who wish to further their professional development through licensure and certification (Steele, 1993).

Advancement in technology is one factor that influences educators to consider distance learning (Davis & Yazak, 1995). Another compelling factor is the potential cost effectiveness of distance education in an era of increased college enrollment and decreasing government funding for higher education (Altekruse & Brew, 2000). The internet connects millions of computers worldwide, allowing access to databases and library materials and facilitating communication between instructors and students. HTML programming capabilities, CD-ROM technology, multimedia presentation of written material, and high-quality graphics have made learning through computer software a viable alternative or supplement to the traditional classroom experience (Bloom & Walz, 2000; Scriven, 1991; Sirkin, 1994).

Synchronous and Asynchronous Learning Paradigms

Two popular, Web-based distance-learning paradigms include synchronous and asynchronous modalities. **Asynchronous** curriculum delivery can occur over the Web using software programs such as Blackboard or Web CT; curricula are delivered through on-line files that are available continuously. Students can interact with the system on their own schedule. **Synchronous** delivery systems have a set time for on-line interaction, sometimes using streaming video to deliver on-line lectures to a prescheduled audience. There are also combinations of the two modalities that create a multimodal interactive curriculum.

Ethical Concerns with Distance Learning

Distance learning brings several ethical concerns for counselor educators. Program integrity, continuity, and sophistication affect the quality of education that a given counselor receives. The available resources that facilitate a program's capacity to accomplish its objectives through distance learning must be considered case by case. It is erroneous to assume that an in vivo course of study will readily translate to a distance-learning format. An outcome research base is necessary to compare the difference between distance-learning programs and exemplary, traditional, university-based programs and to examine the effectiveness of distance learning. Program accreditation standards can be developed from such data to ensure the integrity of counselor education programs.

In traditional university settings, courses can be evaluated through peer review. Course activity between teacher and student can be observed and evaluated by fellow professionals to provide developmental suggestions that enhance an instructor's pedagogy and, ultimately, the quality of the student's education. In a distance-learning setting, the interpersonal dynamic between instructor and student is different than a face-to-face experience. How this difference affects the learning process is not yet known, but it is clear this dynamic cannot be observed for distance learning in the same way it is in the traditional classroom setting. The dynamic difference between in vivo and remote education may also influence the student learning process. This dynamic has not been fully explored. Preliminary data suggest that modalities overall do not impact grades (Stocks & Freddolino, 1998). Students reported that the distance-education format provided a flexibility that was desirable, but it lacked the personal contact of in vivo formats (Keating & Hargitai, 1999). Methods to maintain in vivo, professional feedback that contributes to course quality and development within a distance-learning context should be explored further.

Taped presentations of a distance-learning curriculum do not provide students the opportunity to ask questions and interact contemporaneously with instructors. It is unclear how this may affect the learning process. If a student is having difficulty grasping a concept in a real-time distance-learning presentation, the opportunity for one-to-one interaction for clarification is limited. The logistics of interacting with a classroom or an instructor remotely may inherently be more time consuming than in a traditional classroom setting (e.g., timing of questions, coordinating multiple inquiries, and keeping the course moving in a timely manner). The difficulty associated with cueing an instructor in a remote setting may discourage active and lively class participation. Student-to-student interaction (e.g., breaking into small groups) is limited, although technologically possible. However, these situations introduce a number of factors that affect time, interpersonal interaction, and possibly the willingness to engage others. The effect of these limitations must be clarified before valid comparison of in vivo learning versus distance learning can be made.

If follow-up phone support is available to students, their ability to graphically clarify a concept is limited. People who are uncomfortable with phone communication are at a distinct disadvantage. The effect of video with phone interaction may alleviate some of this concern. Additionally, the expense of such communication may deter students from taking advantage of this assistance. The person-to-person conferences available to students on campus to assist with clarification of difficult material are not available to remote learners. Some courses may more readily lend themselves to remote presentation than others, again necessitating a case-by-case approach to the development of distance-learning curricula.

Some literature suggests that students and faculty generally prefer face-to-face interaction over distance learning (Bland, Morrison, & Ross, 1992). Some would say that simply accessing information in any technologically sophisticated fashion is inferior to an educational environment that includes two-way communication (Garrison, 1990; Law & Sissons, 1985). Most importantly, the personal development of students in counselor education is arguably as important as their professional and academic development. It is difficult for faculty to provide mentoring and role modeling of professional behavior without personal contact with students. All things considered, the development of distance-learning curricula should be carefully thought out.

Suggestions for Ethical Distance-Learning Curricula Development

Davis and Yazak (1995) suggested several areas of focus for the development of accreditation guidelines for distance-learning curricula. They modeled their suggestions after the Southern Association of Colleges and Schools' (Staff, 1993) areas of focus for program accreditation standards, which included mission, curriculum delivery, faculty, resources, student support, and evaluation.

Mission. Faculty should review the mission of their program and institution to consider the long-range strategic effect of distance learning on the fundamental philosophy of the institution and the existing curriculum. Issues such as regional accreditation (proposed catchment area of recruitment), potential student market, admission procedures, and program structure (e.g., time period of course acquisition that maintains program integrity) must be considered. Student skills of self-pacing, goal setting, and self-evaluation may require a greater emphasis in student recruitment. Without the local influence of professors or peers, student motivation becomes critical. Institutions that offer distance-learning curricula have an ethical responsibility to recruit candidates who will thrive in a distance-learning environment.

Curriculum Delivery. Establishing appropriate modes of information dissemination is crucial to the education process. Distance learning presents a number of factors that influence curriculum delivery. Although it may be premature to rule out the viability of certain areas of curricula in distance learning, Eldredge, Gerard, and Smart (1994) suggested that instruction in the areas of counseling skills and testing evaluation "do not lend themselves well to distance education because of the individualized supervision required to assist full skill development" (p. 78). As Davis and Yazak (1995) recommended, "consideration of the characteristics of technical media in relation to the learning requirements of advanced and specialized curriculum is essential" (p. 297).

The presentation of information that is to be organized, generally understood, and memorized, such as historical and theoretical overviews, could perhaps be effectively accomplished through some of the distance-learning techniques already discussed (one-way audiovisual transmission or videotaped curricula). However, course material that requires critical thinking, abstraction, active processing, and synthesis of information may require active instructor and student discussion that does not lend itself to some distance-learning formats (Davis & Yazak, 1995). Discussion of counseling scenarios and complex, ethical problem-solving skills that emerge from such experience could be jeopardized in such formats, which strongly questions the ethical appropriateness of using such approaches in counselor education. Clearly, more research is required to ethically present an entire advanced curriculum exclusively by distance-learning technology.

Faculty. Distance learning presents opportunities to instruct more nontraditional students in remote areas, which presents a new audience to many professional counselor educators. This opportunity may ultimately affect how existing curricula are presented to new audiences. Expertise in technology and troubleshooting are necessary to promote seamless and timely presentation of remote curricula (Davis-Bell, 1991; Fulmer, Hazzard, Jones, & Keene, 1992; Massoumian, 1989; Willis, 1992). "Distance learning faculty must be trained in how to plan lessons that must be precise, well timed, and supported with high-quality visual aids" (Davis & Yazak, 1995). Courses in distance-learning technology and subsequent curriculum development may be necessary for counselor educators in training to facilitate proper use of such technology.

Two more issues need to be addressed with respect to faculty who are developing distance-learning material. First, faculty may share concerns with others who are creating computer-assisted counseling software: distance-learning curriculum development and counseling software development currently are not acknowledged by university administrators in the same spirit as are other quantitative research efforts, although they are equally time consuming. Such efforts must be acknowledged effectively if such technology is to move forward. Second, guidelines for the protection of property rights of materials developed for distance-learning endeavors must be established. If a professor invests a great deal of time in curriculum development, the same ethical rights and restrictions placed on publications should be extended to distance-learning curricula.

Resources. Some distance-learning students, particularly those in remote locations, may not have access to the same resources that students have in a campus setting. Therefore, textbooks used in distance-learning courses should engage the students in active learning. Educators may choose texts with accompanying workbooks that encourage active processing of readings through exercises. Some courses may also require the use of a library or the internet for in-depth study. If such resources are not available at a distance-learning site, and no alternatives exist (e.g., library networking, interlibrary loan services, or facsimile services), courses that require such resources may not be appropriate for a distance-learning curriculum.

Students benefit from speedy instructor feedback on assignments such as quizzes, papers, and exams. In a distance-learning context, rapid turnaround of the student's work is likely to be confounded by proximity. Expedient methods of assignment exchanges are necessary for students to benefit from instructor feedback. In addition to using mail delivery systems and on-line computerized testing, faculty visits to distance classrooms are recommended whenever possible (Barker, 1986; Hodgson, 1986). However, travel to some remote areas may be cost prohibitive, so the nature of the course must determine the optimal instructor feedback and therefore dictate what types of courses will be worth offering through distance learning.

Student Support. Professionals who recruit students to distance-learning programs are ethically responsible for assuring that the recruits have the coping skills necessary to thrive in such an environment. Precourse advisement may help identify students who need remediation before embarking on such an endeavor. Ongoing tutoring services may also be required for students who have taken on more than they are capable of (Davis & Yazak, 1995; Hodgson, 1986).

Students in distance-learning programs need advice on career counseling, course selection, financial aid, registration, and practica/internship placement. Reasonable accommodations for persons with disabilities may also be an issue. Many program-accrediting bodies require a certain advisee-to-faculty ratio for programs to remain accredited. CORE requires a ratio of less than 20:1 (CORE, 2000). The recommended student-to-faculty ratio of CACREP is more rigorous—10:1 (CACREP, 1996). The impact of distance learning upon these requirements, given the temptation to use such technology to educate more students with the same number of faculty members, must be evaluated carefully.

Program Evaluation. Evaluation of distance-learning effectiveness is an ethical responsibility of program developers and is a vital component of program accreditation (Davis & Yazak, 1995; Olcott, 1993). Fenwick (1992) described seven common indicators of quality for distance-learning curricula: (a) attrition rates, (b) work assignment response rates, (c) student course evaluations, (d) quality of the learning package, (e) the learning process, (f) degree of freedom of pace and method, and (g) the level of student independence. Formal feedback from students is even more critical for distance-learning programs because students have comparatively less contact with program faculty (Davis & Yazak). Audio conferencing, phone communication, and e-mail communication can facilitate frequent feedback to distance-learning program developers. The ethical concerns that apply to the electronic media are relevant to distance learning as well. For a review of faculty perceptions of the pros and cons of developing and delivering an on-line course, see Altekruse and Brew (2000), Peterson (2000), and Daniels, Tyler, and Christie (2000).

COMPUTER-ASSISTED INSTRUCTION

Computer-assisted instruction (CAI) uses tutorials to present concepts and examples of instructional tasks. Some program applications can measure performance and present feedback to the learner, whereas other simulations require the learner to use constructs in an applied situation to solve problems (Sampson & Krumboltz, 1991). Like computerized technology in assessment and counseling, CAI has experienced more widespread use as affordability has improved. Although the business world has used CAI extensively, the counseling field has not used it to its fullest potential (Granello, 2000; Lambert, 1988; Sampson & Krumboltz). Computerized assessment and career-counseling software programs have experienced the widest use by, and the greatest financial investment from, large software developers. The financial limitations of individual developers have resulted in restricted development and marketing of CAI software in counseling.

The academic community, particularly those academicians in programs of education, is an excellent resource for CAI development. However, academic institutions traditionally have failed to recognize software development as viable scholarly activity that applies toward promotion and tenure, much like textbook writing (depending upon the tenure-granting institution). This situation inherently limits software development efforts by faculty members, who typically have much to do with limited time and resources.

Although counseling and CAI may be conceptualized as distinct, separate activities, it is also possible to see similarities between them. The definition of CAI in counseling offered by Sampson and Krumboltz (1991) is similar to that of Grencavage and Norcross (1990), who described the commonalities among psychotherapies in computer-assisted counseling. Many of the ethical issues of computer-assisted counseling also apply to CAI in counseling. Additionally, the ethical obligations that educators have to use sound theory and peer review processes in curriculum development and instruction are important to consider in the proliferation of CAI in counseling. For further discussion of computer-assisted instruction in counselor education and supervision, see Granello (2000, pp. 8–11).

"TECHNOCENTERED" AND "TECHNOANXIOUS"

Harris-Bowlsbey (2000), an early pioneer in the development of computer-based, career planning systems, suggested that many warm and caring counselors with enterprising and artistic proclivities may find embracing cybertechnology as foreign and uncomfortable. Counselors' reactions to technology span a continuum from acceptance to anxiety. Brod (1984) dichotomized people's reactions to technology as **technocentered** (comfortable with computer technology) and **technoanxious** (fearful and avoiding computerization of the profession). Counselors' resistance to computerization of various counseling tasks could be explained in part by technoanxiety (Ford, 1993). The benefits to technological advances are numerous and substantial. The best way to ensure the appropriate implementation of progress, both ethically and in addressing people with technoanxiety, is through preservice and in-service training of counseling professionals (ACES, 1999; Ford, 1993; Hammer & Hile, 1985; Meier & Geiger, 1986).

Not all resistance to the computerization of counseling is related to anxiety. There are many ethical concerns associated with the implementation of new technology, so the use of computers and related technology in the counseling field must be carried out carefully after appropriate research. In addition, standards should be set to ensure its continued safe use. The very nature of computerization—its objectivity and relationship to quantifiable data—also brings limitations to situations that require abstract problem solving and clinical judgment. Computerization may restrict the exchange of questions and answers, emphasizing concrete data at the expense of less quantifiable phenomena (Murphy & Pardeck, 1988). Counselors in training must be aware of these limitations before embarking on their own professional practice.

ETHICAL USE OF SOFTWARE

Software **pirating,** or the illegal copying and use of software, is a blatant breach of ethics. The sharing of software between professionals can be considered doing a coworker a favor. Clearly, the motivation is to save several hundred dollars in acquiring a piece of software. However, the unethical reproduction and transfer of computer software results in both increased cost to the consumer and loss of revenue for the author of the product. Because unauthorized reproduction of software is illegal, the ethical integrity of counselors who engage in this behavior is called into question. Software pirating can easily go undetected, increasing the responsibility of counselors to practice the ethical use of electronic media autonomously.

DECISION MAKING IN CONTEXT

As with many quickly growing developments in society, the emergence and acceptance of clear ethical best practices in the professional culture may lag behind the technological advances utilized in practice. As described earlier in this chapter, the ethical standards in counseling have shown important gains in providing some guidance for ethical decision making in matters involving technology. However, there are many situations counselors will encounter in their work with technology that will call upon them to utilize a robust ethical decision-making model to assist them in determining the best ethical course of action.

Consider the application of an ethical decision making model to a dilemma facing a counselor regarding the use of e-mail in counseling. During an initial in-person interview with a client, the client states he would like to use e-mail as the primary modality for counseling services. The client stated that this would be the easiest way for him to access counseling services and, otherwise, he would have a difficult time keeping regular appointments. He lives over 90 minutes from the counseling center. The counselor has no experience with using e-mail in a counseling relationship, but he wants to best serve this client. Should the counselor agree to use e-mail as the main modality of interaction in this counseling relationship?

According to Tarvydas' Integrative Model of Ethical Decision Making, the counselor first needs to identify the stakeholders involved in the situation and consider how each might be affected in this situation. The counselor should examine his own comfort level with using e-mail for counseling services and considering how it might affect the counseling relationship. The client's needs

should be considered paramount; the client predicts he will not be able to access counseling services on a regular basis unless it occurs via e-mail. Systemic considerations might include: third-party reimbursement, specific agency policies, state policies, and standards set by accreditation bodies. The counselor should carefully examine the current ethical standards (see Appendix 10–B and 10–C). After reviewing the current guidelines, the counselor needs to fully consider if he is able to uphold these standards. Taking into account competing empirical findings regarding the use of technology, the counselor should assess how using e-mail as the main contact with the client may affect the counseling relationship. Reflection on personal views towards technology is an essential element of the ethical decision-making process. If the counselor is among the technoanxious he may feel uncomfortable with using technology, which may negatively affect the counseling relationship. Colleagues, supervisors, and other professionals could be consulted. After weighing all factors, the counselor may choose to proceed with caution. However, before beginning services, the counselor will need to establish with the client the nature of the relationship (i.e. how often the sessions will occur, expectations from both parties, billing, etc.). Alternative means of service may be established if the technology is not meeting the client's or counselor's expectations. The counselor should document and evaluate the experience to inform future use of this modality of counseling service provision.

CHAPTER SUMMARY

Technology plays an important role in counseling-related professions. All forms of electronic media used in counseling may contain sensitive material protected by therapist–client confidentiality and privileged communication. Ethical codes that address maintenance of client records mandate that counselors maintain appropriate confidentiality in creating, storing, accessing, transferring, and disposing of all client records.

Counseling professionals use a variety of types of electronic media, including personal computers, faxes, e-mail, and cellular phones. Protocols must be in place to ensure that all types of media are accessible only to ethically appropriate parties. An ethically responsible counseling professional informs clients of the security risks involved when engaging in services provided over the internet.

Computer-assisted counseling exists in a variety of forms, including therapeutic software, on-line counseling, career counseling, rehabilitation software, and behavioral, cognitive, educational, and psychodynamic approaches. Software has been developed to target AIDS education, drug and alcohol abuse, obesity, personal distress, sexual dysfunction, smoking, and stress.

On-line counseling forums represent a recent technological development in computer applications. These forums use the internet, BBSs, and list servers for the public exchange of text-based information. List servers and information databases assist counselors in accessing diverse information quickly. Ethical concerns with on-line counseling include security, access to services, and cost.

Telehealth services are remote electronic consultations between consumers and health care provider, often in remote or rural areas that have a shortage of health professionals.

The application of computers to the area of assessment includes the ability to administer, score, and interpret psychological assessment instruments. Computer-assisted assessment has the benefits of rapid presentation of information and increased reliability in test scoring. However, test administrators may have less vigilance and may overlook situational factors during testing. Some domains of assessment do not transfer well to computerized assessment.

Computer-assisted counselor education includes on-line supervision and virtual practica, distance learning, and synchronous and asynchronous curriculum delivery. Computer-assisted instruction uses tutorials to present concepts and instructional tasks.

INTERNET RESOURCES

Key words: cybercounseling, electronic media, computer-assisted counseling, computer-assisted assessment, distance learning, synchronous learning, asynchronous learning, technocentered and technoanxious, internet or cyberspace, encryption software, Web-based therapy, telehealth services, on-line counseling, e-counseling, on-line forums.

REFERENCES

Ackerman, R. J., & Banks, M. E. (1990). Computers and the ethical treatment of brain-injured patients. *Social Science Computer Review, 8*(1), 83–95.

Aiken, L. R. (2000). *Psychological testing and assessment* (10th ed.). Boston: Allyn & Bacon.

Allen, C. (1995). job.search@internet. *Journal of Career Planning & Employment, 55* (3), 53–55.

Alleman, J. R. (2002). Online counseling: The internet and mental health treatment. *Psychotherapy: Theory, Research, Practice, Training, 39*, 199–209.

Altekruse, M. K., & Brew, L. (2000). Using the web for distance learning. In J. W. Bloom & G. R. Walz, (Eds.), *Cybercounseling and cyberlearning: Strategies and resources for the millennium* (pp. 129–141). Alexandria, VA: American Counseling Association.

American Counseling Association, (2005). *ACA code of ethics.* Alexandria, VA: Author.

American Counseling Association. (1999). Ethical standards for Internet on-line counseling. Available at www.counseling.org.

American Educational Research Association, American Psychological Association, & National Council on Measurement in Education. (1999). *Standards for educational and psychological testing.* Washington, DC: American Educational Research Association.

American Psychological Association. (1986). *Guidelines for computer-based tests and interpretations.* Washington, DC: Author.

American Psychological Association. (1997, November 5). Services by telephone, teleconferencing, and Internet: A statement by the ethics committee of the American Psychological Association. Available at http://www.apa.org.ethics/stmnt01.html.

American Psychological Association of Graduate Students. (1999). Newsletter of APAGS: 1999 APA Telehealth Mini-Convention. Available at http://www.apa.org/apags/sum99/4.html.

Argentero, P. (1989). Computerized psychological testing: An annotated bibliography. *Bollettino di Psicologia Applicata, 190*, 21–38.

Association for Counselor Education and Supervision. (1999). *Recommended technical competencies for counselor education students.* Alexandria, VA: Author.

Barker, K. (1986). Dilemmas at a distance. *Assessment and Evaluation in Higher Education, 11*, 219–230.

Berge, Z. L. (1994). Electronic discussion groups. *Communication Education, 43*, 102–111.

Binder, L. M., & Thompson, L. L. (1994). The ethics code and neuropsychological assessment practices. *Archives of Clinical Neuropsychology, 10*, 27–46.

Binik, Y. M., Servan-Schreiber, D., Freiwald, S., & Hall, K. S. (1988). Intelligent computer-based assessment and psychotherapy: An expert system for sexual dysfunction. *The Journal of Nervous and Mental Disease, 176*, 387–400.

Bland, K., Morrison, G. R., & Ross, S. M. (1992). *Student attitudes toward learning link: A distance education project.* Paper presented at the annual meeting of the Mid-South Educational Research Association, Knoxville, TN.

Bloom, J. W., & Walz, G. R. (Eds.). (2000). *Cybercounseling and cyberlearning: Strategies and resources for the millennium.* Alexandria, VA: American Counseling Association.

Bloom, J. W., & Walz, G. R. (Eds.). (2004). *Cybercounseling and cyberlearning: An encore.* Alexandria, VA: American Counseling Association.

Boles, R. N. (1996, March). The Internet and the job hunt. *Career Planning and Adult Development Network Newsletter, 18*(3), 1–4.

Bouchard, S., Payeur, R., Rivard, V., et al. (2000). Cognitive behavior therapy for panic disorder with agoraphobia in videoconference: Preliminary results. *Cyberpsychology & Behavior, 3*, 999–1007.

Brod, C. (1984). *Technostress: The human cost of the computer revolution.* Don Mills, Ontario, Canada: Addison-Wesley.

Burda, P. C., Starkey, T. W., & Dominguez, F. (1991). Computer-administered treatment of psychiatric inpatients. *Computers in Human Behavior, 7*, 1–5.

Burling, T. A., Marotta, J., Gonzalez, R., Moltzen, J. O., Eng, A. M., Schmidt, G. A., et al. (1989). Computerized smoking cessation program for the worksite: Treatment outcome and feasibility. *Journal of Consulting and Clinical Psychology, 57*, 619–622.

Burnett, K. F., Magel, P. M., Harrington, S., & Taylor, C. B. (1989). Computer-assisted behavioral health counseling for high school students. *Journal of Counseling Psychology, 36*, 63–67.

Burnett, K. F., Taylor, C. B., & Agras, W. S. (1985). Ambulatory computer-assisted therapy for obesity: A new frontier for behavior therapy. *Journal of Consulting and Clinical Psychology, 53*, 698–703.

Butcher, J. N. (Ed.). (1985). Perspectives on computerized psychological assessment [Special issue]. *Journal of Consulting and Clinical Psychology, 53*, 745–838.

Butcher, J. N. (1987). The use of computers in psychological assessment: An overview of practices and issues. In J. N. Butcher (Ed.), *Computerized psychological assessment: A practitioner's guide* (pp. 3–14). New York: Basic Books.

Caplan, B. (1987). *Rehabilitation psychology desk reference*. Rockville, MD: Aspen.

Carr, A. C., Ghosh, A., & Marks, I. M. (1988). Computer-supervised exposure treatment for phobias. *Canadian Journal of Psychiatry, 33*, 112–117.

Celio, A. A., Winzelberg, A., Dev, P., et al. (2002). Improving compliance in on-line, structured self-help programs: Evaluation of an eating disorder prevention program. *Journal of Psychiatric Practice. 8*, 4–20.

Clarke, B., & Schoech, D. (1984). A computer-assisted game for adolescents: Initial development and comments. In M. D. Schwartz (Ed.), *Using computers in clinical practice: Psychotherapy and mental health applications* (pp. 335–353). New York: Hayworth.

Cohen, G. E., & Kerr, B. A., (1998). Computer-mediated counseling: An empirical study of a new mental health treatment. *Computers in Human Services, 15*, 13–26.

Colby, K. M. (1980). Computer psychotherapists. In J. B. Sidorski, J. H. Johnson, & T. A. Williams (Eds.), *Technology in mental health care delivery systems* (pp. 109–117). Norwood, NJ: Ablex.

Colby, K. M. (1986). Ethics of computer-assisted psychotherapy. *Psychiatric Annals, 16*, 414–415.

Colby, K. M., Colby, P. M., & Stoller, R. J. (1990). Dialogues in natural language with GURU, a psychological inference engine. *Philosophical Psychology, 3*, 171–186.

Colby, K. M., Gould, R. L., & Aronson, G. (1989). Some pros and cons of computer-assisted psychotherapy. *The Journal of Nervous and Mental Disease, 177*, 105–108.

Colby, K. M., Watt, J. B., & Gilbert, J. P. (1966). A computer method of psychotherapy: Preliminary communication. *The Journal of Nervous and Mental Disease, 142*, 148–152.

Cook, J. E. & Doyle, C. (2002). Working alliance in online therapy as compared to face-to-face therapy: Preliminary results. *Cyberpsychology and Behavior, 5*, 95–105.

Commission on Rehabilitation Counselor Certification. (2001, June). *Code of professional ethics for certified rehabilitation counselors and CRCC guidelines and procedures for processing complaints*. Rolling Meadows, IL: Author.

Council for Accreditation of Counseling and Related Education Programs. (1996). *CACREP accreditation standards and procedures manual* (Rev. ed.). Alexandria, VA: Author.

Council on Rehabilitation Education. (2000). *Re-accreditation manual for rehabilitation counselor education programs*. Rolling Meadows, IL: Author.

Daniels, H. M., Tyler, J. M., & Christie, B. S. (2000). On-line instruction in counselor education: Possibilities, implications, & guidelines. In J. W. Bloom & G. R. Walz (Eds.), *Cybercounseling and cyberlearning: Strategies and resources for the millennium* (pp. 303–317). Alexandria, VA: American Counseling Association.

Day, S. X., & Schneider, P. (2002). Psychotherapy using distance technology: A comparison of face-to-face, video, and audio treatment. *Journal of Counseling Psychology, 49*, 499–503.

Davidson, R. S. (1985). Applications of computer technology to learning therapy. *Journal of Organizational Behavior Management, 6*, 155–168.

Davis, A., & Yazak, D. (1995). Implementation and accreditation issues in the development of distance learning programs. *Rehabilitation Education, 9*, 293–307.

Davis-Bell, J. (1991). Distance learning: New technology and new potential. *Legislative Reports, 16*(6), 1–10.

Drummond, R. J. (1996). *Appraisal procedures for counselors and helping professionals*. Upper Saddle River, NJ: Prentice Hall.

Duncan, D. M. (1997). *Counseling over the Internet: Ethical and legal considerations*. Presentation at the American Counseling Association's 1997 World Conference, Orlando, FL.

Eldredge, G., Gerard, G., & Smart, J. (1994). A distance education model for rehabilitation counseling. *Journal of Rehabilitation Administration, 18*, 75–79.

Elleven, R. K., & Allen, J. (2004). Applying technology to online counseling: Suggestions for the beginning e-therapist. *Journal of Instructional Psychology, 31*, 223–227.

Erdman, H. P., & Foster, S. W. (1988). Ethical issues in the use of computer-based assessment. In J. W. Murphy & J. T. Pardeck (Eds.), *Technology and human service delivery: Challenges and a critical perspective* (pp. 71–87). New York: Haworth.

Erdman, H. P., Klein, M. H., & Greist, J. H. (1985). Direct patient computer interviewing. *Journal of Consulting and Clinical Psychology, 53*, 760–773.

Eyde, L. D. (Ed.). (1987). Computerized psychological testing [Special issue]. *Applied Psychology: An International Review, 36*, 223–235.

Farrell, A. D., Camplair, P. S., & McCullough, L. (1987). Identification of target complaints by computer interview: Evaluation of the computerized assessment system for psychotherapy evaluation and research. *Journal of Consulting and Clinical Psychology, 55*, 691–700.

Fenwick, J. (1992). *A question of quality*. Paper presented at the International Council for Distance Education 16th World Conference, Bangkok, Thailand.

Ford, B. D. (1988). *An ongoing computerized adjunct to psychotherapy program: Two years plus in a two years minus correctional center*. Paper presented at Counseling as Education Conference, Lakehead University, Thunder Bay, Ontario, Canada.

Ford, B. D. (1993). Ethical and professional issues in computer-assisted therapy. *Computers in Human Behavior, 9*, 387–400.

Ford, B. D., & Vitelli, R. (1992). Inmate attitudes towards computerized clinical interventions. *Computers in Human Behavior, 8*, 223–230.

Fowler, R. D. (1985). Landmarks in computer-assisted psychological assessment. *Journal of Consulting and Clinical Psychology, 53*, 748–759.

French, C. F. (1986). Microcomputers and psychometric assessment. *British Journal of Guidance and Counseling, 14*, 33–45.

French, C. C., & Beaumont, J. G. (1987). The reaction of psychiatric patients to computerized assessment. *British Journal of Clinical Psychology, 26*, 267–278.

French, C., & Beaumont, J. G. (1992). Microcomputer version of a digit span test in clinical use. *Interacting with Computers, 4*, 163–178.

Fulmer, J., Hazzard, M., Jones, S., & Keene, K. (1992). Distance learning: An innovative approach to nursing education. *Journal of Professional Nursing, 8*, 289–294.

Garrison, D. R. (1990). An analysis and evaluation of audio teleconferencing to facilitate education at a distance. *The American Journal of Distance Education, 4*(3), 13–24.

Gates, W., Myhrvold, N., & Rinearson, P. (1995). *The road ahead*. New York: Viking.

Glueckauf, R. L., Pickett, T. C., Ketterson, T. U., Loomis, J. S., & Rozensky, R. H. (2003). Preparation for the delivery of telehealth services: A self-study framework for expansion of practice. *Professional Psychology: Research and Practice, 34*, 159–163.

Goodman, H., Gingerich, W. J., & Shazer, S. (1989). BRIEFER: An expert system for clinical practice. *Computers in Human Services, 5*, 53–68.

Granello, P. F. (2000). Historical context: The relationship of computer technologies and counseling. In J. W. Bloom & G. R. Walz (Eds.), *Cybercounseling and cyberlearning: Strategies and resources for the millennium* (pp. 3–15). Alexandria, VA: American Counseling Association.

Grencavage, L. M., & Norcross, J. C. (1990). Where are the commonalities among the therapeutic common factors? *Professional Psychology: Research and Practice, 21*, 372–378.

Hammer, A. L., & Hile, M. G. (1985). Factors in clinicians' resistance to automation in mental health. *Computers in Human Services, 1*, 1–23.

Hannon, K. (1996, May 13). Upset? Try cybertherapy. *U.S. News & World Report, 81*, 83.

Harrell, T. H., Honaker, L. M., Hetu, M., & Oberwager, J. (1987). Computerized versus traditional administration of the multidimensional aptitude battery-verbal scale: An examination of reliability and validity. *Computers in Human Behavior, 3*, 129–137.

Harris-Bowlsbey, J. (2000). The Internet: Blessing or bane for the counseling profession? In J. W. Bloom & G. R. Walz (Eds.), *Cybercounseling and cyberlearning: Strategies and resources for the millennium* (pp. 39–49). Alexandria, VA: American Counseling Association.

Hartman, D. E. (1986a). Artificial intelligence or artificial psychologist? Conceptual issues in clinical microcomputer use. *Professional Psychology: Research and Practice, 17*, 528–534.

Hartman, D. E. (1986b). On the use of clinical psychology software: Practical, legal, and ethical concerns. *Professional Psychology: Research and Practice, 17*, 462–465.

Heinlen, K. T., Welfel, E. R., Richmond, E. N. & O'Donnel, M. S. (2003). The nature, scope, and ethics of psychologists' e-therapy Web sites: What consumers find when surfing the Web. *Psychotherapy: Theory, Research, Practice, Training, 40*, 112–124.

Hodgson, V. E. (1986). The interrelationship between support and learning materials. *Programmed Learning and Educational Technology, 23*, 56–61.

Honaker, L. M., & Fowler, R. D. (1990). Computer-assisted psychological assessment. In G. Goldstein & M. Hersen (Eds.), *Handbook of psychological assessment* (2nd ed.). Elmsford, NY: Pergamon Press.

Hood, A. B., & Johnson, R. W. (1997). *Assessment in counseling: A guide to the use of psychological assessment procedures* (2nd ed.). Alexandria, VA: American Counseling Association.

Hufford, B. J., Glueckauf, R. L., & Webb, P. M. (1999). Home-based, interactive videoconferencing for adolescents with epilepsy and their families. *Rehabilitation Psychology, 44*, 176–193.

Hughs, A. L., & Ruiz, N. J. (1998, April). Ethics in counseling: Cyberspace and the counseling practice. *Counseling Today, 16*, 22.

International Society for Mental Health Online. (2005). *Mission Statement of the International Society for Mental Health Online*. Retrieved June 06, 2005, from www.ismho.org/mission.htm.

Jandt, F. E., & Nemnich, M. B. (1995). *Using the Internet in your job search*. Indianapolis, IN: JIST Works, Inc.

Keating, A. B., & Hargitai, J. (1999). *The wired professor*. New York: New York University Press.

Keith-Spiegel, P., & Koocher, G. P. (1985). *Ethics in psychology*. New York: Random House.

Kennedy, A. (2005, June). An uneasy alliance. *Counseling Today, 1*, 14, & 16.

Kennedy, J. L. (1995). *Hook up, get hired! The Internet job search revolution*. New York: Wiley.

Kennedy, R., Baltzley, D., Turnage, J., & Jones, M. (1989). Factor analysis and predictive validity of microcomputer-based tests. *Perceptual and Motor Skills, 69*, 1059–1074.

Kilvingham, F. M., Jr., Johnston, J. A., Hogan, R. S., & Mauer, E. (1994). Who benefits from computerized career counseling? *Journal of Counseling and Development, 72*, 289–292.

Koocher, G. P., & Morray, E. (2000). Regulation in telepsychology: A survey of State Attorneys General. *Professional Psychology: Research and Practice, 31*, 503–508.

Kraus, R., Zack, J., & Stricker, G. (2004). *Online counseling: A handbook for mental health professionals*. San Diego, CA: Elsevier Academic Press.

Lambert, M. (1988). Computers in counselor education: Four years after a special issue. *Counselor Education and Supervision, 28*, 100–109.

Lange, A. Schrieken, B. A., van de Ven, J. P., et al. (2000). "Interapy": the effects of a short protocalled treatment of posttraumatic stress and pathological grief through the Internet. *Behavioral & Cognitive Psychotherapy, 28*, 175–192.

Law, M., & Sissons, L. (1985). The challenge of distance education. *New Directions for Continuing Education, 26*, 43–54.

Lawrence, G. H. (1986). Using computers for the treatment of psychological problems. *Computers in Human Behavior, 2*, 43–62.

Lee, C. C. (2000). Cybercounseling and empowerment: Bridging the digital divide. In J. W. Bloom & G. R. Walz (Eds.), *Cybercounseling and cyberlearning: Strategies and resources for the millennium* (pp. 85–93). Alexandria, VA: American Counseling Association.

Levitan, K. B., Willis, E. A., & Vogelgesang, J. (1985). Microcomputers and the individual practitioner: A review of the literature in psychology and psychiatry. *Computers in Human Services, 1*, 65–84.

Lukin, M. E., Dowd, T., Plake, B. S., & Kraft, R. G. (1985). Comparing computerized versus traditional psychological assessment. *Computers in Human Behavior, 1*, 49–58.

Magnusen, K. O., & Magnusen, O. C. (1995). On the leading edge of video interviewing. *Journal of Career Planning & Employment, 55*(4), 45–47.

Maki, D. (1986). Foundations of applied rehabilitation counseling. In T. Riggar, D. Maki, & A. Wolf (Eds.), *Applied rehabilitation counseling* (pp. 3–11). New York: Springer.

Mallen, M. J., Day, S. X., & Green, M. A. (2003). Online versus face-to-face conversations: An examination of relational and discourse variables. *Psychotherapy: Theory, Research and Practice, 40* (1/2), 155–163.

Marino, T. W. (1996, January). Counselors in cyberspace debate whether client discussions are ethical. *Counseling Today, 8,* 8, 20.

Massoumian, B. (1989). Successful teaching via two-way interactive video. *Tech Trends, 34*(2), 16–19.

Matarazzo, J. D. (1985). Clinical psychological test interpretations by computer: Hardware outpaces software. *Computers in Human Behavior, 1,* 235–253.

Matarazzo, J. D. (1986). Computerized clinical psychological test interpretation: Unvalidated plus all mean and no sigma. *American Psychologist, 41,* 14–25.

Matthews, T. J., De Santi, S. M., Callahan, D., Kolblenz-Sulcov, C. J., & Werden, J. L. (1987). The microcomputer as an agent of intervention with psychiatric patients: Preliminary studies. *Computers in Human Behavior, 3,* 37–47.

McLemore, C. W., & Fantuzzo, J. W. (1982). CARE: Bridging the gap between clinicians and computers. *Professional Psychology, 13,* 501–510.

Meier, S. T., & Geiger, S. M. (1986). Implications of computer-assisted testing and assessment for professional practice and training. *Measurement and Evaluation in Counseling and Development, 19,* 29–34.

Merrell, K. W. (1985). Computer use in psychometric assessment: Evaluating benefits and potential problems. *Computer in Human Services, 1* (3), 59–67.

Metanoia. (2001). *E-therapy history and survey.* Retrieved June 12, 2005, from http:www.metanoia.org/imhs/history.htm.

Moncher, M. S., Parms, C. A., Orlandi, M. A., Schinke, S. P., Miller, S. O., Palleja, J., et al. (1985). Microcomputer-based approaches for preventing drug and alcohol abuse among adolescents from ethnic-racial minority backgrounds. *Computers in Human Behavior, 5,* 79–93.

Murphy, J. W., & Pardeck, J. T. (1988). Dehumanization, computers and clinical practice. *Journal of Social Behavior and Personality, 3,* 107–116.

Myrick, R., & Sabella, R. (1995). Cyberspace: A new place for counselor supervision. *Elementary School Guidance and Counseling, 30*(1), 35–44.

National Board of Certified Counselors. (1999). *Code of ethics.* Charlotte, NC: Author.

National Board of Certified Counselors. (2001). *Standards for the ethical practice of Internet Counseling* [Online]. Available: http://www.nbcc.org/ethics/webethics.htm.

National Career Development Association. (1997). *Guidelines for the use of the Internet for provision of career information and planning services.* Columbus, OH: Author.

Newman. R. (2001, March). Professional point: Not a question of 'for' or 'against' *APA Monitor,* 32, (3), 56.

Nickelson, D. W. (1996). Telehealth and the evolving health care system: Strategic opportunities for professional psychology. *Professional Psychology: Research and Practice, 29,* 527–535.

Niemann, H., Ruff, R. M., Baser, C. A. (1990). Computer-assisted attention retraining in head-injured individuals: A controlled efficacy study of an outpatient program. *Journal of Consulting and Clinical Psychology, 58,* 811–817.

Norcross, J. C., Hedges, M., & Prochaska, J. O. (2002). The face of 2010: A Delphi poll on the future of psychotherapy. *Professional Psychology: Research and Practice, 33,* 316–322.

Olcott, D., Jr. (1993). Access to learning: Integrating telecommunications instruction in university extended degree programs. *The Journal of Higher Education, 41,* 16–24.

Park, K., & Lee, S. (1992). A computer-aided aptitude test for predicting flight performance of trainees. *Human Factors, 34,* 189–204.

Peterson, D. B (2003). Ethics and technology. In R. R. Cottone & V. M. Tarvydas, *Ethical and professional issues in counseling* (pp. 169–202). New York: Prentice Hall.

Peterson, D. B., Murray, G., & Chan, F. (1998). Ethics and technology. In R. R. Cottone & V. M. Tarvydas, *Ethical and professional issues in counseling* (pp. 196–235). New York: Prentice Hall.

Peterson, M. (2000). Electronic delivery of career development university courses. In J. W. Bloom & G. R. Walz (Eds.), *Cybercounseling and cyberlearning: Strategies and resources for the millennium* (pp. 143–159). Alexandria, VA: American Counseling Association.

Psychological Corporation. (1997). *Scoring assistant for the Weschler Scales–adult (SAWS–A)* [Computer software]. San Antonio: Author.

Ragusea, A. S. & VandeCreek, L. (2003) Suggestions for the ethical practice of online psychotherapy. *Psychotherapy: Theory, Research, Practice, Training, 40,* 94–102.

Reed, G. M., McLaughlin, C. J., & Milholland, K. (2000). Ten interdisciplinary principles for professional practice in telehealth: Implications for psychology. *Professional Psychology: Research and Practice, 31,* 170–178.

Riley, M., Roehm, F., & Oserman, S. (1996). *The guide to Internet job searching.* Lincolnwood, IL: VGM Career Books.

Rozensky, R. H., Honor, L. F., Rasinski, K., Tovian, S. M., & Hertz, G. I. (1986). Paper-pencil versus computer-administered MMPI's: A comparison of patient's attitudes. *Computers in Human Behavior, 2,* 111–116.

Salyer, S. (1997, July). The dawn of 'virtual therapy' *USA Weekend,* 18–20.

Sampson, J. P., (1986). The use of computer-assisted instruction in support of psychotherapeutic processes. *Computers in Human Behavior, 2,* 1–19.

Sampson, J. P., Jr. (1990). Computer-assisted testing and the goals of counseling psychology. *The Counseling Psychologist, 18,* 227–239.

Sampson, J. P., Jr. (1998). Potential problems and ethical concerns. In J. Harris-Bowlsbey, M. Riley-Kikel, & J. P. Sampson, Jr. (Eds.), *The Internet: A tool for career planning* (pp. 31–37). Columbus, OH: National Career Development Association.

Sampson, J. P., Jr. (2000). Computer applications. In C.E. Watkins, Jr. & V.L. Campbell (Eds.), *Testing and assessment in counseling practice* (2nd ed.) (pp. 517–544). Hillside, NJ: Lawrence Erlbaum.

Sampson, J. P., Jr., Kolodinsky, R. W., & Greeno, B. P. (1997). Counseling on the information highway: Future possibilities and potential problems. *Journal of Counseling & Development, 75,* 203–212.

Sampson, J. P., Jr., & Krumboltz, J. D. (1991). Computer-assisted instruction: A missing link in counseling. *Journal of Counseling and Development, 69,* 395–397.

Sampson, J. P., Jr., Reardon, R. C., Wilde, C. K. Norris, D. S., Peterson, G. W., Strausberger, S. J., et al. (1994). Comparison of the assessment components of 15 computer-assisted career guidance systems. In J. T. Kapes, M. Moran-Mastie, & E. A. Whitfield (Eds.), *A counselor's guide to career assessment instruments* (pp. 373–379). Alexandria, VA: National Career Development Association.

Schinke, S. P., & Orlandi, M. A. (1990). Skills-based, interactive computer interventions to prevent HIV infection among African-American and Hispanic adolescents. *Computers in Human Behavior, 6,* 235–246.

Schinke, S. P., Orlandi, M. A., Gordon, A. N., Weston, R. E., Moncher, M. S., & Parms, C. A. (1989). AIDS prevention via computer-based intervention. *Computer in Human Services, 5,* 147–156.

Schneider, S. J. (1986). Trial of an on-line be-havioral smoking cessation program. *Computers in Human Behavior, 2,* 277–286.

Schneider, S. J., Walter, R., & O'Donnell, R. (1990). Computerized communication as a medium for behavioral smoking cessation treatment: Controlled evaluation. *Computers in Human Behavior, 6,* 141–151.

Schwitzgebel, R. L., & Schwitzgebel, R. K. (1980). *Law and psychological practice.* Toronto: Wiley.

Scriven, B. (1991). Distance education and open learning: Implications for profes-sional development and retraining. *Distance Education, 12,* 297–305.

Selmi, P. M., Klein, M. H., Greist, J. H., Johnson, J. H., & Harris, W. G. (1982). An investigation of computer-assisted cognitive-behavior therapy in the treat-ment of depression. *Behavior Research Methods and Instrumentation, 14,* 181–185.

Selmi, P. M., Klein, M. H., Greist, J. H., Sorell, S. P., & Erdman, H. P. (1990). Computer-administered cognitive-behavioral ther-apy for depression. *American Journal of Psychiatry, 147,* 51–56.

Servan-Schreiber, C., & Binik, Y. M. (1989). Extending the intelligent tutoring system paradigm: Sex therapy as intelligent tu-toring. *Computers in Human Behavior, 5,* 241–259.

Simons, G. (1985). *Silicon shock.* New York: Basil Blackwell.

Sirkin, J. (1994). Learning at a distance. *On Campus, 14*(3), 7–10.

Smith, J. J. (1987). The effectiveness of com-puterized self-help stress coping program with adult males. *Computers in Human Services, 2,* 37–49.

Staff. (1993). *Evaluation consideration for distance learning activities.* Decatur, GA: Southern Association of Colleges and Schools.

Steele, R. L. (1993). Distance learning deliv-ery systems: Instructional options. *Media and Methods, 29*(4), 14.

Stewart, D. (1992). *Student support systems in distance education.* Paper presented at the world conference of the Interna-tional Council for Distance Education, Bangkok, Thailand.

Stocks, T. J., & Freddolino, P. P. (1998). Eval-uation of a World-Wide Web: Overview and basic design principles. *Educational Technology, 37*(3), 7–15.

Stones, M., & Kozma, A. (1989). Multidi-mensional assessment of the elderly via a microcomputer: The SENOTS program and battery. *Psychology and Aging, 4,* 113–118.

Stricker, G. (1996). Psychotherapy in cyber-space. *Ethics and Behavior, 6*(2), 169, 175–177.

Taber, B. J., & Luzzo, D. A. (1999). *A com-prehensive review of research evaluating the effectiveness of DISCOVER in promot-ing career development* (ACT Research Report 99.3). Iowa City, IA: ACT.

Taylor, C. B., Agras, W. S., Losch, M., Plante, T. G., & Burnett, K. (1991). Improving the effectiveness of computer-assisted weight loss. *Behavior Therapy, 22,* 229–236.

U.S. Department of Commerce, National Telecommunications and Information Administration. (1999). *Falling through the net: Defining the digital divide.* Washington, DC: U.S. Government Print-ing Office.

VandeCreek, L., & Knapp, S. (1993). *Tarasoff and beyond: Legal and clinical considera-tions in the treatment of life-endangering patients* (Rev. ed.). Sarasota, FL: Profes-sional Resources Press.

Wagman, M. (1980). PLATO DCS: An inter-active computer system for personal counseling. *Journal of Counseling Psy-chology, 27,* 16–30.

Wagman, M. (1988). *Computer psychother-apy systems.* New York: Gordon and Breach Science Publishers.

Wagman, M., & Kerber, K. W. (1980). PLATO DCS, an interactive computer system for personal counseling: Further development and evaluation. *Journal of Counseling Psy-chology, 27,* 31–39.

Wall, J. E. (2000). Technology-delivered as-sessment: Power, problems, and promise. In. J. W. Bloom & G. R. Walz (Eds.), *Cybercounseling and cyberlearning: Strategies and resources for the millen-nium* (pp. 237–251). Alexandria, VA: American Counseling Association.

Walz, G. R. (1996). Using the I-way for career development. In R. Feller & G. Walz (Eds.), *Optimizing life transitions in tur-bulent times: Exploring work, learning and careers* (pp. 415–427). Greensboro, NC: University of North Carolina, ERIC Clearinghouse on Counseling and Stu-dent Services.

Weiss, D. J. (1985). Adaptive testing by com-puter. *Journal of Consulting and Clini-cal Psychology, 53,* 774–789.

Willis, B. (1992). From a distance. *Educational Technology, 32*(6), 35–37.

Wise, S., & Plake, B. S. (1990). Computerized testing in higher education. *Measurement and Evaluation in Counseling and Development, 23,* 3–10.

Woods, J. F., & Ollis, H. (1996). Labor mar-ket, job information proliferates on-line. *Workforce Journal, 5*(1), 32–44.

Woods, J. F., Ollis, H., & Kaplan, R. (1996). *To spin a web: Job, career, and labor market on the Internet* (Occasional Pa-per No. 8). Washington, DC: National Occupational Information Coordinating Committee.

Wright, J. H., Wright, A. S., Salmon, P., Beck, A. T., Kuykendall, J., Goldsmith, L. J., et al. (2002). Development and initial testing of a multimedia program for computer-assisted cognitive therapy. *American Journal of Psychotherapy, 56,* 76–86.

Wyndowe, J. (1987). The Microcomputerized Diagnostic Interview Schedule: Clinical use in an out-patient setting. *Canadian Journal of Psychiatry, 32,* 93–99.

Youngjohn, J., Larrabee, G., & Crook, T. (1991). First-Last Names and the Grocery List Selective Reminding Test: Two com-puterized measures of everyday verbal learning. *Archives of Clinical Neuropsy-chology, 6,* 287–300.

CHAPTER 11

Ethics and Multiculturalism

Tarrell Awe Agahe Portman

OBJECTIVES

After reading this chapter, you should be able to:

- Discuss the historical scope and importance of multiculturalism in the field of counseling.
- Define multiculturalism and multicultural concepts in counseling.
- Identify critical professional and ethical issues specific to multiculturalism.
- Explain the interrelatedness of ethical decision making and cultural competence.
- Explain how specific ethical concepts are related to multicultural and diversity issues.

INTRODUCTION

"All counseling, and, in fact, all communications are inherently and unavoidably multicultural" (Pedersen, 2001, p. 18). Pedersen made a similar statement in 1987, which used the term cross-cultural counseling. His view has served as the essence of most multicultural dialogue for the past 20 years. **Cross-cultural counseling** is defined as "counseling between individuals from different cultural backgrounds" (Gladding, 2001, p. 34) and has evolved into the term **multicultural counseling,** which is defined as a helping relationship involving two or more individuals with differing socially constructed worldviews (Gladding, Helms & Cook, 1999). The development of multicultural counseling began with attention to counseling services provided by counselors from predominantly majority cultural power groups to oppressed ethnic minority clientele. Since this one-sided beginning, multicultural counseling has evolved into attention on "multicultured" counselors providing services to "multicultured" clientele. For this reason, multiculturalism, with all its various components, is critical in the larger counseling framework, not as a specialty area of the profession but as an integral element of all human interaction. Consideration of multiculturalism and ethics is enmeshed within the self-awareness of each reader. You are encouraged to refer back to the discussions found in Chapter 5 of this text. You may find it helpful to review the basic concepts of values and values in relationships. Indeed, as an essential element for professional inclusion, multiculturalism must be viewed through the personal and professional interactions each professional undertakes (See Box 11–1).

EVOLUTION OF MULTICULTURALISM

Brief Historical Overview

Multiculturalism has evolved from the initial consideration of **culture,** defined as ethnicity and race in testing and assessment procedures, to the intermediate consideration of therapeutic concerns regarding White counselors working with minority clients. Currently, the

212

Box 11–1 • Exploring the Codes

1. How are issues of respecting client rights inclusive of multicultural and diversity perspectives in the ACA, APA, AMHCA, and ASCA codes of ethics?
2. How can a helping professional adhere to ethical codes concerning multiculturalism if they are not practicing in an area with diverse populations?
3. Confidentiality is an important concept in ethics. How will the change in the ACA code of ethics related to respecting client rights be operationalized by practitioners?
4. How are culturally competent professionals considering the ethical issues of engaging in multiple relationships and disclosure of information?
5. What culturally appropriate assessment issues are as considered in the ACA 2005 code of ethics?

concept of **multiculturalism** involves inclusion of all cultures and diverse groups. This evolution began as an ember in the 1950s, addressing issues regarding the significance of culture in the "administration of standard tests" (Jackson, 1995, p. 8). The multicultural fire was fueled by the civil rights movement of the 1960s, which focused attention on how counselors could counsel minority clients who were culturally different, and the neglect of minority issues in counselor preparation programs (Jackson). Multicultural attention began to blaze during the 1970s with more attention to multicultural scholarship, a shift toward inclusion of nonethnic cultural groups, and the creation of a division in the ACA specifically for non-White concerns (currently the Association for Multicultural Counseling and Development, AMCD; Jackson). The 1980s and early 1990s consisted of a controlled fire with a focus on multicultural counseling as a specialty area in the field of counseling (Jackson). By the late 1990s, the flames began to smolder with a few flares of multicultural controversies. Pedersen (2001) described the impact of these controversies on multiculturalism: "The paradigm shift in psychology resulting from these controversies has positioned multiculturalism as a 'fourth force' dimension of psychology and counseling in a historically unique perspective" (p. 18). Thus, multiculturalism began to be represented as the "fourth force" in counseling, holding equal significance with behaviorism, psychodynamism, and humanism as explanations of human behavior (Essandoh, 1996; Pedersen, 2001). Accordingly, a multicultural perspective is seen as "central to the psychodynamic definitions of the conscious, the reinforcing contingencies of behaviorism, and the personal/meaningful comprehension of humanism" (Pedersen, 2001, p. 18).

In the first decade of the 21st century, counselors are witnessing a paradigm rising from the ashes of multiculturalism within the counseling profession. The import of this paradigm is represented through the following commentary by Pedersen (2001):

> One clear indication that multiculturalism is introducing a permanent paradigm shift and not merely a passing fad in counseling is the strength of the multicultural controversies in the field of counseling. By "paradigm shift" I refer to changes in the underlying assumptions about psychology [and counseling] moving from a monocultural to a multicultural basis with profound implications for how psychology [and counseling] is applied in direct service. (p. 15)

QUESTIONS FOR REFLECTION

Take a moment to write down four of your personal fears. Who would you turn to for help facing each of these fears? How might you choose to handle each situation? Now consider four of your friends who are from different cultural backgrounds than your own. To whom might each of your friends turn in the same situations? How might they handle each situation? What are the similarities and differences? After completing the initial task, contemplate how easy or difficult the task was for you. Did you have difficulty selecting friends from culturally different backgrounds? What did you learn about yourself? How will your awareness from this activity transfer to working with clients?

Pedersen (2001) provided a framework of 12 positive advantage statements from his earlier work in support of the multicultural paradigm:

1. Recognizing that all behavior is learned and displayed in a cultural context makes possible accurate assessment, meaningful understanding, and appropriate interventions relative to that cultural context. Interpreting behavior out of context is likely to result in misattribution.

2. People who express similar positive expectations or values through different culturally learned behaviors share the "common ground" that allows them to disagree in their behaviors while sharing the same ultimate positive goal. Not everyone who smiles at you is your friend and not everyone who shouts at you is your enemy.

3. Recognizing the thousands of "culture teachers" each of us has internalized from the friends, enemies, relatives, heroes, heroines, and fantasies helps us understand and identify the sources of our individual identity. As we encounter problems, we are likely to imagine how one or another influential figure we knew might act in a similar situation.

4. Just as a healthy ecosystem requires a diversity in the gene pool, a healthy society requires a diversity of cultural perspectives for its psychological health. By considering many different perspectives in problem solving, we are less likely to overlook the right answer.

5. Recognizing our natural tendency to encapsulate ourselves, cultural diversity protects us from imposing our self-reference criteria inappropriately by challenging our assumptions. We have been taught to "do unto others as you would have them do unto you," imposing our own wants and needs on others.

6. Contact with different cultures provides opportunities to rehearse adaptive functioning skills that will help us survive in the diversified global village of the future. By learning to work with those different from ourselves, we already know we can develop the facility for working with future cultures that we do not yet know.

7. Social justice and moral development require the contrasting cultural perspectives of multiculturalism to prevent any one dominant group from holding the standards of justice hostage. Every social system that has imposed the exclusive will of the dominant culture as the measure of just and moral behavior has ended up being condemned by history.

8. By looking at both similarities and differences at the same time according to the "quantum metaphor," it becomes possible to identify nonlinear alternatives to rigidly absolutist thinking. It is not just the content of our thinking but the very process of thinking itself which can become culturally encapsulated.

9. We are able to continue our learning curve to match the rapid social changes around us by understanding all education as examples of culture shock. We know we have learned something new when we experience a sense of surprise, making education metaphorically similar to a journey.

10. Spiritual completeness requires that we complement our own understanding of Ultimate Reality with the different understandings others have to increase our spiritual completeness. The well-known metaphor that all trails lead to the top of the mountain may indeed apply to our sense of spiritual understanding.

11. The untried political alternative of cultural pluralism provides the only alternative to absolutism on the one hand and anarchy on the other. Our survival in the future will depend on our ability to work with persons who are different from ourselves without sacrificing integrity while at the same time finding common ground.

12. A culture-centered [multicultural] perspective will strengthen the relevance and applicability of psychology by more adequately reflecting the complex and dynamic reality in which we all live. The multicultural perspective resembles the fourth dimension in time as it complements our understanding of three-dimensional space. (pp. 19–20)

These 12 support statements provide a basis for change within the professional counseling organization "meta-worldview" that consists of the collective worldviews of the membership.

Multicultural Terminology

To understand multiculturalism, counselors must have a working understanding of the terminology shifts that have occurred. Terms such as cross-cultural counseling and multicultural counseling have evolved and may be used interchangeably by some authors, but the terms are different. Multicultural counseling may be viewed as the process of professional interaction within a helping relationship. On the other hand, multiculturalism characterizes an individual's or an organization's underlying beliefs, attitudes, and values that are employed for the formulation of attributions of others. **Attributions** are inferences or characteristics assigned to an individual through a "process people use to assign cause and effect to behavior" (Nairne, 1997, p. 592). The assignments of attributions help counselors to explain their own behavior and the experiences of others (Portman, 2001). Perceptions of race, ethnicity, and culture influence the attributions that counselors assign to clients.

QUESTIONS FOR REFLECTION

Consider the following list. Rank each item in the order of importance to you. What factors influenced your rankings? Choose one item and consider what life experiences may have helped in constructing your worldview. Why might someone else have a different ranking from your own? How might the aspirational ethical views of a counselor be influenced by socially constructed worldviews?

1. A sense of belonging to an organized church or temple
2. A respect for older adults and elders
3. A need to be a good representative of your family and community
4. A strong desire to be viewed as independent and self-sufficient
5. A desire to honor others through gift giving

The terms race, ethnicity, and culture have often been used interchangeably (LaFromboise, Foster, & James, 1996). **Race** is an anthropological classification based on physical appearance that some authorities believe should be eliminated from any scholarly discussion on multiculturalism (Gladding, 2001; LaFromboise et al.). **Ethnicity** describes peoples who "share a common origin and a unique social and cultural heritage" (Gladding, p. 45). The term culture accurately articulates the current mindset in the counseling profession. Culture is a psychological construct that is a socially learned set of constructs encompassing "affective styles and values regarding personal control, communication, familial patterns, and societal norms" (Betancourt & Lopez, 1993, p. 631). Similarly, Gladding defined culture as "the shared values, beliefs, expectations, worldviews, symbols, and appropriate behaviors of a group that provide its members with norms, plans, and rules for social living" (p. 34). Differences in such definitions of culture tend to be based on theoretical orientation or internalized value systems. Both definitions agree that culture is the product of social construction to some degree. Each population group has different ways of learning cultural norms and values. Cultural norms may vary both between groups and within groups.

The term **minority** has often been used to describe any identifiable group with differential power and a history of mistreatment (Atkinson & Hackett, 1988; Gladding, 2001; LaFromboise et al., 1996). In earlier literature, the term minority referred to ethnic minority groups in the United States (e.g., African American, American Indian, Asian American, and Hispanic). This terminology has changed to include terms such as *visible racial ethnic groups* and *people of color* (Helms & Cook, 1999). Minority, however, is a mathematical concept. Given the current sociodemographic changes in many communities, traditional minority groups may be the numerical majority, so the term *oppressed populations* may be substituted. However, counselors are reminded that many White ethnic groups were oppressed (e.g., Irish Americans, Polish Americans, Italian Americans, Jews).

Some terminology represents outdated and possibly harmful concepts. Language such as **culturally disadvantaged** and **cultural deficit** was utilized in counselor training programs a few decades ago and may still linger in the minds of counselors and in the archival literature. Currently, these terms are not even listed in *The Counseling Dictionary: Concise Definitions of Frequently Used Terms* (Gladding, 2001). The terms culturally disadvantaged and deficit may cause harm by establishing a psychological assignment of attributions to oppressed group members that inhibits their perceived ability to excel or compete with dominant culture group members. Counselors who embrace a deficit model of interacting with oppressed clients may, in fact, lower their expectations of these clients at the risk of hindering client growth or terminating prematurely. Counselors must recognize these concepts to advocate for their clients.

CASE SCENARIO 11–1

The Counseling Relationship—Client Welfare—Career and Employment Needs

Eduardo is a 38-year-old, self-employed construction worker who has his own roofing crew. He is concerned that he will not be able to continue in his current employment as he ages. He is seeking the help of a career counselor for exploration of possible occupational changes. The counselor explores various skilled labor positions with Eduardo. Eduardo attempts to explain that he has been managing his own roofing business for 18 years, but the counselor ignores his business skills and instead focuses on Eduardo's construction knowledge. Eduardo has the opportunity to purchase an established recycling business with a lucrative clientele and would like to explore his potential skills as a business owner. Without assessing Eduardo's managerial skills, the counselor encourages Eduardo to stay with labor occupations in which other Latinos have been successful. Is the counselor violating any ethical codes by attributing less ability to Eduardo?

YES. The counselor is mandated by ethical codes to work with Eduardo to consider his overall abilities, vocational limitations, physical restrictions, general temperament, interests and aptitude patterns, social skills, education, general qualifications, and other relevant characteristics and needs. The counselor made assumptions because Eduardo is Latino and concluded that Eduardo would not be capable of successfully running his own business. The counselor curtailed exploration of Eduardo's potential based on a cultural deficit perspective.

Counselors must be aware of the linguistic changes within the multicultural literature so as not to misinterpret an author's intended meaning. However, some multicultural terms have remained consistent throughout the literature. One such term is **cultural encapsulation.** Cultural encapsulation was coined by Gilbert Wrenn (1962) and refers to a tendency for people to treat others relative to their own cultural perspective, disregarding important cultural differences. The concept of cultural encapsulation becomes extremely important when examining professional ethical codes and standards due to the process of assigning attributions to clients in determining appropriate treatment or service delivery. If counselors are culturally encapsulated, they view the experiences of their clients through their own socially constructed experiences and perspectives—potentially misattributing client intent and motive. Such professional issues play a significant role in ethical decision making concerning multiculturalism in counseling. Professional counselors must consider their own cultural perspectives, as well as those of their client population. These professional issues hold great significance for the advancement of multiculturalism in counseling.

PROFESSIONAL ISSUES OF SIGNIFICANCE TO MULTICULTURALISM

Professional issues of significance regarding multicultural issues in counseling can be divided into two categories: external and internal factors. External factors are identified as issues that require mandated attention by federal or state governments and influence the sociopolitical structure of American society. Internal factors may include major contributions to the advancement of multiculturalism or issues that may constitute controversies among professional counselors.

External Factors

One of the most challenging political issues to affect multiculturalism in recent years is the change in procedure in the 2000 census conducted by the U.S. Census Bureau. Counseling professionals acknowledged the changing demographic characteristics of the American population long before the 2000 census data were available (Bradt, 1997; Byington, Fischer, Walker, & Freeman, 1997; Pedersen, 1997; Sue, 1996). However, now that the census data are available, the analysis is confounding. Political decisions made by the U.S. Census Bureau changed the manner in which race was reported by the 2000 census. Two changes actually occurred: First, participants were able to select one or more race categories. Second, all respondents were asked if they were of Hispanic or Latino origin. The U.S. government distinguishes between racial groups and Hispanic origin groups. According to the U.S. Census Bureau, "Hispanics may be of any race. The terms 'Hispanic' and 'Latino' are used interchangeably" (Grieco & Cassidy, 2001). Therefore, the numerical information is nondiscrete, or overlapping, in many instances. Counselors must consider the relevance of these changes for the profession—the relevance of any census information for counselors is a matter of preparation to serve possible clientele. Given that counselors are ethically mandated to practice only within the bounds of their competence, they must be proactive in gaining multicultural awareness, knowledge, and skills. Proactive preparation requires being fully informed of potential multicultural client groups. The 2000 census provides such information for counselors.

The Census 2000 data on race provide only descriptive information. Changes in data collection procedures that allowed participants to identify by selecting one or more race categories negate comparison to previous census collections (Grieco & Cassidy, 2001). On the one hand, the change limits using census data to predict population trends. Yet, on the other hand, the descriptive information for multiracial classifications is invaluable for counseling professionals. The census information for all racial groups provides more explicit information that is directly relevant to the counseling profession through the identification of potential multicultural client populations.

Over 281 million people participated in the 2000 census, and 98% identified themselves in the "one race only" categories: White, Black or African American, American Indian and Alaska Native, Asian, Native Hawaiian and Other Pacific Islander, and some other race. Three quarters (75%) of the total group identified themselves as White. The remaining "one race" categories were reported as Black or African American (12%), Asian (4%), American Indian or Alaska Native (0.9%), Native Hawaiian and Other Pacific Islander (0.1%), and some other race (5.5%). The majority of respondents in the "some other race" category were of Hispanic origin (97%)—not considered a standard

TABLE 11–1   Census 2000 Respondents Identifying in the Two or More Race Category

Category	Percentage
White/American Indian and Alaska Native	15.9%
White/Asian	12.7%
White/Black or African American	11.5%
Black or African American/American Indian and Alaska Native	2.7%
White/some other race	32.3%

Source: From E. M. Grieco and R. C. Cassidy. (2001). *Overview of race and Hispanic origin: Census brief 2000.* (Issue Brief No. CZKBe/OH). Washington, DC: U.S. Department of Commerce.

Office of Management and Budget (OMB) race category (Grieco & Cassidy, 2001). These population figures are relevant for counseling professionals because they provide an overview of general clientele possibilities. The need to consider each of these recognized racial groups as potential clients holds relevance for counselor preparation programs for inclusion in the curriculum.

The most relevant findings for counselors may be in the clear identification of respondents in the "two or more races" category. The reporting of multiple racial identification categories in the 2000 census is a major contribution to multiculturalism. Over 6 million people, or 2.4% of the population, identified themselves as being multiracial (Grieco & Cassidy, 2001). These multiracial categories provide much needed insight for the profession concerning implications for future research. The percentages of people in each multiracial classification are noted in Table 11–1. These five categories listed in Table 11–1 account for 75% of all people who identified themselves as multiracial. Census participants selected a combination of two racial identities predominantly over multiracial options. Therefore, counselors must increase their multicultural competence specifically with biracial populations to practice within their boundaries of competence. Counselors must be aware both in practice and in research that attention must be given to biracial individuals' concerns.

Members of the counseling profession must not overlook the importance of the U.S. government descriptions of racial and ethnic groups. The U.S. OMB has designated the five "one race" categories (White, Black or African American, American Indian and Alaska Native, Asian, and Native Hawaiian and Other Pacific Islander) and the four biracial categories (White/American Indian and Alaska Native, White/Asian, White/Black or African American, and Black or

African American/American Indian or Alaska Native) for civil rights monitoring and enforcement (Grieco & Cassidy, 2001).

The exclusion of Latino populations as a racial category in the 2000 census is a professional advocacy issue of relevance to counselors. Attention to this social justice concern may prevent unfair treatment of Latino populations in the future. Therefore, the exclusion of a Hispanic/Latino classification as a racial category needs to be monitored for social advocacy in the counseling profession.

Counselors have an ethical responsibility for multicultural awareness to develop their social advocacy skills and to ensure the welfare of multicultural clients. They must foster active, participatory awareness for informed decision making and promote client welfare. Overall, the majority of external factors may be beyond the control of counselors, but internal factors are open to change within the profession.

Internal Factors

Internal factors are conditions found within the counseling profession that influence multicultural delivery of services. These conditions may promote or impede counselors from fully embracing a multicultural perspective. Four internal factors have been selected to represent current conditions found within the counseling profession: (1) inclusion versus exclusion of population groups, (2) cultural encapsulation, (3) transitioning to new ethical standards, and (4) training issues.

Inclusion Versus Exclusion of Population Groups. Multiculturalism embraces members of ethnic and diverse populations. The inclusion or exclusion of specific population groups is a major internal factor that affects the counseling profession. The question is, "Whom does the profession include under the umbrella of multiculturalism?"

QUESTIONS FOR REFLECTION

1. How does multiculturalism and ethics converge in profession practice?
2. What direction do the ethical codes provide to help professionals become culturally competent?
3. If I don't have exposure to certain cultural groups, how can I become competent?
4. What are the requirements for professional practitioners referring a client based on lack of cultural competence with a particular cultural group?
5. How does a professional adhere to ethical codes and standards of practice that are contradictory to non-majority cultural norms?

6. How does a professional resolve issues of personal religious values that oppose acceptance of diverse sexual orientations and uphold codes of ethics?
7. If a professional fully embraces diversity in perspective and cultural ideology, does this mean a client with a "racist worldview" is protected by ethical codes?
8. Can ethical codes written by members of the dominant majority truly be bias free?
9. Is multiculturalism as an ethical issue a sociopolitical passing fad?
10. Should cultural competence be considered as a gatekeeping assessment in professional preparation programs?
11. As an activity in viewing organizational change, compare the 1995 ACA Code of Ethics and the 2005 ACA Code of Ethics. What changes were made? What would be your opinion on how adequate these changes are?

A controversy does exist within the counseling profession related to the inclusion of diverse viewpoints. This controversy is represented in the following excerpt:

> There are those who would like to define culture broadly to include race, ethnicity, class, affectional orientation, religion, sex, age, and so forth. As such, multicultural counseling would include not only racial and ethnic minorities, but also women, gays and lesbians, and other special populations. There are those who prefer to limit the discussion of multicultural counseling to what has been referred to as "Visible Racial Ethnic Minority Groups"—African Americans, American Indians, Asian Americans, and Hispanics and Latinos. Those who hold this point of view acknowledge that to some extent all counseling is cross-cultural, but the term can be defined so broadly that it dilutes the focus on racial and ethnic concerns (a primary one being racism) and allows counseling professionals to avoid and omit dealing with the four major groups in our society. (Sue, Arredondo, & McDavis, 1992, pp. 477–478)

This debate is well documented in the literature (Arredondo & Toporek, 2004; Gladding, 2001; Patterson, 2004; Pedersen, 2001; Sue et al., 1992; Thomas & Weinrach, 2004; Vontress & Jackson, 2004; Weinrach & Thomas, 2004). In particular controversy over the AMCD Multicultural Counseling Competencies, Weinrach and Thomas (2002) confronted implications of requiring practicing counselors to be multiculturally competent. This one article led to a special issue of the *Journal of Mental Health Counseling*, addressing embracing the Multicultural Counseling Competencies (Pistole, 2004).

Practicing counselors can be affected either overtly or covertly by this controversy as they begin to gain multicultural competence. Overt influences can occur through professional literature or training programs that embrace an exclusionary view of multiculturalisms, which considers only ethnicity as a criterion. Covert influences can occur through exposure to professional growth opportunities, wherein facilitators do not provide a disclaimer regarding their views of inclusion or exclusion of specific groups. Counselors should be aware of the multicultural theoretical continuum that has dichotomous endpoints. A multicultural theoretical continuum presented by Stone (1997) has endpoints ranging from inclusion of only the four major American ethic groups to inclusion of all diverse groups (e.g., people with disabilities, sexual orientation, religion). Counselors must be knowledgeable consumers when presented with multicultural information and resource materials so they can properly interpret and transfer their knowledge to the appropriate clientele. Proponents on both sides of the controversy have valid points. However, ethical codes are relevant for every client, not just a few. Counselors must apply the ethical codes in all circumstances regardless of their underlying theoretical beliefs on who is to be included in multicultural dialogues based on the degree of historical oppression, prejudice, or discrimination faced by their clients' ancestors. Whatever the outcome of this debate among counseling professionals, the reality of the circumstances supported by the 2000 U.S. census is that clients from diverse "ethnographic, demographic, status and affiliational" (Pedersen, 2001, p. 17) backgrounds will present themselves to counselors for services.

Cultural Encapsulation. The concept of cultural encapsulation is not new to the counseling profession as an internal factor. In this view, the counselor embraces and imposes only one set of assumptions that are based on dominant cultural values as being universal, disregarding any cultural variations or influences that may impact client progress (Pedersen, 2001; Wrenn, 1962).

Forty years after Wrenn (1962) coined the term, cultural encapsulation continues to be evident, as described by the following passage:

> The Basic Behavioral Science Task Force of the National Advisory Mental Health Council (1996) in their national plan for behavioral science research identified areas where cultural encapsulation continues to be evident in mental health services. First, anthropological and cross-cultural research has demonstrated that cultural beliefs influence diagnosis and treatment. Second, diagnosis of mental illness differs across cultures. Third, individuals express symptoms differently in each cultural context. Fourth, culturally biased variations in diagnosis follow

the diagnostic categories relevant to the majority population. Fifth, most providers come from majority cultures while most clients come from minority cultures. (Pedersen, 2001, p. 17)

Cultural encapsulation also continues to impact research and training programs (Lonner & Ibrahim, 1996; Paniagua, 1994; Ponterotto, 1988). Even ethical standards are viewed as being culturally encapsulated in dominant culture values (LaFromboise et al., 1996; Pedersen, 1995).

Cultural encapsulation, as an internal factor, may be the most predominant deterrent to the implementation of multiculturalism within the profession. Just as racism can be intentional or unintentional, so too can cultural encapsulation. Yet, even if it is unintentional, the direct delivery of counseling services can be affected (Pedersen, 2001; Ridly, 1995)—for example, treating all people the same regardless of cultural background or the multicultural concept of color blindness.

CASE SCENARIO 11–2

The counseling Relationship—Positive Growth and Development

A 38-year-old female counselor (Irish American, fourth generation) is providing counseling services to Betsy, a 34-year-old female client (Asian American, first generation). Betsy is an only child and resides with her aging parents. Betsy is self-referred. Her presenting issue is difficulty with decision making related to her career as a teacher. Betsy is considering a career change to cosmetology but knows this will upset her parents, who take great pride that their daughter is an American teacher. The counselor encourages Betsy to explore her options in cosmetology. However, the counselor expresses a concern that Betsy's difficulty in making decisions is related to her lack of autonomy from her parents. The counselor begins to explore alternative living arrangements that will help Betsy develop independence. Should the counselor encourage independence and growth that, in the counselor's view, is fostering the client's interest and welfare?

NO. Although the ACA ethics code clearly indicates a counseling relationship involves the counselor encouraging "client growth and development in ways that foster the client's interest and welfare," in a multicultural situation this code is in direct contradiction with the code on "respecting differences." This counselor did not stop and actively pursue information about the client's cultural belief system related to family. The counselor also may have been imposing a dominant worldview upon the client, which embraces independence and autonomy from family that may not be shared in an Asian American worldview. The counselor needs to explore her own values and beliefs related to family and to the possibility of being culturally encapsulated in dominant

cultural values. Culturally competent counselors must be aware of their own biases that may unconsciously enter the counseling relationship.

Transitioning to New Ethical Standards.   Unclear or inadequate inclusion of the language of multiculturalism in professional organization ethical codes and standards of practice has been the norm for many years and requires immediate attention (Bradt, 1997 Pedersen, 1997, 2001). In fact, many assert a serious discrepancy exists between the cultural contexts in which the ethical codes and standards are being applied and the cultural context in which the codes were created (Ivey, 1987; LaFromboise et al., 1996; Pedersen, 1997). This discrepancy was evident in patterns of systematic cultural bias in the 1995 ACA ethics code. As Sue et al. (1992) stated, "Too often, lip service is given to multicultural concerns, without the commitment to translate them into ethical standards and see that they become part of the accreditation criteria" (p. 480).

A limited pattern consisting of three primary concerns emerged from the literature on the need for inclusion of multiculturalism in codes of ethics. Several conclusions were drawn from this analysis:

1. Codes of ethics do not include specific language related to multiculturalism, except superficially. Therefore, the import of counselor inclusion of multicultural concerns is diminished (Bradt, 1997; Pedersen, 1997, 2001; Sue et al., 1992).
2. Codes provide implicit direction related to multiculturalism, which leads practitioners to determine their own interpretations of multicultural competence (Ponterotto & Casas, 1991). Explicit guidelines are not available to practitioners nor to legal authorities determining ethical conduct related to multiculturalism.
3. The codes themselves are framed from a majority worldview stemming primarily from an individualistic perspective (Pedersen, 2001).

In response to these calls for inclusion of multicultural and diverse perspectives in codes of ethics, the ACA Ethics Committee examined the code for its "multicultural content and sensitivity" and made revisions. The resulting 2005 ACA Code of Ethics integrates multicultural and diversity issues throughout. In particular, the 2005 ACA Code of Ethics references cultural consideration to confidentiality and privacy issues, assessment, supervision, curricular infusion, recruitment of diverse faculty and students, and research considerations. In addition, several of the previous guidelines were changed to be more multiculturally sensitive in areas of multiple relationships and beneficial interactions, receiving gifts, cultural alternatives to assisting clients, developmental and cultural sensitivity, and culturally responsive consulting.

Training Issues. After the civil rights movement, counselor training programs were openly criticized for not providing students with the opportunity to learn how to work with multicultural clientele (Jackson, 1995). In fact, the July 1973 APA's conference at Vail, Colorado, provided the impetus for addressing ethical behavior in multicultural counseling through a resolution that suggested that counselors who are not trained or competent to provide services to culturally diverse clients but do so are behaving unethically (Korman, 1974; Pedersen & Marsella, 1982).

The attention from this scholarly dialogue led to the inclusion of multicultural training standards by accreditation bodies such as APA, CACREP, and CORE and eventually to the creation of multicultural competency guidelines through ACA and AMCD. Accrediting standards require multicultural training. Recent research has demonstrated the effectiveness of training in enhancing multicultural competence (Byington et al., 1997). Many training programs offer only one course in multicultural counseling. Others may offer none at all, choosing to opt for an infusion of multicultural issues into the curriculum. It may be both necessary to offer a specific course as well as infuse multicultural content into the curriculum to provide trained, culturally competent counselors to the field. However, accrediting boards recognize few programs, and the programs that are unaccredited are not required to follow the accreditation criterion. The 2005 ACA Code of Ethics incorporates the explicit need for infusion of multicultural content in all training programs. Therefore, the significance of ethical codes becomes more important in ensuring the welfare of multicultural clients.

ISSUES OF SIGNIFICANCE TO MULTICULTURALISM

Ethics

Multicultural professional interaction is becoming pervasive; however, ethical codes and standards of practice of professional organizations may not be adequately inclusive of multiculturalism. The implicit nature of the current ethical codes creates an atmosphere of implied choice and lack of commitment by professional organizations to multiculturalism as a mandated area of concern for counselors (Pedersen, 1997). In essence, implied ethical standards are not enforceable in grievance processes, which limits the profession's ability to protect consumers from being harmed by incompetent multicultural practices. Yet, as these codes are being revised, the current standards serve as guidelines in counselors' professional training and service delivery to all clients.

Each professional must carefully examine the codes and standards necessary to increase counselor awareness of multicultural competency. So, how does a practitioner begin to align implied ethical guidelines with multicultural service delivery?

Basic ethics need to be revisited so that a discussion of basic, ethical decision making can occur (Herlihy & Corey, 1996). Ethical decision making requires reexamination of the distinction between the concepts of mandatory and aspirational ethics. Herlihy and Corey distinguished between mandatory ethics, meaning to function according to minimum legal standards, and aspirational ethics, meaning to function at a higher standard in accordance with the spirit behind the literal meaning of the code. By ascribing to aspirational ethical standards in multicultural counseling, counselors identify fundamental values while recognizing that different cultures may express those values through their own culturally learned behaviors. The expression of learned cultural behaviors surfaces as the basic foundation of multiculturalism. The basic premise involves respecting different cultural worldviews. Accepting a diversity of worldviews and opinions leads to a quandary in ethical decision making—how can a profession mandate respecting diversity and yet clearly establish enforceable behavioral codes of conduct that respect every diverse opinion? Thus, the dilemma of multiculturalism and ethics exists in both mandatory and aspirational ethics. When does the organizational worldview take precedence over the individual practitioner's worldview?

The circular loop created in multicultural ethics may be best served through a discussion on principle and virtue ethics. Jordan and Meara (1990) distinguished between principle and virtue ethics. Principle ethics focuses on rational, objective, universal, and impartial principles mandating actions and choices. Virtue ethics focuses on the counselor's motives, intentions, character, and ethical consciousness. Virtue ethics recognizes the need to interpret principles differently in each cultural context. This complexity in ethical consideration is compounded by the intricacy of cultural worldviews, which may place different levels of importance on the hierarchy of mandatory, aspirational, principle, and virtue ethics. Therefore, clear statements regarding multicultural context and professional responsibility must emerge within future ethical codes. Ponterotto and Casas (1991) highlighted four philosophical premises necessary to translate ethical theory: (1) altruism, (2) responsibility, (3) justice, and (4) caring. These premises assist counselors in making "more purposive and intentional" ethical decisions in multicultural settings (Pedersen, 1995, p. 37).

Pedersen and Marsella (1982) called for "responsible disobedience" of ethical guidelines in multicultural situations that require adherence to the underlying ethical principles represented by specific ethical guidelines at the expense of respect for cultural diversity.

Helms and Cook (1999) actually acknowledged they had instituted responsible disobedience in varying from current ethical standards in multicultural counseling situations. Their statement is presented here as an indication of how counselors must justify reconciling their professional judgments and values with the existing codes of ethics. Helms and Cook stated:

> Some readers may have already reported us to their professional ethics boards for some of the therapeutic practices that we have recommended thus far. However, although we may have straddled the ethical boundaries a bit, we do not believe that we have actually crossed any of them. Perhaps our most distressing recommendation for traditionally trained psychologists is our suggestion that having contact with clients outside of therapy is appropriate. Some of them may argue that such behavior constitutes multiple relationships with clients. The other place therapists sometimes have trouble with our therapy approach is our recommendation that therapists practice fluid terminations when necessary for the client's benefit . . . Our approach merely attempts to ensure that the client does not feel abandoned. (p. 195)

Helms and Cook conducted a deliberate analysis of the ethical codes related to potentially detrimental relationships and respecting diversity. This example of processing ethical codes related to multiculturalism proves a valuable method of self-regulation needed in the profession. Counselors must be cautious in their execution of responsible disobedience or the ethical codes will become diluted and nonfunctioning. Counselors must make a professional decision when one ethical guideline aligns against another. The most efficient outcome will be a congruent set of ethical standards. One strategy for resolving these issues is to use an ethical decision-making model.

Ethical Standards*

Strong (1986), as cited in Sue et al. (1992), defined a multicultural organization as "one which is genuinely committed to diverse representation of its membership; is sensitive to maintaining an open, supportive, and responsive environment; is working toward and purposefully including elements of diverse cultures in its ongoing operations; and one which is authentic in its response to issues confronting it" (p. 7). Organizational systems reflect their collective members' values, attitudes, and beliefs. These factors cycle between the organizational governing principles and the actual behavior and practice of the membership. Thus, change or cyclical movement may occur when the membership begins to express dissatisfaction with current standards or policies. Indeed, this may be ongoing or enmeshed in a paradigmatic shift within the counseling profession—such as that now occurring with multiculturalism in counseling.

The ACA Code of Ethics and Standards of Practice approved by the governing council in April 1995 was a historic move toward inclusion of multicultural statements. Sections on respecting diversity, public responsibility, and relationships with other professionals clearly articulate the language of nondiscrimination and sexual harassment, and respecting cultural differences in an inclusive manner. However, some authors point out there is room for improvement. Pedersen (1995) and Sue (1996) are probably the strongest proponents for multicultural consideration in ethical codes of the counseling profession. Weaknesses exist in both the APA and the ACA ethical guidelines, according to Pedersen (1995). He noted that the ethical codes "lack explicit philosophical principles, assume a dominant culture perspective, and generally minimize or trivialize the role of culture in ethical decision making" (Pedersen, 1995, p. 42).

Pedersen (1995, 1997, 2001) called for organizational change in the area of ethics for the counseling profession. His insight serves as an impetus for change. Pedersen stated that the ACA ethical standards

---

* The ethical standards and code comparisons discussed here are meant to accentuate the strengths and weaknesses in ethics codes in general, even though the 1995 ACA and the 1992 APA codes are discussed to illustrate specific issues. This is not an exhaustive overview of these standards, but merely a general analysis of these codes. It is a useful exercise because these are historic documents that represent the first major attempts by these organizations to infuse multicultural content into their codes. Even as revised codes may be enacted in the future, the same concerns will be relevant to evaluating the multicultural sensitivity of these new documents.

contain a fundamental notion that "what is good for the counselor is good for everyone" (p. 46). This stance forces clients to be at the professional whim of their counselors. According to Pedersen, the ethical codes show a discriminatory bias similar to cultural encapsulation, accompanied by a one-dimensional application of the codes to cultural concerns and an absolute standard for right and wrong (Pedersen, 1995). The "one size fits all" perspective is unacceptable according to the 1995 ACA and 1992 APA codes of ethics, as can be read in both preambles. The 2005 ACA code of ethics is an example of how professional organizations can begin the process of integrating multicultural and diversity issues into the framework of the codes.

CASE SCENARIO 11–3

Research Responsibilities—Use of Human Subjects
A counselor educator joins a student in researching developmental issues of African American children. The researchers have determined that a convenience sampling of children living in a low-income housing unit with a resident population that is 98% African American would be a good source for research participants. The counselor educator contacts the social worker who works with the residents to set up a time to present the study. The social worker informs the researchers that a mandatory meeting has already been scheduled to discuss housing regulations, and the research study could be presented at that time. Should the researchers agree to this mandatory meeting?

NO. There are multiple considerations with this scenario. First, research participation should always be voluntary. Second, a convenience sampling that narrows the participant pool to one small segment of a population is not representative of the general population of African American children. Therefore, the researchers need to consider expanding the research sample to be more representative so as not to add misinformation or overgeneralize findings that may encourage further stereotyping of a cultural group.

Counselors must reexamine the ethical codes and standards of practice by viewing each guideline through the lenses of multiculturalism. Examples of ethical codes and standards that require reexamination fall within five major areas of concern: (1) implicit cultural bias, (2) cultural encapsulation, (3) favoritism toward the dominant culture, (4) issues of professional self-regulation, and (5) a lack of measurable multicultural accountability (LaFromboise et al., 1996; Pedersen, 1995; Sue, 1996).

Implicit Cultural Bias. Implicit cultural bias in codes of ethics may be represented in the preamble and sections on client welfare, multiple relationships, confidentiality, and evaluation and assessment. For instance, the 1995 ACA Code of Ethics preamble stated: "Association members recognize diversity in our society and embrace a cross-cultural approach in support of the worth, dignity, potential, and uniqueness of each individual" (p. 1). This statement implied an individualistic perspective over a collectivistic worldview (Pedersen, 1995). Under client welfare concerning a discourse on counseling plans, counselors are to respect the client's "freedom of choice." The implication of freedom based on individual choice leans heavily toward an individualistic cultural perspective (Pedersen, 1995). Many collectivistic cultural worldviews base personal choice on the potential consequences experienced by the cultural or familial group. The sections in professional organization codes regarding multiple relationships may also ignore the relational values often present in collectivistic cultures (Pedersen, 1995; Sue, 1996). Professional code sections on confidentiality and evaluation, assessment, and interpretation contain generic, well-meaning statements concerning client rights but need to specifically address multicultural and diversity issues. However, in some codes multicultural consideration is only implied and attention to collectivistic cultural differences is not explicit (Pedersen, 1995). These statements have been changed in the 2005 version of the ACA code, which stands as a good illustration for other committees working on ethical codes.

Cultural Encapsulation. Cultural encapsulation permeated the 1995 ACA Code of Ethics and standards. A few examples can be found in sections on nondiscrimination, cultural sensitivity, and research and publication. On the one hand, the nondiscrimination section contains the necessary aspirational statement requesting counselors to respect diversity by attacking discrimination based on an inclusive population multicultural perspective. Yet, on the other hand, this same section does not acknowledge that the counselor needs to appreciate that there may be "simultaneous cultural affiliations" such as in a combination of identities that suffer from discrimination (Pedersen, 1997, p.25). An example would be a fundamental Protestant man who is African American and gay. Counselors must acknowledge the potential for multiple oppression and discrimination of such a client. Counselors must also be aware that their own biases may be confounded in situations wherein clients hold simultaneous cultural affiliations. A similar situation related to counselor roles may occur. The ethical code section on potentially detrimental relationships asserts, "If it becomes apparent that counselors may be called upon to perform potentially conflicting roles, they clarify, adjust or withdraw from roles appropriately" (ACA, 2005, p. 3). In multicultural situations in a collectivistic culture or possibly in geographically diverse situations, roles may overlap and "role diffusion" may be unavoidable (Pedersen, 1997, p. 25). A clear, behaviorally specific statement that outlines expectations could provide much needed guidance in the area of potentially detrimental relationships and collectivistic cultural situations.

Favoritism Toward Dominant Cultural Worldviews. Favoritism toward a dominant worldview is prevalent within codes of ethics and professional training programs, as illustrated in sections relating to personal needs and values of counselors, bartering, and boundaries of professional competence. Counselors' self-awareness concerning their worldview (i.e., values, attitudes, beliefs, and behavior) and its potential effects on diverse clients, as indicated under the section of personal needs and values, provides an example of favoritism toward the dominant culture (Pedersen, 1997). Three factors affect the intent of this ethical code: (1) a low level of cultural self-awareness among counselors, (2) an inability of counselors with low cultural self-awareness to realize their limitations, and (3) counseling practice being heavily weighted in culturally encapsulated values (Pedersen, 1997; Ridley, 1995).

Bartering is discouraged in the ethical codes. The discouragement of bartering favors a monetary economic system based on dominant culture, which may hold different meanings for clients based on their status or cultural background (Pedersen, 1997). An implied consent is integrated into the code making bartering a possibility when the relationship is not exploitive. This again places the responsibility on the counselor to make the determination. However, this guideline may be one example of clear, measurable behavioral guidelines related to counselors participating in a bartering relationship: client request, nonexploitive relationship, clear written contract, and accepted practice in the community. Counselors would benefit if other guidelines held such content.

Issues of Professional Self-Regulation. Professional self-regulation allows counselors the opportunity to monitor their own multicultural behaviors. This may encourage counselors to continue unintentional racism, discrimination, and imposition of their own worldviews when working with clients. Some codes of ethics

assume counselors will be self-regulatory. An examination of several APA codes helps to clarify these issues. One of the general principles is the respect for people's rights and dignity. This principle challenges APA membership to respect client rights in multiple areas and to self-regulate by not knowingly engaging in "unfair discriminatory practices" (APA, 2002). The use of the word "unknowingly" provides a loophole for unintentional racism, discrimination, and imposition of the counselor's worldview. This principle may even appear incongruent with the APA standards on boundaries of competence. However, the boundaries of competence standards contain no language directly related to multicultural competence. Other ethical standards such as those on human differences, nondiscrimination, harassment, and multiple relationships are implied, but are associated with multiculturalism and contain multicultural language for self-regulatory purposes. Thus, counselors must examine implied meanings instead of applying actual guidelines to specific multicultural cases or personal practice.

The APA endorsed guidelines for provision of psychological services to ethnic, linguistic, and culturally diverse populations (APA, 1993; see Appendix J). These guidelines provide a solid foundation for APA members in multicultural awareness and competence; however, they are a separate set of guidelines from the ethical code and therefore appear to be aspirational in nature.

CASE SCENARIO 11–4

Professional Responsibility—Nondiscrimination
Sarah is a school counselor at an affluent elementary school. She has been conducting small groups successfully for 5 years. Parents have been willing to give permission for their children to participate in the groups and often keep Sarah informed of their children's developmental needs. Recently, a group foster home was established within the school district's boundary area. One child from the foster home was selected to participate in a fifth-grade friendship group. A parent called to complain about her child being in a group with "one of those poor kids" and asked that the child from the foster home be removed from her daughter's group. The counselor requested an appointment with the parent to discuss the issue face to face. The parent agreed. At the meeting, the counselor explained her ethical obligation concerning nondiscrimination as a public and professional responsibility. The counselor listened to the parent's complaints. Did the counselor behave in an ethical manner?

YES. The school counselor must serve the needs of every child in her building in a manner that is nondiscriminatory. Socioeconomic status is a diversity issue that is often overlooked.

The counselor listened to the concerns of the parent without imposing her beliefs on the parent and stated her professional responsibilities. The parent maintained the right to refuse services by requesting her child be removed from the group. However, the counselor may have an ethical responsibility to be an advocate for the children in the foster home if this parent's attitude is a reflection of the community at large.

Another critique of ethical codes is the need for specific behaviorally observable statements of competencies or practices that give clear guidance and are enforceable by ethics boards. In 1982, Pedersen and Marsella brought attention to the ethical dilemma in multicultural counseling service delivery. Almost 20 years later, the counseling profession is beginning to reassess ethics related to multiculturalism. This movement appears to be emerging from within the membership. In 1992, AMCD, a division of ACA, published *Multicultural Counseling Competencies and Standards* as a means of providing guidance for counseling professionals (see Appendix K). These multicultural competencies clearly indicate a positive move in the profession. However, professional members of divisional groups of ACA continue to present the need to add explicit statements in ethical codes and standards of practice related to multiculturalism (Burn, 1992; McGinn, Flowers, & Rubin, 1993; Tarvydas & Cottone, 2000). A clear mandate was presented in the 1995 ACA Code of Ethics that: "Counselors practice only within the boundaries of their competence, based on their education, training, supervised experience, state and national professional credentials, and appropriate professional experience. Counselors will demonstrate a commitment to gain knowledge, personal awareness, sensitivity, and skills pertinent to working with a diverse client population" (ACA, 1995, p. 7). This was a positive statement and possibly the strongest multicultural statement in the entire 1995 code. The 2005 ACA Code of Ethics is strengthened by a focus on professional values, as in this preamble statement:

> Professional values are an important way of living out an ethical commitment. Values inform principles. Inherently held values that guide our behaviors or exceed prescribed behaviors are deeply ingrained in the counselor and developed out of personal dedication, rather than the mandatory requirement of an external organization (ACA, 2005).

However, organizations must demonstrate a commitment to multiculturalism to its membership (Sue et al., 1992). This commitment to multiculturalism can be shown in multiple ways: (1) a clear articulation of specific, measurable, behavioral statements of competencies or practices in the ethical codes that provide well-structured guidance to counseling practitioners; (2) the enforcement of multicultural aspects of the codes of ethics in a manner that indicates a solid commitment to multiculturalism by ethics boards; and (3) a strong statement denouncing cultural encapsulation as an accepted practice among helping professionals prominently presented in the preamble and throughout ethical standards.

DECISION MAKING MODELS IN CONTEXT

There are several established ethical decision-making models available to helping professionals (Corey, Corey, & Callanan, 2003; Cottone, 2001; Forester-Miller & Davis, 1996; Hill, Glaser, & Harden, 1995; Keith-Spiegel & Koocher, 1985; Stadler, 1986; Steinman, Richardson, & McEnroe, 1998; Tarvydas, 2004; Welfel, 1998). This author embraces Cottone's Social Constructivism Model of Ethical Decision Making when considering multicultural concerns.

A social constructivist model provides professionals with a framework for exploring their beliefs, values, and worldviews through accumulated knowledge. When an individual acknowledges a social constructivist frame of reference, they may embrace not only the principle of social construction but of social deconstruction or reconstruction as a systemic lifespan development issue. This normalizes self-reflective practices of examining bias, prejudice, and oppressive behaviors.

The social constructivism model of ethical decision making encourages an interpersonal process of consensualizing, and if necessary, may include negotiation and arbitration. Consensualizing is a reciprocal focused discourse involving a minimum of two individuals. The process is inclusive of verbal and nonverbal language, behavior and actions, and in some cases reflecting in silence. (An in-depth discussion of the social constructivism model can be found in Chapter 6.) The following multicultural dilemma is presented as an illustration in applying the social constructivism ethical decision-making model.

Jan, a Norwegian female counselor has been working with John Robert, a Quapaw male lineman for a month. His presenting issue for counseling was his dissatisfaction with his career. John Robert has expressed that this dissatisfaction has to do with paying child support for his five children. The children are living in three different homes with their mothers or grandmothers. When John Robert wishes to discuss this with Jan, he is quickly redirected to focus on his individual career needs. John Robert expresses anger in these moments and accuses Jan of not being culturally sensitive to his needs. He wishes to speak with Quapaw elders to seek advice on cultural methods of handling his frustrations with his career and still representing the tribe as a father. He has asked Jan to allow a Quapaw elder to attend a session with him. Jan refuses, but in further discussion [negotiation] with John Robert agrees to speak to her supervisor and check the ethical codes [consultation with expert opinion]. Jan seeks consultation from her clinical supervisor, Tom [consultation with colleagues]. Tom suggests that the main reason not to bring the elder into a session would be confidentiality; however, if John Robert will sign a waiver, the elder could be considered as an indigenous helper. Tom and Jan agree to meet with John Robert and discuss the issue surrounding confidentiality. Consensus is reached and John Robert signs the waiver to involve the Quapaw elder. An appointment is made to meet with the elder at the tribal administration center [consultation with colleagues].

CHAPTER SUMMARY

Multicultural counseling must be grounded in the underlying premise of multiculturalism. It is the ethical responsibility of helping professionals to provide services to all clients either individually or in groups in a competent manner sensitive to the multiple cultural perspectives of those clients and in a manner that is not biased by the counselor's own multiple cultural perspectives. This ethical responsibility also is assumed by the larger professional organizations and their divisions. These professional organizations must articulate to their memberships that multiculturalism is a necessary assessment criterion for determining client treatment or interventions.

Historically, multiculturalism has been viewed as a separate specialty area in several of the professional helping fields. However, the current multicultural movement appears to be elevating multiculturalism to an equal dimensional status with the movements of behaviorism, psychodynamics, and humanism. This professional stance provides impetus for the increased importance of multiculturalism in the lives of clients and counselors.

The lack of a mutually agreed-upon definition for multiculturalism is a major hindrance to the counseling profession. It is critical for codes of ethics and standards of practice to be explicit in their articulation of multicultural issues so that both mandatory and aspirational ethics may be applied. Given the current revisiting of ethics codes in relation to multicultural integration, the future may hold more inclusive guidelines for helping professions. Multiculturalism in any organization is a separate level of discourse, and scholarly research is needed on this topic within each profession.

REFERENCES

American Counseling Association. (2005). *The ACA Code of Ethics.* Alexandria, VA: Author.

American Counseling Association. (1995). *ACA Code of Ethics and Standards of Practice.* Alexandria, VA: Author.

American Counseling Association. (1991, April). *Multicultural competencies.* Retrieved December 18, 2001, from http://www.counseling.org/multi_diversity/competencies.htm.

American Psychological Association (2002). *Ethical Principles of Psychologists and Code of Conduct.* Washington, D.C.: Author.

American Psychological Association. (1990, August). *Guidelines for provision of psychological services to ethnic, linguistic and culturally diverse populations.* Retrieved December 18, 2001, from http://www.apa.org/pi/guide.html.

American Psychological Association. (1993). Guidelines for providers of psychological services to ethnic, linguistic, and culturally diverse populations. *American Psychologist, 48,* 45–48.

Arredono, P., & Toporek, R. (2004). Multicultural counseling competencies=Ethical practice. *Journal of Mental Health Counseling, 26,* 44–55.

Atkinson, D. R., & Hackett, G. (1988). *Counseling non-ethnic American minorities.* Springfield, IL: Charles C. Thomas.

Betancourt, H., & Lopez, S. R. (1993). The study of culture, ethnicity, and race in American psychology. *American Psychologist, 48,* 629–637.

Bradt, J. (1997). Ethical issues in multicultural counseling: Implications for the field of music therapy. *Arts in Psychotherapy, 24* (2), 137–143.

Burn, D. (1992). Ethical implications in cross-cultural counseling and training. *Journal of Counseling & Development, 70,* 578–583.

Byington, K., Fischer, J., Walker, L., & Freeman, E. (1997). Evaluating the effectiveness of a multicultural counseling ethics and assessment training. *Journal of Applied Rehabilitation Counseling, 28* (4), 15–19.

Corey, G., Corey, M. S., & Callanan, P. (2003). *Issues and ethics in the helping professions* (6th ed.). Pacific Grove, CA: Brooks/Cole.

Cottone, R. R., (2001). A social constructivism model of ethical decision making in counseling. *Journal of Counseling and Development, 79,* 39–45.

Essandoh, P. K. (1996). Multicultural counseling as the "fourth force": A call to arms. *Counseling Psychologist, 24,* 126–137.

Forester-Miller, H., & Davis, T. E. (1996). *A practitioner's guide to ethical decision-making.* Alexandria, VA: American Counseling Association.

Gladding, S. T. (2001). *The counseling dictionary: Concise definitions of frequently used terms.* Upper Saddle River, NJ: Merrill-Prentice Hall.

Grieco, E. M., & Cassidy, R. C. (2001, March). *Overview of race and Hispanic origin: Census Brief 2000* (Issue Brief No. C2KBR/01-1). Retrieved May 29, 2001 from the U.S. Census Bureau via GPO Access www.census.gov/population/www/cen2000/briefs.html. Washington, DC: U.S. Department of Commerce.

Helms, J. E., & Cook, D. A. (1999). *Using race and culture in counseling and psychotherapy.* Needham Heights, MA: Allyn & Bacon.

Herlihy, B., & Corey, G. (Eds.). (1996). *ACA ethical standards casebook.* Alexandria, VA: American Counseling Association.

Hill, M., Glaser, K., & Harden, J. (1995). A feminist model for ethical decision making. In E. J. Rave & C. C. Larsen (Eds.), *Ethical decision making in therapy: Feminist perspectives* (pp. 18–37). New York: Guilford.

Ivey, A. E. (1987). The multicultural practice of therapy: Ethics, empathy, and dialectics. *Journal of Social and Clinical Psychology, 5* (2), 195–204.

Jackson, M. L. (1995). Multicultural counseling: Historical perspectives. In J. G. Ponterotto, J. M. Casas, L. A. Suzuki, & C. M. Alexander (Eds.), *Handbook of multicultural counseling* (pp. 3–16). Thousand Oaks, CA: Sage.

Jordan, A., & Meara, N. (1990). Ethics and the professional practice of psychologists: The role of virtue and principles. *Professional Psychology: Research and Practice, 21* (2), 107–114.

Keith-Spiegel, P., & Koocher, G. P. (1985). *Ethics in psychology.* New York: Random House.

Korman, M. (1974). National conference on levels and patterns of professional training in psychology: Major themes. *American Psychologist, 29,* 441–449.

LaFromboise, T. D., Foster, S., & James, A. (1996). Ethics in multicultural counseling. In P. B. Pedersen, J. G. Draguns, W. J. Lonner, & J. E. Trimble (Eds.), *Counseling across cultures* (pp. 47–72). Thousand Oaks, CA: Sage.

Lonner, W., & Ibrahim, F. (1996). Appraisal and assessment in cross-cultural counseling. In P. Petersen & J. Draguns (Eds.), *Counseling across cultures* (pp. 293–322). Thousand Oaks, CA: Sage.

McGinn, F., Flowers, C., & Rubin, S. E. (1993). In quest of an explicit multicultural emphasis in ethical standards for rehabilitation counselors. *Rehabilitation Education, 7* (4), 261–268.

Nairne, J. S. (1997). *Psychology: The adaptive mind.* Pacific Grove, CA: Brooks Cole.

Paniagua, F. (1994). *Assessing and treating culturally diverse clients: A practical guide.* Thousand Oaks, CA: Sage.

Patterson, C. H. (2004). Do we need Multicultural Counseling Competencies? *Journal of Mental Health Counseling, 26,* 67–73.

Pedersen, P. B. (1995). Culture-centered ethical guidelines for counselors. In J. G. Ponterotto, J. M., Casas, L. A. Suzuki, & C. M. Alexander (Eds.), *Handbook of multicultural counseling* (pp. 34–49). Thousand Oaks, CA: Sage.

Pedersen, P. B. (1997). The cultural context of the American Counseling Association Code of Ethics. *Journal of Counseling & Development, 76,* 23–28.

Pedersen, P. B. (2001). Multiculturalism and the paradigm shift in counseling: Controversies and alternative futures. *Canadian Journal of Counseling, 35* (1), 15–25.

Pedersen, P. B., & Marsella, A. J. (1982). The ethical crisis for cross-cultural counseling and therapy. *Professional Psychology: Research and Practice, 13,* 492–500.

Pistole, M. C. (Ed.). (2004). Entire issue. *Journal of Mental Health Counseling, 26*(1).

Ponterotto, J., & Casas, J. (1991). *Handbook of racial/ethnic minority counseling research.* Springfield, IL: Charles C. Thomas.

Ponterotto, J. G. (1988). Racial/ethnic minority research in the Journal of Counseling Psychology: A context analysis and methodological critique. *Journal of Counseling Psychology, 35*(4), 410–418.

Portman, T. (2001). Sex role attributions of American-Indian women. *Journal of Mental Health Counseling, 23,* 72–84.

Ridley, C. (1995). *Overcoming unintentional racism in counseling and therapy: A practitioner's guide to intentional intervention.* Thousand Oaks, CA: Sage.

Stadler, H. A. (1986). Making hard choices: Clarifying controversial ethical issues. *Counseling and Human Development, 19,* 1–10.

Steinman, S. O., Richardson, N. F., & McEnroe, T. (1998). *The ethical decision-making manual for helping professionals.* Pacific Grove, CA: Brooks/Cole.

Stone, G. (1997). Multiculturalism as a context for supervision: Perspectives, limitations, and implications. In D. Pope-Davis & H. Coleman (Eds.), *Multicultural competencies: Assessment, education and training, and supervision.* Thousand Oaks, CA: Sage.

Strong, L. (1986). *Race relations for personal and organizational effectiveness.* Unpublished manuscript.

Sue, D. W. (1996). Ethical issues in multicultural counseling. In B. Herlihy & G. Corey (Eds.), *ACA ethical standards casebook* (pp. 193–204). Alexandria, VA: American Counseling Association.

Sue, D. W., Arredondo, P., & McDavis, R. J. (1992). Multicultural counseling competencies and standards: A call to the profession. *Journal of Counseling & Development, 70,* 477–486.

Tarvydas, V. M. (2004). Ethics. In T. F. Riggar & D. R. Maki (Eds.), *Handbook of rehabilitation counseling* (pp. 108–141). New York: Springer.

Tarvydas, V. M., & Cottone, R. R. (2000). The code of ethics for professional rehabilitation counselors: What we have and what we need. *Rehabilitation Counseling Bulletin, 43,* 188–196.

Thomas, K. R., & Weinrach, S. G. (2004). Mental health counseling and the AMCD Multicultural Counseling Competencies: A civil debate. *Journal of Mental Health Counseling, 26,* 41–43.

Vontress, C. E., & Jackson, M. L. (2004). Reactions to the Multicultural Counseling Competencies debate. *Journal of Mental Health Counseling, 26,* 74–80.

Weinrach, S. G., & Thomas, K. R. (2004). The AMCD Multicultural Counseling Competencies: A critically flawed initiative. *Journal of Mental Health Counseling, 26,* 81–93.

Weinrach, S. G., & Thomas, K. R. (2002). A critical analysis of the AAMD Multicultural Counseling Competencies: Implication for the practice of mental health counseling. *Journal of Mental Health Counseling, 24*(1), 20–35.

Welfel, E. R. (1998). *Ethics in counseling and psychotherapy: Standards, research, and emerging issues.* Pacific Grove, CA: Brooks/Cole.

Wrenn, G. C. (1962). The culturally encapsulated counselor. *Harvard Educational Review, 32,* 444–449.

PART 5

Ethical Practice with Counseling Specialties

CHAPTER 12

Couple and Family Counseling

OBJECTIVES

After reading this chapter, you should be able to:

- Discuss the major issues in couple and family counseling, including professional identification, licensure, and certification.
- Explain the crucial ethical concerns that arise in the practice of couple and family counseling.

- Compare the applicable ethical codes in couple and family counseling.

INTRODUCTION

Couple* and family counseling is developing and growing as a counseling specialty. It is also recognized by some individuals as a profession, separate from the larger profession of counseling. Marriage and family therapy, represented by the professional organization known as American Association for Marriage and Family Therapy (AAMFT), has its own training standards, accreditation of graduate programs, and licensure. However, many counselor licensure statutes allow for the practice of marriage and family counseling within the purview of the general counseling license. The ACA has taken the position that couple, marriage, and family counseling is a specialty area within the larger counseling profession. Therefore, couple and family counseling is unique—it is viewed by some as a separate profession and by others as a counseling specialty (Gladding, Remley & Huber, 2001). This dual professional identity has it pros and cons. On the negative side, competing professional associations seek members from an overlapping pool of mental health

professionals. Credentials sponsored by the associations also compete, and rivalry and debate exist over the legitimacy of the two professions. On the positive side, two groups are seeking to legitimize the practice of couple and family counseling (or therapy), and two groups are lobbying for such services to be included in health care and other service provider programs. Clients in need of such services are benefited by the effect of two organizations lobbying for their benefits. Regardless, the dual professional identity is confusing, and beginning students in counseling are asked to suspend judgment on which professional association (the AAMFT or the ACA) is right or wrong in the debate over professional identity until a thorough study of the matter is undertaken.

DEFINING THE SPECIALTY, SETTING, AND CLIENTS

The specialty of couple and family counseling has found a home in the IAMFC, an affiliate of the ACA. The IAMFC became a recognized affiliate of the ACA in 1989, and it soon became one of the fastest growing

---

* The term "couple" refers to loving partnerships, including premarital and married couples.

affiliates in the ACA. At present, it is one of the largest affiliate groups of the ACA. In cooperation with several other family therapy organizations, the IAMFC was successful in helping to sponsor the National Credentialing Academy for Certified Family Therapists (NCACFT), a freestanding certification body that identifies qualified family counselors. Counselors who wish to affiliate with other counselors in the area of couple and family counseling can congregate through a professional organization (affiliated with the ACA) and seek certification as recognized and qualified family counselors through the NCACFT.

There are other organizations that seek to represent couple and family therapists. The AAMFT is the largest and most visible. Its membership is composed of individuals who may have educational backgrounds in counseling, social work, medicine, or specifically in marriage and family therapy. In the past, the AAMFT has been an interdisciplinary interest and certifying group. More recently, the AAMFT has sought to carve a niche for a separate profession in the name of "marriage and family therapy." The AAMFT is a recognized leader in advocating for the practice of marriage and family therapy—a visible reminder of the interdisciplinary roots of the professional specialty of couple and family counseling.

Generally, couple and family counselors work in settings that provide services to couples or families, such as family service agencies, clinics, counseling centers, private practices, hospitals, and other general mental health service settings. Unless couple and family counselors are trained in the more general counseling field as a mental health practitioner, they limit their practices to work with couples or families (or in some cases to individuals with serious relationship problems). It is unusual for couple and family counselors to provide individual counseling as a service of preference. The reason they choose to work with couples or families is primarily theoretical—couple and family counselors are directed, to a large degree, by social systems theory, or what has been also identified as systemic-relational theory (Cottone, 1992; Gladding, 2002). Systemic-relational theory is a set of assumptions about the nature of mental health problems. Problems are defined as deriving from relationships, which are viewed as real and assessable processes between people. It is what happens between people that interests the couple and family counselor trained in systemic-relational theory.

The clients of couple and family counselors are couples or families with identified problems of a relational nature. Even if the problem is not identified by clients as relational, the couple and family counselor will probably conceptualize the problem as such. Even in cases of identified patients—individuals viewed as "problems" that need to be fixed—the couple and family counselor will probably redefine the concern as the interpersonal pattern of interaction within which problematic behavior becomes manifest. Even when couple and family counselors see individuals in treatment, they most usually focus the counseling on relationship concerns.

ISSUES OF SIGNIFICANCE TO THE SPECIALTY

Professional Differentiation

The ACA consists of divisions representing groups such as rehabilitation counselors, school counselors, mental health counselors, group counselors, and others. The IAMFC is the only ACA affiliate that specifically addresses concerns of couples, marriages, or families. Couple and family counseling is unique among the counseling specialties represented by the ACA. It is the only specialty with theorists and counselors subscribing to a form of treatment that does not focus attention on the individual. Instead, relationships are the targets of couple and family counseling.

Ethical Issues

Confidentiality and Privileged Communication. Confidentiality, as an antigossip guarantee, is designed to prevent revelation of privately communicated information to other individuals. In the classic one-client and one-counselor relationship, confidentiality is a simple issue of counselor responsibility. Counselors are bound by their ethical codes or legal ethical standards (e.g., ethical standards in licensure statutes) to maintain the information communicated in counseling sessions in confidence—that is, in a way that does not share information with others unless there are extenuating circumstances in which confidentiality would not stand (recognized exemptions). Couple or family counseling, however, presents complications. First, such counseling almost always involves more than one person as a client. Couple and family counselors, by philosophy, often treat relationship "systems" as the unit or target of intervention. Often, therefore, two or more people overhear what other individuals communicate in a session. In this sense, there is no one-to-one confidential relationship.

Most ethical codes and licensure statutes were designed primarily for one-to-one counseling relationships.

However, the AAMFT Code of Ethics does address the issue of more than one person being the unit of treatment. The AAMFT Code of Ethics (2001) states: "Marriage and family therapists have unique confidentiality concerns because the client in a therapeutic relationship may be more than one person. Therapists respect and guard the confidences of each individual client" (Section 2).

Further, the code states:

> When providing couple, family, or group treatment, the therapist does not disclose information outside the treatment context without a written authorization from each individual competent to execute a waiver. In the context of couple, family or group treatment, the therapist may not reveal any individual's confidences to others in the client unit without the prior written permission of that individual (Section 2.2).

The IAMFC standard (B.1) is worded similarly. Essentially, all legally responsible parties in couple or family therapy are required formally to release the information before it can be communicated to other individuals. But not all ethics codes or licensure standards are as clear as the IAMFC or AAFMT ethics codes on this issue. It is especially important for licensed professionals to examine their licensure statutes and any ethical references in those statues. First, the statutes must be examined to ensure that provision of standard services to couples or families is clearly within the purview of the practice of the profession, meaning that the scope of professional practice must clearly reference couples, marriages, relationships, systems, or family work. Second, if couple or family counseling is referenced in the legal definition of professional practice, ethical standards should then be examined in light of the definition of professional practice. Is a confidential relationship described in the statute's ethical guidelines? Does confidentiality extend to relationships beyond the one-on-one counseling relationship? These questions must be addressed in an examination of relevant ethical standards.

Regardless, unique circumstances in couple and family counseling still exist that are worth noting in any discussion of confidentiality and privileged communication. For example, even in a situation wherein legal confidentiality exists by statute for communications made within the context of relationship treatment, certain information may be communicated to a therapist privately by one member of a family or couple in treatment. In fact, Margolin (1982) stated: "Some therapists, in fact, arrange for sessions with individual family members to actively encourage the sharing of 'secrets' to better understand what is occurring in the family"

(p. 791). When one member of a couple or family privately reveals a secret to the counselor (in treatment), the counselor is faced with deciding whether that privately communicated information is confidential in a one-to-one sense. Can that information be communicated subsequently in the context of relationship treatment? What if one member of a couple communicates that he is involved in a secret, extramarital sexual relationship? Obviously this information is crucial to marital counseling, but if it is communicated in a formal counseling setting with no other parties present, it is considered confidential. It is ethically compromising for a counselor to continue relationship counseling with such information (essentially counseling in a way that does not acknowledge the infidelity). Margolin believed that therapists have several options in such a situation: The therapist can choose (a) to keep the secret, (b) to reveal the secret, or (c) to reveal the secret in certain circumstances. But, importantly, *it is crucial that counselors communicate their policy on such matters before counseling is initiated.* Margolin stated, "The most difficult predicament for the therapist would be if she or he failed to convey a policy on confidentiality" (p. 792). The same is true for any communication made by one individual in private to a counselor when that party is involved in relationship treatment with the counselor. Secrets, such as physical or sexual abuse, child molestation, sexual orientation, infection with a sexually transmitted disease, or drug involvement, often are revealed to counselors, and counselors must be prepared to reiterate their policy on confidentiality (with legal exceptions noted) and to follow whatever policy has been communicated and agreed to by the involved parties.

However, there is the additional problem that some secrets may involve illegal activity. For example, adultery is considered a punishable crime in some states. If the counselor keeps a secret of illegal adultery from a spouse, it is possible (although highly unlikely) that the counselor could be charged by the spouse with criminal conspiracy or "alienation of affection" (Cottone, Mannis, & Lewis, 1996; Margolin, 1982). Some argue (Cottone et al., 1996) that counselors must not condone illegal activity by keeping secrets. Counselors are most ethically and legally safe when they maintain a policy that such secrets will be openly discussed in counseling sessions with all involved parties present (or the counselor can choose and communicate a policy to reveal in circumstances wherein there is potential significant personal, physical, or emotional harm to unknowing partners or family members).

Privileged communication, like confidentiality, is more complicated in the context of couple and family counseling. Privileged communication is referenced in statutes most typically as related to one-to-one communication. In other words, communications made by one person in private to a counselor are considered safe from revelation in a legal proceeding, unless there are legal exceptions or the client waives the privilege. But what about cases in which several people are involved in counseling? As with confidentiality, the way the statute is written is critical to interpreting this legal standard. If the statute provides for privileged communication, it must be examined as to whether the privilege extends to all people in a session, or whether it is limited to one-on-one communications made to a counselor. Also, state case law (judgments in past relevant legal cases) is crucial in determining the extent of coverage of privileged communication. Unfortunately, legal standards are often unclear and many states lack definitive case law. Consequently, counselors must act conservatively. Margolin (1982) stated: "Lacking definitive legislation on these issues . . . family therapists cannot comfortably assume that existing privilege statutes protect the communications that occur during family therapy" (p. 794). Clients should know the risks of communicating secrets in circumstances in which there is no clear confidentiality or privileged communication.

Informed Consent.   Vesper and Brock (1991) stated: "The doctrine of informed consent was originally designed to require physicians and surgeons to explain medical procedures to patients and to warn them of any risks or dangers that could result from treatment. The intent of the doctrine was to permit the patient to make an intelligent, informed choice as to whether to undergo the proposed treatment or procedure" (p. 50). There have been times in human history when such a simple concept did not hold weight—a clear example being the Nazi doctors doing experiments on ethnic groups in concentration camps, which lead to a Declaration of Helsinki at the 1964 World Health Conference. The Declaration of Helsinki affirmed informed consent as a central element of research (Cain, Harkness, Smith & Markowski, 2003). As with medical patients, clients of counselors have the right to consent to treatment or research participation (or to refuse to submit to treatment or research; see Caudill, 1998).

Discussions of informed consent are often juxtaposed with discussions of the issue of client competency, which usually refers to the ability of clients to understand and to make judgments or decisions in their best interests. Clients judged to be competent to make decisions in their best interests have a right to be fully informed about the nature of treatments or procedures, the professional's qualifications and experience performing procedures or treatments, the risks and benefits of treatment or procedures, and alternative treatments (Caudill, 1998). Generally speaking, children are considered not competent to make such decisions; parents or guardians must be consulted when a child is involved. Also, when counselors treat people who have disabilities, the elderly, or those legally defined as not competent to make such decisions, they must consult a guardian for approval before initiating treatment. In couple and family counseling, it is accepted procedure to have adult participants (or otherwise competent individuals) sign a statement of consent to treatment once treatment issues have been addressed. However, compromising situations exist. One or more competent parties in the family may refuse to sign the consent form; in such a case, family treatment with all family members present cannot proceed. In effect, the legal and ethical autonomy of the individual overrides that of the majority of the family members. One person's hesitance can lead to a decision to abandon certain types of relationship counseling. Counselors, therefore, should encourage and seek the informed consent of all competent adult participants in couple and family counseling.

Roles and Relationships with Clients.   The historical issue of dual or multiple relationships (e.g., a counselor and client establishing a relationship outside of counseling, whether sexual or nonsexual) in couple and family counseling has aroused some debate in the field (AAMFT, 1993; Ryder & Hepworth, 1990). The reason for the debate probably centers on marriage and family counseling's underlying philosophical position that relationships have great potential in the process of aiding others. Social systems theory posits that relationships are the primary cause of disturbance in individuals and also can affect a positive change in observed behavior, as defined within a specified cultural context. In effect, establishing healthy relationships with clients is basic to the systemic-relational framework. The question of potentially detrimental relationships, then, is an important one. Certain relationships outside of the counseling relationship can be viewed as very helpful to clients.

Obviously, certain types of relationships can be harmful. But should all relationships outside of counseling be considered harmful or potentially harmful? It has been argued (Ryder & Hepworth, 1990; Tomm, 1993) that a closer examination of the issue is warranted because a blanket ban on relationships outside of counseling may prevent the development of some healthy interactions between a counselor and client. For example, Ryder and Hepworth suggested that the AAMFT rule to avoid dual relationships (relationships in addition to the initially contracted therapeutic relationship), which was expanded to nonsexual and apparently nonromantic relationships in 1988, was undesirable. They argued that such a rule masked a complex issue that should be addressed by students in marriage and family therapy. They took the position that it is more important that dual relationship issues be viewed as complex, and they believed the issues of exploitation and power were the crucial concerns. In effect, they argued against a blanket ban on all dual relationships while arguing in favor of a "serious emphasis" in training and supervision programs on the assessment of complex relationship issues.

As a result of the Ryder and Hepworth (1990) article, and a response by Karl Tomm (1993), a highly recognized marriage and family therapy theorist, a 1993 AAMFT conference plenary session was held on the topic, entitled "Dual Relationships: Sex, Power, and Exploitation" (AAMFT, 1993). The plenary allowed for an airing of concerns in a forum where differences of opinion could be and were expressed in a public way. Participants included Ingeborg Haug, Karl Tomm, Linda Terry, and Katharine Wexler. Interestingly, several of the presenters described personal experiences in which they were in violation of the proscription to avoid dual relationships. Tomm described situations wherein he was in violation of the code. He stated:

> When I reviewed the draft of the 1991 code, I realized I was in violation of dual relationship provisions in all three sections—clinical, teaching, and research areas. Clinically, I had colleagues who were in therapy with me—friends I had seen in therapy. In terms of teaching, there were some students and trainees who asked to see me in therapy. I did see them during some important crises they were going through. In the research area, I just completed writing a paper with a couple that I was seeing in therapy and whom I'm still seeing from time to time, and part of this paper was to distinguish the therapeutic moments of our work together—this was obviously a dual relationship.*

* Page numbers are unavailable for the 1993 AAMFT plenary—quotes were transcribed from an audiotape.

Tomm, after consulting colleagues and even the involved parties, came to the conclusion that he had done nothing harmful and that perhaps the code proscriptions to avoid such relationships were in error. Likewise, Linda Terry described situations in which she was involved in friendship relationships with her clinical supervisor and a university trainee. She argued that those friendships brought about "desirable possibilities that would not have been happening without the multiple role relationships." She concluded: "Dual relationships can be growth enhancing at times." Katharine Wexler described several cases of accidental dual relationships—one that proved to be beneficial as described by a client. The presenters essentially provided case examples in which relationships other than the initial professional relationship proved to be harmless or even beneficial to the client or trainee.

There were some persuasive arguments made against a blanket ban on counselor–client or counselor–trainee relationships subsequent to the initial contracted relationship. Tomm made the case that exploitation was clearly the issue. He argued against a linear, causal view of dual relationships and in favor of exploration of "what it is, in fact, that does enhance the possibilities of exploitation and injuries." He proposed that the focus should be on generating "a greater sense of inner responsibility and respect," and how counselors can relate to "clients on the basis of that responsibility and respect." Linda Terry, focusing primarily on the circumstances faced by women and minorities, argued that "continuity and loyalty" in counselor–client relationships are critical, and she pointed out cases in which therapists must go out of their way to communicate these messages. She stated:

> Standards should define ethical responsibilities of therapists to manage interpersonal boundaries with respect for multicontextual influences. Our system underpinnings describe that interpersonal boundaries are managed in terms of the balance of hierarchy and reciprocity, proximity and distance, stability and change, and interpersonal stage.

She essentially made the case for "culturally responsive care" and posed that dual or multiple roles in such circumstances should be viewed as positive.

On the other side of the argument, Ingeborg Haug, speaking as the chair of the AAMFT ethics committee, made a compelling presentation about problems of potentially detrimental relationships. She stated that "two thirds of all complaints against our members alleged dual relationships in various forms, including sexual."

That is a staggering percentage. She argued that "multiple relationships give rise to multiple agendas." Further, she stated that therapists "naively fail to realize there are multiple realities and that our clients' perceptions and experiences can be very different from the therapists'." She described the road from nonsexual, dual relationships to sexual, dual relationships as a "slippery slope" and quoted statistics that showed that "a clear relationship between nonsexual and sexual dual relationships does exist."

The plenary presentations made it clear that counselor–client and counselor–trainee relationships subsequent to the initial contracted relationship are complex. Where there are multiple roles, there are multiple meanings. Some relationships can be entered with ideal intentions; others can be, or can evolve into, detrimental interactions. The question is, "How does a profession, based on a systemic-relational worldview, maximize the beneficial effects of counselor–client and counselor–trainee interactions without risking harm to clients or trainees?"

The issue of dual relationships, which can be viewed as straightforward by many, actually presents a dilemma for those who value relationships as elements in facilitating the emotional health of clients or the professional development of trainees.

The recent revision of the AAMFT Code of Ethics (2001) may have actually created less clarity, unfortunately (Cottone, 2005). Although the new code appropriately bans outright sexual intimacy with clients in a separate standard (Section 1.4), it deletes a provision requiring avoidance of multiple roles, opting for a statement that bans only those multiple roles that have the potential "to impair professional judgment or increase the risk of exploitation" (Section 1.3). The new standard appears to put the burden on the client to prove that the counselor's intent was to exploit, or that the counselor was in some way impaired. The standards to avoid harmful counselor–client interactions or relationships (as described in Chapter 3) are more clear and less equivocal; also, certain (limited) potentially beneficial interactions or relationships are acceptable, so long as clear forethought and written documentation are involved and no harm is done to clients.

Related to training of marriage and family therapists on the issue of sexual attraction and the need to educate future therapists to be ethical in such a situation, Harris (2001) argued that "When it comes to sexual attraction we have a responsibility to educate about and even normalize the process of being attracted to another person. At the same time, we need to promote sound ethical, moral, and clinical practices" (p. 127). Indeed, a dialogue on this matter needs to be reinitiated within the ranks of couple and family counselors.

According to the 2005 IAMFC ethical code, multiple relationships with clients or their family members are to be avoided, "whenever possible" (standard A.9, IAMFC, 2006).

Responsibility. The issue of responsibility to clients, which seems uncomplicated when only one client is being seen in individual treatment, becomes a concern when more than one person is in the counselor's office. Margolin (1982) stated:

> The dilemma with multiple clients is that in some situations an intervention that serves one person's best interests may be counter-therapeutic to another. Indeed, the very reason that families tend to seek therapy is because they have conflicting goals and interests. (p. 789)

Couple and family counselors are in a unique counseling circumstance in which competing interests may enter into therapeutic decision making, if, in fact, the individuals in treatment are viewed as clients to be served. Fortunately, systemic-relational theory provides guidance in supporting the contention that the system of relationships is the focus of treatment. This theoretical focus allows the therapist the flexibility to define the system itself, or the relationship of significance, as the target of treatment. Allegiance, therefore, can be given to the system or the relationships. Margolin described this as relationship advocacy. She stated, "The family therapist then becomes an advocate of the family system and avoids becoming an agent of any one family member" (p. 789). Of course, there are circumstances in which advocating for the system or relationships must be abandoned, such as in cases of child abuse or neglect, or situations in which one party is endangered by the threats or actions of another member in the family. In such situations, relationship advocacy must be abandoned to protect the endangered party (Margolin). For the vast majority of cases, however, relationship advocacy is a legitimate position. Counselors simply define the couple or the family as the unit to which they are responsible and focus their activities on doing what is right for the relationship or the family as a whole. Relationship advocacy is one option of the couple and family counselor that is not available to counselors who provide individual treatment. It is a difference of ethical significance that is theoretically and practically unique to systemic-relational practice.

Values. Huber (1994) stated: "Values are a core component of any professional endeavor and are particularly critical to the professional practice of marriage and family therapy" (p. 225). Values are beliefs about what is desirable. They may be highly individual or they may be shared within a social context. Couple and family counseling poses value dilemmas that are not usually encountered in other types of counseling. For example, a counselor's view of divorce is significant to the tone of marital therapy. Some counselors do all that is possible to guide clients away from consideration of divorce. Other counselors may openly discuss divorce as an option, even early in counseling. Of course, it is implicit in marriage counseling that the marriage is valued. Both the IAMFC and AAMFT ethical codes place value on the well-being or welfare of the family. But to what degree is the individual practitioner bound to a strict, value-driven practice? On the issue of divorce, for example, the AAMFT code specifically states that decisions on marital status are the responsibility of the client (Section 1.8). This appears to give the practitioner latitude in recommending that couples discuss privately their desires related to separation or divorce as options, but it appears also to prevent a practitioner from stating, unconditionally, that a person or couple should seek divorce or separation. Value issues are involved, and beyond the directives of the code, a counselor's values may be highly relevant to what actually occurs in counseling. For example, according to some religions, such as the Roman Catholic religion, divorce is not accepted because marriage is viewed as a sacrament. A Roman Catholic practitioner counseling a Roman Catholic couple may undertake therapy with this overriding religious value directing the options for the couple. Certain values—religious and otherwise—enter into couple and family counseling practice that may be only tangentially or incompletely addressed by a code of ethics. Also, certain value issues relevant to couple and family counseling may not be relevant in other specialties of counseling, and ethical codes covering general practice (e.g., the APA and ACA codes) may not adequately address the value issues at the heart of couple and family counseling.

Other value issues typically encountered by couple and family counselors include judgments about extramarital affairs (sexual or otherwise), sex roles, parenting roles, division of labor in the marital relationship, multicultural or mixed cultural relations, marital sexuality, birth control, involvement with the extended family, decision making and control of resources, and others.

Most textbooks on professional ethics in the human services (e.g., Corey, Corey & Callanan, 2003; Huber, 1994) direct practitioners to assess their values through a process of values clarification and to be alert to circumstances in practice that may activate a value judgment. In situations in which it is apparent that the values of the counselor may be in conflict with those of the couple or family in treatment, the counselor must decide if counseling can be undertaken in a way that is consistent with the family values or whether referral to another counselor is appropriate.

Counselor Competence. Given that the specialty of couple and family counseling is founded on a theoretical framework that is philosophically quite distinct from the foundations of individual psychotherapy (Cottone, 1992), it is imperative that couple and family counselors have special training and supervision in systemic-relational treatment. Both the AAMFT and the NCACFT have set standards for professional marriage and family counselors. The standards are specific in defining the need for a thorough understanding of relationship theory. The standards are also quite demanding regarding adequate supervision: Those who aspire to be specialists in couple and family counseling must obtain supervision under the direction of qualified supervisors. In fact, the AAMFT certifies individuals as "approved supervisors" for the oversight of clinicians in training. It is not enough for a counselor to receive a general counseling degree and then to begin seeing couples or families in practice; practitioners must complete adequate coursework or supervision specifically in couple or family counseling. A counselor providing couple or family counseling without adequate training and competence in this area is vulnerable ethically and legally.

Because procedures and techniques in couple and family counseling vary dramatically from procedures and techniques in individual counseling, practitioners should have more than a cursory understanding of specialty approaches. There is a unique literature in the field of couple and family counseling that may be complementary to, or even incompatible with, good clinical practice in individual counseling. For example, a counselor who treats an individual might be trained to be empathic and acknowledging of the client's perspective. A couple's counselor might be viewed as taking sides if the counselor is overly empathic or acknowledging of one person's perspective, unless the counselor conveys an attitude of neutrality. Family counseling techniques are also designed to facilitate interaction between participants and require an active style of counseling to prevent the counselor from losing control of the process, which can occur easily when there are several active counseling participants. All in all, the practice of couple and family counseling is different to the degree that some practices of individual counseling do not easily or competently apply.

Competency also requires that counselors use up-to-date theory and technique. The practice of couple counseling is being affected significantly by the works of Gottman (e.g., Gottman, 1994), who has done well-controlled empirical research related to marriage success and failure. Some classic myths of marriage have been uncovered by his work. For example, for years it has been believed that similarity of opinions is beneficial to a marriage. Gottman's response was as follows:

> In my research, where I actually observed couples hashing out disagreements and then tracked them down years later to check on how stable their marriages were, I found that couples who initially had complaints about each other's attitudes were among the most stable marriages as the years went on. My research shows that much more important than having compatible views is how couples work out their differences. In fact, occasional discontent, especially during a marriage's early years, seems to be good for the union in the long run. (pp. 23–24)

Teaching couples in their early years to communicate in a way that prevents "hashing out disagreements" may actually be counterproductive to the relationship; following Gottman's ideas, they need to learn to work out their differences, not to avoid them. Couples and family counselors, like all counselors, must ensure that they are current on the literature and applying valid theory and technique.

CODE COMPARISONS

Two ethical codes apply to counselors in the specialty of couple and family counseling. The first is the AAMFT Code of Ethics (AAMFT, 2001); the second is the Ethical Code for the IAMFC (IAMFC, 2005). The IAMFC is a division of the larger ACA; therefore, members of the IAMFC are bound by the more general ACA code, but are directed by the IAMFC code as an aspirational guide. The IAMFC and AAMFT codes are reprinted in Appendices L and M.

Generally, both codes promote the welfare of families and individuals. This is different from more general codes of ethics, which often focus on the

individual in a one-on-one or group counseling context. Both codes, for example, provide for confidentiality of communications made in counseling/therapy. They also require that all competent parties involved in counseling sign a waiver of confidentiality before any information can be released to a third party. Both codes address issues of competence, recognizing that practitioners should not diagnose or treat problems outside the scope of their professional training and supervision, which in this case relates directly to relationship treatment. Both codes recognize ethical concerns related to supervision of students, employees, or supervisees.

The 2001 AAMFT Code of Ethics appears to give equivocal guidance on multiple (outside of counseling) relationship issues that can be potentially confusing to practitioners (Cottone, 2005). There is no outright provision to avoid multiple relationships, but there is no guidance as to what constitutes an acceptable interaction outside of counseling. The IAMFC code, on the other hand, states that multiple relationships should be avoided.

There are other differences in the codes. The IAMFC code has a section specifically dealing with assessment, which reflects the counseling profession's scope of practice, including use of educational and psychological testing devices. AAMFT members may not have training in psychological or counseling assessment. The AAMFT code has a section on advertising and specifically addresses the use of the AAMFT Clinical Member designation, which is recognized nationally as a professional credential. Whereas the AAMFT code addresses "financial arrangements" specifically, the IAMFC code addresses "fees" in its section on the counseling relationships and client well-being. The codes have other similarities and differences, and readers are directed to the codes themselves to analyze their contents (see Box 12–1). Regardless, the professional specialty of couple and family counseling requires knowledge of how treating relationships compounds ethical issues in clinical practice.

ISSUES OF DIVERSITY

Given that couple and family counseling is founded on systemic-relational theory, both positive and negative implications exist from a multicultural perspective. Systemic-relational theory offers a perspective of cause and effect that relieves the individual of blame. Accordingly, it is the system of relationships that is considered causative of what can be observed to be a problem. For

Box 12–1 • Exploring the Codes

How do the standards in the AAMFT (2001) ethics code on the issue of "dual" or "multiple relationships" compare to the standards on roles and relationships with clients discussed in Chapter 3?

Does the ethics code of the IAMFC (2005) address training standards?

Which code is more thorough and comprehensive—the IAMFC or AAMFT ethics code?

What guidance is given to AAMFT "Clinical Members" in using that designation in advertising by the AAMFT (2001) ethics code?

example, if there is a misbehaving child in a family, the family dynamics and patterns of interactions would be analyzed and the child's behavior would be interpreted within the context of the family system. The "cause" of the child's problem would not be identified as being within the individual psychology or learning of the child; rather the family system's patterns of interactions would be implicated. When a relationship is considered problematic, neither individual in the relationship is culpable—blame is placed on the larger relationship pattern. Further, the relationship problem would be interpreted within an encompassing system of relationships within which the problem is imbedded. For example, a couple's concern might be interpreted as a lack of fit between two family systems (the families of origin) interacting through the marital relationship. The influences of family relationships currently and historically would be analyzed in assessing the nature of the problem and a means to solution.

Feminist theorists have attacked this cause-and-effect perspective (Bograd, 1984). In the case of physical abuse of a spouse (about 95% of reported victims being females), to blame the relationship and relational dynamics is, to some degree, to implicate the victim in the abuse (as a part of the sick relationship). Feminist theorists view the systemic position, that a perpetrator is not culpable, as indefensible. The concerns raised by feminist theorists are even more salient when child abuse is the issue. Can a 3-year-old child be viewed in any way as dynamically and relationally "causative" of his or her sexual abuse? To somehow relieve the blame of a child abuser is essentially a double victimization of the child. Several theorists (Cottone, 1992; Cottone & Greenwell, 1992; Dell, 1989) have attempted to accommodate this critique of systemic-relational theory by modifying the theory to account for linear causal processes—processes wherein one individual, in a power position, has straightforward causal influence. The person in power can then be blamed in abusive circumstances.

On the positive side, revision of systemic-relational theory has led to a position that within certain contexts, cause can be viewed as either circular and relational or linear and individual (Cottone & Greenwell, 1992). Systemic-relational theorists are embracing theoretical developments in psychology and biology, which have adopted a position that realities are defined and constructed socially. Such theoretical developments have come forward under the rubric of social constructivism, social constructionism, contextualism, and postmodernism (Cottone, 1992; Gergen, 1985; Hoffman, 1988). Accordingly, a social consensus can be developed around a circumstance, such as abuse, that an individual is culpable (Cottone & McConaghy, 1998). In such circumstances, individual treatment along with relational treatments would be indicated. In this sense, a relational definition of a problem can lead to implication and treatment of an individual.

Additionally, advances in systemic-relational theory allow for an understanding of cultural difference as they arise from socially constructed "realities." When reality is viewed as socially constructed—that is, arising from a consensus in a group—it is then possible to conceive of competing, but equally legitimate, realities (Maturana, 1978). No cultural group or cultural norm can be viewed as better or more valid than any other. Each cultural norm derives from a reality established in the context of social relations within cultural boundaries. Before such advances, systemic-relational theorists depended on theories that defined what was considered right or acceptable in families. For example, Minuchin (1974), a preeminent family therapist, theoretically defined hierarchy in families as important to what is viewed as healthy family organization. Likewise, other theorists defined what they believed to be healthy family organizations or interaction patterns. Currently, counselors are not bound by absolute conceptions of mental health within a family relational framework; rather, they can accommodate cultural diversity in their techniques and approaches to family systems, because no one family norm exists.

DECISION MAKING IN CONTEXT

When a counselor is faced with an ethical dilemma, it is absolutely necessary for the counselor to organize a response in an educated way. Decision-making models assist in this regard. Couple and family counseling certainly is an area of practice that will challenge the counselor with dilemmas because contextual factors come into play like no other area of counseling. For example, competing interests among family members require an approach initially that does not appear to be biased against one person's point of view. Yet value issues enter into such counseling. When using a decision-making model in couple or family counseling, it is wise to view a concern or dilemma from the perspective of each of the involved parties. This is easily accomplished using the Social Constructivism Model or the Tarvydas Integrative Model, because both have strong social components built into the decision process. The rights and responsibilities of each person in the system being counseled must be considered, as well as the rights and responsibilities of the system as a whole. For example, the revelation of a secret by one partner that would negatively affect a marriage must be handled with concern for the revealing party, the unknowing partner, and the relationship as a whole. This requires a balance of ethical responsibilities that ideally enhances the involved individuals and the relationship. Counselors addressing ethical dilemmas in couple and family counseling must be hyperalert to the social factors that may influence a decision.

In 1999, Richard E. Watts published a case study in *The Family Journal* that describes an ethical dilemma involving standards of confidentiality and duty to warn. That case study, (see Box 12–2), is an example of one counselor's attempt to clarify the "ethical course of action." It is a complex and very interesting case. After reading the case, consider the deliberations and try to define what you would do in this situation. What ethics

Box 12–2 • Confidentiality and the Duty to Report: A Case Study

Richard E. Watts

In the course of counseling, marriage and family counselors may experience the dilemma of deciding between the necessity of keeping confidential what clients have shared versus the counselor's duty to report and protect individuals and society in general. In this article, the author presents a case study followed by discussion addressing the issue of confidentiality and the duty to report.

A counselor recently began working with a couple having difficulties in their marriage. The husband is a medical doctor and his wife, a certified public accountant (CPA), runs the business aspects of his practice. During the past 5 years, the couple has lived lavishly and, consequently, developed financial problems. They entered counseling stating that the presenting problem was anger and conflict stemming from their financial difficulties. In a recent session with the couple, the wife shared that about a year ago her husband purposely and terminally overmedicated an elderly patient. The elderly patient was the stepmother of the wife, and because of a recent death, the wife is the lone benefactor of a large insurance policy. The counselor believes the fundamental problem in the couple's relationship is guilt over their conspiracy to terminate the life of the elderly stepmother—especially given the fact that the forthcoming insurance policy payment will cover their debts. However, the counselor is wondering whether she has an ethical or legal responsibility to contact the authorities and report the situation.

This case study addresses the tension between honoring the client's right to confidentiality and the counselor's obligation to a greater societal concern. The counselor's ethical and legal requirements to protect the confidentiality of clients is stated in the ethical codes of counseling professionals, state laws regarding privilege communication, and the constitutional right to privacy. In each case, the privilege or right to confidentiality and privacy belongs to the client. Confidentiality, however, is not an absolute, and there are both ethically and legally mandated exceptions or limits to confidentiality (Ahia & Martin, 1993; American Association for Marriage and Family Therapy, 1991; American Counseling Association [ACA], 1995; Anderson, 1996; Corey, Corey, & Callanan, 1998; Dickson, 1995; Herlihy & Corey, 1996; International Association of Marriage and Family Counselors [IAMFC], 1993; Swenson, 1997).

According to Section A of the ethical code of the IAMFC (1993, p. 75),

> Clients have the right to expect that information shared with the counselor will not be disclosed to others and, in the

continued

Box 12–2 • Confidentiality and the Duty to Report: A Case Study—*continued*

absence of any law to the contrary, the communications between clients and marriage and family counselors should be viewed as privileged. . . . Information obtained from a client can only be disclosed to a third party under the following conditions.

1. The client consents to disclosure by a signed waver.
2. The client has placed him- or herself or someone else in clear and imminent danger.
3. The law mandates disclosure.
4. The counselor is a defendant in a civil, criminal, or disciplinary action arising from professional activity.
5. The counselor needs to discuss a case for consultation or education purposes. These discussions should not reveal the identity of the client or any other unnecessary aspects of the case.

These guidelines are in agreement with the ethical codes of both the ACA (1995) and the American Association for Marriage and Family Therapy (1991).

Regarding the case study under review, however, the ethical codes do not specifically address past criminal activity. Thus, unless the counselor explicitly believes that the doctor and/or his wife may do something similar in the future and therefore constitute a danger to society, the ethical code appears to indicate that she should not break confidentiality. However, exception Number 3 in the IAMFC Code of Ethics, addressing legal concerns, may implicitly be salient to the case study.

Several persons with doctorates in both counseling and law were contacted, including Dr. Bob Crawford, Dr. Ted Remley, and Dr. Carl Swanson. Remley was the general editor for the ACA Legal Series, whereas Crawford (1993) authored and Swanson (Arthur & Swanson, 1993) coauthored two separate volumes in that series.

All three—Crawford, Remley, and Swanson—indicated that whereas the case study addresses a crime from the past (not immediate or future), confidentiality appeared to be the primary concern. Duty to report past crime—even murder—is not clearly delineated in most jurisdictions. Anderson (1996), Arthur and Swanson (1993), and Remley (personal communication, August 1998) state that counselors are under no legal obligation per se to report a client's past or ongoing criminal activity, and to do so may be both unethical and illegal. However, Arthur and Swanson (1993) affirm that criminal behavior that has harmed or threatens harm to others may constitute an exception to confidentiality. The counselor could choose to report the crime and face the possibility of being sued for breach of confidentiality (Anderson, 1996). Given the gravity of the crime, however, Remley (personal communication, August, 1998) stated that he did not believe that any jury would find against the counselor.

The following question arises: If the counselor does not break confidentiality, might she be considered an accessory after the fact should the crime be discovered by authorities? Crawford (personal communication, August 1998) responded:

> To be guilty of this crime, a person must render aid, comfort, and/or shelter to the criminal. A failure to report to the police about the wife's comment here generally is not sufficient to constitute this (or any other) crime. . . . I am not aware of any cases where merely rendering "talk therapy" counseling to a client would constitute comforting the criminal as this term has been defined in previous cases.

Huber (1994) offers a similar conclusion in his discussion of the "accessory after the fact" question.

Duty to report past felony crimes against other persons is a gray area because many jurisdictions do not address the issue with any clarity. However, the fact that the victim in this case study was an elderly woman adds another variable into the discussion. Some states do mandate reporting of current and past incidents of elder abuse (Ahia & Martin, 1993; Anderson, 1996; Arthur & Swanson, 1993; Dickson, 1995; Swenson, 1997).

> In recent years, many states have passed laws requiring mental health professionals to report known or suspected incidents of the abuse of aged or disabled adults. In most cases, these statutes are very similar to child abuse reporting statutes. Once again reporting is generally (though not always) mandatory, those who report are immune from liability, the counselor-privilege does not apply, and there are stiff penalties for failure to report. (Ahia & Martin, 1993, pp. 31–32)

Ahia and Martin (1993), Anderson (1996), Dickson (1995), and Swanson (personal communication, August 1998) all note, however, that mandatory duty-to-report laws regarding past incidents of elder abuse vary depending on state law.

In response to this case study, the following recommendations are offered for counselors. First, because not all states have duty-to-report laws regarding past crimes and because such laws may permit but not require disclosure of these crimes by counseling professionals, it is essential that counselors are cognizant of their own state's statutes prior to breaking confidentiality (Ahia & Martin, 1993; Anderson, 1996; Arthur & Swanson, 1993; Dickson, 1995; Swenson, 1997). "It is imperative that counselors determine the extent of the law in the state(s) in which they practice and make a good faith effort to comply with reporting requirements" (Anderson, 1996, p. 28). The IAMFC ethical code (1993, Section A.5) indicates that counselors may discuss a case for consultation purposes

Box 12–2 • Confidentiality and the Duty to Report: A Case Study—*continued*

but that the identity of the client must not be revealed during the consultation. The ACA ethical code (1995, Section H.2.b) further states that when "uncertain as to whether a particular situation or course of action may be in violation of [the] Code of Ethics, counselors consult with other counselors who are knowledgeable about ethics, with colleagues, or with appropriate authorities" (p. 50). Thus, counselors are well advised to seek consultation from a supervisor, knowledgeable colleagues, or an attorney because they may be subject to liability for failing to report when reporting is mandated—or for reporting when a report is not required (Ahia & Martin, 1993). Sharon Erickson, Sandy Magnuson, Ken Norem, Patricia Stevens, and Anita Thomas—all IAMFC Ethics Committee members—affirm the importance of consultation and emphasized the necessity of documenting that consultation did occur.

Second, Anderson (1996), Sharon Erickson (personal communication, August 1998), and Carl Swanson (personal communication, August 1998) suggest that counselors should urge the client(s) to turn themselves in to the proper authorities. This recommendation is valid regardless of the decision counselors make about breaking confidentiality in order to report the client(s).

Third, Sharon Erickson (personal communication, August 1998) and Anita Thomas (personal communication, August 1998) stated that if a counselor chose to report, he or she would need to refer the client(s) because of the newly created dual relationship; the counselor is now the accuser. However, if counselors choose not to report, they would need to remind clients of the limits of confidentiality throughout the therapeutic relationship.

Finally, whatever action is taken, it is imperative that counselors document the action and include a brief statement explaining their rationale for the action taken. In case of future litigation, the rule of thumb is that whatever is not written (documented) did not occur or does not

exist (Anderson, 1996; Corey et al., 1998; Dickson, 1995; Huber, 1994; Swenson, 1997).

REFERENCES

Ahia, C. E., & Martin, D. (1993). *The danger-to-self-or-others exception to confidentiality*. Alexandria, VA: American Counseling Association.
American Association for Marriage and Family Therapy. (1991). *AAMFT code of ethics*. Washington, DC: Author.
American Counseling Association. (ACA). (1995). *Code of ethics and standards of practice*. Alexandria, VA: Author.
Anderson, B. S. (1996). *The counselor and the law* (4th ed.). Alexandria, VA: American Counseling Association.
Arthur, G. L., & Swanson, C. D. (1993). *Confidentiality and privilege communication*. Alexandria, VA: American Counseling Association.
Corey, G., Corey, M. S., & Callanan, P. (1998). *Issues and ethics in the helping professions* (5th ed.). Pacific Grove, CA: Brooks/Cole.
Crawford, R. L. (1993). *Avoiding counselor malpractice*. Alexandria, VA: American Counseling Association.
Dickson, D. T. (1995). *Law in the health and human services*. New York: Free Press.
Herlihy, B., & Corey, G. (1996). Confidentiality. In B. Herlihy & G. Corey (Eds.), *ACA ethical standards casebook* (5th ed., pp. 205–209). Alexandria, VA: American Counseling Association.
Huber, C. H. (1994). *Ethical, legal, and professional issues in the practice of marriage and family therapy* (2nd ed.). Upper Saddle River, NJ: Merrill/Prentice Hall.
International Association of Marriage and Family Counselors. (IAMFC). (1993). *Ethical code for the International Association of Marriage and Family Counselors*. Alexandria, VA: Author.
Swenson, L. C. (1997). *Psychology and law for the helping professions*. Pacific Grove, CA: Brooks/Cole.

Note: The Family Journal: Counseling and Therapy for Couples and Families, Vol. 7 No. 1, January 1999 64–66. Reprinted with permission. © 1999 Sage Publications, Inc.

decision-making model would you use? What factors described by Watts (1999) enter into your decision? Are there other issues not addressed in the case scenario that you think are of importance?

CHAPTER SUMMARY

The practice of couple and family counseling is unique among the counseling specialties. It is primarily based on a philosophical position that values relationships as being crucial to mental health and observable behavioral difficulties. This philosophical position allows for unique ethical considerations, including concerns over multicultural issues. It also allows for unique solutions to ethical concerns, which would otherwise not be forthcoming from other counseling specialties.

Couple and family counseling is founded on theory that has evolved to be culturally relevant and acknowledges cultural differences.

REFERENCES

American Association for Marriage and Family Therapy. (1991). *AAMFT code of ethics*. Washington, DC: Author.

American Association for Marriage and Family Therapy. (1993). *AAMFT luncheon plenary on "Dual relationships: Sex, power, and exploitation."* Audiotape cassette recording published through the AAMFT Resource Link, Norcross, GA (Call: 1-800-241-7785).

American Association for Marriage and Family Therapists. (2001). *AAMFT code of ethics*. Washington, DC: Author.

Bograd, M. (1984). Family systems approaches to wife battering: A feminist critique. *American Journal of Orthopsychiatry, 54*, 558–568.

Cain, H. I., Harkness, J. L., Smith, A. L., & Markowski, E. M. (2003). Protecting persons in family therapy research: An overview of ethical and regulatory standards. *Journal of Marital and Family Therapy, 29*, 47–57.

Caudill, O. B. (1998, February/March). The hidden issue of informed consent. *Family Therapy News,* Feb/Mar, 7.

Corey, G., Corey, M. S., & Callanan, P. (2003). *Issues and ethics in the helping professions* (6th ed.). Pacific Grove, CA: Brooks/Cole.

Cottone, R. R. (1992). *Theories and paradigms of counseling and psychotherapy*. Needham Heights, MA: Allyn & Bacon.

Cottone, R. R. (2005). Detrimental therapist–client relationships—Beyond thinking of "dual" or "multiple" roles: Relfections on the 2001 AAMFT Code of Ethics. *The American Journal of Family Therapy, 33*, 1–17.

Cottone, R. R., & Greenwell, R. J. (1992). Beyond linearity and circularity: Deconstructing social systems theory. *Journal of Marital and Family Therapy, 18*, 167–177.

Cottone, R. R., Mannis, J., & Lewis, T. (1996). Uncovering secret extramarital affairs in marriage counseling. *The Family Journal, 4*, 109–115.

Cottone, R. R., & McConaghy, J. S. (1998). The systemic view of violence: An ethical perspective. *Family Process, 37*, 51–63.

Dell, P. F. (1989). Violence and the systemic view: The problem of power. *Family Process, 28*, 1–14.

Gergen, K. J. (1985). The social constructionist movement in modern psychology. *American Psychologist, 40*, 266–275.

Gladding, S. T. (2002). *Family therapy: History, theory, and practice* (3rd ed). Upper Saddle River, NJ: Merrill/Prentice Hall.

Gladding, S. T., Remley, T. P., & Huber, C. H. (2001). *Ethical, legal, and professional issues in the practice of marriage and family therapy* (3rd ed.). Upper Saddle River, NJ: Merrill/Prentice Hall.

Gottman, J. (1994). *Why marriages succeed or fail*. New York: Fireside.

Harris, S. M. (2001). Teaching family therapists about sexual attraction in therapy. *Journal of Marital and Family Therapy, 27*, 123–128.

Hoffman, L. (1988). A constructivist position for family therapy. *The Irish Journal of Psychology, 9*, 110–129.

Huber, C. H. (1994). *Ethical, legal, and professional issues in the practice of marriage and family therapy*. Upper Saddle River, NJ: Merrill/Prentice Hall.

International Association of Marriage and Family Counseling. (2006). Ethical code for the International Association of Marriage and Family Counselors. *The Family Journal: Counseling and Therapy for Couples and Families, 14*, 1–7.

Margolin, G. (1982). Ethical and legal considerations in marital and family therapy. *American Psychologist, 37*, 788–801.

Maturana, H. R. (1978). Biology of language: The epistemology of reality. In G. A. Miller & E. Lenneberg (Eds.), *Psychology and biology of language and thought* (pp. 27–63). New York: Academic Press.

Minuchin, S. (1974). *Families and family therapy*. Cambridge, MA: Harvard University Press.

Ryder, R., & Hepworth, J. (1990). AAMFT ethical code: "Dual relationships." *Journal of Marital and Family Therapy, 16*, 127–132.

Tomm, K. (1993). *AAMFT luncheon plenary on "Dual relationships: Sex, power, and exploitation."* Audiotape cassette recording published through the AAMFT Resource Link, Norcross, GA (Call: 1-800-241-7785).

Vesper, J. H., & Brock, G. (1991). *Ethics, legalities, and professional practice issues in marriage and family therapy*. Needham Heights, MA: Allyn & Bacon.

Watts, R. E. (1999). Confidentiality and the duty to report: A case study. *The Family Journal: Counseling and Therapy for Couples and Families, 7*, 64–66.

CHAPTER 13

School Counseling

Donna A. Henderson

OBJECTIVES

After reading this chapter, you should be able to:

- Discuss the scope of a school counseling practice.
- Describe the clients of school counselors.
- Identify critical professional and ethical issues specific to school counseling.

- Discuss the *Ethical Standards for School Counselors*.
- Explain the multicultural and diversity issues specific to school counseling.

INTRODUCTION

Educational institutions in the United States are microcosms that reflect the diversity of demographic, economic, and social variables in our nation. That combination provides school counselors, perhaps more than any other counseling specialty, with the opportunity to serve a wide variety of clients. The varied roles of school counselors, the range of services they provide to students and adults in the educational setting, the dynamic and diverse population with whom they work, and the stimulating settings that schools create all contribute to the complexity of school counseling. This complexity breeds challenging situations that often require immediate action. All of these demanding circumstances necessitate that school counselors know both the ethical implications and the legal consequences of any action they choose.

DEFINING THE SPECIALTY, SETTING, AND CLIENTS

School counseling has evolved as a profession within the past 100 years. In the early 1900s, Jesse Davis established a program in the public schools of Grand Rapids, Michigan. The program was a forerunner of school counseling—a preventative education program to teach character development to students. About the same time, Frank Parsons was building another program in Boston. The focus of that effort was vocational guidance aimed at growth and prevention—helping young people make thoughtful career decisions. From these foundations emerged the steadily growing profession of school counseling. Later, the National Defense Education Act of 1958 provided federal funds for upgrading school counseling programs and for training school counselors. This impetus expanded the numbers and increased the quality of school counselors who have continued to advance the profession and its significance in U.S. schools.

A school counseling program is a critical part of the educational enterprise (see Box 13–1). The American School Counselor Association (ASCA) endorses a developmental, comprehensive approach to school counseling programs that promotes and enhances student learning. ASCA's (1997) position statement describes

Box 13–1 • Exploring the Codes

(See the ACA and APA codes in Appendix A and B and the school counselor's code in Appendix N.)

1. What are the limits of a school counselor's responsibility in working with peer helper programs?
2. To what groups does a school counselor have ethical responsibilities?

3. What are some of school counselors' responsibilities to themselves?
4. In what areas do legal and ethical concerns differ?
5. Which federal laws establish procedures for safeguarding student records?

the programs as systematic, sequential, clearly defined, and accountable. These programs are designed around three interrelated areas of student development: academic development, career development, and personal-social development. The document *Sharing the Vision: The National Standards for School Counseling Programs* (Campbell & Dahir, 1997) provides guidelines for the content and delivery of school counseling programs and outlines the desired learning outcomes relative to these three areas of student development at each grade level. *Academic development* includes the skills, attitudes, and knowledge related to learning throughout life. *Career development* is defined as the foundation of skills, attitudes, and knowledge that enable students to make a successful transition from school into a career. *Personal-social development* relates to the skills, attitudes, and knowledge that help people understand and respect self and others, obtain effective interpersonal skills, understand and practice safety and survival skills, and become contributing members of society. These guidelines provide school counselors with a foundation to organize, implement, and coordinate school counseling programs with the goal of providing "all students with life success skills" (ASCA, 1997).

School counselors find guidance for delivering their programs in *The ASCA National Model: A Framework for School Counseling Programs* (ASCA, 2003b). The guide outlines the foundation of a program including statements of beliefs, philosophy, and mission as well as national standards. The manual explains systems of program delivery, management, and accountability. Forms and guidelines are included to assist with the implementation of a school counseling program.

Thirty states have mandated comprehensive school counseling programs (ASCA, 2005), therefore sanctioning the concept that counselors should focus on all students, in prekindergarten through 12th grade in elementary, middle/junior high, and secondary school settings. Descriptions contained in the national model

(ASCA, 2003b) suggest that school counselors should provide direct services in their schools, using primarily the following interventions:

- *Counseling*—working with individuals and in small groups to help them resolve or cope with their problems and concerns;
- *Classroom instruction*—working collaboratively with teachers to design and implement a planned, developmental program of guidance activities that foster student development;
- *Consultation*—building partnerships with teachers, administrators, parents, and others to devise and implement strategies to help students do well in schools; and
- *Coordination*—leading the organization, managing and evaluating the program, assisting parents in finding needed services for their children, and serving as a liaison to the community.

The school counselor's functions vary across communities as a result of the views of parents, the school board or policy-setting body, the school administration, the teachers, and student needs. Therefore, school counselors may not always be able to define their day-to-day jobs as they wish. For example, some counselors are hired only to do career counseling or individual counseling or to handle scheduling and administrative duties. Furthermore, some school districts restrict personal counseling to only helping students make career decisions, and other districts choose to do without developmental programs in classrooms.

The clients of school counselors also vary according to individual job descriptions. Counselors have their school children as their primary clients, but also work with parents, teachers, and administrators in a consultant role. Counselors who facilitate parenting groups have parents of school children as clients. Some counselors serve as a referral source for teachers and other adults; those adults are the clients of that referral interview. Thus, the variation in school counseling reflects the numerous clients served by the counselor.

Each of the 50 states requires that school counselors be licensed, certified, endorsed, or credentialed in some manner. The requirements for those designations vary significantly from state to state. A summary of the qualifications for each state credential can be found on the ASCA Web site www.schoolcounselor.org. Most often, these standards are defined by the individual state departments of education and adhere to the process followed by teachers in being certified or licensed. In 1995, ASCA resolved that the designation "Professional School Counselor" be used as the title for individuals who engage in the practice of school counseling, provide the services listed previously, have specialized training in school counseling at a minimum master's-degree level, meet state certification standards, and abide by the laws in the states where they are employed. School counselors who meet requirements for the N.C.C. credential become eligible to seek a national credential, National Certified School Counselor, by completing specialized courses and experiences that are specific to school counseling. Additionally, school counselors can seek the designation of master counselor through a process recently established by the National Board for Professional Teaching Standards.

In 1984, the ASCA approved the Ethical Standards for School Counselors as a document for guiding school counselors through the complicated issues of their job (ASCA, 2004b). The most current revision of the standards occurred on June 26, 2004. As stated in the Ethical Standards for School Counselors (ASCA, 2004b), school counselors have responsibilities to each group they serve as well as to themselves. These standards are reprinted in Appendix N at the end of this chapter. Huey (1986) noted that ethical standards are only guidelines and seldom provide concrete answers; each situation must be judged in context. The standards of ASCA are most specific to school counselors and deserve diligent study by practicing counselors.

ISSUES OF SIGNIFICANCE TO THE SPECIALTY

Responsibilities to Students

The primary ethical obligation of the school counselor is to students and their educational, career, emotional, and behavioral needs. Counselors must respect each person as a unique individual. They should refrain from imposing their own personal orientations on the values, plans, decisions, or beliefs of students. School counselors must maintain their knowledge of laws, regulations, and policies that relate to their work and protect the rights of students (ASCA, 2004b).

In the summary of tips to school counselors, the Ethics Committee of ASCA (1999–2001) identified these related points:

- Act in the best interests of the clients at all times.
- Act in good faith and in the absence of malice.
- Increase awareness of personal values, attitudes, and beliefs.
- Refer when personal characteristics hinder effectiveness. (p. 1)

Counseling Process.   Ethical standards stipulate that school counselors inform students about the purposes, goals, techniques, and rules of procedure for counseling in a disclosure statement that is written in terms appropriate to the developmental level of the student. The student should also be informed about the meaning and limits of confidentiality, privileged communication, authoritative restraints if relevant to the setting, and the possibility that the counselor may want to consult with other professionals. This explanation of informed consent should occur when or before a counseling relationship begins. The Ethics Committee of ASCA (1999–2001) also identified the critical necessity of informing clients of potential limitations of the counseling relationship. Glosoff and Pate (2002) suggested counselors recognize informed consent as an ongoing process of clarifying counseling.

Muro and Kottman (1995) suggested that a written disclosure statement to clients makes the process of informed consent more concrete for students in schools. The language should be simple and appropriate for schoolchildren. Kaplan (2001) listed desirable sections that could be included in the disclosure statement or brochure:

- Theoretical framework and treatment approach that the counselor typically uses with clients;
- Confidentiality definition and limits such as clear and present danger of harm to self or others, reporting child abuse, maltreatment and/or neglect; school rules that conflict with confidentiality such as having to report knowledge of alcohol, drugs, or smoking in school;
- The counselor's educational background and training, including degrees and work experiences;
- Guidelines about appointments such as how to contact the counselor, how often students may see

the counselor, guidelines for getting out of class, possibilities for before-or after-school sessions; and

• Acknowledgement by the student's signature that the statement has been read and understood.

O'Connor, Plante, and Refvem (1998) suggested a consent form designed for parents. The form would include these sections:

1. Names of the school; the district, and the form;
2. An explanation of counseling services, a statement about how a parent may withhold consent for counseling services, how to return the form, and notice that permission is assumed if the form is not returned by the due date;
3. Options to check off if desired (group counseling, individual counseling of more than two sessions, referrals, etc.); and
4. A place to sign and date the form.

School counselors may also want to include this information on the school's Web site with instructions for submitting the form on-line.

Where required by law or school district policy, parents must sign consent forms prior to initiation of counseling. Sciarra (2004) pointed out that some schools require parental permission about the first or after a designated number of counseling sessions. He explained the policy of allowing a certain number of sessions before parental permission is needed presents one way to avoid a counselor turning away a student who has an immediate need. Counselors may discover the collaborative relationship that emerges from parents signing a consent to be one advantage of the practice. A more extensive and less specific type of informed consent involves the information provided to parents, teachers, and all other stakeholders about the counseling program. School counselors will want to include a description of their program, its components, and the various activities that will be undertaken, as well as the procedure adults may use to have their questions or concerns addressed.

The ethical standards state that a counselor must safeguard information received in a counseling relationship according to both legal and ethical standards as well as written policies. Counselors can reveal such information to others only with the consent of the parents and the student and in accordance with professional obligations. Records such as case notes that are in the sole possession of the counselor must be separated from the student's educational records. Sole possession records lose that designation when they are shared with

or are accessible to others or if they contain information that is not professional opinion or personal observation. Those notes should be destroyed within a reasonable amount of time, although particular attention may be necessary if those records may be needed by the legal system such as those on child abuse, suicide, sexual harassment, or violence. Hammond and Gantt (1998) reminded counselors that art may also be considered communication and probably requires the same type of protection. Counselors may ask the court not to require the release of confidential information if the disclosure may lead to potential harm to the student. Counselee's records and personal data are similarly protected. Student information stored in computers should receive the same protective care.

When the condition of the student indicates a clear and present danger to the student or to others, the counselor is responsible for informing authorities and parents or guardians. Additionally, the revision of the standards provides guidelines for working with students who are putting a third person at high risk of contracting a communicable, fatal disease such as HIV/AIDS. Costin, Page, Pietrzak, Kerr, and Symons (2002) reviewed the school counselors' knowledge and beliefs about that disease and discovered the need for more education around the implications for counseling in schools. Those researchers admonished practitioners to seek adequate information and to address their personal beliefs about HIV/AIDS in order to understand the inherent risks. In school counseling, unless state legislation forbids disclosing, the ethical standards state that school counselors may reveal information to a clearly identifiable third party who may be at a high risk of contracting a communicable and fatal disease as a result of a relationship with the student. That disclosure comes only after the counselor has recommended that the partner be notified by the student and that the student stop further high-risk behavior. If the student refuses, the counselor first explains the intent to inform the partner of the danger and then seeks legal advice about disclosing.

As noted in the guideline, when confidentiality is broken, the counselor should inform the student of that action. School counselors should disclose confidential information only after careful deliberation and, if possible, after consultation with other professionals (see Isaacs, 1997, and Isaacs & Stone, 1999).

Plans. School counselors and counselees should mutually develop counseling plans that are consistent with the abilities and circumstances of both. The ASCA

Ethics Committee (1999–2001) stated, "Be able to fully explain why you do what you do. A theoretical rationale should undergird counseling strategies and interventions" (p. 1). Providing that type of information allows counselors to help their clients become active partners in the counseling process. As well as being an ethical obligation, involving clients in planning the intervention builds their autonomy and demonstrates the counselor's respect for them (Corey, Corey, & Callanan, 1998). The counseling program emphasizes working together with all students for their developing academic and career goals. Counseling plans should support students' right to choose from an array of postsecondary educational opportunities. Plans should be reviewed regularly and students updated about information they need to make informed choices.

Huey (1986) cautioned that "counselors who work with children need to be particularly careful not to promote acceptance of the counselor's values as the 'right' ones" (p. 321). ASCA ethical standards state that counselors should refrain from imposing their own personal orientations about values, plans, decisions, or beliefs on students and must be careful never to direct a student's decision based on the counselor's ideas of right and wrong. Some of the value-laden issues that school counselors will face include reproductive health care and abortion. Stone (2002) reported that 42 states have laws that require some degree of parental involvement before their child can obtain an abortion. She concluded that school counselors may assist in the decision if they are competent to give such advice and if they proceed in a professional manner. She cited the case of *Arnold v. Board of Education of Escambia County* (1989) as an example of a situation in which a student had an abortion and chose not to inform her parents. The courts found that the school counselor had not coerced the student and was therefore not liable for giving advice. Stone suggested that, because school counselor responsibilities extend to student, parent, and the school, particular care must be taken in such value-laden situations. Her recommendations for school counselors included knowing school board policy; considering the developmental level of the student and that person's ability to make informed, sound decisions; considering parental rights; investigating diversity issues; consulting with a colleague; knowing yourself and your values; and avoiding involvement in a student's medical care.

Situations may arise in which a counselor may choose to express personal values. In such situations, the counselor may explain that these beliefs were established after thought and exploration and may not be right for all people (Huey, 1986). If personal values are so strong that a counselor cannot be effective in a relationship, the counselor should refer the student to another professional for help. The role of values in counseling is complex (see Chapters 5 and 6).

During the course of a counseling relationship, or in other circumstances, the school counselor may refer the counselee to outside resources. Counselors must know about available resources and facilitate the referral transition to minimize interruption of services. Salo and Shumate (1993) stated that the list of referrals should include medical and legal services as well as resources for other mental health services, social service agencies, and others. School counselors must be familiar with state mandates on the limitations as well as the rights of a minor to request and receive health services. Students have the right to discontinue counseling at any time (ASCA, 2004b).

The ethical standards also state that professionals must keep and secure records necessary for providing counseling services. James and DeVaney (1995) stated that school counselors' personal notes should contain factual, concrete, and behaviorally oriented language. Cameron and turtle-song (2002) outlined the process of using the SOAP format to write case notes. The four parts of this data-keeping format include the subjective, objective, assessment, and plan sections. Whatever method the counselor uses as a memory aid, those notes should be kept in a location where privacy can be ensured. Counselors should also destroy their notes after a reasonable amount of time. As noted earlier, if requested to submit the notes by the court, the counselor should consult with an attorney to see if the documents are protected.

Group Work. School counselors who work with groups have ethical considerations specific to that intervention. The *Ethical Guidelines for Group Counselors* (Association for Specialists in Group Work, 1989), Rapin and Keel's (1998) *Best Practice Guidelines*, and the ASCA ethical standards provide direction for school counselors who work with groups. These standards stress the importance of screening potential group members, attending to the safety and growth of each group member, and establishing a norm of confidentiality (see Chapter 16 for a discussion of ethical issues in group counseling).

Terres and Larrabee (1985) and Corey, Corey, Callanan, and Russell (1988) emphasized the possibility for ethical dilemmas in the planning and implementation of groups in schools. At the planning stage, school counselors must determine their competence as group leaders of the specific type of group they will be facilitating. Some topics may be inappropriate for group work in the school setting. Counselors need to determine the appropriateness of the group experience for the specific child and the appropriateness of the specific child to the group and to the group experience. Ritchie and Huss (2000) outlined special considerations in recruiting and screening students for group counseling in schools. Student and parent rights, as well as internal and external constraints of the school setting, also must be considered in planning group counseling in schools. ASCA ethical standards suggest that counselors notify parents about students who are participating in groups if the counselor feels that is appropriate and if that practice is consistent with district policies.

Hines and Fields (2002) outlined prescreening issues such as age, gender, diversity, group fit, and group contribution. They discussed screening problems in the school setting, such as parent permission, confidentiality, and inappropriate referrals. Furthermore they examined various methods for screening and suggestions for a protocol. Their recommendations will alleviate some of the potential difficulties of groups in schools.

To implement groups, counselors should provide information about the purpose of the group, the leader's qualifications, and other facts about the group process both to the participating students and to their parents. Discussing the importance of confidentiality initially and at each meeting may help avoid problems. Some authors recommend asking group members to sign a contract stating they will not discuss outside the group what happens in the group (Corey & Corey, 2001). School counselors should recognize they can guarantee only that they personally will abide by the standard of confidentiality in group counseling, but they should stress to the group members the importance of keeping private the information shared in the group. Group sessions can occur after provisions for space, privacy, participant factors, and session length and duration are determined, with all decisions informed by the developmental stages of the students who are involved. The guidelines provided by Terres and Larrabee (1985) are helpful to school counselors who conduct group counseling. The current ethical standards (ASCA, 2004b) also advise counselors to follow up with group members.

CASE SCENARIO 13–1

Group Work
(written by Juleen Buser, Wake Forest University)

In a group on study skills for elementary students, Jerome, a third-grade student, has been reserved and quiet. The group has worked well together for 3 weeks, but Jerome still appears to be on the outskirts of this unit. You have consistently reinforced the need for confidentiality among the group members and have also alerted students to the limits of that confidentiality.

In one session, Jerome is uncharacteristically talkative and brings up the topic of his brother, who also attends the same school. He begins discussing the many fights and problems that he and his brother have been experiencing at home, giving details about their interactions and his anger at his brother. The group joins in support of Jerome, and you can see that he feels encouraged and more involved in the group than he had been before.

What is your ethical responsibility in this situation? Given Jerome's need for acceptance and belonging in the group, and the fact that you have stressed confidentiality throughout the group meetings, is it responsible to let this session continue as it is, without your intervention?

NO. The current ethical codes for group practice mandate that a professional school counselor "establishes clear expectations in the group setting and clearly states that confidentiality in group counseling cannot be guaranteed. Given the developmental and chronological ages of minors in schools, the counselor recognizes that the tenuous nature of confidentiality for minors renders some topics inappropriate for group work in a school setting" (ASCA, 2004b, p. 2). As confidentiality cannot be completely ensured in a group, and given the reality that Jerome's brother attends the same school, this topic is not suitable for a group on study skills. Jerome's concerns might be better addressed in individual counseling, or in a group specifically tailored for sibling and family distress that involves his brother as well. As a school counselor, it is your responsibility to intervene gently into this group topic to prevent the detailed description of Jerome's fights with his brother; it is also your responsibility, however, not to exacerbate Jerome's isolation from the group. You might say something like, "Jerome, I want to thank you for sharing about your brother today—and I think you can see that the group wants to hear about it and support you. I think we all probably have problems with our brothers and sisters sometimes. But, I am afraid that if we keep talking about that in the group, your brother might hear about it, and it could hurt his feelings. Maybe you and I can talk about it some other time."

After the group, the scheduling of an individual session with Jerome to address this problem would be an appropriate next move.

Roles and Relationships. Whenever a counselor interacts with a client in more than one capacity, potentially harmful relationships can occur (Fisher & Hennessy, 1994). The ethical standards (ASCA, 2004b) state that counselors must avoid these multiple relationships if possible. Corey et al. (1998) stated that, in these situations, incompatible roles have the potential for drastically decreasing the effectiveness of the professional relationship. According to the ethical standards, potentially detrimental relationships to be avoided include counseling relatives, close friends, or associates. In the school setting counselors must be careful to avoid relationships with school personnel that may interfere with the counselor–student relationship. If a counselor finds it impossible to avoid conflicting relationships, he or she must be active in eliminating or reducing the potential for harm in those relationships by using the safeguards of informed consent, consultation, supervision, and documentation. The school counselor must take responsibility for protecting counselees from risk.

Relationships with clients vary from those that are potentially very harmful to those with little potential for harm. Counselors in such a relationship are always obligated to reduce the potential for harm. Counselors need to monitor the relationship closely, gauging the benefits of counseling with the risks of harm or exploitation of the student client. Counselors should also continually evaluate the effectiveness of their counseling and refer the student to another counselor if possible (Fisher & Hennessy, 1994). Counselors should seek consultation or supervision, use informed consent, and document carefully to reduce the potential for harm (Muro & Kottman, 1995). Sexual relationships with student clients are prohibited in the ethical standards of all mental health organizations and are illegal in many states (Kitchener & Harding, 1990).

In determining what action to take in ethical dilemmas presented by potentially detrimental relationships, school counselors should follow these steps:

- Identify the primary client (in most cases, the students in school).
- Identify the ethical issues or dilemma involved.
- Consult the necessary codes and experts.
- Think carefully before acting.

Using the ethical decision-making model presented in Chapter 6 may also help school counselors make responsible and ethical choices. Herlihy and Corey (1992) noted that the harm to clients is derived from the practitioner who exploits the relationship rather than from the duality itself.

Evaluation, Assessment, and Interpretation.   The ASCA Code of Ethics (2004b) requires that counselors adhere to all professional standards in choosing, giving, and interpreting assessment measures. Counselors must be cautious with instruments that have norm groups different from the population with which the measurement is being used. Counselors who use electronically based testing programs should receive specific training in those assessment techniques. Sampson and Pyle (1988) suggested that counselors also are responsible for the accuracy and proper functioning of the computer programs they use. Counselors must ensure the confidentiality of the student data generated in computer testing. Counselors should monitor for the possibility of scoring errors that may be difficult to determine in computer-based testing applications. Overcoming the inadequacies of the generalized test interpretations that accompany the test results is an important counselor obligation, as is the need for follow-up with the computer user.

A counselor is obligated to explain clearly the nature, purposes, and results of assessment instruments to students. Counselors must not misuse results and interpretations and should attempt to prevent others from doing so. Talbutt (1983b) presented practical recommendations for school counselors and testing in schools. She suggested reviewing school policy to become knowledgeable about the counselor's responsibilities related to testing. According to Talbutt (1983b), counselors should follow all regulations and guidelines from state and local boards of education, abide by professional guidelines, keep abreast of current testing information, and be diligent in selecting and interpreting testing instruments. The Association for Assessment in Counseling (2002) provided a monograph that explains more specifically ways to apply standards for educational and psychological testing, and ASCA's (2002c) position statement on high-stakes testing also guides school counselors.

This section of the ASCA ethical standards also directs counselors to use assessment data to assess the effectiveness of the counseling program. Counselors should monitor the impact their work has on closing achievement, opportunity, and attainment gaps in education.

CASE SCENARIO 13–2

Assessment Measures
(written by Juleen Buser, Wake Forest University)

In the elementary school where you work as a counselor, a program for gifted students is in the initial stages of implementation. The school psychologist is administering one aptitude test to all third graders in the coming week and, from this measure, will identify those who will be admitted into the gifted program. Obtaining information on the norm group on which this test is standardized, you realize that it has not been standardized for diverse student populations. You also are aware of several third graders who, although considerably intelligent, are presently experiencing personal problems and will likely be distracted in the coming week when the aptitude test is administered. What is your ethical responsibility as a school counselor regarding this situation?

WHAT YOU SHOULD DO. The current ethical standards clearly state that a professional school counselor "monitors the use of assessment results and interpretations, and takes reasonable steps to prevent others from misusing the information" (ASCA, 2004b, p. 2). Based on these parameters, you have a responsibility to the diverse students and those experiencing personal problems, as their intellectual capabilities have a significant chance of being misrepresented by the assessment measure. As an advocate for the responsible and accurate use of assessment and evaluation procedures, you should bring this matter to the attention of the school psychologist. Suggestions may include the use of several assessment measures with diverse norm groups in identifying gifted students, interpretations that account for the test's norm group so as not to discriminate against diverse students, and behavioral observations so as to monitor the attention and mental state of students who may be emotionally troubled during the testing process (Suzuki & Kugler, 1995).

Computers. Two examples of expanded counseling services to students include computer applications and peer helper programs. The ethical standards specify that the counselor is responsible for explaining the benefits and limitations of computer applications. The use of computers in counseling should be determined by an assessment of the appropriateness of the use of the computer for the student's needs, the student's understanding of the application, and follow-up counseling assistance. All groups should have equal access to computer applications that are unbiased by discriminatory information and values. ASCA's (2000b) position statement on student safety on the internet suggests that school counselors can provide internet guidelines to parents and to school personnel. The counselor takes responsibility for taking reasonable and appropriate measures to protect students from harmful on-line material (ASCA, 2004b). The National Center for Missing and Exploited Children has prepared a document that can be disseminated for that purpose (Net Smartz Workshop, http://www.missingkids.org). The counselor's responsibilities for protecting students extend to all electronic media, including but not limited to facsimile machines, electronic mail, instant messaging, telephones, videoconferencing, and the internet.

ASCA's (2004b) ethical standards charge school counselors with taking appropriate and reasonable measures for protecting student information and educational records stored or transmitted via electronic media. The ethical standards related to using computers in counseling services are enhanced by guidelines offered by Sampson and Pyle (1988), Childers (1988), and Sampson, Kolodinsky, and Greeno (1997). These authors discussed ways of safeguarding stored data by maintaining security procedures, restricting content and access, preserving anonymity when possible, and limiting the time period of storage. If a counselor is using computer applications with a client, the counselor should provide guidelines that include informed consent and release forms specific to computer use. These authors identified potential problems and provided safeguards as solutions. Additional discussions of ethical issues involved in computer use can be found in Chapter 10.

The ethical standards also clarify the responsibilities of school counselors who coordinate peer helper groups. The pertinent standard states that counselors are responsible for the welfare of students in peer programs under their direction. ASCA (2002d) identified the school counselor's role in determining the needs of the school population and for implementing a peer helping program to help meet those needs. Welfel (2002) stated that peer helpers must be chosen carefully, trained well, and supervised closely. The National Peer Helpers Association (2001) Code of Ethics includes the following points:

- A philosophy that upholds the effectiveness of peer helping;
- Commitment to an individual's right to dignity, self-development, and self-direction;
- Guidelines for excellence in program development and implementation; and
- Promotion of realistic expectations of the program.

Responsibilities to Parents

The difficulties of ethical practice often emerge when school counselors try to balance the responsibilities to students with those to parents or guardians. Counselors must determine how to maintain confidentiality for a student as well as provide needed information to parents. The ASCA (2004b) ethical standards stipulate the following counselor obligations to parents:

- To respect the inherent rights and responsibilities of all parents for their children;

- To establish a cooperative relationship with parents, maintaining the confidentiality of their communications with the counselor; and
- To recognize legal and local guidelines when helping parents with family difficulties that interfere with students' effectiveness and welfare.

In some cases, counselors need a clear understanding of the meaning of custody and the legal issues that affect noncustodial parents and their access of information about their child. Wilcoxon and Magnuson (1999) presented definitions and other considerations for school counselors serving non-custodial parents. For example, these authors encouraged school counselors to assist schools in developing guidelines that promote family involvement rather than focusing only on the custodial parent. They recommended that school counselors anticipate difficulties caused by the material decree and design policies and procedures that are not only sensitive to the family but also prevent difficulties in the school setting.

The responsibilities of the school counselor related to parents and confidentiality are as follows:

- To inform parents about the role of the school counselor, emphasizing the importance of confidentiality in that role;
- To give parents "accurate, comprehensive, and relevant information in an objective and caring manner, as appropriate and consistent with ethical responsibilities to the counselee" (ASCA, 2004b, p. 2);
- To make reasonable efforts to honor the wishes of parents and guardians about information concerning the counselee; and
- In cases of divorce or separation to make good-faith efforts in providing both parents with needed information about their child unless a court order stipulates otherwise (ASCA, 2004b).

Balancing the responsibilities to students and to parents presents counselors with ethical dilemmas that often have to be decided case by case. Consultation with another counselor and supervision may be helpful in making those decisions. Welfel (2002) noted that parents are often reassured when they learn that counselors have no intention of working beyond the limits of their competence, that counselors will make reasonable efforts to honor the parents' requests, and that counselors will be respectful of family values. She suggested a brochure or handbook to distribute this information. The ASCA Ethics Committee calls for

counselors to "encourage family involvement, where possible, when working with minors in sensitive areas which might be controversial" (p. 1). Stromberg and colleagues (1993) stated the general rule is that a parent is entitled to general information from the counselor about the child's progress in counseling. School counselors may satisfy parents' requests for information with short updates on the child's progress. Corey et al. (1998) recognized that school counselors must be discrete in the kind and extent of information revealed to parents or guardians.

ASCA's (2004c) position statement on parental consent for services suggests that written information about the school counseling program must be provided to parents. Glosoff and Pate (2002) suggested the information given to parents, teachers, and administrators incorporate the role of the counselor, the possible benefits of the program, and the nature of program activities. Parents can thereby gain a better understanding of the counseling relationship, and the trust among the counselor, the counselee, and the parents will increase. School counselors must obtain parental permission for counseling services if required by local law or policy.

Glosoff and Pate (2002) admonished counselors to approach parents as allies in counseling. In situations when a parent asks for specific information about the content of counseling sessions, the counselor should first ask if the student is willing to give the counselor permission to disclose the content. If the student gives permission, there is no conflict. However, if the student refuses or if the counselor believes that disclosure would be detrimental to the best interest of the student, a more problematic situation exists. In those cases, counselors explain the counseling process and the deleterious effect that disclosure may have on that relationship. Parents should also be assured that if the child were in harm's way, the counselor would impart needed information.

Mitchell, Disque, and Robertson (2002) offered other suggestions for responding to parental demands for confidential information. One strategy is using skills to allow the parent to express their concerns and to convey respect for those worries. The counselor may reframe the concerns to create an alternative viewpoint. Counselors may explain their dilemma, the ethical code, and the importance of confidentiality in the counseling alliance. These authors maintained that the child should be informed of their parents' inquiry. Most importantly, they admonished counselors to prepare procedures and alternatives for responding to difficult situations in advance.

Kaplan (1997) outlined the legal rights of parents and suggestions for preventing challenges to school counseling programs. She proposed that school counselors focus on academics and assure that program activities are designed to support high expectations for all students. She also recommended offering more effective communications to parents, having parent advisory groups, protecting the child's access to all educational programs, and involving parents in decision making relative to their child. Finally, she advocated that school counselors assess the impact of their program on student learning.

Responsibilities to Colleagues and Professional Associates

School counselors have an obligation to establish and maintain a professional relationship with the faculty, staff, and administration. Those relationships help maximize the potential of the school counseling program. School counselors must carefully define the parameters of their professional role by informing colleagues about guidelines regarding confidentiality, public and private information, and consultation. Corey et al. (1998) stated the importance of talking to everyone about matters of confidentiality. Freeman (2000) suggested that ethical counselors maintain open communication lines and provide school personnel with information they need to provide services to students. That exchange of information occurs within the framework of confidentiality and privileged communication guidelines.

Counselors should also be active in cooperating and collaborating with community agencies, organizations, and individuals in the best interests of students and, therefore, establish a network to be used in referring students and their families. Muro and Kottman (1995) suggested providing at least three referral sources. When school counselors do refer students to other professionals, the counselors must provide information that is accurate, objective, and concise in order to assist. If a counselee is being seen by another mental health professional, the school counselor should ask the counselee and parents, where necessary, for permission to talk to the other professional. The school counselor and mental health professional should develop agreements to prevent confusion and conflict for the counselee. School counselors know about the requirement of a release of information and about parents' rights relative to the release of confidential matters.

Responsibilities to School and Community

School counselors have obligations to the school program and to the community as well as to faculty, staff, and administration. The ethical standards (ASCA, 2004b) stipulate those obligations as follows:

- Counselors protect the educational program from anything that is not in the best interests of the students.
- While honoring confidentiality, counselors report to the appropriate authorities any potentially disruptive or damaging conditions that may threaten the school's mission, personnel, and/or property.
- Counselors clearly define their role and functions and report conditions that may impede the effectiveness of the program and services.
- School counselors accept employment only for which they are qualified and recommend only qualified, competent people for counseling positions.
- The school counselor helps develop a positive school environment, an educational program to meet students' developmental needs, and an evaluation process for the counseling program, services, and personnel. The information from the evaluation process of the developmental, standards-based school counseling programs is used for planning programs and services.

Huey (1986) stated "Counselors should adhere to local school policies, whether determined by the principal or the board of education, to the extent possible without compromising their primary responsibility to the client" (p. 321). When conflicts exist between loyalty to the student client and to the employer, Huey suggested a resolution that protects the rights of the student. Counselors may actively try to change existing policies that cause the conflicts.

The Ethics Committee of ASCA (1999–2001) provided this tip for school counselors: "Follow written job descriptions. Be sure what you are doing is defined as an appropriate function in your work setting" (p. 1).

The dilemma of parents' rights in educational control is an ongoing controversy. Parents may continue to challenge the content and activities of school counseling programs. As noted earlier, Kaplan (1997) reviewed the current status of parents' rights and listed ways for counselors to prevent and to respond to parental concerns about affective education. Kaplan (1996) also suggested that bringing parents into the program might prevent problems as well as heighten their sensitivity.

Including parents on an advisory committee would be one way school counselors could provide an opportunity for this involvement.

ASCA's (2002a) position statement on censorship verifies the profession's endorsement of the following activities as part of a counselor's role:

- Supporting academic freedom, access to information, and the right to independent thought;
- Safeguarding student's rights to receive information and services;
- Encouraging growth and academic excellence;
- Recognizing diversity among ideas and students; and
- Providing data to the school and community on the counseling program.

The statement recommends that counselors offer a comprehensive collection of materials that are chosen according to the basic written selection criterion of the school district.

Responsibilities to Self

School counselors also have obligations to themselves and to their ability to accomplish their duties, including operating within the boundaries of their individual professional competence and being aware of their personal strengths and limitations. Counselors who monitor their own psychological health, participate in continuing education, and stay current with literature in the profession, maintain competence in the school counseling setting. Carroll, Schneider, and Wesley (1985) identified formal education, professional training, and supervised experience as the criteria that define competence.

Varhely and Cowles (1991) discussed the counselor's responsibility to engage in self-examination continually. These authors outlined a process for this self-scrutiny. The first step is recognizing that one's personal beliefs, values, and needs may bias behavior in ways that are beyond one's consciousness. As counselors increase their awareness of the impact of their personal worldviews, their thoughtful, ongoing exploration of self is the next step. These two processes lead the counselor to become more aware of cues that may imply a conflict between personal issues and professional responsibilities. By constantly examining their own values, counselors become sensitive to whether they are unconsciously influencing students.

School counselors should monitor their personal performance and effectiveness, always avoiding any inadequacy in professional services or any potential harm to students. Counselors must be aware of their own biases and personal characteristics and their potential effects on students. School counselors must have specific training to ensure they provide appropriate and effective services to people who have differences related to age, gender, race, religion, sexual orientation, and socioeconomic and ethnic backgrounds. Hobson and Kanitz (1996) considered multicultural counseling as an ethical issue for school counselors and challenge school counselors to assess their level of multicultural competence and seek training opportunities to overcome any deficiencies. Counselors should have the knowledge and experiences to improve awareness, knowledge, skills, and effectiveness in working with diverse populations. They must be able to collaborate with students, parents, and school staff in altering attitudes and policies that impede learning. They promote awareness and understanding of diversity and strive to ensure all students have access and opportunities to maximize their potential (ASCA, 2004a).

Continuing education and personal growth are professional obligations of school counselors. Several tips from the Ethics Committee of ASCA (1999–2001) address these responsibilities:

- Function within the boundaries of personal competence. Be aware of personal skill levels and limitations.
- Consult with other professionals. Have a readily accessible support network of professionals.
- Stay up to date with laws and current court rulings.
- Actively attempt to understand the diverse cultural backgrounds of the clients with whom you work. (pp. 1–2)

Responsibilities to the Profession

School counselors have obligations to their profession that include maintaining professionally appropriate conduct, participating in advancing knowledge in the field of counseling, and belonging to professional organizations. School counselors should not use their position to recruit or to gain clients or to receive personal gains. The ASCA standards emphasize that school counselors must abide by ethical standards of the profession as well as other official policy statements and relevant legal mandates.

The Ethics Committee of ASCA (1999–2001) emphasized these points:

- Read and adhere to the ethical standards of your profession. Keep copies of the ethical standards on hand, review them periodically, and act accordingly.
- Join appropriate professional associations. Read association publications and participate in professional development opportunities. (p. 2).

Legal Issues

A consideration of the ethical standards for school counselors would be incomplete without discussing the legal standards that affect school counselors' responsibilities, particularly confidentiality; exceptions to confidentiality, including the duty to warn and reporting child abuse; the Family Educational Rights and Privacy Act; and the Education for All Handicapped Children Act.

School counselors may find the report, *State Minor Consent Laws: A Summary* (2nd ed.; CAHL, 2003), a valuable resource for a state-by-state description of the legal status of minors, their rights to request different types of health services including outpatient mental health services, health privacy and confidentiality statutes, and disclosure to parents, as well as other statutes affecting young people (English & Kenney, 2003). The Alan Guttmacher Institute (www.guttmacher.org/pubs) summarized policies related to young people and has policy briefs and charts that document state laws. Additionally Linde (2003) discussed the implications of a federal regulation that outlines confidentiality of records for substance abuse assessment, referral, diagnosis, and treatment for all, even clients under the age of 18. That mandate has implications that school counselors will want to review. A particularly valuable resource for investigating accurate, contemporary materials is contained in the article written by Guillot-Miller and Partin (2003) on Web-based sites.

Confidentiality

Confidentiality, the assurance to the client that what is said in a counseling relationship will not be revealed, is an ethical responsibility of counselors in all settings. School counselors have unique challenges in trying to honor that obligation because they work with minors. Remley and Herlihy (2005) noted that legal and ethical requirements seldom conflict, but an exception occurs often in counseling minor clients. One difficulty involves defining *minor*. Generally, the legal age of majority, unless designated otherwise, is 18. Therefore, at the age of 18, students are considered legally mature and have control of their own privacy rights (Glosoff & Pate, 2002). Legally, privacy rights before that age belong to the parents (Remley & Herlihy, 2005). Stone (2004) explained the dilemma. She noted the primary function of school is to provide a free and appropriate quality education. When students come to a school counselor, the friction between protecting the child's right to privacy and parent's rights to be informed about what is occurring in their child's life puts the school counselor in the position of protecting the rights of both. Stone and Isaacs (2003) studied over 900 responses from school counselors about situations across school levels in which they might breach confidentiality. Counselors reported their primary responsibility as that of protecting the relationship with students. The researchers suggested that policy makers establish ways to make confidential relationships a priority.

Privileged Communication

Children have an ethical right to privacy and confidentiality. Remley (1985) noted that in the legal structure of the United States, children have some of the protections granted to adults; however, in many ways the protection of children's rights depends on interpretations made by their parents, guardians, or the courts. The legal status pertinent to the discussion of confidentiality is privileged communication, which means that a client is protected from confidential communications being disclosed in a legal proceeding.

Isaacs (1997), Isaacs and Stone (1999), and Glosoff, Herlihy, and Spence (2000) offered a review of privileged communication. Glosoff et al. (2000) found that 45 jurisdictions allowed privileged communication to the counselor–client relationship. In some states that privilege includes school counselors. Herlihy and Sheeley (1987) and Sheeley and Herlihy (1987) summarized their survey of the provision of privileged communication to the clients of school counselors. In approximately 20 states, students in schools are granted the legal right of privileged communication when talking with a school counselor (Taylor & Adelman, 1989). Fischer and Sorenson (1996) reported that 16 states directly grant statutory privilege to school counselors. The restrictions that are placed on the privileged communication vary among the states. School counselors must know whether privilege is granted and examine the limits that exist in the statute.

The level of privilege to which a minor is entitled is a complicated legal determination (Waldo & Malley, 1992) that school counselors must investigate in the state in which they are employed. Additionally, a recent decision by the U.S. Supreme Court in *Jaffee v. Redmond* (1996) has possible implications about privileged communication for all counselors, according to Remley, Herlihy, and Herlihy (1997). In that decision, the Supreme Court ruled that the communications between a master's-level social worker and her client were privileged communication under the Federal Rules of Evidence. The social worker was referred to as "therapist" or "psychotherapist" in the decision, and the activities were referred to as "counseling sessions," "counseling," or "psychotherapy." According to Remley et al., the decision is important for establishing a precedent in an official federal court that provides protection to communications between therapists and their patients. School counselors need to remain informed about how the implications from that decision may extend to minors and to the school setting.

ASCA Position Statement on Confidentiality. Regardless of whether privilege has been mandated to protect student communications with counselors, confidentiality within that relationship is imperative. The position statement on the school counselor and confidentiality (ASCA, 2002b) details the obligations of a school counselor for establishing and maintaining confidentiality in schools and places no age limitation on who is entitled to a confidential relationship. The position paper contains definitions and limitations pertinent to school counselors' practice and should be reviewed carefully. One significant point in the statement is that counselors have a responsibility to protect the privacy of information received from students, parents, and teachers. A critical phrase that is repeated throughout the position statement is "confidentiality must not be abridged by the counselor except where there is clear and present danger to the student and/or other persons" (p. 1).

Employer Policy and Expectations. Tompkins and Mehring (1993) discussed considerations of privilege and confidentiality and stated that the third consideration of counselor–student privacy is the policy and expectation of the employer. Counselors are specialized members of the school community who receive requests from teachers, school administration or staff, and others concerned with the educational enterprise. They must respect, and presumably follow, dictates from the school principal and superintendent (Remley, 1993). Because teachers and administrators are able to reveal all that a child says to them, it is often difficult

for these individuals to understand why school counselors should not do so as well.

CASE SCENARIO 13–3

Responding to the Policies of the School and Maintaining Confidentiality

An elementary school counselor is attending a student assistance team meeting with administrators, teachers, and a school psychologist about a student, Joey, a third grader who is increasingly withdrawn in the classroom. Joey is not completing his work and is not participating in any classroom activities. The counselor has been working with the child, whose single-parent mother has been diagnosed with an inoperable brain tumor. During the school team meeting, the principal asked the counselor to explain what has been happening to Joey. Should the counselor provide this information to the principal and the team?

NO. The counselor should maintain the confidentiality of Joey's communication and simply respond that Joey has been encountering some stressful situations and the effects are obviously being expressed in the classroom. The counselor should continue by saying that perhaps, together, she and the school team could determine strategies to help Joey become more engaged in class.

The competing demands of maintaining confidentiality for the student and some employer policies further complicate the counselor's responsibilities. Before accepting employment, counselors should clarify the policy and expectations of the school.

Options for Counselors in Matters Related to Confidentiality. Several options have been proposed to help school counselors in matters related to confidentiality. Remley and Herlihy (2005) identified some pertinent facts about children and confidentiality:

- Younger children do not have an understanding of the concepts of confidentiality or privacy and are probably not as concerned about confidentiality as the counselor is. Huey (1996) supported that statement.
- On the other hand, preadolescents and adolescents may have a higher desire for privacy. That concern relates to their confusion about identity and other developmental changes.
- Some children at all ages may not be concerned at all about privacy. Counselors should not automatically assume that minors do not want their parents or guardians to know what they are discussing.

- Some children may confide in an adult, thinking that adult will act as an intermediary to resolve their concern.
- Children's limited reasoning capacity may interfere with their ability to make decisions that are in their best interests.

Tompkins and Mehring (1993) and Davis and Ritchie (1993) suggested that counselors:

1. Stay informed about the law and written policy in the area of the practice;
2. Operate within the ethical code of the professional organization;
3. Review expectations and policy before employment is accepted;
4. Operate within their personal limits of expertise; and
5. Keep the best interest of the children their predominant concern.

By providing informed consent for the child and for the parent when dealing with sensitive issues or before engaging in long-term counseling, the counselor should establish a climate of confidentiality. Remley (1985) stated that counselors fulfill their confidentiality responsibilities by informing the child before consulting with anyone about the child's problem, involving the child in the decision-making process and keeping the child informed. The guidelines provided by Zingaro (1983) include some specifics helpful to the practice of school counseling. He suggested that when it is in the best interest of the child for a significant adult to have information, the counselor may respond by telling the adult how he can help the child rather than revealing specific information disclosed by the child. Taylor and Adelman (1989) suggested that counselors should focus on establishing a relationship in which youngsters take the lead in sharing information when appropriate. Those authors provided guidelines for enhancing clients' motivation and choice to resolve their problems by confiding in other adults. Strein and Hershenson (1991) offered suggestions for using a "need-to-know" basis as an alternative guideline to confidentiality when counselors work in situations that are not one-to-one relationships, a common occurrence in schools.

When a parent or guardian demands to know the content of counseling sessions and the counselee strongly resists this disclosure, school counselors may find the following steps suggested by Remley and Herlihy (2005) useful:

1. Discuss the situation fully with the minor and see if the minor will disclose the content of the sessions to the adult. If not,
2. Work to persuade the adult that the child's best interests would not be served by disclosing the information. Telling the adult about the counseling relationship and assuring the adult that information would be revealed if the child were in danger may be helpful. If not,
3. Schedule a joint session with the adult and the minor and assume the role of the mediator. If the conflict has not been resolved yet, choose one of the following:
   a. Inform the child ahead of time and then disclose the content of the sessions to the adult. Remember that the adult may have legal rights to the information.
   b. Refuse to disclose the information. Inform your direct supervisor before doing this, and remember that the adult may have legal rights to the information.

CASE SCENARIO 13–4

Sharing Information on a "Need-to-Know" Basis
How would you respond to this request?

Teacher: *What is going on with Jamie? She has asked to go to your office twice in the last 2 days and she is so testy lately. Every time I speak to her directly, she rolls her eyes and huffs. I hate to stop her from coming to see you, but of course I cannot let her take advantage of my good nature and continue to see you unless I know she has a legitimate reason.*

Should you provide the teacher with the specific circumstances that are creating Jamie's difficulty?

NO. You should phrase your response in such a way that protects Jamie's confidentiality yet tells the teacher some specific actions she can take to assist Jamie. An example of such a response follows.

Counselor: *I know how well you get along with your students and how interested you are in helping them. Jamie does need time with me right now, and I appreciate you letting her come to talk with me when you feel you can. What seems like her frustration with you is probably a result of other concerns. She should be better in time. In the meantime, you might talk with her and arrange a signal to let her know when her reactions are inappropriate so you can have less tense interactions. I remember when you tried that last year with Juan—things went much better for both of you.*

Varhely and Cowles (1991) suggested that an over-looked dilemma in conflicts over confidentiality involves the counselor's personal beliefs, experiences, and values. Counselors must strive to determine their personal beliefs about the rights and responsibilities of children, their needs for belonging and a sense of adequacy, and their personal value system. Without a continual process to develop self-awareness in these areas, counselors may further complicate the difficulties inherent in maintaining confidentiality in school settings.

Exceptions to Confidentiality

Some exceptions to confidentiality relate to protecting children from harm—the duty to warn and reporting child abuse. School counselors should be aware that, as with privileged communication, the statutes that determine a counselor's liability in situations of duty to warn and of reporting child abuse are mandated by the state in which the counselor is practicing. Counselors must do a careful review of legislative updates and judicial opinions in their states to make informed decisions (Hopkins & Anderson, 1990).

Duty to Warn and Protect.   Counselors must determine actions to take in the delicate balance between confidentiality and the duty to warn others on a case-by-case basis (Sheeley & Herlihy, 1989). They may be vulnerable to a lawsuit if they breach confidentiality. However, if counselors could have prevented an incident, they may be sued if a student client is injured, injures someone else, or commits suicide. Counselors should make the decision between breaching confidentiality and warning others with diligence and careful judgment. The first step is to be fully informed about state laws and court decisions. Legal mandates and statutes are continually interpreted and revised; therefore, keeping abreast of the laws and decisions is an ongoing process.

If the school district does not have a policy on confidentiality and its limitations, school counselors should work actively to develop one. That local policy should be adequately disclosed to all students and to all parents.

Capuzzi (2002) outlined a school counselor's legal and ethical challenges when dealing with suicidal children in preventive, crisis, and postvention areas. He described practices related to prevention efforts such as communicating with administrators, providing faculty and staff in-service, preparing crisis teams, offering individual and group counseling options, making parent education available, and giving classroom presentations. If counselors are in the crisis management stage, Capuzzi noted that the adolescent must be assessed,

directed, monitored, and guided in order to prevent the act of self-destruction. Parents must be notified if the person is thought to be potentially suicidal by at least two professionals. Capuzzi also discussed guidelines for postvention. The strategies contained in his article are valuable principles for school counselors.

Sheeley and Herlihy (1989) and Remley and Sparkman (1993) had additional suggestions for school counselors who work with students who may be suicidal. Their suggestions are useful in establishing policy and procedures for this difficult situation:

1. Be able to recognize the warning signs of students with suicidal potential.
2. Have an established plan for dealing with the crisis.
3. Have referral sources for crisis situations.
4. Develop the skills to help students and families if a student threatens suicide.
5. Take action if it is determined that a student is at risk of harming himself of herself.
6. Consider actions that are the least instrusive steps, but that will nevertheless ensure the safety of the person who is suicidal.
7. Consult with colleagues in determining risk as well as the appropriate action to take.
8. Inform school administrators and parents when counselors have determined that a student client is at risk of attempting suicide.
9. If these adults are reluctant to become involved, school counselors have an ethical responsibility to do all they can do to prevent the suicide.

Box 13–2 discusses a court decision in a case involving a student suicide. This decision has strong implications for school counselors to warn parents of the suicidal intentions of students. Eating disorders, substance abuse, reckless sexual behavior, cult membership, criminal activity, self-mutilation, and other dangerous activities may also be viewed as instances of harm to self. School counselors should question the degree to which such behaviors constitute a student's potential for harm to self that might necessitate breaching confidentiality.

Many counselors face the challenge of working with students who purposefully hurt themselves. Self-mutilation has become a prevalent problem. Counselors may be the first professional to work with students who harm themselves. Froeschle and Moyer (2004) argued for maintaining confidentiality in these relationships even with the risk. They noted that students with these self-mutilation behaviors have particular difficulty trusting and expressing their negative emotions. A confidential relationship may help them

Box 13–2 • Duty to Warn of Suicidal Intent

(See the ACA and APA codes in Appendix A and B and the school counselor's code in Appendix N.)

Friends of a middle school student, Nicole, reported to school counselors that she intended to kill herself. The counselors questioned Nicole and she denied making suicidal statements. The counselors did not inform school officials or Nicole's parents. Nicole died in a suicide pact with another student, and her parents sued. On appeal of the original verdict that favored the school personnel, the question of the counselor's duty to warn the parents was considered. The court found "a special relationship sufficient to create a duty of care when an adolescent in a school setting expresses an intention to commit suicide and the counselor becomes aware of such intention" (Fischer & Sorenson, 1996).

---

overcome those difficulties and move to self-disclose. They recommend encouraging students to share their problems with their parents and for counselors to reveal the information if the risk of grater self-harm increases. Eating disorders present a similar dilemma about when to involve parents, as in the following case, which has been submitted by Juleen Buser, a graduate student at Wake Forest University.

CASE SCENARIO 13–5

Confidentiality
(written by Juleen Buser, Wake Forest University)

An eighth-grade middle school student, Stella, confides in you that she is concerned about her friend, Hannah. She says that Hannah has been engaging in erratic and troubling eating patterns for the past several months. According to Stella, Hannah alternates between periods of not eating at all and throwing up her meals and has lost a significant amount of weight. Recognizing signs of an eating disorder, you schedule an individual session with Hannah, in which she denies any serious problem and promises to eat more, if people are concerned. You notice that she appears very thin and express concern. "I know I'm a little skinnier," she says, "but it's probably because out team has been doing a lot of exercise at track practice. And, I just decided to be a vegetarian, so I'm just getting used to eating like that, I guess." You mention a desire to talk with her parents and include them in this conversation, but Hannah reacts angrily to this suggestion and reassures you that she really is fine. She says that she will definitely eat more and gain weight, as long as you don't tell her parents. Hannah does take a self-report measure designed to assess eating disorder risk, and the results reveal no disordered thoughts or behaviors that would be a cause for concern. After deliberation, you decide to take Hannah at her word and maintain the confidentiality of the session, admitting that sports practice and a new diet could explain her weight loss. However, you resolve to keep tabs on Hannah throughout the year to observe any more weight loss or problematic behavior. Was this the correct move?

NO. Individuals with eating disorders frequently deny their behavior and minimize their difficulties (Bardick et al., 2004). Also, interviews and self-report measures are often unreliable in assessing eating disorders, as respondents will not be forthcoming and truthful about their eating beliefs and behaviors. (Bardick et al.) Taking Hannah at her word and maintaining confidentiality could breach several ethical codes, including the duty to warn, parental rights, professional competence, and making appropriate referrals (ASCA, 2004b).

Knowing your limits as a professional is one ethical element to consider, as an accurate assessment of Hannah's eating disorder can likely only come from a specialist in eating disorders (Bardick et al., 2004). The current ethical standards state that a school counselor "functions within the boundaries of individual professional competence and accepts responsibility for the consequences of his/her actions" (ASCA, 2004b, p. 4). Your ethical responsibility in this scenario would thus include a recognition of the limits of your training and the need to make a referral to an eating disorder therapist who can properly assess Hannah's mentality. A school counselor "makes referrals when necessary or appropriate to outside resources" (ASCA, 2004b, p. 2).

This obligation to refer, however, also involves breach of confidentiality, which is required in cases of danger to self or others (ASCA, 2004b, p. 2). Eating disorders are a tricky arena for confidentiality concerns, however, as the danger to self is more gradual and insidious than other disordered behaviors. Yet, as denial is the hallmark of this illness, and malnourishment can impede the rationality of one who is in the throes of an eating disorder (Bardick et al., 2004), breaking confidentiality is an ethically viable move in this case. Stating your concerns to Hannah in a nonjudgmental, objective manner and expressing that you feel the need to contact her parents and look at an outside referral is an appropriate next step (e.g. "I hear you telling me that you are healthy and are taking care of yourself, but I do notice that you have lost a lot of weight in a short time. Maybe it is just the track practice and your new vegetarian diet. But, I just want to be sure that everything is okay, and I would feel better talking to your parents and scheduling a time for you to talk with another counselor"). (Bardick et al., 2004).

Coll (1995) and Sealander, Schwiebert, Oren, and Weekley (1999) discussed the legal and ethical concerns about confidentiality in substance abuse prevention programs. Their review and guidelines may provide additional insights. Federal guidelines (42 U.S.C. 290 dd-3 and ee-3; 42 CFR Part 2) govern the circumstances of disclosure of the records of people who are receiving treatment for substance abuse or who are participating in prevention or referral activities. Generally, the confidentiality of the records is protected. Exceptions are made for medical emergencies, child abuse or neglect, or the endangering of a third party. These are considered situations in which the benefits produced or the harms prevented justify overriding confidentiality. Even in these cases, only information pertinent to the current problem should be revealed. The federal regulations about minors in substance abuse treatment, prevention, or referral programs relate to notification of parents. Linde (2003) explained that, under this federal guideline, students may go from the referral stage through substance abuse treatment without the parent's or guardian's knowledge.

Another situation that may call for breaching confidentiality is when a student client indicates harm to others. The Tarasoff decision was a call for reasonable action by a therapist to protect third parties. In a discussion of this legal duty, Gehring (1982) reviewed and analyzed the court's interpretations of the decision. More recently, Waldo and Malley (1992) concluded that this duty to protect requires several actions on the part of a therapist—not only the duty to warn an intended victim. They explained the four criteria used to assess what might be expected of school counselors in a decision involving the duty to protect:

- A special relationship to the dangerous person or to the potential victim;
- The presence of a clear threat and the imminence of danger;
- The ability to identify potential victim(s); and
- Reasonable care when making decisions.

According to these authors, courts have defined the following obligations of school counselors in such cases: (a) to assemble necessary background information, (b) to confer with a psychiatrist when consultation is needed, and (c) to keep careful records. Seeking professional legal advice is a suggestion but not an obligation. The actions that school counselors may take to protect a person at risk are (a) making referrals by notifying the parents of the student client, (b) notifying a probation officer, (c) notifying the police, (d) designating someone to inform the intended victim, (e) warning the potential victim, (f) detaining the client, and (g) seeking voluntary or involuntary commitment. Counselors may choose one or more of these possibilities (Waldo & Malley, 1992).

Sometimes a threat to harm others may not be explicit. The highly publicized incidents of school violence have caused attention to prevention efforts, a specialty area of school counseling. Hermann and Finn (2002) reviewed the ethical and legal duties of counselors to protect students from violence in schools. They discussed violence prevention activities, risk assessment techniques, and interventions for potential risks. Violence prevention programming, taking every threat seriously, the context of the threat, consultation, and documentation are among the recommendations they have for school counselors.

Assessing the dangerousness of the situation is difficult. In Hermann's (2002) survey of practicing counselors, however, they felt most prepared to report suspected child abuse and to determine whether a person was suicidal. Those were also the legal issues most often being encountered by those counselors. Gross and Robinson (1987) and Thompson, Rudolph, and Henderson (2004) discussed case studies with guidelines and procedures for each situation. Counselors may find these useful practice scenarios.

CASE SCENARIO 13–6

Assessing Dangerousness

As a school counselor, you have been conducting a small group for children whose parents are recently divorced. A 13-year-old from that group, Eleanor, has told a friend that she cannot stand her life with her mother and the live-in boyfriend at home any more. Her mother's boyfriend is "impossible," no one is paying any attention to her, and her father refuses to intervene. Eleanor has said that she isn't sure how she is going to do it, but she's going to end the lives of the people who are making her feel so miserable so that she can go live with her father. Eleanor's friend has told you about these threats. Should you intervene?

YES. You should assess the dangerousness of the situation before determining how to work with Eleanor to resolve the situation. Determine if Eleanor has a specific plan and the plausibility of the plan, whether she has the means to carry out the plan and how accessible those means are, and how pervasive these thoughts are to her. If you determine the threat is credible, you should tell Eleanor that you must report the situation to her parents and possibly to the police. Make the reports and document the actions. Consultation with another professional is advisable. Proceed simultaneously with other actions that are directed at supporting Eleanor in resolving her difficult situation; for example, arrange an agreement with Eleanor for individual counseling to consider alternative actions, arrange a meeting (with Eleanor's permission) with all the parties to work on acceptable solutions to the home situation, or refer Eleanor to another professional for more intensive counseling.

Counselors also deal with two sensitive dilemmas that involve youth sexuality—counseling minors about birth control or abortion and counseling students with AIDS. McWhirter et al. (2004) and Gustafson and Mc-Namara (1987) discussed the difficulties in determining whether to tell parents about the sexual activity of a minor, especially in relation to seeking birth control or abortion information. State laws that mandate reporting, or protect counselors from such reports, are as varied as other laws. In some states, minors can discuss sexually transmitted diseases or pregnancy prevention or cessation with counselors without the legal requirement of parents' notification (Stadler, 1989). Other states mandate notification. Again, counselors can refer to the summary of state laws related to minors provided by English and Kenney (2003). Counselors should remain informed about the legal issues, consult with colleagues, and be deliberate about their decisions.

Talbutt (1983a) reviewed court cases related to abortions. She noted legal and ethical issues in school employees providing abortion information and concluded that counselors should be familiar with their school district's policy and know the laws and current court rulings that have implications for abortion counseling. Urging minors to discuss plans with parents may be both a legal mandate and a counseling goal. Talbutt recognized the need for counselors to establish procedures before taking a crisis approach. The procedure should include family members and local referral agencies.

Likewise, Lynch (1993) provided a thoughtful discussion of the process of counseling someone with AIDS in which counselors balance confidentiality concerns with the duty to protect. Her overview is for those who work in college counseling centers, but the dilemmas she recognized are applicable to other school settings. Both her article and the position statement *The School Counselors and AIDS* (ASCA, 2001) promote positive health education, familiarity with current resources, and prudent adherence to the primary role of counselors. McWhirter et al. (2004) suggested that counselors notify state public health agencies of possible communicable or reported diseases after determining measures to protect confidentiality. Those authors

proposed that such disclosure protects the third person and the client's confidentiality and demonstrates the counselor's measures to prevent harm. Current ASCA ethical standards advise counselors to inform a third party who is at risk for contracting a communicable disease if that person has not already been notified of the danger.

The dilemmas associated with school counselors, their counselees, and issues of confidentiality provoke much discussion. Isaacs (1999) summarized the factors that affect the choices made by counselors to breach confidentiality and suggested the following:

- Determine in advance the kinds of behaviors and issues that might warrant breach;
- Establish a network of peers; and
- Determine alternative actions to breaching confidentiality.

Reporting Child Abuse. All states require some type of reporting of suspected cases of child abuse. As with other state mandates, the specifics of the laws vary from state to state. Counselors should understand the requirements of the laws in their states and the procedures in their districts. Laws are being revised constantly and must be monitored by school counselors. Sandberg, Crabbs, and Crabbs (1988) provided responses to frequently asked questions about legal issues in child abuse.

The Professional School Counselor and Child Abuse and Neglect Prevention, an ASCA (2003a) position statement, outlines various counselor responsibilities beyond the reporting of child abuse. The following information may be found in more detail at www.childhelpusa.org/abuseinfo_signs.htm.

Abuse is the infliction by other than accidental means of physical harm upon the body of a child, continual psychological damage, or denial of emotional needs. Some signs and examples of child abuse are:

- Extensive bruises or patterns of bruises;
- Burns or burn patterns;
- Lacerations, welts, or abrasions;
- Injuries inconsistent with information offered;
- Sexual abuse;
- Emotional disturbances caused by continuous friction in the home, marital discord, or mentally ill parents; and
- Cruel treatment.

Neglect is the failure to provide necessary food, care, clothing, shelter, supervision, or medical attention for a child. According to this statement, children who suffer from neglect include those who are:

- Malnourished, ill clad, dirty, without proper sleeping arrangements, lacking in appropriate health care;
- Unattended, lacking adequate supervision;
- Ill and lacking essential medical attention;
- Irregularly and illegally absent from school;
- Exploited and overworked;
- Lacking essential psychological/emotional nurturance; and
- Abandoned.

Counselors are encouraged to implement activities to educate and to support other school personnel involved in protecting children from abuse and neglect. They are also charged with providing ongoing services to the children or the family in the crisis or to refer them to an appropriate agency. Counselors will want to provide child abuse and neglect prevention programs (Minard, 1993). Remley and Fry (1993) identified the multiple roles of the counselor in reporting child abuse: informant, counselor to the victim or perpetrator, employee, liaison, court witness, and counselor to the family. Clearly, the potential for role conflict, as well as the burden of being a resource for so many people, makes this area a difficult one for school counselors. Counselors must have the qualities of awareness, knowledge, commitment, and effective communication skills to face the process of reporting and preventing child abuse and neglect (Howell-Nigrelli, 1988).

Mitchell and Rogers (2003) discussed the paucity of information on rape, statutory rape and child abuse. *Child sexual abuse* involves a perpetrator who is in a custodial or caretaker role. *Rape* is unlawful sexual activity with a person "without consent and usually by force or threat of injury" (p. 333). In statutory rape, the older person does not have a custodial role and coercion is not part of the definition except in the state of South Carolina. Generally, *statutory rape* is unlawful sexual intercourse with someone who is under the age of consent, usually between 14 and 16 years of age. Some states have an age range between age of consent and a specified number of years of the older partner—usually between 2 to 5 years. These authors reiterated, that all states require child abuse be reported, but rape and statutory rape are not included in that mandate. They suggested that when counselors are in doubt, they present the case as a hypothetical situation and confer with others about their duty. The authors also noted that the states of California, Florida, and Tennessee have revised reporting standards for health workers in cases of rape, and counselors should monitor those trends in revision for their own states.

CASE SCENARIO 13–7

Reporting Suspected Cases of Child Abuse

You are a school counselor who has just met with a student referred to you by her classroom teacher. Based on that session, you arranged an appointment that same morning with your school principal. The meeting leaves you conflicted:

School Counselor: *Mr. B., I need to report this case of suspected abuse to the state reporting agency. Angela Adams has a series of welts on her back that look like the mark of a belt. In addition, she has a large bruise, just darkening, on her shoulder. Her teacher brought her to see me due to these marks, and Angela said she and her dad got into a fight last weekend. She said that her brother looks worse than she does because, "Dad really beat him up."*

Principal: Angela Adams? This is surprising. I met her mom at open house this year, and she and her husband have helped out on several school and community projects. I really doubt that this could be the right story. Angela can be very obstinate, you know. I had her in my office twice last year for not following teacher directives. I think we should wait on this and see if anything further happens. I know the Adam's neighbors. I'll ask if they ever hear anything.

Have you discharged your responsibility to report this suspected child abuse by leaving matters in the principal's hands?

NO. You have both a legal mandate to report suspected abuse and a personal belief that the incident should be reported. If others in the school system do not agree, you should carefully consider the dilemma and be prepared to convince others of your position.

Corporal punishment teaches violence. ASCA (2000) stated that school counselors should not support the use of corporal punishment as a disciplinary tool. Another issue of abuse that is not addressed clearly in the ethical standards is psychological maltreatment in the schools, either by educators or students' peers. Although ASCA provides no position statement and no ethical standards are available, counselors need to monitor the emerging literature about bullying and psychologically abusive teachers (Neese, 1989).

Student Records

Sealander et al. (1999) reviewed the laws that uphold the privacy of student information. FERPA establishes parameters on accessing and disclosing student records. The Drug Abuse Office and Treatment Act (1976) protects the drug and alcohol treatment records of students in any institution that receives federal assistance. The Individuals with Disabilities Education Act further stipulates the care of the records of students in special education. The ACA (1998) compiled a helpful resource that also clarifies federal law on student records.

Family Educational Rights and Privacy Act (FERPA). In November 1974, FERPA, or the Buckley Amendment, became law. The intent of this federal mandate was to provide parents and eligible students (older than age 18) the right to inspect school records and to protect the dissemination of educational records. The act is reprinted in Appendix O. Federal funds may be withheld from school districts that do not adhere to the policies of allowing parents access to records and denying access without parental permission. All U.S. school districts develop a records policy statement and procedures for access and protection to explain how the regulations are implemented. The U.S. Department of Education at 600 Independence, SW, Washington, DC 20202-4605 provides a model policy entitled *Student Records Policies and Procedures for the Alpha School District.* Other model documents and more detailed descriptions are available on the department's Web site, www.ed.gov/offices/OII/fpco/ferpa/. Additionally, the National Center for Education Statistics (2004) produced a guide to protecting student information that may be useful. However, these publications lack specific guidelines for counselors. Walker and Larrabee (1985) and Fischer and Sorenson (1996) presented the following useful information on the application of FERPA guidelines:

- Parents or eligible students should be informed of their rights under this act. This right is extended to custodial and noncustodial parents, unless a court order restrains the access of the noncustodial parent.
- Information about types of educational records that exist and the procedures for accessing those records is disseminated. The content of educational records may include academic progress, test scores, identification data, home background, health information, educational history, anecdotal remarks, case summaries, and recommendations.
- Parents or eligible students may review educational records, request changes, pursue a hearing if the change is disallowed, and add personal statements as explanations, if necessary.

- Personally identifiable information is not released without prior written consent of a parent or an eligible student.
- Parents and eligible students are allowed to see the school's record of disclosure.
- Records made by educators that remain in the sole possession of the maker and therefore are not accessible or revealed to any other individual are not subject to disclosure under this act (Fischer & Sorenson, 1996). This indicates that private notes do not have to be revealed under this federal act.

School counselors who have administrative responsibility for the educational records of children should comply with local policy, state law, and the Buckley Amendment. Remley (1990) discussed whether counselors have a legal or ethical obligation to keep counseling records and the content of the records. He described circumstances in which personnel may be obligated to disclose counseling records and outlined procedures for maintaining, transferring, and discarding counseling records.

The Education for all Handicapped Children Act (PL-94-142). The Education for all Handicapped Children Act is Public Law 94-142. In 1990, that act was amended by PL 101-476 and renamed the Individuals with Disabilities Education Act. The act was revised in 1997. This law guarantees a free and appropriate education in the least restrictive environment possible to all students regardless of the nature and degree of their handicapping conditions. Although the law does not refer to school counselors specifically, they are involved in offering many services to students with handicapping conditions and may be included in the Individual Education Plan (IEP) for students with exceptionalities. School counselors need to be aware of federal guidelines that apply. Henderson (2001) compiled a helpful overview of the Individuals with Disabilities Education Act and Section 504 of the Rehabilitation Act of 1973. These federal laws provide educators with specifics about the eligibility for services, responsibilities, funding, due process, and evaluation and placement procedures.

CODE COMPARISONS

Kaczmarek (2000) discussed ethical and legal complexities in working with minors. She listed references to minors in the ethical codes of the APA, the AAMFT, the ACA, and the ASCA. Her review highlighted three issues: (1) Counselors need to have professional competence to work with children and adolescents and must demonstrate their knowledge of age-related differences that influence the counseling process. (2) The challenges of confidentiality and the boundaries need to be established with the counselee, parent, and counselor. (3) Informed consent is of the utmost importance. The significance of the three concerns—competence, confidentiality, and informed consent—is evident by their presence in all of the listed ethical codes.

School counselors should abide by the codes of ethics of the ACA, the NBCC, the National Peer Helpers Association, the Association for Specialists in Group Work, and the more specific Ethical Standards for School Counselors. The mechanisms for aspirational and mandatory enforcements of ethical standards are described in Chapter 1. Counselors are subject only to the enforcement of the ethical codes of those organizations of which they are members of those credentials they hold, even though they should aspire to the ethical standards endorsed by these organizations. The Ethical Standards for School Counselors differ from the others by clearly delineating specific responsibilities of school counselors to students, parents, colleagues and professional associations, schools and communities, self, and the profession. These responsibilities derive from four basic tenets of the counseling process:

- Each person has the right to receive respect and dignity as a unique human being and to counseling services without prejudice as to person, character, belief, or practice. Counselors advocate for and affirm *all* students regardless of their background.
- Each person has the right to the information and support needed to move toward self-direction and self-development. Counselors give special care to students who have not been given adequate educational services in the past.
- Each person has the right of choice and to understand the meaning of those choices and the future effect of the decisions.
- Each person has the right to privacy and, thereby, the right to expect the counselor–client relationship to comply with all laws, policies, and ethical standards pertaining to confidentiality (ASCA, 2004b).

The specificity of the standards can assist counselors in two important ways: (1) School counselors can prepare themselves to be ethical practitioners. For example, school counselors who inform parents of the counselor role and emphasize the nature of the confidential relationship between the counselor and the student guard the confidentiality of the student while according parents the same privilege. (2) School counselors can educate individuals who have no knowledge about guidelines by providing a reference document. Members of a school board, principals, parent organizations, and others directly involved with schools will benefit by reading the guidelines provided by a national professional organization.

ISSUES OF DIVERSITY

ASCA's (2004a) position statement on cultural diversity encourages school counselors to work within the school setting to increase sensitivity of students, parents, and staff to cultural diversity and to increase awareness of culturally diverse populations. School counselors should also consult with school personnel to identify barriers in attitudes and policies that may inhibit students' learning processes. ASCA suggested that counselors use strategies, activities, and resources in schools, through community outreach, and within the school districts. Counselors should be advocates for sexual harassment victims in schools (McFarland & Dupuis, 2001; Stone, 2000), not only providing a safe place for victims but also working with school officials to adopt a plan of action to eliminate the harassment. Counselors should be well versed in protecting the rights of gay, lesbian, and bisexual students.

CASE SCENARIO 13–8

Diversity Issues and Cultural Values
(written by Juleen Buser, Wake Forest University)
You are a high school counselor and have been seeing Maria, a Latina 12th-grade student, in individual sessions for the past several months. During a session, she tells you, "I've actually decided not to go to community college next year. I'm getting married instead—right after graduation in June! I'm really happy and my whole family is so excited about it."

You are disappointed. Maria has been a good student and has previously been firm in her desire to go to college. You are concerned that her parents are pressuring this marriage for financial reasons. Should you express these concerns to Maria in an individual session, voicing the many benefits of college in comparison to marriage and the importance of not giving into family pressure?

NO. The diversity standards in the current ethical codes mandate that a professional school counselor "expands and develops awareness of his/her own cultural attitudes and beliefs affecting cultural values and biases and strives to attain cultural competence" (ASCA, 2004b, p. 4).

Without a careful examination of the personal values and cultural biases influencing your perspective on Maria's decisions, there is greater chance that any statements you make and any interventions you employ will not be culturally sensitive. Issues such as the understanding of gender roles, acceptable timing of marriage, and commitment to family may be vital components of Maria's decision-making process (Sue & Sue, 2003). To address Maria's decision as a "poor" choice not leading to her personal fulfillment would be to ignore the vast array of cultural values influencing her frame of mind.

A better technique would be to assess your own culturally influenced values, to investigate the values of your diverse client, and then to design an intervention that affirms Maria's culture. A meeting with the parents and with Maria, which would show respect for the family and allow them to participate, would be a viable option. Also, another individual session with Maria in which you talk to her about your confusion in the switch may help her clarify all the implications of her decision. Expressing your concerns in the context of cultural awareness and respect is a more ethically sound intervention than a culturally blind assessment of Maria's decision.

DECISION MAKING IN CONTEXT

School counselors have responsibilities to many people and several institutions. As they make ethical decisions, they must consider federal and state educational law, local school board policies, and the procedural precedents in their school settings. Additionally, they must balance the needs of the particular young person with the rights of the parents and the interest of the school. All these complexities must often be considered quickly, with limited time for reflection. School counselors are advised to memorize a parsimonious yet comprehensive decision-making model, such as those offered in this book by Cottone or by Tarvydas, to help them in the daily situations they must address.

Among all counseling specialties, school counselors work with some of the most ethically complex practices in the profession. The students with whom they work are minors and some may have limited developmental ability to respond to the most serious decisions that face them, thus raising both legal issues and ethical issues of competency in some situations. School counselors also are embedded in a work environment that is unique in requiring a balance between the ethical interests of the student, the student's parents, teachers, and the school administration. Although not all of these parties have the same claim to the school counselor's ethical obligations as the student, depending on the situation, they may have ethical claims that are compelling to various degrees. The counselors, teachers, staff, and administrators all work as a team to provide a safe environment that is conducive to academic and personal progress of the students. Thus they share interests and responsibilities for their care and oftentimes are integrally involved in the interventions the school counselor undertakes with students.

To be of optimal use in school counseling, the ethical decision-making model that school counselors select must explicitly address perspectives, interest, and needs of the multiple parties to the ethical situation and contexts in which the counselor and student find themselves. It also must incorporate the wealth of information and reactions that are generally important to understanding the dilemma. The Social Constructivist Model and the Tarvydas Integrative Model are among those that are able to explore the nuances of school practice to incorporate these considerations. Some of the insights gained by their application will be explored by discussing some considerations that surface by using each to address the following ethical scenario.

Let us assume you are Ms. Goodperson, a high school counselor who has seeing Sara, a junior student, periodically for the last year to assist her in responding to some mild bullying incidents she experienced in the first half of the school year. These incidents had eroded her already weak self-esteem and had made her mildly depressed, and her academic work had deteriorated. Ms. Goodperson and Sara were pleased that their work together was going well, and the incidents had stopped. Most importantly, Sara was much better able to see her strengths herself and rely on the strong, long-term friendships she had established with several of her classmates. At the end of the school year toward the end of your work together, Sara confides in you that she has been told by several of her girlfriends that Mr. Duffy, the band instructor, has had a sexual relationship with two of the girls in the band. She hastens to tell you that she herself was not involved, but said that she has seen Mr. Duffy enter one of the girl's motel room after curfew on the band's road trip to play in a bowl game in January. You question her at length about the story and do believe this behavior may be occurring. She begs you not to reveal that she told you the story but does give you the names of the two girls involved. What should you do? A selection of the most prominent elements from the two decision-making models will be emphasized to assist in illustrating how useful particular types of operations and reflections might be to maintaining a focused and balanced assessment of the situation.

In using the Tarvydas Model during Stage I, one of the components calls upon the counselor to determine who the major stakeholders would be in the particular situation. Clearly, Sara is foremost in your thoughts because she has taken quite a leap of faith in entrusting you with what may be very sensitive information that might be quite distressing to her. Beyond that, the obvious concern would be the effects and perspectives of the students who are reported to have been involved in an inappropriate sexual relationship with Mr. Duffy. However, upon momentary reflection, other concerns surface about detrimental effects upon the potential past and future students who may have been similarly victimized. On the other hand, if this situation is not accurate, Mr. Duffy's life and reputation will be seriously harmed, as well as the potential of the reputation of the school and its teachers if the situation becomes public. Another component in Stage I calls upon the counselor to do some basic fact finding. It would be relatively simple for Ms. Goodperson to find out unobtrusively if there was a band trip during the times mentioned and if Sara and the girl she described as being visited by Mr. Duffy were in attendance. In Stage II, Ms. Goodperson would be pleased to discover that the ASCA standards require school counselors to inform school officials of conditions that are potentially damaging to the school's mission and personnel while honoring counselor–client confidentiality. The ACA ethical standards do not address school-based situations specifically, yet do require the counselor to honor confidentiality of client disclosures. Another potentially crucial stage in this dilemma occurs in Stage III, where the counselor is urged to examine personal biases or blind spots that might impede her ethical judgment. In this case, Ms. Goodperson becomes aware that she has two conflicting reactions that are definitely influencing her. In the first instance, she realizes that she values harmony in her relationships with her colleagues and really likes to please the principal Mrs. Powers, wishing her to think well of her. However, she has very strong loathing for any adult who would take advantage of, or abuse a child. The biggest problem, she realizes in her contextual analysis, will be the potential of the administration to discount the information as the imaginings of a hurt, unpopular girl. Mrs. Powers and the superintendent of schools are very good friends with Mr. Duffy, golfing together regularly and attending the same small community church together. Finally in Stage IV, after constructing an intervention plan to reveal the information to the principal, Ms. Goodperson focuses on the component of the plan that calls upon her to boost her interpersonal skills and strategies to use good personal confrontation preparation and execution skills so that she can steal herself to

professionally and calmly present the dilemma in an assertive, yet open manner. Ms. Goodperson takes care to remain empathic to the principal's need to process the information that is shocking to her, yet resolute in her determination to accurately present the situation from the standpoint of the harm that may be caused to students if it is not given proper credence and investigated. Before you do speak to Mrs. Powers, you tell Sara you will keep her name confidential if you can, but you tell her you will have to report this information to the principal. You report this information to the principal, who questions you regarding the identity of the student who told you. You tell her that you cannot reveal this information unless it is critical, due to your obligations to keep the confidentiality of the student. However you state that you believe the student and think that there is enough information to initiate some type of inquiry without revealing the student's identity.

In the Social Constructivist Model, the social contexts of the situation are the core considerations, thus fitting the issues raised by Sara's dilemma quite well. When Sara's interpretation of the social relationship between Mr. Duffy and the two students is presented, it is clear that Mr. Duffy may have acted based on linkages of vulnerability rather than the more socially accepted linkages of professional responsibility within the professional educator community. That latter community includes Ms. Goodperson, Mr. Duffy, and Mrs. Powers, as well as other fellow teachers and staff. The community social context includes well understood ethical standards that clearly prohibit sexual relationships with students. This professional network would clearly challenge Mr. Duffy's behavior as wrong if it is discovered that the charges are true. However, the competing social network that exists between Mr. Duffy, Mrs. Powers, and the administrator may present a conflicting consensuality, in that those individuals may not accept the interpretation of Mr. Duffy's behavior if the evidence is purely circumstantial. In this case, the interpretation of the situation and its meaning may require negotiation between Mr. Duffy, Ms. Goodperson, and Mrs. Powers, as well as the students who were involved (or allegedly involved) with Mr. Duffy. Some disagreement may result about the behaviors involved and the meaning to the parties in the situation. If there is not an agreement and a consensus of opinion reached regarding whether the behavior involved was a sexual relationship with a minor, then a more formal process of arbitration would likely ensue. The negotiation would also involve the context of the legal system after the situation is clarified because the students involved are minors. If the incident occurred as charged, the behavior of a teacher having a sexual relationship with a minor in most state legal jurisdictions would be considered to be statutory rape. Statutory rape is the subject of a very clear social consensus across diverse social networks as being illegal and unacceptable behavior. If the facts support this interpretation, then the judgment of the community would be leveled against Mr. Duffy within the legal system, and Ms. Goodperson's efforts to enlist the consensus of the professional community to bring it to this conclusion while honoring the obligations of her counselor–client relationship would be vindicated.

dents (Borders & Drury, 1992; Whiston & Sexton, 1998). However, while implementing a counseling program, school counselors may encounter multiple dilemmas in providing services to students, parents, and teachers. The ethical standards of the ASCA outline the responsibilities of counselors to the groups with whom they work. Counselors must know the guidelines and the local, state, and federal laws and procedures; seek consultation; and stay informed of changes to make decisions ethically. By being fully informed, counselors will be prepared in situations that demand careful judgment to protect the best interest of the child.

CHAPTER SUMMARY

School counselors make significant contributions to the educational and personal development of stu-

INTERNET RESOURCES

Key words: school counseling ethics, FERPA, IDEA, educational law

REFERENCES

American Counseling Association. (1998). *Professional counselor's guide to federal law on student records.* Alexandria, VA: Author.

American School Counselor Association (ASCA). (1997). ASCA position statement: The professional school counselor and comprehensive school counseling programs (Rev. Ed.). Alexandria, VA: Author.

American School Counselor Association (ASCA). (2000a). ASCA position statement: The professional school counselor and corporal punishment in the schools (Rev. Ed.). Alexandria, VA: Author.

American School Counselor Association (2000b). *Position Statement: Student safety on the internet.* Alexandria, VA: Author.

American School Counselor Association (ASCA). (2001). ASCA position statement: The professional school counselor and HIV/AIDS (Rev. Ed.). Alexandria, VA: Author.

American School Counselor Association (ASCA). (2002a). ASCA position statement: The professional school counselor and censorship (Rev. Ed.). Alexandria, VA: Author.

American School Counselor Association (ASCA). (2002b). ASCA position statement: The professional school counselor and confidentiality (Rev. Ed.). Alexandria, VA: Author.

American School Counselor Association (ASCA). (2002c). ASCA position statement: The professional school counselor and high-stakes testing. Alexandria, VA: Author.

American School Counselor Association (ASCA). (2002d). ASCA position statement: The professional school counselor and peer helping (Rev. Ed.). Alexandria, VA: Author.

American School Counselor Association (ASCA). (2003a). ASCA position statement: The professional school counselor and child abuse and neglect prevention (Rev. Ed.). Alexandria, VA: Author.

American School Counselor Association (ASCA). (2003b). *The ASCA national model: A framework for school counseling programs.* Alexandria, VA: Author.

American School Counselor Association (ASCA). (2004a). ASCA position statement: The professional school counselor and cultural diversity. (Rev. Ed.). Alexandria, VA: Author.

American School Counselor Association (ASCA). (2004b). *Ethical standards for school counselors* (Rev. Ed.). Alexandria, VA: Author.

American School Counselor Association (ASCA). (2004c). ASCA position statement: The professional school counselor and parent consent (Rev. Ed.). Alexandria, VA: Author.

American School Counselor Association (ASCA). (2005). State comprehensive programs. Retrieved June 8, 2005 from www.schoolcounselor.org.

Association for Assessment in Counseling. (2002). *Applying the standards for educational and psychological testing: What a counselor needs to know.* Alexandria, VA: Author.

Association for Specialists in Group Work. (1989). *Ethical guidelines for group counselors.* Alexandria, VA: Author.

Bardick, A. D., Bernes, K. B., McCulloch, A. R., Witko, K. D., Spriddle, J. W., & Roest, A. R. (2004). Eating disorder intervention, prevention and treatment: Recommendations for school counselors. *Professional School Counselor, 8*(2), 168–174.

Borders, L., & Drury, S. (1992). Comprehensive school counseling programs: A review for policy makers and practitioners. *Journal of Counseling and Development, 70,* 487–498.

Cameron, S., & turtle-song, i. (2002). Learning to write case notes using the SOAP format. *Journal of Counseling and Development, 80,* 286–292.

Campbell, C., & Dahir, C. (1997). *Sharing the vision: The national standards for school counseling programs.* Alexandria, VA: American School Counselor Association.

Capuzzi, D. (2002). Legal and ethical challenges in counseling suicidal students. *Professional School Counseling, 6,* 36–45.

Carroll, M. A., Schneider, H. G., & Wesley, G. R. (1985). *Ethics in the practice of psychology.* Upper Saddle River, NJ: Prentice-Hall.

Center for Adolescent Health and Law, (2003). *State minor consent laws: A Summary* (2nd ed.). Chapel Hill, NC: Author.

Childers, J. H., Jr. (1988). The counselor's use of microcomputers: Problems and ethical issues. In W. C. Huey & T. P. Remley, Jr. (Eds.), *Ethical and legal issues in school counseling* (pp. 262–270). Alexandria, VA: American School Counselor Association.

Coll, K. M. (1995). Legal challenges in secondary prevention programming for students with substance abuse problems. *The School Counselors, 43,* 35–41.

Corey, G., Corey, M. S., & Callanan, P. (1998). *Issues and ethics in the helping professions* (5th ed.). Pacific Grove, CA: Brooks/Cole.

Corey, G., Corey, M. S., Callanan, P., & Russell, J. M. (1988). Ethical considerations in using group techniques. In W. C. Huey & T. P. Remley, Jr. (Eds.), *Ethical and legal issues in school counseling* (pp. 211–222). Alexandria, VA: American School Counselor Association.

Corey, M., & Corey, G. (2001). *Theory and practice of group counseling* (5th ed.). Pacific Grove, CA: Brooks/Cole.

Costin, A. C., Page, B. J., Pietrzak, D. R., Kerr, D. L., & Symons, C. W. (2002). HIV/AIDS knowledge and beliefs among pre-service and in-service school counselors. *Professional School Counseling, 6,* 79–85.

Davis, T., & Ritchie, M. (1993). Confidentiality and the school counselor: A challenge for the 1990s. *The School Counselors, 41,* 23–30.

English, A., & Kenney, K. E. (2003). *State minor consent laws: A summary.* Chapel Hill, NC: Center for Adolescent Health & the Law.

Ethics Committee of the American School Counselor Association (1999–2001). Ethical issues: Tips for school counselors. Retrieved June 5, 2005 from http://www.schoolcounselors.org/ethics/ethicaltips.htm.

Fisher, C. B., & Hennessy, J. (1994). Ethical issues. In J. L. Ronch, W. Van Ornum, & N. C. Stilwel (Eds.), *The counseling sourcebook: A practical reference on contemporary issues* (pp. 175–185). New York: Crossroad.

Fischer, L., & Sorenson, G. P. (1996). *School law for counselors, psychologists, and social workers* (3rd ed.). White Plains, NY: Longman.

Freeman, S. J. (2000). *Ethics: An introduction to philosophy and practice.* Boston: Wadsworth.

Froeschle, J., & Moyer, M. (2004). Just cut it out: Legal and ethical challenges in counseling students who self-mutilate. *Professional School Counseling, 7,* 231–235.

Gehring, D. D. (1982). The counselor's "duty to warn." *The Personnel and Guidance Journal, 61,* 208–210.

Glosoff, H. L., Herlihy, B., & Spence, E. B. (2000). Privileged communication in the counselor–client relationship. *Journal of Counseling and Development, 78,* 454–462.

Glosoff, H. L., & Pate, R. H., Jr. (2002). Privacy and confidentiality in school counseling. *Professional School Counseling, 6,* 20–27.

Gross, D. R., & Robinson, S. E. (1987). Ethics, violence, and counseling: Hear no evil, see no evil, speak no evil? *Journal of Counseling and Development, 65,* 340–344.

Guillot-Miller, L., & Partin, P. W. (2003). Web-based resources for legal and ethical issues in school counseling. *Professional School Counseling, 7,* 52–58.

Gustafson, K. E., & McNamara, J. R. (1987). Confidentiality with minor clients: Issues and guidelines for therapists. *Professional Psychology: Research and Practice, 18,* 503–508.

Hammond, L. C., & Gantt, L. (1998). Using art in counseling: Ethical considerations. *Journal of Counseling and Development, 76,* 271–276.

Henderson, K. (2001, March). An overview of ADA, IDEA, and Section 504: Update 2001. Retrieved July 16, 2001 from http://ericec.org/digests/e606.html.

Herlihy, B., & Corey, G. (1992). *Dual relationships in counseling.* Alexandria, VA: American Association for Counseling and Development.

Herlihy, B., & Sheeley, V. L. (1987). Privileged communication in selected helping professions: A comparison among statutes. *Journal of Counseling and Development, 65,* 479–483.

Hermann, M. A. (2002). A study of legal issues encountered by school counselors and perceptions of their preparedness to respond to legal challenges. *Professional School Counseling, 6,* 12–20.

Hermann, M. A., & Finn, A. (2002). An ethical and legal perspective on the role of school counselors in preventing violence in schools. *Professional School Counseling, 6,* 46–55.

Hines, P. L., & Fields, T. H. (2002). Pregroup screening issues for school counselors. *Journal for Specialists in Group Work, 27,* 358–376.

Hobson, S. M., & Kanitz, H. M. (1996). Multicultural counseling: An ethical issue for school counselors. *The School Counselors, 43,* 245–255.

Hopkins, B. R., & Anderson, B. S. (1990). *The counselor and the law.* Alexandria, VA: American Association for Counseling and Development.

Howell-Nigrelli, J. (1988). Shared responsibility for reporting child abuse cases: A reaction to Spiegel. *Elementary School Guidance and Counseling, 22,* 289–290.

Huey, W. C. (1986). Ethical concerns in school counseling. *Journal of Counseling and Development, 64,* 321–322.

Huey, W. C. (1996). Counseling minor clients. In B. Herlihy & G. Corey (Eds.), *ACA ethical standards casebook* (5th ed.). Alexandria, VA: American Counseling Association.

Isaacs, M. L. (1997). The duty to warn and protect: Tarasoff and the elementary school counselors. *Elementary School Guidance and Counseling, 31*(4), 326–342.

Isaacs, M. L. (1999). School counselors and confidentiality: Factors affecting professional choices. *Professional School Counseling, 99*(2), 258–267.

Isaacs, M. L., & Stone, C. (1999). School counselors and confidentiality: Factors affecting professional choices. *Professional School Counseling, 2*(4), 258–266.

James, S. H., & DeVaney, S. B. (1995). Preparing to testify: The school counselor as court witness. *School Counselor, 43*(2), 97–103.

Kaczmarek, P. (2000). Ethical and legal complexities inherent in professional roles with child and adolescent clients. *Counseling and Human Development, 33,* 1–15.

Kaplan, D. M. (2001). Developing an informed consent brochure for secondary students. Retrieved June 5, 2005 from http://www.schoolcounselor.org/ethics/.

Kaplan, L. S. (1996). Outrageous or legitimate concerns: What some parents are saying about school counseling. *The School Counselor, 43,* 165–170.

Kaplan, L. S. (1997). Parents' rights: Are school counselors at risk? *The School Counselor, 44,* 334–343.

Kitchener, K. S., & Harding, S. S. (1990). Dual role relationships. In B. Herlihy and L. Golden (Eds.), *Ethical standards casebook* (4th ed., pp. 145–148). Alexandria, VA: American Association for Counseling and Development.

Linde, L. (2003). Ethical, legal, and professional issues in school counseling. In B. T. Erford (Ed.), *Transforming the school counseling profession* (pp. 39–62). Upper Saddle River, NJ: Merrill.

Lynch, S. K. (1993). AIDS: Balancing confidentiality and the duty to protect. *Journal of College Student Development, 34*, 148–153.

McFarland, W. P., & Dupuis, M. (2001). The legal duty to protect gay and lesbian students from violence in school. *Professional School Counseling, 4* (3), 171–179.

McWhirter, J. J., McWhirter, B. T., McWhirter, A. M., & McWhirter, E. H. (2004). *At-risk youth: A comprehensive response* (3rd ed.). Pacific Grove, CA: Brooks/Cole.

Minard, S. M. (1993). The school counselor's role in confronting child sexual abuse. *The School Counselor, 41*, 9–15.

Mitchell, C. W., Disque, J. G., & Robertson, P. (2002). When parents want to know: Responding to parental demands for confidential information. *Professional School Counseling, 6*, 156–162.

Mitchell, C. W., & Rogers, R. E. (2003). Rape, statutory rape, and child abuse: Legal distinctions and counselor duties. *Professional School Counseling, 6*, 332–338.

Muro, J. J., & Kottman, T. (1995). *Guidance and counseling in the elementary and middle schools: A practical approach.* Madison, WI: Brown & Benchmark.

National Center for Educational Statistics. (2004). *Forum guide to protecting the privacy of student information: State and local education agencies.* NCES 2003-330. Washington, DC: Author.

National Peer Helpers Association. (2001). Programmatic standards. Retrieved July 10, 2001 from http://www.peerhelping.org.

Neese, L. A. (1989). Psychological maltreatment in schools: Emerging issues for counselors. *Elementary School Guidance and Counseling, 23*, 194–200.

O'Connor, K., Plante, J., & Refvem, J. (1998, March). *Parental consent and the school counselor.* Poster session presented at the annual conference of the North Carolina Counseling Association, Chapel Hill, NC. Cited in S. B. Baker & E. R. Gerler, Jr. *School counseling for the 21st century* (4th ed.). Upper Saddle River, NJ: Merrill.

Rapin, L., & Keel, L. (1998). *Association for specialists in group work best practice guidelines.* http://asgw.educ.kent.edu/best.htm.

Remley, T. P., Jr. (1985). The law and ethical practices in elementary and middle schools. *Elementary School Guidance and Counseling, 19*, 181–189.

Remley, T. P., Jr. (1990). Counseling records: Legal and ethical issues. In B. Herlihy & L. Golden (Eds.), *AACD ethical standards casebook* (4th ed., pp. 162–169). Alexandria, VA: American Association for Counseling and Development.

Remley, T. P., Jr. (1993). What responsibilities do I have for student counseling records? *The American Counselor, 2*(4), 32–33.

Remley, T. P., Jr., & Fry, L. J. (1993). Reporting suspected child abuse: Conflicting roles for the counselor. *The School Counselor, 40*, 253–259.

Remley, T. P., Jr., & Herlihy, B. (2005). *Ethical, legal, and professional issues in counseling* (2nd ed.). Upper Saddle River, NJ: Merrill.

Remley, T. P., Jr., Herlihy, B., & Herlihy, S. B. (1997). The U.S. Supreme Court decision in a *Jaffee v. Redmond:* Implications for counselors. *Journal of Counseling and Development, 75*, 213–218.

Remley, T. P., Jr., & Sparkman, L. B. (1993). Student suicides: The counselor's limited legal liability. *The School Counselor, 40*, 164–169.

Ritchie, M. H., & Huss, S. N. (2000). Recruitment and screening of minors for group counseling. *Journal for Specialists in Group Work, 25*(2), 146–156.

Salo, M. M., & Shumate, S. G. (1993). *The ACA legal series: Vol. 4. Counseling minor clients.* Alexandria, VA: American Counseling Association.

Sampson, J. P., Jr., Kolodinsky, R. W., & Greeno, B. P. (1997). Counseling on the information highway: Future possibilities and potential problems. *Journal of Counseling and Development, 75*, 203–212.

Sampson, J. P., Jr., & Pyle, K. R. (1988). Ethical issues involved with the use of computer-assisted counseling, testing, and guidance systems. In W. C. Huey and T. P. Remley, Jr.(Eds.), *Ethical and legal issues in school counseling* (pp. 249–261). Alexandria, VA: American School Counselor Association.

Sandberg, D. N., Crabbs, S. K., & Crabbs, M. A. (1988). Legal issues in child abuse: Questions and answers for counselors. *Elementary School Guidance and Counseling, 22*, 268–274.

Sciarra, D. (2004). *School counseling: Foundations and contemporary issues.* Belmont, CA: Brooks/Cole.

Sealander, K. A., Schweibert, V. L., Oren, T. A., & Weekley, J. L. (1999). Confidentiality and the law. *Professional School Counseling, 3*(2), 122–127.

Sheeley, V. L., & Herlihy, B. (1987). Privileged communication in school counseling: Status update. *The School Counselor, 34*, 268–272.

Sheeley, V. L., & Herlihy, B. (1989). Counseling suicidal teens: A duty to warn and protect. *The School Counselor, 37*, 89–97.

Stadler, H. A. (1989). Balancing ethical responsibilities: Reporting child abuse and neglect. *The Counseling Psychologist, 17*, 102–110.

Stone, C. B. (2000). Advocacy for sexual harassment victims: Legal support and ethical aspects. *Professional School Counseling 4*(1), 23–30.

Stone, C. B. (2002). Negligence in academic advising and abortion counseling: Courts rulings and implications. *Professional School Counseling, 6*, 28–35.

Stone, C., & Isaacs, M. (2003). Confidentiality with minors: The need for policy to promote and protect. *The Journal of Educational Research, 96*, 140–150.

Stone, C. (2004). Ethical and legal considerations for students, parents, and professional school counselors. In B. T. Erford (Ed.). *Professional school counseling: A handbook of theories, programs & practices* (pp. 57–64). Austin, TX: ProEd.

Strein, W., & Hershenson, D. B. (1991). Confidentiality in nondyadic counseling situations. *Journal of Counseling and Development, 69*, 312–316.

Stromberg, C., and his colleagues in the law firm of Hogan & Harson of Washington, DC (1993, April). Privacy, confidentiality and privilege. The Psychologist's Legal Update. Washington, DC: National Register of Health Service Providers in Psychology. Cited in G. Corey, M. S. Corey, & P. Callanan. (1998). *Issues and ethics in the helping professions* (5th ed.). Pacific Grove, CA: Brooks/Cole.

Sue, D.W., & Sue, D. (2003). *Counseling the culturally diverse: Theory and practice* (4th ed.). Hoboken, NJ: John Wiley and Sons.

Suzuki, L. A., & Kugler, J. F. (1995). *Intelligence and personality assessment: Multicultural perspective.* In J. G. Ponterotto, Casas, L. A. Suzuki, & C. M. Alexander (Eds.). *Handbook of multicultural counseling* (pp. 493–515). Thousand Oaks, CA: Sage Publications.

Talbutt, L. C. (1983a). Current legal trends regarding abortions for minors: A dilemma for counselors. *The School Counselor, 31*, 120–124.

Talbutt, L. C. (1983b). The counselor and testing: Some legal concerns. *The School Counselor, 30*, 245–250.

Taylor, L., & Adelman, H. (1989). Reframing the confidentiality dilemma to work in children's best interests. *Professional Psychology Research and Practice, 20*, 79–83.

Terres, C. K., & Larrabee, M. J. (1985). Ethical issues and group work with children. *Elementary School Guidance and Counseling, 19*, 190–197.

Thompson, C. L., Rudolph, L. B., & Henderson, D. A. (2004). *Counseling children* (6th ed.). Pacific Grove, CA: Brooks/Cole.

Tompkins, L., & Mehring, T. (1993). Client privacy and the school counselor: Privilege, ethics, and employer policies. *The School Counselor, 40*, 335–342.

Varhely, S. C., & Cowles, J. (1991). Counselor self-awareness and client confidentiality: A relationship revisited. *Elementary School Guidance and Counseling, 25*, 269–276.

Waldo, S.L., & Malley, P. (1992). Tarasoff and its progeny: Implications for the school counselor. *The School Counselor 40*, 46–54.

Walker, M. M., & Larrabee, M. J. (1985). Ethics and school records. *Elementary School Guidance and Counseling, 19*, 210–216.

Welfel, E. R. (2002). *Ethics in counseling and psychotherapy: Standards, research, and emerging issues* (2nd ed.). Pacific Grove, CA: Brooks/Cole.

Whiston, S. C., & Sexton, T. L. (1998). A review of school counseling outcome research: Implications for practice. *Journal of Counseling and Development, 76*, 412–426.

Wilcoxon, S. A., & Magnuson, S. (1999). Considerations for school counselors serving noncustodial parents: Premises and suggestions. *Professional School Counseling, 2*(4), 275–280.

Zingaro, J. C. (1983). Confidentiality: To tell or not to tell. *Elementary School Guidance and Counseling, 17*, 261–267.

CHAPTER 14

Mental Health Counseling and Assessment

OBJECTIVES

After reading this chapter, you should be able to:

- Define the specialty of mental health counseling.
- Differentiate the roles and functions of practitioners of mental health counseling from those of practitioners of other counseling specialties.
- Explain the political issues of importance to mental health counselors.
- Discuss the ethical issues specific to the practice of mental health counseling.
- Outline professional credentialing and licensure matters.
- Review the assessment issues related to mental health counseling.
- Apply a decision-making process to an ethical dilemma common to mental health counseling practice.

INTRODUCTION

Mental health counseling, once a fledgling specialty struggling to develop an identity, has become a dominating force in defining how the overall profession of counseling presents itself in the mental health service arena. Mental health counseling is to counseling what clinical psychology has become to psychology. As a specialty, mental health counseling has begun to flex its own muscles politically, separate from the larger, more inclusive filed of counseling. The political activity of counselors affiliated with specialty interests has its good and bad points. For example, it can be argued that mental health counseling is the "tail" that is wagging the larger profession of counseling "dog," meaning the larger profession has begun to follow the specialty's lead, perhaps reluctantly. Mental health counselors, as represented by the American Mental Health Counseling Association (AMHCA), have organized to the extent they are making demands on the organization that rep-

resents counseling as a whole—the ACA. In 1996, there was even a concerted effort by a constituency of AMHCA to disaffiliate from the ACA. At that point, the ACA Governing Council voted to revoke the AMHCA charter (affiliation) if AMHCA failed to comply with ACA bylaws (Governing Council, 1996). Later, under a major reorganization of the ACA, AMHCA, along with a number of other ACA divisions (including the American Rehabilitation Counseling Association and the ASCA), was allowed to solicit freestanding members (members not affiliated with the ACA) and to establish its own governing administration separate from the ACA. The ACA reorganization was a political move to appease certain counseling specialties (with specific political and economic agendas) without jeopardizing the overarching allegiance to the counseling profession as a whole. Although AMHCA members need not be ACA members, they may choose to be members of the ACA as part and parcel of their AMHCA affiliation. ACA members, through ACA channels, may choose to affiliate with and pay dues to AMHCA. These members maintain ACA organizational affiliation, but at the cost of a separate administrative and membership arrangement. This also allows AMHCA to speak for itself on matters of legislation and lobbying.

Beyond influencing the larger profession of counseling, mental health counselors also influence mental health services nationally through efforts to ensure that mental health counselors and their services are available to individuals served by government and private health service providers. Mental health counselors, both through AMHCA and the ACA, have become outspoken advocates for the counseling profession; both groups have lobbied for the inclusion of counseling in laws that oversee health service provision. For example, the AMHCA Public Policy and Legislation Committee published its 2000–2001 federal legislative agenda and listed the following issues: (a) gain Medicare reimbursement for mental health counselors; (b) eliminate discriminatory physician referral and supervision requirements under CHAMPUS/TRICARE (two military medical insurance programs); (c) ensure that mental health counselors are reimbursed by plans participating in the Federal Employee Health Benefits Program; (d) support legislation protecting patient rights regarding access to treatment and confidentiality; and (e) support legislation to name mental health counselors as independent providers in military family service centers.

At about the same time that mental health counseling spread its wings and took flight, it encountered the "wind sheer" of managed care. With the growth of managed care, mental health counselors, like other (competing) mental health professionals, are challenged to provide services under the scrutiny of a managing agency. This is a significant change from the days when mental health professionals just billed their standard fee to an insurance program (for reimbursement that was almost guaranteed). Today, mental health professionals must be on a managed care company's provider list (meeting the company's standards) before most insurance payments are allowed, and referrals are often made through a "case manager." The case manager defines the number of sessions of psychotherapy to be provided within the financial constraints of the managed care contract. A **managed care contract** is an agreement between the managed care company and the provider of counseling services (usually a counselor in independent practice or an agency providing counseling services). The contract usually defines the type of

services that can be provided, the amount of money to be paid for provided services, and other limitations of services. Counselors must agree to abide by the managed care company's contract or they risk being left off the referral panel and not receiving referrals. If a client self-refers and the counselor is not on the managed care panel overseeing the client's benefits, no services are reimbursed by the insurer. Because it has become competitive to be accepted by a managed care company as a provider, the fees for services under managed care are often less than those traditionally billed for services to insurance companies (directly without a managed care mediator) or to individuals paying on their own. In effect, managed care has changed the rules of reimbursement for mental health services.

Regardless, mental health counseling may be well positioned to take a leading role in the mental health enterprise of the future, even with managed care. With managed care's overarching goal of cost containment, the services of master's-degree-trained mental health counselors may be preferable (by cost) to services provided by more expensive doctoral-trained mental health practitioners (e.g., psychologists and psychiatrists). However, as with any service oversight mechanism, there will be limits as to the nature and extent of services to be provided. (See Box 14–1.)

DEFINING THE SPECIALTY, SETTING, AND CLIENTS

Mental health counselors usually work in clinical settings (state, private, or nonprofit clinics, hospitals, and other health service agencies) and in private practice. In the early years of AMHCA, the membership was employed primarily in community mental health centers; however, by the mid 1980s there was a shift to private practice as the predominant employment setting (Hershenson & Power, 1987). Mental health counselors and rehabilitation counselors who specialize in psychiatric rehabilitation also are hired by managed care companies to be case managers, overseeing services provided by their colleagues in the field.

Mental health counselors primarily assess and treat individuals with mental disorders, with an emphasis on promoting healthy development and on coping rather than on "cure" (Hershenson & Power, 1987). Most services are provided to individuals who meet criteria for a diagnosis or diagnoses according to the Diagnostic and Statistical Manual of Mental Disorders, Fourth Edition (DSM–IV), published by the American Psychiatric Association (1994). The DSM–IV provides a detailed

---

Box 14–1 • Exploring the Codes

What section of the American Mental Health Counseling Association (AMHCA, 2000) Code of Ethics (see Appendix P) addresses the use of tests in assessment of clients?

According to the AMHCA ethics code, can a counselor terminate services to a client for nonpayment of fees? What actions should be taken to ensure there is no abandonment of clients in this circumstance?

What should a mental health counselor do if his or her client is being treated by another mental health professional, according to the AMHCA ethics code?

Does the Responsibilities of Users of Standardized Tests, RUST (Association for Assessment, 2003; see Appendix Q) adequately address issues of test selection, especially related to reliability, validity, applicability, and norming?

---

listing of mental disorders classified by larger groupings of disorders, such as mood disorders, anxiety disorders, and schizophrenia and other psychotic disorders. In addition, each disorder is described by its characteristic behaviors, and behavior-specific criteria are listed for a diagnosis to be met. Statistical data are provided on the prevalence of disorders, along with a complete description of associated features, cultural- and age-related factors, the course of the disorder, and predisposing factors. Guidance also is provided for **differential diagnosis,** the process wherein one disorder is considered over another disorder with similar diagnostic signs, symptoms, or course. Mental health counseling is considered the specialty of counseling most suited, by educational and supervised training standards, to serve individuals with mental disorders. However, there is a subtle distinction related to the definition of mental health counseling compared with other "clinical" mental health professions (e.g., clinical psychology; clinical social work). Hershenson and Power stated:

> As its name implies, mental health counseling does not seek to cure illness (implicit in the terms *psychiatric* and *clinical* in the names of . . . most of the other mental health fields), but rather seeks to promote healthy development and coping. It works with both the client and the environment, building on existing strengths wherever possible and using scientifically evaluated methods. (p. 5)

The focus of treatment in the mental health specialty is the developing individual with the mental disorder, not the mental disorder itself. According to Hershenson and Power, the role of the mental health counselor includes (a) prevention of problems, (b) facilitation of healthy growth, (c) remediation of maladaption, (d) rehabilitation, and (e) enhancing and improving the quality of life.

The issues of diagnosis and treatment of mental disorders have been controversial for the field of counseling as a whole. However, in general, the role of the

professional counselor is being expanded to include diagnosis and treatment of mental disorders. Leaders in the field are beginning to recognize the necessity of clearly defining diagnosis and treatment as part of the role and function of the professional counselor. In a monograph on "The Role and Function of the Professional Counselor in the 21st Century," Altekruse, Harris, and Brandt (2000) stated:

> The role of the professionally competent counselor of the 21st century is proposed to be a continued focus on the preventative/developmental model with an added emphasis on diagnosis and treatment strategies. The professionally competent counselor of the future needs the knowledge and skills to work with clients in their respected developmental stages and to provide strategies and approaches that help prevent mental illness. This counselor has the ability and skills to diagnose and treat. (p. 25)

The reality of practice in mental health counseling is such that counselors need to be able to view the client from a developmental, nondiagnostic standpoint (focusing on building strengths) while functioning within a system that supports the diagnosis and treatment of individuals according to psychiatric standards (e.g., the DSM–IV). In fact, when addressing children, a developmental assessment process is wise; a developmental assessment process evaluates the child not against some rigid standard of mental health, but evaluates the child against age-appropriate milestones (see Vernon & Clemente, 2005). So counselors must not only know how to diagnose according to some diagnostic rubric (e.g., DSM–IV), but they must also understand developmental stages. Adequate training of mental health counselors in the practices of diagnosis and treatment is necessary (Altekruse & Sexton, 1995).

To a large degree, the types of clients encountered by the mental health counselor vary by setting. For example, a counselor working in a state, county, or city acute care facility will probably be faced with seriously disturbed individuals who lack resources to obtain medical benefits coverage through private insurers. On the other hand, a counselor working in a private clinic in a rich community may primarily treat clients with adjustment concerns related to everyday living situations. However, mental health counselors must be prepared to serve the full range of mental disorders and to deal with situations involving serious psychopathology. Clients may suffer from mild symptoms of anxiety or depression, or they may be severely disabled by a mental condition such as chronic schizophrenia or bipolar disorder (manic-depressive illness).

Assessment or diagnostic procedures may be undertaken to provide a clear evaluation of the individual's concerns and the effect of the mental disorder on the individual's daily activities. **Assessment** is the process of evaluating a client against a normative standard—a set of criteria for classification—in diagnosis, planning, or treatment. Assessment may also be made against some developmental criterion. Along this line, mental health counselors may assess clients through a diagnostic interview, which typically involves a detailed history of the individual's symptoms, stressors, and family background (see Gladding & Newsome, 2004, for a nice summary of the "client assessment and diagnosis" process). As part of the assessment, a mental status examination may be performed. A **mental status examination** is a structured interview designed to provide a controlled, interpersonal setting for the emergence and observation of symptoms and signs of mental disorders (Cottone, 1992). Treatment usually involves individual psychotherapy, but mental health counselors may also be involved in group treatment. They may choose to specialize further, by focusing on children, adolescents, or adults. They may specialize in working with clients who have one mental disorder (e.g., panic disorder) or one type of mental disorder (e.g., anxiety disorders). Treatment may vary according to the disorder. Regardless, in contrast to psychiatry or clinical psychology, the mental health counselor's emphasis should be on building strengths, facilitating healthy growth, preventing future problems, and rehabilitating the client.

Mental health counselors often work side by side with other mental health professionals in their settings. For example, in a hospital setting, a psychiatrist and social worker may often be assigned to a client, and treatment may follow the dictates of a team decision. Most typically, mental health counselors work with psychiatric nurses, social workers, rehabilitation counselors, psychologists, and psychiatrists. The professional who leads in team decision making is often defined by the rules of the employing organization. Regardless, the mental health counselor works primarily from an "asset-oriented" model rather than from an "illness-oriented" model (Hershenson & Power, 1987), focusing on building the strengths of the individual rather than simply ameliorating symptoms or deficiencies.

At present, AMHCA is the organization that best represents the interests of the mental health counselor. Since its inception, it has been an advocate for the specialty and has facilitated the development of specialty designation through the NBCC. Currently, NBCC offers a specialty designation in mental health counseling. To be certified, NBCC requires that the candidate meet the general requirements for certification as an N.C.C., which is a generic credential. In addition, candidates for the Clinical Mental Health Counselor certificate must complete 60 semester hours of graduate training (the N.C.C. requires only an acceptable master's degree, but does not specify a number of semester hours). Graduate courses are required in areas such as theories of counseling, psychopathology or abnormal psychology, ethics, social and cultural foundations, and group counseling. Three thousand hours of post-master's-supervised experience is required under a supervisor acceptable to the board. In effect, the standards for the Clinical Mental Health Counselor certificate are among the highest in the counseling profession.

As with all members of the ACA, mental health counselors are directed by the ACA's Responsibilities of Users of Standardized Tests (RUST), originally drafted in 1978 but revised in 1987 and 2003 in cooperation with the Association for Assessment in Counseling, a division of the ACA. The RUST spells out specific guidelines of test use decisions, the qualification requirements for those who administer tests, test selection, test administration, scoring, and interpretation. Guidance is also given for communicating test results. The AMHCA Code of Ethics also gives detailed guidance on test selection, administration, and interpretation. Mental health counselors may be called to provide testing as part of the diagnostic or treatment process. For example, if a client is presenting as intellectually challenged, but it is unclear as to whether there is an underlying mental retardation or if the intellectual deficiency is related to a disorder that depresses cognitive functioning (e.g., a severe depression), a mental health counselor may be asked to provide objective test measures to assist the diagnostic process. Such testing may include tests of intelligence or of mood impairment. Other tests, such as those to assess whether there is a pattern consistent with "loss of intelligence" (as in a dementia from aging, disease, or other causes), may be necessary. Mental health counselors, unlike social workers or psychiatrists, have training in objective testing, which is a valuable skill.

QUESTIONS FOR REFLECTION

What is the best way to ensure that licensed professional counselors are well-prepared, competitive, competent, and ethical mental health practitioners? Should graduate program admissions standards be strict? Is it better to have graduated from a program that requires more graduate semester credit hours? Is more supervision during or after graduate training necessary? Should degree programs require stringent entrance or exit examinations? Should licensure standards remain the same or be modified in some way? Consider licensure requirements in your state or a state that is geographically near your state. How do these standards compare to those of other mental health professions? Are the requirements adequate to ensure the health and safety of clients with serious mental disorders who are treated by licensed professional counselors?

ISSUES OF SIGNIFICANCE TO THE SPECIALTY

Professional Differentiation

Mental health counseling has identified itself as the "health" specialty of counseling specialties. Although other specialties in counseling also are involved with medical concerns (e.g., rehabilitation counseling), mental health counseling focuses on the provision of services to prevent and to facilitate healthy development and growth of individuals diagnosed with mental disorders. Mental health counselors focus on building the strengths of people with problems; the focus is on the development of the individual beyond deficiency (Hershenson & Power, 1987). Unique ethical concerns arise due to the medical nature of the settings within which mental health counselors work and due to the nature of the work itself. Like rehabilitation counselors, mental health counselors must be prepared to work with individuals with severe disabilities in need of urgent care.

A major professional issue for the mental health counselor is the inconsistency between specialty training and training required by most states for licensure to do the full range of mental health services. CACREP, the professional accreditation body for graduate counseling programs, requires that mental health counseling

programs must be 60-semester-hour degree programs. The degree program prepares graduates to sit for the specialty examination in mental health counseling—the National Clinical Mental Health Counseling Exam (NCMHCE). However, over 50% of the states that license counselors for independent practice require only 48 (or fewer) semester hours for graduate degrees (see Altekruse, 2001). The examination used by all but six states for licensure is the more general National Counselor Examination (NCE), which does not focus on mental health specialty practice. There are major license portability (reciprocity across states) issues. Even mental health counselors who graduate from CACREP-accredited mental health counseling degree programs and pass the competitive NCMHCE may have problems getting licensed in certain states (where, for example, the NCE is required). The portability issue is a major concern for mental health counselors who are mobile or wish to be licensed by several states; it is also an important matter for the profession as a whole (Altekruse). The ACA's "Model Licensing Law" requires 60-semester-hour degree programs, which is in line with CACREP training in mental health counseling. If more states adopt the ACA model, revising their statutes to be in sync with the professional association's standards, the norm could become the 60-hour degree program.

A related issue is the presentation or advertisement of fraudulent or unaccredited degrees by mental health counselors. Because the profession is a master's-level licensure profession, and master's-level licensed counselors often compete with doctoral-trained professionals in psychology and medicine, there is the potential for presentation or advertisement of fraudulent or unaccredited doctoral degrees. This is a concern that received attention dating back to the 1980s. Dattilio (1989) stated: "What is particularly upsetting is that one of the primary choices of media focus is the mental health field, which appears to have become one of the largest victims of individuals holding 'bogus degrees'" (p. 152). Dattilio further stated: "Most of us would be shocked to see the statistics on those in education, research, and most particularly the clinical practice of counseling and psychotherapy who hold phony or questionable degrees" (p. 152). Several state licensure boards have established rules that licensed professional counselors may not represent their training at the doctoral-degree level unless the doctoral degree is clearly a counseling-relevant degree and is earned from an acceptably accredited college or university. Presenting a bogus or unaccredited doctoral degree as a legitimate credential may be a breach of the AMHCA Code of Ethics, Principle 13, Public Statements, which requires accurate and objective representation of credentials. (See the AMHCA Code of Ethics in Appendix P.)

QUESTIONS FOR REFLECTION

What do you believe will happen in the area of professional credentialing in counseling? Will the 60-hour degree program requirement prevail in licensure standards? Will the more focused mental health counseling examination (the NCMHCE) become the standard examination for practice (versus the NCE)?

Ethical Issues

Privacy.   Privacy issues in mental health counseling are complicated by the presence of a third-party payer, usually an insurance company, sometimes through a managed care overseer or through government or other agencies that fund services. Occasionally, clients pay for counseling out of their own pockets, but not as often as in some specialties of counseling in which clients are sometimes willing to pay for services separate from medical insurance (e.g., marriage counseling). Privacy relates to the "freedom of individuals to choose for themselves the time and the circumstances under which and the extent to which their beliefs, behavior, and opinions are to be shared or withheld from others" (Spiegel, 1979, p. 251). Privacy is an ethical principle that makes private: (a) the fact that a person has sought counseling, and (b) what is communicated in counseling. The client has control over how the information will be used. Privacy and confidentiality, although different concepts, are related; they both involve the right of the client regarding information or behaviors that are shared with a counselor. Whereas privacy issues relate to a constitutional right (Huber, 1994), confidentiality issues address the specific counseling context. Privacy issues extend to such areas as (a) discrete scheduling of sessions to prevent clients from encountering other clients in waiting rooms, (b) billing and administration of case records, (c) use of client information over computers or phone (wireless or otherwise) or through testing services, and (d) other activities that do not necessarily relate to information provided in counseling sessions. Confidentiality is generally understood to deal with the content of counseling sessions. Huber stated: "These [privacy] questions are particularly important when insurance companies and

other third-party payers attempt to gain access to therapy information about clients or when therapists are bound by law and/or professional codes of ethics to break confidentiality" (p. 23). Ethically sensitive counselors do their best to ensure that information about clients is considered private.

In a noteworthy development, the U.S. DHHS issued a major rule related to privacy of individual patient records. Frank-Stromborg (2004) noted:

> Making the Privacy Rules a reality, the Department of Health and Human Services (DHHS) issued its final version of the Privacy Rules on August 14, 2002, under the Health Insurance Portability and Accountability Act (HIPAA) of 1996. As of April 14, 2003, all covered health care entities must comply with the newly implemented national standards. However, compliance for smaller health care entities with annual receipts of $5 million or less is extended until April 14, 2004 (45 CFR chapters 164.534, 164.160.103, 2002). . . . Further the final version means that the government is serious about the newly promulgated rules. In fact, the government is so serious concerning compliance with the Privacy Rules that not only can an employer be penalized with punitive damages, but personal punitive damages can also be a consequence of noncompliance. (p. 2)

The rule "generally gives patients the right to see their records (although not psychotherapy notes), to receive notice of how their records may be disclosed, and to have an accounting of their records that have been released to parties beyond the treating provider" ("New Patient Records Privacy Rule," 2001, p. 1). An article in the *Practitioner Update* of the APA stated:

> Separate patient authorization is required for the release of psychotherapy notes—in addition to consent the patient gives to disclose his or her other records—to parties beyond the treating provider. Psychotherapy notes are the only type of record given heightened privacy protection under this rule. Importantly, a health plan or provider may not make treatment, payment, enrollment or eligibility for benefits conditional on a patient's authorization to release psychotherapy notes. ("New Patient Records Privacy Rule," 2001, p. 1)

All agencies or organizations that receive federal funding may not, by law, release confidential psychotherapy notes, unless there is separate signed client permission to do so. Further, the rule covers material from a private counseling session or a group, joint, or family counseling session. "'Psychotherapy notes' excludes medication prescription and monitoring, counseling session start and stop times, the modalities and frequencies of treatment furnished, results of clinical tests, and any summary of the following items: diagnosis, functional status, the treatment plan, symptoms, prognosis, and progress to date" ("New Patient Records Privacy Rule," 2001, p. 1). The new privacy rules have direct relevance to the related concept of confidentiality because they limit revelation of the content of counseling sessions.

Confidentiality and Privileged Communication. Mental health counselors, more so than any other type of counselor (except rehabilitation counselors), counsel adult clients who are not competent to make judgments about such issues as money management, treatment compliance, or privacy issues. It may be too easy for the unethical practitioner to get the permission of a mentally disturbed individual to share information with other individuals, or even to share the information in legal proceedings. One of the most prevalent traits of individuals with mental disorders listed in the DSM–IV is the presence of poor judgment. Clients who have limitations of judgment or ability must be given special treatment as related to the confidentiality issue because they may release information inadvertently to serve a counselor's agenda rather than their own needs. Ethical counselors ensure that every effort is made to explain fully the relevant issues so clients can understand and make fully informed decisions.

Confidentiality is akin to an antigossip guarantee. Counselors must be alert to the need to keep information learned in counseling as private as legally possible. Because individuals with mental disorders often manifest behaviors that are odd or unusual, their behaviors make for interesting general conversation. At more than one social gathering, counselors have been overheard entertaining others by talking about the strange behaviors of their clients. Such behavior shows poor respect for individuals in serious personal situations and poor regard for the profession that allows counselors the privilege of serving people in need. No matter how seriously disturbed a client's behavior may be, it is incumbent on the counselor to respect the individual and to maintain the privacy of client information.

Pietrofesa, Pietrofesa, and Pietrofesa (1990) described the mental health counselor's responsibility related to the duty to warn endangered parties. They stated, "It is clear that ethically and legally the mental health counselor is required to protect an identifiable victim of a client from harm" (p. 135). They provided steps to be taken when there is potential danger to a client. Costa and Altekruse (1994) also provided guidelines for mental health counselors when duty to warn

is an issue. Their duty-to-warn guidelines included: (a) Get informed consent, (b) plan ahead through consultation, (c) develop contingency plans, (d) obtain professional liability insurance, (e) be selective about clients, (f) involve the client, (g) obtain a detailed history, (h) document in writing, and (i) implement procedure to warn. Further, they provided vignettes of potential dilemmas in working with families and analyses of the circumstances according to three conditions related to duty to warn: a special relationship, a prediction of harmful conduct, and a foreseeable victim. Duty-to-warn situations may arise in mental health counseling because many of the served clients experience acute symptoms of a serious nature that may affect their judgment. In cases of imminent danger, a breach of confidentiality is acceptable (see Box 14–2).

As described in Chapter 3, privileged communication relates to revelation of confidential information in legal proceedings. As with many specialties of counseling, mental health counselors may be called upon to testify at legal proceedings. It is important that mental health counselors know the laws that relate to privileged communication in their states.

The AMHCA Code of Ethics (2000) gives detailed guidance on the matter of confidentiality. The code specifically addresses 14 separate but relevant issues under the heading of confidentiality. The confidentiality "principle" (as it is defined in the AMHCA Code of Ethics) is broad and makes specific reference to such issues as taping (recording) sessions, dealing with minors, working with families, group work, and record keeping (both standard and electronic).

Informed Consent. In a recent actual case, the children of a young woman (diagnosed with a reading disorder, depression, and borderline intelligence) were taken away when she unwittingly signed a form presented to her by a family services agency caseworker. The caseworker had full knowledge of the person's limitations and inability to read and did not inform the woman of the contents of the form fully, even when the woman asked for an explanation. The children later were returned after much legal maneuvering, when it was learned that the client signed a paper she could not read and that was not thoroughly explained to her.

Mental health counselors must be sure that their clients have the capability to consent to treatment. Handelsman, Kemper, Kesson-Craig, McLain, and Johnsrud (1986) found that the readability of consent forms for

Box 14–2 • Recognizing Signs and Taking Action in Cases of Potential Suicide

Recent statistics published by the American Association of Suicidology (AAS) document the staggering toll of suicide in the United States. In 2002, 31,655 individuals completed suicide—the equivalent of one person dying every 16.6 minutes due to suicide. In 2002, suicide was the 11th ranking cause of death in the United States and the 3rd ranking cause of death among youth. Counselors need to be especially alert to the warning signs of suicide, as listed by the AAS. A person may be suicidal if he or she is:

- Someone threatening to hurt or kill him/herself or talking of wanting to hurt him/herself.
- Someone looking for ways to kill him/herself by seeking access to firearms, available pills, or other means.
- Someone talking or writing about death, dying, or suicide, when these actions are out of the ordinary for the person.

Exhibiting any one or more of the following:

- Hopelessness.
- Rage, uncontrolled anger, seeking revenge.
- Acting reckless or engaging in risky activities, seemingly without thinking.
- Feeling trapped—like there's no way out.
- Increasing alcohol or drug use.

- Withdrawing from friends, family, and society.
- Anxiety, agitation, unable to sleep, or sleeping all the time.
- Dramatic mood change.
- No reason for living; no sense of purpose in life.

If someone appears to be threatening suicide, the AAS recommends that you:

- Be direct. Talk openly and matter-of-factly about suicide.
- Be willing to listen. Allow expressions of feelings. Accept the feelings.
- Be nonjudgmental. Don't debate whether suicide is right or wrong.
- Be available, and show interest and support.
- Don't dare him or her to commit suicide.
- Don't act shocked.
- Don't be sworn to secrecy.
- Offer hope that alternatives are available, but do not offer glib reassurance.
- Take action to remove means, such as guns or stockpiled pills.
- Get help from persons or agencies specializing in crisis intervention or suicide prevention.

Source: American Association for Suicidology, 5221 Wisconsin Ave., NW (Second Floor), Washington, DC 20015; phone: (202) 237-2280; Web site: www.suicidology.org.

therapy was difficult—equivalent to an academically oriented periodical. At this level, few clients of even average intelligence can understand a consent document fully. Clients who are emotionally disabled may not be in a state of mind to fully comprehend their rights related to accepting or refusing treatment. Handelsman (2001) outlined general "themes" for "accurate and effective informed consent," and his work provides an excellent context for understanding the process approach to informed consent. He stated, "Think of informed consent as a process rather than an event" (p. 6). A process view of informed consent is welcomed, especially with clients whose capability is in question.

The ACA and APA codes of ethics give guidance on this issue of informed consent. Further, the consent from a legally authorized person is sought for those who are legally incapable of giving informed consent; yet it is a standard that the incapable person is still consulted and informed of the actions to be taken by the therapist, and that person's "assent" is still sought (assent implies

agreement; see the APA and ACA ethics codes). The AMHCA Code of Ethics (2000) states that "In the event that a client is a minor or possesses disabilities that would prohibit informed consent, the mental health counselor acts in the client's best interest" (Principle 1J). These guidelines generally relate to individuals diagnosed as mentally retarded, organically impaired, or seriously emotionally disturbed. It also applies to individuals under adult age as defined in the legal jurisdiction of practice.

Roles and Relationships with Clients.   The AMHCA Code of Ethics (2000) specifically states under a principle titled "Welfare of the Consumer" under the subheading of "Dual Relationships": "Mental health counselors make every effort to avoid dual relationships with clients that could impair professional judgement or increase the risk of harm. Examples of such relationships may include, but are not limited to: familial, social, financial, business, or close personal relationships with the clients" (Principle 1, section F). In section G under the same principle, the code states, "Sexual relationships with clients are strictly prohibited. Mental health counselors do not counsel persons with whom they have had a previous sexual relationship" (Principle 1, section G). Sexual intimacies with former clients are banned for 2 years subsequent to termination of services, with professional scrutiny (for exploitation) of such relations as a qualifying factor.

The term dual relationship is unclear, and the term is not implicitly a negative term, as the standard implies. The AMHCA 2000 standard does not differentiate between professional and nonprofessional dual relationships, and they should be separated for clarity. The ban on sexual relationships with former clients for 2 years appears to be too short a period, and the provision for scrutiny of relationships initiated 2 years subsequent to treatment appears to allow for equivocation, which becomes problematic when enforcement is an issue. A 5-year ban on relationships with former clients appears justified and is less equivocal and is referenced in the new ACA Code of Ethics. The AMHCA standard gives no guidance for potentially beneficial interactions with clients outside of treatment, as does the new ACA Code of Ethics. Overall, there are some inconsistencies between the AMHCA ethics code and the new ACA ethics code. Those AMHCA members who are also members of ACA are bound by both codes, and application of a recognized ethical decision-making model might be beneficial in addressing dilemmas that require negotiation of the two ethics codes on the matter of roles and relationships with clients.

Responsibility. The AMHCA (2000) Code of Ethics states that the "primary responsibility of the mental health counselor is to respect the dignity and integrity of the client. Client growth and development are encouraged in ways that foster the client's interests and promote welfare" (Principle 1, Section A1).

Professional obligation should always start with the client. This is especially true for the mental health counselor, who may be working with individuals who are vulnerable to the whims of others or to agencies involved in the client's treatment. What should a mental health counselor do if a request for additional services is denied by an MCO, when such a denial is to the detriment of the client or even endangers the client or other parties? Obviously, the mental health counselor's primary obligation is to the client. The counselor should make an effort to inform the MCO that actions to deny services may, in fact, endanger individuals or be to the detriment of a client. The counselor should inform the MCO in an appropriate and professional manner, and, if necessary, provide and seek written documentation of correspondence with the MCO. It is imperative that counselors not accede to the insurance company's decisions when serious issues of client survival or welfare are imminent. If unsuccessful in appealing what may appear to be an unwise decision to discontinue treatment by an insurer (managed or not), the counselor must consider treating the client pro bono publico—for the public good (without a fee or for a minimal fee). Principle 1, Section M of the AMHCA (2000) Code of Ethics states: "Mental health counselors contribute to society by devoting a portion of their professional activity to services for which there is little or no financial return." And the ACA Code of Ethics recognizes such work as an aspirational guideline. Regardless, the counselor must be prepared to take the appeal to higher authorities if it is believed that a client has been treated unjustly. Mental health counselors must never confuse their primary responsibility to clients with secondary obligations to paying parties or employers.

Values. Value issues enter into mental health counseling when counselors must make a judgment or take an action that may conflict with their personal values. What should a counselor do when confronted with a client who confesses to repeatedly and seriously sexually abusing children? Treating such an individual may be abhorrent to the counselor, who might prefer to assist and counsel the victims of abuse. Treating abusers or perpetrators may clash with the counselor's most basic values related to children: How can a counselor view perpetrators in a way that allows for fair and competent treatment if their actions are seriously objectionable? Counselors continually must assess their personal values and make appropriate judgments about their own limitations. If counselors find that working with a particular client or a type of client is objectionable, they must assess whether they can serve the client competently and objectively. Obviously, referring the client to another counselor or therapist who specializes in counseling such problems is recommended. But, in some cases, for example, in sparsely populated areas without available mental health alternatives, counselors may have to make judgments to serve clients that they otherwise would refuse to treat. In such cases, counselors are obliged to inform clients of their concerns or feelings, and counseling should proceed only under the full and informed consent of the clients. Many issues may arise in counseling that produce value conflicts (see Chapter 5). In such cases, counselors must be prepared to address the concerns professionally and ethically. Some of the more common value issues that arise in mental health counseling involve (a) abuse of children or defenseless/dependent individuals, (b) pregnancy issues (e.g., abortion), (c) current, recent, or past illegal actions by a patient, (d) sexuality concerns or deviant sexual practices, and (e) alcohol or drug abuse.

Counselor Competence. Counselor competence involves (a) the quality of the provided service, and (b) the boundaries or scope of professional activity. The AMHCA Code of Ethics (AMHCA, 2000) provides a detailed section outlining the principle of competence. High standards are to be maintained, according to the code. Principle 7 of the code, "Competence," reads as follows:

> The maintenance of high standards of professional competence is a responsibility shared by all mental health counselors in the best interests of the public and the profession. Mental health counselors recognize the boundaries of their particular competencies and the limitation of their expertise. Mental health counselors only provide those services and use only those techniques for which they are qualified by education, training or experience. Mental health counselors maintain knowledge of relevant scientific and professional information related to the services they render, and they recognize the need for on-going education. (Principle 7)

Consider the standard of competence in light of a recent news report by the Reuters News Service (2001) about two Colorado therapists who were convicted of "reckless child abuse resulting in death" of a 10-year-old client. The therapists were using a "rebirthing" technique to treat a "reactive attachment disorder." The client was bound in a sheet and told to fight her way out so she could be "reborn" to her adoptive mother. The Reuters article stated: "The girl begged for air and screamed for mercy after she was bound head-to-toe in a flannel sheet during a discredited psychotherapy procedure called rebirthing." Further, the article stated, "the girl begged for air and screamed that she was dying only to have her pleas met with sarcasm from the therapists." She lost consciousness during the procedure and died the next day. The state of Colorado has now banned this sort of treatment. The two therapists were convicted and each was sentenced to 16 years in prison. Obviously, clients should not be physically endangered by a therapeutic technique. Counselors must ensure that the techniques they use have sound empirical and theoretical foundations (based on theory that has stood the test of refereed review in the best counseling journals). The procedure in the Colorado case was dangerous, and it also raises the issue of competency—was this procedure a sound technique and was application of this technique within the scope of the therapists' practice?

Use of new, untested, or controversial techniques is always unwise. It is best to delay use of untested techniques until research supports the technique. The use of "paradoxical technique" is a good example. In this procedure, the counselor directs a client to do something illogical, such as "prescribing the symptom," to procedure a resistance reaction wherein the client resists being symptomatic. Sexton, Montgomery, Goff, and Nugent (1993) stated:

> The use of paradox is a complicated matter and the debate concerning its use is likely to continue. However, consideration of the ethical treatment and the legal issues associated with paradox can help guide the mental health counselor. For example, given the current status of the research, the current enthusiasm for paradoxical therapeutic procedures is not altogether justified. Although there is strong anecdotal evidence, and some controlled experimental evidence of treatment effectiveness, additional well-controlled research is needed to substantiate proponents' claims. At this time, it seems that result of empirical research most clearly support the use of paradox with sleep-onset insomnia and some anxiety disorders. The effects of paradox with other types of concerns, such as family problems, appear to be [sic] less clearly documented empirical support. Furthermore, there appears to be little knowledge of either possible inadvertent effects or of issues such as treatment acceptability. (pp. 271–272)

When counselors are put in the position of having to defend the choice of a professional technique or procedure, they are wise to have chosen techniques that are based on sound empirical or traditional theoretical grounds.

On more general issues related to the scope of professional practice, there are continual "turf battles" over the extent of services to be provided by counselors and other mental health providers. Such a battle raged in Ohio in 1996, when the state attorney general offered a legal opinion allowing licensed professional or clinical counselors to use the term psychological to "describe their work of testing and evaluating people for mental and emotional disorders" ("Ohio," 1996, p. 9). The opinion was opposed by the Ohio Board of Psychology and the Ohio Psychological and School Psychologist Associations. In essence, counselors, by the opinion of the leading law enforcement agency of the state, were told they could use a term that had been associated historically only with the practice of psychology. Some viewed this opinion as a major challenge to psychology in Ohio. Typically, battles over scope of practice of mental health counselors involve the issues of testing, diagnosis, and the use of the term psychotherapy. Counselors are required by licensure laws to practice within the limits of their defined competence and training and consistent with definitions of practice within licensure statutes.

ASSESSMENT

To a large degree, issues of assessment pervade many of the ethical issues addressed in the previous sections. However, the RUST standards, established with the involvement of the Association of Assessment in Counseling (AAC), a division of the ACA, should be consulted for detailed guidelines on assessment matters. The RUST standards were revised in 2003. (The RUST standards are listed in Appendix Q). The RUST standards (section: Qualifications of Test Users) state:

> Qualified test users demonstrate appropriate education, training, and experience in using tests for the purposes under consideration. They adhere to the highest degree of ethical codes, laws, and standards governing professional practice. Lack of essential qualifications or ethical and legal compliance can lead to errors and subsequent harm to clients. Each professional is responsible for making judgments in each testing situation and cannot leave that responsibility either to clients or to others in authority. The individual test user must obtain appropriate training, or arrange for professional supervision and assistance when engaging in testing in order to provide valuable, ethical, and effective assessment services to the public.

The RUST qualifications for test users depend on four factors: (a) purposes of testing, (b) characteristics of tests, (c) settings and conditions of test use, and (d) roles of test selectors, administrators, scorers, and interpreters. The test selected should be based on the purpose of testing, the validity of instruments (how well a test measures what it purports to measure), and other technical standards related to test quality (e.g., reliability—how consistently a test measures what it

purports to measure). The test should be administered in a way that will produce a valid and accurate assessment of the individual. Test scoring should be done in a standardized way against proper norms, if applicable. Interpretation should be according to guidelines in test manuals and as objective as possible. Safeguards should be taken to ensure a client's privacy and to prevent misuse of the test data.

The AMHCA (2000) Code of Ethics provides detailed guidance on Utilization of Assessment Techniques (Principle 4). This ethical category has been expanded in the most recent version of the AMHCA ethics code. It includes three distinct subcategories: (a) test selection, (b) test administration, and (c) test interpretation. The guidance under these categories appears to be comprehensive and consistent with RUST standards.

CODE COMPARISONS

The AMHCA (2000) Code of Ethics (see Appendix P is a vast improvement over the prior (1987) AMHCA ethics code. The prior code was less comprehensive and, at the time, was an aspirational and supplemental code (enforcement was left up to the ACA according to the enforceable ACA Code of Ethics and Standards of Practice). Unfortunately, the 2000 version of the AMHCA ethics code is also aspirational and nonenforceable, and because AMHCA members do not have to affiliate with the ACA (thereby not being bound by the mandatory and enforceable ACA ethics code), there is no professionally binding ethical standard for AMHCA members who do not affiliate with the ACA. The last "principle" of the AMHCA (2000) Code of Ethics reads: "Neither the American Mental Health Counselors Association, its Board of Directors, nor its National Committee on Ethics investigate or adjudicate ethical complaints. In the event a member has his or her license suspended or revoked by an appropriate state licensure board, the AMHCA Board of Directors may then act in accordance with AMHCA's National By-Laws to suspend or revoke his or her membership." The decision of the AMHCA Board of Directors to defer enforcement of its code to the decisions of state licensure boards and ethical codes and standards referenced in licensure statutes renders the AMHCA code of ethics impotent. The lack of enforcement by the AMHCA appears to be a negative by-product of AMHCA administrative separation from the ACA.

Regardless, the RUST standards provide specialized guidance on issues of tests and measurement that are not addressed adequately in the ACA, AMHCA, or

APA codes. Additional standards related to testing are also published by the APA, including the Standards for Educational and Psychological Tests and the Code for Fair Testing Practices in Education.

ISSUES OF DIVERSITY

The issue of deviance or maladjustment is one of the most predominant multicultural issues in mental health counseling. Axelson (1993) described the "cultural model" of maladjustment as defining:

> A normal person as one who is in harmony with self and environment. The definition emphasizes conformity with the cultural requirements, mores, and injunctions of the community. Thus, normality tends to be equated with what is conventional and abnormality with what is viewed as antisocial conduct and/or different behavior. (p. 275)

This view of maladjustment is in contrast to the American Psychiatric Association's (1994) definition in the Diagnostic and Statistical Manual of Mental Disorders, Fourth Edition (DSM–IV). The DSM–IV defines a mental disorder as:

> A clinically significant behavioral or psychological syndrome or pattern that occurs in an individual and that is associated with present distress (e.g., a painful symptom) or disability (e.g., impairment in one or more important areas of functioning) or with a significantly increased risk of suffering death, pain, disability, or an important loss of freedom. In addition, this syndrome or pattern must not be merely an expectable and culturally sanctioned response to a particular event, for example, the death of a loved one. Whatever its original cause, it must currently be considered a manifestation of a behavioral, psychological, or biological dysfunction in the individual. Neither deviant behavior (e.g., political, religious, or sexual) nor conflicts that are primarily between the individual and society are mental disorders unless the deviance or conflict is a symptom of a dysfunction in the individual, as described above. (pp. xxi–xxii)

The cultural definition of maladjustment takes into consideration cultural variation, whereas the DSM–IV definition plays down, minimizes, or subsumes cultural factors by focusing on disorders "in the individual."

For the mental health counselor working in a context that requires diagnosis of mental disorders according to DSM–IV criteria, cultural sensitivity may produce discomfort with standardized procedures. This occurs because the culturally sensitive counselor recognizes that mental disorders may not be equally prevalent across cultural contexts. Should inner-city ghetto inhabitants be diagnosed as "antisocial personality disorders" because they act out of the norm to survive in a difficult environment? Should bulimia or anorexia be interpreted outside of a cultural context that promotes unnaturally thin standards of body weight and attractiveness?

Issues of diversity also are predominant when objective tests are used. Because minorities are usually outnumbered in norm bases, it can be argued that tests, no matter how broadly normed, cannot reflect cultural differences accurately in the development of abilities, interests, aptitudes, or achievement. Although some tests are more culturally sensitive than others, it is imperative that test data are not interpreted out of social or cultural context.

The greatest challenge to culturally sensitive mental health counselors is to view clients in context and to dispute labels that require an internalistic or broadly normative view of mental disorder. As Sue (1996) stated:

> If we believe that many problems reside outside the person (prejudice and discrimination) and not within (person-blame), ethical practice dictates that professionals develop alternative helping roles that are aimed at *system intervention*. The traditional counseling role has been primarily confined to a one-to-one, remediation-oriented, in-the-office form of help, but recognition that problems may reside in the social system dictates use of nontraditional roles. These roles may include adviser, advocate, consultant, change agent, facilitator of indigenous support systems, and facilitator of indigenous healing systems. Most counselor education programs do not train us in these roles, yet they are some of the most effective in multicultural helping. (p. 196)

Whether problems should be viewed as internal or external to individuals is a challenge that may best be met by the profession as a whole. Certainly, counselors should be alert to the pressure to view disorders or measured characteristics according to "clinical" standards at the expense of clients acting to survive in difficult or unusual cultural contexts. The emphasis on client assets and the development of human potential that rests at the base of the mental "health" counselor's philosophy may be an asset when addressing issues of diversity.

DECISION MAKING IN CONTEXT

Ethical dilemmas arise out of the diagnostic process in mental health counseling that might not arise in other specialties of counseling. Related to ethical decision making, consider the following scenario. A mental health counselor is referred a client who is an actress. She is well known locally for her work in the community the- atre. She is in her early 40s. She has had a number of failed love relationships, primarily with men who also work in theatre arts. Her presenting problem is that she is lonely and depressed. At the first session, she presents in a flamboyant way, dressed in colorful and eccentric clothing. As she speaks, she is dramatic, entertaining, and funny. Her affect (emotional tone observed by the coun- selor) is not congruent to her expressed mood (sadness). She comes across as very animated and not shy by any means. She has achieved a degree of fame in the metro- politan area where she lives and works, and she has been the subject of a number of newspaper articles that have praised her work. Yet she has a feeling of empti- ness and despair. Aside from the treatment issues of this case, the counselor is faced with having to provide a diagnosis to a medical insurance company for reim- bursement of treatment services. The counselor must de- cide if the client is presenting with histrionic personality disorder (a serious personality disorder) or whether her social/cultural context should be considered as the pre- dominant factor in her presentation, with consideration of a less severe diagnosis (such as adjustment disorder with disturbance of mood).

From an ethics standpoint, this dilemma derives from the ethical standards of responsibility and com- petence. The counselor is responsible to the client, but the counselor is also obligated to diagnose in a com- petent manner. The 2005 ACA Code of Ethics requires "proper diagnosis," meaning the diagnosis is accurate. But the ACA Code of Ethics also requires "cultural sen- sitivity" when diagnosing mental disorders . . . cultural experiences are considered when diagnosing mental disorders. To discount the serious personality disorder diagnosis means that the counselor must demonstrate significant cultural influence on the client's behavior. The counselor must make a decision with the client's best interest in mind.

There are several components of the Tarvydas In- tegrative Decision-Making Model that are helpful to the dilemma in this case. For example, in Stage I, compo- nent 1 is important—enhancing sensitivity and aware- ness. For the counselor in this situation, it might be wise to study the theatre culture to get an understand- ing of the lifestyle and stressors associated with such work. The counselor might find that there are incredi- ble demands made upon career theatre professionals, and they are faced with stressful daily performances in tense circumstances. They also have little financial sta- bility, as their incomes may depend on the viability of their current show. Given the nature of the career,

these kinds of pressures would impinge even the most resilient personality. As the counselor proceeds through the decision-making components of the Tarvy- das model, two probable courses of action may be de- fined (Stage II component 3)—making the diagnosis strictly on the criteria described in the DSM–IV or con- sidering an alternative explanatory framework for her presentation based on cultural/environmental factors. It is wise to consult other experts on matters such as these (Stage II, component 5). An ethical course of ac- tion must be selected (which may be to hold strictly to the diagnostic criteria), but in Stage III of the Tarvydas model, contextual factors must be weighed. The pre- ferred course of action (to give a less severe diagnosis) may be more acceptable, given the nature of the val- ues of the culture of the client. For example, attention- seeking and dramatic behavior may be viewed as valuable to a person on the stage, whereas, out of that context, it can be viewed as unusual or perturbing. A preferred course of action (Stage III, component 3) may be to give the adjustment disorder diagnosis pro- visionally, with a notation that a more severe person- ality disorder should be ruled out (differentially considered at a later date). In this way, treatment can proceed, but a final diagnosis is not given. Executing the decision then must follow a number of steps (Stage IV), with reevaluation of the client at a later date as a planned step of the decision process.

With the Cottone Social Constructivism Model of Ethical Decision Making, there are a pair of decisions that must be made in this case. A decision to use a less severe diagnosis may come easily based on the early phases of decision making—which typically involve (a) obtaining information from those involved; (b) assessing the nature of relationships (conflicting or adversarial opinions); and (c) consulting valued col- leagues and expert opinion. In this case, because there are no adversarial relationships or other individuals in- volved except the people representing the third-party payer (the MCO), the decision boils down to getting detailed information from the client about her cultural context and then consulting individuals who may be expert at treating individuals in similar circumstances. However, at a later date, the counselor may be faced with a situation where the provisional diagnosis of ad- justment disorder is not allowing for enough pre- scribed treatment for the seriousness of the client's concerns (the MCO assigned too few sessions of ser- vice for a person with a severe personality disorder). At that time, the counselor might have to reassess the prior decision in light of developments in treatment. If the client's concerns are more serious than an adjustment disorder, requiring longer term treatment to resolve treatment goals, then a decision to revise the diagnosis would have to be made—and the decision-making process would be engaged. The second decision might involve negotiation with the insurance managed care representative to ensure that the client receives adequate needed services, regardless of the diagnosis. In the end, some consensus must be established around the nature of the client's concerns and the extent of treatment to be provided. That consensus initially will involve the client and other experts knowledgeable about her circumstance, but later may involve a decision to revise the diagnosis in order to ensure adequate service provision. These clinical decisions are made within the context of the overarching ethical standards of client responsibility and counselor competence (proper diagnosis).

CHAPTER SUMMARY

Mental health counseling has taken a lead in the mental health field and represents a health specialty in counseling. Through specialty certification by means of the NBCC and through development of a specialized code of ethics, mental health counselors have established themselves as a viable and identifiable

specialty. Although the pressures of managed care may affect the practice of mental health counseling, the specialty may also be positioned well to interface with the managed care system. Mental health counselors may find jobs in MCOs as case managers and service providers. Because mental health counselors, like social workers, are primarily master's-level-trained mental health professionals, they may suit the needs of managed care's cost containment efforts by undercutting the rates and salaries of doctoral-level-trained professionals (such as psychologists and psychiatrists). Mental health counseling may be situated ideally to survive the managed care movement in the mental health field. Yet, the field, which has defined itself as a "health" specialty, must also deal with the issue that mental health may be a culturally relative issue, and not just a matter of diagnosing and treating individual deviance.

There are ethical and professional issues unique to mental health practice. The professional identity of the mental health counselor is developing alongside other counseling specialties. Mental health counselors have carved a niche that positions them well to provide services to individuals with diagnosed mental disorders. The developmental model, which lies at the root of mental health counseling practice, may serve the specialty well as the mental health enterprise transitions in the 21st century.

REFERENCES

Altekruse, M. K. (2001). *Counselor portability.* Power point presentation as chair of the American Counseling Association Professionalization Committee. (Available from Dr. Altekruse at UNT, P.O. Box 311337, Denton, TX 76203-1337).

Altekruse, M. K., Harris, H. L., & Brandt, M. A. (2000). *The role and function of the professional counselor in the 21st century.* Unpublished manuscript.

Altekruse, M. K., & Sexton, T. L. (Eds.). (1995). *Mental health counseling in the 90's: A research report for training and practice* (1st ed.). Tampa, FL: The National Commission for Mental Health Counseling.

American Counseling Association. (2005). *American Counseling Association code of ethics.* Alexandria, VA: Author.

American Mental Health Counseling Association. (1987). *Code of ethics of the American Mental Health Counselors Association.* Alexandria, VA: Author.

American Mental Health Counseling Association. (2000). *AMHCA code of ethics.* Alexandria, VA: Author.

American Psychiatric Association. (1994). *Diagnostic and statistical manual of mental disorders* (4th ed.). Washington, DC: Author.

Association for Assessment in Counseling. (2003). *Responsibilities of users of standardized tests.* Alexandria, VA: Author.

Axelson, J. A. (1993). *Counseling and development in a multicultural society.* Pacific Grove, CA: Brooks/Cole.

Costa, L., & Altekruse, M. (1994). Duty-to-warn guidelines for mental health counselors. *Journal of Counseling and Development. 72,* 346–350.

Cottone, R. R. (1992). *Theories and paradigms of counseling and psychotherapy.* Needham Heights, MA: Allyn & Bacon.

Dattilio, F. M. (1989). Fraudulent degrees: A threat to the mental health counseling field. *Journal of Mental Health Counseling, 11,* 151–154.

Frank-Stromborg, M. (2004). They're real and they're here: The new federally regulated privacy rules under HIPAA. *Dermatology Nursing, 16* (1), p. 2 (downloaded version from http://gateway2.ovid.com/ovidweb.cgi).

Gladding, S. T., & Newsome, D. W. (2004). *Community and agency counseling* (2nd ed.). Columbus, OH: Pearson Merrill Prentice Hall.

Governing Council. (1996, August). *Counseling Today,* p. 1.

Handelsman, M. M. (2001). Accurate and effective informed consent. In E. Welfel & E. Ingersoll (Eds.), *The mental health desk reference: A sourcebook for counselor and therapists.* New York: Wiley.

Handelsman, M. M., Kemper, M. B., Kesson-Craig, P., McLain, J., & Johnsrud, C. (1986). Use, content, and readability of written informed consent forms for treatment. *Professional Psychology: Research and Practice, 17,* 514–518.

Hershenson, D. B., & Power, P. W. (1987). *Mental health counseling: Theory and practice.* New York: Pergamon.

Huber, C. H. (1994). *Ethical, legal, and professional issues in the practice of marriage and family therapy* (2nd ed.). Upper Saddle River, NJ: Merrill/Prentice Hall.

New Patient Records Privacy Rule. (2001). New patient records privacy rule takes effect. *Practitioner Update, 9*(1), 1.

Ohio A-G legal opinion allows counselors to call testing and evaluations 'psychological.'

(1996, July/August). *The National Psychologist,* p. 9.

Pietrofesa, J., Pietrofesa, C., & Pietrofesa, J. D. (1990). The mental health counselor and "duty to warn." *Journal of Mental Health Counseling, 12,* 129–137.

Reuters News Service. (2001). Two therapists get 16 years each in death of girl. Published in the *St. Louis Post Dispatch.*

Sexton, T. L., Montgomery, D., Goff, K., & Nugent, W. (1993). Ethical, therapeutic, and legal considerations in the use of paradoxical techniques: The emerging debate. *Journal of Mental Health Counseling, 15,* 260–277.

Spiegel, S. B. (1979). Separate principles for counselors of women: A new form of sexism. *The Counseling Psychologist, 8*(1), 49–50.

Sue, D. W. (1996). Ethical issues in multicultural counseling. In B. Herlihy & G. Corey (Eds.), *Ethical standards casebook* (5th ed.). Alexandria, VA: American Counseling Association.

Vernon, A. & Clemente, R. (2005). *Assessment and intervention with children and adolescents: Developmental and multicultural approaches* (2nd ed.). Alexandria, VA: American Counseling Association.

CHAPTER 15

Career Counseling

Mark Pope • Vilia M. Tarvydas

OBJECTIVES

After reading this chapter, you should be able to:

- Define the specialty of career counseling.
- Differentiate the roles and functions of practitioners of career counseling from those of practitioners of other counseling specialties.
- Address political issues of importance to career counselors.
- Explain the ethical issues specific to the practice of career counseling.
- Outline professional credentialing and licensure matters for career counselors.
- Review the assessment issues of career counseling.
- Apply a decision-making process to career counseling.

INTRODUCTION

The birth and subsequent development of career counseling in the United States occurred during times of major societal change (Brewer, 1942; Pope, 2000a). Career counseling, which was then called "vocational guidance," was born in the United States in the latter part of the 19th century out of societal upheaval, transition, and change. This new profession was described by historians as a "progressive social reform movement aimed at eradicating poverty and substandard living conditions spawned by the rapid industrialization and consequent migration of people to major urban centers at the turn of the 20th century" (Whiteley, 1984, p. 2). Pope (2000a) characterized this time thusly:

> The societal upheaval giving birth to career counseling was characterized by the loss of jobs in the agricultural sector, increasing demands for workers in heavy industry, the loss of "permanent" jobs on the family farm to new emerging technologies such as tractors, the increasing urbanization of the USA, and the concomitant calls for services to meet this internal migration pattern,

> all in order to retool for the new industrial economy. Returning veterans from World War I and those displaced by their return also heightened the need for career counseling. (p. 234)

Career counseling evolved out of the resulting needs to understand the world of work, how to best prepare individuals to enter it, and how to find a suitable match between the demands of the workplace and the skills and needs of individuals within it. Whether those requiring guidance and counseling were students, adults with industrial injuries, or veterans, the need to understand the individual and how that person's needs and skills could be used to find a satisfying and satisfactory match with vocational opportunities became a powerful force behind the career counseling movement.

Over the past 90 years, since the emergence of counseling as an organized profession, there has been significant social and political support for studying the world of work and training professionals to help people make vocational choices and adjust to problems of vocational placement. Career counseling received important legislative support for the emergence and continued growth of information and methods in the field. A description of these federal laws is provided by Pope (2000a) and integrates over 30 separate pieces of federal legislation in the fields of school guidance (e.g., Elementary and Secondary Education Act, 1969), vocational education (Vocational Education Act, 1963 and its Amendments to this Act in 1968 and 1976), workforce development (Manpower Development and Training Act, 1962), employment services (Economic Opportunity Act, 1964), vocational rehabilitation (Vocational Rehabilitation Administration Budget, 1965), social security (Social Security Act, 1967, which created the Work Incentive Program), international trade (Omnibus Trade and Competitiveness Act, 1988), and welfare (Welfare to Work Act, 1997). The evolution of career counseling has been influenced greatly by social and cultural forces affecting the work lives of Americans and the legislation and programs created as a result of these forces.

Frank Parsons (1909) is credited with defining practice in the field of career or vocational guidance through the development of the theoretical model that underlies the trait and factor approaches—approaches that fit a person's specific characteristics to a specific occupation. For example, a bricklayer must have visual spatial ability and gross motor skills, upper body strength, and good hand-eye coordination. These trait and factor theoretical approaches have permeated the development of career counseling (Brown & Brooks, 1991; Lapan, 2004; Salomone, 1996; Scharf, 2002). This model of career counseling identifies three core factors in vocational choice: (a) a clear self-understanding, (b) a knowledge of occupations, and (c) the ability to understand relationships between the self and information about occupations.

The traditional focus of career counseling has been on helping individuals successfully enter the world of work. This theoretical underpinning is shared with counseling psychology, a specialty within psychology that is represented in the APA by Division 17 (Counseling Psychology). Counseling psychology had an early and significant influence on the evolution of vocational counseling and psychology (Whiteley, 1984). Historically, professionals in these areas have done extensive vocational counseling, and their most frequent employment is in educational settings such as colleges and universities. Counseling psychology's research base and the training model have enhanced the knowledge base of career counseling.

Career counseling has increasingly taken a total life-role perspective to understand the place of work within the overall context of people's lives (Brown & Brooks, 1991; Hansen, 1997; Super, 1974). This holistic focus primarily has been pursued through the development of various career-life planning approaches. Career-life perspectives emphasize a wide range of factors that influence career choice, including needs related to work, family, home, and leisure.

It has long been recognized that many clients of career counselors cannot make wise vocational decisions when personal or psychological problems (for which they may need counseling) interfere with the decision-making process. There is an ongoing tension in career counseling concerning the relationship between personal and career counseling (Pope, Cheng, & Leong, 1998). Of course, the degree of focus for all practitioners depends on the needs of their clients, the institutional mission within which they practice, and their individual professional scopes of competency. Salomone (1996) provided a description of the areas of personal and career counseling that clarifies the relationships between these areas of professional practice. **Personal counseling** involves professionals who help clients "understand, accept, and resolve their problems" by using "basic counseling techniques so that their clients can lead more satisfying, well-adjusted lives." In contrast, "**career counseling** focuses on a certain realm of the counselee's life—the world of work" (Salomone, p. 368). It is incorrect to say that career counseling is distinct from personal counseling, because a counselor may assist the client personally as part of the vocational counseling process. It could be said that "it is impossible to do career counseling without simultaneously doing personal counseling" (Salomone, p. 369).

DEFINING THE SPECIALTY, SETTING, AND CLIENTS

As a counseling specialty, career counseling has two structural characteristics important to understanding its organization and professional positioning. First, career counseling was key to establishing the earliest professional organizational structures for the entire counseling movement. Second, career counseling has always taken the lead in establishing standards for the profession. (See Box 15–1.)

Box 15–1 • Exploring the Codes

What section of the NCDA Ethical Standards (1991) (see Appendix R) addresses the use of tests in assessment of clients?

What should a career counselor do if her client is being treated by another mental health professional, according to the NCDA Ethical Standards?

What section of the NCDA Ethical Standards refers to the use of technology in career counseling?

What must career counselors do if they disagree with the general policies and principles of the institution pay-ing them for their services, according to the NCDA Ethical Standards?

What are the responsibilities of career counselors who counsel individuals from a different culture, according to the NCDA Ethical Standards?

What do you believe is the professional role of career management professionals, career coaches, and career development facilitators? Should they be part of the career counseling profession or should they develop their own professional organizations?

Specialty

The National Career Development Association (NCDA), the primary organization that represents career counseling and development professionals, is the oldest counseling organization in the world and has been defining the profession, its ethics, and standards for almost 90 years. The group's ethical standards are reprinted in Appendix R, along with four documents that provide standards for occupational materials. NCDA was established in 1913 as the National Vocational Guidance Association (NVGA) and was a founding division of APGA (now ACA) in 1952 (Engels, 1994; Pope, 2000a).

NCDA/NVGA had always taken the lead in establishing standards for the profession: (1) standards for the practice of vocational guidance, (2) standards for occupational materials, (3) standards for the training of counselors, and (4) standards for vocational counseling agencies (Norris, 1954a, b). In 1982, as a result of the emergence of the private practice career counselor and under heavy pressure from within the profession, NVGA initiated a specific credential for career counseling professionals. The National Certified Career Counselor (NCCC) credential included substantial academic and experiential requirements along with an examination (National Career Counselor Examination). As a precursor to that credential, NVGA promulgated Vocational/Career Counseling Competencies in 1982, which were developed as a "list of competencies necessary for counselors to perform the task of career/vocational guidance and counseling" (NVGA, 1982, p. 1). The competencies were preceded by the American Vocational Association–NVGA Position Paper on Career Development (1973), the American Personnel and Guidance Association (APGA, now ACA) Position Paper on Career Guidance (1975), the ACES Position Paper on Counselor Preparation for Career Development

(1976), the AIR Report on Competencies Needed for Planning, Supporting, Implementing, Operating, and Evaluating Career Guidance Programs (1979), and the APGA Career Education Project (1980) (Pope, 2000a). Pope reported that NVGA then established the National Council for Credentialing Career Counselors in 1983. Using the list of competencies, this independent credentialing body developed the National Career Counselor Examination, which was first administered at the 1984 American Association for Counseling and Development (AACD, now ACA) convention in Houston, Texas. Also in 1984, a letter of intent to affiliate was filed with the new NBCC. The NCCC credential became the first specialty certification area for NBCC.

To hold an NBCC specialty certification, the professional counselor must first attain certification as an NCC, the more general level of counseling certification. Although, at the time, over 800 people held the NCCC specialty credential through NBCC (Engels, Minor, Sampson, & Splete, 1995), in 1999 NBCC officially "retired" the NCCC credential (along with the National Certified Gerontological Counselor [NCGC]). This was done to strengthen the NBCC general practice credential in counseling (NCC) and to begin the process of dismantling its specialty credentialing programs. NCDA then moved quickly to reestablish the NCCC and renamed it the Master Career Counselor (MCC) in 2000 (Pope, 2000b). (See Box 15–2.)

Another credentialing issue was the development of the Career Development Facilitator (CDF) occupation by NCDA and the National Occupational Information Coordinating Committee (NOICC). In the 1980s and 1990s, there was an influx of paraprofessionals into the career development field. Some came as career technicians out of California's school systems; some came as consultants to business and industry through outplacement consulting firms and

Box 15–2 • Special Issue: Credentialing

The National Certified Career Counselor (NCCC) credential offered by NBCC was officially "retired" by NBCC in 1999. Individual career counselors who were holders of the NCCC were allowed to continue to use that certification, but no continuing education units/hours/credits or fees were required.

NCDA immediately established a Task Force on Credentialing Career Services Providers composed of Mark Pope (Chair), A. Dean Porter, Judith Grutter, Frank Karpati, and Norma Zuber. This task force studied this issue through a survey of NCCC and NCDA members, through hearings at the NCDA Global Conferences in Portland (1999) and Pittsburgh (2000), and through study of how other professional associations were handling credentialing issues. Recommendations were presented to the NCDA Board of Directors and Delegate Assembly to establish three new membership categories—the Master Career Counselor, the Master Career Development Professional, and the Fellow.

Each of these membership categories was recommended in response to important constituencies within NCDA. The Master Career Counselor credential was recommended to replace the NCCC for practice career counselors. The Master Career Development Professional was added in response to the growing numbers of Career Development Facilitators (CDFs) who were joining NCDA. CDFs are a paraprofessional occupation developed by NCDA and NOICC to meet the needs of noncounselor career services providers. The Fellow was recommended as a result of the desire to recognize larger numbers of individuals who made significant contributions to the career development profession. Whereas the "NCDA Eminent Career Award" could be awarded to only one person per year, the Fellow could be awarded to more than one person and provided important recognition of the contributions of these professionals.

This comprehensive reform of how career services providers were to be credentialed was fully agreed to in 2000 and implemented in 2001 by NCDA. Both the MCC and MCDP are considered credentials and are certified by NCDA as such.

MASTER CAREER COUNSELOR

The term Master Career Counselor designates a person who has met high standards of practice in the career counseling profession, similar to the AAMFT clinical member and the ABPP diplomate. The MCC is a special membership category as defined in the NCDA Bylaws, and only members of NCDA can be granted and maintain this special status. NCDA confers this title on career counseling practitioners who have met certain standards. Anyone who is both a career counseling practitioner and a member of NCDA is eligible to receive such a status if they meet those standards.

The requirements for the M.C.C. credential are substantially the same as its predecessor—the NCCC—with the exception that there is no requirement to take the National Career Counselor Examination, The MCC requirements include:

- Two-year membership in NCDA (either professional or regular membership).
- Master's degree or higher in counseling or closely related field from a college or university that was accredited when the degree was awarded by one of the regional accrediting bodies recognized by the Council on Postsecondary Accreditation.
- Three years of post-master's experience in career counseling.
- Possess and maintain the NCC, state LPC, RPCC, or licensed psychologist credential.
- Successfully completed at least three credits of coursework in each of the six NCDA competency areas. (Career Development Theory, Individual/Group Counseling Skills, Individual/Group Assessment, Information/Resources, Diverse Populations, Ethical/Legal Issues)
- Successfully completed supervised career counseling practicum or 2 years of supervised career counseling work experience under a certified supervisor or licensed counseling professional.
- Document that at least half of the current full-time work activities are directly career counseling related.
- Members who hold the NCCC are automatically qualified for the MCC credential.

FELLOW

The term Fellow has a long-standing usage within academic societies. A Fellow is a person of professional distinction within an academic institution or society. The status of Fellow is conferred to recognize outstanding and substantial contributions in science, teaching and training, practice, service, policy development, and political action. Few people get elected to this prestigious position—it is considered an honor.

Minimum requirements include:

- Five years of professional membership in NCDA.
- Master's degree or higher in counseling or closely related field from a college or university that was accredited

Box 15–2 • Special Issue: Credentialing—*continued*

when the degree was awarded by one of the regional accrediting bodies recognized by the Council on Postsecondary Accreditation.

- Five years of post-master's experience in career counseling and development.
- Major and significant contributions on career development theory or practice as demonstrated by national and/or international recognition.
- Providing strong and sustained leadership in the career counseling and development profession.
- Engaged in education and training, practice, or research in career counseling and development.
- Sustained commitment to career counseling and development through research, theory, practice, or leadership.

In summary, a Fellow describes a person: (a) whose national and/or international contributions to career counseling and development are considered significant beyond those expected of the successful career counseling and development professional and (b) whose creative leadership (e.g., major conceptual or theoretical models, instruments, techniques, interventions), attested to by others, is worthy or deserving of one of the highest and most prestigious honors that can be accorded by the NCDA.

MASTER CAREER DEVELOPMENT PROFESSIONAL

The Master Career Development Professional (M.C.D.P.) was added to designate a non-counseling career development practitioner who met certain criteria. It designates a person who has met high standards of practice in the career development facilitator profession. The M.C.D.P. is a special membership category as defined in the NCDA By-laws, and only members of NCDA can be granted and maintain this special status. NCDA confers this title on those individuals who are career development practitioners and have met certain standards. Anyone who is both a career counseling practitioner and a member of NCDA is eligible to receive such a status if he meets those standards.

The requirements for MCDP credential include:

- Two-year membership in NCDA (either professional or regular membership).
- Master's degree or higher in counseling or closely related field.
- Three years of post-master's career development experience in training, teaching, program development, or materials development.
- Document that at least half of the current full-time work activities are directly career development related.

---

were hired to provide employment counseling to employees about to be fired. Many of these individuals who were providing career services had little, if any, training in career counseling and yet were providing career development services to corporate clients who were paying large sums of money for their services. NCDA decided to bring those people into the profession rather than ostracize them.

Career counseling is an international phenomenon and NCDA has hundreds of members from outside of the United States (D. Pennington, personal communication, April 28, 2005; Pope, 2003). Further, there are national career development professional associations throughout the world; many are affiliated with the International Association for Educational and Vocational Guidance (IAEVG) and several have developed collaborative status with each other (e.g., NCDA and the Japan Career Development Association). Recently, the NBCC began to certify Global Career Development Facilitators (GCDF) as an international credential.

NCDA, as one of the founding divisions of ACA, had previously fought a long battle within ACA to

maintain "Development" in the NCDA name. Some in NCDA wanted to change the name to the National Career Counseling Association. They also wanted to keep noncounselors outside of the profession. The leadership of NCDA at that time (Ken Hoyt, Jane Goodman, Michael Shanasarian, Mark Pope, and Nancy Schlossberg) was determined not to allow this to happen and to broaden the membership base of the profession by including noncounseling career development professionals as full voting members.

Setting

Career counseling has several types of constituencies that both enrich the practice of career counseling and allow the career counseling professional association to define its organizational base easily. It sometimes has been unclear whether career counseling constitutes a specialty unto itself, or whether it is a specialized or advanced practice area within a number of other professional counseling groups. Even NCDA has noted in its career counseling competencies document (Engels,

1994) that its standards provide guidelines for people interested in a variety of career development occupations, not simply career counseling. These standards state that career counselors should be trained at the master's level or higher with a specialty in career counseling. They further defined 10 competency areas that constitute minimum training for career counseling specialists. Counseling professional groups that might consider themselves to have a specialized background in career counseling, depending on their individual programs of preparation and practice, might include school counselors, counseling psychologists, college counselors, private practice counselors, employment counselors, and rehabilitation counselors.

As the level of professionalization in career counseling has increased, NCDA has strongly promulgated its standards for career counseling and cautioned that it must be differentiated from other career services such as job placement specialists, outplacement consultants, career management professionals, career coaches, and employment agents. Members of the latter occupational groups often provide quite limited or specific career services, rather than working more broadly to place career concerns within a comprehensive approach to increase client career- and self-awareness and development (Engels, 1994). Often the clients for these groups are employers rather than employees or prospective employees. NCDA has acknowledged, however, the following career development specialties and set minimum training and competence standards for each (see Box 15–3):

a. Career counseling (private and public settings);
b. Human resource, career development, and employee assistance specialists (in-house organizational setting, external HR/DC/EAP firms);
c. Career and employment search consultants (private setting);
d. Cooperative education instructors (educational setting);
e. Employment agents (private setting);
f. Outplacement consultants;
g. Job placement specialists (public setting); and
h. School counselors, community college and college counselors, and counselors in postsecondary technical institutes (Engels, 1994).

Clearly, career counselors may practice in a variety of settings that demand proficiency in the core career counseling knowledge and skill areas.

Although many organizations may relate to the specialized practice of career counseling, the core organization that most clearly represents this area is NCDA with its specialty certification (the MCC).

In some instances, the career counseling service is not rendered to an individual, but to a corporation or some other organization, often through a consulting relationship. These and other innovative aspects of career counseling make the professional and ethical demands on this group ever more challenging.

Due to a traditional emphasis on holistic practice, career counselors in private practice are beginning to see themselves as part of a total health team. The composition of the team is dictated by the nature of the treatment setting and needs of the clients. Whether the team is in-house or is physically dispersed, career counselors find themselves frequently working in a collaborative team framework. Thus, it is apparent that career counselors are involved in wide-ranging spheres of professional counseling practice and might affect the lives of many members of our society.

Clients

The practice of career counseling involves a diverse group of clients. When reflecting on the need for career counseling, Crites (1981) remarked that the need for it is even greater than the need for psychotherapy. This observation was proven in a series of Gallup polls that were co-sponsored by NCDA and the NOICC—an agency of the federal government established to coordinate career information among all the various producers and users of such information (Brown & Minor, 1989, 1992; Hoyt & Lester, 1995). These polls documented a tremendous need for career counseling and development services throughout all segments of our society (Pope, 2000a). Economic and political changes—nationally and globally—are creating monumental and rapid changes in business and industry that complicate career choice and career-life development. These elements challenge career counselors to provide career services to an extremely diverse population.

Traditionally, career counselors worked most often in a variety of organizational settings with students who were preparing themselves for a career choice and adults who were entering or reentering the workforce. Career counseling is most often provided in primary and secondary schools, postsecondary institutions (e.g., college counseling or career placement centers), one-stop career centers, employment service settings (both public and private),

Box 15–3 • NCDA Career Counseling Competencies and Performance Indicators (NCDA, 1994)

CAREER DEVELOPMENT THEORY

Theory base and knowledge considered essential for professionals engaging in career counseling and development. Demonstration of knowledge of:

1. Counseling theories and associated techniques.
2. Theories and models of career development.
3. Individual differences related to gender, sexual orientation, race, ethnicity, and physical and mental capacities.
4. Theoretical models for career development and associated counseling and information-delivery techniques and resources.
5. Human growth and development throughout the life span.
6. Role relationships which facilitate life-work planning.
7. Information, techniques, and models related to career planning and placement.

INDIVIDUAL AND GROUP COUNSELING SKILLS

Individual and group counseling competencies considered essential to effective career counseling. Demonstration of ability to:

1. Establish and maintain productive personal relationships with individuals.
2. Establish and maintain a productive group climate.
3. Collaborate with clients in identifying personal goals.
4. Identify and select techniques appropriate to client or group goals and client needs, psychological states, and developmental tasks.
5. Identify and understand clients' personal characteristics related to career.
6. Identify and understand social contextual conditions affecting clients' careers.
7. Identify and understand familial, subcultural, and cultural structures and functions as they are related to clients' careers.
8. Identify and understand clients' career decision-making processes.
9. Identify and understand clients' attitudes toward work and workers.
10. Identify and understand clients' biases toward work and workers based on gender, race, and cultural stereotypes.
11. Challenge and encourage clients to take action to prepare for and initiate role transitions by:
    - locating sources of relevant information and experience,
    - obtaining and interpreting information and experiences, and acquiring skills needed to make role transitions.
12. Assist the client to acquire a set of employability and job search skills.
13. Support and challenge clients to examine life-work roles, including the balance of work, leisure, family, and community in their careers.

INDIVIDUAL/GROUP ASSESSMENT

Individual/group assessment skills considered essential for professionals engaging in career counseling. Demonstration of ability to:

1. Assess personal characteristics such as aptitude, achievement, interests, values, and personality traits.
2. Assess leisure interests, learning style, life roles, self-concept, career maturity, vocational identity, career indecision, work environment preference (e.g., work satisfaction), and other related lifestyle/development issues.
3. Assess conditions of the work environment (such as tasks, expectations, norms, and qualities of the physical and social settings).
4. Evaluate and select valid and reliable instruments appropriate to the client's gender, sexual orientation, race, ethnicity, and physical and mental capacities.
5. Use computer-delivered assessment measures effectively and appropriately.
6. Select assessment techniques appropriate for group administration and those appropriate for individual administration.
7. Administer, score, and report findings from career assessment instruments appropriately.
8. Interpret data from assessment instruments and present the results to clients and to others.
9. Assist the client and others designated by the client to interpret data from assessment instruments.
10. Write an accurate report of assessment results.

continued

Box 15–3 • NCDA Career Counseling Competencies and Performance Indicators (NCDA, 1994)—*continued*

INFORMATION/RESOURCES

Information/resource base and knowledge essential for professionals engaging in career counseling. Demonstration of knowledge of:

1. Education, training, and employment trends; labor market information and resources that provide information about job tasks, functions, salaries, requirements, and future outlooks related to broad occupational fields and individual occupations.
2. Resources and skills that clients utilize in life-work planning and management.
3. Community/professional resources available to assist clients in career planning, including job search.
4. Changing roles of women and men and the implications that this has for education, family, and leisure.
5. Methods of good use of computer-based career information delivery systems (CIDS) and computer-assisted career guidance systems (CACGS) to assist with career planning.

PROGRAM PROMOTION, MANAGEMENT, AND IMPLEMENTATION

Knowledge and skills necessary to develop, plan, implement, and manage comprehensive career development programs in a variety of settings. Demonstration of knowledge of:

1. Designs that can be used in the organization of career development programs.
2. Needs assessment and evaluation techniques and practices.
3. Organizational theories, including diagnosis, behavior, planning, organizational communication, and management useful in implementing and administering career development programs.
4. Methods of forecasting, budgeting, planning, costing, policy analysis, resource allocation, and quality control.
5. Leadership theories and approaches for evaluation and feedback, organizational change, decision making, and conflict resolution.
6. Professional standards and criteria for career development programs.
7. Societal trends and state and federal legislation that influence the development and implementation of career development programs.

Demonstration of ability to:

8. Implement individual and group programs in career development for specified populations.
9. Train others about the appropriate use of computer-based systems for career information and planning.
10. Plan, organize, and manage a comprehensive career resource center.
11. Implement career development programs in collaboration with others.
12. Identify and evaluate staff competencies.
13. Mount a marketing and public relations campaign on behalf of career development activities and services.

COACHING, CONSULTATION, AND PERFORMANCE IMPROVEMENT

Knowledge and skills considered essential in relating to individuals and organizations that impact the career counseling and development process. Demonstration of ability to:

1. Use consultation theories, strategies, and models.
2. Establish and maintain a productive consultative relationship with people who can influence a client's career.
3. Help the general public and legislators to understand the importance of career counseling, career development, and life-work planning.
4. Impact public policy as it relates to career development and workforce plan.
5. Analyze future organizational needs and current level of employee skills and develop performance improvement training.
6. Mentor and coach employees.

DIVERSE POPULATIONS

Knowledge and skills considered essential in relating to diverse populations that impact career counseling and development processes. Demonstration of ability to:

1. Identify development models and multicultural counseling competencies.
2. Identify developmental needs unique to various diverse populations, including those of different gender, sexual orientation, ethnic group, race, and physical or mental capacity.
3. Define career development programs to accommodate needs unique to various diverse populations.
4. Find appropriate methods or resources to communicate with limited-English-proficient individuals.

5. Identify alternative approaches to meet career planning needs for individuals of various diverse populations.

6. Identify community resources and establish linkages to assist clients with specific needs.

7. Assist other staff members, professionals, and community members in understanding the unique needs/characteristics of diverse populations with regard to career exploration, employment expectations, and economic/social issues.

8. Advocate for the career development and employment of diverse populations.

9. Design and deliver career development programs and materials to hard-to-reach populations.

SUPERVISION

Knowledge and skills considered essential in critically evaluating counselor or career development facilitator performance, maintaining and improving professional skills.

Demonstration of ability to:

1. Recognize own limitations as a career counselor and to seek supervision or refer clients when appropriate.

2. Utilize supervision on a regular basis to maintain and improve counselor skills.

3. Consult with supervisors and colleagues regarding client and counseling issues and issues related to one's own professional development as a career counselor.

4. Utilize supervision models and theories.

5. Provide effective supervision to career counselors and career development facilitators at different levels of experience.

6. Provide effective supervision to career development facilitators at different levels of experience by:
   - knowledge of their roles, competencies, and ethical standards,
   - determining their competence in each of the areas included in their certification,
   - further training them in competencies, including interpretation of assessment instruments,
   - monitoring and mentoring their activities in support of the professional career counselor; and scheduling regular consultations for the purpose of reviewing their activities.

ETHICAL/LEGAL ISSUES

Information base and knowledge essential for the ethical and legal practice of career counseling.

Demonstration of knowledge of:

1. Adherence to ethical codes and standards relevant to the profession of career counseling (e.g., NBCC, NCDA, and ACA).

2. Current ethical and legal issues which affect the practice of career counseling with all populations.

3. Current ethical/legal issues with regard to the use of computer-assisted career guidance systems.

4. Ethical standards relating to consultation issues.

5. State and federal statutes relating to client confidentiality.

RESEARCH/EVALUATION

Knowledge and skills considered essential in understanding and conducting research and evaluation in career counseling and development. Demonstration of ability to:

1. Write a research proposal.

2. Use types of research and research designs appropriate to career counseling and development research.

3. Convey research findings related to the effectiveness of career counseling programs.

4. Design, conduct, and use the results of evaluation programs.

5. Design evaluation programs which take into account the needs of various diverse populations, including persons of both genders, differing sexual orientations, different ethnic and racial backgrounds, and differing physical and mental capacities.

6. Apply appropriate statistical procedures to career development research.

TECHNOLOGY

Knowledge and skills considered essential in using technology to assist individuals with career planning. Demonstration of knowledge of:

1. Various computer-based guidance and information systems as well as services available on the internet.

2. Standards by which such systems and services are evaluated (e.g. NCDA and ACSCI).

3. Ways in which to use computer-based systems and internet services to assist individuals with career planning that are consistent with ethical standards.

4. Characteristics of clients which make them profit more or less from use of technology-driven systems.

5. Methods to evaluate and select a system to meet local needs.

vocational rehabilitation settings (both public and private), organizations that serve their own employees (e.g., employee assistance or outplacement programs), and private practice career counseling (Engels, 1994). Thus, the material on ethical issues in school counseling or rehabilitation counseling may also be of particular interest to many career counselors. Within all of these contexts, an increasingly diverse clientele wishes to address its career decisions and career-life planning issues. In addition to the more traditional clients, groups such as middle school and elementary school students, retirees, people whose career development has suffered because of bias or stereotyping, or people who wish to advance in their careers are also seeking career counseling services (Engels).

ETHICAL ISSUES

Confidentiality and Privileged Communication

Any number of complications can arise for career counselors with regard to confidentiality and privileged communication. As with all professional counselors, the trust engendered by the assurance of confidentiality is the most critical element of the counseling relationship. Confidentiality is the ethical obligation that counselors not disclose material that clients reveal during the counseling relationship. Privileged communication is the client's legal or statutory right to protect confidences shared within the counseling relationship from being revealed in a legal proceeding.

Several areas of practice—such as vocational or forensic expert practices—require that career counselors take particular care in observing requirements to guard client confidentiality. They must clearly address confidentiality limitations with all of the individuals involved. The NCDA (1991) Ethical Standards provide a rule that embodies well-accepted advice in such situations. For example, career counselors may be asked to provide information about a person's employability or earnings potential in divorce cases. In this role as forensic expert in these legal cases, there is no intention that the counselor will actually provide counseling to the client, as this is a forensic assessment role only. In such cases, the career counselor must address limits of confidentiality deriving from the forensic assessment role; that is, the career counselor is compelled to testify in such a situation regardless of client permission.

There are many instances of clients having misunderstood the nature of the services provided by a career counselor. Clients may think that information they provided to the professional will be held in confidence, only to be shocked and angered later to discover that it is included in a report or deposition that resulted in a negative outcome for them, such as a loss of benefits. Such anecdotal reports are unfortunate illustrations of a need for greater care in observing the informed consent procedures regarding confidentiality limitations. The client must be informed clearly when the counselor is employed by a third party. Clients must be helped to understand fully how that relationship will influence any information given to the client or how services provided to the client will be limited or changed.

Another potentially devastating and costly misunderstanding on the part of career counselors is the uncritical assumption that privileged communication extends to their practices. Because privileged communication is granted only through statute and legal precedent, the types of professionals covered by this privilege vary by jurisdiction (Cottone, Pullen, & Wilson, 1983). Thus, possessing a national certification, such as M.C.C. or N.C.C.C., does not entitle one to legal privilege for therapeutic communications in and of itself. Career counselors must research the nature of the laws governing the granting of privilege in their own areas of practice and in their geographic locations.

Generally, privileged communication is extended only to licensed professionals. The *Jaffee v. Redmond* (1996) ruling by the U.S. Supreme Court underscored this position (see Chapter 4 for more specific information about privileged communication).

Many career counselors in educational institutions perform their work within a multi- or interdisciplinary team context. Such an arrangement is often considered the intervention of choice, but it does present the counselor with additional factors for consideration of confidentiality. Different team members have varying levels of training and understanding of this ethical obligation and may have a legitimate desire and need to know information the counselor may have about the client. Although, generally, it is acknowledged that professionals may have an appropriate need to communicate information to other people involved in the client's care, the client must be informed clearly and fully of this common limitation of confidentiality at the outset of counseling. Indeed, it is a common and sensible practice to obtain suitable written release of information regarding this and other limitations to confidentiality in a written consent to treatment document (see Chapter 4). It is also wise to discuss with the client sharing information with other professionals. The client should be informed of when, how, to whom, to what extent, and what type of information will be shared with others. This process must be done in such a way as to avoid coercion of clients or the implication that they will not be served if they do not grant blanket permission.

Even when consent is obtained, the career counselor must be circumspect about revealing information to others. The counselor must determine the appropriateness of the disclosure before providing information by asking, "Is it likely that the information that I am about to share with my team member(s) will substantially enhance that person's work with the client?" (Strein & Hershenson, 1991, p. 313). The same analysis should be applied to decisions about including material in case records that will be viewed by these individuals. Strein and Hershenson provided additional benchmark concepts to be considered when fostering confidentiality within a team context. Their recommendations include taking steps to (a) articulate the specific rules the treatment team will follow regarding confidentiality, (b) reinforce the obligation of confidentiality with the team in any circumstance in which it appears that a team member may not realize the confidentiality of the information, and (c) inform the client before material will be shared with members of the team.

Career counselors also should be aware of other important limitations to confidentiality because it would not be unusual to have a number of clients with issues that could limit confidentiality. Examples might include people with psychiatric or addictions disabilities, clients with HIV/AIDS, and clients with correctional histories who might become dangerous to themselves or others. Clients of career counselors may be involved in group treatment or counseling for purposes ranging from job-seeking skills and support groups to more traditional psychotherapeutic adjustment counseling groups. Counselors must inform their clients of confidentiality limitations (although the norm of confidentiality is set, confidentiality cannot be guaranteed in a group context—see Chapter 16 on group counseling). They must also inform clients that the courts generally do not uphold privilege for therapeutic communication in a group setting. It is imperative that the counselor should become skilled and comfortable in providing informed con-

sent opportunities to clients, for it is never possible to anticipate when these issues might arise with any client. Career counselors working in certain specialized settings also must become knowledgeable about specific additional state or federal laws that apply to confidentiality and privilege in those settings. Examples include the access to records of minors by their parents, as required by FERPA (see Chapter 13 for more detailed information), and the laws extending stricter confidentiality to those in treatment in any addictions treatment facility that receives federal funding.

Informed Consent

Informed consent ensures that clients are given sufficient information regarding the treatment or services in which they will be involved in a manner the clients can understand. The intent is to be sure that clients have a sufficient understanding of the circumstances so they can exercise their autonomy and make informed choices. The three required elements of informed consent are (a) capacity, (b) comprehension, and (c) voluntariness (see Chapter 4).

Career counselors may find themselves in situations wherein they are employed by a company to provide outplacement services for an employee who has been fired. If the fired employee has not been fully informed of the limits of confidentiality (e.g., if the employee tells the career counselor she stole money from the company), the counselor is not allowed to inform the employer of any illegal activity.

Career counselors who work in school settings may participate in the development of the IEP as part of the requirement of providing educational services to students with disabilities. Some clients may not have developed decision-making skills, or they may have a limited base of life experiences or other cognitive or psychological limitations. The determination of when a client is legally or ethically competent to provide informed consent is a critical consideration for career counselors and depends on the laws of the state. If a client appears to be under the influence of a drug, the counselor must think carefully about whether informed consent is possible, or whether other measures are needed. The counselor might need to wait until the person is in a better position to provide consent.

Some clients may have a parent or legal guardian who must be involved in the informed consent process. A **legal guardian** is a person who is appointed by the court to make decisions regarding an individual's person or property. This concept presumes the client is incompetent to make these decisions (Anderson & Fearey, 1989). The legal guardian must always consent to services for the client. The new ACA Code of Ethics (ACA, 2005) emphasizes the ethical obligation of counselors to include clients in the decision-making process and to obtain assent from them even if they are not legally capable to give consent.

Roles and Relationships with Clients

Counselor roles and relationships with clients are important and common areas of concern for counselors working in an area of the profession. Career counselors are no exception, and the NCDA (1991) Ethical Standards prohibit engaging in harmful relationships (see Chapter 3). The core issues that make some relationships so potentially dangerous to client and counselor are the power differential between the two parties and a potential loss of objectivity on the part of the counselor. The effects of such relationships may range from harmful to positive or no appreciable effect. However, due to the potential for harm, the counselor should avoid these overlapping roles whenever possible. NCDA strictly prohibits sexual intimacy with current clients because of the strong potential for serious harm to the client in such relationships. With the new ACA Ethical Standards (2005) and its inclusion of "beneficial relationships," NCDA will undoubtedly begin a revision of its own ethics code in the near future.

Herlihy and Corey (1992) provided specific safeguards to assist counselors in managing these potentially detrimental counselor–client relationships:

1. *Informed consent*. The counselor should fully inform the client of all possible risks involved, the limitations of the relationships, and the safeguards in place.
2. *Ongoing discussions*. The counselor should have periodic discussions with all the parties involved in the relationships to identify and work through any conflicts or concerns that develop.
3. *Consultation*. If the counselor does proceed with the potentially detrimental relationship, an ongoing consultation with a colleague should be in place so that all aspects of the situation will be evaluated to guard against overlooking a problem.
4. *Supervision*. If the situation involves a high risk for harm, more continuous supervision may be warranted.
5. *Documentation*. Counselors should document all aspects of the potentially detrimental relationship and issues that arise within the process, including the techniques used to manage the situation.

A major issue in career counseling concerns the emergence of issues that could be described loosely as contiguous professional or nonprofessional relationships—issues that involve conflicts of interest for the counselor. In these situations, counselors provide services that involve a group or team of professionals affiliated with the same client. If one team member has a monetary or business interest in a certain outcome for the client's case, such as an attorney in litigation or a managed care case manager paid through capitation, there may be potential for danger to the client if the counselor begins a noncollegial type of relationship with the first team member. If there is only a professional relationship between the counselor and the other professional, there is no unusual conflict for the counselor in protecting the client's interests. If, however, the counselor is the other professional's lover or business partner, there could be considerable negative pressure exerted on the counselor. Even the appearance of such undue influence is ethically troublesome. Because career counselors pursue various private practice options, the possibilities for business and personal concerns creating multiple and conflicting loyalties is an increasing danger. Consultants and vocational experts are often well known to the hiring organization or professional. This increases the potential for conflicts of interest. Counselors must evaluate such circumstances carefully before entering into or continuing a professional service relationship (Newman, 1993), even if they do not provide direct counseling services. For example, a career counselor is invited to a former client's graduation party. According to the NCDA Ethical Standards, such attendance would be prohibited; however, under the new ACA (2005) Code of Ethics, such attendance would be allowed. This contradiction will likely lead to the revision of the NCDA standards in the next few years. In the meantime, career counselors must apply an appropriate decision-making process when confronted with such ambiguous ethical situations.

Responsibility

The NCDA Ethical Standards clearly assert that the primary responsibility of the counselor is to the client. It is clear, however, that there are secondary responsibilities to other parties in counseling. Career counseling has a long history of practicing primarily within agency or institutional settings. This fact is embodied by standards that enjoin career counselors to respect the rights and responsibilities they owe to their employing agencies and the need to try to resolve disputes with them through constructive, internal processes. NCDA elaborated about the nature of that obligation by stating:

> The acceptance of employment in an institution implies that the career counselor is in agreement with the general policies and principles of the institution. . . . If, despite concerted efforts, the career counselor cannot reach agreement with the employer as to acceptable standards of conduct that allow for changes in institutional policy that are conducive to the positive growth and development of clients, then terminating the affiliation should be seriously considered. (NCDA, 1991, p. 26)

If the ethical values of the institution are in conflict with a career counselor's professional ethics, the career counselor must seriously consider resigning.

All areas of counseling must address issues of counselor stereotyping and treatment system bias and how they affect the rights of clients as counseling attempts to better serve an increasingly multicultural and diverse population of clients (Sue, 1996). Sue stated:

> If we believe that many problems reside outside the person (prejudice and discrimination) and not within (person-blame), ethical practice dictates that professionals develop alternative helping roles that are aimed at system intervention. (p. 196)

This belief—that the context in which an individual functions may be part of the problem—is central to all multicultural counseling.

Values

Any number of value issues could be addressed in the area of career counseling. The richness and complexity of values and the valuing process and how they influence counseling were explored in Chapter 5. At this point, one overriding value of concern might be overlooked for its obviousness—work! The central importance that American society places on work is pervasive and strong. We assume not only that we must value work but also that we must share similar preferences and interpretations regarding what constitutes meaningful and valuable work. Career counseling originated in answer to the powerful societal approbation of this valued role in our culture and the need to give others more effective access to this all-defining status. It is at the very core of the entire vocational counseling process for career counselors to examine the work-related meanings, needs, and interests of their clients and to help them find their niche in this world of work.

Counselors must understand that societal attitudes toward work can affect them in both positive and negative ways as they serve their clients (Gatens-Robinson & Rubin, 1995). Counselors, their agencies, and clients receive support for their career counseling activities as long as the outcomes of the process result in productive or visible economic contributions through work. If a career counselor's client achieves great financial success through dealing drugs or illegally trading stocks, the work of that counselor will not be considered professionally appropriate. If the work obtained by clients is not considered by society (or even counselors themselves) to be valuable, those who find alternative or nonremunerative activities or those who cannot be competitive in the employment market may be devalued. A variety of counseling ethical dilemmas may ensue from our uncritical assumption of values regarding work. Counselors may choose not to work with more difficult vocational clients if the agency rewards only particular types of placements or closures. Counselors may not react positively to clients who choose to work in the home as caregivers to children or elders, or who work only part time to pursue avocational interests. They may pressure clients to take jobs they are not suited for, or are even harmed by, to appear successful. What reactions do vocational counselors have to clients who choose to work in the hidden job market, not reporting income or bartering for payment? These forms of activity may be the only ones preferred or realistically available to the client due to barriers to employment. Counselors may be tremendously conflicted by working with such issues in vocational counseling. These tensions are likely only to increase as changes in the nature of employment and business and industrial structures continue in the 21st century. In addition to the other value issues that confront all counselors, they will be required to lead the professions in interpreting and supporting work-related values in collaboration with their clients.

Counselor Competence

Competence issues occur in the work of all counselors on an ongoing basis. Counselors must develop and practice an approach to quality control in their work that ensures quality and the safety of services they provide to their clients. Counselors must also work within the legal and ethical boundaries of their scopes of practice. Career counselors monitor competence in at least two specific areas of contemporary practice: (a) the integration of a mental health counseling or diagnostic focus with their usual practices, and (b) competence around assessment services.

CASE SCENARIO 15–1

The Case of Ms. Diagnosis

Shelby Diagnosis was the daughter of a prominent banker in a small town in the Midwest. She was referred by her family physician to Carerra Decisiones, M.Ed., L.P.C., M.C.C. for career counseling. Counselor Decisiones did a diagnostic interview with Ms. Diagnosis and reported to the family physician that Ms. Diagnosis was very "clinically depressed" and "had to be treated for that before career counseling would be effective." Ms. Diagnosis stated that she would only go to Counselor Decisiones for treatment of her depression. Counselor Decisiones has a degree that is regionally accredited by the Western Association of Schools and Colleges and CACREP in both community counseling and career counseling. Counselor Decisiones proceeds to treat Ms. Diagnosis for depression and, when those symptoms are under control, she commenced counseling for the career problems for which Ms. Diagnosis had originally been referred. Did Counselor Decisiones do anything that might be considered unethical?

NO. As a licensed professional counselor, Counselor Decisiones was operating well within her profession's scope of practice. Her university and her program were also both appropriately accredited. It might appear as if the counselor has competence only in career counseling, but she has the appropriate training and licenses to address general mental health issues. Further, the fact that she graduated from a CACREP-accredited program means she met competencies in counseling individuals for personal concerns. Finally, assessment is also a core competency of all CACREP-accredited programs. Counselor Decisiones personally must assume that she has had sufficient experience and training to perform these services capably.

The managed care treatment paradigm has grown tremendously through health care reform efforts and the forceful advocacy of the AMHCA for mental health specialization as the core clinical counseling specialization. Both of these forces require all counselors to reevaluate the role of diagnosis and clinical models of practice in their work.

The career counseling tradition is significant in that it is a counseling model that is highly focused on developmental counseling traditions and interventions. Thus, it is at odds with any model based on psychopathological interpretations. Niles and Pate (1989) described the distinction between career counseling and mental health counseling as artificial. They saw the fields as needing to be integrated because mental health and work concerns are inextricably linked in the human experiences brought to counseling. As a result of this reasoning, they made a case for examining how the competence and educational standards of both groups need to be enhanced. They viewed the lack of past career counseling competence standards (knowledge and skill) in standards related to treatment of mental and emotional disorders as distressing. If adding diagnostic and treatment planning competencies will be required of career counselors in the future, this will occasion a redesign of training standards in the field to ensure that practitioners meet minimum levels of knowledge and skill in this complex area. Of course, individual practitioners may reach these levels of capability through their individualized programs of specialized professional experience and preparation. (See the discussion of the ethical considerations in diagnosis in Chapter 8—career counselors are likely to be required to know more about this process in the future.)

The second area of specialized emphasis on counselor competence is assessment and testing. Career counselors spend substantial portions of their time in performing these functions. The use of various vocational assessment devices has been integral to the development of the trait and factor model of career counseling that is at the core of this specialized area. Assessment and testing are primary tools to gain information to be used by client and counselor alike in the career counseling processes (Hood & Johnson, 1991). As such, these tools have tremendous potential for both assistance and harm to clients. Blackwell, Martin, and Scalia (1994) distinguished between testing and assessment. **Testing** is the use of a specific tool to gather information or measure some individual quality or characteristic, such as career interest patterns or aptitudes or educational achievement. **Assessment** refers to the process that involves the coordinated planning of information collection and evaluation to address a client's counseling concern or problem. The assessment function requires a higher level of professional training for proper service (Blackwell et al.).

Career counselors are often involved in using career assessment inventories with clients. These inventories measure career interest patterns, personality, values, career beliefs, work environment, aptitude, achievement, salience, career maturity, and career obstacles. Career counselors who have been trained to use such inventories for personnel selection must always ensure that the examinee's welfare, explicit prior understanding, and agreement determine who will receive the test results. Further, if such results are to be used in research and publication, each of the elements of informed consent must be met.

The issue of who has sufficient knowledge and training to administer the different types and levels of tests properly is a critical counselor competence issue. Tests vary greatly in the complexity of administration and interpretation required for appropriate usage. At one extreme are the individually administered intelligence tests, such as the Wechsler intelligence tests. At the other extreme are simple tests of vocational skills, including typing or language skills such as spelling. Copious work has been done to develop competence standards for the qualifications required of test users and other standards for educational and psychological tests. These standards primarily have exerted an influence in controlling the qualifications of test users. Many of the major test distributors require a statement of qualifications by the purchasers of tests. This statement embodies qualifications developed by the Test User Qualifications Group in consultation with test developers (Hood & Johnson, 1991). The Test User Qualifications Group consists of a number of the professional associations whose members perform assessment and testing services, including ACA and APA. Counselors should review and seek to conform to these qualification requirements for any and all tests that they utilize in their practices. The NCDA Ethical Standards have specific and detailed requirements concerning the ethical obligations of their members in observing the competence standards set for use of these instruments and techniques.

Controversies continue to rage around the attempts of psychology to restrict the ability of nonpsychologists to administer various testing instruments, and they demonstrate the tremendously important role of user competence standards. Several psychology boards have taken a variety of legal actions to restrict other helping professionals from using various tests. States where actions have been taken include California, Georgia, Indiana, Louisiana, and Ohio (Marino, 1996). In 2004, the governor of Indiana refused to approve new guidelines that restricted the use by nonpsychologists of hundreds of inventories, including several inventories used regularly by career counselors. Although this effort is not yet national, there is a disturbing increase in these actions. As a result, various concerned professional groups formed a coalition to develop strategies to deal with this threat to professional autonomy and scope of practice. The group, the Fair Access Coalition on Testing (FACT), is said to represent more than 500,000 professionals (Marino, 1996). The concerns of career counselors have been represented by the leaders of NCDA in the activities of FACT. Although the issues may be resolved in the future, the importance of preserving this essential function of the counselor's role in practice is clear. Career counselors always have worked closely with vocational testing and other types of assessment. The ethical obligations of career counselors should be affirmed by all counselors as they work to preserve this aspect of their services to clients.

Career Counseling Competencies

The NCDA, as a precursor to the development of the N.C.C.C. credential, developed the Vocational/Career Counseling Competencies in 1982 (review Box 15–3). These were developed as a "list of competencies necessary for counselors to perform the task of career/ vocational guidance and counseling" (NVGA, 1982, p. 1). Career counselors need these competencies to provide the professional services expected by the public (Engels, 1994).

Career Counseling has a broad area of practice and a diverse practitioner base, yet has clearly identified standards for what constitutes appropriate professional practice. NCDA has strongly promulgated training standards for the M.C.C. that include: (a) a graduate degree in counseling or in a related professional field from a regionally accredited higher education institution, (b) graduate-level coursework pertinent to the practice of career counseling and related specialties, and (c) supervised counseling experience that includes career counseling (Engels, 1994).

NCDA has developed specific standards for competent computer delivery of career guidance and information systems along with guidelines for the evaluation of printed career information, videos, and software. The Career Information Review Service (CIRS), an NCDA committee, uses these guidelines to annually evaluate career materials. Reviews are also published in various ways by NCDA, including in the *Career Development Quarterly* (NCDA journal), in *Career Developments* (NCDA newsletter), and on the internet at the NCDA Web site (http://www.ncda.org). These guidelines can be found at http://www.ncda.org. NCDA is currently developing its own "seal of approval" for materials judged by CIRS reviewers to meet the guidelines.

The use of various computer-based career guidance and information systems to deliver career counseling services as well as the use of the internet in such delivery are some of the most important issues confronting professional career counseling. NCDA has been a leader in the development of standards for such delivery and published the *NCDA Guidelines for the Use of the Internet for Provision of Career Information and Planning Services* in October 1997. These guidelines can be found at http://www.ncda.org. These guidelines were developed by the NCDA Ethics Committee—David Caulum, Don Doerr, Pat Howland, Spencer Niles, Ray Palmer, Richard Pyle (Chair), David Reile, James Sampson, and Don Schutt. Issues raised by the NCDA Ethics Committee included standards by which such systems and services are evaluated; ways in which to use computer-based systems and internet services to assist individuals with career planning that are consistent with ethical standards; characteristics of clients that make them profit more or less from use of technology-driven systems; and methods to evaluate and select a system to meet local needs.

CODE COMPARISONS

In terms of ethical standards, NCDA indicates that career counselors are expected to follow the ethical guidelines of the organizations pertinent to them, including NCDA, NBCC, ACA, and APA as well as the laws, such as the Code of Federal Regulations, Title 45, Subtitle A, Part 46; FERPA (Buckley Amendment to P. L. 93-380 of the Laws of 1974); and all current federal regulations and various state privacy statutes (NCDA, 1991). The NCDA Ethical Standards were developed by NBCC and adopted with only minor revision by NCDA. Because NCDA is a division of ACA, its members also are subject to discipline through that body; however, over 1,700 members of NCDA have chosen recently not to be dual members with ACA (D. Pennington, personal communication, April 28, 2005). The NCDA Ethics Committee and Professional Standards Committee have yet to issue guidelines for how to handle such ethics complaints.

ISSUES OF DIVERSITY

Cultural issues are addressed in various parts of the NCDA Ethical Standards. Any time there is a cultural

dissimilarity between career counselor and client, the counselor must exercise care in the ensuing interactions (Chung, 2003a, b; Pope, 1995a, b; Pope, 2003; Pope et al., 2004; Sue, Arredondo, & McDavis, 1992).

Individual Versus Collectivist Cultures

One of the most important models to emerge from the multicultural counseling literature over the past 25 years is that of Asante's Afrocentric (collectivist) versus Eurocentric (individualist) model (Asante, 1987). In a collectivist culture, almost all important decisions in a person's life involve both family and community. Clients from collectivist cultures rarely make career decisions without both family and community consultation (Leong, 1992; Pope, 1999; Pope et al., 2004; Pope & Chung, 2000; Pope et al., 1998).

Pope (1999) reported that when clients first present for career counseling, it is important that counselors assess how much involvement of both extended family and community is needed by the clients in their decision-making process. All or selected family and community members may attend each of the group sessions or only selected sessions, depending on the strength of collectivist ideals in the family. Prior to family attendance, it is especially important that the counselor discuss with the client the roles of each family and community member to identify the most important person in the group decision-making process. This person will need the most information and most deference when the client is ready to choose an occupation.

The difficulty in this situation is in sharing information and identifying who is the client. When offering extended family career counseling as developed by Pope (1999), informing all family members, getting agreement, and maintaining the agreement are the keys to effective career counseling.

Assessment

Hartung et al. (1998) addressed the issue of the appropriate use of career assessment instruments with culturally diverse populations. Career assessment instruments should be used only on populations for whom they have been previously normed. Use of these inventories with individuals who are not included in the normative studies is inappropriate.

Pope (1992) identified inappropriate use of assessment with gay and lesbian clients, which included fear of identification/exposure of sexual orientation, especially in the highly sensitive personnel selection area;

bias and prejudice (heterosexism) of the counselor; appropriate interpretation based on identification of client response set; issues of sex-role and sexual orientation stereotyping (male "feeling" types and female "thinking" types); and, generally, the appropriate interpretation of psychological tests with a gay or lesbian client.

Gay and Lesbian Clients

Career counseling with gay and lesbian clients has become a regular topic in the journals of the profession (Pope, 1995a, b, 1996; Pope et al., 2004). The refusal by certain career counselors to provide services to gay and lesbian clients on the basis of the counselor's beliefs (e.g. religious beliefs) is a topic that is discussed in the ethics and career counseling classes of the profession. The NCDA Ethical Standards state:

> Section A.11—NCDA members avoid bringing their personal or professional issues into the counseling relationship. Through an awareness of the impact of stereotyping and discrimination. (e.g., biases based on age, disability, ethnicity, gender, race, religion, or sexual preference), career counselors guard the individual rights and personal dignity of the client in the counseling relationship. (NCDA, 1991)

Gay and lesbian individuals are often the targets of the prejudices of a culture represented by those whose beliefs state that homosexual behavior is a sin or is morally wrong. The refusal of professionals who hold such beliefs to provide quality career counseling services to gay and lesbian clients is troubling. In recent years, NCDA, ACA, and APA have been supportive of the rights of gay and lesbian clients to receive ethical and supportive counseling care by all mental health professionals.

DECISION MAKING IN CONTEXT

Ethical dilemmas in career counseling practice, as in all counseling practice, arise daily. What is important for the professional career counselor is to organize a response in an educated way. Career counseling, as in all counseling, operates in the context of particular clients and all their surrounding and intermingling cultures. In collectivist cultures, for example, decision making is a shared phenomenon, and rarely are decisions about an individual's career accomplished by the person alone. Ethical decision-making models that discount culture and context and focus solely on the individual do a disservice to the person and potentially

undermine the career counseling outcomes. When using a decision-making model in career counseling with individuals from collectivist cultures, it is important to view the career choice from the perspective of each of the identified decision consultants in the social grouping (extended family and community, generally). The Social Constructivism Model and the Tarvydas Integrative Model are two models that have strong social components as part of their decision model. Sensitivity to the issues of the individual, the extended family or community members, and the extended family or community as a whole are critical components to this type of ethical decision-making process. For example, assume that a male freshman college student attending a university in the United States participates in counseling sessions regarding his career choice. The student is from Asia and feels obligated to pursue a career in medicine—a family-informed decision. The student has strong interests in the performing arts and fears that, if he majors in theatre, for example, his choice will be met with anger, rejection, or disdain by family members. The student's social group in the United States is very supportive of his interest in the arts. The student's father has called the career counselor from his country and demanded information about his son's counseling. How should the counselor respond?

According to the Tarvydas Model, "determining the major stakeholders" is a component of Stage I. The counselor must be sensitive to and aware of the decision process in collectivist cultures. Fact finding would be appropriate. The student is consulted and asks for assistance in dealing with his father as a major contributor to the decision process. In Stage II, knowing there is a dilemma related to providing information to the father, the counselor consults laws and ethics standards. FERPA (see Chapter 13) is also consulted. Potential courses of action are defined and consequences are delineated. For example, what are the consequences of openly revealing to the father the student's career choice dilemma? The consequences may be legal, ethical, or relational. A best ethical course of action must be defined. In Stage III, that best ethical course of action must be weighed considering values, personal factors, and prejudices. A preferred course of action may be defined. For example, the counselor may recommend an international conference call with the father or other family members with the son present to discuss the son's concerns. The counselor then, in Stage IV, must plan and execute the decision to invite the father into counseling even through technological means. The counselor might have to implement countermeasures should the father–son relationship become strained through the process. The son's mental health through the process would need to be monitored. The Tarvydas Model is well suited for such a dilemma.

Likewise, Cottone's Social Constructivism Model clearly addresses social influence. In the early stages of addressing the student's dilemma, the counselor would assess the nature of relationships—is there conflicting opinion? Is the relationship adversarial? Experts on Asian culture may be consulted. Assuming some tension and disagreement in the father–son relationship, the counselor might attempt to engage a negotiation process, whereby the father and son and other family members (with the student's permission) might be allowed to interact to address their differences. If they come to some consensus, then the dilemma would be addressed. For example, a double major or a major emphasizing the arts might be acceptable so long as premedical courses are taken and passed with an acceptable (agreed upon) grade. If disagreement persists, an arbitration process consistent with collectivist culture might be explored.

As can be gleaned from this career counseling ethical dilemma, cultural factors may enter into the decision process. The two models applied in this situation are adept at incorporating cultural and relational issues into the decision-making process.

CHAPTER SUMMARY

The focus of career counseling has been on helping individuals successfully enter the world of work. Career counselors increasingly take a total life-role perspective that includes factors related to work, family, home, and leisure.

Personal counseling involves professionals who help clients understand and resolve their problems using basic counseling techniques so clients can lead well-adjusted lives. Career counseling focuses on the work realm of a client's life. Counselors can assist clients personally as part of the vocational counseling process.

NCDA is the primary organization that represents career counseling and development professionals. This group defines the profession, its ethics, and standards. Career counselors practice in a variety of settings and render services to diverse individuals, corporations, and organizations.

Career counselors must take particular care in observing requirements to guard client confidentiality, privileged communication, and informed consent and avoid potentially detrimental counselor–client relationships. Career counselors also must have sufficient knowledge and training to assess clients and administer tests.

INTERNET RESOURCES

Keywords that are useful when conducting internet searches on career counseling issues are: career/vocational counseling, career assessment, career barriers, career beliefs, career coaching, career development, career education, career interests, career management, career planning, employment, jobs, occupations, multicultural career counseling, school guidance, vocational guidance, vocational psychology, work, work adjustment.

REFERENCES

American Counseling Association (2005). *Code of Ethics*. Alexandria, VA: Author.

Anderson, T. P., & Fearey, M. S. (1989). Legal guardianship in traumatic brain injury rehabilitation: Ethical implications. *Journal of Head Trauma Rehabilitation, 4,* 57–64.

Asante, M. K. (1987). *The Afrocentric idea*. Philadelphia: Temple University Press.

Blackwell, T. L., Martin, W. E., & Scalia, V. A. (1994). *Ethics in rehabilitation*. Athens, GA: Elliott & Fitzpatrick.

Brewer, J. M. (1942). *History of vocational guidance*. New York: Harper.

Brown, D., & Brooks, L. (1991). *Career counseling techniques*. Boston: Allyn & Bacon.

Brown, D., & Minor, C. W. (Eds.). (1989). *Planning for and working in America: Report of a national survey*. Alexandria, VA: National Career Development Association.

Brown, D., & Minor, C. W. (Eds.). (1992). *Career needs in a diverse workforce: Implications of the NCDA Gallup survey*. Alexandria, VA: National Career Development Association.

Chung, Y. B. (2003a). Career counseling with lesbian, gay, bisexual, and transgendered persons: The next decade. *Career Development Quarterly, 52,* 78–86.

Chung, Y. B. (2003b). Ethical and professional issues in career assessment with lesbian, gay, and bisexual persons. *Journal of Career Assessment, 11,* 96–112.

Cottone, R. R., Pullen, J. R., & Wilson, W. C. (1983). Counselor licensure, confidentiality, and privileged communication: Implications for private practice in rehabilitation. *Journal of Applied Rehabilitation, 14,* 6–8.

Crites, J. O. (1981). *Career counseling: Models, methods, and materials*. New York: McGraw-Hill.

Engels, D. W. (Ed.). (1994). *The professional practice of career counseling and consultation: A resource document* (2nd ed.). Alexandria, VA: National Career Development Association.

Engels, D. W., Minor, C. W., Sampson, J. P., Jr., & Splete, H. H. (1995). Career counseling specialty: History, development, and prospect. *Journal of Counseling & Development, 37*, 134–138.

Gatens-Robinson, E., & Rubin, S. E. (1995). Societal values and ethical commitments that influence rehabilitation service delivery behavior. In S. E. Rubin & R. T. Roessler (Eds.), *Foundations of the vocational rehabilitation process* (pp. 157–174). Austin, TX: Pro-Ed.

Hansen, L. S. (1997). *Integrated life planning.* San Francisco: Jossey-Bass.

Hartung, P. J., Vandiver, B. J., Leong, F. T. L., Pope, M., Niles, S. G., & Farrow, B. (1998). Appraising cultural identity in career-development assessment and counseling. *Career Development Quarterly, 46*, 276–293.

Herlihy, B., & Corey, G. (1992). *Dual relationships in counseling.* Alexandria, VA: American Counseling Association.

Hood, A. B., & Johnson, R. W. (1991). *Assessment in counseling: A guide to the use of psychological assessment procedures.* Alexandria, VA: American Counseling Association.

Hoyt, K. B., & Lester, J. N. (1995). *Learning to work: The NCDA Gallup survey.* Alexandria, VA: National Career Development Association.

Laffee V. Redmond et al. WL315841 (U.S. June 13, 1996).

Lapan, R. T. (2004). *Career development across the K–16 years.* Alexandria, VA: American Counseling Association.

Leong, F. T. L. (1992). Guidelines for minimizing premature termination among Asian American clients in group counseling. *Journal for Specialists in Group Work, 17*, 218–228.

Marino, T. W. (1996, November). Fair Access Coalition on Testing holds meeting in Washington, DC. *Counseling Today, 13*, 19.

National Career Development Association (1991). *Ethical standards* (revised). Atulsa, OK: NCDA.

National Vocational Guidance Association (1982). *Vocational/career counseling competencies.* Alexandria, VA: NVGA.

Newman, J. L. (1993). Ethical issues in consultation. *Journal of Counseling & Development, 72*, 148–156.

Niles, S. G., & Pate, R. H., Jr. (1989). Competency and training issues related to the integration of career counseling and mental health counseling. *Journal of Career Development, 16*, 63–71.

Norris, W. (1954a). Highlights in the history of the National Vocational Guidance Association. *Personnel and Guidance Journal, 33*, 205–208.

Norris, W. (1954b). *The history and development of the National Vocational Guidance Association.* Unpublished doctoral dissertation, George Washington University, Washington, DC.

Parsons, F. (1909). *Choosing a vocation.* Boston: Houghton Mifflin.

Pope, M. (1992). Bias in the interpretation of psychological tests. In S. Dworkin & F. Gutierrez (Eds.), *Counseling gay men and lesbians: Journey to the end of the rainbow* (pp. 277–291). Alexandria, VA: American Counseling Association.

Pope, M. (1995a). Career interventions for gay and lesbian clients: A synopsis of practice knowledge and research needs. *Career Development Quarterly 44*, 191–203.

Pope, M. (1995b). The "salad bowl" is big enough for us all: An argument for the inclusion of lesbians and gays in any definition of multiculturalism. *Journal of Counseling & Development, 73*, 301–304.

Pope, M. (1996). Gay and lesbian career counseling: Special career counseling issues. *Journal of Gay and Lesbian Social Services, 4*, 91–105.

Pope, M. (1999). Applications of group career counseling techniques in Asian cultures. *Journal for Multicultural Counseling and Development, 27*, 18–30.

Pope, M. (2000a). A brief history of career counseling in the USA. *Career Development Quarterly, 48*, 194–211.

Pope, M. (2000b, Summer). Report on the survey on recognition of career providers. *Career Developments, 4*, 11.

Pope, M. (2003). Career counseling in the 21st century: Beyond cultural encapsulation. *Career Development Quarterly, 51*, 54–60.

Pope, M., Barret, B., Szymanski, D. M., Chung, Y. B., McLean, R., Singaravelu, H., et al. (2004). Culturally appropriate career counseling with gay and lesbian clients. *Career Development Quarterly, 53*, 158–177.

Pope, M., & Chung, Y. B. (2000). From bakla to tongzhi: Counseling and psychotherapy issues for gay and lesbian Asian and Pacific Islander Americans. In D. S. Sandhu (Ed.), *Asian and Pacific Islander Americans: Issues and concerns for counseling and psychotherapy.* Commack, NY: Nova Science Publishers.

Pope, M., Cheng, W. D., & Leong, F. T. L. (1998). The case of Chou: The inextricability of career to personal/social issues. *Journal of Career Development, 25*, 53–64.

Salomone, P. R. (1996). Career counseling and job placement: Theory and practice. In E. M. Szymanski & R. M. Parker (Eds.), *Work and disability: Issues and strategies in career development and job placement* (pp. 365–420). Austin, TX: Pro-Ed.

Scharf, R. S. (2002). *Applying career development theory to counseling* (3rd ed.). Pacific Grove, CA: Brooks/Cole.

Strein, W., & Hershenson, D. (1991). Confidentiality in nondyadic counseling situations. *Journal of Counseling & Development, 69*, 312–316.

Sue, D. W. (1996). Ethical issues in multicultural counseling. In B. Herlihy & G. Corey (Eds.), *ACA ethical standards casebook* (pp. 193–204). Alexandria, VA: American Counseling Association.

Sue. D. W., Arredondo, P., & McDavis, R. (1992). Multicultural counseling competencies and standards: A call to this profession. *Journal of Multicultural Counseling and Development, 20*, 64–88.

Super, D. E. (1974). The broader context of career development and vocational guidance: American trends in world perspective. In E. L. Herr (Ed.), *Vocational guidance and human development* (pp. 63–79). Washington, DC: Houghton-Mifflin.

Whiteley, J. M. (1984). *Counseling psychology: A historical perspective.* Schenectady, NY: Character Research Press.

CHAPTER 16

Group Counseling

OBJECTIVES

After reading this chapter, you should be able to:

- Explain the complexities of group counseling and discuss how those complexities translate to ethical dilemmas.
- Summarize professional identity, training, and credentialing issues in group counseling.
- Summarize crucial ethical issues in group counseling.

- Provide an overview of multicultural issues in group counseling practice.
- Apply a decision-making model to an ethical dilemma in group counseling.

INTRODUCTION

Group counseling raises some interesting ethical dilemmas because treatment involves more than one client. In addition, the clients are usually unrelated (nonfamily members). Ethical issues such as confidentiality, privileged communication, and privacy are crucial concerns in group counseling.

Group counseling is a popular style of counseling. Corey and Corey (2006) stated:

> Psychotherapy groups originated in response to a shortage of personnel trained to provide individual therapy during World War II. At first, the group therapist assumed a traditional therapeutic role, frequently working with a small number of clients with a common problem. Gradually, leaders began to experiment with different roles and various approaches. Over time, practitioners discovered that the group setting offered unique therapeutic possibilities. Exchanges among the members of a therapy group are viewed as instrumental in bringing about change. This interaction provides a level of support, caring, confrontation, and other qualities not

found in individual therapy. Within the group context, members are able to practice new social skills and apply some of their new knowledge. (p. 14)

World War II is an historical marker for the development of group counseling.

Group counseling not only has therapeutic benefits—it has economic benefits for clients—both financial and time related. Group counseling is usually much less expensive than individual counseling; fees for an hour of treatment may be one fourth or one fifth the standard fee for individual therapy. In addition, counselors can treat as many as 8 to 10 people at one time. With constraints of limited government resources, and under the veil of managed care, group counseling and psychotherapy may have an expanded role in the mental health service enterprise.

Although some people view group counseling as a mode of treatment, others view group counseling as having qualities of a separate counseling specialty, requiring specialized training and supervision.

DEFINING THE SPECIALTY, SETTING, AND CLIENTS

Group counseling occurs in a variety of settings: private counseling practices, clinics, college counseling centers, chemical dependency treatment programs, hospitals, schools, and just about any counseling context where there is enough physical space (for three or more individuals) and a pool of available clients. Group counseling usually occurs in a room with chairs arranged in a circular fashion, but the variety of group types and configuration of groupings are unlimited. Some counselors allow clients to sit on the floor or they may recline. Group decision making about how counseling is to be accomplished is common, usually with a defined theme or topic as central to the group task. However, some groups are highly structured and may imitate a classroom-like atmosphere. The directiveness (focus on a specific topic or goal) of groups varies widely, along with the purpose of the group. For example, a group addressing issues of teen drug use may involve open, facilitated discussion, may be educational, or may involve some combination of discussion and didactic activities. A group addressing recovery from trauma may involve open discussion so that individuals can vent their feelings in a supportive environment. There are also differences around the makeup of the group—groups may be organized by such factors such as gender, age, common experiences, conditions of individuals (e.g., physical or mental disorders), or interests. They may be composed of individuals, couples, families, or other groups. The nature of groups varies widely, and the subsequent dynamics of a group vary according to its nature, makeup, and purpose.

Any number of theories of counseling can be used as a theoretical framework for groups (see Corey, 2004; Gladding, 2003). There are groups that are directed by psychoanalytic theory, Gestalt theory, behavioral theory, person-centered theory, or other recognized modes of treatment. Individual therapists who subscribe to one theoretical orientation will tend to apply that theory, and they may apply different theories to different types of groups (say behavioral theory for a group of phobic individuals, or perhaps a person-centered or Gestalt approach for a group seeking self exploration). Regardless, group counselors tend to follow a theory as a template for group practice and procedures.

At the current time, there is no recognized certifying body for group specialists established under the auspices or direction of the APA or the ACA. There is, however, a division of the ACA, the ASGW, which has a Best Practice document specifically written for group work practice.

Members of the ASGW must also be members of the ACA, so they are bound to the mandatory ethical guidelines of the ACA ethics code (which, in sections, specifically addresses group work). The APA has a division (Division 49, Group Psychology and Group Psychotherapy) that serves as a formal organization for psychologists interested in the study and practice of group counseling. Accordingly, group counseling is a specialty that does not meet formal counseling or psychology specialty criteria that involve the credentialing of individuals through a formal specialty board and through specialty designation. In essence, for the professions of counseling and psychology, group counseling represents a specialized mode of treatment.

The American Group Psychotherapy Association (AGPA) is separate from either the ACA or the APA. The AGPA is a freestanding organization that certifies group psychotherapists. In other words, it is not associated with either the profession of counseling or psychology; rather, it is interdisciplinary, having members from a number of mental health professions. The AGPA has a set of ethical guidelines for its certified members, which can be accessed on the internet, for those that have an interest. Regardless, this text focuses on the profession of counseling and the practice of counseling psychology, so the emphasis in this chapter will be on those standards most linked to counseling as a profession.

Group counseling is distinct in treating several clients at the same time. This distinct treatment modality leads to interesting ethical dilemmas, some of which are not adequately addressed by codes of ethics that focus primarily on individual treatment. The ASGW (1998a) Best Practice Guidelines is a useful document that gives added guidance to counselors who use group methods (see Appendix S).

ISSUES OF SIGNIFICANCE TO THE SPECIALTY

Professional Differentiation

Group counseling does not meet the typical criteria for a formal specialty of counseling, even though the ASGW uses the term specialists in its title. Group counseling should be considered a specialized mode of treatment. Whereas specialties such as school counseling or rehabilitation counseling imply a type of setting (schools or rehabilitation agencies, respectively) and a type of client (students or individuals with disabilities, respectively), group counseling has no such boundaries. It can be used with many types of clients in many types of settings. For example, Greenberg (2003) produced a textbook that is a handbook for school counselors doing group counseling in kindergarten through the 12th grade.

It is imperative that group counselors seek supervision and training in group procedures and processes. Even specialized training for certain types of groups is warranted because there are so many variations among groups themselves. Group types range from the "encounter groups" of the 1960s and 1970s, which emphasized personal growth (Rogers, 1970), to a plethora of applications developed since World War II, such as psychodrama groups, behavior therapy groups, and Gestalt therapy groups (see Gazda's [1975] classic text). Generally, individuals who have credentials in a type of therapy (e.g., Gestalt, rational-emotive), who hold credentials in addressing a type of concern (e.g., chemical dependency, sexual dysfunction), and who are trained and experienced in group procedures can supervise group counseling.

To confuse matters more, the ASGW (2000) Professional Standards for the Training of Group Workers defines four specializations in group work, requiring different training beyond receipt of a master's degree (consistent with standards of CACREP, 2001). The specializations are: (a) Task and Work Group Facilitation, (b) Psychoeducational Group Leadership, (c) Group Counseling, and (d) Group Psychotherapy. ASGW recommends at least one course in group procedures plus 10 to 20 hours of experience in groups as core training. In addition, specialization coursework and experience is defined (ASGW, 2000). For example, under the specialization of Group Counseling, coursework includes, but is not limited to, human development, health promotion, and theory and practice of group counseling. The experience requirement is 45 clock hours of supervised practice conducting a counseling group appropriate to the age and clientele of the group leader's specialty area (e.g., school, rehabilitation, mental health).

Related to ethical issues, the Professional Standards (ASGW, 2000) document states: "All graduates of specialization training will understand and demonstrate consistent effort to comply with principles of ethical, best practice, and diversity-competent practice of group work consistent with the program's declared specialization area(s)" (Section III G). The ASGW (1998a) also provided a Best Practice Guidelines document that gives guidance of an ethical nature (see Appendix S).

Group work is a complex area of counseling practice, and although it does not meet criteria for a classic specialty in counseling, it certainly is a specialized mode of treatment that requires focused training through coursework and experience. In fact, it is very important for students of group counseling to learn not only theories that apply to group counseling (e.g., behavioral, existential, cognitive) but also the process and procedures associated with groups. In fact, some textbooks focus more on theory (e.g. Corey, 2004), others focus more on process and practices (e.g., Chen & Rybak, 2004; Corey & Corey, 2006; Jacobs, Masson & Harvill, 2002), and still others address both the theory and the processes and practices of groups (e.g., Gladding, 2003). Actual experience applying theories in the group process and addressing ethical dilemmas in group contexts may be a critical component of training; Gumaer and Forrest (1995) stated, "Knowledge of professional standards by itself is necessary, although not sufficient, to produce ethical behavior by therapists in group practice" (p. 123). Supervised practice addressing ethical dilemmas in group contexts would be ideal. (See Box 16–1.)

Confidentiality and Privileged Communication

Complex ethical circumstances arise in groups that do not arise in other counseling situations. In a recently publicized case in a Midwestern state, a member of an Alcoholics Anonymous group confessed to his group that he had committed murder. The revelation was reported in the newspapers, apparently leaked by other group members. The authorities subsequently investigated the individual who made the revelation. Questions of group counseling confidentiality were raised, and the consensus of the mental health community was that there was no confidentiality except as was voluntarily agreed to by the members of the group.

Box 16–1 • Exploring the Code

What section (or sections) of the ACA (2005) ethics code addresses group counseling?

What is the relationship between the ACA ethics code and the ASGW Best Practice Guidelines? (See Appendix S.)

In the absence of a licensed professional, no protection can be given legally to the information provided in a group. But even in the presence of a licensed professional whose clients are afforded legal confidentiality and privileged communication, the presence of other individuals in a group (nonprofessionals) compromises confidentiality—other group members are not required by law to keep information private or secret. In an article addressing confidentiality in a support group for individuals with AIDS, Posey (1988) described some circumstances unique to group treatment:

> In our group, discussions of confidentiality have been triggered by people dropping in, one member identifying another at a bar, issues of how or whether to leave telephone messages, and how to respond to a member's family and friends at the hospital. Initially, a member distributed names and telephone numbers of the group members but recalled them when members expressed discomfort. Once, a news reporter appeared at a meeting and wanted to sit in, and he guaranteed that identities would be protected. The group agreed to discuss his interest but would not allow him to attend the meeting. (p. 226)

Unusual, and sometimes unpredictable, issues of confidentiality arise in group settings. This is partly because nonprofessional group members may reveal information communicated in a group at their discretion, judgment, or in some cases, misjudgment. The ASGW Best Practice document specifically states: "Group workers have the responsibility to inform all group participants of the need for confidentiality, potential consequences of breaching confidentiality and that legal privilege does not apply to group discussions (unless provided by state statue)" (Section A7).

Group counselors must stress the importance of confidentiality and set a norm of confidentiality regarding all group disclosures. The importance of maintaining confidentiality should be emphasized before the group begins and at various times throughout the group sessions. Participants should also know that confidentiality cannot be guaranteed.

It is important for clients to know that although counselors will act to protect the right to confidentiality of clients, counselors cannot enforce a ban on gossip among other members of the group or between members of the group and outsiders.

Confidentiality is also complicated in groups when other individuals have access to records. For example, if a group of minors is being counseled, the parents of the minors technically have the right to information about the nature and content of counseling (unless there is a legal exemption to parental consent or oversight). Parents even have legal access to case file information. Revelation of group counseling case file information to parents of one or more members of a group (such as a group counseling case note) that references other individuals in the group essentially breaches the confidentiality of the other group members, unless those other group members' parents allow for such revelation.

Group counselors have a special responsibility to ensure that case notes for group counseling are written for each individual in the group. Further, information about other group members should be deleted or omitted from the case files of the group member for whom the case notes are written. This situation is complicated further by federal law. FERPA, which covers all educational institutions that receive federal funding from preschool through university graduate training, clearly states:

> The parents of students [have] the right to inspect and review any and all official records, files, and data directly related to their children, including all material that is incorporated into each student's cumulative record folder. . . . Where such records or data include information on more than one student, the parents of any student shall be entitled to receive or be informed of, that part of such record or data as pertains to their child. (Section 438.[a][1])

Counselors must ensure that records for each client are kept separate and that group case notes do not reference other individuals specifically. In effect, counselors in educational settings must document group counseling case files carefully in light of a legal standard that allows parents full access to such information, even if a parent's child is referenced in another client's case notes.

Regardless of the specific situation in which an issue of confidentiality arises, the counselor must inform each group participant of the limits of confidentiality before that individual consents to treatment (Gregory & McConnell, 1986). The APA and ACA codes and the ASGW (1998a) Best Practice Guidelines all agree that the limits of confidentiality must be discussed with clients. Initiation of groups should not occur until all members of the group are privy to and informed of the limits of confidentiality, and clients should be made to acknowledge such awareness (e.g., by signing a statement of understanding).

Standard exemptions to confidentiality apply in group counseling just as in individual counseling (see Chapter 3). Depending on the state law that applies, counselors must typically breach confidentiality in situations in which there is (a) suspected or substantiated child abuse or neglect, (b) evidence or suspicion that a client intends to do harm to an individual or society (e.g., through an illegal act), (c) a request by a parent or legal guardian, (d) client permission to reveal, (e) the need to confer with other involved professionals, and (f) in other cases covered by law or specific ethical standard.

In an interesting study of confidentiality dilemmas in group psychotherapy, Roback and Purdon (1992) examined how group psychotherapists reported handling serious confidentiality issues. They stated:

> The overall findings of this exploratory study suggest that when confronted with a patient disclosure involving psycholegal issues (criminal behavior, threatened harm to others, potential danger to a child, or past physical abuse of an adolescent), experienced group psychotherapists are highly unlikely to deal with the situation totally within the group context. Rather, they attempt to deal with such incidents by adding private, individual therapy sessions for the patient. However, rarely do they take the incident entirely out of the group context. Realistically, there are groups that are too volatile to manage inflammable patient disclosures such as intended homicide, and patients who are too disturbed (e.g., the agitated paranoid) to be defused within the group context. Competent patient care requires the therapist to be sufficiently flexible to discriminate when the group process will be inadequate for a given situation. (p. 6)

Further, they found that male and female therapists acted differently: "Male group therapists report being more likely to attempt to neutralize patient threats in the group context alone, whereas their female counterparts are more likely to deal with such incidents by augmenting the patient's group sessions with private individual sessions" (p. 6). Beyond ethical considerations, group counseling process issues arise in such conflicts.

The issue of privileged communication, too, is complicated in group treatment circumstances. Privileged communication prevents the revelation of confidential information in a legal proceeding. A counselor cannot be forced to testify on a client's case if the privilege stands—the client owns the privilege. But privileged communication, historically, has been accorded most usually in one-to-one communication circumstances. It may not apply to circumstances in which other individuals are present in counseling. Unless group counseling is specifically addressed in laws that

provide for privileged communication, it is probably wise to assume that group communications will not be considered privileged, and counselors may be required to testify. On the other hand, if group counseling is referenced in the law that provides for privileged communication, counselors may proceed with the intent to hold information that is communicated in group contexts as privileged. However, even in those cases in which group counseling is referenced in laws providing the privilege, there may be no definitive standard as to whether clients will be protected from revelation of private information in a legal proceeding unless there is clear case law in the legal jurisdiction within which the counselor practices. In such cases, clients should know that there is a possibility that information may be vulnerable to revelation in a legal context, although the counselor will make every effort to prevent such revelation. Counselors should study state statutes and case law carefully.

Some statutes provide for privilege under certain circumstances. Many state licensure statutes allow for privileged communication on civil, not criminal, cases only. Most states allow for revelation of suspected or substantiated child abuse or neglect, and state statutes that cover such matters may override any privileged communication provided to clients of counselors. In group settings where such matters are commonly discussed, clients should have prior knowledge of the limits on their privilege.

Individuals who seek group therapy often are involved in individual therapy as well. This occurs in both private practice and in institutional settings. There should be clear guidelines for the sharing of group information among agency employees in institutional settings. Codes of ethics typically require that when there is a relationship between professionals, there should be a formal agreement regarding issues of confidentiality. When a group counselor consults with a client's individual counselor (with the client's permission), the group counselor should be assured that the information communicated will be held in confidence and protected from revelation to outsiders.

Certainly, there are ethical concerns related to the contiguous professional relationship if a counselor is performing both individual and group treatment (for a nongroup matter) with one client (see Glass, 1998). Counselors must be cautious in this circumstance to prevent contamination of group treatment with information from the individual treatment. Counselors should avoid seeing clients in both the group facilitator and individual counselor roles. Concerns also arise if a client participates in individual treatment with another mental health professional. Glass stated:

> Confidentiality questions about what information is to be shared by the two therapists need to be worked out. There is also a danger that the patient will use the individual sessions to drain off affect elicited in the group instead of dealing with it in the group. Using different individual and group therapists will be most productive if the patient consents to allow both therapists to communicate freely with one another throughout the course of treatment. Otherwise the danger is great that the two therapists may find themselves working at cross purposes. (p. 110)

Glass recommended "only one form of treatment at a time" (p. 110) to prevent the ethical dilemmas that arise.

CASE SCENARIO 16–1

A counselor in a small rural mental health center is seeing a client in individual counseling and has also encouraged the client to join a group the counselor runs for individuals with similar issues. The client joins the group, and in the first session, the counselor proceeds to introduce the client, summarizing her concerns to the other group members. Has the counselor done something wrong?

PROBABLY. Unless the counselor got permission from the client before the group meeting to reveal information communicated during individual sessions of counseling, there was a breach of confidentiality. As implied earlier in the chapter, doing both individual and group counseling with a client is an ethical dilemma minefield. Where such an arrangement cannot be avoided, clear ethical boundaries must be defined around the material addressed in the individual sessions and the material addressed by the counselor in group sessions. It would be wise to have a formal written agreement with the client defining any limits of confidentiality across modes of treatment.

Informed Consent

In establishing groups, counselors must play a special role that extends beyond the informed consent of clients agreeing to group treatment. Of course, as with any type of counseling, clients have the right to consent to treatment or to refuse treatment. However, it is also true that an individual can be misplaced in a group that is not consistent with the client's interests or concerns. Obviously, the counselor is obligated ethically to screen clients in or out of groups to ensure appropriate placement. Both the ACA code and the ASGW guidelines emphasize the

importance of screening prospective group members. Corey, Williams, and Moline (1995) stated:

> The purpose of screening is twofold: (a) to determine if an individual is compatible for a particular group and (b) for the person to determine if the group is compatible with his or her personal goals. If both the leader and the prospective member are in agreement with respect to the appropriateness of the group for the member, there is a basis for forming what is likely to become a working group. Proper screening and orientation can occur only if the group counselor is clear about the purpose of the group and is able to provide persons with adequate information prior to joining a group. (p. 164)

Methods of screening include individual interviewing, a group interview with prospective group members, an interview done by a team of leaders, or screening through written questionnaires. Care must be given to prevent a serious misplacement, such as putting a victim of sexual abuse in a group of sexual perpetrators, or placing an abstinent drug abuser in a group that abuses substances. Even more subtle misplacement may occur, and the counselor must be alert to the possible consequences of misplacement and must act to prevent problems by careful group assignment. When it is obvious that a misplacement has occurred, procedures should be in place to provide a formal means for an individual to terminate services in a way that is not harmful to any group participant. Termination procedures should be discussed with members of a group before a group begins. Members should know they may leave the group at any time, but there may be repercussions for premature withdrawal from the group (especially in cases of mandatory treatment). A "trial period" after which members can formally exit the group of their own volition is highly recommended. Certainly, clients should be informed of their obligation to alert the group leader and other group members of their concerns or intentions regarding group attendance.

Coercion is not acceptable; a client's rights have been breached if undue group pressure comes to bear on that client's decision to remain in or participate in group activities. Corey et al. (1995) stated: "Some degree of group pressure is inevitable, and it is even therapeutic in many instances. It is essential for group leaders to differentiate between 'destructive pressure' and 'therapeutic pressure.' People may need a certain degree of pressure to aid them in breaking through their usual forms of resistance" (p. 166). Aside from what can be considered therapeutic pressure, counselors must protect clients from coercion, physical threats, undue pressure, and intimidation.

Ideally, individual clients should screen the group before committing to attend sessions. Counselors have an obligation to provide prospective members with enough information about the group so that they can make fully informed decisions about group attendance. This includes information about the counselor's credentials and background, procedures or rules of the group, the purpose of the group, counselor expectations regarding client behavior, and the rights, responsibilities, and risks of group membership (ASGW, 1998a).

Roles and Relationships with Clients

As with any type of counseling, potentially detrimental counselor–client relationships are to be avoided. When it comes to roles and relationships with clients, group counseling presents some different ethical configurations, however. Although it would be unethical for a counselor to establish a romantic relationship with a group member, can group members establish romantic or other relationships among themselves? The counselor must discourage such activity. The outdated ASGW (1989) code stated that "Group counselors discuss with group members the potential detrimental effects of group members engaging in intimate inter-member relationships outside of the group" (Section 9f), but current standards make no such statement. The current Best Practice Guidelines (ASGW, 1998a) require only that informed consent statements address "implications of out-of-group contact or involvement among members" (Section A.7.). Counselors should discourage potentially detrimental relationships among group members because of their possible negative effects on the group process and possible negative personal outcomes. Obviously, if a member of a group is privy to outside information about another member or is intimately involved with another member, revelations of information that otherwise would be considered private may be made. There is also the potential for covert coalitions among members of a group, which could result in **scapegoating** another member—process wherein one member of a group is placed in an "odd person out" position or is treated by others as a deviant, thereby receiving negative messages from some other members of the group. Scapegoating has been implicated in producing an unhealthy social context, or a two- (or more) against-one scenario (Hoffman, 1981). However, the activities of group members outside of the group cannot be enforced by a group leader, and certainly, a group leader cannot be held responsible for extragroup entanglements. In this regard, counselors can minimize risks by using a contract for treatment that addresses relationships and other issues. Corey et al. (1995) stated: "One way to minimize psychological risks in groups is to use a contract in which leaders specify what their responsibilities are and members specify their commitment to the group by declaring what they are willing to do. If members and leaders operate under a contract that clarifies expectations, there is less chance for members to be exploited or damaged by a group experience" (p. 172). There is great potential benefit through group treatment, but there are added risks.

Some authors (e.g., Brittain & Merriam, 1988) have cautioned counselors against leading two related types of groups—for example, one group of clients and another group of "significant others" to the first group. A counselor should not lead a group of survivors of child sexual abuse and also lead a group of significant others to survivors of child sexual abuse. Running a group for victims and a second group for perpetrators may adversely affect the counselor, as personal value issues and personal "blind spots" may inadvertently affect the counseling process. In such cases, the objectivity of the counselor may be jeopardized (Brittain & Merriam).

Responsibility

Group leaders have a dual responsibility to individual members of the group and to the group itself. The responsibility to the group does not supersede responsibility to individual members of the group. For example, if a counselor recognizes that one member of a group is being scapegoated and believes that the client's continued participation in the group could be detrimental to his or her mental health, the counselor is obligated to protect the individual participant, even if it means that the group membership and process might be negatively affected. Counselors should be equitable in their treatment to all members, and they are directed by the ACA code to protect the welfare of their clients. Implicit in such directives is recognition that when there are conflicts between the needs of the group and the needs of an individual member who is potentially traumatized by the group, the counselor must protect the individual. The group counselor should not abdicate responsibility for the group, but must clearly take action to protect the individual.

The counselor's responsibility to the individual group member is critical when the force of the group can have negative consequences. Glass (1998) said:

Recognizing that powerful forces are generated in groups, and that the leader has only partial control over what occurs, the group therapist faces a complex set of responsibilities. Not only must he or she act ethically, but moreover also create an ethical climate in the group. Some leaders may respond to this challenge by becoming overly controlling and authoritarian in an attempt to insure that the group functions in an appropriate fashion. Unfortunately this undermines the very element which is the group's strength, namely, its collective influence for therapeutic benefit. Conversely, the laissez faire leader who simply encourages the group to "do its own thing" without guidance or direction may be courting disaster. Such leaders often are reluctant to interfere with the functioning of the group out of a belief that groups are inherently wise, offer only good advice, and bring to bear pressures on their members that are ultimately for the individual's own good. Such a leadership approach often results in chaos, where the group never gels into an effective entity, or in harming members through coercive patterns that may emerge in the group. (pp. 99–100)

A group leader must be watchful of serious, personal challenges to a group member that may have detrimental effects (Glass). Leader responsibility and the ability to intervene at critical moments of potential harm are important aspects of group facilitation.

Sometimes groups are led by more than one therapist, which also adds a complicating element to such practice. Haeseler (1992) stated: "The complex transference/countertransference issues in a group can give rise to jealous and aggressive feelings between co-therapists. Such problems, if unresolved, can hinder the therapeutic effectiveness of the group and create an ethical dilemma" (p. 4). The responsibility to the group supersedes any issues between co-therapists, and it is the responsibility of the cotherapist to be alert to potential conflicts and to address those conflicts in a way that does not negatively affect the group process.

When a client ends affiliation with a group, the counselor should follow the formal termination procedures that were established and communicated before the client consented to group treatment. The counselor should make an appropriate referral so the client can receive continued treatment, if necessary.

There are cases, however, in which the needs of the individual and the needs of the group are not in serious conflict yet still require attention. For example, if a group member in a cancer support group raises concerns over disciplining a misbehaving child, the group leader must weigh the needs of the individual against the needs of the group. To focus on the issue of a misbehaving child, which may be tangential to the group purpose, would be a disservice to other group members. In such a case, the counselor would be wise to refer the member to an appropriate treatment source for the child-rearing concern. In this case, neither the individual client nor the group as a whole is placed in a position of lesser priority. Of course, the counselor must ensure that the focus of the group was clearly stated initially so that referral for such a concern does not seem out of the ordinary.

Ethical codes alone are not enough to ensure responsible group counselors. Kotter (1982) suggested self-monitoring related to personal responsibility as important to group leadership. Gregory and McConnell (1986) stated:

> The notion of equal treatment of all group members is often more myth than reality. Therapists like mere human beings are more attracted to some persons than others. Despite efforts to equalize interactions, therapists are prone to give more time, attention, and to be more responsive to group members whom they find personally reinforcing. (p. 60)

Counselors must recognize their own limits and ensure that they do not inadvertently scapegoat members of the group. Counselors, therefore, have a responsibility to self-monitor throughout the group process and to take appropriate corrective action if serious biases reveal themselves.

CASE SCENARIO 16–2

A client in a group has been excessively verbal during group sessions and has monopolized much of the group sessions. It has become increasingly obvious, as communicated by the nonverbal behavior of other group members, that the client's continual verbalizing interferes with the ability of the other clients to process information in the group and to respond in a way that addresses the concerns of others. Other clients often sigh, give "dirty looks" to other group members, or self-distract when the overtalkative member speaks. The counselor realizes that the benefits of the group are being jeopardized. The counselor speaks out in the group and tells the overtalkative client to hold his thoughts while others speak. The client acts perturbed, and the counselor confronts him in front of the group and expresses the observation that the client's verbalizations are negatively affecting the other group members. The overtalkative client begins to tear up, but his behavior is not addressed by the counselor or other members of the group. His tears are never acknowledged by the group members. Has the counselor addressed this concern appropriately?

NO. In such a situation, it is wise for the counselor to meet with the client individually to address the counselor's perceptions of the client's negative effect on the group process. If there are serious personal issues needing attention that cannot be addressed in the group context, the counselor may offer to refer the client for individual counseling. If the counselor can educate the client about the group process and group norms, and the client is willing to try to respond appropriately, then the client can benefit by the individual intervention of the counselor. Regardless, it is unwise for a counselor to confront a client in a group context who is in obvious need of individual counsel about group norms or group etiquette, especially during a time when the client is being scapegoated within the group context or when the client is in distress. In this case, the mental health needs of the individual client outweigh the counselor's responsibility to the group as a whole.

Values

Biases and values may affect the group leader and the group process. Corey, Corey, and Callanan (2003) stated:

> Group counselors are sometimes timid about making their values known, lest they influence the direction that the members are likely to take. Group counselors must consider when it might be appropriate to expose their beliefs, decisions, life experiences, and values. The key issue is that leaders should not short-circuit the members' exploration. Rather, the leader's central function is to help members find answers that are congruent with their own values. (p. 434–435)

Obviously, serious value issues can be avoided by pre-planning and appropriate administration. For example, a group counselor should not be put in a position of leading a group of clients whose behavior is abhorrent or unacceptable to the counselor. A counselor who is a right-to-life (antiabortion) advocate who works in a hospital setting or mental health center should not be required against his or her will by agency or other directives to counsel a group of individuals who are planning to have or have had abortions. A counselor who feels uncomfortable addressing issues of sexuality should not be made to direct a group in which sexual concerns are frequently and appropriately raised. However, there are circumstances in which a counselor may have a value conflict, unrelated to the group purpose, with one or more members of a group. In such cases, the counselor is obligated to address such value differences. The ASGW (1998a) guidelines state that "Group workers assess their values, beliefs and theoretical orientation and how these impact upon the group, particularly when working with diverse and multicultural populations" (Section A.3.). When values conflict, the professional should disclose the conflict and assess the implications of the value conflict and disclosure for the group process.

When value conflicts arise that may affect the group process, the counselor must decide to either proceed or to modify the nature, focus, composition, or leadership of the group.

Counselor Competence

Counselor competence relates to two issues: (a) the quality of provided services and (b) the boundaries or scope of professional activity. This text takes the position that individual counselors must be trained and appropriately credentialed (e.g., licensed) professionals— a somewhat controversial position. A number of self-help groups are led by peers, nonprofessionals, or paraprofessionals (individuals trained usually to the level of a bachelor's degree). Some of the best examples of these are 12-step groups such as Alcoholics Anonymous, Narcotics Anonymous, and Overeaters Anonymous. Some facilities also have paraprofessionals leading groups; this is common in the field of rehabilitation, wherein individuals with bachelor's degrees serve as group educators/counselors for individuals needing guidance on job procurement, social skills, money management, or grooming. It can be argued that there is no need to have a highly trained counselor directing such groups when nonprofessionals and paraprofessionals are able to provide quality services. However, such a response does not take into account issues of ethics other than the obligation to provide quality services. When a professional counselor or psychologist is involved, the client is guaranteed some legal protection (depending on the laws and statutes in the legal jurisdiction). In states where there are licensure statutes with ethical standards, an unlicensed provider or paraprofessional does not accord the group member legal or professional confidentiality (or in some cases, privileged communication). Clients have no recourse if they suspect a breach of privacy or malpractice, unless they sue the agency that directs the nonlicensed provider. Having a professional lead a group is some protection to group members. Attending a group with a nonprofessional group leader puts clients at added risk if there is dissatisfaction with the group or the group leader. When clients seek any service for a fee, they are always wise to learn the credentials of the provider and to address protection or limits under the law.

Is licensure as a counselor or psychologist an acceptable standard for group counseling practice? Licensure in and of itself is no guarantee that a counselor has been adequately trained and experienced in leading groups. Even though group counseling has been defined as a "mode of treatment" (not meeting other criteria for a specialty designation), group counseling still qualifies as a technically sophisticated mode of treatment requiring special training. General credentials are not enough to provide the group leader adequate background in group processes and ethical standards. This is the position of the ASGW (2000). Qualified counselors who plan to lead groups should have a formal graduate course or courses in group theory, procedures, and processes, and they should have supervision in providing group services through practica, internships, and postgraduate training, following the ASGW (2000) Professional Standards for the Training of Group Workers. This ensures that the counselor has adequate knowledge and experience directing groups. This position is consistent with the position of CACREP (2001), which requires accredited graduate programs in counseling to include training in group work. CACREP (2001) requires study of group topics such as (a) group dynamics, (b) group leadership, (c) theories of group counseling, (d) methods of group counseling, (e) approaches used in such group types as task, psychoeducational, and therapy groups, (f) professional preparation standards for group leaders, and (g) ethical considerations. Additionally, the CACREP clinical training standards (e.g., practicum and internship training as part of the degree program) require development of individual counseling and group work skills under supervision. Subsequent to receipt of the degree, ethical counselors who plan to provide group services must seek supervision of group work activity.

CODE COMPARISONS

The ASGW is an affiliate organization of the ACA. The ASGW (1998a) Best Practice Guidelines are aspirational guides—that is, without a mechanism for adherence and in addition to the ACA ethics code. The ACA code is a mandatory code of ethics for all ACA members (including ASGW members). In fact, the introduction of the ASGW Best Practice Guidelines states (see Appendix S):

> The Association for Specialists in Group Work recognizes the commitment of its members to the [ethics code] of its parent organization, the American Counseling Association, and nothing in this document shall be construed to supplant that code. These Best Practice Guidelines are intended to clarify the application of the ACA [ethics code] to the field of group work by defining group workers'

responsibility and scope of practice involving those activities, strategies and interventions that are consistent and current with effective and appropriate professional ethical and community standards. (Preface)

The ASGW guidelines focus on activities of counselors involved in counseling individuals in group contexts and are required reading for counselors involved in group treatment. The guidelines address issues only addressed in a cursory fashion in more general codes and give specific guidance to the practitioner.

ISSUES OF DIVERSITY

In what many consider a milestone publication on the topic of multicultural counseling, Sue, Arredondo, and McDavis (1992) outlined the need for counselors to have a multicultural perspective and presented cross-cultural competencies and standards. Building on the work of Sue and Sue (1990), Sue et al. described the culturally competent counselor as:

> First . . . one who is actively in the process of becoming aware of his or her own assumptions about human behavior, values, biases, preconceived notions, personal limitations, and so forth . . . . Second . . . one who actively attempts to understand the worldview of his or her culturally different client without negative judgments. . . . Third . . . one who is in the process of actively developing and practicing appropriate, relevant, and sensitive intervention strategies and skills in working with his or her culturally different clients. (p. 481)

It is crucial for the group counselor to be culturally sensitive, not only to direct his or her own actions, but to observe any cross-cultural differences among group members that may affect or potentially affect the group process (Glass, 1998).

The ASGW developed Principles for Diversity-Competent Group Workers (1998b), a document that outlines definitions related to cultural difference and principles related to self-awareness, awareness of group members' worldviews, and diversity-appropriate intervention strategies. This document reflects the Association's commitment to multicultural sensitivity in group counseling practice. The conclusion of the document reads as follows:

> This document is the "starting point" for group workers as we become increasingly aware, knowledgeable, and skillful in facilitating groups whose memberships represent the diversity of our society. It is not intended to be a "how to" document. It is written as a call to action

and/or a guideline and represents ASGW's commitment to moving forward with an agenda for addressing and understanding the needs of the populations we serve.

Differences on issues of value arise because "difference" is a "fact" of a multicultural and diverse society. Accordingly, counselors must be alert to how differences manifest themselves in interactions, and they must ensure that actions are neither discriminatory nor disenfranchising of individuals or groups of individuals. Especially in screening group members for participation in groups, counselors must not simply screen out individuals due to differences of culture, race, religion, or sexual orientation, unless failing to do so would be a serious detriment to another group member or members. In fact, counselors are wise to ensure that there is variation among group members along factors of diversity; in this way the counselor may facilitate an acquaintance or acceptance of difference. As biases reveal themselves, trained and culturally sensitive counselors should address them. Sue et al. (1992) stated, as related to counselor interventions: "When they [counselors] sense that their helping style is limited and potentially inappropriate, they can anticipate and ameliorate its negative impact" (p. 483).

On issues of gender, DeChant (1996) and her contributors made some compelling presentations on the nuances of working with women in group contexts in a thought-provoking text entitled *Women and Group Psychotherapy*. They explored topics such as sex-role issues in mixed-gender groups, gender-linked aspects of group behavior, boundary issues, gender-based countertransference in group treatment, and cross-cultural issues for women in groups. This excellent text serves as a scholarly marker about the complexities of group practice in a multicultural society.

There also may be differences in group dynamics among nations or by national origin. Yamaguchi (1986) described some differences between Western culture groups and those in Japan: Group leaders appear to have a more influential role and privacy issues are prominent (consistent with Japanese tradition related to "intimate" information). Counselors who work with culturally different individuals without knowledge of those cultural differences and without making an effort to understand them are counseling in a disadvantaged way. Such a disadvantage may, ultimately, be a disservice or even a detriment to clients.

The ACA and APA codes of ethics are clear on the issue of diversity. Counselors and psychologists do not condone or engage in discrimination. Counselors should actively attempt to understand the diverse cultural backgrounds of the clients with whom they work. In a culture that values equality in a context rich in human diversity, counseling must acknowledge difference nonjudgmentally. Group counselors should facilitate nonjudgmental discourse on cross-cultural issues.

DECISION MAKING IN CONTEXT

Decision making in a group counseling context is complicated by a number of factors. First, group counselors have an obligation, first and foremost, to the individual clients of the group, and additionally, to the group itself. Sometimes counselors are faced with a concern that relates specifically to one or a few members of the group. When the presence of one or more members of a group presents an ethical challenge to the counselor, the counselor must weigh the effect on the group as a whole. For example, assume that a counselor has a history of working with victims of child sexual abuse. The counselor, in one job, facilitated groups for victims of abuse. The counselor, however, is now newly employed in an agency that serves a broad mental health client population (a mental health center). The agency is small, and there are only a few qualified counselors on staff. The counselor, as part of the required job duties, is to counsel a group of adult ex-offenders. The type and nature of the crimes of group members is diverse; however, two of the seven group members have a history of child sexual abuse perpetration. The counselor has made a "best effort" to be fair and receptive to all of the concerns of individual group members, but the counselor is feeling some discomfort related to the two clients with child abusing histories. A decision must be made as to whether the counselor can continue to counsel the group.

The application of a decision-making process is crucial in such a situation. For example, using the Tarvydas Integrative Decision-Making Model for Ethical Behavior, the counselor would follow the decision-making process through the standard stages. At Stage I, the counselor would interpret the situation through awareness and fact finding. The counselor might do research on sexual perpetration with minors to better understand the perspective of these clients. The counselor might also weigh the effect on involved individuals, including the other clients, the agency supervisor, and the agency itself. In formulating an ethical decision (Stage II), the counselor would have to examine applicable ethical standards, including the ACA and APA ethics codes and the ASGW Best Practice Guidelines. Possible courses of action would need to be defined, with consequences for each course of action considered. The supervisor would need to be consulted. And a selection of an ethical course of action would have to be made. Importantly, at Stage III, the additional factors associated with nonmoral values, personal blindspots, or prejudices enter into the final decision equation. In this case, the counselor may have difficulty empathizing with perpetrators of child sexual abuse, especially after having worked with victims. Prejudice may be recognized that may prevent a fair treatment of the concerns of the clients. The preferred course of action, weighing Stage III factors, may be different than the ethical course of action defined in Stage II. If the counselor senses that fair treatment cannot be given, then, regardless of other demands, a decision would have to be made to cease counseling the ex-offenders with histories of child sexual abuse. Other forms of treatment would need to be provided by the agency. On the other hand, if the counselor feels competent, non-discriminatory, and self-assured that scapegoating can be avoided, services can continue in a group format, but the counselor would be well advised to at least address with supervisors (or the clients themselves) his or her concerns on an ongoing basis. In the final stage (Stage IV—planning and executing the selected course of action), the counselor would carry out, document, and evaluate the course of action.

With the Cottone Social Constructivism Model of Ethical Decision Making, the process would involve much more social interaction. The counselor would attempt to construct a decision after consulting a number of individuals, likely including the supervisor, other agency counselors, experts of ethics and of child sexual abuse perpetration, and even the clients themselves. After consulting stakeholders or experts, and after considering the applicable ethics codes and laws, the counselor would attempt to discern a consensus course of action. If conflicting factors prevent definition of an agreeable resolution, the counselor might enter into a negotiation process with involved parties. For example, the counselor might negotiate with agency administrators for a reduced fee (equivalent to a group fee) for child abuse clients in the group to receive individual therapy with another counselor. If

clients were amenable, then they could receive individual treatment for their concerns, while not paying a higher fee. Negotiation may allow for agreement over a course of action that might resolve the problem that otherwise seemed unlikely to be resolved. Of course, the counselor could refuse to continue serving as the group counselor, which may create a situation where arbitration may be necessary. Regardless, the social constructivism model involves social interaction as the means to solve problems.

Decision making when group counseling is involved must weigh the effects on all of the involved clients. If a decision is potentially harmful to any member of the group, then the counselor must seek other options or ensure remedies or means to minimize harm. As can be discerned by this discussion, group counseling has another layer of complexity when ethical dilemmas arise—the complexity of competing interests among group members. Counselors must be aware of that complexity and mindful of its influence on final outcomes.

CHAPTER SUMMARY

Because of the presence of individuals other than a counselor and one client, group counseling poses some interesting ethical dilemmas. The general codes of the APA and the ACA give general guidance related to group work. However, the ASGW provides detailed and specific guidance in addressing issues typically faced in the practice of group counseling. Although group counseling does not clearly meet the criteria of a formal, designated specialty of counseling, it does have unique theory at its base and it has a set of methods or techniques that is not shared with individual, couples, or family therapies. Special training is required of the counselor who plans to provide group counseling services ethically and in the context of a multicultural society.

Specific ethical issues that are relevant to group practice include confidentiality and privileged communication, informed consent, potentially detrimental counselor–client relationships, responsibility, values, and counselor competence.

Counselors must be culturally sensitive and provide culturally competent services. Also, they should anticipate ethical dilemmas arising from the competing interests of clients. They should develop comfort applying decision-making principles to dilemmas as they arise.

REFERENCES

American Counseling Association. (2005). *Code of ethics.* Alexandria, VA: Author.

Association for Specialists in Group Work. (1989). Ethical guidelines for group counselors—ASGW 1989 Revision. *The Journal for Specialists in Group Work, 15,* 119–126.

Association for Specialists in Group Work. (1998a). *Best practice guidelines.* Alexandria, VA: Author.

Association for Specialists in Group Work. (1998b). *Principles for diversity-competent group workers.* Alexandria, VA: Author.

Association for Specialists in Group Work. (2000). *Professional standards for the training of group workers.* Alexandria, VA: Author.

Brittain, D. E., & Merriam, K. (1988). Groups for significant others of survivors of child sexual abuse. *Journal of Interpersonal Violence, 3*(1), 90–101.

Chen, M., & Rybak, C. J. (2004). *Group leadership skills: Interpersonal process in group counseling and therapy.* Belmont, CA: Brooks/Cole–Thomson Learning.

Corey, G. (2004). *Theory and practice of group counseling* (6th ed.). Belmont, CA: Thomson Brooks/Cole.

Corey, G., Corey, M. S., & Callanan, P. (2003). *Issues and ethics in the helping professions* (6th ed.). Pacific Grove, CA: Wadsworth: Brooks/Cole.

Corey, G., Williams, G. T., & Moline, M. E. (1995). Ethical and legal issues in group counseling. *Ethics and Behavior, 5,* 161–183.

Corey, M. S., & Corey, G. (2006). *Groups: Process and practice* (7th ed.). Pacific Grove, CA: Thomson Brooks/Cole.

Council for Accreditation of Counseling and Related Educational Programs. (1994). *CACREP accreditation standards and procedures manual.* Alexandria, VA: Author.

Council for Accreditation of Counseling and Related Educational Programs. (2001). *CACREP accreditation manual.* Alexandria, VA: Author.

DeChant, B. (Ed.). (1996). *Women and group therapy: Theory and practice.* New York: Guilford.

Gazda, G. M. (1975). *Basic approaches to group psychotherapy and group counseling.* Springfield, IL: Charles C. Thomas.

Gladding, S. T. (2003). *Group work: A counseling specialty* (4th ed.). Upper Saddle River, NJ: Merrill Prentice Hall.

Glass, T. A. (1998). Ethical issues in group work. In R. M. Anderson, T. L. Needels, & H. V. Hall (Eds.), *Avoiding ethical misconduct in psychology specialty areas.* Springfield, IL: Charles C. Thomas.

Greenberg, K. R. (2003). *Group counseling in K–12 schools: A handbook for school counselors.* Boston, MA: Allyn & Bacon/Pearson Education.

Gregory, J. C., & McConnell, S. C. (1986). Ethical issues with psychotherapy in group contexts. *Psychotherapy in Private Practice, 4*(1), 51–62.

Gumaer, J., & Forrest, A. (1995). Avoiding conflict in group therapy: Ethical and legal issues in group training and practice.

In *The Hatherleigh Guide to Psychotherapy* (pp. 121–141). New York: Hatherleigh Press.

Haeseler, M. P. (1992). Ethical considerations for the group therapist. *American Journal of Art Therapy, 31,* 2–9.

Hoffman, L. (1981). *Foundations of family therapy.* New York: Basic.

Jacobs, E. E., Masson, R. L., & Harvill, R. L. (2002). *Group counseling: Strategies and skills* (4th ed.). Wadsworth Brooks/Cole.

Kotter, J. A. (1982). Ethics comes of age: Introduction to the special issue. *Journal for Specialists in Group Work, 7*(3), 138–139.

Posey, E. C. (1988). Confidentiality in an AIDS support group. *Journal of Counseling and Development, 66,* 226–227.

Roback, H. B., & Purdon, S. E. (1992). Confidentiality dilemmas in group psychotherapy. *Small Group Research, 23,* 169–185. (Accessed through the MasterFILE Elite database, pp. 1–10)

Rogers, C. (1970). *On encounter groups.* New York: Harper & Row.

Sue, D. W., Arredondo, P., & McDavis, R. J. (1992). Multicultural counseling competencies and standards: A call to the profession. *Journal of Counseling and Development, 70,* 477–486.

Sue, D. W., & Sue, D. (1990). *Counseling the culturally different: Theory and practice.* New York: Wiley.

Yamaguchi, T. (1986). Group psychotherapy in Japan today. *International Journal of Group Psychotherapy, 36*(4), 567–578.

CHAPTER 17

Rehabilitation Counseling

OBJECTIVES

After reading this chapter, you should be able to:

- Describe the specialty of rehabilitation counseling, the historic trends in its evolution, and the political issues of importance to the field.
- Define the standards for a qualified rehabilitation counselor, including professional identity, training, and credentialing.
- Differentiate the roles and functions of rehabilitation counselors from those of other counseling specialties.

- Summarize the ethical issues of concern to rehabilitation counselors.
- Explain the newly revised Code of Professional Ethics for Rehabilitation Counselors and compare it to the ACA Code of Ethics.
- Discuss multiculturalism and diversity in rehabilitation counseling.

INTRODUCTION

The specialty of rehabilitation counseling (RC) has its origins in the tremendous interest in vocational guidance and counseling that began in the early decades of the 20th century. It evolved out of powerful events in the history of the United States: societal changes surrounding the Industrial Revolution and immigration patterns in the late 1800s and early 1900s, the Great Depression, and World Wars I and II. Vocational issues became leading concerns during these critical times. Whether those requiring guidance and counseling were students, adults with industrial injuries, or veterans, the need to understand the individual and how that person's individual needs and skills could be used to find a satisfying and satisfactory match with vocational opportunities became a powerful impetus to this field. From the standpoint of the functions performed and consistent with an emphasis on the socioenvironmental focus of its work, rehabilitation

counseling can be defined as "a profession that assists persons with disabilities in adapting to the environment, assists environments in accommodating the needs of the individual and works toward full participation of persons with disabilities in all aspects of society, especially work" (Szymanski, 1985, p. 3). More recently, rehabilitation counseling has been defined as "a group of professionally prepared and credentialed counselors with specialized knowledge, skills and attitudes who work collaboratively in a professional relationship with persons with disabilities to achieve their personal, social, psychological and vocational goals" (Rehabilitation Counseling Consortium, 2004). The Rehabilitation Counseling Consortium (RCC) is a collaborative consortium of key rehabilitation counseling professional organizations formed in 2004. The definition of rehabilitation counseling adopted by the RCC has also been adopted by its member organizations,

Box 17–1 • Exploring the Codes

According to the CRCC code, to whom does a rehabilitation counselor (RC) owe an obligation if the RC is providing forensic evaluations but has not conducted an examination?

Should an RC who holds a doctoral degree from a field other than counseling use the title "Dr."?

After how many years posttermination may an RC engage in a sexually intimate relationship with a former client?

If disparities exist between laws and the CRCC code, what should the RC do?

According to the CRCC code, for what two purposes should RCs seek peer supervision or consultation?

According to the CRCC code, can RCs diagnose mental disorders?

According to the CRCC code, what three steps are required of an RC prior to disclosing to a third party that a client has a contagious, fatal disease if that third party is at high risk of contracting the disease from the client?

including ARCA, NRCA, NCRE, CORE and CRCC. This latter definition emphasizes both its status as a specialization of counseling and the uniquely collaborative relationship that its professionals maintain with persons with disabilities, as does the CRCC code of ethics which is explored in Box 17–1.

There always has been significant social and political support for studying the world of work and training professionals to help people make vocational choices and adjust to problems of vocational placement. Rehabilitation counseling received significant legislative support for the emergence and continued growth of information and methods in this new field. The evolution of rehabilitation counseling has been influenced greatly by social and cultural forces affecting Americans' work lives and the legislation and programs created as a result of these forces.

As it evolved, rehabilitation counseling increasingly took on a unique identity. Its services and professional development have been tailored to the needs of the populations it has specialized in serving. Historically, rehabilitation counselors have adapted their vocational approaches to meet the needs of people with disabilities across various settings. Clients of rehabilitation counselors may have a wide range of disabling conditions, including physical (e.g., spinal cord injury or epilepsy), sensory (e.g., blindness or deafness), developmental (e.g., mental retardation or autism), cognitive (e.g., traumatic brain injury or learning disability), and emotional disabilities (e.g., schizophrenia or substance abuse). Rehabilitation counselors have had a long-standing tradition that incorporates philosophy and the practical importance of addressing clients holistically, even while addressing vocational concerns. They have long recognized that increasing the client's positive experiences and gains in emotional well-being, or in organizing an efficient, satisfying lifestyle in the community, can significantly enhance the individual's effectiveness and

adjustment on the job. This phenomenon likely is due to the pervasive psychosocial effects of disability on all life areas and the holistic nature of human functioning for all people. This knowledge has resulted in a dual focus on vocational and psychosocial adjustment counseling in rehabilitation counseling.

Since the 1970s, the independent living movement has stimulated use of rehabilitation counseling skills to provide community rehabilitation services for people with disabilities and, thus, has underscored the emphasis on addressing problems across all areas of individual and functional environmental demands. Practitioners of rehabilitation counseling recognize that attitudinal and other social and economic barriers, as well as limited opportunities to access appropriate types of skills training, are often the most severely limiting aspects of disability and design and provide interventions to address these problems.

DEFINING THE SPECIALTY, SETTING, AND CLIENTS

Rehabilitation counseling practitioners most often are trained as generalist rehabilitation counselors and are conversant with the perspectives of both vocational and personal adjustment counseling. They possess basic skills that are useful in both areas. The profession's scope of practice statement has been endorsed by CRCC, CORE, ARCA, NRCA, and NCRE (see Scope of Practice for Rehabilitation Counseling in Appendix U) and involves a blending of the two points of view. The interventions and modalities used within the process of rehabilitation counseling offer a snapshot of the range and intensity of services used by these practitioners (CRCC, 1994):

• Assessment and appraisal;
• Diagnosis and treatment planning;

- Career (vocational) counseling;
- Individual and group counseling treatment interventions focused on facilitating adjustments to the medical and psychosocial impact of disability;
- Case management, referral, and service coordination;
- Program evaluation and research;
- Interventions to remove environmental, employment, and attitudinal barriers;
- Consultation services among multiple parties and regulatory systems;
- Job analysis, job development, and placement services, including assistance with employment and job accommodations; and
- The provision of consultation about, and access to, rehabilitation technology.

Typically, it is only in increasingly specialized practice over the course of their careers that rehabilitation counselors may become more fully involved in one of the most differentiated modes of practice. Leahy (1997) summarized this blending of elements into a unique practice by stating the following:

> It is the specialized knowledge of disabilities and of environmental factors that interact with disabilities, as well as the range of knowledge and skills required in addition to counseling that serves to differentiate the rehabilitation counselor from social workers, other types of counselors (e.g., mental health counselors, school counselors, career counselors) and other rehabilitation practitioners (e.g., vocational evaluators, job placement specialists) in today's service delivery environments. (p. 97)

The discussion of individual scopes of practice in Chapter 3 is important to all counselors in discerning how they develop an appropriate and ethical specialty practice for themselves.

At first glance, rehabilitation counselors may seem to practice within a more restricted or specialized range of clients and settings than do other types of counselors. Nothing could be further from the truth. Rehabilitation counselors work with people who have physical, mental, developmental, cognitive, emotional, and addiction disabilities and help them achieve their personal, career, and independent living goals in the most integrated settings possible (CRCC, 1994). It has been estimated that more than 43 million Americans have disabilities that restrict some of their life activities and prevent them from attaining or maintaining jobs. The diversity of types, degrees, and combinations of disabilities that individuals bring to rehabilitation counselors is immense. Examples of clients served include people who have orthopedic work injuries, brain injuries sustained in an automobile crash, hearing or visual impairments, "invisible" disabilities such as epilepsy, AIDS, or pulmonary disease, developmental disabilities such as mental retardation or cerebral palsy, drug or alcohol addictions, or a psychiatric disorder such as schizophrenia or depression. In recent years, services to individuals with severe disabilities have been emphasized in many settings, and often individuals being served have combinations of several of these disabilities, thus providing more complex issues to the rehabilitation counselors with whom they work.

The primary employment settings for rehabilitation counselors are similarly diverse and include state rehabilitation and Veteran's Administration agencies, alcohol and drug programs, hospitals, independent living centers, educational settings, private rehabilitation companies and private practice settings, halfway houses, supported living and employment agencies, private rehabilitation facilities, and mental health centers. These facilities may be public, private nonprofit, or private for profit.

Due to the traditional emphasis on holistic practice, rehabilitation practice typically is conducted within a rehabilitation team context. The composition of the team is dictated by the nature of the treatment setting and disability-related needs of the clients. Whether the team is in-house or is physically dispersed, rehabilitation counselors have been trained to work within a collaborative team framework. They generally provide the coordination necessary to help the team function for the client's benefit. Often, they also provide the broader case management functions for this process to occur unless another team member has been formally designated to do so. Case management is "focused on interviewing, counseling, planning rehabilitation programs, coordinating services, interacting with significant others, placing clients in jobs and following up with them, monitoring a client's progress, and solving problems" (CRCC, 1994, p. 2). Case managers need to be knowledgeable in both medical and vocational case management, and rehabilitation counselors often perform functions in both of those areas, most frequently in vocational case management. These vocational case management services are often most intensely sought after within the private insurance and Worker's Compensation industry and involve these professionals in long-term disability, bodily injury liability, automobile no-fault claims, disability management, and life-care planning service provision.

In recent years, case management has grown tremendously as an area of advanced practice with a separate credential offered to professionals who have their core professional education and wish to receive acknowledgement of advanced expertise in this particular area of service. Case management as a specific subfield has been intensely stimulated by the demand for professional case managers within the managed care industry. Its growth has been particularly clear since the successful initiation of the Certified Case Manager (C.C.M.) credential by the Commission for Case Manager Certification (CCMC) in 1993. As of this writing, there are over 20,000 C.C.M.s in the United States. Although the majority of those practitioners are nurses by training, a large number of rehabilitation counselors also seek this additional credential.

In recent years, a number of employment settings have begun to emerge as additionally important areas for rehabilitation counseling practice. These areas include employee assistance programs, employer-based disability management programs, school-based transition programs, disabled student services offices in postsecondary educational settings, and agencies that serve people with HIV and AIDS (Leahy & Szymanski, 1995). Recent developments in health care, legislation, technology, and the economic or business community have added demand for other new roles and function to the more traditional roles and functions of this diverse group of practitioners: psychiatric rehabilitation, life-care planning, functional capacity evaluation, genetic counseling, consultation on work motivation and organizational culture, late deafness rehabilitation, human resource management, disability management services, and job redesign.

ISSUES OF SIGNIFICANCE TO THE SPECIALTY

Professional Differentiation

Rehabilitation counseling also has enjoyed prominence within the history of the counseling profession. ARCA and NRCA were founded in 1958, with ARCA as a division of the ACA, and NRCA a division of the National Rehabilitation Association. Rehabilitation counseling established both the first accreditation of professional educational programs and national certification of individual counseling practitioners in the profession of counseling. CORE was incorporated in 1972 by a group that included ARCA and NRCA. CORE is based on an innovative multiple-stakeholder, field-tested approach to accreditation. There are 85 accredited rehabilitation counseling master's-degree programs (CORE, 2004).

Similarly, CRCC, established in 1973, is the oldest and most well-established professional counselor certification. Both the CORE and CRCC processes continue to be at the forefront of credentialing in counseling. The ongoing CORE/CRCC Knowledge Validation Study process provides continuous empirical validation of the professional standards of this professional group. CORE and CRCC are recognized by ACA as parallel to credentialing by CACREP and NBCC, respectively. This position was reaffirmed in 2003 by the ACA Governing Council in a resolution passed at its annual meeting that again endorsed professional parity for rehabilitation counselors (ACA, 2003). By 1993, more than 23,000 professionals had participated in the CRCC certification process in the United States and several foreign countries (Leahy & Holt, 1993). Estimates by the U.S. Bureau of Labor indicate that there are 122,000 rehabilitation counselors among the 526,000 counselors holding jobs in 2002 (BLS, 2004), with rehabilitation counselors accounting for almost one quarter of all counselors in the United States. CRCC reports approximately 15,000 are credentialed as C.R.C.s. This figure of 122,000 rehabilitation counselors compares with 228,000 educational, vocational, and school counselors, 85,000 mental health counselors, 67,000 substance abuse and behavioral disorder counselors, and 23,000 marriage and family therapists. Thus, rehabilitation counselors can be seen as a major force in this nation's counseling community in terms of number as well as historical prominence.

The issue of multiple professional constituencies has expressed itself in rehabilitation counseling. Rehabilitation counseling has arrived at unified professional credentials and standards through collaborative work among its major professional organizations—primarily ARCA and NRCA and the related rehabilitation organizations. This collaboration has resulted in unified accreditation (CORE), certification processes (CRCC), and a code of ethics (reprinted in Appendix T). However, this historical duality of the major organizations has created problems of definition regarding which core identity underlies the profession of rehabilitation counseling—counseling or rehabilitation (Tarvydas & Leahy, 1993).

The first perspective historically casts rehabilitation counselors as counselors who work in a variety of rehabilitation and community counseling agencies with people who have disabilities. This perspective appears to be more aligned with an emphasis on counseling through ARCA and its parent organization, ACA (Salomone, 1996). The counseling point of view is grounded firmly in the developmental and psychoeducational counseling approaches that are so important to the profession. The other perspective adds emphasis on case management or coordination with rehabilitation counselors practicing within more of a functional or medical model. This perspective emphasizes rehabilitation as the profession's core function and is seen as more closely related to NRCA and the National Rehabilitation Association (Salomone) that was its parent group until 2005. It allows for the incorporation of the clinical treatment perspective and allows the use of medical information and collaboration with medical treatment systems that are important to serve clients with certain types of rehabilitation needs. The discussion in Chapter 9 described many of the specialized health care issues that exist for rehabilitation counselors and others working within a medical model of treatment. In many cases, rehabilitation counselors work with people who have mental health disabilities and deal with many of the same issues discussed in Chapter 14 on mental health counseling. In fact, the practice of psychiatric rehabilitation has been a long-term part of rehabilitation counseling training and practice. The Boston University approach is one of the most well-respected, effective, and widespread approaches to psychiatric rehabilitation. It was originated and developed about 35 years ago by rehabilitation counselor Dr. William Anthony and his associates, who continue to provide leadership in this interesting area of practice to rehabilitation counselors and all professions. In addition, the many rehabilitation counselors who work with people who have drug and alcohol abuse disabilities will find Chapter 18 on addictions counseling to be helpful. All rehabilitation counselors have advanced expertise in vocational counseling and through this can be seen as linked to career counseling (see Chapter 15).

In terms of the organizational issues in rehabilitation counseling, Leahy and Szymanski (1995) provided a reality-based analysis by noting that the two organizations (ARCA and NRCA) have often found methods to collaborate on important projects. Active discussions concerning merger began as early as 1979. In 1993, they formed the Alliance for Rehabilitation Counseling (ARC) as a stable, formal structure to continue this process of melding the two perspectives into an effective working structure for professional policy and strategic planning, while still preserving historic ties to their parent groups. The unified code of ethics and scope of practice documents were reviewed and jointly approved through this alliance in conjunction with CRCC. A major effort was undertaken to merge these

two organizations into one, unified organization but failed with the dissolution of the ARC in 2003. This development was undertaken with the intent of strengthening both rehabilitation counseling and the profession of counseling and of improving the representation of the needs of people with disabilities to the general professional, legislative, and lay communities (Leahy & Tarvydas, 2001).

After this unsuccessful attempt at organizational merger, the leadership of the key rehabilitation organizations continued to recognize the need to develop some type of organizational tie that would ensure an effective method for systematic communication and linkage to further the aims of the rehabilitation and disability communities, rehabilitation counselors, and their advocacy agenda. A recent development in the field has attempted to address this need—the formation of RCC in late 2004. This consortium of eight leading organizations in the field of rehabilitation counseling formed a cooperative group to provide a unified voice for rehabilitation counseling and to pool resources and information so that issues of importance to rehabilitation counseling can be addressed through coordinated communication and advocacy efforts across the organizations. The member organizations are ADARA (Professionals Networking for Excellence in Service Delivery with Individuals who are Deaf or Hard of Hearing), ARCA, CARP (Canadian Association of Rehabilitation Professionals), CORE, CRCC, IARP (International Association of Rehabilitation Professionals), NCRE (National Council on Rehabilitation Education), and NRCA. The RCC has agreed to an initial "call to action" to assist rehabilitation counselors in gaining access to the credentials to practice and employment settings for which they are qualified. In order to facilitate this effort and to provide a consistent set of definitions for the field, the RCC adopted definitions for both the rehabilitation counseling professional and the profession (provided earlier in this chapter) that were endorsed by all its member organizations. The formation of the organization and these definitions were first publicly introduced to the profession of counseling as a whole at the January, 2005 meeting of the AASCB.

Clearly, rehabilitation counseling has a broad area of practice and diverse practitioner base, yet has clearly identified standards for what constitutes appropriate professional practice as a result of the long-term collaborative efforts within its professional organizations. For example, the standards for who can be considered a qualified rehabilitation counselor have been established by the professional organizations including

ARCA, NRCA, and the ARC. These standards require that rehabilitation counselors have (a) completed a master's degree in rehabilitation counseling or a closely related program (e.g., counseling), (b) achieved national certification as a C.R.C., and (c) attained the appropriate state licensure (e.g., L.P.C.) in states that require this level of credential for counseling practice and that allow access to licensure for counselors with a rehabilitation counseling background. Both certification and licensure credentials have requirements for supervised professional practice in rehabilitation counseling and for passing a knowledge-based national examination in counseling.

The agencies in the state-federal vocational rehabilitation system are mandated by a federal law to employ qualified staff. In the late 1990s, the federal government took aggressive steps to require that the states observe this requirement. According to the operationalization of qualifications, rehabilitation counselors must meet the requirements to be eligible for certification by CRCC, even though they are not required to become certified. In essence, then, these counselors must have completed a master's degree in rehabilitation counseling or a closely related program and have taken the core courses in rehabilitation counseling. Unfortunately, in most states, employees practicing only within state agencies are exempt from any licensure requirement to practice counseling in that state. Even though quite a number of rehabilitation counselors work in such exempted settings, a recent survey on the ethical beliefs of C.R.C.s revealed that 22% of the respondents were licensed, indicating that a larger proportion of rehabilitation counselors is licensed than might be supposed (Tarvydas et al., 2001). As of the summer of 2005, 48 states plus Puerto Rico and the District of Columbia license counselors, with only California, Guam, Nevada, and the U.S. Virgin Islands being without licensure for counselors. Of these 48 states, 12 that regulate counseling also regulate rehabilitation counseling. These states regulate RCs either through the general credential of Licensed Professional Counselor of Licensed Mental Health Counselor, or separately, as in Louisiana, Massachusetts, and New Jersey (ACA, 2005).

Ethical Issues

Confidentiality and Privileged Communication. Rehabilitation counselors may have particularly pressing issues regarding confidentiality in their work. Issues regarding confidentiality that emerged in a survey of

C.R.C.s (Patterson & Settles, 1992) were (a) maintaining confidentiality in institutional settings, (b) knowing that a client is driving with poorly controlled seizures, (c) recommending to an employer a client who is suspected of abusing substances, (d) sharing information with family members about a client with chronic mental illness, (e) conflicts between Workers' Compensation and state laws related to confidentiality, (f) the requirement to report client information to an agency that results in disciplinary action against the client, (g) learning that a client who has AIDS is not practicing safe sex, and (h) discussing clients with others without signed, written consent.

Many rehabilitation counselors are involved in legal and third-party consultant roles as vocational experts in civil court matters, administrative hearings, and Social Security or Workers' Compensation work (Blackwell, Martin, & Scalia, 1994). Practices involving vocational or forensic expert services often involve **indirect services** provision. CRCC (2001) defined indirect services in its code of ethics as services provided when rehabilitation counselors are employed by a third party, whether or not they engage in direct communication with the client, and where there is no intent to provide rehabilitation counseling services directly to the person with the disability. In such instances, they must clearly address confidentiality limitations with all the individuals involved. Havranek (1997) examined the application of ethical principles in forensic rehabilitation and noted the different demands of this practice in various settings and with specific populations. He further alerted rehabilitation counselors to the necessity of remaining objective despite expectations of the party who may have retained their services. The CRCC Code of Professional Ethics for Rehabilitation Counselors provides a rule that embodies well-accepted advice in such situations in the areas of informed consent and privileged communications, to involved individuals:

> Rehabilitation counselors who are employed by third parties as case consultants or expert witnesses, and who engage in communication with the individual with a disability, will fully disclose to the individual with a disability and/or his or her designee their role and limits of their relationship. (CRCC, 2001, p. 2)

The use of appropriate professional disclosure statements to enhance informed consent is recommended. (See Chapter 4 for elements of written professional disclosure.)

The clarity and timeliness of disclosure of role limitations is crucial to good ethical practice for the rehabilitation counselor. Unless so informed, it is not unreasonable that the client would assume that all information obtained would be held in confidence. If an uninformed client's benefits were cancelled as a result of the rehabilitation counselor's report provided to a third party that employs the rehabilitation counselor, the client justifiably feels that their trust and confidence was violated. Such situations are a common source of ethics complaints. To further assist in encouraging appropriate professional disclosure practice, the new code of ethics notes that "whether direct client contact occurs or whether indirect services are provided, rehabilitation counselors are obligated to adhere to the Code" (CRCC, 2001, Preamble). Rehabilitation counselors are further required to explain the *limitations of confidentiality* and any foreseeable situations that might limit confidentiality at the beginning of counseling and throughout the counseling process.

CASE SCENARIO 17–1

Indirect Services and Client Confusion

James is a new client being seen by Dawn, a vocational rehabilitation counselor working for the RehabCo Insurance Company in its long-term disability policy rehabilitation service program. James, a nurse, has been off on disability with a severe back injury that has resolved into a chronic back pain condition. Several different physicians and clinics made a variety of attempts to provide James with medical services, all resulting in no substantial improvement. James has been out of work for 12 months, and his current physician says that he cannot carry out the physical requirements of his job. Dawn is assigned to assess whether James can benefit from rehabilitation services through a medical and vocational file review. During this process, she interviews James by phone and he states that he is not willing to consider alternative types of employment because he does not want to lose his benefits. James is still hopeful he can return to his old job as a nurse even though his employer is unwilling to consider job modification or light-duty employment. Dawn recommends an independent medical evaluation, after which James is declared medically able to return to work. As a result, James's benefits are terminated. James is angry with Dawn and lodges a complaint that she did not advocate for him. He expected that Dawn would work with him to assist him in returning to work with his previous employer. Was Dawn unethical?

MAYBE. This scenario presents an all-too-frequent situation when rehabilitation counselors provide indirect services on behalf of a third party—the insurance company, in this case. The client who has a disability may not understand what to expect from this professional. The key issues here are whether or not proper professional disclosure and fully informed

consent occurred at the onset of the involvement with James. He should have been fully informed that Dawn was calling only to verify information regarding his medical and vocational status and that she would not be providing direct services to him (professional disclosure). In addition, she should have told him that all information he gave her would be provided to the insurance company to determine the status of his disability claim. Dawn should have clearly explained to James his choices and the consequences of each choice for his benefits (informed consent). If she had done so and truthfully reported her opinion to the insurer based on objective facts, she would have been providing ethically appropriate services to James that unfortunately resulted in an outcome he did not desire.

Rehabilitation counselors should not assume that privileged communication status extends to their practices. Some may erroneously think that their national certification provides privilege to their counselor–client relationships. Rehabilitation counselors must carefully research the legal protections afforded them in their own jurisdictions (see Chapters 3 and 4). In cases where privileged communication is extended to counselors, it is only to those who hold a license in that jurisdiction. Unfortunately, rehabilitation counselors' involvement in the state-by-state counselor licensure movement has been inconsistent and unintegrated compared with that of some counseling specialties, such as mental health counseling. Multidisciplinary or interdisciplinary teams are a frequent aspect of the rehabilitation counseling practice and tradition. They are an important asset to the client's counseling process, but offer an additional challenge to ethical practice. These teams may not necessarily work in physical proximity or have similar levels of training or understanding regarding ethical obligations to the client. Also, the rehabilitation counselor must communicate client information to team members involved in the client's treatment or employment plan. Although this transfer of information is usually standard practice and done to benefit the client, clients must be fully informed of what type of information will be shared and when, how, and with whom it will be shared. Their consent to this disclosure should not be taken for granted nor obtained under pressure to give blanket permission.

Minimal disclosure is another important ethical practice intended to further safeguard client confidentiality. Minimal disclosure requires that even where client consent is given, the rehabilitation counselor reveal only the minimum amount of information necessary. Just being a member of the treatment team does not entitle one automatically to know whether a young man with a spinal cord injury is capable of erection and penile penetration while having sex, or that a student involved in a work-study placement through a high school is a victim of incest. The standard of minimum disclosure also applies to disclosure of case records and other client information provided to other team members or professionals. Whenever disclosure does occur, the rehabilitation counselor must take care that team members have specific rules they follow on confidentiality, that they reinforce the need to preserve client confidentiality, and that the client is informed of this disclosure to the team (Strein & Hershenson, 1991).

Confidentiality issues for rehabilitation counselors may be more prevalent or complex in certain settings or within particular groups of clients, such as those with addictions, psychiatric, correctional, or HIV/AIDS disabilities. Certain types of services, such as group counseling or treatment, present extraordinary challenges to dealing with confidentiality. Rehabilitation counselors may offer group services ranging from skills-training groups for job-seeking or social skills training, to psychosocial treatment-oriented groups that assist in the therapeutic or personal adjustment of their clients. Although the rehabilitation counselor may take appropriate measures to set the expectation of confidentiality among group members, all clients must be informed that confidentiality cannot be guaranteed in a group setting. They must also be told that privileged communication is generally not extended to group counseling by the legal system. Some other confidentiality issues are specific to particular settings. Examples include: (a) legal restrictions placed on access to educational records of minor students provided by FERPA (see Chapter 13), (b) conflicting legal dictates in state and federal law regarding the privacy rights of people who are HIV-positive and the public's need to know about dangerous individuals with fatal, contagious diseases (see Chapter 4 and Anderson & Barret, 2001, for an excellent discussion), and (c) the laws extending stricter confidentiality to those in treatment in any addictions treatment facility receiving federal funding (see Chapters 4, 13, and 18, respectively).

Informed Consent. The intent of informed consent procedures is that clients be provided with the information they need to make informed choices about their own counseling process and rehabilitation plan. The three elements of informed consent necessary to

exercise autonomy through informed choice are: (a) capacity, (b) comprehension, and (c) voluntariness.

Rehabilitation counseling has a longstanding philosophical and political tradition that endorses the ideal of the client participating as an equal partner with the counselor in the counseling process. A keystone right in this movement is the normalization principle—the right of persons with disabilities to have access to informed choices. In fact, Toriello and Leierer (2004) sated that "supporting clients' autonomy during the rehabilitation process may be the defining movement of the current rehabilitation era" (p. 220). **Normalization** is a rehabilitation principle that dictates that people with disabilities "should be treated in a manner that allows them to participate both symbolically and actually in roles and lifestyles that are 'normal' for a person of their age and culture" (Greenspan & Love, 1995, p. 75). This tradition of client participation has become institutionalized in rehabilitation treatment settings in diverse ways, including the powerful accreditation standards for rehabilitation programs such as the Commission on Accreditation of Rehabilitation Facilities (CARF) and the Joint Commission on Accreditation of Healthcare Organizations (JCAHO).

Historically, this point of view is one of the values that differentiates rehabilitation service from the medical treatment model. It received resounding affirmation through the passage of the Rehabilitation Act of 1973, which emphasized consumer involvement of the client in the state-federal vocational rehabilitation process in a number of its provisions. The most striking example of this focus was the mandated involvement in the rehabilitation services planning process through the completion of an Individual Written Rehabilitation Program (IWRP; Rubin & Roessler, 2001). The Rehabilitation Act Amendments of 1998 elaborated on the concept of informed choice by stating: "individuals . . . must be active participants in their own rehabilitation programs, including making meaningful and informed choices about the selection of their vocational goals, objectives, and services" (section 100(a)(3)(c)). In this plan and its contemporary version—the Individualized Plan for Employment (IPE)—the plan is co-developed by counselor and client, written, and reviewed periodically by both as part of the ongoing evaluation of the services plan. The required elements of the plan are (a) a statement of the long-term goals for the client and intermediate steps related to it, (b) a statement of the particular rehabilitation services to be provided, (c) the methods to be used in determining whether the intermediate objectives or the long-term goals are being attained, and (d) information from the client regarding how the client was involved in choosing from among alternative goals (Rubin & Roessler).

It is important that the rehabilitation counselor consider it an aspect of the rehabilitation counseling process to *prepare* clients to participate in this collaborative rehabilitation process on a meaningful basis, rather than just offering an opportunity to decide. This process may involve some preparatory counseling, skill teaching, or motivation-enhancing techniques. Due to their disabilities, some clients may not have had a chance to develop decision-making skills; or they may have a limited base of life experiences or other cognitive or psychological limitations. In a study of counselors' perceptions of barriers to informed choice, participants identified the four most prominent barriers to choice as: (a) unrealistic consumer vocational goals; (b) consumers requesting more services than are necessary to achieve suitable employment; (c) the consumers' desire for the most expensive services rather than reasonable cost/professionally recommended services; and (d) finding ways to balance the expectations of consumers with reality (Patterson, Patrick, & Parker, 2000).

Although rehabilitation philosophy clearly is in support of full informed consent and inclusion, it is a significant ethical challenge to rehabilitation counselors to fulfill the actual intent, rather than just the letter, of these guidelines. The determination of when a client is legally or ethically competent to provide informed consent is a critical consideration for rehabilitation counselors. If a client is a minor, but is psychosocially and cognitively mature, has a traumatic brain injury, or appears to be under the influence of a drug, the counselor must think carefully about whether informed consent is possible or whether other measures are needed. The counselor might need to involve a parent or guardian or wait until the client is in a better position to provide consent. Haffey (1989) and Stebnicki (1997) provided guidance on the assessment of clinical competency for rehabilitation interventions. Haffey differentiated the legal from the clinicoethical issues involved; Stebnicki (1997) utilized a functional assessment approach for determining mental capacity.

The rehabilitation client may have a legal guardian who has been court appointed to make decisions for them if they have been found to be legally incompetent to do this for themselves. There are a number of ways in which the legal requirements of achieving this consent can be reconciled with the ethical responsibility of respectfully allowing clients to participate in the

decision as fully as their abilities allow (Stebnicki, 1999). Therefore, while clients with legal guardians may not be able to provide legal *consent* to a decision, ethically they should be able to *assent* to it. The 2005 revisions to the ACA Code of Ethics reinforces this ethical obligation by directly requiring counselors to gain assent and to make every effort to present information to clients in a form that best allows them to participate as fully as possible in the decision-making process. Often the client can be educated about this process over time. If the client who cannot give legal consent still objects to the course of action, ethically the counselor should seriously consider the situation and whether or not they should proceed. If the client undergoes involuntary commitment or has guardianship instituted on their behalf, the revised Code of Ethics for Rehabilitation Counselors directs the counselor to take such action only after careful deliberation and to advocate for resumption of client autonomy as quickly as possible (CRCC, 2001).

Roles and Relationships with Clients.   Some types of relationships counselors may have with clients outside of the counselor–client relationship may be detrimental to the well-being of the client—even if clients are desirous of pursuing them. The concern about these extra-counseling relationships is based primarily on the existence of a power differential that may impair the objectivity of the rehabilitation counselor (see Chapter 3). Sexual intimacy is strictly prohibited with current clients by the rehabilitation counseling code of ethics because the potential for serious harm to the client in such relationships has been documented as very high. Like the ACA ethics code, the CRCC code discourages sexual relationships with former clients. Both the CRCC and ACA codes allow the potential for such a relationship after a minimum of 5 years have passed. The CRC code requires that the relationship occur only after full examination of its implications and thorough documentation of the evaluation undertaken to ensure it is not exploitative in nature. The counselor is also directed to seek peer consultation prior to entering into the relationship.

CASE SCENARIO 17–2

Allegations of Sex with a Client

Your colleague, Mary, has been hospitalized quite suddenly to have surgery for a ruptured appendix and experienced serious complications. She was quite ill and on medical leave, so you were assigned to cover some of her cases. Two of her clients tell you that Mary has been having sexual relations with them. You do not believe these allegations about Mary because you know her to be a conscientious rehabilitation counselor. On Mary's return, you ask her about these charges, and she replies that she has had a "very close personal relationship" with these individuals. However, she states that it is not a problem because she has provided these clients only limited case management services and purchased some vocationally required adaptive equipment— "I am not counseling them." She assures you that she will not continue the relationships because she realizes that other counselors who do not see clients with disabilities as "equal partners" might misconstrue these relationships. Should you report Mary's behavior?

YES. Mary clearly has engaged in serious, unethical conduct. Sexual contact with current clients is always unethical and is even a felony for licensed professionals in some states. Her position that the ethical standard did not apply because she was not "really" counseling these individuals is seriously inappropriate. The code of ethics makes no such distinction, and case management services are counseling services, delivered as one of a potential range of rehabilitation counseling services. You must immediately report Mary's behavior to your supervisor, who will take steps to evaluate the well-being of these two clients, take appropriate action against Mary, and ensure the safety of any future clients of the agency. Mary herself may have emotional or personal issues for which she might be evaluated and for which she might need help herself. This course of action will be difficult for you because of your friendship and because you do not like being cast in the role of a whistle-blower. However, it is essential that you act, or you yourself will be behaving in an unethical manner.

In rehabilitation counseling, activities with clients outside the office routinely may be incorporated into vocational, independent living skill, or behavioral interventions that may result in additional tensions around the issue of counselor–client relationships. Such situations offer clients the opportunities to challenge boundaries in ways that are not possible in office settings (Knapp & Slattery, 2004). By necessity, many of these interventions take place in natural social, recreational, residential, or vocational settings. For example, social skills training intentionally may simulate some behavioral elements of, but not the emotional content of, relationships such as friend or coworker. For a naive client or an emotionally needy counselor, the climate can create confusion about relationship boundaries. On of the other hand, innovative and constructive intervention styles of mentoring, coaching, and providing a personalized climate for successful achievement, such as that found in a job club, may be beneficial for many

of the nontraditional, diverse clients needing vocational and life skills seen by these specialty counselors. It is important that any out-of-office contact be explicitly linked to the service goals of the client and described to them in this manner; rules for behavior should be established before the work and shared with clients and their families; and this understanding should be reinforced and documented regularly. In order to minimize potential for problems, supervisors should provide specific training regarding the types of problems that may arise in home and community settings, including how staff should respond. They also should provide on-site supervision for staff who work in this manner and an atmosphere that encourages disclosure of any boundary issues that might arise (Knapp & Slattery). Prior to beginning a potentially beneficial interaction, it is the counselor's obligation to document in case records the potential benefit and anticipated consequences of these proposed beneficial interactions. The counselor must also provide the rationale for it, intervene promptly if unintentional harm occurs to the client, and attempt to remedy the harm (ACA, 2005).

Some ethical relationship issues involve situations in which the rehabilitation counselor may have monetary, business, or personal interests with another party to the client's rehabilitation process, but not with the client directly. These other professionals may be such parties as attorneys, claims adjusters, or case managers involved in a long-term disability insurance case. These relationships may be serious conflicts of interest affecting the rehabilitation counselor's judgment. Even if the rehabilitation counselor proceeds ethically, the appearance of such a conflict does exist and should be avoided. An example would be a counselor entering into a sexually intimate relationship with the plaintiff's attorney in a client's Workers' Compensation case, or becoming a business partner of this person. Such conflicting relationships may be difficult to avoid because it seems convenient and natural to hire experts and consultants who are familiar and well known. However, caution should be taken to fully evaluate the potential for conflict of interests and the appearance of conflict, even if no direct rehabilitation counseling services are provided. If there are such conflicts, the rehabilitation counselor should avoid such involvements.

Responsibility. The Code of Professional Ethics for Rehabilitation Counselors clearly asserts that the primary responsibility of the counselor is to the client.

Interestingly, the code defines clients as "individuals with disabilities who are receiving services from rehabilitation counselors" (CRCC, 2001, Preamble) due to the sometimes uncritical use of the term "client" in contemporary counseling and rehabilitation. It is clear that rehabilitation counselors have secondary responsibilities to other parties. For example, rehabilitation counselors are told to recognize that families are usually important to clients' rehabilitation and to enlist the families' understanding and positive involvement in rehabilitation, with client permission. Another relationship that is acknowledged is the rehabilitation counselor's need to "neither place nor participate in placing clients in positions that will result in damaging the interest and welfare of either clients, employers, or the public" (CRCC, 2001, p. 1). It would seem that the imperative need in contemporary counseling is to acknowledge the important moral theme of *interdependence* as the true human condition rather than the traditional and excessive U.S. emphasis on the myth of possessive individualism and independence (Gatens-Robinson & Tarvydas, 1992). This view of interdependence is also more respectful of multiculturally diverse client groups who have a more collectivist worldview, emphasizing central importance of family members for example.

Rehabilitation counseling has had a long history of practicing primarily within agency or institutional settings. This fact is embodied by standards that enjoin counselors to respect the rights and responsibilities that they owe to their employing agencies and the need to try to resolve disputes with them through constructive, internal processes. However, they also have the responsibility to alert the employer to conditions that may be disruptive to their professional practice or limit their effectiveness (CRCC, 2001).

There has been substantial documentation on disability in the sociological, political science, and anthropological literatures that people with disabilities are often denied basic human rights. Even well-meaning individuals and institutions inadvertently deny these individuals equal opportunities for participation and inclusion. For that well-recognized reason, the rehabilitation counseling code of ethics contains a canon on the obligation of counselors to advocate on behalf of their clients and other people with disabilities and to assist in ensuring accessibility of facilities and services. This provision is prominent among professional codes of ethics and has become an important aspect of the self-definition for this professional group. It requires the rehabilitation counselor to "strive to eliminate attitudinal barriers, including stereotyping and discrimination, toward individuals with disabilities and to increase their own awareness and sensitivity to such individuals" (CRCC, 2001, p. 6). The canon goes on to detail the many facets of this advocacy role. The concept is laudatory and was updated at revision of the code from an emphasis on only advocating for clients, to emphasizing the need to empower people with disabilities through providing appropriate information and supporting their efforts at self-advocacy. This change acknowledges the leadership and primary role of people with disabilities in advocating for their own interests and the responsibilities of RCs to assist and teach self-advocacy skills as needed (Vash, 1987).

Although the need to work for the best interests of the rehabilitation client is clear, the exact nature of the balance to be struck between the ethical principles of autonomy and beneficence in actual rehabilitation practice situations is not determined so easily. This tension centers on the temptation of paternalism, which originated within the tradition of medical practice in acute rehabilitation. This tendency toward paternalism is difficult to resolve. It originated in the observations of caregivers that clients, at some early points in their adjustment to disability, might not be able to discern what they might want or need at some later point in their recovery, when they are better equipped emotionally to make stable judgements regarding their needs and wishes. Unfortunately, the beneficence of the caregiver—wishing to influence the process for the good of the client through controlling information and decision making—clashes with the clients' right to autonomous ability to exercise discretion in their own matters (Gatens-Robinson & Tarvydas, 1992). Greenspan and Love (1995) provided a perspective on this issue:

> In disability services, the perception has been that a majority of persons with disabilities (particularly those with cognitive limitations) have sufficiently limited access to autonomy as to justify the substituted decision making of weak paternalism. The reality, however, is that the vast majority of people with disabilities (including cognitive limitations) do have access to autonomy (sometimes with assistance, but more often not). This fact suggests that much of the weak paternalism that is perceived as ethically permissible is, in reality, a form of strong paternalism that should be considered much less acceptable than it is. (p. 80)

The importance of work as a meaningful human activity is a central value shared by both career and rehabilitation counselors (see Chapter 15 for a broader discussion of work values). New employment and

1. **Creaming** Employment networks (ENs) may select consumers with the best chances to be successful in the job market and discourage or be passive with other consumers.

2. **Informed Choice Issues** Consumers may not receive full information concerning the various aspects of the TTW program or ENs that might better serve their needs, or they may be subtly coerced into working with particular ENs. (Note: The regulations do not provide a definition or procedures to be observed related to informed consent even though the law requires it.)

3. **Competency of Staff** Because overhead costs to ENs will be punishing for long periods of time until monies are recouped for services provided, will administration/management provide sufficient staff or fully competent staff to serve the needs of consumers? (Note: Not specifically "qualified staff" related to rehabilitation counselors, but also other team members—such as job placement specialists or job coaches. Will competent benefits counseling be provided to consumers?)

4. **Rehabilitation Systems Competition** There may be concerns about marketing, the payment system, and business practices that will foster competitiveness rather than collaboration in consumer service planning and delivery.

5. **Ticketholder Confidentiality** There may be an increased tendency to erode consumers' confidentiality through such practices as providing ticketholders' names to ENs and one-stop centers and vice versa (without prior consumer consent).

6. **Above All, "Do No Harm"** What will the responsibility be for services to consumers who are adversely impacted by receiving frightening or anxiety-provoking information? What will be the impact to some clients who attempt to work and fail? How will they be assisted? It is in the best interests of ENs to get consumers who are severely disabled off of long-term supports as soon as possible when this may disrupt long-term systems of consumer support that have been reliable and may not be easily reinstituted if needed.

7. **Due Process** What will be the due process rights of consumers (outside of state vocational rehabilitation (VR) systems and Consumer Advocacy Programs) and how will they be provided? Will there be penalties to ENs that flagrantly violate consumer rights?

8. **Honesty of Outcome Data** There will be serious pressures on the agencies and their management to report favorable results for TTW efforts. Will outcome data be collected in such a way that accurately reflects both the positive and negative effects of the program on consumers (e.g., selection of quality-of-life and extraprogrammatic effects of the program as well as the traditional vocational/fiscal indicators).

9. **Professional Disclosure** Will professional staff members provide full disclosure of their qualifications, methods, and the nature of their approach to services (e.g., business-centered versus rehabilitation focus)? Will consumers be informed that "counseling" may not mean counseling in the sense the consumer understands it? It may be focused on education regarding program requirements, not on supporting the consumer or the consumer's psychosocial or vocational issues.

10. **Two-Tier System** Is there a potential that we may end up with the consumers having the most severe disabilities served by the state VR agencies? What are the implications for the consumers and for the agencies?

FIGURE 17–1. Potential Ticket-to-Work Dilemmas

workforce development initiatives by the federal and state government provide a number of ethical challenges to rehabilitation counselors that are not dissimilar to other challenges faced throughout the years of the profession's evolution. Positive legislative reform driven by changes in disability policy has sought to remove barriers to work for people receiving Social Security Disability Insurance (SSDI) and Supplemental Security Income (SSI) through the Ticket to Work (TTW) program and in one-stop career services centers established under the Workforce Investment Act (WIA) of 1998. New pressures were placed on the abilities of rehabilitation counselors to respond to their primary responsibilities to their own clients while at the same

time honoring their responsibility to the welfare of their agencies and the need to serve new populations of clients. Counselors struggle to adapt to new service models, and methods are difficult to reconcile; and many issues are far from resolved and await the process of experience-based refinements of policies and procedures. Such periods of change are stressful for counselors, clients, and all agency personnel. Using the example of the TTW initiative, a number of potentially ethically troublesome issues must be discussed and resolved (see Figure 17–1 for examples of some potential TTW dilemmas for discussion).

In addition to the other value issues that confront all counselors, RCs will be required to lead the professions in interpreting and supporting work-related values in collaboration with their clients.

Counselor Competence.   The work of rehabilitation counselors is extremely diverse, presenting counselors with many challenges to stay competent in the range of skills practiced and to add new skills in areas of evolving practice. It is an ethical requirement of rehabilitation counselors that they continuously monitor their levels of competency and practice only within the limits of their own individual scopes of practice (see Appendix U). One new challenge to evaluating one's individual scope of practice is presented by the increasing involvement of rehabilitation counselors in psychiatric rehabilitation, mental health, and substance abuse counseling areas where diagnosis of mental disorders, is a prominent responsibility. The revised Code of Professional Ethics for Rehabilitation Counselors has a new section that establishes ethical standards for rehabilitation counselors to provide proper diagnosis of mental disorders. In addition, extensive standards address evaluation, assessment, and interpretation of various tests and psychometric instruments.

For some rehabilitation counselors, the issue of adopting a medically based diagnostic paradigm has profound, troubling implications for the long-valued, asset-focused, nonstigmatizing rehabilitation model that centered on functional assessment and not diagnosis of medical problems or pathologies as a basis for treatment. Other rehabilitation counselors do not find the task of reconciling a medical diagnostic framework as a background to functionally based treatment strategies to be problematic. The psychiatric rehabilitation model developed by Anthony, Cohen, Farkas and Gagne (2002) is an example of such a model. The model builds from a medical rehabilitation model used with physical disabilities and allows for medical diagnosis; yet, it emphasizes rehabilitation intervention using a behaviorally oriented, highly supportive, client-directed, and positive model. Additionally, this model has embraced the powerful recovery model that emphasizes transcending the mental illness by identifying meaning and purpose as well as taking charge of one's life (Anthony, 1993).

Rehabilitation counselor educators and CORE should consider the increased demand for diagnostic and treatment planning competency on the part of their graduates in the revision of their curricula and standards. Similarly, individual practitioners wishing to gain or increase these competencies must carefully

create individualized professional development plans that ethically and completely prepare them through such added experiences as coursework, continuing education workshops, and expertly supervised practice.

CASE SCENARIO 17–3

Can I Diagnose?

Sophie is a rehabilitation counselor who graduated 2 years ago from an excellent rehabilitation counselor education program that allowed her to specialize in psychiatric rehabilitation. Since graduation, she has been working in a psychiatric rehabilitation agency that provides a wide range of mental health and rehabilitation services for people with severe and long-term psychiatric disabilities; she found it to be a highly professional environment in which to practice. Recently, the agency was purchased by a larger institution and Sophie was assigned to a new supervisor, Mike. Mike tells her that she will have to begin assessing and diagnosing the new clients who come to the agency, rather than referring clients out for evaluations to establish a diagnosis. The clients' records are reviewed once every 3 months by the consulting psychiatrist, but Sophie is very concerned that this cursory review will not provide sufficient oversight to her fledgling diagnostic attempts. She is worried that this might be unethical and is also concerned about rumors that indicate those who are not "on board" with the new requirements will be fired. Is it unethical for Sophie to begin doing diagnostic evaluations?

PROBABLY. Given the limited information provided, Sophie is not likely to be capable of independently determining psychiatric diagnoses. She may, however, have a reasonable start in learning this skin. The code of ethics does allow for properly prepared individuals to do so with proper care. However, the difficulty is determining what is proper preparation in this area—very little consensus exists. First, counselors need to determine if mental health counselors are licensed in their particular state and the basic requirements for that license, and then actually work toward achieving those requirements. Generally, in addition to a strong basic preparation as a counselor, such credentials require specific courses in psychopathology and specialized assessment as well as diagnosis and treatment planning at a minimum. Beyond that coursework, supervised practice under a properly credentialed, experienced diagnostician is critical. In most states, that is the equivalent of at least 2, if not 3, years of supervised practice. Obviously, supervised practice in diagnostics with diverse types of client conditions is essential. Sophie should contact the state licensure board to gather this basic information and form a professional development plan in consultation with Mike, her supervisor, to permit her to gain this expertise in an appropriate manner.

Sophie is delighted to discover that she had the required courses during her master's education, but she lacks the supervised experience needed for licensure and to do diagnoses. Mike may be willing to provide her with some access to proper supervision, but he states that the agency cannot afford to provide the extensive supervision required. Sophie agrees to contract with a consulting supervisor, an appropriately credentialed psychologist, who is acceptable to her and to the agency to provide the remaining necessary supervision hours. Mike agrees to allow Sophie to see this supervisor on agency time. Although Sophie will have to pay this consultant and ensure that her clients give proper release of information for this consultation, she thinks this investment is well worthwhile to allow her to grow in her professional skills and to learn how to properly assess and diagnose her clients. If some type of satisfactory arrangement had not been reached, and Sophie had still been pressured to diagnose her new clients, she should have considered leaving that position in the agency or even leaving the agency altogether.

The 2001 ethics code for rehabilitation counselors also emphasized new standards for evaluation, assessment, and interpretation of various psychometric instruments. At present, the most authoritative set of guidelines for test users is probably the Standards for Educational and Psychological Testing (AERA, APA, NCME, 1999). Counselors should review and seek to conform to these qualification requirements for any and all tests they utilize in their practices. The CRCC (2001) code of ethics has specific and detailed requirements concerning the ethical obligations of its members in observing the competence standards for the use of these instruments and techniques. In addition, rehabilitation counselors must be knowledgeable of guidelines for the use and release of test data and be aware of relevant federal and state statutes and rules and regulations that relate to release of test data (Blackwell, Autry, & Guglielmo, 2001). For additional discussion of testing in career counseling, see Chapter 15.

CODE COMPARISONS

The ethical practices of rehabilitation counselors are governed by the codes of the organizations to which they belong. However, in rehabilitation counseling, the professional organizations have provided a unified code of ethics through the endorsement by ARCA, NRCA, and CRCC of one code of ethics for all rehabilitation counselors. Of course, rehabilitation counselors who are ARCA members also are subject to enforcement of ethics through ACA, its parent organization. NRCA and ARCA do not provide disciplinary processes to enforce the rehabilitation counseling code within their organizations.

The CRCC does provide active enforcement of the code for all rehabilitation counselors who hold the C.R.C. certification. The CRCC also provides advisory opinions to certificants regarding general ethical concerns to improve ethical practices and assist them in proactively avoiding ethical problems. Saunders, Rudman, and Dew (In review) did a descriptive study of ethics cases adjudicated by CRCC between 1994 and 2004. They found that in the 50 rule violations that were adjudicated, the rules that were most frequently violated were rules that rehabilitation counselors will: obey the laws and statues where they practice ($n = 9$; 18%); not be dishonest or deceitful ($n = 7$; 14%); avoid exploiting clients, student, and subordinates ($n = 7$; 14%); not allow personal problems to lead to inadequate performance ($n = 4$; 8%); maintain moral and ethical standards of behavior ($n = 3$; 6%); and work with their clients in obtaining appropriate potential employment opportunities ($n = 3$; 6%).

In early 1999, CRCC established an Ethics Taskforce to officially examine, review, and update the CRCC Code of Professional Ethics for Rehabilitation Counselors (Tarvydas & Cottone, 2000). The taskforce was directed to consider the core standards from the counseling profession as embodied by the ACA Code of Ethics and Standards of Practice and to develop supplemental standards specifically related to rehabilitation counseling. The rationale for this charge is related directly to the need to: (a). consolidate ethical standards; (b) avoid duplication and inconsistencies; and (c) directly relate the CRCC standards to the general counseling code used as an example or model by other credentialing bodies, such as state licensure boards and other certification agencies. This approach is also informed by analysis of the Scope of Practice for Rehabilitation Counseling (CRCC, 1994). The Scope of Practice reflects an understanding that "the field of rehabilitation counseling is a specialty within the rehabilitation profession with counseling at its core, and is differentiated from other related counseling fields" (CRCC, 1994, p. 1); as such, it is part of the profession of counseling.

The CRCC Ethics Committee undertook an additional analysis of the rehabilitation counseling code during its 1996–1997 work year to review and supplement the ARCA analysis undertaken by the ARCA Ethical Standards Committee in 1994. The committee reviewed ethics literature and the issues raised within the committee during its processing of ethical complaints. Special note was taken of the particular need to provide more emphasis on addressing diversity and multicultural issues, dealing with business and financial issues in practice, client privacy and confidentiality rights, potentially detrimental relationships and relationship boundary issues, among other important areas, and preserving the specific disability-related issues and unique rehabilitation features needed by rehabilitation counselors. The initial draft of the code was refined by the Ethics Committee, underwent a year of public comment and review, was finally adopted in June 2001, and became effective January 1, 2002.

The 2001 code included new standards in a number of areas including sexual intimacies with former clients; dealing with clients who have contagious, fatal diseases; confidentiality issues and other obligations in working with groups and families; expanded consideration of advertising and soliciting clients; sexual harassment; proper diagnosis of mental disorders; expanded considerations for teaching, training, and supervision; use of fees and bartering; importance of ethics consultation; and unwarranted ethics complaints. The 2001 code also was the first ethics code to abandon the term "dual relationship" in favor of the clearer terminology "non-professional relationship" (Cottone, 2005). Two other major changes are the infusion of a major emphasis on multicultural considerations and the addition of an entire section on electronic communication and emerging applications, including computers and internet services. Many of these new areas were a result of the influence of the ACA Code of Ethics and place rehabilitation counseling practitioners in a consistent posture with the mainstream of counseling. However, there remained a number of unique rehabilitation counseling practices that are integral to its specialized requirements, including emphasis on client advocacy and concerns with accessibility; responsibilities in relationships to rehabilitation team members and employers of clients; issues of diminished client autonomy; provision of indirect services; responsibilities to ensure clients that assistants are instructed about client rights to confidentiality; and assurance of confidentiality in alternative communications means. See the edition of the *Journal of Applied Rehabilitation Counseling* for further discussion of code elements (Shaw & Tarvydas, 2001). In this exhaustive process, the Code of Professional Ethics for Rehabilitation Counselors achieved the desired balance of adopting the ethical standards of the general profession of counseling while still retaining the specialized elements of its ethical traditions that are necessary to serve rehabilitation counselors in this unique area of counseling practice. Interestingly, during the recent revision process of the 2005 ACA

Code of Ethics, several of the features unique to the rehabilitation counseling standards were included in the new ACA code. For example, the requirement that counselors gain the assent of clients incapable of giving legal consent to services, provide a qualified interpreter so clients can understand services, and focus attention to their ethical responsibilities in interdisciplinary team work are all similar to those requirements in the rehabilitation counseling code, thus demonstrating the positive synergy between related codes of ethics.

ISSUES OF DIVERSITY

Rehabilitation counseling continues to struggle with the question of how to respond to the widespread movement in society and the professions to build its practice on a foundation of multicultural awareness, knowledge, and competencies. This focus has been prominent in all the helping professions, yet had been slower in developing in rehabilitation counseling. This situation is ironic—rehabilitation counseling is a profession that is heavily invested in a specific, inclusive philosophy. It is based historically on the core rehabilitation, philosophical assumptions of valuing human differences and the basic dignity and worth of all persons. Rehabilitation counselors always have been keenly aware of the difficulties that politically oppressed and socially stigmatized individuals face in having the opportunity to participate fully in their communities and have their basic human needs met. Therefore, it seems ironic that the field's scholars and practitioners were not at the forefront of explicitly incorporating multiculturalism into its professional literature, practice, and standards. The answer may lie partially in this fact—rehabilitation counselors have adopted an explicit, general value system that honors human diversity and are aware of the problems presented by social, vocational, economic, and political barriers to those who are not understood or those who are devalued. This groundwork may have been seen as automatically translating into appropriate competencies and adequate service when rehabilitation counselors serve others from ethnically or racially diverse groups. In more recent years, greater awareness of the more particular needs of people from racially, culturally, or other types of diverse backgrounds has led to serious attempts to infuse a more explicit attention to multicultural issues within rehabilitation practice. The common foundations of the civil rights of persons with disability in the civil rights movement of the 1960s, and the subsequent development of affirmative action, cultural diversity, and disability policy reform, are traced by Middleton, Harley, Rollins, and Solomon (1998). Based on their analysis of these forces, they made the following recommendations:

1. Explore alternative ways to enable the ACA to have a positive impact on racial and ethnic minority populations with disability.
2. Implementation should dominate outcomes. Local choices about how to put a policy into practice should be encouraged as it will have more significance for policy outcomes.
3. Reforms or policies that engage the natural networks of the rehabilitation can support change efforts in a more sustained fashion.
4. Competence matters as much as process. Policies and reforms intending to promote more effective rehabilitation practice must address both and acknowledge that working with multicultural populations requires a specific set of competencies (Middleton et al., 1998, p. 16).

The challenge has been to meet these needs in a serious manner without detracting from the needs of people with disabilities—who come from all of these multicultural backgrounds. Unfortunately, in the contemporary politicoeconomic framework, disadvantaged populations of all types are often pitted against each other for the attention and resources they need.

The growing emphasis on multicultural aspects of practice has also extended to the critique of rehabilitation counseling's core professional institutions and standards. Rehabilitation counseling has lagged behind fields such as counseling psychology and counseling in its attention to infusing multicultural issues into its practice and standards, as noted in earlier rehabilitation literature on multicultural issues and discussed by McGinn, Flowers, and Rubin (1994). When comparing this literature to that of counseling psychology, they found less emphasis had been placed on multiculturalism and the need to incorporate these knowledge and competency elements into services to ethnic minorities. McGinn et al. subsequently turned their attention to analysis of the then-current Code of Professional Ethics for Rehabilitation Counselors and found it seriously lacking. This lack has serious implications in that "by omission, however, the Code may encourage unethical behavior with culturally diverse populations" (Middleton et al., 2000). The obvious conclusion is that: "Although the authors of the Code of Professional Ethics for Rehabilitation Counselors deserve tremendous

credit for their work, the absence of a multicultural perspective in the code suggests a need for modification of the document" (McGinn et al., pp. 264, 266).

In response to this need, the CRCC Ethics Taskforce and Ethics Committee placed more emphasis on diversity and multicultural standards in the revision process that led to the current code of ethics (Tarvydas & Cottone, 2000). The specific mention of multicultural issues is infused in several places throughout the code. However, this focus is heralded early in the code with an entire section on respecting diversity. Among other things, it calls on rehabilitation counselors to "develop and adapt interventions and services to incorporate consideration of clients" cultural perspectives and recognition of barriers external to clients that may interfere with achieving effective rehabilitation outcomes" (CRCC, 2001, p. 1). Types of diversity directly mentioned in the code now include age, color, culture, disability, ethnic group, gender, race, religion, sexual orientation, marital status, and socioeconomic status. Attention to the needs of culturally diverse populations is also explicitly required by the standards in test selection, scoring, and interpretation. Examples of areas of multicultural emphasis in other ethical obligations noted in the code include enhancing diversity and sensitivity to the diversity issues in rehabilitation counselor education and training programs and research and scholarly publications. Nonetheless, it is hoped that these newly revised ethical standards will assist rehabilitation counseling in better fulfilling its obligations to the increasingly diverse and multicultural population of rehabilitation clients it serves.

DECISION MAKING IN CONTEXT

Historically, the practice of rehabilitation counseling began in government agencies with the constraints and assets that are present in large bureaucratic settings. The ethical obligations of rehabilitation counselors who serve their clients in such present-day public agencies with public funds can involve a delicate balancing act, especially during times of scarce resources and declining funding. The rehabilitation counselor is often involved in situations that involve responding to legislative mandates, agency policies, and procedures while balancing the requirements of their professional ethical standards to hold the interests of their clients foremost and to advocate for their clients' well-being. Although contemporary rehabilitation counselors work in diverse types of settings of all types, the experience of those working in governmental settings still presents a fascinating introduction to the balancing act many counselors play in dealing with conflicting agency–client interests.

Consider the situation of rehabilitation counselor Iva Wish, who works at the Everystate Vocational Rehabilitation Services (VRS) agency serving 218 consumers on her caseload. When state-federal funds are not sufficient to serve all clients of the agency, federal law requires all new clients who are not most severely disabled to be placed on a waiting list for services. These clients on the waiting list will be served after the most severely disabled clients have been served, or when increased funding permits clients with less severe disabilities to be served as well. Iva has dreaded this moment, but it has come. Her state legislature has not authorized enough funding to service all clients with the federal matching fund, and her supervisor, Mr. Bythebook, has notified her that Everystate VRS will now be using the waiting list system and serving only the most severely disabled clients. In talking to Mr. Bythebook, Iva and he have agreed that there is really no chance that the clients being placed on the waiting list will receive services this year, and probably not for the next 3 years. Iva and her colleagues have received extensive training and have a great deal of experience in how to evaluate clients to determine how severe their disabilities are and assign them to the most appropriate severity of disability category. They all realize that, for some clients' situations, there are substantial aspects of this process that require their professional judgment and can require a great deal of personal discretion. Iva spends many months making an earnest attempt to fairly apply the criteria to mounting stories of the disastrous results in clients' lives of spending extended time on the waiting list—essentially frozen in time while they wait for a chance to have rehabilitation services that may not come. Meanwhile, Mr. Bythebook requires the counselors to tell the clients on the waiting list that they hope to serve them "soon," so that the clients do not become so frustrated that they begin complaining to their congressional representatives and others. Iva has become increasingly disheartened and disturbed that she in participating in a dishonest enterprise that does not conform to her ethical obligations to her individual clients. Then she meets with Rodney, a young man who has a moderate traumatic brain injury. Rodney has just proudly graduated from high school after much struggle, and he is quite excited about trying to begin working. Iva realizes he probably will not be rated as most severely disabled. As a result, she is concerned that he will become

increasingly discouraged and depressed on the waiting list, as well as losing all the behavioral and memory improvements he has fought so hard to gain during his recent intense school and rehabilitation programs. She must decide if she should "tip the scale" for Rodney and classify him as most severely disabled. What should she do?

By consulting the Social Constructivist model, Iva reflects on the social systems that are involved in this situation. She has always taken seriously the importance of the social consensus that was necessary to create and continually fund the state-federal vocational rehabilitation (VR) system for almost the last 90 years. Mr. Bythebook has frequently emphasized the public trust that has been placed in the VR system to use the funds allotted for the greater good of all needing services. Both he and Iva have known that when the legislature considered procedures to handle times of insufficient funding, the model of justice they adopted in the law was that citizens with disabilities would be served according to their level of need for services rather than in some other manner, such as providing services on a first come, first served basis. However, she also feels responsibility to Rodney individually through the relationship they have formed, and this seems more pressing to her ethically than the abstract group of all clients who need services or all citizens as represented through their legislators. She thinks she may just declare him most severely disabled and hope no one discovers her strategy. After many sleepless nights, Iva realizes that she also has another system to which she is accountable, the agency that hired her, trained her, and counts on her to abide by its rules as provided in the policies and procedures. This relationship is embodied through Mr. Bythebook, and she realizes she "owes it to him" to consult with him regarding her quandary about Rodney. She also realizes she needs to talk to Rodney to get his viewpoint on the situation and its potential effects on him. Finally, she realizes that she could refer Rodney for an evaluation by an expert neuropsychologist who might provide some guidance about how Rodney might be affected and what prevocational activities he might undertake while he waits for services to better prepare him for receiving vocation services. The next morning she consults with Mr. Bythebook to get his interpretation of Rodney's specific situation. He encourages her to follow through on her plan to see where these ideas may lead her. She then calls Rodney and asks him to come in to see her for further discussion and to plan for the neuropsychological evaluation. Thus she has decided to employ several of the components of the Social Constructivist model in obtaining information from those involved, thinking about the nature of the relationships involved in this dilemma to see if there are really conflicting or adversarial opinions, and consulting colleagues or experts for their council and interpretation. This process has the potential for building a social consensus to support negotiating an appropriate solution for Rodney that might serve his needs even if he does spend time on the waiting list.

In the Tarvydas Integrative Model, the process of determining the stakeholders in Stage I also would involve Iva in considering Rodney's interests in relationship to those of the other clients in the agency and society as a whole. In the Stage I fact-finding phase, she may also have placed an emphasis on collecting more information from the family and his school and treatment records to assess the severity of his behavioral and memory problems. She may also have referred him to a neuropsychologist to increase her knowledge of the severity of his disability and potential for depression worsening it.

In Stage II, an interesting aspect involves the application of the ethical principles. Situations involving scarce resources press us to consider issues of distributive justice—by which definition of justice do we distribute these resources when they are limited? Should it be equal shares to all, each according to need, some measure of the person's merit, or some other model? Whereas the legislation does use the "to each according to need" model, Iva's perception is that this stance is not really consistent with the consensus of the people in her community. It seems to her that because, traditionally, people were served in the order they became eligible when resources were not scare, that this has become the expectation and norm of the community. To her, it seems wise to continue this practice. Additionally in Stage II, she reviews the profession's ethical standards that call her both to hold her client's interests as primary and to advocate for her client's appropriate needs. Although she does realize that the code calls on her to abide by the policies of her employer, she does not think that this outweighs the other ethical requirements in this case. At the end of Stage II, therefore, she decides to declare Rodney most severely disabled and eligible for immediate services.

In Stage III, as Iva stops to reflect on her personal biases and the contextual factors, she begins to reconsider her thinking. Although she still questions the wisdom of the legislative waiting list criteria, she notes that she has a powerful need to be liked by her clients

and that this leads her to enjoy "rescuing" by crusading on their behalf so they will be forever grateful to her. She has had a real problem saying "no" to any clients, even at times when she should have for their own good. In terms of the contextual levels, at the team level she also realizes that her colleagues have all had their own struggles with this policy. They would seriously object to her lack of willingness to help them enforce the rules consistently, even when they disappoint clients. They would also say that by taking more resources for her less disabled clients, she was making them look bad and being unfair to their most severely disabled clients. Finally, her supervisor would definitely have difficulty with her actions because he has strong beliefs in being consistent in using resources. He also has concerns that the central office will begin receiving charges of unfair practices from people on the waiting list if they hear of others who received services before them who were less severely disabled than they. As a result, Iva decides to place Rodney on the waiting list and to help him develop some prevocational activities and plans to pursue while he is waiting to be served by VRS. In Stage IV, she moves decisively to form a specific plan and to involve the team members and Mr. Bythebook through consultation to ensure that she maximizes the referrals she is able to make for Rodney to access community resources while he is on the waiting list.

CHAPTER SUMMARY

The counseling specialty of rehabilitation counseling is historically embedded in the vocational guidance, rehabilitation, and counseling movements. It has evolved in response to the specialized needs of its clients and settings of choice. Rehabilitation counseling continues to experience dynamic changes in the ethical and professional issues facing it, as do other counseling specialties. These issues have been better addressed in the 2001 CRCC Code of Professional Ethics for Rehabilitation Counselors. Rehabilitation counseling has been complex in its evolution and influenced by counseling and rehabilitation-based knowledge and skills, as well as developing a strong emphasis on the function of case management. Rehabilitation counseling's scope of practice and the ethical standards reflect these various elements, as do the activities of its professional organizations. Recent developments in the relationship of these organizations include the consolidation around core standards shared with the counseling profession supplemented by foci that are rehabilitation specific.

The ethical issues that are commonly addressed by rehabilitation counselors include confidentiality and privileged communication, informed consent, potentially detrimental counselor–client relationships, responsibility, values, and counselor competence. The changes to the 2001 ethical standards stress greater awareness and emphasis on multicultural perspectives to supplement the traditional emphasis on disability and diversity.

INTERNET RESOURCES

Students wishing to find out more about the ethical issues prominent in rehabilitation counseling may wish to use the following terms to search the internet: advocacy, assent, consumer choice, empowerment, guardianship, informed choice, normalization, paternalism, and substitute decision making.

REFERENCES

American Counseling Association. (2003, June). Rehabilitation and parity. *Counseling Today*, p. 31.

American Counseling Association. (2005). Licensure chart—Requirements for mental health counselor credentials. (On-line). Retrieved August 20, 2005 From http://www.counseling.org//Content/NavigationMenu/JOINRENEW/STATELICENSURECERTIFICATIONDETAILECHART/Licensure_Chart.htm.

American Educational Research Association, American Psychological Association, National Council on Measurement in Education. (1999). *Standards for educational and psychological testing.* Washington, DC: American Educational Research Association.

Anderson, J. R., & Barret, B. (Eds.). (2001). *Ethics in HIV-related psychotherapy: Clinical decision making in complex cases.* Washington, DC: American Psychological Association.

Anthony, W. A. (1993). Recovery from mental illness: The guiding vision of the mental health service system in the 1990s. *Psychosocial Rehabilitation Journal, 16*(4), 11–23.

Anthony, W., Cohen, M., Farkas, M., & Gagne, C. (2002). *Psychiatric rehabilitation* (2nd ed.). Boston: Center for Psychiatric Rehabilitation.

Blackwell, T. L., Autry, T. L., & Guglielmo, D. E. (2001). Ethical issues in disclosure of test data. *Rehabilitation Counseling Bulletin, 44*, 161–169.

Blackwell, T. L., Martin, W. E., & Scalia, V. A. (1994). *Ethics in rehabilitation.* Athens, GA: Elliott & Fitzpatrick.

Bureau of Labor Statistics. (2004). *Counselors.* Retrieved August 23, 2005 from http://bls.gov.coc/ocos067.htm.

Commission on Rehabilitation Counselor Certification (CRCC). (1994). *CRCC certification guide.* Rolling Meadows, IL: Author.

Commission on Rehabilitation Counselor Certification (CRCC). (2001). *Code of professional ethics for rehabilitation counselors.* Rolling Meadows, IL: Author.

Cottone, R. R. (2005). Detrimental therapist-client relationships—Beyond thinking of "dual" or "multiple" roles: Reflections on the 2001 AAMFT Code of Ethics. *The American Journal of Family Therapy, 33*, 1–17.

Council on Rehabilitation Education. (2004). *Profile of CORE-accredited programs.* (On-line). Retrieved August 22, 2005 from http://www.core-rehab.org.

Gatens-Robinson, E., & Tarvydas, V. (1992). Ethics of care, women's perspectives and the status of the mainstream rehabilitation analysis. *Journal of Applied Rehabilitation Counseling, 23*, 26–33.

Greenspan, S., & Love, P. (1995). Ethical challenges in supporting persons with disabilities. In O. C. Karan & S. Greenspan (Eds.), *Community rehabilitation services for people with disabilities* (pp. 71–89). Boston: Butterworth-Heinemann.

Haffey, W. J. (1989). The assessment of clinical competency to consent to medical rehabilitation interventions. *Journal of Head Trauma Rehabilitation, 4*, 43–56.

Havranek, J. E. (1997). Ethical issues in forensic rehabilitation. *Journal of Applied Rehabilitation Counseling, 28*, 11–16.

Knapp, S. E., & Slattery, J. M. (2004). Professional boundaries in non-traditional settings. *Professional Psychology, 35*(5), 553–558.

Leahy, M. J. (1997). Qualified providers of rehabilitation counseling services. In D. R. Maki & T. F. Riggar (Eds.), *Rehabilitation counseling: Profession and practice* (pp. 95–110). New York: Springer.

Leahy, M. J., & Holt, E. (1993). Certification in rehabilitation counseling: History and process. *Rehabilitation Counseling Bulletin, 37*, 71–80.

Leahy, M. J., & Szymanski, E. M. (1995). Rehabilitation counseling: Evolution and current status. *Journal of Counseling & Development, 74*, 163–166.

Leahy, M. J., & Tarvydas, V. M. (2001). Transforming our professional organizations: A first step toward the unification of the rehabilitation counseling profession. *Journal of Applied Rehabilitation Counseling, 32*, 3–8.

McGinn, F., Flowers, C. R., & Rubin, S. E. (1994). In quest of an explicit multicultural emphasis in ethical standards for rehabilitation counselors. *Rehabilitation Education, 7*, 261–268.

Middleton, R. A., Harley, D. A., Rollins, C. W., & Solomon, T. (1998). Affirmative action, cultural diversity, and disability policy reform: Foundations to the civil rights of persons with disability. *Journal for Applied Rehabilitation Counseling, 29*(3), 9–18.

Middleton, R. A., Rollins, C. W., Sanderson, P. L., Leung, P., Harley, D. A., Ebener, D., et al. (2000). Endorsement of professional multicultural rehabilitation competencies and standards: A call to action. *Rehabilitation Counseling Bulletin, 43*, 219–240.

Patterson, J. B., & Settles, R. (1992). The ethics education of certified rehabilitation counselors. *Rehabilitation Education, 6*, 179–184.

Patterson, J. B., Patrick, A., & Parker, R. M. (2000). Choice: Ethical and legal rehabilitation challenges. *Rehabilitation Counseling Bulletin, 43*, 203–208.

Rehabilitation Act Amendments of 1998, 29 U.S.C. §2801 et seq.

Rehabilitation Counseling Consortium. (2004). *Recommendation to form the Rehabilitation Counseling Consortium.* Arlington Heights, IL: Author.

Rubin, S. E., & Roessler, R. T. (2001). *Foundations of the vocational rehabilitation process* (5th ed.). Austin, TX: Pro-Ed.

Salomone, P. R. (1996). Career counseling and job placement: Theory and practice. In E. M. Szymanski & R. M. Parker (Eds.), *Work and disability: Issues and strategies in career development and job placement* (pp. 365–420). Austin, TX: Pro-Ed.

Saunders, J. L., Rudman, R., & Dew, D. (In review). *Ethical complaints and violations in rehabilitation counseling over the past decade: An analysis of Commission on Rehabilitation Counselor Certification data.*

Shaw, L. R., & Tarvydas, V. M. (Eds.). (2001). Special issue—Ethics. *Journal of Applied Rehabilitation, 32*(4), 3–37.

Stebnicki, M. A. (1997, October/November/ December). A conceptual framework for utilizing a functional assessment approach for determining mental capacity: A new look at informed consent in rehabilitation. *Journal of Rehabilitation, 41,* 32–37.

Stebnicki, M. A. (1999). Ethical dilemmas in adult guardianship and substitute decision making. *Journal of Rehabilitation, 43,* 23–27.

Strein, W., & Hershenson, D. (1991). Confidentiality in nondyadic counseling situations. *Journal of Counseling & Development, 69,* 312–316.

Szymanski, E. M. (1985). Rehabilitation counseling: A profession with a vision, an identity, and a future (Presidential address). *Rehabilitation Counseling Bulletin, 29*(1), 2–5.

Tarvydas, V. M., & Cottone, R. R. (2000). The code of ethics for rehabilitation counselors: What we have and what we need. *Rehabilitation Counseling Bulletin, 43,* 188–196.

Tarvydas, V. M., & Leahy, M. J. (1993). Licensure in rehabilitation counseling: A critical incident in professionalization. *Rehabilitation Counseling Bulletin, 37,* 92–108.

Tarvydas, V. M., Leahy, M., Saunders, J., Thielsen, V., Murray, G., & Chan, F. (2001). Beliefs about the ethics of practice among rehabilitation counselors: A national survey. *Journal of Applied Rehabilitation Counseling, 32*(2), 9–18.

Toriello, P. J., & Leierer, S. J. (2004). Predictors of counselors' support for the autonomy of clients with substance abuse issues. *Rehabilitation Education, 18,* 211–222.

Vash, C. (1987). Canon 3—Client advocacy: Fighting another's battles: Is it helpful? Professional? Ethical? *Journal of Applied Rehabilitation Counseling, 18,* 15–17.

CHAPTER 18

Addiction Counseling

Ronald E. Claus • Susan McGuire

OBJECTIVES

After reading this chapter, you should be able to:

- Define the scope of practice of addiction counseling.
- Describe the typical client served by addiction counselors.
- Identify critical professional and ethical issues specific to addiction counseling.

- Identify relevant codes of ethics and compare them.
- Discuss diversity and multicultural issues specific to addiction counseling.
- Apply a decision-making process to an ethical dilemma in addiction counseling.

INTRODUCTION

Addiction counselors serve individuals who abuse or are dependent upon alcohol or other drugs and may also assist individuals who display other compulsive behaviors. Addictive behavior can seriously disrupt the physiological, psychological, and social functioning of the affected individual. In most cases, individuals seek services because a physical addiction or pattern of addictive behavior has caused significant physical, social, or legal consequences. Addiction is the number one public health issue in the United States today. According the Substance Abuse and Mental Health Services Administration (SAMHSA) of the U. S. DHHS, approximately 22.2 million people aged 12 and older needed treatment for an alcohol or illicit drug problem in 2003 (Office of Applied Studies, 2004). Of these 22.2 million people—nearly 10% of the U.S. population—only about 1.2 million received treatment for their addiction problem. Although this chapter acknowledges the broad range of addictive behaviors, it focuses on substance abuse, which is broadly defined here to include diagnoses of the abuse or dependence of alcohol or other mood-altering drugs.

DEFINING THE SPECIALTY, SETTING, AND CLIENTS

Addiction counselors usually work in clinical settings and may work in private practice. In recognition of this counseling specialization, the ACA has an affiliate group, the International Association of Addictions and Offender Counselors (IAAOC), which operates under the ACA ethics code. Two divisions of the APA provide a valuable resource for the addiction counselor, although neither division promulgates an ethical code for addiction counselors. Division 50 (Addictions) promotes advances in training, clinical practice, and research on alcohol, nicotine, and other drugs, as well as a broad range of other addictive behaviors. Division 28

(Pharmacology and Substance Abuse) promotes teaching, research, and dissemination of information regarding the effects of drugs on behavior.

Setting

Substance abuse treatment may be delivered in hospital, residential, or outpatient settings. Hospital-based treatment initially attempts to detoxify the individual who is physically addicted and may suffer withdrawal symptoms. At the detoxification stage, physicians and nurses are involved to oversee the individual's physical response to the cessation of substance use. Medications may ease the discomfort associated with the withdrawal syndrome. Initial detoxification may take from 2 to 4 (or in some cases more) days under close medical oversight. Psychologists or psychiatrists may become involved to assess the mental status of the individual and to make a diagnosis. After detoxification, hospital and residential programs address psychological and social issues.

Psychosocial treatment may be provided by counselors, social workers, case managers, and family counselors. Generally, counselors provide individual counseling, group counseling, and psychoeducation related to substance abuse and other problem areas. Social workers or case managers may provide group treatment and arrange for additional services (e.g., a referral for vocational rehabilitation services or housing assistance). Family counselors may offer couples or family counseling that addresses the relationship problems that are often associated with addiction. However, the substance abuse counselor is often viewed as the front-line professional in providing counseling for individuals in treatment programs.

Outpatient treatment has become the most commonly delivered level of care, as hospital and residential treatment stays have been increasingly limited in the past decade. Clients may begin a substance abuse treatment episode in an outpatient program or may transition to outpatient care after completing a more intensive level of care (e.g., hospitalization). Outpatient treatment is offered at different levels of intensity, ranging from day treatment programs (often 20 hours per week or more) to 1-hour individual or group sessions that occur weekly. These services, intended to help clients adopt and maintain a substance-free lifestyle, generally consist of individual counseling, group therapy, and psychoeducational groups. Case management and family counseling are often available in outpatient programs. Finally, clients may be referred to mutual

help groups, including Alcoholics Anonymous (AA) and Narcotics Anonymous (NA). These self-help fellowships, run by their members, provide an ongoing source of social support for recovery during and after formal addiction treatment.

Addiction counseling is delivered along a continuum of treatment intensities, and many clients are best served by receiving treatment that is stepped from more intensive to less intensive levels of care. The American Society of Addiction Medicine (ASAM) Patient Placement Criteria are the most widely used and comprehensive national clinical guidelines for admission, continued stay, and discharge from treatment. ASAM guidelines, established for adults and adolescents, determine the appropriate level of care based on the potential for physiological "withdrawal" (a biological reaction to the cessation of substance consumption); biomedical conditions and complications; emotional, behavioral, or cognitive conditions and complications; readiness to change; relapse potential; and recovery environment. Several states have modified the ASAM criteria to better fit the needs of publicly funded clients and programs. Further, patient placement may be guided by third-party payer or managed care criteria.

Finally, some clients may benefit from specialized types of treatment. In maintenance treatment for heroin addicts, individuals are given an oral dose of methadone (or another synthetic opiate) administered to block the effects of heroin and to remove the physiological craving for opiates. This stabilized state allows an individual to break away from criminal and drug-seeking behavior, and with appropriate counseling and other social services, to become a productive member of society. Therapeutic communities (TCs) are highly structured residential programs where clients often stay for 6 to 12 months. Clients at TCs typically have relatively long histories of substance abuse problems, have been involved in serious criminal activities, and have seriously impaired social functioning. This approach uses the community as an intervention to promote resocialization into a drug-free, crime-free lifestyle. In recent years, many legally involved clients have been directed or court mandated to treatment for substance-related problems. Most states now require that individuals who are convicted of driving while intoxicated or driving under the influence of another mood-altering substance must seek treatment prior to regaining their driving privileges. The specialized outpatient education and treatment programs developed in response to these legal directives may have unique admission and discharge criteria.

Clients

Distinct criteria have been identified that define substance dependence and substance abuse. The criteria for substance dependence (American Psychiatric Association, 1994) specify a maladaptive pattern of alcohol or other drug use that leads to significant impairment or distress. Individuals receive this diagnosis when three of the following symptoms have occurred: (a) increased tolerance (needing increased amounts to feel intoxicated or get a desired effect); (b) withdrawal (a substance-specific syndrome that manifests itself in symptoms of discomfort when the addictive substance is removed) or substance use to avoid withdrawal; (c) substance taken in larger amounts or over a longer period than was intended; (d) persistent desire or unsuccessful attempts to cut down or control substance use; (e) a great deal of time spent in activities to obtain or use the substance or recover from its effects; (f) important social, occupational or recreational activities given up or reduced because of substance use; or (g) continued substance use despite knowledge of a persistent physical or psychological problem made worse by use. It is important to note that not all of these symptoms must be present for the diagnosis of alcohol or drug dependence. Further, addiction can be identified before physiological dependence develops.

Alcohol or drug abuse, considered a separate condition, is more likely in individuals who have only recently started taking a substance (American Psychiatric Association, 1994). This diagnosis is met when an individual experiences any of the following: (a) a failure to meet major role obligations at work, school, or home due to substance use; (b) recurrent substance use in situations that are physically hazardous; (c) recurrent substance-related legal problems; or (d) continued substance use despite persistent social or interpersonal problems related to the effects of the substance. Some individuals continue to have adverse social consequences related to alcohol or drug use over a long period of time without developing substance dependence.

Numerous studies have examined the course of addiction and the process of recovery. Addiction is a chronic condition, and, after the onset of dependence, substance use often escalates to more severe levels or individuals are likely to experience more severe consequences. Over time, many addicted individuals go through repeated cycles of abstinence followed by a return to substance use. This process has been described as an addiction career, which may vary widely in length, pattern, and outcome (Anglin, Hser, &

Grella, 1997; Hser, Anglin, Grella, Longshore, & Prendergast, 1997). Some researchers contend that addiction is best studied from the perspective of a natural history of a person's life, or as contextually embedded within the social conditions that are meaningful to the individual. From this perspective of addiction as a chronic condition marked by relapse, the addiction counselor sees multiple treatment episodes as part of a process of recovery rather than a series of failed efforts.

Addiction is a treatable disorder, and individuals can learn to control their condition and live productive lives. Like people with other chronic conditions such as diabetes or heart disease, people in treatment for alcohol or drug problems can learn to change their behavior. In general, the more treatment given, the better the results. Many clients will require other services as well, such as medical, family, employment, or mental health services. Studies have shown that treatment works to reduce substance use and crime committed by addicts, and that individuals who have been through treatment are more likely to be employed.

In the late 1970s, practitioners began to recognize that the presence of substance abuse in combination with mental disorders had substantial implications for treatment delivery and treatment outcomes. In recent decades, substance abuse treatment programs typically reported that 50 to 75% of their clients had co-occurring disorders, whereas mental health providers often cited proportions of 20 to 50% (Center for Substance Abuse Treatment, 2005). Addiction may precede the development of a mental illness, but individuals with mental disorders are also prone to develop substance abuse and dependence problems (Evans & Sullivan, 1990). Especially when these issues are unrecognized, individuals with co-occurring disorders often face poorer treatment outcomes, such as higher rates of alcohol or drug relapse, rehospitalization for mental illness, depression, and suicide risk (Drake, Mercer-McFadden, Mueser, McHugo, & Bond, 1998). In recent years, providers have begun to offer integrated treatment services that concurrently address substance abuse and mental health problems. An integrated approach minimizes the risk that clients bounce from one type of treatment to another or that they simply "fall through the cracks" and do not receive the treatment they need. Addiction counselors must be alert to the signs and symptoms of mental illness so that client care may be coordinated with other appropriate professionals. Further information on screening, assessment, treatment strategies, and special issues related to co-occurring disorders is widely available and should be reviewed by the addiction counselor.

ISSUES OF SIGNIFICANCE TO THE SPECIALTY

Professional Differentiation

Individuals who wish to become competent addiction counselors should gain general counseling skills and also seek specialty knowledge about addiction. Counselors providing substance abuse or other addiction treatment should be trained to the master's-degree level, and where required or available, they should meet licensure standards as professional counselors. Several professional certifications or credentials can be sought by counselors wishing to specialize in addiction treatment. One that is closely linked to a professional organization representing counseling professionals is the NBCC specialty designation of Master Addictions Counselor (MAC). This credential requires the broader certification of the sponsoring certifying board (the NCC) and, in addition, candidates must have specialty coursework or continuing education related to addictions, experience under supervision in a setting where addictions are treated, and a passing score on a specialty examination developed by the board. The MAC designation would serve a professional counselor well, identifying that individual as a highly trained counseling professional who has sought additional specialty certification (beyond general counseling criteria) in a field often staffed with individuals who are less professionally trained.

Certification in substance abuse counseling is also offered by national organizations, states, and the military. NAADAC, the Association for Addiction Professionals (formerly known as the National Association of Alcohol and Drug Abuse Counselors), is the largest organization serving addiction counselors, educators, and other health care professionals who specialize in prevention, treatment, and education. NAADAC provides education, clinical training, and professional credentials, which include the MAC, National Certified Addiction Counselor (NCAC I and NCAC II), and the Tobacco Addiction Counselor designations. The MAC offered in collaboration with NBCC, requires a master's degree in counseling or a related field; 500 hours of specific alcoholism or drug abuse counseling training; 3 years full-time supervised experience (2 years of which must be obtained after the master's degree); written verification of counselor competencies in all skill groups by a supervisor or other qualified professional; and a passing score on the nation exam for the MAC. The NCAC certifications require current state certification and also require supervised experience, demonstrated competency with clients, and demonstrated knowledge about addiction via a written examination. To receive the MAC or NCAC certifications, a counselor must also subscribe to the NAADAC Code of Ethics. Finally, most states have developed treatment program standards for addiction treatment and, in recent years, some states have begun to offer licensure for addiction specialists.

A noteworthy observation about the addiction specialty is the high rate of turnover among treatment staff relative to other fields. Recent regional and national estimates of average annual counselor turnover rates at public and private treatment providers ranged from 25%–98% (Carise, McLellan, & Gifford, 2000; Gallon, Gabriel, & Knudsen 2003; Johnson & Roman, 2002). Once they enter the addiction field, counselors tend to remain in the field, although moves from facility to facility are common (Mulvey, Hubbard, & Hayashi 2003). Further, although overall turnover rates are high, some agencies show more staff consistency than others (Johnson & Roman, 2002), suggesting that organizational factors play a role in this phenomenon (Knudsen, Johnson, & Roman, 2003). Individuals interested in addiction counseling should consider organizations that provide a work environment that supports job autonomy and creativity and rewards effective job performance.

Because many individuals who provide addiction counseling are themselves in recovery, there is a historical controversy in the field of addiction treatment related to the qualifications necessary to provide adequate treatment. In response, George (1990) and others (Center for Substance Abuse Treatment, 1998) have recommended that counselors gain specific addiction counseling competencies rather than rely only on academic credentials. Recent findings comparing the effectiveness of recovering and non-recovering counselors suggest that recovery status is not directly related to treatment outcomes. According to Culbreth (2000), clients do not generally perceive differences in treatment effectiveness related to recovery status, nor do they achieve different objective treatment outcomes with recovering counselors. Counselors in recovery may perceive addiction differently and use different treatment methods, and these differences may be relevant to the way recovering and nonrecovering counselors interact with their coworkers, supervisors, and administrators. Culbreth (2000) encouraged counselors to move beyond this historical argument to instead focus on the therapeutic relationship and the counseling process with clients in addiction treatment. To this end, the ACA and NAADAC codes admonish the counselor to place the client's welfare first and prioritize a therapeutic working environment with high standards of professional conduct.

Ethical Issues

Privacy. Conceptually related to confidentiality, privacy issues concern the rights of a client to control personal information. Ethically sensitive counselors work to ensure that information about their clients is considered private. In 2000, the U.S. DHHS released a set of privacy standards for compliance with HIPAA. In many areas, the privacy rule parallels the federal confidentiality requirements, though it also addresses additional areas, especially around business practices. In particular, the rule defines protected health information and lays out patients' rights to access, amend, restrict, and disclose this information. Substance abuse treatment programs must comply with both rules. Generally, this means that addiction counselors will follow federal confidentiality rules and should not disclose client information unless they obtain consent or identify an exception to the rule that allows a disclosure. Counselors should then make sure that the disclosure is also permissible under the Privacy Rule (Substance Abuse and Mental Health Services Administration, 2004).

Confidentiality and Privileged Communication.

Ethically sensitive treatment requires the counselor to protect clients' sensitive personal information in order to respect their autonomy. Due to the social stigma attached to addiction by many, the principle of confidentiality is integral to the ethical provision of care. Confidential communications in the area of addictions counseling is addressed by federal and state laws and regulations. The federal alcohol and other drug confidentiality law requires covered programs to strictly maintain the confidentiality of patient records and limits the release of patient information related to alcohol and drug treatment. These statutes (42 U.S.C. 290dd-2) and the accompanying regulations (42 C.F.R. Part 2) came about through Congress' recognition that safeguards on privacy serve the important purpose of encouraging people with substance abuse problems to seek and succeed at treatment. The lack of privacy could stigmatize clients in their communities and affect the success of substance abuse treatment programs. The law regulates service providers who receive federal funds directly, by way of state distribution, or by way of tax-exempt status. Any provider receiving such

funding is bound by federal confidentiality laws. In addition, state laws generally require confidential relations between individuals treated by licensed professionals. The laws are complex. Addiction counselors are encouraged to become familiar with the rules and their application and advised to take advantage of detailed information sources in order to understand the nuances of the law (e.g., see DHHS, 1994; 1996).

QUESTIONS FOR REFLECTION

Steve has been directed to enter treatment by a judge as an alternative to serving jail time for driving under the influence of alcohol. Your agency has a contract with the court to provide assessment, treatment, and referral services. As counselor, to whom are you responsible, Steve or the court? How should conflicts of interest best be decided?

Consider the degree of autonomy involved in Steve's decision to enter treatment. Is his choice voluntary, given the potential legal consequences that will follow if he declines treatment? How would you apply the concept of informed consent to Steve's case?

Elements of a Valid Consent to Release Confidential Information. In general, a counselor may disclose any information about a client when the client authorizes the disclosure by signing a valid consent form. Valid consent forms, by federal regulation, must include (a) the client's name, (b) the name of the disclosing program, (c) the name and titles of the party receiving the information, (d) the purpose of the information disclosure, narrowly described and corresponding to the information to be released, (e) a statement that the client may revoke the consent at any time, except to the extent that action has been taken in reliance on the consent, (f) a date at which the consent will expire if not revoked, (g) the signature of the client, and (h) the date the consent was signed. A consent is not considered valid unless it contains all of these elements.

QUESTIONS FOR REFLECTION

Wendy, who has been in treatment on many occasions over the past 3 years, requested residential placement and was admitted to your agency. During her first week of treatment, staff discovered that she brought alcohol into the unit and has been sneaking drinks since she was admitted. What action should the staff take? If Wendy were administratively discharged, would the agency bear any moral responsibility if she were to subsequently harm herself or others?

Federal law provides the substance abuse client protection beyond that offered by many licensure statutes on confidentiality or privileged communication. The federal confidentiality codes protect information about any client applying for or receiving services, including assessment, diagnosis, counseling, group counseling, or referral for other treatment and these codes apply to all program personnel. Disclosure does not simply refer to explicit statements about an individual's status in treatment, but also includes implicit disclosures. For instance, staff may not confirm that a particular person is a client, even if the inquirer says he or she is a family member and knows the client is attending treatment. Further, the counselor should not leave messages for a client where another person could hear the message; disclose any information by which a client's identity could be inferred; or permit the police to have access to client records without a valid court order. Information about a client protected by federal confidentiality laws may be disclosed or disseminated only with client consent. Individuals who violate the regulations are subject to a criminal penalty in the form of a fine, may be sued for unauthorized disclosure by the concerned client, and place their professional license and certification at risk.

Exceptions to the Confidentiality Rules. The general prohibition against revealing information that could identify a client does not mean that counselors may never disclose their clients' names. A counselor may disclose identifying information without indicating that a person has ever sought or received alcohol or other drug services, for instance, when a program is part of a larger organization such as a general hospital. Even without consent, client identifying information may be disclosed to medical personnel in an emergency that presents a serious threat and requires immediate medical intervention. Counselors should note that a program may not use the medical emergency rule to contact family members or the police without direct client consent.

If a client commits or threatens to commit a crime either on program grounds or against program staff anywhere, the regulations permit the program to disclose client-identifying information to the police. The law does not permit the release of other client names who may have witnessed the crime without their proper written consent. Of importance, the rule does not allow a counselor to disclose a client's confession of past crimes, unless the crime was committed on the program grounds or against program staff.

In cases of suspected child abuse or neglect, the federal rule allows a counselor to make reports to the appropriate state or local child abuse hot lines, as required by many state laws. However, without client consent or a court order, client files must be withheld from child protection agencies. Another way to avoid disclosing identifying information is to make a disclosure anonymously. For instance, if a client made a serious threat to harm another person and client consent or a court order could not feasibly be obtained, a counselor could make an anonymous phone call to the intended victim or even the police, so long as the client's status at a substance abuse program was not revealed. Counselors should be careful to follow all state laws that require confidential or privileged communication between therapists and clients.

Confidentiality and Group Therapy. An additional concern related to confidentiality and privileged communication in treatment of individuals with addictions centers on the commonly used method of group therapy. According to some state regulations, communications made in a group setting, even if a licensed professional is involved, may not be considered confidential or privileged in the classic sense of these terms. If group treatment is referenced in a licensure statute, the licensed professional is usually bound to keep group discussions confidential. However, because other group members are peers and not professionals, they are not bound by law to keep private any group discussions. Group members may talk about other group members without legal repercussion. They may also report to others, even authorities, information communicated at group meetings. Therefore, if a client confesses a crime in a group meeting, other group members could take this information to authorities, and even testify as to what was said, without legal repercussion. If a counselor is present, the counselor may be bound to confidentiality, given that group counseling is addressed by state law and that the crime does not come under an exception to the statute's confidentiality provision. Counselors may have group members sign an agreement about keeping group-disclosed information confidential, but such agreements may not be legally binding and may serve only as a promise not to discuss group information in other settings. Accordingly, group members should be informed of the limits of their privacy before they enter a group. Likewise, substance abuse clients should know that federal laws provide them extra protections if they seek treatment in a program that is obligated to honor federal confidentiality law. The intricacies of confidentiality and group counseling are described more fully in Chapter 16.

Even when a confidential relationship is formed in an individual or group context, privileged communication may not always stand. Many state laws offer the protection of privileged communication for civil court cases but not for criminal court cases. Counselors should study their state statutes closely in this regard. Counselors may be compelled to testify on criminal allegations, even if a revelation of such was made in a confidential counseling context.

CASE SCENARIO 18–1

An L.P.C. in private practice was informed by the local police that one of his patients had allegedly committed a felony. This particular client, treated in a group setting, had sought treatment to address issues associated with substance abuse problems, and, in fact, the client used his attendance in group therapy as an alibi. Police officers requested the names, addresses, and case files of all clients who attended the group session with the suspect. The counselor refused to provide this information. Did the counselor act appropriately?

YES. In an actual case (State of Missouri v. Anthony Genovese [1999]), a counselor refused to turn over the files of other group clients to authorities, which resulted in the police standing outside of the counselor's office requesting identification from anyone attempting to enter her office. The counselor immediately contacted an attorney, who filed a protest with the police department. The police did leave the entrance of the counselor's office. The counselor was then served with a subpoena to provide all group members' information to the police. Clients of counselors in the state are afforded privileged communication in civil cases, but not criminal cases. The counselor requested that her case files of clients not under investigation be considered confidential and privileged, and the court ruled in her favor. Later, when the original felony charge was tried, the counselor's records of all group members were again subpoenaed. Again, the counselor requested the court view her files as confidential and privileged communications, but this time the court ordered all group members' names, addresses, and phone numbers to be released: They were considered public information and crucial to the defendant's alibi. The counselor appealed this decision, and the court's ruling was overturned in favor of the counselor's actions.

Informed Consent.   Clients have the right to consent to counseling services, and they must be fully informed of the nature of the service, alternative treatments, the qualifications of the professionals involved, or other information that would help them make an educated decision. Informed consent with substance abuse clients is complicated by the fact that treatment services may be sought when a person is not in a condition or state to

make an informed decision. Treatment services may be needed when an individual is under the direct or recent effects of drugs or alcohol or is suffering the consequences of addictive behavior. In those cases, the counselor must ensure that the potential client is competent to make a decision about beginning treatment. An objective method of assessing competence such as a structured clinical interview, routine mental status exam, or breathalyzer test provides the best protection for vulnerable clients (McCrady & Bux, 1999). Further, procedures to maximize the comprehension of consent documents should be considered. Once a client has been treated initially (especially if detoxified), it is incumbent upon the counselor to respect the client's right to further consent to treatment or to withdraw from treatment on his or her own accord.

Mandated Treatment and Coercion.   There are numerous referrals for addictions treatment that can be considered compulsory to a greater or lesser degree. Many states mandate treatment for traffic offenders identified as substance abusers. Judges may also order treatment for other offenders before making rulings about child custody or a criminal sentence. Addiction treatment may be mandated as part of a judicial sentence or condition of parole. In these situations, it must be understood that the client—no matter how the client is referred—still has the right to refuse treatment. It is not the counselor's responsibility to persuade clients sent for compulsory treatment that they must remain in treatment. It is appropriate to explore the alternatives and possible consequences if a client chooses to prematurely terminate counseling. The counselor should then simply report to the referral source, with client consent, that the client has or has not initiated treatment or has ceased treatment. In such cases, it is important for the counselor to obtain consent when treatment begins to release information about the client's compliance with mandated treatment.

Addiction Treatment for Adolescents.   Some states make provisions for minors to receive substance abuse treatment without the consent of parents or guardians. Most often, however, states require the consent of a parent or guardian before treatment can be initiated. In these cases, parents or guardians have the right to review assessment and treatment files. In cases in which minors do not have the right to consent to their own treatment or are not provided confidentiality protection by law, they should be informed from the outset of treatment that the information they provide is subject to review by parents or legal guardians. Informed consent in addiction treatment, then, has some special circumstances that require ethical sensitivity on the part of the counselor.

Roles and Relationships with Clients. As in other counseling areas, acting in roles outside the contracted initial treatment relationship with a client may be problematic, because the counselor often holds a substantial amount of power over the client. Some relationships are clearly inappropriate and harmful to clients. For instance, most ethical codes draw firm distinctions between sexual and nonsexual relationships. The ACA and NAADAC codes prohibit an addiction counselor from having a sexual relationship with a current client. Most ethical codes and ethical standards contained in licensure statutes prohibit such contacts during active treatment and for up to 5 years after treatment has ceased. The ethical standards also mention other types of relationships, including friendship or social relations, business association, and supervision. As in other specialties, the passage of time may affect the ethical ramifications of entering or avoiding such a relationship (Doyle, 1997). In any case, counselors should not harm current or former clients in any of these relationships.

The unique relationship issues in addictions treatment are highlighted by the dilemmas faced by a professional counselor who is also in recovery from addiction. The ACA ethical standards offer general guidelines but do not include specific references to the potentially difficult situations faced by recovering counselors. The dilemmas the counselor will face include issues of confidentiality and anonymity, attending self-help groups with current or former clients, social relationships among self-help members, and employment issues (Doyle, 1997). Within 12-step groups, membership status is protected by anonymity, as detailed in Tradition Twelve of AA (1976): "Anonymity is the spiritual foundation of all our Traditions, ever reminding us to place principles over personalities" (p. 564). When a counselor acts as a client's therapist but is also a peer in a 12-step group, both the client's right to confidentiality and the counselor's anonymity are at risk. Legally, the counselor may not acknowledge in a 12-step group that a client is in treatment. A recovering counselor may see a client at a social gathering, be invited by a client to be a 12-step program "sponsor," or feel unwilling to share personal information in a meeting where a client is present. At these times, the recovering counselor must recognize the treatment needs of the client, consider the counseling relationship, and be aware of his or her own recovery needs.

QUESTION FOR REFLECTION

Danny is a recovering alcoholic with 5 years of sobriety who works as a counselor at the only treatment program in a small town. He regularly attends one of several self-help meetings in the surrounding rural area, which are also attended by many of his clients. What ethical problems does this create for Danny?

Although ethical guidelines do not speak directly to these issues, the ACA ethical code offers general information on counselor roles and relationships. The NAADAC code bars counselors from exploiting relationships with current or former clients for personal gain, including social and business relationships. The counselor can take certain steps to minimize the potential and the impact of these conflicts. Counselors should make use of clinical supervision and develop consulting relationships with professional peers. When possible, recovering counselors should take advantage of the wide range of self-help meetings and other recovery-oriented events so that the potential for dual relationships is minimized; in some communities, self-help groups are available specifically for addiction professionals (Doyle, 1997). In rural areas or with a particular population where nonprofessional roles are more difficult to avoid, treatment agencies may wish to inform clients about expectations for counselor–client interactions that occur outside of treatment (Chapman, 1997).

Responsibility. The responsibility of addiction counselors is first and foremost to their clients. Clients hold the highest priority in terms of the actions of the counselor. In addition, counselors are obligated to their employers and their profession. A counselor may face conflicting or multiple responsibilities, for instance, when clients are mandated to treatment through the legal system. In such a situation, the counselor must address the counseling needs of the clients, maintain confidentiality, and also communicate appropriately with legal representatives, who have a vested interest in a client's progress. If there is a conflict between a counselor's responsibility to a client and to a third party (such as an employer), the counselor must act to rectify the conflict. In the end, the counselor should take actions in accordance with a client's welfare.

A client's welfare is a responsibility of the treating counselor. Counselors must do their best to serve their clients, recognizing that services may not provide the intended purpose. If a counselor recognizes that a client is not benefiting from services, it is the counselor's responsibility to cease treatment and, if necessary, to refer the client to appropriate services provided by other professionals or in other treatment contexts.

Even in cases of family treatment, if an individual with addiction problems is the identified patient and has sought treatment primarily for the addiction, the counselor must advocate for the individual with the addiction. The counselor should not compromise the client's treatment progress even with the intent of serving the larger system of relationships in the family. If treatment is undertaken primarily as a means of assisting in the recovery of the addicted individual, that individual's welfare is the focus of counselor responsibility.

Values. No single treatment approach to addiction stands out as more effective than all others, though there is persuasive evidence that there are a number of different approaches that are better than no intervention (Hester & Miller, 1995; Project MATCH Research Group, 1997). Notably, each addiction treatment approach is guided by a theory or set of beliefs about the etiology and nature of alcohol and drug abuse problems. Individuals treating clients with addictions should clearly define their own values related to the use of alcohol or drugs in society.

The belief that alcohol dependence is a dispositional disease, or a condition rooted in constitutional differences between addicts and others, represents a dominant perspective in the United States since the 1960s (Hester & Miller, 1995). The defining symptom, in this view, is loss of control, or the inability to stop using alcohol once use has started. The disease is understood to be rooted in genetics and physiology, irreversible but possible to arrest through total abstinence from mood-altering substances. By this view, individuals are absolved of responsibility for their addiction and the emphasis is placed on an abnormal response to alcohol found only in certain individuals. The disease model implies that treatment should inform individuals of their condition, bring them to accept their diagnosis, and assist them in remaining abstinent for the remainder of their lives. Recovering addicts may be seen as effective in helping others, and mutual support groups are often used as an ongoing resource.

Spiritual approaches to addiction, typified by AA, are often confused with the disease model. AA itself endorses no particular theory about the etiology of alcoholism, and its writings present an openness to biological, psychological, and social influences in the development of addiction (Alcoholics Anonymous,

1976). According to this view, addiction is a seemingly hopeless condition that people are powerless to overcome on their own. The spiritual view focuses on an individual's need for assistance from a higher power and prioritizes a spiritual path to recovery. Twelve-step program beliefs focus on abstinence as the first step of a recovery process that is based on personal and spiritual growth. The 12-step approach of AA has spread worldwide and has been embraced by individuals dependent on narcotics as well as those who struggle with other addictive behaviors. As a means for individuals with alcohol problems to help others and thereby help themselves, AA itself is properly characterized as a mutual help organization rather than a treatment intervention delivered by counselors.

Many treatment models are based on or draw upon AA concepts. A growing body of evidence indicates that 12-step groups and professional interventions that encourage 12-step program involvement are effective at reducing substance abuse and preventing relapse (Humphreys, Huebsch, Finney, & Moos, 1999; Project MATCH Research Group, 1997; Tonigan, Toscova, & Miller, 1996). Some clients may initially resist attendance but later become engaged and benefit from a 12-step program (Nowinski & Baker, 1992). Other clients, however, may prefer mutual help groups with different philosophical approaches to addiction. To this end, counselors should learn about the 12 steps and 12 traditions of AA and should also investigate alternate groups such as Rational Recovery or Secular Organizations for Sobriety.

Cognitive-behavioral processes in guiding addictive behavior have gained increasing attention in recent years. Behavioral therapies view substance abuse problems as habit disorders and regard loss of control as a learned phenomenon (Marlatt & Gordon, 1985). This approach to addiction, derived from classical conditioning, operant conditioning, and social learning theory, does not exclude the role of genetics in addiction but also does not assign a central role to heritability (McCrady, 1994). Treatment may target positive expectancies or beliefs about the desirable effects of alcohol or other drugs that promote heavier and more frequent use (Brown, 1993). Relapse prevention models (e.g., Marlatt & Gordon) stress the importance of cognitive processes in bringing about or avoiding relapse. Cognitive therapies are often used to address craving and urges, mange co-occurring mood problems, and modify beliefs that promote problematic use (Hester & Miller, 1995). Although at the philosophical level there may be inconsistencies, at the level of practice, AA and behavior therapy may be integrated (McCrady).

Another issue unique to addictions treatment involves the use of specialized techniques that may cause the client some pain or discomfort. These include antidipsotropic medications, which deter the alcoholic from drinking by producing an unpleasant physical reaction if alcohol is ingested (Fuller, 1995), and other aversion therapies (Hester & Miller, 1995). These types of therapies typically produce nausea, apnea, electric shock, or unpleasant imagery. Counselors involved in such programs may experience discomfort themselves over the type of treatment being administered.

The professional counselor should thoroughly review the values inherent to these treatment approaches and weigh them against his or her own beliefs about addiction.

Counselor Competence. It is not enough for a counselor to receive a general or community counseling degree and then to practice primarily as an addiction counselor without receiving additional training and specialized supervision. The intricacies of addiction treatment, especially related to alcohol and drug effects, the process of addiction and recovery, specialized treatment approaches, and adjunctive involvement with 12-step or other self-help groups, requires in-depth knowledge best gained through a combination of academic preparation, an internship or practicum focused on addiction competencies, and supervision under the direction of a counselor well versed in treating addictions. In the addiction field, core competencies have been established in screening, assessment, treatment planning, referral, service coordination, individual and group counseling, psychoeducation, and documentation (Center for Substance Abuse Treatment, 1998).

Other aspects of counselor competence should be considered. Counselors should maintain effective working relationships with other professionals (including physicians, social workers, psychologists, lawyers, judges, probation officers, and vocational rehabilitation counselors) who are almost always involved in cases in which clients receive treatment for addictions. In this way, competence relates to the boundaries of professional practice: Counselors must be cautious not to overstep their professional bounds, because other professionals have integral and important roles in the treatment of individuals with complex addictive disorders. Finally, given the potential for burnout among professionals who serve clients with addiction problems, counselors must be alert to their own limitations. If counselors recognize they are becoming impatient or uncompromising with clients, they should consider

methods of professional rejuvenation, including the use of appropriate supervision, linkage to a professional organization, continuing education, or even a sabbatical from addiction treatment. This is especially true of counselors who are in recovery themselves. The counseling role should not be so stressful as to produce undue distress in the treating professional.

CODE COMPARISONS

ACA members may join the AAOC, and IAAOC members are bound to the ACA ethics code. The IAAOC has an Ethics Committee that is charged with developing aspirational standards of conduct and responsible to communicate ethical problems faced by its membership to the ACA Ethics Committee. Adoption of the NAADAC ethical standards is mandatory for individuals who wish to gain MAC or NCAC status. The NAADAC standards also offer general ethical guidelines to the counselor. Their principled approach to seeking the best interest of the substance abuse client is required reading for those interested in addiction counseling.

ISSUES OF DIVERSITY

Addiction crosses all cultural groups and affects individuals regardless of race or economic status. Among individuals with substance abuse problems, diverse groups may face disparities that stem from stereotyping, marginalization, or racism. Diversity in the treatment of addiction, however, extends beyond the need for racial/ethnic sensitivity to understand the way of life of groups bound together by gender, age, geography, sexual preferences, substance use, and mental illness. Addiction counselors need specialized knowledge to assist those who are intravenous drug users, are medically ill (e.g., with HIV/AIDS), have co-occurring mental disorders, live in rural populations, are younger, or are gay, lesbian, bisexual, or transgender. These diverse groups and others may face cultural barriers to treatment access, present for treatment with unique substance abuse consequences, and face specific challenges in recovery. Cultural competence encompasses the behaviors, attitudes, and policies of the treatment system that allow each professional and agency to work effectively in cross-cultural situations.

Cultural sensitivity implies a basic understanding of the sociocultural factors that affect a client's treatment needs. Sensitivity to the cultural nuances embedded in addictive behavior is critical to establishing a therapeutic alliance with the addicted individual. The culturally competent counselor demonstrates the ability to interpret cultural gradations, can interpret deeper meanings in the client's words and actions, and subsequently makes better treatment decisions based on the client's needs. To these ends, substance abuse treatment agencies may provide interpreter services, recruit counselors that share the background of the client population, and provide training targeted at the elimination of treatment disparities. Addiction counselors should coordinate their services with those of traditional healers, including medical providers and churches, and be prepared to include family and other community members in the treatment process. Finally, counselors should understand the culture of their own organization and examine how it may or may not be welcoming to members of other cultures.

DECISION MAKING IN CONTEXT

Consider the following situation. You are the residential counselor for Rob, a client who, last year, was in your federally funded addiction treatment agency's outpatient program. Your coworker Tracy, who was Rob's outpatient counselor, is aware that he has been readmitted. Tracy stops you in the hall and asks how Rob is doing. What ethical issues, if any, are raised by this question? How would you respond?

In the field of addictions there are added protections for clients if they are in a federally funded program. Certainly, revelation outside of the agency is prohibited without client consent. However, communications with other professionals within an agency is another matter. As you would be directed by the Tarvydas Integrated Ethical Decision-Making Model, or Cottone's Social Constructivism Model, consultation with others on this matter is imperative. Certainly the client is a stakeholder. The client should be consulted, from the very beginning of treatment, how his readmission should be handled with the outpatient staff at the facility. If the client is not concerned about within-agency communication, then the concern is really not an ethical dilemma. Typically, such within-agency communication is addressed in standard agency confidentiality forms. However, the situation is more serious if such within-agency communication was not addressed when treatment was initiated or was not addressed formally in the standard admission forms. Assuming the worst, you must decide how to answer Tracy's enquiry. Certainly, you could put off a response until you have had time to consult with the client on this matter or to consider a course of action subsequent to application of a defensible ethics decision-making model. If the client refuses to let you communicate with employees assigned to other programs at the facility, then you would have to communicate such to Tracy—saying as standard policy, some clients hold their residential treatment confidential. Tracy should understand. If Tracy does not understand your ethical obligation and becames perturbed about your refusal to share information, saying "Come on, you know me—tell me what's going on," then there is a problem at the professional colleague level. If Tracy is not part of the treatment team, and if she is not being formally consulted (see the ACA ethics code sections on "information shared with others" or "consultation"), then sharing information with her without client consent would be an unethical act. Counselors often are hesitant to risk a friendship or colleague relationship over a presumed innocuous act. This is an example of what Tarvydas defined as a "nonmoral value" (valuing social harmony) or a "personal blind spot" ("Tracy will hate me if I don't tell her"). A truly ethically sensitive counselor must be alert to such nonmoral values or blind spots that affect the decision process. With the Cottone Social Constructivism Model, a consensus would need to be established with the client about how to handle such a problem, and then with Tracy to discuss, in general, how to handle cross-program communications about clients.

Regardless, the worst situation would be if you never addressed the issue with the client and simply revealed information to Tracy so as to prevent stress on the professional relationship.

CHAPTER SUMMARY

Working with individuals with addictive behaviors presents challenges that are unique and requires specialized knowledge of addiction and awareness of the ethical intricacies of the field. The competent professional counselor will ensure that a client's ethical and legal rights are respected. Specific state and federal laws speak to alcohol and drug abuse, requiring addiction counselors to be knowledgeable about the legal parameters of their work. Counselors must also be aware of their own limitations and stress levels and should seek consultation, supervision, continuing education, or counseling as appropriate. It is incumbent upon the counselor to acquire and maintain a broad knowledge base about addiction, including information about the physiological, psychological, and social aspects of substance use and recovery, the ethical issues particular to addiction, and the implications for working with diverse groups.

REFERENCES

Alcoholics Anonymous. (1976). *Alcoholics Anonymous.* New York: Author.

American Psychiatric Association (1994). *Diagnostic and statistical manual of mental disorders* (4th ed.). Washington, DC: American Psychiatric Association.

Anglin, M. D., Hser, Y-I., & Grella, C. (1997). Drug addiction and treatment careers among clients in the Drug Abuse Treatment Outcome Study (DATOS). *Psychology of Addictive Behavior, 11,* 308–323.

Brown, S. A. (1993). Drug expectancies and addictive behavior change. *Experimental and Clinical Psychopharmacology, 1,* 1–13.

Carise, D., McLellan, A. T., & Gifford, L. (2000), Development of a "treatment program" descriptor: The addiction treatment inventory. *Substance Use & Misuse, 35*(12–14), 1797–1818.

Center for Substance Abuse Treatment. (1998). *Addiction counseling competencies: The knowledge, skills and attitudes of professional practice* (Technical Assistance Publication (TAP) Series 21), DHHS Publication No. (SMA) 98-3171. Rockville, MD: Substance Abuse and Mental Health Services Administration.

Center for Substance Abuse Treatment. (2005). *Substance abuse treatment for persons with co-occurring disorders* (Treatment Improvement Protocol (TIP) Series 42). DHHS Publication No. (SMA) 05-3992. Rockville, MD: Substance Abuse and Mental Health Services Agency.

Chapman, C. (1997). Dual relationships in substance abuse treatment: Ethical implications. *Alcoholism Treatment Quarterly, 15,* 73–79.

Culbreth, J. R. (2000). Substance abuse counselors with and without a personal history of chemical dependency: A review of the literature. *Alcoholism Treatment Quarterly, 18,* 67–82.

Department of Health & Human Services. (1994). *Confidentiality of patient records for alcohol and other drug treatment* (Technical Assistance Publication (TAP) Series 13). Rockville, MD: U.S. Department of Health & Human Services.

Department of Health & Human Services. (1996). *Checklist for monitoring alcohol and other drug confidentiality compliance* (Technical Assistance Publication (TAP) Series 18). Rockville, MD: U.S. Department of Health & Human Services.

Doyle, K. (1997). Substance abuse counselors in recovery: Implications for the ethical issue of dual relationships. *Journal of Counseling and Development, 75,* 428–432.

Drake, R. E., Mercer-McFadden, C., Mueser, K. T., McHugo, G. J., & Bond, G. R. (1998). Review of integrated mental health and substance abuse treatment for patients with dual disorders. *Schizophrenia Bulletin, 24*(4), 589–608.

Evans, K., & Sullivan, M. J. (1990). *Dual diagnosis: Counseling the mentally ill substance abuser.* New York: Guilford.

Fuller, R. K. (1995). Antidipsotropic medications. In R. K. Hester & W. R. Miller (Eds.), *Handbook of alcoholism treatment approaches* (pp. 123–133). Boston: Allyn & Bacon.

Gallon, S. L., Gabriel, R. M., & Knudsen, J. R. W. (2003). The toughest job you'll ever love: A Pacific Northwest treatment workforce survey. *Journal of Substance Abuse Treatment, 24,* 183–196.

George, R. L. (1990). *Counseling the chemically dependent: Theory and practice.* Boston: Allyn & Bacon.

Hester, R. K., & Miller, W. R. (Eds.) (1995). *Handbook of alcoholism treatment approaches: Effective alternatives* (2nd ed.). Boston: Allyn & Bacon.

Hser, Y-I., Anglin, M. D., Grella, C., Longshore, D., & Prendergast, M. L. (1997). Drug treatment careers: A conceptual framework and existing research findings. *Journal of Substance Abuse Treatment, 14,* 543–558.

Humphreys, K., Huebsch, P. D., Finney, J. W., & Moos, R. H. (1999). A comparative evaluation of substance abuse treatment: V. Substance abuse treatment can enhance the effectiveness of self-help groups. *Alcoholism: Clinical and Experimental Research, 23,* 558–563.

Johnson, J. A. & Roman, P. M. (2002). Predicting closure of private substance abuse treatment facilities. *Journal of Behavioral Health Sciences & Research, 29,* 115–125.

Knudsen, H. K., Johnson, J. A., & Roman, P. M. (2003). Retaining staff at substance abuse treatment centers: Effects of management practices. *Journal of Substance Abuse Treatment, 24,* 129–135.

Marlatt, G. A., & Gordon, J. R. (1985). *Relapse prevention: Maintenance strategies in the treatment of addictive behaviors.* New York: Guilford Press.

McCrady, B. S. (1994). Alcoholics Anonymous and behavior therapy: Can habits be treated as diseases? Can diseases be treated as habits? *Journal of Consulting and Clinical Psychology, 62,* 1159–1166.

McCrady, B. S., & Bux, D. A. (1999). Ethical issues in informed consent with substance abusers. *Journal of Consulting and Clinical Psychology, 67,* 186–193.

Mulvey, K. P., Hubbard, S., & Hayashi, S. (2003). A national study of the substance abuse workforce. *Journal of Substance Abuse Treatment, 24,* 51–57.

Nowinski, J. & Baker, S. (1992). *The twelve-step facilitation handbook: A systematic approach to early recovery from alcoholism and addiction.* San Francisco: Jossey-Bass.

Office of Applied Studies, Substance Abuse and Mental Health Services Administration (2004). *Results from the 2003 National Survey on Drug Use and Health: National findings* (DHHS Publication No. (SMA) 04-3964, NSDUH Series H-25). Rockville, MD: Substance Abuse and Mental Health Services Administration.

Project MATCH Research Group. (1997). Matching alcoholism treatments to client heterogeneity: Project MATCH posttreatment drinking outcomes. *Journal of Studies on Alcohol, 58,* 7–29.

State of Missouri v. Anthony Genovese (April 14, 1999). Associate Circuit Court, County of St. Charles, Missouri, No. CR199-875F.

Substance Abuse and Mental Health Services Administration. (2004, June). *The confidentiality of alcohol and drug abuse patient records regulation and the HIPAA Privacy Rule: Implications for alcohol and substance abuse programs.* Rockville, MD: U.S. Department of Health and Human Services.

Tonigan, J. S., Toscova, R., & Miller, W. R. (1996). Meta-analysis of the literature on Alcoholics Anonymous: Sample and study characteristics moderate findings. *Journal of Studies on Alcohol, 57,* 65–72.

CHAPTER 19

The Ethics of Clinical Supervision

Dennis R. Maki • Janine M. Bernard

OBJECTIVES

After reading this chapter, you should be able to:

- Define clinical supervision and discuss it as an area of specialization and a mainstream activity across all specialties within counseling.
- Discuss the specific ethical codes, standards, and issues relevant to clinical supervision.
- Explain the ethical violations and the legal issues and strategies for their prevention in clinical supervision.

- Discuss issues of diversity in clinical supervision and suggest guidelines for ethical multicultural supervision.
- Apply a decision-making process to issues of supervision.

INTRODUCTION

Clinical supervision is both an area of specialization and a mainstream activity across all specialties within counseling. Clinical supervision earns its status as a specialty due to the sizable literature describing the practice of supervision, research verifying its distinctiveness from counseling, and credentialing/licensing bodies that acknowledge clinical supervision as a separate and specialized professional activity. Unlike other specialties, however, clinical supervision is an area of professional activity that most counselors will encounter in their careers. Thus, although most specialties define one's practice (e.g., addictions counseling), clinical supervision defines one's "professional maturity," so to speak. Although such professional maturity was previously considered both necessary and sufficient, the past 25 years or so have clearly demonstrated that supervision is a unique activity requiring discrete knowledge, skills, and sensitivities. (See Box 19–1.)

Box 19–1 • Exploring the Codes

Which ethical guidelines or Standards for Ethical Practice for Clinical/Counseling Supervisors apply to these issues?

1. Records of the counseling relationship
2. Training in supervision
3. Endorsement
4. Access to the supervisee's performance evaluation
5. Priority for resolving conflicts among the needs of client, supervisee, and agency/program
6. Professional status and conditions of supervision
7. Potentially detrimental relationships
8. Informed consent
9. Cultural issues
10. Laws and legal standards
11. Continuing education

DEFINING THE SPECIALTY, SETTING, AND CLIENTS

The evolution of clinical supervision can be seen as reflecting two paradigms—one ancient and the other parallel to the evolution of the helping professions. For virtually all professions and throughout history, fledging professionals have relied on those senior to them to mentor them to a level of acceptable competence (Bernard & Goodyear, 2004). For most of the history of counseling, this mentoring/apprenticeship paradigm has greatly influenced the practice of clinical supervision. Additionally (and, to some extent, separately), the early practice of clinical supervision paralleled that of counseling and psychotherapy (Leddick & Bernard, 1980). Even within psychoanalysis wherein supervision was stressed early on, clinical supervision took the form of analyzing the supervisee, an intervention that did not necessarily require supervisors to stretch beyond their training as psychoanalysts. Until the mid-1970s, clinical supervision was viewed primarily as an extension of counseling and reflected counseling skills and values. The personal growth of the supervisee was often targeted, and when supervisees floundered in their clinical work, social modeling and counseling were most likely to be the supervisor interventions of choice.

In the mid-1970s to early 1980s, models of supervision that required a conceptual and technical shift away from counseling as a method of supervision began to appear (e.g., Bernard, 1979; Kagan, 1976; Loganbill, Hardy, & Delworth, 1982; Stoltenberg, 1981). Since those early contributions, other models and model refinements have enriched the practice of clinical supervision (e.g., Hawkins & Shohet, 1989; Holloway, 1995; Maki & Delworth, 1995). Additionally, research efforts that address process and relationship variables have helped to illuminate the complex supervision interaction.

Although there are a variety of ways to conduct clinical supervision, the nature of the contract between supervisor and supervisee is foundational and is different from other professional relationships within counseling. Bernard and Goodyear (2004) defined **supervision** as:

> An intervention provided by a more senior member of a profession to a more junior member or members of that same profession. This relationship is evaluative, extends over time, and has the simultaneous purposes of enhancing the professional functioning of the more junior person(s), monitoring the quality of professional services offered to the client(s) that she, he, or they see, and serving as a gatekeeper for those who are to enter the particular profession (p. 8).

This definition distinguishes clinical supervision from counseling, consultation, and administrative supervision. Neither counseling nor consultation is an evaluative relationship. Counselors attempt to assist clients in ways that they request—counseling's success, or lack of success, is ultimately determined by the client. Consultation is a nonhierarchical relationship—it is understood that the advice offered by the consultant can be rejected by the consultee. The key distinction between administrative supervision and clinical supervision is the focus of the activity. The administrative supervisor oversees case management and the professionalism of services offered by counseling staff. However, this person does not focus on the process of counseling itself and, therefore, is not in a position to make a judgment about the counseling or assist in the development of the counselor as clinician.

Most counselors first encounter clinical supervision in their training programs to become entry-level professional counselors, usually as part of a practicum. At this early juncture, standard practice (and requirements of pertinent accrediting bodies) includes both individual supervision and group supervision. (It is beyond the capacity of this chapter to explain the intricacies of these different supervision methods or the many approaches that can be used within each. For coverage of these methods, see Bernard and Goodyear [2004].) Although the clinical supervision within accredited training programs has been regulated and most training programs offer sound supervision, postdegree supervision is far more random. It is still the case that many, if not most, clinical supervisors in the field have not received formal training in supervision. This situation is changing, albeit slowly. Furthermore, the growth of licensure/certification in individual states and national certification have required that counselors receive postdegree supervision. Counselors who do not seek certification or are not required to be licensed may receive virtually no additional clinical supervision once they are employed. This situation results in a heavy responsibility put on new professional counselors to make accurate assessments regarding their competencies and to be aware of a multitude of complicating issues that may affect the counseling process.

Postdegree supervision is usually conducted at a counselor's employment site; for example, a counselor in a community agency is, in most states, expected to acquire licensure as soon as possible. Because a license to practice counseling requires a certain amount of time postdegree under supervision, the agency expects to offer that supervision to the new employee.

Despite the distinctions made earlier, supervisors often have more than one role with supervisees. It is not uncommon for a clinical supervisor to be a counselor's administrative supervisor as well. This is not an ideal situation because it makes it more difficult for trust to be established and for the supervisee to express doubts or vulnerabilities. For example, a supervisor may encourage the supervisee to disclose personal views toward others that may block supervisee development. In doing so, the supervisee may share information that leads the supervisor to conclude that the supervisee is not as mature or introspective as initially thought. This knowledge will most certainly influence the supervisor when it is time to review staff for contract renewal. In this instance, therefore, the clinical and administrative responsibilities of the supervisor are in direct conflict with each other.

Occasionally, counselors seek clinical supervision privately. If it is within the counselor's financial means to do so, this can be the best option because it eliminates any role ambiguity within the workplace. Further, a privately sought clinical supervisor clearly focuses on the supervisee's development and is obliged to act on the gatekeeper role only if the supervisee's counseling is substandard and poses potential harm to clients.

Employment or licensure/certification requirements may mandate supervision, but there are many other reasons why counselors seek clinical supervision throughout their careers. Among these reasons are a desire to develop an expertise in a new clinical area, overall professional development, and a means to avoid professional burnout. It is indicative of those who are most engaged in their professional lives that they continually seek opportunities to learn and to improve their craft. The process of clinical supervision is perhaps most fruitful when approached with the motive of professional development.

Clinical supervision has been performed at some level since the inception of psychotherapy and counseling. For most of this history, however, the practice of supervision did not benefit from standards of practice. The AAMFT formalized standards for training clinical supervisors as early as 1971 (Falvey, 2002). The first counseling group to establish standards for clinical supervision training was the National Academy for Certified Clinical Mental Health Counselors (NACCMHC), the credentialing arm of the AMHCA, which established their Approved Supervisor designation in 1989. The Academy's Approved Supervisor designation was available to C.C.M.H.C.s until the Academy's merger with the NBCC in 1994.

Beginning in the mid-1980s, ACES, through its Supervision Interest Network, sought to professionalize clinical supervision for all specialties within the counseling profession. As a result of their efforts, several key publications emerged that greatly advanced the general knowledge and regard for counselor supervision and its parameters. These publications included the *Standards for Preparation and Practice of Counseling Supervisors* (Supervision Interest Network, 1990), a curriculum guide for training counseling supervisors (Borders et al., 1991), and *Ethical Guidelines for Clinical Supervisors* (ACES, 1993) (see Appendix V). The efforts of the ACES Supervision Interest Network over the years culminated in 1998 when, in collaboration with NBCC, the Approved Clinical Supervisor (A.C.S.) credential was established by NBCC. Although eligibility for the A.C.S. was initially restricted to National Certified Counselors, the NBCC Board passed a resolution in 2000 allowing access to the credential to any mental health professional who meets the training and experience criteria. The A.C.S. stipulates nine content areas that training in clinical supervision must include (see Appendix W). Among these is a focus on legal and ethical tenets that affect supervision. The ACS Code of Ethics (1998) is included in Appendix X. In addition, recent revisions of codes of ethics that previously included little or nothing on supervision now have expanded their coverage or included sections specifically dedicated to the topic (ACA, 2005; ASGW, 1998; CRCC, 2001).

The ACA code now, for example, has a section entitled Supervision, Training, and Teaching, which provides more in-depth and expanded consideration to such things as infusing multiculturalism, broadening the scope of application beyond counselor educators to agencies and private practitioners, requiring training in ethics and supervision with continuing education requirements, and prohibiting the supervision of friends, relatives, or intimates.

Licensure or certification of counselors in individual states has also affected the professionalization of clinical supervision. All jurisdictions (i.e., state boards and the District of Columbia board) that regulate the profession of counseling call for postdegree supervision as a stipulation for licensure/certification. Additionally, 18 states obligate supervisors to have received training in supervision prior to providing supervision (Giordano, 2005). A small number of states currently require either state licensure as a clinical supervisor or a national credential in clinical supervision as a prerequisite to offering supervision to counselors seeking licensure. It is quite likely that this trend will continue and that clinical supervision will be increasingly regulated by counseling licensure boards (Sutton, 2000).

ETHICAL ISSUES

Responsibility

Supervision is an inherently hierarchical relationship, involving supervisor, supervisee(s), and client(s). The professional responsibilities of the supervisor, therefore, are twofold: to enhance the professional functioning of the supervisee and to monitor client care (Bernard & Goodyear, 2004). Although careful case management typically ensures that these two responsibilities are noncontradictory, occasionally this is not the case. This, then, adds a third critical responsibility of clinical supervision—monitoring the fit between the needs of the supervisee and the needs of the client.

Assisting the supervisee to become a better counselor involves assigning clients within the counselor's current level of competence. At the same time, the supervisee must be challenged to learn. This may include assigning clients that represent the upper edge of the counselor's ability and perhaps are beyond the counselor's comfort level. Additionally, the supervisor must be cognizant of different learning styles, cultural issues, and personal characteristics, all of which will influence how efficiently the supervisee will become more expert. Williams (1995) suggested that clinical wisdom be a supervision goal—an ambitious goal indeed! In light of all of these factors, the supervisor must determine what can be accomplished within the time devoted to supervision (e.g., one semester or open ended) and what types of interventions will maximize the desired outcomes. Finally, the supervisor must monitor progress, give regular feedback, and often evaluate the level of competence at the end of the supervision contract.

Clinical supervision will fail if there is insufficient focus on the supervisee. There is no reason to believe that a counselor will become more expert without the kind of feedback routinely offered by supervisors. It is essential that the supervisor not lose sight of the welfare of the client(s) in working with the supervisee. In fact, the original purpose of supervision was to monitor client care (Bernard & Goodyear, 2004). Only later did the scope expand to include a deliberate focus on the supervisee. Professional responsibility continues to dictate that the clinical supervisor monitor the counseling being performed in light of the client's needs as well as

in accordance with training goals. Ultimately, if close supervision is not adequate to ensure that the client is being served at a minimally acceptable level, the supervisor must intervene. As Rubin (1997) aptly stated, "When the supervisor's responsibilities to the evolving supervisee/therapist and the client do not lend themselves to reconciliation, the clinical, ethical and training aspects of the supervisory process all fall on the side of client welfare" (p. 1).

Supervisors have ethical obligations both to clients and to supervisees. However, Bernard and Goodyear (2004) described two major problems with regard to supervisors executing their ethical responsibilities. First, most codes of ethics for practitioners have limited references to supervision. Counselor educators and counseling supervisors often encounter situations that require more specific guidelines than provided by the ACA Code of Ethics and the ACES Ethical Guidelines. Secondly, complex, multidimensional thinking is required by the supervisor's obligations to consider simultaneously the ethical issues that affect both the supervisee and the client. These two problems can lead to ethical issues for both the supervisor and the counselor being supervised. Borders and Brown (2005) noted it is thus important to keep both the ACA Code of Ethics and the ACES Ethical Guidelines.

To address the first problem, ACES and ACS adopted specific supervision codes and standards that (1) ensure ethical and legal protection of clients' and supervisees' rights; (2) meet the training and professional development needs of supervisees in ways consistent with clients' welfare and programmatic requirements; and (3) establish policies, procedures, and standards for implementing programs. To facilitate ethical knowledge and behavior in supervisees, supervisors at a minimum must possess a thorough knowledge of the ethical and regulatory codes in their professions and jurisdictions.

In addition to the ethical codes and standards, ethical principles and decision-making models have been proposed to address the second problem—the multidimensional thinking required by the supervisor to consider simultaneously the ethical issues that affect both the supervisee and their clients. Kitchener (1984) suggested that ethical codes are inadequate for deliberation; instead, ethical principles must be considered when ethical dilemmas surface. Kitchener's five principles can be used to evaluate dilemmas. Specifically, she proposed that consideration of these issues with regard to the principles of autonomy, non-maleficence, beneficence, justice, and fidelity can provide a basis to assess possible harm to the client and growth of the counselor. The ethical decision-making process involves a direct, evaluative process of deciding the morally appropriate option for resolving an ethical dilemma.

Models of ethical decision making have been developed. These models can be adapted to provide a framework for ethical decision making in supervision. These models generally incorporate consideration of the issue or dilemma in relation to the pertinent ethical codes and principles. They provide a cognitive map to process the issue from determination of a potential dilemma to its resolution. One such model to guide this process is the Tarvydas Integrative Decision-Making Model of Ethical Behavior in Counseling (2004), which is presented in detailed form in Chapter 6, along with other models that are used currently. Knowledge of ethical decision-making models, especially when shared by the supervisee, can assist with the multidimensional thinking required by the supervisor to consider simultaneously the ethical issues that affect both the supervisee and their clients.

The following discussion describes the ethical issues that present themselves in the process of clinical supervision. These issues are not unique to clinical supervision; however, the supervisor's obligation to consider simultaneously both the supervisee and the client requires unique considerations. Credit is given to Bernard and Goodyear (2004), whose text has provided a framework and primary reference for the following discussion. Although the discussion is organized by the concept of ethical issues, the primary strategy developed in each section focuses on guidelines provided by codes and standards. The intention here is to direct both supervisor and supervisee in the direction of prevention or containment of ethical issues as they present themselves in the complex, though natural, course of supervision.

Confidentiality

Confidentiality in supervision must be considered from the perspective of both the client and the supervisee. From either perspective, the definition is comparable to confidentiality as traditionally referenced in counseling—that is, "confidentiality involves professional ethics rather than legalism and indicates an explicit promise or contract to reveal nothing about an individual except under conditions agreed to by the source or subject" (Siegel, 1979, p. 251). The following discussion will first consider confidentiality as it relates to the client of the supervisee and then the counselor as supervisee.

Client Confidentiality. Supervisors should make supervisees aware of clients' rights, including protecting clients' right to privacy and confidentiality in the counseling relationship and the information resulting from it. Clients also should be informed that their right to privacy and confidentiality will not be violated by the supervisory relationship (ACES, 1993). Thus, the supervisor must ensure that the counselor has informed clients of their rights to confidentiality and privileged communication. Clients also should be informed of the limits of confidentiality and privileged communication. The general limits of confidentiality are when harm to self or others is threatened; when the abuse of children, elders, or persons with disabilities is suspected; and in cases when a court compels the counselor to testify and break confidentiality. These are generally accepted limits to confidentiality and privileged communication, but they may be modified by state or federal statute.

Supervisors must also be sure that their supervisees keep confidential all client information, except for purposes of supervision. Because supervision allows for third-party discussion, the supervisee must be reminded that this type of discourse cannot be repeated elsewhere (Bernard & Goodyear, 2004). In group supervision, the supervisor must reiterate this point and take the extra precaution of presenting cases using first names only, with as few demographic details as possible (Strein & Hershenson, 1991).

With video, electronic, or live supervision, the supervisor needs to reemphasize the importance of confidentiality. When supervisees tape, they must be reminded they possess confidential documents. Notes should use code numbers rather than names and be guarded with care. Records of the counseling relationship, including interview notes, test data, correspondence, the electronic storage of these documents, and audio- and videotape recordings, are considered confidential professional information. Supervisors should verify these materials are used in counseling, research, and training and supervision of counselors with the full knowledge of the clients and with permission granted by the applied counseling setting that is offering service to the client. This professional information is to be used for full protection of the client. Written consent from the client (or legal guardian, if a minor or a person unable to give voluntary informed consent) should be secured prior to using such information for instructional, supervisory, or research purposes. Policies of the applied counseling setting regarding client records also should be followed (ACES, 1993).

Supervisee Confidentiality. It is the supervisor's responsibility to keep information obtained during supervision regarding the counselor-supervisee confidential and to protect the supervisee's right to privacy. The supervisor must keep and secure supervision records and consider all information gained in supervision as confidential. The supervisee should understand the circumstances under which information obtained in supervision can be revealed. Supervisees can make more informed decisions about what to reveal in supervision if they understand that evaluative information from supervision may be passed along or any particular issues troubling the supervisor may be discussed with colleagues (Sherry, 1991).

Informed Consent

It is essential that both clients and supervisees understand and agree to the procedures of counseling and supervision prior to these activities. Actively involving all parties throughout the decision-making processes or providing for informed consent throughout these processes enhances the likelihood of attaining successful and ethical outcomes for both the client and the counselor being supervised. Informed consent is not a one-time event; rather, it is a continuing concern that needs to be revisited throughout the counseling and supervision process. Bernard and Goodyear (2004) noted that the supervisor has three levels of responsibility: (1) The supervisor must determine that the supervisee has informed clients regarding the parameters of counseling; (2) the supervisor must be sure that the clients are aware of the parameters of supervision that will affect them; and (3) the supervisor must provide the supervisee with the opportunity for informed consent.

Informed Consent with Clients. Counseling and supervision codes of ethics specify that counselors in training or in practice make every effort to ensure clients are aware of the services rendered and the qualifications of the person rendering those services. The supervisor must ensure that supervisees inform clients of their professional status. Supervisors need to ensure that supervisees inform their clients of any status other than being fully qualified for independent practice or licensed. For example, supervisees need to inform their clients if they are a student, intern, trainee or, if licensed with restrictions, the nature of those restrictions (ACES, 1993).

The types of services and the risks and benefits of counseling also need to be discussed. This discussion by the supervisee should include such specifics as the number and length of sessions, the cost for service, and the opportunity for telephone consultations. The type of services the client will be offered, preferred alternatives, and the risk of receiving no treatment should also be explained to ensure informed consent by the supervisee.

Informed Consent Regarding Supervision. Supervisors should have supervisees inform their clients that they are being supervised and explain all the conditions of their supervision. The client must be informed of the supervision procedures, whether sessions will be taped or observed, who will be involved, and how close the supervision will be. Supervisees should provide clients with professional disclosure information and inform them of how the supervision process influences the limits of confidentiality. Client permission must be obtained before students and supervisees can use any information concerning the counseling relationship in the training process (ACA, 2005). Supervisees should also make clients aware of who will have access to records of the counseling relationship and how these records will be used.

Confidentiality should be fully explained as it applies to both the process of counseling and to supervision. This discussion must also include when confidentiality will be breached. Disney and Stephens (1994) noted, "Supervisees place themselves in a position to be sued for invasion of privacy and breach of it if they do not inform their clients that they will be discussing sessions with their supervisor" (p. 50). A written form to alert clients of the conditions of supervision is a strategy to avoid possible misunderstandings later.

Informed Consent with Supervisees. Just as the supervisee has a responsibility to secure the client's informed consent, the supervisor is obligated to ensure that the supervisee understands and consents to the conditions of the supervision. Supervisees should enter the supervisory experience knowing the conditions that dictate their success or advancement. The responsibilities of both the supervisor and the supervisee should be clear. Supervisors should incorporate the principles of informed consent and participation with clarity of requirements, expectations, roles, and rules in the establishment of policies and procedures for their institutions, program, courses, and individual supervisory relationships. Mechanisms for due process appeal of individual supervisory actions should be established and made available to all supervisees. Supervisors should also inform supervisees of the goals, policies, theoretical orientations toward counseling, training, and supervision model or approach on which the supervision is based (ACES, 1993).

Whiston and Emerson (1989) stated all trainees entering a program should be cognizant that personal counseling may be recommended. Trainees should also be informed regarding the choice of supervisor, the form of supervision, the time allotted for supervision, the expectations of the supervisor, the theoretical orientation of the supervisor, and the type of documentation required for supervision. A written agreement can articulate a supervisory relationship in detail to avoid later misunderstandings. It serves to formalize the relationship, educate the supervisee regarding the nature of supervision, provide a model of how to approach informed consent with clients, and provide security for both parties by structuring the relationship (McCarthy et al., 1995).

Due Process

Supervisees have due process rights. Borders (2001) noted that supervisees must be afforded due process, ranging from timely feedback to opportunities for remediation to avenues to report dissatisfaction with supervision. To be ethically and legally sound, supervisors must employ a process that is neither arbitrary nor capricious (Disney & Stephens, 1994). The ACES guidelines are very clear on this issue. Supervisors should incorporate the principles of due process and appeal into the policies and procedures of their institutions, program, courses, and individual supervisory relationships. Mechanisms for due process appeal of individual supervisory actions should be established and made available to all supervisees (ACES, 1993).

The ACES guidelines further specify that supervisors of counselors should meet regularly in face-to-face sessions with their supervisees and provide supervisees with ongoing feedback on their performance. This feedback should take a variety of forms, both formal and informal, and should include verbal and written evaluations. It should be formative during the supervisory experience and summative at the conclusion of the experience. Supervisors should also establish and communicate to supervisees and field supervisors specific procedures regarding consultation, performance review, and evaluation of supervisees (ACES, 1993).

The ACA Code of Ethics addresses the issue of due process with regard to counselor education and train-

ing programs. It states that counselor educators must recognize that orientation is a developmental process that continues throughout the educational and clinical training of students. Counseling faculty should, prior to admission, provide prospective students with information about the counselor education program's expectations: (1) the type and level of skill and knowledge acquisition required for successful completion of the training, (2) program training goals, objectives, and mission and subject matter to be covered, (3) bases for evaluation, (4) training components that encourage self-growth or self-disclosure as part of the training process, (5) the type of supervision settings and requirements of the sites for required clinical field experiences, (6) student and supervisee evaluation and dismissal policies and procedures, and (7) up-to-date employment prospects for graduates.

Counselor education and training programs should integrate academic study and supervised practice. Such programs also are required to clearly state to students and supervisees, in advance of training, the levels of competency expected, appraisal methods, and timing of evaluations for both didactic and experiential components. Supervisors are also required to provide students and supervisees with periodic performance evaluations (ACA, 2005).

Bridge and Bascue (1990) noted the importance of proper documentation of supervision. It is critical that supervisors document the periodic formative as well as the summative evaluations that provide direct feedback to supervisees. Specific competencies and behaviors that are not adequate with behavioral indicators of the target performance to be attained should be noted. The supervision records should be dated and signed. This information should be available to the supervisee so that sufficient time is provided to correct any deficiency. Established notification and grievance procedures should provide recourse for supervisees who are unsuccessful in this process. Evaluations of supervisee performance in universities and in applied counseling settings should be available to supervisees in ways consistent with FERPA (ACES, 1993).

Roles and Relationships with Supervisees

Supervision is complicated when counselors or supervisors take on two or more roles, either professional or personal, simultaneously or sequentially with each other or with the clients served (Herlihy & Corey, 1997). These relationships may be intimate, therapeutic, or social in nature. Examples of such relationships include, but are not limited to, familial, social, financial, business, therapeutic, or close personal relationships with clients or supervisees. Counseling supervisors are required to be aware of the power differential in their relationships with supervisees. If they believe non-professional relationships with a supervisee may compromise the supervisory relationship, they must take precautions similar to those taken by counselors when working with clients. Examples of potentially beneficial interactions or relationships include attending a formal ceremony, hospital visits, providing support during a stressful event, or mutual membership in a professional association, organization, or community. Counseling supervisors should engage in open discussions with supervisees when they consider entering into relationships with them outside of their roles as clinical or administrative supervisors. Before engaging in nonprofessional relationships, supervisors must discuss with supervisees and document the rationale for such interactions, potential benefits or drawbacks, and anticipated consequences for the supervisee. Supervisors also are required to clarify the specific nature and limitations of the additional roles they will have with the supervisee. (ACA, 2005). Borders (2001) noted that these relationships may be a particularly challenging area in supervision because there is a high probability that many supervisors and supervisees will have such relationships. Bernard and Goodyear (2004) noted that these relationships between supervisors and supervisees have proven to be a difficult issue to resolve, as evidenced by much debate in the literature. Such relationships should be anticipated and, when they occur, handled with care (Herlihy & Corey, 1997).

All relevant ethical codes for counseling professionals make some reference to dual relationships between supervisors and supervisees. The factors that make such a relationship unethical are: (1) the likelihood that it will impair the supervisor's judgment, and (2) the risk of exploitation to the supervisee (Hall, 1988). The primary risk factor is a power differential; misuse of this power is exploitive and could cause harm. Kitchener and Harding (1990) identified two additional factors that create the risk of harm: (1) incompatible expectations of the counselor or supervisor in different roles, and (2) incompatible responsibilities of the counselor or supervisor. Whatever the rationale, it is the consensus of the profession that all potentially detrimental relationships should be avoided if at all possible.

The ACES Ethical Guidelines for Counseling Supervisors gives the most attention to these relation-ships. Specifically, these guidelines provide the following directives: Supervisors who have multiple roles (e.g., teacher, clinical supervisor, or administrative supervisor) with supervisees should minimize potential conflicts. Whenever possible, the roles should be divided among several supervisors. When this is not possible, supervisors should convey carefully the expectations and responsibilities associated with each supervisory role. Stoltenberg, McNeill, and Delworth (1998) noted that the supervisor needs to be alert to inappropriate relations between supervisee and client and to avoid multiple relations in supervisory assignments. Specifically, when a nonprofessional or conflicting professional relationship cannot be avoided, counselors and supervisors should take appropriate professional precautions such as informed consent, consultation, supervision, and documentation to ensure that their judgment is not impaired and that no exploitation occurs (ACA, 2005).

Bernard and Goodyear (2004) provided a detailed review of relationship issues related to supervisee-supervisor. The following is drawn from their discussion.

Sexual Attraction. Ellis and Douce (1994) identified sexual attraction between the supervisee-supervisor as one of eight recurring issues in supervision. Ladany, Hill, Corbett, and Nutt (1996) found counselor–client and supervisor–supervisee attractions among the topics that trainees were unwilling to disclose in supervision. This topic needs to be discussed openly and ethically and viewed as a relatively normal part of supervision and therapy. Sexual or romantic interactions or relationships with current students or supervisees are prohibited.

Sexual Harassment. Unlike sexual attraction, sexual harassment is an aberration of the supervision process. It is never acceptable to put the supervisor's own needs and wants in the foreground to the detriment of the professional development needs of the supervisee (Peterson, 1993). The ACA (2005) code clearly states that counselors and supervisors do not engage in sexual relationships with students or supervisees and do not subject them to sexual harassment.

Hidden Consensual Sexual Relationship. Brodsky (1980) asserted, "when one person in a relationship has a position of power over the other, there is no true consent for the acceptance of a personal relationship" (p. 516). Bartell and Rubin (1990) advised, "sexual involvement may further a human relationship, but it does so at the expense of the professional relationship" (p. 446). Supervisors should not participate in any form of sexual contact with supervisees nor engage in any form of social contact or interaction that would compromise the supervisor–supervisee relationship. Again, potentially detrimental relationships with supervisees that might impair the supervisor's objectivity and professional judgment should be avoided or the supervisory relationship terminated (ACES, 1993).

Nonsexual Nonprofessional or Conflicting Professional Relationships. Goodyear and Sinnett (1984) argued that it is inevitable that supervisors and their supervisees will have nonprofessional or conflicting professional relationships. Supervisors should not establish a therapeutic relationship as a substitute for supervision. Personal issues should be addressed in supervision only in terms of the impact of these issues on clients and on professional functioning (ACES, 1993). If students or supervisees request counseling, supervisors or counselor educators should provide them with acceptable referrals. Supervisors or counselor educators should not serve as a counselor to students or supervisees over whom they hold administrative, teaching, or evaluative roles unless this is a brief role associated with a training experience (ACA, 2005). In addition to personal counseling, a supervisor may recommend participation in activities such as personal growth groups when it has been determined that a supervisee has deficits in the areas of self-understanding and problem resolution that impede professional functioning. Again, supervisors should not be the direct provider of these activities for the supervisee (ACES, 1993).

In summary, counselor educators and supervisors should avoid nonprofessional or ongoing professional relationships with students or supervisees in which there is a risk of potential harm to the student or supervisee that may compromise the training/clinical experience or grades assigned. In addition, counselor educators and supervisors do not accept any form of professional services, fees, commissions, reimbursement, or remuneration from a site for student or supervisee placement (ACA, 2005).

Relationships with Former Students. Counselor educators are required to be aware of the power differential in the relationship between faculty and students. Faculty members must foster open discussions with former students when considering engaging in a social, sexual, or other intimate relationship. Faculty members should discuss with the former student how their former relationship may affect the change in relationship (ACA, 2005).

Strategy to Resolve Potentially Detrimental Relationships. Bernard and Goodyear (1998) proposed the following strategy when a potentially detrimental relationship emerges within the context of supervision: (1) The supervisee should get a new supervisor in a manner that will not negatively affect clients being served or the professional growth of the trainee. If it is not possible to replace the supervisor, an additional supervisor should be involved to monitor the supervisory relationship. (2) If it is not possible to remove the supervisor, both the supervisor and the supervisee should document their work together with audio or video examples of the supervisee's work to enable a second opinion. The topics covered in supervision should be recorded; the supervisor should request consultation with colleagues; and if group supervision is used, personal relationships should be made known to the group.

Nonprofessional or conflicting professional relationships confound the already existing supervisory relationship. Peterson (1993) cautioned that these relationship challenges abound in supervisory relationships and cannot be regulated out of existence. The ACA Code of Ethics (ACA, 2005) states that counselors and counseling supervisors must clearly define and maintain ethical, professional, personal, and social relationships with their supervisees and students. Counseling supervisors are required to avoid nonprofessional relationships with current supervisees. If supervisors must assume other professional roles (e.g., clinical and administrative supervisor, instructor) with supervisees, they should work to minimize potential conflicts and explain to supervisees the expectations and responsibilities associated with each role. They will not engage in any form of nonprofessional interaction that may compromise the supervisory relationship. Boundaries in this relationship must be carefully managed because supervisors have considerable power in the relationship.

CASE SCENARIO 19–1

Relationships Matter

Brett, a doctoral student in counselor education, is on a graduate student volleyball team with Jim, a master's student. When Brett sees the list of master's students to supervise, he immediately asks to supervise Jim, without mentioning the volleyball team. Their outside activity is not private, so is there any problem with Brett's decision? What are the ethical issues?

THE ISSUE. This relationship may not cause any issues for Brett or for Jim. At the same time, because there was a choice of supervisees, Brett should not have asked to supervise Jim because of their ongoing athletic team relationship. It is difficult to predict what type of potentially detrimental relationship can become problematic. Furthermore, this could also be seen as a violation of Jim's informed consent rights in that he was not consulted before the choice was made.

Competence

The ACA Code of Ethics (ACA, 2005) states that counselors must practice only within the boundaries of their competence. It further states that, prior to offering clinical supervision services, counselors are required to be trained in supervision methods and techniques. Counselors who offer clinical supervision services are also required to regularly pursue continuing education activities including both counseling and supervision topics and skills. The ACES (1993) guidelines state that supervisors should teach courses or supervise clinical work only in areas in which they are fully competent and experienced. Thus, the capacity of the supervisor to perform the essential functions of both counselor and supervisor is fundamental to the ethical practice of supervision. Competence, existing on a continuum, means having the ability to perform a task at an acceptable level (Cramton, 1981).

Essential Competencies for the Counselor Supervisor. The essential competencies for the counselor supervisor have been established by ACES. The following provides an abstracted listing of these 11 core areas. A detailed description of these competencies can be found in the source document (Supervision Interest Network, 1990).

Supervisors: (1) are effective counselors themselves; (2) demonstrate attitudes and traits consistent with the supervisory role, such as sensitivity to individual differences, motivation, commitment to supervision, and comfort with the authority inherent in the supervisory role; (3) are knowledgeable of and can skillfully apply the ethical, legal, and regulatory dimensions of supervision; (4) demonstrate conceptual knowledge of the professional and personal nature of the supervisory relationship and the impact of supervision on the supervisee; (5) understand and are skilled in the methods and techniques of supervision; (6) understand the process of counselor development and can apply it to supervision; (7) are competent in case conceptualization and management; (8) are competent in client assessment and evaluation; (9) are knowledgeable about oral and written reporting and recording; (10) can evaluate a supervisee's counseling performance fairly and accurately and provide feedback to facilitate growth; and (11) are knowledgeable of the rapidly expanding body of theory and research concerning counseling and counselor supervision and incorporate it in their practice.

Counselor and Supervisor Competence. ACES standards require that the supervisor first be an effective counselor. Importantly, the supervisor must be more advanced than the supervisee in all areas of counseling practice. Counselors must assess their counseling competencies and then determine the kinds of clients they would not supervise, the settings that are out of their scope of expertise, and the kinds of clients they would supervise only working under supervision or in conjunction with a consultant.

Being a competent counselor does not necessarily mean an individual is also a competent supervisor. The ACES guidelines state that supervisors should have training in supervision prior to initiating their role as supervisors. The guidelines go on to state that supervisors should be knowledgeable regarding the ethical, legal, and regulatory aspects of the profession. They also must be skilled in applying that knowledge and in making students and supervisees aware of their responsibilities. Again, as supervisors, professionals must assess their competencies.

Supervisee Competence. Supervisors have the oversight responsibility for supervisees' work in relation to their competence. Supervisors should therefore assess their supervisees' skills and experience to establish the level of their supervisees' competence. Supervisors should then restrict their supervisees' activities to those that are commensurate with their current level of skills and experiences (ACES, 1993). The only way for supervisors to have confidence in their assessment is to use direct forms of supervision, at least on an intermittent basis. The task for supervisors and supervisees is to recognize when they are and are not qualified to serve prospective clients and to accept clients who will challenge them to stretch the boundaries of their competence with consultation.

Stoltenberg et al. (1998) spoke to the ethical mandate to permit supervisees to provide only those services within their competence. They noted that supervisors must select the type and number of clients to match the supervisee's level of competence. Supervisors then need to be vigilant to monitor client welfare and base their level of monitoring on the level of education and experience of the supervisee. In addition, the amount of time supervisors have available to supervise and their competency relative to pertinent issues must be factored into ethical supervisory decisions.

Impairment of Competence. The ACES guidelines speak directly to the issue of supervisee impairment by stating that supervisors, through ongoing supervisee assessment and evaluation, should be aware of any personal or professional limitations of supervisees that are likely to impede future professional performance. Lamb, Cochran, and Jackson (1991) defined the impairment of competence as an inability or unwillingness (a) to acquire and integrate one's repertoire of professional standards into one's repertoire of professional behavior; (b) to acquire professional skills and reach an accepted level of competency; or (c) to control personal stress, psychological dysfunction, or emotional reactions that may affect professional functioning. Any one or combination of these factors requires responsible action on the part of the supervisor.

Supervisors have the responsibility of recommending remedial assistance to the supervisee and of screening from the training program, applied counseling setting, or state licensure those supervisees who are unable to provide competent professional services. These recommendations should be clearly and professionally explained in writing to the supervisees who are so evaluated (ACES, 1993). Stoltenberg and Delworth (1988) described the reciprocal ethical responsibility on the part of supervisees to recognize personal problems that may interfere with their practice, to let the supervisor know of them, and to seek appropriate assistance.

Ultimately, supervisors should not endorse a supervisee for certification, licensure, completion of an academic training program, or continued employment if the supervisor believes the supervisee is impaired in any way that would interfere with the performance of counseling duties. The presence of any such impairment should begin a process of feedback and remediation wherever possible, so the supervisee understands the nature of the impairment and has the opportunity to remedy the problem and continue with professional development (ACES, 1993).

CASE SCENARIO 19–2

Endorsement Recommendations

Alex has been Jaime's post-master's supervisor as part of the requirements for seeking licensure in her state. Alex has been both supportive and challenging in his supervision. Now that Jaime has completed her required hours, she gives Alex an endorsement form for Alex to fill out and file with the state. A week later, Jaime receives an e-mail from Alex that he has studied the form and he does not feel comfortable endorsing her at this time. Alex recommends that Jaime seek additional supervision from another supervisor. What are the ethical issues?

THE ISSUE. Alex might actually believe (and it could be argued) that he is behaving in an ethical manner by withholding endorsement from a supervisee for whom he has marginal confidence. At the same time, Jaime has due process rights that Alex has violated. Because Alex knew that Jaime was interested in seeking licensure, he needed to share his reservations earlier in the supervisory relationship and to stipulate exactly what those reservations were. By doing so, Jaime would have had an opportunity to work on her deficits and perhaps ultimately receive Alex's endorsement. It is also possible that Alex's expectations are higher than reasonable. By informing Jaime sooner about his evaluation, Jaime would have had an opportunity to seek another supervisor with whom to work.

Remaining Competent. Competence is not a static concept; counselors and supervisors need to participate in continuing education activities to maintain their competence (ACA, 2005). In addition, a supervisor must remain competent as both counselor and supervisor. The issue of competence for both the supervisor and the supervisee is central to the most pressing ethical responsibility—that of monitoring client welfare (Sherry, 1991). The ACES code speaks directly to this issue, stating that supervisors should pursue professional and personal continuing education activities such as advanced courses, seminars, and professional conferences on a regular and ongoing basis. These activities should include both counseling and supervision topics and skills. Supervisors are also expected to be active participants in peer review and peer supervision procedures (ACES, 1993).

Supervisors must be committed to continuing education. They need to keep current in their own specialty areas and be aware of advances in the area of clinical supervision. Many professionals become complacent with their degree of competence and wean themselves from professional literature or attendance at professional meetings or workshops (Campbell, 1994). In addition to continuing education, liberal use of consultation with peers is important to prevent the kind of isolation that diminishes competence (Sherry, 1991).

The ethical considerations for supervisor and supervisee are complex and ever present. The ACES Ethical Guidelines for Counseling Supervisors and the ACS

Code of Ethics, in conjunction with the ethical principles and an ethical decision-making model, assist both parties in identifying and strategizing to best ensure client welfare in the course of counselor development. If supervisors and supervisees do not deal with these issues in a proactive, systematic manner, ethical violations can result, with implications for both.

CASE SCENARIO 19–3

Student Disclosures

Alice is the faculty member assigned to Teresa's practicum class. Teresa conceptualizes her cases adequately and seems to have good technical skills, but she is not available emotionally to her clients. In fact, she appears "shut down" in all of her interactions with her clients, with Alice, and with her peers. During one particular supervision session, Alice challenges Teresa more than usual about her affective unavailability. Teresa cries and shares that she was emotionally and sexually abused as a child. She shares that she is in counseling, but, obviously, she still has difficulty trusting others and allowing herself to feel emotions during counseling. She asks Alice to keep her background in confidence. What are the ethical issues?

THE ISSUE. This example is laden with ethical issues. First, there is the issue of informed consent. Was there a supervision contract that made it clear that Alice would not keep in confidence information that was relevant to Teresa's standing in the program? If not, and Alice feels obliged to share this information, she has denied Teresa informed consent. Second, if Alice keeps the confidence, she is in danger of forming an inappropriate, potentially detrimental relationship with Teresa by treating her more like a client than a student. Finally, the issue of competence must be addressed. If Teresa is not able to assess her own feelings or to deal with the feelings of clients, Alice must question her competence at this time. To ignore this limitation in evaluation would be an ethical concern.

ETHICAL VIOLATIONS

It is quite likely that most ethical violations in clinical supervision go unreported. The professional literature points to the fact that ethical violations committed by supervisors occur (e.g., Lamb & Catanzaro, 1998; Lamb, Catanzaro, & Moorman, 2003; Miller & Larrabee, 1995). Yet, there is also evidence that mental health professionals are reluctant to report ethical violations of peers when they become aware of them (e.g., Bernard & Jara, 1986). Lamb et al. (2003) found that 40% of supervisors who had engaged in boundary

violations with supervisees expressed ambivalence about the ethical propriety of their actions and generally felt that their actions had done no harm. Similarly, a study of counseling supervisors (Erwin, 2000) found that 67% of supervisors in the sample received low scores on moral sensitivity when the ethical issue presented to them was ambiguous (having to do with a potentially detrimental relationship). Even when the ethical issue was considered less ambiguous (breach of confidentiality), 35% received low moral sensitivity scores. In light of social modeling, therefore, it should not be surprising that in a national survey of graduate trainees (of clinical psychology), over half of the training directors who responded reported that they had dealt with an ethical transgression of a trainee (Fly, van Bark, Weinman, Kitchener, & Lang, 1997).

Definitions

It is important to distinguish terms when entering the quagmire of unethical behavior of supervisees and supervisors. An **ethical violation** is just that—a behavior that violates the letter or perhaps the spirit of an ethical standard of practice. If a supervisee violates an ethical standard and it becomes known, the consequences will probably occur within the supervisory context. If the supervisee is in a training program, the consequences may range from a confrontation with the supervisor to dismissal from the program, often depending on the egregiousness of the violation (Fly et al., 1997).

An **ethical complaint** is a more formal process and is far more public. A complaint of ethical violation appeals to the professional group that endorses the violated ethical standards. There are three categories of such groups: professional membership associations (e.g., the ACA), voluntary certification organizations (e.g., the CRCC), and state boards for the licensure or certification of counselors. There is nothing to prohibit a complainant from appealing to more that one group. For example, if a supervisor is a member of ACA, a C.R.C., and a licensed clinical mental health counselor in the state of Maine, complaints could be made to ACA, the CRCC, and the state of Maine. Each entity would independently evaluate the complaint to determine its validity and, if valid, impose appropriate sanctions. Professional membership groups and certification groups have jurisdiction only over their members/certificants. State boards are similar unless a mental health professional commits an act specifically prohibited by the law in that state that granted licensure/certification (e.g., practicing without a license, which may or may not be considered an ethical violation). In such a case, the state's attorney general's office can order the mental health professional to "cease and desist." Typically, however, state counseling boards operate similarly to professional membership organizations and certification boards.

Just as a complainant can appeal to different boards, a complainant may also initiate both a complaint and a malpractice lawsuit.

Supervisee Violations

Supervisors are responsible for their own behaviors as well as the behavior of their supervisees. When there is **layered supervision** (e.g., doctoral students supervising master's students who are themselves being supervised by faculty), supervisors must attend to this additional layer. Welfel (1998) cautioned that, in this case, "the professionals who have ultimate responsibility for the client find more and more distance between them and the client" (p. 276). Welfel advised supervisors to develop careful and consistent data-gathering methods to compensate for this vulnerability.

The ethical issue that has received the most attention in the literature (e.g., Hamilton & Spruill, 1999; Lamb & Catanzaro, 1998) is sexual boundary violations between trainees and their clients. The investigation of ethical violations of psychology students (Fly et al., 1997) would justify this concern. Of the eight categories of ethical transgressions, professional boundary transgressions (sexual and nonsexual) ranked as the second most likely trainee transgression, after violations of confidentiality. (These two types of transgressions together represented 45% of the total reported by training directors.) Because it is not uncommon for persons in the mental health fields to have unresolved personal issues of one sort or another, supervisors should be vigilant regarding boundary transgressions. To this point, Jackson and Nuttal (2001) found that three out of five mental health practitioners with severe childhood sexual abuse in their backgrounds reported sexual boundary violations with clients. Jackson and Nuttal strongly recommended that clinicians with this profile avoid private practice and seek ongoing clinical supervision. Supervisors, therefore, need to be prepared to work not only with novice supervisees, but with more seasoned, yet high-risk, clinicians.

Although ethical transgressions with clients are potentially the most worrisome for supervisors, a study conducted by Worthington, Tan, and Poulin (2002) found that some supervisees commit ethical violations within the context of supervision as well. Most supervisee self-reported behaviors revealed in this study would be considered only mildly unethical, yet some behaviors were as egregious as forging a supervisor's signature on case material.

Supervisor Violations

Using primarily the ACES Ethical Guidelines for Counseling Supervisors as their template, Ladany, Lehrman-Waterman, Molinaro, and Walgast (1999) surveyed 151 counselors or psychologists in training regarding the behavior of their supervisors. A startling 51% reported at least one ethical violation by their supervisors. The most frequently violated standards involved adequate performance evaluation, confidentially issues having to do with supervision, and the supervisor's ability/willingness to work with alternative perspectives. Although Ladany et al. found sexual boundary violations to represent only 1.3% of reported breaches, other authors have focused on such violations and have found evidence that they pose some risk within the supervisor–supervisee dyad (e.g., Bonosky, 1995; Lamb et al., 2003; Miller & Larrabee, 1995; Slimp and Burian, 1994).

Preventing Ethical Violations

In light of the findings of Erwin (2000) and Lamb et al. (2003) that supervisors are occasionally ambivalent about ethical matters, it would be wise for supervisors to look for ways to increase their ethical foresight—for themselves and as models for their supervisees. It appears that coursework in ethics is not sufficient to prevent ethical transgressions (Fly et al., 1997), and more attention on ethical behavior needs to be placed within the supervision dialogue itself. This opinion was reiterated by Handelsman, Gottlieb, and Knapp (2005). They asserted that developing a professional ethical identity was a process of acculturating into the culture of psychotherapy, thus requiring time and careful attention.

Hamilton and Spruill (1999) asserted that a decline in concern over transference and countertransference within training programs has increased the risk of boundary violations between supervisees and clients. They also advised supervisors to deal straightforwardly with trainees about sexual attraction between clients and counselors and counselors and supervisors, a strategy also proposed by others (Bridges & Wohlberg, 1999; Samuel & Gorton, 1998). Koenig and Spano

(2003) recommended training in human sexuality to both acknowledge the role sexuality plays in identity and to assist in helping trainees to manage their sexuality in professional contexts. As a monitoring activity that attends to these concerns, Hamilton and Spruill developed an excellent risk management checklist for supervisees and supervisors to help them to identify feelings and motives and to confront inappropriate behaviors (Figure 19–1).

Other authors have suggested the use of professional disclosure statements and formal supervision plans as strategies to reduce the risk of ethical conflicts within supervision (Blackwell, Strohmer, Belcas, & Burton, 2002; Cobia & Boes, 2000). Both of these documents will give the supervisee a great deal of information about the supervisor and about the process of supervision. They serve not only as a guideline for the supervisee, but also as an aid to the supervisor in planning ahead (e.g., choosing an evaluation plan) and covering a variety of issues that could potentially lead to an ethical breach (e.g., informed consent).

LEGAL ISSUES

Any ethical violation becomes a legal issue when a claim of malpractice is made. Such a claim does not mean that a different kind of egregious behavior has been committed. Rather, it simply means that the harmed party has appealed to civil court rather than (or in addition to) a professional body (such as a state counseling board) for reparation. As noted by Montgomery, Cupit, and Wimberley (1999), it is not uncommon for the same claim to result in both a complaint to a regulatory body and a malpractice lawsuit. At the same time, it is safe to assume that there are many more complaints made to regulatory boards than suits for malpractice. Whereas a professional peer review board that would investigate a complaint is interested primarily in whether the professional has breached professional ethics, the civil court's role is quite different. It is restricted by tort law and is an appropriate venue only if negligence can be proved by the defendant to have caused harm.

Malpractice

Although there are two types of torts (i.e., civil wrongs other than breach of contract)—intentional and unintentional (Swenson, 1997)—it is highly unlikely (though possible) that a supervisor would be sued for an intentional tort or deliberately causing harm to a supervisee or client. An example of such a Machiavellian

act might be a supervisor suggesting that a supervisee develop a strategy in counseling that the supervisor believes would increase the suicide risk of the client. Or, less dramatic, a supervisor might place a disliked intern in a clinical setting where the supervisor is fairly sure that the intern will fail. In both of these cases, the offense could be argued under intentional tort.

Virtually all malpractice cases in the mental health professions, however, are negligence cases, and therefore unintentional torts (Swenson, 1997). Disney and Stephens (1994) defined malpractice as "harm to another individual due to negligence consisting of the breach of a professional duty or standard of care" (p. 7). Although the definition seems fairly straightforward, there are actually four elements that must be present for a successful malpractice suit (Ogloff & Olley, 1998): (1) There must be what is called a fiduciary relationship. Within the supervisory context, this means that supervisors can be trusted to be working in the best interests of supervisees and their clients rather than in their own interests (Remley & Herlihy, 2001). In short, there is an acknowledged duty of care based on a professional relationship. (2) The professional (supervisor) must act in a way that falls below the standard established by the profession. (3) The client (and/or supervisee) must suffer some harm. (4) A relationship between the harm and the supervisor's (or supervisee's) act must be established.

It generally is agreed that the crux of liability is whether the professional acted outside the bounds of accepted practice (Ogloff & Olley, 1998; Remley & Herlihy, 2001). Guest and Dooley (1999) made the astute observation that until recently it was difficult to get a handle on "acceptable practice" where clinical supervision was concerned. However, with the emergence of training requirements, standards of practice, and ethical guidelines, supervisors have become more accountable to a standard and, consequently, are more vulnerable to being held liable. At the same time, supervisors who follow sanctioned practice and ethical standards for clinical supervision are protected by their presence.

Direct Liability

Because supervision involves two levels of oversight, liability can be both direct and indirect. **Direct liability** occurs when the harm that is done is a result of supervision itself. Any harm done to the supervisee within supervision would most likely be direct. Results reported by Montgomery et al. (1999) suggested that direct liability is still rare for supervisors, though two reported malpractice suits did, indeed, involve supervisory issues (supervisee performance evaluation and

Therapist Responses to Clients

■ Do you find it difficult to set limits on the demands your client makes of you?

■ Do you accept phone calls from your client at home or your office when the client needs you to (a) help with a "crisis," (b) deal with minor problems, or (c) alleviate his or her loneliness or meet his or her need to talk to someone who "understands"?

■ Do you make statements such as "This is not my usual practice; I ordinarily don't do this, but, in your case . . . " or "Under the circumstances, it seems OK to . . . "?

■ Do you find yourself wanting to rescue your client from some situation or behavior that is detrimental to him or her?

■ Do you find yourself talking about your client to others?

■ Does your client occupy your thoughts outside office hours?

■ Do you hope you will "run into" your client at the grocery store, social settings, and so forth?

■ Is it becoming progressively easier and more satisfying to share intimate details of your own life with your client?

■ Do you find opportunities to talk about nontherapy issues with your client?

■ Do you take care to dress or look more attractive than usual for a particular client?

■ Do you find yourself wondering what the client thinks about you?

■ Do you make excuses to talk with your client by phone?

■ Do you accept friends of your client as therapy clients, and then find yourself spending a lot of the session talking about the original client to the current client rather than focusing on the current client's problems?

■ Do you find yourself looking forward to seeing a particular client (or type of client) and feeling disappointed if he or she cancels the session?

Therapist Needs

■ Does your primary satisfaction come from your work with therapy clients?

■ Do you have more clients than required or more than your fellow practicum students?

■ Are you lonely and feeling as if your needs are not being met by anyone?

■ Do you have a circle of friends with whom you engage in pleasurable social activities?

■ Do you have a circle of friends to whom you can turn for support?

■ Do you have one or more close friends in whom you could confide about fears, anxieties, and self-doubts?

■ What are the important stressors in your life, and what steps are you taking to resolve or to cope with them?

Session Characteristics

■ Do you regularly extend the session for one client but not for others?

■ Do you regularly start the session early, end it late, or both for one client?

■ Do you schedule a particular client at times that afford the opportunity to linger, or to walk out of the clinic together, and so forth?

■ Do you schedule the client after regular office hours because your schedule or the client's schedule does not permit regular office hours?

Accountability

■ Do you find yourself forgetting to document phone calls from your client?

■ Do you find yourself getting defensive about particular clients or certain issues (e.g., you bristle when a supervisor suggests that there is no progress being made and a referral is in order)?

■ Are you reluctant to talk about transference or boundary issues, particularly feelings related to sexual attraction by or to the client?

■ Do you find it difficult to tell your treatment team or supervisor some details related to your client?

■ Is there anything that you "try not to talk about" concerning a particular client?

■ Do you find yourself putting off seeking supervision or consultation about a particular client or issue?

■ Does the tape always run out or mess up at a "sensitive" point in the session? Does the therapy session regularly extend beyond the length of the tape?

■ If you make phone calls, extend sessions, and so forth, how much of this information is recorded in the client's file? Do you find yourself unwilling, or "forgetting," to document information with regard to a particular client?

continued

FIGURE 19–1.   Risk Management: A Checklist for Trainees and Supervisors
Source: Hamilton & Spruill (1999)

Other
- Have the secretaries or other people commented about your behavior toward a client?
- Have you offered to do such things as give the client a ride home, give tutoring in a difficult class, or arrange a meeting outside the therapy hour or place?
- Are you concerned about the client's feelings toward you, or your feelings toward the client?

Checklist for Supervisors
- Have I discussed how to establish a professional therapist-client relationship with my practicum students?
- Have I reviewed the issue of sexual attraction to clients and shared my own experiences with my practicum students? If I am unwilling to share my own feelings, what have I done about this?
- Have I created an atmosphere of openness and willingness to discuss the fears, uncertainties, and so forth of my practicum students?
- Do my practicum students know about boundary violations and the reasons for establishing boundaries?
- Have I discussed the checklist for students with them?

FIGURE 19–1. Risk Management: A Checklist for Trainess and Supervisors—*continued*
Source: Hamilton & Spruill (1999)

a billing/payment issue). When faculty evaluation is claimed, a violation of due process is most likely the grounds on which the suit stands. All areas outlined in clinical supervision standards, however, could potentially lead to a malpractice suit of direct liability, including competence to supervise an individual supervisee (including an inability to work with cultural differences); violations of informed consent, the supervision contract, or confidentiality; or a potentially detrimental relationship.

Direct liability can also be claimed if the harm is done to the client, and the cause of the harm directly traces to the supervisor. For example, if an inadequately informed supervisor suggested an intervention to the supervisee that led to client harm, this could be argued as direct liability. Liability can be argued for actions or omissions of the supervisor (Falvey, 2002). Therefore, a lack of adequate record keeping by the supervisor could lead to additional vulnerability should a client be harmed.

Vicarious Liability

Vicarious liability is perhaps more feared by clinical supervisors. Based on the legal concept of *respondeat superior*, supervisors are considered liable "for the negligent acts of supervisees if these acts are performed in the course and scope of the supervisory relationship" (Disney & Stephens, 1994, p. 15). Falvey (2002) further clarified that three conditions must be met for vicarious liability: (1) Supervisees must agree to work under the direction of the supervisor and act in ways that benefit the supervisor; (2) supervisees must act within a scope

of tasks endorsed by the supervisor; and (3) the supervisor must have the power to control and direct the work of the supervisee. Falvey pointed out that administrative supervisors may be more likely to be considered vicariously liable because of the condition that supervisee acts "benefit the supervisor," as would be the case if a supervisor received part of a fee paid by the client to the supervisee. Finally, Disney and Stephens added one more important component in defining whether an action falls within the scope of supervisory relationships: "whether the supervisor could have reasonably expected the supervisee to commit the act" (p. 16). Ignorance of the supervisee's behavior is not a strong defense if it is reasonable to expect that the supervisor could have predicted the likelihood of the action occurring. The courts do not expect supervisors to be infallible, but they do expect that reasonable care will be applied to the activity of clinical supervision.

Remley and Herlihy (2001) cautioned that exact facts of each situation are different and call for unique interpretations. They underscored the fact that the amount of control that a supervisor has over a counselor would be important to determine in arriving at a judgment of vicarious liability. In this light, they further suggested that supervisors on-site are more likely to be held accountable for a counselor's negligence than those who supervise from elsewhere (e.g., within a university training program setting).

Preventing the Malpractice Lawsuit

It is no surprise to anyone living in the United States that we are presently a litigious culture. Within this broad context, it must be noted that there is no way to make an individual invulnerable to a lawsuit, or as Swenson (1997) asserted, "the courthouse is a place that cannot always be avoided" (p. 165). There are ways to avoid being found guilty of malpractice and this is where supervisors' energies are constructively placed. First and foremost, the supervisor who stays abreast of the field, seeks consultation when necessary, and is particularly vigilant about standards for ethical practice of both counseling and supervision, is highly unlikely to ever be found guilty of malpractice. Although professional regulatory bodies and the courts remain very separate entities, there is evidence that courts typically support decisions made by bodies such as licensing boards (Ogloff & Olley, 1998). Therefore, following the lead of the certification and licensing bodies is totally warranted as a measure to prevent liability.

Falvey, Caldwell, and Cohen (2002) developed a comprehensive supervision documentation system as a strategy for risk management. Their supervision record forms ask the supervisor to review 19 risk management issues (e.g., duty to warn, potentially detrimental relationships) for each supervision session as a means to keep these important matters in the forefront of the supervisor's attention. Although time consuming, this kind of system necessarily leads to increased command over both client and supervisee issues.

Woodworth (2000) concurred that record keeping is an important risk management strategy. She included six other strategies for counselors that are equally relevant to supervisors, including: staying within one's area(s) of competence; attending to communication issues and the therapeutic (or supervisory) relationship; seeking supervision or consultation when needed; carrying liability insurance; staying abreast of ethics and relevant law; and practicing self-care to maintain physical and emotional well-being.

"Avoiding the courthouse," then, involves a unique blend of professional wisdom and human wisdom. In addition to some distinct knowledge, skill, and good work habits, healthy, respectful relationships, and keen, unencumbered self-knowledge add significant protection to the clinical supervisor. In short, insight, integrity, and goodwill are enormous barriers to professional difficulty.

CODE COMPARISONS

Clinical supervision is a unique specialty in that it is not tied to any particular clientele or setting. All counselors receive supervision throughout training, and most receive supervision early in their careers. The ACA has 17 divisions, many of which have separate ethical codes, and counseling has two certifying organizations (NBCC and CRCC), each with separate ethical codes. All of these conceivably refer to the practice of clinical supervision.

Two sets of ethical standards were written specifically for supervision—those of ACES and the ACS. The ACES Ethical Guidelines (1993; Appendix U) are divided into three sections: client welfare and rights; supervisory role; and program administration role. The first two sections are very much in synchrony with the ACS Standards of Ethical Practice (1998; Appendix W). This is not surprising in light of the coordination that took place between ACES and NBCC in creating the A.C.S. designation. The "program administration role" section of the ACES guidelines refers primarily to issues within training programs and the ethical practice of supervision when, for example, off-campus sites are involved, supervisees are also students, and evaluations translate to academic grades. These two publications together are essential for practicing clinical supervisors and underscore the sometimes illusive, yet profoundly important, differences in responsibilities between counselors and supervisors.

Most ethical guidelines for counselors make only cursory reference to supervision and tend to single out one standard (e.g., regarding potentially detrimental relationships) for which to include a statement about supervisors and supervisees. There are five exceptions to this practice: The codes of the ACA, the AMHCA, the ASGW, the IAMFC, and the CRCC have sections devoted to supervision. Members of these organizations should read these guidelines and those of ACES and the ACS prior to conducting supervision.

ISSUES OF DIVERSITY

All practitioners have an ethical mandate to increase their competence in working with diverse populations; supervisors are no exception (Stoltenberg & Delworth, 1988). Cross/multicultural counseling has been defined as "any counseling relationship in which two or more of the participants differ with respect to cultural background, values, and lifestyle" (Sue et al., 1982, p. 47). Sue went on to conclude that if these distinguishing characteristics of the supervisor and the counselor or supervisee are acknowledged and incorporated into practice, it becomes clear that all supervision is, by definition, cross-cultural. Framing supervision cross-culturally acknowledges the diverse backgrounds of each individual in the supervision/counseling triad and promotes culturally sensitive, ethical counseling and supervision practice (Terrell & Cheatman, 1996).

Given this, it would not be ethical for counselors or supervisors to attempt to provide services to culturally diverse clients or supervisees without appropriate training and experience. The ACA Code of Ethics (ACA, 2005) in fact requires counselors to strive actively to understand the diverse cultural backgrounds of their clients and to gain skills and current knowledge in working with diverse client populations. Recognizing the importance of counselor self-awareness, the code also obligates counselors to learn how their own cultural/racial/ethnic identities impact their own values and beliefs about counseling. The importance of recognizing and appreciating parallel diversity issues for the supervisor's self-understanding, knowledge, and skills follows logically from this (Bernard & Goodyear, 1998; Leong & Wagner, 1994). In fact, the ACA code also requires counselor educators to actively infuse multicultural competency in their training and supervision practices. They are to actively train students to gain awareness, knowledge, and skills in the competencies of multicultural practice. Counselor educators should include case examples, role plays, discussion questions, and other classroom activities that promote and represent various cultural perspectives. If supervisors are not equipped adequately to deal with diversity, they are likely to overlook or even reinforce inadvertently biased attitudes and behaviors of their supervisees that could result in potential harm to clients.

Terrell and Cheatman (1996) noted that writers addressing multicultural supervision suggest that multicultural supervision dyads may be more conflicted in nature. They noted that this conclusion might indicate a predisposition on the part of the ethnic minority counselors and majority supervisors to anticipate difficulty in the supervisory relationship. These anticipated difficulties might also be explained by the minority counselors' anticipation of being evaluated by majority supervisors based on criteria rooted in cultural norms not shared in the supervision dyad. Ethical supervision demands that the supervisor be aware of these factors and proceed with sensitivity and a model of multicultural supervision.

Given the cross-cultural nature of all counseling and counseling supervision, the supervisor is involved consistently in cross-cultural supervision of cross-cultural counseling. The challenge for ethical and effective practice is the capacity for the supervisor to share simultaneously the worldview of the counselor and those of the counselor's clients. The culturally effective supervisor is able to generate the widest repertoire of supervisory skills and interventions appropriate to the counselor and the counselor's skill level. This may, in turn, facilitate the counselor's development of the widest repertoire of counseling skills and interventions appropriate to the client and the client's issues. This approach is best ethical practice.

Terrell and Cheatman (1996) outlined the following guidelines for multicultural supervision as a strategy to enhance effective and ethical multicultural supervision.

First, supervisors need to develop an understanding and awareness of self as a cultural being (McCrae & Johnson, 1991) in the supervision process. Supervisors should then undertake self-education about cultural groups that may influence a counselor's worldview. From this perspective, it is suggested that effective cross-cultural supervision should be process oriented rather than client oriented. This method will often include the use of new and creative supervisory interventions to meet the needs of the counselor. This guideline is consistent with Ivey's (1994) call to "cultural intentionality"—generating counseling and supervisory "alternatives from different vantage points, using a variety of skills and personal qualities within a culturally appropriate framework" (p. 19). Supervisees should have the experience of being supervised by culturally different and culturally similar supervisors. Finally, effective multicultural supervision should use multiple or tiered supervisory consultation.

D'Andrea and Daniels (1997) contended supervisors are acting in an ethical manner when they acknowledge their limitations in issues related to multicultural counseling regardless of their supervisory competencies. They noted supervisors should emphasize their interest and commitment to learn about multicultural issues from others, especially from their nonmajority and culturally diverse supervisees. This approach will "often necessitate an increased level of collaboration between supervisor and supervisee" (p. 307).

In the context of supervision, the task becomes one of creating an environment in which supervisees, clients, and supervisors can speak the truth of their respective experiences. Gonzalez (1997) suggested that supervisees find it permissible to be imperfect with regard to multiculturalism and be allowed to reveal ignorance and misunderstandings. In supervision, he suggested supervisors assess what contingencies hinder or facilitate both personal and social constructions that allow for shifts in perspectives, meanings, interpretations, evaluations, and explanations. In this way, he believed, supervisees will not experience guilt but will take personal responsibility for best practice.

Issues of diversity have often been perceived as an obstacle to overcome rather than an opportunity to enhance ethical practice in counseling and supervision. Effective cross-cultural supervisors are sensitive to diversity in both the supervisee–client and supervisor–supervisee relationships. Collaborations between supervisor and supervisee often take place within a multicultural context. This context can involve supervisees and supervisors who are affiliated in a variety of ways with different or similar cultural groups. An attitude of discovery, exploration, and critical thinking in clinical work as opposed to political correctness in approaching multicultural issues has been proposed to enhance the ethical practice of both counseling and supervision (Stone, 1997).

DECISION MAKING IN CONTEXT

Conflicting roles or relationships may occur when a professional assumes two or more roles simultaneously. Concerns about such relationships revolve around issues of possible harm or exploitation of the supervisee or the possible reduction of objectivity on the part of the supervisor. Realizing that professionals who work together share other experiences, the chances of compounding relationships to the supervisory relationship are substantial (Bernard & Goodyear, 1998). It is not uncommon for a counselor to one day be a colleague and then be promoted to supervisor of those who used to be colleagues and friends. The following scenario illustrates an example of such a situation.

An agency that provides substance abuse counseling services to the residents of a rural community has three counselors on staff—you, Sue, and Bob. You and Sue are supervised clinically and administratively by Bob. Prior to becoming supervisor, you and Bob were in an intimate relationship. You now suspect that Sue and Bob are dating. Sue has not been keeping up with her case reports and often arrives late for staff meetings. You notice that Bob overlooks this; yet when you fall behind on your reports, Bob reprimands you and has threatened to deny you your professional development monies if you do not keep your reports current. You are considering what action to take. Bob's relationship with you prior to being promoted to supervisor adds to the complexity of this situation.

Using the Tarvydas Integrative Decision-Making Model, the first step is to interpret the situation through awareness and fact finding. It is important to engage in a reflective process and to sort the personal from the professional aspects of the situation. Awareness of the stakeholders is a place to begin this process. These include the clients each of you serve and the impact of not only late reports, but the potential emotional distraction on the work itself. In addition, Bob and Sue are coworkers, and the effect on the agency and the clinical team is to be considered. It would be important to seek the facts regarding the extent of lateness of your reports as well as to determine if Bob and Sue are dating.

In Stage II, you formulate an ethical decision. The ACA code clearly puts the welfare of clients at the forefront and prohibits sexual relationships between a supervisor and a supervisee. It also speaks to the relationships with other professionals, recognizing that the quality of coworker interactions can influence the quality of services provided to clients. The dilemma, as you see it, is to confront Bob about the injustice you perceive for yourself in the situation, ignore the situation and continue on with your work to the best of your ability, report him to the agency's board, or leave the agency. It would be important to consult with another professional. You decide to talk with a private practitioner who offers consultation and supervision services. After weighing the pros and cons of each course of action, you decide to talk with Bob to ask him about his relationship with Sue and, if true, ask him to stop. In addition, you decide you want to ask him to treat you with fairness with regard to the reports and your professional development monies. This is, in your opinion, the best ethical course of action.

In Stage III, prior to deciding on the preferred course of action, you engage in weighing competing nonmoral values and personal blind spots. Upon reflection, you realize that you have a history of being overly sensitive to injustices. This is compounded by the previous relationship with Bob and the residual feelings you carry, including resentment.

You had believed that you were able to compartmentalize your personal and professional lives, yet now reflect on the impact that your past experiences brings to the current situation. Your relationship with Sue and the fact you believe she is dating Bob also comes to mind. You decide that the preferred course of action is to meet with Bob and discuss your concerns without personalizing the issues.

In Stage IV, you decide that the sequence of activities is to set the time and place for the meeting ahead of time, not to talk to him impromptu. Using "I statements" and assertive communication, you will ask about his relationship, ask him to stop if true, and request that he treat you with fairness in the office.

CHAPTER SUMMARY

Clinical supervision is both an area of specialization and a mainstream activity across all specialties within counseling. Given that supervision is an inherently hierarchical relationship involving supervisor, supervisee(s), and client(s), the ethical and legal considerations are complex. Counseling supervisors encounter situations that challenge the help given by the general ethical standards of the profession at large. To address the problem, ACES and NBCC (ACS) have specific supervision codes and standards. The ACS Standards for the Ethical Practice of Clinical Supervision (1998) and the Ethical Guidelines for Clinical Supervisors (ACES, 1993) are intended to assist supervisors by helping them observe ethical and legal protection of clients' and supervisees' rights. The ethical standards for supervision provide guidelines for best practice.

Supervisors should make supervisees aware of clients' rights, including protecting clients' rights to privacy and confidentiality in the counseling relationship and the information resulting from it. It is also the supervisor's responsibility to keep the supervisee's information confidential and to protect the right to privacy. The supervisee should understand the circumstances under which information obtained in supervision will be revealed.

The client must be informed of the supervision procedures, whether sessions will be taped or observed, who will be involved, and how close the supervision will be. Just as the supervisee has a responsibility to secure the client's informed consent, the supervisor is obligated to ensure that the supervisee understands and consents to the conditions of supervision. Supervisors should incorporate the principles of informed consent and participation; clarity of requirements, expectations, roles, and rules; and due process and appeal into the establishment of policies and procedures of their institutions, programs, courses, and individual supervisory relationships.

Supervision is complicated when supervisors have multiple roles, such as teacher, supervisor, and administrator. All guidelines in the ACA Code of Ethics (ACA, 2005) regarding potentially detrimental relationships between counselor educators and students apply equally to the supervisory relationship. The primary risk factor is a power differential; misuse of this power is exploitive and could cause harm. Potential issues related to the supervisor–supervisee relationship include sexual attraction, harassment, and relationships, as well as acting as counselor or other relationships with supervisees that might impair the supervisor's objectivity and professional judgment.

Being a competent counselor does not necessarily mean one is also a competent supervisor. Counselors must refrain from offering professional services when their physical, mental, or emotional problems are likely to harm clients or others. Supervisors have the responsibility of recommending remedial assistance to the supervisee and of screening from the training program, applied counseling setting, or state licensure those supervisees who are unable to provide competent professional services. Supervisors need to participate in continuing education activities to maintain their competence.

An ethical violation is a behavior that violates the letter or perhaps the spirit of an ethical standard of practice. A complaint of ethical violation appeals to the professional group that endorses the ethical standards that have been violated. Just as a complainant can appeal to different boards, a complainant may also initiate both a complaint and a malpractice lawsuit. Supervisors are responsible for their own behaviors as well as the behaviors of their supervisees. Professional disclosure statements and formal supervision plans are strategies to reduce the risk of ethical conflicts within supervision. Any ethical violation becomes a legal issue when a claim of malpractice is made. Because supervision involves two levels of oversight, liability can be both direct and indirect.

Effective cross-cultural supervisors are sensitive to diversity in both the supervisee–client and supervisor–supervisee relationships. Given the cross-cultural nature of all counseling and counseling supervision, the supervisor is consistently involved in cross-cultural supervision of cross-cultural counseling. The challenge for ethical and effective practice is the capacity for the supervisor to share simultaneously the worldview of the counselor and the counselor's clients.

INTERNET RESOURCES

Recognizing that the internet is a resource to finding information relevant to the ethical practice of clinical supervision, the following key words are provided: clinical supervisor, supervision ethics, counselor education, models of clinical supervision, vicarious liability, direct liability, layered supervision, respondeat superior, impaired professional.

REFERENCES

American Counseling Association. (2005). *The ACA code of ethics.* Alexandria, VA: Author.

Association for Specialists in Group Work. (1998). *Best practice guidelines.* Alexandria, VA: Author.

Association for Counselor Education and Supervision. (1993). ACES ethical guidelines for counseling supervisors. *ACES Spectrum, 53,* 5–8.

Bartell, P. A., & Rubin, L. J. (1990). Dangerous liaisons: Sexual intimacies in supervision. *Professional Psychology: Research and Practice, 21,* 442–450.

Bernard, J. L., & Jara, C. S. (1986). The failure of clinical psychology graduate students to apply understood ethical principles. *Professional Psychology: Research and Practice, 17,* 313–315.

Bernard, J. M. (1979). Supervisor training: A discrimination model. *Counselor Education and Supervision, 19,* 60–68.

Bernard, J. M., & Goodyear, R. K. (1998). *Fundamentals of clinical supervision* (2nd ed.). Boston, MA: Allyn & Bacon.

Bernard, J. M., & Goodyear, R. K. (2004). *Fundamentals of clinical supervision* (3rd ed.). Boston, MA: Allyn & Bacon.

Blackwell, T. L., Strohmer, D. C., Belcas, E. M., & Burton, K. A. (2002). Ethics in rehabilitation counselor supervision. *Rehabilitation Counseling Bulletin, 45,* 240–247.

Bonosky, N. (1995). Boundary violations in social work supervision: Clinical educational and legal implications. *The Clinical Supervisor, 13*(2), 79–95.

Borders, L. D. (2001). Counseling supervision: A deliberate educational process. In D. Locke, J. Myers, & E. Herr (Ed.), *Handbook of counseling* (pp. 417–432), Thousand Oaks, CA: Sage.

Borders, L. D., Bernard, J. M., Dye, H. A., Fong, M. L., Henderson, P., & Nance, D. W. (1991). Curriculum guide for training counseling supervisors: Rationale, development, and implementation. *Counselor Education and Supervision, 31,* 58–82.

Borders, L. D., & Brown, L. L. (2005). *The new handbook of counseling supervision.* Mahwah, NJ: Lawrence Erlbaum Associates.

Bridge, P., & Bascue, L. O. (1990). Documentation of psychotherapy supervision. *Psychotherapy in Private Practice, 8,* 79–86.

Bridges, N. A., & Wohlberg, J. W. (1999). Sexual excitement in therapeutic relationships: Clinical and supervisory management. *The Clinical Supervisor, 18*(2), 123–141.

Brodsky, A. (1980). Sex role issues in the supervision of therapy. In A. K. Hess (Ed.), *Psychotherapy supervision: Theory, research, and practice* (pp. 509–524), New York: Wiley.

Campbell, T. W. (1994). Psychotherapy and malpractice exposure. *American Journal of Forsenic Psychology, 12,* 5–41.

Cobia, D. C., & Boes, S. R. (2000). Professional disclosure statements and formal plans for supervision: Two strategies for minimizing the risk of ethical conflict in post-master's supervision. *Journal of Counseling & Development, 78,* 293–296.

Commission on Rehabilitation Counselor Certification. (2001). *Code of professional ethics for rehabilitation counselors.* Rolling Meadows, IL: Author.

Cramton, R. (1981). Incompetence: The North American experience. In L. E. Trakman & D. Watters (Eds.), *Professional competence and the law* (pp. 158–163). Halifax, Nova Scotia, Canada: Dalhousie University.

D'Andrea, M., & Daniels, J. (1997). Multicultural counseling supervision: Central issues, theoretical considerations, and practical strategies. In D. Pope-Davis & H. Coleman (Eds.), *Multicultural counseling competencies: Assessment, education and training, and supervision.* Multicultural aspects of counseling series, Vol. 7. Thousand Oaks, CA: Sage.

Disney, M. J., & Stephens, A. M. (1994). *Legal issues in clinical supervision.* Alexandria, VA: ACA Press.

Ellis, M. V., & Douce, L. A. (1994). Group supervision of novice clinical supervisors: Eight recurring issues. *Journal of Counseling and Development, 72,* 520–525.

Erwin, W. J. (2000). Supervisor moral sensitivity. *Counseling Education and Supervision, 40,* 115–127.

Falvey, J. E. (2002). *Managing clinical supervision: Ethical practice and legal risk management.* Pacific Grove, CA: Brooks/Cole.

Falvey, J. E., Caldwell, C. F., & Cohen, C. R. (2002). *Documentation in supervision: The focused risk management supervision system.* Pacific Grove, CA: Brooks/Cole.

Fly, B. J., van Bark, W. P., Weinman, L., Kitchener, K. S., & Lang, P. R. (1997). Ethical transgressions of psychology graduate students: Critical incidents with implications for training. *Professional Psychology: Research and Practice, 28,* 492–495.

Giordano, F. (2005, June). Best practices: The development of a best practices policy for counseling supervision standards. International and Interdisciplinary Conference on Clinical Supervision, Buffalo, NY.

Gonzalez, R. C. (1997). Postmodern supervision: Issues for the white supervisor. In D. Pope-Davis & H. Coleman (Eds.) *Multicultural counseling competencies: Assessment, education and training, and supervision. Multicultural aspects of counseling series: Vol. 7.* Thousand Oaks, CA: Sage.

Goodyear, R. K., & Sinnett, E. D. (1984). Current and emerging ethical issues for counseling psychologists. *Counseling Psychologist, 12,* 87–98.

Guest, C. L., Jr., & Dooley, K. (1999). Supervisor malpractice: Liability to the supervisee in clinical supervision. *Counselor Education and Supervision, 38,* 269–279.

Hall, J. E.(1988). Dual relationships in supervision. *Register Report, 15,* 5–6.

Hamilton, J. C., & Spruill, J. (1999). Identifying and reducing risk factors related to trainee–client sexual misconduct. *Professional Psychology: Research and Practice, 30,* 318–327.

Handelsman, M. M., Gottlieb, M. C., & Knapp, S. (2005). Training ethical psychologists: An acculturation model. *Professional Psychology: Research and Practice, 36,* 59–65.

Hawkins, P., & Shohet, R. (1989). *Supervision in the helping professions.* Milton Keynes, UK: Open University Press.

Herlihy, B., & Corey, G. (1997). Codes of ethics as catalysts for improving practice. In B. Herlihy & G. Corey (Eds.), *Ethics in therapy* (pp. 37–56). New York: Hatherleigh.

Holloway, E. L. (1995). *Clinical supervision: A systems approach.* Thousand Oaks, CA: Sage.

Ivey, A. E. (1994). *Intentional interviewing and counseling: Facilitating client development in a multicultural society.* Pacific Grove, CA: Brooks/Cole.

Jackson, H., & Nuttal, R. L. (2001). A relationship between childhood sexual abuse and professional sexual misconduct. *Professional Psychology: Research and Practice, 32,* 200–204.

Kagan, N. (1976). *Influencing human interaction.* Mason, MI: Mason Media, Inc.; Or Washington, DC: American Counseling Association.

Kitchener, K. S. (1984). Intuition, critical evaluations and ethical principles: The foundation for ethical decisions in counseling psychology. *The Counseling Psychologist, 12,* 43–55.

Kitchener, K. S., & Harding, S. S. (1990). Dual role relationships. In B. Herlihy & L. Golden (Eds.), *Ethical standards casebook* (4th ed., pp. 145–148). Alexandria, VA: American Counseling Association.

Koenig, T. L., & Spano, R. N. (2003). Sex, supervision, and boundary violations: Pressing challenges and possible solutions. *The Clinical Supervisor, 22*(1), 3–19.

Ladany, N., Hill, C. E., Corbett, M., & Nutt, E. A. (1996). Nature, extent and importance of what psychotherapy trainees do not disclose to their supervisors. *Journal of Counseling Psychology, 43,* 10–24.

Ladany, N., Lehrman-Waterman, D., Molinaro, M., & Wolgast, B. (1999). Psychotherapy supervisor ethical practices: Adherence to guidelines, the supervisory working alliance, and supervisee satisfaction. *The Counseling Psychologist, 27,* 443–475.

Lamb, D. H., & Catanzaro, S. J. (1998). Sexual and nonsexual boundary violations involving psychologists, clients, supervisees, and students: Implications for professional practice. *Professional Psychology: Research and Practice, 29,* 498–503.

Lamb, D. H., Catanzaro, S. J., & Moorman, A. S. (2003). Psychologists reflect on their sexual relationships with clients, supervisees, and students: Occurrence, impact, rationales, and collegial intervention. *Professional Psychology: Research and Practice, 34,* 102–107.

Lamb, D. H., Cochran, D. J., & Jackson, V. R. (1991). Training and organizational issues associated with identifying and responding to intern impairment. *Professional Psychology: Research and Practice, 22,* 291–296.

Leddick, G. R., & Bernard, J. M. (1980). The history of supervision: A critical review. *Counselor Education and Supervision, 19,* 186–196.

Leong, F. T., & Wagner, N. S. (1994). Cross-cultural counseling supervision: What do we know? What do we need to know? *Counselor Education and Supervision, 34,* 117–131.

Loganbill, C., Hardy, E., & Delworth, U. (1982). Supervision: A conceptual model. *The Counseling Psychologist, 10,* 3–42.

Maki, D., & Delworth, U. (1995). Clinical supervision: A definition and model for the rehabilitation counseling profession. *Rehabilitation Counseling Bulletin, 38*(4), 282–293.

McCarthy, P., Sugden, S., Koker, M., Lamendola, F., Maurer, S., & Renninger, S. (1995). A practical guide to informed consent in clinical supervision. *Counselor Education and Supervision, 35,* 130–138.

McCrae, M. B., & Johnson, S. D. (1991). Toward training for competence in multicultural counselor education. *Journal of Counseling & Development, 70,* 131–135.

Miller, G. M., & Larrabee, M. J. (1995). Sexual intimacy in counselor education and supervision: A national survey. *Counselor Education and Supervision, 34,* 332–343.

Montgomery, L. M., Cupit, B. E., & Wimberley, T. K. (1999). Complaints, malpractice, and risk management: Professional issues and personal experiences. *Professional Psychology: Research and Practice, 30,* 402–410.

Ogloff, J. R. P., & Olley, M. C. (1998). The interaction between ethics and the law: The ongoing refinement of ethical standards for psychologists in Canada. *Professional Psychology: Research and Practice, 39,* 221–230.

Peterson, M. (1993). Covert agendas in supervision. *Supervision Bulletin, 6,* 7–8.

Remley, T. P., Jr., & Herlihy, B. (2001). *Ethical, legal, and professional issues in counseling.* Upper Saddle River, NJ: Prentice-Hall.

Rubin, S. S. (1997). Balancing duty to client and therapist in supervision: Clinical, ethical and training issues. *The Clinical Supervisor, 16*(1), 1–23.

Samuel, S. E., & Gorton, G. E. (1998). National survey of psychology internship directors regarding education for prevention of psychologist–patient sexual exploitation. *Professional Psychology: Research and Practice, 29,* 86–90.

Sherry, P. (1991). Ethical issues in the conduct of supervisions. *The Counseling Psychologist, 19,* 566–585.

Siegel, M. (1979). Privacy, ethics, and confidentiality. *Professional Psychology, 10,* 249–258.

Slimp, P. A. O., & Burian, B. K. (1994). Multiple role relationships during internship: Consequences and recommendations. *Professional Psychology: Research and Practice, 25,* 39–45.

Stoltenberg, C. (1981). Approaching supervision from a developmental perspective: The counselor-complexity model. *Journal of Counseling Psychology, 28,* 59–65.

Stoltenberg, C. D., McNeill, B., & Delworth, U. (1998). *IDM supervision: An integrated developmental model for supervising counselors and therapists.* San Francisco: Jossey-Bass.

Stoltenberg, C. D., & Delworth, U. (1988). Developmental models of supervision: It is development—Response to Holloway. *Professional Psychology: Research and Practice, 19,* 134–137.

Stone, G. L. (1997). Multiculturalism as a context for supervision: Perspectives, limitations, and implications. In D. Pope-Davis and H. Coleman (Eds.), *Multicultural counseling competencies: Assessment, education and training, and supervision.* Thousand Oaks, CA: Sage.

Strein, W., & Hershenson, D. B. (1991). Confidentiality in non-dyadic counseling situations. *Journal of Counseling and Development, 69,* 312–316.

Sue, D. W., Bernier, J. E., Duran, A., Feinberg, L., Pederson, P., Smith E. G., et al. (1982). Position paper: Cross-cultural counseling competencies. *The Counseling Psychologist, 10,* 45–52.

Supervision Interest Network, Association for Counselor Education and Supervision (1990). Standards for counseling supervisors. *Journal of Counseling and Development, 69,* 30–32.

Sutton, J. M., Jr. (2000). Counselor licensure. In H. Hackney (Ed.). *Practice issues for the beginning counselor* (pp. 55–78). Boston, MA: Allyn & Bacon.

Swenson, L. C. (1997). *Psychology and law for the helping professions.* Pacific Grove, CA: Brooks/Cole.

Tarvydas, V. M. (2004). Ethics. In T. F. Riggar & D. R. Maki (Eds.), *Handbook of rehabilitation counseling* (pp. 108–141). New York: Springer.

Terrell, Y. L., & Cheatman, H. E. (1996). Creating a therapeutic alliance: A multicultural perspective. In J. L. DeLucia-Waack (Ed.), *Multicultural counseling competencies: Implications for training and practice.* Alexandria, VA: Association for Counselor Education and Supervision.

Welfel, E. R. (1998). *Ethics in counseling and psychotherapy: Standards, research, and emerging issues.* Pacific Grove, CA: Brooks/Cole.

Whiston, S. C., & Emerson, S. (1989). Ethical implications for supervisors in counseling of trainees. *Counselor Education and Supervision, 28,* 318–325.

Williams, A. (1995). *Visual and active supervision: Roles, focus, and technique.* New York: W. W. Norton.

Woodworth, C. B. (2000). Legal issues in counseling practice. In H. Hackney (Ed.), *Practice issues for the beginning counselor* (pp. 119–136). Boston, MA: Allyn & Bacon.

Worthington, R. L., Tan, J. A., & Poulin, K. (2002). Ethically questionable behaviors among supervisees: An exploratory investigation. *Ethics and Behavior, 12,* 323–351.

PART 6

Conclusion

20 The Ethical Professional Counselor

CHAPTER 20

The Ethical Professional Counselor

OBJECTIVES

After reading this chapter, you should be able to:

- Describe ethical practice in counseling.
- Provide current statistics on ethical complaint adjudication.
- Explain what a counselor should do when confronted with an allegation of ethical misconduct.

- Describe the counselor's response to an ethical challenge in the context of potential legal and professional scrutiny.
- Explain the consequences for clients who are victims of unethical professional conduct.

INTRODUCTION

The study of ethics is like a journey. After individuals first read a code of ethics, they may feel confident about their knowledge and have a sense that nothing can create a serious ethical crisis in their professional lives. However, as the journey progresses, it becomes clearer that the practice of counseling is complex. Often, no easy answers emerge. At the end of the journey, there is the realization that ethical dilemmas do arise, and they challenge even the most sophisticated and ethically sensitive practitioner.

No professional is immune to ethical dilemmas—no matter how ethically sensitive counselors may be, circumstances will always arise that place them in a quandary. It is important, however, that counselors recognize when they are facing a serious ethical challenge. With such recognition, wise counselors protect themselves from a naive decision and a possible breach of ethical standards.

No professional is immune from being accused of ethical misconduct. Complaints against mental health

professionals increased dramatically in the 1990s. Bass et al. (1996) reported a 500% increase in disciplinary actions by state and provincial licensing boards in psychology over a 10-year period. They stated:

> A wide range of behaviors and practices may lead to disciplinary or legal action before a regulatory board, professional association, or court of law. . . . Common problem areas include (a) competence, (b) informed consent and confidentiality, (c) dual relationships, and (d) financial arrangements. (p. 71)

Even counselor educators are concerned about the ethics of educating counselors (Schwab & Neukrug, 1994). Clients and students of counseling are becoming more sophisticated about their rights. Licensure and regulatory boards are more experienced at addressing complaints, and there may be a tendency among licensure board members to assume guilt rather than innocence when a licensed professional is accused (Peterson, 2001). American society is also a litigious culture. It can be expected that a good percentage of counselors will be accused formally of unethical or illegal practice during their careers. Innocent or not, the consequences can be serious.

Professional careers can be ruined by poor decisions made in the moments of an ethical dilemma or in the face of an ethical complaint. (See Box 20–1.)

CONSEQUENCES OF A BREACH OF ETHICAL STANDARDS FOR THE COUNSELOR

The professional consequences of a breach of an ethical standard can range from no formal repercussions to serious repercussions, such as professional and personal censure and the loss of a license to practice. Chauvin and Remley (1996) recommended that once confronted with an allegation of unethical conduct, it is wise for counselors not to discuss the complaint openly with family or friends, to contact their malpractice insurance carrier, and to retain the services of an attorney. Chauvin and Remley stated:

> The immediate reaction of most counselors would be shock and disbelief accompanied by deep sorrow, embarrassment, or extreme anger, or very likely a combination of all three. A first inclination of most counselors would be to call a best friend or family member and describe the details of the accusation and lament the injustice of what has been alleged. A lawyer most likely would advise against such a response. (p. 565)

To consult other individuals (for personal rather than professional reasons) with details of a client's allegation of impropriety is, in effect, a breach of the client's confidentiality and privacy; such action essentially compounds an already tenuous professional situation. Personal needs must be dealt with in a way that will not complicate the situation. Chauvin and Remley recommended that counselors suffering serious emotional pain over an allegation of unethical behavior should seek confidential treatment by mental health professionals. Even then, what is said should be said carefully, because the mental health professional may not be able to guarantee privileged

communications in certain cases (especially those of a criminal nature).

Revelation of serious unethical practice can be devastating to the professional—guilt may prevent an unfettered return to practice. Remorseful counselors will be faced with guilt over possible damage done to any victims involved in the ethical breach. They may feel anxiety over the professional consequences related to licensure board or other certifying board actions. Legal problems may arise, such as malpractice. Malpractice insurance companies, valued by counselors as shields against financial ruin, may be untrusting and unwilling participants in defense of charges of unethical conduct.

There are always cases of professional counselors who are accused falsely of serious ethical misconduct, adding the issue of anger. If cleared of all allegations of misconduct, the exonerated counselors may have done themselves serious professional damage by having communicated to others about the complaint. Trusted colleagues from the past may view them with suspicion or disdain. For their own benefit, counselors are well advised to maintain the secrecy of an ethical complaint against them or be willing to suffer the consequence of professional stigmatization, even in cases of total innocence. In many cases, licensure or certifying bodies will keep the complaint confidential, unless legal standards exist that require public knowledge or public hearing of such complaints (Chauvin & Remley, 1996). It is possible that the complaint will be dismissed by the licensure board as unfounded, without merit, or poorly supported. In cases in which a certifying or licensing authority dismisses a case, the dismissal may signify the end of the charge, unless the client brings legal action (e.g., malpractice charges). According to a 2004 report of the ACA Ethics Committee (Hubert & Freeman, 2004), 33 complaints were received, but only 12 complaints were made against ACA members (therefore the committee had jurisdiction only over these 12 complaints). Of the 12, only 3 were found to have substance. Of the three processed cases, two were dismissed of charges and one was upheld and the member was sanctioned. The chances of being sanctioned on a formal charge of unethical conduct, therefore, is very slight. In effect, counselors should not panic when faced with a charge of unethical conduct; they should address complaints as a professional faced with a matter of professional business. If personal stress somehow affects the practitioner's judgment, professional counsel should be sought from an attorney and a mental health professional.

CONSEQUENCES OF A BREACH OF ETHICAL STANDARDS FOR THE CLIENT

Unethical situations are even more difficult for a client who suffers an injustice. Victimized clients have to deal with the unacceptable actions of the counselor, but they must also deal with a professional system that may be reluctant to discipline one of its own. The legal system may also become involved, and once the legal wheels begin to roll, it is difficult to steer a new direction. Financial and personal commitments may place a strain on the victim of unethical practice. In some cases, there may be degrees of embarrassment or public humiliation. Just the revelation of treatment by a mental health professional may be embarrassing to some individuals. The conduct of the professional also may be embarrassing to the client or may inadvertently or inappropriately reflect on the morals or judgment of the client. Friendships may be strained or destroyed. In the end, the brave victims of serious unethical practice who file formal complaints may place themselves in positions of double or multiple victimization.

FILING A COMPLAINT TO A LICENSURE AUTHORITY

Procedures for filing complaints about unethical practitioners in the mental health field are fairly standard. Licensed professionals practicing in a particular state are bound legally to the ethical and administrative standards of practice as adopted by statute and regulation in that state. These standards and disciplinary procedures are usually available to the public through the state's department of regulation or licensure. Related to psychology licensure, Reaves (1996) stated:

> Virtually all jurisdictions require that complaints concerning psychologists' behavior be in writing. Unless a complaint is determined to be frivolous or made in bad faith, an investigation ensues. In some jurisdictions, trained investigators are employed to perform this task. In smaller jurisdictions, a board member may be assigned as an investigating officer. The method used to investigate a complaint varies with the type or substance of the complaint. For example, an allegation that

a licensee has been convicted of a felony would involve obtaining documentation from the court where the conviction occurred, whereas an allegation of sexual intimacies with a client would likely involve interviews and possible collection of other evidence. (p. 102)

Reaves further noted that a license to practice a profession is considered a "property" and, therefore, a license cannot be taken away without due process of law.

If a professional is accused of unethical conduct and simply admits to the conduct, the case is uncontested. Settlement on such cases may be a matter of the regulatory board's disposition—in such cases the board may make a decision as to the consequences of the unethical conduct. Contested cases, wherein the professional essentially pleads innocent to some or all of the charges, typically leads to a civil court (versus criminal court) hearing or legal proceeding. In such cases, a hearing officer is present and attorneys may be involved. In some jurisdictions, hearings may be open to the public (Chauvin & Remley, 1996). Chauvin and Remley stated, "If a hearing is held, the complainant, the witnesses, and the accused counselor would be given an opportunity to present their positions and would be questioned by the board members" (p. 565). After a hearing, the board most typically makes a decision, which could include the following consequences: reprimand, probation, suspension of a certificate or license, or revocation of a certificate or a license. The counselor or psychologist is allowed to appeal. According to Chauvin and Remley, "After an appeal, if the counselor still disagrees with the board's findings, he or she could sue the board in court in an effort to have the board's decision overturned" (p. 565).

Clients or involved laypersons who desire to file complaints should be provided adequate information to file such complaints. Responsible counselors who are knowledgeable about the questionable or unethical practices of colleagues are obligated by law (in most cases) and by mandatory professional ethical standards to file complaints. Filing of a complaint is required if direct, informal attempts to resolve the issue with the offending professional fail or if the conduct is either serious or repetitive.

It is standard procedure for a complaint to be filed in writing. Any member of the public or the profession may file a complaint, regardless of residence (inside or outside of the state of the alleged ethical violation). Complaints can be based on personal knowledge, public record, or information received from third-party sources. The complainant and the individual filing the complaint (often the same person) must be identified fully in the complaint by name and address and in writing. Complaints typically are logged by the date and nature of the complaint. Each complaint will be acknowledged by the board in writing, and the complainant will be notified of the ultimate disposition of the complaint. Complaints may be dismissed on several grounds, including insufficient evidence or information, noncooperation of the complainant, or inability to prove or to refute charges due to lack of probable corroboration (e.g., hearsay evidence only).

Complainants to licensure boards may file complaints against a suspected unethical practitioner simultaneously with the professional associations to which the practitioner belongs (e.g., the ACA or APA). Counselors are obligated to disclose information about their professional qualifications and affiliations to interested parties. Withholding such information, especially to clients, may be considered a breach of ethics in and of itself, depending on state statute or professional ethical standards. The important issue is the availability of information so that complainants can make informed complaints to appropriate authorities; concerned individuals should not be impeded in their attempts to file complaints.

Counselors who are guilty of unethical conduct and who have the intention of practicing again have a responsibility to "rehabilitate" themselves and to seek guidance so they never repeat their actions (Chauvin & Remley, 1996). There is nothing more repulsive to the public or to professional colleagues than a repeat offender, especially in cases of serious ethical misconduct. In fact, Walden, Herlihy and Ashton (2003), in a survey of former chairs of the ACA Ethics Committee, found that "Former chairs . . . wrote about learning lessons that were, for some, rather disappointing or disillusioning" related to the actions of some professional counselors who harmed their clients. In cases of repeat offenders, it becomes obvious that the unethical practitioner has become a predator, is incompetent, or is simply interested in personal gain. Such activity reflects badly on the profession of counseling, and all professionals have an obligation to prevent such activity.

THE DEVELOPMENT OF THE ETHICAL PROFESSIONAL COUNSELOR

Professional associations such as the ACA and the APA have a special role in helping to develop ethical behavior in practitioners. In a survey of certified counselors who were asked to rate 16 sources of ethical information (Gibson & Pope, 1993), the ACA ethical code, the ACA

Ethics Committee, and the ACA *Journal of Counseling and Development* were given the highest ratings. But good information may not be enough. The development of the ethically sensitive counselor is a complex process. It is not simply a matter of information, education, supervision, and training. As Pettifor (1996) stated:

> Psychologists who maintain high levels of professional conduct are encouraged by aspirational ethics to practice appropriately and . . . the measures they take to maintain competence are voluntary and targeted to specific professional needs. Aspirational ethics are based on moral principles that always place the well-being of the other, the consumer, above self-interest, as opposed to codes of conduct that define minimal levels of acceptable behavior. (pp. 91–92)

Professional training may not be enough. The works of Kohlberg (1964, 1971, 1981) demonstrated that the application of moral thinking stems from a developmental process. It may be that training, no matter how targeted to moral development, may not inspire moral choice adequately in certain counselors. In the end, even the most trained counselor or psychologist may choose to act unethically. Therefore, it is as important to study what prevents unethical conduct as it is to study the correlates of unethical conduct (see Lamb, Catanzaro & Moorman, 2004). It may be that what prevents unethical conduct, as Pettifor implied, is a moral standard and moral directives that supersede even the most powerful motivations to breach an accepted ethical standard. Counselors must have the constitution to make moral choices when other needs enter into decisions.

One approach, deriving from the "positive psychology" movement (Seligman & Csikszentmihalyi, 2000) is to address ethical issues in a positive light—focusing on building strengths against ethical breaches rather than approaching ethics as a crisis and remedial concern. Handelsman, Knapp, and Gottlieb (2002) made a compelling argument for positive ethics:

> Our view of positive ethics encompasses a broad context of ethical behavior—including aspirational elements that range from the personal to the societal in nature—which goes beyond a focus on rules and risk. We propose that the morality of professional actions can be explored without emphasizing the prohibitions or potential sanctions found within psychology's disciplinary codes. At the same time, we are not advocating the abandonment of ethical rules and prohibitions; they do have a basis in morality that psychologists need to understand. Likewise, psychologists should know the laws that govern the practice of psychology and the ways to reduce legal risk. We are suggesting that whereas rules

and good risk management strategies are not antithetical to positive ethics, they are not sufficient to ensure optimal ethical practice. What is necessary is an awareness of several interacting perspectives. (p. 734)

Handelsman et al. (2002) recommended "seven themes of positive ethics," which are: (a) values and virtues; (b) sensitivity and integration; (c) ethics as ongoing self-care; (d) ethical reasoning and decision making; (e) appreciation of the moral traditions underlying ethical principles; (f) prevention of misconduct and promotion of positive behaviors; and (g) sensitivity to larger professional contexts. With the positive psychology movement, there is an opportunity to redefine professional ethics around a positive developmental process rather than a remedial post-crisis event.

Handelsman, Gottlieb, and Knapp (2005) went a step farther in exploring an "acculturation model" of ethics training. In a groundbreaking work, they conceptualized the process of ethics education of psychologists in training as akin to the process of acculturation, a developmental process requiring adaptation strategies. Using Berry's (1980) model of acculturation strategies, Handelsman et al. (2005) outlined the process of ethics training. They concluded: "An acculturation model may help improve the socialization of students, especially in the acquisition of their ethical identity" (p. 64).

On the other hand, some might argue that no matter how ethically focused or sophisticated the profession becomes at ethics training, there always will be practitioners who consciously breach or challenge the limits of ethical behavior. Also, if a profession is struggling—that is, if trained professionals are having difficulty making a living—temptations to sell clients short of ethical services may become more common. In this light, it is important for the leaders of the profession to ensure that ethical professionals are rewarded adequately in their professional practices; otherwise, the fringe ethical behaviors of desperate practitioners may erode the reputation of the profession as a whole.

Ideally, counselors should make the best of their education to take ethics to heart and develop a moral stance. A profession devoted to helping others should facilitate a personal, as well as academic, interest in

defining what is right and wrong in the treatment of individuals in need. The clients of counselors deserve no less.

DECISION MAKING IN CONTEXT

As the popular adage states: "An ounce of prevention is worth a pound of cure." In fact, related to preventing unethical conduct, counselors are well advised to consider decision making an ongoing process of everyday practice, rather than an isolated event when confronted with a dilemma. By being cognizant of the subtleties of ethical practice, a wise counselor builds procedures into his or her daily practice that will act as safeguards against ethical compromises. By being alert to the nuance of ethical practice in the daily decisions that occur in the practice of counseling, big mistakes may be avoided. Counselors can take pride in their practices when they consider the ethical consequences of their policies and procedures as a standard way of operating. Ethics is not an event, it is a way of practice, and decision making should not be viewed as "after the fact" of an ethical challenge.

CHAPTER SUMMARY

This text has been organized to provide the student of counseling and practicing counselors with a clear and concise overview of ethical issues in counseling and psychology. The intent of the book is to provide a thorough and scholarly foundation, defining ethical concepts and practice, legal issues, methods for clarifying values, decision-making models, and contemporaneous and emerging issues. Additionally, the book addresses issues related to some of the largest specialties of counseling. It is hoped that this text will inspire ethically sensitive counselors who will reflect before acting and who will consult with educated colleagues at those moments when ethical dilemmas arise. In the end, ethical counselors are those who have the best interests of their clients at heart and who also respect the rights that derive from being professionals.

REFERENCES

Bass, L. J., DeMers, S. T., Ogloff, J. R., Peterson, C., Pettifor, J. L., Reaves, R. P., et al. (1996). *Professional conduct and discipline in psychology.* Washington, DC: American Psychological Association.

Berry, J. W. (1980) Acculturation as varieties of adaptation. In A. M. Padilla (Ed.), *Acculturation: Theory, models, and some new findings* (pp. 9–25). Boulder, CO: Westview Press.

Chauvin, J. C., & Remley, T. P. (1996). Responding to allegations of unethical conduct. *Journal of Counseling and Development, 74*, 563–568.

Gibson, W. T., & Pope, K. S. (1993). The ethics of counseling: A national survey of certified counselors. *Journal of Counseling and Development, 71*, 330–336.

Handelsman, M. M., Gottlieb, M. C., & Knapp, S. (2005). Training ethical psychologists: An acculturation model. *Professional Psychology: Research and Practice, 36*, 59–65.

Handelsman, M. M., Knapp, S., & Gottlieb, M. C. (2002). Positive ethics. In C. R. Snyder & S. J. Lopez (Eds.), *Handbook of positive psychology* (pp. 731–744). New York: Oxford University Press.

Hubert, R. M., & Freeman, L. T. (2004). Report of the ACA Ethics Committee: 2002–2003. *Journal of Counseling and Development, 82*, 248–251.

Kohlberg, L. (1964). Development of moral character and moral ecology. In M. L. Hoffman & L. W. Hoffman (Eds.), *Review of child development research* (Vol. 1). New York: Russell Sage Foundation.

Kohlberg, L. (1971). Moral development and the education of adolescents. In R. Purnell (Ed.), *Adolescents and the American high school*. New York: Holt, Rinehart & Winston.

Kohlberg, L. (1981). *Philosophy of moral development*. San Francisco: Harper & Row.

Lamb, D. H., Catanzaro, S. J., & Moorman, A. S. (2004). A preliminary look at how psychologists identify, evaluate, and proceed when faced with possible multiple relationship dilemmas. *Professional Psychology: Research and Practice, 35*, 248–254.

Peterson, M. B. (2001). Recognizing concerns about how some licensing boards are treating psychologists. *Professional Psychology: Research and Practice, 32*, 339–340.

Pettifor, J. L. (1996). Maintaining professional conduct in daily practice. In Bass et al. (Eds.), *Professional conduct and discipline in psychology* (pp. 91–100). Washington, DC: American Psychological Association.

Reaves, R. P. (1996). Enforcement of codes of conduct by regulatory boards and professional associations. In Bass et al. (Eds.), *Professional conduct and discipline in psychology* (pp. 101–108). Washington, DC: American Psychological Association.

Schwab, R., & Neukrug, E. (1994). A survey of counselor educators' ethical concerns. *Counseling and Values, 39*, 42–54.

Seligman, M. E. P., & Csikszentmihalyi, M. (2000). Positive psychology: An introduction. *American Psychologist, 55*, 5–14.

Walden, S. L., Herlihy, B., & Ashton, L. (2003). The evolution of ethics: Personal perspectives of ACA Ethics Committee chairs. *Journal of Counseling and Development, 81*, 106–110.

APPENDIX A
ACA Code of Ethics (2005)

ACA CODE OF ETHICS PREAMBLE

The American Counseling Association is an educational, scientific, and professional organization whose members work in a variety of settings and serve in multiple capacities. ACA members are dedicated to the enhancement of human development throughout the life span. Association members recognize diversity and embrace a cross cultural approach in support of the worth, dignity, potential, and uniqueness of people within their social and cultural contexts.

Professional values are an important way of living out an ethical commitment. Values inform principles. Inherently held values that guide our behaviors or exceed prescribed behaviors are deeply ingrained in the counselor and developed out of personal dedication, rather than the mandatory requirement of an external organization.

ACA CODE OF ETHICS PURPOSE

The *ACA Code of Ethics* serves five main purposes:

1. The *Code* enables the association to clarify to current and future members, and to those served by members, the nature of the ethical responsibilities held in common by its members.
2. The *Code* helps support the mission of the association.
3. The *Code* establishes principles that define ethical behavior and best practices of association members.
4. The *Code* serves as an ethical guide designed to assist members in constructing a professional course of action that best serves those utilizing counseling services and best promotes the values of the counseling profession.
5. The *Code* serves as the basis for processing of ethical complaints and inquiries initiated against members of the association.

The *ACA Code of Ethics* contains eight main sections that address the following areas:

Section A: The Counseling Relationship
Section B: Confidentiality, Privileged Communication, and Privacy
Section C: Professional Responsibility
Section D: Relationships with Other Professionals
Section E: Evaluation, Assessment, and Interpretation
Section F: Supervision, Training, and Teaching
Section G: Research and Publication
Section H: Resolving Ethical Issues

Each section of the *ACA Code of Ethics* begins with an Introduction. The introductions to each section discuss what counselors should aspire to with regard to ethical behavior and responsibility. The Introduction helps set the tone for that particular section and provides a starting point that invites reflection on the ethical mandates contained in each part of the *ACA Code of Ethics*.

When counselors are faced with ethical dilemmas that are difficult to resolve, they are expected to engage in a carefully considered ethical decision-making process. Reasonable differences of opinion can and do exist among counselors with respect to the ways in which values, ethical principles, and ethical standards would be applied when they conflict. While there is no specific ethical decision-making model that is most effective, counselors are expected to be familiar with a credible model of decision making that can bear public scrutiny and its application.

Through a chosen ethical decision-making process and evaluation of the context of the situation, counselors are empowered to make decisions that help expand the capacity of people to grow and develop.

A brief glossary is given to provide readers with a concise description of some of the terms used in the *ACA Code of Ethics*.

Section A: The Counseling Relationship

Introduction
Counselors encourage client growth and development in ways that foster the interest and welfare of clients and promote formation of healthy relationships. Counselors actively attempt to understand the diverse cultural backgrounds of the clients they serve. Counselors also explore their own cultural identities and how these affect their values and beliefs about the counseling process.

Counselors are encouraged to contribute to society by devoting a portion of their professional activity to services for which there is little or no financial return (pro bono publico).

A.1. Welfare of Those Served by Counselors
A.1.a. *Primary Responsibility.* The primary responsibility of counselors is to respect the dignity and to promote the welfare of clients.

A.1.b. *Records.* Counselors maintain records necessary for rendering professional services to their clients and as required by laws, regulations, or agency or institution procedures. Counselors include sufficient and timely documentation in their client records to facilitate the delivery and continuity of needed services. Counselors take reasonable steps to ensure that documentation in records accurately reflects client progress and services provided. If errors are made in client records, counselors take steps to properly note the correction of such errors according to agency or institutional policies. (See A.12.g.7., B.6., B.6.g., G.2.j.)

A.1.c. *Counseling: Plans.* Counselors and their clients work jointly in devising integrated counseling plans that offer reasonable promise of success and are consistent with abilities and circumstances of clients. Counselors and clients regularly review counseling plans to assess their continued viability and effectiveness, respecting the freedom of choice of clients. (See A.2.a., A.2.d., A.12.g.)

A.1.d. *Support Network Involvement.* Counselors recognize that support networks hold various meanings in the lives of clients and consider enlisting the support, understanding, and involvement of others (e.g., religious/spiritual/community leaders, family members, friends) as positive resources, when appropriate, with client consent.

A.1.e. *Employment Needs.* Counselors work with their clients considering employment in jobs that are consistent with the overall abilities, vocational limitations, physical restrictions, general temperament, interest and aptitude patterns, social skills, education, general qualifications, and other relevant characteristics and needs of clients. When appropriate, counselors appropriately trained in career development will assist in the placement of clients in positions that are consistent with the interest, culture, and the welfare of clients, employers, and/or the public.

A.2. Informed Consent in the Counseling Relationship

(See A.12.g., B.5., B.6.b., E.3., E.13.b., F.1.c., G.2.a.)

A.2.a. *Informed Consent.* Clients have the freedom to choose whether to enter into or remain in a counseling relationship and need adequate information about the counseling process and the counselors. Counselors have an obligation to review in writing and verbally with clients the rights and responsibilities of both the counselor and the client. Informed consent is an ongoing part of the counseling process, and counselors appropriately document discussions of informed consent throughout the counseling relationship.

A.2.b. *Types of Information Needed.* Counselors explicitly explain to clients the nature of all services provided. They inform clients about issues such as, but not limited to, the following: the purposes, goals, techniques, procedures, limitations, potential risks, and benefits of services; the counselor's qualifications, credentials, and relevant experience; continuation of services upon the incapacitation or death of a counselor; and other pertinent information. Counselors take steps to ensure that clients understand the implications of diagnosis, the intended use of tests and reports, fees, and billing arrangements. Clients have the right to confidentiality and to be provided with an explanation of its limitations (including how supervisors and/or treatment team professionals are involved); to obtain clear information about their records; to participate in the ongoing counseling plans; and to refuse any services or modality change and to be advised of the consequences of such refusal.

A.2.c. *Developmental and Cultural Sensitivity.* Counselors communicate information in ways that are both developmentally and culturally appropriate. Counselors use clear and understandable language when discussing issues related to informed consent. When clients have difficulty understanding the language used by counselors, they provide necessary services (e.g., arranging for a qualified interpreter or translator) to ensure comprehension by clients. In collaboration with clients, counselors consider cultural implications of informed consent procedures and, where possible, counselors adjust their practices accordingly.

A.2.d. *Inability to Give Consent.* When counseling minors or persons unable to give voluntary consent, counselors seek the assent of clients to services, and include them in decision making as appropriate. Counselors recognize the need to balance the ethical rights of clients to make choices, their capacity to give consent or assent to receive services, and parental or familial legal rights and responsibilities to protect these clients and make decisions on their behalf.

A.3. Clients Served by Others

When counselors learn that their clients are in a professional relationship with another mental health professional, they request release from clients to inform the other professionals and strive to establish positive and collaborative professional relationships.

A.4. Avoiding Harm and Imposing Values

A.4.a. *Avoiding Harm.* Counselors act to avoid harming their clients, trainees, and research participants and to minimize or to remedy unavoidable or unanticipated harm.

A.4.b. *Personal Values.* Counselors are aware of their own values, attitudes, beliefs, and behaviors and avoid imposing values that are inconsistent with counseling goals. Counselors respect the diversity of clients, trainees, and research participants.

A.5. Roles and Relationships With Clients

(See F.3., F.10., G.3.)

A.5.a. *Current Clients.* Sexual or romantic counselor-client interactions or relationships with current clients, their romantic partners, or their family members are prohibited.

A.5.b. *Former Clients.* Sexual or romantic counselor-client interactions or relationships with former clients, their romantic partners, or their family members are prohibited for a period of 5 years following the last professional contact. Counselors, before engaging in sexual or romantic interactions or relationships with clients, their romantic partners, or client family members after 5 years following the last professional contact, demonstrate forethought and document (in written form) whether the interactions or relationship can be viewed as exploitive in some way and/or whether there is still potential to harm the former client; in cases of potential exploitation and/or harm, the counselor avoids entering such an interaction or relationship.

A.5.c. *Nonprofessional Interactions or Relationships (Other Than Sexual or Romantic Interactions or Relationships).* Counselor–client nonprofessional relationships with clients, former clients, their romantic partners, or their family members should be avoided, except when the interaction is potentially beneficial to the client. (See A.5.d.)

A.5.d. *Potentially Beneficial Interactions.* When a counselor-client nonprofessional interaction with a client or former client may be potentially beneficial to the client or former client, the counselor must document in case records, prior to the interaction (when feasible), the rationale for such an interaction, the potential benefit, and anticipated consequences for the client or former client and other individuals significantly involved with the client or former client. Such interactions should be initiated with appropriate client consent. Where unintentional harm occurs to the client or former client, or to an individual significantly involved with the client or former client, due to the nonprofessional interaction, the counselor must show evidence of an attempt to remedy such harm. Examples of potentially beneficial interactions include, but are not limited to, attending a formal ceremony (e.g., a wedding/commitment ceremony or graduation); purchasing a service or product provided by a client or former client (excepting unrestricted bartering); hospital visits to an ill family member; mutual membership in a professional association, organization, or community. (See A.5.c.)

A.5.e. *Role Changes in the Professional Relationship.* When a counselor changes a role from the original or most recent contracted relationship, he or she obtains informed consent from the client and explains the right of the client to refuse services related to the change. Examples of role changes include
1. changing from individual to relationship or family counseling, or vice versa;
2. changing from a nonforensic evaluative role to a therapeutic role, or vice versa;
3. changing from a counselor to a researcher role (i.e., enlisting clients as research participants), or vice versa; and
4. changing from a counselor to a mediator role, or vice versa.

Clients must be fully informed of any anticipated consequences (e.g., financial, legal, personal, or therapeutic) of counselor role changes.

A.6. Roles and Relationships at Individual, Group, Institutional, and Societal Levels

A.6.a. *Advocacy.* When appropriate, counselors advocate at individual, group, institutional, and societal levels to examine potential barriers and obstacles that inhibit access and/or the growth and development of clients.

A.6.b. *Confidentiality and Advocacy.* Counselors obtain client consent prior to engaging in advocacy efforts on behalf of an identifiable client to improve the provision of services and to work toward removal of systemic barriers or obstacles that inhibit client access, growth, and development.

A.7. Multiple Clients

When a counselor agrees to provide counseling services to two or more persons who have a relationship, the counselor clarifies at the outset which person or persons are clients and the nature of the relationships the counselor will have with each involved person. If it becomes apparent that the counselor may be called upon to perform potentially conflicting roles, the counselor will clarify, adjust, or withdraw from roles appropriately. (See A.8.a., B.4.)

A.8. Group Work

(See B.4.a.)

A.8.a. *Screening.* Counselors screen prospective group counseling/therapy participants. To the extent possible, counselors select members whose needs and goals are compatible with goals of the group, who will not impede the group process, and whose well-being will not be jeopardized by the group experience.

A.8.b. *Protecting Clients.* In a group setting, counselors take reasonable precautions to protect clients from physical, emotional, or psychological trauma.

A.9. End-of-Life Care for Terminally Ill Clients

A.9.a. *Quality of Care.* Counselors strive to take measures that enable clients
1. to obtain high quality end-of-life care for their physical, emotional, social, and spiritual needs;
2. to exercise the highest degree of self-determination possible;
3. to be given every opportunity possible to engage in informed decision making regarding their end-of-life care; and
4. to receive complete and adequate assessment regarding their ability to make competent, rational decisions on their own behalf from a mental health professional who is experienced in end-of-life care practice.

A.9.b. *Counselor Competence, Choice, and Referral.* Recognizing the personal, moral, and competence issues related to end-of-life decisions, counselors may choose to work or not work with terminally ill clients who wish to explore their end-of-life options. Counselors provide appropriate referral information to ensure that clients receive the necessary help.

A.9.c. *Confidentiality.* Counselors who provide services to terminally ill individuals who are considering hastening their own deaths have the option of breaking or not breaking confidentiality, depending on applicable laws and the specific circumstances of the situation and after seeking consultation or supervision from appropriate professional and legal parties. (See B.5.c., B.7.c.)

A.10. Fees and Bartering

A.10.a. *Accepting Fees From Agency Clients.* Counselors refuse a private fee or other remuneration for rendering services to persons who are entitled to such services through the counselor's employing agency or institution. The policies of a particular agency may make explicit provisions for agency clients to receive counseling services from members of its staff in private practice. In such instances, the clients must be informed of other options open to them should they seek private counseling services.

A.10.b. *Establishing Fees.* In establishing fees for professional counseling services, counselors consider the financial status of clients and locality. In the event that the established fee structure is inappropriate for a client, counselors assist clients in attempting to find comparable services of acceptable cost.

A.10.c. *Nonpayment of Fees.* If counselors intend to use collection agencies or take legal measures to collect fees from clients who do not pay for services as agreed upon, they first inform clients of intended actions and offer clients the opportunity to make payment.

A.10.d. *Bartering.* Counselors may barter only if the relationship is not exploitive or harmful and does not place the counselor in an unfair advantage, if the client requests it, and if such arrangements are an accepted practice among professionals in the community.

Counselors consider the cultural implications of bartering and discuss relevant concerns with clients and document such agreements in a clear written contract.

A.10.e. *Receiving Gifts.* Counselors understand the challenges of accepting gifts from clients and recognize that in some cultures, small gifts are a token of respect and showing gratitude. When determining whether or not to accept a gift from clients, counselors take into account the therapeutic relationship, the monetary value of the gift, a client's motivation for giving the gift, and the counselor's motivation for wanting or declining the gift.

A.11. Termination and Referral

A.11.a. *Abandonment Prohibited.* Counselors do not abandon or neglect clients in counseling. Counselors assist in making appropriate arrangements for the continuation of treatment, when necessary, during interruptions such as vacations, illness, and following termination.

A.11.b. *Inability to Assist Clients.* If counselors determine an inability to be of professional assistance to clients, they avoid entering or continuing counseling relationships. Counselors are knowledgeable about culturally and clinically appropriate referral resources and suggest these alternatives. If clients decline the suggested referrals, counselors should discontinue the relationship.

A.11.c. *Appropriate Termination.* Counselors terminate a counseling relationship when it becomes reasonably apparent that the client no longer needs assistance, is not likely to benefit, or is being harmed by continued counseling. Counselors may terminate counseling when in jeopardy of harm by the client, or another person with whom the client has a relationship, or when clients do not pay fees as agreed upon. Counselors provide pretermination counseling and recommend other service providers when necessary.

A.11.d. *Appropriate Transfer of Services.* When counselors transfer or refer clients to other practitioners, they ensure that appropriate clinical and administrative processes are completed and open communication is maintained with both clients and practitioners.

A.12. Technology Applications

A.12.a. *Benefits and Limitations.* Counselors inform clients of the benefits and limitations of using information technology applications in the counseling process and in business/billing procedures. Such technologies include but are not limited to computer hardware and software, telephones, the World Wide Web, the Internet, online assessment instruments and other communication devices.

A.12.b. *Technology-Assisted Services.* When providing technology-assisted distance counseling services, counselors determine that clients are intellectually, emotionally, and physically capable of using the application and that the application is appropriate for the needs of clients.

A.12.c. *Inappropriate Services.* When technology-assisted distance counseling services are deemed inappropriate by the counselor or client, counselors consider delivering services face to face.

A.12.d. *Access.* Counselors provide reasonable access to computer applications when providing technology-assisted distance counseling services.

A.12.e. *Laws and Statutes.* Counselors ensure that the use of technology does not violate the laws of any local, state, national, or international entity and observe all relevant statutes.

A.12.f. *Assistance.* Counselors seek business, legal, and technical assistance when using technology applications, particularly when the use of such applications crosses state or national boundaries.

A.12.g. *Technology and Informed Consent.* As part of the process of establishing informed consent, counselors do the following:

1. Address issues related to the difficulty of maintaining the confidentiality of electronically transmitted communications.
2. Inform clients of all colleagues, supervisors, and employees, such as Informational Technology (IT) administrators, who might have authorized or unauthorized access to electronic transmissions.
3. Urge clients to be aware of all authorized or unauthorized users including family members and fellow employees who have access to any technology clients may use in the counseling process.
4. Inform clients of pertinent legal rights and limitations governing the practice of a profession over state lines or international boundaries.
5. Use encrypted Web sites and e-mail communications to help ensure confidentiality when possible.
6. When the use of encryption is not possible, counselors notify clients of this fact and limit electronic transmissions to general communications that are not client specific.
7. Inform clients if and for how long archival storage of transaction records are maintained.
8. Discuss the possibility of technology failure and alternate methods of service delivery.
9. Inform clients of emergency procedures, such as calling 911 or a local crisis hotline, when the counselor is not available.
10. Discuss time zone differences, local customs, and cultural or language differences that might impact service delivery.
11. Inform clients when technology-assisted distance counseling services are not covered by insurance. (See A.2.)

A.12.h. *Sites on the World Wide Web.* Counselors maintaining sites on the World Wide Web (the Internet) do the following:

1. Regularly check that electronic links are working and professionally appropriate.
2. Establish ways clients can contact the counselor in case of technology failure.
3. Provide electronic links to relevant state licensure and professional certification boards to protect consumer rights and facilitate addressing ethical concerns.
4. Establish a method for verifying client identity.
5. Obtain the written consent of the legal guardian or other authorized legal representative prior to rendering services in the event the client is a minor child, an adult who is legally

incompetent, or an adult incapable of giving informed consent.

6. Strive to provide a site that is accessible to persons with disabilities.

7. Strive to provide translation capabilities for clients who have a different primary language while also addressing the imperfect nature of such translations.

8. Assist clients in determining the validity and reliability of information found on the World Wide Web and other technology applications.

Section B: Confidentiality, Privileged Communication, and Privacy

Introduction

Counselors recognize that trust is a cornerstone of the counseling relationship. Counselors aspire to earn the trust of clients by creating an ongoing partnership, establishing and upholding appropriate boundaries, and maintaining confidentiality. Counselors communicate the parameters of confidentiality in a culturally competent manner.

B.1. Respecting Client Rights

B.1.a.   *Multicultural/Diversity Considerations.* Counselors maintain awareness and sensitivity regarding cultural meanings of confidentiality and privacy. Counselors respect differing views toward disclosure of information. Counselors hold ongoing discussions with clients as to how, when, and with whom information is to be shared.

B.1.b.   *Respect for Privacy.* Counselors respect client rights to privacy. Counselors solicit private information from clients only when it is beneficial to the counseling process.

B.1.c.   *Respect for Confidentiality.* Counselors do not share confidential information without client consent or without sound legal or ethical justification.

B.1.d.   *Explanation of Limitations:* At initiation and throughout the counseling process, counselors inform clients of the limitations of confidentiality and seek to identify foreseeable situations in which confidentiality must be breached. (See A.2.b.)

B.2. Exceptions

B.2.a.   *Danger and Legal Requirements.* The general requirement that counselors keep information confidential does not apply when disclosure is required to protect clients or identified others from serious and foreseeable harm or when legal requirements demand that confidential information must be revealed. Counselors consult with other professionals when in doubt as to the validity of an exception. Additional considerations apply when addressing end-of-life issues. (See A.9.c.)

B.2.b.   *Contagious, Life-Threatening Diseases.* When clients disclose that they have a disease commonly known to be both communicable and life threatening, counselors may be justified in disclosing information to identifiable third parties, if they are known to be at demonstrable and high risk of contracting the disease. Prior to making a disclosure, counselors confirm that there is such a diagnosis and assess the intent of clients to inform the third parties about their disease or to engage in any behaviors that may be harmful to an identifiable third party.

B.2.c.   *Court-Ordered Disclosure.* When subpoenaed to release confidential or privileged information without a client's permission, counselors obtain written, informed consent from the client or take steps to prohibit the disclosure or have it limited as narrowly as possible due to potential harm to the client or counseling relationship.

B.2.d.   *Minimal Disclosure.* To the extent possible, clients are informed before confidential information is disclosed and are involved in the disclosure decision-making process. When circumstances require the disclosure of confidential information, only essential information is revealed.

B.3. Information Shared With Others

B.3.a.   *Subordinates.* Counselors make every effort to ensure that privacy and confidentiality of clients are maintained by subordinates, including employees, supervisees, students, clerical assistants, and volunteers. (See F.1.c.)

B.3.b.   *Treatment Teams.* When client treatment involves a continued review or participation by a treatment team, the client will be informed of the team's existence and composition, information being shared, and the purposes of sharing such information.

B.3.c.   *Confidential Settings.* Counselors discuss confidential information only in settings in which they can reasonably ensure client privacy.

B.3.d.   *Third-Party Payers.* Counselors disclose information to third-party payers only when clients have authorized such disclosure.

B.3.e.   *Transmitting Confidential Information.* Counselors take precautions to ensure the confidentiality of information transmitted through the use of computers, electronic mail, facsimile machines, telephones, voicemail, answering machines, and other electronic or computer technology. (See A.12.g.)

B.3.f.   *Deceased Clients.* Counselors protect the confidentiality of deceased clients, consistent with legal requirements and agency or setting policies.

B.4. Groups and Families

B.4.a.   *Group Work.* In group work, counselors clearly explain the importance and parameters of confidentiality for the specific group being entered.

B.4.b.   *Couples and Family Counseling.* In couples and family counseling, counselors clearly define who is considered "the client" and discuss expectations and limitations of confidentiality. Counselors seek agreement and document in writing such agreement among all involved parties having capacity to give consent concerning each individual's right to confidentiality and any obligation to preserve the confidentiality of information known.

B.5. Clients Lacking Capacity to Give Informed Consent

B.5.a.   *Responsibility to Clients.* When counseling minor clients or adult clients who lack the capacity to give voluntary, informed consent, counselors protect the confidentiality of information received in the counseling relationship as specified by federal and state laws, written policies, and applicable ethical standards.

B.5.b. *Responsibility to Parents and Legal Guardians.* Counselors inform parents and legal guardians about the role of counselors and the confidential nature of the counseling relationship. Counselors are sensitive to the cultural diversity of families and respect the inherent rights and responsibilities of parents/guardians over the welfare of their children/charges according to law. Counselors work to establish, as appropriate, collaborative relationships with parents/guardians to best serve clients.

B.5.c. *Release of Confidential Information.* When counseling minor clients or adult clients who lack the capacity to give voluntary consent to release confidential information, counselors seek permission from an appropriate third party to disclose information. In such instances, counselors inform clients consistent with their level of understanding and take culturally appropriate measures to safeguard client confidentiality.

B.6. Records

B.6.a. *Confidentiality of Records.* Counselors ensure that records are kept in a secure location and that only authorized persons have access to records.

B.6.b. *Permission to Record.* Counselors obtain permission from clients prior to recording sessions through electronic or other means.

B.6.c. *Permission to Observe.* Counselors obtain permission from clients prior to observing counseling sessions, reviewing session transcripts, or viewing recordings of sessions with supervisors, faculty, peers, or others within the training environment.

B.6.d. *Client Access.* Counselors provide reasonable access to records and copies of records when requested by competent clients. Counselors limit the access of clients to their records, or portions of their records, only when there is compelling evidence that such access would cause harm to the client. Counselors document the request of clients and the rationale for withholding some or all of the record in the files of clients. In situations involving multiple clients, counselors provide individual clients with only those parts of records that related directly to them and do not include confidential information related to any other client.

B.6.e. *Assistance With Records.* When clients request access to their records, counselors provide assistance and consultation in interpreting counseling records.

B.6.f. *Disclosure or Transfer.* Unless exceptions to confidentiality exist, counselors obtain written permission from clients to disclose or transfer records to legitimate third parties. Steps are taken to ensure that receivers of counseling records are sensitive to their confidential nature. (See A.3., E.4.)

B.6.g. *Storage and Disposal After Termination.* Counselors store records following termination of services to ensure reasonable future access, maintain records in accordance with state and federal statutes governing records, and dispose of client records and other sensitive materials in a manner that protects client

confidentiality. When records are of an artistic nature, counselors obtain client (or guardian) consent with regards to handling of such records or documents. (See A.1.b.)

B.6.h. *Reasonable Precautions.* Counselors take reasonable precautions to protect client confidentiality in the event of the counselor's termination of practice, incapacity, or death. (See C.2.h.)

B.7. Research and Training

B.7.a. *Institutional Approval.* When institutional approval is required, counselors provide accurate information about their research proposals and obtain approval prior to conducting their research. They conduct research in accordance with the approved research protocol.

B.7.b. *Adherence to Guidelines.* Counselors are responsible for understanding and adhering to state, federal, agency, or institutional policies or applicable guidelines regarding confidentiality in their research practices.

B.7.c. *Confidentiality of Information Obtained in Research.* Violations of participant privacy and confidentiality are risks of participation in research involving human participants. Investigators maintain all research records in a secure manner. They explain to participants the risks of violations of privacy and confidentiality and disclose to participants any limits of confidentiality that reasonably can be expected. Regardless of the degree to which confidentiality will be maintained, investigators must disclose to participants any limits of confidentiality that reasonably can be expected. (See G.2.e.)

B.7.d. *Disclosure of Research Information.* Counselors do not disclose confidential information that reasonably could lead to the identification of a research participant unless they have obtained the prior consent of the person. Use of data derived from counseling relationships for purposes of training, research, or publication is confined to content that is disguised to ensure the anonymity of the individuals involved. (See G.2.a., G.2.d.)

B.7.e. *Agreement for Identification.* Identification of clients, students, or supervisees in a presentation or publication is permissible only when they have reviewed the material and agreed to its presentation or publication. (See G.4.d.)

B.8. Consultation

B.8.a. *Agreements.* When acting as consultants, counselors seek agreements among all parties involved concerning each individual's rights to confidentiality, the obligation of each individual to preserve confidential information, and the limits of confidentiality of information shared by others.

B.8.b. *Respect for Privacy.* Information obtained in a consulting relationship is discussed for professional purposes only with persons directly involved with the case. Written and oral reports present only data germane to the purposes of the consultation, and every effort is made to protect client identity and to avoid undue invasion of privacy.

B.8.c. *Disclosure of Confidential Information.* When consulting with colleagues, counselors do not disclose confidential information that reasonably could lead to the identification of a client or other person or organization with whom they have a confidential relationship unless they have obtained the prior consent of the person or organization or the disclosure cannot be avoided. They disclose information only to the extent necessary to achieve the purposes of the consultation. (See D.2.d.)

Section C: Professional Responsibility

Introduction

Counselors aspire to open, honest, and accurate communication in dealing with the public and other professionals. They practice in a nondiscriminatory manner within the boundaries of professional and personal competence and have a responsibility to abide by the *ACA Code of Ethics*. Counselors actively participate in local, state, and national associations that foster the development and improvement of counseling. Counselors advocate to promote change at the individual, group, institutional, and societal levels that improve the quality of life for individuals and groups and remove potential barriers to the provision or access of appropriate services being offered. Counselors have a responsibility to the public to engage in counseling practices that are based on rigorous research methodologies. In addition, counselors engage in self-care activities to maintain and promote their emotional, physical, mental, and spiritual well-being to best meet their professional responsibilities.

C.1. Knowledge of Standards

Counselors have a responsibility to read, understand, and follow the *ACA Code of Ethics* and adhere to applicable laws and regulations.

C.2. Professional Competence

C.2.a. *Boundaries of Competence.* Counselors practice only within the boundaries of their competence, based on their education, training, supervised experience, state and national professional credentials, and appropriate professional experience. Counselors gain knowledge, personal awareness, sensitivity, and skills pertinent to working with a diverse client population. (See A.9.b., C.4.e., E.2., F.2., F.11.b.)

C.2.b. *New Specialty Areas of Practice.* Counselors practice in specialty areas new to them only after appropriate education, training, and supervised experience. While developing skills in new specialty areas, counselors take steps to ensure the competence of their work and to protect others from possible harm. (See F.6.f.)

C.2.c. *Qualified for Employment.* Counselors accept employment only for positions for which they are qualified by education, training, supervised experience, state and national professional credentials, and appropriate professional experience. Counselors hire for professional counseling positions only individuals who are qualified and competent for those positions.

C.2.d. *Monitor Effectiveness.* Counselors continually monitor their effectiveness as professionals and take steps to improve when necessary. Counselors in private practice take reasonable steps to seek peer supervision as needed to evaluate their efficacy as counselors.

C.2.e. *Consultation on Ethical Obligations.* Counselors take reasonable steps to consult with other counselors or related professionals when they have questions regarding their ethical obligations or professional practice.

C.2.f. *Continuing Education.* Counselors recognize the need for continuing education to acquire and maintain a reasonable level of awareness of current scientific and professional information in their fields of activity. They take steps to maintain competence in the skills they use, are open to new procedures, and keep current with the diverse populations and specific populations with whom they work.

C.2.g. *Impairment.* Counselors are alert to the signs of impairment from their own physical, mental, or emotional problems and refrain from offering or providing professional services when such impairment is likely to harm a client or others. They seek assistance for problems that reach the level of professional impairment, and, if necessary, they limit, suspend, or terminate their professional responsibilities until such time it is determined that they may safely resume their work. Counselors assist colleagues or supervisors in recognizing their own professional impairment and provide consultation and assistance when warranted with colleagues or supervisors showing signs of impairment and intervene as appropriate to prevent imminent harm to clients. (See A.11.b., F.8.b.)

C.2.h. *Counselor Incapacitation or Termination of Practice.* When counselors leave a practice, they follow a prepared plan for transfer of clients and files. Counselors prepare and disseminate to an identified colleague or "records custodian" a plan for the transfer of clients and files in the case of their incapacitation, death, or termination of practice.

C.3. Advertising and Soliciting Clients

C.3.a. *Accurate Advertising.* When advertising or otherwise representing their services to the public, counselors identify their credentials in an accurate manner that is not false, misleading, deceptive, or fraudulent.

C.3.b. *Testimonials.* Counselors who use testimonials do not solicit them from current clients nor former clients nor any other persons who may be vulnerable to undue influence.

C.3.c. *Statements by Others.* Counselors make reasonable efforts to ensure that statements made by others about them or the profession of counseling are accurate.

C.3.d. *Recruiting Through Employment.* Counselors do not use their places of employment or institutional affiliation to recruit or gain clients, supervisees, or consultees for their private practices.

C.3.e. *Products and Training Advertisements.* Counselors who develop products related to their profession or conduct workshops or training events ensure that the advertisements concerning these products or events are accurate and disclose adequate information for consumers to make informed choices. (See C.6.d.)

C.3.f. *Promoting to Those Served.* Counselors do not use counseling, teaching, training, or supervisory relationships to promote their products or training events in a manner that is deceptive or would exert undue influence on individuals who may be vulnerable. However, counselor educators may adopt textbooks they have authored for instructional purposes.

C.4. Professional Qualifications

C.4.a. *Accurate Representation.* Counselors claim or imply only professional qualifications actually completed and correct any known misrepresentations of their qualifications by others. Counselors truthfully represent the qualifications of their professional colleagues. Counselors clearly distinguish between paid and volunteer work experience and accurately describe their continuing education and specialized training. (See C.2.a.)

C.4.b. *Credentials.* Counselors claim only licenses or certifications that are current and in good standing.

C.4.c. *Educational Degrees.* Counselors clearly differentiate between earned and honorary degrees.

C.4.d. *Implying Doctoral-Level Competence.* Counselors clearly state their highest earned degree in counseling or closely related field. Counselors do not imply doctoral-level competence when only possessing a master's degree in counseling or a related field by referring to themselves as "Dr." in a counseling context when their doctorate is not in counseling or related field.

C.4.e. *Program Accreditation Status.* Counselors clearly state the accreditation status of their degree programs at the time the degree was earned.

C.4.f. *Professional Membership.* Counselors clearly differentiate between current, active memberships and former memberships in associations. Members of the American Counseling Association must clearly differentiate between professional membership, which implies the possession of at least a master's degree in counseling, and regular membership, which is open to individuals whose interests and activities are consistent with those of ACA but are not qualified for professional membership.

C.5. Nondiscrimination

Counselors do not condone or engage in discrimination based on age, culture, disability, ethnicity, race, religion/spirituality, gender, gender identity, sexual orientation, marital status/partnership, language preference, socioeconomic status, or any basis proscribed by law. Counselors do not discriminate against clients, students, employees, supervisees, or research participants in a manner that has a negative impact on these persons.

C.6. Public Responsibility

C.6.a. *Sexual Harassment.* Counselors do not engage in or condone sexual harassment. Sexual harassment is defined as sexual solicitation, physical advances, or verbal or nonverbal conduct that is sexual in nature, that occurs in connection with professional activities or roles, and that either
1. is unwelcome, is offensive, or creates a hostile workplace or learning environment, and counselors know or are told this; or
2. is sufficiently severe or intense to be perceived as harassment to a reasonable person in the context in which the behavior occurred.

Sexual harassment can consist of a single intense or severe act or multiple persistent or pervasive acts.

C.6.b. *Reports to Third Parties.* Counselors are accurate, honest, and objective in reporting their professional activities and judgments to appropriate third parties, including courts, health insurance companies, those who are the recipients of evaluation reports, and others. (See B.3., E.4.)

C.6.c. *Media Presentations.* When counselors provide advice or comment by means of public lectures, demonstrations, radio or television programs, prerecorded tapes, technology-based applications, printed articles, mailed material, or other media, they take reasonable precautions to ensure that
1. the statements are based on appropriate professional counseling literature and practice,
2. the statements are otherwise consistent with the *ACA Code of Ethics,* and
3. the recipients of the information are not encouraged to infer that a professional counseling relationship has been established.

C.6.d. *Exploitation of Others.* Counselors do not exploit others in their professional relationships. (See C.3.e.)

C.6.e. *Scientific Bases for Treatment Modalities.* Counselors use techniques/procedures/modalities that are grounded in theory and/or have an empirical or scientific foundation. Counselors who do not must define the techniques/procedures as "unproven" or "developing" and explain the potential risks and ethical considerations of using such techniques/procedures and take steps to protect clients from possible harm. (See A.4.a., E.5.c., E.5.d.)

C.7. Responsibility to Other Professionals

C.7.a. *Personal Public Statements.* When making personal statements in a public context, counselors clarify that they are speaking from their personal perspectives and that they are not speaking on behalf of all counselors or the profession.

Section D: Relationships With Other Professionals

Introduction

Professional counselors recognize that the quality of their interactions with colleagues can influence the quality of services provided to clients. They work to become knowledgeable about colleagues within and outside the field of counseling. Counselors develop positive working relationships and systems of communication with colleagues to enhance services to clients.

D.1. Relationships With Colleagues, Employers, and Employees

D.1.a. *Different Approaches.* Counselors are respectful of approaches to counseling services that differ from their own. Counselors are respectful of traditions and practices of other professional groups with which they work.

D.1.b. *Forming Relationships.* Counselors work to develop and strengthen interdisciplinary relations with colleagues from other disciplines to best serve clients.

D.1.c. *Interdisciplinary Teamwork.* Counselors who are members of interdisciplinary teams delivering multifaceted services to clients, keep the focus on how to best serve the clients. They participate in and contribute to decisions that affect the well-being of clients by drawing on the perspectives, values, and experiences of the counseling profession and those of colleagues from other disciplines. (See A.1.a.)

D.1.d. *Confidentiality.* When counselors are required by law, institutional policy, or extraordinary circumstances to serve in more than one role in judicial or administrative proceedings, they clarify role expectations and the parameters of confidentiality with their colleagues. (See B.1.c., B.1.d., B.2.c., B.2.d., B.3.b.)

D.1.e. *Establishing Professional and Ethical Obligations.* Counselors who are members of interdisciplinary teams clarify professional and ethical obligations of the team as a whole and of its individual members. When a team decision raises ethical concerns, counselors first attempt to resolve the concern within the team. If they cannot reach resolution among team members, counselors pursue other avenues to address their concerns consistent with client well-being.

D.1.f. *Personnel Selection and Assignment.* Counselors select competent staff and assign responsibilities compatible with their skills and experiences.

D.1.g. *Employer Policies.* The acceptance of employment in an agency or institution implies that counselors are in agreement with its general policies and principles. Counselors strive to reach agreement with employers as to acceptable standards of conduct that allow for changes in institutional policy conducive to the growth and development of clients.

D.1.h. *Negative Conditions.* Counselors alert their employers of inappropriate policies and practices. They attempt to effect changes in such policies or procedures through constructive action within the organization. When such policies are potentially disruptive or damaging to clients or may limit the effectiveness of services provided and change cannot be effected, counselors take appropriate further action. Such action may include referral to appropriate certification, accreditation, or state licensure organizations, or voluntary termination of employment.

D.1.i. *Protection From Punitive Action.* Counselors take care not to harass or dismiss an employee who has acted in a responsible and ethical manner to expose inappropriate employer policies or practices.

D.2. Consultation

D.2.a. *Consultant Competency.* Counselors take reasonable steps to ensure that they have the appropriate resources and competencies when providing consultation services. Counselors provide appropriate referral resources when requested or needed. (See C.2.a.)

D.2.b. *Understanding Consultees.* When providing consultation, counselors attempt to develop with their consultees a clear understanding of problem definition, goals for change, and predicted consequences of interventions selected.

D.2.c. *Consultant Goals.* The consulting relationship is one in which consultee adaptability and growth toward self-direction are consistently encouraged and cultivated.

D.2.d. *Informed Consent in Consultation.* When providing consultation, counselors have an obligation to review, in writing and verbally, the rights and responsibilities of both counselors and consultees. Counselors use clear and understandable language to inform all parties involved about the purpose of the services to be provided, relevant costs, potential risks and benefits, and the limits of confidentiality. Working in conjunction with the consultee, counselors attempt to develop a clear definition of the problem, goals for change, and predicted consequences of interventions that are culturally responsive and appropriate to the needs of consultees. (See A.2.a., A.2.b.)

Section E: Evaluation, Assessment, and Interpretation

Introduction

Counselors use assessment instruments as one component of the counseling process, taking into account the client personal and cultural context. Counselors promote the well-being of individual clients or groups of clients by developing and using appropriate educational, psychological, and career assessment instruments.

E.1. General

E.1.a. *Assessment.* The primary purpose of educational, psychological, and career assessment is to provide measurements that are valid and reliable in either comparative or absolute terms. These include, but are not limited to, measurements of ability, personality, interest, intelligence, achievement, and performance. Counselors recognize the need to interpret the statements in this section as applying to both quantitative and qualitative assessments.

E.1.b. *Client Welfare.* Counselors do not misuse assessment results and interpretations, and they take reasonable steps to prevent others from misusing the information these techniques provide. They respect the client's right to know the results, the interpretations made, and the bases for counselors' conclusions and recommendations.

E.2. Competence to Use and Interpret Assessment Instruments

E.2.a. *Limits of Competence.* Counselors utilize only those testing and assessment services for which they have been trained and are competent. Counselors using technology assisted test interpretations are trained in the construct being measured and the specific instrument being used prior to using its technology based application. Counselors take reasonable measures to ensure the proper use of psychological and career assessment techniques by persons under their supervision. (See A.12.)

E.2.b. *Appropriate Use.* Counselors are responsible for the appropriate application, scoring, interpretation, and use of assessment instruments relevant to the needs of the client, whether they score and interpret such assessments themselves or use technology or other services.

E.2.c. *Decisions Based on Results.* Counselors responsible for decisions involving individuals or policies that are based on assessment results have a thorough understanding of educational, psychological, and career measurement, including validation criteria, assessment research, and guidelines for assessment development and use.

E.3. Informed Consent in Assessment

E.3.a. *Explanation to Clients.* Prior to assessment, counselors explain the nature and purposes of assessment and the specific use of results by potential recipients. The explanation will be given in the language of the client (or other legally authorized person on behalf of the client), unless an explicit exception has been agreed upon in advance. Counselors consider the client's personal or cultural context, the level of the client's understanding of the results, and the impact of the results on the client. (See A.2., A.12.g., F.1.c.)

E.3.b. *Recipients of Results.* Counselors consider the examinee's welfare, explicit understandings, and prior agreements in determining who receives the assessment results. Counselors include accurate and appropriate interpretations with any release of individual or group assessment results. (See B.2.c., B.5.)

E.4. Release of Data to Qualified Professionals

Counselors release assessment data in which the client is identified only with the consent of the client or the client's legal representative. Such data are released only to persons recognized by counselors as qualified to interpret the data. (See B.1., B.3., B.6.b.)

E.5. Diagnosis of Mental Disorders

E.5.a. *Proper Diagnosis.* Counselors take special care to provide proper diagnosis of mental disorders. Assessment techniques (including personal interview) used to determine client care (e.g., locus of treatment, type of treatment, or recommended follow-up) are carefully selected and appropriately used.

E.5.b. *Cultural Sensitivity.* Counselors recognize that culture affects the manner in which clients' problems are defined. Clients' socioeconomic and cultural experiences are considered when diagnosing mental disorders. (See A.2.c.)

E.5.c. *Historical and Social Prejudices in the Diagnosis of Pathology.* Counselors recognize historical and social prejudices in the misdiagnosis and pathologizing of certain individuals and groups and the role of mental health professionals in perpetuating these prejudices through diagnosis and treatment.

E.5.d. *Refraining From Diagnosis.* Counselors may refrain from making and/or reporting a diagnosis if they believe it would cause harm to the client or others.

E.6. Instrument Selection

E.6.a. *Appropriateness of Instruments.* Counselors carefully consider the validity, reliability, psychometric limitations, and appropriateness of instruments when selecting assessments.

E.6.b. *Referral Information.* If a client is referred to a third party for assessment, the counselor provides specific referral questions and sufficient objective data about the client to ensure that appropriate assessment instruments are utilized. (See A.9.b., B.3.)

E.6.c. *Culturally Diverse Populations.* Counselors are cautious when selecting assessments for culturally diverse populations to avoid the use of instruments that lack appropriate psychometric properties for the client population. (See A.2.c., E.5.b.)

E.7. Conditions of Assessment Administration
(See A.12.b., A.12.d.)

E.7.a. *Administration Conditions.* Counselors administer assessments under the same conditions that were established in their standardization. When assessments are not administered under standard conditions, as may be necessary to accommodate clients with disabilities, or when unusual behavior or irregularities occur during the administration, those conditions are noted in interpretation, and the results may be designated as invalid or of questionable validity.

E.7.b. *Technological Administration.* Counselors ensure that administration programs function properly and provide clients with accurate results when technological or other electronic methods are used for assessment administration.

E.7.c. *Unsupervised Assessments.* Unless the assessment instrument is designed, intended, and validated for self-administration and/or scoring, counselors do not permit inadequately supervised use.

E.7.d. *Disclosure of Favorable Conditions.* Prior to administration of assessments, conditions that produce most favorable assessment results are made known to the examinee.

E.8. Multicultural Issues/Diversity in Assessment

Counselors use with caution assessment techniques that were normed on populations other than that of the client. Counselors recognize the effects of age, color, culture, disability, ethnic group, gender, race, language preference, religion, spirituality, sexual orientation, and socioeconomic status on test administration and interpretation, and place test results in proper perspective with other relevant factors. (See A.2.c., E.5.b.)

E.9. Scoring and Interpretation of Assessments

E.9.a. *Reporting.* In reporting assessment results, counselors indicate reservations that exist regarding validity or reliability due to circumstances of the assessment or the inappropriateness of the norms for the person tested.

E.9.b. *Research Instruments.* Counselors exercise caution when interpreting the results of research instruments not having sufficient technical data to support respondent results. The specific purposes for the use of such instruments are stated explicitly to the examinee.

E.9.c. *Assessment Services.* Counselors who provide assessment scoring and interpretation services to support the assessment process confirm the validity of such interpretations. They accurately describe the purpose, norms, validity, reliability, and applications of the procedures and any special qualifications applicable to their use. The public offering of an automated test interpretations service is considered a professional-to-professional consultation. The formal responsibility of the consultant is to the consultee, but the ultimate and overriding responsibility is to the client. (See D.2.)

E.10. Assessment Security

Counselors maintain the integrity and security of tests and other assessment techniques consistent with legal and contractual obligations. Counselors do not appropriate, reproduce, or modify published assessments or parts thereof without acknowledgment and permission from the publisher.

E.11. Obsolete Assessments and Outdated Results

Counselors do not use data or results from assessments that are obsolete or outdated for the current purpose. Counselors make every effort to prevent the misuse of obsolete measures and assessment data by others.

E.12. Assessment Construction

Counselors use established scientific procedures, relevant standards, and current professional knowledge for assessment design in the development, publication, and utilization of educational and psychological assessment techniques.

E.13. Forensic Evaluation: Evaluation for Legal Proceedings

E.13.a. *Primary Obligations.* When providing forensic evaluations, the primary obligation of counselors is to produce objective findings that can be substantiated based on information and techniques appropriate to the evaluation, which may include examination of the individual and/or review of records. Counselors are entitled to form professional opinions based on their professional knowledge and expertise that can be supported by the data gathered in evaluations. Counselors will define the limits of their reports or testimony, especially when an examination of the individual has not been conducted.

E.13.b. *Consent for Evaluation.* Individuals being evaluated are informed in writing that the relationship is for the purposes of an evaluation and is not counseling in nature, and entities or individuals who will receive the evaluation report are identified. Written consent to be evaluated is obtained from those being evaluated unless a court orders evaluations to be conducted without the written consent of individuals being evaluated. When children or vulnerable adults are being evaluated, informed written consent is obtained from a parent or guardian.

E.13.c. *Client Evaluation Prohibited.* Counselors do not evaluate individuals for forensic purposes they currently counsel or individuals they have counseled in the past. Counselors do not accept as counseling clients individuals they are evaluating or individuals they have evaluated in the past for forensic purposes.

E.13.d. *Avoid Potentially Harmful Relationships.* Counselors who provide forensic evaluations avoid potentially harmful professional or personal relationships with family members, romantic partners, and close friends of individuals they are evaluating or have evaluated in the past.

Section F: Supervision, Training, and Teaching

Introduction

Counselors aspire to foster meaningful and respectful professional relationships and to maintain appropriate boundaries with supervisees and students. Counselors have theoretical and pedagogical foundations for their work and aim to be fair, accurate, and honest in their assessments of counselors-in-training.

F.1. Counselor Supervision and Client Welfare

F.1.a. *Client Welfare.* A primary obligation of counseling supervisors is to monitor the services provided by other counselors or counselors-in-training. Counseling supervisors monitor client welfare and supervisee clinical performance and professional development. To fulfill these obligations, supervisors meet regularly with supervisees to review case notes, samples of clinical work, or live observations. Supervisees have a responsibility to understand and follow the *ACA Code of Ethics.*

F.1.b. *Counselor Credentials.* Counseling supervisors work to ensure that clients are aware of the qualifications of the supervisees who render services to the clients. (See A.2.b.)

F.1.c. *Informed Consent and Client Rights.* Supervisors make supervisees aware of client rights including the protection of client privacy and confidentiality in the counseling relationship. Supervisees provide clients with professional disclosure information and inform them of how the supervision process influences the limits of confidentiality. Supervisees make clients aware of who will have access to records of the counseling relationship and how these records will be used. (See A.2.b., B.1.d.)

F.2. Counselor Supervision Competence

F.2.a. *Supervisor Preparation.* Prior to offering clinical supervision services, counselors are trained in supervision methods and techniques. Counselors who offer clinical supervision services regularly pursue continuing education activities including both counseling and supervision topics and skills. (See C.2.a., C.2.f.)

F.2.b. *Multicultural Issues/Diversity in Supervision.* Counseling supervisors are aware of and address the role of multiculturalism/diversity in the supervisory relationship.

F.3. Supervisory Relationships

F.3.a. *Relationship Boundaries With Supervisees.* Counseling supervisors clearly define and maintain ethical professional, personal, and social relationships with their supervisees. Counseling supervisors avoid nonprofessional relationships with current supervisees. If supervisors must assume other professional roles (e.g., clinical and administrative supervisor, instructor) with supervisees, they work to minimize potential conflicts and explain to supervisees the expectations and responsibilities associated with each role. They do not engage in any form of nonprofessional interaction that may compromise the supervisory relationship.

F.3.b. *Sexual Relationships.* Sexual or romantic interactions or relationships with current supervisees are prohibited.

F.3.c. *Sexual Harassment.* Counseling supervisors do not condone or subject supervisees to sexual harassment. (See C.6.a.)

F.3.d. *Close Relatives and Friends.* Counseling supervisors avoid accepting close relatives, romantic partners, or friends as supervisees.

F.3.e. *Potentially Beneficial Relationships.* Counseling supervisors are aware of the power differential in their relationships with supervisees. If they believe nonprofessional relationships with a supervisee may be potentially beneficial to the supervisee, they take precautions similar to those taken by counselors when working with clients. Examples of potentially beneficial interactions or relationships include attending a formal ceremony; hospital visits; providing support during a stressful event; or mutual membership in a professional association, organization, or community. Counseling supervisors engage in open discussions with supervisees when they consider entering into relationships with them outside of their roles as clinical and/or administrative supervisors. Before engaging in nonprofessional relationships, supervisors discuss with supervisees and document the rationale for such interactions, potential benefits or drawbacks, and anticipated consequences for the supervisee. Supervisors clarify the specific nature and limitations of the additional role(s) they will have with the supervisee.

F.4. Supervisor Responsibilities

F.4.a. *Informed Consent for Supervision.* Supervisors are responsible for incorporating into their supervision the principles of informed consent and participation. Supervisors inform supervisees of the policies and procedures to which they are to adhere and the mechanisms for due process appeal of individual supervisory actions.

F.4.b. *Emergencies and Absences.* Supervisors establish and communicate to supervisees procedures for contacting them or, in their absence, alternative on-call supervisors to assist in handling crises.

F.4.c. *Standards for Supervisees.* Supervisors make their supervisees aware of professional and ethical standards and legal responsibilities. Supervisors of postdegree counselors encourage these counselors to adhere to professional standards of practice. (See C.1.)

F.4.d. *Termination of the Supervisory Relationship.* Supervisors or supervisees have the right to terminate the supervisory relationship with adequate notice. Reasons for withdrawal are provided to the other party. When cultural, clinical, or professional issues are crucial to the viability of the supervisory relationship, both parties make efforts to resolve differences. When termination is warranted, supervisors make appropriate referrals to possible alternative supervisors.

F.5. Counseling Supervision Evaluation, Remediation, and Endorsement

F.5.a. *Evaluation.* Supervisors document and provide supervisees with ongoing performance appraisal and evaluation feedback and schedule periodic formal evaluative sessions throughout the supervisory relationship.

F.5.b. *Limitations.* Through ongoing evaluation and appraisal, supervisors are aware of the limitations of supervisees that might impede performance. Supervisors assist supervisees in securing remedial assistance when needed. They recommend dismissal from training programs, applied counseling settings, or state or voluntary professional credentialing processes when those supervisees are unable to provide competent professional services. Supervisors seek consultation and document their decisions to dismiss or refer supervisees for assistance. They ensure that supervisees are aware of options available to them to address such decisions. (See C.2.g.)

F.5.c. *Counseling for Supervisees.* If supervisees request counseling, supervisors provide them with acceptable referrals. Counselors do not provide counseling services to supervisees. Supervisors address interpersonal competencies in terms of the impact of these issues on clients, the supervisory relationship, and professional functioning. (See F.3.a.)

F.5.d. *Endorsement.* Supervisors endorse supervisees for certification, licensure, employment, or completion of an academic or training program only when they believe supervisees are qualified for the endorsement. Regardless of qualifications, supervisors do not endorse supervisees whom they believe to be impaired in any way that would interfere with the performance of the duties associated with the endorsement.

F.6. Responsibilities of Counselor Educators

F.6.a. *Counselor Educators.* Counselor educators who are responsible for developing, implementing, and supervising educational programs are skilled as teachers and practitioners. They are knowledgeable regarding the ethical, legal, and regulatory aspects of the profession, are skilled in applying that knowledge, and make students and supervisees aware of their responsibilities. Counselor educators conduct counselor education and training programs in an ethical manner and serve as role models for professional behavior. (See C.1., C.2.a., C.2.c.)

F.6.b. *Infusing Multicultural Issues/Diversity.* Counselor educators infuse material related to multiculturalism/diversity into all courses and workshops for the development of professional counselors.

F.6.c. *Integration of Study and Practice.* Counselor educators establish education and training programs that integrate academic study and supervised practice.

F.6.d. *Teaching Ethics.* Counselor educators make students and supervisees aware of the ethical responsibilities and standards of the profession and the ethical responsibilities of students to the profession. Counselor educators infuse ethical considerations throughout the curriculum. (See C.1.)

F.6.e. *Peer Relationships.* Counselor educators make every effort to ensure that the rights of peers are not compromised when students or supervisees lead counseling groups or provide clinical supervision. Counselor educators take steps to ensure that students and supervisees understand they have the same ethical obligations as counselor educators, trainers, and supervisors.

F.6.f. *Innovative Theories and Techniques*. When counselor educators teach counseling techniques/procedures that are innovative, without an empirical foundation, or without a well-grounded theoretical foundation, they define the counseling techniques/procedures as "unproven" or "developing" and explain to students the potential risks and ethical considerations of using such techniques/procedures.

F.6.g. *Field Placements*. Counselor educators develop clear policies within their training programs regarding field placement and other clinical experiences. Counselor educators provide clearly stated roles and responsibilities for the student or supervisee, the site supervisor, and the program supervisor. They confirm that site supervisors are qualified to provide supervision and inform site supervisors of their professional and ethical responsibilities in this role.

F.6.h. *Professional Disclosure*. Before initiating counseling services, counselors-in-training disclose their status as students and explain how this status affects the limits of confidentiality. Counselor educators ensure that the clients at field placements are aware of the services rendered and the qualifications of the students and supervisees rendering those services. Students and supervisees obtain client permission before they use any information concerning the counseling relationship in the training process. (See A.2.b.)

F.7. Student Welfare

F.7.a. *Orientation*. Counselor educators recognize that orientation is a developmental process that continues throughout the educational and clinical training of students. Counseling faculty provide prospective students with information about the counselor education program's expectations:

1. the type and level of skill and knowledge acquisition required for successful completion of the training;
2. program training goals, objectives, and mission, and subject matter to be covered;
3. bases for evaluation;
4. training components that encourage self-growth or self-disclosure as part of the training process;
5. the type of supervision settings and requirements of the sites for required clinical field experiences;
6. student and supervisee evaluation and dismissal policies and procedures; and
7. up-to-date employment prospects for graduates.

F.7.b. *Self-Growth Experiences*. Counselor education programs delineate requirements for self-disclosure or self-growth experiences in their admission and program materials. Counselor educators use professional judgment when designing training experiences they conduct that require student and supervisee self-growth or self-disclosure. Students and supervisees are made aware of the ramifications their self-disclosure may have when counselors whose primary role as teacher, trainer, or supervisor requires acting on ethical obligations to the profession. Evaluative components of experiential training experiences explicitly delineate predetermined academic standards that are separate and do not depend on the student's level of self-disclosure. Counselor educators may require trainees to seek professional help to address any personal concerns that may be affecting their competency.

F.8. Student Responsibilities

F.8.a. *Standards for Students*. Counselors-in-training have a responsibility to understand and follow the *ACA Code of Ethics* and adhere to applicable laws, regulatory policies, and rules and policies governing professional staff behavior at the agency or placement setting. Students have the same obligation to clients as those required of professional counselors. (See C.1., H.1.)

F.8.b. *Impairment*. Counselors-in-training refrain from offering or providing counseling services when their physical, mental, or emotional problems are likely to harm a client or others. They are alert to the signs of impairment, seek assistance for problems, and notify their program supervisors when they are aware that they are unable to effectively provide services. In addition, they seek appropriate professional services for themselves to remediate the problems that are interfering with their ability to provide services to others. (See A.1., C.2.d., C.2.g.)

F.9. Evaluation and Remediation of Students

F.9.a. *Evaluation*. Counselors clearly state to students, prior to and throughout the training program, the levels of competency expected, appraisal methods, and timing of evaluations for both didactic and clinical competencies. Counselor educators provide students with ongoing performance appraisal and evaluation feedback throughout the training program.

F.9.b. *Limitations*. Counselor educators, throughout ongoing evaluation and appraisal, are aware of and address the inability of some students to achieve counseling competencies that might impede performance. Counselor educators:

1. assist students in securing remedial assistance when needed,
2. seek professional consultation and document their decision to dismiss or refer students for assistance, and
3. ensure that students have recourse in a timely manner to address decisions to require them to seek assistance or to dismiss them and provide students with due process according to institutional policies and procedures. (See C.2.g.)

F.9.c. *Counseling for Students*. If students request counseling or if counseling services are required as part of a remediation process, counselor educators provide acceptable referrals.

F.10. Roles and Relationships Between Counselor Educators and Students

F.10.a. *Sexual or Romantic Relationships*. Sexual or romantic interactions or relationships with current students are prohibited.

F.10.b. *Sexual Harassment*. Counselor educators do not condone or subject students to sexual harassment. (See C.6.a.)

F.10.c. *Relationships With Former Students*. Counselor educators are aware of the power differential in the relationship between faculty and students. Faculty members foster open discussions with former students when considering engaging in a social, sexual, or other intimate relationship. Faculty members discuss with the former student how their former relationship may affect the change in relationship.

F.10.d. *Nonprofessional Relationships.* Counselor educators avoid nonprofessional or ongoing professional relationships with students in which there is a risk of potential harm to the student or that may compromise the training experience or grades assigned. In addition, counselor educators do not accept any form of professional services, fees, commissions, reimbursement, or remuneration from a site for student or supervisee placement.

F.10.e. *Counseling Services.* Counselor educators do not serve as counselors to current students unless this is a brief role associated with a training experience.

F.10.f. *Potentially Beneficial Relationships.* Counselor educators are aware of the power differential in the relationship between faculty and students. If they believe a nonprofessional relationship with a student may be potentially beneficial to the student, they take precautions similar to those taken by counselors when working with clients. Examples of potentially beneficial interactions or relationships include, but are not limited to, attending a formal ceremony; hospital visits; providing support during a stressful event; or mutual membership in a professional association, organization, or community. Counselor educators engage in open discussions with students when they consider entering into relationships with students outside of their roles as teachers and supervisors. They discuss with students the rationale for such interactions, the potential benefits and drawbacks, and the anticipated consequences for the student. Educators clarify the specific nature and limitations of the additional role(s) they will have with the student prior to engaging in a nonprofessional relationship. Nonprofessional relationships with students should be time-limited and initiated with student consent.

F.11. Multicultural/Diversity Competence in Counselor Education and Training Programs

F.11.a. *Faculty Diversity.* Counselor educators are committed to recruiting and retaining a diverse faculty.

F.11.b. *Student Diversity.* Counselor educators actively attempt to recruit and retain a diverse student body. Counselor educators demonstrate commitment to multicultural/diversity competence by recognizing and valuing diverse cultures and types of abilities students bring to the training experience. Counselor educators provide appropriate accommodations that enhance and support diverse student well-being and academic performance.

F.11.c. *Multicultural/Diversity Competence.* Counselor educators actively infuse multicultural/diversity competency in their training and supervision practices. They actively train students to gain awareness, knowledge, and skills in the competencies of multicultural practice. Counselor educators include case examples, role-plays, discussion questions, and other classroom activities that promote and represent various cultural perspectives.

Section G: Research and Publication

Introduction

Counselors who conduct research are encouraged to contribute to the knowledge base of the profession and promote a clearer understanding of the conditions that lead to a healthy and more just society. Counselors support efforts of researchers by participating fully and willingly whenever possible. Counselors minimize bias and respect diversity in designing and implementing research programs.

G.1. Research Responsibilities

G.1.a. *Use of Human Research Participants.* Counselors plan, design, conduct, and report research in a manner that is consistent with pertinent ethical principles, federal and state laws, host institutional regulations, and scientific standards governing research with human research participants.

G.1.b. *Deviation From Standard Practice.* Counselors seek consultation and observe stringent safeguards to protect the rights of research participants when a research problem suggests a deviation from standard or acceptable practices.

G.1.c. *Independent Researchers.* When independent researchers do not have access to an Institutional Review Board (IRB), they should consult with researchers who are familiar with IRB procedures to provide appropriate safeguards.

G.1.d. *Precautions to Avoid Injury.* Counselors who conduct research with human participants are responsible for the welfare of participants throughout the research process and should take reasonable precautions to avoid causing injurious psychological, emotional, physical, or social effects to participants.

G.1.e. *Principal Researcher Responsibility.* The ultimate responsibility for ethical research practice lies with the principal researcher. All others involved in the research activities share ethical obligations and responsibility for their own actions.

G.1.f. *Minimal Interference.* Counselors take reasonable precautions to avoid causing disruptions in the lives of research participants that could be caused by their involvement in research.

G.1.g. *Multicultural/Diversity Considerations in Research.* When appropriate to research goals, counselors are sensitive to incorporating research procedures that take into account cultural considerations. They seek consultation when appropriate.

G.2. Rights of Research Participants

(See A.2, A.7.)

G.2.a. *Informed Consent in Research.* Individuals have the right to consent to become research participants. In seeking consent, counselors use language that:

1. accurately explains the purpose and procedures to be followed,
2. identifies any procedures that are experimental or relatively untried,

3. describes any attendant discomforts and risks,
4. describes any benefits or changes in individuals or organizations that might be reasonably expected,
5. discloses appropriate alternative procedures that would be advantageous for participants,
6. offers to answer any inquiries concerning the procedures,
7. describes any limitations on confidentiality,
8. describes the format and potential target audiences for the dissemination of research findings, and
9. instructs participants that they are free to withdraw their consent and to discontinue participation in the project at any time without penalty.

G.2.b. *Deception.* Counselors do not conduct research involving deception unless alternative procedures are not feasible and the prospective value of the research justifies the deception. If such deception has the potential to cause physical or emotional harm to research participants, the research is not conducted, regardless of prospective value. When the methodological requirements of a study necessitate concealment or deception, the investigator explains the reasons for this action as soon as possible during the debriefing.

G.2.c. *Student/Supervisee Participation.* Researchers who involve students or supervisees in research make clear to them that the decision regarding whether or not to participate in research activities does not affect one's academic standing or supervisory relationship. Students or supervisees who choose not to participate in educational research are provided with an appropriate alternative to fulfill their academic or clinical requirements.

G.2.d. *Client Participation.* Counselors conducting research involving clients make clear in the informed consent process that clients are free to choose whether or not to participate in research activities. Counselors take necessary precautions to protect clients from adverse consequences of declining or withdrawing from participation.

G.2.e. *Confidentiality of Information.* Information obtained about research participants during the course of an investigation is confidential. When the possibility exists that others may obtain access to such information, ethical research practice requires that the possibility, together with the plans for protecting confidentiality, be explained to participants as a part of the procedure for obtaining informed consent.

G.2.f. *Persons Not Capable of Giving Informed Consent.* When a person is not capable of giving informed consent, counselors provide an appropriate explanation to, obtain agreement for participation from, and obtain the appropriate consent of a legally authorized person.

G.2.g. *Commitments to Participants.* Counselors take reasonable measures to honor all commitments to research participants. (See A.2.c.)

G.2.h. *Explanations After Data Collection.* After data are collected, counselors provide participants with full clarification of the nature of the study to remove any misconceptions participants might have regarding the research. Where scientific or human values justify

delaying or withholding information, counselors take reasonable measures to avoid causing harm.

G.2.i. *Informing Sponsors.* Counselors inform sponsors, institutions, and publication channels regarding research procedures and outcomes. Counselors ensure that appropriate bodies and authorities are given pertinent information and acknowledgement.

G.2.j. *Disposal of Research Documents and Records.* Within a reasonable period of time following the completion of a research project or study, counselors take steps to destroy records or documents (audio, video, digital, and written) containing confidential data or information that identifies research participants. When records are of an artistic nature, researchers obtain participant consent with regard to handling of such records or documents. (See B.4.a, B.4.g.)

G.3. Relationships With Research Participants (When Research Involves Intensive or Extended Interactions)

G.3.a. *Nonprofessional Relationships.* Nonprofessional relationships with research participants should be avoided.

G.3.b. *Relationships With Research Participants.* Sexual or romantic counselor–research participant interactions or relationships with current research participants are prohibited.

G.3.c. *Sexual Harassment and Research Participants.* Researchers do not condone or subject research participants to sexual harassment.

G.3.d. *Potentially Beneficial Interactions.* When a nonprofessional interaction between the researcher and the research participant may be potentially beneficial, the researcher must document, prior to the interaction (when feasible), the rationale for such an interaction, the potential benefit, and anticipated consequences for the research participant. Such interactions should be initiated with appropriate consent of the research participant. Where unintentional harm occurs to the research participant due to the nonprofessional interaction, the researcher must show evidence of an attempt to remedy such harm.

G.4. Reporting Results

G.4.a. *Accurate Results.* Counselors plan, conduct, and report research accurately. They provide thorough discussions of the limitations of their data and alternative hypotheses. Counselors do not engage in misleading or fraudulent research, distort data, misrepresent data, or deliberately bias their results. They explicitly mention all variables and conditions known to the investigator that may have affected the outcome of a study or the interpretation of data. They describe the extent to which results are applicable for diverse populations.

G.4.b. *Obligation to Report Unfavorable Results.* Counselors report the results of any research of professional value. Results that reflect unfavorably on institutions, programs, services, prevailing opinions, or vested interests are not withheld.

G.4.c. *Reporting Errors.* If counselors discover significant errors in their published research, they take reasonable steps to correct such errors in a correction erratum, or through other appropriate publication means.

G.4.d. *Identity of Participants.* Counselors who supply data, aid in the research of another person, report research results, or make original data available take due care to disguise the identity of respective participants in the absence of specific authorization from the participants to do otherwise. In situations where participants self-identify their involvement in research studies, researchers take active steps to ensure that data is adapted/changed to protect the identity and welfare of all parties and that discussion of results does not cause harm to participants.

G.4.e. *Replication Studies.* Counselors are obligated to make available sufficient original research data to qualified professionals who may wish to replicate the study.

G.5. Publication

G.5.a. *Recognizing Contributions.* When conducting and reporting research, counselors are familiar with and give recognition to previous work on the topic, observe copyright laws, and give full credit to those to whom credit is due.

G.5.b. *Plagiarism.* Counselors do not plagiarize, that is, they do not present another person's work as their own work.

G.5.c. *Review/Republication of Data or Ideas.* Counselors fully acknowledge and make editorial reviewers aware of prior publication of ideas or data where such ideas or data are submitted for review or publication.

G.5.d. *Contributors.* Counselors give credit through joint authorship, acknowledgment, footnote statements, or other appropriate means to those who have contributed significantly to research or concept development in accordance with such contributions. The principal contributor is listed first and minor technical or professional contributions are acknowledged in notes or introductory statements.

G.5.e. *Agreement of Contributors.* Counselors who conduct joint research with colleagues or students/supervisees establish agreements in advance regarding allocation of tasks, publication credit, and types of acknowledgement that will be received.

G.5.f. *Student Research.* For articles that are substantially based on students course papers, projects, dissertations or theses, and on which students have been the primary contributors, they are listed as principal authors.

G.5.g. *Duplicate Submission.* Counselors submit manuscripts for consideration to only one journal at a time. Manuscripts that are published in whole or in substantial part in another journal or published work are not submitted for publication without acknowledgment and permission from the previous publication.

G.5.h. *Professional Review.* Counselors who review material submitted for publication, research, or other scholarly purposes respect the confidentiality and proprietary rights of those who submitted it. Counselors use care to make publication decisions based on valid and defensible standards. Counselors review article submissions in a timely manner and based on their scope and competency in research methodologies. Counselors who serve as reviewers at the request of editors or publishers make every effort to only review materials that are within their scope of competency and use care to avoid personal biases.

Section H: Resolving Ethical Issues

Introduction

Counselors behave in a legal, ethical, and moral manner in the conduct of their professional work. They are aware that client protection and trust in the profession depend on a high level of professional conduct. They hold other counselors to the same standards and are willing to take appropriate action to ensure that these standards are upheld.

Counselors strive to resolve ethical dilemmas with direct and open communication among all parties involved and seek consultation with colleagues and supervisors when necessary. Counselors incorporate ethical practice into their daily professional work. They engage in ongoing professional development regarding current topics in ethical and legal issues in counseling.

H.1. Standards and the Law
(See F.9.a.)

H.1.a. *Knowledge.* Counselors understand the *ACA Code of Ethics* and other applicable ethics codes from other professional organizations or from certification and licensure bodies of which they are members. Lack of knowledge or misunderstanding of an ethical responsibility is not a defense against a charge of unethical conduct.

H.1.b. *Conflicts Between Ethics and Laws.* If ethical responsibilities conflict with law, regulations, or other governing legal authority, counselors make known their commitment to the *ACA Code of Ethics* and take steps to resolve the conflict. If the conflict cannot be resolved by such means, counselors may adhere to the requirements of law, regulations, or other governing legal authority.

H.2. Suspected Violations

H.2.a. *Ethical Behavior Expected.* Counselors expect colleagues to adhere to the *ACA Code of Ethics*. When counselors possess knowledge that raises doubts as to whether another counselor is acting in an ethical manner, they take appropriate action. (See H.2.b., H.2.c.)

H.2.b. *Informal Resolution.* When counselors have reason to believe that another counselor is violating or has violated an ethical standard, they attempt first to resolve the issue informally with the other counselor if feasible, provided such action does not violate confidentiality rights that may be involved.

H.2.c. *Reporting Ethical Violations.* If an apparent violation has substantially harmed, or is likely to substantially harm a person or organization and is not appropriate for informal resolution or is not resolved properly, counselors take further action appropriate to the situation. Such action might include referral to state or national committees on professional ethics, voluntary national certification bodies, state licensing boards, or to the appropriate institutional authorities. This standard does not apply when an intervention would violate confidentiality rights or when counselors have been retained to review the work of another counselor whose professional conduct is in question.

H.2.d. *Consultation.* When uncertain as to whether a particular situation or course of action may be in violation of the *ACA Code of Ethics,* counselors consult with other counselors who are knowledgeable about ethics and the *ACA Code of Ethics,* with colleagues, or with appropriate authorities

H.2.e. *Organizational Conflicts.* If the demands of an organization with which counselors are affiliated pose a conflict with the *ACA Code of Ethics,* counselors specify the nature of such conflicts and express to their supervisors or other responsible officials their commitment to the *ACA Code of Ethics.* When possible, counselors work toward change within the organization to allow full adherence to the *ACA Code of Ethics.* In doing so, they address any confidentiality issues.

H.2.f. *Unwarranted Complaints.* Counselors do not initiate, participate in, or encourage the filing of ethics complaints that are made with reckless disregard or willful ignorance of facts that would disprove the allegation.

H.2.g. *Unfair Discrimination Against Complainants and Respondents.* Counselors do not deny persons employment, advancement, admission to academic or other programs, tenure, or promotion based solely upon their having made or their being the subject of an ethics complaint. This does not preclude taking action based upon the outcome of such proceedings or considering other appropriate information.

H.3. Cooperation With Ethics Committees

Counselors assist in the process of enforcing the *ACA Code of Ethics.* Counselors cooperate with investigations, proceedings, and requirements of the ACA Ethics Committee or ethics committees of other duly constituted associations or boards having jurisdiction over those charged with a violation. Counselors are familiar with the *ACA Policy and Procedures for Processing Complaints of Ethical Violations* and use it as a reference for assisting in the enforcement of the *ACA Code of Ethics.*

APPENDIX B
Ethical Principles of Psychologists and Code of Conduct 2002

INTRODUCTION AND APPLICABILITY

The American Psychological Association's (APA's) Ethical Principles of Psychologists and Code of Conduct (hereinafter referred to as the Ethics Code) consists of an Introduction, a Preamble, five General Principles (A–E), and specific Ethical Standards. The Introduction discusses the intent, organization, procedural considerations, and scope of application of the Ethics Code. The Preamble and General Principles are aspirational goals to guide psychologists toward the highest ideals of psychology. Although the Preamble and General Principles are not themselves enforceable rules, they should be considered by psychologists in arriving at an ethical course of action. The Ethical Standards set forth enforceable rules for conduct as psychologists. Most of the Ethical Standards are written broadly, in order to apply to psychologists in varied roles, although the application of an Ethical Standard may vary depending on the context. The Ethical Standards are not exhaustive. The fact that a given conduct is not specifically addressed by an Ethical Standard does not mean that it is necessarily either ethical or unethical.

This Ethics Code applies only to psychologists' activities that are part of their scientific, educational, or professional roles as psychologists. Areas covered include but are not limited to the clinical, counseling, and school practice of psychology; research; teaching; supervision of trainees; public service; policy development; social intervention; development of assessment instruments; conducting assessments; educational counseling; organizational consulting; forensic activities; program design and evaluation; and administration. This Ethics Code applies to these activities across a variety of contexts, such as in person, postal, telephone, internet, and other electronic transmissions. These activities shall be distinguished from the purely private conduct of psychologists, which is not within the purview of the Ethics Code.

Membership in the APA commits members and student affiliates to comply with the standards of the APA Ethics Code and to the rules and procedures used to enforce them. Lack of awareness or misunderstanding of an Ethical Standard is not itself a defense to a charge of unethical conduct.

The procedures for filing, investigating, and resolving complaints of unethical conduct are described in the current Rules and Procedures of the APA Ethics Committee. APA may impose sanctions on its members for violations of the standards of the Ethics Code, including termination of APA membership, and may notify other bodies and individuals of its actions. Actions that violate the standards of the Ethics Code may also lead to the imposition of sanctions on psychologists or students whether or not they are APA members by bodies other than APA, including state psychological associations, other professional groups, psychology boards, other state or federal agencies, and payors for health services. In addition, APA may take action against a member after his or her conviction of a felony, expulsion or suspension from an affiliated state psychological association, or suspension or loss of licensure. When the sanction to be imposed by APA is less than expulsion, the 2001 Rules and Procedures do not guarantee an opportunity for an in-person hearing, but generally provide that complaints will be resolved only on the basis of a submitted record.

The Ethics Code is intended to provide guidance for psychologists and standards of professional conduct that can be applied by the APA and by other bodies that choose to adopt them. The Ethics Code is not intended to be a basis of civil liability. Whether a psychologist has violated the Ethics Code standards does not by itself determine whether the psychologist is legally liable in a court action, whether a contract is enforceable, or whether other legal consequences occur.

The modifiers used in some of the standards of this Ethics Code (e.g., *reasonably, appropriate, potentially*) are included in the standards when they would (1) allow professional judgment on the part of psychologists, (2) eliminate injustice or inequality that would occur without the modifier, (3) ensure applicability across the broad range of activities conducted by psychologists, or (4) guard against a set of rigid rules that might be quickly outdated. As used in this Ethics Code, the term *reasonable* means the prevailing professional judgment of psychologists engaged in similar activities in similar circumstances, given the knowledge the psychologist had or should have had at the time.

In the process of making decisions regarding their professional behavior, psychologists must consider this Ethics Code in addition to applicable laws and psychology board regulations. In applying the Ethics Code to their professional work, psychologists may consider other materials and guidelines that have been adopted or endorsed by scientific and professional psychological organizations and the dictates of their own conscience, as well as consult with others within the field. If this Ethics Code establishes a higher standard of conduct than is required by law, psychologists must meet the higher ethical standard. If psychologists' ethical responsibilities conflict with law, regulations, or other governing legal authority, psychologists make known their commitment to this Ethics Code and take steps to resolve the conflict in a responsible manner. If the conflict is unresolvable via such means, psychologists may adhere to the requirements of the law, regulations, or other governing authority in keeping with basic principles of human rights.

PREAMBLE

Psychologists are committed to increasing scientific and professional knowledge of behavior and people's understanding of themselves and others and to the use of such knowledge to improve the condition of individuals, organizations, and society. Psychologists respect and protect civil and human rights and the central importance of freedom of inquiry and expression in research, teaching, and publication. They strive to help the public in developing informed judgments and choices concerning human behavior. In doing so, they perform many roles, such as researcher, educator, diagnostician, therapist, supervisor, consultant, administrator, social interventionist, and expert witness. This Ethics Code provides a common set of principles and standards upon which psychologists build their professional and scientific work.

This Ethics Code is intended to provide specific standards to cover most situations encountered by psychologists. It has as its goals the welfare and protection of the individuals and groups with whom psychologists work and the education of members, students, and the public regarding ethical standards of the discipline.

The development of a dynamic set of ethical standards for psychologists' work-related conduct requires a personal commitment and lifelong effort to act ethically; to encourage ethical behavior by students, supervisees, employees, and colleagues; and to consult with others concerning ethical problems.

GENERAL PRINCIPLES

This section consists of General Principles. General Principles, as opposed to Ethical Standards, are aspirational in nature. Their intent is to guide and inspire psychologists toward the very highest ethical ideals of the profession. General Principles, in contrast to Ethical Standards, do not represent obligations and should not form the basis for imposing sanctions. Relying upon General Principles for either of these reasons distorts both their meaning and purpose.

Principle A: Beneficence and Nonmaleficence

Psychologists strive to benefit those with whom they work and take care to do no harm. In their professional actions, psychologists seek to safeguard the welfare and rights of those with whom they interact professionally and other affected persons, and the welfare of animal subjects of research. When conflicts occur among psychologists' obligations or concerns, they attempt to resolve these conflicts in a responsible fashion that avoids or minimizes harm. Because psychologists' scientific and professional judgments and actions may affect the lives of others, they are alert to and guard against personal, financial, social, organizational, or political factors that might lead to misuse of their influence. Psychologists strive to be aware of the possible effect of their own physical and mental health on their ability to help those with whom they work.

Principle B: Fidelity and Responsibility

Psychologists establish relationships of trust with those with whom they work. They are aware of their professional and scientific responsibilities to society and to the specific communities in which they work. Psychologists uphold professional standards of conduct, clarify their professional roles and obligations, accept appropriate responsibility for their behavior, and seek to manage conflicts of interest that could lead to exploitation or harm. Psychologists consult with, refer to, or cooperate with other professionals and institutions to the extent needed to serve the best interests of those with whom they work. They are concerned about the ethical compliance of their colleagues' scientific and professional conduct. Psychologists strive to contribute a portion of their professional time for little or no compensation or personal advantage.

Principle C: Integrity

Psychologists seek to promote accuracy, honesty, and truthfulness in the science, teaching, and practice of psychology. In these activities psychologists do not steal, cheat, or engage in fraud, subterfuge, or intentional misrepresentation of fact. Psychologists strive to keep their promises and to avoid unwise or unclear commitments. In situations in which deception may be ethically justifiable to maximize benefits and minimize harm, psychologists have a serious obligation to consider the need for, the possible consequences of, and their responsibility to correct any resulting mistrust or other harmful effects that arise from the use of such techniques.

Principle D: Justice

Psychologists recognize that fairness and justice entitle all persons to access to and benefit from the contributions of psychology and to equal quality in the processes, procedures, and services being conducted by psychologists. Psychologists exercise reasonable judgment and take precautions to ensure that their potential biases, the boundaries of their competence, and the limitations of their expertise do not lead to or condone unjust practices.

Principle E: Respect for People's Rights and Dignity

Psychologists respect the dignity and worth of all people, and the rights of individuals to privacy, confidentiality, and self-determination. Psychologists are aware that special safeguards may be necessary to protect the rights and welfare of persons or communities whose vulnerabilities impair autonomous decision making. Psychologists are aware of and respect cultural, individual, and role differences, including those based on age, gender, gender identity, race, ethnicity, culture, national origin, religion, sexual orientation, disability, language, and socioeconomic status and consider these factors when working with members of such groups. Psychologists try to eliminate the effect on their work of biases based on those factors, and they do not knowingly participate in or condone activities of others based upon such prejudices.

ETHICAL STANDARDS

1. Resolving Ethical Issues

1.01 Misuse of Psychologists' Work
If psychologists learn of misuse or misrepresentation of their work, they take reasonable steps to correct or minimize the misuse or misrepresentation.

1.02 Conflicts Between Ethics and Law, Regulations, or Other Governing Legal Authority
If psychologists' ethical responsibilities conflict with law, regulations, or other governing legal authority, psychologists make known their commitment to the Ethics Code and take steps to resolve the conflict. If the conflict is unresolvable via such means, psychologists may adhere to the requirements of the law, regulations, or other governing legal authority.

1.03 Conflicts Between Ethics and Organizational Demands

If the demands of an organization with which psychologists are affiliated or for whom they are working conflict with this Ethics Code, psychologists clarify the nature of the conflict, make known their commitment to the Ethics Code, and to the extent feasible, resolve the conflict in a way that permits adherence to the Ethics Code.

1.04 Informal Resolution of Ethical Violations

When psychologists believe that there may have been an ethical violation by another psychologist, they attempt to resolve the issue by bringing it to the attention of that individual, if an informal resolution appears appropriate and the intervention does not violate any confidentiality rights that may be involved. (See also Standards 1.02, Conflicts Between Ethics and Law, Regulations, or Other Governing Legal Authority, and 1.03, Conflicts Between Ethics and Organizational Demands.)

1.05 Reporting Ethical Violations

If an apparent ethical violation has substantially harmed or is likely to substantially harm a person or organization and is not appropriate for informal resolution under Standard 1.04, Informal Resolution of Ethical Violations, or is not resolved properly in that fashion, psychologists take further action appropriate to the situation. Such action might include referral to state or national committees on professional ethics, to state licensing boards, or to the appropriate institutional authorities. This standard does not apply when an intervention would violate confidentiality rights or when psychologists have been retained to review the work of another psychologist whose professional conduct is in question. (See also Standard 1.02, Conflicts Between Ethics and Law, Regulations, or Other Governing Legal Authority.)

1.06 Cooperating With Ethics Committees

Psychologists cooperate in ethics investigations, proceedings, and resulting requirements of the APA or any affiliated state psychological association to which they belong. In doing so, they address any confidentiality issues. Failure to cooperate is itself an ethics violation. However, making a request for deferment of adjudication of an ethics complaint pending the outcome of litigation does not alone constitute noncooperation.

1.07 Improper Complaints

Psychologists do not file or encourage the filing of ethics complaints that are made with reckless disregard for or willful ignorance of facts that would disprove the allegation.

1.08 Unfair Discrimination Against Complainants and Respondents

Psychologists do not deny persons employment, advancement, admissions to academic or other programs, tenure, or promotion, based solely upon their having made or their being the subject of an ethics complaint. This does not preclude taking action based upon the outcome of such proceedings or considering other appropriate information.

2. Competence

2.01 Boundaries of Competence

a. Psychologists provide services, teach, and conduct research with populations and in areas only within the boundaries of their competence, based on their education, training, supervised experience, consultation, study, or professional experience.

b. Where scientific or professional knowledge in the discipline of psychology establishes that an understanding of factors associated with age, gender, gender identity, culture, national origin, religion, sexual orientation, disability, language, or socioeconomic status is essential for effective implementation of their services or research, psychologists have or obtain the training, experience, consultation, or supervision necessary to ensure the competence of their services, or they make appropriate referrals, except as provided in Standard 2.02, Providing Services in Emergencies.

c. Psychologists planning to provide services, teach, or conduct research involving populations, areas, techniques, or technologies new to them undertake relevant education, training, supervised experience, consultation, or study.

d. When psychologists are asked to provide services to individuals for whom appropriate mental health services are not available and for which psychologists have not obtained the competence necessary, psychologists with closely related prior training or experience may provide such services in order to ensure that services are not denied if they make a reasonable effort to obtain the competence required by using relevant research, training, consultation, or study.

e. In those emerging areas in which generally recognized standards for preparatory training do not yet exist, psychologists nevertheless take reasonable steps to ensure the competence of their work and to protect clients/patients, students, supervisees, research participants, organizational clients, and others from harm.

f. When assuming forensic roles, psychologists are or become reasonably familiar with the judicial or administrative rules governing their roles.

2.02 Providing Services in Emergencies

In emergencies, when psychologists provide services to individuals for whom other mental health services are not available and for which psychologists have not obtained the necessary training, psychologists may provide such services in order to ensure that services are not denied. The services are discontinued as soon as the emergency has ended or appropriate services are available.

2.03 Maintaining Competence

Psychologists undertake ongoing efforts to develop and maintain their competence.

2.04 Bases for Scientific and Professional Judgments

Psychologists' work is based upon established scientific and professional knowledge of the discipline. (See also Standards 2.01e, Boundaries of Competence, and 10.01b, Informed Consent to Therapy.)

2.05 Delegation of Work to Others

Psychologists who delegate work to employees, supervisees, or research or teaching assistants or who use the services of others, such as interpreters, take reasonable steps to (1) avoid delegating such work to persons who have a multiple relationship with those being served that would likely lead to exploitation or loss of objectivity; (2) authorize only those responsibilities that such persons can be expected to perform competently on the basis of their education, training, or experience, either independently or with the level of supervision being provided; and (3) see that such persons perform these services competently. (See also Standards 2.02, Providing Services in Emergencies; 3.05, Multiple Relationships; 4.01, Maintaining Confidentiality; 9.01, Bases for Assessments; 9.02, Use of Assessments; 9.03, Informed Consent in Assessments; and 9.07, Assessment by Unqualified Persons.)

2.06 Personal Problems and Conflicts

a. Psychologists refrain from initiating an activity when they know or should know that there is a substantial likelihood that their personal problems will prevent them from performing their work-related activities in a competent manner.

b. When psychologists become aware of personal problems that may interfere with their performing work-related duties adequately, they take appropriate measures, such as obtaining professional consultation or assistance, and determine whether they should limit, suspend, or terminate their work-related duties. (See also Standard 10.10, Terminating Therapy.)

3. Human Relations

3.01 Unfair Discrimination

In their work-related activities, psychologists do not engage in unfair discrimination based on age, gender, gender identity, race, ethnicity, culture, national origin, religion, sexual orientation, disability, socioeconomic status, or any basis proscribed by law.

3.02 Sexual Harassment

Psychologists do not engage in sexual harassment. Sexual harassment is sexual solicitation, physical advances, or verbal or nonverbal conduct that is sexual in nature, that occurs in connection with the psychologist's activities or roles as a psychologist, and that either (1) is unwelcome, is offensive, or creates a hostile workplace or educational environment, and the psychologist knows or is told this or (2) is sufficiently severe or intense to be abusive to a reasonable person in the context. Sexual harassment can consist of a single intense or severe act or of multiple persistent or pervasive acts. (See also Standard 1.08, Unfair Discrimination Against Complainants and Respondents.)

3.03 Other Harassment

Psychologists do not knowingly engage in behavior that is harassing or demeaning to persons with whom they interact in their work based on factors such as those persons' age, gender, gender identity, race, ethnicity, culture, national origin, religion, sexual orientation, disability, language, or socioeconomic status.

3.04 Avoiding Harm

Psychologists take reasonable steps to avoid harming their clients/patients, students, supervisees, research participants, organizational clients, and others with whom they work, and to minimize harm where it is foreseeable and unavoidable.

3.05 Multiple Relationships

a. A multiple relationship occurs when a psychologist is in a professional role with a person and (1) at the same time is in another role with the same person, (2) at the same time is in a relationship with a person closely associated with or related to the person with whom the psychologist has the professional relationship, or (3) promises to enter into another relationship in the future with the person or a person closely associated with or related to the person.

A psychologist refrains from entering into a multiple relationship if the multiple relationship could reasonably be expected to impair the psychologist's objectivity, competence, or effectiveness in performing his or her functions as a psychologist, or otherwise risks exploitation or harm to the person with whom the professional relationship exists.

Multiple relationships that would not reasonably be expected to cause impairment or risk exploitation or harm are not unethical.

b. If a psychologist finds that, due to unforeseen factors, a potentially harmful multiple relationship has arisen, the psychologist takes reasonable steps to resolve it with due regard for the best interests of the affected person and maximal compliance with the Ethics Code.

c. When psychologists are required by law, institutional policy, or extraordinary circumstances to serve in more than one role in judicial or administrative proceedings, at the outset they clarify role expectations and the extent of confidentiality and thereafter as changes occur. (See also Standards 3.04, Avoiding Harm, and 3.07, Third-Party Requests for Services.)

3.06 Conflict of Interest

Psychologists refrain from taking on a professional role when personal, scientific, professional, legal, financial, or other interests or relationships could reasonably be expected to (1) impair their objectivity, competence, or effectiveness in performing their functions as psychologists or (2) expose the person or organization with whom the professional relationship exists to harm or exploitation.

3.07 Third-Party Requests for Services

When psychologists agree to provide services to a person or entity at the request of a third party, psychologists attempt to clarify at the outset of the service the nature of the relationship with all individuals or organizations involved. This clarification includes the role of the psychologist (e.g., therapist, consultant, diagnostician, or expert witness), an identification of who is the client, the probable uses of the services provided or the information obtained, and the fact that there may be limits to confidentiality. (See also Standards 3.05, Multiple Relationships, and 4.02, Discussing the Limits of Confidentiality.)

3.08 Exploitative Relationships

Psychologists do not exploit persons over whom they have supervisory, evaluative, or other authority such as clients/patients, students, supervisees, research participants, and employees. (See also Standards 3.05, Multiple Relationships; 6.04, Fees and Financial Arrangements; 6.05, Barter With Clients/Patients; 7.07, Sexual Relationships With Students and Supervisees; 10.05, Sexual Intimacies With Current Therapy Clients/Patients; 10.06, Sexual Intimacies With Relatives or Significant Others of Current Therapy Clients/Patients; 10.07, Therapy With Former Sexual Partners; and 10.08, Sexual Intimacies With Former Therapy Clients/Patients.)

3.09 Cooperation With Other Professionals

When indicated and professionally appropriate, psychologists cooperate with other professionals in order to serve their clients/patients effectively and appropriately. (See also Standard 4.05, Disclosures.)

3.10 Informed Consent

a. When psychologists conduct research or provide assessment, therapy, counseling, or consulting services in person or via electronic transmission or other forms of communication, they obtain the informed consent of the individual or individuals using language that is reasonably understandable to that person or persons except when conducting such activities without consent is mandated by law or governmental regulation or as otherwise provided in this Ethics Code. (See also Standards 8.02, Informed Consent to Research; 9.03, Informed Consent in Assessments; and 10.01, Informed Consent to Therapy.)

b. For persons who are legally incapable of giving informed consent, psychologists nevertheless (1) provide an appropriate explanation, (2) seek the individual's assent, (3) consider such persons' preferences and best interests, and (4) obtain appropriate permission from a legally authorized person, if such substitute consent is permitted or required by law. When consent by a legally authorized person is not permitted or required by law, psychologists take reasonable steps to protect the individual's rights and welfare.

c. When psychological services are court ordered or otherwise mandated, psychologists inform the individual of the nature of the anticipated services, including whether the services are court ordered or mandated and any limits of confidentiality, before proceeding.

d. Psychologists appropriately document written or oral consent, permission, and assent. (See also Standards 8.02, Informed Consent to Research; 9.03, Informed Consent in Assessments; and 10.01, Informed Consent to Therapy.)

3.11 Psychological Services Delivered To or Through Organizations

a. Psychologists delivering services to or through organizations provide information beforehand to clients and when appropriate those directly affected by the services about (1) the nature and objectives of the services, (2) the intended recipients, (3) which of the individuals are clients, (4) the relationship the psychologist will have with each person and the organization, (5) the probable uses of services provided and information obtained, (6) who will have access to the information, and (7) limits of confidentiality. As soon as feasible, they provide information about the results and conclusions of such services to appropriate persons.

b. If psychologists will be precluded by law or by organizational roles from providing such information to particular individuals or groups, they so inform those individuals or groups at the outset of the service.

3.12 Interruption of Psychological Services

Unless otherwise covered by contract, psychologists make reasonable efforts to plan for facilitating services in the event that psychological services are interrupted by factors such as the psychologist's illness, death, unavailability, relocation, or retirement or by the client's/patient's relocation or financial limitations. (See also Standard 6.02c, Maintenance, Dissemination, and Disposal of Confidential Records of Professional and Scientific Work.)

4. Privacy And Confidentiality

4.01 Maintaining Confidentiality

Psychologists have a primary obligation and take reasonable precautions to protect confidential information obtained through or stored in any medium, recognizing that the extent and limits of confidentiality may be regulated by law or established by institutional rules or professional or scientific relationship. (See also Standard 2.05, Delegation of Work to Others.)

4.02 Discussing the Limits of Confidentiality

a. Psychologists discuss with persons (including, to the extent feasible, persons who are legally incapable of giving informed consent and their legal representatives) and organizations with whom they establish a scientific or professional relationship (1) the relevant limits of confidentiality and (2) the foreseeable uses of the information generated through their psychological activities. (See also Standard 3.10, Informed Consent.)

b. Unless it is not feasible or is contraindicated, the discussion of confidentiality occurs at the outset of the relationship and thereafter as new circumstances may warrant.

c. Psychologists who offer services, products, or information via electronic transmission inform clients/patients of the risks to privacy and limits of confidentiality.

4.03 Recording

Before recording the voices or images of individuals to whom they provide services, psychologists obtain permission from all such persons or their legal representatives. (See also Standards 8.03, Informed Consent for Recording Voices and Images in Research; 8.05, Dispensing With Informed Consent for Research; and 8.07, Deception in Research.)

4.04 Minimizing Intrusions on Privacy

a. Psychologists include in written and oral reports and consultations, only information germane to the purpose for which the communication is made.

b. Psychologists discuss confidential information obtained in their work only for appropriate scientific or professional purposes and only with persons clearly concerned with such matters.

4.05 Disclosures

a. Psychologists may disclose confidential information with the appropriate consent of the organizational client, the individual client/patient, or another legally authorized person on behalf of the client/patient unless prohibited by law.

b. Psychologists disclose confidential information without the consent of the individual only as mandated by law, or where permitted by law for a valid purpose such as to (1) provide needed professional services; (2) obtain appropriate professional consultations; (3) protect the client/patient, psychologist, or others from harm; or (4) obtain payment for services from a client/patient, in which instance disclosure is limited to the minimum that is necessary to achieve the purpose. (See also Standard 6.04e, Fees and Financial Arrangements.)

4.06 Consultations

When consulting with colleagues, (1) psychologists do not disclose confidential information that reasonably could lead to the identification of a client/patient, research participant, or other person or organization with whom they have a confidential relationship unless they have obtained the prior consent of the person or organization or the disclosure cannot be avoided, and (2) they disclose information only to the extent necessary to achieve the purposes of the consultation. (See also Standard 4.01, Maintaining Confidentiality.)

4.07 Use of Confidential Information for Didactic or Other Purposes

Psychologists do not disclose in their writings, lectures, or other public media, confidential, personally identifiable information concerning their clients/patients, students, research participants, organizational clients, or other recipients of their services that they obtained during the course of their work, unless (1) they take reasonable steps to disguise the person or organization, (2) the person or organization has consented in writing, or (3) there is legal authorization for doing so.

5. Advertising and Other Public Statements

5.01 Avoidance of False or Deceptive Statements

a. Public statements include but are not limited to paid or unpaid advertising, product endorsements, grant applications, licensing applications, other credentialing applications, brochures, printed matter, directory listings, personal resumes or curricula vitae, or comments for use in media such as print or electronic transmission, statements in legal proceedings, lectures and public oral presentations, and published materials. Psychologists do not knowingly make public statements that are false, deceptive, or fraudulent concerning their research, practice, or other work activities or those of persons or organizations with which they are affiliated.

b. Psychologists do not make false, deceptive, or fraudulent statements concerning (1) their training, experience, or competence; (2) their academic degrees; (3) their credentials; (4) their institutional or association affiliations; (5) their services; (6) the scientific or clinical basis for, or results or degree of success of, their services; (7) their fees; or (8) their publications or research findings.

c. Psychologists claim degrees as credentials for their health services only if those degrees (1) were earned from a regionally accredited educational institution or (2) were the basis for psychology licensure by the state in which they practice.

5.02 Statements by Others

a. Psychologists who engage others to create or place public statements that promote their professional practice, products, or activities retain professional responsibility for such statements.

b. Psychologists do not compensate employees of press, radio, television, or other communication media in return for publicity in a news item. (See also Standard 1.01, Misuse of Psychologists' Work.)

c. A paid advertisement relating to psychologists' activities must be identified or clearly recognizable as such.

5.03 Descriptions of Workshops and Non-Degree-Granting Educational Programs

To the degree to which they exercise control, psychologists responsible for announcements, catalogs, brochures, or advertisements describing workshops, seminars, or other non-degree-granting educational programs ensure that they accurately describe the audience for which the program is intended, the educational objectives, the presenters, and the fees involved.

5.04 Media Presentations

When psychologists provide public advice or comment via print, internet, or other electronic transmission, they take precautions to ensure that statements (1) are based on their professional knowledge, training, or experience in accord with appropriate psychological literature and practice; (2) are otherwise consistent with this Ethics Code; and (3) do not indicate that a professional relationship has been established with the recipient. (See also Standard 2.04, Bases for Scientific and Professional Judgments.)

5.05 Testimonials

Psychologists do not solicit testimonials from current therapy clients/patients or other persons who because of their particular circumstances are vulnerable to undue influence.

5.06 In-Person Solicitation

Psychologists do not engage, directly or through agents, in uninvited in-person solicitation of business from actual or potential therapy clients/patients or other persons who because of their particular circumstances are vulnerable to undue influence. However, this prohibition does not preclude (1) attempting to implement appropriate collateral contacts for the purpose of benefiting an already engaged therapy client/patient or (2) providing disaster or community outreach services.

6. Record Keeping and Fees

6.01 Documentation of Professional and Scientific Work and Maintenance of Records

Psychologists create, and to the extent the records are under their control, maintain, disseminate, store, retain, and dispose of records and data relating to their professional and scientific work in order to (1) facilitate provision of services later by them or by other professionals, (2) allow for replication of research design and analyses, (3) meet institutional requirements, (4) ensure accuracy of billing and payments, and (5) ensure compliance with law. (See also Standard 4.01, Maintaining Confidentiality.)

6.02 Maintenance, Dissemination, and Disposal of Confidential Records of Professional and Scientific Work

a. Psychologists maintain confidentiality in creating, storing, accessing, transferring, and disposing of records under their control, whether these are written, automated, or in any other medium. (See also Standards 4.01, Maintaining Confidentiality, and 6.01, Documentation of Professional and Scientific Work and Maintenance of Records.)

b. If confidential information concerning recipients of psychological services is entered into databases or systems of records available to persons whose access has not been consented to by the recipient, psychologists use coding or other techniques to avoid the inclusion of personal identifiers.

c. Psychologists make plans in advance to facilitate the appropriate transfer and to protect the confidentiality of records and data in the event of psychologists' withdrawal from positions or practice. (See also Standards 3.12, Interruption of Psychological Services, and 10.09, Interruption of Therapy.)

6.03 Withholding Records for Nonpayment

Psychologists may not withhold records under their control that are requested and needed for a client's/patient's emergency treatment solely because payment has not been received.

6.04 Fees and Financial Arrangements

a. As early as is feasible in a professional or scientific relationship, psychologists and recipients of psychological services reach an agreement specifying compensation and billing arrangements.

b. Psychologists' fee practices are consistent with law.

c. Psychologists do not misrepresent their fees.

d. If limitations to services can be anticipated because of limitations in financing, this is discussed with the recipient of services as early as is feasible. (See also Standards 10.09, Interruption of Therapy, and 10.10, Terminating Therapy.)

e. If the recipient of services does not pay for services as agreed, and if psychologists intend to use collection agencies or legal measures to collect the fees, psychologists first inform the person that such measures will be taken and provide that person an opportunity to make prompt payment. (See also Standards 4.05, Disclosures; 6.03, Withholding Records for Nonpayment; and 10.01, Informed Consent to Therapy.)

6.05 Barter With Clients/Patients

Barter is the acceptance of goods, services, or other nonmonetary remuneration from clients/patients in return for psychological services. Psychologists may barter only if (1) it is not clinically contraindicated, and (2) the resulting arrangement is not exploitative. (See also Standards 3.05, Multiple Relationships, and 6.04, Fees and Financial Arrangements.)

6.06 Accuracy in Reports to Payors and Funding Sources

In their reports to payors for services or sources of research funding, psychologists take reasonable steps to ensure the accurate reporting of the nature of the service provided or research conducted, the fees, charges, or payments, and where applicable, the identity of the provider, the findings, and the diagnosis. (See also Standards 4.01, Maintaining Confidentiality; 4.04, Minimizing Intrusions on Privacy; and 4.05, Disclosures.)

6.07 Referrals and Fees

When psychologists pay, receive payment from, or divide fees with another professional, other than in an employer-employee relationship, the payment to each is based on the services provided (clinical, consultative, administrative, or other) and is not based on the referral itself. (See also Standard 3.09, Cooperation With Other Professionals.)

7. Education and Training

7.01 Design of Education and Training Programs

Psychologists responsible for education and training programs take reasonable steps to ensure that the programs are designed to provide the appropriate knowledge and proper experiences, and to meet the requirements for licensure, certification, or other goals for which claims are made by the program. (See also Standard 5.03, Descriptions of Workshops and Non-Degree-Granting Educational Programs.)

7.02 Descriptions of Education and Training Programs

Psychologists responsible for education and training programs take reasonable steps to ensure that there is a current and accurate description of the program content (including participation in required course- or program-related counseling, psychotherapy, experiential groups, consulting projects, or community service), training goals and objectives, stipends and benefits, and requirements that must be met for satisfactory completion of the program. This information must be made readily available to all interested parties.

7.03 Accuracy in Teaching

a. Psychologists take reasonable steps to ensure that course syllabi are accurate regarding the subject matter to be covered, bases for evaluating progress, and the nature of course experiences. This standard does not preclude an instructor from modifying course content or requirements when the instructor considers it pedagogically necessary or desirable, so long as students are made aware of these modifications in a manner that enables them to fulfill course requirements. (See also Standard 5.01, Avoidance of False or Deceptive Statements.)

b. When engaged in teaching or training, psychologists present psychological information accurately. (See also Standard 2.03, Maintaining Competence.)

7.04 Student Disclosure of Personal Information

Psychologists do not require students or supervisees to disclose personal information in course or program-related activities, either orally or in writing, regarding sexual history, history of abuse and neglect, psychological treatment, and relationships with parents, peers, and spouses or significant others except if (1) the program or training facility has clearly identified this requirement in its admissions and program materials or (2) the information is necessary to evaluate or obtain assistance for students whose personal problems could reasonably be judged to be preventing them from performing their training- or professionally related activities in a competent manner or posing a threat to the students or others.

7.05 Mandatory Individual or Group Therapy

a. When individual or group therapy is a program or course requirement, psychologists responsible for that program allow students in undergraduate and graduate programs the option of selecting such therapy from practitioners unaffiliated with the program. (See also Standard 7.02, Descriptions of Education and Training Programs.)

b. Faculty who are or are likely to be responsible for evaluating students' academic performance do not themselves provide that therapy. (See also Standard 3.05, Multiple Relationships.)

7.06 Assessing Student and Supervisee Performance

In academic and supervisory relationships, psychologists establish a timely and specific process for providing feedback to students and supervisees. Information regarding the process is provided to the student at the beginning of supervision.

Psychologists evaluate students and supervisees on the basis of their actual performance on relevant and established program requirements.

7.07 Sexual Relationships With Students and Supervisees

Psychologists do not engage in sexual relationships with students or supervisees who are in their department, agency, or training center or over whom psychologists have or are likely to have evaluative authority. (See also Standard 3.05, Multiple Relationships.)

8. Research and Publication

8.01 Institutional Approval

When institutional approval is required, psychologists provide accurate information about their research proposals and obtain approval prior to conducting the research. They conduct the research in accordance with the approved research protocol.

8.02 Informed Consent to Research

a. When obtaining informed consent as required in Standard 3.10, Informed Consent, psychologists inform participants about (1) the purpose of the research, expected duration, and procedures; (2) their right to decline to participate and to withdraw from the research once participation has begun; (3) the foreseeable consequences of declining or withdrawing; (4) reasonably foreseeable factors that may be expected to influence their willingness to participate such as potential risks, discomfort, or adverse effects; (5) any prospective research benefits; (6) limits of confidentiality; (7) incentives for participation; and (8) whom to contact for questions about the research and research participants' rights. They provide opportunity for the prospective participants to ask questions and receive answers. (See also Standards 8.03, Informed Consent for Recording Voices and Images in Research; 8.05, Dispensing With Informed Consent for Research; and 8.07, Deception in Research.)

b. Psychologists conducting intervention research involving the use of experimental treatments clarify to participants at the outset of the research (1) the experimental nature of the treatment; (2) the services that will or will not be available to the control group(s) if appropriate; (3) the means by which assignment to treatment and control groups will be made; (4) available treatment alternatives if an individual does not wish to participate in the research or wishes to withdraw once a study has begun; and (5) compensation for or monetary costs of participating including, if appropriate, whether reimbursement from the participant or a third-party payor will be sought. (See also Standard 8.02a, Informed Consent to Research.)

8.03 Informed Consent for Recording Voices and Images in Research

Psychologists obtain informed consent from research participants prior to recording their voices or images for data collection unless (1) the research consists solely of naturalistic observations in public places, and it is not anticipated that the recording will be used in a manner that could cause personal identification or harm, or (2) the research design includes deception, and consent for the use of the recording is obtained during debriefing. (See also Standard 8.07, Deception in Research.)

8.04 Client/Patient, Student, and Subordinate Research Participants

a. When psychologists conduct research with clients/patients, students, or subordinates as participants, psychologists take steps to protect the prospective participants from adverse consequences of declining or withdrawing from participation.

b. When research participation is a course requirement or an opportunity for extra credit, the prospective participant is given the choice of equitable alternative activities.

8.05 Dispensing With Informed Consent for Research

Psychologists may dispense with informed consent only (1) where research would not reasonably be assumed to create distress or harm and involves (a) the study of normal educational practices, curricula, or classroom management methods conducted in educational settings; (b) only anonymous questionnaires, naturalistic observations, or archival research for which disclosure of responses would not place participants at risk of criminal or civil liability or damage their financial standing, employability, or reputation, and confidentiality is protected; or

(c) the study of factors related to job or organization effectiveness conducted in organizational settings for which there is no risk to participants' employability, and confidentiality is protected or (2) where otherwise permitted by law or federal or institutional regulations.

8.06 Offering Inducements for Research Participation

a. Psychologists make reasonable efforts to avoid offering excessive or inappropriate financial or other inducements for research participation when such inducements are likely to coerce participation.

b. When offering professional services as an inducement for research participation, psychologists clarify the nature of the services, as well as the risks, obligations, and limitations. (See also Standard 6.05, Barter With Clients/Patients.)

8.07 Deception in Research

a. Psychologists do not conduct a study involving deception unless they have determined that the use of deceptive techniques is justified by the study's significant prospective scientific, educational, or applied value and that effective nondeceptive alternative procedures are not feasible.

b. Psychologists do not deceive prospective participants about research that is reasonably expected to cause physical pain or severe emotional distress.

c. Psychologists explain any deception that is an integral feature of the design and conduct of an experiment to participants as early as is feasible, preferably at the conclusion of their participation, but no later than at the conclusion of the data collection, and permit participants to withdraw their data. (See also Standard 8.08, Debriefing.)

8.08 Debriefing

a. Psychologists provide a prompt opportunity for participants to obtain appropriate information about the nature, results, and conclusions of the research, and they take reasonable steps to correct any misconceptions that participants may have of which the psychologists are aware.

b. If scientific or humane values justify delaying or withholding this information, psychologists take reasonable measures to reduce the risk of harm.

c. When psychologists become aware that research procedures have harmed a participant, they take reasonable steps to minimize the harm.

8.09 Humane Care and Use of Animals in Research

a. Psychologists acquire, care for, use, and dispose of animals in compliance with current federal, state, and local laws and regulations, and with professional standards.

b. Psychologists trained in research methods and experienced in the care of laboratory animals supervise all procedures involving animals and are responsible for ensuring appropriate consideration of their comfort, health, and humane treatment.

c. Psychologists ensure that all individuals under their supervision who are using animals have received instruction in research methods and in the care, maintenance, and handling of the species being used, to the extent appropriate to their role. (See also Standard 2.05, Delegation of Work to Others.)

d. Psychologists make reasonable efforts to minimize the discomfort, infection, illness, and pain of animal subjects.

e. Psychologists use a procedure subjecting animals to pain, stress, or privation only when an alternative procedure is unavailable and the goal is justified by its prospective scientific, educational, or applied value.

f. Psychologists perform surgical procedures under appropriate anesthesia and follow techniques to avoid infection and minimize pain during and after surgery.

g. When it is appropriate that an animal's life be terminated, psychologists proceed rapidly, with an effort to minimize pain and in accordance with accepted procedures.

8.10 Reporting Research Results

a. Psychologists do not fabricate data. (See also Standard 5.01a, Avoidance of False or Deceptive Statements.)

b. If psychologists discover significant errors in their published data, they take reasonable steps to correct such errors in a correction, retraction, erratum, or other appropriate publication means.

8.11 Plagiarism

Psychologists do not present portions of another's work or data as their own, even if the other work or data source is cited occassionally.

8.12 Publication Credit

a. Psychologists take responsibility and credit, including authorship credit, only for work they have actually performed or to which they have substantially contributed. (See also Standard 8.12b, Publication Credit.)

b. Principal authorship and other publication credits accurately reflect the relative scientific or professional contributions of the individuals involved, regardless of their relative status. Mere possession of an institutional position, such as department chair, does not justify authorship credit. Minor contributions to the research or to the writing for publications are acknowledged appropriately, such as in footnotes or in an introductory statement.

c. Except under exceptional circumstances, a student is listed as principal author on any multiple-authored article that is substantially based on the student's doctoral dissertation. Faculty advisors discuss publication credit with students as early as feasible and throughout the research and publication process as appropriate. (See also Standard 8.12b, Publication Credit.)

8.13 Duplicate Publication of Data

Psychologists do not publish, as original data, data that have been previously published. This does not preclude republishing data when they are accompanied by proper acknowledgement.

8.14 Sharing Research Data for Verification

a. After research results are published, psychologists do not withhold the data on which their conclusions are based from other competent professionals who seek to verify the substantive claims through reanalysis and who intend to use such data only for that purpose, provided that the confidentiality of the participants can be protected and unless legal rights concerning proprietary data preclude their release. This does not preclude psychologists from requiring that such individuals or groups be responsible for costs associated with the provision of such information.

b. Psychologists who request data from other psychologists to verify the substantive claims through reanalysis may use shared data only for the declared purpose. Requesting psychologists obtain prior written agreement for all other uses of the data.

8.15 Reviewers

Psychologists who review material submitted for presentation, publication, grant, or research proposal review respect the confidentiality of and the proprietary rights in such information of those who submitted it.

9. Assessment

9.01 Bases for Assessments

a. Psychologists base the opinions contained in their recommendations, reports, and diagnostic or evaluative statements, including forensic testimony, on information and techniques sufficient to substantiate their findings. (See also Standard 2.04, Bases for Scientific and Professional Judgments.)

b. Except as noted in 9.01c, psychologists provide opinions of the psychological characteristics of individuals only after they have conducted an examination of the individuals adequate to support their statements or conclusions. When, despite reasonable efforts, such an examination is not practical, psychologists document the efforts they made and the result of those efforts, clarify the probable impact of their limited information on the reliability and validity of their opinions, and appropriately limit the nature and extent of their conclusions or recommendations. (See also Standards 2.01, Boundaries of Competence, and 9.06, Interpreting Assessment Results.)

c. When psychologists conduct a record review or provide consultation or supervision and an individual examination is not warranted or necessary for the opinion, psychologists explain this and the sources of information on which they based their conclusions and recommendations.

9.02 Use of Assessments

a. Psychologists administer, adapt, score, interpret, or use assessment techniques, interviews, tests, or instruments in a manner and for purposes that are appropriate in light of the research on or evidence of the usefulness and proper application of the techniques.

b. Psychologists use assessment instruments whose validity and reliability have been established for use with members of the population tested. When such validity or reliability has not been established, psychologists describe the strengths and limitations of test results and interpretation.

c. Psychologists use assessment methods that are appropriate to an individual's language preference and competence, unless the use of an alternative language is relevant to the assessment issues.

9.03 Informed Consent in Assessments

a. Psychologists obtain informed consent for assessments, evaluations, or diagnostic services, as described in Standard 3.10, Informed Consent, except when (1) testing is mandated by law or governmental regulations; (2) informed consent is implied because testing is conducted as a routine educational, institutional, or organizational activity (e.g., when participants voluntarily agree to assessment when applying for a job); or (3) one purpose of the testing is to evaluate decisional capacity. Informed consent includes an explanation of the nature and purpose of the assessment, fees, involvement of third parties, and limits of confidentiality and sufficient opportunity for the client/patient to ask questions and receive answers.

b. Psychologists inform persons with questionable capacity to consent or for whom testing is mandated by law or governmental regulations about the nature and purpose of the proposed assessment services, using language that is reasonably understandable to the person being assessed.

c. Psychologists using the services of an interpreter obtain informed consent from the client/patient to use that interpreter, ensure that confidentiality of test results and test security are maintained, and include in their recommendations, reports, and diagnostic or evaluative statements, including forensic testimony, discussion of any limitations on the data obtained. (See also Standards 2.05, Delegation of Work to Others; 4.01, Maintaining Confidentiality; 9.01, Bases for Assessments; 9.06, Interpreting Assessment Results; and 9.07, Assessment by Unqualified Persons.)

9.04 Release of Test Data

a. The term *test data* refers to raw and scaled scores, client/patient responses to test questions or stimuli, and psychologists' notes and recordings concerning client/patient statements and behavior during an examination. Those portions of test materials that include client/patient responses are included in the definition of *test data*. Pursuant to a client/patient release, psychologists provide test data to the client/patient or other persons identified in the release. Psychologists may refrain from releasing test data to protect a client/patient or others from substantial harm or misuse or misrepresentation of the data or the test, recognizing that in many instances release of confidential information under these circumstances is regulated by law. (See also Standard 9.11, Maintaining Test Security.)

b. In the absence of a client/patient release, psychologists provide test data only as required by law or court order.

9.05 Test Construction

Psychologists who develop tests and other assessment techniques use appropriate psychometric procedures and current scientific or professional knowledge for test design, standardization, validation, reduction or elimination of bias, and recommendations for use.

9.06 Interpreting Assessment Results

When interpreting assessment results, including automated interpretations, psychologists take into account the purpose of the assessment as well as the various test factors, test-taking abilities, and other characteristics of the person being assessed, such as situational, personal, linguistic, and cultural differences, that might affect psychologists' judgments or reduce the accuracy of their interpretations. They indicate any significant limitations of their interpretations. (See also Standards 2.01b and c, Boundaries of Competence, and 3.01, Unfair Discrimination.)

9.07 Assessment by Unqualified Persons

Psychologists do not promote the use of psychological assessment techniques by unqualified persons, except when such use is conducted for training purposes with appropriate supervision. (See also Standard 2.05, Delegation of Work to Others.)

9.08 Obsolete Tests and Outdated Test Results

a. Psychologists do not base their assessment or intervention decisions or recommendations on data or test results that are outdated for the current purpose.

b. Psychologists do not base such decisions or recommendations on tests and measures that are obsolete and not useful for the current purpose.

9.09 Test Scoring and Interpretation Services

a. Psychologists who offer assessment or scoring services to other professionals accurately describe the purpose, norms, validity, reliability, and applications of the procedures and any special qualifications applicable to their use.

b. Psychologists select scoring and interpretation services (including automated services) on the basis of evidence of the validity of the program and procedures as well as on other appropriate considerations. (See also Standard 2.01b and c, Boundaries of Competence.)

c. Psychologists retain responsibility for the appropriate application, interpretation, and use of assessment instruments, whether they score and interpret such tests themselves or use automated or other services.

9.10 Explaining Assessment Results

Regardless of whether the scoring and interpretation are done by psychologists, by employees or assistants, or by automated or other outside services, psychologists take reasonable steps to ensure that explanations of results are given to the individual or designated representative unless the nature of the relationship precludes provision of an explanation of results (such as in some organizational consulting, preemployment or security screenings, and forensic evaluations), and this fact has been clearly explained to the person being assessed in advance.

9.11. Maintaining Test Security

The term *test materials* refers to manuals, instruments, protocols, and test questions or stimuli and does not include *test data* as defined in Standard 9.04, Release of Test Data. Psychologists make reasonable efforts to maintain the integrity and security of test materials and other assessment techniques consistent with law and contractual obligations, and in a manner that permits adherence to this Ethics Code.

10. Therapy

10.01 Informed Consent to Therapy

a. When obtaining informed consent to therapy as required in Standard 3.10, Informed Consent, psychologists inform clients/patients as early as is feasible in the therapeutic relationship about the nature and anticipated course of therapy, fees, involvement of third parties, and limits of confidentiality and provide sufficient opportunity for the client/patient to ask questions and receive answers. (See also Standards 4.02, Discussing the Limits of Confidentiality, and 6.04, Fees and Financial Arrangements.)

b. When obtaining informed consent for treatment for which generally recognized techniques and procedures have not been established, psychologists inform their clients/patients of the developing nature of the treatment, the potential risks involved, alternative treatments that may be available, and the voluntary nature of their participation. (See also Standards 2.01e, Boundaries of Competence, and 3.10, Informed Consent.)

c. When the therapist is a trainee and the legal responsibility for the treatment provided resides with the supervisor, the client/patient, as part of the informed consent procedure, is informed that the therapist is in training and is being supervised and is given the name of the supervisor.

10.02 Therapy Involving Couples or Families

a. When psychologists agree to provide services to several persons who have a relationship (such as spouses, significant others, or parents and children), they take reasonable steps to clarify at the outset (1) which of the individuals are clients/patients and (2) the relationship the psychologist will have with each person. This clarification includes the psychologist's role and the probable uses of the services provided or the information obtained. (See also Standard 4.02, Discussing the Limits of Confidentiality.)

b. If it becomes apparent that psychologists may be called on to perform potentially conflicting roles (such as family therapist and then witness for one party in divorce proceedings), psychologists take reasonable steps to clarify and modify, or withdraw from, roles appropriately. (See also Standard 3.05c, Multiple Relationships.)

10.03 Group Therapy

When psychologists provide services to several persons in a group setting, they describe at the outset the roles and responsibilities of all parties and the limits of confidentiality.

10.04 Providing Therapy to Those Served by Others

In deciding whether to offer or provide services to those already receiving mental health services elsewhere, psychologists carefully consider the treatment issues and the potential client's/patient's welfare. Psychologists discuss these issues with the client/patient or another legally authorized person on behalf of the client/patient in order to minimize the risk of confusion and conflict, consult with the other service providers when appropriate, and proceed with caution and sensitivity to the therapeutic issues.

10.05 Sexual Intimacies With Current Therapy Clients/Patients

Psychologists do not engage in sexual intimacies with current therapy clients/patients.

10.06 Sexual Intimacies With Relatives or Significant Others of Current Therapy Clients/Patients

Psychologists do not engage in sexual intimacies with individuals they know to be close relatives, guardians, or significant others of current clients/patients. Psychologists do not terminate therapy to circumvent this standard.

10.07 Therapy With Former Sexual Partners

Psychologists do not accept as therapy clients/patients persons with whom they have engaged in sexual intimacies.

10.08 Sexual Intimacies With Former Therapy Clients/Patients

a. Psychologists do not engage in sexual intimacies with former clients/patients for at least two years after cessation or termination of therapy.

b. Psychologists do not engage in sexual intimacies with former clients/patients even after a two-year interval except in the most

unusual circumstances. Psychologists who engage in such activity after the two years following cessation or termination of therapy and of having no sexual contact with the former client/patient bear the burden of demonstrating that there has been no exploitation, in light of all relevant factors, including (1) the amount of time that has passed since therapy terminated; (2) the nature, duration, and intensity of the therapy; (3) the circumstances of termination; (4) the client's/patient's personal history; (5) the client's/patient's current mental status; (6) the likelihood of adverse impact on the client/patient; and (7) any statements or actions made by the therapist during the course of therapy suggesting or inviting the possibility of a posttermination sexual or romantic relationship with the client/patient. (See also Standard 3.05, Multiple Relationships.)

10.09 Interruption of Therapy

When entering into employment or contractual relationships, psychologists make reasonable efforts to provide for orderly and appropriate resolution of responsibility for client/patient care in the event that the employment or contractual relationship ends, with paramount consideration given to the welfare of the client/patient. (See also Standard 3.12, Interruption of Psychological Services.)

10.10 Terminating Therapy

a. Psychologists terminate therapy when it becomes reasonably clear that the client/patient no longer needs the service, is not likely to benefit, or is being harmed by continued service.

b. Psychologists may terminate therapy when threatened or otherwise endangered by the client/patient or another person with whom the client/patient has a relationship.

c. Except where precluded by the actions of clients/patients or third-party payors, prior to termination psychologists provide pretermination counseling and suggest alternative service providers as appropriate.

History and Effective Date Footnote

This version of the APA Ethics Code was adopted by the American Psychological Association's Council of Representatives during its meeting, August 21, 2002, and is effective beginning June 1, 2003. Inquiries concerning the substance or interpretation of the APA Ethics Code should be addressed to the Director, Office of Ethics, American Psychological Association, 750 First Street, NE, Washington, DC 20002-4242. The Ethics Code and information regarding the Code can be found on the APA web site http://www.apa.org/ethics. The standards in this Ethics Code will be used to adjudicate complaints brought concerning alleged conduct occurring on or after the effective date. Complaints regarding conduct occurring prior to the effective date will be adjudicated on the basis of the version of the Ethics Code that was in effect at the time the conduct occurred.

The APA has previously published its Ethics Code as follows:

American Psychological Association. (1953). *Ethical standards of psychologists.* Washington, DC: Author.
American Psychological Association. (1959). Ethical standards of psychologists. *American Psychologist, 14,* 279–282.
American Psychological Association. (1963). Ethical standards of psychologists. *American Psychologist, 18,* 56–60.

American Psychological Association. (1968). Ethical standards of psychologists. *American Psychologist, 23,* 357–361.

American Psychological Association. (1977, March). Ethical standards of psychologists. *APA Monitor,* 22–23.

American Psychological Association. (1979). *Ethical standards of psychologists.* Washington, DC: Author.

American Psychological Association. (1981). Ethical principles of psychologists. *American Psychologist, 36,* 633–638.

American Psychological Association. (1990). Ethical principles of psychologists (Amended June 2, 1989). *American Psychologist, 45,* 390–395.

American Psychological Association. (1992). Ethical principles of psychologists and code of conduct. *American Psychologist, 47,* 1597–1611.

Request copies of the APA's Ethical Principles of Psychologists and Code of Conduct from the APA Order Department, 750 First Street, NE, Washington, DC 20002-4242, or phone (202) 336-5510.

APPENDIX C
Informed Written Consent for Treatment Checklist

Requirements vary greatly regarding the necessity or the content of an informed written consent for treatment—sometimes referred to as a fact sheet. Agency or institutional policies, state counselor licensing laws and rules, and other binding directives often determine the existence or content of this document. The intent of an informed consent document is to define the basic treatment relationship between counselor and client. Misunderstanding and disappointment, which are often the genesis of a liability claim, can be reduced when clients are made knowledgeable of the ground rules of the counseling relationship. Trust and the therapeutic relationship are enhanced when clients understand what is expected or required of a counselor and of themselves in a successful counseling relationship. The following topics are recommended for consideration when developing an informed written consent for treatment:

1. **Voluntary Participation.** Clients voluntarily agree to treatment and can terminate at any time without penalty.
2. **Client Involvement.** What level of involvement and what type of involvement will be expected from clients?
3. **Counselor Involvement.** What will the counselor provide? How will this be provided? How can the counselor be reached in the event of an emergency?
4. **No Guarantees.** Counselors cannot guarantee results (e.g., become happier, become less tense or depressed, save the marriage, stop drug use, obtain a good job).
5. **Risks Associated With Counseling.** Define what, if any, risks are associated with the counselor's particular approach to counseling.
6. **Confidentiality and Privilege.** Specify how confidentiality will be handled in couple counseling, family counseling, child/adolescent counseling, and group counseling situations. How may confidential and privileged information be released?
7. **Exceptions of Confidentiality and Privilege.** Define specific statutory circumstances where confidentiality and privilege cannot be maintained (e.g., abuse reporting).
8. **Counseling Approach or Theory.** What is the counselor's counseling orientation or theoretical belief system? How will that affect treatment?
9. **Counseling and Financial Records.** What will they include? How long will they be maintained? How will they be destroyed?

10. **Ethical Guidelines.** What standard defines the counselor's practice? How might a client obtain a copy of these guidelines?
11. **Licensing Regulations.** What license does the counselor hold? How may a client check on the status of the license?
12. **Credentials.** What education, training, and experience credentials will the counselor need to provide counseling treatment, including any specialty credentials?
13. **Fees and Charges.** What are the specific fees and charges? How will fees be collected? How are financial records maintained?
14. **Insurance Reimbursement.** What responsibility will the counselor take for filing insurance forms? What fees, if any, are associated with insurance filing? How will co-payments be handled?
15. **Responsibility for Payment.** Who is responsible for payment of counseling charges? How will delinquent accounts be handled? What charges will be assessed for delinquent accounts?
16. **Disputes and Complaints.** How will fee or other disputes be resolved? Provide the address and phone number of the state licensing board for complaints if required by state licensing statute.
17. **Cancellation Policy.** How much notice for cancellation of a scheduled appointment is required? What fees will be charged for late cancellation?
18. **Affiliation Relationship.** Describe independent contractor and/or partnership relationship with any other practitioners in office suite.
19. **Supervisory Relationship.** Describe any required supervisory relationship along with reason for the supervision. Provide supervisor's name and credentials.
20. **Colleague Consultation.** Indicate that, in keeping with generally accepted standards of practice, you frequently consult with other mental health professionals regarding the management of cases. The purpose of the consultation is to ensure quality care. Every effort is made to protect the identity of clients.

Source: From *Legal Aspects of Counseling: Avoiding Lawsuits and Legal Problems* by B. Bertram & A. M. Wheeler, 1994, Workshop materials, Alexandria, VA: American Counseling Association.

Information You Have a Right to Know

When you come for therapy, you are buying a service. Therefore, you need information to make a good decision. Below are some questions you might want to ask. We've talked about some of them. You are entitled to ask me any of these questions if you want to know. If you don't understand my answers, ask me again.

I. THERAPY

A. What is the name of your kind of therapy?
B. How did you learn how to do this therapy? Where?
C. How does your kind of therapy compare with other kinds of therapy?
D. How does your kind of therapy work?
E. What are the possible risks involved? (like divorce, depression)
F. What percentage of clients improve? In what ways? How do you know? (e.g., published research? your own practice experience? discussions with your colleagues?)
G. What percentage of clients get worse? How do you know?
H. What percentage of clients improve or get worse without this therapy? How do you know?
I. About how long will it take?
J. What should I do if I feel therapy isn't working?
K. Will I have to take any kind of tests? What kind?
L. Do you follow a therapy manual with predetermined steps?
M. Do you do therapy over the phone? Over the internet?

II. ALTERNATIVES

A. What other types of therapy or help are there? (like support groups)
B. How often do they work? How do you know?
C. What are the risks and benefits of these other approaches? What are the risks and benefits of NO therapy?
D. How is your types of therapy different from these others?
E. Do you prescribe medication? Do you work with others who do?
F. (If I am taking medications) Will you be working together with the doctor who prescribed my medication? How much do you know about the medications I am taking?

III. APPOINTMENTS

A. How are appointments scheduled?
B. How long are sessions? Do I have to pay more for longer ones?
C. How can I reach you in an emergency?
D. If you are not available, who is there I can talk to?
E. What happens if the weather is bad, or I'm sick?

IV. CONFIDENTIALITY

A. What kind of records do you keep? Who has access to them? (insurance companies, supervisors, etc.)
B. Under what conditions are you allowed to tell others about the things we discuss? (suicidal or homicidal threats, child abuse, court cases, insurance companies, supervisors, etc.)
C. Do other members of my family, or the group, have access to information?
D. How do governmental regulations such as federal HIPAA regulations influence how you handle the confidentiality of my records? Under these regulations, is confidentiality equal for all types of information?

V. MONEY

A. What is your fee?
B. How do I need to pay? At the session, monthly, etc.?
C. Do I need to pay for missed sessions?
D. Do I need to pay for telephone calls, letters, or e-mails?
E. What are your policies about raising fees? (for example, how many times have you raised them in the past 2 years?)
F. If I lose my source of income, can my fee be lowered?
G. If I do not pay my fee, will you pursue legal or debt collection activity? Under what circumstances?

VI. INSURANCE/MANAGED CARE

A. How much and what kind of information will you be required to tell the insurance company about our sessions? (diagnosis, symptoms, etc.)
B. How much influence does the insurance company have on the therapy? (length, goals, etc.)
C. What if I switch insurance companies or lose my insurance? Or what if you stop accepting my insurance?
D. What if you disagree with the insurance company about the best treatment?
E. How would therapy be different if I chose to pay without using insurance?

VII. GENERAL

A. What is your training and experience? Are you licensed by the state? Supervised? Certified?
B. Are you a psychologist? Psychiatrist? Family therapist? Counselor? What are the advantages and limitations of your credentials?
C. Who do I talk to if I have a complaint about therapy that we can't work out? (e.g., supervisor, state licensure board, ACA ethics committee)

I have already given you some written information. This included a contract, privacy statement, brochure, and/or consent form. We have also talked about some aspects of our work together. This information dealt with most of these questions. I will be happy to explain them and to answer other questions you have. This will help make your decision a good one. You can keep this information. Please read it carefully at home. We will also look this over from time to time.

Source: Adapted from "Informed consent revisited: An updated written question format." By A. M. Pomerantz and M. M. Handelsman, 2004, *Professional Psychology: Research and Practice, 35,* pp. 204–205. Copyright 2004 by the American Psychological Association. Adapted with permission.

Feminist Therapy Code of Ethics

(Revised, 1999)

PREAMBLE

Feminist therapy evolved from feminist philosophy, psychological theory and practice, and political theory. In particular, feminists recognize the impact of society in creating and maintaining the problems and issues brought into therapy.

Briefly, feminists believe the personal is political. Basic tenets of feminism include a belief in the equal worth of all human beings, a recognition that each individual's personal experiences and situations are reflective of and an influence on society's institutionalized attitudes and values, and a commitment to political and social change that equalizes power among people. Feminists are committed to recognizing and reducing the pervasive influences and insidious effects of oppressive societal attitudes and society.

Thus, a feminist analysis addresses the understanding of power and its interconnections among gender, race, culture, class, physical ability, sexual orientation, age, and anti-Semitism as well as all forms of oppression based on religion, ethnicity, and heritage. Feminist therapists also live in and are subject to those same influences and effects and consistently monitor their beliefs and behaviors as a result of those influences.

Feminist therapists adhere to and integrate feminist analyses in all spheres of their work as therapists, educators, consultants, administrators, writers, editors, and/or researchers. Feminist therapists are accountable for the management of the power differential within these roles and accept responsibility for that power. Because of the limitations of a purely intrapsychic model of human functioning, feminist therapists facilitate the understanding of the interactive effects of the client's internal and external worlds. Feminist therapists possess knowledge about the psychology of women and girls and utilize feminist scholarship to revise theories and practices, incorporating new knowledge as it is generated.

Feminist therapists are trained in a variety of disciplines, theoretical orientations, and degrees of structure. They come from different cultural, economic, ethnic, and racial backgrounds. They work in many types of settings with a diversity of clients and practice different modalities of therapy, training, and research. Feminist therapy theory integrates feminist principles into other theories of human development and change.

The ethical guidelines that follow are additive to, rather than a replacement for, the ethical principles of the profession in which a feminist therapist practices. Amid this diversity, feminist therapists are joined together by their feminist analyses and perspectives. Additionally, they work toward incorporating feminist principles into existing professional standards when appropriate.

Feminist therapists live with and practice in competing forces and complex controlling interests. When mental health care involves third-party payers, it is feminist therapists' responsibility to advocate for the best possible therapeutic process for the client, including short or long term therapy. Care and compassion for clients include protection of confidentiality and awareness of the impacts of economic and political considerations, including the increasing disparity between the quality of therapeutic care available for those with or without third-party payers.

Feminist therapists assume a proactive stance toward the eradication of oppression in their lives and work toward empowering women and girls. They are respectful of individual differences, examining oppressive aspects of both their own and clients' value systems. Feminist therapists engage in social change activities, broadly defined, outside of and apart from their work in their professions. Such activities may vary in scope and content but are an essential aspect of a feminist perspective.

This code is a series of positive statements that provide guidelines for feminist therapy practice, training, and research. Feminist therapists who are members of other professional organizations adhere to the ethical codes of those organizations. Feminist therapists who are not members of such organizations are guided by the ethical standards of the organization closest to their mode of practice.

These statements provide more specific guidelines within the context of and as an extension of most ethical codes. When ethical guidelines are in conflict, the feminist therapist is accountable for how she prioritizes her choices.

These ethical guidelines, then, are focused on the issues feminist therapists, educators, and researchers have found especially important in their professional settings. As with any code of therapy ethics, the well-being of clients is the guiding principle underlying this code. The feminist therapy issues that relate directly to the client's well being include cultural diversities and oppressions, power differentials, overlapping relationships, therapist accountability, and social change. Even though the principles are stated separately, each interfaces with the others to form an interdependent whole. In addition, the code is a living document and thus is continually in the process of change.

The Feminist Therapy Institute's Code of Ethics is shaped by economic and cultural forces in North America and by the experiences of its members. Members encourage an ongoing international dialogue about feminist and ethical issues. It recognizes that ethical codes are aspirational and ethical behaviors are on a continuum rather than reflecting dichotomies. Additionally, ethical guidelines and legal requirements may differ. The Feminist Therapy Institute provides educational interventions for its members rather than disciplinary activity.

ETHICAL GUIDELINES FOR FEMINIST THERAPISTS

I. Cultural Diversities and Oppressions

A. A feminist therapist increases her accessibility to and for a wide range of clients from her own and other identified groups through flexible delivery of services. When appropriate, the feminist therapist assists clients in accessing other services and intervenes when a client's rights are violated.

B. A feminist therapist is aware of the meaning and impact of her own ethnic and cultural background, gender, class, age, and sexual orientation, and actively attempts to become knowledgeable about alternatives from sources other than her clients. She is actively engaged in broadening her knowledge of ethnic and cultural experiences, non-dominant and dominant.

C. Recognizing that the dominant culture determines the norm, the therapist's goal is to uncover and respect cultural and experiential differences, including those based on long term or recent immigration and/or refugee status.

D. A feminist therapist evaluates her ongoing interactions with her clientele for any evidence of her biases or discriminatory attitudes and practices. She also monitors her other interactions, including service delivery, teaching, writing, and all professional activities. The feminist therapist accepts responsibility for taking action to confront and change any interfering, oppressing, or devaluing biases she has.

II. Power Differentials

A. A feminist therapist acknowledges the inherent power differentials between client and therapist and models effective use of personal, structural, or institutional power. In using the power differential to the benefit of the client, she does not take control or power which rightfully belongs to her client.

B. A feminist therapist discloses information to the client which facilitates the therapeutic process, including information communicated to others. The therapist is responsible for using self-disclosure only with purpose and discretion and in the interest of the client.

C. A feminist therapist negotiates and renegotiates formal and/or informal contacts with clients in an ongoing mutual process. As part of the decision-making process, she makes explicit the therapeutic issues involved.

D. A feminist therapist educates her clients regarding power relationships. She informs clients of their rights as consumers of therapy, including procedures for resolving differences and filing grievances. She clarifies power in its various forms as it exists within other areas of her life, including professional roles, social/governmental structures, and interpersonal relationships. She assists her clients in finding ways to protect themselves and, if requested, to seek redress.

III. Overlapping Relationships

A. A feminist therapist recognizes the complexity and conflicting priorities inherent in multiple or overlapping relationships. The therapist accepts responsibility for monitoring such relationships to prevent potential abuse of or harm to the client.

B. A feminist therapist is actively involved in her community. As a result, she is aware of the need for confidentiality in all settings. Recognizing that her client's concerns and general well-being are primary, she self-monitors both public and private statements and comments. Situations may develop through community involvement where power dynamics shift, including a client having equal or more authority than the therapist. In all such situations a feminist therapist maintains accountability.

C. When accepting third party payments, a feminist therapist is especially cognizant of and clearly communicates to her client the multiple obligations, roles, and responsibilities of the therapist. When working in institutional settings, she clarifies to all involved parties where her allegiances lie. She also monitors multiple and conflicting expectations between clients and caregivers, especially when working with children and elders.

D. A feminist therapist does not engage in sexual intimacies nor any overtly or covertly sexualized behaviors with a client or former client.

IV. Therapist Accountability

A. A feminist therapist is accountable to herself, to colleagues, and especially to her clients.

B. A feminist therapist will contract to work with clients and issues within the realm of her competencies. If problems beyond her competencies surface, the feminist therapist utilizes consultation and available resources. She respects the integrity of the relationship by stating the limits of her training and providing the client with the possibilities of continuing with her or changing therapists.

C. A feminist therapist recognizes her personal and professional needs and utilizes ongoing self-evaluation, peer support, consultation, supervision, continuing education, and/or personal therapy. She evaluates, maintains, and seeks to improve her competencies, as well as her emotional, physical, mental, and spiritual well-being. When the feminist therapist has experienced a similar stressful or damaging event as her client, she seeks consultation.

D. A feminist therapist continually re-evaluates her training, theoretical background, and research to include developments in feminist knowledge. She integrates feminism into psychological theory, receives ongoing therapy training, and acknowledges the limits of her competencies.

E. A feminist therapist engages in self-care activities in an ongoing manner outside the work setting. She recognizes her own needs and vulnerabilities as well as the unique stresses inherent in this work. She demonstrates an ability to establish boundaries with the client that are healthy for both of them. She also is willing to self-nurture in appropriate and self-empowering ways.

V. Social Change

A. A feminist therapist seeks multiple avenues for impacting change, including public education and advocacy within professional organizations, lobbying for legislative actions, and other appropriate activities.

B. A feminist therapist actively questions practices in her community that appear harmful to clients or therapists. She assists clients in intervening on their own behalf. As appropriate, the feminist therapist herself intervenes, especially when other practitioners appear to be engaging in harmful, unethical, or illegal behaviors.

C. When appropriate, a feminist therapist encourages a client's recognition of criminal behaviors and also facilitates the client's navigation of the criminal justice system.

D. A feminist therapist, teacher, or researcher is alert to the control of information dissemination and questions pressures to conform to and use dominant mainstream standards. As technological methods of communication change and increase, the feminist therapist recognizes the socioeconomic aspects of these developments and communicates according to clients' access to technology.

E. A feminist therapist, teacher, or researcher recognizes the political is personal in a world where social change is a constant.

Source: Copyright © 2000, Feminist Therapy Institute, Inc.

APA Statement on Services by Telephone, Teleconferencing, and Internet

A STATEMENT BY THE ETHICS COMMITTEE OF THE AMERICAN PSYCHOLOGICAL ASSOCIATION

The American Psychological Association's Ethics Committee issued the following statement on November 5, 1997, based on its 1995 statement on the same topic.

The Ethics Committee can only address the relevance of and enforce the "Ethical Principles of Psychologists and Code of Conduct" and cannot say whether there may be other APA Guidelines that might provide guidance. The Ethics Code is not specific with regard to telephone therapy or teleconferencing or any electronically provided services as such and has no rules prohibiting such services. Complaints regarding such matters would be addressed on a case by case basis.

Delivery of services by such media as telephone, teleconferencing and internet is a rapidly evolving area. This will be the subject of APA task forces and will be considered in future revision of the Ethics Code. Until such time as a more definitive judgment is available, the Ethics Committee recommends that psychologists follow Standard 2.04c, Boundaries of Competence, which indicates that "In those emerging areas in which generally recognized standards for preparatory training do not yet exist, psychologists nevertheless take reasonable steps to ensure the competence of their work and to protect patients, clients, students, research participants, and others from harm." Other relevant standards include Assessment (Standards 2.01 - 2.10), Therapy (4.01 - 4.09, especially 4.01 Structuring the Relationship and 4.02 Informed Consent to Therapy), and Confidentiality (5.01 - 5.11). Within the General Standards section, standards with particular relevance are 1.03, Professional and Scientific Relationship; 2.04 (a, b, and c), Boundaries of Competence; 1.06, Basis for Scientific and Professional Judgments; 1.07a, Describing the Nature and Results of Psychological Services; 1.14, Avoiding Harm; and 1.25, Fees and Financial Arrangements. Standards under Advertising, particularly 3.01 - 3.03 are also relevant.

Psychologists considering such services must review the characteristics of the services, the service delivery method, and the provisions for confidentiality. Psychologists must then consider the relevant ethical standards and other requirements, such as licensure board rules.

The Practice of Internet Counseling

National Board for Certified Counselors, Inc. and Center for Credentialing and Education, Inc. (Adopted November 3, 2001)

This document contains a statement of principles for guiding the evolving practice of Internet counseling. In order to provide a context for these principles, the following definition of Internet counseling, which is one element of technology-assisted distance counseling, is provided. The Internet counseling standards follow the definitions presented below.

A TAXONOMY FOR DEFINING FACE-TO-FACE AND TECHNOLOGY-ASSISTED DISTANCE COUNSELING

The delivery of technology-assisted distance counseling continues to grow and evolve. Technology assistance in the form of computer-assisted assessment, computer-assisted information systems, and telephone counseling has been available and widely used for some time. The rapid development and use of the Internet to deliver information and foster communication has resulted in the creation of new forms of counseling. Developments have occurred so rapidly that it is difficult to communicate a common understanding of these new forms of counseling practice.

The purpose of this document is to create standard definitions of technology-assisted distance counseling that can be easily updated in response to evolution in technology and practice. A definition of traditional face-to-face counseling is also presented to show similarities and differences with respect to various applications of technology in counseling. A taxonomy of forms of counseling is also presented to further clarify how technology relates to counseling practice.

NATURE OF COUNSELING

Counseling is the application of mental health, psychological, or human development principles through cognitive, affective, behavioral, or systemic intervention strategies that address wellness, personal growth, or career development, as well as pathology.

Depending on the needs of the client and the availability of services, counseling may range from a few brief interactions in a short period of time to numerous interactions over an extended period of time. Brief interventions, such as classroom discussions, workshop presentations, or assistance in using assessment, information, or instructional resources, may be sufficient to meet individual needs. Or, these brief interventions may lead to longer term counseling interventions for individuals with more substantial needs. Counseling may be delivered by a single counselor, two counselors working collaboratively, or a single counselor with brief assistance from another counselor who has specialized expertise that is needed by the client.

FORMS OF COUNSELING

Counseling can be delivered in a variety of forms that share the definition presented above. Forms of counseling differ with respect to participants, delivery location, communication medium, and interaction process. Counseling participants can be individuals, couples, or groups. The location for counseling delivery can be face to face or at a distance with the assistance of technology. The communication medium for counseling can be what is read from text, what is heard from audio, or what is seen and heard in person or from video. The interaction process for counseling can be synchronous or asynchronous. Synchronous interaction occurs with little or no gap in time between the responses of the counselor and the client. Asynchronous interaction occurs with a gap in time between the responses of the counselor and the client.

The selection of a specific form of counseling is based on the needs and preferences of the client within the range of services available. Distance counseling supplements face-to-face counseling by providing increased access to counseling on the basis of necessity or convenience. Barriers, such as being a long distance from counseling services, geographic separation of a couple, or limited physical mobility as a result of having a disability, can make it necessary to provide counseling at a distance. Options, such as scheduling counseling sessions outside of traditional service delivery hours or delivering counseling services at a place of residence or employment, can make it more convenient to provide counseling at a distance.

Table 1 presents a taxonomy of currently available forms of counseling practice. This schema is intended to show the relationships among counseling forms.

TABLE 1 A Taxonomy of Face-to-Face and Technology-Assisted Distance Counseling

Counseling

- Face-to-Face Counseling
- Individual Counseling
- Couple Counseling
- Group Counseling
- Technology-Assisted Distance Counseling
- Telecounseling
- Telephone-Based Individual Counseling
- Telephone-Based Couple Counseling
- Telephone-Based Group Counseling
- Internet Counseling
- E-Mail-Based Individual Counseling
- Chat-Based Individual Counseling
- Chat-Based Couple Counseling
- Chat-Based Group Counseling
- Video-Based Individual Counseling
- Video-Based Couple Counseling
- Video-Based Group Counseling

DEFINITIONS

Counseling is the application of mental health, psychological, or human development principles through cognitive, affective, behavioral, or systemic intervention strategies that address wellness, personal growth, or career development, as well as pathology.

Face-to-face-counseling for individuals, couples, and groups involves synchronous interaction between and among counselors and clients using what is seen and heard in person to communicate.

Technology-assisted distance counseling for individuals, couples, and groups involves the use of the telephone or the computer to enable counselors and clients to communicate at a distance when circumstances make this approach necessary or convenient.

Telecounseling involves synchronous distance interaction among counselors and clients using one-to-one or conferencing features of the telephone to communicate.

Telephone-based individual counseling involves synchronous distance interaction between a counselor and a client using what is heard via audio to communicate.

Telephone-based couple counseling involves synchronous distance interaction among counselors or counselors and a couple using what is heard via audio to communicate.

Telephone-based group counseling involves synchronous distance interaction among counselors and clients using what is heard via audio to communicate.

Internet counseling involves asynchronous and synchronous distance interaction among counselors and clients using e-mail, chat, and videoconferencing features of the Internet to communicate.

E-mail-based individual Internet counseling involves asynchronous distance interaction between counselor and client using what is read via text to communicate.

Chat-based individual Internet counseling involves synchronous distance interaction between counselor and client using what is read via text to communicate.

Chat-based couple Internet counseling involves synchronous distance interaction among a counselor or counselors and a couple using what is read via text to communicate.

Chat-based group Internet counseling involves synchronous distance interaction among counselors and clients using what is read via text to communicate.

Video-based individual Internet counseling involves synchronous distance interaction between counselor and client using what is seen and heard via video to communicate.

Video-based couple Internet counseling involves synchronous distance interaction among a counselor or counselors and a couple using what is seen and heard via video to communicate.

Video-based group Internet counseling involves synchronous distance interaction among counselors and clients using what is seen and heard via video to communicate.

STANDARDS FOR THE ETHICAL PRACTICE OF INTERNET COUNSELING

These standards govern the practice of Internet counseling and are intended for use by counselors, clients, the public, counselor educators, and organizations that examine and deliver Internet counseling. These standards are intended to address practices that are unique to Internet counseling and Internet counselors and do not duplicate principles found in traditional codes of ethics.

These Internet counseling standards of practice are based upon the principles of ethical practice embodied in the NBCC Code of Ethics. Therefore, these standards should be used in conjunction with the most recent version of the NBCC ethical code. Related content in the NBCC Code are indicated in parentheses after each standard.

Recognizing that significant new technology emerges continuously, these standards should be reviewed frequently. It is also recognized that Internet counseling ethics cases should be reviewed in light of delivery systems existing at the moment rather than at the time the standards were adopted.

In addition to following the NBCC® Code of Ethics pertaining to the practice of professional counseling, Internet counselors shall observe the following standards of practice:

INTERNET COUNSELING RELATIONSHIP

1. In situations where it is difficult to verify the identity of the Internet client, steps are taken to address impostor concerns, such as by using code words or numbers. (Refer to B.8)
2. Internet counselors determine if a client is a minor and therefore in need of parental/guardian consent. When parent/guardian consent is required to provide Internet counseling to minors, the identity of the consenting person is verified. (Refer to B.8)
3. As part of the counseling orientation process, the Internet counselor explains to clients the procedures for contacting the Internet counselor when he or she is off-line and, in the case of asynchronous counseling, how often e-mail

messages will be checked by the Internet counselor. (Refer to B.8)

4. As part of the counseling orientation process, the Internet counselor explains to clients the possibility of technology failure and discusses alternative modes of communication, if that failure occurs. (Refer to B.8)

5. As part of the counseling orientation process, the Internet counselor explains to clients how to cope with potential misunderstandings when visual cues do not exist. (Refer to B.8)

6. As a part of the counseling orientation process, the Internet counselor collaborates with the Internet client to identify an appropriately trained professional who can provide local assistance, including crisis intervention, if needed. The Internet counselor and Internet client should also collaborate to determine the local crisis hotline telephone number and the local emergency telephone number. (Refer to B.4)

7. The Internet counselor has an obligation, when appropriate, to make clients aware of free public access points to the Internet within the community for accessing Internet counseling or Web-based assessment, information, and instructional resources. (Refer to B.1)

8. Within the limits of readily available technology, Internet counselors have an obligation to make their Web site a barrier-free environment to clients with disabilities. (Refer to B.1)

9. Internet counselors are aware that some clients may communicate in different languages, live in different time zones, and have unique cultural perspectives. Internet counselors are also aware that local conditions and events may impact the client. (Refer to A.12)

CONFIDENTIALITY IN INTERNET COUNSELING

10. The Internet counselor informs Internet clients of encryption methods being used to help insure the security of client/counselor/supervisor communications. (Refer to B.5)

    Encryption methods should be used whenever possible. If encryption is not made available to clients, clients must be informed of the potential hazards of unsecured communication on the Internet. Hazards may include unauthorized monitoring of transmissions and/or records of Internet counseling sessions.

11. The Internet counselor informs Internet clients if, how, and how long session data are being preserved. (Refer to B.6)

    Session data may include Internet counselor/Internet client e-mail, test results, audio/video session recordings, session notes, and counselor/supervisor communications. The likelihood of electronic sessions being preserved is greater because of the ease and decreased costs involved in recording. Thus, its potential use in supervision, research, and legal proceedings increases.

12. Internet counselors follow appropriate procedures regarding the release of information for sharing Internet client information with other electronic sources. (Refer to B.5)

    Because of the relative ease with which e-mail messages can be forwarded to formal and casual referral sources, Internet counselors must work to insure the confidentiality of the Internet counseling relationship.

LEGAL CONSIDERATIONS, LICENSURE, AND CERTIFICATION

13. Internet counselors review pertinent legal and ethical codes for guidance on the practice of Internet counseling and supervision. (Refer to A.13)

    Local, state, provincial, and national statutes as well as codes of professional membership organizations, professional certifying bodies, and state or provincial licensing boards need to be reviewed. Also, as varying state rules and opinions exist on questions pertaining to whether Internet counseling takes place in the Internet counselor's location or the Internet client's location, it is important to review codes in the counselor's home jurisdiction as well as the client's. Internet counselors also consider carefully local customs regarding age of consent and child abuse reporting, and liability insurance policies need to be reviewed to determine if the practice of Internet counseling is a covered activity.

14. The Internet counselor's Web site provides links to Web sites of all appropriate certification bodies and licensures boards to facilitate consumer protection. (Refer to B.1)

Source: Reprinted with the permission of the Center for Credentialing and Education, an affiliate of the National Board for Certified Counselors, 3 Terrace Way, Suite D, Greensboro, NC 27403-3660.

Ethical Standards for Internet On-Line Counseling

Approved by the ACA Governing Council, October 2005

These guidelines establish appropriate standards for the use of electronic communications over the Internet to provide on-line counseling services and should be used only in conjunction with the latest *ACA Code of Ethics & Standards of Practice*.

CONFIDENTIALITY

a. **Privacy Information.** Professional counselors ensure that clients are provided sufficient information to adequately address and explain the limitations of (i) computer technology in the counseling process in general and (ii) the difficulties of ensuring complete client confidentiality of information transmitted through electronic communications over the Internet through on-line counseling. (See A.12.a., B.1.b., B.1.h.)

1. **SECURED SITES:** To mitigate the risk of potential breaches of confidentiality, professional counselors provide one-on-one on-line counseling only through "secure" Web sites or e-mail communications applications which use appropriate encryption technology designed to protect the transmission of confidential information from access by unauthorized third parties.

2. **NON-SECURED SITES:** To mitigate the risk of potential breaches of confidentiality, professional counselors provide only general information from "non-secure" Web sites or e-mail communications applications.

3. **GENERAL INFORMATION:** Professional counselors may provide general information from either "secure" or "non-secure" Web sites, or through e-mail communications. General information includes non-client-specific, topical information on matters of general interest to the professional counselor's clients as a whole, third-party resource and referral information, addresses and phone numbers, and the like. Additionally, professional counselors using either "secure" or "non-secure" Web sites may provide "hot links" to third-party Web sites such as licensure boards, certification bodies, and other resource information providers. Professional counselors investigate and continually update the content, accuracy and appropriateness for the client of material contained in any "hot links" to third-party Web sites.

4. **LIMITS OF CONFIDENTIALITY:** Professional counselors inform clients of the limitations of confidentiality and identify foreseeable situations in which confidentiality must be breached in light of the law in both the state in which the client is located and the state in which the professional counselor is licensed.

b. **Informational Notices.**

1. **SECURITY OF PROFESSIONAL COUNSELOR'S SITE:** Professional counselors provide a readily visible notice that (i) information transmitted over a Web site or e-mail server may not be secure; (ii) whether or not the professional counselor's site is secure; (iii) whether the information transmitted between the professional counselor and the client during on-line counseling will be encrypted; and (iv) whether the client will need special software to access and transmit confidential information and, if so, whether the professional counselor provides the software as part of the on-line counseling services. The notice should be viewable from all Web site and e-mail locations from which the client may send information. (See B.1.m.)

2. **PROFESSIONAL COUNSELOR IDENTIFICATION:** Professional counselors provide a readily visible notice advising clients of the identities of all professional counselor(s) who will have access to the information transmitted by the client and, in the event that more than one professional counselor has access to the Web site or e-mail system, the manner, if any, in which the client may direct information to a particular professional counselor. Professional counselors inform clients if any or all of the sessions are supervised. Clients are also informed if and how the supervisor preserves session transcripts. Professional counselors provide background information on all professional counselor(s) and supervisor(s) with access to the on-line communications, including education, licensing and certification, and practice area information. (See B.1.g., B.1.i., B.1.j.)

3. **CLIENT IDENTIFICATION:** Professional counselors identify clients, verify identities of clients, and obtain alternative methods of contacting clients in emergency situations.

c. **Client Waiver.** Professional counselors require clients to execute client waiver agreements stating that the client (i) acknowledges the limitations inherent in ensuring client confidentiality of information transmitted through on-line counseling and (ii) agrees to waive the client's privilege of confidentiality with respect to any confidential information transmitted through on-line counseling that may be accessed by any third party without authorization of the client and despite the reasonable efforts of the professional counselor to arrange a secure on-line environment. Professional counselors refer clients to more traditional methods of counseling and do not provide on-line counseling services if the client is unable or unwilling to consent to the client waiver. (See A.12.a., A.12.c., A.12.g.)

d. **Records of Electronic Communications.** Professional counselors maintain appropriate procedures for ensuring the safety and confidentiality of client information acquired through electronic communications, including but not limited to encryption software; proprietary on-site file servers with fire walls; saving on-line or e-mail communications to the hard drive or file server computer systems; creating regular tape or diskette back-up copies; creating hard copies of all electronic communications; and the like. Clients are informed about the length of time for, and method of, preserving session transcripts. Professional counselors warn clients of the possibility or frequency of technology failures and time delays in transmitting and receiving information. (See B.4.a., B.4.b.)

e. **Electronic Transfer of Client Information.** Professional counselors electronically transfer client confidential information to authorized third-party recipients only when (i) both the professional counselor and the authorized recipient have "secure" transfer and acceptance communication capabilities, (ii) the recipient is able to effectively protect the confidentiality of the client confidential information to be transferred, and (iii) the informed written consent of the client, acknowledging the limits of confidentiality, has been obtained. (See B.1.l., B.1.m., B.4.f.)

ESTABLISHING THE ON-LINE COUNSELING RELATIONSHIP

a. **The Appropriateness of On-Line Counseling.** Professional counselors develop an appropriate intake procedure for potential clients to determine whether on-line counseling is appropriate for the needs of the client. Professional counselors warn potential clients that on-line counseling services may not be appropriate in certain situations and, to the extent possible, informs the client of specific limitations, potential risks, and/or potential benefits relevant to the client's anticipated use of on-line counseling services. Professional counselors ensure that clients are intellectually, emotionally, and physically capable of using the on-line counseling services, and of understanding the potential risks and/or limitations of such services. (See A.12.b.)

b. **Counseling Plans.** Professional counselors develop individual on-line counseling plans that are consistent with both the client's individual circumstances and the limitations of on-line counseling. Professional counselors shall specifically take into account the limitations, if any, on the use of any or all of the following in on-line counseling: initial client appraisal, diagnosis, and assessment methods employed by the professional counselor. Professional counselors who determine that on-line counseling is inappropriate for the client should avoid entering into or immediately terminate the on-line counseling

relationship and encourage the client to continue the counseling relationship through an appropriate alternative method of counseling. (See A.11.b., A.11.c., A.12.c.)

c. **Continuing Coverage.** Professional counselors provide clients with a schedule of times during which the on-line counseling services will be available, including reasonable anticipated response times, and provide clients with an alternate means of contacting the professional counselor at other times, including in the event of emergencies. Professional counselors obtain from, and provide clients with, alternative means of communication, such as telephone numbers or pager numbers, for backup purposes in the event the on-line counseling service is unavailable for any reason. Professional counselors provide clients with the name of at least one other professional counselor who will be able to respond to the client in the event the professional counselor is unable to do so for any extended period of time. (See A.11.a.)

d. **Boundaries of Competence.** Professional counselors provide on-line counseling services only in practice areas within their expertise and do not provide on-line counseling services to clients located in states in which professional counselors are not licensed. (See C.2.a., C.2.b.)

e. **Minor or Incompetent Clients.** Professional counselors must verify that clients are above the age of minority, are competent to enter into the counseling relationship with a professional counselor, and are able to give informed consent. In the event clients are minor children, incompetent, or incapable of giving informed consent, professional counselors must obtain the written consent of the legal guardian or other authorized legal representative of the client prior to commencing on-line counseling services to the client (A.2.d).

LEGAL CONSIDERATIONS

Professional counselors confirm that their liability insurance provides coverage for on-line counseling services, and that the provision of such services is not prohibited by or otherwise violating any applicable (i) state or local statutes, rules, regulations, or ordinances; (ii) codes of professional membership organizations and certifying boards; and/or (iii) codes of state licensing boards (A.12.e).

Professional counselors seek appropriate legal and technical assistance in the development and implementation of their on-line counseling services (A.12.f).

Available at ACA's Web site, www.counseling.org.

Source: Reprinted from *Ethical Standards for Internet On-Line Counseling.* American Counseling Association. Reprinted with permission. No further reproduction authorized without written permission from the American Counseling Association.

APPENDIX I

NCDA Guidelines for the Use of the Internet for Provision of Career Information and Planning Services

Approved by the NCDA Board of Directors, October 1997

Developed by members of the NCDA Ethics Committee: Dr. David Caulum, Don Doerr, Dr. Pat Howland, Dr. Spencer Niles, Dr. Ray Palmer, Dr. Richard Pyle (Chair), Dr. David Reile, Dr. James Sampson, and Dr. Don Schutt

INTRODUCTION

Based on readily available capabilities at the time of this writing, the Internet could be used in four ways for the purpose of providing career counseling and/or career planning services to clients. These are:

1. To deliver information about occupations, including their descriptions, employment outlook, skills requirements, estimated salary, etc. through text, still images, graphics, and/or video. In this event, the standards for information development and presentation are the same as those for print materials and audiovisual materials as stated in NCDA's documents on these matters.
2. To provide online searches of occupational databases for the purpose of identifying feasible occupational alternatives. In this event, the standards developed by NCDA and the Association of Computer-Based Systems for Career Information (ACSCI) apply.
3. To deliver interactive career counseling and career planning services. This use assumes that clients, either as individuals or as part of a group, have intentionally placed themselves in direct communication with a professional career counselor. Standards for use of the Internet for these purposes are addressed in this document.
4. To provide searches through large databases of job openings for the purpose of identifying those that the user may pursue. Guidelines for this application are included in this document.

GUIDELINES FOR USE OF THE INTERNET FOR DELIVERY OF CAREER COUNSELING AND CAREER PLANNING SERVICES

"Career planning services" are differentiated from "career counseling" services. Career planning services include an active provision of information designed to help a client with a specific need, such as review of a resumé; assistance in networking strategies; identification of occupations based on interests, skills, or prior work experience; support in the job-seeking process; and assessment by means of online inventories of interest, abilities, and/or work-related values. Although "Career Counseling" may include the provision of the above services, the use of the term implies a deeper level of involvement with the client, based on the establishment of a professional counseling relationship and the potential for dealing with career development concerns well beyond those included in career planning.

Multiple means of online provision of career planning or career counseling services currently exist, the most common of which are e-mail, newsgroups, bulletin boards, chat rooms, and Web sites offering a wide variety of services. Telephone or audiovisual linkages supported by the Internet exist in their infancy, and will likely grow in potential as the technology improves and the costs decline.

1. **Qualifications of Developer or Provider.** Web sites and other services designed to assist clients with career planning should be developed with content input from professional career counselors. The service should clearly state the qualifications and credentials of the developers not only in the content area of professional career counseling, but also in the development of interactive online services.
2. **Access and Understanding of Environment.** The counselor has an obligation to be aware of free public access points to the Internet within the member's community, so that a lack of financial resources does not create a significant barrier to clients accessing counseling services or information, assessment or instructional resources over the internet.

    The counselor has an obligation to be as aware as possible of local conditions, cultures, and events that may impact the client.
3. **Content of Career Counseling and Planning Services on the Internet.** The content of a Web site or other service offering career information or planning services should be reviewed for the appropriateness of content offered in this medium. Some kinds of content have been extensively tested for online delivery due to the long existence of computer-based career information and guidance systems. This includes searching of databases by relevant search variables; display of occupational information; development of a resumé;

assessment of interests, abilities, and work-related values and linkage of these to occupational titles; instruction about occupational classification systems; relationship of school majors to occupational choices; and the completion of forms such as a financial needs assessment questionnaire or a job application.

When a Web site offers a service which has not previously been extensively tested (such as computer-based career guidance and information systems), this service should be carefully scrutinized to determine whether it lends itself to the Internet. The Web site should clearly state the kinds of client concerns that the counselor judges to be inappropriate for counseling over the Internet, or beyond the skills of the counselor.

4. **Appropriateness of Client for Receipt of Services via the Internet.** The counselor has an ethical and professional responsibility to assure that the client who is requesting service can profit from it in this mode. Appropriate screening includes the following:

   a. A clear statement by clients of their career planning or career counseling needs.

   b. An analysis by the counselor of whether meeting those needs via Internet exchange is appropriate and of whether this particular client can benefit from counseling services provided in this mode. A judgment about the latter should be made by means of a telephone or videophone teleconference designed to specify the client's expectations, how the client has sought to meet these through other modes, and whether or not the client appears to be able to process information through an Internet medium.

5. **Appropriate Support to the Client.** The counselor who is providing services to a client via the Internet has ethical responsibility for the following:

   a. Periodic monitoring of the client's progress via telephone or videophone teleconference.

   b. Identification by the counselor of a qualified career counselor in the client's geographic area should referral become necessary. If this is not possible, the web counselor using traditional referral sources to identify an appropriate practitioner, should assist the client in the selection of a counselor.

   c. Appropriate discussion with the client about referral to face-to-face service should the counselor determine that little or no progress is being made toward the client's goals.

6. **Clarity of Contract with the Client.** The counselor should define several items in writing to the client in a document that can be downloaded from the Internet or faxed to the client. This document should include at least the following items:

   a. The counselor's credentials in the field.

   b. The agreed-upon goals of the career counseling or career planning Internet interchange.

   c. The agreed-upon cost of the services and how this will be billed.

   d. Where and how clients can report any counselor behavior which they consider to be unethical.

   e. Statement about the degree of security of the Internet and confidentiality of data transmitted on the Internet and about any special conditions related to the client's

personal information (such as potential transmission of client records to a supervisor for quality-control purposes, or the collection of data for research purposes).

   f. A statement of the nature of client information electronically stored by the counselor, including the length of time that data will be maintained before being destroyed.

   g. A statement about the need for privacy when the client is communicating with the counselor, e.g., that client communication with the counselor is not limited by having others observe or hear interactions between the counselor and client.

   h. If the service includes career, educational, or employment information, the counselor is responsible for making the client aware of the typical circumstances where individuals need counseling support in order to effectively use the information.

7. **Inclusion of Linkages to Other Web Sites.** If a career information or counseling Web site includes links to other Web sites, the professional who creates this linkage is responsible for assuring that the services to which his or hers are linked also meet these guidelines.

8. **Use of Assessment.** If the career planning or career counseling service is to include online inventories or tests and their interpretation, the following conditions should apply:

   a. The assessments must have been tested in computer delivery mode to assure that their psychometric properties are the same in this mode of delivery as in print form; or the client must be informed that they have not yet been tested in this same mode of delivery.

   b. The counselor must abide by the same ethical guidelines as if he or she were administering and interpreting these same inventories or tests in face-to-face mode and/or in print form.

   c. Every effort must be exerted to protect the confidentiality of the user's results.

   d. If there is any evidence that the client does not understand the results, as evidenced by e-mail or telephone interchanges, the counselor must refer the client to a qualified career counselor in his or her geographic area.

   e. The assessments must have been validated for self-help use if no counseling support is provided, or that appropriate counseling intervention is provided before and after completion of the assessment resource if the resource has not been validated for self-help use.

PROFESSIONAL AND ETHICAL GUIDELINES RELATED TO THE USE OF THE INTERNET FOR JOB POSTING AND SEARCHING

1. The posting must represent a valid job opening for which those searching on the Internet have an opportunity to apply.

2. Job postings must be removed from the Internet database within 48 hours of the time that the announced position is filled.

3. Names, addresses, resumés, and other information that may be gained about individuals should not be used for any purposes other than provision of further information about job openings.

UNACCEPTABLE COUNSELOR BEHAVIORS ON THE INTERNET

1. Use of a false e-mail identity when interacting with clients and/or other professionals. When acting in a professional capacity on the Internet, a counselor has a duty to identify him/herself honestly.
2. Accepting a client who will not identify him/herself and be willing to arrange for phone conversation as well as online interchange.
3. "Sharking" or monitoring chat rooms and bulletin board services, and offering career planning and related services when no request has been made for services. This includes sending out mass unsolicited e-mails. Counselors may advertise their services but must do so observing proper "netiquette" and standards of professional conduct.

NEED FOR RESEARCH AND REVIEW

Since the use of the Internet is new for the delivery of career planning and counseling services, it is mandatory that the career counseling profession gain experience with this medium and evaluate its effectiveness through targeted research. The capabilities of Internet delivery of services will expand rapidly as the use of sound and video becomes more feasible. These early guidelines will need constant monitoring and revision as research data become available and additional capabilities become cost feasible.

APA Guidelines for Providers of Psychological Services to Ethnic, Linguistic, and Culturally Diverse Populations

INTRODUCTION

There is increasing motivation among psychologists to understand culture and ethnicity factors in order to provide appropriate psychological services. This increased motivation for improving quality of psychological services to ethnic and culturally diverse populations is attributable, in part, to the growing political and social presence of diverse cultural groups, both within APA and in the larger society. New sets of values, beliefs, and cultural expectations have been introduced into educational, political, business, and health care systems by the physical presence of these groups. The issues of language and culture do impact on the provision of appropriate psychological services.

Psychological service providers need a sociocultural framework to consider diversity of values, interactional styles, and cultural expectations in a systematic fashion. They need knowledge and skills for multicultural assessment and intervention, including abilities to:

1. recognize cultural diversity;
2. understand the role that culture and ethnicity/race play in the sociopsychological and economic development of ethnic and culturally diverse populations;
3. understand that socioeconomic and political factors significantly impact the psychological, political and economic development of ethnic and culturally diverse groups;
4. help clients to understand/maintain/resolve their own sociocultural identification; and understand the interaction of culture, gender, and sexual orientation on behavior and needs.

Likewise, there is a need to develop a conceptual framework that would enable psychologists to organize, access, and accurately assess the value and utility of existing and future research involving ethnic and culturally diverse populations.

Research has addressed issues regarding responsiveness of psychological services to the needs of ethnic minority populations. The focus of mental health research issues has included:

1. the impact of ethnic/racial similarity in the counseling process (Acosta & Sheehan, 1976; Atkinson, 1983; Parham & Helms, 1981);
2. minority utilization of mental health services (Cheung & Snowden, 1990; Everett, Proctor, & Cartmell, 1983; Rosado, 1986; Snowden & Cheung, 1990);
3. relative effectiveness of directed versus nondirected styles of therapy (Acosta, Yamamoto, & Evans, 1982; Dauphinais, Dauphinais, & Rowe, 1981; Lorion, 1974);

4. the role of cultural values in treatment (Juarez, 1985; Padilla & Ruiz, 1973; Padilla, Ruiz, & Alvarez, 1975; Sue & Sue, 1987);
5. appropriate counseling and therapy models (Comas-Diaz & Griffith, 1988; McGoldrick, Pearce, & Giordino, 1982; Nishio & Blimes, 1987);
6. competency in skills for working with specific ethnic populations (Malgady, Rogler, & Constantino, 1987; Root, 1985; Zuniga, 1988).

The APA's Board of Ethnic Minority Affairs (BEMA) established a Task Force on the Delivery of Services to Ethnic Minority Populations in 1988 in response to the increased awareness about psychological service needs associated with ethnic and cultural diversity. The populations of concern include, but are not limited to the following groups: American Indians/Alaska Natives, Asian Americans, and Hispanics/Latinos. For example, the populations also include recently arrived refugee and immigrant groups and established U.S. subcultures such as Amish, Hasidic Jewish, and rural Appalachian people.

The Task Force established as its first priority development of the Guidelines for Providers of Psychological Services to Ethnic, Linguistic, and Culturally Diverse Populations. The guidelines that follow are intended to enlighten all areas of service delivery, not simply clinical or counseling endeavors. The clients referred to may be clients, organizations, government and/or community agencies.

GUIDELINES

Preamble: The Guidelines represent general principles that are intended to be aspirational in nature and are designed to provide suggestions to psychologists in working with ethnic, linguistic, and culturally diverse populations.

1. Psychologists educate their clients to the processes of psychological intervention, such as goals and expectations; the scope and, where appropriate, legal limits of confidentiality; and the psychologists' orientations.
   a. Whenever possible, psychologists provide information in writing along with oral explanations.
   b. Whenever possible, the written information is provided in the language understandable to the client.
2. Psychologists are cognizant of relevant research and practice issues as related to the population being served.

a. Psychologists acknowledge that ethnicity and culture impacts on behavior and take those factors into account when working with various ethnic/racial groups.

b. Psychologists seek out educational and training experiences to enhance their understanding to address the needs of these populations more appropriately and effectively. These experiences include cultural, social, psychological, political, economic, and historical material specific to the particular ethnic group being served.

c. Psychologists recognize the limits of their competencies and expertise. Psychologists who do not possess knowledge and training about an ethnic group seek consultation with, and/or make referrals to, appropriate experts as necessary.

d. Psychologists consider the validity of a given instrument or procedure and interpret resulting data, keeping in mind the cultural and linguistic characteristics of the person being assessed. Psychologists are aware of the test's reference population and possible limitations of such instruments with other populations.

3. Psychologists recognize ethnicity and culture as significant parameters in understanding psychological processes.

a. Psychologists, regardless of ethnic/racial background, are aware of how their own cultural background/ experiences, attitudes, values, and biases influence psychological processes. They make efforts to correct any prejudices and biases.

Illustrative Statement: Psychologists might routinely ask themeslves, 'Is it appropriate for me to view this client or organization any differently than I would if they were from my own ethnic or cultural group?'

b. Psychologists' practice incorporates an understanding of the client's ethnic and cultural background. This includes the client's familiarity and comfort with the majority culture as well as ways in which the client's culture may add to or improve various aspects of the majority culture and/or of society at large.

Illustrative Statement: The kinds of mainstream social activities in which families participate may offer information about the level and quality of acculturation to American society. It is important to distinguish acculturation from length of stay in the United States, and not to assume that these issues are relevant only for new immigrants and refugees.

c. Psychologists help clients increase their awareness of their own cultural values and norms, and they facilitate discovery of ways clients can apply this awareness to their own lives and to society at large.

Illustrative Statement: Psychologists may be able to help parents distinguish between generational conflict and culture gaps when problems arise between them and their children. In the process, psychologists could help both parents and children to appreciate their own distinguishing cultural values.

d. Psychologists seek to help a client determine whether a 'problem' stems from racism or bias in others so that the client does not inappropriately personalize problems.

Illustrative Statement: The concept of 'healthy paranoia,' whereby ethnic minorities may develop defensive behaviors in response to discrimination, illustrates this principle.

e. Psychologists consider not only differential diagnostic issues but also cultural beliefs and values of the clients and his/her community in providing intervention.

Illustrative Statement: There is a disorder among the traditional Navajo called 'Moth Madness.' Symptoms include seizure-like behaviors. The disorder is believed by the Navajo to be the supernatural result of incestuous thoughts or behaviors. Both differential diagnosis and intervention should take into consideration the traditional values of Moth Madness.

4. Psychologists respect the roles of family members and community structures, hierarchies, values, and beliefs within the client's culture.

a. Psychologists identify resources in the family and the larger community.

b. Clarification of the role of the psychologist and the expectations of the client precede intervention. Psychologists seek to ensure that both the psychologist and client have a clear understanding of what services and roles are reasonable.

Illustrative Statement: It is not uncommon for an entire American Indian family to come into the clinic to provide support to the person in distress. Many of the healing practices found in American Indian communities are centered in the family and the whole community.

5. Psychologists respect clients' religious and/or spiritual beliefs and values, including attributions and taboos, since they affect world view, psychosocial functioning, and expressions of distress.

a. Part of working in minority communities is to become familiar with indigenous beliefs and practices and to respect them.

Illustrative Statement: Traditional healers (e.g., shamans, curanderos, espiritistas) have an important place in minority communities.

b. Effective psychological intervention may be aided by consultation with and/or inclusion of religious/spiritual leaders/practitioners relevant to the client's cultural and belief systems.

6. Psychologists interact in the language requested by the client and, if this is not feasible, make an appropriate referral.

a. Problems may arise when the linguistic skills of the psychologist do not match the language of the client. In such a case, psychologists refer the client to a mental health professional who is competent to interact in the language of the client. If this is not possible, psychologists offer the client a translator with cultural knowledge and an appropriate professional background. When no translator is available, then a trained paraprofessional from the client's culture is used as a translator/culture broker.

b. If translation is necessary, psychologists do not retain the services of translators/paraprofessionals that may have a dual role with the client to avoid jeopardizing the validity of evaluation or the effectiveness of intervention.

c. Psychologists interpret and relate test data in terms understandable and relevant to the needs of those assessed.

7. Psychologists consider the impact of adverse social, environmental, and political factors in assessing problems and designing interventions.

a. Types of intervention strategies to be used match to the client's level of need (e.g., Maslow's hierarchy of needs). **Illustrative Statement:** Low income may be associated with such stressors as malnutrition, substandard housing, and poor medical care; and rural residency may mean inaccessibility of services. Clients may resist treatment at government agencies because of previous experience (e.g., refugees' status may be associated with violent treatments by government officials and agencies).

b. Psychologists work within the cultural setting to improve the welfare of all persons concerned, if there is a conflict between cultural values and human rights.

8. Psychologists attend to as well as work to eliminate biases, prejudices, and discriminatory practices.

a. Psychologists acknowledge relevant discriminatory practices at the social and community level that may be affecting the psychological welfare of the population being served.
Illustrated Statement: Depression may be associated with frustrated attempts to climb the corporate ladder in an organization that is dominated by a top echelon of White males.

b. Psychologists are cognizant of sociopolitical contexts in conducting evaluations and providing interventions; they develop sensitivity to issues of oppression, sexism, elitism, and racism.
Illustrative Statement: An upsurge in the public expression of rancor or even violence between two ethnic or cultural groups may increase anxiety baselines in any member of these groups. This baseline of anxiety would interact with prevailing symptomatology. At the organizational level, the community conflict may interfere with open communication among staff.

9. Psychologists working with culturally diverse populations should document culturally and sociopolitically relevant factors in the records.

a. number of generations in the country
b. number of years in the country
c. fluency in English
d. extent of family support (or disintegration of family)
e. community resources
f. level of education
g. change in social status as a result of coming to this country (for immigrant or refugee)
h. intimate relationship with people of different backgrounds
i. level of stress related to acculturation

REFERENCES

Acosta, F. X., & Sheehan, J. G. (1976). Preference towards Mexican American and Anglo American psychotherapists. *Journal of Consulting and Clinical Psychology,* 44(2), 272–279.

Acosta, F., Yamamoto, J., & Evans, L (1982). *Effective psychotherapy for low income and minority patients.* New York: Plenum Press.

Atkinson, D. R. (1983). Ethnic similarity in counseling psychology: A review of research. *The Counseling Psychologists,* 11, 79–92.

Cheung, F. K., & Snowden, L. R. (1990). Community mental health and ethnic minority populations. *Community Mental Health Journal,* 26, 277–291.

Comas-Diaz, L., & Griffith, E. H. (1988). *Clinical guidelines in cross-cultural mental health.* John Wiley.

Dauphinais, P., Dauphinais, L., & Rowe, W. (1981). Effects of race and communication style on Indian perceptions of counselor effectiveness. *Counselor Education and Supervision,* 20, 37–46.

Everett, F., Proctor, N., & Cartmell, B. (1983). Providing psychological services to American Indian children and families. *Professional Psychology: Research and Practice,* 14(5), 588–603.

Juarez, R. (1985). Core issues in psychotherapy with the Hispanic child. *Psychotherapy,* 22(25), 441–448.

Lorion, R. P. (1974). Patient and therapist variables in the treatment of low income patients. *Psychological Bulletin,* 81, 344–354.

Malgady, R. G., Rogler, L. H., & Constantino, G. (1987). Ethnocultural and linguistic bias in mental health evaluation of Hispanics. *American Psychologist,* 42(3), 228–234.

McGoldrick, M., Pearce, J. K., & Giordano, J. (1982). *Ethnicity and family therapy.* New York: Guilford Press.

Nishio, K., & Bilmes, M. (1987). Psychotherapy with Southeast Asian American clients. *Professional Psychology: Research and Practice,* 18(4), 342–346.

Padilla, A. M., & Ruiz, R. A. (1973). *Latino mental health: A review of literature* (DHEW publication No. HSM 73–9143). Washington, DC: U.S. Government Printing Office.

Padilla, A. M., & Ruiz, R. A. & Alvarez, R. (1975). Community mental health for the Spanish-speaking/surnamed population. *American Psychologist,* 30, 892–905.

Parham, T. A., & Helms, J. E. (1981). The influence of Black students' racial identity attitudes on preferences for counselor's race. *Journal of Counseling Psychology,* 28, 250–257.

Root, Maria P. P. (1985). Guidelines for facilitating therapy with Asian American clients. *Psychotherapy,* 22(2s), 349–356.

Rosado, J. W. (1986). Toward an interfacing of Hispanic cultural variables with school psychology service delivery systems. *Professional Psychology: Research and Practice,* 17(3), 191–199.

Snowden, L. R., & Cheung, F. K. (1990). Use of inpatient mental health services by members of ethnic minority groups. *American Psychologists,* 45, 347–355.

Sue, D., & Sue, S. (1987). Cultural factors in the clinical assessment of Asian American. *Journal of Consulting and Clinical Psychology,* 55(4), 479–487.

Zuniga, M. E. (1988). Assessment issues with Chicanas: practical implications. *Psychotherapy,* 25(2), 288–293.

Task Force on the Delivery of Services to Ethnic Minority Populations:

Charles Joseph Pine, Ph.D., Chair
Jose Cervantes, Ph.D.
Freda Cheung, Ph.D.
Christine C. Iijima Hall, Ph.D.
Jean Holroyd, Ph.D.
Robin LaDue, Ph.D.
LaVome Robinson, Ph.D.
Maria P. P. Root, Ph.D.

These guidelines were approved by the Council of representatives in August of 1990 during the 98th Annual Convention in Boston, Massachusetts.

Office of Ethnic Minority Affairs, Washington, D.C.
L. Philip Guzman, Ph.D., Director
Alberto Figuero, Project Coordinator
Debra J. Parks-Perry, Administrative Assistant
Alan P. Alvarez, Student Intern, Syracuse University

The Public Interest Directorate works to advance psychology as a means of promoting human welfare. Programs within the Public Interest Directorate address issues related to aging; AIDS; children, youth, and families; disability; ethnic minorities; lesbians, gay men, and bisexuals; violence; women; urbana initiatives; public interest policy, and other special projects and activities.

Public Interest Directorate
American Psychological Association
750 First Street, NE
Washington, DC 20002
(202) 336-6050
E-mail: publicinterest@apa.org

APPENDIX K

Operationalization of the Multicultural Counseling Competencies

AMCD Professional Standards and Certification Committee

Dr. Patricia Arredondo, Chair
Empowerment Workshops, Inc., Boston

Rebecca Toporek, Sherlon Brown, Janet Jones, Don C. Locke, Joe Sanchez and Holly Stadler

Background

For the past 20 years, the Association for Multicultural Counseling and Development (AMCD) has provided leadership for the American counseling profession, in major sociocultural and sociopolitical domains. Through our vision of the centrality of culture and multiculturalism to the counseling profession, we have created new directions and paradigms for change. One of our major contributions has been the development of the Multicultural Counseling Competencies (Sue, Arredondo & McDavis, 1992).

For the first time in the history of the profession, competencies to guide interpersonal counseling interactions with attention to culture, ethnicity, and race have been articulated. Through the leadership of Dr. Thomas Parham, president of the Association for Multicultural Counseling and Development 1991–92, the Professional Standards and Certification Committee was charged to develop multicultural competencies. On the direction of President Marlene Rutherford-Rhodes (1994–1995), the Committee was asked to provide additional clarification to the revised competencies and to specify enabling criteria as well. This objective has been addressed through this document.

Multicultural Counseling refers to preparation and practices that integrate multicultural and culture-specific awareness, knowledge and skills into counseling interactions. The term *multicultural*, in the context of counseling preparation and application, refers to five major cultural groups in the United States and its territories: African/Black, Asian, Caucasian/European, Hispanic/Latino and Native American or indigenous groups who have historically resided in the Continental USA and its territories. It can be stated that the U.S. is a pluralistic or multicultural society and that all individuals are ethnic, racial, and cultural beings.

All persons can point to one or more of these macro-level, cultural groups as sources of their cultural heritage. For the aforementioned groups named, race and ethnicity are further identifiers although oftentimes the terms are interchanged with culture, introducing confusion. What is noteworthy about cultural groupings is that they point to historical and geographic origins as well as to racial heritage.

- African Americans and Haitians might similarly claim African heritage with etiology tracing back to the African continent. Some individuals might prefer to self-identify in racial terms—black—or based on their country of origin. Thus the term ethnicity or nationality comes into play, and self-descriptors could include Haitian, Nigerian, Afro-American, and so forth.
- Individuals of Asian cultural background—Chinese, Japanese, Korean, Vietnamese—can point to roots on the continent of Asia but all speak different languages and dialects. East Asians are another group coming primarily from India, Pakistan and Iran and other countries not part of the Orient geographically. The term Oriental is considered pejorative and no longer used in multicultural counseling literature.
- Persons racially listed as "White" or Caucasian, are usually of European heritage. In the United States, men of European background have been and continue to hold economic, political and educational power. This is an important factor in the development of the multicultural counseling competencies and the domain of multicultural counseling. As the normative cultural group in the United States, Euro-Americans have been the yardstick by which individuals of the other cultural groups and women have been measured.
- Hispanics/Latinos are similar to and a bit different from the other cultural groups. Generally speaking, they can point to both the North and South American continents for their roots. Central America, although not a continent, is the homeland of many who are classified as Hispanics. Racially, Hispanics are biracial by birth, representing the historical interrelationships of native people/Indians with Europeans and Africans. One slight difference might be noted for individuals from Spain who see themselves as White. The common denominator among Hispanics, regardless of nationality is the Spanish language.

• The Native American or indigenous cultural groups refer to the peoples who populated the United States and its territories prior to the arrival of European settlers. Native Americans further self-define by tribe or nation affiliation. Today, many individuals who might identify primarily as a member of one of the other four cultural groups also claim Native American heritage. In fact, there is a growing body of literature about biracial cultural identity because many individuals claim multiracial or biracial ancestry.

In the original statement of the Multicultural Counseling Competencies (Sue, Arredondo and McDavis, 1992), the point was made that the typical counseling interactions involve a white (Euro-American) counselor with persons of color or others from a similar macrocultural background. This focus will remain with this revised version of the competencies and the explanatory statements. The majority of the examples will be for situations where the counselor is of Euro-American heritage and the client, a *person of color*, or a visible racial, ethnic minority group member (VERG, Helms, 1990), in other words, of one of the other four major cultural groups. While this is the more common dyad, it is not the one referred to in counselor training and supervision texts.

On review of the Multicultural Counseling Competencies, it is noteworthy that the necessary cultural awareness, knowledge and skills recommended for cross cultural, cross racial transactions readily apply when counseling with individuals where there is more "perceived" similarity. The commonly referenced concept comes to mind: *We are all unique; we all share in the diversity of humankind making us more alike; and in this shared identity, we will also find differences.*

In this revision of the Multicultural Counseling Competencies, a distinction is also made between the terms *multicultural* and *diversity*. *Multiculturalism* puts the focus on ethnicity, race and culture. *Diversity* refers to other individual, people differences including age, gender, sexual orientation, religion, physical ability or disability and other characteristics by which someone may prefer to self-define. The term *diversity* emerged in the mid to late '80s in business environments as leaders became aware of *Workforce 2000* (Johnston and Packer, 1987), a text with projections about the people makeup of the future workforce. The authors talked about cultural and demographic diversity and this in turn became shortened to diversity. The problem with the term diversity is that it has been overused, confused with everything from Affirmative Action to political correctness. Both terms, *multiculturalism* and *diversity* have been widely politicized in ways that have been divisive rather than as positive assets of the U.S. population.

Our approach to discussing human diversity will be through the use of the *Personal Dimensions of Identity Model* (Arredondo and Glauner, 1992). We believe this model has more flexibility to examine the intersection of multicultural group identity and other dimensions of the human diversity that make an individual unique.

In undertaking this process of revising and operationalizing the *Competencies*, it became apparent that the focus throughout the document is on interpersonal or clinical counseling. In effect, these competencies are generic or baseline competencies essential to all counseling transactions. Therefore, awareness, knowledge and skills from multicultural perspectives, as defined and described in the *Competencies*, must be part of all counselor preparation and practice. For areas of assessment, evaluation, research, career guidance or other counseling applications, additional competencies need to be developed with a multicultural focus.

Preparation of the Existing Document

The preparation of this document involved a number of steps, with work commencing in September 1994. One of the key reference tools in the process is the Dimensions of Personal Identity Model (Arredondo and Glauner, 1992) (see Figure 1). It serves as a descriptor for examining individual differences and shared identity based on the conceptualization of A, B, and C Dimensions of Personal Identity. This model communicates several premises: a) that we are all multicultural individuals; b) that we all possess a personal, political and historical culture; c) that we are affected by sociocultural, political, environmental and historical events; and that d) multiculturalism also intersects with multiple factors of individual diversity. An explanation of the model follows.

Dimensions of Personal Identity

To look at people as individuals can be challenging. Everyday we give and receive feedback about different aspects about ourselves. Some of these aspects are used to categorize people with labels or terms. Often this categorization or labeling focuses on a visible aspect of a person as though this were the only way to identify the person. How might one feel to be told, "Oh, you're a man. What do you understand about sexual harassment?" or "We are so glad you are now working here. We need the viewpoint of a Latina" or "Why should you care about affirmative action, you're not black." Few of us escape the tendency to buy into the labels of identity, limiting though they may be.

The Dimensions of Personal Identity Model can be utilized as a paradigm to see people more completely as well as an educational tool. It provides a reference point for recognizing the complexity of all persons. The model highlights our different identity-based affiliations, memberships and sub-cultures and, therefore, complements the discussion of multiculturalism.

A Dimension

The A Dimension is a listing of characteristics that serve as a profile of all people. The majority of the dimensions we are born with or into, making most "fixed" and less changeable. For example, our age, gender, culture, ethnicity, race and language are pre-determined. We have no control over these when we are born and there is very little we can do to change most of these dimensions. Some research suggests that sexual orientation is biologically based while other data promote a sociocultural explanation. In the model, sexual orientation appears as an A Dimension characteristic. For some individuals, it has been possible to transcend economic roots. Social class status, however, may persist for generations based on one's culture or society. For example, in India this may appear through the caste system, whereby individuals are born into a caste, complete with its privileges and limitations. In the U.S., social class may play out differently based on historical and familial lineage. One artifact of social class status is the social register, which accords a listing for some at the time of birth. For better or worse, attributions and judgements are made about all of us based on our social status. At times, this is less visible or known. However, appearances are often used to make assessments of individuals' "value". How someone dresses, their "attractiveness" in terms of height, weight, and other physical criteria also interact with A Dimensions. Would a counselor respond similarly to an overweight, White woman as he/she would to a professional, Black woman? How might his/her previous experiences, or lack thereof, with these type of women affect his/her assumptions, comfort and behavior in a counseling encounter?

Note that a number of the A Dimensions also hold "protected class" status based on government classification/Equal Employment Opportunity (EEO) and Title VII of the Civil Rights Act of 1964. The other noteworthy feature of the A Dimension list is that these are characteristics that most readily engender stereotypes, assumptions, and judgments, both positively and negatively. For example, an African American female may be assumed (simply because of her race and gender) to be strong and direct in sharing her thoughts and feelings. Although some people in the general society may view strength and direct behavior as desirable personal characteristics; others may view these characteristics as intimidating and overpowering. An African American woman shared an experience that led to misassumptions based on a lack of cultural awareness:

"I came into work one day feeling pretty tired from staying up all night with my sick three-year-old. I guess you can say I was not very communicative. No one asked how I was or if something was wrong. I didn't think anything of it at the time but later I learned why I was left alone. My coworkers thought my behavior was a statement of my racial identity. They assumed that this was black behavior. I was floored. Of course, when I asked them what made my behavior racial, they could not explain."

Misattributions can readily occur even among people who work together due to a lack of cultural awareness and knowledge and interracial discomfort. In counseling environments, professional counselors, different by ethnicity and race, and often the only person of color, are more often scrutinized because of one or more A Dimensions. Individuals report that they feel the pressure to perform at higher levels than their white counterparts because of their visible difference.

Another example from the A Dimension is that a person speaking English with an accent might be assumed to be less intelligent, more difficult to deal with, or viewed in other negative ways. Often times, immigrant adults experience the impatience and even ridicule of monolingual English speakers when they seek services at a human service agency. Individuals from Jamaica speak English but it might be heard as new and not discernible to a front desk attendant. Chinese language speakers have a different tone when speaking, often to the impatience of medical personnel. One can only wonder how the verbal and non-verbal behavior of the professional staff, from whom clients expect to receive help, will influence an individual's discontinuation of treatment. Literature indicates the extraordinary incidence of dropout among clients of color after an initial visit.

Continuing with the theme of accents, there also are accents typically perceived more positively by Americans. These are British and Australian accents and in turn these individuals may be perceived as more highly desirable and valuable. Lack of awareness, knowledge, experience and respect for cultures that are not of European heritage easily introduces interpersonal barriers to counseling transactions.

Advocates of the Americans with Disabilities Act of 1990 remind the public that everyone is "one accident away from being disabled." Because the effects of an injury are usually irreversible, this is also considered an A Dimension. Consider the perception of a physically challenged woman of Puerto Rican heritage who uses a wheel chair. Is she written-off as a welfare case or assumed to have assets such as bilingual and bicultural experiences?

If placed on a continuum, all of the A Dimensions can bring positive and negative reactions. Because they tend to be more visible, they invite feedback, both wanted and unwanted, from others, thus contributing to self-concept and self-esteem. This lengthy discussion has been made because it is the A Dimensions that invite and challenge counselors to operate from a framework of multiculturalism and cultural competence. Because each person holds a cultural identity from one or more of the five groups cited, and because individuals embody all of the A Dimensions, to be culturally effective, counselors need to see individuals holistically, not in terms of color, ethnicity, culture or accent alone. We are complete packages, as will be described with the B and C Dimensions.

C Dimension

The C Dimension is discussed most because it also encompasses universal phenomena. This Dimension indicates first of all, that all individuals must be seen in a context; we do not exist in a vacuum. The C Dimension grounds us in historical, political, sociocultural and economic contexts indicating that events of a sociopolitical, global and environmental form have a way of impacting one's personal culture and life experiences. The time one is born is an historical moment that will never happen again. In presentations, participants are encouraged to think about the following: 1) *How was your family life at the time of your birth? What was taking place in the local community or in your home country? What was going on in the world?* Reflecting on the questions and the data that emerge provides individuals with a landscape of their personal history.

Individuals who were born during the pre- or post-World War II era have different recollections from their families. Many talk about their fathers being away during their childhood and the relief felt when they returned. African-Americans also share recollections of their parents or grandparents serving in all Black units in the military. Many Americans are unaware that Native Americans, because of their linguistic abilities, were involved in decoding communication among enemy camps. Because U.S. history books are written from a Euro-American, monocultural perspective, the experiences of individuals and families of color are often unreported or minimized. One example is the mode of entry historically experienced in territories today recognized as the United States. Blacks were brought as slaves to the North and South American continents. Native Americans and Mexicans populated the continental territory but were subsumed under American jurisdiction as a result of treaties. In other words, they became conquered people. The island of Puerto Rico was colonized by the Spaniards and today is an American commonwealth. The Japanese and Chinese were brought as laborers to the Northwest to build the new frontier. For millions of people, the U.S. did not represent the land of freedom.

This lack of knowledge can place a counselor at a disadvantage because all s/he can reference is his/her personal experience. Revisionist versions of American history, as they are called, are providing missing information that again highlight some of the experiences of Americans marginalized based on cultural, ethnic and racial differences.

The time at which one was born also indicates the significant political and environmental incidents that may also affect personal identity. Women and persons of color often point to the importance of the Civil Rights Act of 1964 and its consequences for employment, education, and housing. Before the legislation, men and women of color had limited access to the same institutions, job opportunities and housing as their White counterparts. For counselors, knowledge about historical and political realities faced by persons of color should be known when providing career counseling or some other interventions. The work experiences of immigrants must also be inquired about more carefully. Often, accents of limited-English ability may lead to surprise when a counselor learns that Mr. Wu had actually been an accountant in Taiwan or that Senora Garcia had been a school teacher.

Some women, particularly Caucasian, also remark about the women's era of the 70's. The historical, cultural, and sociopolitical contexts into which women are born, however, influence how women of diverse ethnocultural heritages behave, think, and feel. For example, African American women have historically worked outside the home and their history, culture, and sociopolitical realities have influenced their perceptions about working. Often this perception is one of "I will/must work." Because the role of gender is not highlighted in the multicultural texts and literature, it is underscored here. Women, particularly women of color have been portrayed in roles of servitude and secondary status to men. This historical, political and sociocultural reality has marginalized women and that continues to evidence in many contexts, including the counseling profession. As examples, in spite of increases in the number of women who earn doctorates, concerns have been raised about the feminization of the profession and the consequences on earning power. Another example can be pointed to in the field of multicultural counseling. There are very few women who have authored texts or books with a multicultural focus.

In more recent presentations, the Gulf War has been cited as an historical and political event that impacted and continues to impact individuals and their families. At the time it led to many anti-Arab public sentiments, lumping all Middle Eastern peoples into a category labeled *terrorists*. This is also a reminder of the internment of American citizens of Japanese heritage during World War II. Although many of these individuals were contributors to the American society, they were deemed suspect when the war commenced.

Because of technology and the emphasis on acquisitions, many persons who were born or grew up in the late 70's and 80's probably had greater material options than those who were products of the Depression era. There is a different type of story for immigrants and refugees as well. The relationship between their country and the United States, their socioeconomic circumstances, and their racial heritage will all have a bearing on their status, adjustment, and acceptance in this country. For example, a Chicano psychologist shared how he was stopped and questioned as he crossed the Mexican border into San Diego, his home town. Another incident was shared by a Latina professor who was returning from an educational trip from Colombia and entering the country through Puerto Rico. Officials of the INS insisted on questioning her because she looked "Spanish." Their concern was that she was entering illegally.

The C Dimension suggests that there are many factors that surround us over which we have no control as individuals but

which will affect us both positively and negatively. These contextual factors, though not seemingly to have a direct impact, do affect the way people are treated and perceived and how they do this to others. From historical, political and sociocultural perspectives, persons of color have experienced more incidents of oppression, disenfranchisement and legislated discrimination for racial reasons alone. This may also help to explain the phenomenon of learned helplessness and why individuals of color may suffer more experiences that make them the victim of an unfair decision or practice. Counseling from a multicultural perspective indicates developing knowledge of how American history has been experienced differently by persons of color, those who were of lower socioeconomic status, people with less education and access to power, and by women. Oppression is a dynamic that emerges in these discussions because historically power has been used based on an A Dimension to oppress others with different A Dimensions. Where there are victims of homophobia, racism and sexism, there are also beneficiaries. The C Dimension also invites exploration of institutional oppression and how it continues to occur in contemporary society and counseling sites. One example may be calling the Department of Social Services and announcing yourself as a counselor to the receptionist in a situation in which the client has had a lot of difficulty reaching her caseworker, been put on hold indefinitely or told that the case worker will return the call. By announcing the identity of the counselor to the receptionist, the call may be expedited so the client can take care of her business.

Another hypothetical example may be that of a student of color in a large educational institution who approaches a counselor with a complaint about a faculty member, citing racial discrimination and sexual harassment. The student complains that she went through the grievance process but did not feel that it was satisfactorily resolved and was told that the incidents were minor and not adequate to take action. The cultural competent counselor, having been approached by other students in the past with similar complaints against the same faculty member, may choose to intervene in the institution within the institution's policies and procedures for such situations.

B Dimension

The B Dimension is discussed last because theoretically it may represent the "consequences" of the A and C Dimensions. What occurs to individuals relative to their B Dimension is influenced by some of the immutable characteristics of the A Dimension and the major historical, political, sociocultural, and economic legacies of the C Dimension.

Educational experience is one example. Many more women and people of color have pursued higher education in the past 25 years as opportunities and access have become more possible because of Title VII of the Civil Rights Act. As a result of this legislation, colleges and universities can no longer discriminate based on gender, race, religion, etc. With increased levels of education, the work experience and parental status for women looks more varied than it did 25 years ago, although in terms of earning power, it does not equal that of White men. Education and socioeconomic conditions can enhance or limit a person seen only through the lens of an A Dimension. What happens to individuals is not totally within our control in spite of the American myths about self-control and self-reliance. Enabling conditions also play a role in what one can access or even think about. Laurence Graham, a black author and lawyer, spoke to the

Boston Human Resources Association (November 1994) about the reactions of his White peers when they learned he had been accepted to Yale. Rather than offering him congratulations, they stated that he had achieved entry as a result of affirmative action, thus diminishing his achievement. Graham goes on to report that many of his peers, not his par academically, were still admitted to prestigious universities. Why? As Graham notes, they had their own form of affirmative action, entry based on family legacy, connections, etc. The difference was that no one questioned this practice; things just worked that way.

One wonders how a high school counselor might see these two different sets of experiences. How aware and knowledgeable are counselors about the issues of access as they relate to the B Dimensions? For most people of color in this country access has been restricted legislatively and based on interpersonal discomfort and racism. In the CEO ranks, women and persons of color are sparse. Even going to the right schools may not always help. Why? As the literature indicates, organizations tend to hire in their own image, and historically, this has been a certain type of White male. How might this information assist a therapist who sees a woman or person of color who has again been passed over for a promotion? Chances are that encouraging the person to "try harder" will not provide the appropriate empathy. To be culturally competent, counselors need to understand the political power dynamics of the work place and how they perpetuate the dominance of certain groups over others. With this knowledge, counselors can respond more effectively to the reality of the client's experience.

A contemporary example also can be seen when considering individuals who are gay or lesbian. In most work settings, there remains a lack of openness and comfort to be yourself ostensibly denying one the freedom to be totally real. Focusing on only one dimension of a person's totality, limits understanding. For example, an Irish American gay man shares with his family that he is gay. The family expresses their discomfort with their son's lifestyle. The man goes on to reveal to his family that his significant other is an African American. The family asserts that they are uncomfortable with the gay lifestyle but threatens to disown him if he does not give up his African American partner. When counseling from a multicultural perspective, a counselor would know that the racial and gay identity of the men cannot be isolated as two independent dimensions. Both have to be recognized and respected. Counselors would also have to be aware of their own feelings and judgments about interracial and homosexual relationships. To say that one can offer unconditional positive regard does not necessarily mean that one is comfortable or culturally competent to assist the client.

The B Dimension also represents possible shared experiences that might not be observable by stopping with remains with an A Dimension. You cannot tell a person is from Ohio, a single mother, or an avid reader of poetry by looking at that individual out of context. If you see an Asian woman with a child, you might assume she is the mother, although you may not be able to discern her relationship status. Is she straight or gay, an unmarried mother, divorced or married? There are many possibilities for self-definition that go beyond our A Dimensions and in counseling these need to be recognized.

The B Dimension can be a point of connection. In presentations, participants are usually asked about how the B Dimensions relate to them. People from the same organization are invariably surprised when they learn that others attended the same university, were also in the military, or have children under five. There are ways that categories (B Dimensions) can actually foster rapport-building between client and counselor than seems apparent. This may depend, however, on the counselor's position of self-disclosure. Multicultural counseling leaders have reported that rapport building is critical in counseling with persons of color and at times, a counselor's sharing that she has been to the client's home country or knows someone from there may facilitate the connection. Counseling with college age Latina students, experiencing homesickness and guilt for being away from family may be more soothing if the counselor can emphasize with the students about culturally-based expectations for Latinas. This demonstration of "recognizing" the client's dilemma can contribute to relationship development with the client.

A, B, and C Dimensions Summary

The purpose of this model is to demonstrate the complexity and holism of individuals. It suggests that in spite of the categories we may all fit into or that are assigned to us, the combination of these affiliations is what makes everyone unique. Personal culture is comprised of these different dimensions of identity. By definition and in reality everyone is a "multicultural person." The sum is not greater than the parts.

In reference to the Multicultural Counseling Competencies, this model introduces the many ways in which individuals, clients, and counselors alike may self-define. It further suggests that when counseling with persons perceived as different from self in terms of culture, ethnicity or race, working from stereotyped assumptions and focusing only on one A or B Dimension without consideration of the C Dimension will likely lead to miscommunications and the undermining of a potential counseling relationship. Concomitantly, even if one is counseling with a person seemingly more like oneself, these perceived dimensions of sameness, that is gender or race, may not be the most relevant point of connection. There are many dimensions that influence us and assumptions must be questioned regarding which ones are most salient for an individual. It is ultimately up to the client to self-define this. When counseling from a multicultural perspective, culturally competent counselors would know that culture is not to "blame" for a person's problems nor does the presenting problem for a person of color have to be culture or race-based. For example, if counseling an African American couple, a culturally competent counselor would assess the relationship issues primarily and not necessarily ascribe their concerns to race. Over time, the topic of race might be introduced but it should neither be imposed or ignored.

An assumption is often made, although not verbalized, that multicultural counseling is for poor persons of color who use public services. Not only is this erroneous but it does lump all persons of color into one economic class, not the reality at all. Admittedly, there is an over representation of Blacks, Latinos and Native Americans, particularly women and children, living in poverty, but not everyone fits the profile. When counseling at college counseling centers, mental health agencies or private practice, counselors need to check their assumptions about persons of color. They come from varied backgrounds just like White people.

By stepping back and using the Personal Dimensions of Identity (PDI) model as objective criteria, counselors can more readily "see" the range of human potentiality every person possesses. I draw from my experiences, values, and individuality as a woman from Mexican-American heritage who grew up in Ohio, has lived in Boston nearly 25 years, has a doctorate degree in psychology, is a former university professor, married without children, and the owner of a management consulting business. To categorize and see me through one or two A Dimensions only may limit the contributions I can make as a counseling professional in your organization.

From an institutional perspective, the PDI model can assist leaders to become more aware of how the culture of their organization may alienate, marginalize or lose people of color, women and other minority groups if cultural competency is not valued and practiced. The Multicultural Counseling Competencies are designed to promote culturally effective relationships particularly in interpersonal counseling. By applying this paradigm in an institutional setting, it may become better possible to understand the relationship between an organization and its clients/customers. Is the environment friendly to culturally and economically different people?

Increased multicultural competence can enable counselors to provide culturally appropriate counseling as well as to utilize the PDI model more effectively. Through increasing awareness, counselors are better able to understand how their own personal dimensions affect their ability to perceive and understand the personal dimension of their clients. Similarly, greater knowledge enhances the counselor's ability to more accurately understand the various cultures or elements which make up their clients's personal dimensions. Developing greater multicultural counseling skills allows for appropriate interventions, advocacy, and an effective use of culturally appropriate models, such as the PDI model. The shift in counseling paradigms will require counselors to continue to develop themselves, their profession, and institutions along with a much broader spectrum of society.

The revised Multicultural Counseling Competencies and accompanying Explanatory Statements further clarify and define the three domains of *awareness, knowledge and skills.* In this format they go beyond the original document of Multicultural Counseling Competencies (Sue, Arredondo & McDavis, 1992) and take the profession further along in the process of institutionalizing counselor training and practices to be multicultural at the core. With the Explanatory Statements are examples and anecdotes that give life to the competencies. They are operationalized through language that describes the means of achieving and demonstrating a said competency. This new format further underscores the opportunity to utilize multicultural perspectives generically, with all interpersonal counseling.

Multicultural Organizations

The emphasis throughout the Competencies is on individual change. Yet it is obvious that if only individuals change and not the systems in which they work, the textbooks that are used for teaching, the practicum experiences that are provided, the ethical standards and competencies that guide professional practice, and the institutions that set policies and influence legislation, the status quo will remain. We will continue to be segregated professionally and societally.

It is recommended that institutions of higher education, public and private schools, mental health facilities and other settings where counseling is practiced engage in a self-examination process. Assess the cultural appropriateness and relevance of your organizational systems, policies and practices. We encourage organizational leaders to search out the literature that will guide your process to becoming multicultural. It can be done.

Multicultural Counseling Competencies

I. Counselor Awareness of Own Cultural Values and Biases

A. Attitudes and Beliefs

1. Culturally skilled counselors believe that cultural self-awareness and sensitivity to one's own cultural heritage is essential.

    Explanatory Statements
    a. Can identify the culture(s) to which they belong and the significance of that membership including the relationship of individuals in that group with individuals from other groups, institutionally, historically, educationally, etc. (include A, B, and C Dimensions as do the other suggestions in this section).
    b. Can identify the specific cultural group(s) from which counselor derives fundamental cultural heritage and the significant beliefs and attitudes held by those cultures that are assimilated into their own attitudes and beliefs.
    c. Can recognize the impact of those beliefs on their ability to respect others different from themselves.
    d. Can identify specific attitudes, beliefs, and values from their own heritage and cultural learning which support behaviors that demonstrate respect and valuing of differences and those that impede or hinder respect and valuing of differences.

2. Culturally skilled counselors are aware of how their own cultural background and experiences have influenced attitudes, values, and biases about psychological processes.

    Explanatory Statements
    a. Can identify the history of their culture in relation to educational opportunities and its impact on their current worldview (includes A and some B Dimensions).
    b. Can identify at least five personal, relevant cultural traits and can explain how each has influenced cultural values of the counselor.
    c. Can identify social and cultural influences on their cognitive development and current information processing styles and can contrast that with those of others (includes A, B, and C Dimensions).
    d. Can identify specific social and cultural factors and events in their history that influence their view and use of social belonging, interpretations of behavior, motivation, problem solving and decision methods, thoughts and behaviors (including subconscious) in relation to authority and other institutions and can contrast these with the perspectives of others. (A and B Dimensions).

e. Can articulate the beliefs of their own cultural and religious groups around differences, such as sexual orientation, religion able-bodiedness, and so forth, and the impact of these beliefs in a counseling relationship.

3. Culturally skilled counselors are able to recognize the limits of their multicultural competency and expertise.

Explanatory Statements

a. Can recognize in a counseling or teaching relationship, when and how their attitudes, beliefs and values are interfering with providing the best service to clients. (Primarily A and B Dimensions).

b. Can give real examples of cultural situations in which they recognize their limitations and referred the client to more appropriate resources.

4. Culturally skilled counselors recognize their sources of discomfort with differences that exist between themselves and clients in terms of race, ethnicity, and culture.

Explanatory Statements

a. Able to recognize their sources of comfort/discomfort with respect to differences in terms of race, ethnicity and culture.

b. Can identify at least five specific cultural differences, the needs of culturally different clients, and how these differences are handled in the counseling relationship.

B. **Knowledge**

1. Culturally skilled counselors have specific knowledge about their own racial and cultural heritage and how it personally and professionally affects their definitions and biases of normality/abnormality and the process of counseling.

Explanatory Statements

a. Have knowledge regarding their heritage: for example, A Dimensions in terms of ethnicity, language, and so forth, and C Dimensions in terms of knowledge regarding the context of the time period in which their ancestors entered the established United States and/or North American continent.

b. Can recognize and discuss their family's and culture's perspectives of acceptable (normal) codes of conduct and what are unacceptable (abnormal) and how this may or may not vary from those of other cultures and families.

c. Can identify at least five specific features of culture-of-origin and explain how those features impact the relationship with culturally different clients.

2. Culturally skilled counselors possess knowledge and understanding about how oppression, racism, discrimination, and stereotyping affect them personally and in their work. This allows individuals to acknowledge their own racist attitudes, beliefs, and feelings. Although this standard applies to all groups, for White counselors it may mean that they understand how they may have directly or indirectly benefited from individual, institutional, and cultural racism as outlined in White identity development models.

Explanatory Statements

a. Can specifically identify, name, and discuss privileges that they personally receive in society due to their race, socioeconomic background, gender, physical abilities, sexual orientation, and so forth.

b. Specifically referring to White counselors, can discuss White identity development models and how they relate to one's personal experiences.

c. Can provide a reasonably specific definition of racism, prejudice, discrimination and stereotype. Can describe a situation in which they have been judged on something other than merit. Can describe a situation in which they have judged someone on something other than merit.

3. Culturally skilled counselors possess knowledge about their social impact upon others. They are knowledgeable about communication style differences, how their style may clash with or foster the counseling process with persons of color or others different from themselves based on the A, B, and C, Dimensions, and how to anticipate the impact it may have on others.

Explanatory Statements

a. Can describe the A and B Dimensions of Personal Identity with which they most strongly identify.

b. Can behaviorally define their communication style and describe both their verbal and nonverbal behaviors, interpretations of others behaviors, and expectations.

c. Recognize the cultural bases (A Dimension) of their communication style and the differences between their style and the styles of those people different from themselves.

d. Can describe the behavioral impact and reaction of their communication style on clients different from themselves. For example, the reaction of an older (60's) Vietnamese male recent immigrant to continuous eye contact from the young female counselor.

e. Can give examples of an incident where communication broke down with a client of color and hypothesize about the causes.

f. Can give 3–5 concrete examples of situations in which they modified their communication style to compliment that of a culturally different client, how they decided on the modification, and the result of that modification.

C. **Skills**

1. Culturally skilled counselors seek out educational, consultative, and training experiences to improve their understanding and effectiveness in working

with culturally different populations. Being able to recognize the limits of their competencies, they (a) seek consultation, (b) seek further training or education, (c) refer out to more qualified individuals or resources, or (d) engage in a combination of these.

Explanatory Statements

a. Maintain an active referral list and continuously seek new referrals relevant to different needs of clients along A and B Dimensions.

b. Understand and communicate to the client that the referral is being made because of the counselor's limitations rather than communicating that it is caused by the client.

c. Actively consult regularly with other professionals regarding issues of culture in order to receive feedback about issues and situations and whether or where referral may be necessary.

2. Culturally skilled counselors are constantly seeking to understand themselves as racial and cultural beings and are actively seeking a nonracist identity.

Explanatory Statements

a. When receiving feedback the counselor demonstrates a receptivity and willingness to learn.

Strategies to Achieve the Competencies and Objectives (I)

Read materials regarding identity development. For example: a European American counselor may read materials on White or Majority Identity Development, an African American may read materials on Black Identity Development, etc. to gain an understanding of own development. Additionally, reading about others' identity development processes is essential. The following are some resources specifically for European American or White counselors:

- Carter, R. T. (1990). The relationship between racism and racial identity among white Americans: An exploratory investigation. *Journal of Counseling and Development, 69,* 46–50.
- Corvin, S., & Wiggins, F. (1989). An anti-racism training model for White professionals. *Journal of Multicultural Counseling and Development, 17,* 105–114.
- Helms, J. (1990). *White identity development.* New York: Greenwood Press.
- Pedersen, P. B. (1988). *A handbook for development of multicultural awareness.* Alexandria, VA: American Association for Counseling and Development.
- Pope-Davis, D. B., & Ottavi, T. M. (1992). The influence of white racial identity attitudes on racism among faculty members: A preliminary examination. *Journal of College Student Development, 33,* 389–394.
- Sabnani, H. B., Ponterotto, J. G., & Borodovsky, L. G. (1991). White racial identity development and cross-cultural training. *The Counseling Psychologist, 19,* 76–102.
- Wrenn, C. G. (1962). The culturally encapsulated counselor. *Harvard Educational Review, 32,* 444–449.

Other Professional Activities:

Attend annual conferences and workshops such as:

- Annual Conference on Race and Ethnicity in Higher Education sponsored by the *Center for Southwest Studies Oklahoma (1995, Santa Fe)*
- Third World Counselor's Association Annual Conference (Palm Springs, 1995)
- AMCD Annual Western Summit

Engage a mentor from your own culture who you identify as someone who has been working toward becoming cross culturally competent and who has made significant strides in ways you have not.

Engage a mentor or two from cultures different from your own who are willing to provide honest feedback regarding your behavior, attitudes, and beliefs. And, be willing to listen and work toward change!

Film: "The Color of Fear" by Lee Mun Wah
Film: "A Class Divided" by PBS
Film: "True Colors"—20/20 Special
Video: "The Triad Model" by Paul Pederson

II. Counselor Awareness of Client's Worldview
A. Attitudes and Beliefs

1. Culturally skilled counselors are aware of their negative and positive emotional reactions toward other racial and ethnic groups that may prove detrimental to the counseling relationship. They are willing to contrast their own beliefs and attitudes with those of their culturally different clients in a nonjudgmental fashion.

Explanatory Statements

a. Identify their common emotional reactions about individuals and groups different from themselves and observe their own reactions in encounters. For example, do they feel fear when approaching a group of three young African American males? Do they assume that the Asian American clients for whom they provide career counseling will be interested in a technical career?

b. Can articulate how their personal reactions and assumptions are different from those who identify with that group (e.g., if the reaction upon approaching three young African American males is fear, what is the reaction of a young African American male or female in the same situation? What might the reaction be of an African American female approaching a group of White young men?).

c. Can describe at least two distinct examples of cultural conflict between self and culturally different clients, including how these conflicts were used as "content" for counseling. For example, if a Chicana agrees to live at home rather than board at a four year college in order to support her mother. Can a counselor be non-judgmental?

2. Culturally skilled counselors are aware of their stereotypes and preconceived notions that they

may hold toward other racial and ethnic minority groups.

Explanatory Statements

a. Recognize their stereotyped reactions to people different than themselves. (e.g., silently articulating their awareness of a negative stereotypical reaction . . . "I noticed that I locked my car doors when that African American teenager walked by.").

b. Can give specific examples of how their stereotypes (including "positive" ones), referring to the A and B Dimensions, can impact the counselor-client relationship.

c. Recognize assumptions of those in a similar cultural group but who may differ based on A or B Dimension.

B. Knowledge

1. Culturally skilled counselors possess specific knowledge and information about the particular group with which they are working. They are aware of the life experiences, cultural heritage, and historical background of their culturally different clients. This particular competency is strongly linked to the "minority identity development models" available in the literature.

Explanatory Statements

a. Can articulate (objectively) differences in nonverbal and verbal behavior of the five major different cultural groups most frequently seen in their experience of counseling.

b. Can describe at least two different models of "minority identity development" and their implications for counseling with persons of color or others who experience oppression or marginalization.

c. Can identify within-group differences and assess various aspects of individual clients to determine individual differences as well as cultural differences. For example, the counselor is aware of differences within Asian Americans: Japanese Americans, Vietnamese Americans, and so forth; differences between first generation refugees vs. second or third generation; differences between Vietnamese refugees coming in the "first wave" 1975, versus Vietnamese refugees coming to the United States in 1990.

d. Can discuss viewpoints of other cultural groups regarding issues such as sexual orientation, physical ability/disability, gender, and aging.

2. Culturally skilled counselors understand how race, culture, ethnicity, and so forth may affect personality formation, vocational choices, manifestation of psychological disorders, help-seeking behavior, and the appropriateness or inappropriateness of counseling approaches.

Explanatory Statements

a. Can distinguish cultural differences and expectations regarding role and responsibility in family, participation of family in career decision making, appropriate family members to be involved when seeking help, culturally acceptable means of expressing emotion and anxiety, and so forth. (primarily along A Dimension and portions of B Dimension).

b. Based on literature about A Dimensions, can describe and give examples of how a counseling approach may or may not be appropriate for a specific group of people based primarily upon an A Dimension.

c. Understand and can explain the historical point of contact with dominant society for various ethnic groups and the impact of the type of contact (enslaved, refugee, seeking economic opportunities, conquest, etc.) on potential relationships and trust when seeking help from dominant culture institutions.

d. Can describe one system of personality development, the populations(s) on which the theory was developed, and how this system relates or does not relate to at least two culturally different populations.

e. Can identify the role of gender, socioeconomic status, and physical disability as they interact with personality formation across cultural groups.

3. Culturally skilled counselors understand and have knowledge about sociopolitical influences that impinge upon the life of racial and ethnic minorities. Immigration issues, poverty, racism, stereotyping, and powerlessness may impact self esteem and self concept in the counseling process.

Explanatory Statements

a. Can identify implications of concepts such as internalized oppression, institutional racism, privilege, and the historical and current political climate regarding immigration, poverty, welfare (public assistance).

b. Understand the economic benefits and contributions gained by the work of various groups, including migrant farm workers, to the daily life of the counselor and the country at large.

c. Can communicate an understanding of the unique position, constraints and needs of those clients who experience oppression based on an A or B dimension alone (and families of clients) who share this history.

d. Can identify current issues that impact groups of people (A and B Dimensions) in legislation, social climate, and so forth, and how that affects individuals and families to whom the counselor may be providing services.

e. Are aware of legal legislation issues and legal rights that impact various communities and populations (for example, in California it is essential for a counselor to understand the ramifications of the recent passage of Proposition 209 and how that will affect not only undocumented individuals but also families, and *anyone* that has Chicano features, a Mexican American accent, and speaks Spanish. In addition, the counselor must be aware of how this will affect health issues, help-seeking behaviors, participation in education, and so forth).

f. Counselors are aware of how documents such as the book, *The Bell Curve,* and affirmative action legislation impact society's perception of different cultural groups.

C. Skills

1. Culturally skilled counselors should familiarize themselves with relevant research and the latest findings regarding mental health and mental disorders that affect various ethnic and racial groups. They should actively seek out educational experiences that enrich their knowledge, understanding, and cross-cultural skills for more effective counseling behavior.

Explanatory Statements

a. Can identify at least five multicultural experiences in which counselor has participated within past 3 years.
b. Can identify professional growth activities and information which is presented by professionals respected and seen as credible by members of the communities being studied. (e.g., the book *The Bell Curve* may not represent accurate and helpful information regarding individuals from non-White cultures).

2. Culturally skilled counselors become actively involved with minority individuals outside the counseling setting (e.g., community events, social and political functions, celebrations, friendships, neighborhood groups, and so forth) so that their perspective of minorities is more than an academic or helping exercise.

Explanatory Statements

a. Actively plan experiences and activities that will contradict negative stereotypes and preconceived notions they may hold.

Strategies to Achieve the Competencies and Objectives (II)

The following reading list may be helpful for counselors to broaden their understanding of different world views (some of these materials would also be helpful in developing culturally appropriate intervention strategies):

- Atkinson, D., Morten, G., & Sue, D. W. (1989). *Counseling American minorities: A cross-cultural perspective.* Dubuque, IA: Brown.
- Collins, P. (1990). *Black feminist thought: Knowledge, consciousness and the politics of empowerment.* Boston: Unwin Hyman.
- Sue, D. W., & Sue, D. (1990). *Counseling the culturally different: Theory and practice (2nd ed.).* New York: Wiley.

Attend conferences and workshops such as:

- Annual Conference on Race and Ethnicity in Higher Education sponsored by the *Center for Southwest Studies Oklahoma (1995, Santa Fe)*
- Third World Counselor's Association Annual Conference (Palm Springs, 1995)
- AMCD Annual Western Summit

Enroll in ethnic studies courses at local community colleges or universities that focus on cultures different from your own (if none are offered, communicate to that school your expectation that they will offer them in the future).

Spend time in communities different from your own, (e.g., shopping in grocery stores, attending churches, walking in marches).

Read newspapers and other periodicals targeting specific populations different from your own, (i.e., Spanish language newspapers, "Buffalo Soldier", "Lakota Times").

Engage in activities and celebrations within communities different from your own (e.g., Juneteenth, Tet, Cinco de Mayo).

Engage a mentor or two from cultures different from your own who are also working toward cross cultural competency (be sure to discuss with them your contribution to the relationship).

Accept that it is your responsibility to learn about other cultures and implications in counseling and do not expect or rely on individuals from those cultures to teach you.

Learn a second or third language relevant to clients to begin to understand the significance of that language in the transmission of culture.

Seek out and engage in consultation from professionals from cultures relevant to your client population.

Spend time in civil service offices observing service orientation toward individuals of color (Chicano/Latino; African American; Asian American; Native American) and contrast that with service orientation toward white individuals. Also observe any differences on service orientation that may be based on class issues (e.g., someone alone and well dressed versus a woman with children wearing older clothing, somewhat disheveled).

Film: *"The Color of Fear"* by Lee Mun Wah
Film: *"El Norte"*
Film: *"Stand and Deliver"*
Film: *"Roots"*
Film: *"Lakota Woman"*
Film: *"Daughters of the Dust"*

III. Culturally Appropriate Intervention Strategies
A. Beliefs and Attitudes

1. Culturally skilled counselors respect clients' religious and/or spiritual beliefs and values, including attributions and taboos, because they affect worldview, psychosocial functioning, and expressions of distress.

Explanatory Statements

a. Can identify the positive aspects of spirituality (in general) in terms of wellness and healing aspects.
b. Can identify in a variety of religious and spiritual communities the recognized form of leadership and guidance and their client's

relationship (if existent) with that organization and entity.

2. Culturally skilled counselors respect indigenous helping practices and respect help-giving networks among communities of color.

   Explanatory Statements
   a. Can describe concrete examples of how they may integrate and cooperate with indigenous helpers when appropriate.

3. Culturally skilled counselors value bilingualism and do not view another language as an impediment to counseling (monolingualism may be the culprit).

   Explanatory Statements
   a. Communicate to clients and colleagues values and assets of bilingualism (if client is bilingual).

B. **Knowledge**
1. Culturally skilled counselors have a clear and explicit knowledge and understanding of the generic characteristics of counseling and therapy (culture bound, class bound, and monolingual) and how they may clash with the cultural values of various cultural groups.

   Explanatory Statements
   a. Can identify, within various theories, the cultural values, beliefs and assumptions made about individuals and contrast these with values, beliefs, and assumptions of different racial and cultural groups.
   b. Can identify and describe primary indigenous helping practices in terms of positive and effective role in at least five A or B Dimensions, relevant to counselor's client population.

2. Culturally skilled counselors are aware of institutional barriers that prevent minorities from using mental health services.

   Explanatory Statements
   a. Can describe concrete examples of institutional barriers within their organization that prevent minorities from using mental health services and share those examples with colleagues and decision making bodies within the institution.
   b. Can identify and communicate possible alternatives that would reduce or eliminate existing barriers within their institution and within local, state, and national decision making bodies.

3. Culturally skilled counselors have knowledge of the potential bias in assessment instruments and use procedures and interpret findings keeping in mind the cultural and linguistic characteristics of the clients.

   Explanatory Statements
   a. Demonstrate ability to interpret assessment results including implications of dominant cultural values affecting assessment/interpretation, interaction of cultures for those

who are bicultural, and impact of historical institutional oppression.
   b. Can discuss information regarding cultural, racial, gender profile of normative group used for validity and reliability on any assessment used by counselor.
   c. Use assessment instruments appropriately with clients having limited English skills.

4. Culturally skilled counselors have knowledge of family structures, hierarchies, values, and beliefs from various cultural perspectives. They are knowledgeable about the community where a particular cultural group may reside and the resources in the community.

   Explanatory Statements
   a. Are familiar with and use organizations that provide support and services in different cultural communities.
   b. Adequately understand client's religious and spiritual beliefs to know when and what topics are or are not appropriate to discuss regarding those beliefs.
   c. Understand and respect cultural and family influences and participation in decision making.

5. Culturally skilled counselors should be aware of relevant discriminatory practices at the social and community level that may be affecting the psychological welfare of the population being served.

   Explanatory Statements
   a. Are aware of legal issues that impact various communities and populations (for example, in Proposition 187 California described earlier).

C. **Skills**
1. Culturally skilled counselors are able to engage in a variety of verbal and nonverbal helping responses. They are able to send and receive both verbal and nonverbal messages accurately and appropriately. They are not tied down to only one method or approach to helping, but recognize that helping styles and approaches may be culture bound. When they sense that their helping style is limited and potentially inappropriate, they can anticipate and modify it.

   Explanatory Statements
   a. Can articulate what, when, why and how they apply different verbal and nonverbal helping responses based on A and B Dimensions.
   b. Can identify and describe techniques in which they have expertise for providing service that may require minimal English language skills (e.g., expressive therapy).
   c. Can discuss with the client aspects of their religious/spiritual beliefs that have been helpful to the client in the past.

2. Culturally skilled counselors are able to exercise institutional intervention skills on behalf of their clients. They can help clients determine whether a "problem" stems from racism or bias in others (the

concept of healthy paranoia) so that clients do not inappropriately personalize problems.

Explanatory Statements

a. Can recognize and discuss examples in which racism or bias may actually be imbedded in an institutional system or society.

b. Communicate to clients an understanding of the necessary coping skills and behaviors viewed by dominant society as dysfunctional that they may need to keep intact.

c. Can describe concrete examples of situations in which it is appropriate and possibly necessary for a counselor to exercise institutional intervention skills on behalf of a client.

3. Culturally skilled counselors are not averse to seeking consultation with traditional healers or religious and spiritual leaders and practitioners in the treatment of culturally different clients when appropriate.

Explanatory Statements

a. Participate or gather adequate information regarding indigenous or community helping resources to make appropriate referrals (e.g., be familiar with the American Indian community enough to recognize when, how and to whom it may be appropriate to refer a client to indigenous healers).

4. Culturally skilled counselors take responsibility for interacting in the language requested by the client and, if not feasible, make appropriate referrals. A serious problem arises when the linguistic skills of the counselor do not match the language of the client. This being the case, counselors should (a) seek a translator with cultural knowledge and appropriate professional background or (b) refer to a knowledgeable and competent bilingual counselor.

Explanatory Statements

a. Are familiar with resources that provide services in languages appropriate to clients.

b. Will seek out, whenever necessary, services or translators to ensure that language needs are met.

c. If working within an organization, actively advocate for the hiring of bilingual counselors relevant to client population.

5. Culturally skilled counselors have training and expertise in the use of traditional assessment and testing instruments. They not only understand the technical aspects of the instruments but are also aware of the cultural limitations. This allows them to use test instruments for the welfare of culturally different clients.

Explanatory Statements

a. Demonstrate ability to interpret assessment results including implications of dominant cultural values affecting assessment/interpretation, interaction of cultures for those who are bicultural, and the impact of historical institutional oppression.

b. Understand that although an assessment instrument may be translated into another language, the translation may be literal without an accurate contextual translation including culturally relevant connotations and idioms.

6. Culturally skilled counselors should attend to as well as work to eliminate biases, prejudices, and discriminatory contexts in conducting evaluations and providing interventions, and should develop sensitivity to issues of oppression, sexism, heterosexism, elitism, and racism.

Explanatory Statements

a. Recognize incidents in which clients, students and others are being treated unfairly based on race, ethnicity, and physical disability, and take action by directly addressing the incident or perpetrator, filing informal complaint, filing formal complaint, and so forth.

7. Culturally skilled counselors take responsibility for educating their clients to the processes of psychological intervention, such as goals, expectations, legal rights, and the counselor's orientation.

Explanatory Statements

a. Assess the client's understanding and familiarity with counseling and mental health services and provides accurate information regarding the process, limitations, and function of the services into which the client is entering.

b. Ensure that the client understands client rights, issues and definitions of confidentiality, and expectations placed upon that client. In this educational process, counselors adapt information to ensure that all concepts are clearly understood by the client. This may include defining and discussing these concepts.

Strategies to Achieve the Competencies and Objectives (III)

The following reading list may be helpful for building a foundation to develop and apply culturally appropriate interventions:

- Atkinson, D., Morten, G., & Sue, D. W. (1989). *Counseling American minorities: A cross-cultural perspective.* Dubuque, IA: Brown.
- Ibrahim, F. A., & Arredondo, P. M. (1990). Ethical issues in multicultural counseling. In B. Herlihy & L. Golden (Eds.), *Ethical standards casebook* (pp. 137–145). Alexandria, VA: American Association for Counseling and Development.
- Katz, J. (1978). *White awareness: Handbook for antiracism training.* Norman, Oklahoma: Oklahoma.
- LaFromboise, T. D., & Foster, S. L. (1990). Cross-cultural training: Scientist-practitioner model and methods. *The Counseling Psychologist*, 20, 472–489.
- LaFromboise, T. D., & Foster, S. L. (1989). Ethics in multicultural counseling. In P. B. Pedersen, W. J. Lonner, & J. E. Trimble (Eds.), *Counseling across cultures* (3rd ed., pp. 115–136). Honolulu, HI: University of Hawaii Press.

Meet with leaders and heads of organizations that specifically focus on providing service to individuals of certain cultural groups (for example in San Jose, CA, AACI-Asian Americans for Community Involvement) to discuss how you may work cooperatively together and what support you may provide the organization.

Conduct informal research of your clientele, your organizations' clientele, to determine if there are patterns of use or non use along cultural and/or racial lines.

OVERALL STRATEGIES FOR ACHIEVING COMPETENCIES AND OBJECTIVES IN ALL THREE AREAS:

Assess self in terms of Cross Cultural Counseling competencies either by reviewing the competencies and giving examples in each area and/or utilizing any of the following resources regarding assessment instruments:

- Ho, M. K. (1992) *Minority children and adolescents in therapy.* Newbury Park: Sage.
- LaFromboise, T. D., Coleman, H. L. K., & Hernandez, A. (1991). Development and factor structure of the Cross Cultural Counseling Inventory-Revised. *Professional Psychology: Research and Practice, 22,* 380–388.
- Ponterotto, J. G., Rieger, B. P., Barrett, A., & Sparks, R. (1994). Assessing multicultural counseling competence: A review of instrumentation. *Journal of Counseling and Development, 72,* 316–322.

Learn a second or third language relevant to clients.

Communicate to conference organizers and workshop providers that you will attend only if the activity addresses cross cultural aspects of the topic.

Actively communicate in your organization the need for training in cross cultural training relevant to that organization.

Speak up in your organization when you observe that clients, students etc. are being treated unfairly based on race, ethnicity, physical ableness, etc.

Become a member of AMCD, Division 45/APA, or state and local organizations that provide cross cultural exchanges.

REFERENCES

Arredondo, P. And Glauner, T. (1992). *Personal Dimensions of Identity Model.* Boston: Empowerment Workshops.

Graham, L. (November 1994). Comments made in presentation to the Boston Human Resource Association.

Johnston, W. B. and Packer, A. H. (1987). *Workforce 2000: Work and Workers for the 21st Century.* Indiana: Hudson Institute.

Sue, D. W., Arredondo, P. and McDavis, R. J. (1992). Multicultural Counseling Competencies and Standards: A call to the profession. *Journal of Counseling and Development, 70*(4), 477–483.

BIBLIOGRAPHY

Texts and Chapters

Acosta, F. X., Yamamoto, J. and Evans, L. A. (1982). *Effective psychotherapy for low-income and minority patients.* New York, NY: Plenum Press.

Asante, M. (1987). *The Afrocentric idea.* Philadelphia: Temple University Press.

Atkinson, D., Morten, G. and Sue, D. (1989). *Counseling American minorities: A cross-cultural perspective.* (2nd Ed.) Dubuque, IA: W. C. Brown.

Cross, W. E. Jr. (1991). *Shades of Black.* Philadelphia: Temple University Press.

Cross, W. E. Jr. (1995) The psychology of Nigrescence: Revising the Cross model. In J. Ponterotto, M. Casas, L. Suzuki, and C. Alexander (Eds.) *Handbook of multicultural counseling.* Thousands Oaks, CA: Sage.

Cheatham, H. (1990) Empowering Black families. In H. Cheatham and J. Stewart (Eds.) *Black families: Interdisciplinary perspectives.* New Brunswick, N.J.: Transaction.

Ferris, F. (1987). *The central American refugees.* New York: Praeger Publishers.

Freire, P. (1970) *Pedagogy of the oppressed.* New York: Continuum.

Hall, E. T. & Hall, M. R. (1990). *Understanding cultural differences.* Yarmouth, ME.: Intercultural Press.

Helms, J. (1990) *Black and white racial identity: Theory, research, and practice.* Westport, CT: Greenwood.

Helms, J. (1992). *A race is a nice thing to have.* Topeka: Content Communications.

Hofstede, G. (1984). *Culture's consequences.* Cross-Cultural Research and Methodology Series 5. Newbury Park, CA: Sage.

Ivey, A. (1995). Psychotherapy as liberation. In J. Ponterotto, M. Casas, L. Suzuki, and C. Alexander. (Eds.). *Handbook of Multicultural Counseling.* Thousand Oaks, CA: Sage.

Jackson, M. L. (1995). Multicultural counseling: Historical perspective. In J. Ponterotto, M. Casas, L. Suzuki, and C. Alexander (Eds.) *Handbook of Multicultural Counseling.* Thousands Oaks, CA: Sage.

Klein, J (1989). *Jewish identity and self-esteem: Healing wounds through ethnotherapy.* New York: Institute for American Pluralism of the American Jewish Committee.

Kohls, L. R. (1984). *The values Americans live by.* Washington, DC: Meridian House International.

Koslow, D. R. and Salett, E. P. (Eds.). (1989). *Crossing cultures in mental health.* Washington, DC: SIETAR International.

Lee, C. C., & Richardson, B. L. (Eds.). (1991). *Multicultural issues in counseling: New approaches to diversity.* Alexandria, VA: ACA Press.

Locke, D. C. (1992). *Increasing multicultural understanding.* Thousand Oaks, CA: Sage.

Marsella, A. J. and Pedersen, P. B. (Eds.). (1981). *Cross-cultural counseling and psychotherapy.* New York: Pergamon Press.

McGoldrick, M., Pearce, J., and Giordano, J. (1982). *Ethnicity and family therapy.* New York: Guilford.

Nobles, W. (1986). *African psychology: Inward its reclamation, reassension and revitaliation.* Oakland: Black Family Institute.

Padilla, A. M. (Ed.). (1995). *Hispanic psychology.* Thousand Oaks, CA: Sage.

Paniagua, F. (1994) *Assessing and treating culturally diverse clients.* Thousand Oaks, CA: Sage.

Pedersen, P., Draguns, J., Lonner, J., and Trimble, J. (1989). *Counseling across cultures.* (3rd Ed.) Honolulu: University of Hawaii Press.

Pedersen, P., & Ivey, A. (1993) *Culture-centered counseling.* New York: Greenwood.

Ponterotto, J., Casas, M., Suzuki, L. and Alexander, C. (Eds) (1995). *Handbook of multicultural counseling.* Thousand Oaks, CA: Sage.

Sue, D. W., Ivey, A., and Pedersen, P. (Eds.) (1996). *A theory of multicultural counseling and therapy*. Pacific Grove, CA: Brooks/Cole.

Sue, D. W. & Sue, D. (1990) *Counseling the culturally different*. New York: Wiley.

White, J. and Parham, T. (1990). *The psychology of Blacks*. Englewood Cliffs, N. J.: Princeton Hall.

Zambrana, R. E. (Eds.). (1995). *Understanding Latino families*. Thousand Oaks, CA: Sage.

BIBLIOGRAPHY

Articles and Manuscripts

Arredondo, P., Psalti, A. & Cella K. (1993). The woman factor in multicultural counseling. *Counseling and Human Development*, 25, 1–8.

Arredondo-Dowd, P. M. and Gonsalves, J. (1980). Preparing culturally effective counselors. *Personnel and Guidance Journal*, 58, 657–662.

Arredondo-Dowd, P. M. (1981). Personal loss and grief as a result of immigration. *Personnel and Guidance Journal*, 59, 376–378.

Arredondo, P. M., Orjuela, E., & Moore, L. (1989). Family therapy with Central American war refugee families. *Journal of Strategic and Systemic Therapies*, 8, 28–35.

Bennett, M. J. (1986). A developmental approach to training for intercultural sensitivity. *International Journal of Intercultural Relations*, 10, 179–196.

Christiansen, C. P. (1989). Cross cultural awareness development: A conceptual model. *Counselor Education and Supervision*, 28, 270–287.

D'Andrea, M. & Daniels, J. (1991). Exploring the different levels of multicultural counseling training. *Journal of Counseling & Development*, 70, 143–150.

D'Andrea, M. & Daniels, J. (1987). The different faces of racism in higher education. *The NEA Higher Education Journal*.

Fiske, S. T. (1993). Controlling other people. *American Psychologist*, 48, 621–628.

Ford, Jr., D. L. (1978). Cultural influences on organizational behavior. *NTL Institute For Applied Behavioral Science*. 8, 2–8.

Fukuyama, M. A. (1990). Taking a universal approach to multicultural counseling. *Counselor Education and Supervision*, 30, 6–17.

Gaines, S. O., Jr. & Reed, E. S. (1995). Prejudice: From Allport to DuBois. *American Psychologist*, 50, 96–103.

Gibbs, J. T. (1987). Identity and marginality: Issues in the treatment of biracial adolescents. *American Journal of Orthopsychiatry*, 57, 265–278.

Hardiman, R. (1979). *White identity development theory*. Amherst, MA.: New Perspectives, Inc.

Herring, R. D. (1992). Counseling biracial youth within the interracial family. *The New York State Journal of Counseling and Development*, 7, 43–51.

Ibrahim, F. (1985). Effective cross-cultural counseling and psychotherapy: A framework. *The Counseling Psychologist*. 13, 4, 625–638.

Ibrahim, F. A. (1991). Contribution of cultural worldview to generic counseling and development. *Journal of Counseling and Development*, 70, 13–19.

Langman, P. F. (1995). Including Jews in multiculturalism. *Journal of Multicultural Counseling and Development*, 23, 4, 222–236.

Lloyd, A. P. (1987). Multicultural counseling: Does it belong in a counselor education program? *Counselor Education and Supervision*. 26, 164–167.

Locke, D. (1990). A not so provincial view of multicultural counseling. *Counselor Education and Supervision*, 30, 18–25.

McRae, M. B. and Johnson, S. D., Jr. (1991). Toward training for competence in multicultural counselor education. *Journal of Counseling and Development*, 70, 131–135.

Myers, L. J., Speight, S. L., Highlen, P. S., Cox, C. I., Reynolds, A. L., Adams, E. M. and Hanley, C. P. (1991). Identity development and worldview: Toward an optimal conceptualization. *Journal of Counseling & Development*, 70, 54–63.

Nwachuku, U., and Ivey, A. (1991). Culture specific counseling: An alternative approach. *Journal of Counseling & Development*, 70, 106–151.

Ochs, N. G. (1994). The incidence of racial issues in white counseling dyads: An exploratory survey. *Counselor Education and Supervision*, 33, 305–313.

Paradis, F. (1981). Themes in the training of culturally effective psychotherapists. *Counselor Education and Supervision*, 21, 136–151.

Parham, T. (1989) Cycles of psychological Nigrescense. *The Counseling Psychologist*, 17, 187–226.

Pederson, P. B. (1991). Multiculturalism as a generic approach to counseling. *Journal of Counseling & Development*, 70, 6–12.

Ponterotto, J. G. (1991). The nature of prejudice revisited: Implications for counseling intervention. *Journal of Counseling & Development*, 70, 216–224.

Ruiz, A. S. (1990). Ethnic identity: Crisis and resolution. *Journal of Multicultural Counseling and Development*, 18, 29–40.

Seigel, R. (1986). Antisemitism and sexism in stereotypes of Jewish women. *Women and Therapy*, 5, 249–257.

Skillings, J. H. and Dobbins, J. E. (1991). Racism as disease: Etiology and treatment implications. *Journal of Counseling & Development*, 70, 206–212.

Smart, J. F. and Smart, D. W. (1995). Acculturative stress of Hispanics: Loss and challenge. *Journal of Counseling & Development*, 73, 390–396.

Spence, J. (1985). Achievement American style. *American Psychologist*, 40, 1285–1295.

Sue, D., Arredondo, P., & McDavis, R. (1992). Multicultural counseling competencies and standards: A call to the profession. *Journal of Multicultural Counseling and Development*, 20, 64–88.

Sue, S. and Zane, N. (1987). The role of culture and cultural techniques in psychology. *American Psychologist*, 42, 37–45.

Thomas, R. R., Jr. (1990). From affirmative action to affirming diversity. *Harvard Business Review*, March/April, 107–117.

Vontress, C. E. (1969). Cultural barriers in the counseling relationship. *Personnel and Guidance Journal*, 48, 153–180.

Weinrach, S. (1990). A psychosocial look at the Jewish dilemma. *Journal of Counseling & Development*, 68, 548–549.

Whitfield, D. (1994). Toward integrated approach to improving multicultural counselor education, *Journal of Multicultural Counseling and Development*, 22, 239–252.

Wrenn, C. (1962). The culturally encapsulated counselor. *Harvard Educational Review*, 32, 444–449.

Source: Reprinted from *Operationalization of the Multicultural Counselors Competencies*. Association for Multicultural Counseling and Development, a division of the American Counseling Association. Reprinted with permission.

APPENDIX L

Ethical Code for the International Association of Marriage and Family Counselors (2005)

PREAMBLE

The International Association of Marriage and Family Counselors (IAMFC) is an organization dedicated to advancing practice, training, and research in couple and family counseling. Members may specialize in areas such as premarital counseling, marriage counseling, family counseling, sex counseling, intergenerational counseling, separation and divorce counseling, relocation counseling, custody evaluation, and parenting training. Marriage and family counselors may work with special populations, including stepfamilies, nontraditional couples and family systems, multicultural couples and families, disadvantaged families, and dual career couples. In conducting their professional activities, members commit themselves to protect family relationships and advocate for the healthy growth and development of the family as a whole and each member's unique needs. The IAMFC member recognizes that the relationship between the provider and consumer of services is characterized as professional. However, the IAMFC member should remain informed of social and cultural trends as well as scientific and technological changes affecting the foundation of the professional counseling relationship.

This code of ethics provides a framework for ethical practices by IAMFC members and other professionals engaged in couple and family counseling. It is divided into eight sections: the counseling relationship and client well-being, confidentiality and privacy, competence and professional responsibilities collaboration and professional relationships, assessment and evaluation, counselor education and supervision, research and publication, and ethical decision making and resolution. The observations and recommendations presented within these eight areas are meant to supplement the current ethical standards of the American Counseling Association. Although an ethical code cannot anticipate every possible situation or dilemma, the IAMFC ethical guidelines can assist members in ensuring the welfare and dignity of the couples and families who seek services.

The ethical code of the International Association of Marriage and Family Counselors incorporates the ethics of principles and virtues. The code of ethics articulates some specific principles and guidelines, protecting consumers from potentially harmful practices and encouraging professionals to maintain high standards for effective practice. The ethical code also addresses the character of the professional couple and family counselor. Ethics of character or virtue contribute to professional aspirations and values. Each of the eight sections includes aspirations and principles.

SECTION A: THE COUNSELING RELATIONSHIP AND CLIENT WELL-BEING

Marriage and family counselors contribute to the healthy development and evolution of family systems. They are committed to understanding problems and learning needs from multiple contexts. Couple and family counselors, in particular, embrace models of practice based on family dynamics and systems. Professional counselors realize that their perspectives influence the conceptualization of problems, identification of clients, and implementation of possible solutions. Couple and family counselors examine personal biases and values. They actively attempt to understand and serve couples and families from diverse cultural backgrounds. Professional marriage and family counselors are willing to remove barriers to the counseling relationship, act as responsible public servants, and become involved in advocacy in the best interests of couples and families.

1. Marriage and family counselors demonstrate caring, empathy, and respect for client well-being. They promote safety, security, and sense of community for couples and families. Due to potential risks involved, couple and family counselors should not use intrusive interventions without sound theoretical rationale, research support, and clinical consultation or supervision.

2. Marriage and family counselors recognize that each family is unique. Couple and family counselors do not promote bias and stereotyping regarding family roles and functions.

3. Marriage and family counselors respect the autonomy of the families with whom they work. They do not make decisions that rightfully belong to family members. When indicated and possible, couple and family counselors share with clients' clinical impressions and recommendations, decision-making processes, problem-solving strategies, and intervention outcomes.

4. Marriage and family counselors respect cultural diversity. They do not discriminate on the basis of race, gender, disability, religion, age, sexual orientation, cultural background, national origin, marital status, or political affiliation.

5. Marriage and family counselors promote open, honest and direct relationships with consumers of professional services. Couple and family counselors inform clients about the goals of counseling, qualifications of the counselor(s), limits of confidentiality, potential risks and benefits associated with specific techniques, duration of treatment, costs

of services, appropriate alternatives to marriage and family counseling, and reasonable expectations for outcomes.

6. Marriage and family counselors promote primary prevention. They advocate for the development of clients' cognitive, moral, social, emotional, spiritual, physical, educational, relational, and vocational skills. Couple and family counselors promote effective marital and family communication and problem solving skills needed to prevent future problems.

7. Marriage and family counselors have an obligation to determine and inform counseling participants who is identified as the primary client. The marriage and family counselor should make clear when there are obligations to an individual, a couple, a family, a third party, or an institution.

8. Marriage and family counselors who are IAMFC members have a professional duty to monitor their places of employment to make recommendations so the environment is conductive to the positive growth and development of clients. When there is a conflict of interest between the needs of the client and counselor's employing institution, the IAMFC member works to clarify his or her commitment to all parties. IAMFC members recognize that the acceptance of employment implies agreement with the policies and practices of the agency or institution.

9. Marriage and family counselors do not harass, exploit, coerce, or manipulate clients for personal gain. Couple and family counselors avoid, whenever possible, multiple relationships, such as business, social, or sexual contacts with any current clients or their family members. Marriage and family counselors should refrain generally from nonprofessional relationships with former clients and their family members because termination of counseling is a complex process. Couple and family counselors are responsible for demonstrating there is no harm from any relationship with a client or family member. The key element in this ethical principle is the avoidance of exploitation of vulnerable clients.

10. Marriage and family counselors have an obligation to withdraw from a counseling relationship if the continuation of services would not be in the best interest of the client or would result in a violation of ethical standards. If the counseling relationship is no longer helpful or productive, couple and family counselors have an obligation to assist in locating alternative services and making referrals as needed. Marriage and family counselors do not abandon clients. They arrange for appropriate termination of counseling relationships and transfer of services as indicated.

11. Marriage and family counselors maintain accurate and up-to-date records. They make all file information available to clients unless there is compelling evidence that such access would be harmful to the client. In situations involving multiple clients, couple and family counselors provide individual clients with parts of records related directly to them, protecting confidential information related to other clients who have not authorized release. Marriage and family counselors include sufficient and timely documentation in client records to facilitate delivery of services and referral to other professionals as needed.

12. Marriage and family counselors establish fees that are reasonable and customary depending upon the scope and location of their practices. Couple and family counselors in community agencies, schools, and other public settings do not solicit gifts or charge fees for services that are available

in the counselor's employing agency or institution. Culturally sensitive counselors recognize that gifts are tokens of respect and gratitude in some cultures. Marriage and family counselors may receive gifts or participate in family rituals that promote healthy interaction and do not exploit clients.

13. Marriage and family counselors maintain ethical and effective practices as they address the benefits and limitations of technological innovations and cultural changes. Counseling may be conducted or assisted by telephones, computer hardware and software, and other communication technologies. Technology-assisted distance counseling services may expand the scope and influence of marriage and family counseling. However, counselors are responsible for developing competencies in the use of new technologies and safeguarding private and confidential information.

SECTION B: CONFIDENTIALITY AND PRIVACY

Marriage and family counselors recognize that trust is the foundation of an effective counseling relationship. Professional counselors maintain appropriate boundaries so that clients reasonably expect that information shared will not be disclosed to others without prior written consent. Due to the nature of couple and family counseling, safeguards must be established in the counseling process to insure privacy of client disclosures without contributing to dysfunctional family secrets. Clients have the right to know the limits of confidentiality, privacy, and privileged communication.

1. Marriage and family counselors may disclose private information to others under specific circumstances known to the individual client or client family members. Ideally, the client consents to disclosure by signing an authorization to release information. Each person receiving counseling who is legally competent to sign a waiver of right to confidentiality should execute an authorization. The authorization should clearly indicate to whom information will be disclosed under which specific circumstances. The authorization should be time limited, consistent with legal statutes, and limited to the scope agreed by the counselor and client. The client may rescind or withdraw the authorization.

2. Marriage and family counselors inform parents and legal guardians about the confidential nature of the counseling relationship. When working with minor or juvenile clients, as well as adult clients who lack the capacity to authorize release of confidential information, couple and family counselors seek consent from the appropriate custodial parent or guardian to disclose information.

3. Marriage and family counselors inform clients of exceptions to the general principle that information will be kept confidential or released only upon written client authorization. Disclosure of private information may be mandated by state law. For example, states require reporting of suspected abuse of children or other vulnerable populations. Couple and family counselors may have sound legal or ethical justification for disclosing information if someone is in imminent danger. A court may have jurisdiction to order lease of confidential information without a client's permission. However, all releases of information not authorized by

clients should be minimal or narrow as possible to limit potential harm to the counseling relationship.

4. Marriage and family counselors inform clients who may have access to their counseling records, as well as any information that may be released for third-party payment or insurance reimbursement. State and Federal laws may affect record keeping and release of information from client records.

5. Marriage and family counselors store records in a way that protects confidentiality. Written records should be kept in a locked file drawer or cabinet, and computerized record systems should have appropriate passwords and safeguards to prevent unauthorized entry.

6. Marriage and family counselors inform clients if sessions are to be recorded on tape or digital media and obtain written consent authorizing recording for particular purposes. When more than one person is receiving counseling, all persons who are legally competent must give informed consent in writing for the recording.

7. Marriage and family counselors inform clients that statements made by a family member to the counselor during an individual counseling, consultation, or collateral contact are to be treated as confidential. Such statements are not disclosed to other family members without the individual's permission. However, the marriage and family counselors should clearly identify the client of counseling, which may be the couple or family system. Couple and family counselors do not maintain family secrets, collude with some family members against others or otherwise contribute to dysfunctional family system dynamics. If a client's refusal to share information from individual contacts interferes with the agreed goals of counseling, the counselor may terminate treatment and refer the clients to another counselor. Some marriage and family counselors choose to not meet with individuals, preferring to serve family systems.

8. Marriage and family counselors provide reasonable access to counseling records when requested by competent clients. In situations involving multiple clients, counselors provide only the records directly related to a particular individual, protecting confidential information related to any other client.

9. Marriage and family counselors provide reasonable access to counseling records of minor children when requested by parents or guardians having legal rights to custody and health decision making. However, counselors do not become embroiled in custody disputes or parent and child conflicts occasioned by records release. Professional counselors attempt to protect the counseling relationship with children by suggesting limits to disclosure appropriate to the particular situation.

10. Marriage and family counselors maintain privacy and confidentiality in research, publication, case consultation, teaching, supervision, and other professional activities. Ideally, counselors secure informed consent and authorization to release information in all professional activities.

SECTION C: COMPETENCE AND PROFESSIONAL RESPONSIBILITIES

Marriage and family counselors aspire to maintain competency through initial training, ongoing supervision and consultation, and continuing education. They have responsibilities to abide by this ethical code as well as other professional codes related to professional identity and group membership. In particular, couple and family counselors should become active in professional associations such as the International Association of Marriage and Family Counselors and the American Counseling Association to encourage beneficial changes in professionals and the counseling profession.

1. Marriage and family counselors have the responsibility to develop and maintain basic skills in marriage and family counseling through graduate training, supervision, and consultation. An outline of these skills is provided by the current Council for Accreditation of Counseling and Related Educational Programs (CACREP) *Standards for Marital, Couple, and Family Counseling/Therapy Programs.* The minimal level of training shall be considered a master's degree in a helping profession.

2. Marriage and family counselors recognize the need for familiarizing oneself with new developments in the field of marriage and family counseling. They pursue continuing education afforded by books, journals, courses, workshops, conferences, and conventions.

3. Marriage and family counselors accurately represent their education, expertise, training, and experience. Professional counselors objectively represent their professional qualifications, skills, and specialties to the public. Membership in a professional organization, including IAMFC, is not used to suggest competency.

4. Marriage and family counselors insure that announcements or advertisements of professional services focus on objective information that enables the client to make an informed decision. Providing information, such as highest relevant academic degree, licenses or certifications, office hours, types of services offered, fee structure, and languages spoken, can help clients select marriage and family counselors.

5. Marriage and family counselors do not attempt to diagnose or treat problems beyond the scope of their training and abilities. They do not engage in specialized counseling interventions or techniques unless they have received appropriate training and preparation in the methods.

6. Marriage and family counselors do not undertake any professional activity in which their personal problems might adversely affect their performance. Instead, they focus on obtaining appropriate professional assistance to help them resolve the problem.

7. Marriage and family counselors do not engage in actions that violate the legal standards of their community. They do not encourage clients or others to engage in unlawful activities.

8. Marriage and family counselors have the responsibility to provide public information that enhances marriage and family life. Such statements should be based on sound, scientifically acceptable theories, techniques, and approaches. Due to the inability to complete a comprehensive assessment and provide follow-up, members should not give specific advice to an individual through the media.

9. Marriage and family counselors produce advertisements about workshops or seminars that contain descriptions of the audiences for which the programs are intended. Due to their subjective nature, statements either from clients or from the counselor about the uniqueness, effectiveness, or efficiency of services should be avoided. Announcements and advertisements should never contain false, misleading, or fraudulent statements.

10. Marriage and family counselors promoting tapes, books, or other products for commercial sale make every effort to insure that announcements and advertisements are presented in a professional and factual manner.

SECTION D: COLLABORATION AND PROFESSIONAL RELATIONSHIPS

Marriage and family counselors work to maintain good relationships with professional peers within and outside the field of counseling. Consultation and collaboration represent means by which couple and family counselors can remove barriers to underserved populations. Interdisciplinary team-work may be required to best serve clients.

1. Marriage and family counselors are knowledgeable about the roles and functions of other disciplines, especially in the helping professions such as psychiatry, psychology, social work, and mental health counseling. Counselors work to strengthen interdisciplinary relations with colleagues.
2. Marriage and family counselors enter into professional partnerships in which each partner adheres to the ethical standards of their professions. Couple and family counselors should not charge a fee for offering or accepting referrals.
3. Marriage and family counselors do not engage in harmful relationships with individuals over whom they have supervisory, evaluative, or instructional control. They do not engage in harassment or other abuses of power or authority.
4. Marriage and family counselors work to insure the ethical delivery of effective services in any agency or institution in which they are employed. Couple and family counselors engaging in consultation and collaboration take responsibility for the well-being and ethical treatment of clients. Counselors alert administrators about inappropriate policies and practices in institutions they serve.
5. Marriage and family counselors working as subcontractors for counseling services for a third party have a duty to inform clients of limitations that the organization may place on the counseling or consulting relationship.
6. Marriage and family counselors maintain good working relationships with team members and collaborators. They promote healthy boundaries and organizational climate. Couple and family counselors refrain from becoming involved in splitting, triangulation, and indirect forms of communication that could be harmful to colleagues or the organization they share.
7. Marriage and family counselors do not offer services to clients served by other professionals without securing a referral or release. The counselor should be authorized by the client to contact the other professional to coordinate or transfer care. There may be special considerations regarding transfer of care in the termination of an abusive counseling relationship.

SECTION E: ASSESSMENT AND EVALUATION

Marriage and family counselors are highly skilled in relational and interpersonal assessment. They recognize the potential values to clients from appropriate educational, psychological, and vocational evaluation. However, marriage and family counselors are sensitive to misuse and abuse of assessment results. Counselors avoid, whenever possible, evaluation, assessment, or diagnosis that restricts the overall development and freedom of choice of individuals, couples, and families. Recognizing the origins of marriage and family counseling in systems thinking, they avoid, whenever possible, assigning problems to individuals. Instead, professional counselors aspire to identify solutions that promote the well-being of family systems.

1. Marriage and family counselors use assessment procedures to promote the best interests and well-being of the client in clarifying concerns, establishing treatment goals, evaluating therapeutic progress, and promoting objective decision making.
2. Marriage and family counselors recognize that clients have the right to know the results, interpretations, and conclusions drawn from assessment interviews and instruments, as well as how this information will be used. Couple and family counselors safeguard assessment data and maintain the confidentiality of evaluation records and reports.
3. Marriage and family counselors use assessment methods that are reliable, valid, and relevant to the goals of the client. Couple and family counselors using tests or inventories should have a thorough understanding of measurement concepts, including relevant psychometric and normative data. When using computer-assisted scoring, counselors obtain empirical evidence for the reliability and validity of the methods and procedures.
4. Marriage and family counselors do not use inventories and tests that have outdated items or normative data. They refrain from using assessment instruments and techniques likely to be biased or prejudiced.
5. Marriage and family counselors do not use assessment methods that are outside the scope of their qualifications, training, or statutory limitations. They consult with psychologists, mental health counselors, or other professional colleagues in interpreting and understanding particular test results.
6. Marriage and family counselors conducting custody evaluations recognize the potential impact that their reports can have on family members. They are committed to a thorough assessment of both parents. Therefore, custody recommendations should not be made on the basis of information from only one parent. Couple and family counselors only use instruments that have demonstrated reliability, validity, and utility in custody evaluations. They do not make recommendations based solely on test and inventory scores.
7. Members strive to follow current guidelines and standards for testing published or disseminated by the American Counseling Association, American Educational Research Association, American Psychological Association, Association for Assessment in Counseling and Education, National Council on Measurement in Evaluation, and other groups dedicated to professional expertise in assessment.

SECTION F: COUNSELOR EDUCATION AND SUPERVISION

Marriage and family counselors are likely to engage in some training and supervision activities, including peer consultation and supervision. Couple and family counselors recognize potential power imbalances in teacher and student, supervisor and supervisee, and consultant and consultee relationships. They do not abuse power or influence and work to protect students, supervisees, and consultees from exploitation. Marriage and family counselors maintain appropriate boundaries that promote growth and development for all parties. They recognize and respect cultural differences, adjusting their professional efforts to fit the learning needs of trainees.

1. Marriage and family counselors who provide supervision acquire and maintain skills pertaining to the supervision process. They are able to demonstrate for supervisees the application of counseling theory and process to client issues. Supervisors are knowledgeable about different methods and conceptual approaches to supervision.

2. Marriage and family counselors who provide supervision respect the inherent imbalance of power in the supervisory relationship. They do not use their potentially influential positions to exploit students, supervisees or employees. Supervisors do not ask supervisees to engage in behaviors not directly related to the supervision process, and they clearly separate supervision and evaluation. Supervisors also avoid multiple relationships that might impair their professional judgment or increase the possibility of exploitation. Sexual intimacy with students or supervisees is prohibited.

3. Marriage and family counselors who provide supervision are responsible for both the promotion of supervisee learning and development and the advancement of marriage and family counseling. Supervisors recruit students into professional organizations, educate students about professional ethics and standards, provide service to professional organizations, strive to educate new professionals, and work to improve professional practices.

4. Marriage and family counselors who provide supervision have the responsibility to inform students of the specific expectations regarding skill building, knowledge acquisition, and development of competencies. Supervisors also provide ongoing and timely feedback to their supervisees.

5. Marriage and family counselors who provide supervision are responsible for protecting the rights and well-being of their supervisees' clients. They monitor their supervisees' counseling on an ongoing basis and maintain policies and procedures to protect the confidentiality of clients whose sessions have been electronically recorded.

6. Marriage and family counselors who provide supervision maintain ethical standards for counselor supervision. Counselor educators and supervisors may consult publications of the Association for Counselor Education and Supervision to clarify ethical issues in supervisory relationships.

7. Marriage and family counselors who are counselor educators encourage their programs to maintain the current guidelines provided in the CACREP *Standards for Marital, Couple, and Family Counseling/Therapy Programs.* They also encourage training programs to offer coursework and supervision indicated by particular accreditation boards.

8. Marriage and family counselors involved in training and supervision, especially educators and students, should explore ethical principles as well as aspirational goals. Counselor educators should infuse ethical studies throughout the curriculum.

9. Marriage and family counselors refer to the current American Counseling Association *Code of Ethics* as a source document for training and supervision in professional counseling.

SECTION G: RESEARCH AND PUBLICATION

Marriage and family counselors should engage in research and publication that advances the profession of marriage and family counseling. They act to prevent harm to research participants and produce results that are beneficial to couples and families. Couple and family counselors maintain high ethical standards for informed consent and protection of confidentiality when conducting research projects or producing publications. They solicit input from peers, institutional review boards, and other stakeholders to minimize risks and enhance outcomes.

1. Marriage and family counselors shall be fully responsible for their choice of research topics and the methods used for investigation, analysis, and reporting. They must be particularly careful that findings do not appear misleading, that the research is planned to allow for the inclusion of alternative hypotheses, and that provision is made for discussion of the limitations of the study.

2. Marriage and family counselors safeguard the privacy of their research participants. Data about an individual participant are not released unless the individual is informed about the exact nature of the information to be released and gives written permission for disclosure.

3. Marriage and family counselors protect the safety of their research participants. Researchers follow guidelines of a peer review committee or institutional research board. Prospective participants are informed in writing about any potential risk associated with a study and are notified that they can withdraw at any time.

4. Marriage and family counselors make their original data available to other researchers. They contribute to the advancement of the field by encouraging the research and publication efforts of colleagues.

5. Marriage and family counselors only take credit for research in which they make a substantial contribution and give credit to all contributors. Authors are listed from greatest to least amount of contribution.

6. Marriage and family counselors do not plagiarize. Ideas or data that did not originate with the author and are not common knowledge are clearly credited to the original source.

7. Marriage and family counselors are aware of their obligation to be role models for graduate students and other future researchers and act in accordance with the highest standards possible while engaged in research and publication.

8. Marriage and family counselors review materials submitted for research, publication, and other scholarly purposes. They respect the confidentiality and proprietary rights of those who submit their products for review. Counselors engaged in reviews of manuscripts and presentation proposals use valid and defensible standards, act within the limits of their competencies, and refrain from personal biases. In this manner, authors and researchers are supported and the field of marriage and family counseling is advanced.

SECTION H: ETHICAL DECISION MAKING AND RESOLUTION

Marriage and family counselors incorporate ethical practices in their daily work. They discuss ethical dilemmas with colleagues and engage in ethical decision making in all aspects of marriage and family counseling. They hold other counselors to sound ethical principles and encourage professional virtues and aspirations. Couple and family counselors work with other professionals to resolve ethical issues.

1. Marriage and family counselors are responsible for understanding the American Counseling Association *Code of Ethics*, the *Ethical Code of the International Association of Marriage and Family Counselors*, and other applicable ethics codes from professional associations, certification and licensure boards, and other credentialing organizations by which they are regulated.

2. Marriage and family counselors have the responsibility to confront unethical behavior of other counselors or therapists, particularly members of the International Association of Marriage and Family Counselors (IAMFC). The first step should be discussing the violation directly with the caregiver. If the problem continues, the marriage and family counselor may contact the professional organization or licensure board of the counselor or therapist in question. IAMFC members may contact the executive director, president, executive board members, or chair of the ethics committee at any time for consultation on identifying or resolving ethical violations.

3. Marriage and family counselors specify the nature of conflicts between work requirements and other demands of an employing organization and the relevant codes of ethics.

Employment and consultation of couple and family counselors should not compromise ethical standards. They work toward beneficial changes in the organizations of which they are members.

4. Marriage and family counselors do not engage in unwarranted or invalid complaints. Ethics violations are reported when informal attempts at resolution have failed or violations are likely to substantially harm an individual or organization. Couple and family counselors should follow the reporting requirements specified by laws and regulations in their jurisdictions.

5. Marriage and family counselors cooperate with ethics committees and other duly constituted organizations having jurisdiction over the professional charged with an ethics violation. Counselors assist professional associations in promoting ethical behavior and professional conduct.

The members of the Ethics committee who completed the revision of the Ethical Code are the following:

Stephen Southern, *Chair of the Ethics Committee.*

Marvarene Oliver, *Department of Counseling and Educational Psychology, Texas A & M University-Corpus Christi.*

Loretta J. Bradley, *Department of Counselor Education, Texas Tech University.*

Bobbie Birdsall, *Counselor Education Department, Boise State University.*

Source: Reprinted from *The Family Journal: Counseling and Therapy for Couples and Families.* Vol. 14, no. 1, January 2006. Reprinted by Permission.

APPENDIX M
AAMFT® Code of Ethics (2001)

PREAMBLE

The Board of Directors of the American Association for Marriage and Family Therapy (AAMFT) hereby promulgates, pursuant to Article 2, Section 2.013 of the Association's Bylaws, the Revised AAMFT Code of Ethics, effective July 1, 2001.

The AAMFT strives to honor the public trust in marriage and family therapists by setting standards for ethical practice as described in this Code. The ethical standards define professional expectations and are enforced by the AAMFT Ethics Committee. The absence of an explicit reference to a specific behavior or situation in the Code does not mean that the behavior is ethical or unethical. The standards are not exhaustive. Marriage and family therapists who are uncertain about the ethics of a particular course of action are encouraged to seek counsel from consultants, attorneys, supervisors, colleagues, or other appropriate authorities.

Both law and ethics govern the practice of marriage and family therapy. When making decisions regarding professional behavior, marriage and family therapists must consider the AAMFT Code of Ethics and applicable laws and regulations. If the AAMFT Code of Ethics prescribes a standard higher than that required by law, marriage and family therapists must meet the higher standard of the AAMFT Code of Ethics. Marriage and family therapists comply with the mandates of law, but make known their commitment to the AAMFT Code of Ethics and take steps to resolve the conflict in a responsible manner. The AAMFT supports legal mandates for reporting of alleged unethical conduct.

The AAMFT Code of Ethics is binding on Members of AAMFT in all membership categories, AAMFT-Approved Supervisors, and applicants for membership and the Approved Supervisor designation (hereafter, AAMFT Member). AAMFT members have an obligation to be familiar with the AAMFT Code of Ethics and its application to their professional services. Lack of awareness or misunderstanding of an ethical standard is not a defense to a charge of unethical conduct.

The process for filing, investigating, and resolving complaints of unethical conduct is described in the current Procedures for Handling Ethical Matters of the AAMFT Ethics Committee. Persons accused are considered innocent by the Ethics Committee until proven guilty, except as otherwise provided, and are entitled to due process. If an AAMFT Member resigns in anticipation of, or during the course of, an ethics investigation, the Ethics Committee will complete its investigation. Any publication of action taken by the Association will include the fact that the Member attempted to resign during the investigation.

PRINCIPLE I: RESPONSIBILITY TO CLIENTS

Marriage and family therapists advance the welfare of families and individuals. They respect the rights of those persons seeking their assistance, and make reasonable efforts to ensure that their services are used appropriately.

1.1 Marriage and family therapists provide professional assistance to persons without discrimination on the basis of race, age, ethnicity, socioeconomic status, disability, gender, health status, religion, national origin, or sexual orientation.

1.2 Marriage and family therapists obtain appropriate informed consent to therapy or related procedures as early as feasible in the therapeutic relationship, and use language that is reasonably understandable to clients. The content of informed consent may vary depending upon the client and treatment plan; however, informed consent generally necessitates that the client: (a) has the capacity to consent; (b) has been adequately informed of significant information concerning treatment processes and procedures; (c) has been adequately informed of potential risks and benefits of treatments for which generally recognized standards do not yet exist; (d) has freely and without undue influence expressed consent; and (e) has provided consent that is appropriately documented. When persons, due to age or mental status, are legally incapable of giving informed consent, marriage and family therapists obtain informed permission from a legally authorized person, if such substitute consent is legally permissible.

1.3 Marriage and family therapists are aware of their influential positions with respect to clients, and they avoid exploiting the trust and dependency of such persons. Therapists, therefore, make every effort to avoid conditions and multiple relationships with clients that could impair professional judgment or increase the risk of exploitation. Such relationships include, but are not limited to, business or close personal relationships with a client or the client's immediate family. When the risk of impairment or exploitation exists due to conditions or multiple roles, therapists take appropriate precautions.

1.4 Sexual intimacy with clients is prohibited.

1.5 Sexual intimacy with former clients is likely to be harmful and is therefore prohibited for two years following the termination of therapy or last professional contact. In an effort to avoid exploiting the trust and dependency of clients, marriage and family therapists should not engage in sexual intimacy with former clients after the two years following termination or last professional contact. Should therapists engage in sexual intimacy with former clients following two years after termination or last professional contact, the burden shifts to the therapist to demonstrate that there has been no exploitation or injury to the former client or to the client's immediate family.

1.6 Marriage and family therapists comply with applicable laws regarding the reporting of alleged unethical conduct.

1.7 Marriage and family therapists do not use their professional relationships with clients to further their own interests.

1.8 Marriage and family therapists respect the rights of clients to make decisions and help them to understand the consequences of these decisions. Therapists clearly advise the clients that they have the responsibility to make decisions regarding relationships such as cohabitation, marriage, divorce, separation, reconciliation, custody, and visitation.

1.9 Marriage and family therapists continue therapeutic relationships only so long as it is reasonably clear that clients are benefiting from the relationship.

1.10 Marriage and family therapists assist persons in obtaining other therapeutic services if the therapist is unable or unwilling, for appropriate reasons, to provide professional help.

1.11 Marriage and family therapists do not abandon or neglect clients in treatment without making reasonable arrangements for the continuation of such treatment.

1.12 Marriage and family therapists obtain written informed consent from clients before videotaping, audio recording, or permitting third-party observation.

1.13 Marriage and family therapists, upon agreeing to provide services to a person or entity at the request of a third party, clarify, to the extent feasible and at the outset of the service, the nature of the relationship with each party and the limits of confidentiality.

PRINCIPLE II: CONFIDENTIALITY

Marriage and family therapists have unique confidentiality concerns because the client in a therapeutic relationship may be more than one person. Therapists respect and guard the confidences of each individual client.

2.1 Marriage and family therapists disclose to clients and other interested parties, as early as feasible in their professional contacts, the nature of confidentiality and possible limitations of the clients' right to confidentiality. Therapists review with clients the circumstances where confidential information may be requested and where disclosure of confidential information may be legally required. Circumstances may necessitate repeated disclosures.

2.2 Marriage and family therapists do not disclose client confidences except by written authorization or waiver, or where mandated or permitted by law. Verbal authorization will not be sufficient except in emergency situations, unless prohibited by law. When providing couple, family, or group treatment, the therapist does not disclose information outside the treatment context without a written authorization from each individual competent to execute a waiver. In the context of couple, family or group treatment, the therapist may not reveal any individual's confidences to others in the client unit without the prior written permission of that individual.

2.3 Marriage and family therapists use client and/or clinical materials in teaching, writing, consulting, research, and public presentations only if a written waiver has been obtained in accordance with Subprinciple 2.2, or when appropriate steps have been taken to protect client identity and confidentiality.

2.4 Marriage and family therapists store, safeguard, and dispose of client records in ways that maintain confidentiality and in accord with applicable laws and professional standards.

2.5 Subsequent to the therapist moving from the area, closing the practice, or upon the death of the therapist, a marriage and family therapist arranges for the storage, transfer, or disposal of client records in ways that maintain confidentiality and safeguard the welfare of clients.

2.6 Marriage and family therapists, when consulting with colleagues or referral sources, do not share confidential information that could reasonably lead to the identification of a client, research participant, supervisee, or other person with whom they have a confidential relationship unless they have obtained the prior written consent of the client, research participant, supervisee, or other person with whom they have a confidential relationship. Information may be shared only to the extent necessary to achieve the purposes of the consultation.

PRINCIPLE III: PROFESSIONAL COMPETENCE AND INTEGRITY

Marriage and family therapists maintain high standards of professional competence and integrity.

3.1 Marriage and family therapists pursue knowledge of new developments and maintain competence in marriage and family therapy through education, training, or supervised experience.

3.2 Marriage and family therapists maintain adequate knowledge of and adhere to applicable laws, ethics, and professional standards.

3.3 Marriage and family therapists seek appropriate professional assistance for their personal problems or conflicts that may impair work performance or clinical judgment.

3.4 Marriage and family therapists do not provide services that create a conflict of interest that may impair work performance or clinical judgment.

3.5 Marriage and family therapists, as presenters, teachers, supervisors, consultants, and researchers, are dedicated to high standards of scholarship, present accurate information, and disclose potential conflicts of interest.

3.6 Marriage and family therapists maintain accurate and adequate clinical and financial records.

3.7 While developing new skills in specialty areas, marriage and family therapists take steps to ensure the competence of their work and to protect clients from possible harm. Marriage and family therapists practice in specialty areas new to them only after appropriate education, training, or supervised experience.

3.8 Marriage and family therapists do not engage in sexual or other forms of harassment of clients, students, trainees, supervisees, employees, colleagues, or research subjects.

3.9 Marriage and family therapists do not engage in the exploitation of clients, students, trainees, supervisees, employees, colleagues, or research subjects.

3.10 Marriage and family therapists do not give to or receive from clients (a) gifts of substantial value or (b) gifts that impair the integrity or efficacy of the therapeutic relationship.

3.11 Marriage and family therapists do not diagnose, treat, or advise on problems outside the recognized boundaries of their competencies.

3.12 Marriage and family therapists make efforts to prevent the distortion or misuse of their clinical and research findings.

3.13 Marriage and family therapists, because of their ability to influence and alter the lives of others, exercise special care when making public their professional recommendations and opinions through testimony or other public statements.

3.14 To avoid a conflict of interest, marriage and family therapists who treat minors or adults involved in custody or visitation actions may not also perform forensic evaluations for custody, residence, or visitation of the minor. The marriage and family therapist who treats the minor may provide the court or mental health professional performing the evaluation with information about the minor from the marriage and family therapist's perspective as a treating marriage and family therapist, so long as the marriage and family therapist does not violate confidentiality.

3.15 Marriage and family therapists are in violation of this Code and subject to termination of membership or other appropriate action if they: (a) are convicted of any felony; (b) are convicted of a misdemeanor related to their qualifications or functions; (c) engage in conduct which could lead to conviction of a felony, or a misdemeanor related to their qualifications or functions; (d) are expelled from or disciplined by other professional organizations; (e) have their licenses or certificates suspended or revoked or are otherwise disciplined by regulatory bodies; (f) continue to practice marriage and family therapy while no longer competent to do so because they are impaired by physical or mental causes or the abuse of alcohol or other substances; or (g) fail to cooperate with the Association at any point from the inception of an ethical complaint through the completion of all proceedings regarding that complaint.

PRINCIPLE IV: RESPONSIBILITY TO STUDENTS AND SUPERVISEES

Marriage and family therapists do not exploit the trust and dependency of students and supervisees.

4.1 Marriage and family therapists are aware of their influential positions with respect to students and supervisees, and they avoid exploiting the trust and dependency of such persons. Therapists, therefore, make every effort to avoid conditions and multiple relationships that could impair professional objectivity or increase the risk of exploitation. When the risk of impairment or exploitation exists due to conditions or multiple roles, therapists take appropriate precautions.

4.2 Marriage and family therapists do not provide therapy to current students or supervisees.

4.3 Marriage and family therapists do not engage in sexual intimacy with students or supervisees during the evaluative or training relationship between the therapist and student or supervisee. Should a supervisor engage in sexual activity with a former supervisee, the burden of proof shifts to the supervisor to demonstrate that there has been no exploitation or injury to the supervisee.

4.4 Marriage and family therapists do not permit students or supervisees to perform or to hold themselves out as competent to perform professional services beyond their training, level of experience, and competence.

4.5 Marriage and family therapists take reasonable measures to ensure that services provided by supervisees are professional.

4.6 Marriage and family therapists avoid accepting as supervisees or students those individuals with whom a prior or existing relationship could compromise the therapist's objectivity. When such situations cannot be avoided, therapists take appropriate precautions to maintain objectivity. Examples of such relationships include, but are not limited to, those individuals with whom the therapist has a current or prior sexual, close personal, immediate familial, or therapeutic relationship.

4.7 Marriage and family therapists do not disclose supervisee confidences except by written authorization or waiver, or when mandated or permitted by law. In educational or training settings where there are multiple supervisors, disclosures are permitted only to other professional colleagues, administrators, or employers who share responsibility for training of the supervisee. Verbal authorization will not be sufficient except in emergency situations, unless prohibited by law.

PRINCIPLE V: RESPONSIBILITY TO RESEARCH PARTICIPANTS

Investigators respect the dignity and protect the welfare of research participants, and are aware of applicable laws and regulations and professional standards governing the conduct of research.

5.1 Investigators are responsible for making careful examinations of ethical acceptability in planning studies. To the extent that services to research participants may be compromised by participation in research, investigators seek the ethical advice of qualified professionals not directly involved in the investigation and observe safeguards to protect the rights of research participants.

5.2 Investigators requesting participant involvement in research inform participants of the aspects of the research that might reasonably be expected to influence willingness to participate. Investigators are especially sensitive to the possibility of diminished consent when participants are also receiving clinical services, or have impairments which limit understanding and/or communication, or when participants are children.

5.3 Investigators respect each participant's freedom to decline participation in or to withdraw from a research study at any time. This obligation requires special thought and consideration when investigators or other members of the research team are in positions of authority or influence over participants. Marriage and family therapists, therefore, make every effort to avoid multiple relationships with research participants that could impair professional judgment or increase the risk of exploitation.

5.4 Information obtained about a research participant during the course of an investigation is confidential unless there is a waiver previously obtained in writing. When the possibility exists that others, including family members, may obtain access to such information, this possibility, together with the plan for protecting confidentiality, is explained as part of the procedure for obtaining informed consent.

PRINCIPLE VI: RESPONSIBILITY TO THE PROFESSION

Marriage and family therapists respect the rights and responsibilities of professional colleagues and participate in activities that advance the goals of the profession.

6.1 Marriage and family therapists remain accountable to the standards of the profession when acting as members or employees of organizations. If the mandates of an organization with which a marriage and family therapist is affiliated, through employment, contract or otherwise, conflict with the AAMFT Code of Ethics, marriage and family therapists make known to the organization their commitment to the AAMFT Code of Ethics and attempt to resolve the conflict in a way that allows the fullest adherence to the Code of Ethics.

6.2 Marriage and family therapists assign publication credit to those who have contributed to a publication in proportion to their contributions and in accordance with customary professional publication practices.

6.3 Marriage and family therapists do not accept or require authorship credit for a publication based on research from a student's program, unless the therapist made a substantial contribution beyond being a faculty advisor or research committee member. Coauthorship on a student thesis, dissertation, or project should be determined in accordance with principles of fairness and justice.

6.4 Marriage and family therapists who are the authors of books or other materials that are published or distributed do not plagiarize or fail to cite persons to whom credit for original ideas or work is due.

6.5 Marriage and family therapists who are the authors of books or other materials published or distributed by an organization take reasonable precautions to ensure that the organization promotes and advertises the materials accurately and factually.

6.6 Marriage and family therapists participate in activities that contribute to a better community and society, including devoting a portion of their professional activity to services for which there is little or no financial return.

6.7 Marriage and family therapists are concerned with developing laws and regulations pertaining to marriage and family therapy that serve the public interest, and with altering such laws and regulations that are not in the public interest.

6.8 Marriage and family therapists encourage public participation in the design and delivery of professional services and in the regulation of practitioners.

PRINCIPLE VII: FINANCIAL ARRANGEMENTS

Marriage and family therapists make financial arrangements with clients, third-party payors, and supervisees that are reasonably understandable and conform to accepted professional practices.

7.1 Marriage and family therapists do not offer or accept kickbacks, rebates, bonuses, or other remuneration for referrals; fee-for-service arrangements are not prohibited.

7.2 Prior to entering into the therapeutic or supervisory relationship, marriage and family therapists clearly disclose and explain to clients and supervisees: (a) all financial arrangements and fees related to professional services, including charges for canceled or missed appointments; (b) the use of collection agencies or legal measures for nonpayment; and (c) the procedure for obtaining payment from the client, to the extent allowed by law, if payment is denied by the third-party payor. Once services have begun, therapists provide reasonable notice of any changes in fees or other charges.

7.3 Marriage and family therapists give reasonable notice to clients with unpaid balances of their intent to seek collection by agency or legal recourse. When such action is taken, therapists will not disclose clinical information.

7.4 Marriage and family therapists represent facts truthfully to clients, third-party payors, and supervisees regarding services rendered.

7.5 Marriage and family therapists ordinarily refrain from accepting goods and services from clients in return for services rendered. Bartering for professional services may be conducted only if: (a) the supervisee or client requests it, (b) the relationship is not exploitative, (c) the professional relationship is not distorted, and (d) a clear written contract is established.

7.6 Marriage and family therapists may not withhold records under their immediate control that are requested and needed for a client's treatment solely because payment has not been received for past services, except as otherwise provided by law.

PRINCIPLE VIII: ADVERTISING

Marriage and family therapists engage in appropriate informational activities, including those that enable the public, referral sources, or others to choose professional services on an informed basis.

8.1 Marriage and family therapists accurately represent their competencies, education, training, and experience relevant to their practice of marriage and family therapy.

8.2 Marriage and family therapists ensure that advertisements and publications in any media (such as directories, announcements, business cards, newspapers, radio, television, Internet, and facsimiles) convey information that is necessary for the public to make an appropriate selection of professional services. Information could include: (a) office information, such as name, address, telephone number, credit card acceptability, fees, languages spoken, and office hours; (b) qualifying clinical degree (see Subprinciple 8.5); (c) other earned degrees (see Subprinciple 8.5) and state or provincial licensures and/or certifications; (d) AAMFT clinical member status; and (e) description of practice.

8.3 Marriage and family therapists do not use names that could mislead the public concerning the identity, responsibility, source, and status of those practicing under that name, and do not hold themselves out as being partners or associates of a firm if they are not.

8.4 Marriage and family therapists do not use any professional identification (such as a business card, office sign, letterhead, Internet, or telephone or association directory listing) if it includes a statement or claim that is false, fraudulent, misleading, or deceptive.

8.5 In representing their educational qualifications, marriage and family therapists list and claim as evidence only those earned degrees: (a) from institutions accredited by regional accreditation sources recognized by the United States Department of Education, (b) from institutions recognized by states or provinces that license or certify marriage and family therapists, or (c) from equivalent foreign institutions.

8.6 Marriage and family therapists correct, wherever possible, false, misleading, or inaccurate information and representations made by others concerning the therapist's qualifications, services, or products.

8.7 Marriage and family therapists make certain that the qualifications of their employees or supervisees are represented in a manner that is not false, misleading, or deceptive.

8.8 Marriage and family therapists do not represent themselves as providing specialized services unless they have the appropriate education, training, or supervised experience.

Violations of this Code should be brought in writing to the attention of: AAMFT Ethics Committee, 1133 15th Street, NW, Suite 300, Washington, D.C. 20005-2710. Effective July 1, 2001. (telephone 202/452-0109) (email: *ethics@aamft.org*).

APPENDIX N
Ethical Standards for School Counselors (2004)

ASCA's Ethical Standards for School Counselors were adopted by the ASCA Delegate Assembly, March 19, 1984, revised March 27, 1992, June 25, 1998 and June 26, 2004.

PREAMBLE

The American School Counselor Association (ASCA) is a professional organization whose members are certified/licensed in school counseling with unique qualifications and skills to address the academic, personal/social and career development needs of all students. Professional school counselors are advocates, leaders, collaborators and consultants who create opportunities for equity in access and success in educational opportunities by connecting their programs to the mission of schools and subscribing to the following tenets of professional responsibility:

- Each person has the right to be respected, be treated with dignity and have access to a comprehensive school counseling program that advocates for and affirms all students from diverse populations regardless of ethnic/racial status, age, economic status, special needs, English as a second language or other language group, immigration status, sexual orientation, gender, gender identity/expression, family type, religious/spiritual identity and appearance.
- Each person has the right to receive the information and support needed to move toward self-direction and self-development and affirmation within one's group identities, with special care being given to students who have historically not received adequate educational services: students of color, low socioeconomic students, students with disabilities and students with nondominant language backgrounds.
- Each person has the right to understand the full magnitude and meaning of his/her educational choices and how those choices will affect future opportunities.
- Each person has the right to privacy and thereby the right to expect the counselor–student relationship to comply with all laws, policies and ethical standards pertaining to confidentiality in the school setting.

In this document, ASCA specifies the principles of ethical behavior necessary to maintain the high standards of integrity, leadership and professionalism among its members. The Ethical Standards for School Counselors were developed to clarify the nature of ethical responsibilities held in common by school counseling professionals. The purposes of this document are to:

- Serve as a guide for the ethical practices of all professional school counselors regardless of level, area, population served or membership in this professional association;
- Provide self-appraisal and peer evaluations regarding counselor responsibilities to students, parents/guardians, colleagues and professional associates, schools, communities and the counseling profession; and
- Inform those served by the school counselor of acceptable counselor practices and expected professional behavior.

A.1. Responsibilities to Students

The professional school counselor:

a. Has a primary obligation to the student, who is to be treated with respect as a unique individual.
b. Is concerned with the educational, academic, career, personal and social needs and encourages the maximum development of every student.
c. Respects the student's values and beliefs and does not impose the counselor's personal values.
d. Is knowledgeable of laws, regulations and policies relating to students and strives to protect and inform students regarding their rights.

A.2. Confidentiality

The professional school counselor:

a. Informs students of the purposes, goals, techniques and rules of procedure under which they may receive counseling at or before the time when the counseling relationship is entered. Disclosure notice includes the limits of confidentiality such as the possible necessity for consulting with other professionals, privileged communication, and legal or authoritative restraints. The meaning and limits of confidentiality are defined in developmentally appropriate terms to students.
b. Keeps information confidential unless disclosure is required to prevent clear and imminent danger to the student or others or when legal requirements demand that confidential information be revealed. Counselors will consult with appropriate professionals when in doubt as to the validity of an exception.
c. In absence of state legislation expressly forbidding disclosure, considers the ethical responsibility to provide information to an identified third party who, by his/her relationship with the student, is at a high risk of contracting a disease that is commonly known to be communicable and fatal. Disclosure requires satisfaction of all of the following conditions:
    - Student identifies partner or the partner is highly identifiable
    - Counselor recommends the student notify partner and refrain from further high-risk behavior
    - Student refuses
    - Counselor informs the student of the intent to notify the partner
    - Counselor seeks legal consultation as to the legalities of informing the partner

d. Requests of the court that disclosure not be required when the release of confidential information may potentially harm a student or the counseling relationship.

e. Protects the confidentiality of students' records and releases personal data in accordance with prescribed laws and school policies. Student information stored and transmitted electronically is treated with the same care as traditional student records.

f. Protects the confidentiality of information received in the counseling relationship as specified by federal and state laws, written policies and applicable ethical standards. Such information is only to be revealed to others with the informed consent of the student, consistent with the counselor's ethical obligation.

g. Recognizes his/her primary obligation for confidentiality is to the student but balances that obligation with an understanding of the legal and inherent rights of parents/guardians to be the guiding voice in their children's lives.

A.3. Counseling Plans

The professional school counselor:

a. Provides students with a comprehensive school counseling program that includes a strong emphasis on working jointly with all students to develop academic and career goals.

b. Advocates for counseling plans supporting students' right to choose from the wide array of options when they leave secondary education. Such plans will be regularly reviewed to update students regarding critical information they need to make informed decisions.

A.4. Dual Relationships

The professional school counselor:

a. Avoids dual relationships that might impair his/her objectivity and increase the risk of harm to the student (e.g., counseling one's family members, close friends or associates). If a dual relationship is unavoidable, the counselor is responsible for taking action to eliminate or reduce the potential for harm. Such safeguards might include informed consent, consultation, supervision and documentation.

b. Avoids dual relationships with school personnel that might infringe on the integrity of the counselor/student relationship.

A.5. Appropriate Referrals

The professional school counselor:

a. Make referrals when necessary or appropriate to outside resources. Appropriate referrals may necessitate informing both parents/guardians and students of applicable resources and making proper plans for transitions with minimal interruption of services. Students retain the right to discontinue the counseling relationship at any time.

A.6. Group Work

The professional school counselor:

a. Screens prospective group members and maintains an awareness of participants' needs and goals in relation to the goals of the group. The counselor takes reasonable precautions to protect members from physical and psychological harm resulting from interaction within the group.

b. Notifies parents/guardians and staff of group participation if the counselor deems it appropriate and if consistent with school board policy or practice.

c. Establishes clear expectations in the group setting and clearly states that confidentiality in group counseling cannot be guaranteed. Given the developmental and chronological ages of minors in schools, the counselor recognizes the tenuous nature of confidentiality for minors renders some topics inappropriate for group work in a school setting.

d. Follows up with group members and documents proceedings as appropriate.

A.7. Danger to Self or Others

The professional school counselor:

a. Informs parents/guardians or appropriate authorities when the student's condition indicates a clear and imminent danger to the student or others. This is to be done after careful deliberation and, where possible, after consultation with other counseling professionals.

b. Will attempt to minimize threat to a student and may choose to 1) inform the student of actions to be taken, 2) involve the student in a three-way communication with parents/guardians when breaching confidentiality or 3) allow the student to have input as to how and to whom the breach will be made.

A.8. Student Records

The professional school counselor:

a. Maintains and secures records necessary for rendering professional services to the student as required by laws, regulations, institutional procedures and confidentiality guidelines.

b. Keeps sole-possession records separate from students' educational records in keeping with state laws.

c. Recognizes the limits of sole-possession records and understands these records are a memory aid for the creator and in absence of privilege communication may be subpoenaed and may become educational records when they 1) are shared with others in verbal or written form, 2) include information other than professional opinion or personal observations and/or 3) are made accessible to others.

d. Establishes a reasonable timeline for purging sole-possession records or case notes. Suggested guidelines include shredding sole possession records when the student transitions to the next level, transfers to another school or graduates. Careful discretion and deliberation should be applied before destroying sole-possession records that may be needed by a court of law such as notes on child abuse, suicide, sexual harassment or violence.

A.9. Evaluation, Assessment and Interpretation

The professional school counselor:

a. Adheres to all professional standards regarding selecting, administering and interpreting assessment measures and only utilizes assessment measures that are within the scope of practice for school counselors.

b. Seeks specialized training regarding the use of electronically based testing programs in administering, scoring and interpreting that may differ from that required in more traditional assessments.

c. Considers confidentiality issues when utilizing evaluative or assessment instruments and electronically based programs.

d. Provides interpretation of the nature, purposes, results and potential impact of assessment/evaluation measures in language the student(s) can understand.

e. Monitors the use of assessment results and interpretations, and takes reasonable steps to prevent others from misusing the information.

f. Uses caution when utilizing assessment techniques, making evaluations and interpreting the performance of populations not represented in the norm group on which an instrument is standardized.

g. Assesses the effectiveness of his/her program in having an impact on students' academic, career and personal/social development through accountability measures especially examining efforts to close achievement, opportunity, and attainment gaps.

A.10. Technology

The professional school counselor:

a. Promotes the benefits of and clarifies the limitations of various appropriate technological applications. The counselor promotes technological applications (1) that are appropriate for the student's individual needs, (2) that the student understands how to use and (3) for which follow-up counseling assistance is provided.

b. Advocates for equal access to technology for all students, especially those historically underserved.

c. Takes appropriate and reasonable measures for maintaining confidentiality of student information and educational records stored or transmitted over electronic media including although not limited to fax, electronic mail, and instant messaging.

d. While working with students on a computer or similar technology, takes reasonable and appropriate measures to protect students from objectionable and/or harmful online material.

e. Who is engaged in the delivery of services involving technologies such as the telephone, videoconferencing, and the Internet, takes responsible steps to protect students and others from harm.

A.11. Student Peer Support Program

The professional school counselor:

Has unique responsibilities when working with student-assistance programs. The school counselor is responsible for the welfare of students participating in peer-to-peer programs under his/her direction.

B. RESPONSIBILITIES TO PARENTS/GUARDIANS

B.1. Parent Rights and Responsibilities

The professional school counselor:

a. Respects the rights and responsibilities of parents/guardians for their children and endeavors to establish, as appropriate, a collaborative relationship with parents/guardians to facilitate the student's maximum development.

b. Adheres to laws, local guidelines and ethical standards of practice when assisting parents/guardians experiencing family difficulties that interfere with the student's effectiveness and welfare.

c. Respects the confidentiality of parents/guardians.

d. Is sensitive to diversity among families and recognizes that all parents/guardians, custodial and noncustodial, are vested with certain rights and responsibilities for the welfare of their children by virtue of their role and according to law.

B.2. Parents/Guardians and Confidentiality

The professional school counselor:

a. Informs parents/guardians of the counselor's role with emphasis on the confidential nature of the counseling relationship between the counselor and student.

b. Recognizes that working with minors in a school setting may require counselors to collaborate with student's parents/guardians.

c. Provides parents/guardians with accurate, comprehensive and relevant information in an objective and caring manner, as is appropriate and consistent with ethical responsibilities to the student.

d. Makes reasonable efforts to honor the wishes of parents/guardians concerning information regarding the student, and in cases of divorce or separation exercises a good-faith effort to keep both parents informed with regard to critical information with the exception of a court order.

C. RESPONSIBILITIES TO COLLEAGUES AND PROFESSIONAL ASSOCIATES

C.1. Professional Relationships

The professional school counselor:

a. Establishes and maintains professional relationships with faculty, staff, and administration to facilitate an optimum counseling program.

b. Treats colleagues with professional respect, courtesy, and fairness. The qualifications, views and findings of colleagues are represented to accurately reflect the image of competent professionals.

c. Is aware of and utilizes related professionals, organizations, and other resources to whom the student may be referred.

C.2. Sharing Information with Other Professionals

The professional school counselor:

a. Promotes awareness and adherence to appropriate guidelines regarding confidentiality, the distinction between public and private information and staff consultation.

b. Provides professional personnel with accurate, objective, concise and meaningful data necessary to adequately evaluate, counsel and assist the student.

c. If a student is receiving services from another counselor or other mental health professional, the counselor, with student and/or parent/guardian consent, will inform the other professional and develop clear agreements to avoid confusion and conflict for the student.

d. Is knowledgeable about release of information and parental rights in sharing information.

D. RESPONSIBILITIES TO THE SCHOOL AND COMMUNITY

D.1. Responsibilities to the School

The professional school counselor:

a. Supports and protects the educational program against any infringement not in students' best interest.
b. Informs appropriate officials in accordance with school policy of conditions that may be potentially disruptive or damaging to the school's mission, personnel, and property while honoring the confidentiality between the student and counselor.
c. Is knowledgeable and supportive of the school's mission and connects his/her program to the school's mission.
d. Delineates and promotes the counselor's role and function in meeting the needs of those served. Counselors will notify appropriate officials of conditions that may limit or curtail their effectiveness in providing programs and services.
e. Accepts employment only for positions for which he/she is qualified by education, training, supervised experience, state and national professional credentials and appropriate professional experience.
f. Advocates that administrators hire only qualified and competent individuals for professional counseling positions.
g. Assists in developing: (1) curricular and environmental conditions appropriate for the school and community, (2) educational procedures and programs to meet students' developmental needs, and (3) a systematic evaluation process for comprehensive, developmental, standards-based school counseling programs, services, and personnel. The counselor is guided by the findings of the evaluation data in planning programs and services.

D.2. Responsibility to the Community

The professional school counselor:

a. Collaborates with agencies, organizations, and individuals in the community in the best interest of students and without regard to personal reward or remuneration.
b. Extends his/her influence and opportunity to deliver a comprehensive school counseling program to all students by collaborating with community resources for student success.

E. RESPONSIBILITIES TO SELF

E.1. Professional Competence

The professional school counselor:

a. Functions within the boundaries of individual professional competence and accepts responsibility for the consequences of his/her actions.
b. Monitors personal well-being and effectiveness and does not participate in any activity that may lead to inadequate professional services or harm to a student.

c. Strives through personal initiative to maintain professional competence including technological literacy and to keep abreast of professional information. Professional and personal growth are ongoing throughout the counselor's career.

E.2. Diversity

The professional school counselor:

a. Affirms the diversity of students, staff, and families.
b. Expands and develops awareness of his/her own attitudes and beliefs affecting cultural values and biases and strives to attain cultural competence.
c. Possesses knowledge and understanding about how oppression, racism, discrimination, and stereotyping affects her/him personally and professionally.
d. Acquires educational, consultation and training experiences to improve awareness, knowledge, skills, and effectiveness in working with diverse populations: ethnic/racial status, age, economic status, special needs, ESL or ELL, immigration status, sexual orientation, gender, gender identity/expression, family type, religious/spiritual identity, and appearance.

F. RESPONSIBILITIES TO THE PROFESSION

F.1. Professionalism

The professional school counselor:

a. Accepts the policies and procedures for handling ethical violations as a result of maintaining membership in the American School Counselor Association.
b. Conducts herself/himself in such a manner as to advance individual ethical practice and the profession.
c. Conducts appropriate research and report findings in a manner consistent with acceptable educational and psychological research practices. The counselor advocates for the protection of the individual student's identity when using data for research or program planning.
d. Adheres to ethical standards of the profession, other official policy statements, such as ASCA's position statements, role statement and the ASCA National Model, and relevant statutes established by federal, state and local governments, and when these are in conflict works responsibly for change.
e. Clearly distinguishes between statements and actions made as a private individual and those made as a representative of the school counseling profession.
f. Does not use his/her professional position to recruit or gain clients, consultees for his/her private practice or to seek and receive unjustified personal gains, unfair advantage, inappropriate relationships or unearned goods or services.

F.2. Contribution to the Profession

The professional school counselor:

a. Actively participates in local, state and national associations fostering the development and improvement of school counseling.
b. Contributes to the development of the profession through the sharing of skills, ideas, and expertise with colleagues.
c. Provides support and mentoring to novice professionals.

G. MAINTENANCE OF STANDARDS

Ethical behavior among professional school counselors, association members and nonmembers, is expected at all times. When there exists serious doubt as to the ethical behavior of colleagues or if counselors are forced to work in situations or abide by policies that do not reflect the standards as outlined in these Ethical Standards for School Counselors; the counselor is obligated to take appropriate action to rectify the condition. The following procedure may serve as a guide:

1. The counselor should consult confidentially with a professional colleague to discuss the nature of a complaint to see if the professional colleague views the situation as an ethical violation.
2. When feasible, the counselor should directly approach the colleague whose behavior is in question to discuss the complaint and seek resolution.
3. If resolution is not forthcoming at the personal level, the counselor shall utilize the channels established within the school, school district, the state school counseling association, and ASCA's Ethics Committee.

4. If the matter still remains unresolved, referral for review and appropriate action should be made to the Ethics Committees in the following sequence:

state school counselor association
American School Counselor Association

5. The ASCA Ethics Committee is responsible for:
   - educating and consulting with the membership regarding ethical standards
   - periodically reviewing and recommending changes in code
   - receiving and processing questions to clarify the application of such standards; questions must be submitted in writing to the ASCA Ethics chair.
   - handling complaints of alleged violations of the ethical standards. At the national level, complaints should be submitted in writing to the ASCA Ethics Committee, c/o the Executive Director, American School Counselor Association, 1101 King St., Suite 625, Alexandria, VA 22314.

Source: Reprinted by permission of American School Counseling Association.

APPENDIX O
Family Educational Rights and Privacy Act (FERPA)

The Family Educational Rights and Privacy Act (FERPA) (20 U.S.C. § 1232g; 34 CFR Part 99) is a Federal law that protects the privacy of student education records. The law applies to all schools that receive funds under an applicable program of the U.S. Department of Education.

§ 1232g. Family Educational and Privacy Rights

Release date: 2005-08-03

a. Conditions for availability of funds to educational agencies or institutions; inspection and review of education records; specific information to be made available; procedure for access to education records; reasonableness of time for such access; hearings; written explanations by parents; definitions

  1. A. No funds shall be made available under any applicable program to any educational agency or institution which has a policy of denying, or which effectively parents, the parents of students who are or have been in attendance at a school of such agency or at such institution, as the case may be, the right to inspect and review the education records of their children. If any material or document in the education record of a student includes information on more than one student, the parents of one of such students shall have the right to inspect and review only such part of such material or document as relates to such student or to be informed of the specific information contained in such part of such material. Each educational agency or institution shall establish appropriate procedures for the granting of a request by parents for access to the education records of their children within a reasonable period of time, but in no case more than forty-five days after the request has been made.

  B. No funds under any applicable program shall be made available to any State educational agency (whether or not that agency is an educational agency or institution under this section) that has a policy of denying, or effectively prevents, the parents of students the right to inspect and review the education records maintained by the State educational agency on their children who are or have been in attendance at any school of an educational agency or institution that is subject to the provisions of this section.

  C. The first sentence of subparagraph (A) shall not operate to make available to students in institutions of postsecondary education the following materials:
    i. financial records of the parents of the student or any information contained therein;
    ii. confidential letters and statements of recommendation, which were placed in the education records prior to January 1, 1975, if such letters or statements are not used for purposes other than those for which they were specifically intended;
    iii. if the student has signed a waiver of the student's right of access under this subsection in accordance with subparagraph (D), confidential recommendations—
      (I) respecting admission to any educational agency or institution,
      (II) respecting an application for employment, and
      (III) respecting the receipt of an honor or honorary recognition.

  D. A student or a person applying for admission may waive his right of access to confidential statements described in clause (iii) of subparagraph (C), except that such waiver shall apply to recommendations only if
    i. the student is, upon request, notified of the names of all persons making confidential recommendations and
    ii. such recommendations are used solely for the purpose for which they were specifically intended. Such waivers may not be required as a condition for admission to, receipt of financial aid from, or receipt of any other services or benefits from such agency or institution.

  2. No funds shall be made available under any applicable program to any educational agency or institution unless the parents of students who are or have been in attendance at a school of such agency or at such institution are provided an opportunity for a hearing by such agency or institution, in accordance with regulations of the Secretary, to challenge the content of such student's education records, in order to insure that the records are not inaccurate, misleading, or otherwise in violation of the privacy rights of students, and to provide an opportunity for the correction or deletion of any such inaccurate, misleading or otherwise inappropriate data contained therein and to insert into such records a written explanation of the parents respecting the content of such records.

  3. For the purposes of this section the term "educational agency or institution" means any public or private agency or institution which is the recipient of funds under any applicable program.

  4. A. For the purposes of this section, the term "education records" means, except as may be provided otherwise in subparagraph (B), those records, files, documents, and other materials which—

i. contain information directly related to a student; and

ii. are maintained by an educational agency or institution or by a person acting for such agency or institution.

B. The term "education records" does not include—

i. records of instructional, supervisory, and administrative personnel and educational personnel ancillary thereto which are in the sole possession of the maker thereof and which are not accessible or revealed to any other person except a substitute;

ii. records maintained by a law enforcement unit of the educational agency or institution that were created by that law enforcement unit for the purpose of law enforcement;

iii. in the case of persons who are employed by an educational agency or institution but who are not in attendance at such agency or institution, records made and maintained in the normal course of business which relate exclusively to such person in that person's capacity as an employee and are not available for use for any other purpose; or

iv. records on a student who is eighteen years of age or older, or is attending an institution of postsecondary education, which are made or maintained by a physician, psychiatrist, psychologist, or other recognized professional or paraprofessional acting in his professional or paraprofessional capacity, or assisting in that capacity, and which are made, maintained, or used only in connection with the provision of treatment to the student, and are not available to anyone other than persons providing such treatment, except that such records can be personally reviewed by a physician or other appropriate professional of the student's choice.

5. A. For the purposes of this section the term "directory information" relating to a student includes the following: the student's name, address, telephone listing, date and place of birth, major field of study, participation in officially recognized activities and sports, weight and height of members of athletic teams, dates of attendance, degrees and awards received, and the most recent previous educational agency or institution attended by the student.

B. Any educational agency or institution making public directory information shall give public notice of the categories of information which it has designated as such information with respect to each student attending the institution or agency and shall allow a reasonable period of time after such notice has been given for a parent to inform the institution or agency that any or all of the information designated should not be released without the parent's prior consent.

6. For the purposes of this section, the term "student" includes any person with respect to whom an educational agency or institution maintains education records or personally identifiable information, but does not include a person who has not been in attendance at such agency or institution.

b. Release of education records; parental consent requirement; exceptions; compliance with judicial orders and subpoenas; audit and evaluation of federally-supported education programs; recordkeeping.

1. No funds shall be made available under any applicable program to any educational agency or institution which has a policy or practice of permitting the release of education records (or personally identifiable information contained therein other than directory information, as defined in paragraph (5) of subsection (a) of this section) of students without the written consent of their parents to any individual, agency, or organization, other than to the following—

A. other school officials, including teachers within the educational institution or local educational agency, who have been determined by such agency or institution to have legitimate educational interests, including the educational interests of the child for whom consent would otherwise be required;

B. officials of other schools or school systems in which the student seeks or intends to enroll, upon condition that the student's parents be notified of the transfer, receive a copy of the record if desired, and have an opportunity for a hearing to challenge the content of the record;

C. authorized representatives of

i. the Comptroller General of the United States,

ii. the Secretary, or

iii. State educational authorities, under the conditions set forth in paragraph (3), or (ii) authorized representatives of the Attorney General for law enforcement purposes under the same conditions as apply to the Secretary under paragraph (3);

D. in connection with a student's application for, or receipt of, financial aid;

E. State and local officials or authorities to whom such information is specifically allowed to be reported or disclosed pursuant to State statute adopted—

i. before November 19, 1974, if the allowed reporting or disclosure concerns the juvenile justice system and such system's ability to effectively serve the student whose records are released, or

ii. after November 19, 1974, if—

(I) the allowed reporting or disclosure concerns the juvenile justice system and such system's ability to effectively serve, prior to adjudication, the student whose records are released; and

(II) the officials and authorities to whom such information is disclosed certify in writing to the educational agency or institution that the information will not be disclosed to any other party except as provided under State law without the prior written consent of the parent of the student.

F. organizations conducting studies for, or on behalf of, educational agencies or institutions for the purpose of developing, validating, or administering predictive tests, administering student aid programs, and improving instruction, if such studies are conducted in such a manner as will not permit the personal identification of students and their parents by persons other than representatives of such organizations and such information will be destroyed when no longer needed for the purpose for which it is conducted;

G. accrediting organizations in order to carry out their accrediting functions;

H. parents of a dependent student of such parents, as defined in section 152 of title 26;

I. subject to regulations of the Secretary, in connection with an emergency, appropriate persons if the knowledge of such information is necessary to protect the health or safety of the student or other persons; and

J. i. the entity or person designated in a Federal grand jury subpoena, in which case the court shall order, for good cause shown, the educational agency or institution (and any officer, director, employee, agent, or attorney for such agency or institution) on which the subpoena is served, to not disclose to any person the existence or contents of the subpoena or any information furnished to the grand jury in response to the subpoena; and

    ii. the entity or persons designated in any other subpoena issued for a law enforcement purpose, in which case the court or other issuing agency may order, for good cause shown, the educational agency or institution (and any officer, director, employee, agent, or attorney for such agency or institution) on which the subpoena is served, to not disclose to any person the existence or contents of the subpoena or any information furnished in response to the subpoena.

    Nothing in subparagraph (E) of this paragraph shall prevent a State from further limiting the number or type of State or local officials who will continue to have access thereunder.

2. No funds shall be made available under any applicable program to any educational agency or institution which has a policy or practice of releasing, or providing access to, any personally identifiable information in education records other than directory information, or as is permitted under paragraph (1) of this subsection, unless—

    A. there is written consent from the student's parents specifying records to be released, the reasons for such release, and to whom, and with a copy of the records to be released to the student's parents and the student if desired by the parents, or

    B. except as provided in paragraph (1)(J), such information is furnished in compliance with judicial order, or pursuant to any lawfully issued subpoena, upon condition that parents and the students are notified of all such orders or subpoenas in advance of the compliance therewith by the educational institution or agency.

3. Nothing contained in this section shall preclude authorized representatives of

    A. the Comptroller General of the United States,

    B. the Secretary, or

    C. State educational authorities from having access to student or other records which may be necessary in connection with the audit and evaluation of Federally-supported education programs, or in connection with the enforcement of the Federal legal requirements which related to such programs: provided, that except when collection of personally identifiable information is specifically authorized by Federal law, any data collected by such officials shall be protected in a manner which will not permit the personal identification of students and their parents by other than those officials, and such personally identifiable data shall be destroyed when no longer needed for such audit, evaluation, and enforcement of Federal legal requirements.

4. A. Each educational agency or institution shall maintain a record, kept with the education records of each student, which will indicate all individuals (other than those specified in paragraph (1)(A) of this subsection), agencies, or organizations which have requested or obtained access to a student's education records maintained by such educational agency or institution, and which will indicate specifically the legitimate interest that each such person, agency, or organization has in obtaining this information. Such record of access shall be available only to parents, to the school official and his assistants who are responsible for the custody of such records, and to persons or organizations authorized in, and under the conditions of, clauses (A) and (C) or paragraph (1) as a means of auditing the operation of the system.

    B. With respect to thin subsection, personal information shall only be transferred to a third party on the condition that such party will not permit any other party to have access to such information without the written consent of the parents of the student. If a third party outside the educational agency or institution permits access to information in violation of paragraph (2)(A), or fails to destroy information shall be prohibited from permitting access to information from education records to that third party for a period of not less than five years.

5. Nothing in this section shall be construed to prohibit State and local educational officials from having access to student or other records which may be necessary in connection with the audit and evaluation of any federally or State supported education program or in connection with the enforcement of the Federal legal requirements which relate to any such program, subject to the conditions specified in the proviso in paragraph (3).

6. A. Nothing in this section shall be construed to prohibit an institution of postsecondary education from disclosing, to an alleged victim of any crime of violence (as that term is defined in section 16

of title 18), or a nonforcible sex offense, the final results of any disciplinary proceeding conducted by such institution against the alleged perpetrator of such crime or offense with respect to such crime or offense.

B. Nothing in this section shall be construed to prohibit an institution of postsecondary education from disclosing the final results of any disciplinary proceeding conducted by such institution against a student who is an alleged perpetrator of any crime of violence (as that term is defined in section 16 of title 18), or a nonforcible sex offense, if the institution determines as a result of that disciplinary proceeding that the student committed a violation of the institution's rules of policies with respect to such crime or offense.

C. For the purpose of this paragraph, the final results of any disciplinary proceeding—
   i. shall include only the name of the student, the violation committed, and any sanction imposed by the institution on that student; and
   ii. may include the name of any other student, such as a victim or witness, only with the written consent of that other student.

7. A. Nothing in this section may be construed to prohibit an educational institution from disclosing information provided to the institution under section 14071 of title 42 concerning registered sex offenders who are required to register under such section.

B. The Secretary shall take appropriate steps to notify educational institutions that disclosure of information described in subparagraph (A) is permitted.

C. Surveys or data-gathering activities; regulations.
   Not later than 240 days after October 20, 1994, the Secretary shall adopt appropriate regulations or procedures, or identify existing regulations or procedures, which protect the rights or privacy of students and their families in connection with any surveys or data-gathering activities conducted, assisted, or authorized by the Secretary or an administrative head of an education agency. Regulations established under this subsection shall include provisions controlling the use, dissemination, and protection of such data. No survey or data-gathering activities shall be conducted by the Secretary, or an administrative head of an education agency. Regulations established under this subsection shall include provisions controlling the use, dissemination, and protection of such data. No survey or data-gathering activities shall be conducted by the Secretary, or an administrative head of an education agency under an applicable program, unless such activities are authorized by law.

D. Students' rather than parents' permission or consent.
   For the purposes of this section, whenever a student has attained eighteen years of age, or is attending an institution of postsecondary education, the permission or consent required of and the rights accorded to the parents of the student shall thereafter only be required of and accorded to the student.

E. Informing parents or students of rights under this section.
   No funds shall be made available under any applicable program to any educational agency or institution unless such agency or institution effectively informs the parents of students, or the students, if they are eighteen years of age or older, or are attending an institution of postsecondary education, or the rights accorded them by this section.

F. Enforcement; termination of assistance.
   The secretary shall take appropriate actions to enforce this section and to deal with violations of this section, in accordance with this chapter, except that action to terminate assistance may be taken only if the Secretary finds there has been a failure to comply with this section, and he has determined that compliance cannot be secured by voluntary means.

G. Office and review board; creation; functions.
   The Secretary shall establish or designate an office and review board within the Department for the purpose of investigating, processing, reviewing, and adjudicating violations of this section and complaints which may be filed concerning alleged violations of this section. Except for the conduct of hearings, none of the functions of the Secretary under this section shall be carried out in any of the regional officers of such Department.

H. Disciplinary records; disclosure.
   Nothing in this section shall prohibit an educational agency or institution from—
   i. including appropriate information in the education record of any student concerning disciplinary action taken against such student for conduct that posed a significant risk to the safety or well-being of that student, other students, or other members of the school community; or
   ii. disclosing such information to teachers and school officials, including teachers and school officials in other schools, who have legitimate educational interests in the behavior of the student.

I. Drug and alcohol violation disclosures.
   i. In general
      Nothing in this Act or the Higher Education Act of 1965 [20 U.S.C. 1001 et seq.] shall be construed to prohibit an institution of higher education from disclosing, to a parent or legal guardian of a student, information regarding any violation of any Federal, State, or local law, or of any rule or policy of the institution, governing the use or possession of alcohol or a controlled substance, regardless, of whether that information is contained in the student's education records, if—
      (I) the student is under the age of 21; and
      (II) the institution determines that the student has committed a disciplinary violation with respect to such use or possession.
   ii. State law regarding disclosure
      Nothing in paragraph (1) shall be construed to supersede any provision of State law that prohibits an institution of higher education from

making the disclosure described in subsection (a) of this section.

J. Investigation and prosecution of terrorism.
  i. In general
  Notwithstanding subsections (a) through (i) of this section or any provision of State law, the Attorney General (or any Federal officer or employee, in a position not lower than an Assistant Attorney General, designated by the Attorney General) may submit a written application to a court of competent jurisdiction for an ex parte order requiring an educational agency or institution to permit the Attorney General (or his designee) to—
  (I) collect education records in the possession of the educational agency or institution that are relevant to an authorized investigation or prosecution of an offense listed in section 2332b (g)(5)(B) of title 18, or an act of domestic or international terrorism as defined in section 2331 of that title; and
  (II) for official purposes related to the investigation or prosecution of an offense described in paragraph (1)(A), retain, disseminate, and use (including as evidence at trial or in other administrative or judicial proceedings) such records, consistent with such guidelines as the Attorney General, after consultation with the Secretary, shall issue to protect confidentiality.
  ii. Application and approval
  (I) In general—An application under paragraph (1) shall certify that there are specific and articulable facts giving reason to believe that the education records are likely to contain information described in paragraph (1)(A).
  (II) The court shall issue an order described in paragraph (1) if the court finds that the application for the order includes the certification described in subparagraphs (A).
  iii. Protection of educational agency or institution
  An education agency or institution that, in good faith, produces education records in accordance with an order issued under this subsection shall not be liable to any person for that production.
  iv. (4) Record-keeping
  Subsection (b)(4) of this section does not apply to education records subject to a court under this subsection.

APPENDIX P

American Mental Health Counselors Association Code of Ethics (2000)

PREAMBLE

Mental health counselors believe in the dignity and worth of the individual. They are committed to increasing knowledge of human behavior and understanding of themselves and others. While pursuing these endeavors, they make every reasonable effort to protect the welfare of those who seek their services, or of any subject that may be the object of study. They use their skills only for purposes consistent with these values and do not knowingly permit their misuse by others. While demanding for themselves freedom of inquiry and community, mental health counselors accept the responsibility this freedom confers: competence, objectivity in the application of skills, and concern for the best interest of clients, colleagues, and society in general. In the pursuit of these ideals, mental health counselors subscribe to the principles listed throughout this appendix.

CLINICAL ISSUES

Principle 1. Welfare of the Consumer

A. **Primary Responsibility**
   1. The primary responsibility of the mental health counselor is to respect the dignity and integrity of the client. Client growth and development are encouraged in ways that foster the client's interest and promote welfare.
   2. Mental health counselors are aware of their influential position with respect to their clients, and avoid exploiting the trust and fostering dependency of their clients.
   3. Mental health counselors fully inform consumers as to the purpose and nature of any evaluation, treatment, education or training procedure and they fully acknowledge that the consumer has the freedom of choice with regard to participation.

B. **Counseling Plans**
   Mental health counselors and their clients work jointly in devising integrated, individual counseling plans that offer reasonable promise of success and are consistent with the abilities and circumstances of the client. Counselors and clients regularly review counseling plans to ensure their continued viability and effectiveness, respecting the client's freedom of choice.

C. **Freedom of Choice**
   Mental health counselors offer clients the freedom to choose whether to enter into a counseling relationship and determine which professionals will provide the counseling. Restrictions that limit clients' choices are fully explained.

D. **Clients Served by Others**
   1. If a client is receiving services from another mental health professional or counselor, the mental health counselor secures consent from the client, informs that professional of the arrangement, and develops a clear agreement to avoid confusion and conflicts for the client.
   2. Mental health counselors are aware of the intimacy and responsibilities inherent in the counseling relationship. They maintain respect for the client and avoid actions that seek to meet their personal needs at the expense of the client. Mental health counselors are aware of their own values, attitudes, beliefs, and behaviors, and how these apply in a diverse society. They avoid imposing their values on the consumer.

E. **Diversity**
   1. Mental health counselors do not condone or engage in any discrimination based on age, color, culture, disability, ethnic group, gender, race, religion, sexual orientation, marital status or socioeconomic status.
   2. Mental health counselors will actively attempt to understand the diverse cultural backgrounds of the clients with whom they work. This includes learning how the counselor's own cultural/ethical/racial/religious identity impacts his or her own values and beliefs about the counseling process. When there is a conflict between the client's goals, identity and/or values and those of the mental health counselor, a referral to an appropriate colleague must be arranged.

F. **Dual Relationships**
   Mental health counselors are aware of their influential position with respect to their clients and avoid exploiting the trust and fostering dependency of the client.
   1. Mental health counselors make every effort to avoid dual relationships with clients that could impair professional judgement or increase the risk of harm. Examples of such relationships may include, but are not limited to: familial, social, financial, business, or close personal relationships with the clients.
   2. Mental health counselors do not accept as clients individuals with whom they are involved in an administrative, supervisory, and evaluative nature. When acting as supervisors, trainers, or employers, mental health counselors accord recipients informed choice, confidentiality and protection from physical and mental harm.
   3. When a dual relationship cannot be avoided, counselors take appropriate professional precautions such as informed consent, consultation, supervision, and documentation to ensure that judgement is not impaired and no exploitation has occurred.

G. **Sexual Relationships**

Sexual relationships with clients are strictly prohibited. Mental health counselors do not counsel persons with whom they have had a previous sexual relationship.

H. **Former Clients**

Counselors do not engage in sexual intimacies with former clients within a minimum of two years after terminating the counseling relationship. The mental health counselor has the responsibility to examine and document thoroughly that such relations did not have an exploitative nature based on factors such as duration of counseling, amount of time since counseling, termination circumstances, the client's personal history and mental status, adverse impact on the client, and actions by the counselor suggesting a plan to initiate a sexual relationship with the client after termination.

I. **Multiple Clients**

When mental health counselors agree to provide counseling services to two or more persons who have a relationship (such as husband and wife, or parents and children), counselors clarify at the outset which person or persons are clients, and the nature of the relationship they will have with each involved person. If it becomes apparent that counselors may be called upon to perform potentially conflicting roles, they clarify, adjust, or withdraw from roles appropriately.

J. **Informed Consent**

Mental health counselors are responsible for making their services readily accessible to clients in a manner that facilitates the clients' abilities to make an informed choice when selecting a provider. This responsibility includes a clear description of what the client can expect in the way of tests, reports, billing, therapeutic regime and schedules, and the use of the mental health counselor's statement of professional disclosure. In the event that a client is a minor or possesses disabilities that would prohibit informed consent, the mental health counselor acts in the client's best interest.

K. **Conflict of Interest**

Mental health counselors are aware of possible conflicts of interests that may involve the organization in which they are employed and their client. When conflicts occur, mental health counselors clarify the nature of the conflict and inform all parties of the nature and direction of their loyalties and responsibilities, and keep all parties informed of their commitments.

L. **Fees and Bartering**

1. Mental health counselors clearly explain to clients, prior to entering the counseling relationship, all financial arrangements related to professional services, including the use of collection agencies or legal measures for nonpayment.

2. In establishing fees for professional counseling services, mental health counselors consider the financial status of their clients and locality. In the event that the payment of the mental health counselor's usual fees would create undue hardship for the client, assistance is provided in attempting to find comparable services at an acceptable cost.

3. Mental health counselors ordinarily refrain from accepting goods or services from clients in return for counseling service because such arrangements create inherent potential for conflicts, exploitation and distortion of the professional relationship. Participation in bartering is only used when there is no exploitation, if the client requests it, if a clear written contract is established, and if such an arrangement is an accepted practice among professionals in the community.

M. **Pro Bono Service**

Mental health counselors contribute to society by devoting a portion of their professional activity to services for which there is little or no financial return.

N. **Consulting**

Mental health counselors may choose to consult with any other professionally competent person about a client. In choosing a consultant, the mental health counselor should avoid placing the consultant in a conflict of interest situation that would preclude the consultant from being a proper party to the mental health counselor's effort to help the client.

O. **Group Work**

1. Mental health counselors screen prospective group counseling/therapy participants. Every effort is made to select members whose needs and goals are compatible with goals of the group, who will not impede the group process, and whose well being will not be jeopardized by the group experience.

2. In the group setting, mental health counselors take reasonable precautions to protect clients from physical and psychological harm or trauma.

3. When the client is engaged in short term group treatment/training programs, i.e. marathons and other encounter type or growth groups, the members ensure that there is professional assistance available during and following the group experience.

P. **Termination and Referral**

Mental health counselors do not abandon or neglect their clients in counseling. Assistance is given in making appropriate arrangements for the continuation of treatment, when necessary, during interruptions such as vacation and following termination.

Q. **Inability to Assist Clients**

If the mental health counselor determines that their services are not beneficial to the client, they avoid entering or terminate immediately a counseling relationship. Mental health counselors are knowledgeable about referral sources and appropriate referrals are made. If clients decline the suggested referral, mental health counselors discontinue the relationship.

R. **Appropriate Termination**

Mental health counselors terminate a counseling relationship, securing a client's agreement when possible, when it is reasonably clear that the client is no longer benefiting, when services are no longer required, when counseling no longer serves the needs and interests of the client, when clients do not pay fees charged, or when agency or institution limits do not allow provision of further counseling services.

Principle 2. Clients' Rights

The following apply to all consumers of mental health services, including both in- and out-patients and all state, county, local, and private care mental health facilities, as well as clients of mental health practitioners in private practice.

The client has the right:

A. to be treated with dignity, consideration and respect at all times;

B. to expect quality service provided by concerned, trained, professional and competent staff;
C. to expect complete confidentiality within the limits of the law, and to be informed about the legal exceptions to confidentiality; and to expect that no information will be released without the client's knowledge and written consent;
D. to a clear working contract in which business items, such as time of sessions, payment plans/fees, absences, access, emergency procedures, and third-party reimbursement procedures are discussed;
E. to a clear statement of the purposes, goals, techniques, rules of procedure and limitations, as well as the potential dangers of the services to be performed, and all other information related to or likely to affect the ongoing mental health counseling relationship;
F. to appropriate information regarding the mental health counselor's education, training, skills, license and practice limitations and to request and receive referrals to other clinicians when appropriate;
G. to full, knowledgeable, and responsible participation in the ongoing treatment plan to the maximum extent feasible;
H. to obtain information about their case record and to have this information explained clearly and directly;
I. to request information and/or consultation regarding the conduct and progress of their therapy;
J. to refuse any recommended services and to be advised of the consequences of this action;
K. to a safe environment free of emotional, physical, and sexual abuse;
L. to a client grievance procedure, including requests for consultation and/or mediation; and to file a complaint with the mental health counselor's supervisor, and/or the appropriate credentialing body; and
M. to a clearly defined ending process, and to discontinue therapy at any time.

Principle 3. Confidentiality

Mental health counselors have a primary obligation to safeguard information about individuals obtained in the course of practice, teaching, or research. Personal information is communicated to others only with the person's written consent or in those circumstances where there is clear and imminent danger to the client, to others or to society. Disclosure of counseling information is restricted to what is necessary, relevant, and verifiable.

A. At the outset of any counseling relationship, mental health counselors make their clients aware of their rights in regard to the confidential nature of the counseling relationship. They fully disclose the limits of, or exceptions to, confidentiality, and/or the existence of privileged communication, if any.
B. All materials in the official record shall be shared with the client, who shall have the right to decide what information may be shared with anyone beyond the immediate provider of service and be informed of the implications of the materials to be shared.
C. Confidentiality belongs to the clients. They may direct the mental health counselor, in writing, to release information to others. The release of information without the consent of the client may only take place under the most extreme circumstances. The protection of life, as in the case of suicidal or homicidal clients, exceeds the requirements of confidentiality.

The protection of a child, an elderly person, or a person not competent to care for themselves from physical or sexual abuse or neglect requires that a report be made to a legally constituted authority. The mental health counselor complies with all state and federal statutes concerning mandated reporting of suicidality, homicidality, child abuse, incompetent person abuse, and elder abuse. The protection of the public or another individual from a contagious condition known to be fatal also requires action that may include reporting the willful infection of another with the condition.

The mental health counselor (or staff member) does not release information by request unless accompanied by a specific release of information or a valid court order. Mental health counselors will comply with the order of a court to release information but they will inform the client of the receipt of such an order. A subpoena is insufficient to release information. In such a case, the counselor must inform his client of the situation and, if the client refuses release, coordinate between the client's attorney and the requesting attorney so as to protect client confidentiality and one's own legal welfare.

In the case of all of the above exceptions to confidentiality, the mental health counselor will release only such information as is necessary to accomplish the action required by the exception.

D. The anonymity of clients served in public and other agencies is preserved, if at all possible, by withholding names and personal identifying data. If external conditions require reporting such information, the client shall be so informed.
E. Information received in confidence by one agency or person shall not be forwarded to another person or agency without the client's written permission.
F. Service providers have the responsibility to ensure the accuracy and to indicate the validity of data shared with their parties.
G. Case reports presented in classes, professional meetings, or publications shall be so disguised that no identification is possible unless the client or responsible authority has read the report and agreed in writing to its presentation or publication.
H. Counseling reports and records are maintained under conditions of security, and provisions are made for their destruction when they have outlived their usefulness. Mental health counselors ensure that all persons in his or her employ, volunteers, and community aides maintain privacy and confidentiality.
I. Mental health counselors who ask that an individual reveal personal information in the course of interviewing, testing or evaluation, or who allow such information to be divulged, do so only after making certain that the person or authorized representative is fully aware of the purposes of the interview, testing or evaluation, and of the ways in which the information will be used.
J. Sessions with clients may be taped or otherwise recorded only with their written permission or the written permission of a responsible guardian. Even with a guardian's written consent, one should not record a session against the expressed wishes of a client. Such tapes shall be destroyed when they have outlived their usefulness.
K. Where a child or adolescent is the primary client, or the client is not competent to give consent, the interests of the minor or the incompetent client shall be paramount. Where appropriate, a parent(s) or guardian(s) may be included in the counseling process. The mental health counselor must still take measures to safeguard the client's confidentiality.

L. In work with families, the rights of each family member should be safeguarded. The provider of service also has the responsibility to discuss the contents of the record with the parent and/or child, as appropriate, and to keep separate those parts, which should remain the property of each family member.

M. In work with groups, the rights of each group member should be safeguarded. The provider of service also has the responsibility to discuss the need for each member to respect the confidentiality of each other member of the group. He must also remind the group of the limits on and risk to confidentiality inherent in the group process.

N. When using a computer to store confidential information, mental health counselors take measure to control access to such information. When such information has outlived its usefulness, it should be deleted from the system.

Principle 4. Utilization of Assessment Techniques

A. **Test Selection**

1. In choosing a particular test, mental health counselors should ascertain that there is sufficient evidence in the test manual of its applicability in measuring a certain trait or construct. The manual should fully describe the development of the test, the rationale, and data pertaining to item selection and test construction. The manual should explicitly state the purposes and applications for which the test is intended, and provide reliability and validity data about the test. The manual should furthermore identify the qualifications necessary to properly administer and interpret the test.

2. In selecting a particular combination of tests, mental health counselors need to be able to justify the logic of those choices.

3. Mental health counselors should employ only those tests for which they judge themselves competent by training, education, or experience. In familiarizing themselves with new tests, counselors thoroughly read the manual and seek workshops, supervision, or other forms of training.

4. Mental health counselors avoid using outdated or obsolete tests, and strive to remain current regarding test publication and revision.

5. Tests selected for individual testing must be appropriate for that individual in that appropriate norms exist for variables such as age, gender, and race. The test form must fit the client. If the test must be used in the absence of available information regarding the above subsamples, the limitations of generalizability should be duly noted.

B. **Test Administration**

1. Mental health counselors should faithfully follow instructions for administration of a test in order to ensure standardization. Failure to consistently follow test instructions will result in test error and incorrect estimates of the trait or behavior being measured.

2. Tests should only be employed in appropriate professional settings or as recommended by instructors or supervisors for training purposes. It is best to avoid giving tests to relatives, close friends or business associates, in that doing so constructs a dual professional/personal relationship, which is to be avoided.

3. Mental health counselors should provide the test taker with appropriate information regarding the reason for assessment, the approximate length of time required, and to whom the report will be distributed. Issues of confidentiality must be addressed, and the client must be given the opportunity to ask questions of the examiner prior to beginning the procedure.

4. Care should be taken to provide an appropriate assessment environment in regard to temperature, privacy, comfort, and freedom from distractions.

5. Information should be solicited regarding any possible handicaps, such as problems with visual or auditory acuity, limitations of hand/eye coordination, illness, or other factors. If the disabilities cannot be accommodated effectively, the test may need to be postponed or the limitations of applicability of the test results noted in the test report.

6. Professionals who supervise others should ensure that their trainees have sufficient knowledge and experience before utilizing the tests for clinical purposes.

7. Mental health counselors must be able to document appropriate education, training, and experience in areas of assessment they perform.

C. **Test Interpretation**

1. Interpretation of test or test battery results should be based on multiple sources of convergent data and an understanding of the tests' foundations and limits.

2. Mental health counselors must be careful not to make conclusions unless empirical evidence is present to justify the statement. If such evidence is lacking, one should not make diagnostic or prognostic formulations.

3. Interpretation of test results should take into account the many qualitative influences on test-taking behavior, such as health, energy, motivation, and the like. Description and analysis of alternative explanations should be provided with the interpretations.

4. One should not make firm conclusions in the absence of published information that establishes a satisfactory degree of test validity, particularly predictive validity.

5. Multicultural factors must be considered in test interpretation and diagnosis, and formulation of prognosis and treatment recommendations.

6. Mental health counselors should avoid biased or incorrect interpretation by assuring that the test norms reference the population taking the test.

7. Mental health counselors are responsible for evaluating the quality of computer software interpretations of test data. Mental health counselors should obtain information regarding validity of computerized test interpretation before utilizing such an approach.

8. Supervisors should ensure that their supervisees have had adequate training in interpretation before entrusting them to evaluate tests in a semi-autonomous fashion.

9. Any individual or organization offering test scoring or interpretation services must be able to demonstrate that their programs are based on sufficient and appropriate research to establish the validity of the programs and procedures used in arriving at interpretations. The public offering of an automated test interpretation service will be considered a professional-to-professional consultation. The formal responsibility of the consultant is

to the consultee, but his or her ultimate and overriding responsibility is to the client.

10. Mental health counselors who have the responsibility for making decisions about clients or policies based on test results should have a thorough understanding of counseling theory, assessment techniques, and test research.

11. Mental health counselors do not represent computerized test interpretations as their own and clearly designate such computerized results.

D. **Test Reporting**

1. Mental health counselors should write reports in a clear fashion, avoiding excessive jargon or clinical terms that are likely to confuse the lay reader.

2. Mental health counselors should strive to provide test results in as positive and nonjudgmental manner as possible.

3. Mindful that one's report reflects on the reputation of oneself and one's profession, reports are carefully proofread so as to be free of spelling, style, and grammatical errors as much as is possible.

4. Clients should be clearly informed about who will be allowed to review the report and, in the absence of a valid court order, must sign appropriate releases of information permitting such release. Mental health counselors must not release the report or findings in the absence of the aforementioned release or order.

5. Mental health counselors are responsible for ensuring the confidentiality and security of test reports, test data, and test materials.

6. Mental health counselors must offer the client the opportunity to receive feedback about the test results, interpretations, and the range of error for such data.

7. Transmissions of test data or test reports by fax or e-mail must be accomplished in a secure manner, with guarantees that the receiving device is capable of providing a confidential transmission only to the party who has been permitted to receive the document.

8. Mental health counselors should train their staff to respect the confidentiality of test reports in the context of typing, filing, or mailing them.

9. Mental health counselors (or staff members) do not release a psychological evaluation by request unless accompanied by a specific release of information or a valid court order. A subpoena is insufficient to release a report. In such a case, the counselor must inform his/her client of the situation and, if the client refuses release, coordinate between the client's attorney and the requesting attorney so as to protect client confidentiality and one's own legal welfare.

Principle 5. Pursuit of Research Activities

Mental health counselors who conduct research must do so with regard to ethical principles. The decision to undertake research should rest upon a considered judgement by the individual counselor about how best to contribute to counseling and to human welfare. Mental health counselors carry out their investigations with respect for the people who participate and with concern for their dignity and welfare.

A. The ethical researcher seeks advice from other professionals if any plan of research suggests a deviation from any ethical principle of research with human subjects. Such deviation must still protect the dignity and welfare of the client and places on the researcher a special burden to act in the subject's interest.

B. The ethical researcher is open and honest in the relationship with research participants.

1. The ethical researcher informs the participant of all features of the research that might be expected to influence willingness to participate and explains to the participant all other aspects about which the participant inquires.

2. Where scientific or human values justify delaying or withholding information, the investigator acquires a special responsibility to assure that there are no damaging consequences for the participants.

3. Following the collection of the data, the ethical researcher must provide the participant with a full clarification of the nature of the study to remove any misconceptions that may have arisen.

4. As soon as possible, the participant is to be informed of the reasons for concealment or deception that are part of the methodological requirements of a study.

5. Such misinformation must be minimized and full disclosure must be made at the conclusion of all research studies.

6. The ethical researcher understands that failure to make full disclosure to a research participant gives added emphasis to the researcher's abiding responsibility to protect the welfare and dignity of the participant.

C. The ethical researcher protects participants from physical and mental discomfort, harm and danger. If the risks of such consequences exist, the investigator is required to inform the participant of that fact, secure consent before proceeding, and take all possible measures to minimize the distress.

D. The ethical researcher instructs research participants that they are free to withdraw their consent from participation at any time.

E. The ethical researcher understands that information obtained about research participants during the course of an investigation is confidential. When the possibility exists that others may obtain access to such information, the participant must be made aware of the possibility and the plans for protecting confidentiality as a part of the procedure for obtaining informed consent.

F. The ethical researcher gives sponsoring agencies, host institutions, and publication channels the same respect and opportunity for informed consent that they accord to individual research participants.

G. The ethical researcher is aware of his or her obligation to future research workers and ensures that host institutions are given feedback information and proper acknowledgement.

Principle 6. Consulting

A. Mental health counselors acting as consultants must have a high degree of self-awareness of their own values, knowledge, skills and needs in entering a helping relationship that involves human and/or organizational change. The focus of the consulting relationship should be on the issues to be resolved and not on the personal characteristics of those presenting the consulting issues.

B. Mental health counselors should develop an understanding of the problem presented by the client and should secure an agreement with the consultation client, specifying the terms and nature of the consulting relationship.

C. Mental health counselors must be reasonably certain that they and their clients have the competencies and resources necessary to follow the consultation plan.

D. Mental health counselors should encourage adaptability and growth toward self-direction. Mental health counselors should avoid becoming a decision maker or substitute for the client.

E. When announcing consultant availability for services, mental health counselors conscientiously adhere to professional standards.

F. Mental health counselors keep all proprietary information confidential.

G. Mental health counselors avoid conflicts of interest in selecting consultation clients.

PROFESSIONAL ISSUES

Principle 7. Competence

The maintenance of high standards of professional competence is a responsibility shared by all mental health counselors in the best interests of the public and the profession. Mental health counselors recognize the boundaries of their particular competencies and the limitations of their expertise. Mental health counselors only provide those services and use only those techniques for which they are qualified by education, techniques or experience. Mental health counselors maintain knowledge of relevant scientific and professional information related to the services they render, and they recognize the need for ongoing education.

A. MENTAL HEALTH COUNSELORS ACCURATELY REPRESENT THEIR COMPETENCE, EDUCATION, TRAINING AND EXPERIENCE.

B. As teaching professionals, mental health counselors perform their duties based on careful preparation in order that their instruction is accurate, up to date and educational.

C. Mental health counselors recognize the need for continued education and training in the area of cultural diversity and competency. Mental health counselors are open to new procedures and sensitive to the diversity of varying populations and changes in expectations and values over time.

D. Mental health counselors and practitioners recognize that their effectiveness depends in part upon their ability to maintain sound and healthy interpersonal relationships. They are aware that any unhealthy activity would compromise sound professional judgement and competency. In the event that personal problems arise and are affecting professional services, they will seek competent professional assistance to determine whether they should limit, suspend or terminate services to their clients.

E. Mental health counselors have a responsibility both to the individual who is served and to the institution within which the service is performed to maintain high standards of professional conduct. Mental health counselors strive to maintain the highest level of professional services offered to the agency, organization or institution in providing the highest caliber of professional services. The acceptance of employment in an institution implies that the mental health counselor is in substantial agreement with the general policies and principles of the institution. If, despite concerted efforts, the member cannot reach an agreement with the employer as to acceptable standards of conduct that allows for changes in institutional policy conducive to the positive growth and development of counselors, then terminating the affiliation should be seriously considered.

F. Ethical behavior among professional associates, mental health counselors and non-mental health counselors is expected at all times. When information is possessed that raises serious doubts as to the ethical behavior of professional colleagues, whether association members or not, the mental health counselor is obligated to take action to attempt to rectify such a condition. Such action shall utilize the institution's channels first and then utilize procedures established by the state licensure board.

G. Mental health counselors are aware of the intimacy of the counseling relationship, maintain a healthy respect for the integrity of the client, and avoid engaging in activities that seek to meet the mental health counselor's personal needs at the expense of the client. Through awareness of the negative impact of both racial and sexual stereotyping and discrimination, the member strives to ensure the individual rights and personal dignity of the client in the counseling relationship.

Principle 8. Professional Relationships

Mental health counselors act with due regard for the needs and feelings of their colleagues in counseling and other professions. Mental health counselors respect the prerogatives and obligations of the institutions or organizations with which they associate.

A. Mental health counselors understand how related professions complement their work and make full use of other professional, technical, and administrative resources that best serve the interests of consumers. The absence of formal relationships with other professional workers does not relieve mental health counselors from the responsibility of securing for their clients the best possible professional services; indeed, this circumstance presents a challenge to the professional competence of mental health counselors, requiring special sensitivity to problems outside their areas of training, and foresight, diligence, and tact in obtaining the professional assistance needed by clients.

B. Mental health counselors know and take into account the traditions and practices of other professional groups with which they work and cooperate fully with members of such groups when research, services and other functions are shared, or in working for the benefit of public welfare.

C. Mental health counselors treat professional colleagues with the same dignity and respect afforded to clients. Professional discourse should be free of personal attacks.

D. Mental health counselors strive to provide positive conditions for those they employ and to spell out clearly the conditions of such employment. They encourage their employees to engage in activities that facilitate their further professional development.

E. Mental health counselors respect the viability, reputation, and proprietary rights of organizations that they serve. Mental health counselors show due regard for the interest of their present or perspective employers. In those instances where they are critical of policies, they attempt to effect change by constructive action within the organization.

F. In pursuit of research, mental health counselors are to give sponsoring agencies, host institutions, and publication channels the same respect and opportunity for giving informed consent that they accord to individual research participants. They are aware of their obligation to future research workers and ensure that host institutions are given feedback information and proper acknowledgement.

G. Credit is assigned to those who have contributed to a publication, in proportion to their contribution.

H. Mental health counselors do not accept or offer referral fees from other professionals.

I. When mental health counselors violate ethical standards, mental health counselors who know firsthand of such activities should, if possible, attempt to rectify the situation. Failing an informal solution, mental health counselors should bring such unethical activities to the attention of the appropriate state licensure board committee on ethics and professional conduct. Only after all professional alternatives have been utilized will mental health counselors begin legal action for resolution.

Principle 9. Supervisee, Student and Employee Relationships

Mental health counselors have an ethical concern for the integrity and welfare of supervisees, students, and employees. They maintain these relationships on a professional and confidential basis. They recognize the influential position they have with regard to both current and former supervisees, students, and employees. They avoid exploiting their trust and dependency.

A. Mental health counselors do not engage in ongoing counseling relationships with current supervisees, students, and employees.

B. All forms of sexual behavior with supervisees, students, and employees are unethical. Further, mental health counselors do not engage in sexual or other harassment of supervisees, students, employees or colleagues.

C. Mental health counselor supervisors advise their supervisees, students, and employees against offering or engaging in or holding themselves out as competent to engage in professional services beyond their training, level of experience, and competence.

D. Mental health counselors make every effort to avoid dual relationships with supervisees, students and employees that could impair their judgement or increase the risk of personal or financial exploitation. When a dual relationship can not be avoided, mental health counselors take appropriate professional precautions to make sure that judgement is not impaired. Examples of such dual relationships include, but are not limited to, a supervisee who receives supervision as a benefit of employment, or a student in a small college where the only available counselor on campus is an instructor.

E. Mental health counselors do not disclose supervisee confidences except:

1. To prevent clear and eminent danger to a person or persons.
2. As mandated by law.
   a. As in mandated child or senior abuse reporting.

b. Where the counselor is a defendant in a civil, criminal or disciplinary action.
c. Educational or training settings where only other professionals who will share responsibility for the training of the supervisee are present.
d. Where there is a waiver of confidentiality obtained in writing prior to such a release of information.

F. Supervisees must make their clients aware in their informed consent statement that they are under supervision and they must provide their clients with the name and credentials of their supervisor.

G. Mental health counselors require their supervisees, students and employees to adhere to the Code of Ethics. Students and supervisees have the same obligations to clients as those required of mental health counselors.

Principle 10. Moral and Legal Standards

Mental health counselors recognize that they have a moral, legal and ethical responsibility to the community and to the general public. Mental health counselors should be aware of the prevailing community standards and the impact of professional standards on the community.

A. To protect students, mental health counselors/teachers will be aware of diverse backgrounds of students and will see that material is treated objectively and fairly to reflect the multicultural community in which they live.

B. Providers of counseling services conform to the statutes relating to such services as established by their state and its regulating professional board(s).

C. As employees, mental health counselors refuse to participate in an employer's practices that are inconsistent with the moral and legal standards established by federal or state legislation regarding the treatment of employees. In particular and for example, mental health counselors will not condone practices that result in illegal or otherwise unjustified discrimination on the basis of race, sex, religion or national origin in hiring, promotion or training.

D. In providing counseling services to clients, mental health counselors avoid any action that will violate or diminish the legal and civil rights of clients or of others that may be affected by the action.

E. Sexual conduct, not limited to sexual intercourse, between mental health counselors and clients is specifically in violation of this Code of Ethics. This does not, however, prohibit the use of explicit instructional aids including films and videotapes. Such use is within excepted practices of trained and competent sex therapists.

Principle 11. Professional Responsibility

In their commitment to the understanding of human behavior, mental health counselors value objectivity and integrity, and in providing services they maintain the highest standards. They accept responsibility for the consequences of their work and make every effort to ensure that their services are used appropriately.

A. Mental health counselors accept ultimate responsibility for selecting appropriate areas for investigation and the methods relevant to minimize the possibility that their finding will be misleading. They provide thorough discussion of the limitations of their data and alternative hypotheses, especially where their work touches on social policy or might be misconstrued to the detriment of specific age, sex, ethnic, socioeconomic, or other social categories. In publishing reports of their work, they never discard observations that may modify the interpretation of results. Mental health counselors take credit only for the work they have actually done. In pursuing research, mental health counselors ascertain that their efforts will not lead to changes in individuals or organizations unless such changes are part of the agreement at the time of obtaining informed consent. Mental health counselors clarify in advance the expectations for sharing and utilizing research data. They avoid dual relationships that may limit objectivity, whether theoretical, political, or monetary, so that interference with data, subjects, and milieu is kept to a minimum.

B. As employees of an institution or agency, mental health counselors have the responsibility to remain alert to institutional pressures that may distort reports of counseling findings or use them in ways counter to the promotion of human welfare.

C. When serving as members of governmental or other organizational bodies, mental health counselors remain accountable as individuals to the Code of Ethics of the American Mental Health Counselors Association.

D. As teachers, mental health counselors recognize their primary obligation to help others acquire knowledge and skill. They maintain high standards of scholarship and objectivity by presenting counseling information fully and accurately, and by giving appropriate recognition to alternative viewpoints.

E. As practitioners, mental health counselors know that they bear a heavy social responsibility because their recommendations and professional actions may alter the lives of others. They therefore remained fully cognizant of their impact and alert to personal, social, organizational, financial or political situations or pressures that might lead the misuse of their influence.

F. Mental health counselors provide reasonable and timely feedback to employees, trainees, supervisors, students, clients, and others whose work they may evaluate.

Principle 12. Private Practice

A. A mental health counselor should assist, where permitted by legislation or judicial decision, the profession in fulfilling its duty to make counseling services available in private settings.

B. In advertising services as a private practitioner, mental health counselors should advertise the services in such a manner so as to accurately inform the public as to services, expertise, profession, and techniques of counseling in a professional manner. Mental health counselors who assume an executive leadership role in the organization shall not permit their name to be used in professional notices during periods when not actively engaged in the private practice of counseling. Mental health counselors advertise the following: highest relevant degree, type and level of certification or license, and type and/or description of services or other relevant information. Such information should not contain false, inaccurate, misleading, partial, out of context, descriptive material or statements.

C. Mental health counselors may join in partnership/corporation with other mental health counselors and/or other professional provided that each mental health counselor of the partnership or corporation makes clear his/her separate

specialties, buying name in compliance with the regulations of the locality.

D. Mental health counselors have an obligation to withdraw from an employment relationship or a counseling relationship if it is believed that employment will result in violation of the Code of Ethics, if their mental capacity or physical condition renders it difficult to carry out an effective professional relationship, or if the mental health counselor is discharged by the clients because the counseling relationship is no longer productive for the client.

E. Mental health counselors should adhere and support the regulations for private practice in the locality where the services are offered.

F. Mental health counselors refrain from attempts to utilize one's institutional affiliation to recruit clients for one's private practice. Mental health counselors are to refrain from offering their services in the private sector when they are employed by an institution in which this is prohibited by stated policy that reflects conditions of employment.

Principle 13. Public Statements

Mental health counselors in their professional roles may be expected or required to make public statements providing counseling information or professional opinions, or supply information about the availability of counseling products and services. In making such statements, mental health counselors take into full account the limits and uncertainties of present counseling knowledge and techniques. They represent, as accurately and objectively as possible, their professional qualifications, expertise, affiliations, and functions, as well as those of the institutions or organizations with which the statements may be associated. All public statements, announcements of services, and promotional activities should serve the purpose of providing sufficient information to aid the consumer public in making informed judgements and choices on matters that concern it. When announcing professional counseling services, mental health counselors may describe or explain those services offered but may not evaluate as to their quality or uniqueness and do not allow for testimonials by implication. All public statements should be otherwise consistent with this Code of Ethics.

Principle 14. Internet On-Line Counseling

Mental health counselors engaged in delivery of services that involve the telephone, teleconferencing, and the Internet in which these areas are generally recognized. Standards for preparatory training do not yet exist. Mental health counselors take responsible steps to ensure the competence of their work and protect patients, clients, students, research participants, and others from harm.

A. **Confidentiality**

Mental health counselors ensure that clients are provided sufficient information to adequately address and explain the limitations of computer technology in the counseling process in general and the difficulties of ensuring complete client confidentiality of information transmitted through electronic communications over the Internet through on-line counseling. Professional counselors inform clients of the limitations of confidentiality and identify foreseeable situations in which confidentiality must be breached in light of the law in both the state in which the client is located and the state in which the professional counselor is licensed. Mental health counselors shall become aware of the means for reporting and protecting suicidal clients in their locale. Mental health counselors shall become aware of the means for reporting homicidal clients in the client's jurisdiction.

B. **Mental Health Counselor Identification**

Mental health counselors provide a readily visible notice advising clients of the identities of all professional counselor(s) who will have access to the information transmitted by the client. Mental health counselors provide background information on all professional communications, including education, licensing, and certification, and practice information.

C. **Client Identification**

Professional counselors identify clients, verify identities of clients, and obtain alternative methods of contacting clients in emergency situations.

D. **Client Waiver**

Mental health counselors require clients to execute client waiver agreements stating that the client acknowledges the limitations inherent in ensuring client confidentiality of information transmitted through on-line counseling and acknowledge the limitations that are inherent in a counseling process that is not provided face-to-face. Limited training in the area of on-line counseling must be explained and the client's informed consent must be secured.

E. **Electronic Transfer of Client Information**

Mental health counselors electronically transfer client confidential information to authorized third-party recipients only when both the professional counselors and the authorized recipient have "secure" transfer and acceptance communication capabilities; the recipient is able to effectively protect the confidentiality of the client's confidential information to be transferred; and the informed written consent of the client, acknowledging the limits of confidentiality, has been obtained.

F. **Establishing the On-Line Counseling Relationship**

1. **Appropriateness of On-line Counseling** Mental health counselors develop an appropriate in-take procedure for potential clients to determine whether on-line counseling is appropriate for the needs of the client. Mental health counselors warn potential clients that on-line counseling services may not be appropriate in certain situations and, to the extent possible, inform the client of specific limitations, potential risks, and/or potential benefits relevant to the client's anticipated use of on-line counseling services. Mental health counselors ensure that clients are intellectually, emotionally, and physically capable of using on-line counseling services, and of understanding the potential risks and/or limitations of such services.

2. **Counseling Plans** Mental health counselors develop individual on-line counseling plans that are consistent with both the client's individual circumstances and the limitations of on-line counseling. Mental health counselors who determine that on-line counseling is inappropriate for the client should avoid entering into or immediately terminate the on-line counseling relationship and encourage the client to continue the counseling relationship through a traditional alternative method of counseling.

3. **Boundaries of Competence** Mental health counselors provide on-line counseling services only in practice areas within their expertise. Mental health counselors do not provide services to clients in states where doing so would violate local licensure laws or regulations.

G. **Legal Considerations**

Mental health counselors confirm that the provision of on-line services are not prohibited by or otherwise violate any applicable state or local statutes, rules, regulations or ordinances, codes of professional membership organizations, and certifying boards, and/or codes of state licensing boards.

Principle 15. Resolution of Ethical Problems

Neither the American Mental Health Counselors Association, its Board of Directors, nor its National Committee on Ethics investigate or adjudicate ethical complaints. In the event a member has his or her license suspended or revoked by an appropriate state licensure board, the AMHCA Board of Directors may then act in accordance with AMHCA's National By-Laws to suspend or revoke his or her membership.

Any member so suspended may apply for reinstatement upon the reinstatement of his or her licensure.

Source: Revised 2000. Reprinted with permission of the American Mental Health Association.

APPENDIX Q

Responsibilities of Users of Standardized Tests (2003)

Prepared by the Association for Assessment in Counseling (AAC)

Many recent events have influenced the use of tests and assessment in the counseling community. Such events include the use of tests in the educational accountability and reform movement, the publication of the *Standards for Educational and Psychological Testing* (American Educational Research Association [AERA], American Psychological Association [APA], National Council on Measurement in Education [NCME], 1999), the revision of the *Code of Fair Testing Practices in Education* (Joint Committee on Testing Practices [JCTP], 2002), the proliferation of technology-delivered assessment, and the historic passage of the *No Child Left Behind Act* (HR1, 2002) calling for expanded testing in reading/language arts, mathematics, and science that are aligned to state standards.

The purpose of this document is to promote the accurate, fair, and responsible use of standardized tests by the counseling and education communities. RUST is intended to address the needs of the members of the American Counseling Association (ACA) and its Divisions, Branches, and Regions, including counselors, teachers, administrators, and other human service workers. The general public, test developers, and policy makers will find this statement useful as they work with tests and testing issues. The principles in RUST apply to the use of testing instruments regardless of delivery methods (e.g., paper/pencil or computer administered) or setting (e.g., group or individual).

The intent of RUST is to help counselors and other educators implement responsible testing practices. The RUST does not intend to reach beyond or reinterpret the principles outlined in the *Standards for Educational and Psychological Testing* (AERA et al., 1999), nor was it developed to formulate a basis for legal action. The intent is to provide a concise statement useful in the ethical practice of testing. In addition, RUST is intended to enhance the guidelines found in ACA's *Code of Ethics and Standards of Practice* (ACA, 1997) and the *Code of Fair Testing Practices in Education* (JCTP, 2002).

Organization of Document: This document includes test user responsibilities in the following areas:

- Qualifications of Test Users
- Technical Knowledge
- Test Selection
- Test Administration
- Test Scoring

- Interpreting Test Results
- Communicating Test Results

QUALIFICATIONS OF TEST USERS

Qualified test users demonstrate appropriate education, training, and experience in using tests for the purposes under consideration. They adhere to the highest degree of ethical codes, laws, and standards governing professional practice. Lack of essential qualifications or ethical and legal compliance can lead to errors and subsequent harm to clients. Each professional is responsible for making judgments in each testing situation and cannot leave that responsibility either to clients or others in authority. The individual test user must obtain appropriate education and training, or arrange for professional supervision and assistance when engaged in testing in order to provide valuable, ethical, and effective assessment services to the public. Qualifications of test users depend on at least four factors:

1. **Purposes of Testing** A clear purpose for testing should be established. Because the purposes of testing direct how the results are used, qualifications beyond general testing competencies may be needed to interpret and apply data.
2. **Characteristics of Tests** Understanding of the strengths and limitations of each instrument used is a requirement.
3. **Settings and Conditions of Test Use** Assessment of the quality and relevance of test user knowledge and skill to the situation is needed before deciding to test or participate in a testing program.
4. **Roles of Test Selectors, Administrators, Scorers, and Interpreters** The education, training, and experience of test users determine which test they are qualified to administer and interpret.

Each test user must evaluate his or her qualifications and competence for selecting, administering, scoring, interpreting, reporting, or communicating test results. Test users must develop the skills and knowledge for each test he or she intends to use.

TECHNICAL KNOWLEDGE

Responsible use of tests requires technical knowledge obtained through training, education, and continuing professional

468

development. Test users should be conversant and competent in aspects of testing including:

1. **Validity of Test Results**   Validity is the accumulation of evidence to support a specific interpretation of the test results. Since validity is a characteristic of test results, a test may have validities of varying degree, for different purposes. The concept of instructional validity relates to how well the test is aligned to state standards and classroom instructional objectives.
2. **Reliability**   Reliability refers to the consistency of test scores. Various methods are used to calculate and estimate reliability depending on the purpose for which the test is used.
3. **Errors of Measurement**   Various ways may be used to calculate the error associated with a test score. Knowing this and knowing the estimate of the size of the error allows the test user to provide a more accurate interpretation of the scores and to support better-informed decisions.
4. **Scores and Norms**   Basic differences between the purposes of norm-referenced and criterion-referenced scores impact score interpretations.

TEST SELECTION

Responsible use of tests requires that the specific purpose for testing be identified. In addition, the test that is selected should align with that purpose, while considering the characteristics of the test and the test taker. Tests should not be administered without a specific purpose or need for information. Typical purposes for testing include:

1. **Description**   Obtaining objective information on the status of certain characteristics such as achievement, ability, personality types, etc. is often an important use of testing.
2. **Accountability**   When judging the progress of an individual or the effectiveness of an educational institution, strong alignment between what is taught and what is tested needs to be present.
3. **Prediction**   Technical information should be reviewed to determine how accurately the test will predict areas such as appropriate course placement; selection for special programs, interventions, and institutions; and other outcomes of interest.
4. **Program Evaluation**   The role that testing plays in program evaluation and how the test information may be used to supplement other information gathered about the program is an important consideration in test use.

Proper test use involves determining if the characteristics of the test are appropriate for the intended audience and are of sufficient technical quality for the purpose at hand. Some areas to consider include:

1. **The Test Taker**   Technical information should be reviewed to determine if the test characteristics are appropriate for the test taker (e.g., age, grade level, language, cultural background).
2. **Accuracy of Scoring Procedures**   Only tests that use accurate scoring procedures should be used.
3. **Norming and Standardization Procedures**   Norming and standardization procedures should be reviewed to determine if the norm group is appropriate for the intended test takers. Specified test administration procedures must be followed.

4. **Modifications**   For individuals with disabilities, alternative measures may need to be found and used and/or accommodations in test taking procedures may need to be employed. Interpretations need to be made in light of the modifications in the test or testing procedures.
5. **Fairness**   Care should be taken to select tests that are fair to all test takers. When test results are influenced by characteristics or situations unrelated to what is being measured. (e.g., gender, age, ethnic background, existence of cheating, unequal availability of test preparation programs) the use of the resulting information is invalid and potentially harmful. In achievement testing, fairness also relates to whether or not the student has had an opportunity to learn what is tested.

TEST ADMINISTRATION

Test administration includes carefully following standard procedures so that the test is used in the manner specified by the test developers. The test administrator should ensure that test takers work within conditions that maximize opportunity for optimum performance. As appropriate, test takers, parents, and organizations should be involved in the various aspects of the testing process including:

1. **Before administration it is important that relevant persons**
   a. are informed about the standard testing procedures, including information about the purposes of the test, the kinds of tasks involved, the method of administration, and the scoring and reporting;
   b. have sufficient practice experiences prior to the test to include practice, as needed, on how to operate equipment for computer-administered tests and practice in responding to tasks;
   c. have been sufficiently trained in their responsibilities and the administration procedures for the test;
   d. have a chance to review test materials and administration sites and procedures prior to the time for testing to ensure standardized conditions and appropriate responses to any irregularities that occur;
   e. arrange for appropriate modifications of testing materials and procedures in order to accommodate test takers with special needs; and
   f. have a clear understanding of their rights and responsibilities.
2. **During administration it is important that**
   a. the testing environment (e.g., seating, work surfaces, lighting, room temperature, freedom from distractions) and psychological climate are conductive to the best possible performance of the examinees;
   b. sufficiently trained personnel establish and maintain uniform conditions and observe the conduct of test takers when large groups of individuals are tested;
   c. test administrators follow the instructions in the test manual; demonstrate verbal clarity; use verbatim directions; adhere to verbatim directions; follow exact sequence and timing; and use materials that are identical to those specified by the test publisher;
   d. a systematic and objective procedure is in place for observing and recording environmental, health, emotional factors, or other elements that may invalidate test performance and results; deviations from prescribed test administration procedures, including

information on test accommodations for individuals with special needs, are recorded; and

  e. the security of test materials and computer-administered testing software is protected, ensuring that only individuals with a legitimate need for access to the materials/software are able to obtain such access and that steps to eliminate the possibility of breaches in test security and copyright protection are respected.

3. **After administration it is important to**
  a. collect and inventory all secure test materials and immediately report any breaches in test security; and
  b. include notes on any problems, irregularities, and accommodations in the test records.

These precepts represent the basic process for all standardized tests and assessments. Some situations may add steps or modify some of these to provide the best testing milieu possible.

TEST SCORING

Accurate measurement necessitates adequate procedures for scoring the responses of test takers. Scoring procedures should be audited as necessary to ensure consistency and accuracy of application.

1. Carefully implement and/or monitor standard scoring procedures.
2. When test scoring involves human judgment, use rubrics that clearly specify the criteria for scoring. Scoring consistency should be constantly monitored.
3. Provide a method for checking the accuracy of scores when accuracy is challenged by test takers.

INTERPRETING TEST RESULTS

Responsible test interpretation requires knowledge about and experience with the test, the scores, and the decisions to be made. Interpretation of scores on any test should not take place without a thorough knowledge of the technical aspects of the test, the test results, and its limitations. Many factors can impact the valid and useful interpretations of test scores. These can be grouped into several categories including psychometric, test taker, and contextual, as well as others.

1. **Psychometric Factors** Factors such as the reliability, norms, standard error of measurement, and validity of the instrument are important when interpreting test results. Responsible test use considers these basic concepts and how each impacts the scores and hence the interpretation of the test results.
2. **Test Taker Factors** Factors such as the test taker's group membership and how that membership may impact the results of the test is a critical factor in the interpretation of test results. Specifically, the test user should evaluate how the test taker's gender, age, ethnicity, race, socioeconomic status, marital status, and so forth, impact on the individual's results.
3. **Contextual Factors** The relationship of the test to the instructional program, opportunity to learn, quality of the educational program, work and home environment, and other factors that would assist in understanding the test results are useful in interpreting test results. For example, if the test does not align to curriculum standards and how those standards are taught in the classroom, the test results may not provide useful information.

COMMUNICATING TEST RESULTS

Before communication of test results takes place, a solid foundation and preparation is necessary. That foundation includes knowledge of test interpretation and an understanding of the particular test being used, as provided by the test manual.

Conveying test results with language that the test taker, parents, teachers, clients, or general public can understand is one of the key elements in helping others understand the meaning of the test results. When reporting group results, the information needs to be supplemented with background information that can help explain the results with cautions about misinterpretations. The test user should indicate how the test results can be and should not be interpreted.

CLOSING

Proper test use resides with the test user—the counselor and educator. Qualified test users understand the measurement characteristics necessary to select good standardized tests, administer the tests according to specified procedures, assure accurate scoring, accurately interpret test scores for individuals and groups, and ensure productive applications of the results. This document provides guidelines for using tests responsibly with students and clients.

REFERENCES AND RESOURCE DOCUMENTS

American Counseling Association. (1997). *Code of ethics and standards of practice.* Alexandria, VA: Author.

American Counseling Association. (2003). *Standards for qualifications of test users.* Alexandria, VA: Author.

American Educational Research Association, American Psychological Association, National Council on Measurement in Education. (1999). *Standards for educational and psychological testing.* Washington, DC: American Educational Research Association.

American School Counselor Association & Association for Assessment in Counseling (1998). *Competencies in assessment and evaluation for school counselors.* Alexandria, VA: Author.

Joint Committee on Testing Practices. (2000) *Rights and responsibilities of test takers: Guidelines and expectations.* Washington, DC: Author.

Joint Committee on Testing Practices. (2002). *Code of fair testing practices in education.* Washington, DC: Author.

RUST Committee

Janet Wall, Chair
James Augustin
Charles Eberly
Brad Erford
David Lundberg
Timothy Vansickle

APPENDIX R
National Career Development Association Ethical Standards

(Revised 1991)

These Ethical Standards were developed by the National Board for Certified Counselors (NBCC), an independent, voluntary, not-for-profit organization incorporated in 1982. Titled "Code of Ethics" by NBCC and last amended in February 1987, the Ethical Standards were adopted by the National Career Development Association (NCDA) Board of Directors in 1987 and revised in 1991, with minor changes in wording (e.g., the addition of specific references to NCDA members).

PREAMBLE

NCDA is an educational, scientific, and professional organization dedicated to the enhancement of the worth, dignity, potential, and uniqueness of each individual and, thus, to the service of society. This code of ethics enables the NCDA to clarify the nature of ethical responsibilities for present and future professional career counselors.

SECTION A: GENERAL

1. NCDA members influence the development of the profession by continuous efforts to improve professional practices, services, and research. Professional growth is continuous through the career counselor's career and is exemplified by the development of a philosophy that explains why and how a career counselor functions in the helping relationship. Career counselors must gather data on their effectiveness and be guided by their findings.

2. NCDA members have a responsibility to the clients they are serving and to the institutions within which the services are being performed. Career counselors also strive to assist the respective agency, organization, or institution in providing the highest caliber of professional services. The acceptance of employment in an institution implies that the career counselor is in agreement with the general policies and principles of the institution. Therefore, the professional activities of the career counselor are in accord with the objectives of the institution. If, despite concerted efforts, the career counselor cannot reach agreement with the employer as to acceptable standards of conduct that allow for changes in institutional policy that are conducive to the positive growth and development of clients, then terminating the affiliation should be seriously considered.

3. Ethical behavior among professional associates (e.g., career counselors) must be expected at all times. When accessible information raises doubt as to the ethical behavior of professional colleagues, the NCDA member must take action to attempt to rectify this condition. Such action uses the respective institution's channels first and then uses procedures established by the American Counseling Association, of which NCDA is a division.

4. NCDA members neither claim nor imply professional qualifications which exceed those possessed, and are responsible for correcting any misrepresentation of these qualifications by others.

5. NCDA members must refuse a private fee or other remuneration for consultation or counseling with persons who are entitled to their services through the career counselor's employing institution or agency. The policies of some agencies may make explicit provisions for staff members to engage in private practice with agency clients. However, should agency clients desire private counseling or consulting services, they must be apprised of other options available to them. Career counselors must not divert to their private practices, legitimate clients in their primary agencies or of the institutions with which they are affiliated.

6. In establishing fees for professional counseling services, NCDA members must consider the financial status of clients and the respective locality. In the event that the established fee status is inappropriate for the client, assistance must be provided in finding comparable services of acceptable cost.

7. NCDA members seek only those positions in the delivery of professional services for which they are professionally qualified.

8. NCDA members recognize their limitations and provide services or only use techniques for which they are qualified by training and/or experience. Career counselors recognize the need, and seek continuing education, to assure competent services.

9. NCDA members are aware of the intimacy in the counseling relationship, maintain respect for the client, and avoid engaging in activities that seek to meet their personal needs at the expense of the client.

10. NCDA members do not condone or engage in sexual harassment which is defined as deliberate or repeated comments, gestures, or physical contacts of a sexual nature.

11. NCDA members avoid bringing their personal or professional issues into the counseling relationship. Through an awareness of the impact of stereotyping and discrimination (e.g., biases based on age, disability, ethnicity, gender, race, religion, or sexual preference), career counselors guard the individual rights and personal dignity of the client in the counseling relationship.

12. NCDA members are accountable at all times for their behavior. They must be aware that all actions and behaviors of a counselor reflect on professional integrity and, when

inappropriate, can damage the public trust in the counseling profession. To protect public confidence in the counseling profession, career counselors avoid public behavior that is clearly in violation of accepted moral and legal standards.

13. NCDA members have a social responsibility because their recommendations and professional actions may alter the lives of others. Career counselors remain fully cognizant of their impact and are alert to personal, social, organizational, financial, or political situations or pressures which might lead to misuse of their influence.

14. Products or services provided by NCDA members by means of classroom instruction, public lectures, demonstrations, written articles, radio or television programs, or other types of media must meet the criteria cited in Sections A through F of these Ethical Standards.

SECTION B: COUNSELING RELATIONSHIP

1. The primary obligation of NCDA members is to respect the integrity and promote the welfare of the client, regardless of whether the client is assisted individually or in a group relationship. In a group setting, the career counselor is also responsible for taking reasonable precautions to protect individuals from physical and/or psychological trauma resulting from interaction within the group.

2. The counseling relationship and information resulting from it remains confidential, consistent with the legal obligations of the NCDA member. In a group counseling setting, the career counselor sets a norm of confidentiality regarding all group participants' disclosures.

3. NCDA members know and take into account the traditions and practices of other professional groups with whom they work, and they cooperate fully with such groups. If a person is receiving similar services from another professional, career counselors do not offer their own services directly to such a person. If a career counselor is contacted by a person who is already receiving similar services from another professional, the career counselor carefully considers that professional relationship and proceeds with caution and sensitivity to the therapeutic issues as well as the client's welfare. Career counselors discuss these issues with clients so as to minimize the risk of confusion and conflict.

4. When a client's condition indicates that there is a clear and imminent danger to the client or others, the NCDA member must take reasonable personal action or inform responsible authorities. Consultation with other professionals must be used where possible. The assumption of responsibility for the client's behavior must be taken only after careful deliberation, and the client must be involved in the resumption of responsibility as quickly as possible.

5. Records of the counseling relationship, including interview notes, test data, correspondence, audio or visual tape recordings, electronic data storage, and other documents are to be considered professional information for use in counseling. They should not be considered a part of the records of the institution or agency in which the NCDA member is employed unless specified by state statute or regulation. Revelation to others of counseling material must occur only upon the expressed consent of the client; career counselors must make provisions for maintaining confidentiality in the storage and disposal of records. Career counselors providing information to the public or to subordinates, peers, or supervisors have a responsibility to ensure that the content is general; unidentified client information should be accurate and unbiased, and should consist of objective, factual data.

6. NCDA members must ensure that data maintained in electronic storage are secure. The data must be limited to information that is appropriate and necessary for the services being provided and accessible only to appropriate staff members involved in the provision of services by using the best computer security methods available. Career counselors must also ensure that electronically stored data are destroyed when the information is no longer of value in providing services.

7. Data derived from a counseling relationship for use in counselor training or research shall be confined to content that can be disguised to ensure full protection of the identity of the subject/client and shall be obtained with informed consent.

8. NCDA members must inform clients, before or at the time the counseling relationship commences, of the purposes, goals, techniques, rules and procedures, and limitations that may affect the relationship.

9. All methods of treatment by NCDA members must be clearly indicated to prospective recipients and safety precautions must be taken in their use.

10. NCDA members who have an administrative, supervisory, and/or evaluative relationship with individuals seeking counseling services must not serve as the counselor and should refer the individuals to other professionals. Exceptions are made only in instances where an individual's situation warrants counseling intervention and another alternative is unavailable. Dual relationships with clients that might impair the career counselor's objectivity and professional judgment must be avoided and/or the counseling relationship terminated through referral to another competent professional.

11. When NCDA members determine an inability to be of professional assistance to a potential or existing client, they must, respectively, not initiate the counseling relationship or immediately terminate the relationship. In either event, the career counselor must suggest appropriate alternatives. Career counselors must be knowledgeable about referral resources so that a satisfactory referral can be initiated. In the event that the client declines a suggested referral, the career counselor is not obligated to continue the relationship.

12. NCDA members may choose to consult with any other professionally competent person about a client and must notify clients of this right. Career counselors must avoid placing a consultant in a conflict-of-interest situation that would preclude the consultant's being a proper party to the career counselor's efforts to help the client.

13. NCDA members who counsel clients from cultures different from their own must gain knowledge, personal awareness, and sensitivity pertinent to the client populations served and must incorporate culturally relevant techniques into their practice.

14. When NCDA members engage in intensive counseling with a client, the client's counseling needs should be assessed.

When needs exist outside the counselor's expertise, appropriate referrals should be made.

15. NCDA members must screen prospective group counseling participants, especially when the emphasis is on self-understanding and growth through self-disclosure. Career counselors must maintain an awareness of each group participant's welfare throughout the group process.

16. When electronic data and systems are used as a component of counseling services, NCDA members must ensure that the computer application, and any information it contains, are appropriate for the respective needs of clients and is nondiscriminatory. Career counselors must ensure that they themselves have acquired a facilitation level of knowledge with any system they use including hands-on application, search experience, and understanding of the uses of all aspects of the computer-based system. In selecting and/or maintaining computer-based systems that contain career information, career counselors must ensure that the systems provide current, accurate, and locally relevant information. Career counselors must also ensure that clients are intellectually, emotionally, and physically compatible with the use of the computer application and understand its purpose and operation. Client use of a computer application must be evaluated to correct possible problems and assess subsequent needs.

17. NCDA members who develop self-help, stand-alone computer software for use by the general public must first ensure that it is initially designed to function in a stand-alone manner, as opposed to modifying software that was originally designed to require support from a counselor. Secondly, the software must include program statements that provide the user with intended outcomes, suggestions for using the software, descriptions of inappropriately used applications, and descriptions of when and how counseling services might be beneficial. Finally, the manual must include the qualifications of the developer, the development process, validation data, and operating procedures.

SECTION C: MEASUREMENT AND EVALUATION

1. NCDA members must provide specific orientation or information to an examinee prior to and following the administration of assessment instruments or techniques so that the results may be placed in proper perspective with other relevant factors. The purpose of testing and the explicit use of the results must be made known to an examinee prior to testing.

2. In selecting assessment instruments or techniques for use in a given situation or with a particular client, NCDA members must evaluate carefully the instrument's specific theoretical bases and characteristics, validity, reliability, and appropriateness. Career counselors are professionally responsible for using unvalidated information with special care.

3. When making statements to the public about assessment instruments or techniques, NCDA members must provide accurate information and avoid false claims or misconceptions concerning the meaning of psychometric terms. Special efforts are often required to avoid unwarranted connotations of terms such as IQ and grade-equivalent scores.

4. Because many types of assessment techniques exist, NCDA members must recognize the limits of their competence and perform only those functions for which they have received appropriate training.

5. NCDA members must note when tests are not administered under standard conditions or when unusual behavior or irregularities occur during a testing session and the results must be designated as invalid or of questionable validity. Unsupervised or inadequately supervised assessments, such as mail-in tests, are considered unethical. However, the use of standardized instruments that are designed to be self-administered and self-scored, such as interest inventories, is appropriate.

6. Because prior coaching or dissemination of test materials can invalidate test results, NCDA members are professionally obligated to maintain test security. In addition, conditions that produce most favorable test results must be made known to an examinee (e.g., penalty for guessing).

7. NCDA members must consider psychometric limitations when selecting and using an instrument, and must be cognizant of the limitations when interpreting the results. When tests are used to classify clients, career counselors must ensure that periodic review and/or retesting are conducted to prevent client stereotyping.

8. An examinee's welfare, explicit prior understanding, and agreement are the factors used when determining who receives the test results. NCDA members must see that appropriate interpretation accompanies any release of individual or group test data (e.g., limitations of instrument and norms).

9. NCDA members must ensure that computer-generated assessment administration and scoring programs function properly, thereby providing clients with accurate assessment results.

10. NCDA members who are responsible for making decisions based on assessment results must have appropriate training and skills in educational and psychological measurement including validation criteria, test research, and guidelines for test development and use.

11. NCDA members must be cautious when interpreting the results of instruments that possess insufficient technical data, and must explicitly state to examinees the specific purposes for the use of such instruments.

12. NCDA members must proceed with caution when attempting to evaluate and interpret performances of minority group members or other persons who are not represented in the norm group on which the instrument was standardized.

13. NCDA members who develop computer-based interpretations to support the assessment process must ensure that the validity of the interpretations is established prior to the commercial distribution of the computer application.

14. NCDA members recognize that test results may become obsolete, and avoid the misuse of obsolete data.

15. NCDA members must avoid the appropriation, reproduction, or modification of published tests or parts thereof without acknowledgment and permission from the publisher.

SECTION D: RESEARCH AND PUBLICATION

1. NCDA members will adhere to relevant guidelines on research with human subjects. These include:
   a. Code of Federal Regulations, Title 45, Subtitle A, Part 46, as currently issued.
   b. American Psychological Association. (1982). Ethical principles in the conduct of research with human participants. Washington, D.C.: Author.
   c. American Psychological Association. (1981). Research with human participants. American Psychologist, 36, 633–638.
   d. Family Educational Rights and Privacy Act. (Buckley Amendment to P.L. 93-380 of the Laws of 1974).
   e. Current federal regulations and various state privacy acts.
2. In planning research activities involving human subjects, NCDA members must be aware of and responsive to all pertinent ethical principles and ensure that the research problem, design, and execution are in full compliance with the principles.
3. The ultimate responsibility for ethical research lies with the principal researcher, although others involved in research activities are ethically obligated and responsible for their own actions.
4. NCDA members who conduct research with human subjects are responsible for the subjects' welfare throughout the experiment and must take all reasonable precautions to avoid causing injurious psychological, physical, or social effects on their subjects.
5. NCDA members who conduct research must abide by the following basic elements of informed consent:
   a. a fair explanation of the procedures to be followed, including an identification of those which are experimental.
   b. a description of the attendant discomforts and risks.
   c. a description of the benefits to be expected.
   d. a disclosure of appropriate alternative procedures that would be advantageous for subjects.
   e. an offer to answer any inquiries concerning the procedures.
   f. an instruction that subjects are free to withdraw their consent and to discontinue participation in the project or activity at any time.
6. When reporting research results, explicit mention must be made of all the variables and conditions known to the NCDA member that may have affected the outcome of the study or the interpretation of the data.
7. NCDA members who conduct and report research investigations must do so in a manner that minimizes the possibility that the results will be misleading.
8. NCDA members are obligated to make available sufficient original research data to qualified others who may wish to replicate the study.
9. NCDA members who supply data, aid in the research of another person, report research results, or make original data available, must take due care to disguise the identity of respective subjects in the absence of specific authorization from the subject to do otherwise.
10. When conducting and reporting research, NCDA members must be familiar with, and give recognition to, previous work on the topic, must observe all copyright laws, and must follow the principles of giving full credit to those to whom credit is due.
11. NCDA members must give due credit through joint authorship, acknowledgment, footnote statements, or other appropriate means to those who have contributed significantly to the research and/or publication, in accordance with such contributions.
12. NCDA members should communicate to others the results of any research judged to be of professional value. Results that reflect unfavorably on institutions, programs, services, or vested interests must not be withheld.
13. NCDA members who agree to cooperate with another individual in research and/or publication incur an obligation to cooperate as promised in terms of punctuality of performance and with full regard to the completeness and accuracy of the information required.
14. NCDA members must not submit the same manuscript, or one essentially similar in content, for simultaneous publication consideration by two or more journals. In addition, manuscripts that are published in whole or substantial part in another journal or published work should not be submitted for publication without acknowledgement and permission from the previous publication.

SECTION E: CONSULTING

Consultation refers to a voluntary relationship between a professional helper and help-needing individual, group, or social unit in which the consultant is providing help to the client(s) in defining and solving a work-related problem or potential work-related problem with a client or client system.

1. NCDA members acting as consultants must have a high degree of self-awareness of their own values, knowledge, skills, limitations, and needs in entering a helping relationship that involves human and/or organizational change. The focus of the consulting relationship must be on the issues to be resolved and not on the person(s) presenting the problem.
2. In the consulting relationship, the NCDA member and client must understand and agree upon the problem definition, subsequent goals, and predicted consequences of interventions selected.
3. NCDA members must be reasonably certain that they, or the organization represented, have the necessary competencies and resources for giving the kind of help that is needed or that may develop later, and that appropriate referral resources are available to the consultant.
4. NCDA members in a consulting relationship must encourage and cultivate client adaptability and growth toward self-direction. NCDA members must maintain this role consistently and not become decision makers for clients or create a future dependency.
5. NCDA members conscientiously adhere to the NCDA Ethical Standards when announcing consultant availability for services.

SECTION F: PRIVATE PRACTICE

1. NCDA members should assist the profession by facilitating the availability of counseling services in private as well as public settings.
2. In advertising services as private practitioners, NCDA members must advertise in a manner that accurately informs the public of the professional services, expertise, and counseling techniques available.
3. NCDA members who assume an executive leadership role in a private practice organization do not permit their names to be used in professional notices during periods of time when they are not actively engaged in the private practice of counseling.
4. NCDA members may list their highest relevant degree, type, and level of certification and/or license, address, telephone number, office hours, type and/or description of services, and other relevant information. Listed information must not contain false, inaccurate, misleading, partial, out-of-context, or otherwise deceptive material or statements.
5. NCDA members who are involved in partnership or corporation with other professionals must, in compliance with the regulations of the locality, clearly specify the separate specialties of each member of the partnership or corporation.
6. NCDA members have an obligation to withdraw from a private-practice counseling relationship if it violates the NCDA Ethical Standards, if the mental or physical condition of the NCDA member renders it difficult to carry out an effective professional relationship, or if the counseling relationship is no longer productive for the client.

PROCEDURES FOR PROCESSING ETHICAL COMPLAINTS

As a division of the American Counseling Association (ACA), the National Career Development Association (NCDA) adheres to the guidelines and procedures for processing ethical complaints and the disciplinary sanctions adopted by ACA. A complaint against an NCDA member may be filed by any individual or group of individuals ("complainant"), whether or not the complainant is a member of NCDA. Action will not be taken on anonymous complaints.

For specifics on how to file ethical complaints and a description of the guidelines and procedures for processing complaints, contact:

ACA Ethics Committee
c/o Executive Director
American Counseling Association
5999 Stevenson Avenue
Alexandria, VA 22304
Telephone: 1-800-347-6647

APPENDIX S

Association for Specialists in Group Work Best Practice Guidelines (1998)

The Association for Specialists in Group Work (ASGW) is a division of the American Counseling Association whose members are interested in and specialize in group work. We value the creation of community; service to our members, clients, and the profession; and value leadership as a process to facilitate the growth and development of individuals and groups.

The Association for Specialists in Group Work recognizes the commitment of its members to the Code of Ethics and Standards of Practice (as revised in 1995) of its parent organization, the American Counseling Association, and nothing in this document shall be construed to supplant that code. These Best Practice Guidelines are intended to clarify the application of the ACA Code of Ethics and Standards of Practice to the field of group work by defining Group Workers' responsibility and scope of practice involving those activities, strategies and interventions that are consistent and current with effective and appropriate professional ethical and community standards. ASGW views ethical process as being integral to group work and views Group Workers as ethical agents. Group Workers, by their very nature in being responsible and responsive to their group members, necessarily embrace a certain potential for ethical vulnerability. It is incumbent upon Group Workers to give considerable attention to the intent and context of their actions because the attempts of Group Workers to influence human behavior through group work always have ethical implications. These Best Practice Guidelines address Group Workers' responsibilities in planning, performing, and processing groups.

SECTION A: BEST PRACTICE IN PLANNING

A.1. Professional Context and Regulatory Requirements

Group Workers actively know, understand and apply the ACA Code of Ethics and Standards of Best Practice, the ASGW Professional Standards for the Training of Group Workers, the ASGW Best Practice Guidelines, the ASGW diversity competencies, the ACA Multicultural Guidelines, relevant state laws, accreditation requirements, relevant National Board for Certified Counselors Codes and Standards, their organization's standards, and insurance requirements impacting the practice of group work.

A.2. Scope of Practice and Conceptual Framework

These guidelines were approved by the association for specialists in Group Work (ASGW) Executive Board, March 29, 1998.

Prepared by Lynn Rapin and Linda Keel, ASGW Ethics committee Co-Chairs.

Group Workers define the scope of practice related to the core and specialization competencies defined in the ASGW Training Standards. Group Workers are aware of personal strengths and weaknesses in leading groups. Group Workers develop and are able to articulate a general conceptual framework to guide practice and a rationale for use of techniques that are to be used. Group Workers limit their practice to those areas for which they meet the training criteria established by the ASGW Training Standards.

A.3. Assessment

a. Assessment of self. Group Workers actively assess their knowledge and skills related to the specific group(s) offered. Group Workers assess their values, beliefs and theoretical orientation and how these impact upon the group, particularly when working with a diverse and multicultural population.

b. Ecological assessment. Group Workers assess community needs, agency or organization resources, sponsoring organization mission, staff competency, attitudes regarding group work, professional training levels of potential group leaders regarding group work; client attitudes regarding group work, and multicultural and diversity considerations. Group Workers use this information as the basis for making decisions related to their group practice, or to the implementation of groups for which they have supervisory, evaluation, or oversight responsibilities.

A.4. Program Development and Evaluation

a. Group Workers identify the type(s) of group(s) to be offered and how they relate to community needs.

b. Group Workers concisely state in writing the purpose and goals of the group. Group Workers also identify the role of the group members in influencing or determining the group goals.

c. Group Workers set fees consistent with the organization's fee schedule, taking into consideration the financial status and locality of prospective group members.

d. Group Workers choose techniques and a leadership style appropriate to the type(s) of group(s) being offered.

e. Group Workers have an evaluation plan consistent with regulatory, organization and insurance requirements, where appropriate.

f. Group Workers take into consideration current professional guidelines when using technology, including but not limited to Internet communication.

A.5. Resources

Group Workers coordinate resources related to the kind of group(s) and group activities to be provided, such as: adequate funding; the appropriateness and availability of a trained co-leader; space and privacy requirements for the type(s) of group(s) being offered; marketing and recruiting; and appropriate collaboration with other community agencies and organizations.

A.6. Professional Disclosure Statement

Group Workers have a professional disclosure statement which includes information on confidentiality and exceptions to confidentiality, theoretical orientation, information on the nature, purpose(s) and goals of the group, the group services that can be provided, the role and responsibility of group members and leaders, group workers; qualifications to conduct the specific group(s), specific licenses, certifications and professional affiliations, and address of licensing/credentialing body.

A.7. Group and Member Preparation

a. Group Workers screen prospective group members if appropriate to the type of group being offered. When selection of group members is appropriate, Group Workers identify group members whose needs and goals are compatible with the goals of the group.
b. Group Workers facilitate informed consent. Group Workers provide in oral and written form to prospective members (when appropriate to group type): the professional disclosure statement; group purpose and goals; group participation expectations including voluntary and involuntary membership; role expectations of members and leader(s); policies related to entering and exiting the group; policies governing substance use; policies and procedures governing mandated groups (where relevant); documentation requirements; disclosure of information to others; implications of out-of-group contact or involvement among members; procedures for consultation between group leader(s) and group member(s); fees and time parameters; and potential impacts of group participation.
c. Group Workers obtain the appropriate consent forms for work with minors and other dependent group members.
d. Group Workers define confidentiality and its limits (for example, legal and ethical exceptions and expectations; waivers implicit with treatment plans, documentation and insurance usage). Group Workers have the responsibility to inform all group participants of the need for confidentiality, potential consequences of breaching confidentiality and that legal privilege does not apply to group discussions (unless provided by state statute).

A.8. Professional Development

Group Workers recognize that professional growth is a continuous, ongoing, developmental process throughout their career.
a. Group Workers remain current and increase knowledge and skill competencies through activities such as continuing education, professional supervision, and participation in personal and professional development activities.
b. Group Workers seek consultation and/or supervision regarding ethical concerns that interfere with effective functioning as a group leader. Supervisors have the responsibility to keep abreast of consultation, group theory, process, and adhere to related ethical guidelines.
c. Group Workers seek appropriate professional assistance for their own personal problems or conflicts that are likely to impair their professional judgment or work performance.
d. Group Workers seek consultation and supervision to ensure appropriate practice whenever working with a group for which all knowledge and skill competencies have not been achieved.
e. Group Workers keep abreast of group research and development.

A.9. Trends and Technological Changes

Group Workers are aware of and responsive to technological changes as they affect society and the profession. These include but are not limited to changes in mental health delivery systems; legislative and insurance industry reforms; shifting population demographics and client needs; and technological advances in Internet and other communication and delivery systems. Group Workers adhere to ethical guidelines related to the use of developing technologies.

SECTION B BEST PRACTICE IN PERFORMING

B.1. Self-Knowledge

Group Workers are aware of and monitor their strengths and weaknesses and the effects these have on group members.

B.2. Group Competencies

Group Workers have a basic knowledge of groups and the principles of group dynamics, and are able to perform the core group competencies, as described in the ASGW Professional Standards for the Training of Group Workers. Additionally, Group Workers have adequate understanding and skill in any group specialty area chosen for practice (psychotherapy, counseling, task, psychoeducation, as described in the ASGW Training Standards).

B.3. Group Plan Adaptation

a. Group Workers apply and modify knowledge, skills and techniques appropriate to group type and stage, and to the unique needs of various cultural and ethnic groups.
b. Group Workers monitor the group's progress toward the group goals and plan.
c. Group Workers clearly define and maintain ethical, professional, and social relationship boundaries with group members as appropriate to their role in the organization and the type of group being offered.

B.4. Therapeutic Conditions and Dynamics

Group Workers understand and are able to implement appropriate models of group development, process observation and therapeutic conditions.

B.5. Meaning

Group Workers assist members in generating meaning from the group experience.

B.6. Collaboration

Group Workers assist members in developing individual goals and respect group members as co-equal partners in the group experience.

B.7. Evaluation

Group Workers include evaluation (both formal and informal) between sessions and at the conclusion of the group.

B.8. Diversity

Group Workers practice with broad sensitivity to client differences including but not limited to ethnic, gender, religious, sexual, psychological maturity, economic class, family history, physical characteristics or limitations, and geographic location. Group Workers continuously seek information regarding the cultural issues of the diverse population with whom they are working both by interaction with participants and from using outside resources.

B.9. Ethical Surveillance

Group Workers employ an appropriate ethical decision making model in responding to ethical challenges and issues and in determining courses of action and behavior for self and group members. In addition, Group Workers employ applicable standards as promulgated by ACA, ASGW, or other appropriate professional organizations.

SECTION C: BEST PRACTICE IN GROUP PROCESSING

C.1. Processing Schedule

Group Workers process the workings of the group with themselves, group members, supervisors or other colleagues, as appropriate. This may include assessing progress on group and member goals, leader behaviors and techniques, group dynamics and interventions; developing understanding and acceptance of meaning. Processing may occur both within sessions and before and after each session, at time of termination, and later follow up, as appropriate.

C.2. Reflective Practice

Group Workers attend to opportunities to synthesize theory and practice and to incorporate learning outcomes into ongoing groups. Group Workers attend to session dynamics of members and their interactions and also attend to the relationship between session dynamics and leader values, cognition, and affect.

C.3. Evaluation and Follow-Up

a. Group Workers evaluate process and outcomes. Results are used for ongoing program planning, improvement and revisions of current group and/or to contribute to professional research literature. Group Workers follow all applicable policies and standards in using group material for research and reports.
b. Group Workers conduct follow-up contact with group members, as appropriate, to assess outcomes or when requested by a group member(s).

C.4. Consultation and Training with Other Organizations

Group Workers provide consultation and training to organizations in and out of their setting, when appropriate. Group Workers seek out consultation as needed with competent professional persons knowledgeable about group work.

Source: Copyright © 1998 ASGW. Reprinted with permission.

APPENDIX T

Code of Professional Ethics for Rehabilitation Counselors

Adopted in June 2001 by the Commission on Rehabilitation Counselor Certification for its Certified Rehabilitation Counselors. This Code is effective as of January 1, 2002.

PREAMBLE

Rehabilitation counselors are committed to facilitating the personal, social, and economic independence of individuals with disabilities. In fulfilling this commitment, rehabilitation counselors work with people, programs, institutions, and service delivery systems. Rehabilitation counselors provide services within the Scope of Practice for Rehabilitation Counseling (see the Scope of Practice document) and recognize that both action and inaction can be facilitating or debilitating. It is essential that rehabilitation counselors demonstrate adherence to ethical standards and ensure that the standards are enforced vigorously. The Code of Professional Ethics for Rehabilitation Counselors, henceforth referred to as the Code, is designed to facilitate these goals.

The fundamental spirit of caring and respect with which the Code is written is based upon five principles of ethical behavior.[1] These include autonomy, beneficence, nonmaleficence, justice, and fidelity, as defined below:

Autonomy: To honor the right to make individual decisions.
Beneficence: To do good to others.
Nonmaleficence: To do no harm to others.
Justice: To be fair and give equally to others.
Fidelity: To be loyal, honest, and keep promises.

The primary obligation of rehabilitation counselors is to their clients, defined in the Code as individuals with disabilities who are receiving services from rehabilitation counselors. Regardless of whether direct client contact occurs or whether indirect services are provided, rehabilitation counselors are obligated to adhere to the Code. At times, rehabilitation counseling services may be provided to individuals other than those with disabilities, such as a student population. In all instances, the primary obligation remains with the client and adherence to the Code is required.

---

[1] Beauchamp, T. L., & Childress, J. F. (1994). *Principles of biomedical ethics* (4th ed.). Oxford: Oxford University Press. Kitchener, K. S. (1984). Ethics in counseling psychology: Distinctions and directions. *Counseling Psychologists*, 12(3), 43–55.

The basic objective of the Code is to promote public welfare by specifying ethical behavior expected of rehabilitation counselors. The Enforceable Standards within the Code are the exacting standards intended to provide guidance in specific circumstances and will serve as the basis for processing ethical complaints initiated against certificants.

Rehabilitation counselors who violate the Code are subject to disciplinary action. Since the use of the Certified Rehabilitation Counselor (CRC) designation is a privilege granted by the Commission on Rehabilitation Counselor Certification (CRCC), CRCC reserves unto itself the power to suspend or to revoke the privilege or to approve other penalties for a violation. Disciplinary penalties are imposed as warranted by the severity of the offense and its attendant circumstances. All disciplinary actions are undertaken in accordance with published procedures and penalties designed to assure the proper enforcement of the Code within the framework of due process and equal protection under the law.

SECTION A: THE COUNSELING RELATIONSHIP

A.1. Client Welfare

a. **Definition of Client.** The primary obligation of rehabilitation counselors will be to their clients, defined as individuals with disabilities who are receiving services from rehabilitation counselors.

b. **Rehabilitation and Counseling Plans.** Rehabilitation counselors will work jointly with their clients in devising and revising integrated, individual rehabilitation and counseling plans that contain realistic and mutually agreed upon goals and are consistent with abilities and circumstances of clients.

c. **Career and Employment Needs.** Rehabilitation counselors will work with their clients in considering employment that is consistent with the overall abilities, vocational limitations, physical restrictions, psychological limitations, general temperament, interest and aptitude patterns, social skills, education, general qualifications, and cultural and other relevant characteristics and needs of clients. Rehabilitation counselors will neither place nor participate in placing clients in positions that will result in damaging the interest and the welfare of clients, employers, or the public.

d. **Autonomy.**   Rehabilitation counselors will respect the autonomy of the client if actions such as involuntary commitment or initiation of guardianship are taken that diminish client autonomy. The assumption of responsibility for decision-making on behalf of the client will be taken only after careful deliberation. The rehabilitation counselor will advocate for client resumption of responsibility as quickly as possible.

A.2. Respecting Diversity

a. **Respecting Culture.**   Rehabilitation counselors will demonstrate respect for clients' cultural backgrounds.

b. **Interventions.**   Rehabilitation counselors will develop and adapt interventions and services to incorporate consideration of clients' cultural perspectives and recognition of barriers external to clients that may interfere with achieving effective rehabilitation outcomes.

c. **Non-Discrimination.**   Rehabilitation counselors will not condone or engage in discrimination based on age, color, culture, disability, ethnic group, gender, race, religion, sexual orientation, marital status, or socioeconomic status

A.3. Client Rights

a. **Disclosure to Clients.**   When counseling is initiated, and throughout the counseling process as necessary, rehabilitation counselors will inform clients, preferably through both written and oral means, of their credentials, the purposes, goals, techniques, procedures, limitations, potential risks, and benefits of services to be performed, and other pertinent information. Rehabilitation counselors will take steps to ensure that clients understand the implications of diagnosis, the intended use of tests and reports, fees, and billing arrangements. Clients have the right to (1) expect confidentiality will be provided with an explanation of its limitations, including disclosure to supervisors and/or treatment team professionals; (2) obtain clear information about their case records; (3) actively participate in the development and implementation of rehabilitation counseling plans; and (4) refuse any recommended services and be advised of the consequences of such refusal.

b. **Third Party Referral.**   Rehabilitation counselors who have direct contact with a client at the request of a third party will define the nature of their relationships and role to all rightful, legal parties with whom they have direct contact. Direct contact is defined as any written, oral, or electronic communication. Legal parties may include clients, legal guardians, referring third parties, and attorneys actively involved in a matter directly related to rehabilitation services.

c. **Indirect Service Provision.**   Rehabilitation counselors who are employed by third parties as case consultants or expert witnesses, and who engage in communication with the individual with a disability, will fully disclose to the individual with a disability and/or his or her designee their role and limits of their relationship. Communication includes all forms of written or oral interactions regardless of the type of communication tool used. When there is no pretense or intent to provide rehabilitation counseling services directly to the individual with a disability, and where there will be no communication, disclosure by the rehabilitation counselor is not required.

When serving as case consultants or expert witnesses, rehabilitation counselors will provide unbiased, objective opinions. Rehabilitation counselors acting as expert witnesses will generate written documentation, either in the form of case notes or a report, as to their involvement and/or conclusions.

d. **Freedom of Choice.**   To the extent possible, rehabilitation counselors will offer clients the freedom to choose whether to enter into a counseling relationship and to determine which professional(s) will provide counseling. Restrictions that limit choices of clients will be fully explained. Rehabilitation counselors will honor the rights of clients to consent to participate and the right to make decisions with regard to rehabilitation services. Rehabilitation counselors will inform clients or the clients' legal guardians of factors that may affect decisions to participate in rehabilitation services, and they will obtain written consent or will acknowledge consent in writing after clients or legal guardians are fully informed of such factors.

e. **Inability to Give Consent.**   When counseling minors or persons unable to give voluntary informed consent, rehabilitation counselors will obtain written informed consent from legally responsible parties. Where no legally responsible parties exist, rehabilitation counselors will act in the best interest of clients.

f. **Involvement of Significant Others.**   Rehabilitation counselors will attempt to enlist family understanding and involvement of family and/or significant others as a positive resource if (or when) appropriate. The client or legal guardian's permission will be secured prior to any involvement of family and/or significant others.

A.4. Personal Needs and Values

In the counseling relationship, rehabilitation counselors will be aware of the intimacy and responsibilities inherent in the counseling relationship, maintain respect for clients, and avoid actions that seek to meet their personal needs at the expense of clients.

A.5. Sexual Intimacies with Clients

a. **Current Clients.**   Rehabilitation counselors will not have any type of sexual intimacies with clients and will not counsel persons with whom they have had a sexual relationship.

b. **Former Clients.**   Rehabilitation counselors will not engage in sexual intimacies with former clients within a minimum of five years after terminating the counseling relationship. Rehabilitation counselors who engage in such relationship after five years following termination will have the responsibility to examine and document thoroughly that such relations do not have an exploitative nature, based on factors such as duration of counseling, amount of time since counseling, termination circumstances, client's personal history and mental status, adverse impact on the client, and actions by the counselor suggesting a plan to initiate a sexual relationship with the client after termination. Rehabilitation counselors will seek peer consultation prior to engaging in a sexual relationship with a former client.

A.6. Non-Professional Relationships with Clients

a. **Potential for Harm.**   Rehabilitation counselors will be aware of their influential positions with respect to clients, and will avoid exploiting the trust and dependency of clients.

Rehabilitation counselors will make every effort to avoid non-professional relationships with clients that could impair professional judgement or increase the risk of harm to clients. (Examples of such relationships include, but are not limited to, familial, social, financial, business, close personal relationships with clients, or volunteer or paid work within an office in which the client is actively receiving services.) When a non-professional relationship cannot be avoided, rehabilitation counselors will take appropriate professional precautions such as informed consent, consultation, supervision, and documentation to ensure that judgement is not impaired and no exploitation occurs.

b. **Superior/Subordinate Relationships.** Rehabilitation counselors will not accept as clients, superiors or subordinates, with whom they have administrative, supervisory, or evaluative relationships.

A.7. Multiple Clients

When rehabilitation counselors agree to provide counseling services to two or more persons who have a relationship (such as husband and wife, or parents and children), rehabilitation counselors will clarify at the outset which person or persons are clients, and the nature of the relationships they will have with each involved person. If it becomes apparent that rehabilitation counselors may be called upon to perform potentially conflicting roles, they will clarify, adjust, or withdraw from such roles appropriately.

A.8. Group Work

a. **Screening.** Rehabilitation counselors will screen prospective group counseling/therapy participants. To the extent possible, rehabilitation counselors will select members whose needs and goals are compatible with goals of the group, who will not impede the group process, and whose well being will not be jeopardized by the group experience.

b. **Protecting Clients.** In a group setting, rehabilitation counselors will take reasonable precautions to protect clients from physical or psychological trauma.

A.9. Termination and Referral

a. **Abandonment Prohibited.** Rehabilitation counselors will not abandon or neglect clients in counseling. Rehabilitation counselors will assist in making appropriate arrangements for the continuation of treatment, when necessary, during interruptions such as vacations, and following termination.

b. **Inability to Assist Clients.** If rehabilitation counselors determine an inability to be of professional assistance to clients, they will avoid entering or immediately terminate a counseling relationship.

c. **Appropriate Termination.** Rehabilitation counselors will terminate a counseling relationship, securing client agreement when possible, when it is reasonably clear that the client is no longer benefiting, when services are no longer required, when counseling no longer serves the client's needs or interests, or when there is failure to pay fees according to Section J of this document.

d. **Referral upon Termination.** Rehabilitation counselors will be knowledgeable about referral resources and suggest appropriate alternatives. If clients decline the suggested referral,

rehabilitation counselors have the right to discontinue the relationship.

A.10. Computer Technology

a. **Use of Computers.** When computer applications are used in counseling services, rehabilitation counselors will ensure that (1) the client is intellectually, emotionally, and physically capable of using the computer application; (2) the computer application is appropriate for the needs of the client; (3) the client understands the purpose and operation of the computer applications; and (4) a follow-up of client use of a computer application is provided to correct possible misconceptions, discover inappropriate use, and assess subsequent needs.

b. **Explanation of Limitations.** Rehabilitation counselors will ensure that clients are provided information as a part of the counseling relationship that adequately explains the limitations of computer technology.

c. **Access to Computer Applications.** Rehabilitation counselors will provide reasonable access to computer applications in counseling services.

SECTION B: CONFIDENTIALITY

B.1. Right to Privacy

a. **Respect for Privacy.** Rehabilitation counselors will respect clients' rights to privacy and will avoid illegal and unwarranted disclosures of confidential information.

b. **Client Waiver.** Rehabilitation counselors will respect the right of the client or his/her legally recognized representative to waive the right to privacy.

c. **Exceptions.** When disclosure is required to prevent clear and imminent danger to the client or others, or when legal requirements demand that confidential information be revealed, the general requirement that rehabilitation counselors keep information confidential will not apply. Rehabilitation counselors will consult with other professionals when in doubt as to the validity of an exception.

d. **Contagious, Fatal Diseases.** Rehabilitation counselors will become aware of the legal requirements for disclosure of contagious and fatal diseases in their jurisdiction. In jurisdictions where allowable, a rehabilitation counselor who receives information will confirm that a client has a disease known to be communicable and/or fatal. If allowable by law, the rehabilitation counselor will disclose this information to a third party, who by his or her relationship with the client is at high risk of contracting the disease. Prior to disclosure, the rehabilitation counselor will ascertain that the client has not already informed the third party about his or her disease and that the client is not intending to inform the third party in the immediate future.

e. **Court-Ordered Disclosure.** When court ordered to release confidential information without a client's permission, rehabilitation counselors will request to the court that the disclosure not be required due to potential harm to the client or counseling relationship.

f. **Minimal Disclosure.** When circumstances require the disclosure of confidential information, rehabilitation counselors will endeavor to reveal only essential information. To the extent possible, clients will be informed before confidential information is disclosed.

g. **Explanation of Limitations.** When counseling is initiated and throughout the counseling process as necessary, rehabilitation counselors will inform clients of the limitations of confidentiality and will identify foreseeable situations in which confidentiality must be breached.

h. **Work Environment.** Rehabilitation counselors will make every effort to ensure that a confidential work environment exists and that subordinates including employees, supervisees, clerical assistants, and volunteers maintain the privacy and confidentiality of clients.

i. **Treatment Teams.** If client treatment will involve the sharing of client information among treatment team members, the client will be advised of this fact and will be informed of the team's existence and composition.

j. **Client Assistants.** When a client is accompanied by an individual providing assistance to the client (e.g., interpreter, personal care assistant, etc.), rehabilitation counselors will ensure that the assistant is apprised of the need to maintain confidentiality.

B.2. Groups and Families

a. **Group Work.** In group work, rehabilitation counselors will clearly define confidentiality and the parameters for the specific group being entered, explain its importance, and discuss the difficulties related to confidentiality involved in group work. The fact that confidentiality cannot be guaranteed will be clearly communicated to group members.

b. **Family Counseling.** In family counseling, unless otherwise directed by law, information about one family member will not be disclosed to another member without permission. Rehabilitation counselors will protect the privacy rights of each family member.

B.3. Records

a. **Requirement of Records.** Rehabilitation counselors will maintain records necessary for rendering professional services to their clients and as required by laws, regulations, or agency or institution procedures.

b. **Confidentiality of Records.** Rehabilitation counselors will be responsible for securing the safety and confidentiality of any counseling records they create, maintain, transfer, or destroy whether the records are written, taped, computerized, or stored in any other medium.

c. **Permission to Record or Observe.** Rehabilitation counselors will obtain and document written or recorded permission from clients prior to electronically recording or observing sessions. When counseling clients who are minors or individuals who are unable to give voluntary, informed consent, written or recorded permission of guardians must be obtained.

d. **Client Access.** Rehabilitation counselors will recognize that counseling records are kept for the benefit of clients, and therefore provide access to records and copies of records when requested by clients, unless prohibited by law. In instances where the records contain information that may be sensitive or detrimental to the client, the rehabilitation counselor has a responsibility to adequately interpret such information to the client. In situations involving multiple clients, access to records will be limited to those parts of records that do not include confidential information related to another client.

e. **Disclosure or Transfer.** Rehabilitation counselors will obtain written permission from clients to disclose or transfer records to legitimate third parties unless exceptions to confidentiality exist as listed in Section B.1.

B.4. Consultation

a. **Respect for Privacy.** Information obtained in a consulting relationship will be discussed for professional purposes only with persons clearly concerned with the case. Written and oral reports will present data germane to the purposes of the consultation, and every effort will be made to protect client identity and to avoid undue invasion of privacy.

b. **Cooperating Agencies.** Before sharing information, rehabilitation counselors will make efforts to ensure that there are defined policies in other agencies serving the counselor's clients that effectively protect the confidentiality of information.

B.5. Alternative Communication

Rehabilitation counselors will make every effort to ensure that methods of exchanging information that utilize alternative means of communication (i.e., facsimile, cellular telephone, computer, or videoconferencing) will be conducted in such a manner that ensures protection of client confidentiality. If confidentiality cannot be ensured, client or guardian permission must be obtained.

SECTION C: ADVOCACY AND ACCESSIBILITY

C.1. Advocacy

a. **Attitudinal Barriers.** Rehabilitation counselors will strive to eliminate attitudinal barriers, including stereotyping and discrimination, toward individuals with disabilities and to increase their own awareness and sensitivity to such individuals.

b. **Advocacy with Cooperating Agencies.** Rehabilitation counselors will remain aware of actions taken by cooperating agencies on behalf of their clients and will act as advocates of such clients to ensure effective service delivery.

c. **Empowerment.** Rehabilitation counselors will provide the client with appropriate information and will support their efforts at self-advocacy both on an individual and an organizational level.

C.2. Accessibility

a. **Counseling Practice.** Rehabilitation counselors will demonstrate, in their practice, an appreciation of the need to provide necessary accommodations, including accessible facilities and services, to individuals with disabilities.

b. **Barriers to Access.** Rehabilitation counselors will identify physical, communication, and transportation barriers to clients and will communicate information on barriers to public and private authorities to facilitate removal of barriers to access.

c. **Referral Accessibility.** Rehabilitation counselors, as advocates for individuals with disabilities, will ensure, prior to referring clients to programs, facilities, or employment settings, that they are appropriately accessible.

SECTION D: PROFESSIONAL RESPONSIBILITY

D.1. Professional Competence

a. **Boundaries of Competence.** Rehabilitation counselors will practice only within the boundaries of their competence, based on their education, training, supervised experience, state and national professional credentials, and appropriate professional experience. Rehabilitation counselors will demonstrate a commitment to gain knowledge, personal awareness, sensitivity, and skills pertinent to working with a diverse client population. Rehabilitation counselors will not misrepresent their role or competence to clients.

b. **Referral.** Rehabilitation counselors will refer clients to other specialists as the needs of the clients dictate.

c. **New Specialty Areas of Practice.** Rehabilitation counselors will practice in specialty areas new to them only after appropriate education, training, and supervised experience. While developing skills in new specialty areas, rehabilitation counselors will take steps to ensure the competence of their work and to protect clients from possible harm.

d. **Resources.** Rehabilitation counselors will ensure that the resources used or accessed in counseling are credible and valid (e.g., web link, books used in Bibliotherapy, etc.).

e. **Qualified for Employment.** Rehabilitation counselors will accept employment only for positions for which they are qualified by education, training, supervised experience, state and national professional credentials, and appropriate professional experience. Rehabilitation counselors will hire only individuals who are qualified and competent for professional rehabilitation counseling positions.

f. **Monitor Effectiveness.** Rehabilitation counselors will take reasonable steps to seek peer supervision to evaluate their efficacy as rehabilitation counselors.

g. **Ethical Issues Consultation.** Rehabilitation counselors will take reasonable steps to consult with other rehabilitation counselors or related professionals when they have questions regarding their ethical obligations or professional practice.

h. **Continuing Education.** Rehabilitation counselors will engage in continuing education to maintain a reasonable level of awareness of current scientific and professional information in their fields of activity. They will take steps to maintain competence in the skills they use, will be open to new techniques, and will develop and maintain competence for practice with the diverse and/or special populations with whom they work.

i. **Impairment.** Rehabilitation counselors will refrain from offering or rendering professional services when their physical, mental, or emotional problems are likely to harm the client or others. They will seek assistance for problems, and, if necessary, will limit, suspend, or terminate their professional responsibilities.

D.2. Legal Standards

a. **Legal Versus Ethical.** Rehabilitation counselors will obey the laws and statutes of the legal jurisdiction in which they practice unless there is a conflict with the Code, in which case they should seek immediate consultation and advice.

b. **Legal Limitations.** Rehabilitation counselors will be familiar with and observe the legal limitations of the services they offer to clients. They will discuss these limitations as well as all benefits available to clients they serve in order to facilitate open, honest communication and avoid unrealistic expectations.

D.3. Advertising and Soliciting Clients

a. **Accurate Advertising.** Advertising by rehabilitation counselors shall not be restricted. Rehabilitation counselors will advertise or will represent their services to the public by identifying their credentials in an accurate manner that is not false, misleading, deceptive, or fraudulent. Rehabilitation counselors will only advertise the highest degree earned which is in counseling or a closely related field from a college or university that was accredited when the degree was awarded by one of the regional accrediting bodies recognized by the Council on Higher Education Accreditation.

b. **Testimonials.** Rehabilitation counselors who use testimonials will not solicit them from clients or other persons who, because of their particular circumstances, may be vulnerable to undue influence. Full disclosure of uses and the informed consent of the client or guardian will be obtained. Use of testimonials will be for a specified and agreed upon period of time.

c. **Statements by Others.** Rehabilitation counselors will make reasonable efforts to ensure that statements made by others about them or the profession of rehabilitation counseling are accurate.

d. **Recruiting through Employment.** Employed rehabilitation counselors will not use their institutional affiliations or relationship with their employers to recruit clients, supervisees, or consultees for their separate private practices.

e. **Products and Training Advertisements.** Rehabilitation counselors who develop products related to their profession or conduct workshops or training events will ensure that the advertisements concerning these products or events are accurate and disclose adequate information for consumers to make informed choices.

f. **Promoting to Those Served.** Rehabilitation counselors will not use counseling, teaching, training, or supervisory relationships to promote their products or training events in a manner that is deceptive or would exert undue influence on individuals who may be vulnerable. Rehabilitation counselors may adopt textbooks they have authored for instructional purposes.

D.4. Credentials

a. **Credentials Claimed.** Rehabilitation counselors will claim or will imply only professional credentials possessed and are responsible for correcting any known misrepresentations of their credentials by others. Professional credentials include graduate degrees in counseling or closely related fields, accreditation of graduate programs, national voluntary certifications, government-issued certifications or licenses, or any other credential that might indicate to the public specialized knowledge or expertise in counseling.

b. **Credential Guidelines.** Rehabilitation counselors will follow the guidelines for use of credentials that have been established by the entities that issue the credentials.

c. **Misrepresentation of Credentials.** Rehabilitation counselors will not attribute more to their credentials than the credentials represent, and will not imply that other rehabilitation counselors are not qualified because they do not posses certain credentials.

d. **Doctoral Degrees from Other Fields.** Rehabilitation counselors who hold a master's degree in counseling or a closely related field, but hold a doctoral degree from other than counseling or a closely related field, will not use the title "Dr." in their practices and will not announce to the public in relation to their practice or status as a rehabilitation counselor that they hold a doctorate.

D.5. CRCC Credential

a. **Acting on Behalf of CRCC.** Certified Rehabilitation Counselors will not write, speak, nor act in ways that lead others to believe the counselor is officially representing CRCC unless the Commission has granted permission in writing.

b. **Support of Candidates.** Certified Rehabilitation Counselors will not initiate or support the candidacy of an individual for certification by CRCC if the individual is known to engage in professional practices that violate the Code of Professional Ethics for Rehabilitation Counselors.

D.6. Public Responsibility

a. **Sexual Harassment.** Rehabilitation counselors will not engage in sexual harassment. Sexual harassment is defined as sexual solicitation, physical advances, or verbal or nonverbal conduct that is sexual in nature, that occurs in connection with professional activities or roles, and that either (1) the rehabilitation counselor knows or is told the act is unwelcome, offensive, or creates a hostile workplace environment; or (2) is sufficiently severe or intense to be perceived as harassment to a reasonable person within the context in which it occurs. Sexual harassment may consist of a single intense or severe act or multiple persistent or pervasive acts.

b. **Reports to Third Parties.** Rehabilitation counselors will be accurate, timely, and objective in reporting their professional activities and opinions to appropriate third parties including courts, health insurance companies, those who are the recipients of evaluation reports, and others.

c. **Media Presentations.** When rehabilitation counselors provide advice or comment by means of public lectures, demonstrations, radio or television programs, prerecorded tapes, printed articles, mailed material, or other media, they will take reasonable precautions to ensure that (1) the statements are based on appropriate professional counseling literature and practice; (2) the statements are otherwise consistent with the Code of Professional Ethics for Rehabilitation Counselors; and (3) the recipients of the information are not encouraged to infer that a professional rehabilitation counseling relationship has been established.

d. **Conflicts of Interest.** Rehabilitation counselors will not use their professional positions to seek or receive unjustified personal gains, sexual favors, unfair advantage, or unearned goods or services.

e. **Dishonesty.** Rehabilitation counselors will not engage in any act or omission of a dishonest, deceitful, or fraudulent nature in the conduct of their professional activities.

D.7. Responsibility to Other Professionals

a. **Disparaging Comments.** Rehabilitation counselors will not discuss in a disparaging way the competency of other professionals or agencies, or the findings made, the methods used, or the quality of rehabilitation plans.

b. **Personal Public Statements.** When making personal statements in a public context, rehabilitation counselors will clarify that they are speaking from their personal perspectives and that they are not speaking on behalf of all rehabilitation counselors or the profession.

c. **Clients Served by Others.** When rehabilitation counselors learn that their clients have an ongoing professional relationship with another rehabilitation or treating professional, they will request release from clients to inform the other professionals and strive to establish positive and collaborative professional relationships. File reviews, second-opinion services, and other indirect services are not considered ongoing professional services.

SECTION E: RELATIONSHIPS WITH OTHER PROFESSIONALS

E.1. Relationships with Employers and Employees

a. **Negative Conditions.** Rehabilitation counselors will alert their employers to conditions that may be potentially disruptive or damaging to the counselor's professional responsibilities or that may limit their effectiveness.

b. **Evaluation.** Rehabilitation counselors will submit regularly to professional review and evaluation by their supervisor or the appropriate representative of the employer.

c. **Discrimination.** Rehabilitation counselors, as either employers or employees, will engage in fair practices with regard to hiring, promotion, or training.

d. **Exploitative Relationships.** Rehabilitation counselors will not engage in exploitative relationships with individuals over whom they have supervisory, evaluative, or instructional control or authority.

e. **Employer Policies.** In those instances where rehabilitation counselors are critical of policies, they will attempt to affect change through constructive action within the organization. Where such change cannot be affected, rehabilitation counselors will take appropriate further action. Such action may include referral to appropriate certification, accreditation, or state licensure organizations or termination of employment.

E.2. Consultation

a. **Consultation as an Option.** Rehabilitation counselors may choose to consult with professionally competent persons about their clients. In choosing consultants, rehabilitation counselors will avoid placing the consultant in a conflict of interest situation that will preclude the consultant from being a proper party to the counselor's efforts to help the client. If rehabilitation counselors are engaged in a work setting that compromises this consultation standard, they will consult with other professionals whenever possible to consider justifiable alternatives.

b. **Consultant Competency.** Rehabilitation counselors will be reasonably certain that they have, or the organization represented has, the necessary competencies and resources for giving the kind of consulting services needed and that appropriate referral are available.

E.3. Agency and Team Relationships

a. **Client as a Team Member.** Rehabilitation counselors will ensure that clients and/or their legally recognized representative are afforded the opportunity for full participation in their own treatment team.
b. **Communication.** Rehabilitation counselors will ensure that there is fair mutual understanding of the rehabilitation plan by all agencies cooperating in the rehabilitation of clients and that any rehabilitation plan is developed with such mutual understanding.
c. **Dissent.** Rehabilitation counselors will abide by and help to implement team decisions in formulating rehabilitation plans and procedures, even when not personally agreeing with such decisions, unless these decisions breach the Code.
d. **Reports.** Rehabilitation counselors will attempt to secure from other specialists appropriate reports and evaluations, when such reports are essential for rehabilitation planning and/or service delivery.

SECTION F: EVALUATION, ASSESSMENT, AND INTERPRETATION

F.1. Informed Consent

a. **Explanation to Clients.** Prior to assessment, rehabilitation counselors will explain the nature and purposes of assessment and the specific use of results in language the client (or other legally authorized person on behalf of the client) can understand. Regardless of whether scoring and interpretation are completed by rehabilitation counselors, by assistants, or by computer or other outside services, rehabilitation counselors will take reasonable steps to ensure that appropriate explanations are given to the client.
b. **Recipients of Results.** The client's welfare, explicit understanding, and prior agreement will determine the recipients of test results. Rehabilitation counselors will include accurate and appropriate interpretations with any release of test results.

F.2. Release of Information to Competent Professionals

a. **Misuse of Results.** Rehabilitation counselors will not misuse assessment results, including test results and interpretations, and will take reasonable steps to prevent the misuse of such by others.
b. **Release of Raw Data.** Rehabilitation counselors will ordinarily release data (e.g., protocols, counseling or interview notes, or questionnaires) in which the client is identified only with the consent of the client or the client's legal representative. Such data will be released only to persons recognized by rehabilitation counselors as competent to interpret the data.

F.3. Research and Training

a. **Data Disguise Required.** Use of data derived from counseling relationships for purposes of training, research, or publication will be confined to content that is disguised to ensure the anonymity of the individuals involved.
b. **Agreement for Identification.** Identification of a client in a presentation or publication will be permissible only when the client has agreed in writing to its presentation or publication.

F.4. Proper Diagnosis of Mental Disorders

a. **Proper Diagnosis.** Rehabilitation counselors qualified to provide proper diagnosis of mental disorders will take special care when doing so. Assessment techniques (including personal interview) used to determine client care (e.g., locus of treatment, type of treatment, or recommended follow-up) will be carefully selected and appropriately used.
b. **Cultural Sensitivity.** Disability, socioeconomic, and cultural experience of clients will be considered when diagnosing mental disorders.

F.5. Competence to Use and Interpret Tests

a. **Limits of Competence.** Rehabilitation counselors will recognize the limits of their competence and perform only those testing and assessment services for which they have been trained. They will be familiar with reliability, validity, related standardization, error of measurement, and proper application of any technique utilized. Rehabilitation counselors using computer-based test interpretations will be trained in the construct being measured and the specific instrument being used prior to using this type of computer application. Rehabilitation counselors will take reasonable measures to ensure the proper use of psychological assessment techniques by persons under their supervision.
b. **Appropriate Use.** Rehabilitation counselors will be responsible for the appropriate application, scoring, interpretation, and use of assessment instruments, whether they score and interpret such tests themselves or use computerized or other services.
c. **Decisions Based on Results.** Rehabilitation counselors will be responsible for decisions involving individuals or policies that are based on assessment results and will have a thorough understanding of educational and psychological measurement, including validation criteria, test research, and guidelines for test development and use.
d. **Accurate Information.** Rehabilitation counselors will provide accurate information and avoid false claims or misconceptions when making statements about assessment instruments or techniques. Special efforts will be made to avoid utilizing test results to make inappropriate diagnoses or inferences.

F.6. Test Selection

a. **Appropriateness of Instruments.** Rehabilitation counselors will carefully consider the validity, reliability, psychometric limitations, and appropriateness of instruments when selecting tests for use in a given situation or with a particular client.

b. **Referral Information.** If a client is referred to a third party provider for testing, the rehabilitation counselor will provide specific referral questions and sufficient objective data about the client so as to ensure that appropriate test instruments are utilized.

c. **Culturally Diverse Populations.** Rehabilitation counselors will be cautious when selecting tests for disability or culturally diverse populations to avoid inappropriateness of testing that may be outside of socialized behavioral or cognitive patterns or functional abilities.

d. **Norm Divergence.** Rehabilitation counselors will be cautious in using assessment techniques, making evaluations, and interpreting the performance of populations not represented in the norm group on which an instrument was standardized and will disclose such information.

F.7. Conditions of Test Administration

a. **Administration Conditions.** Rehabilitation counselors will administer tests under the same conditions that were established in the test standardization. When tests are not administered under standard conditions, as may be necessary to accommodate modifications for clients with disabilities or when unusual behavior or irregularities occur during the testing session, those conditions will be noted in interpretation.

b. **Computer Administration.** When a computer or other electronic methods are used for test administration, rehabilitation counselors will be responsible for ensuring that programs function properly to provide clients with accurate results.

c. **Unsupervised Test-Taking.** Rehabilitation counselors will not permit unsupervised or inadequately supervised use of tests or assessments unless the tests or assessments are designed, intended, and validated for self-administration and/or scoring.

F.8. Test Scoring and Interpretation

a. **Reporting Reservations.** In reporting assessment results, rehabilitation counselors will indicate any reservations that exist regarding validity or reliability because of the circumstances of the assessment or the inappropriateness of the norms for the person tested.

b. **Diversity in Testing.** Rehabilitation counselors will place test results and their interpretations in proper perspective considering other relevant factors including age, color, culture, disability, ethnic group, gender, race, religion, sexual orientation, marital status, and socioeconomic status.

c. **Research Instruments.** Rehabilitation counselors will exercise caution when interpreting the results of research instruments possessing insufficient technical data to support respondent results. The specific purposes for the use of such instruments will be stated explicitly to the examinee.

d. **Testing Services.** Rehabilitation counselors who provide test scoring and test interpretation services to support the assessment process will confirm the validity of such interpretations. The interpretation of assessment data will be related to the particular goals of evaluation. Rehabilitation counselors will accurately describe the purpose, norms, validity, reliability, and applications of the procedures and any special qualifications applicable to their use.

e. **Automated Testing Services.** The public offering of an automated test interpretation service will be considered a professional-to-professional consultation. The formal

responsibility of the consultant will be to the consultee, but the ultimate and overriding responsibility will be to the client.

F.9. Test Security

Rehabilitation counselors will maintain the integrity and security of tests and other assessment techniques consistent with legal and contractual obligations. Rehabilitation counselors will not appropriate, reproduce, or modify published tests or parts thereof without acknowledgment and permission from the publisher.

F.10. Obsolete Tests and Outdated Test Results

Rehabilitation counselors will not use data or test results that are obsolete or outdated for the current purpose. Rehabilitation counselors will make every effort to prevent the misuse of obsolete measures and test data by others.

F.11. Test Construction

Rehabilitation counselors will use established scientific procedures, relevant standards, and current professional knowledge for test design in the development, publication, and utilization of educational and psychological assessment techniques.

F.12. Forensic Evaluation

When providing forensic evaluations, the primary obligation of rehabilitation counselors will be to produce objective findings that can be substantiated based on information and techniques appropriate to the evaluation, which may include examination of the individual with a disability and/or review of records. Rehabilitation counselors will define the limits of their reports or testimony, especially when an examination of the individual with a disability has not been conducted.

SECTION G: TEACHING, TRAINING, AND SUPERVISION

G.1. Rehabilitation Counselor Educators and Trainers

a. **Relationship Boundaries with Students and Supervisees.** Rehabilitation counselors will clearly define and maintain ethical, professional, and social relationship boundaries with their students and supervisees. They will be aware of the differential in power that exists and the student or supervisee's possible incomprehension of that power differential. Rehabilitation counselors will explain to students and supervisees the potential for the relationship to become exploitive.

b. **Sexual Relationships.** Rehabilitation counselors will not engage in sexual relationships with students or supervisees and will not subject them to sexual harassment.

c. **Supervision Preparation.** Rehabilitation counselors will supervise only within the boundaries of their competence, based on their education, training, supervised experience, state and national professional credentials, and appropriate professional experience. Rehabilitation counselors who are doctoral students serving as practicum or internship supervisors will be adequately prepared and supervised by the training program.

d. **Responsibility for Services to Clients.** Rehabilitation counselors who supervise the rehabilitation counseling services of others will perform direct supervision sufficient to ensure that rehabilitation counseling services provided to clients are adequate and do not cause harm to the client.

e. **Endorsement.** Rehabilitation counselors will not endorse students or supervisees for certification, licensure, employment, or completion of an academic or training program if they believe students or supervisees are not qualified for the endorsement. Rehabilitation counselors will take reasonable steps to assist students or supervisees who are not qualified for endorsement to become qualified.

G.2. Rehabilitation Counselor Education and Training Programs

a. **Orientation.** Prior to admission, rehabilitation counselor educators will orient prospective students to the counselor education or training program's expectations, including but not limited to the following: (1) the type and level of skill acquisition required for successful completion of the training, (2) subject matter to be covered, (3) basis for evaluation, (4) training components that encourage self-growth or self-disclosure as part of the training process, (5) the type of supervision settings and requirements of the sites for required clinical field experiences, (6) student evaluation and dismissal policies and procedures, and (7) up-to-date employment prospects for graduates.

b. **Evaluation.** Rehabilitation counselor educators will clearly state, in advance of training, to students and internship supervisees, the levels of competency expected, appraisal methods, and timing of evaluations for both didactic and experiential components. Rehabilitation counselor educators will provide students and internship supervisees with periodic performance appraisal and evaluation feedback throughout the training program.

c. **Teaching Ethics.** Rehabilitation counselor educators will teach students and internship supervisees the ethical responsibilities and standards of the profession and the students' professional ethical responsibilities.

d. **Peer Relationships.** When students are assigned to lead counseling groups or provide clinical supervision for their peers, rehabilitation counselors educators will take steps to ensure that students placed in these roles do not have personal or adverse relationships with peers and that they understand they have the same ethical obligations as counselor educators, trainers, and supervisors. Rehabilitation counselor educator will make every effort to ensure that the rights of peers are not compromised when students are assigned to lead counseling groups or provide clinical supervision.

e. **Varied Theoretical Positions.** Rehabilitation counselor educators will present varied theoretical positions so that students may make comparisons and have opportunities to develop their own positions. Rehabilitation counselor educators will provide information concerning the scientific bases of professional practice.

f. **Field Placements.** Rehabilitation counselor educators will develop clear policies within their training program regarding field placement and other clinical experiences. Rehabilitation counselor educators will provide clearly stated roles and responsibilities for the student and the site supervisor. Rehabilitation counselor educators will confirm that site supervisors will be qualified to provide supervision and are informed of their professional and ethical responsibilities in this role. Rehabilitation counselor educators will not accept any form of professional services, fees, commissions, reimbursement, or remuneration from a site for student placement.

g. **Diversity in Programs.** Rehabilitation counselor educators will respond to their institution and program's recruitment and retention needs for training program administrators, faculty, and students with diverse backgrounds and special needs.

G.3. Students and Supervisees

a. **Limitations.** Rehabilitation counselors, through ongoing evaluation and appraisal, will be aware of the academic and personal limitations of students and supervisees that might impede performance. Rehabilitation counselors will assist students and supervisees in securing remedial assistance when needed, and will dismiss students or supervisees who are unable to provide competent service due to academic or personal limitations. Rehabilitation counselors will seek professional consultation and document their decision to dismiss or to refer students or supervisees for assistance. Rehabilitation counselors will advise students and supervisees of appeals processes as appropriate.

b. **Self-Growth Experiences.** Rehabilitation counselor educators, when designing training groups or other experiences conducted by the rehabilitation counselor educators themselves, will inform students of the potential risks of self-disclosure. Rehabilitation counselor educators will respect the privacy of students by not requiring self-disclosure that could reasonably be expected to be harmful and student evaluation criteria will not include the level of the student's self-disclosure.

c. **Counseling for Students and Supervisees.** If students or supervisees request counseling, supervisors or rehabilitation counselor educators will provide them with acceptable referrals. Supervisors or rehabilitation counselor educators will not serve as rehabilitation counselors to students or supervisees over whom they hold administrative, teaching, or evaluative roles unless this is a brief role associated with a training experience.

d. **Clients of Students and Supervisees.** Rehabilitation counselors will make every effort to ensure that clients are aware of the services rendered and the qualifications of the students and supervisees rendering those services. Clients will receive professional disclosure information and will be informed of the limits of confidentiality. Client permission will be obtained in order for the students and supervisees to use any information concerning the counseling relationship in the training process.

e. **Professional Development.** Rehabilitation counselors who employ or supervise individuals will provide appropriate working conditions, timely evaluations, constructive consultations, and suitable opportunities for experience and training.

SECTION H: RESEARCH AND PUBLICATION

H.1. Research Responsibilities

a. **Use of Human Participants.** Rehabilitation counselors will plan, design, conduct, and report research in a manner that reflects cultural sensitivity, is culturally appropriate, and is consistent with pertinent ethical principles, federal and state/provincial laws, host institutional regulations, and scientific standards governing research with human participants.

b. **Deviation from Standard Practices.** Rehabilitation counselors will seek consultation and observe stringent safeguards to protect the rights of research participants when a research problem suggests a deviation from standard acceptable practices.

c. **Precautions to Avoid Injury.** Rehabilitation counselors who conduct research with human participants will be responsible for the participants' welfare throughout the research and will take reasonable precautions to avoid causing injurious psychological, physical, or social effects to their participants.

d. **Principal Researcher Responsibility.** While ultimate responsibility for ethical research practice lies with the principal researcher, rehabilitation counselors involved in the research activities will share ethical obligations and bear full responsibility for their own actions.

e. **Minimal Interference.** Rehabilitation counselors will take precautions to avoid causing disruptions in participants' lives due to participation in research.

f. **Diversity.** Rehabilitation counselors will be sensitive to diversity and research issues with culturally diverse populations and they will seek consultation when appropriate.

H.2. Informed Consent

a. **Topics Disclosed.** In obtaining informed consent for research, rehabilitation counselors will use language that is understandable to research participants and that (1) accurately explains the purpose and procedures to be followed; (2) identifies any procedures that are experimental or relatively untried; (3) describes the attendant discomforts and risks; (4) describes the benefits or changes in individuals or organizations that might reasonably be expected; (5) discloses appropriate alternative procedures that would be advantageous for participants; (6) offers to answer any inquiries concerning the procedures; (7) describes any limitations of confidentiality; and (8) instructs that participants are free to withdraw their consent and to discontinue participation in the project at any time.

b. **Deception.** Rehabilitation counselors will not conduct research involving deception unless alternative procedures are not feasible and the prospective value of the research justifies the deception. When the methodological requirements of a study necessitate concealment or deception, the investigator will be required to explain clearly the reasons for this action as soon as possible.

c. **Voluntary Participation.** Participation in research is typically voluntary and without any penalty for refusal to participate. Involuntary participation will be appropriate only when it can be demonstrated that participation will have no harmful effects on participants and is essential to the investigation.

d. **Confidentiality of Information.** Information obtained about research participants during the course of an investigation will be confidential. When the possibility exists that others may obtain access to such information, ethical research practice requires that the possibility, together with the plans for protecting confidentiality, will be explained to participants as a part of the procedure for obtaining informed consent.

e. **Persons Incapable of Giving Informed Consent.** When a person is incapable of giving informed consent, rehabilitation

counselors will provide an appropriate explanation, obtain agreement for participation, and obtain appropriate consent from a legally authorized person.

f. **Commitments to Participants.** Rehabilitation counselors will take reasonable measures to honor all commitments to research participants.

g. **Explanations After Data Collection.** After data are collected, rehabilitation counselors will provide participants with full clarification of the nature of the study to remove any misconceptions. Where scientific or human values justify delaying or withholding information, rehabilitation counselors will take reasonable measures to avoid causing harm.

h. **Agreements to Cooperate.** Rehabilitation counselors who agree to cooperate with another individual in research or publication will incur an obligation to cooperate as agreed.

i. **Informed Consent for Sponsors.** In the pursuit of research, rehabilitation counselors will give sponsors, institutions, and publication channels the same opportunity for giving informed consent that they accord to individual research participants. Rehabilitation counselors will be aware of their obligation to future researchers and will ensure that host institutions are given feedback information and proper acknowledgment.

H.3. Reporting Results

a. **Information Affecting Outcome.** When reporting research results, rehabilitation counselors will explicitly mention all variables and conditions known to the investigator that may have affected the outcome of a study or the interpretation of data.

b. **Accurate Results.** Rehabilitation counselors will plan, conduct, and report research accurately and in a manner that minimizes the possibility that results will be misleading. They will provide thorough discussions of the limitations of their data and alternative hypotheses. Rehabilitation counselors will not engage in fraudulent research, distort data, misrepresent data, or deliberately bias their results.

c. **Obligation to Report Unfavorable Results.** Rehabilitation counselors will make available the results of any research judged to be of professional value even if the results reflect unfavorably on institutions, programs, services, prevailing opinions, or vested interests.

d. **Identity of Participants.** Rehabilitation counselors who supply data, aid in the research of another person, report research results, or make original data available will take due care to disguise the identity of respective participants in the absence of specific authorization from the participants to do otherwise.

e. **Replication Studies.** Rehabilitation counselors will be obligated to make sufficient original research data available to qualified professionals who may wish to replicate the study.

H.4. Publication

a. **Recognition of Others.** When conducting and reporting research, rehabilitation counselors will be familiar with and give recognition to previous work on the topic, observe copyright laws, and give full credit to those to whom credit is due.

b. **Contributors.** Rehabilitation counselors will give credit through joint authorship, acknowledgment, footnote statements, or other appropriate means to those who have contributed significantly to research or concept development in accordance with such contributions. The principal contributor will be listed first and minor technical or professional contributions are acknowledged in notes or introductory statements.

c. **Student Research.** For an article that is substantially based on a student's dissertation or thesis, the student will be listed as the principal author.

d. **Duplicate Submission.** Rehabilitation counselors will submit manuscripts for consideration to only one journal at a time. Manuscripts that are published in whole or in substantial part in another journal or published work will not be submitted for publication without acknowledgment and permission from the previous publication.

e. **Professional Review.** Rehabilitation counselors who review material submitted for publication, research, or other scholarly purposes will respect the confidentiality and proprietary rights of those who submitted it.

SECTION I: ELECTRONIC COMMUNICATION AND EMERGING APPLICATIONS

I.1. Communication

a. **Communication Tools.** Rehabilitation counselors will be held to the same level of expected behavior as defined by the Code of Professional Ethics for Rehabilitation Counselors regardless of the form of communication they choose to use (i.e., cellular phones, electronic mail, facsimile, video, audio-visual).

b. **Imposters.** In situations where it is difficult to verify the identity of the rehabilitation counselor, the client, or the client's guardian, rehabilitation counselors will take steps to address imposter concerns, such as using code words, numbers, or graphics.

c. **Confidentiality.** Rehabilitation counselors will ensure that clients are provided sufficient information to adequately address and explain the limits of: (1) computer technology in the counseling process in general; and (2) the difficulties of ensuring complete client confidentiality of information transmitted through electronic communication over the Internet through on-line counseling.

I.2. Counseling Relationship

a. **Ethical/Legal Review.** Rehabilitation counselors will review pertinent legal and ethical codes for possible violations emanating from the practice of distance counseling and supervision. Distance counseling is defined as any counseling that occurs at a distance through electronic means, such as web-counseling, tele-counseling, or video-counseling.

b. **Security.** Rehabilitation counselors will use encryption methods whenever possible. If encryption is not made available to clients, clients must be informed of the potential hazards of unsecured communication on the Internet. Hazards may include authorized or unauthorized monitoring of transmissions and/or records of sessions.

c. **Records Preservation.** Rehabilitation counselors will inform clients whether the records are being preserved, how they are being preserved, and how long the records are being maintained.

d. **Self-Description.** Rehabilitation counselors will provide information about themselves as would be available if the counseling were to take place face-to-face (e.g., possibly ethnicity or gender).

e. **Consumer Protection.** Rehabilitation counselors will provide information to the client regarding all appropriate certification bodies and licensure boards to facilitate consumer protection, such as links to Web sites.

f. **Crisis Contact.** Rehabilitation counselors will provide the name of at least one agency or counselor-on-call for purposes of crisis intervention within the client's geographical region.

g. **Unavailability.** Rehabilitation counselors will provide clients with instructions for contacting them when they are unavailable through electronic means.

h. **Inappropriate Use.** Rehabilitation counselors will mention at their Web sites or in their initial contacts with potential clients those presenting problems they believe to be inappropriate for distance counseling.

i. **Technical Failure.** Rehabilitation counselors will explain to clients the possibility of technology failure and will provide an alternative means of communication.

j. **Potential Misunderstandings.** Rehabilitation counselors will explain to clients how to prevent and address potential misunderstandings arising from the lack of visual cues and voice intonations from the counselor or client.

SECTION J: BUSINESS PRACTICES

J.1. Billing

Rehabilitation counselors will establish and maintain billing records that accurately reflect the services provided and the time engaged in the activity, and that clearly identify who provided the service.

J.2. Termination

Rehabilitation counselors in fee for service relationships may terminate services with clients due to nonpayment of fees under the following conditions: a) the client was informed of payment responsibilities and the effects of nonpayment or the termination of payment by a third party, and b) the client does not pose an imminent danger to self or others. As appropriate, rehabilitation counselors will refer clients to another qualified professional to address issues unresolved at the time of termination.

J.3. Client Records

a. **Accurate Documentation.** Rehabilitation counselors will establish and will maintain documentation that accurately reflects the services provided and that identifies who provided the service. If case notes need to be altered, it will be done so in a manner that preserves the original note and will be accompanied by the date of change, information that identifies who made the change, and the rationale for the change.

b. **Sufficient Documentation.** Rehabilitation counselors will provide sufficient documentation in a timely manner (e.g., case notes, reports, plans).

c. **Privacy.** Documentation generated by rehabilitation counselors will protect the privacy of clients to the extent that it is possible and appropriate, and will include only relevant information.

d. **Maintenance.** Rehabilitation counselors will maintain records necessary for rendering professional services to their clients and as required by applicable laws, regulations, or agency/institution procedures. Subsequent to file closure, records will be maintained for the number of years consistent with jurisdictional requirements or for a longer period during which maintenance of such records is necessary or helpful to provide reasonably anticipated future services to the client. After that time, records will be destroyed in a manner assuring preservation of confidentiality.

J.4. Fees and Bartering

a. **Advance Understanding.** Rehabilitation counselors will clearly explain to clients, prior to entering the counseling relationship, all financial arrangements related to professional services including the use of collection agencies or legal measures for nonpayment.

b. **Establishing Fees.** In establishing fees for professional rehabilitation counseling services, rehabilitation counselors will consider the financial status and locality of clients. In the event that the established fee structure is inappropriate for a client, assistance will be provided in attempting to find comparable services of acceptable cost.

c. **Bartering Discouraged.** Rehabilitation counselors will ordinarily refrain from accepting goods or services from clients in return for rehabilitation counseling services because such arrangements create inherent potential for conflicts, exploitation, and distortion of the professional relationship. Rehabilitation counselors will participate in bartering only if the relationship is not exploitative, if the client requests it, if a clear written contract is established, and if such arrangements are an accepted practice in the client's community or culture.

J.5. Fees for Referral

a. **Accepting Fees from Agency Clients.** Rehabilitation counselors will not accept a private fee or other remuneration for rendering services to persons who are entitled to such services through the rehabilitation counselor's employing agency or institution. However, the policies of a particular agency may make explicit provisions for agency clients to receive rehabilitation counseling services from members of its staff in private practice. In such instances, the clients will be informed of other options open to them should they seek private rehabilitation counseling services.

b. **Referral Fees.** Rehabilitation counselors will neither give nor receive commissions, rebates or any other form of remuneration when referring clients for professional services.

SECTION K: RESOLVING ETHICAL ISSUES

K.1. Knowledge of Standards

Rehabilitation counselors are responsible for learning the Code and should seek clarification of any standard that is not understood. Lack of knowledge or misunderstanding of an ethical responsibility will not be used as a defense against a charge of unethical conduct.

K.2. Suspected Violations

a. **Consultation.** When uncertain as to whether a particular situation or course of action may be in violation of the Code of Professional Ethics for Rehabilitation Counselors, rehabilitation counselors will consult with other rehabilitation counselors who are knowledgeable about ethics, with colleagues, and/or with appropriate authorities, such as CRCC, state licensure boards, or legal counsel.

b. **Organization Conflicts.** If the demands of an organization with which rehabilitation counselors are affiliated pose a conflict with the Code of Professional Ethics for Rehabilitation Counselors, rehabilitation counselors will specify the nature of such conflicts and express to their supervisors or other responsible officials their commitment to the Code of Professional Ethics for Rehabilitation Counselors. When possible, rehabilitation counselors will work toward change within the organization to allow full adherence to the Code of Professional Ethics for Rehabilitation Counselors.

c. **Informal Resolution.** When rehabilitation counselors have reasonable cause to believe that another rehabilitation counselor is violating an ethical standard, they will attempt to resolve the issue informally with the other rehabilitation counselor if feasible, providing that such action does not violate confidentiality rights that may be involved.

d. **Reporting Suspected Violations.** When an informal resolution is not appropriate or feasible, rehabilitation counselors, upon reasonable cause, will take action such as reporting the suspected ethical violation to state or national ethics committees or CRCC, unless this action conflicts with confidentiality rights that cannot be resolved.

e. **Unwarranted Complaints.** Rehabilitation counselors will not initiate, participate in, or encourage the filing of ethics complaints that are unwarranted or intended to harm a rehabilitation counselor rather than to protect clients or the public.

K.3. Cooperation with Ethics Committees

Rehabilitation counselors will assist in the process of enforcing the Code of Professional Ethics for Rehabilitation Counselors. Rehabilitation counselors will cooperate with investigations, proceedings, and requirements of the CRCC Ethics Committee or ethics committee of other duly constituted associations or boards having jurisdiction over those charged with a violation.

A copy of CRCC's Guidelines and Procedures for Processing Complaints along with a Complaint Form may be obtained from CRCC's Web site at www.crccertification.com or by contacting CRCC at:

CRCC
1835 Rohlwing Road, Suite E
Rolling Meadows, IL 60008
(847) 394-2104, extension 121

Acknowledgements—CRCC recognizes the American Counseling Association for permitting the Commission to adopt, in part, the ACA Code of Ethics and Standards of Practice.

Source: Reprinted by permission of the Commission on Rehabilitation Counselor Certification.

APPENDIX U
Scope of Practice for Rehabilitation Counseling

I. ASSUMPTIONS

- The Scope of Practice Statement identifies knowledge and skills required for the provision of effective rehabilitation counseling services to persons with physical, mental, developmental, cognitive, and emotional disabilities as embodied in the standards of the profession's credentialing organizations.
- The several rehabilitation disciplines and related processes (e.g., vocational evaluation, job development and job placement, work adjustment, case management) are tied to the central field of rehabilitation counseling. The field of rehabilitation counseling is a specialty within the rehabilitation profession with counseling at its core, and is differentiated from other related counseling fields.
- The professional scope of rehabilitation counseling practice is also differentiated from an individual scope of practice, which may overlap, but is more specialized than the professional scope. An individual scope of practice is based on one's own knowledge of the abilities and skills that have been gained through a program of education and professional experience. A person is ethically bound to limit his/her practice to that individual scope of practice.

II. UNDERLYING VALUES

- Facilitation of independence, integration, and inclusion of people with disabilities in employment and the community.
- Belief in the dignity and worth of all people.
- Commitment to a sense of equal justice based on a model of accommodation to provide and equalize the opportunities to participate in all rights and privileges available to all people; and a commitment to supporting persons with disabilities in advocacy activities to enable them to achieve this status and empower themselves.
- Emphasis on the holistic nature of human function which is procedurally facilitated by the utilization of such techniques as:

  1. interdisciplinary teamwork.
  2. counseling to assist in maintaining a holistic perspective.
  3. a commitment to considering individuals within the context of their family systems and communities.

- Recognition of the importance of focusing on the assets of the person.
- Commitment to models of service delivery that emphasize integrated, comprehensive services which are mutually planned by the consumer and the rehabilitation counselor.

III. SCOPE OF PRACTICE STATEMENT

Rehabilitation counseling is a systematic process which assists persons with physical, mental, developmental, cognitive, and emotional disabilities to achieve their personal, career, and independent living goals in the most integrated setting possible through the application of the counseling process. The counseling process involves communication, goal setting, and beneficial growth or change through self-advocacy, psychological, vocational, social, and behavioral interventions. The specific techniques and modalities utilized within this rehabilitation counseling process may include, but are not limited to:

- assessment and appraisal;
- diagnosis and treatment planning;
- career (vocational) counseling;
- individual and group counseling treatment interventions focused on facilitating adjustments to the medical and psychosocial impact of disability;
- case management, referral, and service coordination;
- program evaluation and research;
- interventions to remove environmental, employment, and attitudinal barriers;
- consultation services among multiple parties and regulatory systems;
- job analysis, job development, and placement services, including assistance with employment and job accommodations; and
- the provision of consultation about, and access to, rehabilitation technology.

IV. SELECTED DEFINITIONS

The following definitions are provided to increase the understanding of certain key terms and concepts used in the Scope of Practice Statement for Rehabilitation Counseling.

Appraisal: Selecting, administering, scoring, and interpreting instruments designed to assess an individual's attitudes, abilities, achievements, interests, personal characteristics, disabilities, and mental, emotional, or behavioral disorders as well as the use of methods and techniques for understanding human behavior in relation to coping with, adapting to, or changing life situations.

Diagnosis and Treatment Planning: Assessing, analyzing, and providing diagnostic descriptions of mental, emotional, or behavioral conditions or disabilities; exploring possible solutions; and developing and implementing a treatment plan for mental, emotional, and psychological adjustment or development. Diagnosis and treatment planning shall not be construed to permit the performance of any act which rehabilitation counselors are not educated and trained to perform.

Counseling Treatment Intervention: The application of cognitive, affective, behavioral, and systemic counseling strategies which include developmental, wellness, pathologic, and multicultural principles of human behavior. Such interventions are specifically implemented in the context of a professional counseling relationship and may include, but are not limited to: appraisal; individual, group, marriage, and family counseling and psychotherapy; the diagnostic description and treatment of persons with mental, emotional, and behavioral disorders or disabilities; guidance and consulting to facilitate normal growth and development, including educational and career development; the utilization of functional assessments and career counseling for persons requesting assistance in adjusting to a disability or handicapping condition; referrals; consulting; and research.

Referral: Evaluating and identifying the needs of a counselee to determine the advisability of referrals to other specialists, advising the counselee of such judgments, and communicating as requested or deemed appropriate to such referral sources.

Case Management: A systematic process merging counseling and managerial concepts and skills through the application of techniques derived from intuitive and researched methods, thereby advancing efficient and effective decision-making for functional control of self, client, setting, and other relevant factors for anchoring a proactive practice. In case management, the counselor's role is focused on interviewing, counseling, planning rehabilitation programs, coordinating services, interacting with significant others, placing clients and following up with them, monitoring a client's progress, and solving problems.

Program Evaluation: The effort to determine what changes occur as a result of a planned program by comparing actual changes (results) with desired changes (stated goals), and by identifying the degree to which the activity (planned program) is responsible for those changes.

Research: A systematic effort to collect, analyze, and interpret quantitative or qualitative data that describe how social characteristics, behavior, emotions, cognition, disabilities, mental disorders, and interpersonal transactions among individuals and organizations interact.

Consultation: The application of scientific principles and procedures in counseling and human development to provide assistance in understanding and solving current or potential problems that the consultee may have in relation to a third party, be it an individual, group, or organization.

Source: From the Commission on Rehabilitation Counselor Certification. Reprinted with permission.

APPENDIX V
ACES Ethical Standards

Ethical Guidelines for Counseling Supervisors
Association for Counselor Education
and Supervision

Adopted by ACES Executive Counsel and Delegate Assembly March, 1993

PREAMBLE

The Association for Counselor Education and Supervision (ACES) is composed of people engaged in the professional preparation of counselors and people responsible for the ongoing supervision of counselors. ACES is a founding division of the American Counseling Association for (ACA) and as such adheres to ACA's current ethical standards and to general codes of competence adopted throughout the mental health community.

ACES believes that counselor educators and counseling supervisors in universities and in applied counseling settings, including the range of education and mental health delivery systems, carry responsibilities unique to their job roles. Such responsibilities may include administrative supervision, clinical supervision, or both. Administrative supervision refers to those supervisory activities that increase the efficiency of the delivery of counseling services; whereas, clinical supervision includes the supportive and educative activities of the supervisor designed to improve the application of counseling theory and technique directly to clients.

Counselor educators and counseling supervisors encounter situations that challenge the help given by general ethical standards of the profession at large. These situations require more specific guidelines that provide appropriate guidance in everyday practice.

The Ethical Guidelines for Counseling Supervisors are intended to assist professionals by helping them:

1. Observe ethical and legal protection of clients' and supervisees' rights;
2. Meet the training and professional development needs of supervisees in ways consistent with clients' welfare and programmatic requirements; and
3. Establish policies, procedures, and standards for implementing programs.

The specification of ethical guidelines enables ACES members to focus on and to clarify the ethical nature of responsibilities held in common. Such guidelines should be reviewed formally every five years, or more often if needed, to meet the needs of ACES members for guidance.

The Ethical Guidelines for Counselor Educators and Counseling Supervisors are meant to help ACES members in conducting supervision. ACES is not currently in a position to hear complaints about alleged non-compliance with these guidelines. Any complaints about the ethical behavior of any ACA member should be measured against the ACA Ethical Standards and a complaint lodged with ACA in accordance with its procedures for doing so.

One overriding assumption underlying this document is that supervision should be ongoing throughout a counselor's career and not stop when a particular level of education, certification, or membership in a professional organization is attained.

DEFINITIONS OF TERMS

Applied Counseling Settings—Public or private organizations of counselors such as community mental health centers, hospitals, schools, and group or individual private practice settings.

Supervisees—Counselors-in-training in university programs at any level who work with clients in applied settings as part of their university training program, and counselors who have completed their formal education and are employed in an applied counseling setting.

Supervisors—Counselors who have been designated within their university or agency to directly oversee the professional clinical work of counselors. Supervisors also may be persons who offer supervision to counselors seeking state licensure and so provide supervision outside of the administrative aegis of an applied counseling setting.

1. **Client Welfare and Rights**

    1.01   The primary obligation of supervisors is to train counselors so that they respect the integrity and promote the welfare of their clients. Supervisors should have supervisees inform clients that they are being supervised and that observation and/or recordings of the session may be reviewed by the supervisor.

    1.02   Supervisors who are licensed counselors and are conducting supervision to aid a supervisee to become licensed should instruct the supervisee not to communicate or in any way convey to the supervisee's clients or to other parties that the supervisee is himself/herself licensed.

    1.03   Supervisors should make supervisees aware of clients' rights, including protecting clients' right to privacy and confidentiality in the counseling relationship and the information resulting from it. Clients also should be informed that their right to privacy and confidentiality will not be violated by the supervisory relationship.

    1.04   Records of the counseling relationship, including interview notes, test data, correspondence, the electronic storage of these documents, and audio and videotape

493

recordings, are considered to be confidential professional information. Supervisors should see that these materials are used in counseling, research, and training and supervision of counselors with the full knowledge of the clients and that permission to use these materials is granted by the applied counseling setting offering service to the client. This professional information is to be used for full protection of the client. Written consent from the client (or legal guardian, if a minor) should be secured prior to the use of such information for instructional, supervisory, and/or research purposes. Policies of the applied counseling setting regarding client records also should be followed.

1.05   Supervisors shall adhere to current professional and legal guidelines when conducting research with human participants such as Section D-1 of the ACA Ethical Standards.

1.06   Counseling supervisors are responsible for making every effort to monitor both the professional actions, and failures to take action, of their supervisees.

2. **Supervisory Role**
Inherent and integral to the role of supervisor are responsibilities for:
   a. monitoring client welfare;
   b. encouraging compliance with relevant legal, ethical, and professional standards for clinical practice;
   c. monitoring clinical performance and professional development of supervisees; and
   d. evaluating and certifying current performance and potential of supervisees for academic, screening, selection, placement, employment, and credentialing purposes.

2.01   Supervisors should have had training in supervision prior to initiating their role as supervisors.

2.02   Supervisors should pursue professional and personal continuing education activities such as advanced courses, seminars, and professional conferences on a regular and ongoing basis. These activities should include both counseling and supervision topics and skills.

2.03   Supervisors should make their supervisees aware of professional and ethical standards and legal responsibilities of the counseling profession.

2.04   Supervisors of post-degree counselors who are seeking state licensure should encourage these counselors to adhere to the standards for practice established by the state licensure board of the state in which they practice.

2.05   Procedures for contacting the supervisor, or an alternative supervisor, to assist in handling crisis situations should be established and communicated to supervisees.

2.06   Actual work samples via audio and/or video tape or live observation in addition to case notes should be reviewed by the supervisor as a regular part of the ongoing supervisory process.

2.07   Supervisors of counselors should meet regularly in face-to-face sessions with their supervisees.

2.08   Supervisors should provide supervisees with ongoing feedback on their performance. This feedback should take a variety of forms, both formal and informal, and should include verbal and written evaluations. It should be formative during the supervisory experience and summative at the conclusion of the experience.

2.09   Supervisors who have multiple roles (e.g., teacher, clinical supervisor, administrative supervisor, etc.) with supervisees should minimize potential conflicts. Where possible, the roles should be divided among several supervisors. Where this is not possible, careful explanation should be conveyed to the supervisee as to the expectations and responsibilities associated with each supervisory role.

2.10   Supervisors should not participate in any form of sexual contact with supervisees. Supervisors should not engage in any form of social contact or interaction which would compromise the supervisor-supervisee relationship. Dual relationships with supervisees that might impair the supervisor's objectivity and professional judgment should be avoided and/or the supervisory relationship terminated.

2.11   Supervisors should not establish a psychotherapeutic relationship as a substitute for supervision. Personal issues should be addressed in supervision only in terms of the impact of these issues on clients and on professional functioning.

2.12   Supervisors, through ongoing supervisee assessment and evaluation, should be aware of any personal or professional limitations of supervisees which are likely to impede future professional performance. Supervisors have the responsibility of recommending remedial assistance to the supervisee and of screening from the training program, applied counseling setting, or state licensure those supervisees who are unable to provide competent professional services. These recommendations should be clearly and professionally explained in writing to the supervisees who are so evaluated.

2.13   Supervisors should not endorse a supervisee for certification, licensure, completion of an academic training program, or continued employment if the supervisor believes the supervisee is impaired in any way that would interfere with the performance of counseling duties. The presence of any such impairment should begin a process of feedback and remediation wherever possible so that the supervisee understands the nature of the impairment and has the opportunity to remedy the problem and continue with his/her professional development.

2.14   Supervisors should incorporate the principles of informed consent and participation; clarity of requirements, expectations, roles and rules; and due process and appeal into the establishment of policies and procedures of their institutions, program, courses, and individual supervisory relationships. Mechanisms for due process appeal of individual supervisory actions should be established and made available to all supervisees.

3. **Program Administration Role**
3.01   Supervisors should ensure that the programs conducted and experiences provided are in keeping with current guidelines and standards of ACA and its divisions.

3.02   Supervisors should teach courses and/or supervise clinical work only in areas where they are fully competent and experienced.

3.03   To achieve the highest quality of training and supervision, supervisors should be active participants in peer review and peer supervision procedures.

3.04   Supervisors should provide experiences that integrate theoretical knowledge and practical application. Supervisors also should provide opportunities in which supervisees are able to apply the knowledge they have learned and understand the rationale for the skills they have acquired. The knowledge and skills conveyed should reflect current practice, research findings, and available resources.

3.05   Professional competencies, specific courses, and/or required experiences expected of supervisees should be communicated to them in writing prior to admission to the training program or placement/employment by the applied counseling setting and, in case of continued employment, in a timely manner.

3.06   Supervisors should accept only those persons as supervisees who meet identified entry level requirements for admission to a program of counselor training or for placement in an applied counseling setting. In the case of private supervision in search of state licensure, supervisees should have completed all necessary prerequisites as determined by the state licensure board.

3.07   Supervisors should inform supervisees of the goals, policies, theoretical orientations toward counseling, training, and supervision model or approach on which the supervision is based.

3.08   Supervisees should be encouraged and assisted to define their own theoretical orientation toward counseling, to establish supervision goals for themselves, and to monitor and evaluate their progress toward meeting these goals.

3.09   Supervisors should assess supervisees' skills and experience in order to establish standards for competent professional behavior. Supervisors should restrict supervisees' activities to those that are commensurate with their current level of skills and experiences.

3.10   Supervisors should obtain practicum and fieldwork sites that meet minimum standards for preparing students to become effective counselors. No practicum or fieldwork setting should be approved unless it truly replicates a counseling work setting.

3.11   Practicum and fieldwork classes would be limited in size according to established professional standards to ensure that each student has ample opportunity for individual supervision and feedback. Supervisors in applied counseling settings should have a limited number of supervisees.

3.12   Supervisors in university settings should establish and communicate specific policies and procedures regarding field placement of students. The respective roles of the student counselor, the university supervisor, and the field supervisor should be clearly differentiated in areas such as evaluation, requirements, and confidentiality.

3.13   Supervisors in training programs should communicate regularly with supervisors in agencies used as practicum and/or fieldwork sites regarding current professional practices, expectations of students, and preferred models and modalities of supervision.

3.14   Supervisors at the university should establish clear lines of communication among themselves, the field supervisors, and the students/supervisees.

3.15   Supervisors should establish and communicate to supervisees and to field supervisors specific procedures regarding consultation, performance review, and evaluation of supervisees.

3.16   Evaluations of supervisee performance in universities and in applied counseling settings should be available to supervisees in ways consistent with the Family Rights and Privacy Act and the Buckley Amendment.

3.17   Forms of training that focus primarily on self understanding and problem resolution (e.g., personal growth groups or individual counseling) should be voluntary. Those who conduct these forms of training should not serve simultaneously as supervisors of the supervisees involved in the training.

3.18   A supervisor may recommend participation in activities such as personal growth groups or personal counseling when it has been determined that a supervisee has deficits in the areas of self understanding and problem resolution which impede his/her professional functioning. The supervisors should not be the direct provider of these activities for the supervisee.

3.19   When a training program conducts a personal growth or counseling experience involving relatively intimate self disclosure, care should be taken to eliminate or minimize potential role conflicts for faculty and/or agency supervisors who may conduct these experiences and who also serve as teachers, groups leaders, and clinical directors.

3.20   Supervisors should use the following prioritized sequence in resolving conflicts among the needs of the client, the needs of the supervisee, and the needs of the program or agency. Insofar as the client must be protected, it should understood that client welfare is usually subsumed in federal and state laws such that these statutes should be the first point of reference. Where laws and ethical standards are not present or unclear, the good judgment of the supervisor should be guided by the following list.

   a.   Relevant legal and ethical standards (e.g., duty to warn, state child abuse laws, etc.);
   b.   Client welfare;
   c.   Supervisee welfare;
   d.   Supervisor welfare; and
   e.   Program and/or agency service and administrative needs.

Source: Reprinted by permission of the Association for Counselor Education and Supervision.

APPENDIX W

Required Content Areas for Training in Clinical Supervision

Approved Clinical Supervisor (ACS)

1. *Roles and Functions of Clinical Supervision*—Includes the unique purposes, goals, and foci of supervision, the appropriate conditions for supervision, and the distinction between supervision and other professional roles.

2. *Models of Clinical Supervision*—Includes the major approaches for conceptualizing supervision (e.g., psychotherapy theory-based models of supervision, developmental models, and social models).

3. *Counselor Development*—Includes topics such as individual learning styles, cognitive developmental levels, differences in experience levels, stages of counselor development, and critical transition points, as well as how to create an appropriate educational environment or climate based on developmental differences.

4. *Methods and Techniques in Clinical Supervision*—Includes supervision methods for assessing and intervening with supervisees (e.g., audiotape review, live supervision, self-report), as well as the appropriate use of, and benefits and limitations of, each supervision method.

5. *Supervisory Relationship Issues*—Includes the inter- and intrapersonal variables that affect supervision such as the parameters of a working alliance, conflict within supervision, supervisee anxiety, social influence, and parallel process.

6. *Cultural Issues in Supervision*—Includes the implications of cultural differences and/or similarities between supervisee and supervisor such as race, gender, sexual orientation, and belief systems, and how these impact the process and outcome of supervision.

7. *Group Supervision*—Includes topics such as the structure and processes of group supervision, the unique tasks of the supervisor in the group context, ground rules and stages of group supervision, and the advantages and limitations of the group modality.

8. *Legal and Ethical Issues*—Includes major ethical and legal tenets that affect supervision such as due process, confidentiality, informed consent, dual relationships, competence, duty to warn, and direct and vicarious liability, and the implications of these tenets for supervisees, clients, and the supervisor.

9. *Evaluation*—Includes studies that address the role of evaluation as central to supervision, criteria for evaluation, sources of feedback, the process and outcomes of evaluation, and the role of documentation in evaluation, as well as procedures for the evaluation of the supervision experience.

Source: Reprinted with permission of the National Board for Certified Counselors, Inc. and Affiliates, 3 Terrace Way, Suite D., Greensboro, NC 27403-3660.

APPENDIX X
The ACS Code of Ethics

In addition to following the Code of Ethics of their mental health credentialing body, approved clinical supervisors shall:

1. Ensure that supervisees inform clients of their professional status (e.g., intern) and of all conditions of supervision.

Supervisors need to ensure that supervisees inform their clients of any status other than being fully qualified for independent practice or licensed. For example, supervisees need to inform their clients if they are a student, intern, trainee or, if licensed with restrictions, the nature of those restrictions (e.g., associate or conditional). In addition, clients must be informed of the requirements of supervision (e.g., the audio taping of all clinical sessions for purposes of supervision).

2. Ensure that clients have been informed of their rights to confidentially and privileged communication when applicable. Clients also should be informed of the limits of confidentiality and privileged communication.

The general limits of confidentiality are when harm to self or others is threatened; when the abuse of children, elders or disabled persons is suspected and in cases when the court compels the mental health professional to testify and break confidentiality. These are generally accepted limits to confidentiality and privileged communication, but they may be modified by state or federal statute.

3. Inform supervisees about the process of supervision, including supervision goals, case management procedures, and the supervisor's preferred supervision model(s).

4. Keep and secure supervision records and consider all information gained in supervision as confidential.

5. Avoid all dual relationships with supervisees that may interfere with the supervisor's professional judgment or exploit the supervisee.

Any sexual, romantic, or intimate relationship is considered to be a violation. Sexual relationship means sexual conduct, sexual harassment, or sexual bias toward a supervisee by a supervisor.

6. Establish procedures with their supervisees for handling crisis situations.

7. Provide supervisees with adequate and timely feedback as part of an established evaluation plan.

8. Render assistance to any supervisee who is unable to provide competent counseling services to clients.

9. Intervene in any situation where the supervisee is impaired and the client is at risk.

10. Refrain from endorsing an impaired supervisee when such impairment deems it unlikely that the supervisee can provide adequate counseling services.

11. Supervisors offer only supervision for professional services for which they are trained or have supervised experience. Supervision should not include assistance in diagnosis, assessment, or treatment without prior training or supervision. Supervisors are responsible for correcting any misrepresentations of the qualifications of others.

12. Ensure that supervisees are aware of the current ethical standards related to their professional practice, as well as legal standards that regulate the practice of counseling.

13. Engage supervisees in an examination of cultural issues that might affect supervision and/or counseling.

14. Ensure that both supervisees and clients are aware of their rights and of due process procedures, and that you as supervisor are ultimately responsible for the client.

15. It is considered unethical for an ACS to supervise a relative or immediate family member.

Source: Reprinted with permission of the National Board for Certified Counselors, Inc. and Affiliates, 3 Terrace Way, Suite D, Greensboro, NC 27403-3660.

Glossary

Abuse (child)   the infliction of (by other than accidental means) physical harm upon the body of a child, continual psychological damage, or denial of emotional needs.

Accreditation (general)   the process whereby a college, university, or academic program voluntarily undergoes review by a recognized accrediting body. Accreditation allows for clear recognition of an institution's or a program's nature, intent, and quality. Accreditation is often used to designate that a degree program meets acceptable standards; typically, accreditation is sought by one of the regional accrediting agencies acceptable to the U.S. Department of Education as a legitimate evaluator of the quality of the program.

Accreditation (professional)   the process whereby an educational program meets high standards for preparation of professionals beyond standards required for offering a degree.

Accrediting bodies (professional)   organizations that qualify educational programs as meeting standards beyond those required of colleges or universities to offer degrees. Professional accreditation of graduate counseling degrees occurs through the Council on Accreditation of Counseling and Related Educational Programs (CACREP) or the Council on Rehabilitation Education (CORE). In psychology, the American Psychological Association (APA) accredits doctoral programs.

Active euthanasia   the intentional termination of life, also referred to as mercy killing or assisted suicide.

Advance directives   (1) living wills, which are specific substantive directives regarding medical procedures that should be provided or forgone in specific circumstances; or (2) durable power of attorney (DPA) for health care or proxy directive, giving someone else the right to make such decisions.

Alternative medicine   nontraditional medical approaches that are used instead of traditional medical practices.

Arbitrating   a process wherein a negotiator or negotiators seek the judgment of individuals (alone or in groups) who are socially approved as representatives of sociolegal consensus—arbitrators.

Aspirational ethics   See "Ethics, aspirational."

Assent   the process of consulting with and informing a person incapable of giving legal informed consent regarding his or her preferences regarding the actions to be taken by the counselor to fulfill ethical obligations to this person for informed consent.

Assessment   the process that involves the collection and evaluation of information to address a client's counseling or rehabilitation concern or problem. Typically, an individual is assessed against a normative standard, or a set of criteria, for diagnosis, case planning, or treatment. Objective or projective testing may be involved.

Asynchronous learning   distance learning in which students are not learning at the same time that live instruction occurs (e.g., use of Web-based, software-packaged instruction units).

Attributions (multicultural)   inferences or characteristics assigned to an individual that result in assigning cause and effects to behavior.

Autonomy   the ethical principle that involves having a right to self-determination of choice and freedom from the control of others.

Balancing   involves weighing which ethical or moral principles are more applicable or important in an analysis.

Beneficence   the ethical principle that guides actions consistent with contributing to the well-being of others; it implies doing good to others.

Benevolence   the experience of sharing, helping, and acting generously toward others.

Biomedical ethics   a way of understanding ethical complexity and examining life as it pertains to the biological sciences, medicine, and health care.

Breach of contract   a failure to provide agreed-on services considered to be contracted services.

Burnout   an emotional state experienced by some counselors; characterized by an emotional exhaustion in which the professional no longer has any positive feelings, sympathy, or respect for clients.

CAM   an abbreviation used for "complementary and alternative medicine." (See "Complementary medicine" and "Alternative medicine.")

Capacity   ability, often related specifically to making a rational decision or giving informed consent.

Career counseling   counseling that focuses on a certain realm of the client's life—the world of work.

Case law   legal precedence deriving from past legal judgments, relevant to a law's interpretation in specific circumstances and jurisdictions.

Case manager   an individual who focuses on interviewing, planning rehabilitation, medical, or educational programs; coordinating services; interacting with significant others; placing clients in facilities, organizations, or jobs; following and monitoring a client's progress; and solving problems. Counseling may or may not be a part of case management, depending on the context of employment.

Certification (board)   See "Certification, specialty."

Certification (specialty)   a voluntary means of identifying oneself as a trained and qualified specialist in counseling, psychology, or other professions. Certification usually requires meeting national standards of expertise beyond those required for state licensure.

Civil law   involves the obligation of citizens to one another and the obligation must be asserted by the individual before the obligation is enforced by the government. A civil action may or may not be related to a crime. Typically malpractice, divorce and Workers' Compensation cases are addressed in a civil court.

Competence (client)   the capability of clients to make decisions—a precondition to consent autonomously to services.

Competence (counselor)   a counselor's capability to provide a minimum quality of service within the counselor's (and his or her profession's) scope of practice.

Complaint (ethical)   a formal grievance by an individual (complainant) that expresses dissatisfaction with a counselor's action and appeals to the professional group that endorses the ethical standards that an ethical standard or standards have been violated.

Complementary medicine   nontraditional medical practices that are used with traditional medical practices.

Comprehension   having sufficient information and being able to understand it; a necessary condition of informed consent.

Compulsory therapy   therapy initiated and/or demanded by a third party, usually as a form of rehabilitation or ongoing assessment of a client.

Confidentiality   akin to an antigossip guarantee to clients; the obligation of professional counselors to respect the privacy of clients specifically related to the information communicated during counseling sessions. Legal confidentiality carries the penalty of law should there be a breach of confidentiality. Professional (nonlegal) confidentiality does not carry the weight of law, but it carries the weight of sanctions by the professional associations or certifying organizations with which the counselor affiliates.

Conformity   the following of rules and observation of societal regulations.

Consensualizing   a process whereby at least two individuals act in agreement and in coordination on an issue.

Consultation (professional)   a paid, formal arrangement wherein a consulting counselor obtains a second opinion, advice, or supervision on an issue or issues of concern from a knowledgeable, competent colleague.

Corporal punishment   an act of physical force upon a student for the purpose of punishing the student.

Counseling psychology   a specialty of psychology that focuses on: (a) intact personalities, (b) assets and strengths, (c) emphasis on brief intervention, (d) emphasis on person-environment interactions, and (e) educational and career development of individuals.

Criminal law   the area of law that involves conduct required of all citizens or prohibited to all and that is enforced by the government's legal authorities.

Critical-evaluative level   a level of reasoning that involves three hierarchically arranged stages or tiers of examination to resolve a moral dilemma; involves the evaluation of the implications of laws, ethical principles, and ethical theories for the ethical decision to be made.

Cross-cultural counseling   counseling between two individuals from different cultural backgrounds.

Cultural deficit   an outdated, harmful term used in the past to describe some aspects of attributes of a diverse group from a deficit viewpoint.

Cultural encapsulation   a tendency for people to treat others relative to their own cultural perspective, disregarding important cultural differences.

Culturally disadvantaged   an outdated, harmful term utilized in counseling to describe some aspect of a diverse or multicultural population.

Culture   a socially learned set of psychological constructs encompassing affective styles and values regarding personal control, communication, familial patterns, and societal norms.

Cybercounseling   counseling on the internet.

Differential diagnosis   the process of describing a client whereby one mental disorder is used over another disorder with similar diagnostic signs, symptoms, or course.

Diplomate   the term used by some professions such as psychology to denote the attainment of specialty credentials within a specific area of advanced practice.

Direct liability   liability that occurs when the harm that is done by the supervisor is a result of supervision itself.

Disability   an identifiable physical or mental condition whose functional limitations, when manifested, are recognized and often overcome with appropriate accommodations.

Distance learning   the use of technical equipment or media in place of live teachers to deliver education or training.

Double effect   the circumstance wherein unacceptable consequences such as death are deemed acceptable under certain circumstances; a concept often considered in the context of using medication with a terminally ill patient that is intended to alleviate pain but also hastens or causes death.

Downcoding   giving a client a less serious or severe diagnosis to obtain treatment.

Dual relationship   a professional (treatment or supervisory) relationship and, additionally, a simultaneous or contiguous personal and nonprofessional relationship.

Durable Power of Attorney for Health Care   a proxy directive for health care that allows individuals to select substitute decision makers empowered to make health care decisions on their behalf should they be incapacitated.

Duty to protect   the counselor's responsibility to protect the intended victims of a client or others who may be harmed.

Duty to warn   the counselor's responsibility to inform an endangered party or parties when it is believed a client poses a serious danger to an identifiable, potential victim.

Equivalence (assessment)   psychometric similarity of two different versions of an assessment device.

Ethical climate   one facet of an organizational climate that describes the shared perceptions that colleagues hold concerning ethical procedures and practices occurring within an organization.

Ethical dilemma   a circumstance involving an ethical question that stymies or confuses the counselor because there are: (a) competing or conflicting ethical standards that apply; (b) conflicts between moral and ethical standards; (c) complexities that make the application of specific standards unclear; (d) other circumstances that prevent a clear application of standards.

Ethical principles   higher order norms or fundamental assumptions that develop within society that are consistent with moral principles and constitute higher standards of moral behavior. In counseling, five ethical principles are often referred to: autonomy, beneficence, fidelity, nonmaleficence, and justice.

Ethical standards   established guidelines or rules that apply to counseling practice defined consensually by members of professional counseling organizations (such as the ACA or APA).

Ethical violation   a behavior that violates the letter or perhaps the spirit of an ethical standard of practice.

Ethics   See "Ethics, professional."

Ethics (applied)   See "Ethics, professional."

Ethics (aspirational)   a level of ethical guidance above mandatory ethics that involves consideration of the welfare of clients and the effects of actions on the profession as a whole. Aspirational standards specify ideals for the profession but are not enforceable.

Ethics (mandatory)   the most basic level of professional ethical guidance focusing on compliance with laws and dictates of professional codes of ethics.

Ethics (philosophical)   a branch of study in philosophy concerning theories of what is "good," "right," or "worthy." Philosophical ethics is theoretical.

Ethics (professional)   agreed-on rules or standards established by a profession that define what is acceptable or "good" practice.

Ethics of care   an ethics approach that emphasizes human connectedness, or a relational perspective.

Ethnicity   people who share a common origin and a unique social and cultural heritage.

Eugenics   the use of a scientific strategy for orchestrating human evolution through methods of encouraging transmission of "desirable" traits and discouraging transmission of "undesirable" traits.

Euthanasia   term originally derived from two Greek words meaning "good death"; generally refers to the process of facilitating the painless death of a person who has a terminal/incurable disease. Active euthanasia means there was an intentional act taken to produce the death, sometimes described as mercy killing or assisted suicide. Passive or indirect euthanasia involves the withdrawal or withholding of life-sustaining treatments.

Exploitation   an action by a counselor that benefits the counselor while it compromises the best interest or well-being of a client.

Fidelity   the ethical principle that directs people to keep commitments or promises.

Gene therapy   an approach in which researchers and medical professionals prevent, treat, and cure disease processes through the alteration of an individual's genes.

Genetic testing   specific techniques that are used to seek genetic mutation or an altered gene protein that may indicate a genetic condition or a predisposition.

Genetics   the study of inherited traits.

Genomics   the study of the entire set of human genes.

Hastened death   any process by which people speed up the dying process.

Hierarchical model (four-level)   model of ethical practice that introduces an extended consideration of the contextual forces acting on ethical practice beyond the singular focus on the individual practitioner in relationship to the individual client.

HMO   an abbreviation for "health maintenance organization"; a type of managed care organization.

Holistic care   the use of complementary and alternative methods in health care.

Hospital privileges   the right of a professional to admit and/or to treat patients in a hospital.

Impairment   a covert, often insidious condition that suggests a level of diminished function (obtained by documented evidence) that may be manifested on a continuum by varying degrees of loss of optimal function and may have many causes.

Independence   being free to make one's own decisions and to act autonomously.

Independent practice   the practice of counseling in a private setting based on the right to practice provided by a license of a profession and free from other institutional oversight.

Indirect services   services provided when a counselor is employed by a third party whether or not he or she engages in direct communication with the client, and where there is no intent to provide counseling services directly to the person.

Informed consent   the client's right to agree to participate in counseling, assessment, or professional procedures or services after such services are fully described and explained in a manner that is comprehensible to the client.

Intentionality   acting with a sense of capability and deciding from among a range of alternative actions.

Intuitive level   a level of reasoning that incorporates the richness and influence of the everyday personal and professional moral wisdom of the counselor in the process of ethical decision making.

IPA   an independent practice association which allows consumers to choose independent practitioner but retain a portion of the fee from a provider who may be reimbursed either on a fee-for-service or capitated basis.

Justice   the ethical principle that involves the idea of fairness and equality in terms of access to resources and treatment by others.

Layered supervision   doctoral students supervising master's students who are themselves being supervised by faculty.

Leadership   having responsibility, power, and authority over others, with recognition of such by the others.

Legal guardian   a person who is appointed by the court to make decisions regarding an individual's person and/or property.

Legally mandated ethics   ethics required by law, typically found in counselor or psychology licensure statutes or other state or federal laws that apply to counseling practice.

Licensure   a type of professional regulation that restricts both the use of a professional title, such as "counselor," and the practice of counseling.

Limits of practice   the boundaries that demarcate the acceptable activities associated with a profession.

Living will   specific, substantive directives regarding medical procedures that should be provided or forgone in specific circumstances.

Malpractice   a violation of duty, requiring a determination of what constitutes "good professional practice" as applied to the actions of a professional.

Managed care   provision of health services through medical insurance managed or overseen by a contracted company (a managed care company) that serves as a mediator between insurance carriers and health professionals.

Managed care contract   an agreement between a managed care company and the provider of counseling services; the contract usually defines the type of services that can be provided, the maximum fee, and other limitations of services.

Mandatory ethics   See "Ethics, mandatory."

MCO   an abbreviation used to denote the general term for "managed care organizations."

Mental status examination   a structured interview designed to provide a controlled, interpersonal setting for the emergence and observation of symptoms and signs of mental disorder.

Minority   any identifiable group with differential power and a history of mistreatment.

Mobbing   workplace expulsion through emotional abuse.

Morality (morals)   the principles that guide an individual, sometimes deriving from a religious standard; sometimes referred to as "moral principles."

Morality (philosophical)   the branch of philosophy dealing with the assessment of actions of a person against a theory in philosophical ethics. Philosophical morality always refers to an act.

Multicultural counseling   a helping relationship involving two or more individuals with differing, socially constructed worldviews.

Multiculturalism   an individual's or an organization's underlying beliefs, attitudes, and values that are employed for the formulation of attributions of others in a multicultural context. (See "Attributions.")

Negotiating   the process of discussing and debating an issue wherein at least two individuals indicate some degree of disagreement.

Neglect (child)   the failure to provide necessary food, care, clothing, supervision, or medical attention for a child.

Nonmaleficence   the ethical principle that requires that individuals refrain from any action that might cause harm.

Normalization   a rehabilitation principle that dictates that persons with disabilities should be treated in a manner that allows them to participate both symbolically and actually in roles and lifestyles that are normal for persons of their age and culture.

On-line forums (of counseling)   counseling on the internet; these forums typically offer group interaction on the internet.

Organizational climate   the outward manifestation of culture and the way people would characterize a system's (agency's or business's) atmosphere related to practices and procedures.

Over diagnosis a diagnosis that is more severe than diagnostically justified that ensures adequate insurance coverage for the anticipated treatment.

Passive (indirect) euthanasia See "Euthanasia."

Personal counseling counseling that involves professional helpers who assist clients to understand, accept, and resolve their problems by using basic counseling techniques so that their clients can lead more satisfying, well-adjusted lives.

Pirating the illegal and unethical copying and use of software.

Plagiarism the act of stealing or passing off the ideas or words of another author or person as one's own original work.

Portability the ability of counselors who are licensed in one state to move to another state and have their credentials accepted.

Potentially detrimental counselor–client relationships counselor–client relationships that involve either serious potential or actual harmful or illegal interactions or relationships between counselor and client. This newer term is more clearly descriptive of the ethical issue than the older, increasingly outmoded term, "dual relationships."

PPA an abbreviation for "preferred provider agreement"; used to establish a preferred provider organization relationship.

PPO an abbreviation for "preferred provider organization," a type of managed care organization.

Prima facie Latin phrase meaning that the obligation in question must be considered in every case and set aside only if valid and compelling reasons are present to do so in a specific instance.

Principle ethics objectively applying a system of ethical rules and principles to determine what is the right decision when an ethical dilemma arises. It focuses on the objective, rational, and cognitive aspects of the decision-making process (compare to "Virtue ethics").

Privacy the client's right to keep the counseling relationship to oneself (e.g., as a secret). Privacy is more inclusive than confidentiality, which addresses communications in the counseling context.

Privileged communication a client's right that prevents the revelation of confidential information in a legal proceeding (e.g., a legal hearing or courtroom).

Pro bono publico for the public good (usually meaning providing a service for no fee to those in need).

Professional ethics ethical standards of the professional organizations.

Race an anthropological classification based on physical appearance.

Rational suicide the act of a mentally competent individual, following a sound decision-making process, and without being coerced by others, to end his or her life because of unbearable suffering associated with a terminal illness.

Reciprocity the process whereby a licensed counselor's credentials in one state (licensure) are recognized by another state for licensure purposes without additional imposed requirements.

Recognition the attraction of favorable notice and being considered important.

Relational ethics an approach to ethics that assumes that ethical decisions are primarily influenced by the development of character traits or virtues and concerns itself with cultural, contextual, relational, and emotional intuitive responses to ethical dilemmas.

Residency (specialty) a 3-year or longer, hospital-based training that prepares a physician to practice diagnosis, general treatment, and specialty procedures in a specific area of medical practice.

Responsibility (professional) a counselor's obligation to clients and his or her profession to act in an appropriate and considerate manner.

Revocation (of a professional license) the loss of the right to practice in a licensing jurisdiction.

Scapegoating a process whereby one member of a group is placed in an "odd-person-out" position or is treated by others as deviant, thereby receiving negative messages from other members of the group.

Scope of practice the extent and limits of activities performed by a licensed or certified individual in a profession defined as acceptable practice by the profession. Scope of practice also refers to a recognized area of proficiency or competence gained through appropriate education and experience.

Sliding fee scale requiring clients to pay a certain amount for a service based on their income.

Slippery slope argument an argument that a certain course of action will lead to the progressive erosion of moral restraints.

Social constructivism a philosophical framework that proposes that reality is a creation of individuals in interaction—a socially, consensually agreed-on definition of what is real.

Specialty certification See "Certification, specialty."

Specialty designation certification through a national specialty certifying board.

Specialty residency See "Residency, specialty."

Specifying determining and naming the principles that are involved in a situation being considered.

Subpoena a document issued under authority of a court that compels the appearance of a witness at a legal proceeding. Disobeying a subpoena may result in punishment based on "contempt of court."

Supervision an intervention provided by a more senior member of a profession to a more junior member or members of that same profession. It is evaluative, extends over time, and has the purposes of enhancing the professional functioning of the more junior person, monitoring the quality of services offered to clients, and serving as a gatekeeper for entrance to the profession.

Support   the receiving of encouragement, understanding, and kindness from others.

Suspension (of a professional license)   a temporary loss of the right to practice a profession within a jurisdiction.

Synchronous learning   distance learning in which students learn at the same time that the instruction occurs.

Technoanxious   fearful and avoiding computerization of a profession.

Technocentered   comfortable with computer technology.

Telehealth   remote electronic consultation between consumers and providers in the health care professions.

Testing   use of a specific tool or instrument to gather information or measure some individual quality, characteristic, or level of knowledge.

Third party   an individual or organization that is somehow involved with a case (e.g., a referral source or payor) but is not the counselor or the client.

Upcoding   diagnosing a client with a more serious or severe diagnosis than is diagnostically justified.

UR   an abbreviation for "utilization review."

Value(s)   the quality that makes something desirable, useful, or an object of interest. A value is esteemed, prized, and considered worthwhile. Values also may be viewed as objective, relative to a social context, or relative to an individual (subjective).

Value system   a particular hierarchical rank ordering of the degree of preference for the values expressed by a particular person or social entity.

Valuing   the process of negotiating values with a client or other individual.

Vicarious liability   the legal responsibility of a professional or organization for the potential negligence of another or an employee. In supervision, supervisors are considered liable for the negligent acts of supervisees if these acts are performed in the course and scope of the supervisory relationship.

Virtue ethics   considering the characteristics of counselors themselves as the critical element for responsible practice. (Compare to "Principle ethics.")

Voluntariness   giving consent by acting freely in the decision-making process, such as in giving informed consent.

Web counseling   the practice of professional counseling and information delivery over the internet.

Whistle-blower   a person who identifies an incompetent, unethical, or illegal situation in the workplace and reports it to someone who may have the power to stop the wrong.

Whistle-blowing   the ethical reporting of unethical behavior.

Worldview   view constituted by the observable artifacts, values, and underlying assumptions held by an individual.

Index